ISBN 978-0-265-18756-2
PIBN 10183774

THE

POPES OF ROME;

THEIR CHURCH AND STATE

IN THE

SIXTEENTH AND SEVENTEENTH CENTURIES.

BY

LEOPOLD RANKE,

PROFESSOR EXTRAORDINARY OF HISTORY IN THE UNIVERSITY OF BERLIN.

Translated from the last German Edition.

WITH

AN INTRODUCTORY ESSAY,

BY THE REV. J. H. MERLE D'AUBIGNÉ, D. D.

AUTHOR OF THE HISTORY OF THE REFORMATION IN THE SIXTEENTH CENTURY, ETC. ETC.

VOL. II.

BLACKIE AND SON:

QUEEN STREET, GLASGOW; SOUTH COLLEGE STREET, EDINBURGH;
AND WARWICK SQUARE, LONDON.

MDCCCXLVII.

GLASGOW:
W. G. BLACKIE AND CO., PRINTERS,
VILLAFIELD.

CONTENTS.—VOL. II.

APPENDIX.

LIST OF THE MANUSCRIPTS THAT HAVE BEEN CONSULTED, SUPPLEMENTARY EXTRACTS, AND CRITICAL OBSERVATIONS.

THE ROMAN POPES,

THEIR CHURCH AND STATE, IN THE XVI. AND XVII. CENTURIES.

BOOK SEVENTH.

COUNTER-REFORMATIONS.—SECOND PERIOD. 1590—1630.

I DO not think that I deceive myself or that I overstep the proper limits of history, in believing that I can perceive at this point one of the general laws of human life in operation.

It is unquestionably true, that there are at all times energies of the living mind which thus profoundly move the world. Prepared beforehand in the course of preceding centuries, they rise at their own time, called forth by the agency of vigorous and internally powerful natures, from the unfathomed depths of the human soul. It is their very nature to seek to carry the world along with them and to overpower it. But the more they succeed in doing so, the larger the circle they embrace, the more they come into contact with original independent life, which they cannot so entirely and absolutely subdue and absorb into themselves. Hence it happens, for they belong to the order of interminable creative existences, that they undergo a revolution in themselves. In embracing what is of a nature foreign to their own, they forthwith absorb a part of its essence into themselves; there are developed in them tendencies in particular directions, movements of their very being, which are not seldom inconsistent with their ruling idea. But it cannot fail to happen that in the general advance, these also should wax and thrive. All depends but upon this, that they do not acquire the preponderance; otherwise they would directly destroy the unity and also the fundamental principle of their existence.

Now we saw how powerfully internal contradictions, and profound oppositions of principle, agitated the popedom in its progress towards restoration; nevertheless the theoretical idea carried the day; the higher unity, though not precisely in all the integrity of its ancient comprehensive power, preserved the preponderance, and advanced without intermission to new conquests, at the very time when the internal struggles were going forward, from which it rather drew for that preponderance fresh vigour.

These enterprises now demand our attention. To inquire what was the extent of their success, what the revolutions that resulted from them, what the opposition they met with both from within and from without, is a matter of great consequence to the entire world.

PROGRESS OF THE ROMAN CATHOLIC RESTORATION.

1590—1617.

CHAPTER FIRST.

ENTERPRISES OF ROMAN CATHOLICISM IN POLAND AND THE CONTERMINOUS COUNTRIES.

The opinion has been advanced that the protestants, who even in Poland, as we have seen, had long decidedly held the upper hand, were without doubt in a position likewise to raise a king of their creed to the throne; but that at last, even to them it appeared more advantageous to have a Roman catholic, because in the person of the pope he had a still higher authority, in fact, a judge placed over him.

If this were the case, they drew a severe punishment upon themselves for so unprotestant a sentiment.

For it was precisely by means of a Roman king that the pope was enabled to make war upon them.

Of all the foreign ambassadors the papal nuncios were alone entitled to converse with the king in the absence of a senator. They were well-known personages; they had sufficient talent and adroitness to foster and to improve for their own purposes the confidential footing which was thus placed within their reach.

At the commencement of the eightieth year of the sixteenth century, Cardinal Bolognetto was nuncio in Poland. He complained of the severity of the climate, the cold of which an Italian was doubly susceptible, the damp of close heated apartments, and a general mode of living to which he was quite unaccustomed; notwithstanding all which he accompanied King Stephen from Warsaw to Cracow, from Wilna to Lublin, through the kingdom; at times in a somewhat melancholy mood, but not on that account the less indefatigable; during the time that the troops were in movement, he continued at least to correspond by letters with the king, and upheld the interests of Rome by maintaining an uninterrupted connection with the royal person.

We have a copious narrative of his official conduct, and from it we see what he undertook, and how far he succeeded in his undertakings.[1]

Above all things he urged the king to fill public offices with Roman catholics only, to permit the Roman catholic worship alone in the royal cities, and to re-establish the tithes, measures such as had been adopted at the same period in other countries, and which introduced or indicated the renovation of Roman catholicism.

Now in this his success was incomplete. King Stephen thought he could not go so far; he declared that he was not powerful enough for that.

But therewithal this prince had not only Roman catholic convictions, but an innate zeal likewise for church affairs; in many other things he complied with the nuncio's representations.

The Jesuit colleges in Cracow, Grodno, and Pultusk, owed their establishment to immediate royal support. The new calendar was introduced without difficulty, and the greater part of the regulations of the Tridentine council carried into full effect. But what was of most importance was the king's resolution to give the bishoprics in future to Roman catholics only.[2] Protestants had found their way even to these highest spiritual dignities; the nuncio was now permitted to call them before his judgment seat and to depose them; which was of the more importance, as the episcopal office carried with it a seat and a voice in the senate. This very political importance attached to the spiritual institute the nuncio endeavoured generally to put to good account. Above all things he urged the bishops to adopt united measures at the national diets; these he himself suggested to them, and with the most powerful among them, the archbishop of Gnesen and the bishop of Cracow, he formed a strict personal intimacy, particularly calculated to promote his views. And

[1] Spannocchi: Relatione all' Illmo Rev^{mo} Cardinal Rusticucci, segretario di N. S. Papa Sisto V., delle cose di Polonia intorno alla religione e delle azioni del cardinal Bolognetto in quattro anni ch'egli è stato nunzio in quella provincia.—[Report (rendered) to the Most Illustrious and Most Rev. Cardinal Rusticucci, secretary of our Holy Pope Sixtus V., of the affairs of Poland respecting religion and the proceedings of Cardinal Bolognetto during the four years that he has been nuncio in that province.]

[2] "Sendosi (il re) determinato che nessuno possa tenere chiese chi non sia della vera fede romana."—[(The king) being determined that none should hold churches who are not of the true Roman faith.]

thus he succeeded not only in imbuing the clergy themselves with fresh zeal, but already came to possess a great influence on secular affairs. The English began to agitate about a commercial treaty with Poland, which promised to be very advantageous, particularly for Dantzick; the nuncio was the sole cause of its miscarriage, chiefly because the English wanted to have an express engagement that they should be allowed to conduct business and live in the country, without being incommoded on account of their religion.[1]

Enough, moderate as King Stephen might be, yet under him Roman catholicism first really recovered the footing it had lost.

But this had all the more significancy, as the Zamoisky faction, the most powerful party in the country, and which, through the royal favour, enjoyed, generally speaking, the most important offices,[2] also assumed a Roman catholic complexion, and as it was this party that upon the death of Stephen turned the scale in the election contests. The Zamoiskys placed upon the throne that Swedish prince to whom Catherine Jagellonica[3] had given birth in prison, and who, from his earliest youth, whether from an original bias in his mind, or from his mother's influence,

[1] Spannocchi: "Il che non prima venne agli orecchj del Bolognetto, che andò a trovare S. M^ta^, e con efficacissime ragioni mostrò quanto esorbitante cosa sarebbe stata che avesse concesso per publico decreto una tanto obbrobriosa setta, e come non senza nascosto inganno e speranza d'importantissime conseguenze quella scellerata donna voleva che si dichiarasse cosi per decreto potersi esercitar la setta Anglicana in quel regno, dove tutto il mondo pur troppo sa che si permetta il credere in materia di religione quel che piace a chi si sia: con queste ed altre efficacissime ragioni il re Stefano rimase talmente persuaso che promesse non voler mai far menzione alcuna di religione in qualunque accordo avesse fatto con quella regina o suoi mercanti."—[Which no sooner came to Bolognetto's ears than he went to find his Majesty, and with the most efficacious reasons showed what an exorbitant thing it would be that he should grant by a public decree to so opprobrious a sect, and how not without some secret trick and hope of most important consequences, that wicked woman wished that there should be such a declaration by a decree to the effect that the Anglican sect might have leave to hold (religious) exercises in that kingdom, where all the world, however, knew it were too much for any one whomsoever to be allowed to believe in religious matters whatever he pleased: for which and other most efficacious reasons, King Stephen remained persuaded in such wise as to promise to make no mention whatever of religion in any agreement he had made with that queen or her merchants.]

[2] Spannocchi: "Alle dignità senatorie et all' entrate del regno dicono hoggi non ammettersi se non i dependenti da esso cancelliero, acciò che da nissuno venga impedito di far quello che ad esso ed al re più tornerà di piacere di fare."—[They say that at present none are admitted to senatorial dignities, and to the revenues of the kingdom, except those who depend on the chancellor, in order that no one may interpose hinderances to the doing of that which he and the king may most be pleased to have done.]

[3] The first of the Jagelons seems to have been Ladislas IV., grand duke of Lithuania, &c., who obtained the crown of Poland with Heduvige, daughter of the

or simply from the hope of being raised to the throne of Poland, or from all these causes together, had remained in the midst of a protestant country, immovably attached to the Roman catholic creed. This was Sigismund III., a prince whose disposition was entirely fashioned in conformity with the Roman catholic impulses, which were at that time agitating Europe.

Pope Clement VIII. says in one of his instructions, that while he was cardinal and legate in Poland, he had advised this prince to give all offices connected with the public service, for the future, to Roman catholics only. That advice had often been given before, by Paul IV., by Cardinal Hosius,[1] also by Bolognetto. But now for the first time there was a proper foundation on which to carry it into effect. Sigismund showed himself very soon resolved to adopt a course which neither Sigismund Augustus nor Stephen had pursued. In fact, he laid it down as a principle to promote none but Roman catholics, and Pope Clement was quite in the right when he ascribed the progress of Roman catholicism in Poland most of all to this measure.

The chief attribute of royal power in Poland consisted in the right of appointing to offices. The king had all spiritual and secular appointments, great and small, in his gift, and they were reckoned to amount to 20,000. But what an immense influence now must it have had when Sigismund III. began to fill not only all the ecclesiastical, but all offices in general, with Roman catholics only; when he conferred all the favour of the state, as the Italians once said, and the full rights of citizenship, in the higher meaning of that term, on his co-religionists alone. A man's promotion was all the surer the more he earned the favour of the bishops and Jesuits. The Starost Lewis of Mortangen was mainly indebted for the Pomerellian Waywodeship to his making a present of his house in Thorn to the society of Jesus.

duke of Hungary, and elected Queen of Poland, on condition of her marrying the person who should be chosen by the kingdom's grandees. Jagelon was chosen, and justified the choice by a brilliant reign of forty-eight years. He died at the age of eighty-four, in the year 1434, and was succeeded by his son Ladislas V. Tr.

[1] In a letter of 14th March, 1568, he begs the king, "nullis se deinceps vel honores vel præfecturas vel quæcunque tandem alia munera publice mandaturum nisi qui Christum aperte confessus fuerit, et omni perfidiæ sive Lutheristicæ sive Calvinisticæ sive anabaptistarum nuntium remiserit."—[that for the future he should publicly commit honours, or prefectures, or other offices whatsoever, to none but such as should have openly confessed Christ, and taken leave of all perfidy, whether Lutheran or Calvinistic or of the Anabaptists.]

Upon this, in the Polish-Prussian districts at least, an opposition grew up between the cities and the nobility, which assumed a religious colour. Both had originally embraced protestantism; but from that the nobles now apostatized. The examples of the Kostka, Dzialinsky, and Konopat, who owed their power to their apostasy, exercised a great influence on the rest. The schools of the Jesuits were attended chiefly by the young nobility; and we soon find the pupils of the Jesuits attacking the burgess youth in the cities that remained protestant. But, generally speaking, the new influences laid hold particularly of the nobility. The college at Pultusk had 400 pupils, all belonging to the nobility.[1] The impulse universally pervading the spirit of the age, the instruction of the Jesuits, the newly awakened zeal of the whole body of the clergy, and the favour of the court, all co-operated in determining the Polish nobility to return to Roman catholicism.

But it is evident that farther steps would immediately be taken, and that those who did not now apostatize, would be made to feel the disfavour of the government.

In Poland the Roman catholic clergy specially sought to revive their claim to the ecclesiastical buildings, which had been founded by persons of Roman catholic creed, with the co-operation of bishops, and particularly of the popes, as the inalienable property of the church. In all quarters where the Roman catholic service had been excluded from the parish churches, the bishops commenced suits at law resting on that plea. The law-courts were now filled with zealous Roman catholics; the same processes were commenced against one town after another, and the same judgments were pronounced; it was found of no avail to appeal to the king and to remind him of that agreement by which equal protection was promised to the two confessions. It was answered that equal protection consisted in this very thing, that each party should be assisted in obtaining its rights; that the agreement included no warranty of the ecclesiastical buildings.[2] The Roman catholics in the course of a few years took possession of all the parish churches in the towns: "in the parish churches," exclaimed the Pole, "the old God is worshipped,"

1 Maffei, II. p. 140.

2 The copious letter of the Waywode of Culm, translated by Lengnich, Polish-Prussian History, part IV., p. 291, specially particu arizes these motives.

in the smaller Prussian towns, the evangelical service durst be performed only in a room in the town-house, and of the larger ones, Dantzick alone preserved the parish church.[1]

But at this moment of successful progress, people did not confine themselves to contending with the protestants, they turned their attention also to the Greeks.

Here the king and the pope united their influences. In so far as I can discover, the threat of excluding the Greek bishops from their places, and from the right of voting in the senate, was particularly effective. Suffice it to say that Wladika of Wladimir, and some other Greek bishops, determined, in 1595, to join the Roman catholic church according to the Florentine council. Their deputies repaired to Rome; Roman and royal commissioners appeared in the province; the ceremony of reconciliation was completed; a Jesuit, the king's confessor, gave animation to the scene by preaching a fervid discourse; here too some churches were conceded to the Roman catholics.

This was an uncommon rise for so short a period. "Not long ago," says a papal nuncio, as early as in 1598, "it might have seemed as if heresy was completely to set aside Roman catholicism in Poland; now Roman catholicism is dragging heresy to the grave."

Now if it be asked to what mainly we are to ascribe this result, it was owing above all things to the king's personal sentiments. And these sentiments, in the peculiar position of the sovereign, immediately opened up still more extensive prospects.[2]

[1] See Lengnich: Nachricht von der Religions-änderung in Preussen, § 27.

[2] Among the countries "conterminous to Poland," the author might have included Hungary, which he afterwards briefly notices as part of Germany. What part the Jesuits acted in Hungary, Bohemia, and Moravia, within this period (1590 to 1617), may be learned from the edict of the states of Bohemia, 4th June, 1618—that of those of Bohemia, 6th May, 1619—that of those of Hungary, 19th June, 1619—all banishing them for ever "as public pests." From the last of these we may take the following quotation, in proof of the part they had in the suppression of protestantism in those countries: "The evangelical states of the kingdom of Hungary well remember that the Jesuits, from the time of their coming into Hungary in the reign of the Emperor Ferdinand, excited manifold troubles with their intrigues; yea, they are the more indignant, as it was by the advice and at the instance of the Jesuits that, in the times of Rodolph of most laudable memory, the Turkish war misgave, seeing the Romish bishop, of which the Hungarian states are well aware, very strongly admonished the Emperor Rodolph to make peace with the Turks, and to turn his forces against the heretics, who had been increasing during that Turkish war; which was done, and the Turkish war, that had lasted for sixteen years, was terminated, yet with not small contempt and indignation on the part of all Christendom, but most of the kingdom of Hungary, and with unspeakable loss to the country, many of whose powerful and distinguished families were

ATTEMPT ON SWEDEN.

SIGISMUND had now become king of Sweden, in consequence of the death of his father John in 1592.

It is true that he was neither unlimited in his authority as king, nor even without personal obligations. As early as in 1587, he had subscribed an assurance that he would alter nothing in the ceremonies of the church ; nay, that he would promote no one who was not a protestant; and even now he engaged anew to maintain the privileges alike of the clergy and the laity, to make a man's religion in no case a motive either of hatred or of love to him, and nowise to injure the national church. Not the less were the hopes of all the Roman catholics and the anxieties of all protestants instantly awakened.

The Roman catholics had now secured for themselves all that they had ever so eagerly desired, a king of their own faith in Sweden. Sigismund set out for his hereditary kingdom in July 1593, surrounded with a Roman catholic retinue, in which even the papal nuncio Malaspina failed not to take his place. His journey through the Prussian provinces, was signalized by the promotion of Romanism. In Dantzick, a papal commissioner, Bartholomew Powsinsky, overtook him, having come with a gift of 20,000 scudi, "a small contribution," as it runs in the written instructions given him, "towards the expense which the restoration of Roman catholicism might cost."

These instructions are very remarkable. They show us how unbounded were the hopes of that restoration entertained at Rome, and how absolute were the commands to that effect issued there.[1]

"Powsinsky," so it runs, "a faithful servant of His Holiness, and vassal of His Majesty, is sent to signify to the king the interest felt by the pope in the desirable events that have lately befallen him in his wife's confinement, in the happy result of the last diet, but, above all, in the extreme felicity that he has the

slain, and their property dissipated. - - But the said Jesuit sect, which owed its great and exorbitant progress particularly to the Emperor Matthias, not satisfied with that, insinuated itself into all political business, and penetrated all our most secret councils of the kingdom of Hungary, and made them all misgive by their intrigues with the government, by perverting the meaning of every thing. Yea, this Jesuitical sect have openly proclaimed in their preaching, that heretics should be destroyed and murdered, and dared to add other heavy threatenings tending to the subversion of this kingdom," &c. &c.—See Annales de la Société des soi-disans Jésuites, vol. II. pp. 650—659. TR.

[1] Instruttione al Sr Bartolommeo Powsinsky alla M^a del ro di Polonia e Suetia. (MS. Rom.)

prospect of experiencing in now having an opportunity of restoring catholicism in his native country." The pope did not neglect to suggest some hints for this enterprise.

"There is no doubt," says he, "that in God's special providence, several bishoprics, and among others, even the archi-episcopal see of Upsala, are now vacant.[1] Though the king may pause for a moment before removing the protestant bishops that are still in the country, yet he will without fail supply the vacant sees with Roman catholics. The commissioner has with him a list of Swedish Roman catholics who seem fitted for the purpose. The pope is convinced that these bishops will then think forthwith of procuring Roman catholic parish priests and schoolmasters. All that is required is to give them the possibility of doing so.

"Perhaps," he thinks, "a college of Jesuits might be at once erected in Stockholm. But should this not be the case, the king will certainly take along with him into Poland as many suitable young Swedes as he can find, and have them brought up at his court in the Roman catholic creed, with some of the most zealous bishops, or at the Polish Jesuit colleges."

Here, as in all other quarters, the first object was to recover the command of the clergy. Meanwhile the nuncio had conceived another. He thought of suggesting occasions for the Roman catholics who still remained in Sweden, to prefer complaints against the protestants. The king would then take a position above the two parties, and every innovation might come to have the authority of a judicial decision.[2] The only thing

[1] Intendendosi restar vacante l'arcivescovato di Upsalia, che la divina providenza, per più facilitare le cose del suo servitio, non ha permesso che in due anni sia stato proveduto dal re morto, haverà S. M[ta] particolare pensiere a pigliare un arcivescovo cattolico."—[Understanding that there remains vacant the archbishopric of Upsala, which the divine providence, the more to facilitate what serves to promote its own purposes, has not permitted to have been filled up by the deceased king, His Majesty will think particularly of taking a (Roman) catholic archbishop.]

[2] Ragguaglio dell' andata del re di Polonia in Suetia. (MS. Rom.) "Erano tuttavia nel regno alcune reliquie de' cattolici: et il nuncio seguendo la forma già tenuta da C[l] Madruzzo per fortificar l'autorità dell' imperatore, cercava di costituire il re giudice tra li cattolici e gli heretici di Suetia, inducendo quelli a querelarsi appresso il re dell' insolenza e delle ingiurie di questi."—[Account of the king of Poland's arrival in Sweden. (MS. Rom.) There were always within the kingdom some remains of catholics; and the nuncio, following the form already observed by Cardinal Madruzzo for the purpose of strengthening the authority of the emperor, endeavoured to constitute the king judge between the catholics and the heretics of Sweden, inducing the former to complain to the king of the insolence and the injuries of the latter.]

he had to lament was that Sigismund did not bring along with him a stronger armed force to give effect to his decisions.

Now there is no proof certainly that the king at once adopted the views of the Roman court. In so far as we can perceive from his own declarations, the utmost that he intended was only at first to procure some liberties for the Roman catholics without subverting the protestant constitution. But was he to prove capable of arresting the powerful religious impulse which governed those immediately around him, and whose representatives he took along with him? Can we suppose that he would stop at that point on his reaching it?

The protestants would not wait for this. The aims cherished on the one side, directly called forth, almost unconsciously, their antagonist aims on the other.

Just after the death of John, the Swedish councillors of state, men famous in history, both before that and since; Gyllenstern, Bielke, Baner, Sparre, and Oxenstern, united with the zealous protestant Duke Charles, brother of the deceased, uncle of the young king, and further, one of the sons of Gustavus Wasa, "to acknowledge him in his nephew's absence, as governor of the kingdom, and to promise him obedience in all that he might require to be done for the maintenance of the Augsburg confession in Sweden." In this spirit a council was held at Upsala in March 1593. There the Augsburg confession was proclaimed anew, King John's liturgy was condemned, and all things even in the earlier ritual, that seemed to recall the Roman catholic usages, were moderated; the exorcism was retained only in its milder expressions and for the sake of its moral significancy;[1] a declaration was drawn up that people would endure no sort of heresy whether papistic or Calvinistic.[2] Vacant appointments were now filled up in the same spirit. Many old defenders of

[1] For we must not believe Messenius when he says that it was abolished. The words Faar här uth, were only changed to Wick här ifra, and Duke Charles, who wanted it to be abolished, was opposed: "retinendum esse exorcismum tanquam liberam ceremoniam propter utilem commonefactionem ad auditorium et baptismi spectatores permanantem:"—[that the exorcism was to be retained as a free ceremony, on account of the useful admonition flowing from it to the auditory and lookers on at the baptism:] a view in which Duke Charles acquiesced. Baaz: Inventarium IV. X. 525. In Baaz we find the Acta (minutes) in general in tolerable completeness.

[2] "Concilium definit," it runs farther, "ne hæreticis advenientibus detur locus publice conveniendi."—[The council lays it down that a place for meeting in public should not be given to heretics arriving in the country.]

the liturgy now renounced it; yet this did not avail in the case of all of them, for some were dismissed nevertheless. The bishoprics, on the vacancy of which such magnificent projects had been founded at Rome, were bestowed on Lutherans; the archbishopric of Upsala on the most vehement opponent of the liturgy, M. Abraham Angermannus: by an overwhelming majority, for he had 243 and the next candidate only 38 votes, the clergy placed at their head the most zealous Lutheran they could find.

Under King John there had been maintained to the last a middle state of things, not so keenly opposed to the popedom as elsewhere, and it would have been easy for Sigismund to have modified it according to the wishes of the Roman catholics, but he had now been anticipated on the other side, and protestantism had obtained a firmer hold of the country than it had ever done before.

Nor on this occasion were Sigismund's royal prerogatives spared. Already he was no longer, properly speaking, altogether king, much rather was he regarded as a stranger with pretensions to the crown, as an apostate, who was to be viewed with suspicion, as one who threatened religion. The great majority of the nation, being all of one mind in their protestant convictions, attached themselves to Duke Charles.

The king on his arrival, was perfectly sensible of his isolated position. His hands were tied; he merely sought to stave off the demands that were made upon him.

But while he held his peace and waited, those antagonist principles which had never so directly confronted each other here, entered the lists. The evangelical preachers thundered against the papists; the Jesuit priests, who preached in the chapel-royal did not allow them to remain unanswered. The Roman catholics of the king's suite took possession of an evangelical church at a funeral; hereupon the protestants deemed it necessary to abstain for a time from the use of their desecrated sanctuary. Forthwith acts of violence commenced. The heiducks[1] used force in order to get possession of a chancel that had been shut up; the nuncio was charged with having had stones thrown from

[1] Sclavonian foot soldiers. Tr.

his house at some singing boys belonging to a choir; the embitterment was momentarily increasing.

At last the ceremony of the coronation called the court to Upsala. There the Swedes insisted before all things on the confirmation of the decrees of their council. The king resisted this. He desired only to have toleration for the Roman catholics; he would have been content, had he merely been allowed to entertain the prospect of its being granted at some future time. But these Swedish protestants were immovable. It was asserted that it had been said by the king's only sister that it was his nature to give way at last after a long and resolute resistance, and that she urged them on always to attack him anew.[1] They absolutely insisted that every where, alike in churches and in schools, the one only doctrine of the Augsburg confession should be promulgated.[2] They were headed by Duke Charles. The position which he assumed, gave him a degree of independence and of power such as he could never otherwise have hoped to possess. The personal footing on which he stood with the king, continually became one of greater unpleasantness and acrimony. The king, as has been said, was almost entirely without arms, whereas the duke collected some thousand men on his own estates round the city. At last the estates told the king at once, that they would not do him homage unless he acceded to their demands.[3]

1 The Ragguaglio (Account) calls her "ostinatissima eretica"—[a most obstinate heretic].

2 Messenius VII. 19. "Absolute urgebant ut confessio Augustana qualis sub ultimo Gustavi regimine et primi Johannis in patria viguisset, talis in posterum unica sola et ubique tam in ecclesiis quam in scholis perpetuo floreret."—[They absolutely insisted that the confession of Augsburg, such as it had flourished under the last reign of Gustavus and that of the first John in their country, should thus flourish for ever in time to come alone, sole and universal, both in churches and in schools.] This strict exclusion of popery is hardly to be wondered at when we consider, setting aside all reference to the theological dogmas of that system, that it had caused the deaths of so many hundreds of thousands of innocent protestants in the course of the preceding century, and thought it no crime to engage crowned heads in the foulest perjuries to their subjects. The strictest exclusion of every other form of protestantism but the Augsburg confession, must be referred to the dread of giving scope for the eccentricities of fanatics, but still more, we fear, to that hatred of Calvinism, and exaltation of Lutheran doctrine almost above Scripture, which has all along so weakened the cause of truth. Tr.

3 Supplicatio ordinum: "Quodsi cl. rex denegaverit subditis regiam approbationem horum postulatorum, inhibent nostri fratres domi remanentes publicum homagium esse S. R. M. præstandum."—[The supplication of the orders. But if the most illustrious king shall have refused to his subjects the royal approbation of these demands, our brethren remaining at home forbid that public homage should be rendered to his royal majesty.]

The poor prince found himself in a painful predicament. To accede to what was wanted from him aggrieved his conscience, while to refuse it deprived him of a crown.

In this pressure, he first inquired of the nuncio whether he might not yield, but Malaspina could not be prevailed upon to give his approval.

Upon this the king addressed himself to the Jesuits among his attendants, and these took upon themselves to do what the nuncio durst not venture upon. They declared that, in consideration of the necessity and the manifest jeopardy in which the king was placed, he could concede their demands to the heretics without offending God. The king was not satisfied until he had this decision written out actually in his hands.

Then, only, did he agree to the demands of his subjects. He sanctioned the decrees of Upsala and the exclusive use of the unaltered confession of Augsburg, without the admixture of any foreign doctrine in church or school, and without any person whomsoever being settled in a place who should not be ready to defend the same.[1] He acknowledged the prelates who had obtained their places in opposition to his will.

But could his Roman catholic heart find peace in all this? Could his suite, with their Roman catholic views, be satisfied with a result which they could not but altogether condemn? This of itself was not to be expected.

Steps in fact were taken for having a protest, such as has been adopted in like cases elsewhere.

"The nuncio," it runs in the report which was transmitted to Rome on this affair, and in the words of which I certainly can best elucidate the facts of the case, "was zealously bent on remedying the irregularity that had occurred. He succeeded in having a protest drawn up in writing by the king for the security of his conscience, in which he declared that he had conceded what he had conceded, not of his own will, but solely under the

[1] Yet these words are so conceived as to leave a loophole to escape by. "Ad officia publica nulli promovebuntur in patria qui religionem evangelicam nolunt salvam, quin potius qui eam serio defendere volunt publicis officiis præficiantur."—[None shall be promoted to public offices in our country who do not wish well to the evangelical religion; but, on the contrary, let those rather be placed over public offices who seriously wish to defend it.] Generalis confirmatio postulatorum regis Sigismundi—[King Sigismund's general confirmation of things demanded], in Baaz, p. 537.

force of compulsion. The nuncio further prevailed upon the king to make corresponding concessions to the Roman catholics, so as in Sweden as well as Poland, to be under engagements to both sides, and as was also the case with the German emperor. This the king was content to do."[1]

Rare expedient! Nor was a protest thought enough. In order to get rid in some measure of an obligation which had been undertaken with the sanction of an oath, an oath to the opposite effect was given to the other party: accordingly, obligations were come under to both, and both, when necessity called for it, were to have equal justice done to them.

The Swedes were amazed that the king, after such solemn promises, should immediately confer on the Roman catholics little-dissembled patronage. It might doubtless be traced to that secret engagement. "Even before his departure," our informant goes on to say, with evident satisfaction, "the king conferred offices and dignities on persons of the Roman catholic

1 Relatione dello stato spirituale e politico del regno di Suezia, 1598. "Mandò alcuni senatori Polacchi a darle parte dello stato delle cose in le sue circostanze e conseguenze, e detti patri dichiararono che presupposto la necessità e pericolo nel quale era costituita la M^ta^ S. la potesse senza offender dio concedere alli heretici ciò che ricercavano, e la M^ta^ S. per sua giustificazione ne volle uno scritto da detti patri. - - Hora fatta la coronatione e concessione pose ogni studio il nunzio per applicare qualche remedio al disordine seguito, onde operò per sicurezza della coscienza di S. M^ta^ ch'ella facesse una protesta in scritto, come ella non con la volontà sua ma per pura forza si era indotto a concedere ciò che haveva concesso; e persuase al s^mo^ re che concedesse da parte agli cattolici altrettanto quanto haveva conceduto alli heretici, di modo che a guisa dell'imperatore e del re di Polonia restasse la M^ta^ S. giurata utrique parti. S. M^ta^ si contentò di farlo, et immediatamente mise in esecuzione le dette concessioni: perché avanti la sua partenza diede ufficj e dignità a cattolici, e lasciò in quattro luoghi l'esercitio della religione e fece giurare a quattro governatori, se ben erano heretici, quali lasciò nel regno, che haverebbero protetto la religione e li cattolici.—[Account of the spiritual and political state of the kingdom of Sweden, 1598. He sent to some Polish senators to give him information on the state of affairs in their circumstances and consequences, and the said fathers declared, that assuming the necessity and danger in which his Majesty was placed, he could, without offending God, concede to the heretics what they required, and his Majesty, for his own satisfaction, wished to have a writing from the said fathers. - - Now the coronation and concession having taken place, the nuncio exerted every effort to apply some remedy to the disorder that followed; hence he succeeded in effecting, for the security of his Majesty's conscience, that he should make a protest in writing, that he had not of his own will, but by pure compulsion, been led to concede what he had conceded, and persuaded the most serene king that he should concede on the part of the catholics as much as he had conceded to the heretics, in such wise that, after the fashion of the emperor and the king of Poland, his Majesty should remain sworn *utrique parti* (to both sides). This his Majesty was content to do, and immediately put the said concessions into execution. Accordingly, before his departure, he gave offices and dignities to Roman catholics, and permitted in four places the exercise of that religion, and made four governors, although heretics, whom he left in the kingdom, swear that they would protect religion and the catholics.]

creed. Four stadtholders, albeit they were heretics, he laid under an oath to protect the Roman catholics and their religion. In four different quarters he introduced the use of the Roman catholic worship."

These measures, although they might possibly still the unquiet conscience of a bigot prince, could only exert a mischievous influence on the general course of things.

For it was just owing to this that the Swedish estates, thus kept in constant agitation, threw themselves the more decidedly into opposition.

The clergy reformed their schools on strict Lutheran principles, and appointed a special thanksgiving for the preservation of the true religion against the designs and artifices of the Jesuits; in 1595 a decree was drawn up at the national diet of Südercöping, that all exercise of the Roman catholic ritual where the king might have introduced it, should again be abolished. "We are unanimously of opinion," said the Estates, "that all sectaries that are opposed to the evangelical religion, and that have settled themselves in the country, should within six weeks be removed entirely out of the kingdom;"[1] and these decrees were most strictly carried into effect. The monastery of Wadstena, which had stood for 211 years, and had always kept its place amid so many commotions, was now broken up and destroyed. Angermannus held an ecclesiastical visitation such as had never had its equal. Whoever neglected the evangelical worship was scourged with rods: the archbishop took along with him some strong schoolboys, who carried the punishment into effect under his superintendence:[2] the altars of the saints were pulled down, their relics scattered about, the ceremonies which had in 1593 been declared indifferent, were in 1597 in many places abolished.

The relation between Sigismund and Charles now gave this movement a personal aspect.

Every thing that was done ran counter to the well-known wishes and to the ordinances of the king; in every thing Duke Charles had a preponderating influence. The duke convened

[1] Acta ecclesiæ in conventu Sudercop—[Acts of the church in the Assembly at Südercöping], in Baaz, 567.

[2] While the discipline exercised by the papists on those whom they held to be heretics was barbarous and horrible, this of a Lutheran bishop towards nonconformists can hardly be deemed worse than ludicrous.—Tr.

the diet, contrary to Sigismund's express command; every interference of the latter in the country's affairs, the former endeavoured to set aside; he caused a decree to be drawn up, in virtue of which the king's rescripts should have no force until they had first been confirmed by the Swedish government.[1]

This at once made Charles monarch and master of the country, and forthwith he began to be agitated with the thought of becoming so in name likewise. Among other things, a dream which he had in 1595 suggested this. He dreamt that at an entertainment in Finnland a covered double dish was presented to him; he removed the cover; in the one compartment there were the ensigns of royalty, in the other a dead man's head. Similar thoughts agitated the nation. It was reported through the country that a crowned eagle had been seen at Linköping fighting with an uncrowned one, and that the latter had remained master of the field.

But when matters had advanced thus far, while Protestant principles were enforced with so much severity, and their abettors seemed to raise a claim to the royal power, there was a party striving nevertheless in favour of the king. Some of the grandees who endeavoured to find in his authority a support in opposing the duke, were banished; their adherents remained within the country; the common people were discontented at the abolition of all the ceremonies, and ascribed national disasters to that neglect; in Finnland the stadtholder, Flemming, maintained the royal authority in all its integrity.

This was a state of things which made it on the one hand necessary, and on the other advisable for King Sigismund once more to try his fortunes. It was probably the last moment at which it was possible for him to restore his authority. In the summer of 1598 he set out the second time to take possession of his hereditary kingdom.

He was now, if possible, a still stricter Roman catholic than before. The simple, bigoted prince was persuaded that the

[1] Ausa illustrissimi principis domini Caroli Sudermanniæ ducis adversus serenissimum et potentissimum dominum Sigismundum III. regem Succiæ et Poloniæ suscepta, scripta et publicata ex mandato S. R. Majestatis proprio. Dant. 1598.—[Attempts of the most illustrious prince, Lord Charles, duke of Sudermannia, made against the most serene and potent lord Sigismund III., king of Sweden and Poland, written and published at the express command of his royal Majesty. Dantzick, 1598.]

misfortunes of various kinds that he had met with since his first journey, among others, the death of his wife, had been sent to him on account of the concessions he had then made to the heretics, and with profound sorrow of heart he revealed this painful reflection to the nuncio. He declared that he would rather die than make any concession anew that might stain the purity of his conscience.

But in this an European interest was at the same time involved. Roman catholicism was now making such progress as to regard even an enterprise in so remote a corner of Europe, chiefly in its bearings on a general combination.

Already had the Spaniards, in their struggle with England, cast their eyes at times on the Swedish coasts; they considered that the possession of a Swedish harbour would be of the utmost use to them, and they opened negotiations to that effect. And now no doubts were entertained that Sigismund, on his once making himself master of his own country, would cede to them Elfsborg in West Gothland. There it would be easy to build and maintain a fleet, and have it manned by Poles and Swedes. How very different would it be to make war upon England from such a place than from Spain. Soon they might forget attacking India. Even for the maintenance of the king's authority in Sweden, a league with the catholic king could not be other than advantageous.[1]

But more than this. The Roman catholics took into consideration that they would obtain the ascendancy in Finnland and the Baltic. From Finnland they hoped to make a successful attack on Russia, and by means of their possession of the Baltic, to be able to bring the dukedom of Prussia into their power. The electoral house of Brandenburg had as yet been unable, by any negotiations, to obtain the investiture of it; the nuncio assures us that the king was resolved not to grant it, but to make the dukedom revert to the crown: he tried to strengthen himself there to the best of his power, chiefly, as may be supposed,

[1] Relatione dello stato spirituale e politico. The project was: "che a spese del cattolico si mantenga un presidio nella fortezza che guardi il porto, sopra la quale niuna superiorità habbia il cattolico, ma consegni lo stipendio per esso presidio al re di Polonia.—[that at the expense of the catholic (king) a garrison should be maintained in the fortress to protect the harbour, beyond which the catholic (king) should have no superiority, but should consign the pay for the said garrison to the king of Poland.]

from religious considerations: for never would Brandenburg consent to the restoration of Roman catholicism in Prussia.[1]

If we consider the extent of the prospects that were attached to the king's success, which was not so very unlikely, and the general importance of the result which on either hand awaited the Swedish kingdom, were protestantism to prove victorious, we shall recognise in this a crisis in the general history of the world.

Zamoisky had advised the king to burst in at the head of a powerful army, so as to conquer Sweden by force of arms. King Sigismund, on the contrary, maintained that this was unnecessary; he would not believe that he would be opposed with force in his own hereditary dominions. Meanwhile he had about 5,000 men with him; with these he landed unopposed at Calmar, and from that began to move against Stockholm. There another division of his troops had arrived and been admitted, while a Finnish force marched against Upland.

Meanwhile Duke Charles also had been preparing for hostilities. It would evidently have been all over with his power and with the ascendancy of protestantism, had the king carried the day. While the duke's Upland peasantry repelled the Finns, he himself, with a regular military force, intercepted the king on his march at Stegeborg. He demanded the withdrawal of the royal army, and the reference of the decision to a national diet: in which case he also would disband his people. The king would not agree to this, whereupon the hostile forces rushed into action.

Few in number; insignificant masses; each consisting of but a few thousand men: but the decision that followed was no less important in its results than if it had been brought about by large armies.

Yet all depended on the personal qualities of the princes. Charles, his own counsellor, daring, resolute, a man; and, which

[1] Relatione di Polonia 1598. "Atteso che se rimarrà il ducato nelli Brandeburgesi non si può aspettare d'introdurre la religione cattolica, si mostra S. M[a] risoluto di voler ricuperare il detto ducato."—[Marking that were the dukedom to remain with the Brandenburgs, the introduction of the catholic religion could not be looked for, his Majesty showed himself resolved in his intention of recovering the said dukedom.] This is what King Stephen was ere now to have done. "Ma ritrovandosi con penuria di danari mentre era occupato nelle guerre, ne fu sovvenuto delli Brandeburgesi."—[But being in want of money while engaged in wars, Brandenburg was forgotten.]

was the great matter, in actual possession: Sigismund, dependent on others, weak, good-natured, no soldier; and now reduced to the unhappy necessity of having to conquer the kingdom that belonged to him; lawful heir, it is true, but engaged in a contest with the subsisting order of things.

The troops twice encountered each other at Stangebro. The first time it was rather accidentally than intentionally; the king had the advantage, and he even wanted to stay the slaughter of the Swedes. But the second time, when the Dalecarnians had risen in favour of the duke, and his fleet had arrived, the latter had the superiority: no one stayed the slaughter of the Poles; Sigismund suffered a total defeat, and had to consent to all that was required of him.[1]

He was even brought to such a pass as to deliver up the only faithful subjects he had found, that they might be brought before a Swedish tribunal. He himself promised to submit to the decision of the diet.

This, however, was a mere shift by which to escape from the embarrassments of the moment. Instead of going to the diet, where he could have appeared only in the piteous plight of the vanquished, he took advantage of the first favourable wind to re-embark for Dantzick.

He flattered himself, indeed, with the hope of still obtaining the mastery in his own hereditary kingdom some other time, and at a more fortunate moment: but in point of fact, by thus withdrawing, he abandoned it to itself, and to the overwhelming influence of his uncle, who felt no hesitation, after some delay, to assume the title, as well as the authority, of king; and after that, instead of losing time in Sweden in waiting for war, he carried it into the Polish territories, where it was conducted under various fortunes

VIEWS UPON RUSSIA.

In a short time, however, it seemed as if the miscarriage of this attempt would be compensated by another successful result.

It is well known how often the popes had before this formed

[1] Piasecii Chronicon gestorum in Europa singularium, p. 159. Extracts from the letters of the princes in Geijer: Schwedische Geschichte, II. p. 305.

hopes of gaining Russia,—already had Adrian VI. and Clement VII. done so; then the Jesuit Possevin tried what success he could have with Ivan Wassiljowitsch. Further, in 1594, Clement VIII. sent a certain Comuleo to Moscow, with more than wonted confidence, since he knew the language. But all these attempts went for nothing; still Boris Godunow declared explicitly that "Moscow was now the true orthodox Rome;" he caused himself to be prayed for as "the only Christian sovereign on earth."

So much the more welcome, under these circumstances, was the prospect which presented itself in the most unexpected manner, on the appearance of the false Demetrius.[1]

Demetrius attached himself almost still more to the ecclesiastical than he did to the political interests of Poland.

It was a Roman catholic confessor to whom he first discovered himself. Jesuit fathers were sent to examine him; then the papal nuncio Rangoni took up his cause. The latter declared to him at their first interview, that he had nothing to hope unless he abjured the schismatic religion and adopted the Roman catholic. Demetrius, without much ado, signified his willingness to comply; it was what he had engaged to do already: and

[1] Demetrius Griska Utropoja, a Russian monk, during the reign of Boris, pretended to be prince Demetrius, son of John Basilovitz, and brother of Feodore, the predecessor of Boris. His history presents one of the most singular instances of successful imposture on record, though, perhaps, he ought to be regarded rather as a tool of the papacy, than as acting on his own account. Having left his monastery, he went into Lithuania, and engaged in the service of a nobleman there, who one day happened to maltreat him. On this Griska began to cry, and told his master, that, did he know his birth, he would not treat him so. He then told him that he was the son of the grand duke John; that Boris Godunow had meant to assassinate him, but that he had escaped, while that misfortune had overtaken another boy, whom his friends had put in his place. So artfully did he proceed, that his master took up his case and sent him to the Waywode of Sandomir, who promised him an armed force, sufficient to place him on the throne, *provided he would permit the exercise of the Roman religion in Muscovy.* Finally, he succeeded in displacing Boris, and gained over the mother of the real Demetrius, who, though well aware that her son had been killed, found it her interest to dissemble, besides that she took this opportunity of being revenged on Boris. But the suspicions of the Muscovites being aroused by the impostor's favouritism of strangers and of the Romish religion, they attacked him soon after his marriage with a Romish princess, the daughter of the Waywode of Sandomir. The mother of the real Demetrius having discovered the imposture, Griska was shot, and his body subjected to the grossest insults. Such is an abstract of the account in the supplemental volume to Moreri's *Dictionnaire Historique,* but from a review of all the circumstances, and particularly from the poor runaway monk having been able to gain credit for the tale he told the nobleman, by showing him a cross of gold, ornamented with jewels, as having been given him at his baptism, it seems evident that he was a mere tool of the Roman catholics from the first.—Tr.

his formal change of faith took place the following Sunday.[1] He was in ecstasy on finding that King Sigismund thereupon acknowledged him: he rightly ascribed it to the intercession of the nuncio, and to him he promised to do all in his power for the diffusion and the defence of the Romish faith.[2]

A promise this which turned out forthwith to be of great importance. Yet people in Poland were not quite sure of giving him credit. How astonished were they when, soon after this, the poor miserable refugee entered the palace of the Czars! The sudden death of his predecessor, which the people viewed as a judgment from God, may probably have contributed to this.

And here Demetrius now renewed his engagement. He received into his house the nuncio's nephew with every demonstration of honour; and as his Polish wife soon arrived, accompanied by a numerous court, not only of knights and ladies, but particularly of monks—Dominicans, Franciscans, and Jesuits,[3]—he seemed to lose no time in keeping his word.

But this was the very thing that most ensured his ruin. What obtained him the support of the Poles, withdrew from him the inclinations of the Russians. They said he did not eat or bathe like them; he did not honour the saints; he was a heathen, and had conducted an unbaptized heathen wife to the throne of Moskwa: it was impossible that he could be a son of the Czars.[4]

In consequence of an inexplicable conviction had they acknowledged him; another conviction, which overcame them with still stronger force, induced them to precipitate him again from his elevation.

But here, too, the real moving principle was religion. In Russia, as well as Sweden, there arose a power which, in accord-

[1] Alessandro Cilli: Historia di Moscovia, p. 11. Cilli was present at the act. In Karamsin, X. 109 of the translation, there is a place to be found which is not so closely from Cilli as appears to be the case. Karamsin did not understand Cilli. Not a word of what Karamsin has put into the mouth of Demetrius, is to be found in Cilli.

[2] Cilli: "Con rinnovare insieme la promessa dell' augumento e difesa per quanto havessero potuto le sue forze e nel suo imperio e fuori di quello della santa fede cattolica."—[With the renewal likewise of the promise of the augmentation and defence of the holy catholic faith to the utmost of his ability, both within his dominion and beyond it.]

[3] Cilli, p. 66.

[4] Müller, Sammlung Russischer Geschichte, V. 373, remarks that papers of the pope's writing were found on him.

ance with the source from which it sprang, was opposed to the tendencies of Roman Catholicism.

INTERNAL COMMOTIONS IN POLAND.

WHEN enterprises undertaken against an external enemy miscarry, they ordinarily have the effect of awakening internal dissensions. There now arose in Poland a movement which rendered it doubtful how far the king could reign any longer in the manner in which he had commenced. It had the following causes.

King Sigismund did not always maintain a good understanding with those to whose endeavours he was obliged for having obtained the crown. These had called him to that dignity in opposition to Austria: he, on the contrary, closely attached himself to that power. Twice did he choose a wife for himself from the family line of Gratz: and once he fell under the suspicion of intending to transfer the crown to that house.

Already was the high chancellor Zamoisky discontented on this account. But what still further exasperated him was, that the king, for the very purpose of rendering himself independent of those who had promoted him, had not seldom raised their opponents to important offices, and admitted them to the senate.[1]

For it was chiefly with the senate that Sigismund III. sought to reign. He filled it with men who were personally devoted to him ; he made it likewise purely Roman catholic; the bishops, appointed by the king under the influence of the nuncio, formed there a powerful, and what, indeed, gradually became the ruling party.

But, owing to these very circumstances, there appeared in behalf of the Polish constitution and the religious interests of the country, an extremely important and twofold opposition.

The provincial deputies set themselves in opposition to the

[1] Cilli, Historia delle sollevatione di Polonia 1606-1608, Pistoia 1627,—an author who is so much the more trust-worthy, from his having been long in the service of the king,—mentions at the commencement how powerful Zamoisky was: "Zamoschi si voleva alquanto della regia autorità usurpare :"—[Zamoisky wanted to usurp so much of the royal authority :]—but how the king opposed him, "essendo patrone S. M^{ta} non solo di conferire le dignite del regno, ma anco le stesse entrate." [His Majesty being patron, not only in conferring the dignities of the kingdom, but further, its very revenues.]

senate as a political body. As the latter attached itself to the king, so did the others to Zamoisky,[1] to whom they paid unbounded respect, and who derived from their subserviency an authority almost equal to that of the king. This was a position which must have had an immense charm for an enterprising magnate. After the high chancellor's death, his place was seized upon by the palatine of Cracow, Zebrzydowski.

To this party the Protestants now attached themselves. At last, however, it was the bishops against whom both preferred their complaints, the former because of their secular, the latter because of their spiritual influence. The protestants made it a grievance that in a commonwealth such as that of Poland, based on free accord, well-earned privileges were daily weakened, common people raised to high offices, and that it was meant that men of good nobility should be placed under these. In these complaints they were joined by many Roman catholics.[2]

There can be no question that this religious element imparted a special impulse to the political movement.

After the grievances complained of had often been represented, the subsidies refused, and the diets of the kingdom dissolved,—all to no purpose—the discontented had recourse at last to extreme measures, and summoned the whole of the nobility to the rokoss. Rokoss was a legal form of insurrection: the nobility, on being convened, claimed the right of bringing the king and the senate before them to be tried. At this convention the evangelicals were of so much the more consequence, as they coalesced with the members of the Greek communion.

Meanwhile the king too had his adherents. The nuncio kept the bishops together:[3] the bishops gave the senate the direction it was to follow: a covenant was concluded for the defence of the king and religion: clever advantage was taken of the favourable moment for reviving the old misunderstandings between the

[1] Piasecius: "Zamoyscius, cujus autoritate potissimum nitebatur ordo nunciorum."—[Zamoisky, on whose authority mainly leant the order of the deputies.] From that time forward the provincial deputies were powerful. One part supported the other.

[2] Cilli: "Gli eretici, spalleggiati da cattivi cattolici, facevano gran forza per ottenere la confederatione."—[The heretics, supported by bad catholics, made great efforts to obtain the confederation.]

[3] Cilli: "Il nuntio Rangone con sua destrezza e diligenza tenne e conservò in fede molti di principali."—[The nuncio Rangone, with his skill and diligence, held and preserved many of the chiefs in allegiance.]

laity and the clergy. The king showed himself immovable in the moment of danger: (he thought) he had a just cause and trusted in God.

In fact he maintained the upper hand. In October 1606, he dispersed the rokoss just as a considerable number of the members had gone away. In July 1607, matters came to an open breach. Under the cry Jesu Maria, the royal troops attacked the enemy and defeated him. For some time longer Zebrzydowski kept the field, but in 1608 he was compelled to submit: a general amnesty was proclaimed.

And by this means it happened that the civil government could now follow out still farther the Roman catholic direction which it had once entered on.

Those who were not Roman catholics remained excluded from public offices, and in Rome people proceeded to extol the effect thereby produced.[1] "A protestant prince—a prince who did no more than bestow offices of dignity on both parties in equal shares—would fill the whole land with heresies: private interest is sure to govern mankind. To his own steadfastness the king owes compliance with his will on the part of the nobility."

In the royal cities, too, restraints were laid on the protestant worship: "without open violence," says a papal body of instructions, "the inhabitants are compelled to conversion."[2]

Upon this the nuncio saw to it that the supreme courts should be filled on the principles of the Roman catholic church, and that they should proceed "according to the words of the holy canon-

[1] Instruttione a V. S[ria] M[re] di Torres: "Il re, benchè nato di patre e fra popoli eretici, è tanto pio e tanto divoto e di santi costumi guernito, che dentro a Roma non avrebbe potuto nascere o allevarsene un migliore, imperocchè havendo esso con la longhezza del regnare mutati i senatori eretici, che se tre ne togli erano tutti, gli ha fatto divenire, levatine due o tre, tutti quanti cattolici."—[The king, although from a father and people that were heretics, is so very pious and devout, and so adorned with holy habits, that within Rome there could not have been born or brought up a better, inasmuch as he, having in the course of his reign changed the heretical senators, which, with the exception of three, they all were, he made them become, by raising two or three (to that dignity), all so many catholics.] Their maxim was: "le cose spirituali seguono il corso delle temporali"—[spiritual things follow the course of temporal].

[2] Instruttione a Mr Lancellotti: "La conforti (den Koenig) grandemente a vietare che nelle citte regie che da lei dipendono altro esercitio di religione che il cattolico si comporti, nè permetta che v'abbiano tempj nè sinagoge loro: poiché si vengono per tal dolce modo senza violenza espressa a far convertire o a mutar paese."—[Advise the king strongly to avoid, in the royal cities that depend on him, that there should be allowed any religious exercise but the catholic, or that they should be allowed to have their temples or synagogues: since it is by such mild measures, without express violence, that conversions come to be made or countries changed.]

ical statutes." Mixed marriages were then of particular importance. The highest court of law would admit the validity of none that were not solemnized before the parish priest and some witnesses; but the priests refused to give the benediction to mixed marriages; no wonder if very many submitted to the Roman catholic ritual on this very account, that their children might not be placed in a disadvantageous position. Others were influenced by the possession of church patronages by protestants being disputed. The state possesses a thousand methods of promoting a body of opinions to which it is favourable; here these were all carried as far as they possibly could without actual violence; though little remarked, the change of religion unceasingly went forward.

There is no doubt, too, that this was partly to be attributed to the earnestness and effectiveness with which the nuncios administered ecclesiastical affairs. They were particularly careful that the episcopal sees should be filled with men peculiarly fitted for the office; they visited the monasteries; and did not permit, what had begun to be done, that refractory and turbulent members, whom people elsewhere wished to dismiss, should be sent into Poland; nor did the parish priests escape their attention; they made efforts to introduce psalmody and the instruction of children. They pressed for the establishment of diocesan seminaries.

The Jesuits, in particular, now laboured among them. We find them actively exerting themselves in all the provinces; among the tractable people of Livonia; in Lithuania where they had to combat the remains of the ancient worship of the serpent; among the Greeks where the Jesuits often were the only Roman catholic priests; baptism had sometimes to be given to neophytes of eighteen; they met with very old men who had never received the sacrament; but particularly in Poland proper, where, as a member of the company boasts, "hundreds of learned, orthodox, to-God-devoted men, belonging to the order, are busied by means of schools and religious associations, by word and penning, in extirpating errors and in planting Roman catholic piety."[1]

Here, too, the wonted enthusiasm was aroused in those who

[1] Argentus de rebus societatis Jesu in regno Poloniæ 1615—[Argentus on the affairs of the society of Jesus in Poland 1615]: yet it might have given much more information.

attached themselves to them; but it was combined most unfortunately with the insolence of an overbearing young nobility. The king avoided acts of violence properly speaking; these the pupils of the Jesuits held themselves authorized to commit.

Not seldom did they observe the festival of Ascension day, by raising a storm against the evangelicals, bursting into their houses, plundering and wasting their property; woe to him who was caught or who was even only met upon the street.

As early as in 1606, did the church, and in 1607 the churchyard of the evangelicals in Cracow, become the objects of a furious attack; the bodies of the dead were flung out of the graves; in 1604 the churches of the protestants in Wilna were destroyed, and their priests (ministers) maltreated or put to death; in 1615 there appeared a book at Posen which maintained that the evangelicals had no right to reside in that town; in the year following, the pupils of the Jesuits destroyed the Bohemian church, so that not one stone was left upon another; the Lutheran church was burned. The same things were done in many other quarters; protestants here and there were compelled by constant attacks to alienate their churches. Soon people would no longer be satisfied with attacking the protestants in the towns; the Cracow students burned down the neighbouring churches in the country. In Podlachia an old evangelical preacher of the name of Barkow, was pacing on, aided by his staff, in front of his carriage, when a Polish nobleman who was coming from the opposite direction, ordered his coachman to drive the horses right against him; before the old man could get out of the way he was ridden over and died of his wounds.[1]

But notwithstanding all this, protestantism could not be suppressed. The king was bound by a promise which he had not the power to recall. The barons remained, in so far as themselves were concerned, subject to no restraint, and all of them did not forthwith change their religion. A favourable decision amongst many that were unfavourable, was sometimes pronounced in the courts of law, and one or other church was restored. In the towns of Polish Prussia the protestants still remained the majority. Much less still were the Greeks to be

[1] Wengerscii Slavonia reformata, p. 224, 232, 236, 244, 247.—[Wengerscius's reformed Slavonia, p. 224, &c.]

put aside; the coalition of 1595 had excited disgust rather than imitation. The party of the dissenters, composed both of protestants and Greeks, grew into greater and greater consequence; the towns that had most traffic, the most martial populations, such as the Cossacks, gave a peculiar effect to their demands. This opposition was so much the more powerful, as it daily found a stronger stay in neighbours whom it had been found impossible to subdue, Russia and Sweden.

FARTHER PROGRESS OF THE COUNTER-REFORMATION IN GERMANY.

QUITE other principles were cherished in Germany. There each prince considered that he was fully authorized to regulate religion in his territories according to his own personal principles.

Accordingly the movement that had commenced carried its waves farther onward, without much interference on the part of the imperial government, and without exciting much attention.

The spiritual princes especially considered it a duty to lead back their territories to Roman catholicism.

Already did the pupils of the Jesuits appear among them. John Adam von Bicken, electoral prince of Maintz, from 1601 to 1604, had been reared in the collegium Germanicum at Rome. In the castle of Königstein he once heard the psalmody with which the Lutherans of that time accompanied the remains of their pastors to interment. "May you then," he exclaimed, "honourably consign your synagogue to the grave." The next Sunday a Jesuit mounted the pulpit, and never was it given to a Lutheran preacher again. Thus too did matters proceed in other places.[1] What Bicken had left incomplete, his successor John Schweikard, zealously carried on. He was a man that loved the pleasures of the table, but who withal possessed self-command and displayed uncommon talent. He succeeded in accomplishing the counter-reformation throughout his whole see, and even on the Eichsfelde. He sent a commission to Heiligenstadt, which, within two years, brought back to Roman catholicism two hundred citizens, among whom there were many who had grown gray in the protestant faith. A few there still remained; these he personally admonished "as their father and

[1] Serarius: Res Moguntinæ, p. 973.

pastor," as he said, "from feelings of deep and genuine affection," and prevailed on them too, to come over. He now beheld with no ordinary feelings of satisfaction, a city again Roman catholic, which forty years before had been fully protestant.[1]

And now, too, a like course was pursued by Ernest and Ferdinand of Cologne, both Bavarian princes; and by the electoral prince Lotharius who belonged to the family of Metternich of Treves, a distinguished prince, of an acute intellect, possessing the talent of surmounting the difficulties that lay in his way, prompt in executing justice, vigilant in promoting the interests at once of his country and his family; moreover he was affable and not over severe where religion was not concerned, he tolerated no protestants at his court.[2] To these great names Neithard von Thüngen, bishop of Bamberg, attached himself. On taking possession of his capital, he found that the entire council, with the exception of two members, was protestant. He had given his support before this to Bishop Julius of Würzburg, and now resolved to apply the measures adopted by that prelate to Bamberg. He immediately published his Reformation's-edict for Christmas 1595; it leaves no alternative but that of attending the sacrament of the Supper according to the Roman catholic ritual, or expatriation; and although chapter, nobility and peasantry spoke against him, and the most urgent representations were sent in from the neighbourhood, yet during all the following years in succession, we find the reformations-orders renewed and upon the whole executed.[3] The Bamberger found a rival in Lower Germany, in Theodore von Fürstenberg at Paderborn. In the year 1596 he put all the priests who gave the elements in both kinds at the Supper, into prison. This naturally produced dissension betwixt his nobility and him, and we find the bishop and nobles mutually driving off each other's cattle and horses. Even as respected the town he ended at last by coming to an open feud with it. Unfortunately there appeared there a violent demagogue, who proved notwithstanding unequal to the important position into which he had thrust him-

1 Wolf: Geschichte von Heiligenstadt S. 63. From 1581 to 1601 there were counted up 497 converts, the most were in 1598, when they amounted to 73.

2 Masenius: Continuatio Broweri, p. 474.

3 Jäck: Geschichte von Bamberg, for example III. 212, 199; but fundamentally everywhere, for this history is mainly occupied with the anti-reformation.

self. In 1604 Paderborn was coerced into a renewal of its allegiance. Thereupon the Jesuit college was most splendidly endowed; and in a short time here, too, there went forth an edict that left no choice but the mass or banishment. How entirely Roman catholic do we see Bamberg and Paderborn gradually become.[1]

This rapid and withal so effectual a revolution, brought about in all these countries, must ever be accounted in the highest degree remarkable. Are we to assume that protestantism had never taken proper root in the multitude, or are we to ascribe it to the method pursued by the Jesuits? In point of zeal and address at least they left nothing wanting. They extended their operations in wider and wider circles round all the points at which they had established themselves. They had the art of captivating the multitude; their churches were the most frequented; they uniformly directed their attacks against the chief difficulty they encountered; if there happened anywhere to be a scripture-proof Lutheran, to whose judgment the neighbours so far deferred, they directed all their endeavours to gain him over; which, thanks to their practice in controversy, they seldom failed to do. They showed themselves always ready to aid the needy; they healed the sick and sought to reconcile parties at enmity with each other. They then laid those whom they won over, and who became converts, under solemn oaths. The faithful were to be seen repairing under their banners to all the resorts of pilgrims; and the processions were now joined by persons who had been even zealous protestants.

Nor was it by spiritual princes only, but also by secular, that the Jesuits were sought for. About the end of the sixteenth century, their two great pupils, Ferdinand II. and Maximilian I., stepped forth upon the scene.

It is said that when the young archduke Ferdinand, in the year 1596, celebrated Easter in his capital city of Grätz, he was the only person that took the sacrament of the supper according to the Roman catholic ritual; in the whole city there were but three Roman catholics.[2]

[1] Strunk: Annales Paderborn., lib. XXII. p. 720.

[2] Hansitz: Germania Sacra, II. p. 712. "Numerus Lutheri sectatorum tantus ut ex inquilinis Græcensibus pæne cunctis invenirentur avitæ fidei cultores tres non amplius."—[Such was the number of Luther's followers that three and no more

In point of fact, after the decease of the archduke Charles, the enterprises in favour of Roman catholicism had been going back under a not very powerful government, conducted by the guardians of his successor. The protestants had recovered possession of the churches that were wrested from them; their schools at Grätz had been fortified by new and fortunate appointments; the nobility had appointed a committee for the purpose of resisting all that might be attempted to be done to the prejudice of protestantism.

Notwithstanding this Ferdinand resolved instantly to proceed to the execution and completion of the counter-reformation. In this spiritual and political motives were combined. He said that he, too, would be lord in his own country as well as the elector of Saxony, and the elector of the Palatinate in theirs. If it was suggested to him what dangers might result from an attack by the Turks during internal dissensions, he replied, that people could not count upon divine assistance until after complete conversion. In 1597, Ferdinand passed through Loreto to Rome, on his way to the feet of Clement VIII. He solemnly vowed that he would restore the Roman catholic religion in his hereditary dominions even at the risk of his life, and in this resolve he was confirmed by the pope. So he returned and proceeded to work. In Sept. 1598 his decree went forth, by which he commanded the removal of all the protestant preachers in Grätz within a fortnight.[1]

Grätz was the centre of protestant learning and power. Nothing was left unattempted that might shake the archduke from his purpose; neither entreaties nor warnings, nor even threats; but the young prince was, according to the expression of the historian of Carniola, firm "as a piece of marble."[2] In October a similar proclamation was issued in Carniola, and in December in Carinthia.

And now, indeed, the estates showed themselves extremely

followers of the ancient faith could be found from among all the Greek residents.] The words "pæne cunctis,"—[almost all,] again leaves the matter doubtful.

1 Khevenhiller: Annales Ferdinandei, IV. 1718.

2 Valvassor: Ehre des Herzogthums Krain, Th. 2. Buch 7, p 464; undoubtedly the most important account of this occurrence: "Solche mit Warnung gemischte Bittschrift traf einen festen Marmel an, welchen ihre Feder nicht kunte durchdringen, noch erweichen."—[Such a supplication mingled with warning, struck upon an immovable marble which its feather could neither penetrate nor soften.]

difficult to deal with; even at their particular provincial meetings, for Ferdinand no longer allowed a general one, they refused payment of their subsidies; already were the soldiers on the frontiers in an unsettled state. But the archduke declared that he would sooner lose all that by the grace of God he possessed, than yield a single step. The danger arising from the Turks, who under these circumstances, had already taken Canischa, and advanced in a daily more threatening manner, compelled the estates at last to consent to the taxes without having obtained a single concession.

Upon this the archduke had nothing farther to restrain him. In Oct. 1599 the protestant church in Grätz was closed, and the evangelical worship prohibited under pain of torture and of death. A commission was formed which proceeded into the country attended by an armed force. Styria first, then Carinthia, and at last Carniola too were reformed. From place to place the cry rang in people's ears; "the reformation is coming." Churches were pulled down, preachers banished or thrown into prison, and the inhabitants compelled either to live according to the Roman catholic faith or to leave the country. There were indeed many, for example there were fifty citizens in the small town of St. Veit, who preferred expatriation to apostasy.[1] The emigrants had to pay the tenth penny, which for them was in all cases no small loss.

Such was the grievous harshness of the procedure that was adopted. In return the Romanists had the satisfaction of finding that in 1603 there were reckoned 40,000 communicants, more than there had been previously.

And there was now developed forthwith a more extended operation on all the Austrian territories.

The emperor Rodolph had at first advised his young kinsman against his proposed design; but the success of the latter led the former to imitate him. From 1599 to 1601 we find a Reform-commission actively engaged in Upper Austria, and in 1602 and 1603 in Lower Austria[2] Preachers and teachers who had grown gray in the service of the gospel, had to abandon Lintz and Styria; this was a sore affliction to them; "now when bowed down

[1] Hermann: St. Veit: in the Kaernthnerischen Zeitschrift, V. 3, p. 163.

[2] Raupach: Evangel. Oestreich, I. 215.

with age," exclaims the rector of Styria, "I am thrust into misery!"[1] "Daily," writes one of those that were left behind, "are we threatened with destruction; our adversaries have their eyes upon us, mock at us, thirst after our blood."[2]

In Bohemia people flattered themselves with the idea of being better shielded from wrong by the ancient utraquist privileges, and in Hungary by the independence and power of the estates. But Rodolph seemed now to have no wish to trouble himself with either the one or the other. He had been persuaded that the old utraquists were suppressed, and that the evangelicals had no legal right to the enjoyment of their privileges. In the year 1602, he published an edict which first of all ordered the churches of the Moravian Brethren to be shut, and prohibited their meetings.[3] All others, too, felt that they were in the same case, and did not allow themselves to doubt what they had to expect. Ere long open violence began in Hungary. Basta and Belgioioso, who commanded the imperial troops in that country, removed the churches of Caschau and Clausenburg, and the archbishop of Colocsa endeavoured with their assistance to bring back to Roman catholicism the thirteen towns in Zips. The emperor, in reference to the grievances of Hungary, issued this resolution; "His Majesty, cordially acknowledging the holy Roman faith, desires to extend it likewise in all his dominions, and particularly his Hungarian dominions: he hereby confirms and rectifies all the decrees which from the times of St. Stephen, the apostle of Hungary, have been announced in favour of that faith."[4]

In spite of his advanced age, even the cautious emperor had laid aside his moderation; the Roman catholic princes, one and all, pursued the same policy; to the utmost limits of their power, the stream of Roman catholic opinions more and more widely spread itself out; doctrine and government impelled it onwards; there were no means in the constitution of the empire

[1] "Jam senio squalens trudor in exilium."—[Now while squalid from old age, I am thrust into exile.] Valentine Pruenhueber's Annales Styrenses, p. 326.

[2] Hofmarius ad Lyserum: Raupach, IV. 151.

[3] Schmidt: Neuere Geschichte der Deutschen, III. 260, an extract from the supplements to the apology for the Bohemians of the date 1618, which are often found wanting in later editions.

[4] Art. XXII. anno 1604. In Ribiny: Memorabilia Augustanæ confessionis, I. p. 321.

of opposing it. Much rather so conscious were the Roman catholics of the strength of their efforts, that they began at this important crisis to intermeddle with the affairs of the empire, and to jeopard the hitherto asserted rights of the protestant part of it.[1]

Already, not without the influence of the papal nuncios, and particularly of Cardinal Madruzzi, who first turned his attention in this direction, had changes been admitted in the supreme imperial court, which supplied occasions and means for those ends.

Even the imperial court of justice (Kammergericht) had at last received a more Roman catholic colour towards the close of the sixteenth century; decisions had gone forth which corresponded with the Roman catholic exposition of the peace of Augsburg. Those who had suffered in consequence, had, on the other hand, seized the legal remedy of revision; but the revisions along with the visitations had come to a stand still; the causes accumulated and all lay over undecided.[2]

Amid these circumstances it so happened that the aulic council rose in credit. There at the least people had the prospect of having their cases brought to a final decision; the losing party could not take refuge in a legal remedy which never brought the question at issue to a close. But the aulic council not only was still more decidedly Roman catholic than the supreme court of the empire; it was absolutely dependent also on the court. "The

1 Relatione del nuncio Ferrero 1606—[Report of the nuncio Ferrero 1606] enumerates the results: "Da alcuni anni in qua si è convertito alla nostra santa religione una grandissima quantità d'anime, restorate le chiese, rivocate molte religioni di regolari alli loro antichi monasteri, restituite in buona parte le ceremonie ecclesiastiche, moderata alquanto la licenza degli ecclesiastici, e domesticato il nome del pontefice Romano riconosciuto per capo della chiesa universale."—[From some years in which a very great number of souls have been converted to our holy religion, restored to the church, many orders of the regular clergy recalled to their ancient monasteries, the ecclesiastical ceremonies in a good measure restored, the licentiousness of the clergy somewhat moderated, and the name of the Roman pontiff domesticated, he being recognised as head of the universal church.]

2 Missiv und Erinnerung des Reichskammergerichts am Reichstag von 1608—[Missive and admonition of the supreme imperial court to the imperial diet of 1608] in the Acts of the Imperial diets at Frankfort on the Maine, of which it was kindly permitted to take a preliminary view. The "Kammergericht" declares it "for notorious in the country and empire to what a large and remarkable amount, since the year 86, the revisions of the judgments issued and pronounced by the said "Kammergericht" have accumulated, so that of the same there have been already notified in the imperial college to the amount of an hundred and more of them, probably daily to be looked for.]

aulic council," says the Florentine chargé-d'affaires, Alidosi, "issues no definitive decision, without having communicated it previously to the emperor and to the secret council, who seldom return it to the judges without some alterations."[1]

But what general institutions were there in the empire equal in point of influence to the judicial? To these the unity of the nation attached itself. But even these were now under the influence of Roman catholic sentiments, and at the service of the convenience of the court. Complaints soon began to be heard on all sides of partial judgments, and of illegal violence in giving them effect, when the general danger which threatened to arise from this point, appeared in the case of Donauwerth.

The fact of a Roman catholic abbot in a protestant city, who wanted to hold his processions with more publicity and show than usual,[2] having been interrupted and insulted by the populace, sufficed for the aulic council to visit the city itself with a process aiming at extensive consequences, with mandates, citations, and commissions, and finally to pronounce the ban upon it. A strict Roman catholic prince in the neighbourhood, Maximilian of Bavaria, obtained the commission for giving it complete effect. Not content with occupying Donauwerth, he instantly called hither the Jesuits, allowed the Roman catholic worship only, and proceeded in the usual manner to introduce the counter-reformation.

Maximilian himself viewed this affair in the light of its gene-

[1] Relatione del Sr Rod. Alidosi 1607—1609. "E vero che il consiglio aulico a questo di meno che tutte le definitioni che hanno virtù di definitiva non le pronuntia se prima non dia parte a S. Mta o in suo luogo al consiglio di stato, il quale alle volte o augmenta o toglie o modera l'opinione di questo consiglio, e cosi fatto si rimanda a detto consiglio tal deliberatione e cosi si publica."—[It is true the aulic council has this at least that all the judgments that have the force of being definitive, are not pronounced by it until it has first imparted them to the emperor, or failing him to the council of state, which every time either adds to or takes from, or moderates the opinion of the said council, and when this is done, re-transmits such deliberation to said council, and thus it is announced.]

[2] The report "wegen der Donawerdischen Execution,"—[respecting the execution of Donauwerth,] in the Acts of the Imperial Diet of 4th February 1608 remarks, (and the other accounts and pieces of documentary information agree with it,) that the Abbot had "allein so viel herbracht dass er mit niedergelegten und zusammengewickelten Fahnen ohne Gesang und Klang und zwar allein durch ein sonderes Gaesslein beim Kloster hinab bis ausser der Stadt und ihrem Bezirk gangen, und die Fahnen nicht eher aufrichten und fliegen oder singen und klingen lassen, er sey denn ausser deren von Donawerth grund."—[done no more than gone with lowered and folded flags, without singing or music, and only too by a retired lane from the monastery, out of the town and beyond its circle, and then only allowed the flags to be raised and unfolded, or singing and music to commence; he was accordingly beyond Donauwerth ground.]

ral importance. He wrote to the pope that it might be regarded as a touchstone by which one might perceive the decline that had taken place in the respect commanded by the protestants.

But he deceived himself if he believed that they would submit to it. They very well saw what they had to expect were matters to proceed at this rate.

Forthwith the Jesuits made bold to deny the obligatory force of the peace of Augsburg. In point of principle (they maintained) nothing could have been concluded without the pope's consent; in no event could its validity have continued beyond the date of the Tridentine council; it could only be regarded as a sort of interim.

And even those who owned the validity of this compact, thought nevertheless that at least all the property that had been confiscated by the protestants since it was concluded, must be restored again. They paid no regard to the protestant explanations of its words.

What then, should these views, as had indeed already begun to be the case, be acknowledged by the supreme imperial courts of justice, and should decisions in conformity with them be pronounced and carried into effect?

When the diet met at Ratisbon in 1608, the protestants would proceed to no deliberation, until the peace of Augsburg was confirmed to them absolutely.[1] Even Saxony, though uniformly leaning in other respects to the side of the emperor, now insisted that the processes of the aulic council should be quashed, as being opposed to ancient usage; he urged also the improvement of the judicial system, and not only the renewal of the peace of Augsburg as concluded in 1555, but a pragmatic sanction likewise, by which the Jesuits should be prohibited from uniting against it.

But, on the other side too, the Roman catholics zealously held together; the bishop of Ratisbon had already published beforehand a circular, in which he admonished his co-religionists before

[1] Protocollum im Correspondenzrath, 5 April 1608, in den R. T. U.—[Protocol in the correspondence council, 5th April 1608, in the Archives of the Imperial Diets]: "the chief subject of consultation at the present meeting of the Diet has hitherto remained in suspense on this account, that the orders belonging to the evangelical religion want the confirmation of the peace of religion, and the popish part want to have inserted in the act the clause, that all property confiscated by the evangelical orders since the year 1555 should be restored."

all things to instruct their representatives to engage in a concurrent defence of the Roman catholic faith, "to stand by each other, firm and inflexible like a wall;" only not to temporize; there was no longer cause for fear; staunch and zealous defenders were at hand in distinguished and praiseworthy families. Though the Roman catholics then showed themselves disposed to ratify the peace of Augsburg, they moved the clause nevertheless, "that what contravened the same should be annulled and restitution granted," a clause which plainly comprehended all that the protestants dreaded and wished to avoid.

With such a quarrel in the main affair, it was not to be supposed that in any one point an unanimous resolution should be adopted, or that the aids against the Turks, which the emperor both wished and needed, should be granted him.

Yet it would appear as if this had had an effect on the emperor, and as if it had been even resolved at the court to comply in plain terms with the requisitions of the protestants.

This at least is the tenor of a very remarkable report, which the papal chargé-d'affaires rendered on this diet.

The emperor had not gone thither himself; his place was filled by the archduke Ferdinand. Neither was the nuncio himself at Ratisbon; but he had sent thither as his representative, an Augustinian friar, Fra Felice Milensio, the vicar-general of his order, who endeavoured to maintain the interests of Roman catholicism with more than ordinary zeal.

Now this Fra Milensio, from whom our report proceeded, assures us that the emperor had actually resolved to issue an edict in conformity with the wishes of the protestants. He ascribes it to the immediate influences of Satan; beyond doubt it had proceeded from the members of the emperor's cabinet, one of whom was a Jew, the other a heretic.[1]

[1] "Ragguaglio della dieta imperiale fatta in Ratisbona 1608, nella quale in luogo dell' ecc^{mo} e rev^{mo} Monsr. Antonio Gaetano arcivescovo di Capua nuntio apostolico, rimasto in Praga appresso la M^{ta} Cesarea, fu residente il padre Felice Milensio maestro Agostiniano vicario generale sopra le provincie aquilonari. E certo fu machinato dal demonio e promosso da suoi ministri, di quali erano i due camerieri intimi di Rudolfo, heretico l'uno, Hebreo l'altro, e quei del consiglio ch'eran Hussiti o peggiori."—[Account of the imperial diet held in Ratisbon in 1608, where in place of the most Excellent and Reverend Monsignor Antonio Gaetano, bishop of Capua, apostolic nuncio, who remained in Prague with his imperial Majesty, there was resident Father Felice Milensio, Augustinian doctor, vicar general over the northern provinces. And assuredly it was contrived by the devil and pushed forward by his ministers, of whom there were the two confidential chamberlains of Rodolph, the one a heretic, the other a Jew, and those of the council who were Hussites or worse.]

Let us hear from himself what he now further reports. "On the news of the edict that had arrived," says he, "and which was communicated to me and some others, I repaired to the archduke and asked if such a decree had come to hand. This the archduke admitted.—And now, does your archducal highness think of publishing it? The archduke replied; Such is the command of the imperial privy council; you yourself, most worthy father, must see the state we are in. On this I replied,[1] Your archducal highness would not belie your piety, the piety in which you have been brought up, with which you not long since dared, in the face of so many threatening dangers, to banish heretics without exception from your territories. I cannot believe that your highness will approve, by this new concession, of the loss of the church's property, of the sanctioning of the devilish sect of Luther and, yet worse, of that of Calvin, which has never yet enjoyed open toleration in the empire. The pious prince heard all I had to say; but what is there that we can do? said he. I beseech your highness, said I, to submit the matter to his holiness the pope, and to take no step until we have an answer from him. This was what the archduke did;

1 "Sovenga le, Ser[ma] Altezza, di quella cattolica pietà con la quale ella da che nacque fu allevata e per la quale pochi anni a dietro non temendo pericolo alcuno, anzi a rischio di perdere i suoi stati, ne bandi tutti gli heretici con ordine che fra pochi mesi o si dichiarasserò cattolici o venduti gli stabili sgombrassero via dal paese: sovengale che nella tavola dipinta della chiesa dei padri Capuccini in Gratz ella sta effigiata con la lancia impugnata come un altro Michele e con Luthero sotto i piedi in atto di passarli la gola: et hora essendo ella qui in persona di Cesare, non devo credere che sia per soffrire se perdano i beni dotali della chiesa il patrimonio di Christo, e molto meno che la diabolica setta di Luthero sia con questa moderna concessione confirmata e per peggio quella ancor di Calvino già incorporata la quale non ricevè mai tolleranza alcuna imperiale. Questo e più disse io et ascoltò il piissimo principe. - - Priegola, dissi, a sospender questa materia fino alla risposta del sommo pontefice: e cosi fece differendo i decreti degli huomini per non offendere i decreti di dio."—[Call to remembrance, Most Serene Highness, that catholic piety in which you were born and brought up, and for which a few years ago, not fearing any danger, but at the risk of the loss of your states, you proclaimed to all heretics that within a few months they should either declare themselves catholics, or having sold their property, should go away from the country; reminding him that in the painted tablet in the church of the Capucin fathers in Grätz, he stood represented as grasping a spear, like another Michael, and with Luther under his feet in the act of thrusting it into his neck; and now he being in the person of the emperor, ought not to believe that it should be endured that the church's dowry goods, and Christ's patrimony, should be lost, and much less that Luther's diabolical sect should be confirmed by this modern concession and, worse and worse, that that also of Calvin should now be incorporated which had never received any imperial toleration. This much and more I said, and the most pious prince listened to me. - - Pray, said I, suspend this matter until an answer shall be received from the supreme pontiff; and this he did, delaying the decrees of men that he might do no offence to the decrees of God.]

he made more account of the commands of God than the decisions of men."

If all this was really so, it may easily be seen what an important position this nameless Augustinian friar occupied in our imperial history. At the decisive moment he interposed obstacles to the publication of a concession which would to all appearance have contented the protestants. Instead of it Ferdinand came out with a writ of interposition, which included the possibility of the above clause being introduced as formerly. The protestants at a meeting held on 5th April 1608, combined as one body in a resolution not to comply with it, not to accept it.[1] But as the other party, nevertheless, made no concession, as nothing that could hush their alarm was to be obtained from the emperor or his representative, they proceeded to the most extreme measure; they left the Diet. For the first time no resolution was adopted, far less were any subsidies granted; it was the moment in which the unity of the empire was in point of fact dissolved.

And it was impossible that matters could remain as they were. Each by itself would have been too weak to maintain the position that had been taken up; a union such as had long been already contemplated, deliberated upon, and projected, they now under the pressure of the moment carried into effect. Immediately after the diet a meeting was held at Ahausen, of the two princes of the Palatinate, the elector Frederick and the count palatine of Neuburg, two Brandenburg princes, the margraves Joachin and Christian Ernest, the duke of Würtemberg and the margrave of Baden, and a league was concluded, now known by the name of the Union. They came under a mutual engagement to aid each other in every way, and even with arms, particularly in reference to the grievances that had been laid before the last diet. They immediately prepared themselves for war; each member of the confederation undertook to induce one or other of his neighbours to join the league. Their inten-

[1] Votum der Pfalz im Correspondenzrath—[Vote of the Palatine in the correspondence council]: "That the confirmation of the peace of religion was by no means comprehended in so far as the Interposition's letter went; accordingly it was of no use to the evangelical orders, for the act of 1566 had the very clause which was now the subject of dispute." In the acts of 1557 and 1559 it was not (inserted). The Interposition's letter referred merely to 1566. It was rejected also because it regarded the emperor as judge in religious matters.

tion was, that as the existing state of affairs in the empire gave them no security, they should procure it for themselves and help themselves.

This was an innovation of the most extensive consequence, and so much the more as an occurrence took place in the hereditary possessions of the emperor which very well corresponded to it.

It so happened that the emperor for various reasons had fallen out with his brother Matthias; and in this dissension the Austrian estates, aggrieved in their freedom and religion, saw an opportunity for preserving both and went over to the side of the archduke.

As early as in the year 1606, the archduke, in conjunction with them, concluded a peace with Hungary without consulting the emperor on the subject. They excused themselves on the ground that the emperor neglected public affairs, and that the state of things had compelled them to act as they had done. But as Rodolph now refused to acknowledge this peace they rose, and that, too, directly in virtue of their compact, in open insurrection.[1] First, the Hungarian and Austrian estates concluded with each other an alliance defensive and offensive. They then drew over to them the Moravians, particularly through the influence of one of the Lichtenstein family. They all united, determined to risk property and blood for the archduke. Thus they advanced into the field with their self-elected chief against the emperor, on May 1608, the very day on which the diet at Ratisbon broke up. Rodolph had to submit to transfer to his brother Hungary, Austria, and Moravia.

But now it was natural that Matthias should make concessions to the estates, in return for the services which they had rendered to him. The emperors had for the last forty-eight years avoided the appointment of a palatine in Hungary; a protestant was now promoted to that dignity. Freedom in regard

[1] The compact had this clause: "quodsi propter vel contra tractationem Viennensem et Turcicam - - hostis aut turbator aliquis ingrueret, tum serenissimum archiducem et omnes status et ordines regni Hungariæ et archiducatus superioris et inferioris Austriæ mutuis auxiliis sibi et suppetiis non defuturos."—[But if on account of or against the Vienna and Turkey treaty - - the enemy or any disturber should rush in, then the most illustrious archduke and all the states and orders of the kingdom of Hungary, and of the archdutchy of Upper and Lower Austria, will not be wanting to themselves in the way of mutual assistance and supplies.]

to religion was in the most solemn manner assured not only to the magnates, but also to the towns, to all the estates, nay, even to the soldiers on the frontiers.[1] Not till they had had the *exercitium religionis* [exercise of religion] freely accorded to them in castles and villages, as well as in private houses in the towns, did the Austrians do homage.

That which the Austrians and Hungarians procured by the assault, the Bohemians obtained by the defence. From the very first Rodolph had to submit to great concessions, merely to enable him in any measure to resist his brother; after Hungarians and Austrians had through his brother succeeded in acquiring such important franchises, he, too, could not refuse the Bohemians their demands, whatever the papal nuncio and the Spanish ambassador might say to it. He granted them letters patent which not only repeated the old concessions granted by Maximilian II., but allowed them also to found a jurisdiction of their own for their defence.

How entirely different had the state of the affairs of Germany and the hereditary dominions of a sudden become. The union diffused itself in Germany and watched every assault on the part of Roman catholicism, which it powerfully repelled. The orders in the Austrian provinces had carried out their ancient claims into a well-founded constitutional government. Here withal there was a not unimportant distinction. In the empire, Roman catholicism had again pervaded the territories of the Roman catholic princes; first, on its going beyond this, violently interfering with imperial concerns and jeoparding the existence of free estates, did it encounter resistance. In the hereditary dominions, on the other hand, it was still irresistibly opposed, within the domain of territorial privileges, by the force wielded by the protestant landlords. But, on the whole, it was the same sentiment. It was said, much to the point, in Austria, that one sword must be kept in the sheath by the other.

For the other party, too, placed itself forthwith in a warlike attitude. On the 11th of July 1609, a league was entered into between Maximilian of Bavaria and seven spiritual lords, the bishops of Würzburg, Constance, Augsburg, Passau, and Ratisbon, the provost of Ellwangen and the Abbot of Kempten, for

[1] The article is to be found in Ribiny, I. 358.

their common defence, in which, after the pattern of the old league at Landsperg,[1] the duke of Bavaria obtained extraordinary authority. The three spiritual electors, although retaining a certain independence, soon attached themselves to it. Archduke Ferdinand wanted to be taken in; Spain declared its approval; the pope promised to neglect nothing that he could do for the compact. We doubt that the pope allowed himself, mainly through Spanish influence, to become by and by more and more decidedly involved in the interests of this league.[2]

And thus did two hostile parties confront each other, both prepared for war, each in constant dread of being taken by surprise and attacked, neither able to bring their quarrel to some grand decision.

The consequence was, that in Germany no public difficulty could any more be set aside, no concern of common interest brought to a close.

Steps had to be taken in 1611, for the election of a king of the Romans; but the electoral princes met to no purpose: they could not carry it into effect.

Even after the death of Rodolph in 1612, it was long before any election could be effected. The three secular electors insisted on the introduction of an imperial council, composed on the principle of equality between the two parties, by taking advantage of the election articles of compact; while this demand was opposed by the three spiritual electors. The election was carried through only in consequence of Saxony, who in all these things showed a great devotion to the house of Austria, having gone over to the Roman catholic side.

But what had failed to pass at the electors' council, was only the more impetuously demanded by the union of princes at the diet of 1613; no less decidedly were they opposed by the Roman catholics; there was an end to all further public deliberation; the protestants could no longer submit to the yoke of a majority of (hostile) votes.

In Juliers and Cleves, where, in spite of the changes of tone in the weak government of the last native prince, strong mea-

[1] Maximilian calls to mind this Landsperg compact in a body of instructions to his ambassador on going to Maintz, in Wolf, II. p. 470.

[2] The documents respecting this are still unknown, and until further information is got, the assurance of the Venetian ambassador Mocenigo must suffice.

sures, through the influence of that prince's Lorraine wife, were taken at last for the restoration of Roman catholicism; it now seemed for a time as if protestantism must obtain the upper hand, the next heirs being both protestants. But even here the principle of religious dissension was the more powerful. One of the protestant pretenders passed over to Roman catholicism, and here too the parties set themselves against each other. As they acknowledged no supreme judge, they proceeded, in 1614, to overt hostilities. Each seized, the one with Spanish, and the other with Netherlandish assistance, as much of the country around as he could, and without more ado reformed in his own manner the part that fell to his share.

Attempts, indeed, were made to effect a reconciliation. It was proposed that it should be referred to an electoral diet; but the elector palatine would not hear of it, as he had no confidence in his colleague of Saxony: or to a general composition diet; but this the Roman catholic estates had numberless reasons for opposing. Others had an eye to the emperor: they advised him to recover his authority by the display of a respectable mass of troops. What, however, was to be expected from Matthias; already, in virtue of the very source of his power, he belonged to both parties, but, oppressed by the fetters he had laid on himself, he could rise to no freedom of action. The pope loudly complained of him; declaring him unfit to be invested at such a time with so great an office: he caused representations to be made to him in the strongest expressions, and was surprised only that the emperor took it all so easily. At a later period the Roman catholics were not so dissatisfied with him. The very zealots declared that he had become more useful to their church than could have been believed. But in the affairs of the empire he had no power. In the year 1617, he made an attempt to dissolve both covenants. But immediately upon that the union acquired fresh vigour, and the League might be said to have been founded anew.

OFFICE OF NUNCIO IN SWITZERLAND.

THERE had now matured itself in Switzerland, as had been the case there for a considerable period, only in a more peaceful manner, a state of equipoise between the two parties.

It was now long since the various territories of Switzerland had been declared independent: in framing the statutes of the diets, religious matters never durst once be dealt with. At the commencement of the 17th century, the hope of overpowering the protestants was no longer for a moment cherished on the side of the Roman catholics; the former were not only more powerful and richer, they had also men of greater skill and more practised in business.[1]

The nuncios, who fixed upon Lucerne as their chief place of residence, indulged no illusion with regard to this state of things; they are the very persons who notice it. Nevertheless, even with all this narrowing of the sphere of their operations, in the midst of Roman catholics they never ceased to occupy a very important position.

Their principal business was to keep the bishops to their duty.[2] The bishops of the German nation inclined to consider themselves

[1] Informatione mandata dal Sr Cardl d'Aquino a Monsr Feliciano Vescovo di Foligno per il paese de' Suizzeri e Grisoni,—[Notices sent the Lord Cardinal d'Aquino to my Lord Feliciano, bishop of Foligno, for the country of Switzerland and the Grisons (Informationi Politt.IX.), further adds: "Li cantoni cattolici sino a questi tempi sono tenuti più bellicosi che i cantoni heretici, ancora che quelli siano più potenti di genti al doppio e di denari: ma hoggi li cattolici si mostrano tanto affettionati e mutati da quelli antichi Suizzeri che se non fosse particolare gratia del Signore, humanamente parlando, poco o veruno avvantaggio haverebbero questi sopra gli avversarii heretici, e non sarebbe securo senza ajuto straniero il venir a rottura con essi, oltre che li medesimi protestanti hanno persone più dotte, prattiche, giudiciose, e potenti in ogni affare."—[The catholic cantons down to this time are accounted more warlike than the heretical cantons, although these are as powerful again in people and in money: but at this day the catholics show themselves so affected and changed from those ancient Swiss, that, but for the special grace of God, humanly speaking, these would have little or no advantage over the heretical adversaries, and without foreign aid there would be no safety in coming to a rupture, besides that these same protestants have among them persons at once more learned, practical, judicious, and powerful in all affairs.]

[2] Relatione della nuntiatura de' Suizzeri: "L'esperienza mi ha mostrato che per far frutto nella nuntiatura non è bene che i nuntii si ingerischino nelle cose che possono fare i vescovi e che spettano a gli ordinarii, se non in sussidio e con vera necessità: perchè mettendosi mano ad ogni cosa indifferentemente, non solo essi vescovi si sdegnano, ma si oppongono spesse volte e rendono vana ogni fatica del ministro apostolico, oltre che è contro la mente di monsignore e delli canoni che si metta mano nella messe aliena, mandandoli i nuntii per ajutare e non per distruggere l'autorità degli ordinarii."—[Report on the Swiss nuncioship: Experience has shown me, that in order to derive any fruit from the nuncioship, it is not well that the nuncios should interfere in things which may be done by the bishops, and which belong to the ordinaries, unless in the way of assistance, and when there is a real necessity: for if they put their hands to every thing indifferently, not only will these bishops take offence, but they will ofttimes set themselves in opposition, and neutralize all the labours of the apostolic minister, besides that it is contrary to the mind of monsignor and the canons that they should put their hands to another's harvest, charging the nuncios to assist, not to destroy the authority of the ordinaries.]

as princes: the nuncios perpetually represented to them that they were so, yet merely in virtue of their spiritual calling, and this they urged upon their attention. In point of fact we find much appearance of life in the Swiss church; visitations carried on, synods arranged, monasteries reformed, seminaries founded. We see the nuncios endeavouring to maintain a good understanding between the spiritual and the civil power, and, by mildness and persuasion, tolerably successful in attaining their object. They succeed in preventing the rushing in of protestant publications, even although they have to come to the determination of allowing the people to retain their bibles and German prayer-books. Jesuits and Capuchin friars we see actively engaged, and with great success. Fraternities of the Virgin Mary are instituted, comprising old and young; preaching and the confessional are zealously attended: pilgrimages to miracle-working images come again into vogue: and the very severity which some here and there practise on themselves, has occasionally to be tempered.[1] The nuncios know not how sufficiently to laud the services they receive, particularly from the Italian Capuchins.

Conversions accordingly follow as a matter of course. The nuncios take the converts under their own charge, support them, and recommend them; and try to establish funds in their favour from the contributions made by the faithful under the superintendence of the prelates. Sometimes they succeed in recovering lost jurisdictions, upon which measures are eagerly adopted for restoring the mass in these. In this, the bishop of Basle and the abbot of St. Gall show themselves particularly zealous.

In all this the nuncios were exceedingly aided by the circumstance of the king of Spain having formed a party in Roman catholic Switzerland. The adherents of Spain, such as the Lusi in Unterwalden, the Amli in Lucerne, the Bühler in Schwytz, and so forth, we find in general among the most devoted to the Roman see. The nuncios fail not to take advantage of these leanings to the best of their ability. They are careful to show every mark of respect that they can think of; patiently hear out the longest and most tedious discourse; are lavish in giving titles,

[1] An example will be found in Literæ annuæ societatis Jesu 1596, p. 187. "Modus tamen rigido illi jejunio est a confessario adhibitus."—[A restraint is laid on that rigid fasting by the confessor.]

and profess the utmost admiration for the ancient feats of the nation, and for the wisdom of their republican institutions. They find it specially necessary to keep their friends together by inviting them to entertainments at set times; they even return every invitation and mark of respect that is shown them with a present: presents seem here beyond every thing effective; whoever is named a knight of the golden spurs, and receives withal a gold chain and medal, feels himself everlastingly obliged to them. They have only to guard against promising what they are not sure of being able to perform: if they can do more than they engaged for, the greater the amount of obligation they are supposed to confer. Their domestic economy we find had to be always well regulated, and no room allowed for scandal.

Such now was the state of matters, that Roman catholic interests, even throughout Switzerland in general, were in a fair condition and quietly advancing.

There was but one point where the opposition between protestants and Roman catholics within one and the same territory, coinciding with an unsettled state of political relations, could give occasion for danger and conflict.

In the Grisons the government was actually protestant; among their rural districts on the contrary, the Italian and particularly the Valteline, were immovably Roman catholic.

Hence in this quarter perpetual causes of mutual irritation. The government allowed no foreign priests in the valley: it had forbidden even attendance at foreign Jesuit schools: it never so much as once gave permission to the bishop of Como, to whose diocese the Valteline belonged, to exercise his episcopal functions there. On the other hand, even the natives beheld with the utmost dissatisfaction protestants in their country, and that, too, as its lords and masters. In their own secret thoughts they held still to the Italians, to the orthodox Milan. From the collegium Helveticum in that city, where alone six places were set apart for the valley, young theologians ever went forth anew, inflamed with zeal for their creed.[1]

[1] Rel^ne della nuntiatura: "Il collegio Elvetico di Milano è di gran giovamento, et è la salute in particolare della Val Telina, che quanti preti ha, sono soggetti di detto collegio, e quasi tutti dottorati in theologia."—[Account of the nuncioship: the Helvetic college of Milan is of great assistance, and is the salvation in particular of the Valteline, all whose priests have come from that college, and are almost all doctors in theology.]

But this was the more dangerous from the fact, that France, Spain, and Venice, were all doing their utmost to form parties in the Grisons; parties which not unfrequently encountered each other with open violence, and thrust each other out of place. In 1607, first the Spanish, then the Venetian faction, took possession of Cuir. The one broke up the alliances, the other restored them. The Spanish had the sympathies of the Roman catholics, the Venetians those of the protestants; and these then determined the general policy of the country. The future mainly depended on the side that France would adopt. The French had pensioned adherents throughout the whole, not only of Roman catholic, but also of protestant Switzerland; and they enjoyed an influence of old standing in the Grisons. About the year 1612 they espoused the Roman catholic interests: the nuncio succeeded in gaining over their friends to the side of Rome. the alliance with Venice was even formally renounced.

These party contests would of themselves deserve little attention, did they not derive a higher importance from the opening or closing of the mountain passes in the confederacy to one or the other power, depending on them. We shall see that they threw some weight into the scale in the general relations of politics and religion

REGENERATION OF ROMAN CATHOLICISM IN FRANCE.

The chief question that now remains is what position France, on the whole, assumed as respected religion.

We perceive, at the first glance, that the protestants still continued to constitute an extremely powerful body.

Henry IV. had granted them the edict of Nantes, which not only confirmed them in the possession of the churches they occupied, but gave them also a participation in the public institutions for learning, placed them on a parity with the Roman catholics in the chambers in the parliaments, gave them a great many guarantee towns; and, in general, afforded them an extent of independence, with respect to which it was questionable how far it comported with the idea of the state. About the year 1600, the consistorial districts of the French protestants were reckoned as amounting to 760; all regularly organized. Four thousand of the nobility attached themselves to that confession; and it was supposed that without difficulty it could bring 25,000 fighting men into the field. It possessed nearly 200 fortified places. All this presented a power sufficient to command more than respect, and which could not be insulted with impunity.[1]

But beside them, and opposed to them, there arose a second power, presented by the corporation of the Roman catholic clergy in France.

The large possessions of the French clergy gave that body of itself a certain independence; but this independence was placed in evidence, and brought home to their own consciousness, by their having been drawn into a participation in the national debt.[2]

For this participation was not so wholly a matter of compulsion, as that the obligations it involved had not to be renewed from time to time under the forms of a voluntary resolution.

Under Henry IV. the assemblies that met for that purpose, acquired a regular form. They were to be held every ten years: always in May, when the days are long and admit of much being done; never at Paris, to prevent dissipation; and every two years smaller conventions were to be held, for the purpose of auditing the accounts.

Evidently it was not to be expected that these assemblies, particularly the larger ones, would confine themselves to their financial duties. Already had the discharge of these emboldened them to proceed to more comprehensive resolutions. In the years 1595 and 1596, they resolved to renew the meeting of provincial councils, to oppose the inroads of the civil jurisdiction in the exercise of the clergy's official functions, to tolerate no simony, and which was still more to the purpose, the king, after some

1 Badoer: Relatione di Francia, 1605.

2 In the Mémoires du Clergé de France, tom IX.—Recueil des contrats passés par le clergé avec les rois,—[Memoirs of the clergy of France, vol. IX.—collection of contracts entered into by the clergy with the kings,]—we find the official documents relating thereto from 1561 downwards. At the assembly held at Poissy that year, for instance, the clergy engaged not only to pay interest on an important part of the national debt, but to liquidate that part of the debt itself. This liquidation never took place: on the other hand, the obligation to pay interest still remained. It consisted mainly of the debts which had been contracted at the Hotel de Ville of Paris: the interest went to that city, and became a settled annual rent from the clergy. It will be seen why Paris, even had it not been so thoroughly Roman catholic as it was, yet would never have permitted the ruin of the clergy, and never durst consent to the destruction of ecclesiastical property, over which it held a hypothec, *i. e.*, which was its security for the debt.

hesitation, gave his consent to this.[1] The rule was, that the clergy should make general representations upon churches and church discipline. The king found it impossible to escape this; it never came to a close without their receiving new acts of favour. At the next assembly, accordingly, the clergy began with inquiring what effect had been given to these.

The position of Henry IV. consequently became very peculiar, being thus placed betwixt two corporations; both having a certain independence, both holding their assemblies at stated times, and assailing him with mutually opposing representations, with which in fact, on neither side, could he easily refuse to comply.

His general intention, no doubt, was to maintain an equipoise betwixt them, and not to allow them to become involved in a fresh conflict: but if we ask to which of the two sides he was most biased, and to which he gave the greatest assistance, it was evidently the Roman catholic, albeit that his own rise was to be traced to the protestants.

Henry showed truly as little gratitude as thirst for revenge; he was more concerned about gaining new friends than about rewarding and granting favours to old ones.

Had not the protestants, in point of fact, already been obliged to extort that edict from him? He granted it to them only at a crisis when he was hard pressed by the arms of Spain, and when they likewise assumed a very warlike position.[2] Now too they used their franchises in the same temper wherewith they had acquired them. They formed a republic on which the king had but little influence; from time to time they even spoke of choosing for themselves another and that a foreign protector.

The clergy on the other hand clung to the king; they made no demands for money; on the contrary, they supplied money; nor could their independence be dangerous, since no other but the king held in his hands the nominations to places. In so far as the position of the protestants apparently involved a limita-

[1] Relation des principales choses qui ont ésté résolues dans l'assemblée générale du clergé tenue à Paris ès années 1595 et 1596, envoyée à toutes les diocèses.—[Account of the chief matters which have been resolved in the general assembly of the clergy held at Paris in the years 1595 and 1596, transmitted to all the dioceses.] Mémoires du clergé, tom. VIII. p. 6.

[2] This incontestably follows from the representation given by Benoist, Histoire de l'édit de Nantes, I. 185.

tion of the royal authority, the extension of that authority was manifestly connected with the progress of Roman catholicism.[1]

As early as 1598, the king declared to the clergy that it was his object to make the Roman catholic church as prosperous as it had been a century before; he besought them only to be patient and to trust him; Paris had not been built in a day.[2]

The rights conferred by the concordat were now exercised in quite a different manner from what they had been before; benefices were no longer bestowed on women and children; in appointing to places in the church the king looked very seriously to the learning, mental qualifications, and edifying lives of the candidates.

"In all external matters," says a Venetian, "he shows himself personally devoted to the Roman catholic religion, and averse to that which is opposed to it."

It was in accordance with this course of procedure that he recalled the Jesuits. He conceived that their zeal must contribute to the restoration of Roman catholicism, and through that to the extension of the royal power, as he now understood it.[3]

Yet all this would have gone but a short way towards accomplishing his object, had not the internal regeneration of the Roman catholic church in France made a powerful advance at this period. In fact, in the course of the two first decads of this

1 Niccolò Contarini: "Il re, se ben andava temporeggiando con le parti, e li suoi ministri e consiglieri fussero dell'una e l'altra religione, pur sempre più si mostrava alienarsi dagli Ugonotti e desiderarli minori: la ragione principal era perchè tenendo essi per li editti di pace molte piazze nelle loro mani, delle quali ben trenta erano di molto momento, senza di queste li pareva non essere assolutamente re del suo regno."—[The king, though he went on temporizing with the parties, and his ministers and councillors belonged to both religions, yet always showed himself more alienated from the Huguenots, and to wish them less powerful; the chief reason was because of their holding by the edicts of pacification many places in their hands, of which full thirty were of much consequence, without which he appeared not to be absolutely king of his kingdom.]

2 Mémoires du clergé, tom. XIV. p. 259.

3 Contarini: "Per abbassamento del quale (del partito degli Ugonotti) s'imaginò di poter dar gran colpo col richiamar li Gesuiti, pensando anco in questa maniera di toglier la radice a molte congiure."—[In order to keep down which (the means of the Huguenots) he thought he should be able to strike a great blow by recalling the Jesuits, thinking further in this way to cut off by the root many conspiracies.] He gave for answer to the parliaments that if they would but place his life out of danger, the exile of the Jesuits might last for ever. (Why does the author confine himself in the text to the statement of an honourable reason for the recall of the Jesuits, while he mentions only in a somewhat doubtfully conceived note the grand reason, affording one of the most important lessons in modern history, that the king felt himself exposed at every moment to assassination as long as the Jesuits were not taken into favour? Tr.)

century, it assumed a new form. Let us further glance at this revolution, and particularly at the renovation of conventual discipline in which it presents itself.

The old orders, Dominicans, Franciscans and Benedictines, were reformed with great zeal.

These were emulated by the female sisterhoods. The Feuillantines[1] underwent such excessive penances that on one occasion, within a single week, fourteen perished in consequence; the pope himself had to exhort them to moderate their severity.[2] In Portroyal a community of goods, silence, and nightly watching were again introduced; there the mystery of the eucharist was worshipped day and night without intermission.[3] The nuns of Calvary observed the rule of St. Benedict without any mitigation; by continual prayer at the foot of the cross they sought to practise a kind of penance for the affronts put upon the tree of life by the protestants.[4]

St. Theresa at that time reformed, in a somewhat different sense, the order of the Carmelite nuns in Spain. She too enjoined the strictest seclusion, seeking even to limit the visits of relations at the grating, and even the father confessor was not left without superintendence. However she did not consider severity the end to be attained. She endeavoured to call forth such a tone of mind in the soul as should bring it nearer to the divine. She found also that no seclusion from the world, no self-denial, no chastisement, kept the mind within the limits that were necessary for it, if something else did not come to its aid; but that labour, say domestic employments and female handiwork, was the salt for preserving the soul of a woman from ruin, and by which the door was closed on idle roving thoughts. Yet, this work, as she further enjoined, was not to be costly, or ingenious, or done at certain stated times; further, it was not of itself to occupy the mind. Her object was to promote the peace of a soul conscious of being itself in God, of a soul, as she says, "which lives constantly as if it were standing in God's sight,

[1] So called from a monastery of St. Bernard, called Feuillans, where John de la Barrière founded a new order in the time of Gregory XIII. Tr.

[2] Helyot: Histoire des Ordres monastiques, V. p. 412.

[3] Felibien: Histoire de Paris, II. 1339; a work especially valuable for the history of this restoration, and which is often based on original accounts.

[4] La Vie du véritable père Josef, 1705, p. 53, 73.

and which knows nothing so distressing as not to enjoy his presence;" she wished to produce what she calls the prayer of love; "where the soul forgets itself and perceives the voice of the heavenly master."[1] It was an enthusiasm which at least by her was conceived after a pure, exalted, and simple manner, and which made the greatest impression in the whole Roman catholic world. Very soon the conviction gained ground, even in France, that people needed something more than merely doing penance. A special agent, Peter Berulle, was sent to Spain, who at last, though not without encountering difficulties, transplanted the order into France, where it very soon struck root and bore the fairest fruits.

The establishments of Francis de Sales were also conceived in this milder spirit. He himself used to go about all his employments with an unclouded peace of mind, without violent effort or hurry. Aided by his friend, Mère Chantal, he founded the order of the Visitation, expressly for such persons as were debarred by the weakness of their physical constitution, from entering the more severe associations. In the rule he prescribed, not only did he avoid penance properly so called, and dispense with the more difficult duties, he also warned his followers against all inward unreasonable requirements; without putting much strain on their thoughts they were to place themselves in the sight of God, and not to desire enjoying him more than he himself should grant; that under the guise of ecstasy we were apt to be led away by pride; we ought to walk only along the common path of the virtues. On this account he charged his nuns before all things with the care of the sick. The sisters were to go forth, always by twos, the one a superior, the other an associate, and visit the indigent poor in their own houses. The idea of Francis de Sales was, that we should pray with works and by labour.[2] His order diffused a benevolent activity throughout all France.

It will easily be seen that in this course of things there is a

[1] Diego de Yepes: Vita della gloriosa vergine S. Teresa di Giesu, fondatrice de' Carmelitani scalzi, Roma, 1623, p. 303. Constituzioni principali, § 3, p. 208. The Exclamaciones o meditaciones de S. Teresa con algunos otros tratadillos, Bruselas, 1682, display her inspiration in almost too lofty a flight for our feelings.

[2] For example in Gallitia's Leben des h. Franz von Sales, II. 285. But his meaning appears in the clearest and most attractive manner in his own writings, particularly in the Introduction to a devout life.

transition from severity to moderation, from ecstatic excitement to peace, from the practice of penance in seclusion from the world, to the discharge of a social duty.

Forthwith the Ursuline nuns too were received into France, an order whose fourth vow bears that they will devote themselves to the instruction of young women, and which discharged this vow with amazing zeal.

Like tendencies, as will at once be seen, appeared in full vigour in the congregations instituted for the male sex.

John Baptist Romillon, who had twice before his 26th year borne arms against Roman catholicism, but had then gone back to it, instituted, in concert with a like-minded friend, the brothers of Christian doctrine who laid anew the foundations of elementary instruction in France.

We have already mentioned Berulles, one of the distinguished clergymen of that age in France. From his early youth he had shown a most sincere zeal in qualifying himself for the service of the church; for that purpose he had daily, as he says, kept before his eyes "the truest and deepest sentiment of his heart, which was, "to strive after the utmost perfection." It may perhaps have been connected with the difficulties that he found in this course, that to him nothing seemed so necessary as the erecting of an institution for the education of clergymen immediately for the service of the church. In this he took Philip Neri for his model; he too founded priests of the oratory. He would tolerate no vows, but permitted only simple obligations, being magnanimous enough to desire that every one that could not perceive in himself the spirit for such a vocation, should withdraw again. In fact his institute, too, now made uncommon progress; by its mildness it drew to it young men of rank to educate; and Berulle soon saw himself at the head of a splendid, powerful and learned body of youths. Episcopal seminaries and learned schools came to be transferred to him; and a new and fresh spirit actuated the clergy who issued from the institute. It educated a great number of important preachers, and from this time forward the character of French preaching became fixed.[1]

And at this place can we forget the congregation of St. Maur?

1 Tabaraud: Histoire de Pierre de Berulle, Paris, 1817.

While the French Benedictines attached themselves to the reformation of that order that had been effected in Lorraine, to their other obligations they added that of devoting themselves to the education of the young nobility and to learning. At the very commencement there appeared then among them that praiseworthy person, Nicholas Hugo Menard, who gave their studies the direction to ecclesiastical antiquities, and to which we are indebted for so many works of high value.[1]

Soon, too, there was introduced into France, by means of Mary Medici, the compassionate brethren, the institution of that indefatigable attendant on the sick, Johannes a Deo[2] a Portuguese, to whom a Spanish bishop in a moment of admiration gave this surname; there they adopted a still stricter rule; but their success was only so much the greater, so that in a short time we find no fewer than thirty hospitals founded by them.

But what an undertaking is it, to alter the tone of religious feeling throughout a whole kingdom, and to allure it onwards in the direction of faith and learning. In the lower walks of society, among the country people, with the very country priests even, the old abuses still continued in many quarters to be in vogue. At last there appeared also amid the general stir, that great apostle of the common people, Vincent de Paul, the founder of the congregation of the mission, whose members, passing from one place to another, were to carry the religious impulses to the remotest corner of the land. Vincent, himself the son of a peasant, was meek, full of zeal and practical sense.[3] The order, too, of the Sisters of charity was indebted to him for its origin, an order in which the weaker sex, while still at an age in which it might make every pretension to domestic felicity and worldly splendour, devotes itself to waiting on the sick and often on the outcasts of society, without so much as daring to express

[1] Filipe le Cerf: Bibliothèque historique et critique des auteurs de la congrégation de S. Maur, p. 355.

[2] Approbatio congregationis fratrum Johannis Dei, 1572, Kal. Jan.—[Approval by the congregation of the brothers of Johannis Dei, 1572, January 1st.] (Bullar. Cocquel. IV. III. 190.)

[3] Stolberg: Leben des heiligen Vincentius von Paulus. Münster 1818. This worthy Stolberg should only not have considered his hero as "a man by whose means France was renewed" (p. 6, p. 399).

in other than in a cursory way, the religious sentiments which are the source of all true activity.[1]

These efforts are such as happily have ever been ready to appear anew in Christian countries; having for their objects education, instruction, preaching, learned studies, and beneficence. Nowhere will they succeed without a combination of manifold energies with religious enthusiasm. Elsewhere we see them left to the energy of the ever rising generation, to the needs of society. Here for the time being an attempt is made to give an immovable foundation to associations, and a fixed form to religious impulses, in order to devote all to the immediate service of the church, and unobtrusively to rear up coming generations in the same disposition.

In France the greatest results were soon manifest. Already under Henry IV. the protestants saw themselves hampered and placed in jeopardy by an activity so penetrating and so extensively diffused; for some time they made no farther progress; but soon they suffered losses; even as early as under Henry IV. we find them complaining that desertion had commenced in their ranks.

And yet Henry IV. had already been compelled by his policy to grant favours to them, and to oppose the unreasonable demands of the pope, who wished that they, for example, should be excluded from all public situations.

Under Mary Medici, however, the line of policy that had till

1 After reading the above flattering accounts of the efforts made at this time by Romanists in France, to rival the moral superiority of the Reformed, to whom the highest compliment was paid in giving the title of ceux de la réligion to their whole body, as being no less marked by a strict regard for religious duties than if they had been bound by the vows of a religious order, these orders being popularly called religious, the reader may well ask how, in spite of such efforts, made by such persons, the general tone of morals in Roman catholic France was so wretchedly low during the earlier and middle part particularly, of that very seventeenth century. We would answer, that it was a morality which, however self-denying and devout, was not based on doing homage to Jehovah by implicit deference to his written word, that it did not spring from a pure scriptural faith, but was mingled in its motives with much superstition, idolatry, and pride, and that by being conducted by persons of both sexes who renounced domestic life, it may be distinguished at once from the morality that runs through the New Testament, nay, the whole Bible, by its artificiality and remote bearing on families. But the full force of this can best be understood by comparing the Saint Francis de Sales, Saint Theresas, &c. with a simple protestant father of a family, who though never ranked among the great wonder-working saints, did more, we doubt not, in diffusing the practice of the Christian virtues throughout France, by making them flourish in the domestic circles of the Reformed, than all the saints did put together. See an account of de Coligny's domestic character at the close of his Memoirs, Edinburgh, 1844. Tr.

then been pursued was laid aside; a much closer intimacy was maintained with Spain; a decidedly Roman catholic temper obtained the ascendancy in all internal and external affairs. And as it had the preponderance at the court, so also in the assembly of the states. Not only the publication of the Tridentinum, but also the restoration of ecclesiastical property in Bearn were expressly demanded by the two first estates in 1614.

Now it was at that time a great mercy to the protestants, among whom, too, there was much ecclesiastical life and activity, in order that they might not see it all suppressed, that they still remained so strong politically, and so well prepared for action. As the government had united with their adversaries, they found in powerful malcontents, who in France never were nor ever will be wanting, a stay to fall back upon and to assist them: some time elapsed before they could be directly attacked.

GENERAL WAR.—TRIUMPH OF ROMAN CATHOLICISM.
1617—1623.

CHAPTER SECOND.

OUTBREAK OF THE WAR.

VARIOUS as the circumstances may be which thus develope themselves, yet they, nevertheless, all combine to produce one great result. Roman catholicism has powerfully advanced in all quarters; but everywhere also has it encountered a mighty resistance. In Poland it has proved incapable of crushing its antagonists, from these having found an invincible support in the neighbouring kingdoms. In Germany a closely compacted opposition has dashed itself against the invading dogma and returning priesthood. The king of Spain has had to make up his mind to grant the United Netherlands a truce, virtually amounting to little short of a formal recognition. The French Huguenots are well provided against any attack by the possession of fortresses, by having troops ready for war, and effective financial arrangements. In Switzerland we see the equipoise between the parties already long established, and that even regenerated Roman catholicism is unable to unsettle it.

Europe we behold divided into two worlds, which at every point encompass, confine, encounter and conflict with each other.

On making a general comparison between them, the Roman catholic side presents first of all a greater unity by far. Doubtless we are well aware that there was no lack of internal animosities, but these for the first time are hushed into a calm. Above all, a good and even confidential understanding exists between France and Spain; that being the case, it is no great matter that symptoms of the old refractoriness of Venice or of Savoy occasionally manifest themselves; even such dangerous attempts as the conspiracy against Venice, pass over without producing any violent shock. Pope Paul V., taught by the impressive lessons of his first experiences, showed himself calm and temperate; he knew how to preserve unbroken the peace between the Roman catholic powers, and would now and then suggest a measure of general policy. The protestants, on the other hand, not only, generally speaking, had no common centre; since the death of the English Elizabeth and the accession of James I., who had all along observed a somewhat equivocal policy, they had not even on their side a single prominently powerful state. Lutherans and Reformed confronted each other with feelings of mutual aversion, which necessarily led to opposite political measures. But even the Reformed were at variance among themselves; episcopalians and puritans, Arminians and Gomarists, contended with furious hatred; in the Huguenot assembly held at Saumur in 1611, a schism broke out which could never again be radically healed.

We certainly cannot trace this difference to an inferior vivacity of religious movement within Roman catholicism; we have seen the very reverse. The following reason rather suggests itself. In Roman catholicism there was not that energy of exclusive doctrine which prevailed in protestantism; there were important controverted questions that were left undetermined; enthusiasm, mysticism, and that profound mood of the mind which never arrives at any clearness of conception, all which must ever be expected to re-appear from time to time among the results of religious tendencies, found admission with Roman catholicism, were regulated and made available in the form of monastic asceticism, but on the other hand protestantism repelled these, condemned them, and thrust them away. Owing precisely to this rejection, such a peculiarity of disposition, thus abandoned to itself, broke away among protestants into a variety of sects, and sought its own paths, partial yet free.

Corresponding to this, literature in general on the Roman catholic side, had acquired much more form and regularity. We may say that it was under the auspices of the church that in Italy the modern classical forms first established themselves; in Spain there was an approach to them as far as the mind of that nation ever would permit; already there began a like development in France, where at a later period it so completely set itself in operation and produced such splendid results. Malherbe appeared, the author who first willingly subjected himself to rules, with a full consciousness of what he was doing, abandoned all licence,[1] and now gave a new effect to the monarchical Roman catholic sentiments, which he cherished, by the epigrammatic precision with which he expressed himself. A manner somewhat prosaic, it is true, but according to the French mind popular and elegant. In the Germanic nations, even on the Roman catholic side, this literary taste could not at that time as yet become dominant; it first appeared only in Latin poetry, where, however, even with our Balde, otherwise a man of distinguished talents, it really at times has much the effect of a parody; in the vernacular all continued, as yet, to be the utterance of nature. But much less still could this imitation of the antique establish itself among these nations on the protestant side. Shakespeare places before the eye the purport and spirit of the romantic in imperishable forms; antiquity and history had to be the handmaids of his muse. From the shop of a German shoemaker there went forth dark, formless, and unfathomable, yet with a resistless force of attraction, works of German thought, fulness, and religious contemplation, which have nowhere their equal.

1 With respect to Malherbe's intellectual character and his mode of composition, there will be found some new and remarkable additions to the biography of the poet of Racan, in the Mémoires or rather the Historiettes de Tallemant des Reaux, published by Monmerqué, 1834, I. p. 195.

Yet I will not attempt to describe the contrast presented by these two mental worlds, thus confronting each other; in order to take in the whole, we must have devoted more attention to the protestant side. All that is permitted me is to give relief to a single principle which directly operated towards the production of the result itself.

The monarchical tendencies now predominated in Roman catholicism. Ideas of popular rights, of legal resistance and king-murder, such as were abetted thirty years before even by zealous Roman catholics, were no longer opportune. There was now no important opposition on the part of a Roman catholic population against a protestant prince; people even bore with James I. of England; those theories no longer found any application.[1] Already did the consequence follow, that the religious ever more closely attached itself to the dynastic principle; to this was added, if I mistake not, that the monarchical personages on the Roman catholic side displayed a certain superiority in weight. At least this we may venture to say of Germany. There was still living the old bishop Julius of Würzburg, who had made the first thorough attempt at a counter-reformation amongst us; the electoral prince Schweikard of Maintz administered his chancellorship with a talent which was enhanced by a warm heartfelt sympathy and once more procured for it again great influence;[2] the two other Rhenish electors were resolute active men; at their side there appeared the manly, shrewd, indefatigable Maximilian of Bavaria, an expert administrator, full of lofty political projects, and Archduke Ferdinand, a man not to be shaken in his creed, which he embraced with all the fervour

[1] The author strangely shuts his eyes to the obvious reasons that must have induced the papacy to adopt this new policy at that time. On the one hand, its success in the conversion of a Bourbon dynasty must have led it to hope to bring over the Stuarts, a hope realized in James's grandsons; and on the other, the failure of the gunpowder plot, and the damage that the discovery of that atrocious attempt had manifestly done to the papacy in England, must have furnished the strongest grounds, even to the Jesuits and especially to them, to avoid every thing in word or deed that could remind people of the principles that suggested it. And yet even though papal doctors may cease to teach, and papal intriguers cease to conspire, their religion will ever foster enough of bigotry and fanaticism among its members, to produce in all others a reasonable and justifiable alarm. Tr.

[2] Montorio: Relatione di Germania 1624: "di costumi gravi, molto intento alle cose del governo cosi spirituale come temporale, molto bene affetto verso il servigio di cotesta santa sede, desideroso del progresso della religione, uno de' primi prelati della Germania."—[of serious habits, very attentive to the affairs of his government, alike spiritual and temporal, very well affected to the service of this holy see, desirous of seeing religion make progress, one of the first prelates of Germany.]

of a strong soul; almost all of them pupils of the Jesuits, who still understood how to call forth powerful impulses in the minds of their pupils; reformers also on their own side, who by means of much effort and mental activity had brought things to the condition in which they stood.

The protestant princes, on the other hand, were rather heirs than founders; they were already the second or third generation. In a very few of them only were there signs, I know not if we can say of vigour and inward power, certainly of ambition and love of agitation.

On the other hand, there now appeared among the protestants open leanings to republicanism, at least to an aristocratical freedom. In many quarters, in France, in Poland, in all the Austrian territories, a powerful nobility, with protestant convictions, was engaged in open conflict with the Roman catholics. The republic of the Netherlands, then rising daily to greater prosperity, presented a splendid example of what such an aristocracy might accomplish. There were certainly at that time in Austria, discourses to the effect that people must throw off the government of the reigning family, and adopt some such constitution as that of Switzerland or of the Netherlands. In the success of those endeavours lay the sole possibility of the German imperial cities rising again to greater importance, and they warmly interested themselves in them. The internal constitution of the Huguenots was already republican; indeed it was not without democratical elements. Among the English puritans these elements were already thwarting a protestant king. There is still extant a short paper belonging to this period, from an imperial ambassador in Paris, in which the attention of the European princes is forcibly directed to the common danger threatening them from the rise of such a spirit.[1]

The mind of the Roman catholic world was at this moment of one uniform character, classical, monarchical; that of the protestant world was divided, romantic, republican.

[1] Advis sur les causes des mouvements de l'Europe, envoyé aux roys et princes pour la conservation de leurs royaumes et principautés, fait par Messir Al. Cunr. baron de Fridembourg, e présenté au roy très-chréstien par le comte de Furstemberg, ambassadeur de l'empereur.—[Notice on the causes of the movements of Europe, transmitted to kings and princes for the preservation of their kingdoms and principalities, composed by Messir Al. Cunr. baron of Fridemburg, and presented to the most Christian king by Count von Furstemberg, ambassador from the emperor.] To be found in the Mercure François, tom. IX. p. 342.

In the year 1617 every thing already gave token of the approach of a decisive struggle between them; on the Roman catholic side, people, it would seem, felt superior in force to their adversaries; it is undeniable that they were the first to move.

In France, on the 15th of June, 1617, an edict was issued which the Roman catholic clergy had already long demanded, but the court, out of respect for the power and for the chiefs of the Huguenots, had constantly refused, and by virtue of which ecclesiastical property in Bearn was to be restored. Luines allowed himself to be brought into this measure, for although the protestants had at first reckoned on him,[1] he had gradually attached himself to the Jesuit popish party; forthwith, trusting to this disposition on the part of the supreme government, the populace, sometimes at the sound of the tocsin, in various quarters attacked the protestants; the parliaments took part against them.

Once more did the Polish prince Wladislow rise up in the certain expectation that he would now obtain possession of the throne of Moscow. It was supposed instead of that, that with this preparation there were connected views against Sweden, and the war between Poland and Sweden was resumed without delay.[2]

But by far the most important result was preparing in the hereditary dominions of the house of Austria. The archdukes had been reconciled and had come to a mutual good understanding; with the great good sense which that house has often shown in critical conjunctures, the rest had given up to the archduke Ferdinand the claims which necessarily accrued to them on the death of the emperor Matthias, who had left no posterity; and in a short time the archduke was in fact recognised as successor

[1] This may be seen among other things from a letter of Duplessis Mornay, Saumur, 26 April 1617: "sur ce coup de majorité"—[on this stroke by the majority], as he calls the putting to death of the marshal d'Ancre. La Vie de du Plessis, p. 465.

[2] Hiärn: Esth-Lyf-und Lettländische Geschichte, p. 418. "The Swedes knew that their king in Poland - - had sent his son into Russia with a powerful military force, for the purpose of surprising the fortresses that the Muscovites had surrendered to Sweden, in order that should he succeed in this stroke, he might be better able to attack the kingdom of Sweden; for he had been promised assistance for the recovery of the kingdom of Sweden, both at the national diet in Poland from the orders, and from the house of Austria; wherefore he turned all his thoughts more to that than to any thing else."

to the thrones of Hungary and Bohemia. This was certainly only a compromising of personal claims, yet it involved a point of general importance.

From so determined a zealot as Ferdinand, nothing was to be expected but that here likewise he would endeavour, without delay, to obtain an exclusive predominance for his creed, and thereafter direct the collective force of those countries to the diffusion of Roman catholicism.

This threatened all the protestants in his hereditary dominions, in Germany and in Europe, with one common danger.

Hence it was that opposition rose first at this very point. The protestants, who had thrown themselves against the forward pressure of Roman catholicism, were not only prepared for resistance; they had courage enough to convert the defence forthwith into an attack.

The elements of European protestantism concentrated themselves in the elector Frederick of the Palatinate. His consort was the daughter of the king of England, and niece to the king of Denmark; his uncle was Prince Maurice of Orange, and the duke of Bouillon, chief of the French Huguenots of the less pacific party, was nearly related to him. He himself stood at the head of the German union. A serious prince, he possessed sufficient self-command to keep himself free from the bad customs which then prevailed at the German courts, and had it much more at heart to discharge the duties devolving on him as a sovereign, and assiduously to attend the sittings of his privy council; of a somewhat melancholy humour, proud, and full of lofty thoughts.[1] During his father's time, there were tables in the dining saloon for the councillors and nobility; these he caused

[1] Relatione di Germania 1617: "Federico V. d'età di anni 20, di mezzana statura, d'aspetto grave, di natura malinconico, di carnaggione buona, uomo di alti pensieri, e rare volte si rallegra, e coll' appoggio dell' accasamento fatto con la figliuola del re d'Inghilterra e di altri parenti e confederati aspirarebbe a cose maggiori se segli appresentasse occasione a proposito: onde essendo ben conosciuto suo naturale per il colonnello di Scomburg già suo ajo, seppe cosi ben valersene accomodandosi al suo umore, che mentre visse fu più d'ogni altro suo confidente."—[Account of Germany, 1617. Frederick V. twenty years of age, of middle stature, of a grave aspect, of a melancholy nature, of a good complexion, a man of deep thoughts, and seldom diverts himself, and with the aid of his marriage with the daughter of the king of England, and of other relations and confederates, he would aspire to greater things if a suitable opportunity offered; whence his natural disposition being well known to Colonel Schomburg, formerly his tutor, he has known how to take good advantage of it, by accommodating himself to his humour, and during all his life has been more his confident than any one else.]

to be removed; and dined only with princes and persons of the highest rank. There was cherished at this court a warm presentiment of having a great political destiny to fulfil; innumerable extensive alliances were eagerly formed; as long as no blow was seriously struck, there could be no clear idea formed of what was likely to happen, or of what the future might bring along with it; scope was left for indulging the rashest projects.

Such was the tone prevailing at the court at Heidelberg when the Bohemians, who, particularly under the influence of their apprehension of the religious jeopardy we have mentioned, had fallen into an even more violently fermenting variance with Austria, resolved to cast off Ferdinand, although he already had received their homage, and to transfer their crown to the elector palatine.

The elector Frederick paused for a moment before accepting it. Never had it been heard of that one German prince should deprive another of a crown that fell legitimately to that other! But all his friends, Maurice, who never liked the truce with Spain, the duke of Bouillon, Christian von Anhalt, who surveyed the whole drift of European policy, and was fully convinced that no one would have either the spirit or the power to oppose the thing when done, and all his most trusty councillors, urged him on: the immeasurable prospect before him, ambition, and religious zeal, combined to hurry him along: so he accepted the crown (August 1619). What immense results would have followed had he maintained his position! The power of the house of Austria in eastern Europe would have been broken, and the progress of Roman catholicism for ever checked.

And already in all quarters powerful sympathies began to stir in his favour. In France there appeared a general movement among the Huguenots: the inhabitants of Bearn resisted the royal order above mentioned; the assembly at Loudun espoused their cause; nothing could have been more desirable for the queen-mother than to gain over this opposition, now ready for war; already Rohan was on her side, and had engaged for the rest passing over to it.

As amid the perpetual fluctuations in the Grisons the Roman catholic Spanish party had been once more put down, and the protestant had risen into power; the tribunal at Davos received with satisfaction the ambassador of the new king of Bohemia, and promised to keep the passes in their country closed for ever against the Spaniards.[1]

Let us not forget to observe, that along with all this, the republican tendencies also began forthwith to show head. Not only did the Bohemian estates maintain a natural independence with respect to the king whom they had elected, attempts were made in all the hereditary dominions of Austria to imitate them. the imperial cities of Germany conceived new hopes, and in fact it was from this quarter that Frederick was assisted with the largest supplies in money that he ever had.

But on that very account, and influenced at once by religious and political considerations, the Roman catholic princes now combined more energetically than ever.

Maximilian of Bavaria and Ferdinand, who was fortunate enough at this crisis to be appointed emperor, formed the closest alliance; the king of Spain made preparations for giving effective assistance; Pope Paul V. allowed himself to be induced to make very respectable and welcome payments in the way of subsidies.

As at the stormy season of the year the wind sometimes suddenly veers about, so did the tide of prosperity and of achievement now turn at once in favour of the other side.

The Roman catholics succeeded in gaining over to their side the electoral prince of Saxony, one of the most powerful protestant princes, but a Lutheran, who heartily detested every movement proceeding from Calvinism.

This already inspired them with a certain hope of coming off victorious. A single battle, at Weissenberg,[2] on the 8th of November, 1620, gave a death-blow to the power of the palatine Frederick and to all his projects.

For the union gave no adequate succour to their chief. It might be that that republican element appeared dangerous even to the combined princes: they did not wish to abandon the Rhine

[1] The bearings of this incident, to which no importance was afterwards attached, were felt by those who were living at the time. See Fürstl. Anhaltische Geh. Canzlei Fortsetzung, p. 67.

[2] In the original "at the white hill." Tr.

to the Dutch: they dreaded the analogies which their constitution might suggest in Germany. The Roman catholics in upper Germany also instantly won for themselves the preponderance there. The upper palatinate was seized upon by the Bavarians, the lower palatinate by the Spaniards; and so soon as April, 1621, the union was dissolved. All that moved or showed head in favour of Frederick, was put to flight or shattered to pieces. In a moment, immediately after the utmost danger, the Roman catholic principle became omnipotent in upper Germany and in the Austrian provinces.

Meanwhile in France, too, a great decision of the contest was fought out. After a successful battle which the royal government had gained against the factions of the court that opposed it, and the party of the queen-mother, with whom certainly the Huguenots stood in close contact,[1] the papal nuncio insisted that advantage should be taken of so favourable an opportunity for making an attempt against protestantism in general; he would hear of no delay; he thought that what began with being once put off in France, would never be done:[2] he carried Luines and the king along with him. In Bearn the old factions of the Beaumonts and Grammonts, which had opposed each other for centuries, were still in existence; and to their quarrel was it owing that the king invaded their country without a check, dissolved its armed forces and its constitution, and restored the dominion of the Roman catholic church. It is true, that in France proper the protestants now took measures for espousing the cause of their brethren, but in 1621 they were every where defeated.

A Valteline chief, also, called James Robustelli, having gathered round him some Roman catholic outlaws, who had been banished from that country, together with some bandits from the Milanese and Venetian territories, formed the design of putting an end to the dominion of the Grisons, whose protestant tendency was felt to be so oppressive to that district of country. A Capuchin father inflamed this force, bloodthirsty

[1] Even Benoist says, II. 291: "Les Réformés n'auroient attendu que les premiers succès pour se ranger au même parti (de la reine)."—[The Reformed would have waited only for the first success in order to range themselves with the same party (that of the queen).]

[2] Siri: Memorie recondite, tom. V. p. 148.

enough of itself, to all the zeal of religious fanaticism. In the course of the night of 19th July, 1620, they burst into Tiranno. In the gray of the morning the bells were heard to ring, and the protestants having at this alarm run out of their houses, they were attacked, overpowered, and one and all put to death. And as in Tiranno, so immediately after in the whole valley. It was in vain that the inhabitants of the Grisons more than once proceeded from the lofty mountains to reconquer the dominion they had lost; they were beaten on every attempt. In 1621, the Austrians from the Tyrol, and the Spaniards from the Milan territory, burst even into the Grisons properly so called. "The shaggy mountains resounded with the death-shrieks of the murdered, and were fearfully lit up with the flames that rose from the lonely dwellings." The passes and the whole country were taken possession of.

This vigorous and violent advance awakened all the hopes of the Roman catholics.

The papal court represented to the Spanish, that the Dutch were at variance among themselves, and were now without allies, so that there could not be a fitter opportunity for renewing the war against the old rebels: it succeeded in convincing the Spaniards of this.[1] The chancellor of Brabant, Peter Peckius, appeared at the Hague on the 25th of March, 1621, and instead of the renewing of the truce, which was just expiring, he proposed the acknowledgment of the legitimate prince.[2] The states-general declared this monstrous suggestion unjust, unlooked-for, nay, inhuman;—hostilities of course recommenced. Here, too, the Spaniards had at first the advantage. They took Juliers from the Dutch, an achievement which formed a grand concluding stroke to their enterprises on the Rhine. They now occupied the left bank of the river from Emmerich to Strasbourg.

So many were the successes, all happening at one point of time, in such a variety of quarters, the results of such manifold preparation, but which, viewed in the light of the world's gene-

[1] Instruttione a Mre Sangro. "Là onde S. M^tà^ non può voltare le sue forze in miglior tempo ovvero opportunità."—[There then his Majesty could not direct his forces in better time or opportunity.]

[2] In words he proposed a union, "sub agnitione dominorum principumque legitimorum"—[under acknowledgment of the legitimate lords and princes]. See proposal and reply in Leonis ab Aitzema historia tractatuum pacis Belgicæ, p. 2 & 4.

ral development, form, in fact, but one. Let us now consider what is the most important point for us, the use that was made of them.

GREGORY XV.

AT the procession which took place in celebrating the battle at Weissenberg, Paul V. had a stroke of apoplexy, and that was soon followed by a second, of which he died, 28th January, 1621.

The new election was carried through, generally speaking, much like those that preceded it. Paul V. had reigned so long that nearly the whole college had been renewed under him; by far the greater number of cardinals, accordingly, were dependants of his nephew, Cardinal Borghese. The latter, after some vacillations, found the man in whose favour all his dependants united, namely, Alexander Ludovisio of Bologna, who was elected forthwith on the 9th of February, 1621, and assumed the name of Gregory XV.

He was a little phlegmatic man, who at an earlier period had acquired the reputation of being an expert negotiator, one who understood how to conduct matters without parade, and quietly to proceed to the attainment of his object:[1] but now he was bent down with age, weak, and sickly.

For that crisis in a struggle affecting the interests of the world at large, in which people were now placed, what was to be expected from a pope whom others had often refrained from trusting with difficult affairs, from an apprehension that they might thus give the last shock to his frail frame.[2]

But at the side of this dying graybeard there appeared a young man of five-and-twenty, his nephew, Lewis Ludovisio, who forthwith took possession of the papal government, and

[1] Relatione di IV. ambasciatori 1521 (1621?)—[Account given by the ambassadors, 1621]: "di pelo che avvicinasi al biondo. La natura sua è sempre conosciuta placida e flemmatica, lontana dall' imbarraciarsi in rotture, amicissimo d'andare in negotio destreggiando et avanzando li proprj fini."—[his hair approaching to white. His disposition has always been known to be placid and phlegmatic, far from involving himself in quarrels, most friendly to proceeding in business so as to manage and advance his own ends.]

[2] Rainier Zeno: Relatione di Roma, 1623,—[Rainier Zeno's account of Rome, 1623]: "aggiungendosi all' età cadente una fiacchissima complessione in uno corpicivolo stenuato e mal affetto—[adding to declining years a very feeble constitution, in a lean and sickly little body].

showed all the mind and hardihood that the state of things could ever require.

Lewis Ludovisio was a magnificent and showy person; he did not neglect the amassing of wealth, forming advantageous family alliances, and obtaining favours and promotions for his friends; he lived and let live, but therewithal he had an eye likewise to the grand interests of the church. His very enemies admit that he had a real talent for conducting affairs, a mind of fine discernment, which in the most perplexing complications could discover a satisfactory issue, and all that cool self-possession which enables a man to perceive a possible result in the darkness of the future, and to steer towards it.[1] Had not his uncle's feebleness, which did not allow him to count upon any long duration of his power, laid some restraint upon him, no deference for any thing in the world would have influenced him.

It was a point of great consequence that the nephew, as well as the pope, was absorbed with the idea that the salvation of the world was to be found in the extension of Roman catholicism. Cardinal Ludovisio had been brought up by the Jesuits, and was their great patron: the church of St. Ignatius at Rome was erected in a great measure at his expense: he reckoned it of some consequence that he was protector of the Capuchins, and thought it the most important protectorship he had: he devoted himself with predilection and devotion to the most superstitious order of Roman catholic opinions.[2]

If we would represent to ourselves the spirit of the new government in general, we need but to call to mind that it was Gregory XV. under whom the Propaganda was instituted, and the founders of the Jesuits, Ignatius and Xavier, canonized.

1 Rainier Zeno: "E d'ingegno vivacissimo: l'ha dimostrato nel suo governo per 'abondanza dei partiti che in ogni grave trattatione gli suggerivano suoi spiriti nati per comandare, i quali se bene in molte parti aberravano dell' uopo della buona politica, nondimeno l'intrepidezza, con la quale si mostrava pronto ad abbracciare ogni ripiego appreso da lui per buono, poco curandosi di consigli di chi gli haveria potuto esser maestro, davano a credere che la sua natura sdegnava una privata conditione." —[He is of a most lively genius: has shown this in his government by the abundance of resources which in all serious deliberations his spirits, born to command, suggested to him; although in many things he deviated from the scope of sound policy, nevertheless the intrepidity with which he showed himself ready to embrace whatever remedy he apprehended to be good, caring little for the counsels of those who should have been able to teach him, led to the belief that his nature disdained a private condition.]

2 Giunti: Vita e fatti di Ludovico Ludovisio, MS.—[Giunti's life and actions of Lewis Ludovisio, MS.]

The origin of the Propaganda lies properly in a previous ordinance of Gregory XIII., by whom a body of cardinals was charged with the direction of missions in the East, and orders given for the printing of catechisms in the less known languages.[1] Yet the institution was neither firmly founded, nor furnished with the necessary means, nor even very comprehensive. Now there was flourishing at this time in Rome, a great preacher called Girolamo de Narni, who commanded general reverence by a life which procured for him the reputation of a saint, and who in the pulpit displayed a fulness of thought, solidity of expression, and majesty of delivery, which captivated every body. Bellarmin, on one occasion, as he came from hearing Narni preach, said he thought that one of St. Augustine's three wishes had been granted to him, that, namely, of hearing St. Paul preach. Cardinal Ludovisio likewise was ready to befriend him; he supplied the money required for printing his sermons. It was this Capuchin who first of all projected the extension of that institution.[2] By his advice a congregation came to be founded with all the formalities, for the purpose of superintending the direction of missions in all parts of the world; and it was to meet at least once a month in the presence of the pope. Gregory XV. made the first appointment of funds; the nephew contributed somewhat from his private resources; and as the institution met an actually existing necessity, it enjoyed from day to day a more splendid success. Who knows not what the Propaganda has done for universal philology? But it has generally, and perhaps with the most success in the earlier times of its existence, sought to follow out its vocation in a very superior manner.

To this point of view the canonization of these two Jesuits attaches itself. "At the time," says the bull, "that new worlds were discovered, and when, in the old, Luther had raised himself to attack the catholic church, the spirit of Ignatius Loyola was awakened to form a society which devotes itself espe-

[1] Cocquelines: Præfatio ad Maffei Annales Gregorii XIII., p. V.—[Preface to Maffeus's Annals of Gregory XIII., p. V.]

[2] Fr. Hierothei: Epitome historica rerum Franciscanarum, etc., p. 362: "publicis suasionibus et consiliis privatis"—[Fr. Hierotheus: Historical epitome of the affairs of the Franciscans, &c., p. 362: by public persuasions and private counsels] Friar Girolamo caused the pope. Compare Cerri: Etat présent de l'église Romaine, p. 289. There, too, there is to be found a copious description of the institution and the growth of its capabilities.

cially to the conversion of the heathen and to the bringing over of heretics. But above all the other members, Francis Xavier made himself worthy of being called the apostle of the newly discovered nations. On this account both have now been admitted into the catalogue of the saints: churches and altars where people present their offerings to God, shall be dedicated to them."[1]

And now proceeding in the spirit that was embodied in these acts, the new government took instant steps for the purpose of following up with conversions the victories achieved by the Roman catholics, and to justify and consolidate the conquests they had made, by the re-establishment of religion. "All our thoughts," says one of the first papers containing instructions issued by Gregory IV., "we must direct to this object, how to derive the utmost advantage possible from the happy turn and triumphant position of affairs;" a purpose in which he had the most brilliant success.

GENERAL DIFFUSION OF ROMAN CATHOLICISM.—BOHEMIA AND THE AUSTRIAN HEREDITARY DOMINIONS.

THE attention of the papal government was first directed to the growing success of Roman catholic opinions in the Austrian provinces.

While Gregory XV. doubled the subsidies which had hitherto been paid to the emperor,[2] and promised him at the same time an extraordinary present of no inconsiderable amount, albeit, as he said, he hardly had enough of money remaining to support life, he strongly urged him not to delay a single moment in following up his victory with the utmost promptitude, and at the same time to set to work and re-establish the Roman catholic religion.[3] Only by that re-establishment could he express his thanks to the God of victory. He proceeds upon the principle

[1] Bullarium Cocquelines V. 131, 137.

[2] From 20,000 guldens to 20,000 scudi. The present (amounted to) 200,000 scudi. He had wished therewith even to maintain regiments under papal authority.

[3] Instruttione al Vescovo d'Aversa 12 April 1621: "Non è tempo di indugi nè di coperti andamenti."—[It is no time for delays nor for covert proceedings.] Bucquoi, in particular, was considered at Rome to be by far too dilatory. "La prestezza apportarebbe il rimedio di tanti mali, se dal conte di Bucquoi per altro valoroso capitano ella si potesse sperare."—[Promptitude would bring a remedy for such great evils, if it could be looked for from the Count of Bucquoi, otherwise a valiant captain.]

that by rebellion the nations had incurred the necessity of being subjected to severer restraint; they must be obliged by force to abandon their offences against God.

The nuncio sent by Gregory XV. to the emperor, was Charles Caraffa, so well known in German history. The two reports of his still extant, the one printed, the other in manuscript, enable us to know with certainty what measures he adopted for the attainment of those objects.

In Bohemia, which was the first scene of his activity, he began by seeing to the removal of the protestant preachers and schoolmasters, "who were guilty of offending the divine and human majesty."

This he found not quite so easy to accomplish; the members of the imperial government at Prague considered it as yet to be dangerous. Only on Mansfeldt being driven out of the upper Palatinate, all danger from without removed, and some regiments that had been enlisted at the desire of the nuncio, marched into Prague on December 13th, 1621, were such measures ventured on. But even then the two Lutheran ministers were spared, out of respect for the electoral prince of Saxony. The nuncio, as the representative of a principle which pays no respect to persons, would not hear of this; he complained that the whole people hung upon such folk, so that a Roman catholic priest had nothing to do, he could not find a livelihood.[1] In October, 1622, he at last carried his point, and the Lutheran preachers also were banished. It seemed for a moment as if the fears of the government council were to be realized; the elector of Saxony issued a threatening document, and assumed a hostile attitude in the most important questions; the emperor himself once told the nuncio that too much haste had certainly been shown, and that it would have been better to have waited for a fitter opportunity.[2] Yet means were contrived to keep Ferdinand to these

[1] Caraffa Ragguaglio MS.: "Conducevano in disperatione i parochi catolici per vedersi da essi (Luterani) levarsi ogni emolumento."—[Caraffa's MS. statement. The Roman catholic rectors were thrown into despair at seeing all emolument taken away by these (Lutherans).] The printed Commentarii have nevertheless a more ostensible reason: "quamdiu illi hærebant, tamdiu adhuc sperabant sectarii S. Majestatem concessuram aliquando liberam facultatem," p. 130.—[As long as they stuck (to the place), so long the sectarians still hoped that his Majesty would grant them full freedom of worship.]

[2] Caraffa Ragguaglio: "Sua M[ta] mi si dimostrò con questo di qualche pensiere ed usci a dirmi che si haveva havuta troppa prescia e che saria stato meglio cacciare

measures; the old bishop of Würzburg represented to him that "a glorious emperor should not quail before dangers; and that it would even stand him in better stead, to fall into the power of men than into the hands of the living God." The emperor yielded. The nuncio came off in triumph, for Saxony at last submitted to the removal of the preachers, and withdrew his opposition.

By this means the way was smoothed for what followed. In the place of the protestant preachers there came—for there was still a sensible want of secular clergy—Dominicans, Augustinians, Carmelites; from Gnesen there arrived a complete colony of Franciscans; then the Jesuits took care that there should be no want of them; on the arrival of a letter of the Propaganda, in which they were requested to undertake to fill the places of the parish priests, they were found to have done so already.[1]

And now the only question that could remain was whether, so far at least, the national utraquist[2] ritual in conformity with the determinations of the council of Basel, might not be suffered to continue. The government council and the governor himself (prince Lichtenstein) were for this;[3] they gave permission that Maunday Thursday, 1622, should once more be observed by having the communion in both kinds; and forthwith a voice was heard from the people, that they ought not to allow this

quei predicanti in altro tempo dopo che si fosse tenuto il convento in Ratisbona. Al che io replicai che Sua Maestà poteva havere più tosto errato nella tardanza che nella fretta circa questo fatto, poichè se il Sassone fosse venuto al convento, di che non ammettono che egli avesse avuta mai la volontà, si sapeva per ognuno che haverebbe domandato a S. M[ta] che a sua contemplazione permettesse in Praga l'esercizio Luterano che già vi era."—[Caraffa's statement. His Majesty upon this to me seemed to have some doubts, and went out to tell me that there had been too much haste, and that it would have been better to turn out these preachers at another time, after the convention which was to have been held at Ratisbon. To that I replied that his Majesty may have rather erred in dilatoriness than in haste, as respected this that had been done, for if Saxony were to come to the convention, whose good will they did not admit that he had ever had, every one knew that he would have it demanded of his Majesty, that in compliance with his views, the Lutheran exercise, such as was already there, should be permitted in Prague.]

1 Cordara: Historia societatis Jesu, tom. VI. lib. VII. p. 38.

2 Utraquists or Calixtins; a sect of the Hussites, in Bohemia, who differed from the Roman catholics principally in giving the cup in the Lord's supper to laymen. Tr.

3 According to the accounts hitherto admitted, for example, in Senkenberg's Fortsetzung der häberlinschen Reichshistorie Bd 25, p. 156, Note k, we should believe the reverse of Lichtenstein. Yet that were altogether a mistake, as is seen from what is said by Caraffa. The nuncio, on the other hand, found support from Plateis.

ancient national custom to be wrested from them. But by no representation was the nuncio to be induced to give his consent; he was immovably resolved to carry out the views of the Curia; he well knew that the emperor would at last approve; and in fact he succeeded in bringing out a declaration from the latter, to the effect that his civil government had nothing to do with mixing itself up with religious affairs. Upon this the mass came to be everywhere celebrated according to the Roman ritual alone; in Latin, accompanied with the sprinkling of holy water and invocation of the saints; the communion in both kinds was no longer to be thought of; the boldest defenders were imprisoned; finally, the symbol of utraquism, the great chalice with the sword at the Thein church, the sight of which would have kept alive old recollections, was taken down. On the sixth of July, when people would at another time have been celebrating the memory of John Huss, all the churches were kept carefully closed.

The government with its political resources now came to the aid of this most rigid enforcement of Roman dogmas and customs. The confiscations brought a considerable part of the landed property into the hands of Roman catholics; the acquisition of real property by protestants was virtually rendered impossible;[1] the council was changed in all the royal cities; no member whose Roman catholicism was suspected would have been tolerated there; the rebels were pardoned as soon as they repented; the refractory, on the other hand, those who were not to be convinced, and who would not yield compliance with the admonitions of the clergy, had soldiers quartered in their houses, "in order that," to use the very words of the nuncio, "their distress might enlighten their minds."[2]

The effect produced by this joint application of force and teaching, exceeded even the nuncio's expectations. He was

[1] Caraffa: "con ordine che non si potessero inserire nelle tavole del regno, il che apportò indicibile giovamento alla riforma per tutto quei tempo."—[with orders that they should not have it in their power to be inscribed in registers of the kingdom, a thing which brought unspeakable assistance to the reformation during all that time.]

[2] "Acciò il travaglio desse loro senso ed intelletto"—[in order that anxiety might give them sense and understanding]; which was afterwards repeated even in the printed works: "cognitumque fuit solam vexationem posse Bohemis intellectum præbere"—[and it was known that vexation alone could give the Bohemians understanding].

amazed at the numbers that frequented the churches in Prague, many a Sunday morning from two to three thousand individuals, and how becoming, devout, and externally Roman catholic their behaviour! He concludes from this that Roman catholic recollections had never been entirely obliterated there; as might be seen, for example, from the huge cross on the bridge not having been allowed to be removed even by the consort of King Frederick; the reason no doubt was that protestant convictions had in fact in this quarter never penetrated the masses. The conversions went on without intermission. In 1624 the Jesuits alone had brought back 16,000 souls to the Roman catholic church.[1] In Tabor, where protestantism seemed to prevail exclusively, fifty families went over as early as Easter, 1622, and were followed by all the rest in Easter, 1623. How completely Roman catholic had Bohemia become with the time.

In Moravia, too, all now went on as in Bohemia, and there, indeed, the object aimed at was attained so much the more expeditiously, in as much as Cardinal Dietrichstein, being at once governor of the country and bishop of Olmütz, exercised in this spirit the ecclesiastical and civil government simultaneously. Here there was but one special difficulty to be overcome. The nobility refused to allow the Moravian brethren to be taken from them, persons whose services in house and land were invaluable, and the districts cultivated by whom were the most flourishing in the country;[2] nay, they found advocates in the emper-

1 Caraffa: "messovi un sacerdote catolico di molta dottrina, e poi facendosi missioni di alcuni padri Gesuiti"—[a catholic priest of much learning being placed there, and then missions conducted by some Jesuit Fathers].

2 Ragguaglio di Caraffa: "Essendo essi tenuti huomini d'industria e d'integrità venivano impiegati nella custodia de' terreni, delle case, delle cantine e de' molini, oltre che lavorando eccellentemente in alcuni mestieri erano divenuti ricchi e contribuivano gran parte del loro guadagno a' signori de' luoghi ne' quali habitavano, sebbene da qualche tempo indietro havevano cominciato a corrompersi essendo entrata tra di loro l'ambizione e l'avarizia con qualche parte di lusso per comodità della vita. Costoro si erano sempre andati augumentando in Moravia, perciocchè oltre a quelli che seducevano nella provincia e ne' luoghi convicini, havevano corrispondenza per tutti li luoghi della Germania, di dove recorrevano alla loro fratellanza tutti quelli che per debito o povertà disperavano potersi sostentare, e specialmente veniva ad essi gran numero di poveri Grisoni e di Suevia lasciandosi rapire da quel nome di fratellanza e sicurtà di havere sempre del pane, che in casa loro diffidavano potersi col proprio sudore guadagnare, onde si sono avvanzati alle volte sino al numero di centomila."—[These being considered to be persons of industry and integrity, came to be employed in the custody of landed estates, houses, cellars, and mills; besides, as they wrought excellently at some handicrafts, they had become rich and contributed a great part of their gains to the landlords of the places which they inhabited, albeit that for some time past they have begun to be corrupted, there having entered

or's privy council itself. But even here the nuncio and the principle triumphed notwithstanding. About 15,000 were removed.

In the Glatz country the young count Thurn had once more led the protestant standards to victory, but the Poles came to the assistance of the imperialists, whereupon the country was overpowered, the city likewise captured, and the Roman catholic worship restored with the usual vigour. Some sixty preachers were banished from the country; no insignificant number of the faithful followed them; for this their property was confiscated; the mob apostatized to Roman catholicism.[1]

Under these circumstances the endeavours to restore Roman catholicism in Austria proper, which had failed so often, and had so often been repeated, were finally renewed with decisive success.[2] First, those preachers that had been accused of rebellion, and then all the rest were banished; supplied with a pittance for their journey, these poor people slowly wended their way up the Danube, followed by the contemptuous cry; "where is now your strong tower?"[3] The emperor straightway declared to the estates of the country, without reserve, "that he had wholly and absolutely charged himself and his posterity with the disposition of matters relating to religion." In October 1624, a commission appeared which appointed a certain term for the inhabitants,

among them ambition and avarice, as well as some measure of luxury in regard to the conveniences of life. These have always gone on augmenting in Moravia, in as much as besides those that seduce in the province and neighbouring places, they have correspondence with all parts of Germany, from whence recourse is had to the brotherhood by all who from debt or poverty despair of being able to support themselves, and in particular there comes to them a great number of poor people from the Grisons and from Suabia, being allowed to please themselves with that title of brotherhood, and to be sure of always having bread which at their homes they are doubtful of being able to gain by the sweat of their own brow, whence they have advanced constantly even to the number of a hundred thousand.]

1 Köglers Chronik von Glatz, I. III. 92.

2 It had been the first thought of the emperor, even before the battle of Prague when Maximilian invaded the Upper Austrian territory; he urged the latter to displace the preachers without delay, "thus the pipers will be sent away and the dance left off."—See his letter in Breier's Continuation of Wolf; Maximilian IV. 414. In 1624 the Jesuits had the University of Vienna put entirely into their hands. "Imperator societatem academiæ intexuit et in unum quasi corpus conflavit, data illi amplissima potestate docendi literas humaniores, linguam latinam, græcam, hebraicam, philosophiam denique omnem ac theologiam." Monitum ad statuta acad. Vindob. recentiora. Kollar, Anal. II. p. 282.—[The emperor has interwoven the society into the academy, and thrown them as it were into one body, having given it most ample power of teaching humanity, Latin, Greek, Hebrew, in fine the whole body of philosophy and divinity. Monitum to the more modern statutes of the Vienna academy. Kollar's Annals, II. p. 282.]

3 Referring doubtless to the well-known hymn by Luther, commencing, "A strong tower is our God." Tr.

within which they had either to conform to the Roman catholic ritual or to leave the country. Some connivance was still shown for a very short time to the nobility personally

Though Hungary too had been subdued, such a violent course could not be adopted there; still the march of events, government favour, and, above all, the efforts of Archbishop Pazmany, brought about a change there also. Pazmany had a remarkable talent for writing his mother tongue. His book, intituled Kalauz,[1] full of genius and learning, was to his countrymen irresistible. He was endowed also with the gift of eloquence; he had by his personal efforts induced about fifty families to apostatize. Among these we find such names as Zrinyi, Forgacz, Erbödy, Balassa, Jakusith, Homonay, Adam Thurzo. Count Adam Zrinyi alone expelled twenty protestant pastors, and replaced them with Roman catholic priests. Under these influences public affairs, too, in Hungary took a different turn. At the national diet of 1625, the Roman catholic and Austrian party had the majority. One of the converted, an Esterhazy, in conformity with the wishes of the court, was appointed Palatine.

But let us mark the precise difference here. The transition (from popery to protestantism) was a much more voluntary act in Hungary than in the other provinces; the magnates, in making it, did not give up a single right they had; these rights might rather be considered as acquired anew. In the Austrian Bohemian territories, on the contrary, the entire independence of the estates, their strength and power, had been thrown into the forms of protestantism; the transition with them, if not in every individual case, yet in general was compulsory; with the restoration of Roman catholicism the absolute power of the government immediately supervened.

THE EMPIRE.—TRANSFERENCE OF THE ELECTORATE.

WE know to how much farther an extent proceedings had already been carried in the empire than in the hereditary dominions (of the house of Austria); nevertheless the new events that had taken place produced there likewise an indescribable effect.

The counter-reformation once more obtained a fresh impulse and a new field.

[1] Hodoegus Igazságra vezérlö Kalauz. Presb. 1613, 1623.

After Maximilian had taken possession of the Upper palatinate, he proceeded without delay to change its religion; he divided the country into twenty stations, in which fifty Jesuits went to work; the churches were compelled to be given up to them, the exercise of the protestant religion was generally prohibited; the more the probability increased that the country would continue Bavarian, the more the inhabitants yielded compliance.[1]

The Lower palatinate, too, was considered by the victors as their own property. Maximilian even made a present of the library at Heidelberg to the pope!

Previous to the conquest of the country, to add a word about this in passing, the pope, through the nuncio Montorio in Cologne, had applied to the duke for this favour; the duke, with his usual alacrity, had given a promise, and on the first arrival of the news that Heidelberg was taken, Montorio availed himself of the right he had thus acquired. He had been told that the manuscripts in particular were of inestimable value, and all he asked of Tilly was that they should be protected amid the general pillage.[2] Then the pope sent Dr. Leone Allacci, scribe to the Vatican, to Germany to take possession of the books. Gregory XV. considered it a matter of the highest consequence. He declared it to be one of the most fortunate occurrences in the course of his pontificate, and one that would prove honourable and useful to the holy see, to the church, and to the sciences; for the Bavarian name, too, it would be glorious that so precious a trophy should be preserved to everlasting remembrance, in that great theatre of the world, Rome.[3]

Moreover, here too, the duke displayed an indefatigable reforming zeal; in this he surpassed the Spaniards, good Roman catholics as they were.[4] The nuncio was in ecstasy at seeing

[1] Kropff: Historia societatis Jesu in Germania superiori, tom. IV. p. 271.—[Kropff's History of the Jesuits in Upper Germany, vol. IV. p. 271.]

[2] Relatione di Mr Montorio ritornato nunzio di Colonia 1624.—[Report of Monsignor Montorio on his return as nuncio from Cologne, 1624.] See the passages given in the Appendix.

[3] "Che cosi pretioso spoglio e così nobil trofeo si conservi a perpetua memoria in questo teatro del mondo."—[Which, as a precious spoil and a noble trophy, should be preserved in this theatre of the world.] Instruttione al dottore Leon Allatio per andare in Germania per la libreria del Palatino.—[Instruction to Dr. Leo Allacci for going into Germany, for the library of the Palatine.] We shall prove its genuineness in the Appendix.

[4] Montorio: "Benchè nelle terre che occupano i Spagnuoli non si camini con quel fervore con quale si camina in quelle che occupa il Sr Da di Baviera alla con-

the mass celebrated, and conversions taking place in Heidelberg, "whence the doctrinal standard of the Calvinists, the far-famed catechism, had gone forth."

Meanwhile the elector Schweikard reformed the[1] Bergstrasse, of which he had taken possession, and the margrave William Upper-baden, which, after a long lawsuit, was recognised as his, although his ancestry was hardly legitimate, not to say equal in birth (to the title): he had already expressly promised it to the nuncio Caraffa.[2] Even in territories not immediately affected by political events, the old efforts were put forth with renovated zeal. In Bamberg,[3] in Fulda, on the Eichsfeld, in Paderborn, where twice in succession Roman catholic bishops occupied the see; particularly in the country about Münster, where Meppen, Vechta, Halteran, and many other circles were made Roman catholic. Archbishop Ferdinand established missions in almost all the towns, and in Coesfield, "for the bringing back of the ancient catholic religion, to which so many had become indifferent," she founded a college of Jesuits.[4] We find Jesuit missionaries as far as Halberstadt and Magdeburg. They settled in Altona for the purpose of first acquiring the languages, and then pressing forward into Denmark and Sweden.

Thus we see these Roman catholic efforts powerfully diffused from Upper to Lower Germany, from the south to the north. Meanwhile a fresh attempt was also made to carry by force a new position in the general concerns of the empire.

Immediately after the league was concluded, Ferdinand II.

versione de' popoli."—[Although in the lands occupied by the Spaniards, people do not proceed to the conversion of the inhabitants with the fervour shown by the duke of Bavaria.]

1 A district of country lying contiguous to the road of the same name, leading from Heidelberg to the vicinity of Darmstadt. The district is very fruitful, and hence is sometimes called the German paradise. Tr.

2 Caraffa: Germania restaurata, p. 129.

3 Particularly by John George Fuchs of Dornheim, who also brought back to Roman catholicism twenty-three parsonages belonging to the nobility. See Jäck's Geschichte von Bamberg, II. 120.

4 A letter of one of his assistants, John Drachter, dean at Dülmen, sounds exceedingly strange: "ungern hab ich J. Ch. D. einen grossen Anzhall der hirnlosen Schaifen überschreiben willen, und mich uf die heutige Stunde noch lieber bearbeitet noch alle mit einander mit swebender Furcht in den rechten Schaifstall hineinzujagen, wie dann och Balthasar Bilderbeck und Gaspar Karl mit zwen Füssen schon hineingestiegen."—[I have been unwilling to address to you a great many silly sheep, and would more readily have employed myself at the present time in driving them all, one after another, with perplexity and fear into the right sheep fold, as Balthasar Bilberbeck and Gaspar Karl also have already walked into it with two feet.]

had given a promise to Duke Maximilian, that in the event of its success the electorship of the palatinate should be transferred to him.[1]

There can be no question as to the object mainly contemplated on the side of the Roman catholics in this project. The majority of votes which that party possessed in the council of the princes, had been met hitherto by the equality of votes possessed by the protestants in the electoral college; but should the transference take place, then any such trammel would be for ever got rid of.[2]

The papal court had from of old maintained the most intimate good understanding with Bavaria, and Gregory XV. too made this affair peculiarly his own.

By the very first nuncio that he sent into Spain, he caused the king to be admonished, upon the count palatine being utterly ruined, to assist in the transference of the electorate, as a step that would secure the imperial crown to the Roman catholics for ever.[3] The Spaniards were not quite so ready to agree to it. They were engaged in the most important negotiations with the king of England, and scrupled to offend him in the person of his son in law, that very count palatine Frederick, to whom the electorate belonged. So much the keener did Pope Gregory become. He was not satisfied with having the nuncio only; in 1622 we find that expert Capuchin friar, brother Hyacinth, who enjoyed the special confidence of Maximilian, at the Spanish court with a commission from the pope.[4] It was with the ut-

1 Emperor's letter to Balthasar de Zuniga, 15 October 1621, printed by Sattler: Würtemberg Geschichte, VI. p. 162.

2 Instruttione a Mr Sacchetti nuntio in Spagna—[the instruction to Monsignor Sacchetti, nuncio in Spain] speaks of the giving back of the Palatinate as an "irreparabile perdita della reputazione di questo fatto e della chiesa cattolica, se il papa ci avesse condisceso, con indicibil danno della religione cattolica e dell' imperio: che tanti e tanti anni hanno bramato, senza poterlo sapere, non che ottenere, il quarto elettor cattolico in servitio ancora del sangue Austriaco."—[irreparable loss of reputation from this being done, and of the catholic church, if the pope had acceded to it, together with an unspeakable loss to the catholic religion and to the empire: which have for so many years desired, without being able to know, or to effect, that the fourth elector should be a catholic, and further in the service of the blood of Austria.]

3 Instruttione a Monsr Sangro.—[Instruction to Monsignor Sangro.] He was admonished, "di infervorare S. Mta, acciò non si lasci risorgere il Palatino, e si metta l'elettorato in persona cattolica, e si assicuri l'impero eternamente fra cattolici."—[to urge his Majesty that he do not suffer the palatine to rise again (from his defeat), and to place the electorate in the hands of a Roman catholic, and to secure the empire for ever among Roman catholics.]

4 Khevenhiller, IX. p. 1766.

most reluctance that any farther countenance was given to the project there. The utmost that the king would allow himself to say at last, was that he would rather see the electorate vested in the Bavarian family than in his own. This satisfied brother Hyacinth; he hastened with the above declaration to Vienna, in order to remove from the emperor's mind the scruples he might entertain respecting Spain. He was then aided there by the wonted influence of Cardinal Caraffa, and the pope himself came to his assistance with a new letter. "See there," exclaims the pope to the emperor in that letter, "the gates of heaven are opened; the heavenly hosts urge thee on to earn so great an honour; they will fight for thee in thy camp." The emperor was influenced withal by a singular consideration which well marks his character. He had long ere now contemplated the transference, and had expressed his views respecting it in a letter which had fallen into the hands of the protestants and came to be known amongst them. The emperor, in consequence of this, thought himself virtually bound to carry his purpose into effect. He deemed it necessary to his own dignity to hold fast to a wish that he had once cherished, all the more strictly the more people had come to know about it. Enough, he fully resolved to take steps for effecting the transference at the next electoral diet.[1]

The only question that now remained was, whether the princes of the empire also would give their approbation. As to this, most depended on Schweikard of Maintz, and the nuncio Montorio at least assures us that that cautious prince was at first against it, that he declared that the war would only be renewed more fearfully than it had raged already: moreover, that if people would have a change, the count palatine of Neuburg having nearer right, it was impossible to pass him over. The nuncio does not say by what reasons he at last brought the prince over to his opinion. His words are, "in four or five days which I spent with him at Aschaffenburg, I obtained the wished for resolution." This is all that we can perceive: in the event of the war being renewed, strenuous assistance from the pope was promised.

But the resolution of the electoral prince of Maintz was in this case decisive. He was followed in his opinion by his two

[1] Caraffa: Germania restaurata, p. 120.

Rhenish colleagues. Although Brandenburg and Saxony still persisted in their opposition—that of Saxony was removed likewise by the archbishop of Maintz[1]—although the Spanish ambassador, too, now directly declared against it,[2] the emperor, notwithstanding, proceeded without flinching to effect his design. On the 25th of February 1623, he transferred the electorate to his victorious ally; yet, in the first instance, it was only to be a personal possession: the palatine heirs and agnates were to have their right reserved to them entire for the future.[3]

Meanwhile, even under this restriction, an immense deal was gained, above all, the preponderance in the supreme court of the empire, whose assent now gave a legal sanction to every new resolution in favour of Roman catholicism.

Maximilian saw well how much in this matter he was obliged to Pope Gregory XV. "Your holiness," he writes, "has not only furthered this business, but through your suggestions, your authority, and your zealous endeavours, has directly brought it about. Altogether and absolutely must it be ascribed to the favour and vigilance of your holiness."

"Thy letter, O son," replied Gregory XV., "hath filled our breast with a stream of delight as if with heavenly manna: at last may the daughter of Zion shake the ashes of grief from her head, and clothe herself in festive raiment."[4]

[1] Montorio calls Schweikard, "unico instigatore a far voltare Sassonia a favore dell'imperatore nella translatione dell'elettorato:"—[the sole instigator in making Saxony turn in favour of the emperor in the translation of the electorate].

[2] See Onate's declaration and the vehement letter of Ludovisio against giving back the electorate to a blaspheming Calvinist, in Khevenhiller X. 67, 68.

[3] The president Henault, under the year 1622, says: "The Spaniards divert the attention of James I. (*amusent Jacques I.*) by the hope of giving the infanta in marriage to the prince of Wales," &c. Now if the marriage was all along on their part a mere feint, and if the dispensation was procured from the pope merely to throw the odium of the rupture on England when the deception practised with regard to the palatinate became evident, the Spanish ambassador's opposition must have been dissembled, and the emperor might well proceed unflinchingly to execute his project, since he must have known Spain to be really in favour of it. The deceptions practised by the papacy and Roman catholic governments on the protestant during this whole period—may we not say, down to the present day?—will probably never be fully known till the day when all secret things shall be brought to light, but even from the little that may be seen of them, they are perfectly astonishing for their want of principle, astuteness, and, alas! also for their success.—Tr.

[4] Giunti, Vita di Ludovisio Ludovisi, ascribes the chief merit to the nephew. "Da S. Sta e dal Cle furono scritte molte lettere anche di proprio pugno piene d'ardore et efficacia per disporre Cesare, et in oltre fu mandato Mor Verospi auditore di rota, e doppo il P. F. Giacinto di Casale cappuccino."—[Many letters were written by his Holiness and by the Cardinal, with his own hand, too, full of ardour and efficacy, in order to dispose the emperor, and besides Monsignor Verospi, auditor of the Rota, was despatched, and afterwards father F. Hyacinth di Casale, capuchin.]

III.—FRANCE.

At the same moment the great turn in the state of matters in France commenced.

If we inquire to what the losses sustained by protestantism in 1621 are mainly to be ascribed, the answer seems to be, that they were caused by its own dissensions and by the apostasy of the nobles. Very possibly this may have been connected with those republican efforts which had a municipal and a theological foundation, and were unfavourable to the influence of the nobility. The nobles may have thought it more advantageous to adhere to the king and the court, than to allow themselves to be governed by preachers and burgomasters. Enough—already, in 1621, the warranty cities were delivered up by their governors, who seemed to emulate each other in their eagerness to do so; each only sought to bargain for a favourable post to himself. This was repeated in 1622. La Force and Chatillon received marshal's batons on separating from their fellow religionists: old Lesdiguières became Roman catholic;[1] and even led part of an army against the protestants: their example hurried many more into apostasy.[2] Under these circumstances, nothing but a most unfavourable peace could be concluded in 1622. Nay, people durst not even flatter themselves that it would be observed. At an earlier period, when the protestants were powerful, the king had often transgressed and broken the stipulations: was he likely to observe these now, after they had lost their power? Everything was done that the peace had interdicted: the protestant form of worship was in many quarters prevented: the Reformed were forbidden to sing psalms on the street, or in their shops: their university privileges were circumscribed.[3] Fort Louis, which it had been promised should be demolished, was preserved: there followed an attempt to bring the election of the magistrates in the protestant towns into the hands of the king:[4]

[1] Mémoires de Deageant, p. 190, and at many other places very well worth notice with respect to this apostasy.

[2] Liste des gentilhommes de la religion réduits au roi, [list of men of noble birth belonging to the religion (*i. e.* protestants) who have been brought back to the king] in Malingre's Histoire des derniers troubles arrivés en France, p. 789. Rohan, too, made his terms: unfortunately, however, the articles agreed to, as they stand in the Mercure de France, VII. p. 845, are not authentic.

[3] Benoist, II. 419.

[4] Rohan: Mém. l. III.

by an edict likewise of the 17th of April 1622, a commissioner was appointed for the assemblies of the Reformed; after these had once allowed so great an invasion of their long established franchises, the government interfered in concerns that were purely ecclesiastical: the Huguenots were prevented by the commissioners from accepting the decrees of the Synod of Dort.

They ceased to have any further independence: they could no longer offer any effective resistance. Conversions spread throughout their whole territory.

The Capuchins filled Poitou and Languedoc with missions:[1] the Jesuits, who maintained new institutions in Aix, Lyons, Pau, and many other quarters, were making the greatest progress in town and country: their fraternities of the Virgin Mary contrived to obtain general notice and approbation, by the assiduity of their attentions to the wounded in the last war.[2]

Franciscans also distinguished themselves, such as that father Villele of Bourdeaux, of whom it is almost mythically related, that after he had brought over the whole town of Foix to his side, an old man of above a hundred years of age had again conformed to Roman catholicism, though he was the very person that, once on a day, had received the first protestant minister from the hands of Calvin, and had conducted him to Foix. The protestant churches were pulled down; and the triumphant *patres* caused the expelled ministers to be attended by trumpeters, as they passed from town to town.[3]

Enough, the work of conversion went on vigorously, including high and low, and even the learned: these last being particularly influenced by the proof that the ancient church, even before the council of Nice, invoked the saints, prayed for the dead, and had a hierarchy, and many Roman catholic customs.[4]

[1] Instruttione all'arcivescovo di Damiata, MS.

[2] Cordara: Historia societatis Jesu, VII. 95, 118.

[3] Relation catholique inserted in the Mercure françois, VIII. 489.

[4] There must have been a marvellous undecidedness in their protestantism to have allowed them to be so easily seduced. That corruption began long before the council of Nice is notorious. Similar statements seem, however, at the present day even, to be perfectly credited; it being not uncommon to hear it said, that the Roman catholic church is fundamentally pure in doctrine and correct in practice; that it is only in the lapse of ages and by the degeneracy of mankind that her doctrines have been perverted, or smothered with rubbish. Arguments founded upon such statements concerning the condition of the church during the times of the fathers, always stop short a step in the journey backwards into antiquity in search of purity; another step in the same direction and the New Testament would be

There are still extant reports by some of the bishops, from which we can calculate the numerical proportion of the adherents of the two creeds, as it came to be fixed amid these circumstances. In the diocese of Poictiers the half of the inhabitants in some towns were protestants, for example, in Lusignan and St. Maixant: in others, such as Chauvigny and Niort, a third: a fourth in Loudun: in Poitiers itself, only a twentieth part: a much smaller proportion in the country.[1] For the furtherance of the conversions the bishops kept up a direct intercourse with the see of Rome: to it they made their reports and laid their wishes before it: the nuncio was instructed to bring before the king's notice what they should indicate to him, and to preface it with words of his own. In this they often entered into particulars. The bishop of Vienne, for example, finds the missionaries particularly kept in check by a protestant preacher in St. Marcellin, who had shown that he was not to be driven off the field: the nuncio was commissioned to urge the court to have him removed. He was to support the bishop of St. Malo, who complained that no Roman catholic worship was allowed to be held in a castle in his diocese. For the bishop of Xaintes he was to procure an expert converter, who was pointed out to him by name. The bishops were occasionally required, in the case of their encountering obstacles, to specify more particularly what might be done, in order that the nuncio might make corresponding representations to the king.[2]

reached, which alone can be held as the test by which to judge the doctrine or the practice either of churches or individuals.—Tr.

1 Relatione del vescovo di Poitiers, 1623, MS.

2 Instruttione all'arcivescovo di Damiata: a single instance will suffice.—" Dalla relatione del vescovo di Candon si cava, che ha il detto vescovo la terra di Neaco, ove sono molti eretici, con una missione di Gesuiti, li quali in danno s'affaticano se con l'autorità temporale il re non da qualche buon ordine: ed ella potrà scrivere al detto vescovo che avvisi ciò che può fare Sua M^{ta}, perché nella relatione non lo specifica. Da quella del vescovo di S. Malo s'intende che in un castello e villa del marchese di Moussaye è solo lecito di predicare a Calvinisti: però sarebbe bene di ricordare alla M^{ta} del re che levasse i predicatori acciocchè i missionarj del vescovo potessero far frutto: il castello e villa non è nominato nella relatione, e però si potrà scrivere al vescovo per saperlo. Il vescovo di Monpellier avvisa di haver carestia d'operarj, e che dagli eretici sono sentiti volontieri i patri Cappuccini, onde se gli potrebbe procurare una missione di questi padri.—[From the report of the bishop of Candom it comes out that the said bishop has the estate of Neaco, where there are many heretics, with a mission of Jesuits, who labour at a disadvantage, unless, with the temporal authority, the king gives out some good orders: and it (the temporal authority) might write to the bishop, who may advise what might be done by his Majesty, since that is not particularly mentioned in the report. From that of the bishop of St. Malo, it appears, that in a castle and small town of the marquis of

Thus there was an intimate union of all the spiritual powers with the pope and with the Propaganda, which, as we have remarked, was perhaps most effective in its earliest years: zeal and a lively activity follow in the wake of a successful decision in an appeal to arms: the court, seeing a great political interest involved in it, puts forth its sympathy: the whole exhibiting a period in which the subversion of protestantism in France was finally accomplished.

IV.—THE UNITED NETHERLANDS.

But this progress was not confined to countries where the government was Roman catholic: it was manifest at the same moment in countries under protestant sway.

One is confounded at reading in Bentivoglio that in those very towns of the Netherlands which had offered so heroic and long-continued a resistance to the king of Spain, mainly on religious grounds, perhaps the majority of the leading families professed Roman catholicism:[1] but what is much more striking, a circumstantial account of the year 1622 even informs us of the augmentation and advances of Roman catholicism under such unfavourable circumstances. The priests were persecuted and expelled, notwithstanding which their numbers increased. In the year 1592, the first Jesuit came into the Netherlands; in 1622, there were reckoned 22 members of that order there. From the colleges at Cologne and Louvain, new labourers were constantly going forth, so that in 1622 there were 220 secular priests employed in the provinces, but they were far from being adequate to the wants of the country. According to that account, the number of Roman catholics in the archdiocese of Utrecht had risen to 150,000, in the diocese of Haarlem, to which Amster-

Moussayes,* leave is given to preach to the Calvinists alone: wherefore it were well to memorialize to the king's majesty that he should take away the preachers, so that the bishop's missionaries may produce some effect: the castle and town are not named in the report, and therefore the bishop might be written to, that they be known. The bishop of Montpellier intimates that he is in need of labourers, and that, as the Capuchin fathers are willingly listened to by the heretics, a mission of the said fathers might be procured for him.]

[1] Relatione delle provincie ubbidienti, parte II., c. II.—[Account of the provinces that have retained their obedience, part II., ch. II.], where religion in Holland falls under notice.

* The Moussaye family deserve to be honourably recorded as unflinching protestants at a time of very general apostasy. The "Proces Verbaux" (Minutes) of the Gallican church show that they never ceased to furnish matter of complaint on the part of the clergy to the court, by their steadfast adherence to the religion of the Bible as opposed to that of Rome. Tr.

dam belonged, to 100,000 souls: Leuwarden had 15,000, Gröningen 20,000, Deventer 60,000 Roman catholics: the vicar-apostolic, who was sent at that time from the Roman see to Deventer, administered confirmation to 12,000 persons in three towns and some villages. The numbers given by this account must be much exaggerated; still it is evident that even that pre-eminently protestant country had uncommonly strong Roman catholic elements. Even some of the episcopal sees which Philip II. had attempted to introduce, were from that time forward recognized by the Roman catholics.[1] This state of things might even have been the grand incentive with the Spaniards in leading them to renew the war.

V.—RELATION TO ENGLAND.

MORE peaceful prospects had meanwhile opened up in England. The son of Mary Stuart had united the British crowns, and, in a more decided manner than ever, he was now making an approach to the Roman catholic powers.

Even before James I. had ascended the throne of England, Clement VIII. had intimated to him that "he prayed for him as the son of a mother so rich in virtues; he wished him all temporal and spiritual welfare, he hoped yet to see him become Roman catholic." His accession was celebrated at Rome with solemn prayers and processions.

This approach was what James durst not have ventured fully to reciprocate, even had he been inclined to do so. But he went so far as to permit Parry, his ambassador at Paris, to enter into a confidential understanding with Bubalis, the nuncio there. The nuncio came forward with a letter from the cardinal nephew Aldobrandino, in which he exhorted the English Roman catholics to obey King James as their king and natural lord, nay, even to pray for him: Parry met this with a body of instructions from James, in which the king engaged to allow peaceable

[1] Compendium status in quo nunc est religio catholica in Holandia et confœderatis Belgii provinciis—[compendium of the state which the catholic religion now presents in Holland and the confederate provinces of Belgium], 2 Dec. 1622: "his non obstantibus—laus Deo—quotidie crescit catholicorum numerus, præsertim accedente dissensione hæreticorum inter se."—[notwithstanding these things—praise be to God—the number of the catholics is constantly increasing, specially aided by the dissensions of the heretics among themselves.]

Roman catholics to live without any burdens being imposed on them.[1]

In point of fact the mass again began to be openly held in the north of England; the puritans complained that within a short period 50,000 English had gone over to Roman catholicism; James is said to have replied that "on their side they might convert an equal number of Spaniards or Italians."[2]

This success might have given occasion for the Roman catholics to stretch their hopes too high. As therewithal the king still kept himself on the other side, as the old acts of parliament were again carried into effect, and new persecutions followed, they fell into so much the greater exasperation and ferment:—all which burst forth frightfully in the gunpowder plot.

Upon that the king even could nowise admit of any further toleration. The severest laws were passed and executed: domiciliary visits, imprisonment, and fines were denounced; priests, and especially Jesuits, were banished and persecuted; it was thought necessary to use the utmost rigour in bridling in such enterprising enemies.

But when the king was questioned privately, his expressions were very moderate. He directly told a Lorraine prince, who, not without the privity of Paul V., paid him a visit, that betwixt the two confessions there was in the end no great difference. It is true, he considered his own as the best; he adopted it from conviction, not from political reasons; but willingly would he listen to another. As he thought the calling of a council would be attended with too many difficulties, yet he would willingly see a convention of learned men brought about, for the purpose of attempting a reconciliation. Would the pope advance but one step to him, he would take four on the other side. He, too, owned the authority of the fathers: he valued Augustine above Luther, St. Bernard above Calvin: nay, he saw in the Romish church, even as it was at present, the true church, the mother of all others, it only needed purification:—he agreed, what he certainly would never have said to a nuncio,

[1] Breve relatione di quanto si è tratto tra S. Sta ed il re d'Inghilterra.—[Brief account of as much as was treated of between His Holiness and the king of England.] (MS. Rom.)

[2] And no doubt they might easily have done so, under an equal relaxation of the laws against protestantism in Spain and Italy. The monarch's taunt was silly in the extreme. Tr.

but might confide to a friend and kinsman, that the pope is the head of the church, the supreme bishop.[1] It would therefore be doing him great injustice, were he to be signalized as a heretic and schismatic: a heretic he was not, for he believed just what the pope believed, only that the latter included something more in his creed; and he was no schismatic, for he considered the pope to be the head of the church.

With such sentiments, and connected with these an aversion towards the puritanical side of protestantism, the king would certainly prefer being on a friendly understanding with the Roman catholics, to holding them in check by making them feel his power, and keeping them in constant jeopardy.

In England they still continued to be powerful and numerous. In spite of great reverses and losses, or rather directly in consequence of these, Ireland was in a state of constant fermentation; it was of great consequence to the king that he should be relieved of this opposition.

Now the reader must be aware that the English and Irish Roman catholics attached themselves to Spain. The Spanish ambassadors in London, active, clever, and magnificent, had procured for themselves an extraordinary number of adherents: their chapel was always full, the holy week was celebrated with great pomp: the ambassadors took their co-religionists in crowds along with them: as a Venetian remarks, they were looked upon much in the same light as the legates of the apostolical see.

I am not afraid of being in error when I assume that it was this bond of relationship above all, that led King James to entertain the idea of marrying his heir to a Spanish princess.[2] He hoped that he should thereby make sure of the Roman catholics,

[1] "Che riconosce la chiesa Romana etiando quella d'adesso per la vera chiesa e madre di tutte, ma ch'ella aveva bisogno d'esser purgata, e di più ch'egli sapeva che V. Sta è capo di essa chiesa e primo vescovo :"—[That he recognized the church of Rome, even that of the present day, for the true church and mother of all, but that it had need of being purified; and still more, that he knew that his holiness is head of the church and first bishop]: expressions that can in no wise be reconciled with the principle of the English church, as subscribed, however, by that monarch elsewhere. (Relatione del S^r^ di Breval al papa.)

[2] Relatione di D. Lazzari 1621, ascribes this project to the king's timidity: "havendo io esperimentato per manifesti segni che prevale in lui più il timore che l'ira" —[for I have found out by manifest tokens that fear is more prevalent in him than anger]. Moreover, "per la pratica che ho di lui (del re) lo stimo indifferente in qualsivoglia religione"—[from the intercourse I have had with him (the king), I consider him indifferent as to what religion he professes].

and gain over to his own family that favour which they were now devoting to the royal family of Spain. Foreign relations added a new motive for his doing so. He cherished the hope that the house of Austria, on being nearly allied to him, would show itself more favourable to his son-in-law of the Palatinate.

It only remains to be inquired whether the match could be carried into effect. In the difference of religion there lay an obstacle which, in those days, it was truly no easy matter to remove.

This world, this present order of things, will ever be found surrounded with a fantastical element which expresses itself in poetry and romantic narratives, and then comes easily to react upon life in youth. As the negotiations that had been commenced were protracted from day to day and month to month, the prince of Wales conceived the romantic idea, along with his trusty friend and contemporary, Buckingham, to set off and to fetch his bride himself.[1] The Spanish ambassador, Gondamar, seems not to have been altogether without participation in this enterprise. He had told the prince that his presence would put an end to all difficulties.

How amazed was the English ambassador at Madrid, Lord Digby, who had till then been conducting the negotiations, on being called one day out of his chamber to see two cavaliers who wanted to speak with him, to recognize in those two cavaliers the son and the favourite of his king!

And now certainly the utmost earnestness was shown in endeavouring to remove the grand religious difficulty.

For this there was required the papal consent, and King James had not been afraid to open direct negotiations on the subject with Paul V. Yet that pope would accede only under the condition that the king should grant complete religious liberty to the Roman catholics in his territories. On the other hand, such was the impression made on Gregory XV. by the demonstration implied in the prince's journey, that he even thought forthwith that smaller concessions might be accepted. In a letter to the prince,

[1] Papers relative to the Spanish match, in Hardwicke Papers, I. p. 399. They comprise a correspondence between James I. and the two travellers, which makes one feel the greatest interest in the persons who correspond. James's failings appear at least to have been very human. His first letter commences, "My sweat boys and dear ventrous knights worthy to be put in some new romanso." "My sweat boys," is the usual address, while they write, "dear dad and gossip."

he expresses to him his hope, "that the old seed of Christian piety, such as had once flourished in English kings, would now live again in him; in no event could he desire, since he thought of uniting himself in marriage with a catholic maiden, to oppress the catholic church." The prince replied that he would never exercise any hostility towards the Romish church; he would endeavour to bring it about, "as we all," says he, "acknowledge one triune God, and one crucified Christ, that we shall all unite in one faith and in one church."[1] It will be seen how near the mutual approach was on both sides. Olivarez asserted that when the pope was applied to in the most urgent manner about the dispensation, he declared to him that the king could refuse the prince nothing that was in his kingdom.[2] The English Roman catholics too were urgent with the pope; they represented that the refusal of the dispensation would bring along with it a new persecution for them.

Upon this the parties came to an agreement as to what the king was to engage for.

Not only was the infanta with her suite to be allowed the exercise of her religion in a chapel where the court resided, the first education also of the princes that might be born of the marriage, was to be left to her: no penal law was to have any application to them, nor was their right of succession to the crown to be at all invalidated by their continuing to be Roman catholics.[3] The king promised in general, "not to disturb the private exercise of the Roman catholic religion, not to compel the Roman catholics to any oaths inconsistent with their creed, and instead of that to provide that the laws against the Roman catholics should be repealed by the parliament."

In August, 1623, King James swore to observe these articles,

1 Often printed: I have adopted it as found in Clarendon and the Hardwicke papers, where it was copied from the original.

2 In the first burst of his delight, he even said after Buckingham's report (20th March), that if the pope would not give a dispensation for a wife, they would give the infanta to thy son's (son ?) baby as his wench.

3 The most important, and the source of much mischief. The article runs thus: "quod leges contra catholicos Romanos latæ vel ferendæ in Anglia et aliis regnis regi magnæ Britanniæ subjectis non attingent liberos ex hoc matrimonio oriundos, et libere jure successionis in regnis et dominiis magnæ Britanniæ fruantur."—[that the laws against Roman catholics passed or to be passed in England and other kingdoms subject to the king of Great Britain, shall not affect the children to be born of this marriage, and that they shall freely enjoy the right of succession in the kingdoms and dominions of Great Britain.] (Merc. Franc., IX., Appendice II. 18.)

and there seemed to remain no further doubts that the marriage would be carried into effect.

Public rejoicings now took place in Spain; the court there received congratulations; formal intimation of the marriage was sent to the ambassadors; the infanta's maids of honour and confessor were instructed not to drop a single expression against the marriage.

King James reminded his son, amid his delight at this auspicious alliance, not to forget his nephews, who were wrongfully deprived of their inheritance, or his sister, now bathed in tears. The case of Westphalia was zealously taken up. A proposal was made to draw the imperial line and the house of Westphalia also into this new connection: the son of the ex-elector palatine was to be married to a daughter of the emperor's; and that no offence might be done to Bavaria, it was suggested that an eighth electorate should be erected. The emperor opened forthwith negotiations on this scheme with Maximilian of Bavaria, who, we find, was not opposed to it, and only made the demand that the palatine electorate that had been transferred to him should remain in his hands, and the eighth to be newly erected, given to the palatinate. This did not amount to much, in as far as Roman catholicism was concerned. The Roman catholics were to enjoy religious liberty in the restored palatinate: they would have continued to command a majority of votes in the electoral college.[1]

Thus did that power which, under its former government, formed the grand bulwark of protestantism, pass into relations of amity with those old enemies, to whom it seemed to have vowed irreconcilable hatred—the pope and Spain. The Roman catholics soon began to be treated quite in a different manner in England. Domiciliary visits and persecutions ceased; the swearing of certain oaths was no longer required; Roman catholic chapels raised their heads to the indignation of the protestants; those puritanical zealots who condemned the marriage were punished. King James did not doubt that he should yet before winter embrace his son and his young wife, and also his favourite: all his letters express a heartfelt longing to do so.

It is evident what advantages must already have accrued from

[1] See Khevenhiller, X. 114.

the execution of that article: but the alliance itself led to the expectation of very different and immeasurable results. What force had failed to effect, namely, the acquisition of an influence on the administration of the government in England, seemed now to have been attained in the most pacific and natural manner.

VI.—MISSIONS.

At this place, in the consideration of this splendid progress in Europe, we may well direct our regards also to the more remote quarters of the world into which Roman catholicism, by dint of kindred impulses, had powerfully advanced.

Even in the very first idea that called forth the discoveries and conquests of the Spanish and Portuguese, there was involved a religious principle: this had all along accompanied and animated them: and it was strongly manifested in the kingdoms that grew out of them, both in the East and in the West.

At the commencement of the seventeenth century we find the proud fabric of the Roman catholic church fully erected in South America, including five archbishoprics, twenty-seven bishoprics, 400 monasteries and convents, innumerable parochial charges and doctrinas.[1] Magnificent cathedrals raised their heads; the most splendid perhaps was that of Los Angeles. The Jesuits taught mathematics and the liberal arts, while a theological seminary was attached to their college of San Ildefonso at Mexico. All the theological courses were taught at the universities of Mexico and Lima. We find that the Americans of European descent distinguished themselves by more than ordinary acuteness; they only regretted being too far removed from the regards of the royal favour to admit of their being rewarded according to their desert. Meanwhile the begging orders in particular had begun to diffuse Christianity in regular progress over the South American continent. Conquest had converted itself into mission, and mission became civilization; the friars taught the natives at once to sow and to reap, to plant trees and to build houses, to read and to sing. For that accordingly they were looked up to with deep submission. When the priest arrived in his parish he would be welcomed with the pealing of bells and music; flowers were strewed along the road; the women held

1 Herrera descripcion de las Indias, p. 80.

out their children that he might give them his blessing. The Indians manifested great delight in the external services of divine worship. They were not wearied with serving at mass, singing vespers and attending the choral office; they had a talent for music, and took an innocent delight in decking out a church with ornaments. For the simply and blamelessly fantastic seems to have made the strongest impression upon them.[1] In their dreams they beheld the joys of paradise. The queen of heaven appears to the sick in all her splendour, young female attendants encircle her and bring refreshments to the starving. Or she reveals herself all alone; and teaches her worshippers a song about her crucified son, "whose head droops like the stalk of yellow corn."

Such are the principles which Roman catholicism here employed. The monks only lament that the bad examples and violence of the Spaniards corrupted the natives, and stood in the way of their conversion.

Much the same process was now going on in the East Indies, within the limits of the Portuguese dominions. Roman catholicism obtained a central position of great importance in Goa; thousands were converted from year to year; as early as in 1565 there were reckoned to be about 300,000 new Christians about Goa, and in the hills of Cochin and at Cape Comorin.[2] But the general state of matters was altogether different. Arms as well as doctrine were here encountered by a vast, peculiar, unvanquished world; ancient religions, whose worship laid fetters upon the mind and soul, was intimately combined with the manners and intellectual habits of the nations comprised in it.

1 Compendio y descripcion de las Indias ocidentales, MS. "Tienen mucha caridad con los necessitados y en particular con los sacerdotes: que los respetan y reverencián como ministros de Christo, abraçcan los mas de tal suerte las cosas de nuestra santa fe, que solo el mal exemplo que los demos es causa de que no aya entre ellos grandes santos, como lo experimente el tiempo que estuve en aquellos reynos." —[They have much kindness for the necessitous and for the priests in particular; so that they respect and revere these as the ministers of Christ, thus the most of them embrace the things of our holy faith, so that nothing but the bad example that we set them is the cause that there are no great saints among them, as was proved the time that I was in those kingdoms.] The literæ annuæ provinciæ Paraquariæ missæ a Nicolao Duran, Antv. 1636,—[yearly letters of the province of Paraguaria (Paraguay?) sent by Nicolas Duran, Antwerp, 1636,] are particularly remarkable, for there the Jesuits kept the Spaniards at a distance.*

2 Maffei Commentarius de rebus Indicis, p. 21.

* The success of the Jesuit Missions in Paraguay has been much vaunted. But while it appears from Professor Ranke's text that the Indians were at the best brought up like children, in what would be a childish idolatry, if idolatry were not in every case a very awful sin, the results that followed on the removal of the Jesuits, prove that even the civilization they had introduced had no moral power to sustain it, and was itself childish and unsatisfactory. Tr.

It was the natural tendency of Roman catholicism to extend its conquests over even this world.

This idea lay at the bottom of all the exertions of Francis Xavier, who arrived in the East Indies as early as in 1542. He traversed India far and wide. He prayed at the tomb of the apostle Thomas at Meliapoor; he preached from a tree to the people at Travancore; taught at the Moluccas spiritual songs, which were afterwards repeated by boys at the market and fishermen on the sea; yet he was not born to perfect his wish; his favourite words were, Amplius! Amplius![1] His zeal as a converter was likewise a kind of passion for travelling; he soon reached Japan; he had thoughts of tracing out in China the native seat and origin of the peculiarities of character which he met with there, when he died.[2]

It was to be expected from what we know of human nature, that his example, the difficulty attending the undertaking, rather provoked to imitation than deterred from the attempt. Men were employed in the most manifold ways in the East during the first decades of the 17th century.

In Madura we find father Nobili from the year 1606. He was amazed to see how little progress had been made by Christianity in a long period, and thought that it could be accounted for only by the Portuguese having addressed themselves to the Parias.[3] Christ came to be considered as a god of the Parias! Very different was the manner in which he proceeded to the assault, for instead of that he held that an effective conversion must commence with the higher classes. He explained at his first arrival that he belonged to the best of the nobility, he had along with him testimonies to that effect, and attached himself to the Brahmins. He dressed and lived like them, subjected himself to their penances, learned Sanscrit, and proceeded according to their ideas.[4] They entertained the idea that there

[1] Still more! Still more! Tr.

[2] Maffei Historiarum Indicarum lib. XIII. et XIV.

[3] That is, the lowest class. Tr.

[4] "Juvencius: Historiæ societ. Jesu, pars V. tom. II. lib. XVIII. § IX. n. 49. "Brachmanum instituta omnia cærimoniasque cognoscit: linguam vernaculam, dictam vulgo Tamulicam, quæ latissime pertinet, addiscit: addit Baddagicam, qui principum et aulæ sermo, denique Grandonicam sive Samutcradam, quæ lingua eruditorum est, cæterum tot obsita difficultatibus, nulli ut Europæo bene cognita fuisset ad eam diem, atque inter ipsosmet Indos plurimum scire videantur qui hanc utcunque norint etsi aliud nihil norint."—[Juvenci's History of the Society of

had been in former days in India four ways of truth, of which one had been lost. He asserted that he had come to point out to them this lost, but most direct, and the spiritual path to immortality. In 1609 he had already gained over seventy Brahmins. He guarded himself well against wounding their prejudices; he even tolerated their distinctive marks, and only gave them a different meaning; he separated the different castes in the churches; the expressions which used previously to be employed in exhibiting the doctrines of Christianity he exchanged for others that were more elegant, and in a literary point of view more genteel. In every thing he proceeded with so much tact that he soon saw himself surrounded by hosts of converts. Although his method excited much scandal, yet it seemed the only one properly fitted to further the object in view. Gregory XV. expressed his approval of it in 1621.

Not less remarkable were the efforts put forth at this time at the court of the emperor Akbar.

It will be recollected the old Mogul Khans, the conquerors of Asia, long maintained a peculiarly undecided position among the various religions which divided the world. It seems almost as if the emperor Akbar cherished a like disposition. While he called the Jesuits to him, he told them, "that he had sought to make himself acquainted with all the religions of the earth; now he wanted to inform himself about the Christian, with the aid of the fathers whom he revered and prized." Jerome Xavier, nephew of Francis, filled the first settled post at his court in the year 1595; the risings among the Mahomedans contributing to dispose the emperor to look with favour on the Christians. Christmas was observed with the utmost solemnity at Lahore in 1599; the manger was exhibited for twenty days in succession; numerous catechumens proceeded to church with palms in their hands and were baptized. The emperor read with much satisfaction a life of Christ which had been composed in Persian; and had an image of the mother of God, designed after the model of

Jesus, part V. vol. II. book XVIII. § IX. n. 49. He knows all the institutions and ceremonies of the Brahmins; he learns the vernacular, commonly called the Tamul, which very widely prevails, he adds the Baddagic spoken by the princes and the court, finally the Grandonic or Sanskrit, which is the language of the learned, but beset with so many difficulties as never to have been well known to any European till that day, and among the very Indians those seem to know most who any way know it, although it be all they know.]

the Madonna del popolo in Rome, brought into his palace, that he might show it also to his wives. From this the Christians certainly concluded more than they ought to have done; still they made great progress; after Akbar's death in 1610, three princes of the royal blood solemnly received baptism. They rode to the church on white elephants, and were received by father Jerome with trumpets and kettle-drums. By degrees, though here, too, there appeared a changeableness of disposition, no doubt according as the political relations of the country with the Portuguese were favourable or otherwise, it seemed as if a certain degree of stability would be attained as respected Christianity. In 1621 a college was founded in Agra and a station in Patna. Further, in 1624, the emperor Dschehangir gave hopes that he himself was about to come over to Christianity.

At the same time the Jesuits had already penetrated into China. They endeavoured to gain access to the population of that empire, so remarkable for their proficiency in the arts and sciences and their reading habits, by explaining to them the discoveries of the west and the sciences. Ricci owed his first introduction to his teaching mathematics, and to his appropriating and reciting passages from the writings of Confucius, marked by their genius. The present of a clock which he made to the emperor, procured him admission into Pekin, and nothing afterwards raised him so much in the imperial favour and good graces as his drawing for him a map, which far surpassed all the attempts of the Chinese in that department. It was characteristic of Ricci, that on his receiving the commands of the emperor to paint ten such tablets on silk, and to hang them up in his chamber, he took the opportunity thus given him of doing something also for Christianity, and introduced in the vacant spaces of the maps Christian symbols and sayings. Such in general was his method of imparting instruction; he usually began with mathematics and ended with religion, and his scientific endowments procured respect for his religious doctrines. Nor was it only those immediately taught by him that he gained over, many mandarins, too, whose dress he assumed, went over to him; and as early as in 1605 a fraternity of the Virgin Mary was founded at Pekin. Ricci died prematurely in 1610, worn out not so much by excessive labour, but chiefly by the innumerable visits, the long dinner hours, and all the other social duties of China; but even after his death there were others who adopted the counsel he had given, which was "to proceed to work without attracting observation or making a noise, and on so stormy a sea to creep along the coast," and who followed his scientific example. In the year 1610 there was an eclipse of the moon, in predicting which there was the difference of a full hour between the calculations of the native astronomers and the Jesuits; and the latter being found once more to be in the right, they began to be treated with great respect.[1] Not only were they together with some Mandarins who had been instructed by them, charged with the correction of the astronomical tables, Christianity itself was brought into notice. The first church in Nankin was consecrated in 1611: in 1616 there were Christian churches in five provinces of the empire; in consequence of the opposition which they not seldom experienced, it was of the utmost consequence that their pupils should write books which should enjoy the approbation of the learned. They contrived to avert threatened storms. They followed, too, as closely as possible the customs of the country, and for this in the year 1619 they received the pope's sanction as to various practices. And thus not a year passed in which there were not thousands of converts; their opponents gradually died off; in 1624 Adam Schall had made his appearance; the minute description of two eclipses which occurred that year, and a writing by Lombardy upon the earthquake, gave them fresh respect.[2]

[1] Jouvenci has devoted his whole 19th book to the enterprises in China, and has added to it a treatise at p. 561: "Imperii Sinici recens et uberior notitia"—[A later and fuller account of the Chinese empire] which is still worthy of perusal.

[2] Relatione della Cina dell'anno 1621. "Lo stato presente di questa chiesa mi pare in universale molto simile ad una nave a cui e li venti e le nuvole minaccino di corto grave borasca, e per ciò li marinari ammainando le vele e calando le antenne fermino il corso, e stiano aspetttando che si chiarasca il cielo e cessino li contrasti de' venti: ma bene spesso avviene che tutto il male si resolve in paura e che sgombrate le furie de' venti svanisce la tempesta contenta delle sole minaccie. Cosi appunto pare che sia accaduto alla nave di questa chiesa. Quattro anni fa se le levò contro una gagliarda borasca, la quale pareva che la dovesse sommergere ad un tratto: li piloti accommodandosi al tèmpo raccolsèro le vele delle opere loro e si ritirarono alquanto, ma in modo che potevano essere trovati da chiunque voleva l'aiuto loro per aspettare donec aspiret dies et inclinentur umbræ. Sin' hora il male non è stato di altro che di timore."—[Account of China for the year 1621. The present state of this church seems to me on the whole very like a ship which both winds and clouds threaten shortly with a severe storm; and accordingly the mariners taking in the sails and lowering the yards lie too, and stand waiting till the sky shall clear and the war of the winds cease; but it often happens that the whole mischief ends in fear, that the fury of the winds passes off and the tempest vanishes,

The Jesuits pursued a different course in Japan, a country at once fond of war and torn by perpetual dissensions. From the very first they had attached themselves to a party. In 1554 they had been fortunate enough to declare for that which carried the day; they were sure of its favour, and by means of it they made great progress. As early as in 1579, the Christians there were reckoned at 300,000. Father Valignano, who died in 1606, a man with whose counsels Philip II. willingly concurred in East Indian affairs, founded 300 churches and thirty Jesuit houses in Japan.

Nevertheless this very connection maintained by the Jesuits with Mexico and Spain, excited at length the jealousy of the native powers; they had no longer the same success as formerly in the civil wars; the party to which they had attached themselves was worsted; frightful persecutions were denounced against them from and after the year 1612.

But they held out remarkably well. Their converts openly called for death by martyrdom; they instituted a martyr fraternity, in which the members mutually animated each other to the endurance of all kinds of suffering; that year they noted as the martyr-era; however much the persecutions increased, say their historians, still there were new converts every year.[1] They allege that from 1603 to 1622, the Japanese who came over to Christianity, amounted exactly to 239,339.

In all these countries, accordingly, the Jesuits maintained a character no less accommodating than persevering and unflinching; they made progress to such an extent as never could have been expected; they succeeded in triumphing, so far at least,

content with having only threatened. Such exactly seems to have been the case with this ship. Four years ago a violent tempest rose against it, such as seemed likely to sink it at one stroke; the pilots suiting themselves to the weather gathered in the sails of their operations and withdrew for a little, yet so as that they could be found by whoever should call for their assistance, *donec aspiret dies et inclinentur umbræ* (until the weather should prove favourable and the shadows decline.) Thus far the evil has been confined to fear.]

[1] Lettere annue del Giappone dell'anno 1622—[The yearly letters from Japan for the year 1622] give instance: "I gloriosi campioni che morirono quest' anno furono 121: gli adulti che per opera de' padri della compagnia a vista di cosi crudele persecutione hanno ricevuto il santo battesimo arrivano al numero di 2236 senza numerar quelli che per mezzo d'altri religiosi e sacerdoti Giapponesi si battezorno." —[The glorious champions who died this year amounted to 121: the adults who by the labours of the fathers of the company have received holy baptism, amount to 2236, without counting those that have been baptized by the instrumentality of other religious orders and Japanese priests.]

over the resistance of those elaborately contrived national religions which lord it over the East.

Therewithal they had not neglected to think about uniting the Christians of the East with the Roman church.

In India itself there had been discovered that ancient Nestorian communion, known under the name of Thomas Christians; and as these held, not the pope at Rome, about whom they knew nothing, but the patriarch of Babylon (at Mosul) to be their head and the pastor of the universal church, arrangements were speedily made for drawing them into communion with the Roman church. In these there was no lack either of force or persuasion. In 1601 the leading men seem to have been gained over; and a Jesuit was installed as their bishop. The Roman ritual was printed in the Chaldee tongue; the errors of Nestorius were anathematized at a provincial council; a Jesuit college raised its head at Cranganore, and those who had been most obstinate in their opposition till then, gave their consent at the new instalment of the bishop in 1624.[1]

It is evident that this was mainly brought about by the political preponderance of the Spanish Portuguese power. In Abyssinia, too, it exercised at the same period the greatest influence.

Earlier attempts had all proved unavailing. First, in the year 1603, on the Portuguese of Fremona having rendered the Abyssinians effective services in a battle with the Caffres, they and their religion came to be looked up to with much respect. Just then Father Paez appeared; a clever Jesuit, who preached in the language of the country, and procured for himself access to the court. The victorious prince wanted to form closer ties with the king of Spain, mainly with the view of obtaining support against his enemies in the interior; Paez represented to him that his only means of effecting this lay in relinquishing his schismatical doctrine and passing over to the Roman church. He made the stronger impression on him from the Portuguese having shown in fact both loyalty and valour in the internal commotions of the country. Disputations were arranged; it was an easy matter to triumph over the ignorant monks; the bravest man in the empire, Sela Christos, a brother of the emperor Seltan Segued (Socinius), was converted; numberless others followed

[1] Cordara: Historia soc. Jesu, VI. IX. p. 535.

his example, and an alliance was straightway formed with Paul V. and Philip III. The representatives of the established religion naturally bestirred themselves against this; in Abyssinia as well as Europe, civil wars assumed a religious complexion; the Abuna and his monks ranged themselves uniformly on the side of the rebels, Sela Christos, the Portuguese and the converts on that of the emperor. Battles were fought year after year with alternations of success and jeopardy; at last the emperor and his party came off victorious. It proved likewise the triumph of Roman catholicism and the Jesuits. In 1621 Seltan Segued decided those ancient controversies that had been raised about the two natures in Christ, according to the views of the Roman church; he prohibited prayers to be offered up for the Alexandrine fathers; Roman catholic churches and chapels were erected in his towns and gardens.[1] In 1622, after having confessed himself to Paez, he received the supper according to the Romish ritual. Long before this application had been made to the Roman court for a Latin patriarch, but some hesitation was felt there as long as any doubts remained as to the opinions and the power of the emperor. But now he had vanquished all his adversaries, and could not have shown more docility and submission. On the 19th of December, 1622, Gregory XV. appointed a Portuguese who had been suggested to King Philip, Dr. Alfonso Mendez, of the society of Jesus to be patriarch of Ethiopia.[2] On Mendez arriving at last, the emperor solemnly engaged to obey the pope of Rome.

Meanwhile men's eyes were directed to all the Greek Christians in the Turkish empire. The popes sent out mission after mission. The Roman *professio fidei* was introduced among the Maronites by some Jesuits; we find a Nestorian Archimandrite at Rome in 1614, who abjured the doctrine of Nestorius in the name of a whole multitude of those who had been attached to it; in Constantinople, a Jesuit mission was established, which obtained, through the influence of the French ambassador, a certain degree of stability and support, and which, among other things, succeeded, in 1621, in removing, at least for some time, the patriarch, Cyril Lucaris, who leant to protestant opinions.

[1] Juvencius, p. 705. Cordara, VI. 6, p. 320. Ludolf calls the emperor Susneus.

[2] Sagripanti: Discorso della religione dell Etiopia—[Discourse on the religion of Ethiopia] MS. from the atti consistoriali—[Consistorial proceedings].

Here we behold an activity immeasurable in its results, and embracing the world! which pressed on at once into the Andes and into the Alps, sent out its spies and pioneers to Thibet and Scandinavia, and in England and in China made approaches to the civil government: and yet, over the whole of this unbounded theatre, it was fresh, and complete, and indefatigable: the impulse that moved in the centre, animated every workman on the most distant frontier, and that, too, perhaps more warmly and thoroughly than elsewhere.

CHAPTER III.

MUTUAL OPPOSITION OF POLITICAL RELATIONS.—NEW TRIUMPHS OF ROMAN CATHOLICISM. 1603—1628.

WHAT imposes limits on a power when in a state of rapid aggrandizement, is not always, indeed, is never, mere opposition from without: such opposition, generally speaking, if not directly called forth, is yet greatly favoured by internal dissensions.

Had Roman catholicism remained united in sentiment, and continued to combine all her resources in speeding onwards to her aim, we do not well see how that part of Europe embraced by Germany and the North, engaged in a great measure as it already was in her interests, and entangled in the meshes of her policy, could in the long run have held out against her.

But, after having reached this degree of power, was it not to be expected that there would be a reappearance in Roman catholicism of those earlier contrarieties which, after all, had only been superficially reconciled, and had remained in constant activity within?

What was most peculiar in the progress of religion during this period was, that in all quarters that progress rested on a preponderance of political and military power. Missions followed in the wake of wars. Hence it happened that with the former there were combined the greatest political changes, which even as such, could not fail to be of some consequence, and to call forth reactions which could not be calculated upon beforehand.

Of all these changes, without doubt, by far the most important now was that the German line of the house of Austria, which, after having been so hampered hitherto by the troubles in its hereditary territories, as to intervene less than might have been expected in general affairs, rose at once to the independence, importance, and force of a great European power. One consequence of the aggrandizement of German Austria, was that Spain, too, which ever since the time of Philip II. had maintained a pacific posture, roused herself with fresh warlike ardour, and revived her former hopes and claims. These two, ere long, entered into a direct alliance, arising out of the transactions relating to the Grisons: the passes through the Alps were taken possession of by Spain on the side of Italy, and by Austria on that of Germany: and there, on the lofty mountain tops, they seemed to hold out their hands to each other, and mutually to encourage each other to enterprises to be undertaken in common in all directions of the world.

There was certainly involved in this position, on the one hand, a great prospect for Roman catholicism itself, as the system to which both dynasties were devoted with an inviolable attachment; but on the other hand, too, it brought with it great risk of internal dissension. How much jealousy did not the Spanish monarchy awaken under Philip II.! But with how much greater force and solidity did the collective might of the family now lift itself in consequence of the augmentation of its German resources. It could not but necessarily arouse the old antipathies in a still higher degree.

Symptoms of this first appeared in Italy.

The lesser Italian states, having no independence of their own, both needed, and most keenly felt their need at this time of an equal balance of power. Their being now caught as it were in the middle between the two great monarchies, and cut off by the occupation of the Alpine passes from all foreign aid, they looked upon as nothing short of being directly threatened. Without much regard for the advantages that might accrue to their religious creed from that combination, with the view of undoing it, they turned to France, the only power, indeed, that could assist them. Louis XIII., too, dreaded the loss of his influence in Italy. Immediately after the peace of 1622, before he had returned to his capital, he concluded a treaty with Savoy and Venice, in virtue of which the house of Austria was to be compelled, by means of a junction of all their forces, to restore the passes and fortresses in the Grisons.[1]

This object, it is true, contemplated but a single point, yet it might easily jeopard the relations of Europe in general.

Gregory XV. saw perfectly the danger which, from this point, threatened the peace of the Roman catholic world, the progress of religious interests, and, through that, the revival of the papal authority; and now—for to him the connection existing between the two was most evident—he displayed all the same zeal he had shown in calling forth missions and conversions, in endeavouring to prevent the breaking out of hostilities.

Respect for the papal see, or rather a feeling of the unity of the Roman catholic world, was still so warmly cherished, that Spain, as well as France, declared her readiness to leave the decision of the case to the pope. Nay, so far did they defer to him, that, until there should be a fuller adjustment, the fortresses which were the means of stirring up so much jealousy, were placed in his hands as a deposit, and he allowed to garrison them with his troops.[2]

Pope Gregory hesitated for a moment whether he should enter into this active, and, no doubt, also costly participation in distant affairs; but as it was evident how much the peace of the Roman catholic world depended on it, he ordered at last some companies to be enlisted, and sent them off to the Grisons under the command of his brother, the duke of Fiano. The Spaniards had wished to occupy at least Riva and Chiavenna; but these, too, they now surrendered to the papal troops.[3] Archduke Leopold of the Tyrol at last declared himself ready to deliver over to them those territories and strongholds, to which he himself preferred no claim on the ground of their being possessions of his own.

And by this means, in fact, the danger which had first thrown the Italian states into commotion, seemed to be removed. But the grand affair was to provide for the promotion of Roman ca-

[1] Nani: Storia Veneta, p. 255.

[2] Dispaccio Sillery, 28th Nov. 1622. Corsini, 13, 21, Genn. 1623, in Siri: Memorie recondite, tom. V. p. 435, 442. Scritturá del deposito della Valtellina, ib. 459.

[3] Siri: Memorie recondite, V. 519.

tholic interests by further arrangements. The plan was conceived, that while the Valteline was not to be allowed to fall into the hands of the Spaniards, so neither was it to be suffered again to pass under subjection to the Grisons: for in that case how easily might the Roman catholic restoration of the valley be interrupted: but that being placed on an independent footing, it should be added as a fourth to the three old Rhætian confederacies. From a regard to the same object it was thought desirable that the alliance of the two Austrian lines, which seemed necessary to the progress of Roman catholicism in Germany, should not be completely broken up. The passes by Worms and the Valteline were to remain open to the Spaniards; it being fully understood that this was to be for the purpose of troops passing into Germany, not of their being allowed to come into Italy.[1]

Matters had advanced thus far: nothing, it is true, was concluded, but all was ripe for being finally settled, when Gregory XV. died,—8th July, 1623. He had still the satisfaction of seeing those quarrels composed, and the advance of his church proceed without a check. In the negotiations, moreover, there was something even said about a new alliance between the Spaniards and the French, for the purpose of making attacks on Rochelle and Holland.

Such results were far, however, from being realized after Gregory's death.

The new pope, Urban VIII., for one thing, did not enjoy, as yet, that confidence which rests on the proved exhibition of absolute impartiality: besides which, the apprehensions of the Italians had by no means been pacified by the treaty; but what was most important of all, the helm of public affairs in France came to be held by men like Vieuville and Richelieu, who readopted the opposition against Spain, no longer as a method of aiding foreigners who applied for assistance, but of their own unfettered disposition, as a leading feature in French policy.

In this there was less caprice, perhaps, than one is apt to suppose. France, as well as the Austrian-Spanish power, was in process

[1] Art. IX. of the draught of the Convention.

CARDINAL RICHELIEU.

BLACKIE & SON, GLASGOW, EDINBURGH & LONDON.

preferred giving his son in marriage to a French princess, and to her he made the same religious concessions that had been promised in the case of Spain.

And so, upon this, immediate preparations were made for war. Richelieu drew up a most comprehensive plan, such as had never before his time appeared in European policy, but which was peculiarly characteristic of himself. He thought of subverting the Spanish-Austrian power at one blow, by a general attack on all sides.

He himself, in league with Savoy and Venice, was to fall upon Italy, and paying no regard to the pope, he caused French troops to make an unexpected irruption into the Grisons, and to expel the papal garrisons from the fortresses.[1] Together with the English alliance, he had renewed the Dutch likewise. The Hollanders were to attack South America, and the English the coasts of Spain. Through the intervention of King James, the Turks put themselves in motion, and threatened to fall upon Hungary. But the grand blow was to be struck in Germany. The king of Denmark, who had long been in a state of preparation, at length resolved to lead the forces of that kingdom and Lower Germany into the field, in support of his kinsman, the count palatine. Not only was he promised help from England, Richelieu engaged to pay a contribution of a million of livres towards defraying the expense.[2] Backed by both, Mansfeld

[1] Relatione di IV. ambasciatori, 1625. "Il papa si doleva che mai Bettune gli aveva parlato chiaro, e che delle sue parole non aveva compreso mai che si dovessero portare le armi della lega contra li suoi presidii."—[Account by the IV. ambassadors, 1625. The pope complained that Bethune had never spoken clearly to him, and that he had never understood from his words that the arms of the league were to be carried against his garrisons.] The common policy of France.

[2] Extract from Blainville's instructions in Siri, VI. 62. "Nel fondo di Alemagna"—[From the bottom of Germany Mansfield was to co-operate with him] (Siri, 641). Relatione di Caraffa: "(I Francesi) hanno tuttavia continuato sino al giorno d'hoggi a tener corrispondenza con li nemici di S. M^{ta} Ces^{a} e dar loro ajuto in gente e danari se ben con coperta, quale però non è stata tale che per molte lettere intercette e per molti altri rincontri non si siano scoperti tutti l'andamenti e corrispondenze: onde prima e doppo la rotta data dal Tilly al re di Danimarca sempre l'imperatore nel palatinato inferiore e nelli contorni d'Alsatia v'ha tenuto nervo di gente, dubitando che da quelle parti potesse venire qualche ruina."—[The French) have all along to this day continued to hold a correspondence with the enemies of his imperial majesty, and to aid them with men and money, covertly indeed, yet not so much so but that all the proceedings and corespondence have been revealed by many intercepted letters and many other indications: whence first and after the rout given by Tilly to the king of Denmark, the emperor has kept a strong force in the lower palatinate and on the frontiers of Alsace, dreading lest some disaster should come from that quarter.]

was to set out at the king's side, and endeavour to find his way into the hereditary dominions of Austria.

The two leading Roman catholic powers made preparations accordingly for so universal an attack by the one upon the other.

There can be no question that this could not fail to check directly the progress of Roman catholic interests. Granting that the French league was of a political nature, yet just owing to the close connection between ecclesiastical and political relations, protestantism must have viewed it as eminently fitted to promote her cause. It gave her time to recover breath. A new champion appeared for her in Lower Germany, in the king of Denmark, with fresh unspent energies and supported by the grand combination of European policy. A triumph on his side must have caused a retrogression in all the successes of the archducal house and in the Roman catholic restoration.

The difficulties, nevertheless, involved in an enterprise generally come to light only when the attempt is begun. Splendid as Richelieu's talents might be, yet he proceeded too hastily with the work to which his inclinations attached importance, and which he saw before him, whether with a full consciousness of its bearings or from a blind presentiment, as an object of life; his project gave rise to dangers that in the first instance threatened himself.

Not only did the German protestants, the opponents of the house of Austria, take fresh courage, those of France also, Richelieu's own adversaries, again recovered heart under the new political combination. They even said that they might hope, should events turn out for the worst, to have their peace made with the king by means of his present allies.[1] Rohan headed an insurrection on land and Soubize at sea. In May 1625 the Huguenots were up in arms in all quarters.

And simultaneously with this the cardinal was confronted by perhaps still more formidable enemies on the other side. With all his bias towards France, Urban VIII. had too much self-respect notwithstanding, to bear with patience the expulsion of his garrisons from the Grisons.[2] He caused troops to be enlisted

[1] Mémoires de Rohan, p. I. p. 146: "espérant que s'il venoit à bout, les alliés et ligués avec le roi le porteroient plus facilement à un accommodement."—[hoping that should matters come to an extremity, those who were in alliance and league with the king would bring him more readily to an accommodation.]

[2] Relatione di P. Contarini: "S. Sta (he speaks of the first time after the arri-

and directed towards the Milanese territory, with the avowed object of combining with the Spaniards in an expedition for the recovery of the fortresses that had been lost. Very possibly, little importance was to be attached to such threats of war. But so much the greater was that of the ecclesiastical influence which was conjoined with them. The complaint of the papal nuncio that the most Christian king intended being the auxiliary of heretical princes, found an echo in France. The Jesuits appeared with their ultramontane doctrines, and Richelieu had to stand warm attacks from the high church party.[1] It is true that he found support on the other side in the Gallican principles, and was defended by the parliaments; notwithstanding which he durst not venture to have the pope long for an enemy. The Roman catholic principle was too closely bound up with the restored royalty; and who could answer to the cardinal for the impression that might be produced in the mind of his prince by spiritual admonitions?

In France itself, accordingly, Richelieu saw himself assailed, and that too by both the opposite parties at once. Whatever he might have been able to effect against Spain, still the position he had taken up was untenable, and he had to quit it with all possible expedition.

And as in the attack he had threatened, he displayed the genius of universal comprehension, of bold penetrating design, so he showed at the present crisis that perfidious fickleness which first employs allies as mere tools, and then casts them off, —a quality which characterized him during life.

He first induced his new confederates to assist him against Soubize. He himself had no naval force; but with the assistance of protestant military resources from foreign lands, with Dutch and English ships, he overpowered his protestant adversaries at home. He availed himself of their mediation to force the Huguenots into a disadvantageous agreement. They made no doubt that as soon as he had rid himself of these enemies, he would renew the general attack.

val of the news) sommamente disgustata, stimando poco rispetto s'havesse portato alle sue insegne, del continuo e grandemente se ne querelava."—[His Holiness (he speaks &c.) supremely disgusted, considering that little respect had been shown to his flag, of which he constantly and grievously complained.]

1 Mémoires du cardinal Richelieu: Petitot 23, p. 20.

But how were they astounded when, instead of this, their ears were suddenly saluted with the news of the peace of Monzon concluded between Spain and France in March 1626. A papal legate was on this account sent off to both courts. It is true that he seemed to have no real influence in what was agreed upon, yet at all events he kept alive the Roman catholic principle. While Richelieu made tools of the protestants under show of the strictest confidence, he with still greater zeal entered into negotiations with Spain for their destruction. With respect to the Valteline he combined with Olivarez in effecting that that district should return, indeed, under the government of the Grisons, but with an unfettered share in the appointments to public offices, and without any restrictions on the freedom of Roman catholic worship.[1] Those Roman catholic powers which seemed to have been just on the eve of commencing a struggle for life and death, now stood in a moment again re-united.

To this was added the rise of misunderstandings betwixt the French and English about the execution of the engagements that had been entered into in the marriage-contract (between Charles I. and the sister of Louis XIII).

Of necessity then a cessation of all those anti-Spanish enterprises followed.

The Italians, with whatever unwillingness, had to consent to what they had no means of changing. Savoy concluded a truce with Genoa; Venice congratulated herself that no invasion of Milan had ere now taken place, and disbanded her militia. It has been asserted at least that the wavering conduct of the French further prevented the relief of Breda in the year 1625, so that to them must be ascribed the loss of that important fortress which fell into the hands of the Spaniards. Yet the grand and decisive disaster occurred in Germany.

The forces of Lower Germany had assembled around the king of Denmark, under the shield, as was thought, of that general alliance against Spain; Mansfeld advanced towards the Elbe. In preparing to meet them the emperor had put forth redoubled

[1] Du Mont V. 2, p. 487, § 2, "qu'ils ne puissent avoir par ci-après autre religion que la catholique - - § 3, qu'ils puissent élire par élection entre eux leurs juges, gouverneurs et autres magistrats tous catholiques;"—[that they may have no religion thenceforward but the catholic - - § 3, that they may choose out by election among themselves their judges, governors, and other magistrates, all catholics.] Some limitations then follow.

efforts, being perfectly aware how much depended on the result.

When the blow was to be struck, the alliance was no more: the French subsidies were not paid, the support from England was quite too long of arriving; the imperial troops were more inured to war; the consequence was that the king of Denmark lost the battle of Lutter and was thrown back on his own country; that Mansfeld too was driven as a refugee into the Austrian provinces, which he had hoped to march through as a conqueror and a restorer.

This was a result which could not fail to produce effects as universal in their operation as its causes had been.

First of all, as respected the imperial territories. We may indicate these in a few words. The last movement undertaken here in behalf of protestantism, in hope of a general combination, was extinguished; the nobles, who had hitherto remained exempt from all personal hardship, were compelled to apostatize. The emperor declared on St. Ignatius's day, 1627, that after the lapse of six months, he would no longer tolerate any one, even of the nobility and equestrian order, in his hereditary kingdom of Bohemia, who should not agree with him and with the apostolic church in the catholic faith in which alone we can be saved;[1] similar edicts were promulgated in Upper Austria, in the year 1628, in Carinthia, Carniola and Styria, and some time after in Lower Austria. In vain was it even to beg for some delay; the nuncio Caraffa represented that these petitions could only be traced to the hope of some general turn in the scale of fortune. From that time we must date those territories having first been completely Roman catholic. What an opposition eighty years before that, did the nobility make to the archducal house! Now

[1] Caraffa: Relatione MS. "Havendo il Sr Cardinale ed io messo in consideratione a S. M^ta^ che come non si riformassero i baroni e nobili eretici, si poteva poco o nulla sperare della conversione delli loro sudditi e per conseguenza havriano potuto ancora infettare pian piano gli altri, piacque a S. M^ta^ di aggiungere al S^r^ C^le^ ed agli altri commissarj autorità di riformare anche li nobili."—[Caraffa's Manuscript report. The lord cardinal and I having placed before his Majesty for his consideration, that as the heretical barons and nobility did not reform themselves, little or nothing could be hoped for in the way of the conversion of their dependents, and consequently that they would have it in their power by fair and soft methods to infect others, that his Majesty may be pleased to give further authority to the lord cardinal and other commissioners to reform the nobility also.]

the monarchical government of the country, orthodox, triumphant, and absolute, towered above all opposition.

And still more extensive were the effects consequent on the new victory in the rest of Germany. Lower Saxony was taken possession of; the imperial troops reached all the way to the Kattegat; they held possession of Brandenburg and Pomerania. Mecklenburg was in the hands of the imperial general; so many of the chief posts of protestantism were thus overpowered by a Roman catholic army.

Tokens immediately appeared of the use that was proposed to be made of this position of affairs. An imperial prince was postulated to be bishop of Halberstadt; and then, in virtue of his apostolic plenitude of power, the pope appointed the same person archbishop of Magdeburg. Now it was not to be doubted that on a Roman catholic archducal government being established there, it would introduce the restoration of Roman catholicism in the whole diocese, with all the rigour shown by the other spiritual princes.

Meanwhile the anti-reformations went forward in Upper Germany with new zeal. One needs only to look at the catalogue of acts issued by the imperial chancery for these years as given by Caraffa; how many admonitions, decrees, decisions, public orders, all in favour of Roman catholicism.[1] The young count of Nassau Siegen, the young counts palatine of Neuburg, the master of the Teutonic order, undertook new reformations; in the upper palatinate even the nobility were coerced into Roman catholicism.

The old lawsuits brought by the spiritual lords against the secular orders for the recovery of confiscated ecclesiastical property, now took a different course from formerly. How was Würtemberg alone made to suffer! All the old complainants, the bishops of Constance and Augsburg, the abbots of Mönchsreit and Kaisersheim pressed against the ducal house with their claims, so that its very existence was endangered.[2] The bish-

1 "Brevis enumeratio aliquorum negotiorum quæ - - in puncto reformationis in cancellaria imperii tractata sunt ab anno 1620 ad annum 1629,"—[Brief enumeration of some matters of business which - - in the article of the reformation were treated of in the chancery of the empire from 1620 to 1629,] in the appendix to Germania sacra restaurata, p. 34.

2 Sattler: Geschichte von Würtenberg unter der Herzogen, Th. VI. p. 226.

ops in all quarters carried their point against the cities, the bishop of Eichstädt against Nürnberg, the chapter of Strasburg against the city there; Hall in Suabia, Memmingen, Ulm, Lindau, together with many other cities were compelled to restore to the Roman catholics the churches that had been taken from them.

If people now began every where to urge the letter of the peace of Augsburg, how much the greater inducement was there for a more general application of its principles as now understood.[1]

"After the battle of Lutter," says Caraffa, "the emperor seemed as if he had awoke from a long sleep; delivered from a great cause of apprehension which had hampered both his predecessors and himself, he conceived the idea of bringing back all Germany to the standard of the peace of Augsburg."

Besides Magdeburg and Halberstadt, Bremen, Verden, Minden, Camin, Havelberg, Schwerin, almost all North-German sees were given back to Roman catholicism. This had uniformly been the remote object which the pope and the Jesuits had held in view in the brightest moments of their success. But about this very thing the emperor had his scruples. He had doubts, says Caraffa, not respecting the justice, but respecting the possibility of carrying it into effect. But the zeal of the Jesuits, and most of all of the father confessor Lamormain, the favourable opinion of the four Roman catholic electors, the unwearied support he received from that papal nuncio, who himself, indeed, informs us that it had cost him a month's exertion to bring it about, removed at last all scruples. Already in August, 1628, the edict for restitution was drawn up exactly as it appeared afterwards.[2] Before being promulgated it was first to be submitted to the consideration of the Roman catholic electoral princes.

But with this there was conjoined a still more extensive plan;

[1] Senkenberg: Fortsetsung der Häberlinschen Reichsgeschichte, Bd. 25, p. 633.

[2] This appears to have been the date of the draught from Caraffa: Commentar de Germ. sacra restaurata p. 350. He remarks that the edict was drawn up in 1628 and published in 1629; he then goes on to say: "Annuit ipse deus; dum post paucos ab ipsa deliberatione dies Cæsarem insigni victoria remuneratus est."—[God himself assented, for within a few days after that deliberation he rewarded the emperor with a signal victory.] He refers to the victory of Wolgast, which was fought on the 22d of August.

hopes were entertained of amicably gaining over the Lutheran princes. The attempt was to be made, not by divines, but by the emperor or some of the Roman catholic princes of the empire. It was contemplated to start from this point, that the ideas of Roman catholicism entertained by the people of northern Germany were erroneous, and that the unaltered Augsburg confession differed in but a slight degree from genuine Roman catholic doctrine; as for the elector of Saxony, it was hoped that he might be gained over by surrendering to him the patronage of the three archbishoprics in his territory.[1] Nor did they despair of being able to stir up the hatred of the Lutherans against Calvinism, and then to take advantage of that passion for the complete restoration of Roman catholicism.

This idea was warmly laid hold of at Rome and worked out into a feasible project. Urban VIII. nowise intended to rest content with the terms laid down by the peace of Augsburg, which no pope indeed had ever approved.[2] Nothing short of a full restitution of all ecclesiastical property and the bringing back of the entire mass of protestants could satisfy him.

This pope, however, at this fortunate conjuncture, had allowed himself to entertain what if possible was a still bolder idea, the project of an attack upon England. As if from a kind of natural necessity, this design had re-appeared from time to time in the grand Roman catholic combinations. The pope now hoped to make the return of a good understanding between the two crowns subservient to its execution.[3]

[1] Even as early as in 1624 hopes were entertained at Rome of the conversion of this prince. Instruttione a mons^r Caraffa. "Venne ancora qualche novella della sperata riunione con la chiesa cattolica del signor duca di Sassonia, ma ella svani ben presto: con tutto ciò il vederlo non infenso a' cattolici e nemicissimo de' Calvinisti ed amicissimo del Magontino e convenuto nell' elettorato di Baviera ci fa sperare bene: laonde non sarà inutile che S. S^{tà} tenga proposito col detto Magontino di questo desiderato acquisto."—[Instructions to Monsignor Caraffa. There arrived further some news about the hoped-for reunion of the Lord duke of Saxony with the catholic church, but it soon died away; notwithstanding, his being seen to be no deadly enemy to the catholics and most hostile to the Calvinists, and most friendly to the elector of Maintz, and his having agreed to the electorate of Bavaria, give grounds for hopes in that quarter; hence it will not be without use for his Holiness to concert with the said Maintz about this wished-for acquisition.]

[2] "A cui," says the pope of the Passau compact in a letter to the emperor, "non haveva giammai assentito la sede apostolica."—[To which the apostolic see has never assented.]

[3] In Siri's Memorie VI. 257, there is a notice of this, though a very incomplete

He first represented to the French ambassadors how grossly France was insulted by the total neglect in England of the promises that were made at the marriage (of Charles with the king's sister): that Lewis XIII. must either compel the English to fulfil their engagements, or wrest the crown from a prince who, heretic as he was before God, and promise-breaker in the sight of man, must be deemed unworthy to possess it.[1]

He next turned to the Spanish ambassador, Onate. The pope conceived that Philip IV. was already called upon, as a trusty knight, to take up the cause of the queen of England, his own near connection. She was his sister-in-law, and now aggrieved in her conscience on account of her faith.

On finding that he might venture to cherish hopes of success, the pope committed the negotiation to Spada, his nuncio at Paris.

Among those who commanded most influence in France, this idea was most warmly espoused by Cardinal Berulle, who had conducted the negotiation relative to the marriage. He calculated how the vessels of the English might be taken possession of on the French coasts, and even how the English fleets might be burnt in their own harbours. In Spain, Olivarez entered into this project without much delay. It is true that former instances of faithlessness might have made him cautious, and another statesman who stood high in the government, Cardinal Bedmar, for that reason gave his voice against it: but the idea

one. Even the information in Richelieu's Mémoires, XXIII. 283, is very partial. Much more copious and authentic is the account to be found in Nicoletti, which we make use of here.

[1] The pope says in Nicoletti; "Essere il re di Francia offeso nello stato, pel fomento che l'Inghilterra dava agli Ugonotti ribelli: nella vita, rispetto agli incitamenti e fellonia di Sciales, il quale haveva indotto il duca di Orleans a macchinare contro S. M[ta], per lo cui delitto fu poscia fatto morire: nella riputazione, rispetto a tanti mancamenti di promesse: e finalmente nel proprio sangue, rispetto agli strapazzi fatti alla regina sua sorella: ma quello che voleva dire tutto, nell' anima, insidiando l'Inglese alla salute di quella della regina ed insieme a quella del christianissimo stesso, e di tutti coloro che pur troppo hebbero voglia di fare quello infelice matrimonio."—[That the king of France was injured in his state, by England fomenting rebellion among the Huguenots; in his life, because of the instigations employed with Sciales, and the felony committed by that person who had instigated the duke of Orleans to enter into machinations against his Majesty, for which crime he was afterwards put to death; in his reputation, because of so many breaches of engagement; and, finally, in his own blood, because of the acts of ill usage inflicted on the queen his sister: but that which comprised every thing, in his soul, the English laying snares for the salvation of that of the queen, and at the same time that of his most Christian majesty himself, and of all those who had been but too anxious for that inauspicious marriage.]

was too magnificent and too comprehensive for Olivarez, who in all things loved what was splendid, to be diverted from it.

The negotiation was conducted with the utmost secrecy. The very French ambassador in Rome, to whom the first overtures had been made, heard nothing of their farther progress.

Richelieu drew up the articles of compact: Olivarez improved them: and so improved they satisfied Richelieu. They were ratified on the 20th of April. The French engaged to make military preparations immediately, and to put their harbours in a proper state. The Spaniards were ready to proceed to the attack even before the year 1627 had expired; they were then to be assisted the following spring by the French in full force.[1]

It does not clearly appear, from the accounts we have, how Spain and France were to divide the spoil: all we perceive is, that here, too, regard was paid to the pope. Berulle revealed to the nuncio in the deepest confidence, that in the event of success, Ireland was to fall to the share of the papal see: after which the pope might govern the country by means of a viceroy. This proposal was received by the nuncio with extraordinary satisfaction: only he besought his holiness not to allow a word to be said on the subject: lest it might seem that worldly views had entered into their calculations.

But Germany and Italy, too, were thought of in this scheme.

It still seemed possible to overcome by force the preponderance of the English and Dutch maritime power, by means of a gene-

[1] Lettere del nunzio, 9 Aprile, 1627. "Tornò a Parigi il prefato corriere di Spagna con avvisi che il re cattolico contentavasi di muoversi il primo, come veniva desiderato da Francesi, purchè da questi si concedessero unitamente le due offerte altre volte alternativamente proposte, cioè che il christianissimo si obligasse di muoversi nel mese di maggio o di giugno dell anno seguente e che presentemente accomodasse l'armata cattolica di alcune galere ed altri legni. Portò anche nuova il medesimo corriere che il conte dùca haveva in Ispagna staccata la pratica e dato ordine che se ne staccasse una simile in Fiandra col re d'Inghilterra, il quale offriva al cattolico sospensione d'armi per tre anni o altro più lungo tempo tanto a nome del re di Danimarca quanto degli Olandesi."—[Letters from the nuncio, 9th April 1627. The said courier returned to Paris from Spain with advices that the catholic king was content to move first, as had been desired by the French, since these had agreed to both offers together, which at another time had been proposed as alternatives, to wit, that the most Christian king should engage to put his forces in movement by the month of May or June of the following year, and for the present should accommodate the catholic armament with some galleys and other ships. Moreover, the same courier brought news that the conde-duke had broken off in Spain the negotiation with the king of England, who had offered to the catholic king a suspension of arms for three years or any longer period, in the name at once of the king of Denmark and of the Dutch, and that he had given orders for a similar negotiation to be broken off in Flanders.]

ral combination for the purpose. It was suggested that an armed company should be formed, under whose protection a direct intercourse might be established between the Baltic, Flanders, the French coasts, Spain, and Italy, without any share being given to these two maritime powers. The emperor straightway laid proposals to this effect before the Hans towns: the Infanta at Brussels desired, moreover, that a harbour in the Baltic might be procured for the Spaniards:[1] a negotiation on this subject was opened with the grand duke of Tuscany, who, by means of such a company, might draw the Spanish and Portuguese trade to Leghorn.[2]

Matters were not, indeed, carried at present thus far. Owing to the complexity of its bearings, the affair took a very devious course, yet such as to conduct at last to a result extremely favourable to the Roman catholic tendencies.

While people were projecting such extensive schemes for an attack upon England, it so fell out that they had actually to meet an attack from England.

In July, 1627, Buckingham appeared on the coasts of France with a magnificent fleet; he landed on the island of Rhé, and took possession of the whole, with the exception of the citadel of St. Martin, to which he forthwith laid siege; and called upon the Huguenots to defend anew their franchises and their religious independence, which were certainly placed in greater and greater jeopardy from day to day.

English historians commonly account for this expedition by tracing it to a strange passion entertained by Buckingham for Queen Anne of France. But whatever connection it may have had with such a passion, a very different and surely the real reason for it lay in the grand course of affairs. Was Buckingham to wait in England for the contemplated attack? It was undoubtedly better for him to anticipate it, and to carry the

[1] Pope Urban says this in a body of instructions to Ginetti, in Siri. Mercurio II. 984.

[2] Scrittura sopra la compagnia militante, MS. in Archivio Mediceo, [Paper on the militant company, MS. in the Medicean MSS.] contains a deliberation about the feasibility of this scheme: "Si propone che i popoli delle città anseatiche entreranno nella compagnia militante per farne piacere all'imperatore, e che i Toscani non abbino a ricusare come chiamati da sì gran monarchi."—[It is proposed that the inhabitants of the Hanseatic cities should enter into the militant company for the sake of pleasing the emperor, and that the Tuscans could not well refuse, as being called to do so by such great monarchs.]

war into France.[1] There could not be a more favourable moment. Lewis XIII. was dangerously ill, and Richelieu engaged in a struggle with powerful factions. After some delay, the Huguenots did in fact take up arms anew: their brave and able generals once more took the field

Buckingham needed now but to have conducted the war more effectively, and to have been better supported. In all his letters Charles I. owns that this was not sufficiently done. As matters were managed, the assailants were soon found to be no longer fit to cope with Cardinal Richelieu, whose genius developed its resources with double vigour at moments of the greatest difficulty, and who never displayed more resolution, unflinching courage, or indefatigable activity. Buckingham saved himself by a retreat. His attempt, which might have brought the French government into extreme jeopardy, had then no other consequence but that of pouring the collective strength of the country, under the cardinal's direction, with fresh force upon the Huguenots.

Rochelle was unquestionably the grand centre of Huguenot power. Already, at an earlier period, when he resided hard by in his bishopric of Luçon, Richelieu had pondered the possibility of taking the place, and now he saw himself called upon to direct such an enterprise: he resolved to carry it into execution, cost what it might.

Strange to say, nothing contributed so much to his assistance in this, as the fanaticism of an English puritan.

Buckingham had at last prepared once more to raise the siege of Rochelle. To this his honour was engaged; his future position in England and the world depended upon it; nor is there a doubt that he had strained his utmost energies to insure success. Such was the very moment chosen by that fanatic, under

[1] It may be asked whether Buckingham had received any intimation of this most secret project? This, however, is extremely probable. For how seldom is a secret so perfectly concealed that not a hint of it escapes. At least the Venetian ambassador, Zorzo Zorzi, who came to France about the time when these concerted schemes were in progress, became at once aware of them. "Si aggiungeva che le due corone tenevano insieme machinationi e trattati di assalire con pari forze e dispositioni l'isola d'Inghilterra."—[There was added that the two crowns held machinations and negotiations together about an attack with equal forces and dispositions on the island of England.] Hence it is very improbable that no word of it had reached England: the Venetians stood in the closest terms with England: they even came to be suspected of having suggested the expedition against the isle of Rhé." (Relatione di Francia, 1628.)

the impulse of revenge and mistaken religious zeal, to assassinate Buckingham.

In every great crisis, it is necessary that powerful men make an enterprise their own personal concern. The siege of Rochelle was, as it were, a duel between the two ministers. Now Richelieu alone survived. There was nobody in England to step into Buckingham's place and make his honour an object of heartfelt concern. The English fleet appeared in the roads, but without undertaking any thing properly. It is said that Richelieu was aware that this would not be done. He persisted immovably in his purpose, and in October, 1628, Rochelle surrendered.

After the chief fortress had fallen, the neighbouring places despaired of holding out: their only care was but to obtain tolerable terms.[1]

And thus from all these political developments, which at first seemed favourable to the protestants, there resulted at last another decisive triumph for Roman catholicism and powerful advance on its side. North-eastern Germany and south-western France, after having made so protracted a resistance, were both vanquished. The only concern that seemed to remain now was the perpetual subjection of the vanquished foes by laws and efficient institutions.

The assistance granted by Denmark to the Germans and by England to the French, had rather contributed to their ruin than otherwise: it had first brought upon them the enemy, who proved an overmatch for them: these very powers were already endangered or attacked. The imperial troops pushed on towards

[1] Zorzo Zorzi : Relatione di Francia, 1629. "L'acquisto di Rocella ultimato sugli occhi dell'armata Inglese, che professava di sciogliere l'assedio et introdurvi il soccorso, l'impresa contro Roano, capo et anima di questa fattione, i progressi contro gli Ugonotti nella Linguadocca colla ricuperatione di ben 50 piazze hanno sgomentato i cuori e spozzato la fortuna di quei partito, che perdute le forze interne e mancategli le intelligenze straniere si è intieramente rimesso alla volontà e clemenza del re."—[Zorzo Zorzi's Report from France, 1629. The acquisition of Rochelle, accomplished before the eyes of the English armament, which professed to raise the siege and introduce supplies; the expedition against Rohan, who was the head and soul of this faction; the proceedings against the Huguenots in Languedoc, with the recovery of full fifty places, have disheartened and weakened that party, so that, having lost internal force, and despairing of union with foreign powers, they have absolutely surrendered themselves to the king's will and clemency.] He remarks that the Spaniards, though they came certainly late, and with only fourteen vessels, yet did actually come to take part in the siege of Rochelle. Their coming over he ascribes to the "certezza del fine" [certainty of a termination], and to the "participar agli onori" [wish to share in the honour].

Jutland. And in 1628, negotiations were still carried on between Spain and France, having for their object the same common attack on England.

CHAPTER IV.

MANTUAN-SWEDISH WAR.—TURN IN THE TIDE OF AFFAIRS.

At a first view, the course of human affairs, the progress of a development which has once commenced, presents the appearance of immutability.

But upon a further inspection, it often becomes manifest that the fundamental bearing on which every thing rests, is frail and flimsy, well nigh personal, some bias or some aversion, and not so difficult to be shaken and subverted.

If we ask what it was that mainly brought about this new and great advantage for the Roman catholic restoration, we shall find that this was not so much the military forces commanded by Tilly and Wallenstein, or the military preponderance of Richelieu over the Huguenots, as the renewal of a friendly understanding between France and Spain, from being that without which neither the former nor the latter could have produced much effect.

Even as early as 1626, all independent resistance on the part of protestantism had ceased: nothing had encouraged it to attempt such a movement, but a quarrel between the Roman catholic powers: on these being reconciled its ruin was inevitable.

But no one could shut his eyes to the ease with which that mutual concord might be disturbed.

Within the bounds of Roman catholicism there were two antagonist springs of action, each equally the result of necessity; the one was religion, the other policy.

The former urged to mutual concert, to the extension of the faith, and the postponement of all other objects. The latter constantly impelled the great powers to a contest of rivalry for the possession of pre-eminence in point of influence and authority.

We cannot venture, indeed, to say that the balance of power in Europe was already subverted by the course of events. The equipoise rested at that period on the antagonism between France on the one hand and Austria and Spain on the other; and France, too, had in the course of those occurrences gained immensely in point of strength.

But practical policy depends no less on what is perceived when looking forward into the future, than on a present pressure. The natural course of things seemed inevitably about to lead to a state of general danger.

The fact of the old protestant north-German territories being overwhelmed by the forces of Wallenstein, opened up the prospect of a possible restoration of that imperial supremacy in the empire, which for centuries, excepting perhaps a moment in the life of Charles V., had been but a shadow, to real power and substantial significance. Were the Roman catholic restoration to go on as it had begun, this result was sure to follow.

Now France had no equivalent for this to expect; after having reduced the Huguenots to subjection, nothing further remained for her to gain. But it was the anxious forebodings of the Italians that were chiefly excited. They considered the revival of a mighty empire, that had so many claims to assert in Italy, and which stood so intimately related to the detested government of the Spaniards, as pregnant with danger, nay, not to be endured.

The question recurred anew, were the Roman catholic efforts to be continued without any regard being paid to this, and once more to gain the advantage; or would political views preponderate, and interpose a check upon those efforts.

While the stream of the Roman catholic restoration was pouring itself in full force over France and Germany, a movement appeared in Italy which could not fail to resolve that question.

MANTUAN SUCCESSION.

Just about the close of the year 1627, died Vincent II. Gonzaga, duke of Mantua, without leaving heirs of his body. His next agnate was Charles Gonzaga, duke of Nevers.

Now this succession, considered in itself, presented no difficulties: there could be no valid objection to the rights of the next of kin. But it involved a political change of great importance.

Charles Nevers had been born in France, and could be looked upon only as a Frenchman: it was supposed that the Spaniards would not submit to see a Frenchman attain to power in upper Italy, which from of old they had endeavoured, with peculiar jealousy, to secure against all French influence.

If, at this remote distance of time, we search into the real merits of the case, we shall find that no one, either at the Spanish or the Austrian court, thought of excluding him. Indeed he was also connected with the archiducal family; the empress was a Mantuan princess, and always much in his favour; "there was no perverse desire," says Khevenhiller, who was employed in Mantuan affairs, "at first to resist his claims; much rather was it made a matter of deliberation how he might be brought to devote himself to the interests of the archiducal house."[1] Olivarez too has given his express assurance to this effect; he relates how, on the arrival of the intelligence that Don Vincent was dangerously ill, it was resolved that a courier should be dispatched to the duke of Nevers, with an offer that he should take peaceable possession of Mantua and Montserrat, under the protection of Spain.[2] It is possible, indeed, that conditions were laid down for him, and that securities would have been desired from him; but there was no thought of depriving him of his rights.

It is singular to observe how this natural development was prevented.

No one in Italy would give the Spaniards credit for such honest dealing. None would believe, notwithstanding all the assurances they had previously given to that effect, that they

[1] Annales Ferdinandei, XI. p. 30.

[2] Francesco degli Albizi, negotiator di mons[r] Cesare Monte: "S. M[ta]," says Olivarez, "in sentire la grave indispositione del duca Vincenzo ordinò che si dispacciasse corriero in Francia al medesimo Nivers promettendogli la protettione sua acciò egli potesse pacificamente ottenere il possesso di Mantova e del Monferrato: ma appena consegnati gli ordini, si era con altro corriere venuto d'Italia intesa la morte di Vincenzo, il matrimonio di Retel senza participatione del re etc."—[His Majesty, says Olivarez, on hearing of the serious illness of duke Vincenzo, gave orders for a courier being despatched to France to the said Nevers, with a promise of his protection, in order that he might enter peaceably into possession of Mantua and Montferrat; but hardly had these orders been given when intelligence came with another courier from Italy, of the death of Vincenzo, the marriage of Rhetelois, without the king's being made a party to it, &c.]

would not oppose the succession of Nevers to his inheritance.[1] The Spanish plenipotentiaries in Italy had now incurred the suspicion of endeavouring to possess themselves of an unlimited power, even in defiance of law and justice; and at the present conjuncture people could not divest themselves of the idea that they would seek to promote to the dukedom some member of the Gonzaga family more devoted to themselves.

But we confess that a wish on the part of the Italians to see Mantua in the hands of a prince naturally allied to France, and independent of Spain, had much to do with this opinion. They refused to believe that Spain would at all consent to what, to them in the anti-Spanish interest, was so desirable. Of this they convinced the legitimate line of heirs itself, and the latter deemed it best to put itself in possession in the first place, in any way that it could.

It may be said that the case resembled that in an animal organization; the malady within only wanted an occasion, some attacked point, to break out externally.

In the most profound secrecy, and before Duke Vincent had yet breathed his last, young Gonzaga Nevers, duke of Rhetelois, arrived in Mantua. A Mantuan minister of state, of the name of Striggio, who was attached to the anti-Spanish party, had prepared every thing there beforehand. The old duke made no difficulty of acknowledging the rights of his kinsman. There was still a young woman remaining of the native line, granddaughter of Philip II. of Spain, by his younger daughter, who had married into the house of Savoy, and it seemed of much consequence that the young duke should marry her. Accidental circumstances had delayed the match and Vincenzo was already dead,[2] when the young lady was taken one night out of the convent in which she had been educated, conducted to the palace, and there without much loss of time, the marriage was

[1] "Nè si deve dar credenza,"—[No faith ought to be attached,] says among others, Mulla, the Venetian ambassador in Mantua, in 1615, "a quello che si è lasciato intender più volte il marchese di Inoiosa, già governator di Milano, che Spagnoli non porterebbono, quando venisse il caso, mai altri allo stato di Mantoa che il duca di Nivers:"—[to what has been repeatedly given out by the Marquis of Inoiosa, now governor of Milan, that the Spaniards would not suffer, on the case happening, any others in the state of Mantua but the duke of Nevers.] But why not? We have nothing but the fact before us that the governor says it, and the Italians disbelieve it; nevertheless it is even so.

[2] Nani Storia Veneta l. 7, p. 350, Siri Memorie recondite VI. 309, quote this fact; the latter from one of Sabran's letters to the French court.

settled and solemnized. Then for the first time the death of the duke was made known, Rhetelois greeted as prince of Mantua, and homage paid to him as such. An envoy from Milan was kept off until all had been done, and was then informed of it, not without a kind of sneer.

Intelligence of these proceedings arrived at Vienna and Madrid, simultaneously with the notice of the duke's decease.

It will be admitted that they were highly fitted to enrage and exasperate such mighty potentates, who delighted in maintaining a kind of religious majesty. So near a relative married without their consent, nay, without their knowing of it; and an important fief taken possession of without the slightest respect being paid to the lord superior! Yet the two courts on this occasion adopted different measures.

Olivarez, with all the pride of a Spaniard, doubly proud as the minister of so mighty a king, filled at all times, too, with towering self-conceit, was now most averse to making approaches to the duke; he resolved, if he did nothing more, at least, as he expressed it, to mortify him.[1] And was not the display the latter had made of himself openly hostile? After such a proof of his disposition, was it safe to entrust him with the important city of Montferrat, which was considered as an outer bulwark of Milan? The duke of Guastalla made claims upon Mantua, and the duke of Savoy on Montferrat. The Spaniards now formed a connection with both these parties; arms were taken up, and the duke of Savoy entered Montferrat from the one side and Don Gonzalez de Cordova, governor of Milan, from the other. The French had already found admittance into Casale. Don Gonzalez hastened to besiege it. He the less doubted being able soon to have it in his power, as he reckoned on an understanding with those who were within.

The emperor did not go about matters in such haste. He

[1] Nicoletti: "Vita di papa Urbano,"—[Life of Pope Urban,] from a despatch of the nuncio Pamfilio: "Dichiaravasi il conte duca che per lo meno voleva mortificare il duca di Nivers per lo poco rispetto portato al re nella conclusione del matrimonio senza parteciparlo: mà a quel segno potesse giungere la mortificatione, non poteva il nuntio farne congettura, e tanto più che le ragioni che avevano mosso il papa a concedere la dispensa, erano acerbamente impugnate dal medesimo conte duca."—[The count duke declared that he wished at least to mortify the duke of Nevers, for the small respect shown to the king in concluding the marriage without his participation; but by what mark he could inflict that mortification the nuncio could make no conjecture, and the more because the reasons that had led the pope to grant the license, were bitterly impugned by the said count duke.]

was convinced that God would protect him as long as he pursued the path of righteousness. He disapproved of the conduct of the Spaniards and sent to Don Gonzalez warning him to desist. On the other hand he meant to exercise his rights, as lord paramount, with perfect freedom. He pronounced Mantua to be sequestrated, until it should be decided to which of the different claimants the inheritance belonged. As the new duke of Mantua, who had now entered on his dukedom, would not submit, the severest mandates were issued against him.[1]

But while these measures differed in their source and character, yet they coincided in their effects. Nevers saw himself threatened no less by the legal claims of the German line of the house of Austria, than by the violent course pursued by the Spanish line. And while he thought to escape from danger, he brought it directly upon his head.

And at first, in fact, his prospects were but poor. It is true that some of the Italian states looked on his case as identified with their own; they omitted nothing that was likely to make him hold fast by the determination to resist; but as for doing any thing effectually of themselves in his behalf, their resources were inadequate.

[1] The views of the imperial houses appear from Pallotta's despatches, 10 June 1628; according to an excerpt in Nicoletti. "Il nunzio ogni di più accorgevasi che era malissima l'impressione contro il duca di Nivers, che havesse disprezzato il re di Spagna e molto più l'imperatore conchiudendo matrimonio senza sua participazione col possesso dello stato senza investitura, anzi senza indulto imperiale, che fosse nemico della casa d'Austria, che avesse intelligenza e disegno co' Francesi di dare loro mano nell' invasione dello stato di Milano: e che non di meno S. M[ta] Ces[a] havesse grandissima inclinatione alla pace, e con questo fine havesse fatto il decreto del sequestro per levare l'armi dalle mani di Spagnuoli e di Savojardi stanti le ragioni che pretendevano Guastalla, Savoja, Lorena e Spagna negli stati di Mantova e Monferrato: che dapoi il duca havesse di nuovo offeso l'imperatore col disprezzo de' commissarj non dando loro la mano dritta e non gli ammetttendo in Mantova, e sopra tutto col appellazione e protesta che l'imperatore fosse caduto dalla ragione e superiorità di detti feudi."—[The nuncio was daily better and better informed that there was a very bad impression against the duke of Nevers, that he had shown contempt for the king of Spain, and still more for the emperor, by concluding the marriage without his participation, together with his taking possession of the state without investiture, nay, even without imperial indult; that he was an enemy of the house of Austria, that he kept intelligence and plotted with the French to assist them in the invasion of the state of Milan; and that notwithstanding his imperial Majesty had the utmost desire for peace, and for that end had issued the decree of sequestration, that there might be no pretext for the Spaniards and the Savoyards having recourse to arms, as no prejudice was done to the grounds alleged by Guastalla, Savoy, Lorraine and Spain, as having right to Mantua and Montferrat; that thereafter the duke had given fresh offence to the emperor, by the contempt shown to the commissioners in not giving them a courteous reception, and admitting them into Mantua, and above all, in the appeal and protest, that the emperor had lost the right and superiority of the said fief.]

Richelieu, indeed, had promised also not to suffer him to sink, if he could but hold out until France should come to his assistance. But the question remained, when might this be safely calculated upon as likely to happen.

The bearings of the case of Mantua were developed while the siege of Rochelle was still in progress, and at a very critical moment. Until that fortress had fallen Richelieu could take no step whatever. He durst not venture on such a risk as again to enter into hostilities with Spain, as long as that step might give occasion to a formidable rising among the Huguenots.

But, further, his earlier experiences compelled him to take another view. For the sake of no advantage durst he quarrel with the devout, seriously Roman catholic party in his native country. He durst not venture upon a breach with the pope, or even to pursue a line of policy which might be displeasing to him.

Once more an immense deal depended on the pope. His position, the nature of his office, required him to do his utmost for the maintenance of peace in the Roman catholic world. As an Italian prince he had an undoubted influence on his neighbours. France even, as we saw, was influenced by the measures he adopted. Every thing depended on whether he was to obviate the breaking out of dissension, or himself to become a party in the quarrel.

In previous complications, Urban VIII. had found his policy introduced, and its course indicated beforehand. Here for the first time, his peculiar character came fully out, in such a manner, too, as to determine at the same time the course of the world's affairs.

URBAN VIII.

AMONG other strangers who owed their rise to the possession of considerable wealth, to the trade of Ancona, which was tolerably prosperous in the 16th century, the Florentine family, Barberini, were distinguished for skilful calculation and successful results. A scion of that family, called Maffeo, born at Florence in 1568, was on the premature decease of his father brought to Rome, the residence at that time of an uncle who had acquired a certain position at the Curia. Maffeo, too, began his career at the Curia; he owed his promotion to the opulence of his family, but at the same time displayed distinguished talents besides. Every step that he rose, his colleagues in office acknowledged a certain superiority in him; it was chiefly through a nuncioship in France, in which he acquired the full attachment of the French court, that high views opened out still farther before him. Upon the death of Gregory XV. the French party, from the very first, destined him for the pontificate. The aspect of the conclave differed from the preceding in this respect, that the last pope had reigned but for a short period. Although he had nominated a considerable number of cardinals, yet those created by his predecessor still continued quite as numerous, so that the nephew of the pope before the last, and of the last one, confronted each other in the conclave with apparently equal strength. Maffeo Barberino had given each of them to understand that he was the opponent of the other; it has been affirmed that on that account he was supported by both, and by each too out of hatred for the other. Yet what unquestionably contributed more to that result, was his having uniformly shown himself ready to defend the jurisdictional pretensions of the Roman curia, and his having thus raised himself in the estimation of the greater number of cardinals. Suffice it to say that, aided at once by his own merits and by foreign support, Maffeo carried the election, and at the tolerably fresh age of 55, rose to the papal dignity.

The court very soon perceived a strong contrast between him and his more recent predecessors. Clement VIII. was usually found occupied with the works of St. Bernard, Paul V. with the writings of the blessed Justinian of Venice; on the business table of the new pope Urban VIII., on the other hand, lay the latest poems or drawings of fortifications.

It will generally be found that the decided bias of a man's character is received during the first bloom of manhood; the period at which he first begins to take an active part in public affairs or in literature. The youth of Paul V., who was born in 1552, and of Gregory XV., born in 1554, belonged to an epoch in which the principles of the Roman catholic restoration were advancing in a full unbroken tide, and they themselves were imbued with those principles. The first active labours of Urban VIII., born in 1568, coincided, on the other hand, with the times of the opposition of the papal principality to Spain, and the re-establishment of a Roman catholic France. We find now, too, that the bias of his character went by predilection in those directions.

Urban VIII. considered himself as chiefly a secular prince.

He cherished the idea that the church state must be secured by means of fortifications, and make itself formidable by its own weapons. On being shown the marble monuments of his ancestors, he said that he would set up iron ones for himself. On the frontiers of the Bolognese territory he built Castelfranco, which has been called Fort Urbino, although the military object to be gained by it, was so far from suggesting itself at once, that the Bolognese suspected it to be intended to serve against them, rather than in their defence. In Rome, he began, from the year 1625, to strengthen the castle of St. Angelo with new breastworks, and lost no time in storing it with munitions of war and victuals, as if an enemy had been at the gates; over the Monte Cavallo he drew the high wall that encloses the papal gardens, without making any account of some magnificent remains of antiquity in the gardens of the Colonna family, being thereby levelled with the ground. In Tivoli he formed an establishment for the manufacture of arms.[1] The vacant apartments in the

[1] A. Contarini: Rel[ne] di 1635. "Quanto alle armi, i papi n'erano per l'addietro totalmente sproveduti, perchè confidavano più nell' obligarsi i principi con le gratie che nelle difese temporali. Hora si è mutato registro, et il papa presente in particolare vi sta applicatissimo. A Tivoli egli ha condotto un tal Ripa Bresciano, suddito di V. Ser[ta], il quale poi di tempo in tempo è andato sviando molti operai della terra di Gardon. Quivi costui fa lavorare gran quantità d'arme, prima facendo condurre il ferro grezzo dal Bresciano et hora lavorandone qualche portione ancora di certe miniere ritrovate nell' Umbria: di che tutto diedi avviso con mie lettere a suo tempo, che m'imagino passassero senza riflessione. Di queste armi ha il papa sotto la libreria del Vaticano accomodato un' arsenale, dove con buon ordine stanno riposti moschetti, picche, carabine e pistole per armare trentamila fanti e cinquemila cavalli, oltre buon numero che dalla medesima fucina di Tivoli si è mandato a Ferrara e Castelfranco in queste ultime occorrenze."—[A. Contarini's Report for 1635. As for arms, the popes in times past were absolutely unprovided with them, for they trusted more to laying princes under obligations by conferring favours on them, than to temporal defences. Now the register is altered, and the present pope in particular is paying the utmost attention to this. At Tivoli he has engaged a certain Ripa Bresciano, a subject of your Serenity, who has gone from time to time removing many of the works on the estate of Gardon. There this person has now a great quantity of arms manufactured, first making the rough iron to be brought from Bresciano, and now working up with it some portion farther of certain minerals found in Umbria; of all which I gave you advice in my letters at its own time, which I suppose might pass without reflection. The pope has fitted up an arsenal of these arms under the Vatican library, where there are deposited in good order, muskets, pikes, carrabines and pistols, sufficient for arming thirty thousand infantry and five thousand cavalry, besides a good number sent from the said forge at Tivoli to Ferrara and Castelfranco during these late occurrences.]

Vatican library were set apart as an arsenal. There was a superabundance of soldiers, and the parade grounds of the supreme spiritual power in Christendom, the peaceful circuit of the eternal city, resounded with military noises. A free port also he considered as indispensable in every well-ordered state, and Civita Vecchia was at much expense rendered suitable for that purpose. Only the result corresponded more to the state of things than to the pope's design. The Moors of Barbary sold there the booty they had taken from Christian merchant vessels. Such was the purpose subserved at last by the earnest efforts of the chief pastor of Christendom.

In all these things, however, Pope Urban acted with unlimited absolutism. In the earlier years of his reign at least, he still farther extended the absolute method of government adopted by his predecessors.

If it was suggested to him that he might advise with the college, he would at once reply that he alone understood more than all the cardinals put together. Meetings of the consistory were held but seldom, and even then few had the courage to speak their sentiments freely. The congregations met as usual, yet no questions of any importance were laid before them, and little regard was paid to the decrees that they might perhaps draw up.[1] Even for the administration of the state Urban formed no proper *consulta* as his predecessors had done. His nephew Francis Barberino was quite right during the first ten years of his pontificate, in refusing to undertake the responsibility of any measure that might have been adopted, whatever may have been its nature.

The foreign ambassadors were annoyed at being able to dispatch so little business with the pope. At audiences he spoke most himself,[2] he lectured, and went on talking on the same

1 "Le congregationi servono," says Alvise Contarini, "per coprire talvolta qualche errore."—[The congregations serve often to palliate some blunder.]

2 Pietro Contarini: Rel^ne^ di 1627. "Abbonda con grande facondia nelli discorsi, è copioso nelli suoi ragionamenti di cosè varie, argomenta e tratta nelli negotj con tutte le ragioni che intende e sa, a segno ché le audienze si rendono altrettanto e più lunghe di quelle de' precessori suoi: e nelle congregationi dove interviene segue pur il medesimo con grande disavvantaggio di chi tratta seco, mentre togliendo egli la maggior parte del tempo poco ne lascia agli altri; et ho audito io dire ad un card^lo^ che andava non per ricever l'audienza ma per darla al papa, poichè era certo che la Sta S. più avrebbe voluto discorrere che ascoltarlo: e molte volte è accaduto che alcuni entrati per esporre le proprie loro istanze, postosi egli nei discorsi, se ne sono usciti senza poter de' loro interessi dirle cosa alcuna."—[He abounds in great elo-

subject with those that followed, that he had begun with in speaking to those who went before. On all occasions he had to be listened to, and admired, and treated with the utmost respect, even when he refused a favour. Many unfavourable answers to requests were given under other popes, but that from a principle, whether of religion or of policy; in the case of Urban one could observe the influence of personal humour. One never could tell whether he had a yea or a nay to expect. The quick-witted Venetians discovered, by watching his behaviour, that he liked contradiction, that from an almost involuntary bias of his temper he took a fancy for the reverse of what was proposed to him; so that in endeavouring to obtain what they wanted, they used the method of starting objections themselves. While the pope looked about for something to oppose to these objections, he naturally fell into what was proposed, and to which, otherwise, no reasonings in the world would ever have brought him.

This was a peculiarity of temper which can display itself even in subordinate spheres, in its own way, and at that time not unfrequently appeared in the Italians and Spaniards. It regarded a public position as if it were nothing more than a tribute due to merit and personal character. In administering a public office, accordingly, it was far more influenced by personal motives than by a regard for what the case required; not much otherwise than with an author who from being inflated with a high idea of his own talents, keeps less to the object before him, than he gives free scope to the play of his caprice.

What if Urban himself belonged to this class of authors! Such poems of his as are still extant, show wit and dexterity. Yet how seldom do we find sacred subjects treated in them! The hymns and the sayings, alike of the Old and the New Testament, must be accommodated to the Horatian metres, the song

quence of discourse, he is copious in reasoning on various matters, he argues and treats in affairs with all the arguments that he understands and knows, to such a degree that audiences are given so much the oftener, and are held longer than those of his predecessors: and at the congregations in which he takes a part, the same thing happens to the great disadvantage of those who treat with him, whilst by engrossing most part of the time to himself he leaves little to others: and I have heard it said to a cardinal that he was going not to receive an audience but to give it to the pope, for he was certain that his Holiness would rather choose to discourse to him, than to hear what he had to say: and it has often happened that people that have gone in for the purpose of explaining their requests, in consequence of his setting himself to speak, have come away without being able to say a word about their interests.]

of praise of old Simeon in two Sapphic strophes! Hence it naturally follows that the peculiarities of the original are altogether lost; the meaning must suit itself to a form, which of itself is incompatible with it, merely because the composer prefers its being so.

But these talents, the brilliant colouring they threw around the person of the pope, the athletic health he enjoyed, only increased in him that self-conceit with which his elevated position had otherwise imbued him.[1]

I know of no pope who had this weakness to such a degree. An objection was once stated to him, taken from the old papal constitutions: he replied, that the utterance of a living pope was worth more than the ordinances of a hundred dead ones.

He repealed the decree of the people of Rome, that no statue should ever again be erected to a pope during his lifetime, with these words: "that such a decree could not apply to such a pope as he was."

The manner in which one of his nuncios had conducted himself in difficult circumstances having been praised to him, he replied, "the nuncio has acted according to his instructions."

Such was the man—so imbued with the idea of making himself a great monarch, with such a leaning to France, derived at once from his previous labours in that country, and the promotion he had experienced there, finally, so self-willed, so energetic, and so inflated with self-conceit—who at this critical moment had obtained the direction of the supreme spiritual power in Roman catholic christendom.

On his determination, on the line of conduct he might pursue in the midst of the Roman catholic powers, an immense deal depended as respected the progress or the arrest of the universal restoration (of Romanism) with which people were now occupied.

[1] This was remarked from the very first. Relatione de' quattro ambasciatori, 1624: "Ama le proprie opinioni e si lascia lusingare dal suo genio, a che conseguita una salda tenacità dei proprj pensieri: - - è sempre intento a quelle cose che possono ringrandire il concetto della sua persona."—[Report of the four ambassadors, 1624: He loves his own opinions, and allows himself to be flattered by his own genius; to which is added stiffness in holding to his own ideas: - - he is always intent on whatever can enhance the conceit of his own person.]

Already, however, there had often been remarked in this pope aversion towards Spain and Austria.[1]

Even as early as in 1625, Cardinal Borgia complained of the difficulty of overcoming this dislike: "the king of Spain could not obtain the smallest act of grace; every thing was refused to him."

Cardinal Borgia asserted that Urban VIII. did not willingly settle the affair of the Valteline: the king had professed his readiness to give up the passes in dispute; to this the pope paid no regard.

Thus, too, it is not to be denied that Urban was so far to blame for the rupture of the proposed alliance between the houses of Austria and Stuart. In completing the dispensation which his predecessor had drawn up, he added to the previous conditions, that public churches should be erected for the Roman catholics in every province: a demand which never could be agreed to, considering the greater proportion that there was of a susceptible protestant population, and which the pope himself receded from afterwards, on the occasion of the French matrimonial alliance. In fact, he seemed to view with unwillingness the augmentation of power which Spain would have acquired by that connection with England. A negotiation was carried on with the utmost secrecy by the nuncio resident in Brussels, about a marriage between the electoral prince of the palatinate, not with an Austrian, but with a Bavarian princess.[2]

And in the Mantuan complication which now started up, the pope had no less essential a part. The secret marriage of the young princess with Rhetelois, on which all depended, could not have been accomplished without a dispensation from the pope. It was obtained from Pope Urban without his having so much as put a single question to the nearest relatives, to the emperor, or to the king, and it arrived just at the fitting moment.

1 Marquemont (Lettres, in Aubery's Mémoires de Richelieu, I. p. 65) remarks this from the very first. It will not be found difficult, says he, to deal with the pope. His leaning is for the king and for France: but from prudential motives he will satisfy the other princes. The pope became aware, forthwith, of the aversion of the Spaniards.

2 The nuncio's emissary was a Capuchin friar, called Francis della Rota. Russdorf, Négociations, I. 205, is particularly minute on the subject of his negotiations.

In this manner did the pope's peculiar disposition already lie open to the light of day. Like the other Italian princes, he wished above all things to see placed in Mantua a prince who should be disconnected with Spain.

He did not wait even until he had received any kind of solicitation from Richelieu. As his applications to the imperial court remained without fruit, the proceedings adopted there becoming, on the contrary, more and more hostile, and as the siege of Casale went on, the pope himself turned to France.

He presented the most urgent entreaties, setting forth that the king might send an army into the field even before the capture of Rochelle: that an enterprise in the Mantuan affair would be no less pleasing in the sight of God than the siege of that main bulwark of the Huguenots: only let the king once appear in Lyons and declare for the freedom of Italy, and the pope, too, would not delay placing an army in the field, and uniting his forces with the king.[1]

From this side, accordingly, Richelieu, on the present occasion, had nothing to dread on reviving again that opposition to Spain which had miscarried three years before. But he wished to proceed with the utmost caution; he had none of the pope's eager haste; he would not allow himself to be distracted while engaged with the siege that captivated his love of glory

The more decided was he, as soon as Rochelle had fallen. "Monsignore," he said to the papal nuncio, whom he had immediately ordered to be called, "we shall now not lose a moment further: the king will take up the Italian affair with all his energies."[2]

In this manner did that animosity towards Spain and Austria which had already been so often excited, start up more powerfully than ever. The jealousy of Italy once more called forth the ambition of France. The state of things seemed so urgent that Louis XIII. would not even wait for the return of spring. While it was as yet but the middle of January, 1629, he set out from Paris and took the way towards the Alps. In vain did the duke of Savoy, who, as we said, remained attached to

[1] Extracts from Bethune's despatches of the 23d of September and 8th of October, 1628, in Siri: Memorie, VI. p. 478.

[2] Dispaccio Bagni, 2 Nov. 1628.

Spain, oppose him: his passes, which he had caused to be barricaded, were carried by storm at the first assault; Susa was taken; by the month of March he had to come to terms; the Spaniards, in fact, found themselves compelled to raise the siege of Casale.[1]

Thus did the two leading powers of Roman catholic christendom confront each other anew in arms. Richelieu again adopted his boldest schemes for attacking the Spanish-Austrian power.

If we compare the two periods, however, we shall find that in this he now proceeded on a far more solid and more tenable footing than in his previous enterprises connected with the Grisons and the Palatinate. At that time, the Huguenots had been able to seize the favourable moment for renewing a war with him within France. Not that they were yet completely crushed, but since they had lost Rochelle, they no longer gave cause for anxiety: their defeats and losses went on without interruption, so that they were now incapable even of making a diversion. And perhaps it is of still more consequence that Richelieu now had the pope in his favour. In the former enterprise, the opposition in which he was involved in regard to it with the Roman see, perilled even his position in the interior of France, whereas Rome itself suggested the present attempt, as being for the interest of the papal principality. Richelieu found it advisable on the whole, to attach himself as closely as possible to the popedom: in the controversy between Romish and Gallican doctrines, he now kept to the former and denied the latter.

In all this, how important were the results that arose from the opposition of Urban VIII. to the house of Austria!

With the religious development, with the progress of the Roman catholic restoration, there were interwoven political changes, which constantly gave effect to their own principle, and now set themselves in direct opposition to that of the church.

The pope entered the lists with that very power which had made the re-establishment of Roman catholicism a matter of the most eager interest.

[1] Recueil de diverses relations des guerres d'Italie, 1629.—[Collection of the various accounts of the wars of Italy, 1629.] Bourg en Bresse, 1632.

The question now remains, what course would be pursued by this power, and particularly by the emperor Ferdinand, in whose hands chiefly lay the grand work of the re-establishment, when called to face so powerful and threatening an opposition.

THE POWER OF THE EMPEROR FERDINAND II. IN 1629.

To the emperor it was just as if nothing had happened.

He could not, indeed, under existing circumstances, promise himself any kind of favour from the pope: in the smallest matters, for example, in the case of the abbey of St. Maximian, nay, in the most devout suggestions, as when, among other things, he wished to see admitted into the Roman kalendar, St. Stephen and St. Wenceslaus, because of the one being so much revered in Hungary, and the other in Bohemia, he met with opposition, and received nothing but unfavourable answers. Not the less, on the 6th of March, 1629, did he cause the edict of restitution to be promulgated in the empire. It was as it were the final judgment pronounced in a great lawsuit, which had now been carried on for more than a century. The evangelical body had judgment given against them out and out: the Roman catholics had it decided completely in their favour: "nothing further remains for us," said the emperor, "but to take up the cause of the injured party, and to send out our commissioners to demand back from their illegal possessors all archbishoprics, bishoprics, prelatures, monasteries, and convents, and other spiritual property, that have been confiscated since the compact of Passau." The commissioners appeared immediately; one was specially appointed for each circle of the empire, and set to work forthwith; the most reckless executions commenced. And with this at least was the pope not to be appeased, or to be moved to some favour and liking for the emperor? Pope Urban took it all as a mere discharge of duty. The emperor prayed that in the first instance, at least, he might be empowered to nominate persons to the ecclesiastical appointments obtained by means of the edict of restitution; this the pope refused to grant him, for, said he, I must not violate the concordat: it is observed even in France.[1] There is almost a sneer in this reference, for the

[1] Lettera di segretaria di stato al nuntio Pallotta li 28 Aprile, 1629.—[Letter of the secretaryship of state to the nuncio Pallotta, 28th April, 1629.] The pope appointed Peter Lewis Caraffa, his nuncio at Cologne, to go to Lower Saxony, "under

French concordat secured to the king the very right which the emperor desired. The emperor wished to have it in his power to change the regained monasteries into colleges, particularly for Jesuits; the pope replied that the monasteries must first of all be delivered over to the bishops.

The emperor meanwhile proceeded on his course, without paying regard to the disfavour shown him by the pope; he considered himself as the great champion of the Roman catholic church.

He caused three armies at once to take the field.

The first came in aid of the Poles against the Swedes, and in fact did so far restore the military fortunes of the Poles. Yet that was not its only object; it was thought, that at the same time Prussia might, in that campaign, be restored to the empire and to the order from which it had been wrested.[1]

Another army marched against the Netherlands, to assist the Spaniards in that quarter. It spread itself over the moors from Utrecht towards Amsterdam, and nothing but an accident, the surprisal of Wesel, prevented it from achieving the greatest successes.

Meanwhile, a third army assembled at Memmingen and Lindau, for the purpose of marching into Italy, and putting an end to the Mantuan affair with the sword. The Swiss could not be induced to grant a passage as a favour, but they were compelled to do so; Luciensteig, Chur, together with all the passes in the Grisons as far as the Lago di Como, were taken in an instant: this army, 35,000 strong, then descended along the Adda and the Oglio. The duke of Mantua was once more called upon to submit. He declared, in reply, that he stood under the safeguard of France, and that they must negotiate in that quarter. While the Germans were now moving against Mantua, and the Spaniards against Montferrat, the French ap-

pretence of being sent for the restitution of church property, and thought also of giving him the power, apart from there being any need for it, of using it in the controversies of the clergy among themselves."

1 Mémoires et négotiations de Rusdorf, II. 724. "Comiti Negromontano (Schwarzenberg) Viennæ nuper claris verbis a consiliariis et ministris Cæsaris dictum fuit, imperatorem scilicet sibi et imperio subjecturum quidquid milite suo in Borussia occuparit et ceperit."—[Count Schwarzenberg was lately told at Vienna, in fine words, by the emperor's councillors and ministers, that the emperor would, doubtless, subject to himself and the empire whatever his forces might occupy and take in Prussia.]

peared again the second time. On this occasion likewise, they achieved some successes, having taken Saluzzo and Pinerolo: but in the main affair they accomplished nothing: they could not even compel the duke of Savoy anew to comply with their wishes. The Spaniards began to besiege Casale, and the Germans, after a short cessation of hostilities, Mantua:[1] they were an overmatch by far for the other side.

No wonder if, in such a state of things, people now began to talk in Vienna itself of the old imperial supremacy, "that the Italians were yet to be shown that there still was an emperor, and that they would yet be called to a reckoning."

Venice, in particular, had brought on itself the hatred of the house of Austria. People judged at Vienna, that were Mantua once taken, the terra firma of Venice, too, could no longer hold out. It could not fail to be taken possession of in the course of a few months, and then the imperial fief might be demanded back. The Spanish ambassador went even beyond this. He compared the Spanish-Austrian power with the Roman, and the Venetian with the Carthaginian. *Aut Roma*, he exclaimed, *aut Carthago delenda est.*[2]

And here, too, people called to mind the secular claims of the empire against the popedom.

Ferdinand II. contemplated having himself crowned: he required that the pope should come to Bologna or to Ferrara, to meet him: the pope dared neither promise nor refuse, and tried to help himself with a *reservatio mentalis* (mental reservation).[3] Mention was made of the feudal rights of the empire over Urbino and Montefeltro, and the papal nuncio was informed, without more ado, that Wallenstein, on coming into Italy, would make further inquiry into the subject. In point of fact, that was Wallenstein's object. He had been ere now opposed to the Italian war; but he now declared that as he saw that the

[1] The eleventh book dell' istoria di Pietro Giov. Capriata discusses the individual steps in this occurrence.

[2] Either Rome or Carthage must be destroyed. TR.

[3] Se bene Urbano una volta usci coll' ambasciatore Savelli che bisognando si saria trasferito a Bologna o Ferrara, non intese però dire in correspettività di quello che espresse il principe di Eckenberg.—[If, indeed, Urban on one occasion came to this issue with the ambassador Savelli, that in case of need he should transfer himself to Bologna or Ferrara, he did not therefore mean to say so in relation to what had been expressed by the prince of Eckenberg.]

pope with his allies wanted to crush the house of Austria, he was for it.[1] He hinted that it was a hundred years since Rome had been plundered, and that it must now be much richer than it was then.

Meanwhile France was not to be spared. The emperor thought of recovering the three lost bishoprics by dint of arms: his plan being to take Cossacks from Poland and to send them to France. The dissensions of Louis XIII. with his brother and his mother, seemed to present a desirable opportunity for doing so.

And thus did the house of Austria occupy a position in which it followed out its efforts against the protestants in the boldest manner, but at the same time powerfully kept down and controlled the Roman catholic opposition and even the pope.

NEGOTIATIONS WITH SWEDEN.—ELECTORAL DIET OF RATISBON.

IN earlier times, as often as a case of this kind was merely seen at a distance and dreaded only, all that yet remained independent in Europe would have coalesced, but now it had actually occurred. The Roman catholic opposition looked round for assistance from beyond the boundaries of Roman catholicism; no longer from jealousy, but for deliverance from jeopardy and in self-defence. But to what quarter could it turn? England was fully occupied at home in consequence of the broils betwixt king and parliament, and was, moreover, negotiating anew with Spain: the Netherlands were actually invaded by the enemy:

[1] The opinion generally entertained of the pope at Vienna, may be learned from Palotta's letter of 10th August, 1628. "E stato qui rappresentato da' maligni, che son quelli che vogliono la guerra, che lo stato di Milano sta in grandissimo pericolo, essendo cosa sicura che papa Urbano havendo vastissimi pensieri sia di cattivo animo verso la casa d'Austria, che perciò si habbia da temere di S. Sta non meno che di Veneziani e di Francesi havendo gli stati cosi vicini al ducato di Milano e potendo in un tratto mettere potente esercito in campagna: e di più gli stessi maligni hanno rappresentato per cosa già stabilita che S. Sta vuole in ogni modo far fare re de' Romani il re di Francia, ed in confermazione di ciò hanno allegato che essendo la Sta S. nunzio in Francia dicesse alla regina che s'egli arrivava ad esser papa, voleva procurare di fare re de'Romani il suo figliuolo, il quale ancora era fanciullo." —[It has been represented here by malignant persons, that is, by those who wish for war, that the state of Milan is in the utmost jeopardy, it being certain that Pope Urban, having the vastest thoughts, bears ill will towards the house of Austria, that, therefore, there is ground of apprehension in his Holiness not less than in the Venetians, and the French having states thus near to the duchy of Milan, and being able at a stroke to send a powerful army into the field: and, further, these same malignant persons have represented it as quite an established fact, that the pope wishes anyhow to make the king of France king of the Romans; and in confirmation of this have alleged that when his Holiness was nuncio in France, he had told the queen that should he ever happen to become pope, he wished to bring it about that her son should be king of the Romans, he being still an infant.]

the protestants of Germany were either beaten or overawed by the imperial armies: the king of Denmark had been compelled to accede to a disadvantageous peace. There was none left but the king of Sweden.

While the protestants had been beaten in all quarters, Gustavus Adolphus alone had gained victories. He had conquered Riga, the whole of Livonia as far as the Dünamünd, and of Lithuania, as the Poles expressed it, as much as he desired. Then, in 1626, he appeared in Prussia, chiefly, as he said, to pay a visit to the clergy in the bishopric of Ermeland. He had possessed himself of Frauenburg and Braunsberg, the headquarters of restored Roman catholicism in those parts, and afforded a new and powerful stay to the oppressed protestants among their inhabitants. All eyes were turned upon him. "Above all other men," writes Rusdorf as early as 1624, "I prize this victorious hero; I revere him as the sole safeguard of our cause, as the terror of our common enemy: I follow his glory, which is exalted above envy, with my prayers."[1] Gustavus Adolphus, it is true, had now experienced a loss upon the moors of Stumm, and had well nigh himself been taken prisoner, but the chivalrous courage with which he broke through the enemy, invested him even with fresh glory, and he never ceased to keep the field.

To this prince the French now addressed themselves. First they mediated a truce between him and the Poles, and it is, indeed, very possible that the emperor's design upon Prussia helped to give a friendly tone, if not to the king, at least to the magnates of Poland.[2] After this, they came nearer their main design, which was to draw the king of Sweden into Germany. They confined themselves withal to merely insisting on the insertion in the compact of some stipulations in favour of Roman catholicism. With this reservation they declared their readiness to assist the king, who had to bring a considerable force

[1] Rusdorf, Mémoires, II. 3. "Ejus gloriam invidiæ metas eluctatam, excelsam infracti animi magnitudinem, et virtutis magis ac magis per merita enitescentis et assurgentis invictum robur cum stupore adoro et supplici voto prosequor."—[I adore with amazement and follow with suppliant vow his glory, which has struggled beyond the barriers of envy, the lofty grandeur of his unbroken mind, and the unvanquished strength of a virtue that shines out more and more by its deserts.]

[2] Rusdorf, II. 724. "Poloniæ proceres, si unquam, vel nunc maxime pacem desiderabunt."—[The magnates of Poland, if ever, now chiefly wished for peace.]

GUSTAVUS ADOLPHUS

into the field, with a corresponding sum of money. Hereupon, after some delay, King Gustavus went into the proposed agreement. In his instructions he avoids all mention of religion, placing the object of the alliance simply in the restoration of the German estates to their ancient privileges, the removal of the imperial troops, and the security of the sea and of commerce.[1] An agreement was drawn up in which the king engaged to tolerate the Roman catholic worship where he might find it, and in religious matters, as it is expressed, to act according to the laws of the empire. This was necessary for the sake of the pope, to whom notice of it was immediately communicated. Some formalities, it is true, still stood in the way of the completion of the compact; it was considered to be definitely settled, however, by summer 1630.[2] The papal nuncio in France maintains that Venice engaged to pay a third part of the subsidies.[3] I have had no means of discovering what ground there was for this assertion, it corresponds at least with the state of circumstances at the time.

But could one venture indeed to hope that Gustavus Adolphus was in fit case alone to break down the preponderance of the imperial army and to beat it in the field. Nobody trusted that he could. It seemed desirable above all things to bring

1 Tenor mandatorum quæ S. R. Maj. Sueciæ clementer vult ut consiliarius ejus - - Dn. Camerarius observare debeat, Upsaliæ, 18 Dec. 1629.—[Tenor of the instructions which his royal Majesty of Sweden, in his clemency, desires that his councillor . - - the Lord Chamberlain, should observe, Upsala, 18th December, 1629.] Moser's patriotic Archives, vol. VI. p. 133.*

2 Bagni, 18 Giugno [18th June] 1630. He quotes the article, which occurs also in the compact of 6th January, 1631, with a slight difference, as follows: "Si rex aliquos progressus faciet, in captis aut deditis locis, quantum ad ea quæ religionem spectant, observabit leges imperii."—[If the king make any progress (*lit.* progresses) he shall observe the laws of the empire, as for those things that respect religion, in places taken by or surrendered to him.] He shows, also, how that was to be understood. "Le quali leggi" [which laws], he adds, "dicevano dovere intendersi della religione cattolica e della confessione Augustana [they said, were to be understood of the catholic religion and the Augsburg confession]. So that Calvinism seems to have remained excluded.

3 Bagni, 16 Luglio [16th July] 1630. "Sopragiunsero" [there were added], it runs in the extract, "nuove lettere del Bagni coll' aviso che alla prefata confederatione fra il re di Francia e lo Sueco erasi aggiunta la republica di Venetia, la quale obligavasi a contribuire per la terza parte"—[fresh letters from Bagni, with advice that to the foresaid confederacy between the kings of France and Sweden, Venice had been added, and had come under an obligation to contribute the third part].

* But it must by no means be thought that he had not another and far higher end at heart. His grand purpose may be learned from the admirable prayer which he offered up on landing on the island of Rugen, and in which he calls God to witness that he came for the sake of God's honour, and for some comfort and assistance to His afflicted Church. Tr.

about in Germany itself some movement that might co-operate with the expedition he was about to undertake.

And here undoubtedly the protestants might safely be reckoned upon. Whatever line of policy might be suggested to individual princes by a regard for their personal interests or fears, yet men's minds had become completely overpowered by that fermentation which penetrates into the depths of common life, and precedes great storms. I shall mention but one idea that prevailed at the time. On the edict of restitution coming to be carried into effect here and there, and the Jesuits were already giving hints that they intended to pay no regard whatever to the Augsburg peace, the protestants intimated that before they could carry matters thus far, the utter subversion of the empire of the German nation would take place: "sooner would they cast off law and manners, and convert Germany again into its ancient wolds and wildernesses."

But even on the side of the Roman catholics, there were symptoms of discontent and dissension.

It cannot be told what a commotion was caused among the clergy by the Jesuits having it in contemplation to possess themselves of the restored conventual property. The Jesuits declared that there were no longer any Benedictines: that they had all apostatized, and were altogether incapable of entering again into the lost possessions. On the other hand, their own merits were brought into question by the opposite side: people would not hear of conversions having been effected by them: what were apparently such were said to be the mere effects of compulsion.[1]

1 Although the true facts of the case are not to be learned from the violent controversial writings, accusations, and defences that appeared on the subject, yet they present the points in dispute. "E verissimo," says the papal nuncio, in a letter written in cipher, "che i padri Gesuiti hanno procurato e procurano col favore dell'imperatore, che non può esser maggiore, di non solo soprastare agli altri religiosi, ma di escluderli dove essi v' hanno alcun interesse o politico o spirituale."—[It is most true that the Jesuit fathers have procured and are procuring, with the emperor's favour, which cannot be greater than it is, not only a place above the other religious (orders), but the exclusion of these where they have any interest, either political or secular.] I find, however, that the emperor, devoted as he was to the Jesuits, was disposed, in 1629, to a simple restitution to the old orders. This we learn from Peter Lewis Caraffa, nuncio at Cologne. But already at this critical moment, the Jesuits had carried their point at Rome. There a decree followed in July 1629: "che alcuna parte (dei beni ricuperati) potesse convertirsi in erezioni di seminarj, di alunnati, di scuole e di collegj tanto de' padri Gesuiti, quali in gran parte furono motori dell'editto di Cesare, come di altri religiosi:"—[that any part (of the recovered property) may be converted into the erection of seminaries, of academies, of schools, and colleges, as well of the Jesuit fathers, who in a great

Ere the church property had as yet been restored, they introduced among the religious orders dissensions and brawling about the claims to its possession, and about the right of collation between the emperor and the pope.

But to these misunderstandings on religious matters there were added secular ones of a still more extensive nature. The imperial soldiers were felt to be an intolerable burthen; in their marches they exhausted both the country and the people; while the soldier maltreated the burghers and peasantry, the commander in chief used the princes no better; Wallenstein allowed himself to use the most insolent language. Even the emperor's old allies, the heads of the league, and above all Maximilian of Bavaria, were discontented with the present and anxious about the future.

Such was the state of things when Ferdinand, in order to have his son elected king of the Romans, assembled the Roman catholic electors at Ratisbon in the summer of 1630. All other concerns of public importance could not fail on this occasion to come under discussion.

The emperor clearly saw that he must make some concessions. It was his intention to do so in the affairs of Germany; he showed a disposition to suspend the edict of restitution with respect to the territories of Brandenburg and the electorate of Saxony, to compromise matters as respected the Palatinate and Mecklenburg, and again to conciliate Sweden, negotiations for which were already set on foot, and meanwhile he proposed to direct his main force against Italy, to bring the Mantuan war to an end, and to compel the pope to acknowledge his ecclesiastical pretensions.[1]

measure were promoters of the edict of the emperor, as of other religious orders.] The Jesuit schools would have been diffused over all the north of Germany.

1 Dispaccio Pallotta, 2 Ag. 1630, gives among the points that come under consultation: " 1° se si doveva sospendere o tirare avanti l'editto della ricuperatione de' beni eccl^{ci}; 2° se havendosi da procedere avanti, si avesse da sospendere quanto a quelli che erano negli stati dell' elettori di Sassonia e di Brandenburgo: ed inclinavasi a sospenderlo; 3o quanto ai beneficii e beni eccl^{ci} che si erano ricuperati, pretendevasi che alli imperatori spettasse la nominazione - - 6° trattavasi di restituire il ducato di Mechelburgh agli antichi padroni, siccome il palatinato almeno inferiore al palatino, con perpetuo pregiuditio della religione cattolica, come era seguito con Danimarca."—[1. Whether they should suspend or proceed with the edict for the recovery of ecclesiastical property; 2. Supposing that they were to proceed with it, whether they should suspend it as far as respected that which lay in the states of the electors of Saxony and Brandenburg: and there was an inclination to suspend it; 3. As for the benefices and church estates that were recovered, it was

He might believe, that as he had to do with German princes, he could effect most by compliancy in German affairs. Nevertheless the state of things was not so simple as he supposed.

The Italian French opposition had already found its way among the Roman catholic electoral princes, and was endeavouring to make use of the discontented among them for its own purposes.

First, there appeared in Ratisbon the papal nuncio Rocci, and it may well be supposed that he would turn every thing to account in thwarting the execution of the emperor's Italian and antipapal designs.

The pope had instructed him to put himself before all things on a friendly footing with the electoral prince of Bavaria, and in a short time he mentions that this friendly footing was kept a profound secret;[1] he brought the Roman catholic electors to unite in a declaration that in all church affairs they would continue to act along with him, and in particular would preserve entire the jurisdiction and the reverence due to the papal see.

But in order to give a decisive turn to the affair, there came to his assistance Richelieu's trusty friend, father Joseph. Never certainly was the thorough craftiness of this Capuchin friar more busily exercised, more efficient, or to those who were privy to it, more manifest than on this occasion. M. St. Leon who accompanied him to Ratisbon, and gave his name to the embassy, said of him, "the friar indeed has no soul, but instead of it he has a shallow wit and jocose humour, in which all who treat with him must join."

Now by means of these agents that Italian French opposition to the emperor made his very German allies in a short time fully its own. Nothing was done towards restoring peace between the empire and Sweden, or for the quieting of the protestants; the pope never could have approved of the suspension of the edict of restitution. On the other hand the electoral princes pressed for

alledged that the nominations belonged to the emperor - - 6. There was a discussion about restoring the dukedom of Mecklenburg to the old proprietors as well as the palatinate, at least the lower, to the palatine, with perpetual prejudice of the Roman catholic religion, as was done with regard to Denmark.]

[1] Dispaccio Rocci 9 Sett. 1630. "E questa corrispondenza riusci molto fruttuosa, perchè Baviera di buon cuore operò che in quel convento non si trattò delle operationi sopra mentovate."—[And this mutual understanding proved most advantageous, for Bavaria heartily endeavoured to prevent the proceedings above mentioned from being treated of in that convention.]

the restoration of peace in Italy, and called for the dismissal of the imperial commander in chief, who assumed all the airs of an absolute dictator.

And so powerful was this influence, so skilfully was it made to bear, that the potent emperor, in the zenith of his might, yielded without resistance, and unconditionally.

While the negotiations were in progress at Ratisbon, his troops had taken Mantua; he could consider himself as master of Italy, and yet at that very moment he consented to cede Mantua to Nevers, under condition of the empty formality of his asking pardon. But perhaps the other demand was still more significant. The German princes, France, and the pope were one and all threatened by the commander in chief, with whom personally the success of the imperial arms was associated! We cannot wonder if they hated him and wanted to be rid of him. The emperor, for the sake of peace, gave him up.

At the moment when he might have lorded it over Italy, he allowed that prize to slip from his grasp! At the moment of his being attacked by the most formidable, and, in the conduct of a war, the ablest foe in Germany, he discarded the only general capable of defending him. Never did policy and negotiation produce greater consequences.

SWEDISH WAR.—POSITION OF THE POPE.

AND now was the first real beginning of the war. Gustavus Adolphus, it cannot be denied, opened it under the most favourable auspices. For had not the imperial army been assembled in the name of Wallenstein, and was it not devoted and beholden to him personally? The emperor even dismissed a part of it; he subjected the requisitions made by the generals which had formerly been left to their discretion, to an abatement prescribed by the circles of the empire.[1] It must be allowed that in dismissing the general, the emperor at the same time ruined his army, deprived it of its moral force. Torquato Conti, an Italian, who had previously been in the papal service, was to lead it against the enemy who had now recovered heart and was full of ardour. It

[1] Adlzreitter III. XV. 48: "Cæsar statuit ne in posterum stipendia pro tribunorum arbitrio, sed ex circulorum præscripta moderatione penderentur."—[They decreed that in future the pay should not depend on the caprice of the officers, but on the moderation prescribed by the circles.]

was in the nature of things that this command met with no success. The new imperial army showed itself to be no longer what the old had been; nothing was to be seen but indecision, agitation, alarm, and loss; Gustavus Adolphus drove it fairly off the field, and established himself on the lower Oder.

It was thought at first in Upper Germany that this was of little consequence to the rest of the empire; Tilly, meanwhile, was going on very deliberately with his operations on the Elbe. His finally taking Magdeburg was thought by the pope a great victory, and the brightest hopes were founded on it. A commissioner was forthwith appointed at Tilly's suggestion, "for the purpose of arranging the concerns of the archbishopric according to the laws of the catholic church."

But it was just this that had the effect of attaching all the protestant princes that had as yet been undecided, to Gustavus Adolphus, and while Tilly sought to prevent such a result of leading them to enter into an hostility with the league which no longer permitted a distinction to be made between the leaguist and the imperial populations.[1] The battle of Leipsic followed; Tilly was knocked on the head, and the protestant troops poured themselves over the leaguist as well as the imperial territories; Würzburg and Bamberg fell into the hands of the king, and the protestants of the remote north encountered on the Rhine those old champions of Roman catholicism, the troops of Spain; there, near Oppenheim, we see their skulls mingled together; Maintz was taken; all the oppressed princes attached themselves to the king; the banished count palatine appeared in his camp.

It now followed as a necessary consequence, that an enterprise which had been called forth and approved by the Roman catholic opposition, from political views, could not fail to turn out for the advantage of protestantism. The overpowered and oppressed party again saw itself at one stroke victorious. It is true, the king granted his protection in general to the Roman catholics, as he was bound to do by his engagements to his allies; but yet

[1] It could not have been the mere taking of Magdeburg that excited this profound disgust, but the unparalleled atrocities with which it was followed, and the cold-blooded cruelty of the imperial general. History records that 20,000 persons of both sexes and all ages were destroyed, the city burned down, and women of all ranks driven into the woods and made the victims of the brutal passions of the soldiers, while the general remained perfectly indifferent to all remonstrance. Tr.

he declared withal that he came to deliver his co-religionists from oppression of conscience;[1] he took the evangelical ministers who lived under Roman catholic governments, for example in Erfurt, into his special safeguard; he likewise permitted people everywhere to profess the Augsburg confession, the banished pastors returned to the palatinate, and along with the victorious army Lutheran preachers traversed the empire anew.

Thus strangely complicated was the policy of Urban VIII. In so far as the king attacked and overcame the power of Austria, he was the natural ally of the pope; equally in Italian affairs did he show himself so; under the influence of the losses sustained in Germany, the emperor, in 1631, complied in the Mantuan affair with conditions still more unfavourable than those of the year before at Ratisbon. Nay, there even existed indirect, if not direct, ties between the papal see and the protestant powers, now advancing again in full career of victory. "I speak of this on good grounds," says Alvise Contarini, who had been at the French and afterwards at the Roman court, "I was present at all the negotiations; the pope's nuncios uniformly favoured Richelieu's enterprises, both as respected his keeping his place, and in so far as he endeavoured to ally Bavaria and the League with France; as far as respected his alliance with Holland and the protestant powers in general, they held their peace, in order that they might not say that they approved of it. Other popes would probably have made this a matter of conscience; the nuncios of Urban VIII. thereby obtained increased respect and personal advantages."[2]

Loud and bitter were the complaints of the emperor; "first had the Roman court prevailed on him to issue the edict of restitution, and now it abandoned him in the war which it had occasioned; the pope had thwarted the election of his son as king of the Romans; he instigated the electoral prince of Bavaria, by what he advised and what he did, to follow a separate line of policy and to ally himself with France; that it was idle to apply to Urban for assistance, such as former popes had so often afforded in money or troops; he even refused to condemn the

[1] Letter of the king to the town of Schweinfurt in Chemnitz: Schwedischer Krieg Th. I. p. 231.

[2] Al. Contarini: Relatione di Roma, 1635.

alliance of the French with heretics, or to declare this to be a religious war."[1] In 1632 we find the imperial ambassadors at Rome reiterating before all things the last request; still, said they, might the declaration of his Holiness produce the utmost effect; still it may not be altogether so impossible to expel the king of Sweden; he had not above 30,000 men.

To this the pope replied, with more learning than warmth of sympathy; "with thirty thousand men Alexander conquered the world."

He persisted that it was no religious war; that it related to political matters only; that, besides, the papal exchequer was exhausted; he could do nothing.

The members of the Curia and the inhabitants of Rome were amazed. In the midst of the flames that burst from Roman catholic churches and monasteries, thus they expressed themselves, "the pope stands cold and motionless as ice. The king of Sweden has more zeal for Lutheranism than the holy Father has for the only saving catholic faith."

Once more the Spaniards proceeded to make a protest. As Olivarez had done to Sixtus V., Cardinal Borgia now appeared before Urban VIII. solemnly to protest against the conduct of his Holiness. There followed perhaps a still more violent scene than before. While the pope fell into a boiling rage and interrupted the ambassador, the cardinals that were present, took part with the one or the other side. The ambassador had to be content with giving in his protest in writing.[2] But with this the zealous religious party was not satisfied; there was soon mooted,

1 Aluise Contarini: "Gli Alemanni si pretendono delusi dal papa, perchè dopo aver egli reiteratamente persuaso l'imperatore di ripetere dagli eretici i beni ecclesiastici d'Alemagna ch' erano in loro mani, origine di tante guerre, resistesse S. Sta poi alle reiterate spedizioni di card^li^ e d'amb^ri^ nelle assistenze di danaro, nel mandar gente e bandiere con l'esempio de' precessori, nel publicar la guerra di religione, nell' impedire colle scomuniche gli appoggi ai medesimi heretici della Francia: anzi nel medesimo tempo ritardata l'elettione del re de' Romani, confortato il duca di Baviera con la lega cattolica all' unione di Francia, assistendo lo medesimo di danari e di consiglio per sostenersi in corpo separato. Il papa si lagna d'esser tenuto eretico et amatore di buoni progressi de' protestanti, come tal volta in effetto non li ebbe discari."—[Translated in the text excepting the last sentence; The pope is grieved at being accounted heretical, and a lover of the successful proceedings of the protestants, and often, indeed, in point of fact they are not disagreeable to him.]

2 "Nella quale," says Cardinal Cecchini in his autobiography, "concludeva che tutti li danni che per le presenti turbolenze erano pervenire alla christianità, sarano stati attribuiti alla negligenza del papa."—[In which I concluded that all the mischiefs which were to happen to Christendom through these troubles will be attributed to the negligence of the pope.]

particularly at the instigation of the former cardinal nephew Ludovisio, the idea of calling a council in opposition to the pope.[1]

But what a fire would this have kindled! Affairs already took a turn which left no doubt as to their real character, and which could not fail to give a different tone to the papal policy.

Urban VIII. flattered himself for some time, that the king would conclude a neutrality with Bavaria and restore to their territories the spiritual princes that had fled. But every attempt to reconcile interests so diametrically opposed to each other, proved all too soon an utter failure. The Swedish arms rolled onwards to Bavaria; Tilly fell; Münich was taken; Duke Bernhard pushed on to the Tyrol.

Upon this there was no longer room to doubt what the pope and Roman catholicism had to expect from the Swedes. How completely had the state of things been altered in a moment. As there had even been hopes entertained of making the protestant sees in the north of Germany again Roman catholic, so now there was revived in the king the plan of converting the sees of southern Germany that were now in his hand, into secular principalities. He talked already of his dukedom of Franconia; he showed some intention of establishing his royal court at Augsburg.

Two years before this the pope had to dread the arrival of the Austrians in Italy; he was threatened with an attack on Rome. The Swedes now appeared on the frontiers of Italy; with the name of king of the Swedes and Goths, as Gustavus Adolphus called himself, recollections were associated which were now revived on both sides.[2]

RESTORATION OF THE BALANCE BETWEEN THE TWO RELIGIOUS PROFESSIONS.

AND now I shall not relate the story of the struggle which for the space of sixteen years extended over Germany. Enough, if we have apprehended how that powerful advance of Roman

[1] Al. Contarini speaks of "orecchio che si prestava in Spagna alle pratiche di Ludovisio per un concilio."—[the ear that was given in Spain to the evil designs of Ludovisio for a council.]

[2] Nevertheless Al. Contarini affirms: "L' opinione vive tuttavia che a S. Sta sia dispiaciuta la morte del re di Suezia e che più goda o per dir meglio manco tema i progressi de' protestanti che degli Austriaci."—[The opinion constantly prevailed that the death of the king of Sweden would be displeasing to his Holiness, and that he liked better or, to speak more correctly, he dreaded less the successes of the protestants than of the Austrians.]

catholicism, which had contemplated taking possession of our fatherland for ever, just as it was making preparations for extirpating the protestant opinions at their source, was checked in its career and experienced a triumphant resistance. It may be said in general, that Roman catholicism, considered as a unity, could not bear its own triumph. The head of the church thought himself compelled, for political reasons, to oppose the powers that had done most to contend for his spiritual authority, and to enlarge it. Roman catholics, in accord with the pope, called up the still unsuppressed energies of protestantism, and cleared the way for their being exercised.

Schemes of such magnitude as those cherished by Gustavus Adolphus, when at the acme of his power, could not, indeed, be accomplished after the premature death of that prince, not certainly on that account, for the successes of protestantism were in no wise to be ascribed to its own power alone. Roman catholicism, however, was incapable, even when it had summoned up its energies better, when Bavaria had re-attached itself to the emperor, and when even Urban VIII. paid subsidies anew, of ever again overpowering protestantism.

People soon came to be convinced of this, at least in Germany. The peace of Prague already rested on such an assumption. The emperor allowed his edict of restitution to drop; the electoral prince of Saxony and the states that concurred with him, abandoned the idea of the restoration of protestantism in the (emperor's) hereditary dominions.

It is true that Pope Urban opposed all that might be concluded to the prejudice of the edict of restitution, and in the emperor's ecclesiastical council he had the Jesuits on his side, and particularly Father Lamormain, who, accordingly, was often enough commended for this as a worthy confessor, as a man beyond the influence of all worldly considerations;[1] but he was opposed by the majority, consisting of the Capuchins Quiroga and Valerian, and Cardinals Dietrichstein and Pafmany; these maintained, were the Roman catholic religion kept up in its

[1] Lettera del card[l] Barberino al nuntio Baglione, 17 Marzo 1635: "essendo azione da generoso Christiano e degno confessore di un pio imperatore, ciò che egli ha fatto rimirando più il cielo che il mondo."—[Letter from Cardinal Barberino to the nuncio Baglione, 17th March 1635: being the work of a generous Christian and worthy confessor of a pious emperor, that which he has done having more respect for heaven than for the world.]

purity, in the hereditary dominions, liberty of conscience might be granted in the empire. The peace of Prague was proclaimed in all the pulpits at Vienna; the Capuchins gloried in the share they had had in this "honourable and holy" work, and appointed special solemnities to be observed on account of it; hardly could the nuncio prevent a Te Deum from being sung.[1]

While Urban VIII. although he had practically contributed so much to the entire failure of the schemes of Roman catholicism, nevertheless in theory would relinquish no claim to which he pretended, all that he effected was that the popedom took up a position beyond the sphere of the world's living and real interests. Nothing shows this more manifestly than the instructions he transmitted to his legate Ginetti at Cologne, on the first attempt being made to effect a general pacification in 1636. In these the hands of the ambassador were quite tied up, in regard to all the important points that bore absolutely, and throughout, on the questions to be settled. One of the most pressing necessities, for example, was the restoration of the palatinate. Not the less on that account was the legate instructed to oppose the

[1] From Baglioni's correspondence which is excerpted in Nicoletti's 6th volume, for example, 14th April 1635. "Disse un giorno il conte di Ognate che assolutamente il re di Spagna non havrebbe dato ajuto alcuno all'imperatore se non in caso che seguisse la pace con Sassonia: di che maravigliandosi il nunzio disse che la pietà del re cattolico richiedeva che si cumulassero gli ajuti non seguendo detta pace, la quale doveva piuttosto disturbarsi trattandosi con eretici, ed applicare l'animo alla pace universale coi principi cattolici. Fulli risposto che ciò seguirebbe quando la guerra si fosse fatta per la salute delle anime e non per la ricuperazione de' beni ecclesiastici, ed il padre Quiroga soggiunse al nunzio che l'imperatore era stato gabbato da quelli che l'havevano persuaso a fare l'editto della ricuperazione de' beni ecclesiastici, volendo intendere de' Gesuiti, e che tutto erasi fatto per interesse proprio: ma avendo il nunzio risposto che la persuasione era stata interposta con buona intenzione, il padre Quiroga si accesse in maniera che proruppe in termini esorbitanti, sicchè al nunzio fu difficile il ripigliarlo perchè maggiormente non eccedesse. Ma Ognate passò più oltre, dicendo che l'imperatore non poteva in conto alcuno ritirarsi dalla pace con Sassonia per la necessità in cui trovavasi, non potendo resistere a tanti nemici, e che non era obbligato a rimettervi l'havere de' suoi stati hereditarj ma solamente quelli dell' imperio, che erano tenuissimi, e che non compliva di tirare avanti con pericolo di perdere gli uni e gli altri."—[Count Ognate said one day that absolutely the king of Spain had not given any aid to the emperor, unless in the event of the peace with Saxony following: at which the nuncio marvelling, said that the piety of the catholic king required that the aids should be multiplied in the event of that peace not following, which (piety) ought rather to disturb itself in negotiating with heretics, and to apply the mind to universal peace with the Roman catholic princes. Fulli replied that that would follow had the war been waged for the salvation of souls, and not for the recovery of church property, and Father Quiroga replied to the nuncio that the emperor had been deceived by those who had persuaded him to issue the edict for the recovery of church property, meaning it to be understood of the Jesuits, and that all had been done from a regard to their own interests; but the nuncio having rejoined that the persuasion had been interposed with a good intention, Father Quiroga got so angry as to break out

restitution of the palatinate to any not catholic prince.[1] What had already been found manifestly unavoidable at Prague, namely, the making of some concessions to the protestants with respect to ecclesiastical property, was subsequently still more so; notwithstanding which the legate was exhorted to be specially zealous in seeing to nothing being conceded in respect to ecclesiastical property, that might prove to the advantage of protestants. But the pope would not even approve of the concluding of a peace with the protestant powers. The legate was not to give it his support, if the Dutch were to be included in the pacification; he was to set his face against every transference to the Swedes, all that was talked of at the time was only a harbour; "the divine compassion would soon find means for removing that nation out of Germany."

The Roman see could not, consistently with common sense, cherish the hope any longer of overpowering the protestants; still it is of great significancy that, although against its will, yet through its obstinate maintenance of impracticable pretensions, it made itself incapable of exercising any real influence on the relation between the faithful of its own communion and the protestants.

It is true that the Roman see despatched still more ambassadors to the congress met for peace. Ginetti was followed by Machiavelli, Rosetti, and Chigi. Ginetti, it is said, was very penurious, and thereby impaired his efficiency; Machiavelli was only, properly speaking, to obtain rank, by going, so as to capacitate him for occupying a higher position; Rosetti was not suited to the French; thus has the insignificance of their influence been explained;[2] the truth is, that the affair itself, the position the pope had assumed, made any effective interposition on the part of the nuncios impossible. Chigi was fitted for his task and well liked, yet he effected nothing. A peace was concluded before his eyes such as the Roman see had expressly condemned.

into most violent language, so that it was difficult for the nuncio to reprove him, to the end that he might not exceed still more. But Ognate went further, saying that the emperor could not on any account withdraw from the peace with Saxony, from the necessity in which he found himself, being unable to stand out against so many foes, and that he was not obliged to send here the wealth of his hereditary estates, but only of those of the empire, which were very small, and that it was not meet that he should go on at the risk of losing both the one and the other.]

[1] Siri: Mercurio II. p. 987.

[2] Pallavicini: Vita di papa Alessandro VII. MS.

The elector palatine, in fact all the expelled princes, were restored. Matters fell far short of allowing the determinations of the edict of restitution to be thought of. Many sees were immediately secularized and abandoned to the protestants. Spain resolved at last to recognize the independence of the Dutch, those rebels against pope and king. The Swedes retained an important portion of the empire. The Curia could not even approve of the peace between the emperor and France, because it comprised stipulations with respect to Metz, Toul, and Verdun, by which its rights were weakened. The popedom found itself under the lamentable necessity of protesting, and desired at least to give expression to those principles to which it had found it impossible to give effect. But this had been already anticipated. The religious determinations of the peace of Westphalia were opened with the declaration, that in these no regard was to be paid to opposition from any one, be he who he might, whether belonging to laity or clergy.[1]

By the peace, that great suit at law between protestants and Roman catholics was at last brought to a decision, though very differently from what had been attempted in the edict of restitution. The Roman catholics, if we are to assume 1624 as the normal year, to which things should have been brought back, preserved great acquisitions; on the other hand, the protestant side obtained that indispensable parity which had been so long withheld from them. According to that principle all the mutual bearings in the empire were regulated.

How vain, besides, was it to think any longer at that time of enterprises, such as had been ventured on and had succeeded at an earlier period.

Much rather did the results of the German contest re-act immediately on the neighbouring countries.

Although the emperor had been enabled to uphold Roman catholicism, in all its integrity, in his hereditary dominions, yet he had to make concessions to the protestants in Hungary; in 1645 he found himself constrained to restore to them no inconsiderable number of churches.

And now that Sweden had risen to a position of universal consequence, could Poland ever think of renewing its old claims to

[1] Osnabrückischer Friedenschluss V. Articul. § 1.

that country? Wladislaw IV. even gave up his father's zeal for conversions, and became a merciful king to the dissenters.

In France itself, Richelieu showed favour to the Huguenots after they had been deprived of their political independence. But he gave a far more effective support to the protestant principle in shaking to its foundation that leading Roman catholic power, the Spanish monarchy, by carrying on a war against it, in which it had to struggle for its very existence. This quarrel (between Spain and France) was the only one that the pope could have composed without the smallest scruple. But while all others were actually set at rest, this remained undetermined, and perpetually distracted the interior of the Roman catholic world.

The Dutch had participated most successfully in the war against Spain, down to the peace of Westphalia. It was the golden age of their power and opulence. But while they obtained the preponderance in the east, they at the same time powerfully checked the progress of the Roman catholic missions there.

In England alone did Roman catholicism, or at least something analagous to it in its outward forms, seem at times as if it would gain admission into the country. We find envoys from the English court at Rome and papal agents in England; the queen, who enjoyed at Rome a kind of official recognition,[1] exercised an influence over her husband which seemed likely to extend even to religion; and already there were approaches made to Rome in various ceremonies. Nevertheless even here the reverse of this followed. Charles I. scarcely ever departed in heart from the protestant system of doctrine, but even the slightest approaches he made to the Roman catholic ritual proved his ruin. It seemed as if the violent excitement which had produced such long-continued, universal, and unintermitted attacks, in the protestant world in general, had concentrated itself in the English puritans. Ireland tried in vain to shake off their domin-

[1] Nani: Relatione di Roma 1640: "Con la regina d'Inghilterra passa communicatione de' ministri con officii e donativi di cortesia, e si concede a quella M^ta^ nominatione di cardinali a pare degli altri re." Spada: Relatione della nunziatura di Francia 1641: "Il S^r^ conte Rossetti, residente in quel regno, bene corrisponde nell' ossequio gli ordini del S^r^ card^l^ Barberini protettore tutti pieni dell' ardore e zelo di S. Em^za^."—[Nani: Report from Rome in 1640: Communications pass between the ministers and the Queen of England, together with civilities and presents, and the nomination of cardinals is conceded to her majesty the same as to other monarchs. Spada: Report of the nuncioship from France, 1641: The count Rosetti, residing in that kingdom, well agrees, by his assiduous compliance, with the orders of Lord cardinal Barberini protector, orders full of the ardour and zeal of his eminency.]

ion, and to organize itself as a Roman catholic country; its subjection only became the more severe. In the aristocracy and the commons of England there was matured a secular power, the rise of which forms a marked feature in the returning prosperity of protestantism in Europe at large.

Thus, however, there now came to be laid on Roman catholicism, limitations which can never be removed. It has had settled boundaries appointed to it, and never more can it seriously contemplate a conquest of the world such as it once proposed to itself.

Nay, the spiritual development itself has taken a direction which renders this impossible.

We behold those impulses which jeoparded the higher unity, obtain the preponderance; the religious element repressed, and political views governing the world.

For the protestants did not owe to themselves their deliverance. It was mainly a schism in the bosom of Roman catholicism, by means of which they succeeded in re-establishing themselves. In 1631 we find the two great Roman catholic powers in league with the protestants, France openly, Spain covertly at least. It is certain that the Spaniards at that time had entered into an understanding with the French Huguenots.

But just as little did the protestants keep together. Not that the Lutherans and the Reformed only contended with each other; that was always the case; but the different bodies of the Reformed, although beyond all doubt they had a common cause to fight for, went forth to attack each other in this war. The maritime power of the French Huguenots was eventually broken up, only through the support which their fellow-religionists and old allies had resolved to afford to the French crown.

Even the supreme head of Roman catholicism, who had taken the lead hitherto against the protestants, the pope at Rome, put at last these highest interests of ecclesiastical government aside; he became a party to an attack on those who had most zealously urged on the re-establishment of Roman catholicism; he pursued a course which was dictated by a mere regard for secular sovereignty. He went back to the policy that had been abandoned ever since the time of Paul III. It will be remembered that protestantism was promoted by nothing so much in the former half of the 16th century, as by the political struggles of the popes. It was just these to which, humanly speaking, protestantism was now indebted for its deliverance, for its preservation.

But this example must necessarily have had an effect on the remaining powers. German Austria, which had so long unwaveringly retained its orthodoxy, at last adopted the same policy; the position it assumed after the peace of Westphalia, was based on its intimate alliance with the most of Germany, with England, and with Holland.

If we inquire into the remoter causes of this phenomenon, we should be in the wrong did we seek them in a depression and arrest of spiritual impulses; I conceive that we must look elsewhere for the meaning and significancy of this event.

For once had the great spiritual contest completed its operation in men's minds.

In the primitive times Christianity was more a matter of implicit surrender, of simple acceptation, of a faith unaffected by doubts; now it had become a matter of conviction, and of conscious acquiescence. It is of great consequence that a man should have to choose between different creeds; that he can reject, apostatize, pass from the one to the other. The man himself is laid claim to, his unfettered self-determination is challenged. Hence it followed that Christian ideas penetrated still more deeply and fully into all life and thought.

Then to this there was added another important element.

It is very true that the increase of internal antagonisms disturbed the unity of the collective whole; but, if we do not deceive ourselves, it is still another law of life, and at the same time a more exalted and a greater development, which was thus prepared amid the urgency of the general strife; religion came to be embraced by the nations according to one or other of the various modifications that had taken place in its dogmatic structure; religious doctrine had become fused in one mass with feelings of nationality, as if it were a common property, an attribute of the government or of the people. It had been gained by arms, maintained amidst infinite dangers, and became part of their flesh and blood.

Hence it has arisen that states on both sides formed an ecclesiastical and a political individuality; already, on the Roman catholic side, according to the measure of their devotedness to the see of Rome, and the toleration or exclusion of all who were not Roman catholics; but still more perhaps on the side of the protestants, where deviations from the symbolical books that were sworn to, the mingling of the Lutheran and the Reformed creeds, and the greater or less considerable approach to the episcopal constitution, form the groundworks of so many manifest differences. In every country the first question is, What is the dominant religion? Christianity appears under manifold forms. However great the contrasts these present, no one part can dispute with another the fact of it likewise having the foundation of the faith. Much rather are these various forms guaranteed by means of compacts and pacifications in which all participate, and which are as it were the fundamental laws of one commonwealth. The idea can never more be entertained of elevating one or other confession to universal dominion. All now depends on this, how each particular state and nation shall best be enabled to develope its energies, while proceeding upon its own political religious principles. On that now reposes the future destiny of the world.[1]

1 The author speaks as if the Author of all good, and the Source of all truth, had given the sanction of his authority to the political religious principles, alike of those nations who adhere most closely to Divine Revelation, and of those who most widely depart from that standard; as if Italy and Spain had to seek their happiness only in the development of their energies on papal principles, instead of exchanging these for the protestant principle of implicit deference for the revealed will of God. In this we need not say how utterly he departs from eternal truth, and is refuted by glaring facts. Tr.

BOOK EIGHTH.

THE POPES ABOUT THE MIDDLE OF THE SEVENTEENTH CENTURY.—LATER EPOCHS.

AFTER the effort made by the popes to renew their secular empire, and in which, whatever may have been their success for a time, they failed at last, the position they occupy and the interest we take in them undergo a general change. Our attention comes to be chiefly drawn to the relations of the principality, its administration, and its internal development.

As if passing from some lofty mountain where vast and distant prospects stretched before us, we had entered some valley which confines and gives narrow limits to the view, so now we proceed from a survey of those general events in the history of the world in which the popedom had once more played so important a part, to the consideration of the particular concerns of the states of the church.

The states of the church received their first completion in the time of Urban VIII. Let us begin with that event.

LAPSING OF URBINO AS A FIEF TO THE PAPAL SEE.

THE dukedom of Urbino comprehended seven towns and nearly 300 castles: it possessed a line of coast at once fertile and convenient for trade, and towards the Apennines a salubrious and pleasant hill country.

The dukes of Urbino, like those of Ferrara, attracted notice sometimes by feats of arms, sometimes by literary efforts, sometimes by the liberal and splendid hospitality of their[1] court. Guidubaldo II. formed four court establishments in 1570: besides his own, there was one specially for his consort, and another for the princes and princesses. All four were brilliant, eagerly visited by the native nobility, and open to foreigners.[2] According to ancient manners, every stranger was hospitably received in the palace. The revenues of the country never could have sufficed for so much expense: they amounted, even when the corn-trade of Sinigaglia was thriving, to no more than about 100,000 scudi. But the princes, at least nominally and by title, were always in foreign military service; the happy position of the country in the middle of Italy, had the effect of making the neighbouring states emulate each other in securing their devotedness by favours, by military pay, and subsidies.

It was remarked in the country itself, that the prince brought more into it than he cost.

It is true that here, as well as everywhere else, attempts were made to augment the taxes: but these attempts were attended with so many difficulties, especially in Urbino itself, that at last, partly from good-will, partly from inability to do better, the government submitted to take what had been wont to be given. Law and privilege, too, remained untouched. Under the safeguard of this family, San Marino preserved its inoffensive freedom.[3] In short, while everywhere throughout the rest of Italy the power of the prince became more free, more licentious, and more powerful, here it remained subject to its old restraints.

Hence it followed that the inhabitants became extremely attached to their dynasty; and they were all the more devoted to it, as their union with the states of the church would have

[1] Bernardo Tasso has bestowed a splendid eulogy on them in the 47th book of his Amadigi:—

> Vedete i quattro a cui il vecchio Apennino
> ornerà il petto suo di fiori e d'erba- - -

[2] Relatione di Lazzaro Mocenigo ritornato da Guidubaldo duca d'Urbino, 1570. "Vuole alloggiar tutti li personaggi che passano per il suo stato, il numero de' quali alla fine dell'anno si trova esser grandissimo."—[Report of Lazarus Mocenigo on his return from Guidubaldo duke of Urbino, 1570. He wishes to lodge all personages passing through his state, the number of whom, by the end of the year, proves very great.]

[3] "Ha humore d'esser republica "—[It has the humour of being a republic], says a Discorso a N. S. Urbano VIII. sopra lo stato d'Urbino [a discourse to our Lord Urban VIII. about the state of Urbino], by S. Marino. Yet by passing over to the States of the Church it extended its privileges.

led unquestionably to the total abolition of all ties of old standing, of all their ancient franchises.

Hence it became a matter of the utmost importance to the country that the line of the ducal house should be perpetuated.

Francis Maria, prince of Urbino, resided for some time at the court of Philip II.[1] There it is told of him, he formed a connection with a Spanish lady, in which he was perfectly serious, and proposed to marry her. But his father Guidubaldo was quite opposed to the match: he desired above all things to see in his family a daughter-in-law not inferior to himself in point of birth. So he compelled his son to return and bestow his hand on the Ferrarese princess, Lucretia.

They seemed a singularly well-matched couple. The prince was remarkable for mental and bodily endowments, practised in feats of arms, and not without some scientific acquirements, particularly those relating to war; while the princess was clever, commanding, and agreeable. Men's hopes were sanguine that the marriage would be sure to give permanency to the family, and the cities in the principality strove which should do most honour to the spouses by receiving them with triumphal arches and beautiful presents.

But it was unfortunate that the prince was just twenty-five, while the princess, on the other hand, was already about forty years old. The father had overlooked this in his eagerness to palliate his refusal to consent to the Spanish match, which, however, had made no favourable impression at the court of Philip II., by so exalted, splendid, and rich an alliance. Yet it turned out worse than he could have supposed. After the death

[1] In the Amadigi he appears still very youthful, and is right quaintly pourtrayed:—

> Quel piccolo fanciul, che gli occhi alzando
> par che si specchi nell'avo e nel padre
> e l'alta gloria lor quasi pensando.

Mocenigo describes him at the time of his marriage. "Giostra leggiadramente, studia et è intelligente delle matematiche e delle fortificationi: tanto gagliardi sono i suoi esercitii—come giuocare alla balla, andare alla caccia a piedi per habituarsi all'incommodo della guerra—e così continui che molti dubitano che gli abbino col tempo a nuocere."—[He tilts with ease, studies, and has some knowledge of the mathematics and fortification: his exercises are such only as show a brave spirit—such as playing at tennis, going to the chase on foot, to accustom himself to the hardships of war—and this so constantly that many fear they may come at last to hurt his health.]

of Guidobaldo, Lucretia had to return to Ferrara: the idea of having any posterity was out of the question.[1]

We have remarked already what a decisive influence Lucretia of Este had on the fortunes and on the dissolution of the dukedom of Ferrara. In the concerns of Urbino, too, we now find her most inauspiciously implicated. At the very time that Ferrara was taken possession of, it seemed a matter of certainty that Urbino also would lapse (to the popedom), and the more, as in this case there were no agnates to claim the right of succession.

Nevertheless, once more the face of things was changed. Lucretia died in February 1598, so that Francis Maria was left at liberty to marry again.

The whole country was in ecstasy on its being understood soon after, that their worthy lord, who, from year to year hitherto, had governed mildly and peacefully, and whom they all loved, really entertained hopes, though now well up in years, that his lineage would not end with himself. All made vows for the happy delivery of the new duchess, and when the time came, the nobles of the country and the magistrates of the towns met in Pesaro, where the princess was to be confined. At the time of the birth being expected, the court in front of the palace and the adjacent streets were filled to overflowing with people. At length the duke appeared at a window. "God," he called aloud, "God has given us a son." The news was received with indescribable acclamations of joy. The towns built churches and erected pious institutions in fulfilment of their vows.[2]

But how treacherous are the hopes that are founded on men! The prince was remarkably well educated; he showed signs of literary talent at least; and the old duke had the happiness to be able to marry him to a princess of Tuscany, after which

[1] Mathio Zane, Relatione del duca d'Urbino, 1574 [Mathio Zane's account of the duke of Urbino, 1574], makes Lucretia already "Signora di bellezza manco che mediocre, ma si tien ben acconcia : - - si dispera quasi di poter veder da questo matrimonio figliuoli." [A lady of beauty less than mediocre, but she sets herself off to advantage : - - she despairs, it would seem, of being able to see children by this marriage.]

[2] La devoluzione a S. Chiesa degli stati di Francesco Maria II. della Rovere, ultimo duca d'Urbino, descritta dall' ill^{mo} Sr Antonio Donati nobile Venetiano.— [The devolution to the Holy Church of the states of Francis Maria II. della Rovere, last duke of Urbino, described by the most illustrious Lord Anthony Donati, a Venetian nobleman.] (Inff. Politt., also printed already.)

he withdrew to the peaceful retreat of Castel-durante, and handed over the government to his son.

But hardly had the prince become master of his own actions and of the country, than he became intoxicated with his power. A taste for theatrical amusements began then for the first time to prevail in Italy; and the young prince became so much the more the slave of this passion, from having fallen in love with an actress. By day he indulged himself like Nero in the gratification of driving a chariot; at night he himself would appear upon the boards: and these were followed by a thousand other extravagancies. The worthy burgesses looked sadly at each other, nor knew they whether to lament or to rejoice when, in 1623, the prince, after passing a wild and frantic night, was one morning found dead in bed.

Upon this old Francis Maria had to resume the government; full of regret at his now being the last of the Roveres, and his family soon about to disappear altogether, but doubly and trebly disheartened from his having to conduct public affairs without any relish for the task, and to hold out under bitter ill treatment in transactions with the Roman see.[1]

At first he had cause to apprehend that the Barberini would get into their hands the daughter whom his son had left, a child of a year old. In order to remove her once for all beyond the reach of their solicitations, he had her betrothed to a prince of the house of Tuscany, and instantly sent off to that neighbouring country.

But another untoward occurrence immediately took place.

As the emperor, too, laid claim to some part of the territory of Urbino, Urban VIII., to secure his own claims, insisted on having a declaration from the duke, to the effect that all he possessed he held as a fief of the papal see. With this Francis Maria long refused to comply; it went against his conscience to do so; at last, however, he gave such a declaration: "but he never after that," says our informant, "looked up: he felt that what he had done had laid a burden on his soul."

Soon thereafter, he had to consent to the officers who had the command of his fortresses, taking oaths of fidelity to the pope.

[1] P. Contarini: "trovandosi il duca per gli anni e per l'indispositione già cadente prosternato et avvilito d'animo."—[the duke finding himself already failing from years and indisposition, and his mind prostrate and desponding.]

At last—which, in fact, was the best course he could adopt—he handed over the government of the country, without reserve, to the pope's vice-gerents.

Weary of life, enfeebled by age, bent down with anguish of heart, after having lived to see all his confidential friends die off, the duke found his only consolation in religious exercises. He died in 1631.

Thaddeus Barberini instantly hastened to the spot to take possession of the country. The allodial inheritance went to Florence. The territory of Urbino, too, was organized after the model of the other districts in the states of the church, and soon we find the same complaints prevailing there which the government of the priests used to call forth generally.[1]

Let us now take a general view of this administration, and begin with the most important of its elements, that on which all else is dependent—the finances.

INCREASE OF THE DEBT OF THE STATES OF THE CHURCH.

ALTHOUGH Sixtus V. diminished the expenditure, and amassed a treasure, yet he at the same time increased the revenues and imposts, and upon the credit of these borrowed a vast amount of debt.

To curtail expense and to accumulate money was not every one's concern. The necessities, also, alike of the church and of the state, became from year to year more urgent. Recourse was had at times to the treasure: yet so strict were the conditions attached to its application, that that could be done only on rare occasions. Strange to say, it was far more easy to make loans than to use the money people had lying by them, and most rashly and recklessly did the popes pursue this course.

It is very remarkable to observe how the relative amounts of the revenues and of the capital and interest of the debt, stand in the different years for which we possess authentic statements.

In 1587, the revenues amounted to 1,358,456 scudi, the debts to six millions and a half of scudi. About the half of the re-

[1] Aluise Contarini in 1635 found the inhabitants very much dissatisfied: "Quei sudditi s'aggravano molto della mutatione, chiamando tirannico il governo de' preti, i quali altro interesse che d'arrichirsi e d'avanzarsi non vi tengono."—[The subjects were much afflicted at the change, charging with tyranny the government of the priests, who had no interest at heart there but that of enriching and advancing themselves.]

venues, 715,913 scudi, was set apart for paying the interest of the debt.

In 1592, the revenues had risen to 1,585,520 scudi, the debts to 12,242,620 scudi. Already had the debt increased in a much greater ratio than the revenues had done; 1,088,600 scudi, that is, about two-thirds of the receipts was set apart for the interest of the debt in offices and luoghi di monte.[1]

This proportion had already become so hazardous that it must have given rise to serious apprehensions. People would willingly have proceeded at once to lower the rate of interest: a proposal was made to take a million out of the castle, with which to pay back their capital to such of the fundholders as should oppose a reduction of the interest. The net income would thus have been materially augmented. Nevertheless, the bull of Sixtus V., and the anxiety felt lest there should be any wasteful expenditure of the treasure, prevented measures of this kind being taken, and people were compelled to keep to the course on which they once had entered.

It may be thought, perhaps, that the acquisition of so productive a country as the dukedom of Ferrara would have secured a special alleviation; yet this was not the case.

Already, in 1599, the interests had crept up to near three-fourths of the total income of the state.

But in 1605, at the commencement of the administration of Paul V., only 70,000 scudi of the sums paid into the exchequer remained unappropriated to the payment of interest.[2] Cardinal du Perron assures us that the pope could not live for half a year on his regular income, although the disbursements at the palace were very moderate.

So much the less did it become possible to avoid the accumulation of debt upon debt. We see from authentic statements,

[1] Detailed account of the papal finances for the first year of the pontificate of emen VIII., without any particular title. Bibliot. Barb. No. 1699, on eighty leaves. t

[2] Per sollevare la camera apostolica discorso di M. Malvasia, 1606. "Gli interessi che hoggi paga la sede apostolica assorbono quasi tutte l'entrate, di maniera che si vive in continua angustia e difficoltà di provedere alle spese ordinarie e necessarie, e venendo occasione di qualche spesa straordinaria non ci è dove voltarsi."—[Discourse of M. Malvasia for the alleviation of the apostolic exchequer. The interests now paid by the apostolic see absorb, it may be said, all the receipts, in such wise that people live in continual straits and difficulty of providing for ordinary expenses and necessaries, and on the occasion of any extraordinary expense, they know not where to turn to.]

how regularly Paul V. had recourse to this measure: in November, 1607; twice in January, 1608; in March, June, and July, 1608; twice in September of that year, and so on through all the years of his government. The loans were not large, according to our ideas; the petty necessities of the government, as they occurred, were met by establishing and selling new luoghi di monte to a larger or smaller amount. They were secured sometimes on the customs at Ancona, sometimes on the dogana of Rome, or of one of the provinces, sometimes on an enhancement of the price of salt, sometimes on the post-office revenue. They increased gradually, yet grievously. Paul V. alone funded above two millions of debt in luoghi di monte.[1]

But this would have been found impossible, had not a circumstance of a peculiar kind come in aid of that pope.

Power always attracts money. As long as the Spanish monarchy was pursuing its career of rapid aggrandizement, and made its influence felt all over the world, the Genoese, who were at that time the richest capitalists, invested their money in the royal loans, and went on doing so without minding the violent reductions and encroachments of Philip II. Gradually, however, as the grand movement declined, and its wars and wants ceased, they drew their money back again. They turned to Rome, which had meanwhile assumed again so powerful a position in the world, and to which the collective treasures of Europe streamed anew. Under Paul V. Rome became perhaps the leading money market of Europe. The Roman luoghi di monte were in particular request. As they yielded a considerable interest and presented sufficient security, their market value rose at times to 150 per cent. To whatever extent the pope might found them, he always procured plenty of purchasers.

Thus, then, it so happened that the debts increased incessantly. At the commencement of the reign of Urban VIII. they ran to 18 millions. The receipts, according to the system of the Roman court, had to increase proportionally: they were calculated, at the commencement of that reign, to amount to 1,818,104 sc. 96 baj.[2] I do not find precisely how much of this

[1] Nota de' luoghi di monte eretti in tempo del pontificato della felice memoria di Paolo V. 1606—1618.—[Note of the luoghi di monte erected in the time of the pontificate of the happy memory of Paul V. 1606—1618.]

[2] Entrata et uscita della sede apostolica del tempo di Urbano VIII.—[Income and expenditure of the apostolic see from the time of Urban VIII.]

went to the payment of interest; yet it must have been by far the greater part. On looking into the details of the accounts we find the sums received but too often exceeded by the demands upon them. In the year 1592 the dogana of Rome brought in 162,450 sc.; in 1625, it produced 209,000 sc.; but at that time 16,956 sc. went into the coffers of the exchequer; and now the assignations exceeded the receipts by about 13,260 sc. The salt monopoly at Rome had by this time risen from 27,654 to 40,000 sc.; but in 1592 there was a surplus left over of 7482 sc., while in 1625 there was a deficiency of 2321 sc., 98 baj.

It will be seen how small was the possibility of the system attaining its limit, even when economy was practised.

How much less under such an administration as that of Urban VIII., who was so often impelled by political jealousy to make military armaments and to erect fortifications.

It is true that Urbino was acquired, but then, especially at first, it produced very little. After the deduction of the allodial estates, the revenues amounted only to 40,000 sc. On the other hand, the entering upon possession was attended with much expense, no insignificant concessions having then been made to the heirs.[1]

As early as in 1635, Urban VIII. had raised the debt to thirty millions of scudi, to meet the demands occasioned by which he had already either introduced anew, or had augmented, ten different imposts. But with all that, he was far from accomplishing his object. Combinations appeared which led him to go much further, to which, however, we had better turn our regards after having first directed them to another development.

FOUNDING OF NEW FAMILIES.

If we inquire now, whither all those revenues went, and to what they were applied, it is certainly undeniable, that they went in a great measure to support the general efforts of Roman catholicism.

Armies such as Gregory XIV. sent into France, and which his successors, too, had for some time after to keep on foot, the

[1] Remark of Francis Barberini to the nuncio in Vienna, where the emperor grounded claims on that acquisition.

active interest taken by Clement VIII. in the Turkish war, subsidies such as those so often granted under Paul V. to the League and to the house of Austria, which Gregory XV. afterwards doubled, and which Urban VIII., at least so far, transferred to Maximilian of Bavaria, must have cost the Roman see uncommonly large sums.

The necessities, also, of the states of the church often made an extraordinary expenditure necessary; such were the conquest of Ferrara under Clement VIII., the preparations of Paul V. against Venice, and all the military equipments of Urban VIII.

To this were added the magnificent architectural works undertaken sometimes for the beautifying of the city, sometimes for the fortifying of the state, and in which every pope emulated the memory of his predecessors.

But there grew up, moreover, an established practice which contributed not a little to the accumulation of that mass of debts, and which, it must be confessed, benefited neither christendom, nor the state, nor yet the city, but the families of the popes alone

The practice had been generally introduced, and is connected with the relation borne by the priesthood to an extremely complex family constitution, for the surplus of the ecclesiastical revenues to be shared, as a matter of course, by the relations of each individually.

The popes of that time were prevented by the bulls of their predecessors from investing their relations with principalities, as used so often to be done formerly: but therewithal they did not abandon the general usage of the clerical order: they now made it only so much more a matter of concern to procure for them hereditary respect by means of wealth and landed property.

They took care, in doing this, to put forward certain reasons for their justification, starting from the principle that they had never by any vow bound themselves to poverty, and having once concluded that they might regard the surplus of the fruits arising from the ecclesiastical office as their own property, they thought likewise that they had a right with this surplus to make a present to their relations.

But what operated far more powerfully than any views of this kind, was birth and blood, and the natural inclination of mankind to leave behind them something that will last after they themselves are dead.

The first to discover the form afterwards adopted by others, was Sixtus V.

One of his grand nephews he raised to the cardinalship, allowed him to take a part in the administration of affairs, and gave him an ecclesiastical revenue of 100,000 scudi; the other he married to one of the Sommaglia family, and raised him to the marquisate of Mentana, to which were afterwards added the principality of Venafro, and the countship of Celano in the Neapolitan territories. The Peretti family, after that, maintained a high rank for a long period; it repeatedly appears in the college of cardinals.

But the Aldobrandini became far more powerful.[1] We have seen what an influence was exercised by Peter Aldobrandino during his uncle's government. He had already in 1599, nearly 60,000 scudi of ecclesiastical revenues, and how much must they have been augmented after that. The fortune left him by Lucretia d'Este formed a splendid addition to his means. He bought an estate; besides which we find he had money lying in the bank of Venice. But however much he might accumulate, all had to go at last to the family of his sister and her husband, John Francis Aldobrandino. John Francis was warder of St. Angelo, governor of the Borgo, captain of the guard, and general of the church. He, too, even by the year 1599, had 60,000 scudi of income; he often obtained ready money from the pope. I find a calculation according to which Clement VIII., during the thirteen years of his reign, had made presents to his nephews in general to the amount of upwards of a million in cash. They were so much the more opulent, as John Francis was a good manager. He bought the property of Ridolfo Pio, which had never brought the latter above 3000 sc., and raised the annual revenue derived from it to 12,000 c. The marriage of his daughter Margaret with Rainuccio Farnese was not carried

[1] Niccolo Contarini: Storia Veneta: "Clemente VIII. nel conferir li beneficii ecclesiastici alli nepoti non hebbe alcun termine, et andò etiandio di gran lunga superiore a Sisto V. suo precessore, che spalancò questa porta."—[Niccolo Contarini: Venetian History: Clement VIII. never ended conferring ecclesiastical benefices on his nephews, and even went far beyond his predecessor, Sixtus V., who first threw open that door.]

through without a heavy expense: it brought the bridegroom, in addition to some profitable favours, a dowry of 400,000 scudi:[1] although this alliance, as we have seen, did not prove so cordial afterwards as had been hoped.

And now the Borgheses pursued the same course as the Aldobrandini with almost still more haste and recklessness.

Cardinal Scipio Cafarelli Borghese had as much commanding influence over Paul V. as Peter Aldobrandino ever had over Clement VIII., and, indeed, he likewise amassed still greater wealth. In the year 1612 the benefices that had been handed over to him were already reckoned to produce a yearly revenue of 150,000 scudi. He endeavoured to lessen the envy which so much wealth and power necessarily called forth, by benevolence and a courtly and complaisant behaviour, yet we cannot feel surprised that in this he did not quite succeed.

The secular offices were bestowed on Mark Anthony Borghese, whom the pope likewise invested with the principality of Sulmona in Naples, together with palaces in Rome, and the finest country seats around. He loaded his nephews with presents. We have a list of these for the whole period of his government, down to the year 1620. They consisted sometimes of precious stones, sometimes of plate; splendid room-hangings were occasionally taken directly from the stores of the palace and sent to the nephews; sometimes carriages, sometimes even muskets and falconets were given them; but the principal article is always bullion. It appears that they obtained, down to the year 1620, in all, 689,727 sc., 31 baj. in bullion, in luoghi di monte 24,600 sc. according to their nominal value, and in offices, reckoned according to the sum it would have cost to buy them, 268,176 sc.: which also amounts, accordingly, as in the case of the Aldobrandini, to about a million.[2]

But the Borgheses, too, did not neglect likewise to invest their money in real property. In the Campagna of Rome they

[1] Contarini: "Il papa mostrando dolore di esser condotto da nepoti da far cosi contro la propria conscienza, non poteva tanto nasconder nel cupo del cuore che non dirompesse la soprabondanza dell'allegrezza."—[The pope, while affecting to be grieved at being led by his nephews to act thus against his own conscience, could not conceal so much in the depth of his own heart as that the superabundance of his joy did not break out.]

[2] Nota di danari, officii e mobili donati da papa Paolo V. a suoi parenti e concessioni fattegli. MS.—[Note of the money, offices, and movables presented by Pope Paul V. to his relations, and concessions made to them. MS.]

got into their hands about 80 estates: the Roman nobility having allowed themselves to be induced to alienate their ancient property and patrimonies by the good prices paid to them, and by the high rate of interest borne by the luoghi di monte in which they invested the purchase-money. They established themselves in many other quarters besides in the states of the church, the pope therewithal favouring them with special privileges. Sometimes they obtained the right of restoring the banished, or of holding markets, or their subjects were favoured with exemptions; they were exempted from payment of the gabel or salt-tax: they brought out a bull, by virtue of which their properties never were to be confiscated.

The Borgheses became the wealthiest and most powerful race that had ever arisen in Rome.

But by this means the system of nepotism had now come in such a manner into vogue, that even a short reign found means for securing a splendid provision.[1]

There is no doubt that Cardinal Lewis Ludovisio, the nephew of Gregory XV., exercised a more unlimited authority than any of the previous nephews had done. Fortunately for him, during his administration two of the most important offices of the Curia, the vice-chancellorship and the chamberlainship, became vacant and fell into his hands. He obtained above 200,000 sc. of ecclesiastical revenues. Secular power, the generalship of the church and several other lucrative offices fell next to the pope's brother, Don Horatius, senator at Bologna. As the pope did not promise to live long, so much the greater haste was shown in making provision for his family. In a short time they received luoghi di monte to the amount of 800,000 scudi. The dukedom of Fiano was bought for them from the Sforzi, and the principality of Zagarola from the Farneses. Already did the young Niccolo Ludovisio venture to make pretensions to the most brilliant and the richest marriage. By a first

1 Pietro Contarini: Relatione di 1627. "Quello che possiede la casa Peretta, Aldobrandina, Borghese e Ludovisia, li loro principati, le grossissime rendite, tante eminentissime fabriche, superbissime supellettili con estraordinarii ornamenti e delizie, non solo superano le conditioni di signori e principi privati, ma s'uguagliano e s'avanzano a quelle dei medesimi re."—[That which is possessed by the houses of Peretto, Aldobrandino, Borghese, and Ludovisio, their principalities, their immense revenues, so many distinguished fabrics, most superb furniture, together with extraordinary ornaments and delicacies, not only surpass the condition of private lords and princes, but equal and exceed that of kings themselves.]

marriage he brought Venosa, by a second Rombino, into his family. In this, further, he was particularly aided by the favour of the king of Spain.

Emulating such splendid examples, the Barberini now threw themselves into the same course. By the side of Urban VIII. there rose his elder brother, Don Charles, as general of the church, a grave and experienced man of business, who was sparing of his words, and at the commencement of his good fortune would not allow himself to be dazzled by it, nor to be tempted to indulge an empty pride, and now he contemplated before all things the founding of a great family estate.[1] "He knew," it runs in the account of 1625, "that the possession of money distinguishes a man from the general mass of his fellows: and did not consider it seemly that one who had once been nearly related to a pope, should appear in limited circumstances after his death." Don Charles had three sons, Francis, Anthony, and Thaddeus, who could not now miss rising at once to a position of great consequence. The two first devoted themselves to clerical offices. Francis, who, by his discretion and kindness, won the general confidence of all around him, and understood at the same time how to fall in with his uncle's humours, was invested with the leading direction of affairs: a post which, although on the whole he acted with moderation, could not fail of itself, in so long a course of years, to lead to the acquisition of considerable wealth. In the year 1625, he had a yearly income of 40,000 scudi, and as early as in 1627, one of nearly 100,000 scudi.[2] It was not altogether with his good-will that Anthony

[1] Relatione de' quattro ambasciatori 1625. "Nella sua casa è buon economo et ha mira di far danari, assai sapendo egli molto bene che l'oro accresce la riputatione agli uomini, anzi l'oro gli inalza e gli distingue vantaggiosamente nel cospetto del mondo."—[Account by the four ambassadors, 1625. In his house he is a good economist, and contemplates making money, as he knows well enough that gold very much enhances a man's reputation, also that gold raises him and distinguishes him advantageously in the sight of the world.]

[2] Pietro Contarini 1627. "E di ottimi, virtuosi e lodevoli costumi, di soave natura, e con esempio unico non vuole recever donativi o presente alcuno. Sarà nondimeno vivendo il pontefice al pari d'ogni altro cardinale grande e ricco. Hor deve aver intorno 80,000 sc. d'entrata di beneficii eccl^{ci}, e con li governi e legationi che tiene deve avvicinarsi a 100^{m} sc."—[He is a man of excellent, virtuous, and laudable manners, of a sweet nature, and with a single exception does not wish to receive donatives or any presents. Nevertheless during the life of the pope he will, equal to any other cardinal, be great and rich. At present he ought to have about 80,000 sc. of income from ecclesiastical benefices, and together with the governorships and legations which he holds, he ought to have near 100,000 scudi.]

too was named a cardinal, and only under the express condition that he should take no part in the government. Anthony, though of a feeble body, was ambitious, obstinate, proud; and in order at least not to be eclipsed by his brother in all things, he busied himself in getting into his hands a number of places and large revenues, which, even so early as in 1635, ran to 100,000 scudi. For one thing, he obtained no fewer than six Maltese benefices *in commendam*, which could not have been very agreeable to the knights of that order. He also received presents, yet at the same time he gave much away; and was studiously open-handed, for the purpose of attaching to himself a body of adherents from among the Roman nobility. Don Thaddeus, the middle one of the three brothers, was selected for the founding of a family by means of the acquisition of hereditary possessions. He obtained the dignities of the secular nephew, and after his father's death became general of the church, warder of St. Angelo, and governor of the Borgo. Already, in 1635, he had been invested with so many estates, that he too enjoyed a yearly revenue of 100,000 scudi,[1] and to these new ones were constantly added. Don Thaddeus lived very retired and was most exemplary in his household economy. In a short time, the regular income of the three brothers, taken altogether, was reckoned at half a million scudi a year. The most important offices were in their hands. As Anthony obtained the chamberlainship, so did Francis obtain the vice-chancellorship and Don Thaddeus the prefecture, which fell vacant upon the decease of the duke of Urbino. People will have it that in the course of this pontificate, the Barberini received the incredible sum of 105 millions scudi.[2] "The palaces," the author of this information goes on to say, "for example, the palace of the four fountains, a royal work, the vineyards, the pictures, the

1 That is, the revenues of the real property ran to that amount: "per li novi acquisti" [for the new acquisitions], says Al. Contarini, "di Palestrina, Monterotondo e Valmontone, fatto vendere a forza dai Colonnesi e Sforzeschi per pagare i debiti loro."—[of Palestrina, Monterotondo, and Valmontone, which the Colonneses and Sforzeschis were obliged to sell for payment of their debts.]

2 Conclave di Innocenzo X. "Si contano caduti nella Barberina, come risulta da sincera notitia de partite distinte, 105 milioni di contanti."—[The sums that fell into the hands of the Barberini family, as results from an impartial note of the different particulars, amount to 105 millions of scudi.] This sum is so incredible that it may well be accounted a slip of the pen. Yet it is found put down in the same way in several manuscripts, among others, in the Foscarini at Vienna, and in my own.

statues, the wrought silver and gold, the precious stones, that were bestowed on them, are beyond what can be believed or expressed." The pope himsef felt scruples at times about so rich an endowment of his race, and in the year 1640 he appointed a commission in due form, to inquire into its lawfulness.[1] This commission first of all laid down the principle, that with the popedom there was combined a principality, from the overplus or savings of which the pope may make gifts to his relations. From that it proceeded to discuss the circumstances of this principality, in order to determine to what extent the pope might venture to go. After having taken every thing into calculation, it gave it as its judgment that the pope, with a good conscience, might found a patrimonial estate with a net income of 80,000 scudi, and over and above this, may found an estate for a younger branch of his house besides; the daughters' portions he might venture to carry to the amount of 180,000 scudi. Vitelleschi, too, the general of the Jesuits, for the Jesuits must have their hand in every thing, having been asked his opinion, considered these conclusions moderate, and gave them his approval.

In this manner, from one popedom to another, did new families constantly spring up and obtain hereditary wealth and influence: they entered immediately into the rank of the high aristocracy of the country, a distinction willingly accorded to them.

Naturally there could not fail to be jarrings among them. The antipathies between those who went before and those who followed, which formerly appeared in the factions of the conclave, were now exhibited in the nephews. The new family that had attained to power, jealously maintained its supreme dignity, and, generally speaking, denounced hostilities, nay, even persecutions, against its immediate predecessor. However much the Aldobrandini had done towards the elevation of Paul V., they were not the less thrust aside by his relations, treated with ill-will, and visited with expensive and hazardous law-suits:[2] they called

[1] Niccolini treats of this. I have seen, too, a short paper specially on the subject, intituled: "Motivi a far decidere quid possit papa donare, al 7 di Luglio 1640," —[Grounds on which to decide to what extent a pope may make donations, 7th July, 1640,] by a member of the said commission.

[2] An example will be found in the Vita del C[l] Cecchini. See the Appendix.

him the great ingrate. Just as little favour did the nephews of Paul V. find with the Ludovisi; while Cardinal Ludovisio himself had to leave Rome immediately on the accession of the Barberini to power.

For the Barberini, too, now showed much ambition in the advantage they took of the power which they acquired from the possession of the papal government, over the native nobility and the Italian princes. Urban VIII. bestowed on his secular nephew the dignity of a prefect of Rome, because there were titular honours combined with that office which seemed likely for ever to secure to that family its precedency above the rest.

With this, nevertheless, there was at last connected a movement, which was not, indeed, of consequence to the world at large, but which makes an important epoch for the position of the popedom as well with respect to the states of the church as to Italy in general.

WAR OF CASTRO.

THE highest rank among the papal families not actually in power, was always maintained by the Farneses, in as much as they had not only, like the rest, risen to opulence as landed proprietors, but had also come into the possession of a not unimportant principality; and it had never been easy for the reigning nephews to keep that family in submission and due subordination. When Duke Edward Farnese came to Rome in 1639, all possible honours were paid to him.[1] The pope caused lodgings to be provided for him, appointed noblemen to wait on him, and even gave him assistance in his money affairs. The Barberini feasted him and made him presents of pictures and horses; yet with all this they failed to make a complete conquest of him.

[1] Deone: Diario di Roma, tom. I. " E fatale a sig[ri] Barberini di non trovare corrispondenza ne' beneficati da loro. Il duca di Parma fu da loro alloggiato, accarezzato, servito di gentil'huomini e carrozze, beneficato con la reduttione del monte Farnese con utile di grossa somma del duca e danno grandissimo di molti poveri particolari, corteggiato e pasteggiato da ambi li fratelli card[li] per spatio di più settimane, e regalato di cavalli, quadri et altre galanterie, e si parti da Roma senza pur salutarli."—[Deone's Roman journal, vol. I. It is fatal to the lords Barberini not to find their favours reciprocated by those who have enjoyed them. The duke of Parma was lodged by them, caressed, served with men of noble birth, and provided with carriages, benefited by the reduction of the monte Farnese, thus giving the duke the advantage of a large sum, and to the very heavy loss of many poor individuals, courted and feasted by both the brothers cardinals for the space of more than seven months, and presented with horses, pictures, and other braveries, and left Rome without so much as taking leave of them.]

Edward Farnese, an able, clever, self-conceited prince, cherished to a great degree that ambition of those times which found gratification in a jealous attention to petty distinctions. He could not be brought to recognise as he ought to have done, the dignity of a prefect in Thaddeus, and to concede to him the rank that was combined with it. Even when visiting the pope he would make an annoying display of his profound sense of the high rank of his family, and even of his own personal accomplishments. At length misunderstandings arose which were so much the harder to remove, that they were grounded on an insurmountable personal impression.

Hence it became a serious question, how the duke was to be attended on his departure. Edward required being treated with the same attentions as were bestowed on the grand duke of Tuscany; -that is, that the reigning nephew, Cardinal Francis Barberini, should himself give him convoy. To this the latter would consent on the sole condition of the duke paying him a formal visit on taking leave at the Vatican, and Edward held that he was under no obligation to do so. To this there were added some difficulties started in regard to his money transactions, so that his self-love, thus doubly mortified, burst into a flame. After having taken farewell of the pope in a few words, in which further he complained of the nephews, he left the palace and the city without having even taken leave of Cardinal Francis. He hoped thus to mortify him to the very heart.[1]

But the Barberini, in possession as they were of an absolute authority in that country, possessed likewise the means of still more sensibly revenging themselves.

[1] Among the many controversial pieces in this affair which are still extant in manuscript, I find the following particularly peaceable and worthy of belief: Risposta in forma di lettera al libro di duca di Parma [Reply in the form of a letter to the book of the duke of Parma], in the 45th volume of the Informationi: "Il duca Odoardo fu dal papa e ringraziollo, soggiunse di non si poter lodare del Sr C^le^ Barberino. Dal papa gli fu brevemente risposto che conosceva l'affetto di S. Em^za^ verso di lui. Licentiatosi da S. Beat^ne^ senza far motto al S^r^ cardinale se n'andò al suo palazzo, dovendo se voleva esser accompagnato da S. Em^za^ rimanere nelle stanze del Vaticano e licentiarsi parimente da S. Em^za^, come è usanza de' principi. La mattina finalmente partì senza far altro."—[Duke Edward was at the pope's and thanked him, adding that he could not be satisfied with the lord cardinal Barberino. It was briefly replied on the part of the pope, that he was aware of his Eminency's feelings towards him. Having taken leave of his Beatitude without paying his respects to the lord cardinal, he went to his palace, whereas if he had wished to be accompanied by his Eminency, he ought to have remained in the Vatican apartments, and to have taken leave equally of his Eminency, as is usual with princes. Finally, he went off next morning without doing anything further.]

The money-dealing that had developed itself in the state, found admission and imitation also in all the princely houses constituting its aristocracy: they had all of them established monti, and their creditors were secured upon the rents of their estates, just as the papal creditors were on the revenues of the exchequer: the luoghi di monte passed in like manner from hand to hand. Yet these monti would hardly have found credit, had they not been under the control of the supreme government: it being only under the special approbation of the pope that they durst be established or modified. Thus it came to be among the privileges of the reigning family, that by the exercise of such a control it acquired a material influence over the domestic concerns of all the rest: the reductions of the monti to a lower rate of interest formed a matter of daily regulation, and depended on its good-will and friendly disposition.

Now the Farneses, like the rest, were burdened with very considerable debts. The old monte Farnese originated in the wants and expenditure of Alexander Farnese in the Flanders campaigns: a new one had been established: indults of the popes had augmented the mass, and while new luoghi had been contracted for at lower rates of interest, and the old remained unextinguished, the various operations, however, being conducted by different and mutually jealous mercantile houses, every thing had fallen into confusion.[1]

But in addition to all this, it now so happened that the Barberini adopted certain measures which proved most detrimental to the duke.

The two Farnese montes were secured on the rents of Castro

1 Deone, T. I. "Fu ultimamente l'uno et l'altro stato, cioè Castro e Ronciglione, affittato per 94^{m} scudi l'anno a gli Siri. Sopra questa entrata è fondata la dote dell' uno e dell' altro monte Farnese, vecchio cioè e nuovo. Il vecchio fu fatto dal duca Alessandro di 54^{m} scudi l'anno, denari tutti spesi in Fiandra: al quale il presente duca Odoardo aggiunse somma per 300^{m} scudi in sorte principale a ragione di 4½ per cento: e di più impose alcuni censi: di modo che poco o nulla rimane per lui, si che se li leva la tratta del grano, non ci sarà il pago per li creditori del monte, non che de' censuarii."—[Deone, vol. I. Both estates, that is to say, Castro and Ronciglione, were ultimately let to the Siri for 94,000 sc. a year. On that revenue was secured the interest of both the monti Farnesi, that is, both the old and the new. The old one had been created by Duke Alexander Farnese, requiring for payment of interest 54,000 scudi a year, the money having been all spent in Flanders, to which the present duke Edward added a sum amounting to 300,000 scudi in capital lots, bearing interest at the rate of 4½ per cent., and he further has burthened the estate with certain mortgages: in such wise that little or nothing remains for himself, so that if the corn trade be taken away, there will not be wherewithal to pay the monte creditors, nor the mortgagees.]

and Ronciglione. The Siri, who farmed the revenues of Castro, paid the duke 94,000 sc., out of which the interests of the monti could even still have been paid. But it was only in consequence of certain favours bestowed by Paul III. on his family that the rents ran so high. Pope Paul had for that purpose transferred the grand highway of the province from Sutri to Ronciglione, and granted that district greater freedom for exporting its corn than other provinces possessed. These favours the Barberini now resolved to recall. They transferred the grand highway again to Sutri: and in Montalto di Maremma, where the corn from Castro used to be put on board ship, they published a notice prohibiting export.[1]

The results that were contemplated instantly showed themselves. The Siri, who were already pinched by those operations of the duke, and who now had a resource to lean upon in the palace—it has been maintained at the special instigation, moreover, of certain prelates who had a kind of secret partnership in their business,—refused to fulfil their contract, and ceased to pay the interests of the monte Farnese. The montists, thus suddenly deprived of their income, pressed their rights, and applied for redress to the papal government. The duke, seeing himself so purposely wronged, scorned to take any steps with the view of conciliating them. But the montists complained so warmly, urgently, and generally, that the pope thought he was authorized to put himself in possession of the hypothec, in order to assist so many Roman citizens in obtaining their rents. With this design he despatched a small military force to Castro. There he was not altogether unopposed: "We have been compelled," he exclaims among other things, with a strange burst of indignation, in his monitorium, "to cause four cannon shots to be given, by which, too, one of the enemy has been left on the field."[2] He took possession of Castro on the 13th of October,

1 In this they defended themselves by the words of the bull of Paul III., in which only the "facultas frumenta ad quæcunque etiam præfatæ Romanæ ecclesiæ e nobis immediate vel mediate subjecta conducendi"—[power of exporting corn to any parts also of the said Roman church held immediately or mediately of us] was given;—meanwhile there had grown up nevertheless a free export to all quarters generally.

2 It was at a bridge. "Dictus dominus Marchio, ex quo milites numero 40 circiter, qui in eisdem ponte et vallo ad pugnandum appositi fuerunt, amicabiliter ex eis recedere recusabant, immo hostiliter pontificio exercitui se opponebant, fuit coactus pro illorum expugnatione quatuor magnorum tormentorum ictus explodere, quorum formidine hostes perterriti fugam tandem arripuerunt, in qua unus ipsorum inter-

1641, and did not even mean to confine himself to this. In January, 1642, he pronounced the excommunication over the duke, who had not allowed himself to be disturbed by that capture; he was declared to have lost all his feudalities; troops took the field for the purpose of depriving him of Parma and Placentia. The pope would not hear of any pacification; he declared that "there was no room for such a thing between the liege lord and his vassals: he would humble the duke; he had money, courage, and soldiers; God and the world were on his side."

But the affair, by this procedure, became a matter of more general importance. The Italian states had already for a long while been jealous of the repeated extensions of the states of the church. They would not suffer his possibly laying his hands on Parma, as had been done with Urbino and Ferrara: and the Estes had not as yet relinquished their Ferrarese claims, nor the Medici certain pretensions they made to Urbino. All of them had been offended by the arrogant acts of Don Thaddeus; the Venetians were doubly so, owing to Urban VIII. having shortly before caused to be obliterated an inscription in the Sala Regia, in which they were commended on account of their fabled defence of (Pope) Alexander III.; a proceeding which they considered to be a gross insult:[1] to this were added some general political considerations. The preponderance of France now roused the same fears and suspicions among the Italians, that that of Spain had previously excited. In all quarters the Spanish monarchy suffered the heaviest losses, and the Italians dreaded that a general revolution of affairs might take place among them also, should Urban VIII., whom they reckoned to be a decided ally of France, have his power enhanced. For all these reasons they resolved to oppose him. Their troops assembled in the Modenese territory. The Barberini had to abandon the idea of passing through it; the papal forces sent against the allies took up their quarters round Ferrara.

fectus remansit."—[The said lord Marchio, upon a party of soldiers about 40 in number, who had been posted at the same bridge and rampart for their defence, refusing to retire from them in a friendly way, was compelled to fire four shots of heavy artillery in order to dislodge them, frightened at which the enemy at last took flight, in which one of them was left slain.]

[1] I will touch upon this in the Appendix.

Accordingly we here find a repetition to a certain degree of the opposition between the French and the Spanish interests which agitated Europe in general. But how much weaker were the moving causes, the resources and the efforts, here brought to a kind of contest!

An expedition, undertaken on his own responsibility by the duke of Parma, who now saw himself, without much ado on his side, defended and yet laid under no restraint, reveals to us at once the singularity of the position in which the parties found themselves placed.

Without either artillery or infantry, and with only 3000 cavalry, Edward burst into the states of the church. Fort Urbano, that had been built at such expense, and the assembled militia, which had never contemplated meeting an armed enemy. did not check his course. The Bolognese shut themselves up within their walls, while the duke passed on without so much as obtaining a sight of the papal troops. Imola opened her gates to him; he waited on the papal officer in command, and exhorted the city to remain true to the papal see. For he maintained that it was not against Rome, not even against Urban, had he taken up arms, but only against his nephews; he marched onwards under the banners of the church's standard-bearer, on which were to be seen figures of St. Peter and St. Paul, and in the church's name he required a free passage for his troops. In Faenza the gates had been put in a state of defence, but when the governor saw the enemy, he let himself down from the wall by a rope, for the purpose of having a personal interview with the duke, the result of which was that the gates were thrown open. The same was the case at Forli. The inhabitants of all these towns looked calmly from their windows as their enemy passed along the streets. The duke proceeded over the hills to Tuscany, and then starting from Arezzo he burst anew into the states of the church. Castiglione da Lago and Citta del Pieve opened their gates to him; he pushed on without halting, filling the country with the terror of his name.[1] This consternation prevailed most at Rome, where the pope dreaded the fate of Clement VII. He made an attempt to arm his Romans. But he found it necessary to repeal a tax, and a collection had to be

1 A detailed account of this enterprise in Siri's Mercurio, tom. II. p. 1289.

made from house to house, in which specious arguments had to be used before even a small force of cavalry could be equipped. Had the duke of Parma appeared at this moment, a few cardinals would unquestionably have been sent to him at the Ponte molle, and he would have had all his demands conceded.

But withal he was no soldier. Who can tell what considerations, what reflections, restrained him? He allowed himself to be led into negotiations, from which he could expect no good whatever. The pope had time to recover breath. He fortified Rome with all the zeal inspired by a sense of danger.[1] He sent a fresh army into the field, which very soon drove out of the states of the church the duke, whose forces, besides, did not hold together. When all cause for alarm had ceased, Urban made anew the hardest conditions; the prince's ambassadors left Rome; even in peaceful Italy people once more began to prepare to try the chances of civil war.

First of all, in May 1643, the allies invaded the territory of Ferrara. The duke of Parma took a few fortified places, including Bondena and Stellata; the Venetians and the Modenese combined their forces and pushed on farther into the country. But the pope, too, as we have said, had meanwhile put forth all his resources in preparing to oppose them; he had 30,000 infantry and 3000 cavalry; the Venetians had doubts about the expediency of attacking so fine a force; they drew back, and in a short while we find the troops of the church pressing forward into the Modenese territory and the Polesine of Rovigo.[2]

The grand duke of Tuscany then threw himself to no purpose upon Perugia; the pope's troops even made inroads here and there into the duke's territory.

1 Deone: "Si seguitano le fortificationi non solo di Borgo, ma del rimanente delle mura di Roma, alle quali sono deputati tre cardinali, Pallotta, Gabrieli et Orsino, che giornalmente cavalcano da una porta all'altra: e si tagliano tutte le vigne che sono appresso le mura per la parte di dentro di Roma, cioè fanno strada tra le mura e le vigne e giardini con danno grandissimo de' padroni di esse: e cosi verrà anche tocco il bellissimo giardino de' Medici, e perderà la particella che haveva nelle mura di Roma."—[There follow the fortifications not only of the Borgo but the remainder also of the walls of Rome, to superintend which, three cardinals, Pallotta, Gabrieli and Orsino, are deputed, who daily ride about from the one gate to the other: and all the vines near the wall on the side within Rome are cut down, that is, they are forming a street betwixt the walls and the vineyards and gardens, to the very great loss of the proprietors; and thus there will farther come to be broken in upon the exquisite garden of the Medici, and there will be lost the small part that it has in the wall of Rome.]

2 Frizzi: Memorie per la storia di Ferrara, V. p. 100.

How strangely were these movements characterized; on both sides so utterly inefficient and nerveless, if we compare them with the contemporaneous conflicts in Germany, and with the ever memorable Swedish expedition from the Baltic to the neighbourhood of Vienna, from Moravia to Jutland! And yet they were not even purely Italian; foreigners served on both sides; the larger proportion of the allied army was composed of Germans; while Frenchmen formed the majority in that of the church.

Meanwhile this Italian war, too, had the same result; the country was exhausted, and the papal treasury in particular fell into a state of the utmost embarrassment.[1]

Many, indeed, were the devices to which Urban VIII. had recourse in his efforts to procure the money he stood in need of. Already in September 1642, the bull of Sixtus V. was submitted to a new deliberation, and thereafter it was resolved in the consistory to take 500,000 scudi from the castle.[2] Naturally this could not go far, so sums of money began to be taken on loan from the remainder of that treasure, that is to say, it was laid down as a first rule to pay back to the same at some future time, what was now taken from it. We have seen already that personal taxation was one of the measures adopted, and it was often repeated; the pope intimated to the conservators how much money he wanted; whereupon the inhabitants, not even excluding foreigners, had each his quota imposed upon him. But the excise duties continued at all times to be the grand resource. At first these were not very sensibly felt, as, for example, in the

[1] Riccius: Rerum Italicarum sui temporis narrationes, Narr. XIX. p. 590: "Ingens opinioneque majus bellum exarsit, sed primo impetu validum, mox senescens, postremo neutrius partis fructu, imo militum rapinis indigenis exitiale, irritis conatibus prorsus inane in mutua studia officiaque abiit."—[Ricci's Narrations of the Italian affairs of his time, Narration XIX. p. 590. A war burst forth huge and beyond belief, but at the first outburst full of energy, presently declining in vigour, finally profitable to neither party, nay, destructive to the natives in consequence of the rapines of the soldiers, becoming utterly vain from fruitless efforts, it passed away at last in mutual endeavours to please and advantage each other.]

[2] Deone 20 Sett. 1642: "Havendo il papa fatto studiare da legisti e theologi di potere conforme la bolla di Sisto V. cessare denari dal tesoro del castel Sant' Angelo, il lunedi 22 del mese il papa tenne consistoro per il medesimo affare. - - Fu risoluto di cessare 500m scudi d'oro, a 100m per volte, e non prima che sia spesi quelli che al presente sono ancora in essere della camera."—[Deone 20 Sept. 1642: The pope having submitted to the judgment of lawyers and divines, whether, in conformity with the bull of Sistus V., one might divert money from the treasury of the castle of St. Angelo, on Monday the 22d of the month the pope held a meeting of consistory about the said affair. - - It was resolved to take out 500,000 scudi, by 100,000 at a time, and not until there shall first be spent what remained still on hand in the treasury.]

case of an excise on bruised corn for feeding fowls; but heavier burthens soon followed, affecting the indispensable necessaries of life, such as firewood, salt, bread, and wine;[1] now it was that these experienced their second great advance, having been raised in 1644 to 2,200,000 scudi. As a matter of course, every new impost was forthwith capitalized; was made the basis of a monte which was sold. Cardinal Cesi, who had previously been treasurer, reckoned that in this manner 7,200,00 scudi of new debts were created, although there was only 60,000 scudi in the treasure. The whole expense of the war was stated to the Venetian ambassador in 1645 at above 12 millions.[2]

People began to feel more and more every moment how serious a matter this was; credit came at last to be quite exhausted; and it was evident that by degrees every resource must be drained out. The war, too, did not always succeed to a wish. In a skirmish at Lagoscuro, on the 17th of March, 1644, Cardinal Antony owed his escape from being taken prisoner only to the swiftness of his horse.[3] As the pope found himself becoming weaker and weaker every day, he was under the necessity of thinking of peace.

The French undertook the task of mediating between the parties. The Spaniards had so little power at the papal court, and had lost besides so much of their authority elsewhere, that on this occasion they were quite left out.

Previous to this the pope had often been heard to say, that he knew well the object of the Venetians was to kill him with vexation, but they should not succeed in doing so; he should know how to hold out against them; yet he now saw himself compelled

1 Deone 29 Nov. 1642: "Si sono imposte 3 nuove gabelle, una sopra il sale oltre l'altre, la 2ª sopra le legna, la 3ª sopra la dogana, la quale in tutte le mercantie che vengono per terra, riscuote 7 per cento, per acqua 10 per cento. Si è cresciuto uno per cento d'avvantaggio, e si aspettano altre 3 gabelle per le necessità correnti, una sopra le case, l'altra sopra li censi, la terza sopra li casali, cioè poderi nella campagna."—[Three new gabelles were laid on, one on salt, besides the other, the 2d on wood, the 3d on the dogana, applicable to merchandise conveyed by land carriage charged at 7 per cent, that conveyed by water at 10 per cent. There is an addition of one per cent more, and there are expected three new gabelles to meet the current necessities, one on houses, another on mortgages, the third on "casali," that is, manorial estates in the country.]

2 "Relatione de' IV. ambasciatori: "L'erario si trova notabilmente esausto, essendoci stato affermato da più Cli, aver spesi i Barberini nella guerra passata sopra 12 milioni d'oro."—[Reports by the four ambassadors. The treasury is notably exhausted, it having been affirmed by several cardinals, that the Barberini had spent in the late war above 12 millions of gold.]

3 Nani: Storia Veneta, lib. XII. p. 740.

to concede all their demands; to absolve the duke of Parma from the excommunication he had pronounced against him, and to reinstate him in Castro. He never had thought that it would come to this, and felt the disappointment most acutely.

Then there came something else to afflict him. It appeared to him anew that he might have exceeded what was proper in the favours bestowed on his nephews, and that this would burthen his conscience in the sight of God. Once more he called on some divines, in whom he reposed particular confidence, and among whom were Cardinal Lugo and Father Lupis, a Jesuit, to meet for consultation in his presence. The answer was; that as the nephews of his Holiness had made themselves so many enemies, it was equitable, and even necessary for the honour of the apostolic see, to leave them the means of maintaining themselves in undiminished respect, in defiance of those enemies, even after the pope's decease.[1]

Such were the painful doubts, and such the bitter disappointment, wherewith the pope met the approaches of death. His physician has stated that at the moment of his having to sign the peace of Castro, he was so overcome by distress as to fall into a swoon; and then took the disease of which he died. He implored heaven to revenge him on the godless princes who had forced him into a war. He died on the 29th of July, 1644.

Hardly had the papal see ceased to occupy the central point in European affairs, when it suffered a defeat in its Italian concerns, in those of its own state, such as it had not experienced for a long period.

Pope Clement VIII. likewise, it is true, had fallen out with the Farneses, and at last granted them pardon. Nevertheless, he did so only because he wished to have the assistance of the other Italian princes, in revenging himself on the Spaniards. Very different was the state of things now. Urban VIII. had attacked the duke of Parma with all his forces; the combined resources of Italy had exhausted his, and compelled him to submit to an unfavourable peace. It was not to be denied that the popedom had been left for once decidedly at a disadvantage.

INNOCENT X.

THE reaction that followed, revealed itself in the next con-

[1] Nicoletti: Vita di papa Urbano, tom. VIII.

clave.[1] The nephews of Urban VIII. introduced eight and forty cardinals, creatures of their uncle; never had there been so strong a faction. Not the less did they soon perceive that they could not carry the election of the man of their choice, Sacchetti; the scrutinies daily turned out more and more unfavourably. To prevent a declared opponent from obtaining the tiara, Francis Barberini decided at last upon favouring Cardinal Pamfili, who was at least of Urban VIII.'s creation, although leaning strongly to the Spanish side, and although the French court had expressly forbidden his being elected. On the 16th of Sept. 1644, Cardinal Pamfili was elected. He called himself Innocent X., in remembrance, it was thought, of Innocent VIII., under whose reign his family had come to Rome.

But once more, on this event, did the policy of the Roman court undergo a change.

The allied princes, and particularly the Medici, to whom the new pope ascribed his elevation, now gained an influence over the government with which they had just been contending; the Venetian inscription in the Sala Regia was restored again;[2] and at the first promotion that took place, hardly any but the friends of Spain were promoted. The whole Spanish party acquired a fresh accession of strength, and again equally balanced the French, at least in Rome.

The Barberini were the first to feel this complete turn in the tide of affairs. It can no longer now be clearly ascertained how

1 Ever the old violent state of things during a vacancy in the popedom. J. Nicii Erythræi Epist. LXVIII. ad Tyrrhenum III. non. Aug. 1644. "Civitas sine jure est, sine dignitate respublica. Tantus in urbe armatorum numerus cernitur quantum me alias vidisse non memini. Nulla domus est paulo locupletior quæ non militum multorum præsidio muniatur: ac si in unum omnes cogerentur, magnus ex eis exercitus confici posset. Summa in urbe armorum impunitas, summa licentia: passim cædes hominum fiunt: nil ita frequenter auditur quam, hic vel ille notus homo est interfectus."—[Sixty-eighth epistle of J. Nicius of Erythræ to Tyrrhenus, 5th Aug. 1644. The state is without law, the commonwealth without dignity. There is such a number of armed men to be seen in the city as I do not remember having ever seen elsewhere. Not a house a little richer than others but is defended by a guard of many soldiers; and were all to be collected together in one body, they would make a large army. There is the utmost impunity in using arms in the city, and the utmost licentiousness; men are slain here and there, and nothing is oftener heard than that this or the other person of note has been killed.]

2 Relatione de' IV. ambasciatori, 1645. "Il presente pontefice nel bel principio del suo governo ha con publiche dimostrationi registrate in marmi detestato le opinioni del precessore, rendendo il lustro alle glorie degli antenati di VV.EE."—[The present pontiff, in the fine commencement of his government, with public demonstrations, registered in marble, expressed his detestation of the opinions of his predecessor, restoring the lustre of the glories of the ancestors of your eminencies.] This shows what importance they attached to it.

much of all that was laid to their charge, was well founded. They were said to have indulged themselves in invasions of justice, and to have violently appropriated foreign benefices, but their main offence seems to have been embezzling the public money. The pope resolved to call his predecessor's nephews to account, in regard to their money transactions during the war of Castro.[1]

At first the Barberini thought they might secure their safety by placing themselves under the protection of France, and as Mazarin had risen in their family and through their promotion, he now did not allow them to be at a loss for support. They put the French arms on their palaces, and formally committed themselves to the safeguard of France. But Pope Innocent declared that he was there for the purpose of maintaining justice, and although Bourbon should stand at the gates, he must discharge his duty.

Upon this Antony took to flight first, his jeopardy being most imminent, in October 1645; some months afterwards Francis too, and Thaddeus with his children, removed themselves out of the way.

The pope caused their palaces to be occupied, their offices to be distributed, their luoghi di monte to be sequestrated, in which proceedings he had the support of the people of Rome. On the 20th of February 1646, a meeting was held at the capitol. It was the most splendid that had been seen within the memory of man, a part being taken in it by persons distinguished by their rank and titles. A proposal was made that the pope should be prayed to repeal the most oppressive at least of the imposts of Urban VIII., the tax upon flour. The relations of the Barberini, alarmed lest, on the tax being repealed, the debt that had been secured upon it might be paid off out of their property, opposed this suggestion. Donna Anna Colonna, the wife of Thaddeus Barberino, caused a paper to be read, in which she reminded the people how well Urban VIII. had deserved of the

[1] Relatione delle cose correnti, 25 Maggio 1646. MS. Chigi. "I Barberini, come affatto esclusi dal matrimonio del novello pontefice, cominciorono a machinar vastità di pensieri stimati da loro nobili. Il papa continuò ad invigilare con ogni accuratezza, che la discamerata camera fusse da loro sodisfatta."—[Account of current affairs, 25 May 1646. Chigi MS. The Barberini, as being completely excluded from the marriage of the new pope, began to contrive a number of plans much thought of by their nobles. The pope continued to see to it with the utmost care, that the disexchequered exchequer should be satisfied (replenished?) by them.]

city, and of his zeal for the maintenance of justice, and declared it unbecoming to protest against the lawful taxes laid on by a pope of such merits. Not the less was the resolution carried; Innocent X. complied with it at once; the deficit thus occasioned, as had been rightly foreseen, was covered by confiscating the property of Don Thaddeus.[1]

Well then, while the whole family of the preceding pope was thus warmly attacked and prosecuted, the question occurs, for this had now become the most important interest in every pontificate, how the new pope would conduct himself. In the history of the popedom in general, it is an important circumstance, that in this respect matters were no longer as before; although the scandal caused by the court became, properly speaking, more offensive.

Pope Innocent lay under obligations towards his sister-in-law, Donna Olympia Maidalchina of Viterbo, specially on account of her having brought a considerable fortune into the house of Pamfili. He gave her great credit for not having married again, after the death of his brother, her husband.[2] He himself had owed his promotion to this. He had long committed to her the management of the family concerns; no wonder if now she obtained an influence over the administration of the popedom.

She very soon began to have great deference paid to her. To her first would an ambassador on his arrival pay a visit; cardinals would have her bust placed in their apartments, as one would set up the bust of his prince there, and foreign courts sought to gain her favour by means of presents. As all others who had any request to make to the Curia, took the same course—it was even alleged that she caused a monthly tax to be paid her from the petty offices she procured—riches flowed in upon her. In a short time she raised a great establishment; gave feasts and theatrical entertainments, travelled, and purchased estates. Her daughters were married into the most distinguished and the most

1 The passages from Deone's Journal in the Appendix.

2 Bassi: Storia di Viterbo, p. 331. At first she even stood high in point of reputation. "Donna Olimpia," say the Venetian ambassadors of 1645, "è dama di gran prudenza e valore, conosce il posto in cui si trova di cognata del pontefice, gode la stima e l'affettione della Sta S., ha seco molta autorità."—[Donna Olympia is a lady of great prudence and worth; she knows the position she holds as a near connection of the pope's; she enjoys the esteem and affection of his Holiness, and has much authority with him.]

opulent families; the one to a Ludovisi, the other to a Guistiniani. As for her son Don Camillo, who was a person of but mean abilities, she had at first thought it most accordant with circumstances for him to become a clergyman, and externally at least to assume the position of a cardinal nephew;[1] but as there appeared an opportunity for obtaining a splendid marriage likewise for him, the hand of the richest heiress in Rome, Donna Olympia Aldobrandina, being now at liberty in consequence of her husband's death, he returned to the condition of a layman and formed that connection.

Don Camillo had now attained by this step to the utmost possible felicity. His wife was not only rich, but was still in the bloom of life, and full of grace and spirit, compensating for his defects by distinguished personal qualities. But she, too, wished to reign. Between the mother-in-law and the daughter-in-law there was not a moment's peace. The pope's house was filled with the contentions of two women. At first the newly-married couple had to withdraw, but this they would not long endure; they came back against the pope's will, and then the dissension that prevailed was manifest to all the world. Donna Olympia Maidalchina once appeared, for instance, during the carnival, in a splendid equipage on the Corso; her son and his wife stood at a window, and as soon as their mother's carriage came in sight, they went away. Every body noticed this, and it became the talk of all Rome.[2] The different parties endeavoured to obtain influence with the rivals.

Unfortunately the peculiar temper of Pope Innocent was better fitted to promote dissensions of this kind than to remove them.

In himself he was no common character. In his earlier career, in the Rota, as nuncio and as cardinal, he had shown him-

1 From the very first every body was surprised at this: "Io stimo," says our Deone 19th Nov. 1644, "che sia opera della S^ra^ donna Olimpia che ha voluto vedere il figlio cardinale e desidera più tosto genero che nuora."—[I suppose that this was the doing of her Ladyship Donna Olympia, who wanted to see her son a cardinal, and wished to have a son-in-law rather than a daughter-in-law.]

2 Diario Deone. At another time he relates as follows: "Mercordì la tarda (Ag. 1648) la S^ra^ Olimpia con ambidue le figliuole con molta comitiva passò per longo il corso: ogn' uno credeva che ella andasse a visitare la nuora, ma passò avanti la casa senza guardarla."—[Late on Wednesday (Aug. 1648) Lady Olympia with her two sons (in law) passed along the Corso with a great retinue; every one supposed she was going to visit her daughter-in-law, but she passed before the house without looking at it.]

self active, irreproachable, and sincere. His exertions were thought the more extraordinary, from his having attained the age of seventy-two when he was elected; "therewithal," it was boasted of him, "labour does not fatigue him; he is as fresh after it as before it; he finds gratification in talking to people, and he hears every one out." He presented a contrast to the haughty reserve of Urban VIII., by the affability and blandness of his temper. He made the maintenance of order and peace in Rome a matter of special concern; showing himself ambitious of upholding the security of property and person by day and by night, and allowing no ill treatment on the part of superiors towards their inferiors, or of the strong towards the weak.[1] He compelled the barons to pay their debts. As the duke of Parma still continued to delay satisfying his creditors, and the pope could never show himself in Rome without people calling to him, that he might see justice done to the montists, as, moreover, even the bishop of Castro, as was believed, had been put to death by the contrivance of the ducal government, most effectual steps were at last taken in this affair also. The estates of the Farneses were anew exposed to sale; soldiers and police officers proceeded to Castro to take possession of it in the name of the montists.[2] On this occasion, too, the duke showed resistance; he attempted to burst into the states of the church. But this time he found no one to come to his aid. Innocent X. was no longer dreaded by the Italian princes; he rather, as we have seen, became their ally. Castro was taken and demolished; the duke had to submit to hand over the administration of that country to the papal exchequer, which came under an obligation in return, to satisfy his creditors; he even consented to an agreement, that he should forfeit possession of the country, should

1 Relatione di Contarini, 1648. "Rimira solamente con applicatione alla quiete dello stato ecclesiastico e particolarmente di Roma, acciò goda ciascheduno delle proprie facoltà e della libertà del praticare la notte e non rimanga l'inferiore tiranneggiato dal superiore."—[See the text.]

2 Diario Deone 16 Giugno 1649. "Il papa in questo negotio sta posto totalmente, e mi disse: 'non possiamo andare per le strade di Roma, che non si venga gridato dietro, che facciamo pagare il duca di Parma. Sono sette anni che non paga, e di questa entrata devon viver molti luoghi pii e vedove e pupilli.' "—[Deone's Journal, 16th June 1649. The pope is entirely occupied with this affair, and said to me, We cannot pass through the streets of Rome but people call out from behind that we should make the duke of Parma pay. Seven years are past since he paid, and many pious families, and widows and orphans, have to live on this (as their) income.] It will be seen that his motives were not objectionable.

the Farnese monti not be extinguished within eight years. The capital amounted to about 1,700,000, the accumulated interests to about 400,000 scudi. The duke did not seem to be in a condition to raise so large a sum; so that the agreement, which, moreover, was again brought about under Spanish mediation, could only be regarded as a compulsory renunciation, and not at all as one granted freely.

In all these affairs Innocent appears energetic, able, and resolute; but he suffered under one defect, which rendered it difficult to remain on good terms with him, and which even imbittered his own life to him. This was that he had no steady lasting confidence in any one. Favour and disfavour alternated with him according to the impressions of the moment.

This was felt among others by the datary Cecchini. After having long enjoyed the papal favour he found himself all at once suspected, attacked, accused, and superseded by a sub-official, one Mascambruno, who was afterwards alleged to have committed the most extraordinary forgeries.[1]

But still more disagreeable intrigues found admission into the papal family itself, which was already divided at any rate. After the marriage of Don Camillo Pamfili, Innocent X. had no longer any papal nephew, and yet for a long while this had formed even a regular part of the pope's court establishment. One day he felt a particular fit of benevolence come over him, on Don Camillo Astalli, a distant relation of his family, being presented to him; and this young man he resolved to elevate to the dignity of cardinal-nephew. He received him into his house, gave him apartments in the palace and a share in public business. And this elevation of Astalli he openly proclaimed by means of public solemnities and the firing of the castle guns.

Yet the consequence was nothing but unmixed fresh dissension.

The pope's other relations considered themselves placed on the back ground; the very cardinals whom Innocent had previously nominated were put out of temper, by the circumstance of a new

[1] Vita del C[l] Cecchini scritta da lui medesimo. "Scrittura contro mons[r] Mascambruno, con laquale s'intende che s'instruisca il processo che contro il medesimo si va fabricando;"—[Life of Cardinal Cecchini, written by himself. Writing against monsignor Mascambruno, which he intends shall serve for instructing the process that is in course of being raised against the same;] and the still more detailed writing, Pro R. P. D. Mascambruno. MS.

comer having been preferred to them;[1] but Donna Olympia Maidalchina was particularly dissatisfied. She had recommended the young Astalli; she had proposed his being created a cardinal; yet never had she suspected that matters would have been carried thus far.

First, she herself was removed. The secular nephew and his wife, who, as a contemporary expresses it, "was as much exalted above ordinary women as he stood below ordinary men," entered the palace.

But the natural and secular nephew and the ecclesiastical and adopted one did not long agree. The elder Olympia was soon recalled, to keep the house in order; and in a short while she regained her wonted influence.[2]

The busts of the pope and his sister-in-law stand in one of the apartments of the Villa Pamfili. On comparing them with each other, and contrasting the traits in that of the woman, breathing spirit and decision of character, with the mild and inexpressive countenance of the pope, one is convinced that it was not only possible but even unavoidable that he should have been ruled by her.

But after her re-admission, she would not even endure that the advantages accompanying the position of a nephew should go to any family but her own. Because Anstalli would not divide the power with her as she desired, she never rested until he had lost the pope's favour, was quite undermined and supplanted, and obliged to quit the palace, until, in short, she had again become undisputed mistress of the establishment. On the other hand, propitiated with presents, she now even entered into a strict alliance with the Barberini, who meanwhile had returned.

1 Diario Deone 10 Sett. 1650. "Discorre la corte che'l papa ha perduto il beneficio conferito a tutte le sue creature, che si tengono offese che papa babbia preferito un giovane senza esperienza a tutti loro, tra quali sono huomini di molto valore, segno che tutti l'ha per diffidenti overo inetti alla carica."—[It is said at court that the pope has lost the benefit on all those who have been created (cardinals) by him, that they have taken offence at his having preferred a young man without experience to all of them, among whom are men of great worth, intimating that he holds them all distrustful or unfit for the burthen.] In a paper, Osservationi sopra la futura elettione 1652—[Observations on the future election 1652] much also is said on the subject. "Io credo che sia solamente un capriccio che all' improviso gli venne - - conoscendo appena mon^r Camillo Astalli."—[I believe that it was solely a whim that came upon him at unawares - - for he hardly knew monsignor Camillo Astalli.]

2 Pallavicini: Vita di papa Alessandro VII. "La scaltra vecchia passò con breve mezzo dall' estremo della disgratia all' estremo della gratia."—[Pallavicini: Life of Alexander VII. The cunning old dame passed, with a brief interval, from the extremity of disfavour to the extremity of favour.]

How grievously must all these alternations of favour and disfavour, and such unceasing broils in his nearest and most intimate circle, have afflicted the poor old pope! Even an open breach cannot utterly extirpate the inward longings of the mind; it only renders uneasy and painful what was intended to lead to cheerfulness and enjoyment. Over and above this, the old man became sensible at last that he was but the tool of a woman's ambition and avarice; this he disapproved and would gladly have put a stop to it, yet for such an effort he felt he had neither strength nor resolution; besides that he knew not how he could do without her. His pontificate, the course of which was not else marked with any particularly untoward occurrences, might otherwise have been classed among the fortunate ones; yet this morbid state of things in his family and palace has brought it into disrepute. Innocent X. became thereby, still more than nature had made him, peevish, changeable, capricious, and burthensome to himself;[1] in his last days even we find him occupied with the deprivation and fresh dismissal of his surviving relations; in this state of chagrin he died on the 5th of January, 1655.

The corpse lay three days without any of those connected with him, to whom according to the usage of the court that task is committed, having made any preparations for his burial. Donna Olympia said that she was a poor widow, and that it was more than she was able for; no one else considered himself under obligations of duty to the deceased. At length a canon who had once been in the papal service, but had been dismissed long before, laid out half a scudo in seeing to the last honours being done to him.

But let it not be supposed that these domestic broils had only personal consequences.

It is manifest that the government by nephews, which in the preceding pontificates had exercised so complete an authority in the state and so powerful an influence in the church, after having

[1] Pallavicini: "Fra pretiosi arredi oggetto fetente e stomachevole - - proruppe a varie dimostrationi quasi di smanie. - - Assai temuto, niente amato, non senza qualche gloria e felicità ne' successi esterni, ma inglorioso e miserabile per le continue o tragedie o comedie domestiche."—[Amid costly furniture and nasty loathsome objects - - he broke out into various displays apparently of madness. - - Sufficiently feared, by no means loved, not without some glory and felicity in external successes, but inglorious and miserable from the continued recurrence of domestic tragedies or comedies.]

experienced such a check in the latter years of Urban VIII., would never more appear upon the scene, and was approaching its final subversion.

ALEXANDER VII. AND CLEMENT IX.

THE next conclave likewise presented an unusual aspect. The nephews had always appeared hitherto with numerous hosts of devoted creatures, for the purpose of lording it over the new election; but Innocent X. had left behind him no nephew that had kept together the cardinals of his choice, or that had formed them into a faction. These had not owed their promotion, nor could feel themselves under any obligations to Astalli, who had held the helm of affairs but for a short time, and had never exercised any commanding influence. For the first time, for several centuries, the new cardinals entered the conclave with unlimited freedom to vote as they chose. It was represented to them that they ought of their own accord to unite under one head; they are said to have answered that each of them had a head and feet of his own. They were for the most part distinguished men, of independent character; who took care likewise to keep together—they were distinguished by the title of the squadrone volante,[1] (the flying squadron)—but would now no longer follow the beck of a nephew, but acted according to their own convictions and judgment.

While Innocent X. yet lay on his death-bed, one of these, called Cardinal Ottobuono, exclaimed, "We must look out for a truly honest man," "Do you want a truly honest man," replied Azzolini, who was one of them, "there stands one such," pointing to Chigi.[2] Chigi, moreover, had not only gained the reputation of being an able and well-meaning person, but he had particularly distinguished himself as an opponent of the abuses of the form of government that had hitherto prevailed, which, it must be confessed, had never been more crying. Nevertheless, he found that these friends of his were confronted by powerful opponents, particularly among the French. While Mazarin,

[1] Pallavicini names the following as confederates: Imperiale, Omodei, Borromei Odescalco, Pio, Aquaviva, Ottobuono, Albizi, Gualtieri, Azzolini. It was the Spanish ambassador that introduced the name Squadrone.

[2] "Se vogliamo un uomo da bene, quegli è desso, et additò C[1] Chigi, che era indi lontano alquanto nella medesima camera."—[See the text.]

on being driven out of France by the troubles of the Fronde, was making preparations on the frontiers of Germany for putting himself in possession of the power that he had lost, he had not found that assistance in carrying out his plans which he had thought he might reckon upon, from Chigi, who was then nuncio at Cologne, and had entertained a personal ill-will to the latter ever since. Hence it happened that great exertions were required; the election struggles were once more protracted to a great length; at last, however, the new members of the college, that is, the Squadronists, carried the day. Fabio Chigi was elected on the 7th of April, 1655, and took the name of Alexander VII.

The new pope had already imposed upon him, by the leading idea that had led to his elevation, the duty of pursuing a different system of government from that of his predecessors, and he seemed likewise resolved to do so.

For a long while he would not allow his nephews to come to Rome, and boasted that he did not allow a penny to go into their pockets; so that Pallavicini, who was at that time writing his history of the council of Trent, forthwith introduced a passage into his work in which he predicted the everlasting renown to be enjoyed by Alexander the VII., particularly on account of this self-denial with respect to his kindred.[1]

Yet it never could be an easy matter to abandon a custom that had once thoroughly established itself; it would not, nay, never could have prevailed, had there not been something recommendable and natural about it; at every court there are people to

[1] "Populus," he says in his biography of Alexander VII. "qui præ multis vecti galibus humeris sibi ferre videbatur recentiores pontificias domos tot opibus onustas, huic Alexandri S^{mi} magnanimitati mirifice plaudebat; - - inexplicabili detrimento erat et sacro imperio distributione minus æqua beneficiorum et perpetuis populi oneribus."—[The people who, because of the many taxes, seemed to bear upon their shoulders the more recent pontifical families, loaded with so much wealth, marvellously applauded this magnanimity of Alexander VII.; - - it was of unspeakable loss likewise to the sacred empire, owing to the partial distribution of benefices, and the perpetual burthens of the people.] Relatione de' IV. ambasciatori, 1655. "E continenza sin ora eroica quella di che S. Sta si mostra armata, escludendo dall' adito di Roma il fratello, i nepoti e qualunque si pregia di congiontione di sangue seco: et è tanto più da ammirarsi questa parsimonia d'affetti verso i suoi congiunti quanto che non è distillata nella mente dalle persuasioni, ma è volontaria e natavi per propria elettione."—[The self-denial has been heroic hitherto, which his Holiness shows himself armed with, excluding from coming to Rome his brother, his nephews, and whosoever boasts of being related to him by blood: and there is so much the more to be admired in this parsimony of affection towards his kindred, from its not having been infused into his mind by persuasions, but is spontaneous, and the native result of his own choice.]

be found who cry up such customs, and attach themselves to what is sanctioned by use and wont, however glaring the abuse may be.

By degrees one person after another represented to Alexander the VII., that it was not decent for a pope's relations to remain as simple burgesses of a city, neither in point of fact was it possible; that in Siena people abstained not from paying princely honours to his family, and he might readily thereby involve the holy see in a misunderstanding with Tuscany; not content with confirming this, others added that the pope would present a still better example, did he take his relations into favour, while at the same time he contrived to restrain them within proper bounds, than were he absolutely to keep them at a distance;—but there is no doubt that the greatest impression was made by Oliva, the rector of the Jesuits' college, who directly declared that the pope would be guilty of sin, if he did not call his nephews to him; that the foreign ambassadors would never have so much confidence in a mere minister as in the pope's blood relations; that the holy Father would be so much the worse informed, and could administer his office to the less advantage.[1]

So many reasons were hardly required to induce the pope to do what he was already inclined to: on the 24th of April, 1656, he proposed as a question in the consistory, Whether it seemed good to his brethren the cardinals, that he should employ his relations in the service of the papal see. None venturing to say nay, they arrived shortly afterwards.[2] Don Mario, the pope's brother, obtained the most lucrative offices, the superintendence of the annona, and the administration of justice in the Borgo; Flavio, Mario's son, became cardinal padrone, and in a short time had 100,000 scudi of ecclesiastical revenues: another brother of the pope, of whom he had been particularly fond, being by this time dead, his son Augustine was selected for the founding of a family: he was gradually provided with the finest estates,

[1] Scritture politiche, &c. "Un giorno Oliva prese occasione di dire al padre Luti"—[Political writings, &c. One day Oliva took occasion to say to Father Luti] Father Luti had been brought up with the pope, often visited him, and wished that the nephews should be sent for—"che il papa era in obligo sotto peccato mortale di chiamare a Roma i suoi nepoti"—[that the pope was obliged under mortal sin to call up his nephews to Rome]. He then adduced the above reasons.

[2] Pallavicini: "In quei primi giorni i partiali d'Allessandro non potean comparir in publico senza soggiacere a mordaci scherni."—[In those first days Alexander's partisans could not appear in public without subjecting themselves to biting taunts.]

the incomparable Ariccia, the principality of Farnese, the palace at the piazza Colonna, besides many luoghi di monte, and was married to a Borghese.[1] Nay, this favour reached even to more distant relations; for example, to the commendator Bichi, who appears at times in the Candian war, and it was extended to the Siennese generally.

And thus did all things seem to have become quite as they used to be. This, however, was not the case.

Flavius Chigi was far from possessing the same authority as Peter Aldobrandini, or Scipio Cafarelli, or Francis Barberino had done; neither did he make any effort to obtain it, the sweets of government had no charm for him: he rather envied his secular relation, Augustine, whose lot seemed to be the real enjoyment of life, without much effort or labour.

Nay, Alexander VII. himself was far from reigning any longer with the absolute and undivided authority of his predecessors.

While Urban VIII. was yet alive, a congregation di stato was established, in which the most important general concerns of the state were, after due consultation, to be decided upon, yet at that time it was of no great importance. Under Innocent X. it soon became much more influential. Pancirolo, its secretary, and the first distinguished person holding that office that laid the foundation of the respect it subsequently commanded, had down to his death the largest share in the government of Innocent X.: and he before all others obtained credit for preventing any nephew from establishing himself during that period in the government. Chigi himself had for some time been invested with this office. Rospigliosi now obtained it. He had already

1 Vita di Alessandro VII., 1666 : "Il principato Farnese, che vale 100,000 scudi, la Riccia, che costa altrettanto, il palazzo in piazza Colonna, che finito arriverà ad altri 100^{m} sc., formano bellissimi stabili per Don Augustino, et aggiuntovi i luoghi di monte et altri officii comprati faranno gli stabili di una sola testa più di mezzo milione, senza le annue rendite di 25^{m} scudi che gode il commendator Bichi, e senza ben 100$_{m}$ e più sc. d'entrata che ogni anni entrano nella borsa del C^{l} Chigi."—[The principality of Farnese, which is worth 100,000 sc.; Riccia, which cost as much; the palace in the Piazza Colonna, which, when finished, will come to another 100,000 sc.; form a very fine fortune for Don Augustine, and adding to it the luoghi di monte and other offices that have been procured, make up a fortune for one sole person of above half a million, not counting the annual revenue of 25,000 sc. enjoyed by the commendator Bichi, nor full 100,000 sc. and more of income which goes yearly into the purse of C^{l} Chigi.] These are naturally calculations, such as might be put forth at that time in the talk of the day, and to which we must not attach any higher value.

had foreign affairs completely in his hands. Next to him Cardinal Corrado of Ferrara had much influence in matters of ecclesiastical immunity; Monsignore Fugnano had the direction of the religious orders, and theological questions were decided by Pallavicino. The congregations which had little weight under previous popes, again rose to respect and influence, and acquired an efficiency of their own. Already people might be heard saying, that the power of pronouncing absolutely and personally belonged to the pope in spiritual matters only; that in all secular affairs, on the other hand, as when he would begin a war, conclude a peace, alienate a territory, or impose a tax, he must consult the cardinals.[1] In fact Pope Alexander VII. took but little active interest in the administration of the state. For two months in the year he went into the country to Castelgandolfo, where accordingly business was studiously avoided; when at Rome the afternoons were devoted to literature; authors appeared and read aloud their works; the pope liked to suggest improvements. Even in the forenoon it was difficult to succeed in obtaining an audience from him on business properly so called. "I served," says Giacomo Quirini, "Pope Alexander forty-two months; I perceived that he had only the name of pope, not the use of the popedom. No further trace was found of those peculiar qualities which he displayed as cardinal, of that intellectual vivacity, talent for discrimination, decision in difficult emergencies, and facility of utterance; business was put away, he thought only of living in undisturbed serenity of soul."[2]

Alexander was sensible at times of this state of things and disapproved of it. When his negotiations misgave, he would lay the blame on the interested conduct of the cardinals. In his very delirium, shortly before his death, it was observed that he spoke of it.

[1] Giac. Quirini: "I cardinali, particolarmente Cl Albicci, pretendevano che il papa potesse disporre d'indulgenze, - - ma per pace e guerra, alienatione di stati, impositione di gabelle dovrebbe ricorrere ai cardinali."—[The cardinals, particularly Cl Albicci, held that the pope could dispose of indulgences, - - but for peace and war, alienations of states, and the imposing of taxes, he ought to have recourse to the cardinals.]

[2] "Datosi quel capo alla quiete dell' animo, al solo pensiere di vivere, e con severo divieto ripudiato il negotio."—[that head having given itself up to the quiet of the mind, to solitude and thoughtfulness of life, and rejecting business with a stern resolution to forbid its approach.]

But as this arose from the natural course of things, so now it continued going on from bad to worse.

Those cardinals of the squadrone who had contributed most to the election of Alexander VII., and during his whole reign had preserved a great authority, turned the scale also in the new conclave after his death. The only difference was, that on this occasion they were on a better understanding with France. On the 20th of June, 1667, Rospigliosi, who had till now been secretary of state, was raised to the papal throne under the name of Clement IX.[1]

All were of one mind in considering him the best and the most benevolent of men anywhere to be found. True, he was not so active as he was well disposed: he was compared to a tree of luxuriant growth, which produces abundance of foliage and blossoms, but no fruit; all those moral excellencies, however, which are based on the absence of faults, purity of morals, discretion, and moderation, he possessed in a high degree. He was the first pope who really restrained himself in bestowing favours on his nephews. They were not directly kept at a distance; they obtained the usual places, and even founded a new family, but this was solely owing to an occasion having presented itself for marrying a young Rospigliosi to a wealthy heiress, a Pallavicina of Genoa. The favours they enjoyed from their uncle were extremely moderate: they appropriated to themselves none of the public resources, unless some luoghi di monte which were given them; they did not divide amongst them the management of public affairs, or the powers of government.

Now the greatest change of system was involved in this. Hitherto, whenever a new pope ascended the throne, persons holding public offices were either one and all, or for the most part, changed: on this was based the character of the court and the direction in which it was to move: Clement IX. first abolished

[1] Quirini: "Dalle pratiche di volanti, ch' in vero ebbero il merito della presente elettione, successe che Chigi con mal regolato consiglio e fuori di tempo et ordine si dichiarò in sala regia nell' entrare in cappella allo scrutinio, che acconsentiva alla nomina di Rospigliosi. - - Ottoboni innanzi dell' adoratione fu dichiarato prodatario, Azzolini segretario di stato."—[From the measures taken by the *volanti*, who in truth had the merit of the present election, it so happened that Chigi, with an ill-regulated council, and out of time and order, declared in the royal saloon, in going into the chapel to the scrutiny, that he assented to the nomination of Rospigliosi. - - Ottoboni, previous to the adoration, was declared prodatarius, and Azzolini secretary of state.]

this; he would have no man dissatisfied, he confirmed all official persons as he found them, with the exception of a few in the highest situations.[1] In these he put such cardinals as Ottobuono and Azzolini, members of the squadrone, who had guided the last elections, and persons of weight irrespective of their offices. He was far from persecuting the nephews of former popes, as had been usual in so many pontificates: Flavius Chigi's recommendations were not much less effective with him than under Alexander: favours, furthermore, passed through his hands: all things, in short, remained as usual.

How much did the pope's countrymen, the people of Pistoja, find themselves disappointed. They had calculated on favours, such as so many of the Siennese had just been receiving: it was said that such of them as were in Rome had already assumed airs of gentility, and had begun to swear on the faith of a nobleman; but how bitter must have been their surprise on finding the places they had hoped to have, not even vacated, far less bestowed upon them.

It is true that Clement IX., too, did not omit that display of liberality with which the popes were wont to signalize their ascension to the throne: he even went to unusual lengths in this respect, having given away above 600,000 sc. in the course of the first month of his reign. But this was for the benefit neither of his countrymen nor even of his kindred, to whom representations were even made about the neglect of their interests,[2] but it was divided among the cardinals, the leading members of the Curia. It was supposed forthwith that there had been some low game in the conclave in the way of stipulations, but no clear trace of this can be discovered.

1 Grimani: Relatione. "I suoi corteggiani sono mal sodisfatti, per non haver voluto rimuovere alcuno de' ministri et officiali di quelli dell' antecedente pontefice, come sempre costumarono di far gli altri pontefici."—[His attendants are dissatisfied on account of his not having been pleased to remove any one of the ministers and officials among those of the preceding pope, as other popes had always been wont to do.] Already it was alleged against him, that he allowed his nephews to be without proper supports. "Quelli che havevano ricevute le cariche di Alessandro VII., benchè non rimossi da Clemente, conserveranno l'obligatione agli eredi di Alessandro."—[Those who received charges from Alexander VII., although not removed by Clement, will continue to feel the obligation to Alexander's heirs.]

2 "Considerandogli che con tanta profusione d'oro e d'argento una lunga catena per la povertà della loro casa lavoravano." (Quirini.)—[They taking into consideration, that amid this profusion of gold and silver, a long train were labouring in consequence of family poverty.]

It much rather bespeaks the general development of society as fully matured during this period throughout the whole of Europe.

Never has there been a time more favourable to the aristocracy than the middle of the seventeenth century: when, over the entire circuit of the Spanish monarchy, there had again fallen into the hands of the highest nobility those powers of government which preceding kings had taken from them; when the English constitution acquired, amid the most perilous struggles, that aristocratic character which it has maintained down to our own times ; when the French parliaments persuaded themselves that they might play the same part as the English had done; when in all parts of the German territory the nobility had acquired a decided preponderance, with an exception here and there, in which some bold prince strenuously put forth independent efforts; when the estates in Sweden aimed at an inadmissible limitation of the supreme power; and the Polish nobility succeeded in acquiring a complete autonomy. Such likewise was the case in Rome. The papal throne was surrounded by a numerous, powerful, and rich aristocracy; the families already formed imposed limits on those that were rising; and the ecclesiastical government was passing from the self-determination and imperious hardihood of monarchy, to the deliberation, the calmness, and the slowness of an aristocratical constitution.

Under these circumstances the court put on a new aspect. Amid that uninterrupted influx of strangers who came to seek their fortune there, in the everlasting change of upstarts, there appeared a remarkable calm; there had been formed a stationary population, in which changes took place much less frequently. Let us glance for a moment at this population.

ELEMENTS OF THE POPULATION OF ROME.

Let us commence with the highest circles, to which we have just alluded.

There there were still flourishing those ancient and renowned Roman families, the Savelli, the Conti, the Orsini, the Colonnas, and the Gaetani. The Savelli still possessed their ancient jurisdiction of the Corte Savella, with the privilege of saving one criminal every year from capital punishment;[1] the ladies of the family, according to immemorial custom, either never left their palace at all, or only in a close-shut carriage. The Conti preserved in their ante-chambers the portraits of the popes that had sprung from the family. The Gaetani, not without self-satisfaction, cherished the remembrance of Boniface VIII.; they thought, and people were inclined to admit, that the spirit of that pope rested upon them. The Colonnas and Orsini boasted that during whole centuries no peace was ever concluded between the princes of Christendom, in which they had not been included by name.[2] But however powerful they might have been formerly, they were indebted for their importance now, chiefly to their intimacy with the curia and with the popes. Although the Orsini had the finest estates, which should have given them an income of 80,000 sc., yet, owing to an ill-calculated liberality, they had sunk much in point of wealth, and required the support to be derived from ecclesiastical offices. The constable, Don Philip Colonna, was enabled to repair his worldly fortune first, by obtaining leave from Urban VIII. to lower the rate of interest on his debts, and by means of the church livings to which four of his sons had been promoted.[3]

For it had long been usual for the families that were only rising into distinction, to enter into close intimacy with those ancient princely houses.

For a considerable time under Innocent X. there existed, as it were, two factions, in two great sets of family connections. With the Pamfili there were united the Orsini, Cesarini, Borghesi, Aldobrandini, and Giustiniani; on the other side, there

[1] Discorso del dominio temporale e spirituale del sommo pontefice, 1664.—[Discourse on the temporal and spiritual dominion of the supreme pontiff, 1664.]

[2] Descrittione delle famiglie nobili Romane [Description of noble Roman families], MS. in the St. Mark's library, VI. 237 and 234.

[3] Almaden: Relatione di Roma. "Il primogenito è Don Federico, principe di Botero: il secondo Don Girolamo cardinale, cuore del padre e meritamente per esser signore di tutta bontà: il terzo Don Carlo, il quale dopo diversi soldi di Fiandra e di Germania si fece monaco ed abate Casinense: il quarto Don Marc Antonio, accasato in Sicilia: il quinto Don Prospero, commendatore di S. Giovanni: il sesto Don Pietro, abbate secolare, stroppio della persona, ma altrettanto fatica d'ingegno."—[Almaden's Report from Rome. The eldest is Don Frederick, prince of Botero; the second is Don Girolamo, cardinal, the father's delight, and deservedly, because of his being a lord possessed of all goodness: the third, Don Charles, who, after holding various lucrative offices in Flanders and Germany, made himself a monk and abbot of Casino: the fourth, Don Mark Anthony, married in Sicily: the fifth, Don Prospero, commendator of St. John's: the sixth, Don Peter, secular abbot, lame in person, but so much the more the work of genius.]

were the Colonneses and the Barberini. By means of the reconciliation of Donna Olympia with the Barberini, the connection became general: it comprised all the leading families.

In this very circle we now observe a change. The reigning family used formerly on every occasion to play the leading part, to supplant those that had preceded it, and, by the acquisition of greater wealth, to cast them into the shade. This was now no longer possible: partly because the older families had, by intermarriages or by good management, become too rich to permit it; partly, too, because the treasures of the popedom were in the course of being gradually exhausted. The Chigi could no longer dream of such a thing as to surpass their predecessors: the Rospigliosi were far from attempting it: it was thought quite enough if they succeeded in being admitted among them.

In any production whatever of men's minds, any point of manners, any custom, every social community will pourtray, and, so to speak, reflect itself as if in a mirror. The most remarkable product of this Roman society and its modes of intercourse, was the court ceremonial. Generally speaking, there had never been an epoch in which stricter regard was paid to etiquette than now: it indicates the aristocratical tendencies of this age in general; its being carried to such perfection at Rome in particular, may have arisen from that court claiming precedence of every other, and seeking to express this in certain outward forms;[1] and, also, from the ambassadors of France and Spain having contended from of old about precedence. There were here, accordingly, numerous disputes about rank; between the ambassadors and the higher officers of state, for example, the governor; between the cardinals who sat together in the Rota and the rest who did not; between so many other corporations of official persons; between the different families, for example, between the Orsini and Colonna. In vain had Pope Sixtus V. decided that on all occasions the oldest person of the two houses should have the precedence: if this was a Colonna, then the Orsini did not appear; if an Orsino, then the Colonnas kept out of the way; but to these even the Conti and Savelli conceded the precedency of rank only with reluctance, and under

1 These attempts are complained of among others, 1627, Feb. 23d, by the French ambassador, Bethune, in Siri's Memorie, rec. VI. p. 262.

unceasing protests. Distinctions were laid down with the utmost precision; the pope's relations, for example, on entering the papal apartments, had both leaves of the folding doors thrown open to them, while other barons or cardinals had to be contented with the opening of one. A singular mode of paying respect to others had been introduced: it was usual to stop one's coach on meeting the carriage of a person of higher rank, of a patron. It was said to have been first introduced by the Marquis Mattei, who paid this compliment to Cardinal Alexander Farnese: the latter, too, then ordered his to stop, and a few words were interchanged.[1] The example was soon followed by others. The ambassadors received this token of respect from their countrymen, so that, however inconvenient, it came to be a general custom and common duty. Self-love attaches itself with the utmost force even to what is of no importance: it supplies an excuse for not giving up the smallest point of etiquette to relations or equals.

Let us proceed one step further.

In the middle of the 17th century, there were reckoned to be in Rome about fifty noble families 300 years old, five and thirty that were 200 years old, and sixteen that were 100 years old. None were allowed to pass for older than that, and in general they might be traced to a mean and humble origin.[2] A great part of them were originally settled in the Campagna. Unhappily, however, as we have already noticed, they allowed themselves, at the time when the luoghi di monte bore a high rate of interest, to be induced to sell their estates chiefly to the nephew-families, and to invest the purchase-monies in the papal monti. At first this seemed no unimportant advantage. The nephews gave good prices, sometimes beyond the proper value: the interests from the luoghi di monte, which were drawn without trouble,

[1] In the Barberini (library) I saw a special memoir on this: "Circa il fermar le carrozze per complimento, e come s'introdusse in uso."—[About the stopping of coaches as a compliment, and how the custom came in.]

[2] Almaden: "La maggior parte delle famiglie oggi stimate a Roma nobili vengono da basso principio, come da notaro, speziale che sarebbe da sopportare, ma dell' arte puzzolente della concia di corame. Io benché sappia particolarmente l'origine, non però lo scrivo per non offendere alcuno."—[The greater part of the families now reckoned noble at Rome came of a low origin, as from a notary, an apothecary, which would be endurable, but also from the stinking trade of tanning leather. Although I am particularly acquainted with the original (of those families), I do not relate it in writing, that I may not give offence to any one.]

exceeded in value the surplus produce after the most careful cultivation of the ground. Nevertheless, how soon did they come to feel that real property had been transformed into perishable capital. Alexander VII. found himself compelled to reduce the monti, whereby credit was shaken, and the value of the luoghi materially declined. There was not a family that did not lose by it.

But by the side of these there rose up numerous other new races. Each of the cardinals and prelates of the curia naturally pursued, according to the proportion of his means, precisely the same course as the popes did. They, too, neglected not to enrich their nephews, and to found families from the surplus of their ecclesiastical revenues. Others raised themselves by means of the appointments they held in the administration of justice. Not a few rose to distinction as bankers in conducting the business of the dataria. There are reckoned in our time fifteen Florentine, eleven Genoese, nine Portuguese, and four French families, that rose in this way to eminence, more or less, according to their fortune and talents: some among these, whose reputation no longer depended on the business of the day, were money kings—under Urban VIII., the Guicciardini and the Doni, to whom the Giustiniani, Primi, and Pallavicini, joined themselves.[1] Likewise, without any business of that sort, respectable families were constantly coming in, not only from Urbino, Rieti, and Bologna, but also from Parma and Florence. The establishment of the monti and the saleable offices led to this. For a long while the luoghi di monte were much in request as an investment, particularly the vacabili, which formed a sort of life annuity, and on that account bore interest at 10½ per cent., but which not only, as a matter of course, were transferred from older to younger persons, but even when this had been neglected to be done, were directly inherited: the Curia offered their assistance towards this without difficulty. Nor was it otherwise with the saleable offices. Upon the death of the holders they ought to have reverted to the exchequer; and it

1 Almaden: "Non passano ancora la seconda generatione di cittadinanza Romana, - - son venute da Fiorenza e Genova coll' occasione del danaro - - molte volte mojono nelle fascie."—[They are not yet past the second generation of Roman citizenship, - - they are come from Florence and Genoa, on the occasion of having money matters to transact - - they frequently go off into partnerships.]

was for this reason that the return they afforded was in so large a proportion to the capital originally paid in; yet, in point of fact, it was a mere pure annual-rent, in as much as the holder was not obliged to discharge any official duties; without much difficulty, however, in this case likewise transferences could be effected.[1] Many an office remained for a whole century without ever falling vacant.

The union of the public functionaries and of the montists in colleges, gave them a certain representation, and although their rights came gradually to be taken from them, still they retained an independent position. The aristocratical principle so remarkably mixed up with the credit and public debt system, which penetrated this whole state, was likewise calculated to favour these parties. Foreigners found them occasionally very arrogant.

Now around so many distinct families, all possessed of property, struggling to rise in the world, and gradually becoming more and more established, the lower class of the people crowded in continually increasing numbers, and in a firmer manner.

There are still extant returns of the population of Rome, on comparing which in various years, a very remarkable result comes out, as regards the manner in which that population was formed. Not that upon the whole it rose rapidly in amount; this cannot be said; in the year 1600 we find nearly 110,000, fifty-six years thereafter, somewhat above 120,000 inhabitants; an increase which is not at all extraordinary, but here another circumstance presents itself which deserves our notice. At an earlier period the mass of the inhabitants of Rome used to be extremely fluctuating; under Paul IV. the number of souls fell from 80,000 to 50,000; in the course of a few decades afterwards, it rose to above 100,000. This is owing to most of it having been composed of the unmarried men who formed the court, and had no permanent settlement there. The population now fixed itself in settled families, a change which had commenced even towards the close of the sixteenth century, though

1 To suppose that such a wanton sacrifice of the public interest could have been gratuitously perpetrated, seems incredible. No doubt, considerations, like fines on the renewal of leases at a nominal rent, were given, which, however, as they do not appear in the public accounts, must have been paid to, or shared among individuals. Tr.

it chiefly took place in the first half of the seventeenth. Rome had

in the year	1600,	109,729 inhabitants, and	20,019 families.
	1614,	115,643	21,422
	1619,	106,050	24,380
	1628,	115,374	24,429
	1644,	110,608	27,279
	1653,	118,882	29,081
	1656,	120,596	30,103.[1]

It will be seen that the number of the inhabitants at large even falls off in some years; on the other hand, the number of families goes on regularly increasing. In the course of these six and fifty years it increased by more than ten thousand; a fact which certainly becomes the more significant, from the increase of the inhabitants in general being no more than just about that number. The host of unmarried men, coming and going, became less considerable, while, on the contrary, the mass of the population acquired a fixed character. In this state, with insignificant deviations arising from diseases and the natural filling up of the voids they cause, it has remained ever since.

After the return of the popes from Avignon, and the healing up of the schism, the city, which had been threatening to sink into a village, grew in bulk around the curia as its centre. Yet it was with the power and wealth of the papal families, from the time that neither internal troubles nor external enemies were any longer dreaded, from the time that the incomes people drew from the revenues of the state or of the church secured an undisturbed enjoyment, that a numerous settled population first came into being. Its prosperity and its possessions must uniformly be ascribed, whether through direct bestowment or indirect advantages, to the importance of the church and of the court; properly speaking, all were upstarts like the nephews themselves.

Hitherto those already established, continually received fresh numbers and vigour from new settlers who crowded in, particularly from the native towns of every new pope; but the form which the court now assumed, prevented this from being any longer the case. Under the influences of that grand power of

[1] The statements from which these numbers are taken, are in manuscript in the Barberini library. A later one from 1702 to 1816 is to be found in the Cancellieri del tarantismo di Roma, p. 73.

operating upon the world at large, which the Roman see had gained by means of the restoration of Roman catholicism in general, the capital likewise was fundamentally modified; then were those Roman families founded that are flourishing to this day; since the extension of the spiritual empire received a check, the population ceased with the lapse of time to increase. It may be said to have been a production of that epoch.

Nay, the modern city in general, such as it now enchains the attentions of travellers, belongs in a great measure to the same period of the Roman catholic restoration. Let us for a moment glance at it also.

BUILDINGS ERECTED BY THE POPES.

We have noticed the magnificent architectural achievements of Sixtus V., and seen with what views, ecclesiastical and religious, he projected them.

In this he was followed by Clement VIII. To him belong some of the most beautiful chapels in the churches of St. John and St. Peter; he founded the new residence in the Vatican; the pope and the secretary of state occupy to this day the apartments which he built.

But Paul V. in particular made it his ambition to emulate the Franciscan. "Throughout the whole city," says a contemporary biography of him, "he has levelled superficial inequalities; where corners and turnings intercepted the view, he has opened extensive prospects; he has cleared the ground for large squares, and given them a still nobler appearance by the projection of new buildings; the water which he has introduced no longer plays through a tube, it rushes out in a stream. The splendour of his palaces is rivalled by the beautiful variety of the gardens he has laid out. The whole interior of his private chapels glitters with gold and silver; and they are not so much ornamented with precious stones as filled with them. The public chapels rise like basilics, the basilics like temples, the temples like mountains of marble."[1]

We see that the charm of his works does not lie in beauty and symmetry, but in the splendid and the colossal, in which they speak for themselves.

[1] Vita Pauli V. compendiose scripta. MS. Barb.—[Life of Paul V. compendiously written. Barberini MS.]

In the church of St. Mary the greater, he erected over against the chapel of Sixtus V. a far more splendid one, built throughout of the most costly marble.

The water called after him the Aqua Paolina, he brought to the Janiculus, from a spot no less than five and thirty miles off, a still greater distance than that from which Sixtus V. had brought his; it is seen bursting forth from afar, opposite the fontana and Moses of Sixtus V., with nearly five times the strength of that fountain, and in four powerful branches. Who has not been here to visit these heights so famous of old, as having once been attacked by Porsena, and now presenting nothing but vineyards, orchards, and ruins. Here the eye commands both the city and country, as far as those distant hills which evening envelopes in a wondrously tinted haze, as with a transparent veil. The solitude of the place is nobly enlivened by the din of the rushing water. What, indeed, distinguishes Rome from all other cities is the superabundance of water and the multitude of fountains. To this charm the Aqua Paolina certainly contributes most. It feeds the incomparable fountains of Peter's place. It is conducted under the Ponte Sisto to the city, properly so called; the wells at the Farnese palace and many more beyond that, are also supplied from it.

While Sixtus V. erected the dome of St. Peter's, Paul V. undertook to complete the building in general.[1] This he executed, according to the prevailing taste of the time, on the largest scale. At the present day one would much rather see the original plan of Bramante and Michael Angelo followed out; on the other hand, what Paul V. undertook to do, completely satisfied the taste of the seventeenth and eighteenth centuries. True, the dimensions are enormous; who would consider that façade beautiful? But all is lively, appropriate, and magnificent. The colossal size of the building, the square, the obelisk, and the surrounding objects viewed as a whole, impress the mind with a

[1] Magnificentia Pauli V., seu publicæ utilitatis et splendoris opera a Paulo vel in urbe vel alibi instituta. MS. "Unius Pauli jussu impensisque instructa ejus templi pars cum reliquis ab omnibus retro pontificibus exstructis partibus merito conferri potest."—[The magnificence of Paul V., or the works of public utility and splendour begun by Paul in the city and elsewhere. MS. That part of the temple which has been prepared by the command and at the expense of Paul alone, may deservedly be compared with the parts that have been built by all the pontiffs that went before him.]

feeling of the gigantic, being the very idea which was contemplated, and which obtrudes itself irresistibly and indelibly.

Short as was the duration of the government of the Ludovisi, yet they founded for themselves imperishable memorials in the church of St. Ignatius and their villa in the city. Niccolo Ludovisio possessed at one time no fewer than six palaces, all of which he kept in good repair or beautified.

Urban VIII. is recalled to our remembrance not only in many churches, such as St. Bibiana, St. Quirico and St. Sebastian on the Palatine hill, but, as was to be expected from his personal predilections, still more in palaces and fortifications. After he had surrounded St Angelo with ramparts and ditches, and, as he boasts on one of his coins, had armed, fortified, and completed that fortress, he led the walls, according to a plan suggested by Cardinal Maculano, who was skilled in architecture, round the Vatican and the Belvedere gardens, as far as the Porta Cavalleggieri. There other fortifications commenced which were to embrace the Lungara, the Trastevere, and the Janiculus, and to reach as far as the priory on Mount Aventine. The Porta Portuense may be ascribed, mainly at least, to Urban VIII. Within this circuit he first felt himself secure. The bridge communicating between the papal residences and the castle he carefully restored.[1]

Pope Innocent X. likewise was an assiduous builder; as may be seen on the capitol, the two sides of which he endeavoured to harmonize with each other; in the Lateran church, where he has gained the merit of having spared the old forms, more than was usual at that time; but most of all, on the Piazza Navona. It was remarked, that when he passed over Peter's square, he never could avert his eyes from the fountains that Paul V. had constructed there.[2] Willingly would he have emulated that pope, and adorned his favourite square with others still more beautiful. To this Bernini applied all the resources of his art. An obelisk was brought over from the circus of Caracalla, and the arms of

1 From the Diario of Giacinto Gigli, which was unluckily pilfered from me at Rome, being the chief loss my collection has sustained; the Cancellieri del tarantismo di Roma, p. 55, enabled me to print off the passages relating to this.

2 Diario Deone 4 Luglio 1648. But he equally remarks: "la quale (la fontana di papa Paolo, there being then but one) difficilmente potrà superare nè in bellezza nè in quantità d'acque."—[the which (the fountain of Pope Paul) he will not easily surpass either in beauty or in quantity of water.]

the pope's family were put upon it. Houses were pulled down in order to give the place a new aspect; the church of St. Agnes was renewed from the foundation; then there rose at no great distance the Pamfili palace, richly furnished with statues, paintings, and costly internal arrangements. He converted the vineyard which his family possessed on the other side of the Vatican, into one of the most beautiful of villas, including within itself every thing that could make a life in the country agreeable.

In Alexander VII. we perceive the modern taste for regularity. How many houses did he pull down in order to obtain straight streets. The Salviati palace was doomed to fall, in order to form the square of the collegio Romano: the Colonna square, too, where his family palace was erected, was remodelled by him. He renewed the Sapienza and the Propaganda. But his chief memorial is unquestionably to be found in the colonnades with which he surrounded the upper part of Peter's square —a colossal work of 284 pillars and 88 pilasters. Whatever may have been said against them from the very first and in later times,[1] still it is undeniable that they have been conceived in harmony with the idea of the whole, and contribute their own impression to that produced by the vast and serenely-pleasing character of the square.

Thus gradual was the rise of the city which has ever since been the resort of such immense numbers of strangers. It was at the same time filled with treasures of every kind. Numerous libraries were collected; not only were the Vatican, or the monasteries of the Augustinians and of the Dominicans, the houses of the Jesuits and of the fathers of the Oratory, furnished with them, but the palaces also: people emulated each other in heaping together printed works, and in collecting rare manuscripts. Not that the sciences were very zealously cultivated; people

[1] Sagredo: "I colonnati che si vanno intorno alla piazza erigendo, di quatro ordini di questi restar cinta dovendo, tutti in forma ovata, i quali formeranno tre portici coperti con tre magnifici ingressi, e sopra da un corridore che sarà d'altro ordine di picciole colonne e di statue adornato, il papa pretende che servir debbano per ricevere della pioggia e del sole alle carrozze."—[The colonnades in course of being erected within the square, of four rows of which the enclosure is to remain composed, all in an oval shape, which will form three covered porticoes with three magnificent entrances, and above that a corridor, which will be of another row of small pillars, and adorned with statues, the pope holds out that they ought to serve as a shelter to the carriages from the rain and the sunshine.] At that time the expense had already run to 900,000 scudi, which were taken from the building fund of St. Peter's.

studied to be sure, but in a leisurely way, less for the discovery of something new, than to appropriate and elaborate what was already known. Among all the academies that rose up year after year, one or two were devoted to the investigation of nature, to botany perhaps, although without anything that could properly be called success:[1] but all the rest, the Good-humoured,[2] the Orderly, the Virginal, the Phantastic, the Uniform, and whatever other strange names they might give themselves, occupied themselves solely with poetry and eloquence, exercises of intellectual skill, confined within a narrow range of thought, yet giving scope to many fine energies. Nor was it with books only that the palaces were adorned, but also with ancient and modern works of art, statues, relievos, and inscriptions. At the time we speak of, the houses of the Cesi, Giustiniani, Strozzi, Massini, and the gardens of the Mattei were in most repute; with which may be classed collections such as that of Kircher at the Jesuits' college, no less the wonder of the age. Still, it was rather curiosity and antiquarian lore that gave occasion for these collections than a taste for the forms or any profound comprehension of antiquity. It is remarkable that at bottom people thought on this subject as Sixtus V. did. They were still far from showing that attention to the remains of ancient times, and that care for their preservation, which these have found at a later period. What could be expected when among other privileges of the Borgheses, we find one to the effect that they should not incur any penalty for any sort of demolition they might commit. One can hardly now believe what was permitted even in the seventeenth century. The baths of Constantine, among others, had been preserved through so many vicissitudes in a tolerably perfect state, and certainly the merits of their builder should alone have led to their preservation after the Christian church had obtained the ascendancy; notwithstanding, under Paul V. they were levelled to the ground, and, according to the taste of that time, converted into a palace and garden, which were afterwards exchanged for the Villa Mondragone in

[1] I refer to the Lincei, founded by Frederick Cesi in 1603, which, nevertheless, did not properly effect much more than the Italian edition of Hernandez's Natural History of Mexico. Tiraboschi: Storia della letteratura Italiana, VIII. p. 195.

[2] For thus would we translate the *Umoristi*, conformably with the information given by Erythræus, which is very well put together by Fischer, Vita Erythræi, p. l. li.

Frascati. Even the temple of Peace, at that time likewise in tolerable preservation, found no mercy with Paul V. He conceived the odd idea of casting a brazen statue of colossal size, representing the virgin and child, and of having it placed at such a height, that the whole city might be overlooked by this, its protectress. All that was wanted was a pillar of unusual altitude. Such he found at last in the temple of Peace. Without troubling himself with the thought that it there formed part of an entire building, and that standing by itself, it would be distinguished rather by grotesqueness and oddity, than by beauty and fitness, he had it removed and crowned with the colossal statue, as it appears at the present day.

Even were all not to be true that has been told of the Barberini, yet it is undeniable that in general their proceedings were dictated by this very taste. Under Urban VIII. it was actually contemplated at one time to pull down that incomparable monument of republican times, the only genuine one in good preservation, the monument to Cæcilia Metella, in order that the travertin marble of which it was composed might be used in the Fontana di Trevi. Bernini, the most renowned sculptor and architect of that time, and to whom the execution of the Fontana had been committed, made this proposal, and the pope gave him permission by a brief to execute it. The work of destruction had already commenced, when the people of Rome, who loved their antiquities, came to the knowledge of the matter, and violently opposed it. For the second time they saved from demolition this, their most ancient possession. It was necessary to desist to prevent a riot.[1]

But all was of a piece. The epoch of the restoration had developed its own peculiar ideas and impulses: these we see struggling to reign without a rival, even in art and literature, neither comprehending nor recognising any thing foreign to them, and resolved to destroy what they cannot subjugate.

Not the less on this account was Rome always a leading city in the cultivation of the human faculties, unequalled in the variety of learning it embraced, and in the practice of art, such as was preferred by the taste of that age: still as productive as ever in music, for the style of the cantata, so well suited to con-

[1] Deone minutely details this.

certs, went on, hand in hand, with the chapel style: it threw the travellers into raptures. "A man must have been neglected by nature," exclaims Spon, who came to Rome in 1674, "if he find no gratification in one or other of the branches."[1] He mentions what these branches are: the libraries, where the rarest works are studied; the concerts in the churches and the palaces, where the finest voices may be heard every day; so many collections for ancient and modern sculpture and painting; so many glorious buildings of all dates, whole villas covered over with bas-reliefs and inscriptions, of which he alone had made fresh copies of thousands; the presence of so many foreigners from all countries and of all tongues; nature enjoyed in gardens charming as paradise; and whoever, he adds, loves the exercises of piety, such will find a whole life long provided for in the churches, relics, and processions.

No doubt other places presented intellectual movements of a higher kind; but the completeness of the Roman world, its being so enclosed within itself, the abundance of wealth and calm enjoyment combined with the security and the satisfaction which were secured to the faithful by the continual view of the objects of their reverence, all put forth an ever-powerfully attractive charm, sometimes operating more by means of one, sometimes more by means of another motive, and sometimes without its being possible to say which was most powerful.

Let us represent to ourselves this attractive charm in the most striking example, which at the time produced a vigorous re-action on the Roman court.

DIGRESSION ON QUEEN CHRISTINA OF SWEDEN.

We have often already found ourselves called upon to direct our attention to Sweden.

That country where Lutheranism first politically revolutionized the whole constitution; where the anti-reformation, in so unusual a manner, found both representatives and opponents in persons of the highest rank; and from which, afterwards, there mainly proceeded the grand decision of the contest that fills so large a space in the history of the world, in that very country Roman catholicism, even under the new form it had assumed,

1 Spon et Wheler: Voyage d'Italie et de Grèce, I. p. 39.

QUEEN CHRISTINA.

OF SWEDEN

BLACKIE & SON, GLASGOW, EDINBURGH & LONDON.

now made the most unexpected conquest. It drew over to its side the daughter of the great champion of the protestants, Queen Christina of Sweden. The manner in which this happened is in itself, and also specially for us, a matter that well deserves consideration.

Let us begin with the position which the young queen occupied in her own country.

Upon the death of Gustavus Adolphus, in Sweden, as in Austria in 1619, in Portugal in 1640, and during the same epoch in so many other quarters, the question came to be momentarily mooted, whether the monarchical power might not as well be thrown off altogether, and a republican constitution adopted.[1]

This proposal, it is true, was rejected: people paid their homage to the daughter of the deceased king; but owing to her being a child of six years of age, and to there being no one of the royal race capable of holding the reins of government, they fell into the hands of a few. The anti-monarchical tendencies of the time found an approving response in Sweden, as did already the proceedings of the Long parliament in England, but still more the movements of the Fronde in France, from their having been so much more decidedly aristocratical. "I clearly perceive," said Christina on one occasion even in the senate, "that a wish prevails here for having Sweden to become an elective monarchy or an aristocracy."[2]

But this young princess had no intention of allowing the

[1] La vie de la reine Christine faite par elle-même [Life of Queen Christina written by herself], in Arckenholtz's Mémoires pour servir à l'histoire de Christine, tom. III. p. 41 [Memoirs for the history of Christina, vol. III. p. 41]: "On m'a voulu persuader qu'on mit en délibération en certaines assemblées particulières s'il falloit se mettre en liberté, n'ayant qu'un enfant en tête, dont il étoit aisé de se défaire, et de s'ériger en république."—[They would have had me persuaded that it was a subject of deliberation at certain private meetings, whether people should not place themselves at liberty, having only a child at their head, of whom it was easy to rid themselves and to erect a republic.] Compare Arckenholtz's notes.

[2] A remarkable proof of this aristocratical tendency is to be found in the sentiments entertained on the subject of the constitution by the greater part of the orders and the "good patriots," in the year 1644, which had appeared shortly before. See Geijer's Swedish History, III. 357. Of the five high functionaries of the kingdom, none was to be placed in office otherwise than by three candidates being proposed by the orders, of whom one was to be chosen. One only, out of three proposed by the order of knights, was to be elected marshal of the country. A consistorium politico-ecclesiasticum, with a president and assessors, was demanded, to be appointed according to the free choice of the orders, and so forth.

royal power to be abolished; she strenuously endeavoured to be, in the full sense of the word, queen. From the instant that she entered upon the government in 1644, she devoted herself to business with marvellous assiduity. Never would she neglect attending a meeting of the senate; we find her on one occasion attacked with fever, so that she had to be let blood, but attended the sitting notwithstanding. Nor did she neglect preparing herself beforehand to the best of her power, reading through state papers many pages long, and mastering their contents; in the evening before retiring to rest, and in the morning as soon as she awoke, pondering the points in dispute.[1] She knew how to propose the questions that arose out of these with great skill; she would avoid giving any hint as to the side to which she inclined; and after hearing all the members state their opinions, she expressed her own, which was always founded on good reasons, and were generally preferred. The foreign ambassadors were amazed at the power she contrived to procure for herself in the senate,[2] although she herself was never contented with it. She had a large personal share in an event of such universal historical importance as the conclusion of the peace of Westphalia. The officers of the army, even one of her ambassadors at the congress, were against that step: and in Sweden, too, there were persons who did not approve of the concessions made to the Roman catholics, particularly in the Austrian hereditary dominions: but she was not for always challenging fortune anew: never had

1 Paolo Casati al papa Alessandro VII. sopra la regina di Suecia. MS. "Ella m'ha più d'una volta assicurato di non aver mai portato avanti alcun negotio grave a cui non avesse quasi due anni prima pensato, e che molte hore della matina, dopo che s'era svegliata da quel poco sonno che era solita di prendere, impiegava nel considerare i negotii e conseguenze loro benchè lontane."—[Paul Casati to Pope Alexander VII. about the queen of Sweden. MS. She has more than once assured me that she had never brought forward any business of serious consequence which she had not first thought over for about two years, and that she employed many hours in the morning, after waking from the little sleep she was wont to take, in considering affairs and their consequences, however remote.]

2 Mémoires de ce qui est passé en Suede tirêz des dépêsches de Mr Chanut, I. p. 245. (1648, Févr.) "Il est incroyable comment elle est puissante dans son conseil, car elle ajoute à la qualité de reine la grace, le crédit, les bienfaits, et la force de persuader."—[Memoirs of what has passed in Sweden, taken from the despatches of M. Chanut, I. p. 245. (1648, Feb.) It is incredible what power she exercises in her council, for she adds to the quality of queen, grace, credit, kind acts, and the force of persuasion.] In a copy of these memoirs, which appeared as early as 1675, marginal notes are found in the queen's handwriting, and in these, indeed, we find rather the expression of a later melancholy, than a minute recollection of the first years of her government; by these, however, at all events, Chanut's statements must be modified.

Sweden been so glorious or so powerful; and she saw enough to gratify her self-complacency in confirming this state of things, and again restoring peace to Christendom.

While she restrained for the present, to the best of her ability, the arbitrary power of the aristocracy, just as little could the latter venture to flatter themselves with the prospect of coming any nearer their object in future: young as she was she very soon brought forward a proposal for the succession to the crown being settled on her kinsman, the count palatine Charles Gustavus. She thought the prince did not venture to hope this; she herself carried the measure in spite of the reluctance of the senate who would not even take it into consideration, and of that of the estates, who complied in this matter merely out of respect for her: in point of fact, it was altogether her idea, and in spite of all difficulties she carried it into effect. The succession was irrevocably settled.[1]

Now it is doubly remarkable that with all this zealous attention to business, she applied to study with a kind of passion. When as yet but a child, no part of her time was pleasanter to her than the hours devoted to her lessons. This might arise from her living with her mother, who absolutely resigned herself to grief for the loss of her husband, and daily looked forward with impatience to the moment when she would be released from those gloomy chambers of sorrow. But she also possessed extraordinary talents, particularly for acquiring languages; she relates that she had learned most of those she knew, properly speaking, without teachers;[2] a circumstance which involves the more as she could actually use some of them with the ease of a native. As she grew in years she became more and more captivated with the charms of literature. It was the epoch when learning was gradually emancipating itself from the fetters of theological dis-

[1] Règne de Christine jusqu'à sa résignation—[Reign of Christina to the period of her resignation], in Arckenholtz, III. 162, notes.

[2] La Vie de Christine écr. p. e. m. p. 53. "Je savois à l'âge de quatorze ans toutes les langues, toutes les sciences, et tous les exercises dont on vouloit m'instruire. Mais depuis j'en ai appris bien d'autres sans le secours d'aucun maître: et il est certain que je n'en eus jamais ni pour apprendre la langue Allemande, la Françoise, l'Italienne, ni l'Espagnole."—[Life of Christina written by herself, p. 53. At the age of fourteen I knew all the languages, all the sciences, and all the exercises that people had wished to teach me. But after that I learned many others without assistance from any master; and it is certain that I never had any for learning the German, French, Italian or Spanish tongues.]

putes, and in which generally acknowledged reputations were rising above both parties. She was ambitious of drawing celebrated persons within her circle, and of enjoying their instructions. First, there came some German philologers and historians, for instance Freinsheim, at whose request she remitted to his native city, Ulm, the greater part of the war assessment imposed upon it.[1] These were followed by Netherlanders; Isaac Vossius brought the study of the Greek writers into vogue; she made herself mistress in a short time of the most important authors of antiquity, and she was even no stranger to the fathers of the church. Nicolaus Heinsius even boasts of it as his chief felicity, that he had been born in the time of the queen; as his second that he had become known to her; as the third and the greatest, he desired that posterity should learn that he had not altogether displeased her. She employed him chiefly in procuring for her costly manuscripts and rare books from Italy, a commission which he executed with intelligence and success. The Italians forthwith complained that ships began to be laden with the spoils of their libraries, and that the aids to learning were taken from them to be carried to the remotest north.[2] In 1650 Salmasius appeared; the queen had sent him word that if he did not come to her, she would be obliged to go to him; he staid for a whole year in the palace. At last even Descartes was induced to pay her a visit; every morning by five o'clock he had the honour of seeing her in her library; it was maintained that she had contrived to trace his ideas, to his own astonishment, out of Plato. Certain it is that alike in her conversations with the learned, and in her conferences with the senate, she showed the superiority derived from the most felicitous memory, quickness of comprehension and penetration. "She has a most extraordinary mind," exclaims Naudæus with astonishment; "she has seen every thing, read every thing, knows every thing."[3]

1 Harangue panégyrique de Freinsheimius à Christine, 1647,—[Panegyrical Harangue of Freinsheim to Christina, 1647,] in Arckenholtz, II. second appendix, p. 104.

2 Compare Granert: Königin Christina und ihr Hof—[Queen Christina and her court], p. 379, 407.

3 Naudé à Gassendi, 19th Oct. 1652. "La reine de laquelle je puis dire sans flatterie qu' elle tient mieux sa partie ès conférences qu' elle tient assez souvent avec Messieurs Bochart, Bourdelot, du Fresne et moi, qu' aucun de la compagnie, et si je vous dis que son esprit est tout à fait extraordinaire, je ne mentirai point, car elle a tout vu, elle a tout lu, elle sait tout."—[Naudé to Gassendi, 19th Oct. 1652.

Wonderful production of nature and of fortune. A young woman free from all frivolity; she does not attempt to conceal that one of her shoulders is higher than the other; she had been told that her beauty chiefly consisted in the rich profusion of her hair, yet to that she did not pay the most ordinary attention; she was a stranger to all the petty cares of life; she never troubled herself about her table, never complained about her food, and drank nothing but water; neither had she ever set herself to any female employment; on the other hand she was delighted to hear it said that she had been supposed to be a boy at her birth, that in her earliest years, during the firing off of artillery, instead of being frightened she had clapped her hands and proved herself to be a true soldier's child; she rode on horseback with the utmost boldness, one foot in the stirrup she bounded along; while at the chase she could bring down the game at the first shot; she studied Tacitus and Plato, and sometimes understood the meaning of these authors even better than philologists by profession; young as she was, yet she had understanding enough of herself to form a remarkably sound opinion even in state affairs, and to defend it out and out among senators who had grown gray in the experience of the world; she threw the fresh vigour of native shrewdness into the work; above all things she was thoroughly impressed with the high importance which her birth gave her, and with the necessity of governing by herself; she never addressed any ambassador to her minister; she would not suffer any of her subjects to wear foreign orders, or one of her flock, as she said, to allow itself to be marked by a strange hand; she knew how to assume a bearing, before which generals who had made Germany tremble, were compelled to be silent; had a new war broken out, she would without fail have put herself at the head of her troops.

With such a temper, with so commanding and determined a character, the thought of marrying, of giving a man rights to her person, was already intolerable to her; she considered that by the settlement of the succession, she had removed the obliga-

The queen, of whom I may say without flattery that she maintains her part at the conferences she holds pretty often with Messieurs Bochart, Bourdelot, du Fresne and me, better than any one of the company, and if I tell you that her mind is altogether extraordinary I should speak the truth, for she has seen every thing, has read every thing, she knows every thing.]

tion to do so which her country might have claimed from her; after her coronation she declared that she would sooner die than be married.[1]

But could, indeed, a condition of this kind in general be preserved? It had something crampt and overstrained; it was wanting in the equipoise of a healthy temperament, in the tranquillity of a natural existence, having all the sources of satisfaction in itself. It was not a turn for business that thus eagerly impelled her onwards; ambition and the self-conceit natural to a princess, urged her in that direction; she found no gratification there. Neither did she love her country, its sources of enjoyment nor its customs; its ecclesiastical or its civil constitution; nor yet its past history, of which she had formed no proper estimate; the state ceremonies; the tedious discourses to which she was obliged to listen, every function in which there was involved a claim on herself personally, were the objects of her direct dislike; the circle of education and learning to which her fellow-countrymen were confined seemed to her contemptible. Had she not possessed that throne from her infancy, it might perhaps have appeared to her a desirable object to aim at; but now that she had been queen as far back as she could remember, those longing faculties of the mind which prepare for a man his future fortunes, had taken a direction that averted her affections from her own country. Her life began to be governed by fancy and a love of singularity; she was unrestrained by any personal considerations; she only thought of opposing to the impressions of accident or of the moment, the ascendancy of the moral propriety which suited her position; she was indeed a woman of lofty mind, high-spirited, full of elasticity and energy, magnanimous, but also ungovernable, violent, of set purpose unwomanly, nowise amiable, undutiful, and that not only towards her mother, for she did not even spare the sacred memory of her father when she wished to give a biting retort; it seemed, indeed, at times as if she knew not what she said.[2]

1 "Je me serois," she says moreover in her autobiography, p. 57, "sans doute mariée si je n'eusse reconnue en moi la force de me passer des plaisirs de l'amour;" —[I should certainly have married had I not perceived in myself sufficient force of mind to enable me to dispense with the pleasures of love;] and here she is the more to be believed as that work is at the same time a sort of confession.

2 No other judgment can be formed with respect to her conversation with her mother in Chanut III., 365, May 1654.

High as was her position in society, the effects of such behaviour could not fail to recoil upon herself; so much the less, accordingly, did she feel herself contented, at home, and happy.

Hence it now happened that this spirit of dissatisfaction attached itself chiefly to religious matters, with regard to which the course of things was as follows.

In her Memoirs the queen dwells with particular predilection on her preceptor Dr. John Matthiä, whose simple, pure and mild soul attracted and charmed her from the very first, and who was her first confidential friend even in the smallest matters.[1] Immediately on its becoming evident that none of the existing religious communions was to overpower the other, there began to manifest itself here and there among well-disposed persons, a tendency to unite. Matthiä too cherished this desire, and published a book in which he mooted the question of a union between the two protestant churches. Now the queen was very much of his opinion; she formed the design of founding a theological academy which should co-operate towards a union of the two confessions. But against this there immediately arose a storm of opposition from the unbridled zeal of some determined Lutherans. The book was attacked with indignation by a superintendent of Calmar; the estates became parties in opposing it. The bishops bid the council of state remember to watch over the religion of the country; the high chancellor repaired to the queen and addressed such representations to her as made tears of disappointment start into her eyes.[2]

Here she may have thought that she could very clearly observe that it was not a pure zeal that had set the Lutherans in commotion. She supposed that people would fain have practised an illusion on her with the name of God, only for the purpose of leading her to some pre-contemplated aim. The manner in which they spoke to her of God seemed unworthy of the Deity.[3]

[1] "Très capable," she says in her autobiography, p. 51, "de bien instruire un enfant tel que j'étois, ayant une honnêteté, une discrétion et une douceur qui le faisoient aimer et estimer."—[Very capable of instructing such a child as I was, having an honesty, a discretion and a gentleness which made him at once esteemed and loved.]

[2] Axel Oxenstiern's letter of 2 May 1647, in Arckenholtz IV. Ap. n. 21, and still more that of Count Brahe, ibid. IV. p. 229. The work of Matthiä is that intituled, "Idea boni ordinis in ecclesia Christi"—[The idea of good order in the church of Christ].

[3] "Je crus," she says in one of the notes communicated by Galdenblad, "que

Those tedious preachers, who were constantly wearying her with their prolixity, and whom in compliance with the rules of the country she was obliged to hear, now became intolerable to her. She often showed her impatience, she would move her chair, play with her little dog; so much the longer, and the more pitilessly, did they endeavour to detain her.

In this disposition of mind into which she now had fallen, and in which she became estranged at heart from the received religion of the country, she now became confirmed by the arrival of men of learning from abroad. Some of these were Roman catholics; others, such as Isaac Vossius, gave occasion for their being accounted sceptical; Bourdelot, who had most influence with her, having cured her easily and successfully of a dangerous illness, quite a man for the court, full of knowledge, remarkable for his conversational powers, and free from all pedantry, ridiculed every thing, polyhistories and national religions, and passed directly for a deist.

The young princess fell gradually into a state of hopeless scepticism. It seemed to her as if all positive religion were but of man's invention, as if every argument were equally valid against one as against another; as if, finally, it were all one to which a person might belong.

Meanwhile she did not proceed directly to cast off all religion; she was not without some convictions which it was impossible to shake; in her isolated position as a princess on her throne, she could not dispense with thoughts about God; nay, she almost thought that she stood one step nearer to him; "thou knowest," she exclaims, "how often I have besought thee in a language unknown to common minds, for grace to enlighten me, and have vowed to obey thee although at the cost of life and fortune." This she soon associated with her other ideas; "I renounced," said she, "all other love and devoted myself to this."

She was particularly impressed with a saying of Cicero, that all the religious beliefs of mankind might be false, but it was impossible that more than one could be true. But was it possible that God could have left mankind without the true religion?

les hommes vous faisoient parler à leur mode et qu' ils me vouloient tromper et me faire peur pour me gouverner à la leur;"—[I believed that men made you speak after their own fashion, and that they wanted to deceive me and to frighten me, so as to govern me as they pleased;] in Arckenholtz, tom. III. p. 209.

It seemed to her as if it were to accuse Him of tyranny, to suppose that he had established in the soul and conscience of mankind a feeling of the want of religious support, and still had not troubled himself about providing the means for satisfying that want.[1]

The question was just only which was the true religion.

Here we need not look for reasons and proofs. Queen Christina has herself confessed that she never could perceive any error in protestantism in the things of faith.[2] But as her aversion to it had sprung from an original feeling of no great depth, and enhanced by circumstances only, so she threw herself with quite as inexplicable a bias, and with a perfect sympathy, to the side of Roman catholicism.

She was nine years old when she received for the first time some more precise information on the subject of the Roman catholic church, and was told among other things that in it the unmarried state was accounted meritorious. "Ah," she exclaimed, "how fine that is; this is the religion I will embrace."

For this she was seriously reprehended, but only persisted in her opinion the more obstinately.

To this there were added further impressions of a like nature. "When one is a Roman catholic," she would say, "he has the comfort of believing what so many noble minds have believed during sixteen hundred years; of belonging to a religion that has been confirmed by millions of miracles and millions of martyrs;" "which finally," she would add, "has produced so many wonderful virgins, who surmounted the weaknesses of their sex and devoted themselves to God."

The constitution of Sweden is based on protestantism; it lies at the foundation of the glory, the power, and the political position of that country; but upon her it was imposed as a kind of

[1] Pallavicini: Vita Alexandri VII. The passage to be found in the appendix.

[2] During a later visit to Sweden, she was earnestly pressed no longer to despise the religion for which her father had died. She answered in such a manner that she did not attribute to protestantism the smallest error, much less any heresy, but grounded her refusal to comply, upon the scorn that would accompany any relapse. Wagenseil in Arckenholtz II. 300: "Ita respondisse reginam, non ut cujusquam hæresios vel minimi erroris ecclesiam protestantium insimularet."—[That the Queen thus answered, not as if she charged the protestant church with any heresy or the smallest error.] The words do not appear to me to admit of an equivocal explanation, whether considered in a philological or historical point of view. Wherefore should the author have said it, if he did not intend to convey that meaning?

necessity. Revolted by a thousand casualties, untouched by its spirit, she capriciously broke away from it. That opposed to it, and of which she had but an indistinct knowledge, attracted her. That the popes should have an infallible authority seemed to her an order of things quite accordant with the goodness of God; and on that she threw herself from day to day with a fuller determination of purpose. It seemed as if the natural longing of a female soul for an object to which to devote itself, here found the satisfaction it desired; as if faith sprang up in her heart, as love would have done in another's, a love of unconscious affection, condemned by the world, and therefore to be kept a secret, but on that account only the deeper rooted, in which a woman's heart finds gratification when resolved to sacrifice every thing to it.

At least Christina had recourse, in seeking to approach the Roman court, to a secret artifice, such as in any other case would have occurred only in affairs of love or ambition; and at the same time she contrived an intrigue with the view of becoming a Roman catholic. In this she showed herself quite a woman.

The first person to whom she gave any hint of her leaning was Antonio Macedo, a Jesuit, and confessor to the Portuguese ambassador, Pinto Periera.[1] Periera spoke Portuguese only, and employed his confessor to act at the same time as interpreter. The queen took a singular delight, during the audiences she gave to the ambassador, and while he thought only of treating about state affairs, in entering into religious controversies with his interpreter, and in confiding to him, in the presence of a third party who understood not a word that passed, her most secret and most daring thoughts.[2]

[1] It has sometimes been stated that the author of her conversion was a certain Godfrey Franken. According to the account of the matter in Arckenholtz, I. 465, the first idea of sending Franken to Stockholm occurred on the return of Salmasius from hence, which took place in 1651. Macedo, however, was there already in 1650. His claim is undeniable.

[2] Pallavicini: "Arctius idcirico sermones et colloquia miscuit, non tunc solum quum ad eam Macedus ab legato mittebatur, sed etiam ipso præsente, qui nihil intelligens animadvertebat tamen longiores inter eos esse sermones quam res ferrent ab se interpreti propositæ et sibi ab interprete relatæ."—[She therefore mingled conversations and conferences more closely, not only on occasions when Macedo was sent to her by the ambassador, but also when the latter was himself present, who, understanding nothing, yet perceived that the conversations betwixt them were longer than the things would bear that were by him proposed to the interpreter, and related by the latter to him.]

Macedo suddenly disappeared from Stockholm. The queen sent after him, as if she had ordered him to be sought for, but she herself had despatched him to Rome, there to lay her purpose in the first instance before the general of the Jesuits, and to beg that he would send her a few confidential members of the order.

In February, 1652, these actually arrived in Stockholm. They consisted of two young men, who gave themselves out to be Italian noblemen on a tour, and upon this were admitted to her table. She suspected at once who they were: as they proceeded immediately before her into the dining-room, she said in a low voice to one of them, that he might possibly have a letter for her: the person addressed said yes, without turning round; she merely inculcated silence on him in pointed terms, and then sent her most trusted servant, John Holm, immediately after dinner, to fetch the letter, and the next morning to bring themselves, in the most profound secrecy, to the palace.[1]

In the royal palace of Gustavus Adolphus, deputies from Rome held a meeting with his daughter, to treat with her on the subject of her coming over to the Romish church. Here the grand charm for Christina lay in nobody having the least idea of what was in progress.

The two Jesuits at first contemplated observing the order of the catechism, but soon perceived that here this would be out of place. The queen put quite different questions in the way of objection from what are found there. Whether there were really any difference between good and evil, or if all depended on the usefulness or the hurtfulness of what was done: how the doubts were to be removed that people might raise against the assumption of a Providence; whether man's soul were really immortal; whether it were not most advisable to follow externally the religion of one's own country, and to live according to the laws of reason. The Jesuits do not mention what replies they gave to these questions: they suppose that during the conference thoughts had suggested themselves that never had occurred to them before, and which they had then

[1] Relatione di Paolo Casati al papa Alessandro VII.—[Report made by Paul Casati to Pope Alexander VII.] Extract in Appendix.

forgotten again: that the Holy Ghost operated in the queen. In fact, she was already under the influence of a decided bias, which made up for all that was wanting in reasons, and even in conviction itself. They most frequently fell back on that highest principle, that the world could not have been left without the true religion: to which assertion was added, that among those presented to our choice the Roman catholic was the most reasonable. "Our chief endeavour," say the Jesuits, "was to demonstrate that the points of our holy faith were elevated above reason, but were in no wise opposed to it." The chief difficulty lay in the invocation of saints, and the worshipping of images and relics. "But her majesty," they proceed to say, "apprehended with a penetrating mind the entire force of the reasons that we laid before her; otherwise much time would have been necessary." She spoke to them also about the difficulties that would arise, were she to make up her mind to change her religion, in carrying that step into effect. These at times appeared insurmountable, and one day, on her seeing the Jesuits again, she declared to them that they had better return home again, that it was an undertaking that could not be accomplished: she could hardly, too, ever become altogether Roman catholic at heart. The worthy *patres* were amazed; they urged every argument that seemed likely to keep her to her former purpose; pressed God and eternity on her consideration, and declared her doubts to be a temptation of Satan. It is perfectly characteristic of her, that at this moment she at once became more resolved than ever she had been at any previous conference. "What would you say," she suddenly began, "if I am nearer becoming a Roman catholic than you suppose?" "I cannot describe the feeling," says the Jesuit who relates the circumstance, "that we experienced; we felt as if we had risen from the dead." The queen asked if the pope might not give her leave to receive the supper once a-year according to the Lutheran practice. "We answered, no; then, said she, there is no help for it, I must resign the crown."

Now to this her thoughts were daily more and more directed on other accounts.

The affairs of the country did not always succeed to a wish. Confronting the powerful aristocracy, which always held fast together, the queen, with a circle of persons drawn from so many different countries, with the successor to the throne, whom she had forced upon the country, and count Magnus de la Gardie, on whom she bestowed her confidence, but whom the old Swedish nobility never would acknowledge as their equal in point of birth, formed a party which came to be regarded as almost foreign. Her unbounded liberality had drained the finances, and the moment was seen approaching when every resource would be found exhausted. So early as in October 1651, she had intimated to the estates that it was her intention to resign. It was at the very time that she despatched Antonio Macedo to Rome. Once more, however, she allowed herself to be induced to recede from this step. The chancellor of the kingdom represented to her that she need not at all be influenced by the financial pressure, that it would be provided forthwith that the splendour of the crown should not suffer.[1] She saw well, too, that this step would not appear so heroic to the world as she had supposed. When, shortly after, Prince Frederick of Hesse contemplated a similar proceeding, she expressly warned him against it; not directly on religious grounds, she only reminded him that whoever changed his creed would be hated by those whom he had abandoned, and despised by those whom he joined.[2] By degrees, however, these considerations ceased to influence herself. It was in vain that she endeavoured to form a party by repeated new appointments to places in the royal council, which she raised from 28 to 39 members. The respect entertained for Oxenstiern, which had been for some time on the decline, rose again by means of family alliances, the influence of habit, and what in that family seemed hereditary, its talents; so that on several important questions, such as, for example, the division of Brandenburg, the queen remained in the minority. Count Magnus de la Gardie, too, lost her favour. The want of money began to be sensibly felt, and often there

[1] Pufendorf Rerum Suecicarum lib. 23, p. 477.

[2] Lettre de Christine au Prince Fréderic, Landgrave de Hesse, in Arckenholtz, I. p. 218. "Pouvez-vous ignorer combien ceux qui changent sont haïs de ceux des sentiments desquels ils s'éloignent, et ne saurez-vous pas par tant d'illustres exemples qu'ils sont méprisés de ceux auprès desquels ils se rangent?"—[Can you be ignorant how much those who change are hated by those who hold the sentiments from which they withdraw, and know you not, by so many illustrious examples, that they are despised by those on whose side they range themselves?]

was not enough to meet the daily wants of her household establishment.[1] In point of fact, did it not seem better for her to stipulate for a yearly revenue, and with that to live abroad according to her heart's desires, without so many remonstrances from over-zealous preachers, who in her life and conduct saw nothing but a rash and venturesome curiosity, an apostasy from the religion and the manners of the country? Affairs were already proceeding untowardly, and she felt herself unhappy when the secretaries of state approached her. Already it was with reluctance that she associated herself with any one but the Spanish ambassador, Don Antonio Pimentel, who took part in all her social intercourse and gratifications, in the meetings of the Amaranthine order which she founded, and whose members had to bind themselves to a kind of celibacy. Don Antonio was aware of her Roman catholic project: he informed his master of it, who promised to receive the princess into his states, and to introduce the subject of her change of faith to the pope.[2] The Jesuits above mentioned, who meanwhile had gone back to Italy, had already taken some preparatory steps there.

On this occasion she was not to be dissuaded by any representations. Her letter to the French ambassador, Chanut, shows how little she reckoned on being applauded for what she was about to do. But she assures him that that gave her no concern. She would be happy, strong in herself, without fear before God and man, and from the haven she had reached would look out upon the sufferings of those who were beaten about by the storms of life. Her sole concern now was to secure her income in a way that should prevent its being taken from her again.

The ceremony of abdication took place on the 24th of June,

[1] Motivi onde si crede la regina di Suezia aver presa la risolutione di rinonciare la corona,—[Motives that are thought to have led the queen of Sweden to resolve to renounce the crown,] in Arckenholtz, II., App. No. 47, probably from Raym. Montecuculi.

[2] Pallavicini, Vita Alexandri VII. "Aulæ Hispanicæ administri, cum primum rem proposuit Malines (who had been sent hither), omnino voluissent ab regina regnum retineri, ob emolumenta quæ tum in religionem tum in regem catholicum redundassent, sed cognito id fieri non posse nisi læsâ religione, placuit regi patronum esse facti tam generosi."—[The ministers of the Spanish court, on the thing being laid before them by Malines, were very desirous that the kingdom should be retained by the queen, on account of the advantages that would thus accrue both to religion and to the catholic queen, but on its being known that that could not be without injury to religion, the king was pleased to become the patron of so generous a deed.]

1654. Much offence as had been given by the government of the queen, still both the aristocracy and the common people were affected at this renunciation of her country by the last scion of the house of Wasa. Old Count Brahe refused to take the crown from her again, which he had three years before placed on her head: he held the bond between prince and subject to be indissoluble, and such an act to be unlawful.[1] The queen had to take the crown from her head herself: he took it first from her hand. Stript of the insignia of royalty, the queen, in a plain white dress, received the parting homage of the estates. Among the rest there appeared the speaker of the estate of the peasantry. He knelt down before the queen, shook her hand, kissed it again and again; tears burst from his eyes; he wiped them off with his handkerchief, and, without having said a word, turned round and went to his place.[2]

Meanwhile her whole mind and measures were directed to going abroad; she would not linger a moment longer in a country in which she had abdicated the supreme authority to another. She had already sent away her jewels; and while the fleet was preparing that was to take her to Wismar, she seized the first favourable opportunity, disguised herself, with a few confidants, in order to escape the annoying superintendence which her former subjects exercised over her, and to repair to Hamburg.

And now she commenced her tour through Europe.

After having secretly embraced Roman catholicism in Brussels, she made an open profession to that effect in Inspruck, and then, invited by the prospect of the papal benediction, she hastened to Italy. She presented crown and sceptre to the Virgin Mary at Loretto. The Venetian ambassadors were amazed at the preparations made in all the cities belonging to the states of the church for giving her a splendid reception; Pope Alexander, whose ambition was flattered by so brilliant a conversion having taken place in his reign, exhausted the apostolic treasury in order that the event might be fitly solemnized, and she en-

1 "It is opposed to God, to the general rights of the people, and to the oath whereby she became engaged to the kingdom of Sweden and to her subjects,—it was no honourable man who gave your majesty such advice." See Life of Count Peter Brahe in Schlözer's Swedish Biography, II. p. 409.

2 Whitelocke's Narrative.

tered Rome not as a penitent, but as if on a triumph.[1] In the years that immediately followed we find her often engaged in travelling: we meet with her in Germany, several times in France, even in Sweden. She never kept herself so far aloof from political efforts as she at first contemplated: she negotiated at one time in good earnest, and not without some prospect of success, about obtaining the crown of Poland, by which she might at least have remained Roman catholic: at another, she drew on herself the suspicion of intending to seize upon Naples in the French interest: the necessity she was under of looking after her pension, which too often failed to be punctually paid, seldom allowed her the enjoyment of perfect tranquillity. Her not wearing a crown, and yet assuming full power as mistress of her own actions, as if she wore one, particularly in the sense she attached to royalty, had sometimes very doubtful consequences. Who could excuse the horrid sentence which she pronounced in her own cause at Fontainbleau over Monaldeschi, a member of her household, and which she left to be executed by his accusers and personal enemies? She allowed him only an hour to prepare for death.[2] The treachery of which the wretched man had been guilty towards her, she viewed as high treason: to have placed him for trial before a court of justice, whatever court it might be, she considered beneath her dignity. "To own no superior," she exclaimed, "is better worth than to govern the world." She despised even public opinion. That execution had excited general disgust, particularly in Rome, where the contention in her domestic establishment was better known to the public than to herself; yet this did not prevent her from hastening back thither. Where else could she have

1 Relatione de' IV. ambasciatori: "Il sospetto che prese papa Innocentio che il ricevimento dovesse costarli caro ritardò il suo arrivo in Roma: e contento quel buon pontefice del risparmio del danaro lasciò la gloria intiera al suo successore d'accomplire a questa memoranda funtione. Intorno a ciò ritrovammo al nostro giongere in Roma occupate le maggiore applicationi della corte, et al ritorno ci si fece vedere tutto lo stato della chiesa involto in facende et a gara l'una città dell' altra chi sapeva fare maggiore ostentatione di pomposi accoglimenti."—[Report by the IV. ambassadors. The suspicion felt by Pope Innocent that the reception would cost him dear, delayed her arrival in Rome; and that good pope, contented with the saving of money, left to his successor all the glory of discharging this memorable function. With respect to that, on our arrival in Rome we found the court assiduously occupied, and on returning hither the whole state of the church might be seen absorbed, one city emulating another, in striving which should make the greater show in giving a pompous reception.]

2 Pallavicini: in the Appendix.

lived but in Rome? She would have fallen into perpetual feuds with every secular power that had a character of a piece with her pretensions. Even with the popes, with Alexander VII. himself, whose name she had added to her own at the time of her change of creed, she was often involved in bitter disputes.

By degrees, however, her manners became milder, and her condition more sedate; she succeeded in paying some regard to herself; she understood what was required of her by the peculiarities of her place of residence, where, in other respects, the ecclesiastical government of aristocratical privileges and personal independence opened a wide field for her activity. She took a greater and greater part in the splendour, the occupations, the social life of the Curia, and by degrees became very peculiarly identified with that corporation in its collective capacity. The collections she had brought out of Sweden she now enlarged at so much cost, and with so much taste and success, that she surpassed the native families, and elevated this pursuit from the level of mere curiosity to one of higher importance for learning and art. Such men as Spanheim and Havercamp have thought it worth their while to illustrate her coins and medals, and Sante Bartolo applied his practised hand to her engraved stones and cameos. The Correggios of her collection of paintings have always been the finest ornaments of those picture galleries into which the change of times introduced them. The manuscripts of her library have contributed not a little to maintain the renown of the Vaticana, to which they were afterwards bequeathed. Acquisitions and possessions of this sort supply a source of harmless enjoyment to every-day life. She took a warm part likewise in scientific pursuits. It is much to her honour that she patronized, to the best of her ability, the poor persecuted Borelli, who, at an advanced age, was compelled again to betake himself to teaching; and that at her expense he printed his famous and still unsurpassed work on the mechanism of animal movements, a work which has also been of so much consequence to the development of physiology. Nay, I think we may venture to assert, that even she herself, in the further progress of her faculties, that her mind, when more mature, exerted an effective and imperishable influence, particularly upon Italian literature. It is notorious what perversities obtained at that time in the tautological, far-fetched, meaningless poetry and eloquence of Italy. Queen Christina had too highly cultivated and too richly endowed a mind to be ensnared by such a style; to her it was disgusting. In 1680 she established an academy in her own house, for political and literary essays, where the chief rule was, that the modern tumid style, so overloaded with metaphors, should be abandoned, and that sound sense and the examples of the Augustan and Medicean ages should alone be followed.[1] One feels peculiarly struck when stumbling on the works of this academy in the Albani library at Rome, at finding the essays of Italian abbes improved by the hand of a northern queen; nevertheless, this was a fact of no small importance. From her academy there went forth such men as Alexander Guidi, who had previously followed the common style, but ever after his forming a part of the queen's circle, resolved to cast it off, and associated himself with some friends for the purpose of utterly extirpating it where possible. The Arcadia, an academy which has had the credit of accomplishing this, arose out of the society instituted by Queen Christina. In general, it is not to be denied that the queen, amid so many influences pressing upon her from all sides, preserved a noble independence of mind. She had no idea of submitting to the demand generally made on converts, or which they voluntarily imposed on themselves for the sake of making a display of ostentatious piety. Roman catholic as she was, and often as she would repeat her conviction of the pope's infallibility, and of the necessity of believing all that he and the church might command, still she had a genuine dislike to bigots, and abominated the guidance of father confessors, which at that time regulated one's whole life. She would

1 Constituzioni dell' academia reale [Rules of the royal academy], in Arckenholtz, IV. p. 28, § 28. "In quest' academia si studj la purità, la gravità e la maestà della lingua Toscana: s'imitino per quanto si può i maestri della vera eloquenza de' secoli d'Augusto e di Leone X., - - e però si dia bando allo stile moderno turgido ed ampolloso, ai traslati, metafore, figure, &c."—[In this academy the object of study is the purity, weight, and majesty of the Tuscan tongue; the utmost possible imitation of the masters of true eloquence of the ages of Augustus and Leo X., - - and, therefore, banishment is pronounced on the turgid and bombastic modern style, on transpositions, metaphors, figures, &c.] Another paragraph (11) forbids all eulogies on the queen, which, too, was very necessary. In the fourth volume of Nicoletti's Urban VIII., there is a description of this academy, in which the chief point shown is, that the leading members were Angelo della Noce, Joseph Suarez, Jo. Francis Albani (afterwards pope), Stephen Gradi, Ottavio Falconieri, Stephen Pignatelli, who lived in family with Cardinal Francis Barberino.

allow nothing to deprive her of the enjoyment of carnival, concert, comedy, and whatever else Roman life might offer, above the internal movements of an intellectual and animated social circle. She was fond, it is well known, of satire, and was delighted with Pasquin. We find her uniformly implicated likewise in the intrigues of the court, the broils among the papal families and the factions that prevailed among the cardinals. She attached herself to the Squadronist party, at the head of which stood her friend Azzolini, a man whom others besides her considered the most richly gifted member of the curia, but whom she at once declares to be a pious, incomparable, godlike man, and whom alone she considered superior to the old lord high chanceller Axel Oxenstiern. She meant to leave a memorial of him in her memoirs. Unhappily but a small part of these has ever come to light, which, however, is fraught with an earnestness, a truthfulness in her converse with herself, and a taste at once free and fixed, that silence calumny. A no less remarkable production is to be found in the apophthegms and detached thoughts which we possess as the work of her leisure hours.[1] With much taste for the world, much insight into the workings of the passions, such as experience only can give, the most refined remarks upon them, and at the same time a decided turn for what is real and substantial, a living conviction of the spontaneity and nobility of the mind, a just estimate of earthly things, neither too low nor too high a standard, and a disposition which seeks to satisfy only God and itself. That great movement of the mind which towards the close of the seventeenth century developed itself in all the departments of human activity, and thus opened a new era, ran its course in this princess. For this her residence at the centre of European cultivation and the leisure of private life, if not absolutely necessary to her, were at least highly advantageous. She was passionately fond of the circle she found there, and thought she could not live beyond the atmosphere of Rome.

ADMINISTRATION OF THE STATE AND CHURCH.

HARDLY was there another place in the then known world,

[1] We have them in two editions that vary somewhat from each other: Ouvrage de loisir de Christine reine de Suede—[Work of the leisure of Christina queen of Sweden] in the Appendix to the second volume of Arckenholtz, and Sentimens et

where one could find so much cultivated society, such manifold efforts in literature and art, so much calm intellectual gratification, and in general a life so stored with interests that at once engaged men's sympathies and employed their minds. Government was little felt; the ruling families shared in reality both its splendour and its power. The spiritual demands of the church, too, could no longer be carried out in practice in all their severity; they already found a marked resistance in the manner of thinking prevailing in the world. It was more an epoch of enjoyment; the personal qualities and spiritual impulses that had risen up in the course of time, moved on in luxurious quietude.[1]

But it became another question how church and state were likely to be governed in such a condition of things.

For there is no doubt that the court, or rather the prelature, which properly comprised only the members of the curia in the full enjoyment of their office, had this administration in their hands.

The institution of the prelature had matured itself, in its modern forms, as early as the reign of Alexander VII. In order to become a referendario di segnatura, on which all else depended, a man required to be doctor juris, to have been employed three years with an advocate, to have attained a certain age, to possess a certain amount of fortune, and, moreover, to be without scandal. The age was at first twenty-five years, the fortune a fixed income of 1000 scudi; Alexander introduced the somewhat aristocratical alteration of having the requisite age made as low as twenty-one only, while, on the other hand, evidence was to be given of a fortune amounting to 1500 scudi of fixed income. Whoever met these requirements, was admitted by the prefetto di segnatura, and charged with the task of reporting upon two lawsuits before the assembled segnatura.[2] Thus he was installed, and became capable of being appointed to all other offices. From the governorship of a town or province one rose

dits mémorables de Christine—[Memorable sentiments and sayings of Christina] in the Appendix to his fourth volume.

[1] It is manifest from what follows, that the above advantages were engrossed by the worldly and selfish few, at the expense of the oppressed and suffering many. Tr.

[2] Discorso del dominio temporale e spirituale del S. Pontefice Romano, 1664. MS.—[Discourse on the temporal and spiritual dominion of the Holy Roman pontiff, 1664. MS.]

to the office of nuncio or vicelegate, or he obtained a place in the rota, in the congregations; then followed the cardinalship and legation. Ecclesiastical and civil powers were combined even in administering the highest offices. When the legate appeared in a town, some of the bishop's ecclesiastical titles to respect were placed in abeyance; the legate, as representing the pope, blessed the people. A perpetual interchange of ecclesiastical and secular offices took place among the members of the curia.

Here let us stay for a little to review first the secular side of the administration of the state.

In this all depended on the necessities of the government, the demands made on the subjects, the state of the finances.

We have seen what a ruinous augmentation took place in the public debt under Urban VIII., particularly owing to the war of Castro; but even still loans could be effected, the luoghi di monte maintained a high price, and with a recklessness that allowed no halt, the popes proceeded along the course they had once entered upon.

Innocent X. found in 1644, 182,103¾, and left behind him, in 1655, 264,129½ of luoghi di monte, so that the capital corresponding to this had risen from eighteen to above twenty-six millions. Although he had with this sum paid off debts in another quarter, and redeemed capital sums, still there remained an immense augmentation of the general amount, which was reckoned at his death, at forty-eight millions of scudi. He had been fortunate enough to draw an increased revenue from the taxes laid on by Urban VIII., and on that had founded new monti.

Meanwhile, on Alexander's entering upon the government, it became evident that any further augmentation of the taxes was impracticable; loans had already become so much the custom that they could no longer be dispensed with; Alexander resolved to look for a new resource in the reduction of the interests.

The vacabili, which bore interest at the rate of 10½ per cent, stood at 150; he resolved to call them all in. Although he paid for them at the current rate, he gained a great advantage, as the chamber in general borrowed at 4 per cent, and hence even by repaying them with borrowed money, yet in future, instead of 10½ he had to pay only 6 per cent of interest.[1]

[1] Had the vacabili, however, been really made annuities as they were designed to

After this Alexander conceived the idea of reducing all the nonvacabili that bore above 4 per cent to that rate.[1] But as, in doing this, he did not trouble himself about the current value which stood at 116, but according to the actual words of his engagment, merely paid back a hundred for the luogho and no more, he thus further reaped a very considerable advantage. All these interests were secured, as we have seen, upon taxes, and probably it might have been contemplated at first to remit the most oppressive; but as the old modes of management were retained, that was not to be accomplished; a reduction in the price of salt was soon followed by a rise in the flour tax; and the entire amount of that gain came to be swallowed up by the civil administration, or by the prevailing nepotism. The aggregate amount of savings effected by the above reductions, must have come to near 140,000 scudi, the new application of which, as interest, would involve an augmentation of the debt to the amount of about three millions.

Clement IX., too, could contrive no better method of conducting the government than by having recourse to new loans. But he soon found himself brought into such a predicament as to have to lay his hands at last on the revenues of the dataria, which had always till then been spared, and which were charged with the daily maintenance of the papal court. On these he founded 13,200 new luoghi di monte. In 1670 the papal debts had run up to nearly fifty-two millions.

Hence it now likewise followed that whatever willingness there might be to grant relief, the public burthens, already most op-

have been, this immediate advantage must have been obtained at the cost of a heavy permanent loss. Tr.

1 Pallavicini: Vita di Alessandro VII. "Perciocchè in nessun altro paese d'Italia la rendita del danaro aveasi tanto pingue e tanto sicura, pian piano era succeduto che quei luoghi del primitivo lor prezzo di 100 fussero cresciuti nella piazza al valor di 116. Hor la camera valendosi del suo diritto, come avrebbe potuto qualsivoglia privato, rendeva il prezzo originario di 100, non permettendo la vastità della somma, nè persuadendo la qualità de' padroni, in gran parte ricchi e forastieri, che ad aggravio de' poveri, alle cui spalle stanno tutti i publici pesi, il pontefice usasse più la liberalità usata da lui nell' estintione de' monti vacabili."—[Pallavicini's Life of Alexander VII. In as much as in no other country of Italy the return for money was so abundant and so secure, it gradually came about that those luoghi, from their original price of 100, had increased in the market to the price of 116. Now the chamber availing itself of its right as any private individual could have done, paid back the original price of 100, the vastness of the sum (Pallavicini reckons it at 26 millions) not permitting, and the rank of the owners, great part being rich persons and foreigners, not persuading the pontiff, at the expense of the poor, on whose shoulders lay all the public burdens, to employ more of his wonted liberality in the extinction of the monti vacabili.]

pressive to a non-producing country, which took no part in the general commerce of the world, could be diminished only in an inconsiderable and transient manner.

It formed the ground of another complaint that the monti belonged to foreigners as well as natives, so that many profited by receiving the interest who had contributed nothing to the taxes. It was calculated that 600,000 scudi were annually remitted to Genoa; the country thus became debtor to a foreign territory, and it was impossible that this could be favourable to its free development.

And with this there was connected a still more deeply operative effect. How could those who received the revenues, who possessed the money, fail to acquire a powerful influence over the state and its administration?

The great mercantile houses came to have a direct share in the business of the state. In addition to the treasurer there was always a banking house where the money was received and paid out; the coffers of the state were, properly speaking, at all times in the hands of bankers. But there were also farmers of the revenues and treasurers in the provinces. So many offices were purchasable; they had the means of getting them into their own hands. Be it remembered, moreover, that no inconsiderable fortune was required in order to be advanced to the curia. About the year 1665, Florentines and Genoese were occupying the most important posts in the administration. The spirit of the court took so mercantile a turn, that by degrees the promotions depended far less on merit than on money. "A merchant with his purse in his hand," exclaims Grimani, "is always preferred at last. The court swarms with hirelings, whose sole object is money, who have the feelings of merchants, not of statesmen, and have no elevation of thought about them."[1]

[1] Antonio Grimani. "Per la vendita della maggior parte degli officii più considerabili si viene a riempire la corte d' uomini mercenarj e mercanti, restanti indietro quelli che potrebbero posseder tali officii per merito e per virtù, male veramente notabile che smacca il credito concepito della grandezza della corte Romana, non avendo detti mercenarj d' officii involto l' animo che in cose mecaniche e basse e più tosto mercantili che politiche."—[By the sale of the greater part of the more considerable offices, the court came to be filled with mercenary men and merchants, those remaining behind, whose merit and virtue gave them claims to such offices, an evil truly to be noted which vilifies the opinion entertained of the grandeur of the Roman court, these said official mercenaries having minds solely engrossed with mechanical and low objects, and much more mercantile than political.]

This came now to be of the more importance, as there was no longer any independence in the country. Bologna alone displayed at times an effective resistance, so that it was even contemplated once at Rome, to erect a citadel there. Other communities, it is true, occasionally assumed an attitude of resistance; the inhabitants of Fermo once refused to submit to the corn which they supposed they might require for themselves, being taken out of their territory;[1] in Perugia the people would not pay the arrears of their taxes; but these movements were easily put down by the court commissaries general, who then introduced just so much severer a system of subordination; even the administration of communal property gradually became subjected to the measures of the court.

The institution of the Annona presents a remarkable example of the ordinary character of this administration.

As it had become a general principle throughout the sixteenth century to impose trammels on the export of the indispensable commodities of life, the popes too adopted measures for that end, mainly with the view of preventing an enhancement of the price of bread. Yet the functions of the prefetto dell' annona, to whom this branch of the administration was entrusted, were originally very limited. These were first extended by Gregory XIII. Without the prefetto's leave the corn that had been gathered in, could neither be exported out of the country altogether, nor removed even from one district into another. But this leave was granted only in the event of the corn being to be had on the 1st of March, under a certain price. Clement VIII. fixed this price at 6, Paul V. at 5½ scudi for the rubbio. There was a special tarif established for the price of bread, which was regulated by the variations in the price of corn.[2]

But now it was found that the demand for corn at Rome was increasing year after year. The number of inhabitants was increasing; the cultivation of the campagna was falling off. The

1 Memoriale presentato alla Sta di N. Sre papa Innocentio dalli deputati della città li Fermo per il tumulto ivi seguito alli 6 di Luglio 1648. MS.—[Memorial presented to the Holiness of our Lord pope Innocent, by the deputies of the city of Fermo, owing to the tumult that took place there on the 6th of July 1648. MS.] See Bisaccioni Historia delle guerre civili, p. 271, where, besides England, France, Poland, and Naples, Fermo too is introduced.

2 In the work intituled Nicola Maria Nicolai's Memorie, leggi et osservationi sulle campagne e sull' annone di Roma 1803, there is to be found in vol. II. a long series of papal regulations on those matters.

decay of that district is specially to be dated from the former half of the seventeenth century. If I mistake not, it may be traced to two causes; in the first place, to the alienation already mentioned of small possessions, by their original proprietors to great families; for the land requires the most careful cultivation, such as is usually bestowed upon it by the small proprietor only, who devotes to it himself and his whole income; and in the second place to the increasing deterioration of the air. Gregory XIII. extended the cultivation of corn-land, Sixtus V. endeavoured to destroy the lurking-places of the banditti, and thus the former had deprived the lower districts towards the sea of their trees and underwood, and the latter had cleared the high grounds of their forests.[1] Neither the one nor the other could be put to any use; the aria cattiva extended and contributed to render the campagna a desert. The return in produce fell off from year to year.

Now this disproportion between the supply and demand gave occasion to Pope Urban VIII. to make the superintendence more stringent, and to extend the rights of the prefetto. By one of his first enactments he absolutely prohibited the exportation of corn, cattle, or oil, alike from the states in general, and from one district into another; and he empowered the prefetto to fix the price of corn at the Campofiore, according to the produce of each harvest, and to prescribe to the bakers the weight of the loaf in proportion to the same.

By this means the prefetto became omnipotent, and neglected not to turn to his own advantage and that of his friends, the function accorded to him. The monopoly of corn, oil and meat, including all the most indispensable articles of consumption, was placed directly in his hands. We are not told that the cheapness of these articles was much promoted thereby; exportation was even conceded to favoured persons, and what was chiefly felt, was only the pressure that took place in forestalling and selling. It was at once perceived that agriculture suffered a still further decline.[2]

1 Relatione dello stato di Roma presente—[Account of the state of Rome at present] or Almaden. See Appendix.

2 Pietro Contarini 1627: "Il pontefice avendo levato le tratte concessi a diversi da suoi precessori - - hora vendendole ne cava bona somma di danaro: non vole i prezzi troppo vili nè grano forestiero: l' arte del campo viene ad abbandonarsi per

This, generally speaking, was the period whence we may date the complaints that prevailed with respect to the universal decline of the states of the church, complaints which have, since that time, never ceased to be made. "In travelling hither and thither," say the Venetian ambassadors of 1621, whom I first find giving expression to them, "we have observed that there is great poverty among the peasantry and common people, not to say much pinching among the other classes: a fruit of the sort of government they live under, and particularly of the insignificant trade of the country. Bologna and Ferrara have a certain splendour in their palaces and nobility; Ancona is not without some traffic with Ragusa and Turkey; all the remaining towns are sunk very low." In 1654, the opinion very generally prevailed, that an ecclesiastical government is ruinous.[1] Already, too, the inhabitants began bitterly to complain. "The imposts of the Barberini," exclaims a contemporary biographer, "have exhausted the country, and the avarice of Donna Olympia the court; a better state of things was expected from the virtue of Alexander VII., but all Sienna has poured itself out on the states of the church for the purpose of draining them to the dregs."[2] And there was no abatement of the demands.

The administration was once compared by a cardinal to a horse, which, after being fatigued with running, is spurred on afresh, and makes another effort to proceed, until it becomes quite exhausted and falls. This period of utter exhaustion seems now to have arrived.

il poco o niun guadagno che ne traggono."—[The pontiff having taken away the export licence granted to sundry persons by his predecessors - - by selling it now derives from it a good sum of money: he wishes that there should neither be too low prices nor foreign corn: agriculture comes to be abandoned on account of the little or no profit it bears.]

1 Diario Deone, tom. IV. 1649, 21 Ag. "E dovere di favorir la chiesa: però veggiamo che tutto quello che passa a lei, è in pregiudicio del publico, come che le terre sue subito sono dishabitate e le possessioni mal coltivate, si vede in Ferrara, in Urbino, in Nepe, in Nettuno, et in tutte le piazze che sono passate nel dominio della chiesa."—[Deone's Journal, vol. IV. 1649, 21st Aug. It is made a duty to favour the church: wherefore we see that all that goes to it is to the prejudice of the public, so that its lands suddenly become uninhabited, and its possessions ill cultivated, as is to be seen in Ferrara, in Urbino, in Nepe, in Nettuno, and in all the places through which we passed in the church's dominions.]

2 Vita di Alessandro VII.: "Spolpato e quasi in teschio ridotto dalle gabelle Barberine lo stato ecclesiastico e smunta la corte dall' ingordigia di Olimpia confidavano generoso ristoro della bontà d'Alessandro."—[The ecclesiastical state picked to the bone, and, as it were, reduced to a skull by the taxes of the Barberini, and the court exhausted by the greed of Olympia, trusted to the generous restoration to be derived from the goodness of Alexander.]

There had grown up the worst spirit that can animate a body of public officials: every man looked upon the commonwealth mainly as an object of personal advantage, often only of his avarice.

In what a frightful manner did bribery and corruption break in!

At the court of Innocent X., Donna Olympia procured offices for applicants under the condition of their paying her a monthly acknowledgment. Nor was she the only one to do so. Donna Clementia, sister-in-law of the datarius Cecchino, acted in the same way. Christmas, in particular, was the grand harvest-time for presents. Because Don Camillo Astalli, on one such occasion, would not allow Donna Olympia to share in his presents, although he had given hopes that he would do so, the former felt the utmost indignation, and thus the foundation was laid for Astalli's ruin. Into what falsifications was not Mascambruno hurried by bribery! To the decrees which he laid before the pope he added false summaries of contents; and as the pope read only the summaries, he subscribed his name to things of which he had no suspicion, and which covered the Roman court with ignominy.[1] Nothing can be more deplorable than to read that Don Mario, the brother of Alexander VII., was enriched, among other things, by the administration of justice in the Borgo.

For, unhappily, the judicial functions also were infected with this disorder.

We have a statement of the abuses that had found their way into the law court of the Rota, presented to Pope Alexander by a man who had been in his employment during a period of 28 years.[2] He reckons that there was not an auditor of the Rota that did not receive Christmas presents to the amount of 500

[1] Pallavicini attempts to excuse it on the ground that the proceedings in the Dataria were written "di carattere francese, come è restato in uso della dataria dapoi che la sedia fu in Avignone,"—[in the French character, as has been in use by the Dataria ever since the seat (of the popes) was at Avignon,] which the pope, accordingly, did not easily read.

[2] Disordini che occorrono nel supremo tribunale della rota nella corte Romana e gli ordini con i quali si potrebbe riformare, scrittura fatta da un avvocato da presentarsi all Sta di N. S^{re} Alessandro VII.—[Disorders that occur in the supreme tribunal of the Rota in the Roman court, and the regulations by which they might be reformed, a writing drawn up by an advocate for presentation to the Holiness of our Lord Alexander VII.] MS. Rang. at Vienna, No. 23.

scudi. People who could not find access to the auditor in person, could reach at least his relations, assistants, and servants.

Not less corrupting, however, was the operation of the injunctions issued by the court or by the great. The judges would even excuse at times to the parties themselves the unjust judgments they pronounced: they declared that justice suffered violence.

Now what sort of administration of justice could this be considered? There were four months of holidays: the remaining months were likewise given to dissipation and idleness; decisions were improperly delayed, and bore at last every mark of undue haste. Appeals served nó good purpose. The case, it is true, would be handed over to other members of the court; but what was there to prevent these from being just as much subjected to such influences as the former? Besides they even allowed their minds to be guided by the judgment already pronounced.

These were evils which extended from the supreme court of justice to all the rest, and to the administration of justice and of the government in the provinces.[1]

They are pressed on the attention of Pope Alexander by Cardinal Sacchetti in the most urgent manner, in a document which is still extant: the oppression of the poor, whom no man helps, by the powerful: the corruption of justice through the intercession of cardinals, princes, and dependants of the palace, in favour of particular parties; the delay of causes which might be despatched in a few days, for years, and tens of years; the violent treatment experienced by those who apply for redress from an inferior to a higher magistrate; the mortgages and executions wherewith the payment of taxes is enforced; revolting measures fitted only to make princes detested, and to enrich their servants: "sufferings, most holy Father," he exclaims, "which are worse than those of the Hebrews in Egypt! people that have not been conquered with the sword, but that happen to belong to the Roman see, either in consequence of their having been presented

[1] Disordini: "Con le male decisioni di questo tribunale supremo (della rota) si corrompe la giustitia a tutti gli altri minori, almeno dello stato ecclesiastico, vedendosi da giudici dare sentenze con decisioni si fatte."—[With the bad decisions of this supreme court (of the rota), justice is corrupted among all the minor courts, at least in the ecclesiastical state, it being seen to by the judges that they pronounce sentence in conformity with such decisions.]

to it by princes, or by having voluntarily placed themselves under its rule, are treated more inhumanly than the slaves in Syria or in Africa. Who can perceive it without shedding tears!"[1]

Such was already the state of things in the civil government of the church in the middle of the seventeenth century.

And now let us see if there be any good ground to believe, that the administration of the church could have been preserved from similar abuses?

That, equally with the administration of the civil government, depended on the court, and from the spirit of the court received its general impulsion.

Certain limitations were, no doubt, imposed on the curia in this department. In France, the crown possessed the most important prerogatives; and in Germany, the chapters preserved their independence. In Italy and Spain, on the other hand, it was more at liberty to act as it pleased; and, in point of fact, it there took unscrupulous advantage of its lucrative rights.

In Spain, the Roman court had the power of appointing to all the less important, and in Italy even to all the higher offices and benefices. It is hardly to be believed what sums flowed in to the dataria from Spain, through the expediting of appointments, the spolia, and the revenues acquired during vacancies. But the curia drew probably still more profit from its connection with Italy, regarded as a whole, for the members were directly benefited by the richest bishoprics and abbacies, and by many priories, commendatorships, and other benefices.

And can it even be said that this was all!

But along with rights, which of themselves were somewhat

[1] Lettre du cardinal Sacchetti écrite peu avant sa mort au pape Alexandre VII. en 1663, copie tirée des Manuscritti della regina di Suezia,—[Letter of Cardinal Sacchetti, written shortly before his death, to Pope Alexander VII., in 1663, copy taken from the manuscripts of the queen of Sweden], in Arckenholtz's Mémoires, tom. IV. App. No. XXXII.: a most instructive document, confirmed by too many others, for example, by a scrittura sopra il governo di Roma—[writing on the government of Rome], of the same period (Bibl. Alt.): "I popoli, non avendo più argento nè rame nè biancherie nè matarazze per sodisfare alla indiscretione de' commissarj, converrà che si venderanno schiavi per pagare i pesi camerali."—[The populations, having no more silver, or copper, or linens, or bedding, wherewith to satisfy the indiscretion of the commissaries, would agree to sell themselves as slaves, to pay the burthens imposed by the chamber.]

suspicious, there were connected the most ruinous abuses. I shall mention one only, which, it must be owned, was, no doubt, the worst. The practice was introduced, and about the middle of the seventeenth century became quite common, of burthening the benefices that were given away, with a pension in favour of some one or other member of the curia.

This was expressly forbidden in Spain: as the benefices themselves could be given to natives only, so any pension that they might be burdened with, could have been in their favour only. But in Rome, people contrived to evade these enactments. The pension was made out in the name of a native or naturalized Spaniard: but the latter bound himself by a civil contract to pay yearly a fixed sum into a Roman banking house, in favour of the person whom it was chiefly sought to favour. Now in Italy, this respect for appearance used never once to be thought of; and the bishoprics were often intolerably burdened. Monsignor de Angelis, bishop of Urbino, complained in 1663, that from that rich bishopric he drew no more than 60 scudi a-year; he had already offered to renounce it, but the court refused to accept his resignation. For a number of years nobody could be found to undertake the sees of Ancona and Pesaro, under the hard conditions imposed on them. In 1667, there were counted twenty-eight bishops and archbishops who had been loosed from their office, for non-payment of their pensions. This disorder extended, too, from the bishoprics to the parochial cures. The occupant even of the richest parochial living, often found but a sorry subsistence; nay, the poor incumbents sometimes saw their very perquisites burdened.[1] Many became broken-hearted

[1] The spiteful Basadona says: "Bisogna conchiudere che ogni beneficio capace di pensione rimanga caricato come l'asino di Apulejo, che non potendo più sostenere il peso meditava di gettarsi in terra, quando il veder caduto il compagno e tosto de' vetturini scorticato hebbe per bene di sopportare l'insopportabil soma."—[We must conclude, that every benefice capable of bearing a pension, remains burthened like the ass of Apuleius, which, when unable any longer to bear the weight it carried, thought of throwing itself on the ground, when, seeing its companion fallen and immediately flayed by the drivers, he thinks it well to support the insupportable load.] All contemporary writers are agreed in their representations of the evil itself. The practice was likewise re-introduced for incumbents to resign their livings to others, but reserving part of the revenues. Deone, Diario 7 Genn. 1645—[Deone, in his journal, under 7th January, 1645], after mentioning the archbishopric of Bologna, which Cardinal Colonna relinquished to Albregati, goes on to say: "con questo esempio si è aperta la porta d'ammettere le risegne: e cosi stamane si è publicata la risegna della chiesa di Ravenna fatta dal card[l] Capponi nella persona di mons[r] Tungianni suo nipote con riserva di pensione a suo favore e dopo la morte sua d'una

and left their places; but time always brought fresh candidates; nay, these strove with each other which should offer the curia the largest pension!

But what sort of people must these not have been! Nothing could follow but the ruin of the country clergy, and the neglect of the common people.

Far better was it, indeed, that the people in the protestant church from the very first had abolished superfluities, and now at least order and justice were maintained.

Certainly the wealth of the Roman catholic church and the rank in the world to which a man was raised by obtaining a place in it, had the effect of leading the aristocracy to devote themselves to it. Pope Alexander had even made it a maxim to promote chiefly men of good birth; he entertained the strange notion, that as it gratified the rulers of this world to see themselves surrounded with servants of high descent, so God also must be gratified by his service being conducted by persons elevated in point of rank above others. But this certainly was not the way by which the church raised itself in the early centuries of its history; nor was it that by which it (the Roman catholic church) had been restored in later times. The monasteries and congregations, on the other hand, much as they had contributed to the resumption of Roman catholicism, fell into contempt. The nephews had no liking for any one that lay under monastic vows, just because unceasing court could not be paid to them by such. In every case, where several candidates appeared, the secular clergy, as the general rule, and even although inferior in point of merit and learning, were preferred. "People seem to hold," says Grimani, "that an insult is put on the episcopate, or even on the purple, when given away to a brother of the monastery." He remarks, that they were no longer very sure of venturing to exhibit themselves at court, seeing that they had nothing to look for there but ridicule and insult. Symptoms already began to appear of none but people of the meanest parentage being disposed to enter the monas-

buona parte al card[l] Pamfilio."—[with this example, the door, indeed, is opened for admitting resignations, and thus this morning there has been made public the resignation of the church of Ravenna made by Cardinal Capponi in the person of Mons[r] Tungianni, his nephew, under reservation of a pension in his favour, and after his death, of a good part (of it) to Cardinal Pamfilio.]

teries. "Even a bankrupt shopkeeper," he exclaims, "reckons himself too good to wear the cowl."[1]

After the monasteries had thus virtually lost their internal importance, no wonder that the idea already began to be entertained, that they were superfluous. It is very remarkable that this idea first revealed itself in Rome; that there it was first thought necessary to lay restraints on the monastic life. As early as 1649, Innocent X. prohibited by a bull all new receptions into any of the regular orders, until a calculation should be made of the income possessed by the various monasteries, and until the number of persons whom they could maintain was determined.[2] Still more important is a bull of 15th October, 1652. In it the pope complains that there were so many small monasteries, in which the offices could not be performed by day or by night, nor could spiritual exercises be kept up, nor the rules respecting confinement within the cloisters observed, and which were retreats for disorderly conduct and crime: the number of these had now increased beyond all due measure; at one stroke he abolished them all, for it was necessary that the tares should be separated from the wheat.[3] Already people be-

1 To this Grimani adds: "Si toglie ad ognuno affatto la voglia di studiare e la cura di difendere la religione. Deteriorandosi il numero de' religiosi dotti et esemplari, potrebbe in breve soffrirne non poco detrimento la corte: onde al mio credere farebbono bene i pontefici di procurar di rimettere i regolari nel primo posto di stima, partecipandoli di quando in quando cariche, - - e cosi nelle religioni vi entrerebbero huomini eminenti."—[Any desire for study, any concern for the defence of religion, is taken quite away from every one. In consequence of the falling off in the number of learned and exemplary men, the court may, in a short time, suffer no small loss from it: hence, in my opinion, the pontiffs would do well to set about putting the regular clergy in the first posts of honour, and giving them a part now and then in public charges, - - and thus eminent men will enter the religious orders there.]

2 The journal describes, under 1st of January, 1650, the impression made by this constitution: "Non entrando quella ragione ne' cappuccini et altri riformati che non possedono entrata, temono che la prohibitione sia perpetua, e cosi cred' io, fin a tanto che il numero de' regolari hoggi eccessivo sia ridotto a numero competente e la republica da loro non venga oppressa."—[As this reasoning did not embrace the Capuchins, and other reformed orders that had no revenues, it is feared that the prohibition may be perpetual, and so, I believe, until the number of the regular clergy, nowadays excessive, be reduced to a competent extent, and the commonwealth not come to be oppressed by them.]

3 Constitutio super extinctione et suppressione parvorum conventuum, eorumque reductione ad statum secularem, et bonorum applicatione, et prohibitione erigendi nova loca regularia in Italia et insulis adjacentibus. Idibus Octobris 1652.—[Constitution on the extinction and suppression of small convents, and their reduction to a secular condition, and on the application of their property, and prohibition against erecting new regular places (*i. e.* convents) in Italy and the adjacent islands. 15th Oct. 1652.]

gan to think, and that, too, first of all at Rome, of relieving the financial embarrassments even of foreign states, by the sequestration, not of monasteries, but of whole orders. When Alexander VII., shortly after his ascending the throne, happened to be asked by the Venetians to assist them in the war of Candia against the Turks, even he suggested to them the abolition of some of the orders in their territories. They were rather opposed to this, as these orders offered a provision for the poorer nobili. But the pope carried his purpose into effect. The existence of these convents, said he, tends rather to scandalize the faithful than to edify them; that he acted as a gardener would do, who cuts away the useless branches from the vine to make it the more fruitful.[1]

Yet it could not be said that particularly splendid abilities were now to be found only among those who received promotion. We find a general complaint in the seventeenth century about the want of distinguished persons.[2] Men remarkable for their talents were often excluded even from the prelature, on account of their being too poor to comply with the conditions attached to their reception.[3] Success in life, however, depended far too much on the favour of the nephews, who allowed themselves to be approached only by means of a suppleness and servility that could not be propitious to the free development of the nobler gifts of genius. This had an effect on the whole body of the clergy.

It is certainly a striking fact, that in the most important branches of theological study, it may be said that no Italian authors of eminence appeared, neither in scripture-exposition, where the productions of the 16th century were merely repeated, nor in morals, although that department was much cultivated

[1] Relatione de' IV. ambasciatori, 1656. See Appendix.

[2] Grimani: "Tolto l'economia esteriore ogni altra cosa si deteriora; - - - d'huomini di valore effettivamente scarseggia al presente la corte al maggior segno." —[Excepting the external economy, everything else is getting worse; - - - the court in the greater degree really stands in need of men of worth.]

[3] Relatione di Roma sotto Clemente IX. "Portando lo stile che le cariche si transferiscono solamente a prelati e che la prelatura si concede solo a quelli che hanno entrata sufficiente per mantenere il decoro, ne siegue però che la maggior parte di soggetti capaci ne resta esclusa."—[Account of Rome under Clement IX. While the way leads thus, that public charges are transferred solely to prelates, and the prelature is conceded only to those who have a sufficient income for maintaining decorum, it follows, accordingly, that the greater number of capable subjects remain excluded from them.]

in other quarters, nor in dogmatic theology. Already, in the congregations, foreigners alone appeared on the arena in the disputes about the means of grace; and in those that followed concerning free-will and faith, the Italians took but little part. After Girolamo da Narni, no distinguished preacher appeared in Rome. In the journal referred to, from 1640 to 1650, composed as it was by so strict a Roman catholic, this is remarked with astonishment. "With the arrival of fast-days," it goes on to say, "comedies cease in the saloons and houses, and commence in the churches and pulpits. The holy employment of preaching serves but for purposes of vain-glory or flattery. Metaphysics are introduced, of which the speaker understands little and his hearers nothing. Instead of teaching and rebuking, the preacher makes the church ring with panegyrics, for the sole purpose of furthering his own promotion. Already, too, when a preacher has to be chosen every thing depends no longer on merit, but only on connections and private favour."

The conclusion is, that that great internal impulse which had previously prevailed in the court, the state, and the church, and which had given these their strict religious character, was now extinct; the tendencies indicated by the restoration and conquest had now gone by; other motives came to influence the course of things, which at last ran only upon power and personal enjoyment, and secularized afresh all that was spiritual.

The question occurs, what direction was taken, under these circumstances, by a society that had been so specially founded on the principles of the restoration as the order of Jesuits.

THE JESUITS IN THE MIDDLE OF THE SEVENTEENTH CENTURY.

THE principal alteration in the internal structure of the society of Jesus, consisted in the transference of power into the hands of the professed.

The professed, who took the four vows, were at first but few in number; disconnected with the colleges, and subsisting upon alms, they had confined themselves consequently to the exercise of spiritual authority; posts requiring secular activity, that is, those of rectors, provincials, and those in the colleges generally, had been occupied by the coadjutors. But now this was changed The professed themselves occupied posts in the administration;

they shared in the college revenues, and became rectors and provincials.[1]

Now the first consequence resulting from this was, that the stricter tendencies of personal devotion which had hitherto maintained their vigour chiefly through the profession houses being kept entirely apart, became gradually more and more relaxed. From the first reception of a member, his ascetic training could not be so narrowly looked to; Vitelleschi, in particular, admitted many who had no proper call; and the highest posts were eagerly sought after, merely because they secured at once spiritual authority and secular power. But, moreover, this combination showed itself altogether hurtful in its general effects. Formerly, the professed and the coadjutors had maintained a mutual surveillance over each other; now practical weight and spiritual pretension were united in the same persons. Men even of the most limited capacities, considered themselves great geniuses, because nobody ventured any longer to oppose them. Having arrogated to themselves the possession of an exclusive dominion, they began quietly to take the enjoyment of the wealth which in the lapse of time was acquired by the colleges, and to make the augmentation of it the chief object of their thoughts, leaving the official management, properly so called, of the colleges and churches to younger people.[2] They assumed likewise a very independent bearing even as respected the general.

The extent of this change may be seen, among other things, in the nature and the fortunes of the generals, the sort of persons chosen as chiefs, and how matters were conducted with these.

[1] In a collection, Scritture politiche, morali e satiriche sopra le massime, istituti e governo della compagnia di Gesu—[of documents political, moral, and satirical, on the maxims, institutes, and government of the company of Jesus] (MS. Rom.), there is to be found a copious memoir of nearly 400 pages: Discorso sopra la religione de' padri Gesuiti e loro modo di governare—[Discourse on the religion of the Jesuit fathers and their mode of government]—written between 1681 and 1686, by an apparently deeply initiated person,—from which the notices that follow have chiefly been taken.

[2] Discorso. "Molti compariscono, pochi operano: i poveri non si visitano, i terreni non si coltivano. - - Escludendo quei pochi, d'ordinario giovani, che attendono ad insegnare nelle scuole, tutti gli altri, o che sono confessori o procuratori o rettori o ministri, appena hanno occupatione di rilievo."—[Discourse. Many make a show, few work; the poor are not visited, the lands are not cultivated. - - Excepting a few, ordinarily young men, who attend to the teaching of the schools, all the rest, whether confessors, or procurators, or rectors, or ministers, hardly have any fragmentary occupations.]

What a difference between Mutio Vitelleschi and his predecessor Aquaviva, so remarkable for self-command, subtlety, and firmness! Vitelleschi was naturally mild, tolerant, placable; his acquaintances called him the angel of peace; and he found it a subject of consolation on his death-bed that he never had injured any one. Striking traits of an amiable disposition, but which made him inadequate for the government of an order so widely diffused, so active, and so powerful. He was unable to preserve strictness of discipline even in the matter of dress, far less, of course, to oppose effectually the demands of determined ambition. Under his administration, extending from 1615 to 1645, the revolution we have referred to, took effect.

The same spirit was shown in the manner in which affairs were conducted by his next successors; Vincent Caraffa (1649) a man who even disdained having any personal attendance, and who was all meekness and piety,[1] but who could effect nothing either by his example or by his admonitions; Piccolomini, (1651) who now cast off that disposition to adopt decisive measures which was natural to him, and thought of nothing but complying with the wishes of his brethren of the order.

For already it was no longer advisable to think of attempting any change in this respect. Alexander Gottofredi, from January to March, 1651, would willingly have done so, and endeavoured at least to set bounds to the ambition that was struggling for its own advancement; but the two months of his administration sufficed to make him generally hated, so that his death was hailed as deliverance from a tyrant. And still more decided was the dislike which the next general, Goswin Nickel, drew on himself. It could not be said that he contemplated any radical reforms; generally speaking, he allowed matters to go on as they

[1] Diario Deone 12 Giugno 1649. "Martedi mattina mori il generale de' Gesuiti: fu di poche lettere, ma di santità di vita non ordinaria: quanto alla sua persona, egli non ha mai voluto carrozza al suo servigio, nè esser differentiato da qualsivoglia minimo tra di loro nel trattar del vitto o vestito: quanto agli altri, voleva che i padri Gesuiti fossero e vivessero da religiosi lasciando i trattati politici e 'l frequentare le corti, nel che havendo trovato difficoltà impossibile gli hanno cagionato il sedia della morte."—[Deone's Journal, 12 June 1649. The General of the Jesuits died on Tuesday morning. He was of little literature, but of no ordinary sanctity of life: as regards his person, he never wished to have a carriage at his service, nor to be differently treated from any, the least considerable among them, nor to make any account of food and clothing; as for others, he wished that the Jesuit fathers should be and should live as religious, (that is, as persons bound by vows) forsaking political schemes and frequenting courts, in which having found insurmountable difficulty, they became the cause of his death.]

were, only he was wont to insist obstinately on the views which he had once adopted, and in his manners and conduct was rough, repulsive, and wanting in due respect for others. But by this he soon offended the self-love of powerful members of the order so profoundly, and so sensibly, that the congregation general of 1661, took steps against him, such as might have been thought impossible, if we consider the monarchical character of the institute.

They first applied to Pope Alexander VII. for permission to appoint, as an adjunct to their general, a vicar with the right of succeeding him. This was easily obtained, the court even suggesting a candidate for the office, in the person of that Oliva who first recommended the calling in of the pope's nephews, and the members wore obsequious enough to elect that favourite of the palace. The only question that remained was under what form the government should be transferred from the general to the vicar. Deposition was a word which people could not prevail upon themselves to pronounce. To obtain the thing while the expression was avoided, the question was proposed, whether the vicar should have a cumulative power, that is, together with the general, or a privative, that is, without him. The congregation naturally decided for the privative; it virtually declared by that decision, that the general who had been such till then, should be deprived of all his power, and that it should be absolutely transferred to the vicar.[1]

Thus it came to pass that the society, based as it was on the principle of unconditional obedience, supplanted its very chief, and that, too, without his having, properly speaking, incurred the guilt of any offence. It is manifest to what an extent the aristocratical tendencies were beginning to predominate in that order as well as elsewhere.

Oliva was a man that liked external peace, good living, and political intrigue. He had a villa, not far from Albano, where he cultivated the rarest exotics. Even when he was in the city, he would, from time to time, retire to the noviciate house of St.

[1] See the detailed account in the contemporary Discorso. "Venendo noi," the author ends by saying, "in tal tempo a Roma ed andando a fargli riverenza (a Nickel) - - conchiuse con dire queste parole: Io mi trovo qui abandonato e non posso più niente."—[We having arrived about this time at Rome, and having gone to pay him (Nickel) reverence - - he concluded with the following words: I find myself forsaken here, and have it no longer in my power to do any thing.]

Andrew, where he gave audiences to no one. The most exquisite dishes only were placed on his table; he never went out on foot; the apartments he occupied were already carried to refinement in point of comfort; he enjoyed his position and the power that it gave him; such a man assuredly was little fitted to revive the old spirit of the order.

The latter, in fact, was daily departing farther and farther from the principles on which it had been founded.

Was it not bound before all things to defend the interests of the Romish church, and had it not been virtually instituted for that purpose? But the intimate ties we have seen it form with France and the house of Bourbon, had now modified it in such a way, that in the competition between Roman and French interests that was gradually appearing, it almost uniformly adopted the side of the latter.[1] Jesuit works were occasionally condemned at Rome by the inquisition, for excessive warmth in defending the rights of crowned heads. The superior of the French Jesuits avoided intercourse with the papal nuncio, in order to avoid the suspicion of entertaining ultramontane sentiments. Nor could the Roman see otherwise boast of the obedience of the order at that time; in missions, for example, papal regulations were almost always cast to the wind.

Further, it was a fundamental principle with the society, that the members were to renounce all secular ties, and to devote themselves to spiritual duties alone. How had not this principle been maintained at other times with such strictness that every entrant renounced his whole property! First, that step was delayed for a while; it was then taken indeed, but only conditionally, in as much as the member possibly might be expelled; at length the practice was introduced of members transferring their property to the society: it being clearly understood, however, that this transference should be made to the precise college which each severally entered, in such wise that

[1] Relatione della nuntiatura di Monsr Scotti, nunzio alla M^ta del re X^mo, 1639—1641: "I Gesuiti, che dovrebbero essere come altre volte defensori della santa sede, più degli altri la pongono in compromesso. - - Professano totale ritiratezza (dalla nuntiatura), dubbiosi sempre nell' accostarsi al nuntio di non perdere appresso ministri regj."—[Account of the nuncioship of Monsignor Scotti, nuncio to the Most Christian king, 1639—1641. The Jesuits, who ought, as in other times, to be the defenders of the holy see, jeopard it more than any others. - - They profess absolute withdrawment (from the nuntiatura), being always doubtful in accosting the nuncio, lest they should lose influence with the king's ministers.]

a man even retained the management of his property after having thus transferred it, only under another title.[1] The members of colleges, here and there, having more time at their command than their relations who lived in the midst of society, managed the affairs of the latter, collected their money, and conducted their lawsuits.[2]

But not only in the case of individuals, in colleges as corporations, also, this mercantile spirit began to prevail. Under the pretence of securing their prosperity, because large donations had ceased, the members endeavoured to accomplish this by means of some kind of industry. The Jesuits held there was no difference between cultivating the ground as the most ancient monks had done, and engaging in business, as they sought to do. The collegio Romano allowed cloth to be woven at Macerata, first for their own use alone, then for all the colleges in the province, finally for the public in general: it was sent for sale to the fairs. In consequence of the close ties that bound the different colleges together, a system of doing business for one another grew up. The Portuguese ambassador in Rome was directed to draw what money he might require, from the Jesuits who came from Portugal. In the colonies, in particular, they traded with success: a net-work, formed of the connections of the order, extended over both continents, having Lisbon for ist central point.

This was a spirit which, after having been once called forth, necessarily re-acted on all the internal bearings of the institution.

It had always remained a fundamental principle, that instruc-

[1] Vincentii Carrafæ epistola de mediis conservandi primævum spiritum societatis. "Definitis pro arbitrio dantis domibus sive collegiis in quibus aut sedem sibi fixurus est aut jam animo fixerit, - - anxie agunt ut quæ societati reliquerunt, ipsimet per se administrent."—[Vincent Carrafa's letter on the means of preserving the primitive spirit of the society. The houses or colleges being defined according to the choice of the donor, in which he is either about to fix a place for himself or has already fixed it in his own mind, - - they anxiously drive at having the administration to themselves of what they have given to the society.]

[2] Epistola Goswini Nickel de amore et studio perfectæ paupertatis. "Illud intolerabile, si et lites inferant et ad tribunalia confligant et violentas pecuniarum repetitiones faciant, aut palam negotiantur ad quæstum, - - specie quidem primo aspectu etiam honesta, caritate in consanguineos, decepti."—[Epistle of Goswin Nickel on the love and study of perfect poverty. It is intolerable, if they commence lawsuits, and fight out claims before the judges, and make violent repetitions of money, or openly trade for the purpose of making gains, deceived by what, at first sight, indeed, seems honourable, namely, by affection for relations.]

tion should be given gratuitously. But presents were taken of receiving pupils, and also on the occasion of particular holidays, which occurred several times in the year:[1] scholars possessed of property were in special request. Yet the consequence of this was, that these felt a certain degree of independence, and would no longer comply with the strictness of the old discipline. A Jesuit that had raised a stick against a pupil, received from him a stab for doing so; and a young man in Gubbio, who had thought himself too roughly treated by the father prefetto, murdered the latter in return. Even in Rome the disturbances in the college were the constant subject of conversation, both in the city and in the palace. The teachers were, on one occasion, blockaded for a whole day by their scholars; and the rector, in compliance with their demands, had at last actually to be dismissed. These things were symptomatic of a general struggle between the old regulations and the new tendencies. The latter, in the end, virtually maintained their ground. The Jesuits were incapable of any longer preserving the influence with which, at an earlier period, they had governed men's minds.

In fact, however, they no longer had a mind to subject the world to themselves, and to imbue it with a religious spirit; much rather had their own spirit fallen under the influence of the world: their only endeavour was to render themselves indispensable to mankind, in whatever way they could succeed in doing so.

To this object they adjusted not only the rules laid down by the institute, but religious and moral doctrines also. To the work of confession, through which they exercised so immediate an influence on the inmost motives of individual minds, they

1 Discorso. "Per lo meno l'anno due volte, cioè al natale e nel giorno della propria festa, si fanno le loro offerte ovvero mancie, le quali ascendono a somma considerabile. - - Il danaro poi di queste offerte o che venga impiegato in argenti, quadri o tappezzerie, calici o altri addobbi somiglianti, tutto ridonda in utilità de' collegi medesimi. Avegna che i rettori locali se ne servono indifferentemente, dal che ne derivano infinite offensioni, poco o nulla stimano i lamenti de' proprj scolari."—[Discourse. Twice a-year at least, that is, on the birth-day (of the donor) and the day of the proper festival (of the college, I suppose, *i. e.* on the feast of the saint to whom it is dedicated. Tr.), they make their offerings, or drink-money gifts, which amount to a considerable sum. - - The money, then, of these offerings, or what comes in the shape of articles of silver plate, pictures, or tapestry, or such like furniture, all goes to the use of the said colleges. It may happen that the local rectors make use of these indifferently, from which there arise infinite offences; they care little or nothing for the complaints of their own scholars.]

gave a direction which justly demands the attention of all times.

On this subject we have unquestionably authentic documents. They have expounded, in numerous and extensive works, the principles observed by themselves in confession and absolution, and which they offer to others. They are essentially the same, in general, with those that have been so often objected to them. Let us endeavour to comprehend at least the leading principles, proceeding upon which they made the whole territory their own.

In the confessional, however, every thing must infallibly depend on the idea a man may conceive of transgression—of sin.

They explained what sin is, by calling it a spontaneous departure from the command of God.[1]

And in what, we further inquire, consists this spontaneity? They reply, in a discernment of the sin, and in a full consent of the will.[2]

This principle they adopted from an ambitious desire of proposing something new, endeavouring, at the same time, to reconcile it with the usages of ordinary life. With all the subtlety of the schoolmen, and with a comprehensive regard to occurrent cases, they carried it out to the most revolting consequences.

According to their doctrine, it is enough that a man only does not intend to commit sin as such; he has the more ground to hope for pardon the less he thinks of God in doing what is wrong, and the more violent the passion by which he feels himself impelled: habit, nay, even a wicked example, in as much as they control the freedom of the will, suffice for exculpation. How much, by this means, is the sphere of transgression narrowed! No one would love sin for its own sake alone. But besides this, they recognise grounds for exculpation of a different kind still. For

[1] Fr. Toledo's definition: "voluntarius recessus a regula divina"—[a voluntary departure from the divine rule].

[2] Busembaum, Medulla theologiæ moralis lib. V. c. II. dub. III., thus expresses himself: "Tria requiruntur ad peccatum mortale (quod gratiam et amicitiam cum Deo solvit), quorum si unum desit, fit veniale (quod ob suam levitatem gratiam et amicitiam non tollit): 1. ex parte intellectus, plena advertentia et deliberatio, 2. ex parte voluntatis, perfectus consensus, 3. gravitas materiæ."—[Three things are required to constitute mortal sin (which dissolves favour and friendship with God), and of these should one be wanting, it becomes venial (which, because of its lightness, does not take away (God's) favour and friendship): 1. on the part of the understanding, full advertency and deliberate purpose; 2. on the part of the will, perfect consent; 3. importance of the thing that is done.]

example, duelling is certainly forbidden by the church; nevertheless, the Jesuits find, that should any one, by avoiding a duel, risk being accounted a coward, the loss of an office, or the favour of his prince, he is not to be condemned because he accepts a challenge.[1] To swear falsely is in itself a grievous sin, but whoever, say the Jesuits, swears outwardly only, without an inward intention of doing so, he will not be bound thereby: he jests indeed, but does not swear.[2]

These doctrines are to be found in books that expressly profess to be moderate. Who would pursue still further, now that those times are gone by, the search after wider deviations from what is right, on the part of a subtlety that annihilated all morality, and in which one such teacher strives, with literary emulation, to outdo another? But it is not to be denied that even the most rugged precepts of individual doctors became very dangerous, owing to another principle of the Jesuits, the doctrine of probability. They maintained that, in doubtful cases, a man may venture to follow an opinion of the soundness of which he himself is not convinced, provided, beforehand, that it be defended by some respectable author:[3] they held it not only allowable to follow the most tolerant teachers, but they even advised people to do so. People were to despise scruples of conscience; nay, the true way for a man to rid himself of these, was for him to follow the mildest opinions, even though they should be less sure.[4] How did the most secret self-determination become thereby quite an external act. In the Jesuit directories, all the pos-

[1] "Privandus alioqui ob suspicionem ignaviæ, dignitate, officio vel favore principis."—[To be deprived otherwise, on account of the suspicion of cowardice, of dignity, office, and the favour of the prince.] Busembaum, lib. III. tract. IV. cap. I. dub. V. art. I. n. 6.

[2] "Qui exterius tantum juravit, sine animo jurandi, non obligatur, nisi forte ratione scandali, cum non juraverit sed luserit." (Lib. III. tract. II. cap. II. dub. IV. n. 8.)—[He who has sworn only externally, without the intention of swearing, is not bound, unless, perhaps, by reason of the scandal, since he has not sworn, but merely jested. (Book III. tract II. ch. II. doubt IV. n. 8.)]

[3] Aphorismi confessariorum s. v. dubium. "Potest quis facere quod probabili ratione vel auctoritate putat licere, etiamsi oppositum tutius sit: sufficit autem opinio alicujus gravis autoris."—Aphorisms of confessors under the word *doubt*. Any one may do what he thinks lawful on probable grounds or authority, although to do the opposite may be safer: the opinion, however, of any grave author is sufficient.]

[4] Busembaum, lib. I. c. III.: "Remedia conscientiæ scrupulosæ sunt, 1. scrupulos contemnere, 4. assuefacere se ad sequendas sententias mitiores et minus etiam certas."—[Busembaum, book I. ch. III.: The remedies for a scrupulous conscience are, 1. To despise scruples. 2. To accustom one's self to follow milder and even less sure opinions.]

sible contingencies of life are treated of, much in the spirit of method usually adopted in systems of civil law, and tested according to the degree of their excusability; a man needs only to look up for his case there, and to regulate himself accordingly, without any conviction of his own, and then he is sure of absolution before God and the church. A slight declination of the thoughts from a particular point, disburdens from all moral blame. The Jesuits themselves, with a certain degree of candour, are amazed at times to see how light the yoke of Christ becomes through their doctrines.

THE JANSENISTS.

All life must ere this have died out in the Roman catholic church, had there not at the same moment appeared likewise an opposition to such destructive doctrines, and to the whole development connected with them.

Already even, most of the other orders were on bad terms with the Jesuits. The Dominicans had quarrelled with them on account of their deviations in doctrine from Thomas Aquinas; and the Franciscans and Capuchins because of the exclusive power which they arrogated to themselves in the missions in farther Asia: sometimes they were attacked by the bishops, whose authority they abridged; sometimes by the parish priests, whose official duties they invaded. Often, too, in the universities, at least in France and the Netherlands, they had adversaries to contend with. But all this formed no effective opposition, such as could only spring from a conviction deep in its source, and taken up with fresh spirit.

For at last, even the moral doctrines of the Jesuits came to be closely connected with their dogmatical propositions. In the former, as well as the latter, they allowed an ample scope to the freedom of the will.

But this was now the very point to which the greatest resistance which the Jesuits in general have ever experienced, attached itself. It revealed itself in the following manner.

During those years in which the controversies on the means of grace kept the theological world in the Roman catholic church in great contention, among the students at Louvain there were two young men, Cornelius Janse, from Holland, and John du

Verger, a Gascon, who, with a conviction in which they were perfectly agreed, had adopted the side of the stricter doctrines, doctrines which had never, indeed, been suppressed in Louvain, and conceived a violent antipathy to the Jesuits. Verger was of higher rank and ampler means than his friend, whom he took with him to Bayonne. There they plunged into the constantly-repeated study of the works of Augustine, and conceived such an enthusiastic admiration for the doctrines of that church-father on grace and free-will, as determined the character of their whole future lives.[1]

Jansenius, who became a professor at Louvain, and bishop of Ypres, pursued rather the theoretical; Verger, who obtained the abbacy of St. Cyran, rather the practical and ascetic method, for the purpose of bringing these doctrines again into vogue.

Yet the book in which Jansenius copiously and systematically developed his convictions, under the title—Augustinus, is a very important one, not only because of the boldness with which it impugns the Jesuits in their dogmatical and moral tendencies, but because it does so by giving all the freshness of living thoughts to the ancient formulas on grace, sin, and forgiveness.

Jansenius starts from the point that the will of man is not free; that he is fettered and held in bondage by lusting after earthly things; that by his own power he is incapable of rising out of this condition; that grace must come to his assistance, grace which is not so much the forgiveness of sins as the deliverance of the soul from the bonds of concupiscence.[2]

1 Synopsis vitæ Jansenii [Sketch of the life of Jansenius], prefixed to the Augustinus: "In Cantabriam deinde migravit, ubi eruditissimorum virorum consuetudine et familiari studiorum communione in SS. Patrum et præsertim Augustini intelligentia magnos progressus fecisse, sæpe testatus est."—[He then migrated into Biscay, where he has often testified that while enjoying the acquaintance and familiar fellowship in study of most learned men, he made great progress in understanding the holy fathers, and particularly Augustine.]

2 Corn. Jansenii Augustinus, tom. III. lib. I. cap. II.: "Liberatio voluntatis non est peccati remissio, sed relaxatio quædam delectabilis vinculi concupiscentialis, cui innexus servit animus quoad per gratiam infusa cœlesti dulcedine ad suprema diligenda transferatur."—[The liberation of the will is not the remission of sin, but a certain delightful relaxation of the concupiscential bond, enchained by which the mind is in bondage, until, by a celestial sweetness infused by grace, it is carried over to the love of the supreme good.] Thus, also, does Pascal understand this doctrine. "Dieu change le cœur de l'homme par une douceur céleste qu'il y répand." Les Provinciales, l. XVIII. tom. III. p. 413.—[God changes man's heart by a heavenly sweetness which he sheds over it. Provincial Letters, letter XVIII. vol. III. p. 413.]

Here we see at once his distinctive view. He makes grace enter by the higher and purer gratification which the soul experiences in things divine. The effectual grace of the Saviour, says he, is nothing but a spiritual delight, by which the will is induced to desire and to perform what God has decreed. It is the unspontaneous movement instilled into the will by God, through which goodness pleases a man, and he is induced to strive after it.[1] He repeatedly inculcates that what is good must be done, not from dread of punishment, but from love of righteousness.

And now, proceeding from this point, he rises to the higher question, what this righteousness is?

He answers, God himself.

For God must not be thought of as if he were corporeal, or under any form whatever, not even that of light; we must contemplate him and love him as the eternal truth, the source of all truth and wisdom, as righteousness, not in so far as that is the attribute of a character, but in so far as realized to our thoughts as an idea, as a supreme inviolable rule. The rules of our actions emanate from the eternal law: they are a reflection of his light: whoever loves righteousness, loves God himself.[2]

Man does not become good by directing his mind to this or that virtue, but by fixing his regards on the unchangeable, simple, supreme good, which is truth, which is God himself. Virtue consists in the love of God.

And it is just in this love that the deliverance of the will consists: its ineffable sweetness annihilates the charm of sinful desires: there arises a voluntary and blissful necessity of not sinning but living well,[3] the true free-will, that is, a will delivered from evil and filled with good.

1 Tom. III. lib. IV. c. I.

2 Tom. III. lib. V. c. III.: "Regulæ vivendi et quasi lumina virtutum immutabilia et sempiterna non sunt aliud quam lex æterna quæ in ipsa Dei æterni veritate splendet, quam proinde diligendo non aliud diligit nisi ipsum Deum seu veritatem et justitiam ejus incommutabilem, a qua promanat et ex cujus refulgentia lucis fulget quidquid velut justum et rectum approbamus."—[The rules of living, and as it were the unchangeable and eternal lights of the virtues, are nothing but the eternal law which shines forth in the very truth of the eternal God; which, therefore, in loving a man, loves nothing else but God himself, or his immutable truth and justice, from which there emanates, and from whose refulgence there shines forth, whatever we approve as just and right.]

3 Tom. III. lib. VII. c. IX.: "voluntas felix, immutabilis et necessaria non peccandi recteque vivendi."—[Vol. III. book VII. ch. IX.: a blissful, immutable, and necessary willingness, not to sin, but to live rightly.]

In this work it is amazing to how high a degree the developments of doctrine are kept philosophically clear, even in the learned zeal of a hostile discussion: the fundamental ideas are at once moral and religious, speculative and practical; to the external self-satisfaction of the Jesuit doctrine, it opposes strict retirement within a man's own self, the ideal of an activity that vents itself in love to God.

But while Jansenius was still occupied with the composition of this work, his friend was already attempting, first of all, to exhibit in his own life, and then practically to extend among those around him, the ideas that lay at its foundation.

St. Cyran, for so had Verger now come to be called, had provided for himself a learned, ascetic solitude in the midst of Paris, and there, in a course of indefatigable study of holy scripture and of the fathers of the church, he endeavoured to imbibe their spirit. The peculiarity of the doctrine in which he agreed with Jansenius, must have led him first of all to the sacrament of penance. He was dissatisfied with the regulations for penitents laid down by the (Roman) church; and was heard, indeed, to say, that the church had been purer at its commencement, as brooks are near their source; and that but too many Gospel truths were now obscured.[1] His requirements, on the contrary, sounded very severe. Self-humiliation, patience, dependance on God, absolute renunciation of the world,[2] the devotion of all a man's active energies, to the love of God, this alone to him seemed Christianity. So profound an idea had he of the necessity of an inward change, that according to his doctrine, grace must precede penance. "When God means to deliver a soul, he begins internally: if the heart be but once changed, if true contrition be but once experienced, all else follows; absolution can but indicate the first beam of grace: as a physician has but to follow the motions and internal operations of nature, so must the physician of the soul follow the operations of grace." He often repeats that he himself had travelled over the whole path from temptation and sin, to contrition, prayer, and exaltation. He opened his mind to but few; whenever he did so he was

1 Extracts from his examination in Reuchlin's Geschichte von Portroyal [History of Portroyal], I. p. 451.

2 "S'humilier, souffrir et dépendre de Dieu est toute la vie Chrétienne."—[Self-humiliation, suffering, and dependence on God, is the whole Christian life.]

sparing of his words, his countenance beaming with the expression of peace; but as he threw his whole soul into what he said, as he always waited for an occasion and inward call, in himself as well as in others, he made an irresistible impression: those who listened to him felt themselves involuntarily changed, and tears would burst from their eyes before they were aware.[1] Very soon some distinguished men attached themselves to him as decided proselytes: Arnauld d'Andilly, who stood on intimate terms with Cardinal Richelieu and Queen Anne of Austria, and was employed on the most important affairs; whose nephew, too, le Maitre, admired at that time as the first speaker in the parliament, and who had the most splendid career before him, yet now withdrew at once to a hermitage near Paris. Angelique Arnauld, whom we have already had occasion to mention, and her nuns of Portroyal, clung to St. Cyran with the unbounded deference usually felt by pious women for their prophets.

Jansenius died before he had seen his book in print: and St. Cyran, immediately after his first conversions, was thrown into prison by Richelieu, who had a natural dislike to such personal efficiency; but these untoward events did not check the progress of their doctrines.

Jansenius's book, alike from its inherent merit and from its boldness as a polemical work, gradually produced a general and deep impression.[2] St. Cyran continued to put forth his activity in making converts from his prison; the respect he commanded was increased by the unmerited sufferings which had befallen him, and which he bore with great resignation; so that on regaining his liberty on the death of Richelieu, he came to be looked upon as a saint, another John the Baptist. He died, indeed, a few months after (on the 11th of October, 1643), but he had founded a school which saw the gospel in his doctrines and those of his friend: "his disciples," says one of them, "went forth like eaglets under his wings: heirs of his virtues and his

[1] Mémoires pour servir à l'histoire de Portroyal par Mr. Fontaine, I. p. 225. Racine: Histoire de Portroyal, p. 134.

[2] Gerberon: Histoire du Jansénisme, I. 63: "Les théologiens de Paris s'appliquèrent tellement à l'étude de l'Augustin d'Ipres, où ils reconnoissoient celui d'Hippone, - - qu'on commençoit à n'entendre plus parmi ces théologiens que les noms de Jansénius et de S. Augustin."—[Gerberon: History of Jansenism, I. 63. The divines of Paris applied themselves so to the study of the Ypres Augustine, in whom they recognized him of Hippo, - - that among those divines there began to be no other names heard but those of Jansenius and St. Augustine.]

piety, who transmitted again to others what they had received from him. Elijah left Elisha behind him, who continues to carry on his work."

If we attempt to point out the relation in which the Jansenists stood to the prevailing ecclesiastical parties in general, they manifestly remind us of protestantism. They urged with quite the same zeal the necessity of holy living; they endeavoured no less to give a new form to theology, by removing the excrescencies of scholasticism. But, in my opinion, we must not venture on that account to pronounce them, remotely even, a kind of unconscious protestants. The main difference, viewed historically, lies in their willingly submitting to a principle, to which protestantism, from the first, was not to be brought back; they remained attached to those most eminent fathers of the Latin church, who had been abandoned in Germany ever since 1523, namely, Ambrose, Augustine and Gregory; and only added to these some of the Greek fathers, particularly Chrysostom; in the works of these fathers, they thought they possessed a pure unadulterated tradition, from which, further, St. Bernard never deviated, but which, posterior to that "last of the fathers," became obscured through the intrusion of the Aristotelian doctrines. Hence we find them far removed from that energetic zeal, wherewith the protestants went back directly to the doctrines of Holy Scripture, their conscience being satisfied with the first formations which became the groundwork of the later system. They remained satisfied that the visible church, notwithstanding momentary obscuration and disfigurement, still is of one spirit, yea, of one body with Christ, and is infallible and imperishable; they held very earnestly to the episcopal hierarchy; they lived in the belief that Augustine had been inspired by God, for the purpose of communicating to the world, in its fulness, the doctrine of grace, which constitutes the essence of the new covenant; in their apprehension, Christian theology in him received its completion; that theology they desired but to comprehend in its root, to understand in its essence; yet Pelagian opinions had often, down to that time, been held as Augustinian—Luther had been awakened by Augustine, but had then gone back without reserve to the first source of information, Scripture, the word of God; confronting him Roman catholicism, had held fast to the entire system that had grown up in the course of ages; the Jansenists endeavoured to give currency to Augustine's conception, as being that which comprised all that went before, and laid the foundation of what followed. Protestantism rejects tradition; Roman catholicism clings to it, while Jansenism seeks to purify it, to restore its original character, and thereby thinks to regenerate alike doctrine and life.

Forthwith there assembled in the solitude of Port-royal des Champs, to which le Maitre had first retired, no inconsiderable society around him, all agreed in the profession of those principles. It is not to be denied that in the first instance there was something contracted about it, for it was chiefly composed of members and friends of the Arnauld family. Le Maitre alone drew about him four of his brothers; their mother who had given them their peculiar disposition of mind, was an Arnauld. St. Cyran's oldest friend, to whom he had bequeathed his heart, was Arnauld d'Andilly; he, too, at length joined the society; his youngest brother, Anthony Arnauld, was the author of the first work of any consequence in its favour. These were followed by a great many other relations and friends. The convent of Port-royal in Paris also, was almost exclusively in the hands of that family. Andilly relates that his mother, who at length likewise entered there, had around her twelve daughters and granddaughters.[1] This reminds us that it was chiefly the elder Anthony Arnauld, from whom all these were descended, that by his splendid pleading in 1594, led to the decision that the Jesuits should leave Paris. A dislike to the order had become as it were hereditary in the family.

But how soon and how nobly was that narrow circle enlarged. Many others attached themselves to it, attracted solely by the tie of a congenial taste. An influential preacher in Paris, called Singlin, an adherent of St. Cyran's, was particularly active in their behalf Singlin had this singular quality, that while it was only with difficulty that he could express himself in common conversation, no sooner did he mount the pulpit than he displayed an overpowering eloquence.[2] Those who most eagerly clung to him, he sent to Port-royal, where they were cordially

[1] Memoires d'Arnauld d'Andilly, I. p. 341.

[2] Mémoires de Fontaine, II. p. 283.

welcomed. They consisted of young clergymen and men of learning, thriving merchants, men of the most distinguished families, physicians who already occupied important positions in society, members of other orders, all nevertheless such as nothing but an inward impulse and a decided agreement in sentiment could have induced to take this step.

And now in this retirement, just as if in a convent kept together voluntarily, and without the obligation of formal vows, there was much time given no doubt to religious exercises; the church was sedulously attended; there was much solitary and social prayer; there were agricultural labours also, and one or other member of the society engaged in some handicraft; but literary engagements constituted the chief occupation of the place; the Port-royalists formed a sort of academy.

While the Jesuits stored up learning in enormous folios, or lost themselves in the perverse scholasticism of artificial systems of morals and theology, the Jansenists addressed themselves to the nation.

They began by translating the Holy Scriptures, the church fathers, and Latin prayerbooks; in this they happily contrived to avoid the old French forms which had injured the works of this kind that had hitherto appeared, and to express themselves with an attractive clearness. An educational institution which they established near Port-royal, furnished them with an occasion for composing school-books for the ancient and modern languages, and in logic and geometry; and these proceeding from a fresh apprehension of the object to be attained, supplied new methods for ordinary use, the advantage of which came to be universally acknowledged.[1] Mingled with these there then appeared other works, controversial writings of an acuteness and precision which intellectually annihilated their enemies; works of deep devotion, such as the hours of Port-royal, which came to be greedily received, and after the lapse of a century, are still as new and as much in request as at their first appearance. Minds of such eminent scientific capacity as Pascal, coryphæi of French poesy, such as Racine, men of learning of the most comprehensive range of study, such as Tillemont, went forth from

[1] Notice de Petitot, prefixed to the Memoirs of Andilly, I., otherwise a surprisingly partial work.

among them. Their efforts, as we see, extended far beyond the circle of theology and asceticism that had been marked out by Janse and Verger. We should not, indeed, venture too far, should we assert, that this union of men, rich in mental endowments, full of noble aims, who in their intercourse with each other developed, altogether of themselves, a new tone of expression and of communicating knowledge, has exercised in general a very remarkable internally-beneficial influence on the literature of France, and hence on that of Europe, and that the literary lustre of the age of Louis XIV. may so far be traced to it.

Now, however, how must not the spirit that lay at the foundation of all these productions, have by their means opened a way for itself into the nation? It found adherents in all quarters. The parish priests, by whom the Jesuit confessional had long been detested, particularly attached themselves to them. At times, for example under Cardinal Retz, it seemed not unlikely that they would find their way to the ranks of the superior clergy; important situations were given them. Forthwith we find that they had patrons, not only in the Netherlands and France, but even in Spain: while Innocent X. was still reigning, a Jansenist preacher was to be heard from the pulpit in public at Rome.[1]

The question there before all others now was, how these opinions would be looked upon by the Roman see.

POSITION OF THE ROMAN COURT WITH RESPECT TO THE TWO PARTIES.

THERE had now recommenced, only under somewhat different

[1] Deone, tom. IV. "Fu citato per il sant' officio Monsieur Honorato Herzan (Hersent), dottor della Sorbona di Pariggi, per la predica che fece in San Luigi nel giorno della festa, nella quale sostenne e difese l' opinione di Jansenio con esaltarlo per unico interprete di S. Agostino, non specificandolo ma però delineandolo che da ciascheduno era inteso. Egli si ritirò in casa dell' ambasciator di Francia e di là a Pariggi. Il suo libro è prohibito, et il maestro del sacro palazzo ne ha havuto qualche travaglio per haverne permessa la stampa: egli si scusa con dire che veniva dedicato al papa et era in lingua francese, la quale egli non intende, però contenendo il libro l' opinione favorevole all' opinione loro contro l'opinione de' Gesuiti."—[There was summoned to appear before the holy office, Monsieur Honorato Herzan (Hersent), doctor of the Sorbonne at Paris, for the sermon he had preached in the church of St. Louis on the feast day, in which he maintained and defended the opinion held by Jansenius, extolling him at the same time as the sole interpreter of St. Augustine, not naming him, but describing him in such a manner that every body understood him. He withdrew to the house of the French ambassador, and from that to Paris. His book is prohibited, and the master of the sacred palace has got himself into some trouble for having permitted it to be printed; he excuses himself by saying that it came with a dedication to the pope, and was in the French tongue, which he does not understand, the book, in fine, containing the opinion favourable to their opinion against the opinion of the Jesuits.]

forms, that same controversy, which, forty years before, neither Clement VIII. nor Paul V. had ventured to determine.

I am not sure that Urban VIII. or Innocent X. would have shown more decision, had there not unluckily appeared in the work of Jansenius a passage at which the Roman see, on other grounds, took great offence.

In his third book, on the state of innocence, Jansenius has occasion to speak of a position laid down by Augustine, which, it could not be denied, had been condemned by the court of Rome. He hesitates for a moment, at a loss which to follow, the church-father or the pope. But, after some hesitation, he observes,[1] that the Roman see occasionally condemns a doctrine merely for the sake of peace, without meaning thereby to declare exactly that it is false; he then bluntly determines in favour of the Augustinian dogma.

His adversaries naturally took advantage of this passage; they pointed to it as an attack on papal infallibility; further, Urban VIII. was prevailed upon to pronounce his displeasure on a book which, to the disparagement of the apostolic authority, contained positions that had been condemned by preceding popes.

With this declaration, however, he effected little. The Jansenist doctrines diffused themselves not the less powerfully, and in France there appeared a general separation into two parties. The opponents of Port-royal held it necessary to draw forth another and a more precise condemnation from the Roman see. To that end they comprised the fundamental doctrines of Jansenius as they understood them, in five propositions, and called on Pope Innocent X. to pronounce his apostolical judgment upon them.[2]

And upon this steps were taken at the Roman court for hav-

[1] De statu naturæ puræ, III. c. XXII. p. 403. "Quodsi," he adds, "vel tunc ostendi potuisset hanc aliasque nonnullas propositiones ab Augustino doctorum omnium coryphæo traditas, nunquam, arbitror, hujusmodi decretum ab apostolica sede permanasset."—[On the state of pure nature, III. chap. XXII. p. 403. But if (he adds) it could even then have been shown that this, and some other propositions, had been delivered by Augustine, the coryphæus of all doctors, never, in my opinion, would a decree of this kind have emanated from the apostolic see.]

[2] Pallavicini: Vita di Alessandro VII: "acciochè ben informato dichiarasse ciò che devea permettersi o proibirsi intorno cinque principali propositioni di quell' autore."—[Pallavicini's Life of Alexander VII.: in order that, after being well informed, he might declare what ought to be permitted or prohibited with respect to the five chief propositions of that author.]

ing a formal investigation made. A congregation was named, consisting of four cardinals, under whose supervision thirteen theological consultors undertook this task.

Now these propositions were so prepared, that at the first glance they contained obvious heterodoxies, but on a closer examination they might at least so far bear an orthodox meaning.[1] Different views forthwith appeared among the consultors. Four of them, that is, two Dominicans, Luca Wadding, a Minorite, and the general of the Augustinians, thought the condemnation unadvisable. But the other nine were in favour of it.[2] All now depended on how far the pope would agree with the majority.

Innocent X. was averse to agitating the question at all. Already in itself he detested puzzling theological investigations; but he anticipated besides, that on which ever side he might declare himself, the results would be untoward. He could not decide in defiance of the verdict of so large a majority. "When he came to the edge of the ditch," says Pallavicini, "and measured with his eye the extent of the leap, he drew back and was not to be persuaded to advance farther."

But these scruples were not felt by all the court. Immediately at the side of the pope, stood a secretary of state, Cardinal Chigi, who was incessantly inflaming him. While still at Cologne Chigi had met with the book and read it; already had the above passage filled him while there with devout indignation, so that he had tossed it away from him; in this repugnance to it he had been strengthened by some of the German regular clergy; he had taken an active part in the congregation appointed to examine the case, and had contributed his own share towards its result; now he urged the pope not to be silent on this occasion; silence would be interpreted as permission; he must not allow the doctrine of papal infallibility to fall into discredit; and that this was just one principal vocation of the apostolic see, to decide where the faithful were in doubt as to what to believe.[3]

1 Racine: Abrégé de l' histoire ecclésiastique, tom. XI. p. 15.—[Racine's Abridgement of Church History, vol. XI. p. 15.]

2 Pallavicini, who was himself one of the consultors, communicates these details. He says of the pope: "Il suo intelletto alienissimo delle sottigliezze scolastiche."—[His intellect is most alien to scholastic subtleties.]

3 Pallavicini's communications.

Innocent, as we know, was a man that allowed himself to be led by sudden impressions, and in a luckless hour he was overpowered by the representation that had been made to him of the danger to which the papal infallibility was exposed. He the more readily took this to be an inspiration from above, as it happened to be the day of St. Athanasius. On the 1st of June, 1653, he published his bull, in which he condemned those five propositions as heretical, blasphemous, and execrable. He declared that with this he hoped to restore peace to the church; that he had nothing more at heart than that the vessel of the church should sail onwards as on a quiet sea, and reach the haven of salvation.[1]

But how completely different was it fated that the result should be!

The Jansenists denied that they could find the propositions in Jansen's book, and still more, that they were understood by them in the sense in which they had been condemned.

Now first was it manifest in what a false position the Roman court had placed itself. The French bishops urged in Rome to have it declared that those propositions were really condemned in the meaning held by Jansenius. Chigi, who meanwhile had ascended the throne under the name of Alexander VII., could so much the less refuse this from his having taken so large a part himself in the condemnation that had been pronounced: he gave forth that declaration in plain and formal terms, "that the five propositions had certainly been taken from Jansen's book, and had been condemned as understood by him."[2]

But this, too, the Jansenists were prepared to meet. They replied, that a declaration of this sort exceeded the limits of the papal power: that the papal infallibility did not extend to a judgment upon facts.

Thus there was added to the dogmatical controversy a question relative to the limits of the papal authority; in their unde-

1 In Coquel. VI. III. 248. We see from Pallavicini that it was drawn up by Chigi, and chiefly by Albizi, assessor of the Inquisition.

2 In Coquel. VI. IV. 151. "Quinque illas propositiones ex libro præmemorati Cornelii Jansenii episcopi Iprensis cui titulus Augustinus excerptas ac in sensu ab eodem Jansenio intento damnatas fuisse declaramus et definimus."—[We declare and determine that those five propositions have been excerpted from the book of the before-mentioned Cornelius Jansenius, bishop of Ypres, intituled Augustinus, and that they have been condemned in the meaning intended by the said Jansenius.]

niable opposition to the Roman catholic see, the Jansenists uniformly contrived, however, to maintain the character of good Roman catholics.

This party, too, was now no longer to be set aside. Preparatory measures were occasionally taken on the side of the crown for that purpose; formularies, embodying the meaning of the condemnatory bull, were issued, and were to be subscribed by all ecclesiastical persons, even by schoolmasters and by nuns. The Jansenists made no difficulty of condemning the five propositions, which, as has been said, admitted of a heterodox interpretation; they only refused to acknowledge, by an unconditional subscription, that they were contained in Jansenius, and that they were the doctrines of their master; nor could any persecution induce them to do so. The effect of this constancy was, that their numbers and credit daily increased; and soon numerous defenders of their views might be found even amongst the bishops.[1]

In order that peace might be restored, externally at least, Clement IX., in 1668, had to declare himself satisfied with a subscription which even a Jansenist could give. He contented himself with a condemnation of the five propositions in general, without insisting that they were actually taught by Jansenius.[2]

[1] Letter of nineteen bishops to the pope, 1st Dec. 1667. "Novum et inauditum apud nos nonnulli dogma procuderunt, ecclesiæ nempe decretis quibus quotidiana nec revelata divinitus facta deciduntur, certam et infallibilem constare veritatem."—[Some among us have coined a new and unheard-of doctrine, namely, that certain and infallible truth appears in the decrees of the church, by which facts of daily occurrence, and not divinely revealed, are decided.] Yet this is properly the acknowledged opposition of the question of right and fact.

[2] The last formulary of Alexander VII. (15th Feb. 1665) runs thus: "Je rejette et condamne sincèrement les cinq propositions extraites du livre de Cornelius Jansenius intitulé Augustinus, et dans le sens du même auteur, comme le saint siège apostolique les a condamnées par les susdites constitutions."—[I sincerely reject and condemn the five propositions extracted from the book of Cornelius Jansenius, intituled Augustinus, and in the meaning of the same author, as the holy apostolic see has condemned them by the said constitutions.] On the other hand there is the more circumstantial declaration of peace: "Vous devez vous obliger à condamner sincèrement, pleinement, sans aucune réserve ni exception tous les sens que l'église et le pape ont condamnés et condamnent dans les cinq propositions."—[You should oblige yourself to condemn sincerely, fully, and without reserve or exception, all the senses which the church and the pope have condemned, and do condemn, in the five propositions.] This is followed by a second article: "Déclarons que ce seroit faire injure à l'église de comprendre entre les sens condamnés dans ces propositions la doctrine de St Augustin et de St Thomas touchant la grace efficace par elle-même nécessaire à toutes les actions de la piété chrétienne et la prédestination gratuite des élus."—[We declare that it would be insulting to the church to comprise among the meanings condemned in these propositions the doctrine of St. Augustine and

This, in fact, implies a virtual yielding on the part of the Roman court: he not only dropt the claim to decide on the matter of fact, but he likewise provided that his condemnatory judgment on Jansenius should remain quite without effect.

And from that time the party of St. Cyran and Jansen rose to even greater strength and importance, tolerated as it was by the curia, maintaining a good understanding with the royal court,—the well-known minister of state, Pomponne, was a son of Andilly,—and favoured by some of the great. Now first did their literary assiduity act upon the nation. But together with their aggrandizement, notwithstanding the pacification, a warm opposition to the Roman see began to spread; they knew right well that they should not have leave to subsist, were the course of affairs to accord with its designs.

RELATION TO THE CIVIL POWER.

FROM another quarter, too, there had already sprung up at that time an opposition, at least not less dangerous, and which went on constantly extending and increasing in animosity.

In the seventeenth century, the Roman see began to attend to the preservation of its jurisdictional rights, I know not if it can be said with greater energy and effect, but certainly more systematically and uncompromisingly than before. Urban VIII., who owed his elevation, among other things, to the respect he commanded as a zealous abettor of these pretensions,[1] founded a special immunity congregation. To a few cardinals, who already, in the ordinary course of things, had formed ties with the reigning powers, as youthful prelates who might look for promotion according to the zeal they exhibited in this depart-

St. Thomas touching grace efficacious by itself, necessary to all the actions of Christian piety, and to the free predestination of the elect.]

1 Relatione de' IV. ambasciatori, 1625: "Professa sopra tutte le cose haver l'animo inflessible e che la sua independenza non ammetta alcuna ragione degl' interessi de' principi. Ma quello in che preme con insistenza et a che tende l'impiego di tutto il suo spirito è di conservare e di accrescer la giuirisdittione ecclesiastica. Questo medesimo concetto fu sempre sostenuto dal pontefice nella sua minor fortuna, e ciò è stato anche grandissima causa della sua esaltatione."—[Professing, above all things, inflexibility of purpose, and that his independence should never admit any argument founded on the interests of princes. But that in which he pressed with insistency, and to which he directed the entire employment of his mind, was the preservation and increase of the ecclesiastical jurisdiction. This same conceit was always kept up by the pontiff before his fortunes rose so high, and was also one very great cause of his exaltation.]

ment, he committed the charge of keeping a vigilant eye over all the encroachments committed by monarchs in matters of spiritual jurisdiction. The attention bestowed on this became thereafter much closer and more regular, the exhortations to vigilance more urgent; official zeal and interest more combined; in the public opinion of the court it was considered a sign of piety to maintain a jealous watch over every article of those ancient rights.[1]

But would the states (of Europe) willingly submit to this more vigilant superintendence? The feeling of religious union that had been awakened in the struggle with protestantism, had again become cold; the objects of universal effort were internal strength and political compactness; the consequence was, that the Roman court fell into the bitterest dissensions with all the Roman catholic states.

The very Spaniards occasionally endeavoured to circumscribe the active influences of Rome, for example, on Naples, and to attach to the inquisition there some assessors on the part of the state! Some hesitation was felt at Rome about yielding to the emperor the patriarchate of Aquileja, to which he had claims, from alarm lest he should take advantage of it for acquiring a greater ecclesiastical independence. The estates of the German empire, in the election articles of 1654 and 1658, endeavoured, by stringent regulations, to circumscribe the jurisdictions of the nuncios and the curia;. Venice was in incessant agitation about the influence of the court on the appointments to ecclesiastical places in the country, about the pensions, the usurpations of the nephews; Genoa at one time, Savoy at another, found occasion to recall their ambassadors from Rome; but the French church, as was already involved in the principles of its restoration, presented

[1] Joh. Bapt. de Luca S. R. E. Cardinalis: Relatio curiæ Romanæ, 1683. Disc. XVII. p. 109. "Etiam apud bonos et zelantes ecclesiasticos remanet quæstio, an hujus congregationis erectio ecclesiasticæ immunitati et jurisdictioni proficua vel præjudicialis fuerit, potissime quia bonus quidem sed forte indiscretus vel asper zelus aliquorum, qui circa initia eam regebant, aliqua produxit inconvenientia præjudicialia, atque asperitatis vel nimium exactæ et exorbitantis defensionis opinionem impressit apud seculares."—[Even with good and zealous ecclesiastics the question remains, whether the erection of this congregation were more beneficial or prejudicial to ecclesiastical immunity and jurisdiction, chiefly because a zeal, good indeed, but possibly indiscreet or rude in some who about the commencement conducted it, produced some prejudicial inconveniences, and impressed laymen with an idea of asperity, and of an excessively rigid and exorbitant defence.] A very important concession, however, from a cardinal.

the most animated opposition.[1] The nuncios find no end to the complaints they think it necessary to make, particularly about the limitations imposed on the ecclesiastical jurisdiction; ere they had taken a single step, appeals would be lodged; the power over marriages was withdrawn from them, under the pretence of an abduction being projected; they were excluded from jurisdiction in penal processes; clergymen were sometimes executed without having been first degraded; the king, without any consideration for them, promulgated edicts about heresy and simony; the tenths had gradually become a perpetual impost. The more considerate members of the curia even now perceived in these usurpations the preludes to a schism.

The peculiar relation into which people were thrown by these dissensions, was necessarily connected likewise with other circumstances, chiefly with the political bearing assumed by the Roman court.

From respect to Spain, neither Innocent nor Alexander had ventured to acknowledge Portugal, which had broken off from that monarchy, or to give canonical institution to the bishops appointed there. Almost the whole regular episcopacy of Portugal died out: ecclesiastical property was in a great measure given up to the officers of the army: king, clergy, and laity left off their former submissiveness.

But, moreover, the popes, after Urban VIII., leant to the Spanish-Austrian side.

It cannot be matter of surprise, that the preponderance of France very soon displayed a character that threatened the general freedom. To this was added that those popes owed their elevation to Spanish influence, and both were personal opponents of Cardinal Mazarin.[2] This animosity constantly expressed

[1] Relatione della nuntiatura di Francia di Monsr Scotti, 1641, 5 Aprile.—[Account of the French nuncioship of Monsignor Scotti, 1641, 5th April.] He has a special section, dell' impedimenti della nuntiatura ordinaria: " Li giudici regj si può dire che levino tutta la giurisdittione eccl^ca in Francia alli prelati."—[on the impediments to the ordinary nuncioship: The king's judges, it may be said, deprive the prelates of all ecclesiastical jurisdiction.]

[2] Deone: Ottobre 1644. " Si sa veramente che l'esclusione di Panfilio fatta da cardinali Francesi nel conclave non era volontà regia nè instanza del C^l Antonio, ma opera del C^l Mazzarini, emulo e poco ben affetto al C^l Panziroli, il quale prevedea che doveva aver gran parte in questo ponteficato."—[It is known for certain, that the exclusion of Panfilio by the French cardinals in the conclave, was not the royal wish nor pressed by Cardinal Anthony, but the doing of Cardinal Mazarin, a rival of, and little, indeed, inclined to favour Cardinal Panziroli, who foresaw that he ought to have a large share in that pontificate.] As was also actually the case.

itself with greater and greater force: in truth he could not forgive the cardinal for having allied himself with Cromwell, and for having long been led by personal motives to throw obstacles in the way of peace with Spain.

Another consequence of this, however, was, that in France the opposition to the Roman see was constantly becoming more deeply rooted, and burst out from time to time in violent explosions. How severely did even Alexander come to experience this!

A dispute that had broken out in Rome betwixt the suite of the French ambassador Crequy and the Corsican city guard, and in which Crequy himself at last was insulted, gave the king an opportunity of interfering in the dissensions between the Roman see and the houses of Este and Farnese, and of finally ordering troops to march straight into Italy. The poor pope tried to help himself by means of a secret protest: but before the eyes of the world he had to concede all the king required in the treaty concluded at Pisa. The popes are notorious for their love of eulogistic inscriptions; it has been said that they will not allow a stone to be placed in a wall without having their name traced on it: but Alexander, in his own capital, had to allow a pyramid to be erected in the most frequented square, the inscription on which was to perpetuate his humiliation for ever.

This act could not fail of itself deeply to lower the authority of the popedom.

But besides this, the respect it commanded had already, about the year 1660, begun again to decline. The papal see had still had influence enough to take the first steps in the peace of Vervins, to promote it by its negotiations, and to bring it to a conclusion; at that of Westphalia it had been represented by its envoys, but had even then seen itself obliged to protest against conditions to which the other parties had agreed; at the peace of the Pyrenees it no longer took even any ostensible part, people avoided admitting its envoys; hardly was any regard shown in the articles of pacification to its interests.[1] How soon was this

[1] Galeazzo Gualdo Priorato della pace conclusa fra le due corone 1664—[G. G. P. on the peace concluded between the two crowns, 1664], at p. 120 has Osservationi sopra le cause per le quali si conclude la pace senza intervento del papa.—[Observations on the causes whereby peace was made without the pope's interven-

followed by pacifications in which papal fiefs were disposed of, without so much as asking for the pope's consent.

TRANSITION TO LATER EPOCHS.

It must ever be thought extremely remarkable, and opens up to us a view in the course of human affairs in general, that the popedom, at the moment of its failing in the accomplishment of its plans for the recovery of its general dominion, began likewise to experience an internal decline.

In that period of progress which we have traced, the whole restoration was founded. It was then that doctrines were renovated, ecclesiastical prerogatives more powerfully centralized, the Roman catholic monarchs drawn in as allies, the old orders revived and new ones founded, the resources of the states of the church consolidated, the curia reformed in taste and spirit, and every thing directed to the one end of restoring the government and the Roman catholic faith.

This, as we have seen, was no new creation: it was a re-animation by the force of new ideas, which abolished some abuses, and only carried along with it with fresh impulsion the living elements already existing.

But there is no doubt, that a restoration of this sort is more exposed than a fundamentally new creation to a decline of the motives that animate it.

The first check experienced by the ecclesiastical restoration was in France. The papal power could make no progress by keeping to the beaten path; it had to submit to see a church, although Roman catholic, yet removed from under the influence which it contemplated, acquire consistency and distinction; and with this church it had to condescend to enter into an accommodation.

Then, in connection with this, there forthwith happened also to spring up in the very bosom of the church, strong oppositions of sentiment, controversies on the most important points of faith, and on the relation that ought to subsist between the spiritual and secular powers; in the curia nepotism grew up in the most perilous manner; the financial resources, instead of being fully

tion.] We see that the bad footing between the pope and Mazarin was a well-known affair at that time.

applied to their proper object, went mostly to enrich individual families.

Still, however, a grand general purpose was constantly kept in view, towards which advances were made with extraordinary success. In these higher efforts all oppositions were reconciled, controversies on points of doctrine and ecclesiastical and secular claims were silenced, dissensions among the powers of Europe composed, the progress of common enterprises kept in check: the curia was the directing centre of the Roman catholic world, and conversions went on in the grandest style.

But we see how it happened that the aim was not attained, but by means of internal dissensions and external opposition the papacy was thrown back upon themselves.

Now from this time, too, all the relations of the state and of its social development assumed a different aspect.

In the spirit of conquest and opposition that devotes itself to some great object, there is at the same time involved devotedness: it cannot accord with a narrow selfishness; there now appeared in the curia a spirit of enjoyment, of eagerness to possess. There was formed an association of annuitants, who conceived they had a good right to the revenues of the civil and ecclesiastical government. Though all the while making a ruinous abuse of this right, yet they clung to it as eagerly as if the very existence of the faith were involved in it.

But from this very cause it happened that an implacable opposition arose from opposite quarters.

A doctrine had sprung up, which, originating in a new view of the deep things of religion, was condemned and persecuted by the Roman see, but could never be suppressed. The states (of Roman catholic Europe) assumed an independent bearing; they threw themselves loose from any respect for the papal policy: in their social concerns they claimed a power of self-government, which constantly left less and less influence to the curia, even as respected ecclesiastical affairs.

Now it is upon these two points that the farther history of the popedom rests.

Epochs succeed, in which, displaying far less of an unfettered activity, it thinks only, while attacked now on the one side, now on the other, of defending itself, every successive moment, as it best may.

In the usual course of things force and energy attract attention, and events can be properly understood only by being viewed on the side of their practical efficacy; nor does it fall within the scope of this book to describe the most recent epochs. Yet they will always exhibit a highly remarkable spectacle, and as we began with taking a review of earlier times, we cannot well close our labours without attempting, although but in a few slight sketches, to pass the more recent under review.

The assault, however, commenced on the side of the states. It is most intimately connected with the separation of the Roman catholic world into two hostile parties, the Austrian and the French, that the pope was no longer capable of either overpowering or of pacificating. The political position assumed by Rome, determined at the same time the measure of ecclesiastical submissiveness that she found. We have already seen how that commenced, let us now observe how it further developed itself.

LOUIS XIV. AND INNOCENT XI.

EXCELLENT Roman catholic as was Louis the XIV., yet it seemed to him intolerable that the Roman see should follow not only an independent policy, but one, too, often opposed to his own.

As had been the case with Innocent and Alexander, and if not with Clement IX., at least with the circle that surrounded him, Clement X. too, (1670 to 1676) and his nephew Pauluzzi Altieri leaned to the side of the Spaniards.[1] For this Louis XIV. revenged himself by making incessant assaults on the ecclesiastical power.

He arbitrarily confiscated church property; suppressed one or other of the monastic orders, and claimed the privilege of burthening church benefices with military pensions. The right of enjoying the revenues of a bishopric, and of appointing to the

1 Morosini: Relatione di Francia, 1671. "Conosciuta naturale partialità del card[l] Altieri per la corona cattolica rende alla X[ma] sospetta ogni sua attione. Il pontefice presente è considerato come un imagine del dominio che risiede veramente nell' arbitrio del nipote."—[Morosini's Account of France, 1671. The knowledge of Cardinal Altieri's natural partiality for the catholic crown, renders all his doings suspicious to the most Christian king. The present pontiff is considered as but a shadow of the government, which lies really at the absolute disposal of the nephew.]

livings in its gift, during its being vacant, a right so well known under the name of the regale, he tried to extend to provinces where it had never been sanctioned; and he inflicted the severest wound on the Roman annuitants, by exercising a parsimonious superintendence over the remittances of money to that court.[1]

Thus did he proceed now, too, under Innocent XI., who on the whole observed the same policy; but in him he found resistance.

Innocent XL, from the house of Odescalchi of Como, had come to Rome in his 25th year, armed with sword and pistol, with a view of devoting himself to some one or other secular employment, perhaps to the military service in Naples. The advice of a cardinal who saw through his character better than he knew it himself, prevailed with him to devote himself to the career presented by the curia. This he did with so much devotion and earnestness, and gradually earned for himself such a reputation for ability and good dispositions, that during the sitting of the conclave the people called out his name from the portico of St. Peter's, and public opinion felt gratified when he came forth from the church adorned with the tiara, (21 Sept. 1676.)

He was a man who in calling for his servants would do it conditionally, only if they had nothing to detain them, of whom his confessor affirmed that he had never perceived any thing in him that could withdraw the soul from God; mild and gentle in his disposition, but whom the same conscientiousness that characterized his private life, now likewise impelled to fulfil the obligations of his office, without any respect for persons or consequences.

How vigorously did he attack the evils, particularly of the financial administration. The disbursements had risen to 2,578,106 scudi, 91 baj; while the receipts, including the dataria and spolia, brought in only 2,408,500 scudi, 71 baj; exhibiting so grievous a deficiency, amounting yearly to 170,000 scudi, as threatened to lead to a public bankruptcy.[2] That matters did

[1] Instruzione per Monsr arcivescovo di Patrasso, 1674. "Questo fatto arrivato alla corte sicome eccitò lo stupore e lo scandalo universale cosi pervenuto alla notitia di N. S[re] mosse un estremo cordoglio nell' animo di S. Beat[ne]."—[Instruction for Monsignor the archbishop of Patrasso, 1674. This proceeding having reached the court, as it excited astonishment and universal scandal, so on its coming to the knowledge of our Lord (the pope) it raised extreme grief in the mind of his Beatitude.]

[2] Stato della camera nel presente pontificato di Innocenzo XI.—[State of the exchequer in the present pontificate of Innocent XL] MS. (Bibl. Alb.)

not proceed to this extremity is undoubtedly to be ascribed to the meritorious conduct of Innocent XI. He at last absolutely abstained from nepotism. He declared that he loved his nephew Don Livio, who deserved as much on account of his modesty, but on that very account he would not have him in the palace. He immediately applied to the public service all the official emoluments and revenues that used to belong to the nephews; and he did the same too with many other places whose existence was more a burthen than otherwise. He abolished innumerable abuses and exemptions; and at last, as the state of the money market permitted, he unhesitatingly reduced the monti from four per cent to three per cent.[1] After the lapse of some years he succeeded, in fact, in raising the receipts to no inconsiderable excess above the disbursements.

And with the same decision of purpose the pope now opposed the attacks of Louis XIV.

A few bishops of Jansenist opinions who opposed the above extension of the right of the regale, had on that account been subjected to oppression and vexation from the court; among these the bishop of Pamiers had for some time to live upon charity. They addressed themselves to the pope, and Innocent without delay took up their cause.[2]

Once and again he warned the king to shut his ears to flatterers, and to abstain from assaulting the franchises of the church; he might come to be the cause of the fountain of divine favour being dried up over his whole kingdom. Receiving no answer he repeated his warning a third time; but now, he added, he would not again write, nevertheless he would no longer be content with warnings, but would avail himself of all the resources that God had placed within his power. In this he would fear no danger, no storm that might assail him; he gloried in the cross of Christ.[3]

It has always been a maxim of the French court, by means of

[1] In a manuscript of 763 pages, of the year 1743, Erettione et aggionte de' monti camerali,—[Erections and additions of the exchequer monti,] may be found the decrees and briefs relating to this. In a brief to the treasurer Negroni, dated 1684, Innocent first declares his object, "d' andar liberando la camera del frutto di 4 p. c.—che in questi tempi è troppo rigoroso."—[to proceed with the relieving of the exchequer from the interest of 4 per cent, which in these times is too high.]

[2] Racine: Histoire ecclésiastique, X. p. 328.

[3] Brief of 27 Dec. 1679.

the papal power to control its clergy, and by means of its clergy to restrain the influences put forth by the papal power. But never had a monarch a more absolute command over his clergy than Louis XIV. The discourses with which he was greeted on solemn occasions, breathe a spirit of submission without a parallel. "We hardly dare venture," is the language of one of them,[1] "to make demands, from an apprehension that we may set a limit to your Majesty's ecclesiastical zeal. The sad liberty we have of stating our grievances, is now changed into a sweet necessity for praising our benefactor." The prince of Condé thought that had the king been pleased to pass over to the protestant church, the clergy would be the first to follow him.

And at least as respected the pope, the clergy unhesitatingly stood by their king; year after year they promulgated more and more decided declarations in favour of the royal authority. At last there followed the general assembly of 1682. "It was summoned to meet and it was dissolved," says a Venetian ambassador, "according to the convenience of the council of state, and by its suggestions it was guided."[2] The four articles which it drew up, have passed ever since for the manifesto of the liberties of the Gallican church. The first three repeat old assertions; independence of the ecclesiastical power on the part of the secular, the superiority of a council above the pope, the inviolability of the Gallican usages. But the fourth is specially worthy of observation, because it also limits ecclesiastical authority. "Even in questions relating to the faith, the pope's decision is not be-

[1] Remontrance du clergé de France (assemblée à St. Germain en Laye en l'année 1680) faite au roi le 10 Juillet par l' illme et rév^{me} J. Bapt. Adheimar de Monteil de Grignan. Mém. du clergé tom. XIV. p. 787.—[Remonstrance of the clergy of France (assembled at St. Germain, en Laye, in the year 1680) made to the king on the 10th of July, by the most illustrious and most reverend J. Bapt. Adheimar de Monteil de Grignan.] See Mém. du Clergé tom. XIV. p. 787.

[2] Foscarini: Relatione di Francia, 1684. "Con non dissimile dipendenza segue l' ordine eccl^{co} le massime e l' interesse della corte, come l' ha fatto conoscere l' assemblea sopra le vertenze della regalia, unita, diretta e disciolta secondo le convenienze ed ispirationi del ministero politico. Provenendo dalla mano del re l' esaltatione e fortuna de' soggetti che lo compongono, dominati sempre da nuove pretensioni e speranze, si scorgono più attaccati alle compiacenze del monarca che gli stessi secolari."—[Foscarini's Report on France, 1684. With no dissimilar dependence, the ecclesiastical order follows the maxims and the interests of the court, as has been shown by the assembly on the diverting of the regalia, brought together, directed and dissolved according to tne convenience and inspirations of the ministry of state. As the elevation and fortune of the subjects composing it proceed from the hands of the king, being ever under the influence of new pretensions and expectations, they show more regard in their conduct to the good pleasure of the monarch than do the laity themselves.]

yond the possibility of being improved, as long as it remains without the assent of the church." We see the two powers support each other. The king was pronounced to be exempted from the interferences of the secular, and the clergy from the unlimited authority of the spiritual government of the popedom. Contemporaries considered that although people in France were still, indeed, within the Roman catholic church, they were on the very threshold of going out of it. The king elevated these maxims to a sort of articles of faith and symbolical book. They were to be taught ever after in all schools, and nobody could obtain a degree in the faculties of law or theology, without swearing to his profession of them.

But the pope too had his weapons. The king promoted the authors of the declaration, and the members of that assembly before all others to episcopal appointments; but Innocent refused to give them spiritual institution. They might enjoy the revenues, but they received no ordination; they dared not exercise any spiritual function of the episcopate.

This complication was further increased by the circumstance of Louis XIV. at that moment, and chiefly, too, for the purpose of manifesting his thorough orthodoxy, having proceeded to extirpate the Huguenots in the frightful manner related in history. He believed that he should thereby render great service to the Roman catholic church. It has likewise been said, indeed, that Pope Innocent was of one mind with him in reference to that proceeding.[1] But this in fact was not the case. The Roman court would have nothing to do at this period with a conversion effected by armed apostles; "Christ had not availed himself of such a method; people must be led into the temple, not driven into it."[2]

1 Bonamici, Vita Innocentii; in Lebret: Magazine VIII. p. 98, and Lebret's note; "Nor is it to be denied," &c.

2 Venier: Relatione di Francia, 1689: "Nell' opera tentata nella conversion degli Ugonotti dispiacque al re, non riportar dal pontefice lode che sperava, e ricevè il papa in mala parte che fosse intrapresa senza sua participatione et eseguita con i noti rigori, - - publicando che non fosse proprio fare missioni d' apostoli armati, e che questo metodo nuovo non fosse il migliore, giachè Christo non se n' era servito per convertire il mondo: in oltre parve importuno il tempo di guadagnar gli eretici all' ora che erano più bollenti le controversie col papa."—[Venier: Report on France, 1689. In what was attempted in the conversion of the Huguenots, the king was displeased at not having had bestowed on him by the pope the praise he merited, and the pope took it in bad part that he should have undertaken the enterprise without his participation, and followed it out with the known rigours, - - proclaiming

And new broils now perpetually occurred. In 1687, the French ambassador entered Rome with so strong a retinue, consisting even of several squadrons of cavalry, that it would have been no easy matter to have disputed with him the right of asylum, which the ambassadors claimed at that time, not only for their palace, but likewise for the adjacent streets. With an armed force he bearded the pope in his own capital. "They come with horse and chariot," said Innocent, "but we will go forth in the name of the Lord." He pronounced the censures of the church on the ambassador; and the church of St. Louis, in which the latter had attended a solemn high mass, was laid under the interdict.[1]

The king then likewise proceeded to take extreme measures. He appealed to a general council, caused Avignon to be occupied, and the nuncio to be imprisoned in St. Olon; it was thought that he meditated creating Archbishop Harlay of Paris, who if not the prime mover in all these steps, at least approved of them, patriarch of France.

Thus far were matters carried; the French ambassador at Rome excommunicated, the papal nuncio in France kept a prisoner, thirty-five French bishops without canonical institution, a papal territory taken possession of by the king; in all this the schism had in fact already broken out. Not the less on that account did Innocent XI. refuse to yield a single step.

If we ask to what he trusted for support in this inflexibility, it was not to the effect of his censures in France, not to the mighty influence of his apostolical authority; but it was above all to that general resistance which had been aroused in Europe to the enterprises of Louis XIV., threatening as these were to the existence of its liberties; to which resistance the pope too now gave his adhesion.

He supported Austria in its Turkish war to the best of his

that it was not fit to send out missions of armed apostles, and that this new method was not the best, since Christ had not made use of it in converting the world: further, the time appeared unseasonable for gaining heretics, just as the controversies with the pope were most keenly agitated.]

[1] Legatio marchionis Lavardini Romam ejusque cum Romano pontifice dissidium, 1697.—[Embassy of the Marquis of Lavardin and his quarrel with the Roman pontiff, 1697.] A refutation of Lavardin which discusses this event with much calmness and shrewdness. It belongs to a catalogue of striking public writings that were called forth by the encroachments of Louis XIV. in Germany, the Netherlands, Spain, and Italy.

power;[1] and the fortunate result of that campaign placed the whole party and the pope too in a new attitude.

It were no easy matter, certainly, to prove that Innocent, as has been said, stood in immediate alliance with William III., and was personally in the secret of the latter's designs upon England.[2] But with so much the greater confidence may we venture to assert that his ministers were privy to it. All that the pope was told was that the prince of Orange would take the chief command on the Rhine, and defend the rights of the empire as well as of the church against Louis XIV.; towards that he engaged to contribute considerable subsidies. But his secretary of state, Count Cassoni, had, as early as the end of 1687, precise information that the plan of the discontented in England was to dethrone King James, and to transfer the crown to the princess of Orange. The count was ill served, and the French had found a traitor among his domestics. From among the papers which the latter had found an opportunity of inspecting in his master's most secret cabinet, the courts of France and England received the first intelligence respecting these plans. Astounding complication! At the Roman court there met the threads of an alliance, which had for its object and for its result, the deliverance of protestantism in Western Europe from the last great danger that threatened it, and to gain the English throne for ever for that profession.[3] Granting that Innocent

[1] Relatione di Roma di Giov. Lando, 1689. The subsidies are here rated at two millions scudi.

[2] Also in the Mémoires sur le règne du Fréderic I., roi de Prusse, par le comte de Dohna,—[Memoirs of Frederick I. king of Prussia, by the count de Dohna,] p. 78, we find this assertion. The letters are said to have come through the queen of Sweden to his father; "qui les fesoit passer par le comté de Lippe, d' où un certain Paget les portoit à la Haye."—[who passed them by the county of Lippe, from whence a certain Paget carried them to the Hague.] In spite of the details of this piece of information, one must question their truth when we observe that Queen Christina was all this while on ill terms with the pope. Looking to the relation in which she stood to others as indicated by her correspondence, I hold it impossible that the pope, who once remarked with a shrug, "è una donna,"—[she is a woman,] would have trusted her with such a secret. Therewithal there might have been secret Roman dispatches.

[3] The Lettre écrite par le Cl d'Etrées, ambassadeur extraord. de Louis XIV., à M. de Louvois, 18 Dec. 1687, Œuvres de Louis XIV., tom. VI. p. 497,—[Letter written by the Cardinal d'Etrées, ambassador extraordinary of Louis XIV., to M. de Louvois, 18th Dec. 1687, Works of Louis XIV. vol. VI. p. 497,] little as it has been noticed, yet decisively settles this circumstance. It will be seen how soon James II. was informed. Young Lord Norfolk, then living incognito at Rome, sent off a courier to him immediately. Mackintosh (History of the Revolution, II. 157) assumes that James in the middle of May 1688, was convinced of the views of the

XI., as has been said, knew even nothing of this whole scheme, still it is undeniable, that he attached himself to an opposition that was in a great measure based on protestant resources and motives. The resistance he made to the candidate for the archbishopric of Cologne, that was favoured by France, was in the interests of that opposition, and mainly contributed to the commencement of hostilities.

Of hostilities which, nevertheless, in relation to France, had very fortunate consequences for the papal principle. If the pope, by his policy, promoted protestantism, the protestants in return, by preserving in its integrity the balance of power in Europe against the "exorbitant potentate," co-operated towards bringing the latter into compliance with the spiritual claims of the popedom.

It is true that Innocent XI. no longer lived to witness this. But the very first French ambassador that appeared in Rome after his death (10th August, 1689) renounced the right of asylum; the king's conduct became altered, he restored Avignon and began to negotiate.

This was so much the more necessary, as the new pope, Alexander VIII., however widely he may have departed from the rigorous example of his predecessor in other respects, yet on this point maintained his fundamental principles. Alexander declared anew the decrees of 1682[1] to be vain and invalid, null and void, having no binding power, even in the case of their having been confirmed with an oath; day and night he thought of the subject with a heart surcharged with bitter reflections;

Prince against England. But as early as the 10th or 11th of March, he said to the papal nuncio, "il principe avere in principal mira l'Inghilterra"—[that the prince had England for his principal object]. Lettera di Monsr d'Adda, ibid. p. 346.) It was his misfortune not to believe his own self.

[1] "In dictis comitiis anni 1682 tam circa extensionem juris regaliæ quam circa declarationem de potestate ecclesiastica actorum ac etiam omnium et singulorum mandatorum, arrestorum, confirmationum, declarationum, epistolarum, edictorum, decretorum quavis auctoritate sive ecclesiastica sive etiam laicali editorum, nec non aliorum quomodolibet præjudicialium præfatorum in regno supradicto quandocunque et a quibusvis et ex quacunque causa et quovis modo factorum et gestorum ac inde secutorum quorumcunque tenores, 4 Aug. 1690."—[The tenours of the acts of the said assembly of 1682, as well about the extension of the right of the regale, as about the declaration concerning the ecclesiastical power, and also of all and singular mandates, arrêts, confirmations, epistles, edicts, and decrees, published by whatever authority, ecclesiastical or even lay; as also of other foresaid acts, in whatsoever way prejudicial, in the said kingdom, at what time soever, by whom soever, from what cause soever, and in what manner soever done and carried on, and their consequences, 4th Aug. 1690.] Cocquel., IX. p. 38.

he was constantly giving expression to his feelings in tears and sighs.

Upon the death of Alexander VIII. the French used every endeavour to secure the transmission of the popedom to some peaceably-disposed and placable person;[1] which they succeeded in doing when Anthony Pignatelli—Innocent XII.—was made pope (12th July, 1691).

Nevertheless, even this pope was just as little disposed to abate aught of the dignity of the papal see, as there was little occasion for doing so, in as much as the allied arms employed Louis XIV. in so serious and threatening a manner.

Negotiations went on for two years. Innocent rejected more than once the formulas proposed to him by the French clergy. At last, however, they had in fact to declare that all that had been advised and concluded in that assembly, must be regarded as not advised and concluded; "casting ourselves at the feet of your Holiness, we confess our unutterable grief at what has been done."[2] It was only after such an unreserved retractation that Innocent gave the canonical institution.

It was only under these conditions that peace was restored. Louis XIV. wrote to the pope that he had recalled his ordi-

[1] Domenico Contarini: Relatione di Roma, 1696. "Tenendosi questa volta da Francesi bisogno d'un papa facile e d'animo assai rimesso e che potesse facilmente esser indotto a modificare la bolla fatta nell' agonia di Allessandro VIII. sopra le propositioni dell' assemblea del clero dell' anno 1682, diedero mano alla elettione di esso."—[The French, at this time having much need of a pope of an easy temper and sufficiently pusillanimous, and that could readily be induced to modify the bull rendered in the agony of Alexander VIII. on the propositions of the assembly of the clergy of 1682, gave their assistance in having him elected.]

[2] It has been asserted, indeed, and among others, Petitot (Notice sur Portroyal, p. 240) is of opinion that this document is an invention of the Jansenists, "pour répandre du ridicule et de l'odieux sur les nouveaux évêques"—[for the purpose of throwing ridicule and odium on the new bishops]; but in the first place there never has been any other formula produced on the other side, and then the above has been uniformly recognised, at least indirectly, by the Roman historians, for example in Novaes, Storia de' pontefici, tom. XI. p. 117; finally, at that very time it came to be generally held for genuine, even at the court, without contradiction. Domenico Contarini says: "Poco dopo fu preso per mano da Francesi il negotio delle chiese di Francia proponendo diverse formule di dichiarazione, - - materia ventilata per il corso di due anni e conclusa ed aggiustata con quella lettera scritta da vescovi al papa che si è diffusa in ogni parte."—[Shortly after, there was taken up by the French the affair of the churches of France, by proposing divers forms of declaration, - - a subject talked of for the course of two years, and concluded and adjusted with that letter written by the bishops to the pope, which has been circulated in all quarters.] Now, that was just the formula referred to. Any other has never been known. Daunou also, Essai historique sur la puissance temporelle des papes—[Historical essay on the temporal power of the popes], II. p. 196, communicates the letter as authentic.

nance respecting the observance of the four articles. It is evident that once more the Roman see maintained the plenitude of its claims, even in the face of the mightiest monarch.

But had not a grievous detriment already been inflicted by assertions, fraught with such decided animosity, having enjoyed for a long while an authority sanctioned by the laws and government? They had been promulgated with a deal of noise, as decrees of the kingdom: they were retracted privately, quite in a quiet way, in the form of a letter, and the retractation was further the act of but a few, who happened just at the time to be much in need of the favour of the Roman court. Louis XIV. allowed it to pass, but no man would venture to believe that he had recalled the four articles, although it was sometimes viewed in that light, even in Rome. Long subsequent to this, he would not allow such a thing as that the Roman court should refuse the institution to persons holding the four articles. He declared that he had merely repealed the obligation to teach them; but just as little was any man to be prevented from professing them.[1] And we have still further to remark, that it was in no wise through any force of its own, that the Roman court had maintained its ground, but only in consequence of a grand political combination, only through France in general having been driven back within closer limits. How then had these circumstances been altered, had there been no one any

[1] The words of the king in his letter to Innocent XII., Versailles, 14 Sept. 1693, are: " J'ai donné les ordres nécessaires afin que les chose scontenues dans mon édit du 22 Mars 1682 touchant la déclaration faite par le clergé de France (à quoi les conjonctures passées m'avoyent obligé) ne soyent pas observées."—[I have given the necessary orders in order that the things contained in my edict of 22d March, 1682, touching the declaration made by the clergy of France (to which past conjunctures have obliged me) be not observed. In a letter of 7th July, 1713, of which we are informed by Artaud (Histoire du Pape Pie VII. 1836, tom. II. p. 16), there are the following words relating to that time : " On lui (au Pape Clement XI.) a supposé contre la vérité, que j'ai contrevenu à l'engagement pris par la lettre que j'écrivis à son prédécesseur, car je n'ai obligé personne à soutenir contre sa propre opinion les propositions du clergé de France, mais il n'est pas juste que j'empêche mes sujets de dire et de soutenir leurs sentiments sur une matière qu'il est libre de soutenir de part et d'autre."—[He (Pope Clement XI.) was made to believe, contrary to the truth, that I have acted contrary to the engagement I had taken in the letter I wrote to his predecessor, for I have obliged no one to support, contrary to his own opinion, the propositions of the clergy of France, but it is not just that I should hinder my subjects from expressing and defending their opinions on a subject which one is free to hold either way.] It will be seen that Louis XIV., even in his last days, was not so bigoted a Romish devotee as he has been assumed to be. He says peremptorily, " je ne puis admettre aucun expédient"—[I cannot admit any expedient].

longer willing to take the Roman see under its safeguard against the assailing party.

SPANISH SUCCESSION.

THE dying out of the Spanish line of the house of Austria, was also an event of the utmost importance to the popedom.

The antagonism between the Spanish monarchy and France, which determined the character of European policy in general, likewise formed at last the basis of freedom and power of independent action in the papal see: through the maxims adopted by Spain, the states of the church had reposed in the lap of peace for the space of half a century. Whatever else might happen, it was at all times hazardous to introduce uncertainty into a state of things to which all the usages of the present time had a reference

But much more hazardous was it for the right of inheritance to give rise to a contest which threatened to result at last in a general war—a war, too, the grand theatre of which would necessarily be Italy. The pope himself could hardly escape from the necessity of taking a side in it, without his being able to flatter himself that he could contribute any thing effectual to secure the victory for the side he might espouse.

I find it was reported,[1] that Innocent XII., who by this time was reconciled with France, advised Charles II. of Spain to nominate the French princes to the inheritance, and that this advice of the holy father had mainly influenced the provisions of the testament on which so much depended.

At all events the Roman see abandoned the anti-French po-

[1] Morosini: Relatione di Roma, 1707. "Se il papa abbia avuto mano o partecipatione nel testamento di Carlo II., io non ardirò d'asserirlo, nè è facile di penetrare il vero con sicurezza. Bensi addurrò solo due fatti. L'uno che questo arcano, non si sa se con verità, fu esposto in un manifesto uscito alle stampe in Roma ne' primi mesi del mio ingresso all' ambasciata, all ora' che dall' uno e l'altro partito si trattava la guerra non meno con l'armi che con le carte. L'altro che il papa non s'astenne di far publici elogj al christ^mo d'essersi ritirato dal partaggio ricevendo la monarchia intiera per il nepote."—[Morosini: Report on Rome, 1707. Whether the pope has had any hand or participation in the testament of Charles II., I will not venture to assert, nor is it easy with safety to penetrate the truth. I will adduce only two facts as true. The one is, that this secret, it is not known whether truly, was set forth in a manifesto published in Rome during the first months of my entering on the embassy, at a time when war was carried on by both parties, no less with arms than with papers. The other is, that the pope does not refrain from eulogizing in public the most Christian king for having withdrawn himself from the partition, receiving the entire monarchy (of Spain) for his grandchild.]

licy which it had pursued, almost without exception, since the time of Urban VIII.: it might regard it as the slighter change and the smaller evil, for the entire monarchy, without partition, to go to a prince belonging to a house so pre-eminently Roman catholic in its conduct at that time. Clement XL, John Francis Albani, elected 16th November, 1700, openly commended the determination of Louis XIV. to take the succession; he despatched a letter of congratulation to Philip V., and granted him subsidies from ecclesiastical property, quite as if no doubts prevailed with respect to his rights.[1] Clement XI. might be regarded as a pupil, and justly as a representative of the Roman court, which he had never quitted; the affability of his manners, his literary talents, and his irreproachable life, had procured for him general popularity:[2] he had contrived to insinuate himself equally into the good graces of all the last three popes, different as they were, and to make himself necessary to them; rising to eminence by a practised, useful, and yet never unaccommodating capacity. Although he once said, that when cardinal he had always known how to give good advice, but that when pope he knew not which way to turn, this might have been meant to convey that he felt himself better fitted to adopt and carry forward an impulse communicated to him than to form and carry into effect a free determination of his own. When, among other things, he took up, from his very accession, the jurisdictional questions with fresh vigour, he only followed public opinion and the interests of the curia. So now did he trust also to the good fortune and the power of the great king. He had no doubt that Louis XIV. would come off victorious. On the occasion of the expedition directed from Germany and Italy against Vienna in 1703, which seemed likely to bring matters to a close, as the Venetian ambassador assures us, he could not conceal the joy and satisfaction he had received from the progress of the French arms.

1 Buder: Leben und Thaten Clemens XI. tom. I. p. 148.

2 Erizzo: Relatione di Roma, 1702. "In fatti pareva egli la delizia di Roma, e non eravi ministro regio nè natione che non credesse tutto suo il cardinale Albani. Tanto bene," he adds, "sapeva fingere affetti e variare linguaggio con tutti."—[Erizzo: Report on Rome, 1702. In short he seemed the delight of Rome, and there was not a royal minister or nation there that would not believe Cardinal Albani to be altogether theirs. So well, he adds, did he know how to feign affection and to vary his language with all.]

But at this very moment fortune suddenly changed; those German and English opponents of the king, to whom Innocent XI. had attached himself, but from whom Clement XI. had become estranged, obtained victories such as had never been known before; the imperial armies, united with the Prussian, poured on towards Italy; they had no idea of sparing a pope that had conducted himself so equivocally; and again was there a revival of those ancient claims of the empire that had never been thought of since the time of Charles V.

Not to enter into all the bitter contentions in which Clement XI. became involved,[1] at last the imperialists appointed a certain term for the acceptance of their proposals for peace, among which the most important was his recognizing the Austrian pretender (to the Spanish crown). The pope looked about him for assistance in vain. He waited till the appointed day, on allowing which to elapse without complying with their offers, the imperialists threatened a hostile attack on state and city, 15th January, 1709; nor till the last hour of that day, at eleven o'clock at night, did he give his signature. He had previously congratulated Philip V., and now found himself compelled to recognize his opponent, Charles III., as catholic king.[2]

In this, not only did the authority of the popedom, as supreme arbiter in settling differences, receive a severe check, but its political freedom and independence were wrested from it. The French ambassador left Rome with the declaration, that it was no longer the seat of the church.[3]

The position of the world, too, in general assumed a new aspect. It was protestant England at last, that decided the question with respect to the final destination of the Spanish and ca-

[1] For example, about the quartering of soldiers in Parma and Placentia; where the clergy even were obliged to pay their share of the war-contributions. Accord avec les députés du duc et de la ville de Plaisance 14 Dec. 1706, art. IX., que pour soulager l'état tous les particuliers, quoique très-privilégiés, contribueroient à la susditte somme.—[Agreement of the deputies of the duke and city of Placentia, 14th Dec. 1706, art. IX., that in order to alleviate the pressure on the state all individuals, although very much privileged, should contribute towards the said sum.] Even this the pope would not suffer. The imperial claims were thereupon renewed with redoubled earnestness. Contre-déclaration de l'empereur—[Counter-declaration of the emperor] in Lamberty, V. 85.

[2] This condition, kept secret at first, was made known by a letter from the Austrian ambassador to the duke of Marlborough, in Lamberty, V. 242.

[3] Lettre du Maréchal Thessé au pape, 12 Juillet 1709.—[Marshal Thessé's letter to the pope, 12th July, 1709.]

tholic monarchy; what influence, then, could the pope exercise over the great events of the time?

At the peace of Utrecht, countries which he looked upon as his fiefs, such as Sicily and Sardinia, were given away to new princes, without his being so much as consulted on the subject.[1] The convenience of the great powers took the place of the infallible decision of the supreme spiritual pastor

Nay, peculiar misfortunes fell to the lot of the papal see on this occasion.

It had always been one of the chief objects of its policy, to possess an influence over the Italian states, and to give effect, where possible, to an indirect sovereignty over them.

But now not only had German Austria established itself in Italy, in almost open warfare with the pope; the duke of Savoy too, in opposition to him, succeeded in acquiring royal power and ample new possessions.

And thus matters were carried still further.

In order to reconcile the contending houses of Bourbon and Austria, the powers of Europe complied with the wish of the queen of Spain to have Parma and Placentia made over to one of her sons. For the period of two centuries the papal rights of superiority over this dukedom had never been called in question: the princes had received feudal possession and paid tribute; but now that this right came to be of fresh importance, now that there was the prospect of an early extinction of the male line of the house of Farnese, no further regard was paid to it. The emperor bestowed the country as a fief on an infanta of Spain, while nothing remained for the pope but to give in his protest, to which nobody paid any attention.[2]

But the peace between the two houses proved but of momentary duration. In 1733, the Bourbons renewed their claims upon Naples, which was in the possession of Austria: the Spanish ambassador, too, proffered to the pope the palfrey and tribute. Pope Clement XII. would now have willingly allowed matters to remain as they were: he named a commission of

1 How suspicious the conduct of Savoy was, see Lafitau, Vie de Clément XI., tom. II. p. 78.

2 Protestatio nomine sedis apostolicæ emissa in conventu Cameracensi.—[Protest in the name of the apostolic see, emitted in the convention at Cambray.] See Pousset, Supplément au corps diplomatique de Dumont, III. II. p. 173.

cardinals, which decided in favour of the imperialist claims. But on this occasion, too, the fortune of war ran counter to the papal judgment; the Spanish arms were victorious. Clement had in a short time to adjudge the investiture of Naples and Sicily to the same infanta whom he had, with so much vexation, seen take possession of Parma.

It is true that the final result of all these contests was not so very unlike what the Roman court had originally contemplated; the Bourbon family had spread over Spain and a great part of Italy: but under what totally different circumstances had this taken place from what was originally intended.

The decisive word, at the most important moment, proceeded from England; and the Bourbons penetrated into Italy in open contradiction to the papal see: the separation of the provinces, which it had been sought to avoid, had just taken place, and had filled Italy and the states of the church incessantly with hostile weapons. Hereby the secular authority of the papal see was annihilated in its own immediate circle.

This, accordingly, must have powerfully re-acted also on those questions regarding ecclesiastical rights which were so closely connected with political circumstances.

How grievously had Clement XI. even now to feel all this!

His nuncio was more than once removed out of Naples: in Sicily, those clergy whose opinions leant to the side of Rome, were on one occasion apprehended in a body and sent off to the states of the church;[1] forthwith it began to be made an object in all the Italian territories to allow none but natives to obtain ecclesiastical dignities:[2] the nunciatura came to a close likewise in Spain,[3] and Clement XI. thought himself even compelled to bring the leading Spanish minister, Alberoni, before the Inquisition.

These embroilments had a wider and wider range from year to

[1] Buder, Leben und Thaten Clemens XI., tom. III. p. 571.—[Buder's Life and Acts of Clement XI., vol. III. p. 571.]

[2] From Lorenzo Tiepolo, Relatione di Roma, 1712—[L. Tiepolo's Report on Rome, 1712], we see that the imperialists in Naples as well as Milan already had it in contemplation, "che li beneficii ecclesiastici siano solamente dati a nationali, colpo di non picciolo danno alla corte di Roma se si effettuasse."—[that the church livings should be given solely to natives, a blow that would in no small degree injure the Roman court, were it effected.]

[3] San Felipe, Beiträge zur Geschichte von Spanien, III. 214.—[San Felipe's contributions to the History of Spain, III. 214.]

year. The Roman court no longer possessed the force and inward energy requisite for keeping the faithful of its own fold united together.

"I must confess," says the Venetian ambassador Moncenigo, in 1737, "there is something contrary to nature when one surveys the Roman catholic governments in a body involved in quarrels of such importance with the Roman court, that no reconciliation can be thought of that must not damage that court in its vital force. Whether it be from people being more enlightened, as so many assume, or from a spirit of violent oppression of the weak, certain it is that the princes (of Roman catholic Europe) are hastening with rapid strides to deprive the Roman see of all its civil prerogatives.[1]

One needed but raise his eyes at Rome and look about him, in order to be convinced that all was at stake, if offers of peace were not immediately held out.

Blessings have been poured on the memory of Benedict XIV. —Prospero Lamberti, 1740-1758—for having come to the resolution of conceding the points which were considered indispensable.

It is well known how little Benedict XIV. allowed himself to be dazzled by the consequences attached to the dignified office he held, or to be inflated with self-confidence. While pope, he was never false to his naturally facetious vivacity, and love of Bolognese witticisms. He would stop in the midst of business, step up to his attendants, deliver himself of some conceit that had struck his fancy, and go back to his table to resume his work.[2] He ever kept above things (instead of allowing himself to be overborne by them), and after a liberal survey of the relation in which the papal see stood to the European powers, saw what should be retained and what abandoned. He was too good

[1] Aluise Moncenigo IV.: Relatione di Roma, 16 Apr. 1737. See the Appendix.

[2] Relatione di F. Venier di Roma, 1744: "Asceso il papa al trono di S. Pietro, non seppe cambiare l'indole sua. Egli era di temperamento affabile insieme e vivace, e vi restò: spargeva fin da prelato li suoi discorsi con giocosi sali, ed ancor li conserva: - - dotato di cuore aperte e sincero trascurò sempre ogn' una di quelle arti che si chiamano romanesche."—[F. Venier's Report on Rome, 1744. The pope, having ascended the throne of St. Peter, knew not how to alter his natural disposition. He was of a temper at once affable and lively, and remained so; from the time of his being a prelate he interspersed his discourse with witty sayings, and still preserved the habit: - - endued with an open and sincere heart, he neglected every one of those arts that are called 'romanesque.']

a canonist and also too much of a pope, to allow himself in this respect to be carried too far.

Certainly the most extraordinary act of his pontificate was the concordat which he concluded with Spain in 1753. He prevailed on himself to renounce that right of presenting to the smaller benefices which the curia had always possessed there, although now under violent opposition. But was the court to lose the important advantages in money which it had hitherto derived, without any compensation? Was the papal government likewise to lose at one stroke all its influence on the clergy personally? Benedict compromised the matter as follows. Of those benefices, fifty-two were set apart by name, to remain in the gift of the pope, "wherewith he might reward such of the Spanish clergy as should earn a claim to them by their virtuous conduct, purity of manners, learning, or by services rendered to the Roman see."[1] The loss sustained by the curia was estimated in money. It was found to amount to 34,300 scudi. The king engaged to pay a capital sum, the interest of which, at 3 per cent., should amount to as much: that is, 1,143,330 scudi. Thus all-equalizing money showed its mediating power at last, even in ecclesiastical affairs.

With most of the other courts likewise, Benedict XIV. concluded arrangements in which he submitted to concessions. The right of patronage which the king of Portugal already possessed, was extended, and to the other ecclesiastical honorary titles which he had earned there was added that of "Most Faithful." The court of Sardinia—doubly dissatisfied because the concessions it had obtained at favourable conjunctures, had been revoked under the last pontificate—was pacified by means of concordat-instructions, issued in 1741 and 1750.[2] In Naples,

1 "Acciò non meno S. Sta che i suoi successori abbiano il modo di provedere e premiare quegli ecclesiastici che per probità e per illibatezza de' costumi o per insigne letteratura o per servizi prestati alla s. sede se ne renderanno meritevoli."—[So that not less than his Holiness, his successors may have the means of providing for and rewarding such of the clergy,] &c.; see the text. Words of the concordat among other places in the English Committee report, 1816, p. 317. From an instruction of Caravajal's (printed in Cantillo Tratados de Paz, p. 425), it appears that the views of the Roman court had originally gone much farther. Besides the official negotiation there was a secret one carried on through the confidential minister, Ensenada. The pope himself drew up the concordat; Ensenada transmitted the money before it had as yet been subscribed.

2 Risposta alle notizie dimandate intorno alla giurisdittione ecclesiastica nello stato di S. M[ta.] Turino, 5 Marzo 1816, ibid. p. 250.—[Reply to the notices required

where, even under the auspices of the imperial government, particularly through the instrumentality of Gaetano Argento, a school for jurisprudence had been formed, which made the disputed points in ecclesiastical law its leading study, and which warmly resisted the papal claims,[1] Benedict XIV. allowed the rights of the nunciatura to be limited in no inconsiderable degree, and the clergy to be subjected to the payment of a proportion of the taxes. To the imperial court was conceded that diminution of the number of commanded holidays which at its time caused so much surprise; while the pope merely allowed labour to be done on these days, the imperial court scrupled not to make it compulsory.

In this fashion did the Roman catholic courts once more reconcile themselves with their ecclesiastical chief; peace was once more restored.

But might one indeed venture to persuade himself that with this all was done? Was the contest between state and church, based as it almost seemed to be on an internal necessity of Roman catholicism, likely to be arranged by such shallow compromises? It was impossible that these could do more than suffice for the moment at which they appeared. Forthwith new and far more violent storms announced their approach on the excited deep.

CHANGE IN THE GENERAL POSITION OF THE WORLD.—INTERNAL FERMENTATION.—SUPPRESSION OF THE JESUITS.

Not only in Italy, in the south of Europe, but in the political posture of affairs in general, the greatest revolution had been accomplished.

Where were now the times in which, and not indeed without reason, the popedom ventured to entertain the hope of making the conquest anew of Europe and the world?

Three non-catholic powers had risen up among the five great monarchies which, in the midst of the eighteenth century, were already determining the course of the world's history. We have mentioned what attempts were made by the popes at ear-

respecting the ecclesiastical jurisdiction in his Majesty's state. Turin, 5th March, 1816], in the above Committee Report, p. 250.

[1] Giannone: Storia di Napoli, VI. 387.

lier periods to overpower Russia and Prussia from Poland, and England from France and Spain. Those very powers now had their share in the dominion of the world; nay, one may say with truth, that at that period they had the preponderance over the Roman catholic half of Europe.

Not perhaps that there had been a triumph of one system of doctrine over the other, of the protestant over the Roman catholic; the controversy between them was no longer waged in that field, but the change had come in by means of national developments, the fundamental grounds of which we have perceived above: the states on the non-Roman catholic side displayed a superiority over the Roman catholic on general points. The monarchical disposition of the Russians, by tending to make their empire compact, had triumphed over the easily disunited aristocracy of Poland,—the industry, the practical sense, the good seamanship of the English had done the same over the remissness of the Spaniards and the fluctuating policy of the French, always dependent on casual changes in their internal circumstances,—the energetic organization and military discipline of Prussia, had equally triumphed over the principles of a federative monarchy as then presented in Austria.

Now although this preponderance was not in any wise of an ecclesiastical nature, yet it could not fail to exercise a necessary reaction on ecclesiastical affairs.

First, this arose at once from religious parties rising into eminence along with the states with which they were connected. Russia, for example, without further ado, placed bishops of the Greek church in the united provinces of Poland;[1] the elevation of Prussia gradually re-inspired the German protestants with a consciousness of independence and power such as they had not felt for a long while; the more decidedly the protestant government of England rose to the command of the sea, the more the Roman catholic missions necessarily fell into the shade and lost their efficiency, which, indeed, was based of old on political influence.

But in a wider sense, too, even before the expiration of the second half of the seventeenth century, when England was implicated in the policy of France, when Russia was virtually se-

[1] Rulhière: Histoire de l'anarchie de Pologne, I. 181.

parated from the rest of Europe, and when the combined government of Brandenburg and Prussia was just rising for the first time to eminence, the Roman catholic powers, France, Spain, Austria, and Poland, governed the European world, even though at variance among themselves. It must, methinks, have gradually forced itself on one's conviction, that this state of things had become very much changed; the self-confidence natural to a politico-religious system circumscribed by no superior power beyond itself, must have vanished. The pope was now first convinced that he no longer stood at the head of the government that lorded it over the world.

But, lastly, should we pay no regard to the originating causes of this change? Every defeat, every loss will, on the side of the beaten party, if not driven to despair, call forth some internal change, some imitation of the adversary that has proved his superiority, some rivalry with him. The strictly monarchical. military-commercial tendencies of the non-Roman catholic world now forced their way into the Roman catholic states. Yet, as it was undeniable that the disadvantage into which they had fallen, was connected with their ecclesiastical constitution, this movement accordingly first threw itself on that side.

But here it met with other powerfully fermenting elements, which meanwhile had burst forth on the territory of faith and opinion within the circle of Roman catholicism.

The Jansenist contentions, whose origin we have been contemplating, had been renewed with redoubled vehemence since the commencement of the eighteenth century. They had their source in the highest places of society. The chief influence in the supreme ecclesiastical council in France used to be exercised by the king's confessor, generally a Jesuit, and the archbishop of Paris. From that quarter La Chaise and Harlay, in close alliance with each other, directed the proceedings of the crown against the popedom. Their successors, le Tellier and Noailles, were not so well agreed. Slight differences of opinion may have furnished the first occasion for their discord; the one holding more strictly to the Jesuit, Molinist, the other, more tolerant, to the Jansenist views; but their differences gradually led to an open breach: the nation was rent by a schism which began in the cabinet of the king. The confessor succeeded not only in keeping himself in power and in gaining over the king, but also in inducing the pope to publish the bull Unigenitus, in which the Jansenist doctrines of sin, grace, justification, and the church were anathematized, even in the less austere expression of them, sometimes word for word, as it was assumed they were to be found in Augustinus, and far more extensively than in the five propositions above mentioned.[1] It was the final determination of the old questions respecting the faith that had been agitated by Molina; the Roman see, after so long a delay, at last, without hesitation, adopted the Jesuit side. It certainly succeeded thereby in attaching to its interests that powerful order, which has ever since, what it by no means formerly always did, uniformly abetted, with the utmost warmth, the ultra-montane doctrines and the claims of the papal government; it succeeded also in remaining on good terms with the French government, which, indeed, had called forth the above decision; soon such persons only as submitted to the bull, were placed in public situations. But on the other side, too, there arose the most violent opposition: among the learned, those who adhered to Augustine—in the religious orders, those who held by Thomas Aquinas—in the parliaments, which viewed every new act of the Roman court as an injury done to the Gallican church; and now at last, the Jansenists became the eager partisans of these franchises: with an ever-advancing courage they matured a doctrine on the subject of the church, which ran counter to the Roman on that point; nay, under the safeguard of a protestant government, they gave effect forthwith to their idea: there arose an archiepiscopal church at Utrecht, which held itself to be in general Roman catholic, yet withal absolutely independent of Rome, and waged an incessant warfare on the Jesuit ultra-montane tendency. It were well worth the pains to trace out the development, ex-

1 The Mémoires secrets sur la bulle Unigenitus, I. p. 123—[Secret memoirs on the bull Unigenitus], describe the first impression it produced. "Les uns publioient qu'on y attaquoit de front les premiers principes de la foi et de la morale; les autres qu'on y condamnoit les sentiments et les expressions des saints pères; d'autres qu'on y enlevoit à la charité sa prééminence et sa force; d'autres qu'on leur arrachoit des mains le pain céleste des écritures: les nouveaux réunis à l'église se disoient trompés," etc. etc.—[Some proclaimed that the first principles of the faith and of morality were directly attacked in it; others that the sentiments and expressions of the holy fathers were condemned in it; others that charity was deprived in it of its pre-eminence and its force; others that the heavenly bread of the scriptures was snatched from their hands: those who had been recently re-united to the church, said they were deceived, &c. &c.]

tension, and practical influence of these opinions over all Europe. In France the Jansenists were oppressed, persecuted, and excluded from public offices; but, as usually happens, this did them no damage in the main point: during the persecutions, a large proportion of the public declared in their favour. Had they but avoided throwing discredit even on their well-founded doctrines, by their extravagancies in giving credit to miracles! But at all events they preserved a close association with greater purity of morals and a deeper faith, which every where smoothed the way for them. We find traces of them in Vienna and in Brussels, in Spain and Portugal,[1] and in every part of Italy.[2] They disseminated their doctrines throughout all Roman catholic christendom, sometimes openly, oftener in secret.

There can be no doubt that it was this dissension among the clergy, among other things, that opened the way for the rise of a far more dangerous spirit.

It will ever be a remarkable phenomenon what influence the religious efforts of Louis XIV. produced upon the French mind, nay, upon that of Europe in general. In his eagerness to extirpate protestantism, and even to annihilate all departures from strict orthodoxy within the Roman catholic church, he had employed the most extreme violence, had outraged the laws of God and man, his whole efforts had been directed to giving his kingdom a thorough and orthodox Roman catholic character. But hardly had death closed his eyes, when all was reversed. The spirit that had been forcibly repressed, broke away from all restraint.

The disgust caused by the proceedings of Louis XIV., led directly to the rise of opinions which declared war not only against Roman catholicism, but against all positive religion in general. From year to year these increased in internal force, and spread more and more widely. The kingdoms of Southern Europe were founded on the closest union of church and state. Here a spirit matured itself, which carried opposition to the

[1] It may be seen in Llorente's Histoire de l'Inquisition, III. pp. 93-97—[History of the Inquisition, vol. III. pp. 93-97], how much the Inquisition under Charles III. and Charles IV. had to do with real or pretended Jansenists.

[2] For example, very early in Naples; as early as in 1715 it was believed that the half of people of any measure of reflection were Jansenists. See Keyssler Reisen [Keyssler's Travels], p. 780.

church and to religion into a system, in which were comprehended all notions respecting God and the world, all political and social principles, and all the sciences,—a literature of opposition which captivated men's minds in spite of themselves, and subjected them to a yoke that nothing could shake off.

It is manifest how little accord there was between these tendencies; the reforming, in conformity with its nature, was monarchical; which cannot be said of the philosophical, for that very soon uniformly set itself in opposition to the state; the Jansenists held fast to convictions which were viewed by both with indifference, if not with hatred; but at first they contributed to bring about the same results as the others. They produced that spirit of innovation, which spreads the more extensively, the less it has any precise aim, and the more it lays claim to the whole of futurity, and daily derives fresh force from the abuses of the existing order of things. This spirit now seized the Roman-catholic church. It certainly had its foundation in general, consciously or unconsciously, in what has been called the philosophy of the eighteenth century; the Jansenist theories gave it an ecclesiastical form and bearing, and it derived an active impulse from the necessities of the civil governments and the opportuneness of the moment. In all countries, and at all courts, there were formed two parties, the one of which waged hostilities with the curia and the accredited constitution and doctrines of the day, while the other sought to keep things as they were, and to preserve the prerogatives of the general church.

The last was represented most especially in the Jesuits; that order appeared as the main bulwark of the ultra-montane principles; and it was first against it that the storm directed its fury.

Even in the eighteenth century the Jesuits were still very powerful; as at an earlier period, chiefly from their possessing the confessional seat of the great and of monarchs, and conducting the instruction of youth, their enterprises, whether in the field of religion, although not carried on, it must be allowed, with all the old energy, or in that of commerce too, still embraced the world. They now held unwaveringly to the doctrines of ecclesiastical order and subordination; and what in any wise ran counter to these, direct infidelity, Jansenist views, tendencies to reform, all were involved, according to them, in the same anathema.

First they were attacked on the field of opinion—of literature. It is certainly not to be denied, that to the numbers and the force of the foes that pressed upon them, they opposed rather a stubborn persistance in the doctrines they had once embraced, indirect influence with the great, and an eagerness to consign their adversaries to damnation, than the genuine weapons of the intellect. One can hardly comprehend how it could happen that neither they themselves nor others of the faithful that made common cause with them, produced a single original and effective book in their defence, while the world was deluged with the works of their adversaries, and the convictions of the public firmly moulded by them.

But after being once beaten on this field of doctrine, science, and intellect, neither could they any longer keep themselves in possession of power.

About the middle of the eighteenth century, the helm of affairs, in opposition to both these tendencies, came to be held in almost all Roman catholic countries by reforming ministers: in France by Choiseul,[1] in Spain by Wall and Squillace, in Naples by Tanucci, in Portugal by Carvalho; all men who made it the object of their lives to keep down the preponderance of the clerical element in the social system. In their persons the church opposition was represented and became powerful; their personal position depended upon it, and open hostility became so much the more unavoidable, as the Jesuits, by means of personal counteraction and of their influence in the highest circles, thwarted their measures.

As yet there was no idea of extirpating the order: all that was at first contemplated was their removal from courts, and the depriving them of their credit, and, where possible, of their wealth. To this it was believed that even the Roman court

[1] In the appendix to Mad. du Hausset's memoirs there will be found an essay, de la destruction des Jésuites en France [on the destruction of the Jesuits in France], in which Choiseul's aversion to the Jesuits is traced to the circumstance of the general having once given him to understand in Rome, that he knew what had been said at a supper in Paris. But that is a story which is repeated in various ways, and hardly has much in it. Matters lay somewhat deeper.

might be induced to lend its aid. The schism that rent the Roman catholic world, had at length, in a certain sense, made its appearance there also; there was a strict and a tolerant party; Benedict XIV., who represented the latter, had long been dissatisfied with the Jesuits, and had often openly condemned their conduct in regard to missions.[1]

After Carvalho, amid the agitation caused by the factions at the Portuguese court, had in spite of the Jesuits, who endeavoured to subvert him, come off absolute master of the government, and even of the royal will, he called upon the pope to reform the order.[2] He insisted most, as was natural, on the view of the case that presented most room for scandal, the mercantile turn that the society had taken, which, moreover, had very much thwarted him in his commercial efforts. The pope felt no scruples in entertaining his proposal. The bustling assiduity of the order in secular business was disgusting to himself, and so, at the suggestion of Carvalho, he charged a friend of his and a Portuguese, Cardinal Saldanha, with a visitation of the order. In a short while this visitor issued a decree seriously reprimanding the Jesuits for their commercial dealings, and authorizing the royal functionaries to confiscate all merchandise belonging to those spiritual persons.

And meanwhile the society had already been assailed on the same side in France. The bankruptcy of a commercial house connected with Father Lavallette at Martinique, which led to a great many other failures, gave occasion for those who had suffered by these failures, to carry their complaints before the law courts, and these zealously took the case in hand.[3]

Had Benedict XIV. remained longer in life, there is much ground to suppose, that although he might not perhaps have abolished the order, he would have subjected it to a thorough and fundamental reform.

At this moment, however, Benedict XIV. died, and there went forth from the conclave as pope, 6th July, 1758, a man of an opposite character, namely, Clement XIII.

[1] This he had already done as Prelate Lambertini. Mémoires du père Norbert, II. 20.

[2] On the Jesuit side this strife of factions is very graphically described in a History of the Jesuits in Portugal, translated by Murr from an Italian manuscript.

[3] Vie privée de Louis XV., IV. p. 88.—[Private Life of Louis XV., v. IV. p. 88.]

Clement was a man of a pure soul and pure intentions; one that prayed much and fervently, and whose highest ambition it was to be one day pronounced a saint. Therewithal, however, he entertained the opinion, that all the claims of the popedom were sacred and inviolable; he deeply lamented that any of them had ever been dropped; he was resolved to make no concessions of any kind; nay, he lived in the conviction that all might yet be gained, and the sullied splendour of Rome restored again by a determined conservatism.[1] In the Jesuits he beheld the most faithful defenders of the papal see and of religion; he approved of them just as they were, and thought they had no need of reformation. In all this he was confirmed by the circle with which he was surrounded, and which joined in his devotions.

It cannot be said that Cardinal Torregiani, in whose hands lay chiefly the administration of the papal power, was in like manner penetrated with spiritual sentiments. He much rather bore the character of having, for example, a personal interest in the farming of the papal revenues, and in general, of being fond of power for its own sake. But was it not of great consequence on these accounts likewise, to maintain the order in its integrity? All the influence, wealth, and authority, on account of which the Jesuits were hated by the jealous viceroys in America, and ministers struggling for pre-eminence in Europe, they laid at last at the feet of the Roman see. Torregiani made their cause his own, and his doing so strengthened his position at court in return. The only person capable of subverting him, the papal nephew, Rezzonico, dreaded lest by so doing he should injure the church of God.[2]

But as matters stood in the world, this zeal, springing from a diversity of motives, could have no effect but that of mak-

[1] See Collection of the most remarkable writings relative to the abolition of the Jesuits, 1773, I. p. 211. How much the general opinion was on the other side, may be seen, among other things, from Winkelmann's letters.

[2] Carattere di Clemente XIII. e di varj altri personaggi di Roma.—[Character of Clement XIII. and of various other personages at Rome.] Manuscript in the British Museum, 8430: "La diffidenza che (il papa) ha di se medesimo e la soverchia umiliazone che lo deprime lo fa differire ai sentimenti altrui che sono per lo più o sciocchi o interessati o maligni. - - Chi lo dovrebbe scuotere non si move. - - "—[The distrust that he (the pope) has of himself, and the excessive humility that depresses him, makes him defer to the sentiments of others, who are, for the most part, silly persons, or interested, or malignant. - - He who ought to move him never stirs. - -]

ing the attacks still more vehement, and of directing them at the same time against the Roman see.

In Portugal, one cannot yet see clearly how far deservedly or not, the Jesuits came to be involved in the investigation made into an attempt on the life of the king:[1] one blow followed after another; finally they were expelled with merciless violence, and transported to the coasts of the states of the church.

Meanwhile in France they had fallen, in consequence of the above lawsuit, into the power of the parliaments, by which they had been hated from the first. Their cause was conducted with a deal of noise: at last the whole society was adjudged to be liable for the fulfilment of Lavalette's engagements. But people did not stop at this point. The constitution of the Jesuit order was subjected anew to scrutiny, and doubts were cast on the lawfulness of its existence in the kingdom in general.

The points on which the result depended in this affair, are remarkable and characteristic.

Two things in particular were objected against the order: its persistence in impugning the four Gallican maxims, and the unlimited power of the general.

The former of these, however, now formed no insurmountable difficulty. The general of the Jesuits was not opposed to the members of the order being at least tacitly permitted to abstain from impugning the four maxims, and in fact, we find in the negotiations of the French clergy of 1761, that they offered to regulate themselves according to these in their expositions of doctrine.

But it was quite otherwise with the latter objection.

The parliaments, a commission nominated by the king, and

[1] In the judgment of 12th January, 1759, weight was attached chiefly to certain "legitimate suspicions" against the "perverse regular clergy of the Society of Jesus." The principal are: their ambitious desire to possess themselves of the reins of the government of the kingdom (§ 25), their arrogance previous to the attempt, their despondency after its failure (§ 26), finally, and indeed far more aggravating, their great intimacy with the principal person among the accused, Mascarenhas, with whom, previously, they had been on bad terms. Father Costa was alleged to have said, that in slaying the king, "a man would not even commit a venial sin." (§ 4.) But it has been remarked, on the other hand, that the confessions on which these statements rest, were extorted by torture, and that the proceedings of the trial in general are full of marks of precipitation and informalities. The sentence never indeed can be justified juridically. Compare von Olfers on the attempt to murder the king of Portugal, 3d Sept. 1758, Berlin, 1839. According to a letter given by Smith in his memoirs of the Marquis of Pombal, I. 287, Cardinal Acciguoli, on his return from Portugal, declared explicitly, "that the Jesuits were undoubtedly the authors of the attempted assassination." II. M. Dom Joseph.

even the majority of an assembly of the French clergy, convened by Cardinal Luynes,[1] unanimously concurred in the following judgment,—that the obedience which, in conformity with the statutes, the general resident in Rome was authorized to require, was irreconcileable with the laws of the kingdom and with the duty of subjects in general.[2]

It was not with the intention of annihilating the order, but much rather with that of rescuing it, where possible, from ruin, that the king caused it to be proposed to the general, that a vicar should be nominated for France, who should fix his residence there, and should be bound to obey the laws of the country.

Had such a person as Aquaviva been now at the head of its affairs, there is no doubt that some expedient or other, some compromise of differences, would have been thought of. But the society had at this time the most inflexible chief, Lorenzo Ricci, who felt nothing but the injustice that was done to him. The point attacked appeared to him to be the most important, both ecclesiastically and politically. His encyclical letters still extant, show at what an immense value he estimated personal discipline in the duty of obedience, in all the severity preached up by Ignatius. Besides this it was suspected in Vienna, that the only object aimed at by the various kingdoms, was to render themselves independent of the government of the church; and the request made to the general of the Jesuits seemed to confirm this suspicion. He replied, that to so essential a change of the constitution it was beyond his power to consent. The pope was then applied to, and Clement XIII. replied that that constitution had been formally approved all too clearly by the holy council of Trent, and by too many solemn acts of his predecessors, to admit of his being able to alter it.[3] They rejected every modification. It was quite Ricci's sentiment: *sint ut sunt, aut non sint* [let them be as they are, or cease to be].

The result was, that they were to cease to be. The parlia-

1 St. Priest, Chute des Jésuites—[Fall of the Jesuits], p. 54.

2 Praslin's letter, 16th Jan. 1762, in Flassan's Hist. de la diplomatie Française—[History of French diplomacy], VI. 498. The whole account is very instructive.

3 Account of the Jesuits in Wolf: Geschschte der Jesuiten, III. 365. book is of no use except with regard to the abolition of the order.

ment, which had now no further obstacle to obstruct its course, declared (6th Aug. 1762) that the institute of the Jesuits ran counter to all ecclesiastical and civil authority, and was calculated for the purpose first of rendering itself independent by means secret and open, direct and indirect, and ultimately of even usurping the government: it pronounced that the order should be irrevocably and for ever excluded from the kingdom. True, the pope intimated at a meeting of the consistory that this decree was null and void;[1] but matters had already advanced so far, that he durst not venture to give publicity to the allocution in which he did this.

And this movement spread incessantly over all countries subject to the Bourbon sway. Charles III. of Spain came to be convinced that it was a plan of the Jesuits to advance his brother Don Louis in his stead to the throne;[2] upon this, with all the determined love of secrecy that generally characterized him, he caused every thing to be had in readiness, and the houses of the Jesuits, on one and the same day, to be shut up all over Spain. This example was followed in Naples and Parma without delay.

In vain were all the pope's admonitions, entreaties, and obtestations. At last he made yet a further effort. On the duke of Parma going so far as even to forbid recourse to the Roman tribunal, as well as all bestowing of benefices within the country on any but natives, the pope summoned up courage to publish a monitorium, in which he denounced spiritual censures against that vassal of his.[3] Once more were spiritual weapons

[1] "Potestatem ipsam Jesu Christi in terris vicario ejus unice tributam sibi temere arrogantes totius societatis compagem in Gallico regno dissolvunt, etc."—[Rashly arrogating to themselves the very power given by Jesus Christ solely to his vicar on earth, they dissolve the entire bond of the society in the Gallic kingdom, &c.] Daunou has this judicial paper, II. 207.

[2] Letter of the French ambassador, which has been transferred from the Italian work, Delle cagioni dell' espulsione de' Gesuiti, in Lebret's Geschichte der Bulle In cœna Domini, IV. 205. A Relatione al conte di Firmian, 1767, 7 Apr. (MS. of Brera) assures us that the Jesuits, nevertheless, had a pre-intimation. "Non fu senza forte motivo che poco prima di detta espulsione dimandarono al re la conferma de' loro privilegi e del loro instituto, il che solamente in oggi si è saputo."—[It was not without strong grounds, that shortly previous to the said expulsion, they called upon the king for a confirmation of their privileges, and of their institute, which is only at present certainly known.] They had removed their money and papers out of the way. But so great did the advantage gained by the crown appear to Charles III., that after the affair was over, he said he had conquered a new world.

[3] Botta: Storia d' Italia, tom. XIV. p. 147.—[Botta's History of Italy, vol. XIV. p. 147.]

wielded, and an attempt made at defence in the way of returning the assault. But it had the worst consequences: the duke replied in a way that the mightiest would not have ventured on some centuries sooner: the Bourbons made common cause with each other. They occupied Avignon, Benevento, and Pontecorvo.

Such was the direction in which the hostility of the Bourbon courts developed itself. From persecuting the Jesuits they directly proceeded to make an attack upon the Roman see. It was actually proposed that Rome should be attacked with a military force, and reduced by starvation.

To whom was the pope now to turn for help? All the Italian states, Genoa, Modena, Venice, sided against him. Once more he directed his eyes to Austria, and wrote to the empress Maria Theresa, that she was his only consolation on the earth: she could not possibly permit such a thing as that his old age should be oppressed with acts of violence.

The empress replied, as Urban VIII. did on one occasion to the emperor Ferdinand, that it was an affair of state and not of religion, and that it would be injustice on her part to interfere.

The spirit of Clement XIII. was broken. At the commencement of 1769, the ambassadors of the Bourbon courts, one after another, made their appearance; first the Neapolitan, then the Spanish, last of all the French, requiring the irrevocable suppression of the whole order.[1] The pope summoned a meeting of the consistory for the 3d of February, at which he seemed willing at least to take the matter into consideration. But it was not fated that he should outlive such profound depression. The evening before the meeting he had a convulsion fit, of which he died.

The position assumed by the courts was too threatening, their influence too powerful, for them not to carry their object in the conclave that now followed, and to promote to the triple crown such a person as they needed.

Of all the cardinals, the mildest and most moderate unquestionably was Lorenzo Ganganelli. In his younger days one of his masters had said of him, that it was no wonder he loved

[1] Continuazione degli annali d' Italia di Muratori, XIV. 1, p. 197.—[Continuation of Muratori's Annals of Italy, XIV. 1, p. 197.]

music, for in himself all was harmony.[1] Thus was his character further developed in innocent companionship, retirement from the world, solitary studies, which carried him ever deeper and deeper into the mystery of true theology. As he soon passed from Aristotle to Plato, who gave greater contentment to his soul, so he passed from the schoolmen to the early fathers of the church, and from these again to the Holy Scriptures, which he seized with all the fervour of a mind convinced of the divine revelation of the Word; at whose hand he then became penetrated with that still and pure mysticism which sees God in everything, and devotes itself to the good of its neighbour. His religion was not zeal, persecution, thirst for power, polemics, but peace, humility, and inward intelligence. The everlasting contention of the papal see with the governments of the Roman catholic states, which distracted the church, he heartily detested. His moderation did not spring from weakness, or any imposed necessity, but flowed spontaneously from inherent kindliness.

From the bosom of religion there was developed a disposition of mind which, however it might differ in its origin from the worldly tendencies of the court, yet coalesced with these, though proceeding from another side.

Ganganelli carried his election in the conclave mainly through the influence of the Bourbons, and immediately at the suggestion of the Spanish and French cardinals. He called himself Clement XIV.

The Roman curia, as has been mentioned, was, like other bo-

[1] Aneddoti riguardanti la familia e l'opere di Clemente XIV.—[Anecdotes regarding the family and the works of Clement XIV.], in the Lettere ed altre opere di Ganganelli, Firenze, 1829—[Letters and other works of Ganganelli, Florence, 1829]. As far as respects these works and letters, they may indeed have been interpolated, but in the main I consider them genuine: 1. because the defence that has been made of them in the Ringratiamento dell' editore all' autor dell' anno literario—[Thanks of the editor to the author of the literary world], is, on the whole, natural and satisfactory, although previous to the publication an unwarrantable use was made of it; 2. because persons entitled to credit, Cardinal Bernis for example, assure us that they had seen the originals; the person who originally collected them was the Florentine man of letters, Lami; according to a letter of the abbe Bellegarde in Potter's Vie de Ricci, I. p. 328, those who possessed the originals and who had given out copies, confirmed their genuineness; 3. because they bear the stamp of an originality, of a character of a peculiar kind, and which preserves its consistency in all conditions of life, such as no fictitious writer could have fabricated. We see in them a living man. Least of all can these letters have proceeded from Caracciolo. One needs but read his Vie de Clement XIV.—[Life of Clement XIV.] to be convinced how far all his remarks are below what originated with Clement XIV. The good to be found in that work is but an effect of the Ganganellian spirit.

dies, split into two parties: the zelanti, who sought to preserve entire all old privileges, and the party of the crowns, the royalists, who considered that the safety of the church was to be found in a wise spirit of concession. The latter came into power in the person of Ganganelli, and the same change took full effect in Rome that had appeared at all other monarchical courts.

Ganganelli's first step was not to permit the public reading of the bull—*In cœna Domini;* he still further extended the concessions that had been made by Benedict XIV. to the king of Sardinia, and the recognition of which had been refused since that time; on the very day of his taking possession of his dignity, he declared that he would send a nuncio to Portugal; he suspended the operation of the monitorium that had been issued against Parma; he then took up in good earnest the case of the Jesuits. A commission of cardinals was constituted; the archives of the Propaganda were carefully examined; the reasons on both sides were seriously weighed. Clement XIV., indeed, had been all along unfavourably disposed. He belonged to the order of Franciscans, which had already been constantly at war with the Jesuits, particularly in regard to missions; he held the doctrinal views of the Augustinians and Thomists, so entirely opposite to those of the society; indeed he was not altogether free from Jansenist sentiments. In the course of the investigation there appeared a number of points of complaint which were perpetually repeated, and which could be put out of the way by no argumentation on the other side; the Jesuits were charged with mixing themselves up with worldly affairs, and in ecclesiastical matters, with contention and quarrelling, both with the regular and secular clergy; with the toleration of heathen customs in the missions; with scandalous maxims in general; with the procuring of great wealth, and that too by commercial dealings. To any general measure applicable to the entire institute it had often been objected, that it had been approved by the council of Trent; the commission examined the canon and found merely mention made of the institute, no express confirmation of it. Then, however, Clement did not doubt that that which one of his predecessors had founded in other times, might be revoked by him in his. It is true, indeed, that still it cost him a severe struggle; he had even been led to entertain some anxiety about his life. But now the peace of the church was not to be restored in any other way; the Spanish court in particular vehemently insisted on its demands; without compliance no restoration of the territories that had been taken was to be thought of. The papal decision followed on the 21st of July 1773. "Inspired, as we trust, by the Holy Ghost, urged by a sense of duty to restore the harmony of the church, convinced that the society of Jesus can no longer subserve the uses for which it was appointed, and on other grounds of prudence and governmental wisdom, which we keep undisclosed in our own mind, we abolish and extirpate the society of Jesus, its offices, houses, institutes."[1]

This was a step of immense consequence.

First of all, in so far as it bore upon the protestants. For the contest with them the institute was originally calculated, and from its very foundation regulated:—the very form of its dogmatical theology rested mainly on contrast to Calvin;—this was the character which the Jesuits had renewed and confirmed in the persecutions of the Huguenots down to the close of the 17th century. But this contest had now come to a final close; no actual object presented itself any longer even to the most studious self-delusion; in the grand concerns of the world the non-Roman catholics possessed an undeniable preponderance, and the Roman catholics were endeavouring much rather to move towards them than to draw them to themselves. In this, I should suppose, lay the chief and the deepest reason for the abolition of the order. It was a warlike institution which no longer suited a state of peace. As it would not yield by a single hairbreadth, and obstinately rejected all reform, of which in another respect, likewise, it stood much in need, it may be said to have pronounced sentence upon itself. It is a circumstance of great importance that the papal see was incapable of preserving an order, which had been founded for the purpose of combating the protestants; that a pope, and that too, at the same time, from personal inducement, surrendered it.

But this step produced its most immediate effect on Roman

[1] Brief: Dominus ac redemptor. Continuazione degli annali, tom. XIV, P. II. p. 107.

catholic countries. The Jesuits owed the ill will with which they were regarded, and their subversion, mainly to their having contended for the strictest view that could be entertained of the Roman see's supremacy; and when the latter left them to their fate, it itself likewise abandoned the strictness of that view and its consequences. The struggles of the opposition obtained an undoubted triumph. The annihilation at one blow, and without any preparatory measures, of the society that had chiefly occupied itself with the education of youth, and that was constantly operating within so extensive a range, could not but shake the Roman catholic world to its foundation, to the point where the new generations form their character.[1] On the fall of the outer defences, the assaults of a triumphant opinion on the inner fortress were sure to be commenced with still greater animation. The movement increased from day to day, the desertions took a more and more extended range; which was to be expected from the ferment having now appeared in the very kingdom, whose existence and power were most intimately associated with the results of the Roman catholic efforts at the epoch of its re-establishment, that is, in Austria.

JOSEPH II.

THE intention of Joseph II. was to combine together and to take absolutely into his own hands the whole resources of his monarchy. How then could he have approved of the influences exerted by Rome and the connection maintained by his subjects with the pope. Whether it was that he was most surrounded by Jansenists or by infidels,[2] there is no doubt that here too they assisted each other as in the attack on the Jesuits; he waged an incessant and destructive war on all institutions that held together, and were based on the idea of an external unity in the church. Out of above 2000 monasteries and convents, he allowed only about 700 to remain: of the associations of nuns those only received mercy at his hands that were directly useful;.and even in those that he spared he no longer tolerated any

[1] Montbarey, Mémoires, I. p. 225.

[2] What Van Swieten believed may be referred to this. But that there was also at Vienna, at that time, a very fully developed Jansenistic tendency, is shown among other proofs by the life of Fessler. See Fessler's Rückblicke auf seine siebzigjährige Pilgerschaft, p. 74, 78, and at other places. Compare Schlözer's Staatsanzeigen, IX. 33, p. 113.

ties with Rome. He looked upon the papal dispensations as foreign merchandise, and would allow no money to leave the country in return for them: he openly announced himself administrator of the church's temporalities.

Ganganelli's successor, Pius VI., thought forthwith that the only means of restraining the emperor from going to extreme measures, in respect to doctrine perhaps as well as other things, lay in the impression he hoped to make upon him at a personal interview; he went himself to Vienna, and no one will venture to say that the mild dignity and graciousness of his appearance left no lasting impression. Nevertheless, in the main, Joseph went straight on without wavering. The monastery at which he had taken solemn farewell of the pope, had an intimation made to it immediately thereafter, that it was to be abolished. Pius VI. had at last to make up his mind to relinquish to the emperor the appointment to the episcopal sees even in Italy.

Thus did the antipapistical struggles now force their way from the side of Austria too into Italy. Leopold, in so far as we can judge, himself a man of Jansenist sentiments, reformed the churches of Tuscany without paying any respect to the Roman see. Not far from the capital of (Roman catholic) Christendom, the synod of Pistoja promulgated in its decrees a veritable manifest of union between the Gallican and Jansenist principles. Naples, which through Queen Caroline, stood intimately connected likewise with that side, abolished the last remaining traces of feudal connection with the Roman see.

On the German churches likewise the emperor's measures had an indirect effect. The spiritual electors after having been so long on a good understanding with the Roman see, began at last to set themselves against it. In them were united the interests of territorial princes, which put an end to the secret conveying away of money, and of persons invested with ecclesiastical dignities, who desired to re-establish their own authority.[1] According to their Ems declaration, "written," says a Roman prelate, "with a pen dipt in the gall of Paul Sarpi," the Roman primacy was to be contented in future with the rights that were

[1] Compare the Coblentz article for the year 1769, in the Zeitschrift: Deutsche Blätter für Protestanten und Katholiken. Heidelberg, 1839, Heft I. p. 39.

conceded to it in the first centuries.[1] The German canonists had done them distinguished service by their previous labours; and along with these there were other teachers of jurisprudence who attacked the entire fabric of the Roman catholic church in Germany, the political power of its hierarchy and its civil administration.[2] Men of learning, as well as the people at large, were carried away with a thirst for innovation. The inferior clergy and the bishops, the bishops and the archbishops, and these last and the pope, were all opposed to each other. Every thing prognosticated a change.

THE REVOLUTION.

But before matters went thus far, before Joseph had as yet succeeded in accomplishing all his reforms, the most violent explosion took place in the abyss of the elements fermenting in France.

It is self-evident, that the dissensions of the clergy among themselves, the antagonism of two hostile parties in all religious concerns, the incapability of men in power to defend themselves on the territory of opinion and literature, the general dislike which, not altogether without their own fault, they had brought on themselves, indescribably contributed to the development of the event that governs recent times—the French Revolution. The spirit of opposition that had risen from the interior of Roman catholicism while embarrassed within itself, had been constantly acquiring greater firmness and consistency. Step after step it kept advancing; amid the storms of 1789 it succeeded in obtaining possession of the government, a government which considered itself destined utterly to subvert whatever was ancient, and to make a new world; in the general subversion accordingly, that was denounced against the most Christian monarchy, the ecclesiastical constitution received one of the severest blows.

All things tended to the same result: financial embarrass-

[1] Bartolommeo Pacca: Memorie Storiche sul di lui soggiorno in Germania—[Historical memoirs of his sojourn in Germany], p. 33.

[2] For example, Friedrich Carl v. Moser: ueber die Regierung der geistlichen Staaten in Deutschland—[on the government of the ecclesiastical states in Germany], 1787. His chief suggestion is at page 161, that "prince and bishop should again be separated."

ment, the interests alike of individuals and municipalities, indifference or hatred towards the existing religion: at last a member of the superior clergy themselves made the proposition that they should acknowledge the right of the nation, that is, of the civil government, and, in the first instance, of the national convention, to dispose of the ecclesiastical estates. Until that time these estates had been considered to be special property, not of the French church alone, but of the church at large, and the consent of the pope was requisite before any alienation could take place. But how remote now were the times and the ideas that had given rise to notions of this sort! The convention, after a short debate, assumed the right of disposing of this property, that is, of alienating it, and that, too, with a still more unlimited authority than had been contemplated when it was first proposed. But it was impossible to stop at this point. As by the sequestration of the property, which was proceeded with without delay, the relations that had subsisted hitherto necessarily came to a close, it became requisite forthwith to make a new arrangement, such as took effect in the civil constitution of the clergy. The principle of the revolutionized state was transferred to ecclesiastical things;[1] the settlement of the clergy, instead of being as prescribed in the concordat, was to be by popular election; instead of the independence secured to them by the possession of real property, they were to receive salaries; all the dioceses were altered, the religious orders were abolished, vows revoked, connection with Rome dissolved; the receiving of a bull was to be held as one of the most heinous offences. The attempt of a Carthusian to restore the exclusive dominion of the Roman catholic religion, had only the effect of accelerating these decrees. The whole clergy were to bind themselves to observe them, by solemnly swearing to that effect.

It is not to be denied that this course of things was accomplished under the co-operation of the French, and the assent of the other Jansenists. They saw with satisfaction that the power

1 Very systematically, according to the doctrine of the elder church historians: "Tota ecclesiarum distributio ad formam imperii facta est."—[The whole distribution of the churches has been made according to the form of the empire.] Camus: Opinion sur le projet de constitution du clergé, 31 Mai 1790.—[Opinion on the project for the constitution of the clergy, 31st May 1790.]

of Babylon, as in their hatred they called the Roman curia, suffered so severe a blow, and that the clergy, from whom they had experienced so many persecutions, were subverted. Even their theoretical convictions tended to this, "for while the clergy were deprived of their wealth, they would be compelled to acquire for themselves real merit."[1]

The Roman court flattered itself for a moment with the prospect of this movement being checked by an internal re-action, and this the pope did every thing in his power to bring about. He rejected the new constitution, anathematized the bishops that had sworn to it, endeavoured by encouragement and praise to fortify in their opposition the still numerous party that had thrown itself into an attitude of resistance; and at last he even pronounced the ban upon the most influential and distinguished members of the constitutional clergy.

But it was all to no effect; the revolutionary tendency kept the place it had won; the civil war that raged within the country, and which had been excited mainly by religious impulses, turned out for the advantage of the new state of things. Well had it been for the pope had he but had his disappointments brought to a close at this point, had France been content to throw off its connection with him.

But meanwhile the general war, which was so fundamentally to alter the condition of Europe, had broken out.

With all that resistless fury, with a mixture of enthusiasm, avarice, and terror, which had been displayed in the strife within France, the revolutionary government burst the frontiers of that country, and poured itself into those beyond.

The adjacent territories to France, Belgium, Holland, and Germany on the upper Rhine, just where the ecclesiastical constitution had its chief seat, it revolutionized in a manner analogous to itself. The campaign of 1796 made it mistress of Italy also; revolutionary states sprang up in all quarters; and it already threatened the pope in his state and in his capital.

Without properly taking an active interest in the coalition,

[1] Letters of Gianni and several other abbots in Potter: Vie de Ricci—[Potter's Life of Ricci], II. p. 315. Wolf, Geschichte der katolischen Kirche unter Pius VI.—[Wolf, History of the catholic church under Pius VI.], has at vol. VII. page 32, a chapter on the part taken by the Jansenists in the new constitution, which, however, turned out to be very slight.

he had merely thrown the weight of his spiritual weapons on that side. But in vain did he seek to take advantage of his neutrality.[1] His territories were overrun and stirred up to insurrection; exorbitant exactions and renunciations, such as none of his predecessors had ever experienced, were imposed on him.[2] And with all this, matters were not yet brought to a close. The pope was not the same kind of enemy as the rest. During the war he had even summoned up sufficient courage to reject the Jansenist-Gallican doctrines of Pistoja by the bull *Auctorem fidei:* the unyielding attitude he assumed, and those condemnatory briefs of his, continued still powerfully to affect the interior of France: the French government now demanded as the price of peace, that he should revoke these and acknowledge the civil constitution.

But Pius VI. was not to be moved to this. To have yielded here, would have seemed to him a departure from the foundation of the faith, an act of treason to his office.[3] He replied to the proposals, "after having called upon God for his assistance, inspired as he believed with the Holy Ghost, he refused to yield to these conditions."

For a moment the revolutionary governments seemed to recollect themselves—a compact was struck even without these concessions—but it was only for a moment. From contemplating an entire separation from the pope, they proceeded to entertain the idea of directly annihilating him. The Directory found the regimen of the priests in Italy incompatible with its own. On the first occasion that offered, that of a casual commotion among the people, Rome was invaded and the Vatican occupied. Pius VI. besought his enemies to allow him to die likewise there, being where he had lived; he being already above eighty years

1 Authentische Geschichte des Franzözischen Revolutionskrieges in Italien, 1797.—[Authentic History of the French revolutionary war in Italy, 1797.] The pope had declared that religion forbade a resistance that might occcasion the shedding of blood.

2 In the Mémoires historiques et philosophiques sur Pie VI. et son pontificat, tome II.—[Historical and philosophical memoirs on Pius VI. and his pontificate, vol. II.], the loss of the Roman state is reckoned at 220 millions of livres.

3 Memoria diretta al principe della pace—[Memoir addressed to the prince of Peace], in Tavanti: Fasti di Pio VI. tom. III.—[Annals of Pius VI. vol. III.], p. 335. "S. Santità rimase stordita, veggendo che si cercava di traviare la sua conscienza per dare un colpo il più funesto alla religione."—[His Holiness was confounded, seeing that it was sought to mislead his conscience in order to give the most fatal blow to religion.]

of age. He was told in reply, that he could die any where; the room he usually occupied was plundered before his eyes; even his smallest necessaries were taken from him; the ring he wore was taken from his finger; and at last he was removed to France, where he departed this life in August, 1799.

In fact, it might seem as if the papal government had come to its final close. Those tendencies of ecclesiastical opposition which we have seen commence and rise into vigour, had now prospered to such a point as to venture to entertain the idea of aiming at such a result.

TIMES OF NAPOLEON.

EVENTS occurred, however, which prevented this.

The chief result of the hostility which the pope experienced at the hands of the revolutionary governments was, that the rest of Europe, whatever even may have been its sentiments otherwise, took him under its protection. The death of Pius VI. happened at the very time in which the coalition once more was triumphant, and thus it became possible for the cardinals to meet in St. George's at Venice, and to proceed to the election of a pope, Pius VII. (13th March 1800).

It is true that the revolutionary power triumphed soon after, and won for itself a decisive preponderance, even in Italy. But at that very time, a great change took place in that power itself. After having passed through so many metamorphoses, effected amid the storms of the pressing moment, it took a direction towards monarchy. A person of extraordinary vigour appeared, with the idea of a new universal empire in his head; and, which for us here is the main concern, who in the review of the general subversion that had taken place, and from the experience that the East had given him, was convinced that, in order to the accomplishment of his projects, as in the case of so many other forms of the old states, he required before all things unity of religion and hierarchical subordination.

While still on the battle-field of Marengo, Napoleon deputed the bishop of Vercelli to open negotiations with the pope for the re-establishment of the Roman catholic church.

Such a tender, extremely captivating as it no doubt was in some respects, involved, however, much that was dangerous.

It was evident that the re-establishment of the Roman catholic church in France, and its alliance with the pope, could be purchased only with extraordinary concessions.

To this Pius VII. was resolved to submit. He at once sanctioned the alienation of the ecclesiastical possessions—a loss of 400 millions of francs in real property—the reason that influenced him being, as he expressed it, that fresh troubles would break out were he to refuse, but that he would much rather go the utmost lengths that religion would at all permit; he consented to a new organization of the French clergy, who were now to be paid and appointed by the government; he was content that he should have restored to him the right of canonical institution within the same range, and without limitation of the right of refusal, as was possessed by the earlier popes.[1]

There now actually followed, what no one shortly before could have expected, the re-establishment of Roman catholicism in France, and the subjection anew of that country to spiritual authority. The pope was in ecstasy "at the churches being cleansed from profanation, the altars again set up, the banner of the cross unfurled anew, legitimate pastors placed over the people, so many souls that had strayed from the right way restored to unity and reconciled to themselves and to God." "How many motives," he exclaimed, "for rejoicing and thankfulness!"

But could any one venture to conclude, that together with the concordat of 1801 there was accomplished at the same time a cordial union of the old ecclesiastical government with the new revolutionary state?

Concessions were made on both sides; notwithstanding these each party remained obstinately attached to its own principles.

The restorer of the Roman catholic church in France contributed most, immediately thereafter, towards effecting the complete overthrow of the proud fabric of the German church, and the transference of its estates and lordships to secular princes, equally without respect to their being Roman catholic or protestant. People at the court of Rome were amazed beyond measure. "According to the old decretals," said they, "he-

1 Lettera apostolica in forma di breve—[Apostolic letter in the form of a brief], in Pistolesi: Vita di Pio VII., tom. I. p. 143, with a general comparison of the variations of the publication as it appeared in France.

resy drew upon itself the loss of property, but the church must now look on while its own property is divided out among heretics."[1]

And meanwhile, for Italy likewise a concordat was drawn up in the spirit of that for France. There, too, the pope had to assent to the sale of the ecclesiastical property, and to abandon to the civil government the appointments to benefices; nay, there were so many new and trammelling conditions, all in favour of one side, appended to this agreement, that Pius VII., under these circumstances, refused to publish it.[2]

But it was chiefly in France itself that Napoleon gave effect, with the greatest zeal, to the rights of the civil government at the expense of the church; he considered the declaration of 1682 to be a fundamental law of the kingdom, and caused it to be commented upon in the schools; besides he would have no vows, no monks; the regulations with respect to marriage, as adopted in his civil code, were at variance with Roman catholic principles as respected its sacramental import: the organic articles, which from the very first he appended to the compact, were conceived quite in an anti-Roman spirit.

When the pope, notwithstanding all this, resolved, at the emperor's entreaty, to cross the Alps and give the sanction of the church to his coronation with the holy oil, he was influenced by the consideration that, however much or little people may have contributed to it even on the side of France, he might flatter himself with the hope "of effecting something for the advantage of the Roman catholic church, and completing the work that had been begun."[3] In this he reckoned upon the influence of personal conferences. He took with him the letter of Louis XIV. to Innocent XII., in order to convince Napoleon that that monarch had already allowed the declaration of 1682 to fall to the ground. In the first statement, drawn up in Italian, which he then delivered to the government in Paris, he even formally made war on that declaration, and endeavoured to di-

1 Instruction to a Nuncio at Vienna—unfortunately without a date, probably of 1803—in Daunou: Essai II. p. 318.

2 Coppi: Annali d' Italia, tom. III. p. 120.

3 Allocutio habita in consistorio secreto, 29 Oct. 1804.—[Allocution delivered in the secret consistory, 29th Oct. 1804.] In Italian in Pistolesi: Vita di Pio VII., tom. I. p. 193.

vest the new concordat of the limitations of the organic articles.[1] Nay, his aims and expectations went farther still. In a minute memorial he stated the necessities of the pontificate, together with the losses it had sustained in the course of the preceding half century, and urged the emperor after the example of Charlemagne, to restore to it the territories that had been taken possession of.[2] So highly did he estimate the service he had rendered to the revolutionary monarchy.

But how sorely did he find himself deceived! In the very act of crowning the emperor, a tinge of melancholy was perceived in him. Of all he had desired and contemplated even after that, he never obtained the smallest part. Much rather was this the very time when the emperor's projects revealed themselves in their whole extent.

The constituent Assembly had endeavoured to cast off its connection with the pope; the Directory had wished to annihilate him; Bonaparte's idea was to preserve him, but at the same time to keep him in a state of subjection, and to make him the mere instrument of his omnipotence.

He caused it to be proposed to the pope, if we are rightly informed, at that very time, that he should remain in France, and reside in Avignon or Paris.

He is said to have replied, that to meet the case of his being kept a prisoner, he had drawn up an abdication in regular form, and had deposited it at Palermo, beyond the reach of French decrees.

The pope could at that moment have found protection only under the dominion of the English fleet.

It is true the pope was now allowed to return to Rome, and left in possession of his previous independence; but from that hour there broke out the most untoward misunderstandings.

Napoleon very soon declared, in plain terms, that like his predecessors of the second and third dynasties, he was the eldest

[1] Extrait du rapport de Mr. Portalis—[Extract from the report of Mr. Portalis], in Artaud's Pie VII., t. II. p. 11.

[2] Printed in Artaud, p. 31. Compare Napoleon's letter, 22d July, 1807. "Le pape s'est donné la peine de venir à mon couronnement. J'ai reconnu dans cette démarche un saint prélat; mais il voulait que je lui cédasse les légations."—The pope took the trouble of coming to my coronation. In this step I recognized a holy prelate; but he wanted me to cede the legations to him.] See Bignon's Histoire de France sous Napoléon: Deuxième époque, I. p. 158.—[History of France under Napoleon, second epoch, I. p. 158.]

son of the church who bore the sword for her protection, and could not endure that she should stand associated with heretics and schismatics, such as the Russians and the English. He was particularly fond of being looked upon as the successor of Charlemagne, from which, nevertheless, he drew another doctrine than that drawn by the Roman court. He assumed that the church state was a gift of Charles to the pope, but on that very account the latter lay under the obligation of not departing from the policy of the empire; this too was what he would not suffer.[1]

The pope was amazed at such an unreasonable demand, as that he must consider the enemy of another as his enemy. He replied that he was the common pastor, the father of all, the minister of peace, and that such a demand had already shocked him; "He must be Aaron the prophet of God, not Ishmael whose hand was against every man, and every man's hand against him."

Napoleon, however, went straight on to his object without heeding the pope. He caused Ancona and Urbino to be occupied, and upon the rejection of his ultimatum, in which he had claimed among other things the nomination of a third of the cardinals, he ordered his troops to march on to Rome; the cardinals that were not favourable to him were expelled, and so was the secretary of state to the pope twice; but as all this had no effect upon the pope, at last his own person was not spared, and he too was sent off from his palace and capital. A decree of the senate then pronounced the union of the states of the church

[1] Schoell Archives historiques et politiques (Paris, 1819)—[Schoell's historical and political Archives] contain, in the 2nd and 3rd vols., a "Précis des contestations qui ont eu lieu entre le saint siége et Napoléon Buonaparte accompagné d' un grand nombre de pièces officielles."—[Brief view of the contests that took place between the holy see and Napoleon Buonaparte, accompanied with a great many official documents.] The correspondence communicated here, in all its extent, reaches from 13th Nov. 1805 to 17th May 1808. Notwithstanding, in Bignon's Histoire de France depuis la Paix de Tilsit—[History of France since the Peace of Tilsit] 1838, I. chap. 3, p. 125, we meet with the following passage: "Les publications faites depuis 1815, ne se composent guère que de pièces dont la date commence in 1808."—[The publications that have appeared since 1815, are hardly composed of any thing but documents, the date of which commences in 1808.] And farther on: "Jusqu'à présent son caractère (de Pie VII.) n'est pas suffisamment connu. On ne le connoîtra bien qu'en l'appréciant d'après ses actes."—[To this day his character (that of Pius VII.) is not sufficiently known. It can be properly known only by appreciating it according to his acts.] In point of fact, however, we knew these acts already. Bignon has added but little to the public documents given by Schoell.

with the French empire. The secular sovereignty was declared to be incompatible with the exercise of spiritual prerogatives; the pope was for the future to be formally bound to observe the four Gallican principles; he was to draw an income from real property, almost like a feudal tenant of the empire; the state was to undertake the cost of the college of cardinals.[1]

This was a plan, it will be seen, which would have subjected the whole spiritual government of the church to the empire, and placed it indirectly at least in the hands of the emperor.

But how was it to be brought about, what however was indispensable, that the pope should be prevailed upon to consent to this degradation? Pius VII. had availed himself of the last moment of his freedom to pronounce the excommunication. He refused canonical institution to the bishops that had been nominated by the emperor. Napoleon was not so absolutely master of his clergy as not to feel the effects of this, sometimes from one side, sometimes from another, and indeed from that of Germany too.

But this very resistance contributed at last to the overpowering of the pope. The consequences were much more severely felt by the ecclesiastical head who sympathized with the internal condition of the church than by the secular, to whom even spiritual affairs were but an engine of state, in themselves indifferent.

In Savona, whither the pope had been taken, he was lonely, cast upon himself, without any adviser. The good man was at last prevailed upon, by means of earnest and almost extravagant representations of the distraction of the church, which would follow upon his refusal of the institution, although with poignant grief and with vehement reluctance, nevertheless, properly speaking, to surrender this right. For what else was implied in his transferring it to the metropolitans, as often as he himself should put off exercising it for more than six months, on any other ground but that of personal unworthiness. "He renounced the right in which, nevertheless, his last weapon for defence was really to be found."

Nor was that all that was expected from him. With an in-

[1] Thibaudeau: Histoire de la France et de Napoléon. Empire, tom. V. p. 221. —[Thibadeau's History of France and of Napoleon. The Empire, vol. V. p. 221.]

tolerable haste, which his bodily weakness made him feel more keenly, he was conducted to Fontainebleau. There he was beset with new assaults and with the most urgent demands, that he would completely restore the peace of the church. At last matters were brought so far in fact, that the pope submitted even on the remaining and decisive points. He yielded to the request that he should reside in France; he now adopted the most essential of the determinations of the senatus-consultum above mentioned. The concordat of Fontainebleau, 25th January 1813, is conceived on the pre-supposition that he was no more to return to Rome.[1]

In this the autocrat of the revolution had, in point of fact, accomplished what no previous Roman catholic prince had even so much as seriously ventured to contemplate. The pope consented to subject himself to the French empire. His authority would on all sides have been an engine in the hands of this new dynasty; it would have served to confirm the internal obedience and the relations of dependence in the Roman catholic states that had not yet been reduced to subjection. The popedom would have returned so far to the position in which it stood under the German emperors while in the plenitude of their power, in particular, under the Salier Henry III. But it would have had far heavier fetters. There was a certain antagonism to the church in the power that now lorded it over the pope; yet fundamentally it was but another metamorphosis of that spirit of ecclesiastical opposition which had developed itself in the eighteenth century, and which was characterized by so strong a disposition to downright infidelity. To this hostile power the popedom would have been subjected and placed in a state of vassalage to it.

Notwithstanding, on this occasion likewise, matters were not destined to proceed thus far.

THE RESTORATION.

The empire, which was now to have its hierarchical centre in the pope, continued constantly involved in doubtful hostilities with invincible enemies. The pontiff in his solitude received no

[1] Bart. Pacca: Memorie storiche del ministero de' due viaggi in Francia, etc.—[Historical memoirs of the ministry by two travellers in France, &c.], p. 323. Historisch politische Zeitschrift, I. IV. 642.

certain tidings of the alternations of success in this contest. At the moment of his yielding at last, after so long a resistance, Napoleon had failed in his final and greatest enterprise against Russia; and by all the consequences that necessarily followed that failure, his power was shaken to its foundations. Europe already entertained the almost forlorn hope of regaining her freedom. When the pope, to whom, after his submission, some of the cardinals ventured to return, came to the knowledge of this state of things, he too felt again re-assured: he recovered his breath, and it seemed to him as if every advance of the allied powers were an act of deliverance.

When Prussia rose, shortly after the call to arms from the king appeared, Pius VII. took courage so far as to recall the concordat above mentioned; on the congress of Prague having met, he ventured forthwith to cast a glance beyond the frontiers of the empire that surrounded him, and to remind the emperor of Austria of his rights. After the battle of Leipsic he regained his confidence so far as to decline an offer then made to him, of restoring part of his territory; after the allies had passed the Rhine, he declared that he would negotiate no more until his complete restoration took place. Events now unfolded themselves with the utmost rapidity; when Paris was taken by the allies, he had already reached the frontiers of the states of the church; and on the 24th of May, 1814, he again entered Rome. The world entered upon a new era, and a new era opened up also for the Roman see.

The periods of ten years that have last elapsed, have derived their character and essential features from the struggle between the tendencies of the revolution, still powerfully influencing men's minds, and the ideas to which the old states now, after the triumph they had achieved, returned with redoubled earnestness, as to their original and fundamental principles: in this antagonism the supreme spiritual power of the Roman catholic church, as is evident, necessarily assumed an important position.

First of all, it was aided by the idea of secular legitimacy, and that, indeed, still more almost, from the side of its ecclesiastical opponents, than from its own adherents and the professors of its creed.

The triumph was that of the four great allied powers, among which three were non-Roman catholic, over one who thought to have made his capital the centre of Roman catholicism, and by means of which the pope was set at liberty, and put in a position that enabled him to return to Rome. The pope's desire to recover the whole states of the church, was first laid before the three non-Roman catholic monarchs who happened just then to be met in London. How often in earlier times had the resources of these territories been strained for the purpose of annihilating protestantism in England or in Germany, or of diffusing Roman catholic doctrines over Russia or Scandinavia! And now it was necessarily to be through the intercession of these non-Roman catholic powers that the pope was to succeed in regaining possession of his territories. In the allocution in which Pius VII. communicated to the cardinals the happy results of his negotiations, he expressly commends the services of the monarchs "who did not belong to the Romish church; the emperor of Russia, who had taken his rights into consideration, and bestowed particular attention on the subject; both the king of Sweden and the prince-regent of England; so also the king of Prussia, who, during the whole course of his negotiations, declared himself in his favour."[1] Differences of creed were for the time put in oblivion: political considerations alone were attended to.

We have often had occasion already to note these tendencies in the last century and a half. We saw what were the states in which Innocent XI. found support and assistance in his contentions with Louis XIV. When the Jesuits were devoted to destruction by the Bourbon courts, they found favour and protection in the north, in Russia and in Prussia; and the circumstance of these courts having, in 1758, taken possession of Avignon and Benevento, produced a political ferment in England. At no time, however, has this singular position of parties with respect to each other appeared more remarkably than in the events of the last years.

[1] "Ne' possiamo non fare un gran conto dei meriti verso di noi di Federigo (Guil.) re di Prussia, il cui impegno fu constantemente in nostro favore nel decorso tutto delle trattative de' nostro affari."—[We cannot but make much account of the merits towards us of Frederick (William) king of Prussia, whose engagement was constantly in our favour, throughout the whole course of the negotiating of our affairs.] Allocution of the 4th of Sept. 1815, in Nicolesi, II., p. 144.

Now, however, that the pope had again acquired an independent position among the princes of Europe, he could think without molestation about the renovation of spiritual obedience. One of the first acts by which he notified his new administration of office, was his solemnly restoring the Jesuits. On Sunday the 7th of August, 1814, he himself read mass in the church del Jesu, at the altar of Ignatius Loyola, heard another mass, and then caused a bull to be published, whereby he authorized the surviving members of the society of Jesus, again to live according to the rules of Loyola, to admit novices, to found houses and colleges, and to devote themselves to the service of the church in preaching, confession, and education: (alleging that) it would be a violation of his duty, while on the stormy sea and momentarily threatened with death and shipwreck, were he to decline the aid of powerful and experienced rowers, who even offered themselves for that purpose.[1] He restored to them whatever remained of their ancient property, and promised them compensation for what had been alienated. He conjured all secular and spiritual governments to be favourable to the order, and willing to promote its interests. It was manifest that he hoped to be able to exercise his spiritual authority, not within the limited sphere imposed by the last times of the 18th century, but in the spirit of his earlier predecessors. And in fact, how could he have ever found a more propitious or more inviting moment for that purpose. The restored civil governments of the south of Europe seemed, as it were, to repent of their previous refractoriness; they thought that they had thus let loose the spirit by which they themselves had been subverted; they now viewed the pope as their natural ally, and hoped, by means of spiritual influence, to triumph the more easily over the internal enemies by whom they saw themselves surrounded. The king of Spain called to mind that he bore the title of a catholic king, and declared that he would render himself deserving of it: he recalled the Jesuits, whom his grandfather had so eagerly banished; he renewed the court of the nuncio, and edicts issued by the grand inquisitor were again sent forth. In Sardinia, there were new bishoprics founded: in Tuscany, monasteries and convents were restored: Naples, after some struggles,

[1] Bull: Sollicitudo omnium ecclesiarum.

submitted to a concordat, in which a very effective direct influence over the clergy of the kingdom was accorded to the Roman curia. Meanwhile, in France, the chamber of 1815 looked on the salvation of that nation as involved in the re-establishment of the ancient French church, "that work," as one of the speakers expressed himself, "of heaven, of time, of kings, and of the men of former days;" but therewithal the question was only in the main, about the necessity of restoring to the clergy their practical influences on the state, on society in general and individual families, on public life and public education; not a word was any longer said about those franchises, of which the Gallican church had either factiously possessed itself, or expressly reserved: by the new concordat now drawn up, it was subjected to a dependence on Rome, such as it had experienced at no preceding period.

It lay, indeed, in the nature of things, that with so decided a course, a triumph could not at once be achieved over the spirit of the Romanesque nations after it had developed itself amid totally different prospects. In France there was an insurrection of the old antipathies against the hierarchy, with loud calls for war against the new concordat: the legislative power was constituted there in such a manner as made it for ever idle to think of carrying out the plans of 1815. The violent proceedings of the Ferdinandean government in Spain, aroused an equally vehement re-action there: a revolution broke out which, while it contended with the absolute monarch who could offer it no resistance, displayed at the same time a decided anti-clerical tendency. One of the first acts of the new cortes was the redismissal of the Jesuits; soon there followed a decree abolishing the whole religious orders in a body, alienating their property, and applying it to the extinction of the national debt. And similar commotions immediately took place in Italy: they penetrated into the states of the church, which became full of the same elements: the carbonari had even at one time fixed the day for a general rising in the church's territories.

Once more, however, did the restored princes find support and assistance in the great powers which had won the last triumphs in war: the revolutions were stifled; it is true that on this occasion the non-Roman catholic governments did not take an immediate part in these repressions; but they were not opposed at least by some, and were approved by others.

And meanwhlie, even in the non-Roman catholic kingdoms too, Roman catholicism obtained a new organization. Positive religion, of whatsoever profession, was held to be the best support of civil obedience. Care was taken, in all quarters, to arrange the dioceses anew, to found new bishoprics and archbishoprics, to institute Roman catholic seminaries and schools. What a totally different aspect did the Roman catholic ecclesiastical system in the provinces of Prussia, that had once been incorporated with the French empire, now assume from what it once had. The ecclesiastical opposition bestirring itself here and there against the ancient ordinances of the Roman catholic church, found no support in the protestant states. On the contrary, even the Roman court concluded compacts with protestant as well as Roman catholic governments, and found itself reduced to the necessity of conceding to them a certain degree of influence in the election of bishops. That influence, too, came at times to be actually applied to the promotion of the most ecclesiastically zealous men to the most important situations. It might seem as if, in the higher regions of society, the controversy about creeds had been for ever laid aside. In civil life it was perceived to be daily disappearing more and more. Protestant literature gave a recognition to old Roman catholic institutions, which it would have been impossible for it to have done in earlier times.

Symptoms, however, had begun to show, that these expectations of peace had been too bold, too inconsiderate, and hasty.

Much rather has the strict Roman catholic principle which clings to Rome and is represented in Rome, gradually become involved, more or less warmly and consciously, in a contest with the protestant civil governments.

Over such a government it achieved a grand victory in the year 1829, in England.

During the wars of the revolution, the English government, which for a century had been exclusively protestant, made approaches to the Romish see. Pius VII. had been elected under the auspices of the triumph achieved in 1799 by the coalition, in which England played so distinguished a part. We have mentioned how this pope further, also, enjoyed the support afforded by the power of England, and could not bring himself to engage in any measures of hostility against it. In England, likewise, people no longer found it so necessary as it was at an earlier period, that a religious connection with the pope should exclude a man from all proper political rights, from all capability of holding civil offices. Already had Pitt felt this and expressed it:[1] nevertheless, as may readily be imagined, every innovation on the established habit of keeping to the tried principles of the constitution, experienced for a long period invincible resistance. But for once the spirit of the age, with its repugnance to all exclusive privileges, made itself bear with effect on this as well as other questions. Then in pre-eminently Roman catholic Ireland, associations, partly religious, partly political, symptoms of a refractory spirit and disturbances, began, in a certain measure, to gain the ascendancy, so that at length the great general who had triumphantly withstood so many enemies, and who then held the reins of government, had to declare that he could no longer govern unless this concession was made. Accordingly, those oaths of office, by which alone, at the time of the restoration and revolution in England, people thought they could secure the protestant interest, were moderated or abolished. How often previous to this, had Lord Liverpool declared, that were these measures to pass, England would cease to be any longer a protestant state: that even should they not all at once be followed by any great consequences, yet it was impossible to foresee what might be their future results.[2] Nevertheless, they were adopted, they were ventured upon.

And a still more splendid and more unlocked-for triumph was immediately afterwards achieved in Belgium.

1 "Mr. Pitt is convinced," so it runs in his letter to George III., 31st January, 1801, "that the grounds on which the laws on exclusion now remaining were founded, have long been narrowed,—that those principles, formerly held by the catholics, which made them be considered as politically dangerous, have been for a course of time gradually declining,—that the political circumstances under which the exclusive laws originated, arising from the conflicting power of hostile and nearly balanced sects - - and a division in Europe between catholic and protestant powers are no longer applicable to the present state of things."

2 Speech of Lord Liverpool, 17th May, 1825. "Where was the danger in having a popish king or a popish chancellor, if all the other executive officers might acknowledge the pope? It was said,—that a catholic might be prime minister, and have the whole patronage of the church and state at his disposal. - - If the bill were to pass, Great Britain would be no longer a protestant state."

In the kingdom of the Netherlands, ever since the moment of its establishment, there had been symptoms of a mutual aversion betwixt the north and the south, which threatened to rend them asunder again, and which, from the very first, threw itself chiefly into ecclesiastical concerns. The protestant king adopted the ideas of Joseph II.: in that spirit he erected higher and lower schools, and administered in general his share in the ecclesiastical government. The opposition encountered him with educational institutions, conducted in a different spirit, and of set purpose resigned itself to the most repulsive hierarchical efforts. A Roman catholic liberal opinion and party was formed, which, taking its ground here, as in England, on the general rights of man, daily assumed higher and higher pretensions; first obtained concessions, emancipation, for example, from the school system just mentioned, and at last, when the favourable moment appeared, completely threw off the hated dominion (of the house of Orange). It succeeded in founding a kingdom in which the priests again attained to a high degree of political importance. Even the most decidedly liberal ideas contributed most to their advantage. The low qualification which admitted the poorer class in town and country, being the class which they could easily influence, to a participation in public affairs, enabled them to guide the elections: by means of the elections they have since then ruled the chambers, and by means of the chambers, the kingdom. They are to be seen in Brussells as at Rome, on the public promenades, plump and full of pretension; in short, they enjoy their triumph.

The Roman court, in so far as we know, took an immediate and usurping part in neither of these events, however advantageous for its authority they might be. In a third, on the contrary, that of its dissensions with Prussia, it appeared as a negotiator. Here the tendencies of the protestant state and the Roman catholic hierarchy, which might seem to have coalesced since the restoration, but had, some time thereafter, separated from each other, now ran into opposite courses with the most perfect consciousness of what they were doing, and became involved in a contest which justly engaged the attention of the world, and is fraught with the utmost importance. The pope, leagued with both archbishops of the kingdom, rose in opposition to an ordinance of the king, designed to regulate the relations between the families of the mixed population in regard to religion. In the midst of Germany he found willing organs and powerful support.

Collateral with these grand results an internal consolidation has taken place in Roman catholicism.

The principle of an unlimited subordination under the see of Rome, has again obtained the ascendancy in the ecclesiastical institute: the ideas of popedom, bishopric, and priesthood, however various the notions they seem to admit at other times, have now, as it were, become fused together; the order of Jesuits, which presents itself as the quintessence of the restoration, has obtained anew, not only riches and local authority, but an influence also, which embraces the world; and this quiet, yet all-pervading revolution, has been met and furthered by tendencies the most diverse in themselves; first of all, by the favour of those governments that desire that there should be an unlimited ecclesiastical authority; still more, afterwards, by the bias of the age to political opposition wanting an auxiliary; at times, by a real religious want; oftener, too, by the calculations of a partial selfishness: so that enthusiastic minds have once more conceived the idea, that all that has ever been lost may yet be regained.

But if we cast our eyes over the various kingdoms of the world, it would appear that this progress, far from offering such extensive prospects, has rather already called forth the opposition and hostility of antagonist civil powers.

In the north, in the frontier lands towards the followers of the Greek church, the Roman catholic church has met with an irreparable loss, such as it has not experienced since the times of the Reformation: two millions of united Greeks, under the precedence of their bishops, have been brought back to the Greek church, to which their fathers belonged.

In the southern kingdom, which is distinguished by the title of "Catholic," Spain, the possessions of the clergy, which, as the pope says in one of his allocutions,[1] "were allowed to remain in their hands even under the dominion of infidels," have been confiscated by a revolutionary government: and a dis-

[1] In the consistory of 2d March 1841.

pute, has broken out on the subject, which even a return of friendly sentiments on both sides will not easily settle.

The revolution of July in France, must be regarded as, of itself involving a defeat of the strict (Roman catholic) opinion in church affairs: it is notorious that the religious zeal of Charles X. had the chief share in bringing about his fall. Since that time, indeed, the extended constitutional privileges, of which all could avail themselves, have given scope and opportunity even for the extension of hierarchical efforts: but even these growing capabilities, and, in particular, the claim preferred by the clergy to a direct education, have reminded the existing state there, that not only is it based on franchises and individual rights, but, still more, that the exercise of these in a spirit that runs counter to its fundamental principle, may prove exceedingly dangerous to it. Seldom has the chamber of deputies been seen more unanimous than in the resolutions against the attempted organization of the Jesuits: so that Rome, in fact, has retreated a step before them.

In Belgium, acquired as it was from the first with so much tact and forethought, liberal opinions, nevertheless, now advancing on their own account, are acquiring more and more influence from year to year.

In Germany, the insisting on an exclusive Roman catholic orthodoxy which renewed every thing ancient, has produced a notable reactionary blow. After hundreds of thousands had been invited and brought together to worship an extremely doubtful relic,[1] a slight demonstration on the other side, without any properly positive meaning, has brought to light in the middle ranks of Germany, a disposition to apostatize from Rome, stronger than any one had suspected. It is, no doubt, closely connected with the obstacles opposed to mixed marriages, which people congratulated themselves at Rome for having carried into effect, but which were opposed to the general sentiments of the nation.

German protestants, too, of whom it was continually repeated, that their existence as a church was declining, and that it was

1 Our readers are surely of opinion that there could be no doubt whatever that the relic adverted to, the pretended coat of our Lord, lately exhibited at Treves, was a monstrous cheat. The expression "überaus zweifelhaften," if used out of politeness, is more than the patrons of such an imposition deserve.—Tr.

approaching its final dissolution, have awoke to a consciousness of their original power and their common interest. The attempt made by a Roman catholic government to force upon its troops in military service, the practice of Roman catholic ceremonies, has been found impracticable.

In England, the protestant spirit bestirs itself even against the measures which the government, advancing along the course on which it has once entered, conceives that it is necessary to adopt for the religious settlement of Ireland, with an energy which makes it doubtful whether now, under the altered circumstances of the reformed and hitherto popular parliaments, measures like those of 1829 could still be carried.

For in these, as well as other movements of the age, there is an incessant conflicting of eager energies, advance and retreat, assault and defence, action and re-action. Not a moment resembles another; different elements unite and separate again; every excess is followed by its opposite; and the remotest objects act upon each other. Whilst, moreover, political considerations linger more in individual kingdoms and nations, the ecclesiastical interest has this peculiarity, that one of the most powerful principles of the popedom possesses a great representative body, which insinuates itself and makes encroachments in all kingdoms and nations. Even around the restored popedom, men's minds are divided in opinion, and nations and states assume anomalous positions; not, indeed, any longer with the energetic faith of former times, which created and annihilated: any such force resides neither in the assault nor the defence, neither in the Jesuits nor in their enemies; yet not without a real reference to the weightiest and profoundest needs of individuals and of society, and which is very characteristic, under the incessant influence of past times operating on living contemplation. All the antagonisms that have ever agitated the world on this territory, have again advanced into the arena; of councils and ancient heretics, of the medi-æval power of the emperor and the popes, of reformation ideas and the inquisition, of later churches and modern civil government, of Jansenism and the Jesuits, of religion and philosophy; and over these moves the life of these our days, susceptible and excursive, driving in vehement dissension towards unknown ends, no longer compressed and bound by powerful natures, fickle and self-confident, and in a state of universal fermentation.

It is not certainly to be expected that hierarchical efforts will again take possession of the world, and prove capable of establishing a kind of priestly dominion: they are opposed by energies all too powerful and bound up with the deepest sentiments of man's inmost soul.

But in the course that ecclesiastical things have taken, there is no prospect such as may lead us to expect that the negative spirit, that especially which would do away with all religion, will be so soon subdued. Much rather does infidelity nourish itself on hierarchical usurpation. It cannot, indeed, be said, in general, that the Roman see, while placed itself, all along the protestant frontiers, in a state of readiness to strike a blow, to renew afresh the ancient controversies between church and state, has contributed much towards the restraining of the revolutionary spirit. In the most immediate neighbourhood of Rome, at the very foot of the Vatican, it has more than once bestirred itself, and could be repressed only by means of foreign power.

Betwixt these two antagonist influences will the formation of the personal sentiments of mankind for some time yet certainly fluctuate.

Not only the religious soul, the mind, too, that takes a comprehensive view of things, meanwhile feels its need of entertaining a prospect beyond the sphere of contention and dispute.

We do not deceive ourselves if we fancy we can perceive that, in spite of these, men of deeper minds on both sides, are returning to the eternal principles of pure inward religiousness, with an ever-increasing consciousness, penetration, and freedom from the trammels of a narrow regard for ecclesiastical forms! The full apprehension of the spiritually-positive that lies at the bottom of all forms, and which, in its whole import, can be expressed by none of them, when it succeeds, must at last, indeed, reconcile all enmities. We cannot relinquish the hope that, emerging from the ocean of dissentient opinions, there will yet one day arise the unity of a knowledge of God, at once pure, and not, on that account, the less certain of attaining its purpose.[1]

[1] "The knowledge of man," says Lord Bacon, "is as the waters, some descending from above, and some springing from beneath; the one informed by the light of nature, the other inspired by divine revelation:" and surely we may add that not till man shall seek the latter as well as the former, and that, too, at its proper source, submitting withal to its lessons, without confounding them with those of his own wisdom, under whatever shows of authority these may be propounded,—not till then can the unity and purity contemplated by our author possibly be attained. Tr.

OF THE MANUSCRIPTS THAT MAY

SPECIMEN ACTS.

SECTION FIRST.

TO THE COUNCIL OF TRENT.

AD S. D^m Nostrum Pontificem Maximum Nicolaum V conformatio curie romane loquentis edita per E. S. oratorem Joseph. B. doctorem cum humili semper recommendatione. (1453.) Bibl. Vatic. nr. 3618.—[To our holy supreme pontiff Nicolas V., the Roman curia represented as speaking, published by E. S., orator, doctor of the blessed Joseph, always with a humble recommendation. (1453.) Vatican Library, No. 3618.]

A lament over the well-known conspiracy of Stephen Porcaris, which does not directly communicate more precise information with respect to it, yet sets before us some of the main features in the state of things at that time. Take an instance which bears particularly on the architectural enterprises of Nicolas V.

Arces fortificat muris turrimque superbam
Extruit - - - ne quisque tyrannus ab alma
Quem queat urbis valeat pepam

[With walls he fortifies each castled height,
And builds a tower magnificently great,
Lest any tyrant should have power to chase
The pope, defenceless, from the bounteous
place.]

How often had preceding popes been compelled to desert their city! Nicolas built in order to defend himself against enemies from within and from without.

Further on we find the relation in which Rome stood to other Italian cities.

- - Si tu perquiris in omnibus illam (libertatem)
urbibus Italiæ, nullam mihi crede profecto
invenies urbem quæ sit majore per omnem
libertate modum quam nunc tua Roma fruatur.
Omnis enim urbs dominis et pace et bello coacta
præstita magna suis durasque gravata gabellas
solvit, et interdum propriam desperat habere
justitiam, atque ferox violentia civibus ipsis
sæpe fit, ut populus varie vexatus ab illis
fiat, sit hoc onere pauper de divite
at tua Roma sacro nec præstita nec si
vim
nec grave vectigal nec pondera cogitur ulla
solvere pontifici nil humiles minimasque
las:
præterea hic dominus tribuit justissimus almam
justitiam cuicunque suam, violentaque nulli
infert: hic populum prisco de paupere ditem
efficit, et placida Romam cum pace gubernat.

[Ask them through all the Italian cities round,
Where most of this true liberty is found,
Believe me, all will in their turns confess,
That thine own Rome doth most of it possess,
In all its kinds. For every city ruled
By its own lords, in peace and war befooled,
To meet the calls of tax and due must toil,
Yet hardly knows what justice is the while.
Often oppression fierce and violence
So overwhelm and vex the citizens,
That rich men are impoverished, and the poor
Are crushed by miseries unknown before.
Far otherwise thy Rome, nor charge severe,
Nor tyrant force, nor heavy tax, need fear,
She never is compelled to pay the least
Tribute or impost to her sacred priest,
And yet the pontiff, justest of the just,
Faithful to execute his solemn trust,
'Twixt man and man sees justice always done,
And offers violence himself to none.
He makes the poor in opulence increase,
And governs Rome with joy-inspiring peace.]

APPENDIX.

LIST OF THE MANUSCRIPTS THAT HAVE BEEN CONSULTED, SUPPLEMENTARY EXTRACTS, AND CRITICAL OBSERVATIONS.

SECTION FIRST.

TO THE COUNCIL OF TRENT.

1.

Ad S. Dm Nostrum Pontificem Maximum Nicolaum V. conformatio curie romane loquentis edita per E. S. oratorem Joseph. B. doctorem cum humili semper recommendatione. (1453.) Bibl. Vatic. nr. 3618.—[To our holy supreme pontiff Nicolas V., the Roman curia represented as speaking, published by E. S., orator, doctor of the blessed Joseph, always with a humble recommendation. (1453.) Vatican Library, No. 3618.]

A lament over the well-known conspiracy of Stephen Porcaris, which does not directly communicate more precise information with respect to it, yet sets before us some of the main features in the state of things at that time. Take an instance which bears particularly on the architectural enterprises of Nicolas V.

Arces fortificat muris turrimque superbam
Extruit - - - ne quisque tyrannus ab alma
Quemque armis valeat papam depellere Roma.

[With walls he fortifies each castled height,
And builds a tower magnificently great,
Lest any tyrant should have power to chase
The pope, defenceless, from the bounteous place.]

How often had preceding popes been compelled to desert their city! Nicolas built in order to defend himself against enemies from within and from without.

Farther on we find the relation in which Rome stood to other Italian cities.

- - Si tu perquiris in omnibus illam (libertatem)
urbibus Italiæ, nullam mihi crede profecto
invenies urbem quæ sic majore per omnem
libertate modum quam nunc tua Roma fruatur.
Omnis enim urbs dominis et pace et bello coacta
præstita magna suis durasque gravata gabellas
solvit, et interdum propriam desperat habere
justitiam, atque ferox violentia civibus ipsis
sæpe fit, ut populus varie vexatus ab illis
fasce sub hoc onerum pauper de divite fiat;
at tua Roma sacro nec præstita nec similem vim
nec grave vectigal nec pondera cogitur ulla
solvere pontifici ni humiles minimasque gabellas:
præterea hic dominus tribuit justissimus almam
justitiam cuicunque suam, violentaque nulli
infert: hic populum prisco de paupere ditem
efficit, et placida Romam cum pace gubernat.

[Ask then through all the Italian cities round,
Where most of this true liberty is found,
Believe me, all will in their turns confess,
That thine own Rome doth most of it possess,
In all its kinds. For every city ruled
By its own lords, in peace and war befooled,
To meet the calls of tax and due must toil,
Yet hardly knows what justice is the while.
Often oppression fierce and violence
So overwhelm and vex the citizens,
That rich men are impoverished, and the poor
Are crushed by miseries unknown before.
Far otherwise thy Rome, nor charge severe,
Nor tyrant force, nor heavy tax, need fear,
She never is compelled to pay the least
Tribute or impost to her sacred priest,
And yet the pontiff, justest of the just,
Faithful to execute his solemn trust,
'Twixt man and man sees justice always done,
And offers violence himself to none.
He makes the poor in opulence increase,
And governs Rome with joy-inspiring peace.]

He charges the Romans with coveting the old Roman freedom. The fact, too, that the papal government was milder than the sovereignty of civic chiefs, is established beyond a doubt, and contributed much towards the acquisitions made by the ecclesiastical state.[1] Our author thinks the opposition of the citizens to the church as unpardonable, seeing that it secured to them so many spiritual and secular benefits.

quibus auri copia grandis argentique ferax, æternaque vita salusque, provenit, ut nulli data gratia tam ardua genti.	with whom are always rife Both gold and silver, while eternal life, Their souls' salvation is to them made sure, Blessings beyond what others can secure.

The pope is recommended to provide still better for his safety, never to go to St. Peter's without a guard of 300 armed men; but therewithal to aim at possessing the affection of the inhabitants, to support the poor, particularly poor people of good descent, "vitam qui mendicare rubescunt"—[who blush to support life by begging];

—succurre volentibus artes exercere bonas, quibus inclyta Roma nitescat.	—succour the willing to expend Their lives in arts that Rome's renown extend.

which hardly needed to be said to Nicolas V. This little work, moreover, is referred to in the Vita Nicolai V. a Domenico Georgio, conscripto Romæ, 1742, p. 130.—[Life of Nicolas V. by Dominick George, written at Rome in 1742, p. 130.]

2.

Instructiones datæ a Sixto IV. RR. PP. Dnis J. de Agnellis protonotario apostolico et Antº de Frassis s. palatii causarum auditori ad M. Imperatoris. 1 Decis 1478.—[Instructions given by Sixtus IV. to the Rev. fathers Lords J. de Agnelli, apostolic prothonotary, and Anthony de Frassis, auditor of causes to the sacred palace, proceeding on an embassage to the Emperor's Majesty. 1st December, 1478.] Bibl. Altieri [Altieri Libr.], VII. G. 1, 99.

The earliest body of instructions that I have met with among the manuscripts that have come into my hands. It begins, "Primo salutabunt Serenissimum Imperatorem."—[They will first salute the most serene emperor.]

The assault of the Pazzi on the Medici occurred on the 26th of April, 1478. It threw all Italy into commotion. "Ecclesia justa causa contra Laurentium mota, clamant Veneti, clamat tota ista liga."—[The church being justly incensed against Lorenzo, the Venetians exclaim, the whole of that League exclaims.]

The ambassadors were to prevent the emperor from giving credit to a certain James de Medio whom the Venetians had sent as their deputy to the Imperial court. "Est magnus fabricator et Cretensis: multa enim referebat suis quæ nunquam cogitaveramus neque dixeramus."—[He is a great fabricator (of lies) and a Cretan: for he told many things to his countrymen which we never had thought of nor had said.] They were to apply to the emperor about his mediation. This the king of France had offered, but the pope might prefer procuring that honour for the emperor.

"Velit scribere regi Franciæ et ligæ isti, ostendendo quod non recte faciunt, et parum existimant deum et honorem pontificis, et quod debent magis favere ecclesiæ justitiam habenti quam uni mercatori, qui semper magna causa fuit, quod non potuerunt omnia confici contra Turcum quæ intendebamus parare, et fuit semper petra scandali in ecclesia dei et tota Italia."	[He might be willing to write to the king of France and to that league, showing that they are not acting rightly, and make too little account of God and the honour of the pontiff, and that they ought rather to favour the church with justice on her side than a merchant, who had always been a great cause of their not having been able to carry into effect against the Turk what we minded to prepare, and was always a rock of offence in the church of God and in all Italy.]

The case was so much the more perilous for the pope, as it was contemplated to oppose his secular encroachments with a council. "Petunt cum rege Franciæ concilium in Galliis celebrari in dedecus nostrum."—[They seek with the king of France to have a council held in the Gauls to our disgrace.]

This reminds us of the attempt certainly made somewhat later, to have a council assembled. The archbishop of Kraina had acquired thereby a certain reputation. To this John von Müller has devoted a few pages of his Swiss History (p. 286). Only, in the account he gives, the secular occasion for it does not sufficiently appear. Cardinal Andreas was not quite so spiritual as it would seem, according to Müller. The ambassadors from Florence and Milan went to look for him at Basel; they came in the name of the whole league that had taken the field against Sixtus. They found in him, we have their report, great worldly experience (gran pratica et experientia del mundo—[great practice and experience of the world]), and a vehement hatred of the pope and his nephews. "E huomo per fare ogni cosa purche e' tuffi el papa e 'l conte."—[He is a man capable of doing anything, if but the pope and the counts are put down.] S. Baccius Ugolinus Laurentio Medici in Basilea a dì 20 Sept. 1482, in Fabroni Vita Laurentii, II. 229. Thus we perceive that, even at this time, there was an ecclesiastical opposition on the part of the princes from secular motives. They had ecclesiastical weapons, too, and these they opposed to those of the popes.

1 Small thanks for this, when we remember that all Christendom was laid under contribution for the pope.—Tr.

3.

Relatione fatta in pregadi per Polo Capello el cavalier venuto orator di Roma, 1500, 28 Sett. —[Report presented in the Senate by Polo Capello, knight, on his coming as ambassador from Rome, 28th September, 1500.]

This is the first report, that I have found, by a Venetian ambassador on the papal court. It nowhere appears in the Venetian archives, and it would seem, that at that time the reports were not as yet delivered in writing. It is to be found in the Chronicle of Sanuto, who, generally speaking, records all that was laid before the senate, the *pregadi.*

Polo Capello engages to treat of four things: the cardinals—the disposition entertained by the pope towards the king of France and to Venice—the objects aimed at (el desiderio) by his Holiness—from which might be augured what was to be expected from him; but as this distribution of his subject is not based on any very precise distinction, he does not strictly observe it.

He remarks, first of all, that neither Venice nor France were on good terms with the pope: the former because he had possessed himself of part of the Milanese territory, and made people fear that he might seize upon all Italy; but the latter because the king did not keep his promises to the pope. Here we find the conditions of the league between the king and the pope. The pope granted the king the dispensation for separation from his wife. In return the king engaged to give the pope's son, Cæsar Borgia, a state with a revenue of 28,000 francs, a wife of the blood royal (Navarre?), and the renunciation of any Neapolitan attempt of his own, except in favour of Borgia, "— del regno di Napoli non se impazzar se non in ajutar il papa." So that we see that the pope had even then an eye to Naples. But these promises were not kept. The matrimonial alliance promised to Cæsar was not altogether desirable; the pope went so far as even to purchase, on the security of the dowry, an estate of 12,000 francs, but the young bride remained in France. Nothing but the king's superiority in point of force, kept the pope to his duty. "Quando il Sr Lodovico intrò in Milan," says Capello, very emphatically, "publice diceva (il papa) mal del roy."—[When Lord Louis entered Milan, he (the pope) publicly traduced the king.] He was enraged at the French not offering him their assistance in expelling Bentivogli from Bologna.

While this passage gives us a better insight into the internal spring of the papal policy at that time, it is followed by a delineation of personal qualities which is of much value.

The author comes first to speak of the death of the son-in-law of Alexander VI. Cæsar had already wounded him.

"Per dubio mandò a tuor medici di Napoli: stè 33 dì ammalato, et il c^l Capua lo confessò, e la moglie e sorella, ch' è moglie del principe de Squillaci altro fiol di papa, stava con lui et cusinava in una pignatella per dubio di veneno, per l'odio li haveva il ducha di Valentinos, et il papa li faceva custodir per dubio esso ducha non l'amazzasse, e quando andava il papa a visitarlo, il ducha non vi andava se non una volta e disse: quello non è fatto a disnar si farà a cena. Or un zorno, fo a dì 17 Avosto, intrò in camera che era za sublevato, e fe ussir la moglie e sorella: intrò Michiele cussi chiamato, e strangolò ditto zovene. - - "

"Il papa ama et ha gran paura del fiol ducha, qual è di anni 27, bellissimo di corpo e grande, ben fatto e meglio che re Ferandin: amazzò 6 tori salvadegi combatendo a cavallo a la zaneta, et a uno li taiò la testa a la prima bota, cosa che paresse a tutta Roma grande. E realissimo, imo prodego, e il papa li dispiace di questo. Et alias amazzò sotto il manto del papa, M. Peroto, adeo il sangue li saltò in la faza del papa, qual M. Peroto era favorito del papa. Etiam amazzò il fratello ducha di Gandia e lo fe butar nel Tevere.—Tutta Roma trema di esso ducha non li faza amazzar."

[In doubts (of his safety) he sent for physicians from Naples: he continued 33 days unwell, and Cardinal Capua confessed him, and the wife and the sister, who is wife of the prince of Squillace, another son of the pope's, remained with him and prepared his food in a saucepan for fear of poison, because of the hatred with which he was regarded by the duke of Valentinois, and the pope caused him to be guarded, in dread of the said duke murdering him, and when the pope went to visit him, the duke went not thither except once, and said, What is not done at dinner will be done at supper. But one day, it was the 17th of August, he entered the room, after he had risen, and made the wife and sister go out: Michael entered, as if called, and strangled the said youth.]

[The pope loves and stands in great dread of his son, the duke, who is twenty-seven years of age, remarkably handsome and tall, well made and better than king Ferdinand (the last king of Naples, that is, Ferdinand, who passed for being particularly handsome): he killed six wild bulls, fighting on horseback with the *gianetta*, and cleft the head of one of them at the first blow, which all Rome thought was a great feat. He is most regal, very prodigal, and the pope is displeased with him for this. And at another time he assassinated, under the mantle of the pope, M. Peroto, so that the blood spurted on the face of the pope, which M. Peroto was a favourite of the pope. He murdered, likewise, his brother, the duke of Gandia, and had him thrown into the Tiber. All Rome trembled at the thought of being murdered by the said duke.]

Roscoe, in the Life of Leo X., has endeavoured to clear the memory of Lucretia Borgia from the scandalous charges that have been heaped upon it. To the accusations brought

against her earlier life, he has opposed a multitude of favouraolc testimonies to the latter part of it. But even the German translator of his work has not been convinced by these. It is his opinion that she had first after that undergone a change for the better. The report before us is remarkable, besides, on this account, that it gives a favourable testimony for Lucretia, taken from the earlier period. It says: "Lucrezia la qual è savia e liberal."—[Lucretia, who is wise and generous.] Cæsar Borgia was rather her enemy than her lover. He took her sermoneta, which she had received from the pope; he said, she is a woman, she knows not how to keep it: "è donna, non lo potrà mantenir."

4.

Among the various documents to be found in Sanuto's fifth volume, the following seems to me the most important.

Questo è il successo de la morte di papa Alexandro VI.—[This is what happened at the death of Pope Alexander VI.]

"Hessendo el c[l] datario dno Arian da Corneto stato richiesto dal pontefice chel voleva venir a cena con lui insieme con el duca Valentinos a la sua vigna et portar la cena cum S. Sta, si imaginò esso cardinal questo invito esser sta ordinado per darli la morte per via di veneno per aver il duca li soi danari e beneficii, per esser sta concluso per il papa ad ogni modo di privarlo di vita per aver il suo peculio, come ho ditto, qual era grande, e procurando a la sua salute penso una sola cosa poter esser la via di la sua salute. E mando captato tpio (tempo?) a far a saper al schalcho del pontefice chel ge venisse a parlar, con el qual havea domestichezza. El qual venuto da esso cd[l], se tirono tutti do in uno loco secreto, dove era preparato duc. X m. d'oro, e per esso c[l] fo persuaso ditto schalco ad acetarli in dono e galderli per suo amor. El qual post multa li acceptò, e li oferse etiam il resto di la sua faculta, perche era richissimo card[l], a ogni suo comando, perchè li disse chel non poteva galder detta faculta se non per suo mezo, dicendo: vui conoscete certo la condition del papa, et io so chel ha deliberato col ducha Valentinos ch'io mora e questo per via di esso schalco per morte venenosa, pregandolo di gratia che voia haver pieta di lui e donarli la vita. Et dicto questo, esso schalcho li dichiari il modo ordinato de darli il veneno a la cena, e si mosse a compassione promettendoli di preservarlo. Il modo era chel dovea apresentar dapoi la cena tre schatole di confecion in taola, una al papa, una al d[to] card[l] et una al ducha, et in quella del card[l] si era il veneno. E cussi messe ditto card[l] ordine al prefato schalcho del modo che dovea servir, e far che la scutola venenata, dovea aver esso card[l], di quella il papa manzasse e lui si atosegaria e moriria. E cussi venuto il pontefice a la cena al zorno dato l'hordine col ducha preditto, el prefato c[l] se li butto a li piedi brazzandoli et strettissimamente baxandoli, con affectuosissime parole supplicando a S. S[ta], dicendo, mai di quelli piedi si leveria si S. Beat. non li concedesse una gratia. Interrogato del pontefice, qual era facendo instanza, se levasse suso, esso c[l] respondeva chel voleva aver la gratia el dimanderia et haver la promessa di fargela da S. Sta. Hor dapoi molta persuasion, il papa stete assai admirativo vedendo la perseverantia del d[to] c[le] e non si voler levar, e li promisse di exaudirlo: al qual card[l] sublevato disse: patre santo, non è convenicnte che venendo il signor a caxa del

[The cardinal datary, lord Arian da Corneto, having been informed by the pontiff, that he wished to come to supper with him, together with the duke de Valentinois, at his vineyard, and to bring the supper with his holiness, the cardinal imagined that this invitation had been arranged with the view of taking his life by poison, in order that the duke might have his fortune and his benefices, from the pope having come to the conclusion of by all means depriving him of life, in order to have his private property, which, as I have said, was large, and while looking about how he could save his life, he thought that one thing only could secure his safety. And he sent, having taken (time?) word to the pontiff's carver, for him to come to speak with him as he had a favour for him. And the latter having come to the said cardinal, the two went aside together to a secret place, where ten thousand ducats in gold had been got ready, and the said carver was persuaded by the cardinal to accept of them as a present, and to keep them out of love for him. The which he accepted after much being said, and he offered him even the rest of his wealth, for he was a very rich cardinal, to whatever extent he might command it, for he told him he could not keep that wealth unless by his intervention, saying, "You certainly know the nature of the pope, and I know that he has determined, along with the duke of Valentinois, that I must die, and that through the agency of the carver by a death by poison, beseeching him for mercy's sake that he would have compassion on him and give him his life." And after this was said, the carver told him in what manner it had been determined to give him poison at supper, and he was moved with compassion, and promised to preserve him. The method was that he was to put after supper three dishes of confectionary on the table, one for the pope, one for the said cardinal, and one for the duke, and the poison was to be in that presented to the cardinal. And so the said cardinal gave instructions to the carver aforesaid as to the manner in which he was to serve, and to do so in such wise that the poisoned dish which the cardinal was to have, should be eaten by the pope, and that he should poison himself and die. And so the pope having come to supper on the appointed day with the foresaid duke, the said cardinal threw himself at his feet, embracing and most familiarly kneeling to him, supplicating

servo suo, dovesse el scrvo parimente confrezer (?) con el suo signor, e perho la gratia el dimandava era questa zusta e honesta che lui servo dovesse servir a la mensa di S. S[ta], e il papa li fece la gratia. E audato a cena al hora debita di meter la confecion in tavola, fo per il schalcho posta la confezion avenenata ne la scutola secondo el primo ordine li havea dato il papa, et il c[l] hessendo chiaro in quella non vi esser venen li fece la credenza di dicta scatola e messe la venenata avante il papa, e S. S. fidandosi del suo schalcho e per la credenza li fece esso c[l], judico in quella non esser veneno e ne manzo allegramente, e del altra, chel papa fusse avenenata si credeva e non era, manzo ditto c[l]. Hor al hora solita a la qualita del veneno sua S[ta] commenzo a sentirlo e cussi sen'e morto: el card[l], che pur haveva paura, se medicino e vomito, e non have mal alcuno ma non senza difficulta. Valete."

his holiness in most affectionate terms, and saying that never would he rise from those feet unless his Beatitude should grant him a favour. On being asked by the pope, who was pressing him to rise, the said cardinal answered that he wished to have to favour he should ask for, and to have a promise to do it from his Holiness. Then after much persuasion, the pope was surprised enough at seeing the perseverance of the said cardinal, and that he would not rise, and promised to comply with his request, whereupon the cardinal, having risen, said: Holy father, it is not fitting that the master coming to the house of his slave, the slave should be put on an equality with (?) his master, and accordingly the favour he had to ask of him was this just and honest one, that he, the slave, should serve at the table of his Holiness, and the pope complied. And having come to supper, at the time for placing the confectionary, the poisoned confects were put by the carver into the dish according to the first order that the pope had given to him, and the cardinal, well knowing which contained no poison, tasted of the said dish and put the poisoned one before the pope; and his Holiness confiding in his carver, and trusting to the cardinal's having tasted it, concluded that in that there was no poison, and ate of it heartily, and of the other which the pope believed to be poisoned, but which was not, the said cardinal ate. Now at the time that the poison, according to its quality, usually operated, his Holiness began to feel its effects and died of it: the cardinal, who however felt afraid, took medicine and vomited, and escaped without bad effects, but not without difficulty. Farewell.]

A document concerning the death of Alexander, which, if not authentic, is at least very worthy of notice; of all those we have it is perhaps the best.

5.

Sommario de la Relatione de S. Polo Capello, venuto orator di Roma, fatta in collegio 1510.—[Summary of the Report of S. Polo Capello, ambassador arrived from Rome, made in the college in 1510.]

After the great misfortune that befell the Venetians in consequence of the League of Cambray, they first succeeded gaining over pope Julius II. anew.

Polo Capello adduces some hitherto unknown motives which led to this result. The pope was afraid of the consequences that might attend a projected meeting between Maximilian and the king of France. "Dubitando perche fo ditto il re di Romani e il re di Francia si voleano abboccar insieme et era certo in suo danno."—[Being alarmed at its being said that the king of the Romans and the king of France wished to confer together, and he was certain to his disadvantage.] For some time, indeed, he called on the Venetians to give up the towns which, in virtue of the League, should fall to the German king; but when he saw that Maximilian's enterprise came to so bad an end, he pressed this no farther. He had a very poor opinion of him. "E una bestia," said he, "merita piu presto esser rezudo ch' a rezer altri."—[" He is a beast," said he, "and deserves sooner to be rejected himself than to reject others."] On the other hand, it greatly redounded to the honour of the Venetians, whose name was already considered in Rome as blotted out, that they maintained themselves. The pope gradually determined to grant absolution.

Capello had much respect for his character. "E papa sapientissimo, e niun pol intrinsechamente con lui, e si conseja con pochi, imo con niuno."—[The pope is very wise, and no one intrinsically influences him, and he consults with few, nay, with none.] The influence of Cardinal Castel de Rio was very indirect: "parlando al papa dirà una cosa, qual dita il papa poi considererà aquella," [while conversing with the pope, he will say a thing, which being said, the pope will think over it.] At that very time the cardinal was opposed to the Venetians, and yet the pope concluded his agreement with them. Capello considers that he was very well off in respect of money; that he might have had 700,000 ducats if not a million, in his treasury.

6.

Sommario di la relatione de Domenego Trivixan, venuto orator di Roma, in pregadi, 1510.—[Summary of the report of Domenego Trivixan, on his arrival ambassador from Rome, delivered in the Senate, 1510.]

Trivisan gives at greater length in the senate what Capello had stated in the college. Yet there is this difference, that the former explains the secret motives, the latter is more concerned about giving a general description. Even this, however, deserves notice.

He agrees with his colleague in his calculation of the papal treasure, only adding, that the pope had destined the money for a war against the infidels. "Il papa è sagaze praticho: ha mal vecchio galico e gota, tamen è prosperoso, fa gran fadicha: niun pol con lui: alde tutti, ma fa quello li par. È tenuto e di la bocha e di altro per voler viver piu moderamente."—[The pope is sagacious and expert; he has long suffered from liver complaint and the gout, yet he is vigorous, and undergoes much fatigue. Nobody overrules him: he hears all, but does as he pleases. He is bound both by the mouth and by another to be willing to live more moderately.] (Does this mean that he himself asserted that for the future—perhaps in drink—he would be more moderate?) "A modo di haver quanti danari il vole: perche come vacha un beneficio, non li da si non a chi (ha) officio e quel officio da a un altro, si che tocca per esso (trie durch) assai danari; ed è divenudo li officii sensari piu del solito in Roma."—[He has a method of acquiring as much money as he pleases: for when a benefice becomes vacant, he bestows it only on one who (has) an office, and this office he gives to another, so that, by this means, he gets enough of money, and offices have become higher in value than usual in Rome.] That is, the offices people have would obtain this higher value at the brokers in offices.

"Il papa a entrada duc. 200,000 di ordinario, et extraordinario si dice 150,000 (d. h. die Päpste haben gewöhnlich so viel): ma questo a di do terzi piu di extraordinario e di ordinario ancora l'entrade." [The pope has 200,000 ducats of ordinary revenue, and the extraordinary is said to be 150,000 (the meaning is, that the popes have generally so much), but this pope has now two-thirds more of extraordinary revenues and of ordinary also.] so that he would have about a million. He proceeds at once to explain this:—"Soleano pagare il censo carlini X. al ducato e la chiesia era ingannata: era carlini XIII.½ el duc.; vole paghino quello convien, et a fatto una stampa nova che val X. el duc., e son boni di arzento, del che amiora da X. a XIII.½ la intrada del papa. e diti carlini novi si chiamano juli."—[They used to pay the taxes at the rate of X. carlins for the ducat, and the church was defrauded; there was XIII.½ carlins in a ducat; he desires that they should pay what is proper, and has made a new coinage of the value of X. to the ducat, and they are good silver coins, from which the pope's revenues are improved from X. to XIII.½; and the said new carlins are called juli.] Here we see the origin of the small money in use at the present day. For the paoli of the present day not till lately supplanted the juli in name and use. The carlins which formed the coin that people reckoned by had become so depreciated that great losses were sustained thereby at the exchequer. In the interests of the exchequer Julius II. made good coins.

"Item è misero: a pocha spesa. Si acorda col suo maestro di caxa: li da el mexe per le spexe duc. 1500 e non piu. Item fa la chiexia di S. Piero di novo, cosa bellissima, per la qual a posto certa cruciata, et un solo frate di S. Francesco di quello habia racolto diti frati per el mondo li portò in una bota duc. 27 m., si che per questo tocca quanti danari el vuol. A data a questa fabrica una parte de l'intrada di S. M. di Loreto e tolto parte del vescovado di Recanati."

[Also, he is a miser: he lives at little expense. He bargains with his house steward; he gives him 1500 ducats a month for the expenses, and no more. Also, he is rebuilding the church of St. Peter, a most beautiful thing, for which he has set apart certain cruciata and a single Franciscan friar, from what the said friars had collected throughout the world, brought him, in one payment, 27,000 ducats; indeed for this he has as much money as he pleases. He has given to that building a part of the revenues of St My of Loreto, and taken part of the bishopric of Recanati.]

7.

Summario de la relatione di S. Marin Zorzi, dotor, venuto orator di corte, fata in pregadi a dì 17 Marzo, 1517.—[Summary of the report of S. Marin Zorzi, doctor (of laws), on his arrival as ambassador from the court, made in the senate, 17th March, 1517.]

Marin Zorzi was elected ambassador to the court of Leo X. on the 4th of January, and, after declining that office, was again elected to it. Though it is true that commissions were given to him, bearing upon Francis I.'s expedition, as Paruta says (lib. iii. p. 109), he must first have gone to Rome at the commencement of the year 1515.

His report refers to that period. It is the more important as he proposed to report what he had not ventured to write. "Referirà (says the Sommario, which seems to have been written afterwards,) di quelle cose che non a scritto per sue lettere, perche *multa occurrunt quæ non sunt scribenda*."—[It will report respecting things which he has not written by his letters, because there occur many things which are not proper to be written.]

These chiefly relate to the pope's negotiations with Francis I., which even Paruta did not know, and respecting which, so far as I know, we have here the best information.

There has been, ere now, something said at times about a desire on the part of pope Leo to procure a crown for his brother Julian. But it has never yet appeared how that was to be effected. Zorzi assures us, that at that time Leo proposed to the king of France, "che del reame di Napoli saria bon tuorlo di man di Spagnoli, e darlo al magnifico Juliano suo fradello."—[That it were well to take the kingdom of Naples out of the hands of the Spanish, and to give it to Julian the magnificent, his brother.] He adds—

"E sopra questo si fatichoe assai, perche el non si contentava di esser ducha so fradello, ma lo volea far re di Napoli: il christianissimo re li aria dato il principato di Taranto e tal terre: ma il papa non volse, e sopra questo venneno diversi oratori al papa, mons' di Soglie e di Borsi, et il papa diceva: quando il re vol far questo accordo, saremo con S. M. Hor si stette sopra queste pratiche: il ch^{mo} re havendo il voler che 'l papa non li saria contra, deliberò di venir potente, et cussi venne: et il papa subito si ligò con l'imperator, re catholico, re de Inghilterra e Sguizzari."

[And about this he gave himself enough of trouble, for he was not content with his brother being a duke, but wished to make him king of Naples: the most Christian king would have given him the principality of Tarentum, and so many estates: but the pope did not want that, and upon this there came divers ambassadors to the pope, Mon: de Soglie and de Borsi, and the pope said: "Should the king consent to this arrangement, we shall then side with his Majesty." Now people came to a stop about these negotiations. The most Christian king, having a mind that the pope should not be opposed to him, thought about coming with a high hand, and so he did: and the pope suddenly leagued himself with the emperor, the catholic king, the king of England and the Swiss.]

Some of Canossa's letters, printed in the Archivio storico Italiano in the year 1844, assert that this was seriously spoken of; yet, as one sees, the report of it was not so unheard-of "among domestic and foreign historians" as the editor supposed.

I have already communicated, in the text or in notes, the notices that bear on the time during which the campaign lasted.

But how much the pope was opposed in his sentiments to the French, appears from this, that he at once, on the occasion of Maximilian's enterprise of the next year, not only censured the Venetians for showing themselves so decidedly French: "O che materia," says he, "a fatto questo senato a lassar le vostre gente andar a Milano, andar con Francesi, aver passa 8 fiumi, o che pericolo è questo."—[Oh, what a thing has been done by this senate in allowing your troops to go to Milan, to go with the French, to have passed eight rivers; oh, how dangerous is this!]—but he even secretly supported Maximilian: "Il papa a questo subito mandò zente in favor del imperador e sotto man dicendo: M. Ant. Colonna è libero capitano a soldo del imperador."—[The pope upon this suddenly sent off troops in favour of the emperor, and under hand, saying: M. Ant. Colonna is a free captain in the pay of the emperor.] Meanwhile the ratification of the resolutions of Bologna was delayed. The king sent ambassadors upon ambassadors to demand it. At last the pope, on the other hand, sent his to France, and the articles were sealed.

Francis I. soon had an opportunity of revenging himself for this. The duke of Urbino presented an unexpected resistance to the pope. The ambassador of the latter assures us: "Il re non si tien satisfacto del papa: è contento Francesco Maria prosperi.—[The king does not hold himself satisfied with the pope; he is content that Francis Maria should prosper.]

He then gives a closer portraiture of the pope. "A qualche egritudine interior de repletion e catarro ed altra cosa, non licet dir, videl. in fistula. E hom da ben e liberal molto, non vorria fatticha s'il potesse far di mancho, ma per questi soi si tuo faticha. E ben suo nepote è astuto e apto far cosse non come Valentino ma poco mancho."—[He has some inward ailment arising from repletion and catarrh, and something else, which must not be spoken of, that is, *in fistula*. He is a good sort of man, and very open-handed; he would avoid all labour if he could, but owing to this his people have a double share of labour. And, indeed, his nephew is shrewd, and fit for practical business, not like Valentinois, but a little deficient.] He means Lorenzo Medici. He then absolutely asserts, what others deny—Vettori, for example—that Lorenzo Medici eagerly endeavoured to obtain Urbino. Julian, two days before his death, besought the pope to spare Urbino, where he had enjoyed so much kindness after his expulsion from Florence. The pope paid no regard to his request. He said, "non é da parlar deste cose."—[He was not there to speak about such things.] "Questo feva perche de altra parte Lorenzin li era attorno in volerli tuor il stato."—[This was because on the other hand Lorenzo was then about him, wishing him to take the state.]

Among the pope's advisers we next find Julius Medici, afterwards Clement VII., of whose talents, however, he forms no such high estimate as others: "è hom da ben, hom di non molte facende, benche adesso il manegio di la corte è in le sue mani, che prima era in S. M^{a} in Portego;"—[he is a good enough person, a man of no great powers of business, albeit that at present the management of the court is in his hands, which first was in those of S. Maria in Portego;] then Bibbiena, whom he considers disposed to favour Spain, as he had been enriched with Spanish benefices; finally, the said Lorenzo—"qual a animo gaiardo"—[who has a brave spirit].

Lorenzo leads him to speak of Florence. He says a word about the constitution, but adds: "Hora non si serva piu ordine: quel ch'el vol (Lorenzin) è fatto. Tamen Firenze è piu francese che altrimente, e la parte contraria di Medici non pol far altro, ma non li piace questa cosa."—[Now due order is no longer maintained: whatever he (Lorenzo) wishes, is done. Yet Florence is more disposed to favour France than otherwise, and the party opposed to the Medici, can make no alteration, but this does not please it.] The land militia—the *ordinanze* (rank and file)—had been dimiuished. The revenues were as follows:—(1.) 74,000 duc. from the customs, collected at the gates and in the city;—(2.) 120,000 duc. from the subject towns;—(3.) 160,000, duc. from balzello—a direct impost, a kind of tythes.

This brings him to the pope's revenues, which he reckons in general at 420,000 duc.: and so he returns to the expenditure and personal qualities of the pope.

"E docto in humanità e jure canonicho, e sopra tutto musico excellentissimo, e quando il canta con qualche uno, li fa donar 100 e piu ducati: e per dir una cosa che si dimenticò (by the author who speaks), il papa trahe all' anno di vacantie da duc. 60,000 e piu, ch' è zercba duc. 8,000 al mese, e questi li spende in doni, in zuogar a primier di che molto si diletta."

[He is learned in humanity and the canon law, and above all a most excellent musician, and when he sings with any one, he gives him 100 duc. and more: and to say what was forgotten (by the author who speaks), the pope draws annually from vacancies about 60,000 ducats and more, which is about 8,000 duc. a-month, and this he spends in presents, in playing at premier (a kind of cards), which he was very fond of.]

These notices, it will be perceived, are very graphic, and are communicated with much naiveté, and in an easy conversational manner. The reader's interest is carried along with them.

8.

Sommario di la relatione di Marco Minio, ritornato da corte, 1520 Zugno. Sanuto, Tom. XXVIII.—[Summary of the report of Marco Minio, on his return from the court in June 1520. Sanuto, vol. xxviii.]

Marco Minio was Zorzi's successor; his report is unfortunately very short. He begins with the revenues, which he considers as inconsiderable:—

"Il papa a intrada per il papato pocha: son tre sorte de intrade: d' annate traze all' anno 100 m. duc., ma le annate consistorial, ch' è episcopati e abbattie, la mita è de cardinali; di officj traze all' anno 60 m.; di composition 60 m. Non a contadi (contanti), perche e liberal, non sa tenir danari, poi li Fiorentini e soi parenti non li lassa mai aver un soldo, e diti Fiorentini è in gran odio in corte, perche in ogni cosa è Fiorentini. Il papa sta neutral fra Spagna e Franza: ma lui orator tien pende da Spagna, perche è sta pur messo in caxa da Spagnoli, etiam assumpto al papato. Il cardinal di Medici suo nepote, qual non è legitimo, a gran poter col papa: è hom di gran manegio:"—it will be seen that since Zorzi's time his reputation had increased—"a grandissima autorità, tamen non fa nulla se prima non dimanda al papa di cose di conto; hora si ritrova a Firenze a governar quella città; il cardinal Bibbiena è appresso assa del papa, ma questo Medici fa il tutto."

[The pope derives little revenue from the popedom: there are three kinds of revenue; from the annates he draws 100,000 ducats a-year, but of the consistorial annates, which are bishoprics and abbacies, a half belongs to the cardinals: from the offices he draws 60,000 ducats a-year; and from compositions 60,000. He has no ready money, for he is liberal, he cannot keep money; then the Florentines and his relations never allow him to keep a farthing, and the said Florentines are much disliked at court, for in everything there are Florentines. The pope holds a neutral position betwixt Spain and France: but the ambassador considers him a dependant of Spain on account of his having been restored to his native country by the Spaniards, and even raised to the popedom. Cardinal Medici his nephew, who is illegitimate, has much influence with the pope; he is a man of much skill in negotiation—(it will be seen that since Zorzi's time his reputation had increased)—he has the utmost authority, yet he does nothing without first asking the pope's leave when the matter is important: at present he is at Florence engaged in the government of that city: Cardinal Bibbiena is often enough with the pope, but this Medici does everything.]

The ambassador assures his countrymen that the pope entertains tolerably favourable sentiments towards them. It is true he does not wish to see Venice become greater, but for no disadvantage in the world would he suffer it to perish.

9.

Diario de Sebastiano de Branca de Telini. Bibl. Barber. n. 1103.—[Diary of Seb. de Branca de Telini. Barberini Library, No. 1103.]

Sixty-three leaves, from the 22d of April, 1494, to 1513, run into the time of Leo X. It is not, indeed, to be compared with Burcardus, and as the least was known to the author, it cannot at all be used for the purpose of rectifying the same. He saw only what everybody else likewise saw.

Thus he describes the entrance of Charles VIII., whose army he estimates at from 30,000 to 40,000 men. He considers the king the most ill-looking person he had ever seen; while his people, on the other hand, he thought the handsomest in the world: "la piu bella gente non fu vista mai." He must not be taken at his word; he likes this way of expressing himself. (He relates that a man had paid as much as 300 ducats for a horse.)

Cæsar is the most terrible person that ever lived. The times of (pope) Alexander were distinguished for atrocities, dearths, and taxes. "Papa Alessandro gittao la data a tutti li preti e a tutti li officiali per tre anni e tutte le chiese di Roma e fora di Roma — — per fare la cruciata contro il Turco, e poi la dava allo figliuolo per fare meglio la guerra."—[Pope Alexander squandered what was given to all the priests, and to all the officials, for three years, and all the churches in Rome and out of Rome — — for carrying on a crusade against the Turk, and then gave it to his son, that the war might be better conducted.] According to him, Cæsar gave audiences to nobody but his executioner, Michilotto. All his servants went about gaily dressed: "vestiti di broccado d'ore e di velluto fino alle calze: se ne facevano le pianelle e le scarpe"—[clothed in brocade of gold and velvet to their stockings: their shoes and slippers were made of it].

He is a huge admirer of Julius II.: "No lo fece mai papa quello che have fatto papa Julio." —[No pope ever did what has been done by pope Julius.] He reckons up the towns he had taken, yet he supposes that by his wars he was chargeable with the death of 10,000 men.

Leo comes next. He began with promises: "Che i Romani fossero franchi di gabella, ed officii e beneficii che stanno nella cittade di Roma fossero dati alli Romani: ne fecero grand' allegrezze per Roma."—[That the Romans should be freed from the tax called gabel, and the offices and benefices which were comprised within the city of Rome were to be given to the Romans: he by this caused great satisfaction throughout Rome.]

Private persons occasionally occur; thus here, for example, we become acquainted with the boldest and most renowned procurator: Bent° Moccaro, il piu terribile nomo (mæchtigste, gewaltigste) che mai fusse stato in Roma per un uomo privato in Roma."—[Bent° Moccaro, the most terrible man (most powerful and violent) that had ever been in Rome, for a private man in Rome.] He lost his life by means of the Orsini.

Even in this otherwise unimportant work there is reflected, as in a glass, the spirit of the times—the spirit of the different governments,—times of terror, of conquest, and of mildness, under Alexander, Julius, and Leo. Other diaries, as that for example of Cola Colleine, from 1521-1561, contain, on the other hand, nothing of importance.

10.

Vita Leonis X. Pontificis Maximi per Franciscum Novellum Romanum, J. V. Professorem. Bibl. Barberina.—[Life of Leo X., supreme pontiff, by Francis Novella, Roman, Professor of Civil and Canon Law. Barberini Library.]

"Alii (says the author) longe melius et haec et alia mihi incognita referre et describere poterunt."—[Others (says the author) could relate and describe both these and other things unknown to me, much better.] Very true. His little work is thoroughly insignificant.

11.

Quaedam historica quae ad notitiam temporum pertinent pontificatuum Leonis X., Adriani VI., Clementis VII. Ex libris notariorum sub iisdem pontificibus.—[Some historical notices bearing upon a proper notion of the times of the popedom of Leo X., Adrian VI., Clement VII. From the books of the notaries under those pontiffs.] Excerpted by Felix Contellorius. Bibl. Barberina. 48 leaves.

Short sketches of the tenor of instruments: e. g. "Leo X. assignat contessinae de Medicis de Rodulfis ejus sorori duc. 285 auri de camera ex introitibus dohanarum pecudum persolvendos."—[Leo X. assigns to the countess di Medici di Rodulphi, his sister, 285 golden ducats from the treasury, to be paid out of the receipts of the customs on sheep.]

I have availed myself here and there of these sketches. Perhaps humanly the most remarkable, and which has remained hitherto unmentioned, is the following statement from a brief of 11th June, 1529:—"Some jewels belonging to the papal see had been removed into the charge of Bernard Bracchi. At the time of the capture of the city, Bracchi thought it advisable to bury them in a garden. He informed one person alone of his having done so, a certain Jerome Bacato of Florence, so that some one might know of it in case of any mischance happening to himself. In a short time Bracchi was seized by the Germans, and received very rough treatment. Jerome supposed forthwith that his friend had died under the torture, and from a like anxiety communicated his secret to another person. But this last was not so incommunicative: the Germans heard of the hidden treasure, and by renewed and more violent tortures, they compelled Bracchi at last to point out the place. In order to redeem this treasure Bracchi came under an obligation to pay 10,000 ducats. Jerome looked upon himself as a traitor, and killed himself from shame and rage.

12.

Sommario di la relation fatta in pregadi per S. Aluixe Gradenigo, venuto orator di Roma, 1523 Mazo.—[Summary of the Report made in the senate by S. Aluixe Gradenigo, on his arrival as ambassador from Rome, March 1523.] Sanuto, tom. xxxiv.

First about the city, which he too finds increased in a short time by about 10,000 houses; of its constitution: the conservators claim the rank of ambassadors, which the latter refuse them. Julius Medici had risen still higher in reputation. "Hom di summa autorità e richo cardinale, era il primo appresso Leon, hom di gran ingegno e cuor: il papa (Leone) feva quello lui voleva."—[A man of the highest authority, and a rich cardinal, he ranked next after Leo, a man of great genius and spirit: the pope (Leo) did whatever he desired should be done.] He describes Leo X., "Di statura grandissima, testa molto grossa, havea bellissima

man: bellissimo parlador: prometea assa ma non atendea.—Il papa si serviva molto con dimandar danari al imprestido, vendeva poi li officii, impegnava zoie, raze del papato e fino li apostoli per aver danaro."—[Of very large stature, he has a huge head, and a most beautiful hand: the finest speaker: he promises enough but forgets to observe his promises.—The pope has been much in use to ask for money on loan; he then sold offices, and pledged jewels, the glories of the popedom, and even the (silver) apostles, to get money.[1]] He reckons the secular revenues at 300,000, and the spiritual at 100,000 ducats.

He considers Leo's policy thoroughly anti-French. If appearances were ever otherwise, he must have dissembled. "Fenzeva esse amico del re di Francia."—[He feigned being a friend to the king of France.] But at that time he was openly opposed to France, for which Gradenigo adduces the following reason. "Disse che m[r] di Lutrech et m[r] de l'Escu havia ditto che 'l voleva che le recchia del papa fusse la major parte restasse di la so persona."—Does it mean that there should be nothing left to the pope but his ears? A gross jest indeed, and absurd withal, which Leo took very ill. On the arrival of the news of the taking of Milan, Leo is said to have remarked that it was but half of the war.

Leo left the papal exchequer so exhausted, that the wax candles that had been intended for the funeral ceremonies of cardinal S. Giorgio, who died shortly before him, had to be taken for his own.

The ambassador waited till the arrival of Adrian VI. He describes the latter's moderate and rational mode of life, and remarks that at first he maintained a neutrality.

"Disse: il papa per opinion soa, ancora che'l sia dipendente del imperador, è neutral, ed a molto a cuor di far la trieva per atender a le cose del Turco, e questo si judica per le sue operation cotidiane come etiam per la mala contentezza del vicere di Napoli, che venne a Roma per far dichiarar il papa imperial, e S. S[a] non volse, onde si partì senza conclusion. Il papa è molto intento a le cose di Hungaria e desidera si fazi la impresa contra infideli, dubita che 'l Turco non vegni a Roma, pero cerca di unir li principi christiani e far la paxe universal, saltem trieve per tre anni."

[It is said, that in his own opinions the pope is neutral, notwithstanding his being dependant on the emperor, and has much at heart the making of a peace in order to attend to the affairs of the Turk, and this is thought to be the case from his daily proceedings, as also from the discontentment of the viceroy of Naples, who came to Rome to get the pope to declare himself imperial, and His Holiness would not do so; hence he went away without effecting his object. The pope is very attentive to the affairs of Hungary, and desires that an enterprise should be undertaken against the infidels, is afraid lest the Turk should come to Rome, therefore wishes to unite the chiefs of Christendom, and to have an universal peace, or at least a truce for three years.]

13.

Summario del viazio di oratori nostri andono a Roma a dar la obedientia a papa Hadriano VI.—[Summary of the journey which our ambassadors made to Rome to do obeisance to pope Adrian VI.]

The only report which gives the interest of the narrative of a journey, and also pays attention to objects of art.

The ambassadors describe the prosperity of Ancona, the fertility of the Mark; in Spello they were well received by Horace Baglione; and so they came to Rome.

They describe an entertainment given them by a landed proprietor, cardinal Cornelio. Their account of the music given while they were at the table, is worth notice. "A la tavola vennero ogni sorte de musici, che in Roma si atrovava, li pifari excellenti di continuo sonorono, ma eravi clavicembani con voce dentro mirabilissima, liuti e quatro violoni."—[All kinds of musicians to be found in Rome came to the table, excellent lute-players sounded continually, but there were there harpsichords with a most wonderful voice within, lutes and four violins.] Grimani too gave them an entertainment: "Poi disnar venneno alcuni musici, tra li quali una donna brutissima che cantò in liuto mirabilmente."—[After dinner came some musicians, among whom an exceedingly deformed woman sang to the lute most wonderfully.]

They then visited the churches. At that of the Holy Cross men were employed in making some decorations about the doors; "alcuni arnesi e volte di alcune porte di una preda raccolta delle anticaglie:"—[some ornaments and vaulted masonry of some gates from spoil collected from the antique:]—each little stone that the men were here working at, deserved in their opinion, to be set in gold and worn on the finger. — The Pantheon. An altar was just then in the course of construction, at the foot of which was the grave of Raphael. They were shown decorations in imitation of gold, that seemed equal to Rhenish guldens. They are of opinion, that were it real gold, pope Leo would not have left it there. They are amazed at the pillars, larger than theirs of St. Mark. "Sostengono un coperto in colmo, el qual è di alcune travi di metallo."—They support a dome over head, which is formed of several beams of metal.]

1 Italian scholars, from different parts of Italy, have been consulted as to the meaning of the words *raze* and *apostoli*. One suggests reading *rose* for *raze*. I have ventured on preferring *razi*, as the Venetian for *raggi*. As to the word *apostoli*, writs of appeal sent from the church courts to Rome, being called in the canon law *apostoli*, the passage may imply that Leo simoniacally sold the ecclesiastical jurisdiction. This is the suggestion of an accomplished Italian; but he thinks, at the same time, that a more literal interpretation is probably more correct, and that the word may mean relics of saints and apostles. I have assumed the existence of *silver images* of the apostles.—Tr.

They surrender themselves with great *naiveté* to the admiration of antiquity. I know not whether this book is likely to fall into the hands of antiquaries. The following description of the Colosseum is at least very striking:—

"Monte Cavallo è ditto perche alla summità del colle benissimo habitato vi è una certa machina de un pezo di grossissimo muro (eine rohe Basis), sopra un di cantoni vi è uno cavallo di pietra par de Istria molto antiquo e della vetustà corroso e sopra l' altro uno altro, tutti doi dal mezo inanzi zoe testa, collo, zampe, spalle e mezo il dorso: appresso di quelli stanno due gran giganti, huomini due fiate maggiori del naturale, ignudi, che con un brazzo li tengono: le figure sono bellissime, proportionate e di la medesima pietra di cavalli, bellissimi sì i cavalli come gli huomeni, sotto uno di quali vi sono bellissime lettere majuscule che dicono opus Fidie e sotto l' altro opus Praxitelis."

[Monte Cavallo is so called because at the summit of the hill, which is very well inhabited, there is a certain contrivance of a piece of very rough wall (a rough base), over one of the corners there is a horse of what appears to be Istrian stone, very ancient, and corroded with age; and over the other (corner) another (horse), both of them from the middle perfect models, their heads, necks, paws, shoulders, and the half of their backs: beside which stand two great giants, two men sculptured larger than life, naked, holding them with one arm; the figures are most beautiful, finely proportioned, and of the same stone as the horses; most beautiful are the horses as well as the men, under one of which are most beautiful majuscule letters which tell us that it is the work of Phidias, and under the other the work of Praxiteles.]

They repair to the capitol, where, among many other fine statues, they find "uno villano di bronzo che si cava un spin da un pe, fatto al natural rustico modo: par a cui lo mira voglia lamentarsi di quel spin, cosa troppo excellente."—[a bronze peasant taking a thorn from a foot, sculptured after nature in a rustic fashion: it seems to one that his whole soul is absorbed in the distress caused by that thorn; an excellent thing.] At the Belvedere they go first of all to see the Laocoon. The German infantry have often been charged with having made it necessary to restore an arm to this work of art. But we here find that the arm was wanting previous to the taking of the city. "Ogni cosa è integra, salvoche al Laocoonte gli manca il brazzo destro."—[Every thing is entire, except that Laocoon wants his right arm.] They are in an extacy of admiration. They say of all (the figures): "non gli manca che lo spirito."—[nothing is wanting but life.] They describe the children remarkably well:—

"L' uno volendosi tirare dal rabido serpente con il suo brazello da una gamba nè potendosi per modo alcuno ajutar, sta con la faccia lacrimosa cridando verso il padre e tenendolo con l'altra mano nel sinistro brazzo. Si vede in sti puttini doppio dolore, l'uno per vedersi la morte a lui propinqua, l'altro perche il padre non lo puol ajutare e si languisce."—

[The one wishing to draw himself away from the rabid serpent with his little arm at one leg, unable in any way to help himself, stands with his weeping face crying towards his father, and holding him with the other hand in the left arm. A double grief is seen in those two boys; the one on account of the near approach of death, the other because his father cannot assist him, and he is pining away.]

They add that king Francis, at the conference of Bologna, had applied to the pope for this work (of art), but he would not allow his Belvedere to be deprived of it, and had a copy made of it for the king. The boys are already finished. But though the artist were to live 500 years, and worked a hundred at it, it would not turn out equal to the original. They found also at the Belvedere a young Flemish artist, who had executed two statues of the pope.

They now come to the subject of the pope and the court. The most important notice they communicate is that cardinal Volterra, who had hitherto dispossessed the Medici, had been apprehended, in consequence of a correspondence of his having been intercepted in which he encouraged the king of France now to ask an attack upon Italy, as he never would find a more favourable opportunity. It was just that that raised Medici again. The imperial ambassador Sessa stood by him. This occurrence may likely have given the decisive occasion for the turn taken by Adrian's policy.

14.

Clementis VII. P. M. Conclave et Creatio. Bibl. Barb. 4. 70 Bl.—[Conclave and Creation of Clement VII., supreme pontiff. Barb. Lib. 4. 70 leaves.]

We find the following note on the title: "Hoc conclave sapit stylum Joh. Bapt. Sangae civis Romani qui fuit Clementi VII. ab epistolis."—[This conclave savours of the style of John Bapt. Sanga, Roman citizen, who was Clement VII.'s secretary for letters.] But this conjecture may be unhesitatingly rejected. Another MS. of the Barberini Library, which bears the title "Vianesii Albergati Bononiensis commentarii rerum sui temporis,"—[Commentaries of the affairs of his own time by Vianesius Albergati of Bologna,) contains nothing but this conclave. It forms the first part of the Commentaries, of which meanwhile, there is no continuation to be found. We may assume that the conclave above mentioned had Vianesius Albergati for its author.

But who was this author? Mazzuchelli has several Albergati, but not this one.

In a letter of Girolamo Negros we find the following anecdote:—A Bolognese intimated to pope Adrian that he had an important secret to communicate to him, but he was in want of money to pay for his coming to him. Messire Vianesio, a friend and favourer of the Medici, interceded for him. The pope at length told the latter that he might lay out the twenty-four ducats which the Bolognese required, and that he should have them back again. Vianesio did this, and his man arrived. He was introduced with the utmost secrecy: "Holy Father," he began, "if you would conquer the Turks, you must fit out a great armament by land and sea." He said nothing more. "*Per Deum!*" [By G——!][1] said the pope, in exceeding ill humour at this, "this Bolognese of yours is a great cheat; but if he has deceived me it shall be at your cost." He never returned him the twenty-four ducats. Probably this was our author. Even in our little work he says that he had been the negotiator between the Medici and the pope: *me etiam internuntio*. He was well acquainted with Adrian, whom he already had had means of knowing in Spain.

Yet he has erected for him the most inglorious monument that can be conceived. We may form some idea from it of that whole hatred which Adrian awakened in these Italians: "Si ipsius avaritiam, crudelitatem et principatus administrandi inscitiam considerabimus, barbarorumque quos secum adduxerat asperam feramque naturam, merito inter pessimos pontifices referendus est."—[If we consider his avarice, cruelty, and ignorance of administering the principality, and the rough and wild nature of the barbarians whom he brought with him, he may deservedly be reckoned among the worst popes.] He is not ashamed to give the most pitiful pasquils on the deceased, one, for example, where he is compared first to an ass, then to a wolf, "post paulo faciem induit lupi acrem,"—[a little after he puts on the fierce countenance of a wolf,]—nay, at last with Caracalla and Nero. But if we come to proofs, the poor pope becomes even justified by what Vianesio relates.

Adrian had a room in the Torre Borgia, the key of which he always carried about with him, and which used to be called the most holy; on his death this room was eagerly opened. As he had received much and spent little, it was supposed that his treasure would be found here. Nothing was found but books and papers, a few rings of Leo the X., but hardly any money. It was admitted at last, "male partis optime usum fuisse"—[that he had made the best use of things which he had badly obtained].

The complaints raised by the author about the delays in public business might be better founded. The pope would say, "cogitabimus, videbimus"—[we will think of it—we will see]. He gave instructions indeed to his secretary; but only after long delays did the latter give instructions to the auditor of the chamber. That was a well-meaning person, but one who never brought business to a close, and entangled himself in his own activity. "Nimia ei nocebat diligentia."—[Too much diligence was hurtful to him.] Adrian was applied to anew. He would repeat: "cogitabimus, videbimus."

So much the more does he extol the Medici and Leo X., his kindly disposition, the security people enjoyed under his reign, and his architectural works.

From this I conclude that Raphael's Arazzi (tapestry) was originally intended for the Sistine chapel.

"Quod quidem sacellum Julius II. opera Michaelis Angeli pingendi sculpendique scientia clarissimi admirabili exornavit pictura, quo opere nullum absolutius extare aetate nostra plerique judicant, moxque Leo X. ingenio Raphaelis Urbinatis architecti et pictoris celeberrimi auleis auro purpuraque intextis insignivit, quae absolutissimi operis pulchritudine omnium oculos tenent."

[Which chapel, indeed, Julius II. adorned with painting admirably done by Michael Angelo, who was most celebrated as a painter and sculptor, a work than which nothing more perfect is thought by most to exist in our times, and straightway Leo X., aided by the genius of Raphael of Urbino, that most celebrated architect and painter, made it further remarkable with halls covered over with gold and purple, which charm the eyes of all men with the beauty of the most exquisite workmanship.]

15.

Instruttione al Card' Revmo di Farnese, che fu poi Paul III., quando andò legato all' Impre Carlo V. doppo il sacco di Roma.—[Instructions to the most Rev. Cardinal Farnese, who was afterwards Paul III., on his proceeding as ambassador to the emperor Charles V., after the sack of Rome.]

I found these instructions first in the Corsini library, No. 467, and thereupon obtained a copy in the written characters of the middle of the 16th century.

It was known to Pallavicini: he refers to it in his Istoria del concilio di Trento, lib. II. c. 13.—[History of the council of Trent, book II. ch. 13.] Yet, as it is evident from the following heads, he had made less use of it than his words would imply. He takes his narrative from other sources.

As these Instructions are not only of great consequence as respects papal affairs, but for the whole policy of Europe at so important a crisis, and comprise many weighty matters not acknowledged elsewhere, in the earlier editions of this work, I thought it advisable to print them entire. But since that this has been done also in the Papiers d' état du Cardinal Granvelle,—[Cardinal Granvelle's State papers,] vol. I. p. 280—310, a collection

1 It would appear that Adrian, so celebrated as a pious and virtuous pope, was a profane swearer.—Tr.

indispensable to every one who occupies himself seriously with the history of this period. I think the reader will be content with my leaving out a document which he can find elsewhere—perhaps a little modernized; but who will contend about that—and with my taking advantage of the space thus acquired to make the rest more readable by employing a larger type.

Let me only repeat here the introductory remarks on the occasion, and the arrangement of the instructions.

In June 1526, the pope published a brief, in which he succinctly narrated all his complaints against the emperor. To this the latter very warmly replied in 1526. The state paper, which appeared at that time under the title, "Pro divo Carolo V., - - apologetici libri, - -" (in Goldast Politica Imperialia, p. 984,) contains a detailed refutation of the pope's assertions. To those writings these Instructions are now to be added. It will be seen that they consist of two different parts: in the one of which the pope personally is spoken of in the third person: composed probably by Giberto or some other confidential minister of the pope, and is of the utmost importance with respect to the earlier occurrences under both Leo and Clement; and a second, which is shorter, beginning with the words *per non entrare in le cause per le quali fummo costretti,* (Pap. d' ét. p. 303) in which the pope speaks in the first person, and which was probably drawn up by himself. Both are calculated for the purpose of justifying the measures of the Roman court, and on the other hand of placing in the worst light the proceedings of the viceroy of Naples. One must not believe them to the letter on all individual points; here and there we find misrepresentations of facts: but in general not only the papal, but also a great deal of the Spanish policy is involved in them. We find, for instance, that as early as in 1525, people thought of the acquisition of Portugal to Spain.

16.

Sommario dell' Istoria d' Italia dall' anno 1512 insino a 1527, scritto da Franceso Vettori.—[Summary of the history of Italy from the year 1512 to 1527, by Francis Vettori.]

This is an exceedingly remarkable little work, written by a sensible man who was deeply initiated in the affairs of the house of Medici and those of all Italy, the friend of Machiavel and Guicciardini. I found it in the Corsini library at Rome, yet could only excerpt from it. Otherwise I should have had it printed, which it eminently deserves to be.

The plague of 1527 drove Francis Vettori from Florence, and he wrote this review of the most recent events at his country house.

He chiefly occupies himself with Florentine affairs. He approximates an opinion similar to that formed by those friends of his. When he mentions the order of things which the Medici gave to his native city in 1512, so that cardinal Medici, afterwards Leo X., had every thing at his command ("si ridusse la città, che non si facea se non quanto volea il cardinal de Medici,")—[the city was reduced to such a condition, that nothing was done but in so far as cardinal Medici chose]; he adds, men may call this tyranny, but for his part he knew of no state, whether monarchy or republic, that had not somewhat tyrannical in it. "Tutte quelle republiche e principati de' quali io ho cognitione per historia o che io ho veduto mi pare che sentino della tiraunide."—[All republics and principalities that I have any knowledge of from history, or that I have seen, seem to me to smell of tyranny.] The example of France or of Venice might be objected to him. But in France the noblesse had the preponderance in the state, and enjoyed the benefices; in Venice the 3,000 men were seen lording it over 100,000, not always righteously; between king and tyrant there is no difference but that a good governor deserves to be called a king—a bad one a tyrant.

Notwithstanding the near relation in which he stood to both Medicean popes, he is far from being convinced of the Christian nature of the papal government.

"Chi considera bene la legge evangelica, vedrà i pontefici, ancora che tenghino il nome di vicario di Christo, haver indutto una nova religione, che non ve n' è altro di Christo che il nome: il qual comanda la povertà e loro vogliono la richezza, comanda la humilità e loro vogliono la superbia, comanda la obedientia e loro vogliono comandar a ciascuno."

[He who well considers the law of the gospel will see that the popes, albeit nominally Christ's vicars, have introduced a new religion, which has nothing of Christ but the name: he enjoins poverty and they desire riches, he enjoins humility and they will have pride, he enjoins obedience and they would command everybody.]

It will be seen how much this worldly character and its contrariety to the spiritual principle, prepared the way for protestantism.

Vettori ascribes the election of Leo mainly to the opinion entertained of his good nature. Two awe-inspiring popes had preceded, and people had had enough of them. So they chose Medici. "Havea saputo in modo simulare che era tenuto di ottimi costumi."—[Having contrived to affect in his behaviour being a man of the best habits.] Bibbiena contributed most to this result, as he knew the inclinations of all the cardinals, and contrived to gain them over, against their own interests. "Condusse fuori del conclave alcuni di loro a promettere, e nel conclave a consentire a detta elettione contra tutte le ragioni."—[He led some of them out of the conclave to promise, and in the conclave to consent to the said election, against all reasons.]

He details remarkably well the expedition of Francis I. in the year 1515, and Leo X.'s conduct during the same. Its having no ill consequences as respected the pope, he attributes chiefly to the tact of Tritarico, who entered the French army at the moment when the king was about to mount his horse at Marignano, in order to oppose the Swiss, and who afterwards conducted the negotiations in the ablest manner.

The Urbino commotion followed. I have already stated the reasons alleged by Vettori in behalf of Leo.

"Leone disse, che se non privava il duca dello stato, el quale si era condotto con lui e preso danari et in su l' ardore della guerra era convenuto con li nemici nè pensato che era suo subdito, nè ad altro, che non sarebbe sì piccolo barone che non ardisse di fare il medesimo o peggio: e che havendo trovato il ponteficato in riputatione lo voleva mantenere. Et in verità volendo vivere i pontefici come sono vivuti da molte diecine d' anni in qua, il papa non poteva lasciare il delitto del duca impunito."

[Leo said that had he not taken his state from the duke who had come under an engagement to serve him, and had taken money, and in the very heat of the war had made terms with the enemies, neither considering that he was his subject, nor besides that there would not be a baron, however insignificant, who should not dare to do the same or worse, and that having received the popedom in a state of good repute, he desired to preserve it sound. And in truth, the pontiffs desiring to live as they had lived for many decads of years in this way, the pope could not allow the duke's misdeed to go unpunished.]

Vettori besides wrote in particular a life of Lorenzo Medici the I. He praises him more than any other author has done, and places his political administration of Florence in a new and peculiar light. What he says in that biography, and in the above Sommario, form the mutual complements of each other.

He treats also of the election of the emperor which fell within that period. He considers that Leo encouraged the king of France in his efforts only because he was already aware that the Germans would not elect him emperor. He reckoned that Francis I., merely to prevent the election of Charles, would give his interest to some German prince. I find the unexpected notice, which, I confess, I would not not have at once admitted—that the king did in fact at last strive to promote the election of Joachim of Brandenburg. "Il re . . haveva volto il favore suo al marchese di Brandenburg, uno delli electori, et era contento che li danari prometteva a quelli electori che eleggevano lui, dargli a quelli che eleggevano dicto marchese."—[The king . . had turned his favour to the margrave of Brandenburg, one of the electors, and was content that the money he had promised to those who elected him, should go to those who elected the said margrave.] At least the conduct of Joachim at that election was very extraordinary. This whole history, which has been marvellously misrepresented, both intentionally and unintentionally, deserves at length to receive for once the elucidation it requires.

Vettori considers Leo's alliance with Charles beyond conception irrational. "La mala fortuna di Italia lo indusse a fare quello che nessuno uomo prudente avrebbe facto."—[The evil fortune of Italy led him to do that which no prudent man would have done.] He imputes it especially to the advice of Jerome Adorno. He does not come to speak of the considerations natural to the Medici family.

With respect to the death of the pope he relates some particulars which I have adopted. He does not believe there was any poisoning. "Fu detto che morì di veneno, e questo quasi sempre si dice delli uomini grandi e maxime quando muojono di malattie acute."—[It was said that he had died of poison, and this is as it were always said of great men, and especially when they die of acute diseases.] He thinks there was more matter for wonder in Leo's having lived so long.

He maintains that Hadrian refused at first to do anything against the French: that it was on receiving a pressing letter from the emperor that he first agreed to contribute some little towards opposing them.

It would carry us too far were I to put down the remarks made in this piece on the further course of affairs; it is deserving of attention were it for nothing but the opinions expressed by the author. In these, as we have said, he very nearly resembles Machiavelli. He has quite as bad an opinion of mankind. "Quasi tutti gli uomini sono adulatori e dicono volontieri quello che piaccia agli uomini grandi, benche sentino altrimenti nel cuore."—[Almost all are flatterers, and say willingly what pleases the great, although at heart they may think otherwise.] Francis the I.'s not observing the peace of Madrid, he declares was the most glorious and the noblest thing that had been done for many centuries. "Francesco," says he, "face una cosa molto conveniente, a promettere assai con animo di non observare, per potersi trovare a difendere la patria sua."—[Francis did a very convenient thing, in promising enough with no intention of performance, in order that he might find the means of defending his country.] This view of the matter is worthy of a place in the book (of Macchiavelli's) called the Prince.

But in yet another respect, Vettori shows that he had a kindred spirit with the great authors of that epoch. The piece of writing before us is full of originality and spirit, and only the more attractive from its being brief. The author says only as much as he knows. But that is of great importance. It would require a more extensive work to do him justice.

17.

Sommario di la relatione di S. Marco Foscari venuto orator del sommo pontefice a dì 2 Marzo 1526.—[Abbreviate of the report given in by S. M. Foscari, ambassador, on his coming from the supreme pontiff, the 2d of March 1526.] In Sanuto, vol. 41.

Marco Foscari belonged to the embassy that did homage to Hadrian. Hence he appears to have remained in Rome till 1526.

He says something of Hadrian's times also, but for Clement the VII. is of so much the more weight in as much as he maintained a constant and animated intercourse with him, during the intimate connection subsisting at that time between Venice and the pope.

He describes Clement as follows:—

"Hom prudente e savio, ma longo a risolversi, e di qua vien le sue operation varie. Discorre ben, vede tutto, ma è molto timido: niun in materia di stato pol con lui, alde tutti e poi fa quello li par: homo justo et homo di dio: et in signatura, dove intravien tre cardinali e tre referendarii, non farà cosa in pregiuditio di altri, e come el segna qualche supplication, non revocha piu, come feva papa Leon. Questo non vende beneficii, nè li da per symonia, non tuo officii con dar beneficii per venderli, come feva papa Leon e li altri, ma vol tutto passi rectamente. Non spende, non dona, nè tuol quel di altri: onde è reputa mixero. E qualche murmuration in Roma, etiam per causa del card[l] Armelin, qual truova molte invention per trovar danari in Roma e fa metter nove angarie e fino a chi porta tordi a Roma et altre cose di manzar. . . . . E continentissimo, non si sa di alcuna sorte di luxuria che usi. . . . Non vol buffoni, non musici, non va a cazare. Tutto il suo piacere è di rasonar con inzegneri e parlar di aque."

[He is a prudent and wise man, but long in coming to a resolution, and changes when matters have to be carried into effect. He discourses well, sees everything, but is very timorous: no one has any power over him in matters of state, he hears all, and then does what seems to him best: he is a just man, and a man of God: and in the segnatura, where three cardinals and three referendaries have seats, he will do nothing to the prejudice of others; and when he signs any supplication, he never revokes what he has done, as Leo used to do. This pope does not sell benefices nor give them away simoniacally, he does not take offices with the right of presenting to benefices for the sake of selling them, as Leo and others did, but desires that everything should be done in a right and regular manner. He does not squander, he does not give away, nor does he take ought from another: hence he is thought miserly. There is some murmuring at Rome, even on account of cardinal Armelin, who has found out many contrivances for raising money in Rome, and causes new burthens to be laid even on those who bring thrushes and other eatable things to Rome—he is most continent: it is not known that he indulges in any luxury. . . He does not like jesters or musicians, he does not go about visiting. His whole delight lies in conversing with eminent persons and talking about waters.]

He then proceeds to speak of his advisers. To his nephew the pope would allow no influence; even Giberto had not much to say in state affairs: "il papa lo alde, ma poi fa al suo modo" [the pope hears him, but then takes his own way]; he also considers that Giberto, "devoto e savio," [who was devout and wise,] was French; Schomberg, "libero nel suo parlar," [who was loose in his conversation,] imperial. Zuan Foietta was also a great partisan of the emperors: he was less frequently with the pope after the latter became leagued with France. Foscari mentions also the pope's two secretaries, Jac. Salviati and Fr. Vizardini (Guicciardini): he considers the latter the more able of the two, but quite in the French interest.

It is remarkable that the pope stood on no better terms with the French than with the Imperialists: he knew well what he had to expect from them in the event of their being victorious. With Venice alone he found himself really allied. "Conosce, se non era la Signoria nostra, saria ruinado e caza di Roma."—[He knows that but for our Signoria, Rome too would be ruined.]

Both mutually fortified themselves in their Italian intentions, and in these saw their honour involved. The pope was proud of having withheld Venice from entering into terms with the emperor; on the other hand, our ambassador now directly maintains that he was the person to whom Italy owed her freedom: that the pope had already made up his mind to acknowledge Bourbon as archduke of Milan, when he so warmly dissuaded him from doing so, that he changed his resolution.

He asserts that the pope wanted to grant the emperor the dispensation that was required for his marriage only under certain conditions, which the foregoing instructions do not intimate, but that the emperor had contrived to obtain it without these.

In looking at this report, one special remark suggests itself. As the ambassadors were afterwards directed to draw up and give in their reports in writing, this was done by M. Foscari as well as the rest. Now it is remarkable how much tamer a production the second report is than the first. The latter was presented immediately after the occurrences had taken place, from the fresh recollection of them; so many other great events appeared thereafter, that the remembrance of the former had already become faint. Hence we see how much we are indebted to the diligence of the indefatigable Sanuto. This is the last report that I have come to the knowledge of from his Chronicle. There follow others which were kept back in private copies revised by the authors.

18.

Relatione riferita nel consiglio de pregadi per il clarissimo Gaspar Coutarini, ritornato ambasciatore dal papa Clemente VII. e dal impre Carlo V., Marzo 1530.—[Report given in to the council of Pregadi (the senate) by the most illustrious Gaspar Contarini, ambassador returned from pope Clement VII., and from the emperor Charles V., March 1530.] Informationi Politiche XXV. Berlin Library.

This is the same Gaspar Contarini, in praise of whom we have had so much to say in our history.

After having once conducted an embassy to Charles V.—the report which he rendered thereon is amongst the rarest: I have seen a single copy of it in Rome at the Albani,—he was in 1528 deputed to the pope, ere the latter had come back to Rome after so much misfortune and long absence. He accompanied him from Viterbo to Rome, from Rome to the coronation of the emperor at Bologna. There he took part in the negotiations.

He here reports on all he had met with in Viterbo, Rome, and Bologna: the only thing to be objected to him is his being so brief.

Contarini's embassy took place just at that important conjuncture in which the pope was gradually inclining again to the alliance with the emperor, such as the Medici had formerly held with him. The ambassador soon observed to his surprise that the pope, though he had been so grievously injured by the Imperialists, put almost more confidence in them than in the allies: in this he was fortified chiefly by Musettolo, "huomo," as Contarini says, "ingegnoso e di valore assai, ma di lingua e di audacia maggiore" [a man of genius and of worth enough, but of still more loquacity and audacity]; as long as the fortune of war was doubtful, the pope came to no determination; but when the French were defeated, and the Imperialists gradually found themselves ready to give up the places they possessed, no doubts could any longer be entertained. Already in the spring of 1529, the pope was on good terms with the emperor: in June they concluded their alliance, the conditions of which Contarini could obtain a sight of only with difficulty.

Contarini describes individuals also.

The pope was rather large and well-built. At that time he had not yet properly recovered from the effects of so many mischances, and from a severe illness. "He has neither much love," says Contarini, "nor vehement hatred; he is choleric, but so governs himself that none would suppose him so. He desired, indeed, to remedy the evils that oppressed the church; yet for this end he takes no proper means. No certain judgment can be formed with respect to his inclinations. It seemed for a long while as if he had the interests of Florence a little at heart, yet he now allows an imperial army to be led before that city.

Several changes took place in Clement the VII.'s ministry.

The datary Giberto still had at all times the peculiar confidence of his master, but after the measures that had been adopted under his administration, had come to so bad an issue, he withdrew of his own accord. He devoted himself to his bishopric of Verona. Niccolo Schomberg, on the other hand, had again, by means of a mission to Naples, come to have the management of the most important affairs. Contarini considers him very imperial, a man of good understanding, beneficent, but vehement. James Salviati too had much in his power; at that time he was still accounted French.

Short as this document is, yet it gives much information.

19.

Instructio data Caesari a revmo Campeggio in dieta Augustana 1530.—[Instructions given to the Emperor by the most Rev. Campeggio, at the diet of Augsburg 1530.] (MS. Rom.)

Down to this date political affairs were of most importance, but the ecclesiastical gradually draw attention. At the very first we meet with the blood-breathing proposal for the suppression of the Protestants which I have mentioned: here even called an "Instruction."

In conformity with the position he occupies and the commission of the apostolic see, says the cardinal, he would suggest the measures which, according to his judgment, should be adopted.

He describes the position of affairs as follows. "In alcuni luoghi della Germania per le suggestioni di questi ribaldi sono abrogati tutti li christiani riti a noi dagli antichi santi padri dati: non piu si ministrano li sacramenti, non si osservani li voti, li matrimonii si confundono e nelli gradi prohibiti della legge."—[In some parts of Germany, in consequence of the suggestions of some ribald souls, all the Christian rites bequeathed to us by the ancient holy fathers are abrogated: the sacraments are no longer administered, vows are not observed, marriages are confounded, and within the degrees prohibited in the law,] and so on, for it were superfluous to transcribe this Capucinade.

He reminds the emperor that this sect would bring him no such augmentation of his power as had been promised him. In the steps which he counsels him to take, he promises him his spiritual support.

"Et io, se sarà bisogno, con le censure e pene ecclesiastiche li proseguirò, non pretermettendo cosa a far che sia necessaria, privando li heretici beneficiati delli beneficii loro e separandoli con li excommunicationi

[And I, if need be, will prosecute them with ecclesiastical censures and penalties, omitting the doing of nothing that may be necessary, depriving beneficed heretics of their benefices, and separating them with ex-

dal cattolico gregge, e V. Cels. col suo bando imperiale justo e formidabile li ridurrà a tale e si horrendo esterminio che ovvero saranno costretti a ritornare alla santa e cattolica fede ovvero con la loro total ruina mancar delli beni e della vita. . . Se alcune ve ne fossero, che dio nol voglia, li quali obstinatamente perseverassero in questa diabolica via. . . quella, (V. M.) potrà mettere la mano al ferro et al foco et radicitus extirpare queste male e venenose piante."

communications from the catholic flock, and your Highness with your most just and dreadful imperial ban will reduce them to such and so horrible an extermination, that either they will be constrained to return to the holy and catholic faith, or to their utter ruin forfeit both property and life. . . Should there be any, which God forbid, that shall obstinately persevere in this diabolical course, . . your Majesty will put your hand to sword and fire, and radically extirpate these mischievous and venemous plants.]

To the kings of England and of France too, he proposes the confiscation of the property of heretics.

In the main, however, he confines himself to Germany: he shows how it was thought one might venture to interpret the articles of Barcelona, to which he chiefly refers:—

"Sarà al proposito, poiche sarà ridotta questa magnifica e cattolica impresa a buono e dritto camino, che alcuni giorni dipoi si eleggeranno inquisitori buoni e santi, li quali con summa diligentia et assiduità vadino cercando et inquirendo, s'alcuni, quod absit, perseverassero in queste diaboliche et heretiche opinioni nè volessero in alcun modo lasciarle, . . et in quel caso siano gastigati e puniti secundo le regole e norma che si osserva in Spagna con li Marrani."

[It will be to the purpose when this magnificent and catholic enterprise shall be brought into a good and straight course, that some days afterwards there be elected some good and holy inquisitors, who, with the utmost diligence and assiduity, shall go about searching and enquiring if any, *quod absit* (which may it not be) persevere in these diabolical and heretical opinions, nor will anywise relinquish them, . . and in that case they shall be chastised and punished according to the rule and principle observed in Spain with respect to the Marranos.]

Happily all were not of this opinion. Nor do such efforts any longer hold a prominent place in our documents.

20.

Relatio viri nobilis Antonii Suriani doctoris et equitis, qui reversus est orator ex curia Romana, presentata in collegio 18 Julii 1533.—[Report of the noble Anthony Suriano, doctor and knight, who has returned from acting as ambassador at the Roman curia, presented in the college 18th July 1533.] (Archivio di Venetia.)

"Among the most important matters," he begins by saying, "which ambassadors accredited to monarchs have to observe, are their personal qualities."

He describes Clement VII.'s character first.

He is of opinion that, considering the sedate manner of life of this pope, the assiduity with which he attended to the giving of his audiences, and his careful observance of ecclesiastical ceremonies, one might suppose that he was of a melancholic constitution; yet that those who knew him judged him to be of a sanguine temperament, and only cold at heart; so that he was slow in deciding, and allowed himself easily to change his determinations.

"Io per me non trovo che in cose pertinenti a stato la sia proceduta cum grande dissimulatione. Ben cauta: et quelle cose che S. Sta non vole che si intendano, piu presto le tace che dirle sotto falso colore."—[For my part I do not find, that in state affairs his Holiness has acted with much dissimulation. Certainly he is cautious: and what things his Holiness does not wish to be understood, he prefers being silent upon, to speaking of them under false colours.]

Among Clement VII.'s ministers, those mentioned in the preceding reports were no longer influential; they are not so much as once mentioned: on the other hand, James Salviati came forward, who chiefly had to direct the administration of the Romagna, and of the states of the Church in general. With regard to these, the pope committed himself entirely to him. True, the pope saw that he certainly had his own personal advantage too much in his eye; he had ere now even complained of this at Bologna; he tolerated him, however, in public affairs.

But on this very account was Salviati hated by the pope's other connections. They thought he stood in their way; they blamed him if Clement showed himself less liberal to them than they expected:—"Pare che suadi al papa a tener strette le mani nè li subministri danari secundo è lo appetito loro, che è grande di spender e spander."—[It appears that he advises the pope to hold his hands tight, and not to supply money according to their appetite, which is great, for spending and wasting.]

But the others also were but too much at variance among themselves. Cardinal Hippolyto Medici had become rather worldly. The pope would occasionally say only, "He is a foolish d—l, the fool will not be a priest:" L' è matto diavolo, el matto non vole esser prete; but it was exceedingly vexatious to him when Hippolyto actually made attempts to dispossess duke Alexander of Florence.

Cardinal Hippolito lived in close friendship with the young Catharine Medici, who here appears as *duchassina*. She is his "cusina in terzo grado, con la quale vive in amor grande, essendo anco reciprocamente da lei amato, nè piu in altri lei si confida nè ad altri ricorre in li sui bisogni e desiderj salvo al dicto cardinal"—[cousin in the third degree, with whom he lives in much affection, being again loved by him in return, nor does she trust in any one, nor have recourse to any one but the said cardinal in her wants and wishes.]

Suriano describes this child who was called to occupy so important a position in society: "Di natura assai vivace, monstra gentil spirito, ben accostumata: è stata educata e gubernata cum le monache nel monasterio delle murate in Fiorenza, donne di molto bon nome e sancta vita: è piccola de persona, scarna, non de viso delicato, ha li occhi grossi proprj alla casa de' Medici."—[Of sufficient vivacity of disposition, she shows a fine spirit and good habits. She has been educated and governed with the nuns in the monastery *delle murate* in Florence, ladies of excellent reputation and sanctity of life: she is small in person, lean, not of delicate features, she has the large eyes peculiar to the Medici family.]

People paid their court to her from all quarters. The duke of Milan, the duke of Mantua, and the king of Scotland, wanted to marry her: one thing thwarted one of these, and something else another. The French marriage had not yet been decided upon. In accordance with his irresolute nature, says Suriano, "the pope spoke of it sometimes with more, sometimes with much less eagerness."

He thinks that the pope too certainly went into the alliance with France, in order that he might gain over the French party in Florence to his interests. Beyond this he treats of foreign relations but briefly and with reserve.

21.

Relatione di Roma d' Antonio Suriano—[Report on Rome by Anthony Suriano]—1536. MS. Foscar. at Vienna. St Mark's Libr. at Venice.

The copies of this report fluctuate between the dates 1535 and 1539. I consider 1536 to be the proper date: first, because the emperor's return to Rome is mentioned in it, that having taken place in April 1536; next, because we find a letter of Sadolet's to Suriano, from Rome, November 1536, which shows that the ambassadors had left Rome again by that time.

That is a letter—Sadoleti Epp. p. 383—the tenor of which is highly honourable to Suriano: "Mihi ea officia praestitisti quae vel frater fratri, vel filio praestare indulgens pater solet, nullis meis provocatus officiis."—[You showed me those kind offices which one brother usually does for another, or an indulgent father for his son, although not urged to this by any good offices of mine.]

Three days after the communication of the preceding report—21st July, 1533—Suriano was again nominated to the embassy in Rome.

The new report opens out the farther progress of the events that had already been introduced, and in particular the conclusion of the French marriage, which, however, was not agreeable to all the pope's connections: "non voglio tacere che questo matrimonio fu fatto contra il volere di Giac. Salviati e molto piu della Sra Lucretia sua moglie, la quale etiam con parole ingiuriose si sforzò di dissuadere S. Stà"—[I do not wish to conceal that this marriage has been carried through against the wishes of Giac. Salviati, and much more against those of the lady Lucretia, his wife, who even tried with upbraiding words to dissuade the pope from it]—no doubt because the Salviati were now partisans of the emperor's. Farther (he speaks of) that remarkable meeting of king Francis with Clement, which we have mentioned. There the pope acted with extreme prudence; he gave out no written assurance. "Di tutti li desiderii s'accommodò Clemente con parole tali che gli facevano credere S. Stà esser disposta in tutte alle sue voglie senza pero far provisione alcuna in scritture."—[Clement met all that was desired with such words as induced the belief that his Holiness was disposed in all things to his wishes, yet without making any provision in writing.] The pope wished that there should be no war, none at least in Italy; all he wanted was to keep the emperor in check: "con questi spaventi assicurarsi del spavento del concilio."—[with these fears to secure himself from the dread of the council.]

By degrees the council became the chief object of the papal policy. Suriano discusses the views which the Roman court cherished with regard to it at the commencement of Paul III.'s reign. Already, said Schomberg, it was to be granted under the sole condition that whatever came before it should first of all be weighed, advised, and brought to a conclusion, by the pope and cardinals.

SECTION SECOND.

CRITICISMS ON SARPI AND PALLAVICINI.

The Tridentine Council—in the preparation made for it, its calling, dispersion for the first and second time, and call to meet again, with all the motives that contributed towards it—fills a large space in the history of the sixteenth century. I need not here discuss what immense importance it was of for the final establishment of the Roman Catholic and its relation to the Protestant creed. It is thus properly the central point of the theological-political quarrels that mark that century.

It has also been the subject of two original historical representations, both copious, and, in themselves, important works.

But not only are these directly opposed to each other, but the world has quarrelled no less about the historians than about the matters they relate: to this very day, with one party Sarpi is accounted veracious and credible, Pallavicini fictitious and false; while the other insists that Pallavicini is to be absolutely believed, while Sarpi is declared to be almost proverbially a liar.

We are seized with a sort of dread on approaching these voluminous works. It were no easy matter of itself to master their contents did they merely relate to authentic facts, but how immensely is this difficulty increased when we must guard at every step against being misinformed by the one or the other, and drawn into a labyrinth of intentional deceptions.

It is impracticable, notwithstanding, to test their authenticity, step by step, by facts better known from other quarters: for on these facts where shall we find impartial information? Even could we find it, fresh folios would be required in order to wind up matters in this way.

Nothing further remains but that we try to arrive at a right view of the methods severally pursued by the authors before us.

For all is not usually exclusively historical that presents itself in the works of historians, especially in works so extensive and so full of matter: after having got together the mass of his information, the individual man first appears in the way and manner in which he masters and prepares his materials, and in the man himself at last consists the unity of the work. Even in these folios, so terrifying to one's industry, there lurks a poet.

Storia del Concilio Tridentino di Pietro Soave Polano.—[History of the Tridentine Council, by Pietro Soave Polano.] First edition, free from foreign additions, at Geneva, 1629.

This work was first published in England by Dominis of Spalatro, an archbishop who had passed over to Protestantism. Although Father Paul Sarpi never acknowledged the work for his, there can be no doubt of his being the author. We perceive from his letters that he was occupied with such a history; there is to be found at Venice a copy which he had ordered to be made with corrections by his own hand; and it may be said that he was at once the only man, in all time, who could have composed a history such as that which lies before us.

Fra Paolo stood at the head of a Roman Catholic party opposed to the pope. Its opposition originated in views of state, but at many points, particularly through the adoption of Augustinian principles, it approached protestant views: sometimes it even fell under the suspicion of protestantism.

Nevertheless Sarpi's work is not therefore at once to be suspected. There were in the world, confessionally, only the decided adherents and the decided opponents of the Council of Trent: from the former there was nought but eulogy, from the latter nought but reprobation to be expected: Sarpi did not quite belong to either of the opposite parties. He was under no necessity of defending the council out and out, neither had he any occasion to reprobate it at all hands. His position enabled him to survey things with an unbiassed vision; in the midst of an Italian Roman Catholic republic alone he could collect the materials that were necessary for this.

Now, if we would have a right view of the manner in which he went to work, we must first bear in mind in what manner great historical works, down to his time, were composed.

Authors had not as yet proposed to themselves either the collection of materials into a homogeneous completeness, a task besides so difficult, nor even first to subject them to a critical examination, to press for direct information, nor, finally, intellectually to elaborate the whole matter in hand.

How few, to this day, put themselves to so much trouble! Men were content, in those days, not so much with making those authors who had a general character for authenticity the groundwork of their histories, as with directly adopting them: they filled up what was incomplete in their narratives, where that was practicable, with new materials, which they had collected for the purpose, and intercalated at the proper places. The main endeavour then was to give these materials an uniform style.

Thus Sleidan consists of documents relating to the history of the Reformation, as he could best procure them, and which he then arranged in methodical order, without much criticism, and converted them, by means of the varnish of his latinity, into one homogeneous whole.

Thuanus (De Thou) has, without scruple, transferred into his pages long passages from other historians. He has, for example, taken Buchanan's Scottish History to pieces, and intercalated these at different places. English history he has borrowed from materials sent him by Camden, German from Sleidan and Chytraeus, Italian from Adriani, Turkish from Busbequius and Leunclavius.

This is a method in which there is some saving of originality, according to which one often reads what is really the work of another, as if it were that of the author whose name appears on the title, and which at the present day, in particular, the writers of French memoirs have adopted anew. These last, indeed, are altogether without excuse. Their appropriate tendency should certainly be to communicate what is original.

To return to Sarpi: In the first positions he lays down in his work, he sets before us how he stood. "My object is to write the history of the Council of Trent. For although several celebrated historians of our age have touched in their works upon some of its individual points, and John Sleidan, a very minute historian, has related, with great diligence, the previous occurrences which gave occasion to it—le cause antecedenti—yet were all these put together, they would not present a complete narrative. As soon as I had begun to concern myself with the affairs of mankind, I felt a great desire to obtain a complete knowledge of that history; after having collected all that I found written on the subject, and the documents, too, printed or manuscript, in circulation with respect to it, I began to search out, among the remains of the prelates and others who had taken part in the council, the notices they might have left behind, as well as the votes they had given, as committed to writing by themselves or others, and the information by letters that was transmitted from that city. In this I have spared neither pains nor labour. I have also had the good fortune to procure a sight of whole collections of the notes and letters of persons who took a large share in those negotiations. After having collected so many materials, presenting superabundant matter for a narrative, I resolved to put them together."

Here Sarpi has described his situation with eminent simplicity. We behold him, on the one hand, in the midst of the historians, whose accounts he arranges in their proper order, but which he did not consider sufficient; on the other hand, provided with manuscript materials wherewith to complete what might be wanting in the former.

Sarpi unfortunately has named in detail neither the one nor the other (of these original sources); neither was that the method of his predecessors: as we have seen, he confines his whole endeavour to weave out of the notices he had found, a regularly composed, pleasant history, and complete in itself.

Meanwhile, without descending to particulars, we can easily recognise who were the historians whose printed works he made use of: first of all Jovius and Guicciardini, then Thuanus and Adriani, but chiefly the author whom he also names, Sleidan.

For example, in the collective view of affairs at the period of the Interim, and after the transference of the council to Bologna, he has had Sleidan, and only in a few instances the originals adduced by that historian, but beyond these nothing but Sleidan before him.

It is well worth our while, and must take us one step farther, to observe how he here proceeds.

He not unfrequently directly translates from Sleidan—somewhat freely, it is true, still he translates: for instance, in the emperor's negotiations with the princes on the subject of their preliminary submission to the Council of Trent: Sleidan, lib. xix. p. 50.

"Et Palatinus quidem territatus fuit etiam, nisi morem gereret, ob recentem anni superioris offensionem, uti diximus, cum vix ea cicatrix coaluisset: Mauricius, qui et socerum landgravium cuperet liberari et nuper admodum esset auctus a Caesare, faciundum aliquid sibi videbat. Itaque cum Caesar eis prolixe de sua voluntate per internuncios promitteret, et ut ipsius fidei rem permitterent flagitaret, illi demum Octobris die vigesimo quarto assentiuntur. Reliquae solum erant civitates: quae magni rem esse periculi videbant submittere se concilii decretis indifferenter. Cum iis Granvellanus et Hasius diu multumque agebant: atque interim fama per urbem divulgata fuit, illos esse praefractos, qui recusarent id quod principes omnes comprobassent: auditae quoque fuerunt comminationes, futurum ut acrius multo quam nuper plectantur. Tandem fuit inventa ratio ut et Caesari satisfieret et ipsis etiam esset cautum. Etenim vocati ad Caesarem, ut ipsi responsa principum corrigant non suum esse dicunt, et simul scriptum ei tradunt, quo testificantur quibus ipsi conditionibus concilium probent. Caesar, eorum audito sermone, per Seldium respondet, sibi pergratum esse quod reliquorum exemplo rem sibi permittant et caeteris consentiant."—Sarpi, lib. iii. p. 283.

[And the Palatine indeed was even afraid, unless he complied, on account of the recent offence of the year before, as we said, when that wound had hardly closed: Maurice, who wished also that his father-in-law, the landgrave, should be liberated, and who had lately been very much aggrandized by the emperor, thought that something must be done. Accordingly, on the emperor making them promises at great length as to his good will, by interchanges of messengers, and beseeching them to leave the matter to his good faith, they at last, on the 24th of October, gave their assent. The rest were only the free cities, which saw that it would be very dangerous for them to yield indifferently to the decrees of the council. Granvelle and Hasius wrought much and long with them; and meanwhile the report was spread through the city that they were perversely obstinate who refused what all the princes had approved: threats were also heard that they would be punished much more sharply than before. At length a method was found out which both satisfied the emperor and was safe for them. For on being summoned to the emperor, they said, that it was not for them to correct the answers of the princes; and at the same time they gave in a writing, by which they testified upon what conditions they approved of a council. The emperor, having heard their answer, replied through Seldius, that it would be most agreeable to him if, following the example of others, they would leave the matter to him, and agree with the rest.]—Sarpi, lib. iii. p. 283.

"Con l'elettor Palatino le preghiere havevano specie di minacce rispetto alle precedenti offese perdonate di recente: verso Mauricio duca di Sassonia erano necessità, per tanti beneficii nuovamente havuti da Cesare, e perche desiderava liberare il lantgravio suo suocero. Perilche promettendo loro Cesare d'adoperarsi che in concilio havessero la dovuta sodisfattione e ricercandogli che si fidassero in lui, finalmente consentirono, e furono

[With the elector Palatine prayers had the semblance of threats, from their bearing on preceding offences lately forgiven: with re-

seguiti dagli ambasciatori dell' elettore di Brandeburg e da tutti i prencipi. Le città ricusarono, come cosa di gran pericolo, il sottomettersi indifferentemente a tutti i decreti del concilio. Il Granvela negotiò con gli ambasciatori loro assai e longamente, trattandogli anco da ostinati a ricusar quello che i prencipi havevano comprobato, aggiongendo qualche sorte di minacce di condannargli in somma maggiore che la già pagata. Perilche finalmente furono costrette di condescendere al voler di Cesare, riservata però cautione per l' osservanza delle promesse. Oude chiamate alla presenza dell' imperatore, et interrogate se si conformavano alla deliberatione de' prencipi, risposero che sarebbe stato troppo ardire il loro a voler correggere la risposta de' prencipi, e tutti iesieme diedero una scrittura contenente le conditioni con che avrebbono ricevuto il concilio. La scrittura fu ricevuta ma non letta, e per nome di Cesare dal suo cancellario furono lodati che ad essempio degli altri havessero rimesso il tutto all' imperatore e fidatisi di lui: e l'istesso imperatore fece dimostratioue d'haver lomolto grato. Così l'una e l'altra parte voleva esser ingannata."

gard to Maurice, duke of Saxony, they had the force of necessity, because of so many benefits lately received from the emperor, and because he wished to liberate the landgrave, his father-in-law. Accordingly, on the emperor engaging that he would use his interest in seeing that in the council they should have all due satisfaction, and requesting that they would entirely confide in him, they finally gave their consent, and were followed by the ambassadors of the elector of Brandenburg and by all the princes. The cities refused, as involving great danger, to subject themselves indifferently to all the decrees of the council. Granvelle negotiated enough with their ambassadors at great length, treating them as obstinate, to refuse that which had been consented to by the princes, adding some sort of threats of condemning them in a larger sum than they had already paid. Accordingly, in the end, they were constrained to comply with the emperor's wishes, with the reservation, however, of its being under the condition of the promises being observed. Whence, being called into the presence of the emperor, and asked whether they conformed to the final opinion of the princes, they replied that it would be too bold in them to wish to correct the answer of the princes; and all in a body gave in a writing containing the conditions on which they would consent to receive the council. The writing was received, but not read, and in the name of the emperor, they were by his chancellor commended for having followed the example of the others, in remitting all to the emperor, and confiding in him: and the emperor himself made a show of being very grateful. Thus both parties wished to be deceived.]

In this translation it is obvious at once that Sarpi does not strictly adhere to the facts laid before him. It is not said by Sleidan that Granvelle threatened the towns: what the German notices as a common report, the Italian puts into the mouth of the minister. The expedient fallen upon with respect to the cities is more clearly expressed in the original than in the translation. What we find here occurs in numberless other places.

Beyond this, however, we have on this nothing farther to remark; one has only to bear always in mind, that he has before him a somewhat arbitrary paraphrase of Sleidan, though not every here and there, yet material alterations occur in it.

For one thing, Sarpi has no correct idea of the constitution of the empire. He has, properly, at all times in his eye, a constitution consisting of three orders, clergy, secular grandees, and cities. He not seldom alters his author's expression according to this peculiar and erroneous idea. For instance, at p. 108, lib. xx., Sleidan inquires what were the votes given on the interim in the three colleges:—1. The electoral: the three spiritual electors are for it, but not the secular: "Reliqui tres electores non quidem ejus erant sententiae, Palatinus imprimis et Mauricius, verum uterque causas habebant cur Caesari non admodum reclamarent."—[The other three electors were not indeed of that opinion, especially the Palatine and Maurice, but both had causes for not opposing the emperor.] 2. The college of the princes: "Caeteri principes, qui maxima parte sunt episcopi, eodem modo sicut Moguntinus atque collegae respondent." 3. "Civitatum non ita magna fuit habita ratio."—[The other princes, consisting mostly of bishops, reply in the same manner as Mayutz and his colleagues. 3. No great account was made of the cities.] Now Sarpi makes out of this (lib. iii. p. 300): The spiritual electoral princes speak their mind just as in Sleidan: "Al parer de' quali s'accostarono tutti i vescovi: i prencipi secolari per non offendere Cesare tacquero: et a loro esempio gli ambasciatori delle città parlarono poco, nè di quel poco fu tenuto conto."—To whose opinion all the bishops adhered: the secular princes, in order not to offend the emperor, held their peace: and, following their example, the ambassadors of the cities spoke little, nor was any account made of that little.] What in Sleidan is said of two electoral princes, is here made to apply to all the electoral princes. It appears as if the bishops in particular had given their votes, the whole odium is thrown upon them. The high importance which the council of the electoral princes obtained in those times is completely misapprehended. In the very passage above quoted, Sarpi asserts that the princes had gone over to the sentiments of the electoral princes. In point of fact, however, they had given an opinion of their own, which differed in very many particulars from that of the electoral princes.

But it is of still more importance that Sarpi, while he transfers the notices he finds, or with these combines excerpts, and translates what he derives from other quarters, withal interweaves his narrative likewise with his own remarks. Let us observe what kind of re marks these are. The subject is well worth attention.

For example, the worthy Sleidan repeats (lib. xx. p. 58), without the least artifice, a proposal of the bishop of Trent, in which this threefold demand is made: the re-establishment of the council at Trent, the sending of a legate into Germany, and such a mode of voting as would be followed in the case of a vacancy in the (Roman) see. This Sarpi translates word for word, but then he intercalates the following observation: "The third point was added," says he, "to remind the pope of his advanced age and approaching death, and this to bring him to greater compliancy, for he surely would not leave the dissatisfaction of the emperor as a legacy to his successors.

Such is the general style of his remarks: one and all they are imbued with gall and bitterness. "The legate summoned the meeting, and first spoke his opinion: for the Holy Ghost, who usually influences the legates according to the ideas of the pope, and the bishops according to the ideas of the legates, acted on this occasion as he is wont to do."

According to Sleidan, the Interim was sent to Rome, "for there was something conceded in it even to the protestants." According to Sarpi, the German prelates urged this: "for," says he, "they have endeavoured from of old to maintain the respect in which the authority of the pope is held, in as much as it alone forms a counterpoise to that of the emperor, whom, but for the pope, they would find irresistible, particularly were the emperor but once to com pel them to do their duty, according to the practice of the ancient Christian Church, and to lay restraints on the abuses of the so-called ecclesiastical liberty."

In general we see well how much Sarpi differs from the compilators that had hitherto appeared. What he extracts from the works of others, is full of spirit and life. In spite of the foreign material, his expression has an easy, pleasant, and equable flow. There is no perceptible passing from one author to another. But therewithal it must be admitted that his narrative bears the colour of his opinions—of systematic opposition, of aversion or of hatred to the Roman court. So much the greater is the impression it produces.

But, as has been said, Sarpi further had quite a different body of materials besides printed authors. By far the most important part of his book, is what he drew from those other sources.

He himself distinguishes the *interconciliary* and preparatory events from the proper history of the council. He says, he means to treat the former more in the form of an annual, the latter in that of a daily register. Another difference consists in this, that for the former he has kept for the most part to familiar and well known authors; for the latter, on the other hand, he has drawn from fresh documentary sources of his own.

The next question that meets us is, what may be the nature of these.

Now I cannot believe that in minute particulars it was much that he could obtain from such persons as that secretary of the first legate to the council, Oliva, or from Ferrier, the French ambassador in Venice, who also had been at the council; even with respect to Oliva, Sarpi commits a gross blunder, by making him leave the council sooner than was actually the case, because the French acts were very soon printed; yet the influence of these men, as they belonged to the discontented, would all go to strengthen the aversion felt by P. Sarpi to the council. On the other hand, the Venetian collections presented him with original papers in great abundance: letters of the legates, such as Monte's; of secret agents, such as Visconti's; despatches from nuncios, such as Chieregato; copious diaries kept at the council; *lettere d' avisi*, and countless other more or less authentic memorials. In this he was fortunate enough to have made use of documents that have never since come to light, and which Pallavicini, notwithstanding the magnificent support he received, yet knew not how to procure for himself—for which history, in its researches, will in all time coming be directed to his work.

And now there only remains the new question, what use he has made of these.

To a certain extent, he has unquestionably transferred them directly into his own pages, with a slight retouching of them. Courayer assures us that he had had in his hands a manuscript report on the congregations of the year 1563, which had been made use of by Sarpi, and almost copied by him: "que notre historien a consultée et presque copiée mot pour mot."

I have in my possession a manuscript "Historia del s. Concilio di Trento scritta per M. Antonio Milledonne, secr. Veneziano."—[History of the sacred Council of Trent, written by M. Anthony Milledonne, Venetian Secretary.] Known also to Foscarini (Lett. Venez. I., p. 351) and Mendham—by a contemporary very well-informed author, and, notwithstanding all its brevity, by no means unimportant for the later sittings of the council.

I now find that Sarpi has occasionally adopted it word for word. For example:—

Milledonne: "Il senato di Norimbergo rispose al nontio Delfino, che non era per partirsi dalla confessione Augustana, e che non accettava il concilio, come quello che non aveva le conditioni ricercate da' protestanti. Simil risposta fecero li senati di Argentina e Francfort al medesimo nontio Delfino. Il senato	Sarpi, p. 450: "Il noncio Delfino nel ritorno espose il suo carico in diverse città. Dal senato di Norimberg hebbe risposta, che non era per partirsi dalla confessione Augustana, e che non accetterà il concilio, come quello che non haveva conditioni ricercate da' protestanti. Simili risposte gli fecero li senati

di Augusta e quello di Olma risposero, che non potevano separarsi dalli altri che tenevano la confessione Augustana."

d'Argentina e di Francfort. Il senato d'Augusta e quello d'Olma risposero, che non potevano separarsi dagli altri che tengono la lor confessione."

Sarpi does not follow only where Milledonne has fallen into eulogy, even although altogether without insidious intention.

Milledonne: "Il card[l] Gonzago prattico di negotii di stato, per aver governato il ducato di Mantova molti anni doppo la morte del duca suo fratello fino che li nepoti erano sotto tutela, gentiluomo di bell' aspetto, di buona creanza, libero e schietto nel parlare, di buona mente, inclinato al bene. Seripando era Napolitana, arcivescovo di Salerno, frate eremitano, grandissimo teologo, persona di ottima coscienza e di singolar bontà, desideroso del bene universale della christianità."

[Cardinal Gonzago treats of affairs of state, from having governed the duchy of Mantua many years after the death of the duke his brother, as long as his nephews were in their minority,—a gentleman of fine appearance, good credit, liberal and sincere in speech, of a good disposition, and inclined to good. Seripando was a Neapolitan, archbishop of Salerno, an eremite friar, a very great theologian, a person of the best conscience and of singular goodness, desirous of the universal good of Christendom.]

Sarpi is much more chary in speaking of these men:—"Destinò al concilio," he says, for example, "fra Girolamo, card[l] Seripando, theologo di molta fama," [He set apart for the council friar Girolamo cardinal Seripando, a divine of great fame]; that is enough for him.

Visconti's letters, which Sarpi had before him, were afterwards printed, and, at the first glance we find, on comparing them, that here and there he keeps very close to them. Take, for instance, Visconti, Lettres et Négotiations, tom. ii. p. 174.—[Visconti's Letters and Negotiations, vol. ii. p. 174.]

"Ci sono poi stati alcuni Spagnuoli, liquali parlando dell' istituzione de' vescovi e della residenza havevano havuto ordine di affirmare queste opinioni per vere come li precetti del decalogo. Segovia seguì in queste due materie l'opinione di Granata, dicendo ch'era verità espressa la residenza ed istituzione delli vescovi essere de jure divino e che niuno la poteva negare, soggiungendo che tanto più si dovea fare tal dichiarazione per dannare l'opinione de gli heretici che tenevano il contrario. Guadice, Aliffi e Montemarano con molti altri prelati Spagnuoli hanno aderito all' opinione di Granata e di Segovia; ma piacque al signore dio che si fecero all'ultimo di buona risoluzione."

[Here there were then some Spaniards, who in speaking of the institution of bishops and of residence, had orders given them to affirm that these opinions were as true as the precepts of the decalogue. Seville followed on these two subjects the opinion of Granada, saying that it was plain truth that the residence and institution of bishops are of divine appointment and what no one could deny, adding that so much the more ought they to make such a declaration in order to condemn the opinion of the heretics who held the contrary. Cadiz, Aliffi, and Montemarano, with many other Spanish prelates, adhered to the views of Granada and Seville; but it pleased the Lord God that they brought themselves at last to a good determination.]

Sarpi, viii. 753: "Granata disse, esser cosa indegna haver tanto tempo deriso li padri trattando del fondamento dell' instituzione de' vescovi e poi adesso tralasciandola, e ne ricercò la dichiarazione de jure divino, dicendo maravegliarsi perche non si dichiarasse un tal punto verissimo et infallibile. Aggionse che si doveano prohibire come heretici tutti quei libri che dicevano il contrario. Al qual parer adherì Segovia, affermando che era espressa verità che nissuno poteva negarla, e si doveva dichiarare per dannare l'openione degli heretici che tenevano il contrario. Seguivano anco Guadice, Aliffe et Monte Marano con gli altri prelati Spagnuoli, de' quali alcuni dissero, la loro openione esser così vera come li precetti del decalogo."

[Granada said, that it was an unworthy thing to have so long derided the fathers by taking up the fundamental principle of the episcopal institution and then instantly passing it over, and he called for the declaration of its being *de jure divino,* saying that he wondered at their not having declared that point most true and infallible. He added, that they ought to prohibit as heretical all books that maintained the contrary. To which view there adhered Seville, affirming that it was plain truth, which no one could deny, and that it ought to be declared by condemning the opinion of the heretics who maintained the contrary. There further followed Cadiz, Aliffe, and Monte Marano, with the other Spanish prelates, some of whom said that their opinion was as true as the precepts of the decalogue.]

It will be seen that Sarpi is no ordinary transcriber: the farther we compare him with the sources whence he draws, the more do we perceive how well he understood how to complete the connection, and to give relief to the expression by a slight turn in the phraseology; but at the same time he obviously tries to give greater force to the expression to the disadvantage of the council.

As it would be impossible to suppose otherwise, he treats the unprinted just as he treats the printed materials.

But one can understand that this at times very much influences the conception formed of matters of fact, as, among other instances, appears in the description of the most important of our German religious conferences, that of Ratisbon in 1541.

Here he again keeps nearest to Sleidan: no doubt he had likewise in his eye the report that Bucer drew up of that conference.

In the use he makes of these German sources, he commits anew the faults above adverted to. The orders gave the emperor at that diet an answer to his proposals twice. Both times they were themselves disunited. The electoral college was in favour of the emperor's intentions, the college of the princes was against it. Yet there was this difference, that the princes yielded the first time, yet they did not do so the second; they then handed in an answer, declining compliance.

Sleidan endeavours to explain the opposition of the college of the princes by remarking, that there were so many bishops in that college; a very important point certainly, as respects the constitution of the empire. But Sarpi quite does away with the real state of matters by persisting in calling the college of princes directly bishops. Speaking of the first reply, he says, "I vescovi rifiutarono" [the bishops refused]; of the second, "I vescovi con alcuni pochi prencipi cattolici" [the bishops, with some few catholic princes]; which, accordingly, as has been said, quite misrepresents the constitution of the empire.

Meanwhile, we have no wish to dwell longer on this. The main affair is what use he made of original and more secret sources, with regard to which he might venture to believe, that they might still remain for a long time unknown.

For the history of that diet, he had the instructions communicated to Contarini, and which Cardinal Quirini afterwards caused to be printed also from a Venetian MS.

Here we have first to remark, that what he found in these instructions he here and there interweaves into the conferences which the legate held with the emperor.

For example, in the instructions, we find as follows:—"Eos articulos in quibus inter se convenire non possunt, ad nos remittant, qui in fide boni pastoris et universalis pontificis dabimus operam ut per universale concilium vel per aliquam viam aequivalentem non praecipitanter, sed mature et quemadmodum res tanti momenti exigit, finis his controversiis imponatur, et remedium quod his malis adhibendum est quam diutissime perdurare possit."—[Let them remit to us those articles on which they cannot agree among themselves, and we, on the faith of a good pastor and universal bishop, will do our endeavour that either by a general council or some equivalent method, not precipitately but maturely, and as a matter of such moment demands, an end may be put to these controversies, and that the remedy which is to be applied to these evils may last as long as possible.]

Sarpi makes Contarini require, "ogni cosa si mandasse al papa, il qual prometteva in fede di buon pastore et universal pontefice di fare che il tutto fosse determinato per un concilio generale o per altra via equivalente con sincerità e con nissun affetto humano, non con precipitio, ma maturamente."—[that everything should be remitted to the pope, who promised on the faith of a good pastor and universal bishop, to do all that should be determined by a general council, or by some other equivalent method, with sincerity, and without any human affection, not precipitately but maturely.]

The instructions proceed at another place as follows:—

"Si quidem ab initio pontificatus nostri, ut facilius hoc religionis dissidium in pristinam concordiam reduceretur, primum christianos principes ad veram pacem et concordiam per literas et nuntios nostros saepissime hortati sumus, .. mox ob hanc candem causam concilium generale .... christianis regibus et principibus etiam per proprios nuntios significavimus, ... multaque in Germania religionis causa non ea qua decuit auctoritatem nostram, ad quam religionis judicium cognitio et examen spectat, reverentia tractari et fieri, non absque gravi dolore animi intelleximus, tum temporum conditione moti, tum Caesareae et regiae majestatum vel earum oratorum pollicitationibus persuasi, quod ea quae hic fiebant boni alicujus inde secuturi causa fierent, partim patientes tulimus," etc.

[In as much as since the commencement of our pontificate, in order that this religious dissension might be the more easily brought back to ancient concord, first we very frequently exhorted Christian princes by our letters and nuncios, to true peace and concord, ... presently for the same cause a general council .... was intimated by us to Christian kings and princes, even by special nuncios, ... and we learned not without grievous mental disquietude, that many things were handled and done in Germany on account of religion, without that reverence which was befitting our authority, to which belongs the judgment, cognisance and examination of religion, yet, influenced both by the state of the times, and by the promises of imperial and royal majesties or their ambassadors, that the things done here had been done for the sake of some good that was to follow, we have so far patiently borne with it, etc.]

To this Sarpi adds:—

"Sicome la Sta S. nel principio del pontificato per questo medesimo fine haveva mandato lettere e nuntii a prencipi per celebrar il concilio, e poi intimatolo, e mandato al luogo i suoi legati, e che se haveva sopportato che in Germania tante volte s'havesse parlato delle cose della religione con poca riverentia dell' autorità sua, alla quale sola spetta trattarle, l'haveva fatto per essergli

[Inasmuch as His Holiness at the commencement of his pontificate for this same purpose had sent letters and nuncios to the princes, in order to the celebrating of a council, and had then intimated it, and had sent his legates to the place, and that if he had borne with religious matters having been spoken of so often in Germany with little reverence for his authority, to which alone it

dalle Mta S. data intentione e promesso che cio si faceva per bene."

[...belongs to treat of such things, he had done so from his Majesty having intended and promised that this was done for good.]

Enough—it is evident that the explanations which Sarpi puts into the mouth of Contarini, are taken directly from the instructions given to the latter; and once that we know how the matter stands, we can readily excuse him. Nevertheless, it is not to be denied that in proceeding thus, the truth is occasionally confounded with error. In the course of the daily alterations in events, the legate had his instructions altered. Reasons which were calculated for the case of those points only on which the parties could not agree being to be sent to Rome, are allowed by the author to be proposed by him (Contarini) at a time when it was required in Rome that he should submit to the approval of the Roman court all those points besides on which the parties were already agreed.

But to this first departure from strict accuracy, seen in the author's applying to one state of things words of the instructions intended for another, he further adds others still more important.

The pope, in the instructions, declares himself specially opposed to a national council:—

"Majestati Caesareae in memoriam redigas, quantopere concilium illud sit semper detestata, cum alibi tum Bononiae palam diceret nihil acque perniciosum fore et apostolicae et imperiali dignitatibus quam Germanorum nationale concilium, illa nulla meliore via quam per generale concilium obviam iri posse confiteretur: quin imo etiam S. M. post Ratisbonensem dietam anno domini 1532 habitam pro sua singulari prudentia omni studio semper egit ne qua imperialis dieta hactenus sit celebrata ac ex ea occasione ad concilium nationale deveniretur."

[You will remind his imperial Majesty how much he always detested that council, and how, both elsewhere and at Bologna, he said that nothing would be so pernicious, at once to the apostolical and imperial dignities, than a national council of the Germans, and openly confessed that in no better way could it be obviated than by a general council: moreover his Majesty, also, after the diet that was held at Ratisbon in 1532, as was to be expected from his singular prudence, ever strenuously endeavoured to prevent any imperial diet being held from that time forth, and occasion being taken from it for proceeding to hold a national council.]

This Sarpi, too, gives word for word, and avowedly, indeed, as taken from the instructions; still it is with a notable addition.

"Che raccordasse all' imperatore quanto egli medesimo havesse detestato il concilio nationale essendo in Bologna, conoscendolo pernicioso all' autorità imperiale: poiche i sudditi preso animo dal vedersi concessa potestà di mutare le cose della religione pensarebbono ancora a mutare lo stato; e che S. M. dopo il 1532 non volse mai più celebrare in sua presenza dieta imperiale per non dar occasione di domandar concilio nationale."

[That he should remind the emperor how much he himself had detested a national council when he was at Bologna, acknowledging how pernicious it would be to the imperial authority; since subjects, emboldened at seeing power conceded to them for changing the things of religion, would think also of changing the state; and that his Majesty after 1532 did not wish that an imperial diet should any more be held in his presence, so that he might not give occasion for demanding a national council.]

Who would not suppose that the emperor had himself expressed the idea that a nation readily changed its form of government, if it had once changed its religion? But this I cannot believe on the author's mere assertion. Nothing to that effect is found in the instructions. It is an idea that obtained currency after the events of a later period.[1]

I do not think my criticisms will appear too petty and minute. How shall we ascertain how far a man speaks the truth but by comparing him with the original sources which he had had before his eyes?

I find a farther inaccuracy, still stronger than the above.

In the very first conference which he puts down as having taken place between Contarini and the emperor, he intermixes the words of the instructions: those important words to which also we have referred.

The pope excuses himself for not having given the cardinal such extensive discretionary powers as had been wished for him by the emperor and the king:—

"Primum quia videndum imprimis est, an protestantes . . . . . in principiis nobiscum conveniant, cujusmodi est hujus sanctae sedis primatus tanquam a deo et salvatore nostro institutus, sacros. ecclesiae sacramenta, et alia

[First, since it is to be seen, in the first place, whether the protestants . . . . . shall agree with us in principles, of such a kind as that of the primacy of this holy see as instituted by God and our Saviour, the sacred holy

1 Many readers will think this hypercriticism. The instructions plainly point to the emperor's having openly expressed apprehension lest the *state* as well as religion should suffer from the discussions of a national council. But what *civil* evil could he dread, if not a change in the forms of government? Sarpi, therefore, merely takes the very innocent liberty of stating the emperor's apprehension more fully. Nor are we sure that he means to put this development of it in the emperor's mouth. *Poichè* is translated *simulatque* in Latin by F. Alunno (1547), in his "La Fabrica del Mondo," and as a semicolon divides the first clause of the sentence from the second, as well as the second from the third, it would appear that the second need not any more be put in the emperor's mouth than the third, which states a fact not a saying.—Tr.

quaedam quae tum sacrarum literarum auctoritate tum universalis ecclesiae perpetua observatione hactenus observata et comprobata fuere et tibi nota esse bene scimus: quibus statim initio admissis omnis super aliis controversiis concordia tentaretur."

[sacraments of the church, and some other things that have hitherto been observed and approved both by the authority of the holy scriptures and by the perpetual observation of the universal church, and which we know to be well known to you: which things being once admitted at the beginning, an agreement might be attempted on all other controversies.]

Sarpi makes Contarini say—

"Che S. Sta gli aveva data ogni potestà di concordare co' protestanti, purche essi ammettino i principii, che sonno il primato della sede apostolica instituito da Christo, et i sacramenti sicome sono insegnati nella chiesa Romana, *e le altre cose determinate nella bolla di Leone,* offerendosi nelle altre cose di dar ogni sodisfattione alla Germania."

[That his Holiness had given him full powers to agree with the protestants, provided main points were admitted, namely, the primacy of the apostolic see, as instituted by Christ, and the sacraments as taught in the church of Rome, *and the other things determined in the bull of Leo,* offering to give every satisfaction to Germany in other matters.]

The difference here is manifest. The entire possibility of a successful result lay in the indefiniteness of the papal expressions. The conference could have had no conceivable object, had there been no room left for such a prospect, but according to Sarpi, this, properly speaking, vanishes altogether. The pope will not have "quaedam quae tibi nota esse bene scimus," [something which we know to be well known to you,] he demands the recognition of what is laid down in Leo X.'s bull, that is, the condemnation of the Lutheran doctrines. This was what never could have been accomplished.

In general, Sarpi will not acknowledge that the papal see showed any kind of compliancy whatever. According to him Contarini had to defend the papal authority in the most rigorous forms. With Sarpi he starts at once from this point. The pope could by no means share with any man the office of determining doubtful points of faith: to him alone was the privilege given of never erring, in the words, "Ego rogavi pro te, Petre."—[I have prayed for thee, Peter.] Matters these, of which, in the Instructions at least, not a word is to be found.

For in general Sarpi viewed the popedom in the light of his own time. After the restoration had been accomplished, it became much more dictatorial and inflexible than it had been in the days of jeopardy and pressure. But it was in that plenitude of power and unbroken self-confidence, that it presented itself to the eyes of Sarpi. What he experienced and felt he then transferred to earlier times. All the pieces of information, and the documents he could lay his hand upon, he interpreted in this sense, which to him was so natural, and was based on the position of his native city, his party in that city, and his own personal position.

We have yet another historical work of Paul Sarpi on the subject of the Venetian Roman dissensions of 1606: "Historia particolare delle cose passate tra 'l summo pontefice Paolo V. e la Ser^{ma} Rep^{a} di Venetia, Lion 1624," [Particular history of the matters that passed between the supreme pontiff Paul V., and the most Serene Republic of Venice, Lyons 1624,] which on the whole is written in a kindred spirit. Masterly in point of description, and truthful upon the whole, still it is a party writing. We find little or nothing in Sarpi about the dissensions of the Venetians among themselves, which broke out on that occasion, and formed so important a feature of internal history. According to him one would suppose that they were all of one mind. He constantly speaks of the *princeps;* so he designates the Venetian civil government. This fiction, accordingly, does not admit of his going into a minute description of internal affairs. He skips over the things that were not so creditable to Venice; for example, the delivering up of the prisoners which we have mentioned, as if he did not know why it was that they were first handed over to the ambassador, and then, with other words, to the cardinal. Nor does he mention that the Spaniards were for the exclusion of the Jesuits. He entertained an implacable dislike to both, and shut his eye to the fact of their interests happening in this case to clash.

Now it is nearly the same with the history of the Council. The sources of information are industriously collected,—remarkably well elaborated—superior talent shown in the use that is made of them; neither can it be said that they are falsified, that they are often and essentially perverted, but they are worked up in the spirit of a decided opposition.

By this Sarpi led the way anew to another side. To that work of compilation he gave the unity of the general tendency; his work is condemnatory, sneering, hostile: it is the first example of a history which makes ceaseless fault-finding accompany the whole development of its subject: far more decidedly than de Thou, who first merely touched on that method; in this Sarpi found afterwards innumerable followers.

Istoria del concilio di Trento scritta dal padre Sforza Pallavicino della compagnia di Gesu. 1664.—[History of the council of Trent by father Pallavicino, of the Company of Jesus, 1664.]

Such a book as Sarpi's history, so richly furnished with details till then unknown, full of wit and evil-speaking, on so important an occurrence, which in its consequences exercised a commanding influence over those times, could not fail to make the deepest impression.

The first edition appeared in 1619; up to 1622, a Latin translation appeared four times; besides these there were a German and a French translation.

The Roman court was all the more bent on having it refuted, as in point of fact it contained so many errors which were obvious to all persons more intimately acquainted with the occurrences of that period.

A Jesuit, Terentio Alciati, prefect of the studies in the Collegio Romano, busied himself forthwith with the amassing of materials for a refutation which at the same time should form a complete work. His book bore the title "Historiae Concilii Tridentini a veritatis hostibus evulgatae elenchus;"[1] [Confutation of the History of Trent published by the enemies of truth;] he collected an enormous mass of materials, but died in 1651, before he had worked these into a book.

The Jesuit general Nickel selected for that task another brother of the order who had already so far given proof of literary talent, Sforza Pallavicini; he relieved him of other engagements: "like a *condottiere*[2] of soldiers," says Pallavicini himself, the general appointed him to that work.

Pallavicini brought out this work in three thick quartos, the first of which appeared in 1656.

It is one which really comprises an uncommonly rich body of materials, and for the history of the 16th century—for it starts from the first rise of the Reformation—is of the utmost importance. Public archives were opened for the author, and he had free access to all the available materials contained in the Roman libraries. He could avail himself not only of the acts of the council to the utmost extent, but also of the correspondence of the legates with Rome, and a vast medley of other documentary pieces of information. Far from making any secret of his originals, he rather makes a parade of their titles on the margin of his book: they are very numerous.

Now his first business is to confute Sarpi. At the end of each volume he appends a catalogue of the "errors in facts," of which he maintains that he has convicted his opponent: he reckons up 361. But innumerable others, he adds, which he has also refuted, are not mentioned in that catalogue.

He says in his preface, that "he will not permit himself to engage in petty skirmishes: whoever would attack him, might advance in regular order of battle, and confute his whole book, as he had confuted Paul Sarpi." But what a formidable task were that! We cannot be tempted to proceed in such a fashion.

We must be content, as we have said, only to do as much as may enable one to form an idea of Pallavicini's method, by giving some examples of it.

Now, as he drew his materials from so many secret records, and, properly speaking, formed the whole book by interweaving them into one tissue, the first thing of importance is to have an idea of the use he makes of these.

This we shall find we can do best in those cases where the original documents, of which he availed himself, were afterwards printed. I have been so fortunate also as to have inspected a whole range of documents, never yet printed, and which he quotes. We must now proceed to compare the originals with his elaboration of them.

This I will do, in some points, *seriatim*.

1. And here it must, first of all, be owned, that the written instructions and papers which lay before Pallavicini, are often quite satisfactorily excerpted and employed by him. I have, for example, compared a body of instructions which the Spanish ambassador obtained in November, 1562; the answer which the pope returned to him in March, 1563; the fresh instructions with which the pope provided his nuncio, with the extracts in Pallavicini, and have found them in general quite to the same purport. Pallav. xx. 10, xxiv. 1. He has availed himself of his right to venture upon some transpositions that do no prejudice to truth. It is true, indeed, that he softens some strong expressions; for example, when the pope says that he had re-opened the council only in consequence of his reliance on the king's assistance, under the conviction that the king was to be his right arm, and would be a guide and leader to him in all his projects and proceedings—"il fondamento che facessimo nell' promessa de S. M^{ta} e de' suoi ministri di doverci assistere ci fece entrare arditamente nell' impresa, pensando di avere S. M^{ta} per nostro braccio dritto e che avesse a esserci guida o conduttiero in ogni nostra azione e pensiero"—he makes him say only that he would not again have opened the council, had he not cherished the confident expectation that the king would be his arm and his leader. Here, as the substance of the thing remains, there can be no real ground for censure. On Visconti being sent to Spain, and another ambassador to the emperor, Sarpi supposes (viii. 61) that their commission to propose a meeting was a mere feint; but this is quite too refined a suspicion; the proposal of a congress, or of a conference, as it was then called, is one of the points most urgently pressed in the instructions. Pallavicini is unquestionably quite in the right when he insists upon this.

2. Pallavicini, however, is not in every instance the better informed of the two. When Sarpi relates that Paul III., at the conference of Busseto, made the proposal to the emperor Charles V., of bestowing Milan upon his nephew, who was married to a natural daughter of the emperor's, Pallavicini devotes an entire chapter to refute him. He will not believe the historians in whose works, besides, this appears. "How then," he exclaims, "could the pope have dared to write letters to the emperor in such a tone as he did employ in writing to him?"

1 So it runs in Mazzuchelli.

2 The *condottieri* were soldiers of fortune, who raised as well as commanded troops for those who employed them. —Tr.

Con qual petto avrebbe ardito di scrivere a Carlo lettere così risentite? The emperor might have charged him with shameless dissimulation (simulatione sfacciata). As Pallavicini is so vehement, one must suppose that here he writes *bona fide*. Not the less has the matter its foundation in truth, as Sarpi relates it. This appears past all contradiction, from the despatches of the Florentine ambassador. (Dispaccio Guicciardini, 26 Giugno 1543.)

Further, on this subject, still more ample details are found in a manuscript life of Basto. We may mention a *discorso* of cardinal Carpi, which is precisely to the same effect. Nay, even in the year 1547, the pope had not quite laid aside this idea: "Le cardinal de Bologne au roy Henry II."—[The cardinal of Bologna to king Henry II.]—In Ribier ii. 9. "L'un—le papa—demande Milan, qu' il jamais n'aura; l'autre—l'empereur—400,000 sc., qu'il n'aura sans rendre Milan."—[The one—the pope—asks for Milan, which he will never get; the other—the emperor—400,000 scudi, which he will never get without delivering up Milan.] Notwithstanding this, Paul III. wrote those letters.

But the question still remains, whether Pallavicini, when he goes wrong, uniformly does so bona fide. This cannot have been the case in all instances. It occasionally happens that his documents are not so orthodox and (Roman) catholic as himself. While affairs were as yet only taking their course, and represented on all sides every possibility of a different development, they could not be viewed so rigorously as afterwards, when all had again become firmly established. Such a compromise as the peace of religion was, could never be approved by the (Roman catholic) orthodoxy of the 17th century; Pallavicini laments the "detrimenti gravissimi" [most grievous losses] which it cost the Roman see; he compares it to a palliative cure, which only brings on a more dangerous crisis. Nevertheless, he found the report of a nuncio upon it, who clearly saw its necessity. This was bishop Delfino of Liesina. Pallavicini quotes the report which had been rendered by this bishop to cardinal Caraffa, and in fact makes use of it. But how does he do this?

All the reasons wherewith Delfino demonstrates the vital necessity for such an agreement he changes into grounds of exculpation adduced by Ferdinand for himself.

The nuncio says: At this time there was no prince and no city which would not have traded with its neighbour. He names them—the land was going to wreck, as if they formed an opposition diet—Brandenburg, Hesse, and Saxony write from Naumburg, that they will keep themselves united. The king had besought the emperor rather to make peace with France, and to fix his regards on Germany; yet he refused to do so. In the midst of such an unhealthy state of things, the constituted orders met; the king now sanctioned the points on which both parties had united; so joyfully had they done this (si allegrimente) that never since the days of Maximilian has Germany been so quiet as it is now.

Now Pallavicini, too, touches on all this (l. xiii. c. 13), but how much is it weakened by its being put into the mouth of a prince, who seeks only to exculpate himself.

"Scusavasi egli di cio con addurre che haveva richiesto d'ordini specificati l'imperatore, confortandolo alla pace di Francia, . . . ed havergli ricordato esser questa l'unica arme per franger l'orgoglio de' protestanti," etc.	[Exculpating himself of this with the allegation that he had requested the emperor's specific orders, exhorting him to peace with France, . . . and had reminded him that that was the sole weapon by which the pride of the protestants could be broken, &c.]

Let us contrast with these twisted expressions the words of Delfino: "Il ser^{mo} re vedendo questi andamenti," [The most serene king, beholding these proceedings] (the religious dissensions) "scrisse a S. M^{ta} Cesarea esortandolo alla pace col christianissimo, accioche ella possa attendere alle cose di Germania a farsi ubedire," etc.—[had written to his Imperial Majesty, exhorting him to peace with the Most Christian King, in order that he might attend to the affairs of Germany and make himself obeyed, &c.]

It is beyond doubt a great, and in a book that boasts so much of its authenticity, an intolerable inaccuracy, for the author to turn the statement of a nuncio into the exculpation of a prince; but the worst of it is, that thereby the true view of what took place is obscured. In general the whole original documents are made use of, and changed from the style of the 16th into that of the 17th century, but they are misused.

4. Without going beyond the relations of the pope with Ferdinand I., we find some further matters calling for remark. It is known that our emperor pressed for a reform that was not very agreeable to the pope. In the course of the first months of the year 1563, Pius twice despatched nuncios—first Commendone, then Morone—to Inspruck, where the emperor was at the time, to induce him to relinquish his opposition. These were very remarkable missions, and of great consequence as respected the council. It is interesting to observe how Pallavicini (xx. 4) reports upon them. We have Commendone's report (relation) of 19th February, 1563, which he also had before him.

Now here we have first to notice, that he infinitely weakens the expressions that were employed at the imperial court, and the prospects entertained there. Of the union in which the emperor stood at that time with the French and the cardinal of Lorraine, he makes Commendone say: "Rendersi credibile che scambievolmente si confirmerebbono nel parer e si prometterebbono ajuto nell' operare."—[It was to be believed that they would mutually confirm each other in opinion, and promise each other assistance in carrying matters into effect.] Commendone expresses himself quite otherwise. At the imperial court people not only thought of seeking reform in common with the French—"pare che pensino trovar modo e ferma di haver più parte et autorità nel presente concilio per stabilire in esso tutte le loro petitioni giuntamente con Francesi"—[it seems they contemplated finding a mode and form for having a greater part in the present council for the securing in it of all their petitions conjointly with the French.]

But many other things Pallavicini directly omits. People at the emperor's court were of opinion that with somewhat more of a disposition to make concessions and of serious reform, much might have been accomplished with the protestants.

"La somma è che a me pare di haver veduto non pur in S. M[ta] ma nelli principali ministri, come Trausen e Seldio, un ardentissimo desiderio della riforma e del progresso del concilio con una gran speranza quod remittendo aliquid de jure positivo et reformando mores et disciplinam ecclesiasticam non solo si possono conservare li cattolici ma guadagnare e ridurre degli heretici, con una opinione et impressione pur troppo forte che qui siano molti che non vogliano riforma."

[The sum of the matter is, that it seems to me I have seen, not indeed in his Majesty, but in the principal ministers, such as Trausen and Seldius, a most ardent desire for reform and for the progress of the council, with a great hope that by remitting somewhat from positive law, and reforming manners and church discipline, they could not only preserve the (Roman) catholics, but bring back the heretics, with an opinion and impression quite too strong, that there were many that had no wish for a reform.]

I will not inquire who those protestants might be, of whom, in the event of a methodical reform, it was to be expected that they would return to (Roman) catholicism; but these reasons were much too offensive to the court prelates to admit of his communicating them. People spoke of the difficulties that were met with in the council: Seld laconically replied: "Oportuisset ab initio sequi sana consilia."—[Sane counsels ought to have been followed from the very first.] Pallavicini mentions the complaints about difficulties, but says nothing of the reply.

To make up for that, however, he gives in full a judgment pronounced by the chancellor in favour of the Jesuits.

Enough—he dwells on whatever is agreeable to him; what might not be pleasing to himself and the curia, he affects to know nothing about; or he tries to give a good turn to the matter. For example, the legates opposed the intention of the bishops to exclude from the *vox decisiva* [voting on the question], the generals of religious orders and abbots: "*per non sdegnar tante migliara de' religiosi*, frà quali in verità si trova oggi veramente la theologia"—[in order not to give offence to so many thousands of monks and friars, among whom, in truth, theology is to be found at this day.] (Registro di Cervini, Lettera di 27 Decem. 1545. Epp. Poli, iv. 229.) Now from this, Pallavicini brings out a very honourable view of the matter: "il che desideravano," [which thing they desired] (that is, the admission of the generals of orders), "perche in effetto la theologia, con la quale si doveva decidere i dogmi, resedeva ne' regolari, ed era opportuno e dicevole che molti de' giudici havessero intelligenza esquisita di articoli da giudicarsi"—[because, in fact, the theology wherewith dogmas ought to be decided, had its seat among the regular clergy, and it was seasonable and plausible that many of the judges should possess an exquisite comprehension of the articles to be submitted to their judgment.] (VI. II. 1, p. 576.)

5. It cannot fail but that that must impair the view of the subject.

For example, still in the year 1547, the Spaniards gave in certain Reformation articles, known under the name of Censures. The translation of the council followed shortly after, and there can be no question that the Censures contributed much to that being done. It was certainly of the utmost importance that the immediate dependants of the emperor Charles, at the moment of his triumph, presented such extraordinary demands. Sarpi has them in all their extent, lib. ii. p. 262. He also follows them up briefly by giving the pope's replies. But such vehement demands on the part of orthodox prelates, do not meet Pallavicini's views. He says that here Sarpi relates much of which he can find nothing; he finds only the reply made by the pope to certain reforming projects that had been made by many of the fathers and had been intimated to him by the presidents, lib. ix. c. 9, "sopra varie riformazioni proposte da molti de' padri."—[On various reforms proposed by many of the fathers.] He takes good care not to state what these were. To do that might damage his refutation of the human (worldly) motives, to which Sarpi ascribes the transference of the council from Trent to Bologna.

6. In this reticence, this setting aside of what it did not suit him to introduce, he now goes very far (lit. is very strong).

In Book III., for example, he twice quotes a Venetian report drawn up by Suriano. He says of it, that the author gives his assurance that he possesses an exquisite and unquestionably accurate acquaintance with the treaties betwixt Francis and Clement, nor has he any idea of controverting him on this point (iii. c. 12, No. 1). He adopts sketches communicated by him, directly into his own narrative, for instance, that Clement shed tears of vexation and despondency on hearing of the imprisonment of his nephew by the emperor—enough, he believes what he says. He alleges too, that this Venetian stood directly opposed to his fellow-countryman Sarpi. Sarpi says, to wit: "Il papa negotiò confederazione col re di Francia, la quale si concluse e stabilì anco col matrimonio di Henrico secondogenito regio e di Catharina."—[The pope negotiated alliances with the king of France, which were further wound up and confirmed with the marriage of Henry, the king's second born, and Catharine.] Upon this Pallavicini flares up into a passion. "The pope," says he, "made no alliance with the king, as P. Soave so fearlessly asserts." He appeals to Guicciardini and Soriano. Now what says Soriano? He traces at great length how and where the pope's prepossession in favour of the French began, what a decidedly political colour it had; finally, he speaks also of the negotiations at Bologna. Now he certainly denies that matters went the length of a proper treaty; but all that he denies is that there was any draft of the same in writing. "Di tutti li desiderii (del re) s'accommodò Clemente con parole tali che gli fanno credere, S. Sta esser disposta in tutto alle sue voglie, senza però far provisione alcuna in scrittura." —[Clement complied with all the king's desires, using such words as made him believe that His Holiness was disposed in every thing to meet his wishes, without, however, making any provision in writing.] He afterwards relates that the king had pressed for the fulfilment of the promises that had there been made to him. "S. Mta chrma dimandò che da S. Stà le fussino osservate le promesse" [His Most Christian Majesty demanded that the promises should be kept by His Holiness]; being what, according to that author, was partly the cause of the pope's death. Here we find the singular case of what is not true being in a certain measure more true than the truth. There is no room for doubt: Sarpi is wrong when he says that any treaty was concluded; what is so called never was effected. Pallavicini is right when he denies it; but on the whole Sarpi comes by much the nearest to the truth. There was the closest union, but only by word of mouth, not in writing.

7. Something similar occurs in the use made of Visconti's letters. Sarpi sometimes adopts more from these than stands expressed in words. For example, he says, vii. 657, speaking of the decree about residence, that the cardinal of Lorraine spoke at great length and indistinctly, and that people could not make out whether he was favourably inclined to such a decree, generally speaking, or not. On this he is keenly attacked by Pallavicini. "Si scorge apertamente il contrario."—[The contrary is evident.] (xix. c. 8.) In refuting it he even alleges the authority of Visconti. Let us hear Visconti himself: "Perchè s'allargò molto, non poterò seguire se non pochi prelati."—[As he enlarged greatly, none but a few prelates could follow him.] (Trento, 6 Dec. in Mansi, Misc. Baluzii, iii. p. 454.) Thus it remains true that people could not follow him, did not properly understand his meaning. Further, Pallavicini is enraged at Sarpi for giving it to be understood that the cardinal did not appear in a congregation because he wanted to leave the French the opportunity of expressing themselves with perfect freedom: he pretended to make the report of the death of the king of Navarre his excuse. Pallavicini declares with vehemence that that was his true and only motive. "Nè io trovo in tante memorie piene di sospetto, che ciò capitasse in mente a persona."—[I do not find in so many memoirs full of suspicion, that this ever suggested itself to any one.] (Ib.) How? Had nobody ever entertained any suspicion about that staying away? Visconti says in a letter published by Mansi, elsewhere: "Lorena chiamò questi prelati Francesi, e gli commise che havessero da esprimere liberamente tutto quello che haveano in animo senza timor alcuno. E sono di quelli che pensano che il cardinal se ne restasse in casa per questo effetto."—[Lorraine called these French cardinals and communicated to them that they should have to speak out there freely, all that they might have a mind to say, without any fear. And there were some who thought that the cardinal staid at home for that purpose.] Visconti certainly says nothing about the cardinal assuming that death (of the king of Navarre) as a pretext; though it might have occurred somewhere in other letters, inasmuch as Sarpi evidently had before him still other sources of information. Nevertheless, the point at issue, that it was suspected that the cardinal purposely staid at home, is certainly to be found in the correspondence as plain as words can make it. What are we to say, since Pallavicini unquestionably saw them?

8. Generally speaking, Pallavicini makes it his sole object to confute his opponent, without having it at all at heart to bring out the truth. Nowhere is this more manifest than in the case of the colloquy at Ratisbon, which we have treated so copiously above. Pallavicini likewise knew that paper of instructions, as may readily be supposed; he held them as secret, which they really were. But from the manner in which he handles them, we acquire a complete knowledge of them. He makes a violent attack on Sarpi; he upbraids him for making the pope declare that he would grant the protestants satisfaction if they would but agree with him in the already established points of catholic doctrine: "che ove i Luterani convenissero ne' punti già stabiliti della chiesa romana, si offeriva nel resto di porger ogni sodisfattione alla Germania."—[That when the Lutherans should agree to the already settled points of the Roman church, he offered for the rest to give every satisfaction to Germany.] He considers this directly opposite to the truth. "Questo è dirimpetto contrario al primo capo dell' instruttione."—[This is directly contrary to the first head of the instructions.] How? The opposite of this was true. In the pope's instructions it runs thus: "Videndum est an in principiis nobiscum conveniant, . . . quibus admissis omnis super aliis controversiis concordia tentaretur," [It is first to be seen whether they will agree with us in principles, . . . which being admitted all concord might be attempted on other controversies,] and the other words as above quoted. It is true that Sarpi has committed a fault here: he restricts the legate more than he was really restricted; he says too little of the pope's willingness to make concessions: instead of disclosing this, as it was manifest Pallavicini would have it that he says too much, he throws himself there into a distinction between articles of faith and other things which had not been made in the bull; he adduces a number of things which were true, but not solely true, and which cannot do away with those words, after their once occupying the place they do in the paper of instructions. In non-essentials he is strictly correct; what is essential he completely misrepresents. We sometimes meet with an attempt at convicting him of deliberate falsification. For example (l. iv. xiii.): "Mentisce Soave con attribuire ad arte de' pontefici l'essersi tirato il convento in lungo senza effetto."—[Soave lies in attributing to the papal arts the tedious prolongation of the conven-

tion (in Worms, 1540-1), without anything being effected.] But that, however, is, in point of fact, the result of Morone's whole correspondence on the meeting, as it now lies before us. Suffice it to say, that Pallavicini acts like an advocate who has undertaken to defend his sorely assaulted client in all matters, and out and out. He tries to place him in the best light; he brings forward all that is likely to promote his cause; what, according to his conception, is likely to prejudice him, he not only sets aside, but directly denies it.

It would be impossible to accompany him in all the lengthened discussions on which he enters; it suffices that we have in some measure recognised his manner.

It must be confessed, that from this there is to be gathered not the most gratifying result as respects the history of the council.

It has been said, indeed, that the truth comes out from the two works put together. At the most, this assertion must be very much confined to the subject as a whole, and to general points; in particulars it is not the case.

They both deviate from the truth; it is certainly the case, that it lies in the middle; but it cannot be learned from guess-work;—it is again something positive and new; it can be apprehended, not by any compromise of parties, but only by contemplating what was actually done.

As we have seen—Sarpi says that there was a treaty concluded at Bologna; this Pallavicini denies; now no guessing in the world can bring out the fact, that the treaty was verbally agreed upon, never drawn out in writing; which, it will be seen, certainly reconciles the contradiction.

They both misrepresent the instructions given to Contarini; you can never balance between the two accounts; it is only by having the original before you that the truth comes plainly to light.

They present minds of a totally opposite character. Sarpi is acute, penetrating, spiteful; his arrangement is exceedingly skilful; his style pure and simple (ungesucht); and although the (academy della) Crusca would not admit him into the catalogue of classic authors, apparently on account of some provincialisms which he has, still he is really a treat, after the pomp of words through which one has to toil in other quarters; his style adapts itself to the matter itself; in respect of description, he is certainly the second among the modern historians of Italy: I rank him immediately after Machiavelli.

Pallavicini, too, is not without talent. He often makes ingenious comparisons; he often conducts his defence not unskilfully. But his talent has something heavy and oppressive about it: it is, in the main, a talent that makes phrases and thinks about subterfuges: his style is redundant in words. Sarpi is clear and transparent to the very bottom; Pallavicini, not without fall and flow, but muddy, broad, and fundamentally shallow.

Both are, to the heart's core, partisans; both, in fact, are without the true mind of an historian, which is to apprehend the object in all its truth, and to bring it into the light. Sarpi has certainly talent, but he will do nothing but complain; Pallavicini has also talent, although in a much lower degree, but at any cost he insists on defending.

Neither can one obtain a complete view of the matter (of which they treat) even from both viewed together. It remains even to be noted, that Sarpi has much which Pallavicini, notwithstanding all the archives that were opened to him, had not contrived to fall upon. I shall instance only the memoir of the nuncio Chieregato on the deliberations at the court of Adrian, a document of much importance, and against which Pallavicini makes exceptions that signify nothing. Pallavicini passes over much, too, from a kind of incapacity: he has not the acuteness to perceive how much depends upon a thing, and so he allows it to pass. On the other hand, Sarpi again was deprived of innumerable pieces of information which Pallavicini had: he saw but a small part of the correspondence of the Roman court with the legates. His defects arise for the most part from the want of original sources of information.

Often, however, neither of them had important memorials. For the history of the whole latter part of the council, a small report of cardinal Morone, who discharged the duties of ambassador in the last decisive embassy to Ferdinand I., is of the utmost weight. It remains, without having been taken advantage of by either.

Nor must it be supposed that Rainaldus or Le Plat fully supplies this deficiency. Rainaldus often merely excerpts from Pallavicini. Le Plat often follows him or Sarpi, word for word, and takes from the Latin translations of their works those things, as authoritative memorials, on which he found nothing more authentic himself. He has fewer unprinted (authorities) than was to be expected. In Mendham's "Memoirs of the Council of Trent," there is much that is new and good; for instance, we find, at page 181, an extract from the Acta of Paleotto; as well as his introductions even to individual sessions, as (for instance) to the 20th; but the requisite pains have not been bestowed on the final elaboration of the work.

Would any one take in hand to write a new history of the council of Trent—a thing which meanwhile, since these matters have now lost much of their interest, is not so readily to be expected—he must commence altogether from the beginning. He must bring together the negotiations that properly belong to it; the discussions of the congregations, of which but very little has become authentically known; he must also procure the despatches of one or other of the ambassadors that were present. Not till then would he be able to have a complete view of the subject matter, and to review the two opposite authors that have written upon it. This, however, is an undertaking which will never be accomplished, in as much as those who might perhaps accomplish it, do not wish for it, and those who would wish for it, have it not in their power to do it.

SECTION THIRD.

TIMES OF THE RESTORATION DOWN TO SIXTUS V.

We return to our manuscripts, in which, even when fragmentary, we find at all events genuine and unfalsified information.

22.

Instructio pro causa fidei et concilii data episcopo Mutinae, Pauli IH. ad regem Romanorum nuntio destinato.—[Instructions for the cause of the faith and the council given to the bishop of Modena, nuncio of Paul III., appointed to go to the king of the Romans.] 24 Oct. 1536. (MS. Barb. 3007, 15 leaves.)

This furnishes a conclusive proof how necessary the Roman court found it to recollect itself, and to look to its reputation. The nuncio had, among other things, the following rules prescribed to him. He was neither to be too liberal, nor too parsimonious and greedy; to be neither too serious nor too sprightly: he was not to publish his spiritual functions by notices affixed to the church-doors: he might thereby make himself ridiculous: whoever wanted him might find him without that; he was to abandon his official fees only under special circumstances, but was never to collect money too eagerly,—to contract no debts,—to pay for what he got at inns.

"Nec hospitii pensione nimis parce vel fortasse etiam nequaquam soluta discedat, id quod ab aliquibus nuntiis aliis factum plurimum animos eorum populorum in nos irritavit. .. In vultu et colloquiis omnem timorem aut causae nostrae diffidentiam dissimulet. .. Hilari quidem vultu accipere se fingant invitationes, sed in respondendo modum non excedant, ne id forte mali iis accidat quod cuidam nobili Saxoni, camerario secreto q. Leonis X. (Miltitz) qui ob Lutheranam causam componendam in Saxoniam missus, id tantum fructus reportavit, quod saepe, perturbatus vino, ea effutire de pontifice et Romana curia a Saxonibus inducebatur non modo quae facta erant, sed quae ipsi e malae in nos mentis affectu imaginabantur et optabant, et ea omnia scriptis excipientes postea in conventu Vormatiensi nobis publice coram tota Germania exprobrabant.

[Nor to leave an inn with too parsimonious a payment of the reckoning, or perhaps even without paying at all, the doing of which by some other nuncios has exceedingly incensed the minds of those peoples against us. .. In countenance and in conversations to dissemble all fear or distrust of our cause. .. Let them affect receiving invitations with a cheerful countenance, but let them observe moderation in answering them, lest the same mischief should happen to them as once befell a noble Saxon, quondam privy chamberlain to Leo X., (Miltitz) who having been sent into Saxony to bring the Lutheran affair to a settlement, produced no better result than that often, when flushed with wine, he was led by the Saxons to blab out respecting the pontiff and the Roman curia not only things that had actually been done, but things also which from the evil disposition of their minds towards us, they imagined and wished, and putting all these things down in writing, they afterwards brought them out as charges against us publicly in the face of all Germany, at the diet of Worms.]

We see also from Pallavicini i. 18, that the behaviour of Miltitz had given him a very bad reputation in the recollection of the Roman court.

This paper of instructions, which, moreover, Rainaldus knew, and has in a great measure incorporated into his work, (xxi. 19,) is further remarkable for giving the names of some little known defenders of (Roman) catholicism in Germany, Leonh. Marstaller, Nicol. Appel, Joh. Burchard, preacher of an order, "qui etsi nihil librorum ediderit contra Lutheranos, magnae tamen vitae periculo ab initio usque hujus tumultus pro defensione ecclesiae laboravit."—[Who although he has published none of the books against the Lutherans, yet at the great peril of his life has, from the very commencement of this tumult, laboured in the defence of the church.] Among the better known, Lewis Berus, who had fled from Basel to Freiburg in Breisgau, is chiefly famed and recommended to the nuncio, "tum propter sanam et excellentem hominis doctrinam et morum probitatem, tum quia sua gravitate et autoritate optime operam navare poterit in causa fidei."—[as well on account of the man's sound and excellent doctrine and moral probity, as because by his weight and authority he can admirably give his assistance in the cause of the faith.] It is known that Ber contrived to make himself respected even among the Protestants.

23.

Instruttione mandata da Roma per l'elettione del luogo del concilio.—[Instructions sent from Rome for the choice of the place for the council.] (1537.) Informationi politt. T. xii.

Paul III.'s opinion was certainly now in favour of the calling of a council: in these Instructions he gives his assurance that he was fully resolved on it (tutto risoluto). Only he wanted it to be convened in Italy. He was equally content that it should meet at Placentia or Bologna, places belonging to the Church, the common mother of all; and he would have been most pleased with a city belonging to the Venetians, as these too were the common friends of all. His reason is, that the Protestants felt no eagerness about the council, as might be seen from the conditions that were proposed by them: here likewise the idea occurs, which afterwards acquired so high an historical importance, that the council was only an affair of the Roman Catholics among themselves.

Moreover, he gives notice to the emperor of his efforts to accomplish an internal reform. "Sarà con effetto e non con parole."—[It will be effectual, and not confined to words.]

24.

Instruttione data da Paolo III. al c[l] Montepulciano destinata all' imperatore Carlo V. sopra le cose della religione in Germania, 1539.—[Instructions given by Paul III. to Cardinal Montepulciano appointed to go to the emperor Charles V. about the affairs of religion in Germany, 1539.] (Bibl. Corsini, nr. 467.)

Withal, however, it was manifest that the longing for a reconciliation first of all appeared in Germany. It broke out now and then on both sides, in opposition to the pope. At the convent at Frankfort the imperial ambassador John Wessel, archbishop of Lund, made very important concessions to the Protestants—a fifteen months' truce, during which all the judicial proceedings of the imperial court of justice (kammergericht) should be stayed; and he promised them a religious conference without the pope having any part in it. This was naturally in the highest degree hateful to Paul III.: the cardinal Montepulciano, afterwards Marcellus II., was therefore despatched into Germany for the purpose of thwarting so un-(Roman) catholic a settlement.

The instructions first of all impute the compliancy of the archbishop of Lund to improper personal motives: to presents, promises, and ampler prospects. "La communità d'Augusta gli donò 2500 fiorini d'oro, poi gli fu fatta promissione di 4000 f. singulis annis sopra il frutto del suo arcivescovato di Lunda occupato per quel re Luterano."—[The community of Augsburg presented him with 2500 golden florins; then a promise was given to him of 4000 florins a-year (secured), on the revenues of his archbishop of Lund, occupied by that Lutheran king (of Denmark). He wanted to remain on good terms with the duke of Cleves and with queen Maria of Hungary. For before all was that sister of the emperor, at that time stadtholder in the Netherlands, complained of as having a strong leaning to the protestants. "Secretamente presta favore alla parte de' Luterani, animandogli ove può, e con mandarli huomini a posta disfavoreggia la causa de' cattolici."—[She secretly shows favour to the Lutheran party, encouraging them where she had it in her power, and by purposely sending men to them she disfavours the cause of the (Roman) catholics.] She had had an envoy at Schmalkalde and expressly dissuaded the electoral prince of Treves from entering the (Roman) catholic league.

Maria and the archbishop, to wit, represented the anti-French and anti-Romish leaning of the imperial court. She wished to see Germany united under the emperor. The archbishop declared that that depended altogether on some religious concessions being made: "che se S. M[ta] volesse tolerare che i Luterani stassero nei loro errori, disponeva a modo e voler suo di tutta Germania."—[that if his majesty would but bear with the Lutherans remaining in their errors, he might dispose of all Germany according to his own method and pleasure.]

The pope replied that there were quite other means of bringing matters to a close in Germany. Let us hear what he says.

"Annichilandosi dunque del tutto per le dette cose la dieta di Francfordia, et essendo il consiglio di S. M[ta] Cesarea et altri principi christiani, che per la mala dispositione di questi tempi non si possa per hora celebrare il concilio generale non ostante N. S. già tanto tempo lo babbia indetto et usato ogni opera e mezzo per congregarlo, pare a S. B[ne] che sarebbe bene che S. M[ta] pensasse alla celebratione di una dieta imperiale, per prohibire quelli inconvenienti che potriano nascere massimamente di un concilio nationale, il quale facilmente si potria fare per cattolici e Luterani per la quiete di Germania quando i cattolici havendo visto infiniti disordini seguiti per causa di alcun ministro della Cesarea e Regia M[ta] vedessero anche le Maestà loro esser tardi alli rimedj: nè detto concilio nationale sarebbe meno dannoso alla Cesarea e Regia Maestà, per le occulte cause che sanno, che alla sedia apostolica: non potria non partorire scisma in tutta la christianità così nel temporale come nello spirituale. Ma S. Sta è di parere che si celebri tal dieta in evento che S. M[ta] si possa trovare presente in Germania o in qualche luogo vicino a la congre-

[Annihilating, accordingly, altogether for the said causes, the diet of Frankfort, and it being the counsel of his imperial majesty and other Christian princes, that, on account of the evil disposition of these times, the general council cannot now be celebrated, notwithstanding that our lord has already so long since summoned it to meet, and used every effort and means for assembling it, it appears to his beatitude that it were well that his majesty should think of celebrating an imperial diet, for the purpose of preventing the inconveniences that might arise chiefly from a national council, which might easily be done (held?) by (Roman) catholics and protestants for the quiet of Germany, when the (Roman) catholics having seen the infinite disorders that have followed, because of some minister of the imperial and royal majesties, shall have further perceived that their majesties are slow to apply remedies: nor would the said national council be less detrimental to the imperial and royal majesties from the secret causes of which they are aware, than to the apostolic see; it could not fail to produce a schism throughout all christendom,

gatione: altrimenti se S. M^{ta} Cesarea distratta da altre sue occupationi non potesse trovarsi così presto, è d'opinione che la dieta non s'indichi, nè che S. M^{ta} si riposi nel giudicio altrui, quantunque sufficienti e buoni che procurassero e sollecitassero fare detta dieta in assenza di S. M^{ta}, per non incorrere in quei disordini che sono seguiti nelle altre diete particolari ove non si è trovato S. M^{ta}, e tra questo mezzo con fama continuata da ogni banda di voler venire in Germania e fare la dieta e con honeste vie et esecutioni trattenere quei principi che la sollecitano e l'addimandano: mentre che S. M^{ta} venendo da buon senno la indichi poi e celebri, et interea vedendo S. M^{ta} quanto bene et utile sia per portare la propagatione della lega cattolica, attenda per hora a questa cosa principalmente, e scriva al suo oratore in Germania e parendoli ancora mandi alcun' altro che quanto più si può procurino con ogni diligenza e mezzo d'accrescere detta lega cattolica acquistando e guadagnando ogn' uno, *ancora che nel principio non fossero così sinceri nella vera religione*, perche a poco a poco si potriano poi ridurre, e per adesso importa più il togliere a loro che acquistare a noi: alla quale cosa gioveria molto quando S. M^{ta} mandasse in Germania quella più quantità di denari ch'ella potesse, perche divulgandosi tal fama confirmarebbe gli altri, che più facilmente entrassero vedendo che li primi nervi della guerra non mancariano. E per maggiore corroboratione di detta lega cattolica S. Sta sisolverà di mandare una o più persone a quei principi cattolici per animarli, similmente con promissioni di ajuto, di denari et altri effetti, quando le cose s'incammineranno di sorte, per il beneficio della religione e conservatione della dignità della sede apostolica e della Cesarea M^{ta}, che si veda da buon senno la spesa dover fare frutto: nè in questo si partirà dal ricordo di S. M^{ta}: nè sarebbe male tra questo mezzo sotto titolo delle cose Turchesche mandare qualche numero di gente Spagnuola et Italiana in quelle bande con trattenerli nelle terre del re de' Romani suo fratello, accioche bisognando l'ajuto fosse presto in ordine."

alike in the temporal and spiritual department. But his holiness is of opinion that such a diet should be held in the event of his majesty being able to be present in Germany or somewhere in the vicinity of the meeting; otherwise, should his majesty, called away by his other occupations, find it impossible to be thus at hand, he is of opinion that the diet should not be summoned, and that his majesty should not trust to the judgment of others, however capable and good, who should seek and solicit the having of the said council to meet in his majesty's absence, so as not to incur the disorders that ensued on the other special diets where his majesty was not present, and meanwhile by continuing the report on all sides of his intending to come to Germany, and to hold the diet, and by honest ways and practices those princes should be kept in good humour who solicit and call for it; while his majesty, on his arrival, should then prudently summon it and hold it, and meanwhile that his majesty sees how well and useful it would be to carry on the propagation of the (Roman) catholic league, he should attend at present to that matter principally, and write to his ambassador in Germany, and on his arrival should further commission some one else, so that as soon as possible they should procure with all diligence and every means, the increase of the said (Roman) catholic league, by acquiring and gaining over every one, *albeit that at first they might not be so sincere in the true religion*, in order that by little and little they might then be brought back, and for the present it was of more consequence that they should be withdrawn from them than acquired to us: to which it would much assist were his majesty to send as much money into Germany as he can, because the report of this being spread will confirm others, who will more readily engage on seeing that the chief sinews of war are not wanting. And for the greater strengthening of the said (Roman) catholic league, that his majesty should resolve to send one or more persons to these (Roman) catholic princes to encourage them, together with promises of aid in money and other supplies, when matters shall proceed in such wise, for the benefit of religion and the preservation of the dignity of the apostolic see and of his imperial majesty, that it may be rationally assumed that the expense ought to bear fruit; nor in this should his majesty be forgetful. Nor will it be amiss, meanwhile, under the show of the Turkish affairs, to send a certain number of Spanish and Italian troops into those parts, to be kept on foot in the territories of his brother the king of the Romans, so that in case of need, regular assistance might at once be had.]

Pallavicini was acquainted with this as well as the preceding paper of instructions (lib. iv. cap. 14). We see, from what he says, that they were originally suggested by the last received notices respecting Germany, particularly those obtained from the letters of Aleander, who gained for himself in these negotiations so equivocal a reputation. Rainaldus, too, has excerpted them, although this very instance shows how useful it is to consult the originals. The above rather obscure passage runs thus in Rainaldus:—"Interea omni studio catholicorum foedus augere atque ad se nonnullos ex adversariis pellicere niteretur, mitteret etiam aurum militare ut foederatis adderet animos fluctuantesque ad se pertraheret." [Meanwhile he should strive with all his endeavours to augment the league of the Roman Catholics, and to allure to himself some of the adversaries, that he should send also military gold, so as to add courage to the members of the league, and to draw the fluctuating over to himself.]

25.

Instructiones pro rev[mo] dom[no] episcopo Mutinensi apostolico nuntio interfuturo conventui Germanorum Spirae, 12 Maji, 1540, celebrando.—[Instructions for the most Rev. Lord Bishop of Modena, apostolic nuncio, who is to be present at the Convention of the Germans, to be held at Spires on the 12th of May, 1540. (Barb. 3007.)]

Nevertheless religious conferences were held. Here we see the light in which these were contemplated in Rome.

"Neque mirum videatur alicui si neque legatis neque nuntiis plenaria facultas et autoritas decidendi aut concordandi in causa fidei detur, quia maxime absurdum esset et ab omni ratione dissentaneum, quin imo difficile et quam maxime periculosum, sacros ritus et sanctiones, per tot annorum censuras ab universali ecclesia ita receptas ut si quid in his innovandum esset id nonnisi universalis concilii decretis vel saltem summi pontificis ecclesiae moderatoris mature et bene discussa deliberatione fieri debeat, paucorum etiam non competentium judicio et tam brevi ac praecipiti tempore et in loco non satis idoneo committi. . . .

"Debet tamen rev. dom. nuntius domi suae seorsim intelligere a catholicis doctoribus ea omnia quae inter ipsos et doctores Lutheranos tractabuntur, ut suum consilium prudentiamque interponere et ad bonum finem omnia dirigere possit, salva semper sanctissimi Domini Nostri et apostolicae sedis autoritate et dignitate, ut saepe repetitum est, quia hinc salus universalis ecclesiae pendet, ut inquit D. Hieronymus. Debet idem particulariter quadam cum dexteritate et prudentia catholicos principes, tam ecclesiasticos quam saeculares, in fide parentum et majorum suorum confirmare, et ne quid in ea temere et absque apostolicae sedis autoritate, ad quam hujusmodi examen spectat, innovari aut immutari patiantur, eos commonefacere."

[Nor let it seem strange to any one that neither to legates nor nuncios are full power and authority given to decide or agree in the matter of faith; for it would be most absurd and altogether irrational, nay more, difficult and hazardous in the highest degree, for the sacred rites and sanctions, through the judgments of so many years so admitted by the church universal, that were any innovation to take place, it ought not to be done unless by the decrees of a general council, or at least by the mature and fully discussed deliberation of the supreme pontiff, the moderator of the church, to be committed to the judgment of a few persons, those even not competent, in so short a time and so hurriedly, and in an insufficiently convenient place. . . . .

The most rev. lord nuncio ought, however, at his own house to learn from (Roman) catholic doctors all things that are to be treated of between them and the Lutheran doctors, so as to be able to interpose his own advice and judgment, and direct every thing to a good result, saving always the authority and dignity of our most sacred lord and of the apostolic see, as has often been repeated, seeing that on this hangs the salvation of the universal church, as saith the demigod[1] Jerome. He ought, particularly, with some skill and prudence, to confirm catholic princes, both ecclesiastical and secular, in the faith of their parents and their forefathers, and should admonish them not to suffer any innovation or change to be made in that, rashly and without the authority of the apostolic see, to which the examination of such a thing belongs.]

26.

Instructio data rev[mo] card[li] Contareno in Germaniam legato.—[Instructions given to the most rev. cardinal Contarini, sent as legate into Germany.] 28th January, 1541.

Already printed, and often touched upon. The Roman court, at last, in this allows itself to show some compliancy.

Betwixt 1541 and 1551, there follows in our collection a not insignificant number of letters, advices, instructions, comprehending all Europe, and not seldom throwing a new light on historical occurrences, yet which cannot be here minutely sifted; as indeed the book which these extracts might farther elucidate is not designed to give an account at large of that period. Without much scruple, I confine myself to the more important.

27.

1551, die 20 Junii in senatu Matthaeus Dandulus eques ex Roma orator.—[20th June, 1551, Matthew Dandolo, ambassador (returned) from Rome, in the Senate.]

Such is the title of the report presented by Matthew Dandolo—who, we see from the letters of cardinal Polo (ed. Quir. ii. p. 90), was brother-in-law to Gaspar Contarini—after a residence of twenty-six months in Rome. He promises to be short:—"Alle relationi non convengono delle cose che sono state scritte se non quelle che sono necessarie di esser osservate."—[Things that have been put in writing are not suitable for reports, unless it be those that are necessary to be observed.]

He treats, first, of the last days of Paul III.—I have already related the most important part of this. He then speaks of the conclave: all the cardinals are mentioned by name. Dandolo states that he arrived along with members of the college of the university of Padua. We see how well off he must have been in point of information. He proceeds to give a tabular view of the papal finances: "Il particolar conto, io l'ho avuto da essa camera."—[The particular account I have had from the chamber itself.]

1 D. *i. e.* Divus Hieronymus, commonly translated saint; but as there is the closest analogy between the placing of certain mortals among the saints, by the papacy, and the making demigods of their heroes by the ancients, so that in Latin the former borrows its very terms from the latter, these should certainly be retained in a translation.—TR.

"I. La camera apostolica ha d'entrata l'anno: per la thesaureria della Marca 25000 sc., per la salara di detta provincia 10000, per la thesauriera della città d'Ancona 9000, — d'Ascoli 2400, — di Fermo 1750, — di Camerino 17000, — di Romagna et salara 31331, — di Patrimonio 24000, — di Perugia et Umbria 35597, — di Campagna 1176, per Norsia 600, per la salara di Roma 19075, per la doana di Roma 92000, per la gabella de cavalli in Roma 1322, per le lumiere 21250, per l'ancoraggio di Civita vecchia 1000; per il sussidio triennale: dalla Marca 66000, da Romagna 44334, da Bologna 15000, da Perugia et Umbria 43101, da Patrimonio 18018, da Campagna 21529; da censi di S. Pietro 24000, dalla congregatione de frati 23135, da vigesima de Hebrei 9855, da maleficj di Roma 2000. Summa . . . 559473

Da dexime del stato ecclesiastico quando si pongono 3000 sc., da dexime di Milano 40000, — del regno 37000, — dalla gabella della farina 30000, — dalla gabella de contratti 8000 = 220(?)000. Ha il datario per li offici che vacano, compositioni et admissioni 131000, da spoglie di Spagna 25000 = . . . (?) 147000

Summa delle entrate tutte 706(?)473 senza le 5 partite non tratte fuora, che stanno a beneplacito di N. Signore.

II. La camera ha di spesa l'anno: a diversi governatori, legati, roche 46071 scudi, alli officiali di Roma 145815, a diverse gratie 58192, in Roma al governatore Bargello, guardie camerali et altri officii 66694, al capitano generale 39600, alle gallere 24000, al populo Romano per il capitolio 8950, al maestro di casa il vitto della casa 60000, a diversi extraordinarii in Roma 35485, al signor Balduino cameriere 17000, al signor Gioan Battista 1750, alla cavalleria quando si teneva l'anno 30000, al N. S. per suo spendere et per provisioni da a cardinali e tutto il datariato 232000. Summa in tutto questo exito 70(6?)5557 sc.

[I. The apostolic chamber possesses, of yearly revenues:—

	Scudi.
For the treasury of the Mark,	25,000
The saltworks of that province,	10,000
The treasury of the city of Ancona,	9,000
" " Ascoli,	2,400
" " Fermo,	1,750
" " Camerino,	17,000
" of the Romagna and saltworks,	31,331
" " Patrimony (of the Church),	24,000
" of Perugia and Umbria,	35,597
" of the Campagna,	1,176
For Norsia, ...	600
" the saltworks of Rome, .	19,075
" customs of Rome, .	92,000
" horse tax in Rome, .	1,322
" lights, . . .	21,250
" anchorage dues of Civita Vecchia, . .	1,000
" triennial subsidy—	
of the Mark, .	66,000
of the Romagna,	44,334
of Bologna, .	15,000
of Perugia & Umbria,	43,101
of the Patrimony,	18,018
of the Campagna,	21,529
From the *censi* of St. Peter, .	24,000
" congregation of friars,	23,135
" twentieth of the Hebrews,	9,855
" malefactors of Rome,	2,000
Total amount,	559,473
From the tithes of the ecclesiastical state when they yielded 3000 sc.; from the tithes of Milan, 40,000; from the kingdom, 37,000; from the gabelle on flour, 30,000; from the gabelle of contracts, 8000 = 220(?)000. The datario has, per the offices that fall vacant, compositions and admissions, 131,000; from the Spoglia of Spain, 25,000 = .	(?) 147,000
Total amount of all the revenues,	706(?)473

Exclusive of the 5 divisions not drawn out, which depend on the good pleasure of our Lord.

II. The chamber has yearly payments as follows:—

To sundry governors, legates, roche,	46,071
To the officials of Rome, .	145,815
For various gratuities, . .	58,192
In Rome, to the governor Bargello, guards of the chamber, and other offices, . . .	66,694
To the captain general, . .	39,600
" galleys, . .	24,000
" people of Rome for the capitol,	8,950
" master of the household, the household expenses (*lit.* food)	60,000
To various extraordinary payments in Rome, . . .	35,485
To Signor Baldwin, . .	17,000
To Signor John Battista, . .	1,750
To the cavalry, when they are kept up, for a year, . .	30,000
To our Lord (the pope) for his own expenditure, and for provisions given to the cardinals and all the datariato, . . .	232,000
The total amount of all which is,	70(6?)5,557

He concludes with some remarks on the personal character of Julius III.:—

"Papa Giulio, Ser^ma^ S^ig^ria^, gravissimo e sapientissimo cons°, è dal Monte Sansovino, picciol luogo in Toscana, come già scrissi alle Ecc^e^ V^e^. Il primo che diede nome e qualche riputatione alla casa sua fu suo avo, dottore e molto dotto in legge, e fu al servitio del duca Guido de Urbino, dal quale mandato in Roma per negotii del suo stato lì acquistò gratia molta, sicche col molto studio che in detta facultà fece il suo nepote, acquistò tanto di gratia et riputatione che el fu il cardinal de Monte: de chi po fu nipote questo. Arrivato in corte per il primo grado camerier di papa Julio secondo, fu poi arcivescovo di Siponto, et in tal grado venne qui alle Ecc^e^ V^e^ a dimandargli Ravenna et Cervia, quandoche elle le hebbeno doppo il sacco di Roma: et col multo suo valore nel quale el si dimostrò et nelle lettere di legge et nei consigli havuti molti et per l'auttorità molta di suo zio, che fu il cardinal de Monte, doppo morto lui, fu fatto cardinal questo. Et fatto papa si prese subito il nome di Julio, che fu il suo patron, con una perfettion (presuntion?) di volerlo imitare.

"Ha Sua S^tà^ 64 anni a 28 di Ottobre, di natura collerica molto, ma ancho molto benigna, sicche per gran collera che l'abbi la gli passa inanzi che compisse di ragionarla, sicche a me pare di poter affirmare lui non portar odio nè ancho forse amore ad alcuno, eccetto però il cardinal di Monte, del quale dirò poi. A Sua Santità non volsero mai dar il voto li cardinali nè di Marsa (?) nè di Trento, et furono li subito et meglio premiati da lei che alcun' altro di quei che la favorirono. Il più favorito servitore di molti anni suo era lo arcivescovo di Siponto, che lei essendo cardinale gli diede l'arcivescovato e da lui fu sempre ben servita, sicche si credea che subito la lo farebbe cardinale, ma lui si è rimasto in minoribus quasi che non era quandoche lei era cardinale, che poi fatto papa o poco o nulla si è voluto valer di lui, sicche el poverino se ne resta quasi come disperato." . . .

[Pope Julius, most serene signory, most grave and sapient council, is from Monte Sansovino, a small place in Tuscany, as I have already written to your excellencies. The first person that gave a name and some reputation to his family was his grandfather, a doctor, and very learned in the laws, who was in the employment of duke Guido of Urbino, by whom having been sent to Rome on the business of his state, he acquired much favour, so that, together with the assiduous study his grandson devoted to that faculty (of law) he acquired so much favour and reputation as to be (made) cardinal del Monte, of which (place) that grandson afterwards became (cardinal).[1] On his arrival at court, his first step was that of chamberlain to pope Julius II.; thereafter he was archbishop of Siponto; and when holding that rank, he came here to your excellencies to demand Ravenna and Cervia, seeing that they fell into your hands after the sack of Rome; and because of the great value (of his services), of which he gave evidence both in the letter of the laws and in the many consultations that were held, and by means of the great authority of his uncle, who was cardinal de Monte, on the death of the latter he was made that cardinal. And when made pope, he at once took the name of Julius, who had been his patron, with the (presumption?) of wishing to imitate him.

His holiness will be sixty-four years old on the 28th of October, of a very choleric nature, but also very benevolent, so that with the great choler he has, he runs on before being pleased to reason; so that to me it seems one may affirm that he bears no ill will, and, perhaps, no affection to any one, except indeed the cardinal del Monte, of whom I shall speak afterwards. Neither the cardinal of Marsa (?) nor the cardinal of Trent would ever give a vote for his holiness, and they were at once and better rewarded by him than any of the rest who favoured him. His most favourite servant, for many years, was the archbishop of Siponto, so that when his holiness was cardinal he gave him the archbishopric, and was always well served by him; and so it was believed that he would at once make him a cardinal, but he has been left *quasi in minoribus*, which he was not as long as his holiness was a cardinal, for after being made pope he wishes to make little or no account of him, so that the poor man remains as if in despair.]

Our manuscript is unfortunately too defective to admit of our copying any further, especially as the notices it gives often fall on matters of no importance.

28.

Vita di Marcello II. scritta di propria mano del signor Alex. Cervini suo fratello.—[Life of Marcellus II., written with his own hand, by signor Alex. Cervini, his brother.] Alb. No. 157.

There is still extant a very serviceable little work on pope Marcellus II. by Peter Polidore, 1744. Of the sources whence that author drew his materials, the very first he adduces is this biography by Alexander Cervini. Unfortunately, however, it was so early as in 1598 in a great measure spoilt, on the occasion of a fire in the family dwelling-house at Monte-

1 The Venetian Italian of this sentence seems to be extremely elliptical. I know not how far I may have hit the meaning. Tr.

pulciano. A fragment only remains. I extract from it the following passage, relating to the attempt to improve the kalendar, and which is not to be found in Polidore:—

"Havendolo adunque il padre assuefatto in questi costumi et essercitatolo nella grammatica, rettorica, aritmetica e geometria, accadde che anche fu esercitato nell' astrologia naturale più ancora che non haverebbe fatto ordinatamente, e la causa fu questa: la Sta di N. Signore in quel tempo, Leone X., per publico editto fece intendere che chi aveva regola o modo di correggere l'anno trascorso fino ad all' hora per undici giorni, lo facesse noto a S. Sta: onde Mr Riccardo già detto (vater des papstes), siccome assai esercitato in questa professione, volse obbedire al pontefice, e però con longa e diligente osservatione e con suoi stromenti trovò il vero corso del sole, siccome apparisce nelli suoi opusculi mandati al papa Leone, con il quale e con quella gloriosissima casa de Medici teneva gran servitù e specialmente con il magnifico Giuliano, dal quale aveva ricevuti favori et offerte grandi. Ma perche la morte lo prevenne, quel Signore non seguì più oltre il disegno ordinato che Mr Riccardo seguitasse, servendo la persona Sua Ecca in Francia e per tutto dove essa andasse, come erano convenuti. Nè la Santità di N. Signore potette eseguire la publicatione della correttione dell' anno per varii impedimenti e finalmente per la morte propria, che ne seguì non molto tempo doppo."

[The father, accordingly, having inured him to these habits, and exercised him in grammar, rhetoric, arithmetic, and geometry, it happened, also, that he was exercised in natural astrology still more than he would have been in the ordinary course of things, and the cause was this: The holiness of our lord—at that time Leo X.—announced, by a public edict, that whoever might have a rule or method of correcting the year, which had, up to that time, gone wrong by eleven days, should notify the same to his holiness; hence Mr. Ricardo, above mentioned (the pope's father), as being already practised in this profession, wished to comply with the pontiff's request, and, accordingly, by long and diligent observation, and with the aid of his instruments, found the true course of the sun, as it appears in his *opusculi* (sketches) sent to pope Leo, with whom and with the most glorious house of Medici, he maintained great service, and especially with Julian the Magnificent, from whom he had received great favours and offers. But in as much as death overtook him, that signor did not follow out any further the prescribed design pursued by Mr. Ricardo, while serving personally his excellency in France, and wherever else he might go, as they had agreed. Nor was the holiness of our lord (the pope) able to carry out the publication of the correction of the year on account of various obstacles, and, finally, on account of his own death, which followed not long after.]

Still we see how the mind of the Italians, in the times of Leo X., laboured even in this field; and that the famous bishop of Fossombrone, who, in the Lateran council of 1513, recommended attention to be paid to the correction of the kalendar, was not the only person who thought of that.

29.

Antonio Caracciolo Vita di Papa Paolo IV. (2 vol. fol.)—[Antony Caracciolo's Life of Pope Paul IV. (2 folio vols.)]

Antony Caracciolo, Theatiner, Neapolitan, and a collector all his life long, could not neglect to apply his assiduity to the most renowned of the Neapolitan popes, the founder of the Theatiners, Paul IV. For this we are exceedingly obliged to him. He has collected a number of notices which, but for him, would have been lost. His book forms the basis of the copious work of Charles Bromato, Storia di Paolo IV. Pontefice Massimo, Rom. 1748, which presents, in two thick and close-printed quarto volumes, a superabundantly rich collection of materials.

Meanwhile, as could not fail to happen with the rigorous censorship maintained in the Roman Catholic Church, Bromato durst in nowise adopt all (the information) that his originals offered to him.

I have often referred to a detailed "Information" of J. P. Caraffa to Clement VII., on the circumstances of the church, which was composed in 1533. Bromato (i., p. 205) makes a long extract from it. But he also leaves out a great deal, and that just the most notable (part of it); for example, on the spread of Lutheran opinions in Venice.

"Si supplica S. Sta, che per l'honore di Dio e suo, non essendo questa città la più minima nè la più vil cosa della christianità et essendovi nella città e nel dominio di molte e molte migliara d'anime commesse a S. Sta, sia contenta da persona fedele ascoltare qualche cosa del loro bisogno, il quale, ancorche sia grande, pure se ne dirà per hora qualche parte. E perche, come l'apostolo dice, sine fide impossibile est placere Deo, comminciarete da questa, et avisarete S. Sta come si sente degli errori e dell' heresie nella vita e nei costumi di alcuni, come è in non fare la quaresima e non confessarsi etc, e nella dottrina di alcuni, che publicamente ne parlano e tengono e

[His holiness is besought, by the honour of God and his own honour, that city not being the most inconsiderable nor the most worthless of Christendom, and there being in that city and dominion many many thousands of souls committed to his holiness, to be content as a faithful person, to listen to somewhat of its needs, the which, albeit they be great, nevertheless are not likely to be spoken of at the present time in any quarter. And since, as the apostle says, without faith it is impossible to please God, you will begin with that, and will notify to his holiness how there may be perceived errors or heresies in the life and habits of some, how it is with re-

communicano ancora con gli altri de' libri prohibiti senza rispetto. Ma sopra tutto direte che questa peste, tanto dell' heresia Luterana quanto d'ogni altro errore contra fidem et bonos mores, da due sorti di persone potissimamente si va disseminando et aumentando, cioè dagli apostati e da alcuni frati massime conventuali: e S. Sta deve sapere di quella maledetta nidata di quelli frati minori conventuali, la quale per sua bontà fermando alcuni suoi servi ha incominciato a mettere in iscompiglio: perche essendo loro stati discepoli d'un frate heretico già morto, han voluto far onore al maestro. . . . E per dire quello che in cio mi occorse, pare che in tanta necessità non si debba andare appresso la stampa usata: ma siccome nell' ingruente furore della guerra si fanno ogni dì nuove provvisioni opportune, così nella maggior guerra spirituale non si deve stare a dormire. E perche S. Sta sa che l'officio dell' inquisitione in questa provincia sta nelle mani de' sopradetti frati minori conventuali, li quali a caso s'abbattono a fare qualche inquisitione idonea, come è stato quel maestro Martino da Treviso, della cui diligenza e fede so che il sopradetto di buona memoria vescovo di Pola informò S. Sta, et essendo hora lui mutato da quello in altro officio, è successo nell' inquisitione non so chi, per quanto intendo, molto inetto: e però bisogneria che S. Sta provvedesse parte con eccitar gli ordinarj, che per tutto quasi si dorme, e parte con deputare alcune persone d'autorità, mandare in questa terra qualche legato, se possibile fosse, non ambitioso nè cupido, e che attendesse a risarcire l' honore e credito della sede apostolica e punire o almeno fugare li ribaldi heretici da mezzo de' poveri christiani: perche dovunque anderanno, porteranno seco il testimonio della propria nequitia e della bontà de' fedeli cattolici, che non li vogliono in lor compagnia. E perche la peste dell' heresia si suole introdurre e per le prediche e libri hereticali e per la lunga habitatione nella mala e dissoluta vita, della quale facilmente si viene all' heresia, par che S. Sta potria fare in cio una santa, honesta et utile provvisione."

spect to not observing Lent, and not confessing, &c., and, in the doctrine of some, that they openly speak of, hold, and communicate with others, prohibited books, without paying respect to the prohibition. But, above all, you will say that this pest, as well of the Lutheran heresy as of every other error against the faith and good manners, is mainly diffused and augmented by two sorts of persons, that is to say, by apostates and some friars chiefly belonging to monasteries: and his holiness ought to know of that cursed nest of those conventual friars minorites, which, in consequence of his good nature stopping (the proceedings of) some of his servants, have begun to throw things into disorder: because that they, having been disciples of an heretical brother already dead, have been desirous of doing honour to their master. . . . And, to say what has occurred to me in this matter, it appears that in a case of such necessity one must not proceed after the usual method: but, as at the first violent approach of the fury of war, all new means of providing for the exigency are adopted, so in the more important matter of a spiritual war we must not allow ourselves to go to sleep. And in as much as his holiness knows that the office of the inquisition is placed in this province in the hands of the said conventual minorite friars, who carelessly refrain from making any proper inquisition, such as that of the able Martin of Treviso, of whose diligence and fidelity I know that the above mentioned bishop of Pola, of good memory, informed his Holiness, and he having now been transferred from that to another office, there has succeeded him in the inquisition, I know not whom, (but) so far as I understand, a very unfit person. And therefore it will be needful for his holiness to provide, partly by stirring up the ordinaries, who seem every where to be asleep, partly by deputing some persons of authority to send into this country some legate, if possible, neither ambitious nor greedy, and that he should attend to the repairing of the honour and credit of the apostolic see, and should punish, or at least to drive into banishment, ribald heretics from among poor Christians: for wherever they shall go, they will carry with them a testimony to their own wickedness, and to the goodness of faithful catholics, who will not have them in their company. And for as much as the pest of heresy is usually introduced both by preaching and by heretical books, and by long continuance in a bad and dissolute life, from which one passes easily into heresy, it seems that his holiness might in this respect take safe, honest, and useful measures.]

Caracciolo's work further contains many other more or less important notices, which, for the rest, would have remained unknown, and which a more extensive work could not have ventured to let pass. The Italian biography is quite distinct from another of his writings—Collectanea Historica di Polo IV.—it is quite a different and a far more serviceable work. Yet there are found in the Collectanea some things that re-appear in the *Vita;* for example, the account of the changes adopted by Paul IV., after the removal of his nephews to a distance.

30.

Relatione di M. Bernardo Navagero alla S^ma^ Rep^ca^ di Venetia tornando di Roma ambasciatore appresso del Pontefice Paolo IV. 1558.—[Report of M. Bernardo Navagero to the Most Serene Republic of Venice, on returning as ambassador from Pope Paul IV. 1558.]

This is one of the Venetian reports which has found general circulation. Pallavicini has already made use of it, and has even been attacked on that account; Rainaldus, too (Annales eccles. 1557, No. 10), refers to it, not to mention later authors.

It no doubt deserves this honour in a high degree. Bernardo Navagero enjoyed in Venice the respect due to a man of learning. We see from Foscarini (dell. lett. Ven. p. 255), that he was proposed for the office of historiographer of the Republic: during his previous embassies to Charles V., Henry VIII., and Soliman, he had become practised alike in the conduct of difficult affairs and in the observation of distinguished characters. He came to Rome immediately after the accession of Paul IV.

Navagero distinguishes three things as required of an ambassador: intelligence, and for this penetration is requisite; negotiation, which requires tact; reporting (to his government), which requires judgment, that he may say what is necessary and useful.

He starts from the choice and the power of a pope. He is of opinion, that would the popes make it their serious object to imitate Christ, they would become far more formidable. He then describes "li conditioni," as he says, "di Paolo IV., e di chi lo consiglia," [the condition of Paul IV., and of those who counselled him], that is, first of all, of his three nephews. I have made use of his delineation, but in the general judgment one cannot agree with the author. He thinks that even Paul IV. only wanted to aggrandize his family. Had he written later, after the driving off of his nephews, such a judgment would not have satisfied him. That very moment was the grand turning point of the papal policy from secular to spiritual views. From personal descriptions, Navagero passes to an account of the war between Paul IV. and Philip II., which is no less felicitously composed, and full of clever observations. There follows a review of the foreign relations, and of the most probable result of a future election. It is only with great caution that Navagero proceeds to discuss this subject: "piu," says he, "per sodisfare alle SS. VV. EE. che a me in quella parte" [more to satisfy your Excellencies than me in that part]. Yet he has not done it ill. Among the two in whom he observed the greatest likelihood of success, he names in fact the one who was elected, Medici, although, to be sure, he thinks the other, Puteo, still more likely to be chosen.

"But now," says he, "I am here again; I again behold the countenance of my prince, the enlightened republic, for whose service nothing will be too great for me not to dare, nothing so mean that I shall not take it upon me." The expression of devotion heightens the colouring of the description.

31.

Relatione del Cl^mo^ M. Alvise Mocenigo Cav^re^ ritornato della corte di Roma 1560.—[Report of the most illustrious M. Alvise Mocenigo, knight, on his return from the court of Rome. 1560.] (Arch. Ven.)

For seventeen months Mocenigo remained with Paul IV.; the conclave lasted four months and eight days; he then for seven months discharged the duties of ambassador at the court of Pius IV.

He first pourtrays the ecclesiastical and secular administration, the administration of justice and the court under Paul IV. Here he makes a remark which I have not ventured to make use of: "I cardinali," he says, "dividono fra loro le città delle legationi (nel conclave): poi continuano in questo modo a beneplacito delle pontefici."—[The cardinals, he says, divide among them the cities of the legations (in the conclave): they then continue in that order at the good pleasure of the popes.] Can this be the origin of the administration of the state by ecclesiastics, which was gradually introduced?

Nor does he forget to speak of antiquities, of which Rome, as the descriptions of Boissard and Gamacei testify, possessed then a greater abundance than ever: "In cadaun loco, habitato o non habitato, che si scava in Roma, si ritrovano vestigie e fabriche nobili et antiche, et in molti luoghi si cavano di bellissime statue. Di statue marmoree, poste insieme, si potria fare un grandissimo esercito."—[In every place, inhabited or uninhabited, that is excavated in Rome, there are found remains and noble and antique buildings, and in many places most beautiful statues are dug up. The marble statues, placed all together, would make a very large army.]

Then he comes to the disturbances that broke out on the death of Paul IV., and which, even after they had apparently been quieted, continued to re-appear in a thousand disorders.

"Cessato c'ebbe il popolo, consorsero nella città tutti falliti e fuorusciti, che non si sentiva altro che omicidii, si ritrovavano alcuni che non 8, 7 e fin 6 scudi si pigliavano il carico d'amazzar un' uomo, a tanto che ne furono in pochi giorni commesse molte centenara, alcuni per nimicizia, altri per lite, molti per ereditar la sua roba et altri per di-

[When there was a cessation of the disorders among the people (of Rome), all the bankrupt persons and outlaws came flocking into the city, so that nothing was seen but murders: some were found who undertook for 8, 7, and even 6 scudi to kill a man, to such an extent that some hundreds of murders were committed within a few days, some

verse cause, di modo che Roma pareva, come si suol dire, il bosco di Baccaro."

[from personal enmities, some on account of law suits, many for the sake of inheriting property, and others for various other causes, so that Rome seemed, as one should say, a very bedlam.]

The conclave was very pleasant: there were banquets given every day: Vargas was there for whole nights: at least "alli busi del conclave" [at the noisy meetings of the conclave]; but the person who made the pope was duke Cosmo of Florence.

"Il duca di Firenze l'a fatto papa: lui l'a fatto poner nei nominati del re Filippo e poi con diversi mezzi raccommandar anco dalla regina di Franza, e finalmente guadagnatogli con grand' industria e diligenza la parte Carafesca."

[The duke of Florence has made him pope: he effected his being placed among king Philip's nominees, and then by various means his being recommended further by the queen of France, and finally he gained over to his side, with much industry and diligence, the Caraffa party.]

How completely fallen to nothing those intrigues that are spoken of by the histories of the conclaves. The authors of those histories, usually members of the conclaves themselves, saw only the reciprocal contacts of personalities known to themselves; all the influences exerted from without remained concealed from their view.

The report closes with a portraiture of Pius IV., carried as far as his peculiar qualities had at that time been developed.

32.

Relatione del C^{lmo} M. Marchio Michiel K^{r} e Proc. ritornato da Pio IV. summo pontefice, fatta a 8 di Zugno 1560.—[Report of the most illustrious M. Marchio Michiel, knight and procurator, on his return from Pius IV., chief pontiff, made 8th June, 1560.]

This is the report of a congratulatory embassage which was only 39 days absent from Venice; it cost 13,000 ducats. As a report, it is very feeble. Michiel recommends submissiveness to Rome: "Non si tagli la giurisdition del papa, e li signori avogadori per non turbare l'animo di S. S^{tà} abbino tutti quelli rispetti che si conviene, i quali ho visto che molte volte non si hanno."—[The jurisdiction of the pope does not faulter, and the forensic (?) signors, in order not to disturb the mind of his holiness, pay all those attentions that are proper, and which I have seen are many times not paid.]

33.

Dispacci degli ambasciatori Veneti 18 Maggio—21 Sett. 1560. Inform. politt. tom. viii. 272 leaves. Ragguagli dell' ambasciatore Veneto in Roma 1561. Inform. politt. tom. xxxvii. 71 leaves.]—Despatches of the Venetian ambassadors, 18th May—21st September, 1560. Political Notices, vol. viii. Advices of the Venetian ambassador in Rome, 1561. Political Notices, vol. xxxvii.]

The advices, too, are despatches of January and February 1561, all from Mark Anthony de Mula, who for some time filled the post of an ambassador. (See Andreae Mauroceni Historia Venet. lib. viii., tom. ii., 153.) They are full of information; interesting for the temporary circumstances and the natural character of pope Pius. The last fortunes of the Caraffa family come prominently forward; and it appears that Philip H. now wanted to rescue those old friends of his. This was even charged upon him at court as a crime. Vargas replied, that Philip II. now for once forgave them: "quel gran re, quel santo, quel cattolico non facendo come voi altri"—[that great king, that saint, that catholic, not doing as ye others do]. The pope, on the contrary, loaded them with the severest reproaches: "havere mosse l'arme de Christiani, de Turchi, e degl' eretici . . . . e che le lettere che venivano da Francia e dagli agenti in Italia, tutte erano contrafatte"—[that they had stirred up the arms of Christians, Turks, and heretics . . . . that the letters that came from France and from the agents in Italy were all counterfeit], &c. The pope thinks he would give 100,000 scudi that they were innocent. But the horrible things they had done were not to be tolerated in Christendom.

I abstain, however, from excerpting from letters. It is enough to have indicated the nature of their contents.

34.

Extractus processus cardinalis Caraffae.—[Extract, Cardinal Caraffa's process.] Inff. tom. ii. f. 465-516, with this note appended to it:—"Haec copia processus formati contra cardinalem Caraffam reducta in summam cum imputationibus fisci eorumque reprobationibus perfecta fuit die xx. Nov. 1560."—[This copy of the process formed against Cardinal Caraffa, reduced to a summary, with accounts charged by the exchequer and the statements disproving these, was completed on the 20th of November, 1560.]

From the ninth article of the defence, under the word *heresy*, we see that Albert of Brandenburg sent a certain colonel Frederick to Rome to conclude a treaty with Paul IV. The colonel had an audience of Paul himself, but the cardinal of Augsburg (Otto von Truchsess) made so many representations against him, that he was at last sent away from Rome. To

this there is attached—"El successo de la muerte de los Garrafas con la declaracion y el modo que murieron y el di y hora, 1561."

35.

Relatione di Girolamo Soranzo del 1563. Roma. (Arch. Ven.)—[Report of Girolamo Soranzo, for 1563. Rome. (Venetian Archives.)]

The date 1561, which the copy in the archives bears, is unquestionably incorrect. According to the authentic catalogue of the embassies, Girolamo Soranzo was elected as early as 22d September, 1560, owing to Mula having accepted a post from pope Pius IV., and having fallen, on that account, under the displeasure of the republic: but he was received into favour again, and first upon Mula being appointed a cardinal in the year 1562, did Soranzo take his departure. Accordingly, he makes frequent references to the council which in 1561 had not yet sat.

Girolamo Soranzo remarked, that the reports were at once agreeable and useful to the Senate: "e volontieri udite e maturamente considerate" [you both listen willingly and consider maturely]: he has drawn them up with diligence and affection. It is well worth while to listen to his description of Pius IV.

"Della qualità dell' animo di Sua Beatitudine dirò sinceramente alcune particulari proprietà, che nel tempo della mia legatione ho potuto osservare in lei et intender da persone che ne hanno parlato senza passione. Il papa, come ho detto di sopra, ha studiato in leggi; con la cognitione delle quali e con la pratica di tanti anni nelli governi principali che ha havuto, ha fatto un giudicio mirabile nelle cause così di giustitia come di gratia che si propongono in segnatura, in modo che non s'apre la bocca che sa quello si può concedere e quello si deve negare, la quale parte è non pur utile ma necessaria in un pontefice per le molte et importanti materie che occorre trattar di tempo in tempo. Possiede molto bene la lingua latina e s'ha sempre dilettato di conoscer le sue bellezze, in modo che, per quanto mi ha detto l'illustrissimo Navagiero, che ne ha così bel giudicio, nei concistorj, dove è l'uso di parlar latino, dice quello che vuole e facilmente e propriamente. Non ha studiato in theologia, onde avviene che non vuole mai propria autorità pigliar in se alcuna delle cause commesse all' ufficio dell' inquisitione: ma usa di dire che non essendo theologo si contenta rimettersi in tutte le cose a chi si ha il carico: e se bene si conosce non esser di sua satisfatione il modo che tengono gl'inquisitori di procedere per l'ordinario con tanto rigore contra gl'inquisiti, e che si lascia intendere che più gli piaceria che usassero termini da cortese gentilhuomo che da frate severo, nondimeno non ardisce e non vuole mai opponersi ai giudicii loro, nei quali interviene poche volte, facendosi per il più congregationi senza la presenza sua. Nelle materie e deliberationi di stato non vuole consiglio d'alcuno, in tanto che si dice non esser stato pontefice più travagliato e manco consigliato di S. Sta, non senza meraviglia di tutta la corte che almeno nelle cose di maggior importantia ella non voglia avere il parere di qualche cardinale, che pur ve ne sono molti di buon consiglio: e so che un giorno Vargas lo persuase a farlo, con dirle che se bene S. Sta era prudentissima, che però unus vir erat nullus vir, ma ella se lo levò d'inanzi con male parole: et in effetto si vede che, o sia che ella stima esser atta di poter risolver da se tutte le materie che occorrono, o che pur conosca esser pochi o forse niuno cardinale che non sia interessato con qualche principe, onde il giudicio non può esser libero e sincero, si

[Of the mental qualities of his beatitude, I will say sincerely what are some of their peculiarities, which, during the period of my embassy, I could observe in him and heard from persons who spoke of him dispassionately. The pope, as I have said above, has studied in the laws; with the knowledge of which, and with so many years' practice in the principal governorships he has had, he shows an admirable judgment in such causes as those of justice as well as grace which appear before the segnatura, so that he never opens his mouth without knowing what can be conceded and what ought to be refused, which part is not only useful but necessary in a pontiff, owing to the many and important matters that fall to be treated from time to time. He has an excellent command of the Latin tongue, and has always taken pleasure in acquainting himself with its beauties, so that, by what has been told me by the most illustrious Navagiero, who has so fine a judgment in that matter, in the consistories where Latin is usually spoken, he expresses himself at pleasure readily and with propriety. He has not studied in theology, hence it is that he never wishes on his own authority to take upon himself any of the causes committed to the office of the Inquisition; but is wont to say, that not being a theologian, he is content to remit himself in all these things to him who has the charge; and if he knows himself well, it is not to his satisfaction the manner adopted by the inquisitors in proceeding ordinarily with so much rigour against those who have been brought before it, and that he has let it be understood that he would be better pleased would they act like a courteous gentleman rather than a severe friar; nevertheless he does not dare, and does not desire to set himself to oppose their judgments, in which he rarely intervenes, the congregations being held, for the most part, without his being present at them. In matters of state and political deliberations he wants no man's advice, so much so, that it is said there never has been a pontiff more hard worked and less counselled than his holiness, not without the wonder of the whole court that at least in matters of greater importance he does not wish to have the opinion of any cardinal, though there be many there fit to give good advice: and I know that one day Vargas persuaded him to do so, telling him that albeit his holiness was most prudent, yet "unus vir erat nullus vir,"

vede, dico, che non si vuole servire d'altri che dal card[l] Borromeo e dal sig[re] Tolomeo, i quali essendo giovani di niuna o poca sperienza et esseguenti ad ogni minimo cenno di S. S[ta], si possono chiamar piutosto semplici esecutori che consiglieri. Da questo mancamento di consiglio ne nasce che la Beat[e] Sua, di natura molto presta per tutte le sue attioni, si risolve anco molto presto in tutte le materie, per importanti che le sieno, e presto si rimuove da quello che ha deliberato: perche quando sono pubblicate le sue deliberationi e che li venga poi dato qualche advertimento in contrario, non solo le altera, ma fa spesso tutto l'opposito al suo primo disegno, il che a mio tempo è avvenuto non una ma molte volte. Con i principi tiene modo immediate contrario al suo precessore: perche quello usava di dire il grado del pontefice esser per metter sotto i piedi gl'imperatori et i re, e questo dice che senza l'autorità de' principi non si può conservare quella del pontefice: e percio procede con gran rispetto verso di cadauno principe e fa loro volentieri delle gratie, e quando le niega, lo fa con gran destrezza e modestia. Procede medesimamente con gran dolcezza e facilità nel trovar i negotii indifferentemente con tutti: ma se alcuna volta segli domanda cosa che non sente, se mostra vehemente molto e terribile, nè patisce che segli contradica: nè quasi mai è necessaria con S. Sta la destrezza, perche quando si è addolcita, difficilmente niega alcuna gratia: è vero che nell' essecutione poi si trova per il più maggior difficultà che nella promessa. Porta gran rispetto verso i rev[mi] cardinali, e fa loro volentieri delle gratie, nè deroga mai ai soi indulti nelle collationi de' beneficii, quello che non faceva il suo precessore. E vero che da quelli di maggior autorità par che sia desiderato che da lei fusse dato loro maggior parte delle cose che occorrono a tempo di tanti travagli di quello che usa di fare la S. Sta: onde si dogliono di vedere deliberationi di tanta importantia passar con cosi poco consiglio, e chiamano felicissima in questa parte la Serenità Vostra. Alli ambasciatori usa S. Beat[ne] quelle maggior dimostrationi d'amore et honore che si possi desiderare, nè lascia adietro alcuna cosa per tener li ben satisfatti e contenti: tratta dolcemente i negotii con loro, e se alcuna volta s'altera per causa di qualche dimanda ch'ella non senta o altra occasione, chi sa usare la destrezza, l'acquieta subito, e fa in modo che se non ottiene in tutto quanto desidera, ha almeno in risposta parole molto cortesi: dove quando segli vuol opponere, si può esser certo di non aver nè l'uno nè l'altro: e però Vargas non è mai stato in gratia di S. Sta, perche non ha proceduto con quella modestia ch'era desiderata da lei. Finito che ha di trattar li negotii con li ambasciatori, fa loro parte cortesemente, parla delli avvisi che ha di qualche importantia, e poi entra volentieri a discorrere de lo presente stato del mondo: e con me l'ha fatto in particulare molto spesso, come si può ricordar V. Sta, che alcune volte ho empito i fogli dei suoi ragionamenti. Con i suoi famigliari procede in modo che non si può conoscere che alcuno ha autorità con lei, perche li tratta tutti egualmente, non li

[one man was no man]; but he sent him off with ill words; and, in fact, it is evident, that either it is that he thinks himself fit to determine by himself all the matters that come before him, or that he knows there are few, perhaps no cardinals that are not in the interest of some prince, whence their judgment cannot be unfettered and candid; it is evident, I say, that he does not wish to be served unless by cardinal Borromeo and signor Tolomeo, who being youths of no, or a small experience, and complying with the slightest hint from his holiness, may rather be called simple executors than counsellors. From which want of advice it results that his holiness, naturally very prompt in all he does, further makes up his mind very promptly in all matters, however important they may be, and quickly resiles from the resolution he has taken: whereby, when his resolutions have been published, and there then comes to be given him some advice to the contrary, he not only alters his measures, but often does the very opposite to his first design, a thing which in my time has happened not once but often. With the princes, he pursues a method directly the contrary of that of his predecessor; for that pope used to say, that the dignity of the pontiff was to put emperors and kings beneath his feet; and this one says that without the authority of the princes, that of the pontiff cannot be maintained; and therefore he acts with great respect towards every prince, and willingly grants them favours; and when he denies these he does so with great tact and modesty. He proceeds likewise with great suavity and readiness in conducting business indifferently with all: but should he be asked at any time for something he does not approve, he shows himself very and terribly vehement, and will not suffer himself to be contradicted: nor is it as if tact were never necessary with his holiness, for if once he be softened down, he finds it hard to refuse any favour: it is true, that in executing a thing there is greater difficulty found for the most part than in promising. He treats the most Rev. Cardinals with great respect, and willingly confers favours on them, nor ever derogates from their indults in the collations of benefices, which was not done by his predecessor. It is true that to some of greater authority it appears desirable that he should give them a larger share of the affairs that occur at a time of such labours, than what his holiness is in use to do; whence they are grieved to see deliberations of so much importance pass with so little consultation, and in this respect they call your serenity most fortunate. Towards ambassadors, his beatitude makes those greater demonstrations of love and honour which are to be desired, and omits nothing to satisfy and keep them contented: he conducts business with them in a mild manner, and if at any time he loses his temper on account of some demand that he does not like, any one who has a little tact, speedily appeases him, and can so manage, that if he does not in all things obtain what he wants, he gets at least very courteous words in reply: whereas, when one would set himself to oppose him, he may be certain of getting neither

dando libertà di far cosa alcuna che non sia conveniente, nè permettendo che se la piglino da loro medesimi, ma li tiene tutti in. così bassa e povera fortuna che dalla corte saria desiderato di veder verso quelli più intimi camerieri et altri servitori antichi dimostratione di maggior stima et amore. Fa gran professione d'esser giudice giusto, e volentieri ragiona di questo suo desiderio che sia fatta giustitia, e particolarmente con gli ambasciatori de' principi, con li quali entra poi alle volte con tal occasione a giustificarsi della morte di Caraffa e delle sententie di Napoli e Monte come fatte giustamente, essendoli forse venuto alle orecchie esser stato giudicato dalla corte tutta ch'esse sententie e particularmente quella di Caraffa siano state fatte con severità pur troppo grande et extraordinaria. E naturalmente il papa inclinato alla vita privata e libera, perche si vede che difficilmente si può accomodare a procedere con quella maestà che usava il precessore, ma in tutte le sue attioni mostra piutosto dolcezza che gravità, lasciandosi vedere da tutti a tutte l'hore et andando a cavallo et a piedi per tutta la città con pochissima compagnia. Ha una inclinatione grandissima al fabbricare, et in questo spende volentieri e largamente, sentendo gran piacere quando si lauda le opere che va facendo: e par che habbi fine lasciar anco per questa via memoria di se, non vi essendo hormai luogo in Roma che non habbi il nome suo, et usa di dire il fabbricare esser particularmente inclinatione di casa de Medici: nè osserva S. Beat^{ne} quello che è stato fatto dalli altri suoi precessori, che hanno per il più incominciato edificii grandi e magnifici lasciandoli poi imperfetti, ma ella ha piutosto a piacere di far acconciar quelli che minacciano rovina e finir gl'incominciati, con farne anco de' nuovi, facendo fabbricar in molti luoghi dello stato ecclesiastico: perche fortifica Civita Vecchia, acconcia il porto d'Ancona, vuol ridur in fortezza Bologna: in Roma poi, oltra la fortificatione del borgo e la fabbrica di Belvedere e del palazzo, in molte parti della città fa acconciar strade, fabbricar chiese e rinovar le porte con spesa così grande che al tempo mio per molti messi nelle fabbriche di Roma solamente passava 12 m. scudi il mese e forse più di quello che si conviene a principe, in tanto che viene affermato da più antichi cortigiani non esser mai le cose passate con tanta misura e così strettamente come fanno al presente. E perche credo non babbia ad esser discaro l'intendere qualche particulare che tiene S. Beat^{ne} nel vivere, però satisfarò anche a questa parte. Usa il pontefice per ordinario levarsi, quando è sano, tanto di buon' hora così l'inverno come l'estate ch'è sempre quasi inanzi giorno in piedi, e subito vestito esce a far esercitio, nel quale spende gran tempo: poi ritornato, entrano nella sua camera il rev^{mo} Borromeo e mons^{r} Tolomeo, con i quali tratta, come ho detto, S. S^{tà} tutte le cose importanti così pubbliche come private, e li tiene per l'ordinario seco doi o tre hore: e quando li ha licentiati, sono introdutti a lei quei ambasciatori che stanno aspettando l'audientia: e finito che ha di ragionar con loro, ode S. S^{tà} la messa, e quando l'bora non è tarda, esce fuori a dare audientia ai

the one nor the other: and accordingly Vargas has never been in favour with his holiness, on account of his not proceeding with the modesty that was desired of him. After he has finished treating of matters of business with ambassadors, he politely converses with them, speaks of the news of any importance that he has received, and then begins of his own accord to talk about the present state of the world; and this he has done with me very often, as your serenity may recollect that I have sometimes filled whole leaves with his reasonings. With his familiar friends he conducts himself in such a manner that it cannot be known whether any one has any authority with him, for he treats all alike, not giving them any liberty to do anything that is unsuitable, nor permitting them to take it of themselves, but keeps them all in such a low and poor fortune, that the court would like to see demonstrations of greater esteem and affection paid to those more intimate chamberlains and other old servants. He makes a great profession of being a just judge, and willingly discourses about this desire of his that justice should be done, and particularly with the ambassadors of monarchs, with whom he invariably enters on such occasions into a justification of himself for the death of Caraffa and of the condemnation of Naples and Monte, as done justly, it having, perhaps, come to his ears that it had been thought by the whole court that those sentences, and particularly that of Caraffa, had been pronounced with by far too great and extraordinary a severity. The pope is naturally inclined to a private and untrammeled life, for it is seen that he can with difficulty accommodate himself to proceed with that majesty which was usual with his predecessor, but in all his actions he shows rather affability than gravity, allowing himself to be seen by everybody at all times, and going on horseback or on foot through the whole city, with a very small retinue. He has an excessive passion for building, and in this spends willingly and largely, taking great delight when he is praised for the operations he is proceeding with: and it appears that he aims at leaving also in this way a memorial of himself, there not being a spot in Rome which has not his name, and he is wont to say that the Medici family are particularly addicted to building, nor does his beatitude do like other popes, his predecessors, who have for the most part commenced grand and magnificent edifices, and then left them unfinished, but he has more at heart the repairing of such as threaten to come down, and the finishing of those once commenced, together with the erection of new buildings which he is carrying on in many places in the ecclesiastical state: for he is fortifying Civita Vecchia, is repairing the harbour of Ancona, and wants to convert Bologna into a fortress: in Rome, then, besides the fortification of the *Borgo*, and the building of the Belvedere and the palace, in many parts of the city he is causing streets to be repaired, is building churches, and renewing the gates at so vast an expense, that for many months, in my time, in the buildings in Rome alone, he spent 12,000 scudi a-month,

cardinali et ad altri: e poi si mette a tavola, la qual, per dir il vero, non è molto splendida, com'era quella del precessore, perche le vivande sono ordinarie e non in gran quantità et il servitio è de'soliti soi camerieri. Si nutrisce di cibi grossi e di pasta alla Lombarda bene più di quello che mangia, et il vino è greco di somma molto potente, nel quale non si vuole acqua. Non ha piacere che al suo mangiare si trovino, secondo l'uso del precessore, vescovi et altri prelati di rispetto, ma piutosto ha caro udir qualche ragionamento di persone piacevoli e che babbino qualche umore. Ammette alla sua tavola molte volte de cardinali e degli ambasciatori, et a me in particulare ha fatto di questi favori con dimostrationi molto amorevoli. Dapoi che ha finito di mangiare, si ritira nella sua camera, e spogliato in camicia entra in letto, dove vi sta per l'ordinario tre o quattro hore: e svegliato si ritorna a vestire, e dice l'ufficio et alcune volte da audientia a qualche cardinale et ambasciatore, e poi se ne ritorna al suo esercitio in Belvedere, il quale non intermette mai l'estate fin l'hora di cena e l'inverno fin che si vede lume."

and perhaps more, according to original estimates, so that it was affirmed by some of the oldest courtiers that things had never been conducted with so much order, and so strictly as they are at present. And as I believe that it will not be disagreeable to hear some particulars relating to his beatitude's way of life, I will accordingly say something on that head. The pontiff usually rises, when in good health, so early both in winter and summer, that he is almost always on foot before day-break, and after dressing in haste, goes out to take exercise, in which he spends much time: then on his return, the most Rev. Borromeo and Monsr. Tolomeo enter his chamber, with whom, as I have said, his holiness talks over matters of importance, whether public or private, and he ordinarily keeps them with him for two or three hours: and after parting with them, ambassadors waiting for an audience are introduced, and when done with what he has to say to them, his holiness hears mass, and if the hour be not too late, goes out to give audiences to cardinals and others: he then sits down to dinner, which, to say the truth, is not very splendid, as was that of his predecessor, for the viands are ordinary, and in no great quantity, and the service is done by his usual domestics. He eats gross dishes, and most indeed of what he eats is Lombardy pastry; the wine is Greek, and of great strength, in which he wants no water. He has no pleasure in having to dine with him, as his predecessor used to have, bishops and other prelates in a ceremonious way, but prefers listening to the discourse of pleasant persons, and such as have some humour. He often admits to his table cardinals and ambassadors, and to myself in particular, has often done these favours with very affectionate demonstrations. As soon as he has finished eating he retires to his chamber, and undressing to his shirt, goes to bed, where he remains ordinarily three or four hours: and on awaking dresses himself again, and says the office, and occasionally gives an audience to some one or other, cardinal or ambassador, and then returns to take exercise in the Belvedere, which he does in summer until the supper hour, and in winter as long as the light lasts.]

Soranzo gives many other notices deserving attention, from their bearing on the history of that time. For example, he very well explains the otherwise hardly intelligible going over of the king of Navarre to the Roman Catholics. That prince had been assured in Rome, that even should Philip II. not indemnify him for the part of Navarre which he had lost, by giving him Sardinia, the pope would at all events give him Avignon. No divines, says the ambassador, were employed to make him change his opinions; the negotiation sufficed.

36.

Instruttione del re cattolico al C^l^ M^r^ d' Alcantara suo ambasciatore di quello ha da trattar in Roma. Madr. 30 Nov. 1562. (MS. Rom.)—[Instructions given by the king of Spain to the cardinal of Alcantara, his ambassador, as to the matters to be treated of in Rome. Madrid, 30th Nov. 1562.]

Together with the pope's answers. Satisfactorily excerpted in Pallavicini xx. 10, as far as the following passage, which he has somewhat misunderstood:—

"Circa l' articolo della communione sub utraque specie non restaremo di dire con la sicurtà che sapemo di potere usare con la M^ta^ Sua, che ci parono cose molto contrarie il dimandar tanta libertà e licenza nel concilio et il volere in un medesimo tempo che noi

[With respect to the article of the communion under both kinds, we shall not cease saying, with the confidence that we know we may use with his majesty, that here there appear to be great contradictions, to ask for so much liberty and license in the council,

impediamo detto concilio e che prohibiamo all' imperatore, al re di Francia, al duca di Baviera et ad altri principi che non possano far proponere et questo et molti altri articoli che ricercano attento, che essi sono deliberati et risoluti di farli proponere da suoi ambasciatori e prelati, etiam che fosse contro la volontà dei legati. Sopra il che S. M^{ta} dovrà fare quella consideratione che le parerà conveniente. Quanto a quello che spetta a noi, havemo differita la cosa fin qui, e cercaremo di differirla più che potremo, non ostante le grandi istanze che circa cio ne sono state fatte: e tuttavia se ne fanno dalli sudetti principi, protestandoci che se non se gli concede, perderanno tutti li loro sudditi, quali dicono peccar solo in questo articulo e nel resto esser buoni cattolici, e di più dicono che non essendogli concesso, li piglieranno da se, e si congiungeranno con li settarii vicini e protestanti, da quali quando ricorrono per questo uso del calice, sono astretti ad abjurare la nostra religione: sicche S. M^{ta} può considerare in quanta molestia e travaglio siamo. Piacesse a dio che S. M^{ta} cattolica fosse vicina e potessimo parlare insieme ed anche abboccarsi con l'imperatore—havendo per ogni modo S. M^{ta} Cesarea da incontrarsi da noi—che forse potriamo acconciare le cose del mondo, o nessuno le acconcierà mai se non dio solo, quando parerà a Sua Divina Maestà."

and at the same time to desire that we should impede the said council and prohibit the emperor, the king of France, the duke of Bavaria, and other princes, so that they cannot cause to be proposed both this and many other articles that require attention, until they have been discussed, and until the proposal of them has been resolved upon by his ambassadors and prelates, even though it should be contrary to the wish of the legates. Upon this his majesty ought to bestow the consideration he may think proper. As for what respects us, we have deferred the matter till now, and will try to defer it to the utmost, notwithstanding the pressing instances that have been made about this to us: and nevertheless these continue to be made about it by the above said princes, protesting that, if the concession is not made, they will lose all their subjects, who say that they offend only in this article, and for the rest are good catholics; and moreover say, that if it be not conceded to them, they will take of themselves, and will join with the neighbouring sectaries and protestants, by whom, on their having recourse to this use of the cup, they are compelled to abjure our religion: so that his majesty may see in what a state of trouble and auxiety we are. Would to God that his majesty were at hand, and that we might converse together, and, farther, have a conference with the emperor—by having in any way his imperial majesty face to face with us—so that we might, perhaps, put the affairs of the world in a better state, or none will mend them but God alone, when it shall seem fit to his Divine Majesty.]

37

Instruttione data al Sr Carlo Visconti mandato da papa Pio IV. al re cattolico per le cose del concilio di Trento.]—Instructions given to Signor Carlo Visconti, sent by Pope Pius IV. to the king of Spain about the business of the council of Trent.] Subscribed, Carolus Borromaeus, ultimo Oct. 1563.—[last of Oct. 1563.]

This is not contained in the collection of the nuncio's letters, which reaches only to September, 1563, and is remarkable for discussing the motives for closing the council. Pallavicini xxiv. 1. 1. has, in a great measure, taken in these instructions, although in a different order from that in which they are written. Further, it was, perhaps, the most remarkable point of the instructions that it was contemplated that the council should take up the case of England, and that this was refrained from only out of respect for Philip II.:—

"Non abbiamo voluto parlare sin ora nè lasciar parlare in concilio della regina d'Inghilterra (Maria Stuart), con tutto che lo meriti; nè meno di quest' altra (Elizabeth), e cio per rispetto di S. M^{ta} Cattolica.—Ma ancora a questa bisognerebbe un di pigliare qualche verso, e la M^{ta} S. dovrebbe almeno fare opera che li vescovi et altri cattolici non fossero molestati."

[We have not wished to speak in the council, until permitted, of the queen of England (Mary Stuart), however the subject may deserve it; nor less of that other (Elizabeth), and this from respect for the king of Spain.—But still it; will be necessary that some side should be taken, and his majesty ought at least to do his endeavour that the bishops and other (Roman) catholics should not be molested.]

It is evident that Philip was considered to be laid under a certain obligation to take up the cause of the Roman Catholics of England.

38.

Relatione in scriptis fatta dal Commendone ai signori legati del concilio sopra le cose ritratte dell' imperatore. 19 Febr. 1563.—[Report in writing made by Commendone to the lords legates of the council on the matters represented by the emperor. 19th February, 1563.]

"La somma è che a me pare di aver veduto non pur in S. M^{ta} ma nelli principali ministri, come Trausen e Seldio, un ardentissimo desiderio della riforma e del progresso del concilio con una gran speranza quod remit-

[In fine, it seems to me that I could perceive, not indeed in his majesty, but in his principal ministers, such as Trausen and Seld, a most ardent desire for reform and for the progress of the council, together with a great

tendo aliquid de jure positivo et reformando mores et disciplinam ecclesiasticam non solo si possono conservare li cattolici ma guadagnare e ridurre degli heretici, con una opinione o impressione pur troppo forte che qui siano molti che non vogliano riforma."

hope that by remitting somewhat of positive law, and by reforming manners and church discipline, not only might the (Roman) catholics be preserved, but some of the heretics gained and brought back, together with an opinion, or an impression, certainly excessive, that there were many here who don't want reform.]

The activity of the Jesuits had, in particular, made an impression.

"Seldio disse, che li Gesuiti hanno hormai mostrato in Germania quello che si può sperare con effetto, perche solamente con la buona vita e con le prediche e con le scuole loro hanno ritenuto e vi sostengono tuttavia la religione cattolica."

[Seld said that the Jesuits have now effectually shown what may be hoped for, in as much as solely by means of their good life, and preaching, and schools, they have preserved and still uphold the (Roman) catholic religion there.]

39.

Relatione summaria del cardinal Morone sopra la legatione sua 1564 Januario.—[Summary Report by cardinal Morone on his legation in January, 1564.] (Bibl. Altieri vii. F. 3.)

This would require to be communicated *verbatim*. Unfortunately I did not find myself in a position to take a copy. Accordingly the reader must be contented with the extract which I have inserted in the third Book.

40.

Antonio Canossa: On the attempt to murder Pius IV. Compare i., p. 258.

41.

Relatione di Roma al tempo di Pio IV. e V. di Paolo Tiepolo ambasciatore Veneto.—[Paul Tiepolo the Venetian ambassador's Report from Rome, at the time of Pius IV. and V., first found in manuscript at Gotha, afterwards in many other collections.] 1568.

This Report is in almost all the copies dated in the year 1567, yet Paul Tiepolo expressly says that he had been thirty-three months with Pius V., who was elected in January, 1566; so that it must date posterior to September, 1568. The *Dispacci*, too, of this ambassador, the first that were preserved in the Venetian archives, come down likewise to that year.

Tiepolo describes Rome, the ecclesiastical state and its administration, also the spiritual power, which, as he says, punishes with interdicts and rewards with indulgences. He then compares Pius IV. and V. in point of piety, integrity, liberality, manners, and general natural disposition. Venice found the former a very mild, the latter a very strict and severe pope. Pius V. complained unceasingly of the limitations of ecclesiastical rights in which Venice indulged itself; that it laid taxes on monasteries and convents, and dragged priests before its courts; he complained about the *avogadores*. In spite of these misunderstandings, the comparison made by Tiepolo ends altogether in favour of the severe and to the disadvantage of the mild pope. In this ambassador, too, one can perceive the impression which the personal qualities of Pius V. generally produced over the whole Roman catholic world.

This report, as we have said, has found its way to many places. It has likewise been transferred occasionally into printed works. But be it well observed how. In the *Tesoro Politico*, i. 19, we find a *Relatione di Roma*, in which all that Tiepolo says of Pius V. is transferred to Sixtus V. Traits of character, nay, even actions, ordinances, and so forth, are, without more ado, taken from the one pope and applied to the other. This report, thus thoroughly falsified, has then been incorporated in the Elzevir *Respublica Romana*, where it is found, word for word, at page 494, under the title, "De statu urbis Romae et pontificis relatio tempore Sixti V. papae, anno 1585."—[Account of the state of the city of Rome and of the pope at the time of pope Sixtus V. in the year 1585.]

42.

Relatione di Roma del Cl^mo^ Sr Michiel Suriano K. ritornato ambasciatore da N. S. papa Pio V. 1571.—[Report from Rome of the Most Illustrious Signor Michael Suriano, Knight, on his return as ambassador to our Lord Pope Pius V. 1571.]

Michael Suriano, in whom, as Paruta says, the study of literature set business talents in a clearer light, (Guerra di Cipro I., p. 28,) was Tiepolo's immediate successor.

He describes Pius V. as follows:—

"Si vede che nel papato S. Santità non ha atteso mai a delitie nè a piaceri, come altri suoi antecessori, che non ha alterato la vita nè i costumi, che non ha lasciato l'essercitio dell' inquisitione che haveva essendo privato, et lasciava più presto ogn' altra cosa che quella, riputando tutte l' altre di manco

[It is evident that in the popedom his holiness never gives his attention to luxuries and gratifications like others that have preceded him; that he has made no change in his life or habits, that he has not left off the management of the inquisition, which he had as a private individual, and would aban-

stima et di manco importantia: onde benche per il papato fosse mutata la dignità et la fortuna, non fu però mutata nè la volontà nè la natura. Era S. Sta di presenza grave, con poca carne magra, et di persona più che mediocre ma forte et robusta: havea gl' occhi piccoli ma la vista acutissima, il naso aquilino, che denota animo generoso et atto a regnare, il colore vivo et la canitie veneranda: caminava gagliardissimamente, non temea l' aere, mangiava poco e bevea pochissimo, andava a dormire per tempo: pativa alcune volte d'orina, et vi rimediava con usar spesso la cassia et a certi tempi il latte d'asina et con viver sempre con regola et con misura. Era S. Sta di complession colerica et subita, et s'accendeva in un tratto in viso quando sentiva cosa che le dispiacesse: era però facile nell' audientie, ascoltava tutti, parlava poco et tardo et stentava spesso a trovar le parole proprie et significanti al suo modo. Fu di vita esemplare et di costumi irreprensibili con un zelo rigoroso di religione, che haveria voluto che ogn' un l'havesse, et per questo corregea gl'ecclesiastici con riserve et con bolle et i laici con decreti et avvertimenti. Pacca professione aperta di sincerità et di bontà, di non ingannare, di non publicar mai le cose che gli eran dette in secretezza et d'esser osservantissimo della parola, tutte cose contrarie al suo predecessore: odiava i tristi et non poteva tollerarli, amava i buoni o quei che era persuasa che fosser buoni: ma come un tristo non potea sperar mai di guadagnar la sua gratia, perche ella non credea che potesse diventar buono, così non era senza pericolo un buono di perderla quando cadea in qualche tristezza. Amava sopra tutte le cose la verità, et se alcuno era scoperto da S. Sta una sol volta in bugia, perdeva la sua gratia per sempre, et fu visto l'essempio nel sig^r Paolo Ghisilieri suo nipote, il quale scacciò da se per averlo trovato in bugia, come S. Sta medesima mi disse, et per officii che fusser fatti non volse mai più receverlo in gratia. Era d'ingegno non molto acuto, di natura difficile et sospettosa, et da quella impression che prendea una volta non giovava a rimoverlo niuna persuasione di ragione di rispetti civili. Non avea isperienza di cose di stato, per non averle mai pratticate se non ultimamente: onde nei travagli che portan seco i maneggi di questa corte et nelle difficoltà che sempre accompagnan la novità dei negotii, un che fosse grato a S. Santità et in chi ella havesse fede era facilmente atto a guidarla a suo modo, ma altri in chi non havea fede non potea essere atto, et le ragioni regolate per prudenza humana non bastavano a persuaderla, et se alcun pensava di vincere con auttorità o con spaventi, ella rompeva in un subito et metteva in disordine ogni cosa o per lo manco gli dava nel viso con dir che non temeva il martirio et che come Dio l'ha messo in quel luogo così poteva anco conservarlo contra ogni auttorità et podestà humana. Queste conditioni et qualità di S. Santità, se ben son verissime, però son difficili da credere a chi non ha auto la sua pratica et molto più a chi ha auto pratica d'altri papi: perche pare impossibile che un huomo nato et nutrito in bassa fortuna si tenesse tanto sincero: che resistesse così arditamente

don anything sooner than it, thinking everything else of no value or importance; whence, albeit that by the popedom his rank and fortune were changed, yet there was no alteration in his will or natural character. His holiness was a man of grave aspect, meagre from want of flesh, rather above the ordinary size, but strong and robust: he had small eyes, but most acute powers of vision, an aquiline nose, denoting a generous mind and aptitude for government, a lively complexion, and venerable white hair: he walked most vigorously, was not afraid of the open air, ate little and drank very little, went to bed by times: he sometimes suffered from strangury, and by way of remedy often took cassia, and occasionally ass's milk, and lived always regularly and moderately. His holiness was of a quick and choleric temper, and his face flared up in a moment when he met with anything that displeased him: he was withal good-natured in audiences, heard all, spoke little and slowly, and often struggled hard to find proper and significant terms to express the matter in his own way. He was of an exemplary life and blameless morals, with a rigorous zeal for religion, which would have had every one to have the same, and for this he corrected the ecclesiastics with reservations and bulls, and the laity with decrees and warnings. He made an open profession of sincerity and goodness, of never deceiving people, of never divulging matters committed to him in secrecy, of most strictly keeping his word, in all these things presenting a contrast to his predecessor. He hated rogues and could not bear them, loved good people or such as he thought to be so: but as a rogue never could look for his favour, because he did not believe such a one would ever become good, so a good man was not beyond the risk of losing his favour on falling into any impropriety of conduct. He loved truth above all things, and if any one was but once detected by his holiness in a lie, he lost favour with him for ever, and this was seen in the case of Signor Paul Ghisilieri, his nephew, whom he expelled from his presence for having been found in a lie, as his holiness himself told me, and for all the good offices that may have been done, would never more take him into favour. He was not of a very acute genius, was of an untoward and suspicious disposition, and no persuasive of reasons of policy availed at all for the removal of an impression he had once taken. He was not experienced in state affairs, not having had any practice in that way till late in life; accordingly, amid the annoyances involved in the negotiations of this court, and amid the difficulties that always attend the novelty of affairs, one who should be agreeable to his holiness, and in whom he would feel confidence, would find it easy to guide him in his own way, but others in whom he had no confidence, were incapable of this, and reasons regulated by human prudence were not enough to persuade him, and if any one thought to overcome him by addressing himself to his respect for authority and his fears, he would break away of a sudden and throw all into disorder, or at the least have given it him in

a i maggior prencipi et più potenti: che fosse tanto difficile nei favori et nelle gratia et nelle dispense et in quell' altre cose che gl' altri pontefici concedean sempre facilmente: che pensasse più all' inquisitione che ad altro, et chi secondava S. Santità in quella, potesse con lei ogni cosa: che nelle cose di stato non credesse alla forza delle ragioni nè all' auttorità de i prencipi esperti, ma solamente alle persuasioni di quei in chi havea fede: che non si sia mai mostrato interessato nè in ambitione ne in avaritia, nè per se nè per niun de suoi: che credesse poco ai cardenali et gl' avesse tutti per interessati o quasi tutti, et chi si valea di loro con S. Santità, se nol facea con gran temperamento et con gran giudicio, si rendea sospetto et perdea il credito insieme con loro. Et chi non sa queste cose et si ricorda delle debolezze, della facilità, de i rispetti, delle passioni et degl' affetti de gl' altri papi, accusava et strapazzava gl' ambasciatori, credendo non che non potesser ma che non volessero o non sapessero ottener quelle cose che s' ottenevano facilmente in altri tempi.

the face, saying, that he was not afraid of martyrdom, and that as God had placed him there, so he could still keep his post against all human authority and power. These peculiarities of his holiness, although most true, yet are hard to be believed by such as have not had experience of them, and much more by such as have had to do with other popes: for it seems impossible that a man born and brought up in so low a condition, should keep himself so pure: that he should resist so ardently the greater and more powerful monarchs; that he should be so chary in favours, and graces, and dispensations, and other things which other popes have always granted readily: that he should think more about the Inquisition than ought else; and that whoever seconded his holiness in that, might do anything with him: that in state affairs he should not trust to the force of reasons, nor to the authority of experienced princes, but solely to the persuasions of those in whom he has confidence: that he has never shown himself led by ambition or avarice, either for himself or for any one else: that he should trust the cardinals little, and hold them all, or nearly all, to be selfish persons: and that whoever makes use of them with his holiness, unless he does it with great moderation and judgment, incurs suspicion, and loses credit as well as they. And he that knows these things and remembers the weakness, the facile disposition, the petty fears, the passions, and the capricious affections of other popes, accuses and despises the ambassadors, believing, not that they cannot, but that they will not obtain, or that they know not the way to obtain those things that were of easy procurement in other times.]

We can readily believe the ambassador, that with a pope of such a temper he had no easy post to occupy. For example, on Pius V. being made aware that people in Venice would not publish the bull in Coena Domini, he burst into a violent passion: "Si perturbò estremamente, et accesso in collera disse molte cose gravi et fastidiose."—[He was extremely troubled, and in a flaming passion said many severe and haughty things.] Circumstances, under which affairs became doubly difficult. Suriano in fact lost the favour of his republic. He was recalled, and a great part of this Report is written with the view of justifying his proceedings, in which, however, we cannot now accompany him.

43.

Informatione di Pio V. Inform. polit. Bibl. Ambros. F. D. 181.—[Notice of Pius V. Political notices in the Ambrosian Library. F. D. 181.]

Anonymous, it is true, but the production of some one intimately acquainted with the subject, and confirmatory of other descriptions. It is singular, that notwithstanding all the strictness of this pious pope, yet factions prevailed in his family. The older servants were opposed to the younger, who attached themselves more to the house steward, Monsignor Cyrillo. In general the latter was of easy access for the most part: "Con le carezze e col mostrar di conoscere il suo valore facilmente s' acquistarebbe: ha l' animo elevatissimo, grande intelligenza con Gambara e Correggio, e si stringe con Morone."—[What with flatteries, and letting people know his importance, he easily acquired wealth: he had a most haughty spirit, was on an intimate footing with Gambara and Correggio, and attached himself to Morone.]

44.

Relatione della corte di Roma nel tempo di Gregorio XIII. (Bibl. Cors. nr. 714.)—[Report from the court of Rome in the time of Gregory XIII. (Corsini Libr. No. 714.)] Dated 20th Feb., 1574.

Anonymous, but not the less full of information, and having the stamp of authenticity. The author finds it difficult to pass a judgment on courts of princes: "Dirò come si giu-

dica nella corte e come la intendo"—[I will say what is thought at the court, and how I understand matters.] He gives the following description of Gregory XIII.:—

"Assonto che è stato al pontificato in età di 71 anni, ha parso c' habbi voluto mutare natura: et il rigore che era solito biasimare in altri, massimamente nel particulare del vivere con qualche licenza con donne, n' è stato più rigoroso dell' antecessore e fattone maggiori esecutioni: e parimente nella materia del giuoco si è mostrato rigorosissimo, perche havendo certi illustrissimi principiato a trattenersi nel principio del pontificato con giuocare qualche scudo, li riprese acremente, ancorche alcuni dubitarono che sotto il pretesto del giuoco si facessero nuove pratiche di pontificato per un poco di male c' hebbe S. Sta in quel principio: e da questo cominciò a calare quella riputatione o oppinione che si voleva far credere dall' illustrissimo de' Medici, d' haver lui fatto il papa e doverlo governare, la qual cosa fece chiaro il mondo quanto S. Sta abhorrisce che alcuno si voglia arrogare di governarlo o c' habbi bisogno d' essere governato, perche non vuole esser in questa oppinione di lasciarsi governare a persona. Perche in effetto nelle cose della giustitia n' è capacissimo e la intende e non bisogna pensare di darli parole. Ne' maneggi di stati S. Sta ne potria saper più, perche non vi ha fatto molto studio, e sta sopra di se alle volte irresoluto, ma considerato che v' habbi sopra, n' è benissime capace e nell' udire le oppinioni discerne benissime il meglio. E patientissimo e laboriosissimo e non sta mai in otio e piglia ancora poca ricreatione. Da continuamente audientia e vede scritture. Dorme poco, si leva per tempo, e fa volontieri esercitio, e li piace l' aria, quale non teme, per cattiva che sia. Mangia sobriamente e beve pochissimo, ed è sano senza sorte alcuna di schinelle. E grato in dimostrationi esteriori a chi gli ha fatto piacere. Non è prodigo nè quasi si può dire liberale, secondo l' oppinione del volgo, il quale non considera o discerne la differentia che sia da un principe che si astenghi dall' estorsioni e rapacità a quello che conserva quello che ha con tenacità: questo non brama la roba d' altri e gli insidia per haverla. Non è crudele nè sanguinolento, ma temendo di continuo delle guerre sì del Turco come degli heretici, li piace d' haver somma di denari nell' erario e conservarli senza dispensarli fuori di proposito, e n' ha intorno a un millione e mezzo d' oro: è però magnifico e gli piacciono le grandezze, e sopra tutto è desideroso di gloria, il qual desiderio il fa forse trascorrere in quello che non piace alla corte: perche questi reverendi padri Chiettini, che l' hanno conosciuto, se li sono fatti a cavaliere sopra, con dimostrarli che il credito et autorità che haveva Pio V. non era se non per riputatione della bontà, e con questo il tengono quasiche in filo et il necessitano a far cose contra la sua natura e la sua volontà, perche S. Sta è sempre stato di natura piacevole e dolce, e lo restringono a una vita non consueta: et è oppinione che per far questo si siano valsi di far venire lettere da loro padri medesimi di Spagna e d' altri luoghi, dove sempre fanno mentione quanto sia commendata la vita santa del papa passato, quale ha acquistata tanta gloria con la riputatione della bontà e delle riforme, e

[As soon as he had been raised to the pontificate, at the age of 71, he seems to have wished to change his nature: and in the strictness which he used to blame in others, chiefly in the particular of living too freely with women, he has been stricter than his predecessor, and has given greater effect to his severity; and, in like manner, in the case of gambling, he has shown himself extremely strict, in as much as, on certain most illustrious persons having begun to amuse themselves at the commencement of the pontificate with playing for a few scudi, he sharply reprehended them, although some were afraid lest, under the pretext of gambling, there should be new devices of the popedom practised on account of a little evil that his holiness had at that commencement: and from this there began to be a decline in that reputation and opinion which people wished to have believed of the most illustrious Medici, that he had made him pope and ought to govern him, which thing made it clear to the world how much his holiness abhorred any one wishing to pretend to govern him, or that he had need of being governed, in as much as he disliked the idea of allowing himself to be governed by any one. For, in fact, in the affairs of justice he is most capable, and understands the subject, and has no need of being advised. In dealing with states, his holiness could not know more, not having made them a subject of much study, and uniformly remains unresolved; but, having considered what he has before him, he shows great capacity, and in hearing opinions excellently discerns the best. He is most patient and laborious, is never idle, and, further, takes little recreation. He is constantly giving audiences and seeing papers. He sleeps little, rises early, enjoys taking exercise, and likes the open air, which he never dreads, however bad the weather be. He eats soberly and drinks very little, and is healthy, without any sort of *schinelle.* He is grateful in outward demonstrations to those who have done him agreeable services. He is not prodigal nor what, in the opinion of the common people, would be called liberal, who don't consider nor perceive the difference between a prince that abstains from extortions and rapaciousness, and one who tenaciously keeps what he has: this (pope) covets not the property of another, nor plots how to have it. He is not cruel nor sanguinary, but, being in constant apprehension of wars, both with the Turk and with the heretics, he likes to have a quantity of money in the treasury, and to keep it there without spending it to no purpose, and has about a million and a half of gold: in fine, he loves magnificence, is pleased with grand things, and, above all, is fond of glory, which passion he allows perhaps to appear in things that don't please the court: for these reverend Chietine fathers, who have known him, have set themselves to ride over him, by making it appear to him that Pius V.'s credit and authority were entirely due to his reputation for goodness, and with this they hold him, as it were, in leading strings, and oblige him to do things con-

con questo modo perseverano loro in dominare et bavere autorità con S. Beat^{ne}: e dicesi che sono ajutati ancora dal vescovo di Padova, nuntio in Spagna, creatura di Pio V. e di loro. Brama tanto la gloria che si ritiene e sforza la natura di fare di quelle dimostrationi ancora verso la persona del figliuolo quali sariano riputate ragionevoli et honeste da ogn' uno per li scrupoli che li propongono costoro: et in tanta felicità che ha havuto S. Sta di essere asceso a questa dignità da basso stato, è contrapesato da questo oggetto e dall' bavere parenti quali non li sodisfanno e che a S. Sta non pare che siano atti o capaci de' negotii importanti e da commetterli le faccende di stato."

trary to his nature and wishes, seeing his holiness has always been of an affable and gentle disposition, and they constrain him to a life to which he is unaccustomed: and people have the notion that to accomplish this they avail themselves of having letters made to come from their own fathers from Spain and other places, wherein there is constant mention made of the commendations bestowed on the holy life of the last pope, how he acquired so much glory from the reputation of goodness and of reformations, and in this way they persevere in dominating and having authority with his beatitude; and it is said that they are further assisted in this by the bishop of Padua, nuncio in Spain, and a creature of Pius V. and them. So covetous is he of glory, that he restrains himself and forces nature from making such demonstrations even to the person of his son as would be thought reasonable and honourable by every body, under the influence of the scruples which these suggest to him: and with all the good fortune his holiness has had in having risen to this dignity from a low condition, he is counterbalanced in that object, and from having relations who do not give him satisfaction, and who do not appear to his holiness fit or capable of managing affairs of importance, and of having committed to them what has to be done for the state.]

He then proceeds to describe the cardinals. He remarks of Granvelle that he did not maintain his credit. He followed his own gratifications, and was thought greedy: in the affairs of the League he had well nigh made a breach between the king and the pope. Commendone, on the contrary, is highly praised. "Ha la virtù, la bontà, l'esperienza con infinito giudicio."—[He has virtue, good nature, experience, together with infinite soundness of judgment.]

45.

Seconda Relatione dell' ambasciatore di Roma, clar^{mo} M. Paolo Tiepolo K^{r} 3 Maggio 1576.—[Second Report of the ambassador from Rome, the most illustrious Paul Tiepolo, Knight, 3d May, 1576.]

The above anonymous report mentions Tiepolo also in the highest terms. He passed for a clear-headed and able man.

"E modesto e contra il costume de' Veneziani è corteggiano e liberale, e riesce eccellentemente, e sodisfa molto, e mostra prudenza grande in questi travagli e frangenti a sapersi regere."

[He is modest, and, contrary to what is usual with the Venetians, is courteous and affable, appears to great advantage in company, is very agreeable, and shows great prudence in knowing how to govern himself amid these toils and troubles.]

When, for instance, the Venetians withdrew from the league formed against the Turks, he was placed in a difficult position. It was thought that the pope would propose, in the consistory, that the Venetians should be excommunicated, and some cardinals were preparing to oppose any such project. "Levato Cornaro (a Venetian) nessuno fo che in quei primi giorni mi vedesse o mi mandasse a veder, non che mi consigliasse, consolasse e sollevasse."—[Excepting Cornaro (a Venetian) there was not a single person at first who saw me, or sent for me to see him, not one to offer me advice, to console and support me.] Tiepolo assigns, as the true ground of the separate peace, that, after the Spaniards had promised to be prepared for war in April, 1573, they declared, in that month, that they would be ready with their armaments at soonest in June. It greatly contributed to the softening down of the pope that Venice finally resolved to make his son one of the Venetian *nobili*. The terms in which Tiepolo speaks of this son of the pope's, are particularly worth noting.

"Il s^{r} Giacomo è figliuolo del papa: è giovane anchor esso di circa 29 anni, di belle lettere, di gratiose maniere, di grande et liberal animo et d'un ingegno attissimo a tutte le cose dove egli l'applicasse. Non bisogna negar che'l primo et si può dir solo affetto del papa non sia verso di lui, come è anco ragionevole che sia: percioche nel principio del pontificato, quando egli operava più secondo

[Signor Giacomo is the pope's son: he is a young man still, about twenty-nine years of age; is well versed in literature, gracious in his manners, of a great and liberal mind, and possessed of a genius perfectly adapted to everything to which he may apply it. There is no denying that the pope's first, and it may be said his only partiality, was for him, as was reasonable that it should; for, at the com-

il suo senso, lo creò prima castellano et dapoi governator di s. chiesa con assegnarli per questo conto provisioni di cerca Xm. ducati all' anno et con pagarli un locotenente, colonnelli et capitani, accioche egli tanto più honoratamente potesse comparer: ma dapoi, come che si fosse pentito di esser passato tanto oltre verso un suo figliuolo naturale, mosso per avvertimenti, come si affermava, di persone spirituali, che li mettevano questa cosa a conscientia et a punto d'honore, incominciò a ritirarsi con negarli i favori et le gratie che li erano da lui domandate et con far in tutte le cose manco stima di lui di quello che prima avea fatto: anzi come che doppo averlo palesato volesse nasconderlo al mondo, separandolo da lui lo fece partir da Roma et andar in Ancona, dove sotto specie di fortificar quella città per un tempo lo intertenne, senza mai provederlo d'una entrata stabile et sicura colla quale egli dopo la morte sua avesse possuto con qualche dignità vivere et sostenersi: onde il povero signore, dolendosi della sua fortuna che lo havesse voluto innalzar per doverlo poi abbandonare, si messe più volte in tanta desperatione che fuggendo la pratica et conversatione di ciascuno si retirava a viver in casa solitario, continuando in questo per molti giorni, con far venir anchora all' orecchie dell' padre come egli era assalito da fieri et pericolosi accidenti, per vedere se con questo havesse possuto muover la sua tennerezza verso di lui. In fine troppo può l'amor naturale paterno per spingere o dissimulare il quale indarno l'uomo s'adopera. Vinto finalmente et commosso il papa dapoi passato l'anno santo volse l'animo a provederli et a darli satisfatione, et prima si resolse da maritarlo."

[mencement of his pontificate, when he acted more according to his own feelings, he made him first warder and then governor of the holy church, with an assignation to him on that score of a yearly provision of about 10,000 ducats, and with pay for a lieutenant, colonels, and captains, in order that he might make the better figure; but afterwards, as if he had repented of having gone too far towards a natural son, influenced, as has been affirmed, by the warnings of spiritual persons, who pressed the matter upon him as a point of conscience and of honour, he began to retract by refusing the favours and acts of grace that his son asked from him, and by making much less account of him in all things than he had done at first; also, as if, after having introduced him to the world, he wished to conceal him from it, by separating himself from him, he made him leave Rome and go to Ancona, where he kept him for a time, under the pretext of fortifying that city, without however providing him with any such stable and secure income as might enable him, after the pope's death, to live and maintain himself with any dignity: whence the poor Signor, lamenting his fortune, which seemed to have intended to exalt him only to abandon him afterwards, was often rendered so desperate, that shunning intercourse and converse with every body, he would withdraw and live in a house alone, continuing there for many days, contriving farther that there should come to his father's ears what cruel and dangerous accidents had befallen him, in order to see whether this might not move a return of tenderness towards him. In the end, the natural love of a father proved the more powerful, to expel or dissemble which a man's efforts are vain. Overcome at last, and moved to a return of affection, after the expiration of a year, the pope wished, with a holy mind, to provide for him and to give him satisfaction, and first he resolved to have him married.]

On Gregory's XIII.'s administration of the state also, and particularly with respect to the cardinal of Como, Tiepolo communicates some interesting information.

"Partisce il governo delle cose in questo modo, che di quelle che appartengono al stato ecclesiastico, ne da la cura alli d^{ni} cardinali sui nepoti, et di quelle che hanno relatione alli altri principi, al cardinal di Como. Ma dove in quelle del stato ecclesiastico, che sono senza comparation di manco importanza, perche non comprendono arme o fortezze, al governatore generale reservate, nè danari, de' quali la camera apostolica et il tesorier generale ne tien cura particolare, ma solamente cose ordinarie pertinenti al governo delle città et delle provincie, non si contentando delli d^{ni} nepoti ha aggiunta loro una congregatione di quattro principali prelati, tra' quali vi è monsignor di Nicastro, stato nuntio presso la Serenità V^{ra}, colli quali tutte le cose si consigliano per doverle poi referir a lui: in quelle di stato per negotii colli altri principi, che tanto rilevano et importano non solo per la buona intelligentia con lor ma ancora per beneficio et quiete di tutta la christianità, si rimette in tutto nel solo cardinal di Como, col quale si redrecciano li ambasciatori dei principi che sono a Roma et li nuntii apostolici et altri ministri del

[He divided the affairs of the government as follows, giving those appertaining to the ecclesiastical state to the lords cardinals his nephews, and those that related to other princes to the cardinal of Como. But where in those of the ecclesiastical state, things are incomparably of less importance, as they comprise neither arms nor fortresses, these being reserved to the governor-general, nor money matters, which are committed to the special care of the apostolic chamber and treasurer general, but solely ordinary matters relating to the government of the cities and provinces, not contenting himself with the lords' nephews, he has added to them a congregation of four leading prelates, among whom there is monsignor di Nicastro, who has been nuncio with your serenity, with whom all things are duly weighed, in order to their being afterwards referred to him: in affairs of state for negotiations with other monarchs, which are of so much consequence and importance not only as respects the maintenance of a friendly footing with others, but also as they affect the benefit and peace of all Christendom, he commits himself en-

papa che sono alle corti, perche a lui solo scrivono et da lui aspettano li ordini di quello che hanno da fare. Egli è quello che solo consiglia il papa, et che, come universalmente si tiene, fa tutte le resolutioni più importanti, et che da li òrdini et li fa eseguire. Sogliono ben alcuni cardinali di maggior pratica et autorità et qualcun' altro ancora da se stesso raccordare al papa quello che giudica a proposito, et suole ancora alle volte il papa domandar sopra alcune cose l'opinione di qualcuno et di tutto il collegio di cardinali ancora, massimamente quando li torna bene che si sappia che la determination sia fatta di conseglio di molti, come principalmente quando si vuol dare qualche negativa, et sopra certe particolari occorrentie ancora suole deputar una congregatione di cardinali, come già fo fatto nelle cose della lega et al presente si fa in quelle di Germania, del concilio, et di altre: ma nel restretto alle conclusioni et nelle cose più importanti il cardinal di Como è quello che fa et vale. Ha usato il cardinal, seben cognosce saver et intender a sofficientia, alle volte in alcune cose andarsi a consigliare col cardinal Morone et cardinal Commendon, per non si fidar tanto del suo giudicio che non tolesse ancor il parer d'huomini più intelligenti et savii: ma in fatto da lui poi il tutto dipende. Mette grandissima diligentia et accuratezza nelle cose, et s'industria di levar la fatica et i pensieri al papa et di darli consigli che lo liberino da travagli presenti et dalla spesa, poiche nessuna cosa pare esser più dal papa desiderata che'l sparagno et la quiete. Si stima universalmente ch'esso abbia grande inclinatione al re cattolico, non tanto per esser suo vassallo et per haver la maggior parte delli sui beneficii nei sui paesi, quanto per molti comodi et utilità che in cose di molto momento estraordinariamente riceve da lui, per recognition de' quali all' incontro con destri modi, come ben sa usar senza molto scoprirsi, se ne dimostri nelle occasioni grato. Verso la Serenità Vostro posso affermar ch'egli sottosopra si sia portata assai bene, massimamente se si ha respetto che ne i ministri d'altri principi non si può ritrovar tutto quello che si vorria, et che ben spesso bisogna contentarsi di manco che di mediocre buona volontà."

tirely to the cardinal of Como, with whom the ambassadors of the princes that are in Rome, and the apostolic nuncios and other ministers of the pope that are at the courts address themselves, for to him alone they write, and look to him for being ordered what they have to do. He is the pope's sole counsellor who, as is universally maintained, makes all the more important resolutions, gives orders and sees to their being executed. Some cardinals indeed, of greater experience and authority, and further, some besides these, are wont of themselves to remind the pope of what he thinks fit to be done, and further, the pope is uniformly wont to ask on every subject the opinion of each cardinal, and also of the whole college of cardinals, chiefly when it is of advantage to him that it should be known that the determination come to has been advised by many, as chiefly when he wants to refuse something, and further, upon certain particular occurrences he is wont to depute a congregation of cardinals, as he did formerly in the affairs of the league, and as is done at present in those of Germany, of the council and other matters: but looking to conclusions restrictively, and in all matters of importance, the cardinal of Como is the man who does the thing and carries weight. The cardinal, although sufficiently capable of knowing and understanding (what should be done), is wont to go at all times, in all cases, to consult with cardinal Morone and cardinal Commendone, that he may not trust so much to his own judgment as not to avail himself likewise of the opinions of the more intelligent and wise: but in point of fact, everything, after all, depends on him. He shows the utmost diligence and accuracy in affairs, and sets himself to save the pope fatigue and anxiety, and to give him advices that save him from present labour and from expense, for nothing seems more to be desired by the pope than thrift and tranquillity. It is the universal opinion that he has a great leaning in favour of the catholic king, not so much owing to his being his vassal, and from having the greater part of his benefices in his territories, as on account of the many acts of accommodation and utility he receives from him out of the ordinary way in matters of much moment, in acknowledgment of which he shows himself grateful, on occasions, by ingenious methods, such as he well knows how to use without their being much noticed. Towards your serenity, I may say that, generally speaking, he has conducted himself pretty well, particularly if we consider, that with the ministers of other monarchs all that they want is not to be obtained, and that very often they have to be contented with the want of good will rather than with a moderate degree of it.]

Although this report has had far less circulation than the former, yet, in point of fact, it is no less important and instructive as respects the times of Gregory XIII. than that other is for those of Pius IV. and Pius V.

46.

Commentariorum de rebus Gregorii XIII., lib. I. et II.—[Books I. and II. of Commentaries on the affairs of Gregory XIII. (Bibl. Alb.)

Unfortunately incomplete. The author, cardinal Vercelli, promises, on coming, after some preliminary observations, to speak of Gregory's pontificate, to treat of three things: the war

against the Turks, the war of the protestants against the kings of France and Spain, and the controversies about the jurisdiction of the church.

Unfortunately, we find in the 2d book only the war against the Turks down to the Venetian peace.

We know the connection that subsisted betwixt the events that took place in the East and the affairs of religion: our author not unhappily contrasts the developments of the year 1572. The news had come to hand that Charles IX. was supporting the attacks of the protestants in the Netherlands.

"Quod cum Gregorius moleste ferret, dat ad Gallorum regem litteras quibus ab eo vehementer petit ne suos in hoc se admiscere bellum patiatur: alioquin se existimaturum omnia haec illius voluntate nutuque fieri. Rex de suis continendis magnae sibi curae fore pollicetur, id quod quantum in se est praestat: verum ejusmodi litteris, quae paulo minacius scriptae videbantur, nonnihil tactus, nonnullis etiam conjecturis eo adductus ut se irritari propeque ad bellum provocari putaret, ne imparatum adorirentur, urbes quas in finibus regni habebat diligenter communit, duces suos admonet operam dent ne quid detrimenti capiat, simulque Emanuelem Allobrogum ducem, utriusque regis propinquum et amicum, de his rebus omnibus certiorem facit. Emanuel, qui pro singulari prudentia sua, quam horum regum dissensio suis totique reipublicae christiane calamitosa futura esset, probe intelligebat, ad pontificem haec omnia perscribit, eumque obsecrat et obtestatur, nascenti malo occurrat, ne longius serpat atque inveteratum robustius fiat. Pontifex, quam gereret personam minimum oblitus, cum regem Gallorum adolescentem et gloriae cupidate incensum non difficillime a catholicae fidei hostibus, quorum tunc in aula maxima erat autoritas, ad hujusmodi bellum impelli posse animadverteret, reginam tamen ejus matrem longe ab eo abhorrere dignitatisque et utilitatis suae rationem habituram putaret, mittit eo Antonium Mariam Salviatum, reginae affinem eique pergratum, qui eam in officio contineat, ipsiusque opera facilius regi, ne reip. christianae accessionem imperii et gloriam quae ex orientali expeditione merito expectanda esset invideat funestumque in illius visceribus moveat bellum, persuadeat."

[Gregory taking this very ill, sends letters to the king of the French, vehemently insisting that he should not allow his subjects to mix themselves up with that war, otherwise that he would consider all things done according to his will and suggestion. The king promises to do his utmost in restraining his subjects, which he performs to the best of his ability; yet being not a little huffed at such letters, which seemed written in rather too threatening a style, led moreover by some conjectures even to suppose that he was insulted and almost provoked to war, he diligently fortifies his frontier towns lest they should be attacked unawares, admonishes his generals to see to it that he received no damage, and, at the same time, informs Emanuel, duke of the Allobroges (Savoy), the neighbour and friend of both kings, of all these things. Emanuel, who, as might be expected from his singular prudence, well perceived how calamitous the dissension of these two kings would be to his own subjects and to the whole Christian commonwealth, writes of all this to the pope, and beseeches and adjures him to counteract the growing evil, lest it should creep on and acquire strength from inveteracy. The pontiff, far from forgetting what person he bore, on perceiving that the king of the French, a young man burning with a thirst for glory, might not, with very much difficulty, be led by the enemies of the (Roman) catholic faith, who had the greatest authority at court at that time, into such a war, yet thought that the queen his mother, from regard to dignity and expediency, would be utterly averse to it, sends thither Antonio Maria Salviati, a relation of the queen's, and much liked by her, to keep her to her duty, and that, with her assistance, he might more easily persuade the king not to envy that accession of empire and glory to the Christian commonwealth which was deservedly looked for from the Eastern expedition, nor to raise a deadly war in its own bowels.]

In so far the pope had certainly an indirect participation in the massacre of St. Bartholomew. He had to make every effort to prevent the outbreak of war between Spain and France. It were much to be wished that we possessed this work, at least where it treated of the religious broils.

I have quoted the above passages, because the very first lines show that it belongs to the sources made use of by Maffei in his Annals of Gregory XIII., supreme pontiff. Compare i. p. 27 in Maffei.

"Scrisse a Carlo risentitamente, che se egli comportava che i sudditi e ministri s'intromettessero in questa guerra per distornarla, egli tutto riconoscerebbe da lui e dalla mala sua intenzione. E per l'istesso fine operò che li signori Veneziani gli mandassero un' ambasciadore con diligenza. Rispose Carlo modestamente, ch'egli farebbe ogni possibile perchè i suoi nè a lui dovessero dar disgusto nè agli Spagnuoli sospetto di quello ch'egli non aveva in pensiero. Ma non restò però

[He wrote sharply to Charles, that if he suffered his subjects and ministers to intermeddle in that war for the purpose of thwarting it, he would impute everything to him and to his ill intentions. And in order to the same end, he got the Venetian lords to send an ambassador to him with all diligence. Charles replied modestly, that he would do his utmost that his subjects should not give any disgust either to him or to the Spaniards—a suspicion which he had never thought of.

di dolersi con Emanuele duca di Savoja della risentita maniera con che gli aveva scritto il pontefice: parendogli che si fosse lasciato spingere dagli Spagnuoli che avessero voglia essi di romperla: et ad un tempo cominciò a presidiare le città delle frontiere."

But he did not, therefore, refrain from complaining to Emanuel, duke of Savoy, of the captious manner in which the pope had written to him; being of opinion that he had allowed himself to be urged on to do so by the Spaniards, who had themselves wished to break with him; and all at once he put garsons in the frontier towns.]

For the rest, I find also that Maffei here and there is a completed extract from the above manuscript. Yet therewithal I will not, in the slightest degree, detract from Maffei's work, to which I am indebted for much information, and which, although not quite impartial, is calmly written, full of matter, and, upon the whole, to be depended upon.

47.

Relatione di mons^{r} rev^{mo} Gio P. Ghisilieri a papa Gregorio XIII., tornando egli dal presidentato della Romagna. S. I. p. 393.—[Report of Monsignor the most rev. G. P. Ghisilieri to pope Gregory XIII., on his return from the Presidentship of the Romagna. S. i. p. 393.]

48.

Discorso over ritratto della corte di Roma di mons^{r} ill^{mo} Commendone all' ill^{mo} s^{r} Hier. Savorgnano. (Bibl. Vindob. Codd. Rangon. nr. 18, fol. 278-395.)—Discourse or description of the court of Rome, by the most illustrious Monsignor Commendone to the most illustrious Signor Jerome Savorgnano.]

According to all appearance, this work belongs to the times of Gregory. Commendone's name I cannot answer for; but the person from whom it comes is always a man of talent, deeply initiated in all the secret relations of Roman life.

He defines the court as follows:—

"Questa republica è un principato di somma autorità in una aristocratia universa di tutti i christiani collocato in Roma. Il suo principio è la religione. Conciosia," he continues, "che la religione sia il fine e che questa si mantenga con la virtù e con la dottrina, è impossibile che alterandosi le conditioni degli uomini non si rivolga insieme sotto sopra tutta la republica."

[This republic is a principality having its seat in Rome, of the highest authority in an universal aristocracy of all Christians. Its principle is religion. Conscious (he farther goes on to say) that religion is the end, and that this maintains itself by virtue and learning, it is impossible that changes in the conditions of men should not react at the same time on the whole Christian commonwealth.]

He proceeds to treat chiefly of this conflict between spiritual and secular efforts. Above all things, he inculcates great prudence:

"Molto riguardo di tutti i movimenti e gesti della persona: casa, servitori, cavalcature convenienti, amicitie e honorate e virtuose, non affermando cosa che non si sappia di certo."

[Much attention to all personal movements and acts: house, servants, suitable riding horses, honourable and virtuous friendships, affirming nothing not certainly known.]

The court requires "bontà, grandezza del' animo, prudentia, eloquentia, theologia" [goodness, magnanimity, prudence, eloquence, theology]. Yet all is uncertain.

"Deve si pensar che questo sia un viaggio di mare, nel quale benche la prudentia possa molto e ci renda favorevole la maggior parte de' venti, nondimeno non gli si possa prescriver tempo determinato o certezza alcuna d' arrivar. Alcuni di mezza estate in gagliarda e ben fornita nave affondano o tardano assai, altri d'inverno in debole e disarmato legno vanno presto."

[One ought to think that this is a voyage at sea, in which, although prudence may do much, and may render favourable the greater part of the winds, nevertheless it is impossible to prescribe a set time, or any certainty of arriving at port. Some, in summer, and in a gallant and well-furnished ship, go to the bottom, or are tardy enough in their voyage; others, in winter, and in a frail and ill-furnished bark, arrive at once.]

SECTION FOURTH.

SIXTUS V.

I.—Criticism on this Pope's Biographers, Leti and Tempesti.

Vita di Sisto V. pontefice Romano scritta dal signor Geltio Rogeri all' instanza di Gregorio Leti. Losanna 1669.—[Life of Sixtus V., Roman pontiff, written by Signor Geltio Rogeri, at the instance of Gregorio Leti. Lausanne, 1669.] 2 vols.; afterwards, under less singular titles, in 3 volumes.

The reputation of an individual, the view taken of an event, are usually determined far more by popular writings, which procure for themselves a general reception, than by more important historical works which, besides, often allow themselves to be too long waited for. The public does not truly ask whether what is set before it be really founded on facts; it is content if the memorial, in so far as expressed in language, is presented to it in a readable book, often varied and diversified, yet withal somewhat terse in style.

Such a book is Leti's biography of Sixtus V., perhaps the most effective of all the works of that prolific writer: it has exhibited the idea of pope Sixtus, which has ever since prevailed in the general opinion of the world.

When a man first sets about to study such books, he finds himself extremely embarrassed with them. One cannot deny them a certain degree of veracity, one dare not set them altogether aside, yet it is equally evident that they are not much to be trusted; but, generally speaking, one cannot determine how far precisely our confidence in them may safely go.

We first find ourselves in a capacity to form a right judgment in this respect when we discover what were the author's sources of information, and can form an idea of the manner and method of his making use of them.

As we advance in our study we arrive at last at the sources whence Leti drew his materials: —we cannot forego the necessity of comparing his account of matters with them.

1. In the whole life of Sixtus V., there is nothing more famous than the way by which he is said to have attained to the popedom, the way in which he conducted himself in the conclave. Who knows not how the tottering cardinal, leaning over his staff, as soon as he was made pope, instantly stood erect and vigorous, threw away his staff, and threatened with the exercise of his power, those very persons from whom he had obtained it by deception. Leti's account has found admission throughout the whole world. We ask where he got it.

With respect to every election of a pope, there are writings extant bearing upon the motives, or rather the intrigues that preceded them; and upon the election of Sixtus V. also, we find a so-called conclave, drawn up impartially, as most of them are, and composed with an intimate acquaintance with personal peculiarities: "Conclave nel quale fu creato il card' Montalto che fu Sisto V."—[The conclave at which cardinal Montalto was created, who was Sixtus V.]

At the very first glance we perceive on comparing them, that Leti had this writing particularly in his eye. It will be observed that, properly speaking, he merely paraphrases it.

Concl. MS.:—"Il lunedì mattina per tempo si ridussero nella capella Paulina, dove il cardinal Farnese come decano celebrò messa e di mano sua communicò li cardinali: dipoi si venne secondo il solito allo scrutinio, nel quale il cardinal Albani hebbe 13 voti, che fu il maggior numero che alcun cardinale havesse. Ritornati i cardinali alle celle, si attese alle pratiche, et Altemps cominciò a trattare alla gagliarda la pratica di Sirleto, ajutato da Medici e delle creature di Pio IV., per la confidenza che bavevano di poter di qualsivoglia di loro disponere: ma subito fu trovata l' esclusione, scoprendosi contra di lui Este, Farnese e Sforza."

[On Monday morning an early meeting was held in the Pauline chapel, where cardinal Farnese, as dean, celebrated mass and gave the communion with his own hand to all the cardinals: after which they proceeded as usual to the scrutiny, in which cardinal Albani had 13 votes, being the most that any cardinal had. On the cardinals having returned to their cells, negotiations commenced and Altemps began vigorously to conduct the negotiation in favour of Sirlet, aided by Medici and the cardinals created by Pius IV., each confidently anticipating that they would be able to decide the matter: but all of a sudden it was found that Sirleto was excluded, Este, Farnese and Sforza appearing against him.]

Leti:—"Lunedì mattina di buon' hora si adunarono tutti nella capella Paolina, ed il cardinal Farnese in qualità di decano celebrò la messa e communicò tutti i cardinali: e poi si diede principio allo scrutinio, nel quale il cardinal Albano hebbe 13 voti, che fu il numero maggiore. Doppo questo li cardinali se ne ritornarono alle lor celle per

[Early on Monday morning all met in the Pauline chapel, and cardinal Farnese as dean celebrated mass, and gave the communion to all the cardinals: and then for the first time the scrutiny began, in which cardinal Albano had 13 votes, which was the greater number. After this the cardinals went back to their cells to dinner, and after dinner there began

pransare, e doppo il pranso si attese alle pratiche di molti: ma particolarmente Altemps comincid a trattare alla gagliarda le pratiche di Guglielmo Sirleto Calabrese, ajutato dal cardinal Medici e dalle creature di Pio IV., per la confidenza che haveva ogni uno di loro di poterne disporre: ma in breve se gli fece innanzi l' esclusione, scoprendosi contro di lui Este, Farnese e Sforza."

negotiations on the part of many: but in particular Altemps began vigorously to conduct negotiations in favour of William Sirleto of Calabria, aided by cardinal Medici and the cardinals created by Pius IV., each confidently anticipating that they would be able to decide the matter: but in a short time his exclusion became evident, Este, Farnese, and Sforza appearing against him.]

Thus it is as regards the main facts; thus, too, as to accessary circumstances. For example, in the MS. it runs—

"Farnese incapricciato et acceso di incredibile voglia di essere papa, comincia a detestare publicamente la pratica et il soggetto, dicendo: Io non so come costoro lo intendono di volere far Sirleto papa. Leti:—Il primo che se gli oppose fu Farnese, incapricciato ancor lui ed acceso d' incredibile voglia d' esser papa: onde parendo a lui d' esserne più meritevole, come in fatti era, cominciò publicamente a detestare la pratica ed il soggetto, dicendo per tutti gli angoli del conclave: Io non so come costoro l'intendono di voler far papa Sirleto."

[Farnese, prepossessed and inflamed with an incredible wish to be pope, began openly to express his detestation of the negotiation and the subject, saying, I know not what those can mean who would make Sirleto pope. Leti:—The first to oppose him was Farnese, he further being prepossessed and inflamed with an incredible wish to be pope: therefore thinking himself much more worthy of being pope, as in fact he was, he began openly to express his detestation of the negotiation and the subject, saying in all the corners of the conclave: I know not what those can mean who would make Sirleto pope.]

Nor less as respects occasional observations. For example, the MS. says, as to one whom cardinal Alessandrino, at least his disguise, had scandalized: "Ma dio, che haveva eletto Montalto papa. non permesse che si avertisse a quello che principalmente avertire si dovea, nè lasciò che Farnese nè suoi si svegliassero a impedire la pratica, credendo che non fosse per venire ad effetto dell' adoratione, ma solo per honorare Montalto nello scrutinio."—[But God, who elected Montalto, did not suffer this to be noticed by the person who ought principally to have done so, and did not allow Farnese or his friends to be on the alert in opposing the negotiation, believing that matters would not have gone the length of the adoration, but that it was only meant to honour Montalto in the scrutiny.] Although so pious a remark is not what was to be looked for from Leti; yet it suits him to transcribe it, and to adopt it in his book. He transcribes it, bating a few slight alterations, word for word.

Is this not rather a justification of the oft arraigned faithfulness of Leti, than a charge against him?

But let us come to the one case which here prompts a doubt: the behaviour of the cardinal. It is remarkable that on this sole point Leti does not agree with his original.

Leti says: "Montalto se ne stava in sua camera e non già nel conclave, fingendosi tutto lasso et abandonato d' ogni ajuto humano. Non usciva che raramente, et se pure andava in qualche parte, come a celebrare messa, o nello scrutinio della capella, se ne andava con certe maniere spensierate."—[Montalto confined himself to his chamber, and never appeared in the conclave, feigning to be quite worn out and forsaken of all men. He seldom went out, and if he chanced to go anywhere, as for instance to celebrate mass, or to the scrutiny in the chapel, it was with the airs of one who took no interest in what was passing.]

The original says on the contrary: "Sebene non mostrava una scoperta ambitione, non pretermetteva di far poi tutti quelli officii che il tempo et luogo richiedevano, humiliandosi a cardinali, visitandoli et offerendosi, ricevendo all' incontro i favori e l'offerte degli altri."—[Although he did not manifest an open ambition, he did not omit doing all those offices which time and place required, humbling himself to the cardinals, visiting them, and offering himself, receiving on the other hand the favours and offers of others.]

The original says that even previous to the conclave he did this with Farnese, and thereafter with Medici and Este: it relates how on the evening preceding his election, he called on cardinal Madruzzi, and on the morning before it, on cardinal Altemps, and received from them the assurance that he would be elected. In a word, the original represents Montalto as active, vigorous, and in good health: nay, his being of so fresh an age, and so lively, was a motive for his being elected. The whole story of his dissembled weakness and retiringness, which has been so famous, is an addition of Leti's; but whence did he take it; did he merely follow the common rumour of a tale that grew up of itself, or had he it from some other written work?—We shall yet come upon it.

2. A second element in the general reputation of Sixtus, is formed by the impression produced by his financial regulations. This too is so far based upon Leti. In the 2d part of the book (p. 289), there appears a statement of the papal receipts and disbursements, which has found a certain credit even among the most intelligent and learned persons. "Rendite ordinarie c'havea la sede apostolica nel tempo che Sisto entrava nel pontificato." —[Ordinary revenues of the apostolic see at the time when Sixtus entered on the pontificate.] His figures, at least, people generally thought they might venture to trust.

Here too, meanwhile, it is evident at once that things are not as Leti represents them. When Sixtus V. ascended the throne in April 1585, the contracts were still in force that Gregory XIII. had made with the farmers of the revenues for nine years. Of these we have an authentic statement under the title "Entrata della reverenda camera apostolica sotto il pontificato di Notre Sig^{re} Gregorio XIII., fatto nell' anno 1576."—[Revenues of the Rev. apostolic chamber under the pontificate of our lord, Gregory XIII., drawn up in the year 1576]: very minute, in which first the sum contracted for, then that part of it which was alienated; last of all, the remainder is given by itself. Now with this statement Leti's returns tally very ill. He states the income of the dogana of Rome at 182,450 scudi, while it brought only 133,000: of all the sums he mentions there is not one right. But what can have been the source of his account? It cannot have been purely imaginary. There is another before us dated two years after the death of Sixtus V. With this Leti's statement agrees in almost all items as well as in its arrangement: in both, for instance, it runs seriatim thus: "Dogana di Civita Vecchia 1,977 scudi, di Narni 400, di Rieti 100, gabella del studio di Roma 26,560, gabella del quadrino a libra di carne di Roma 20,335, and so on. But what a conclusion is here! In these items there are comprised almost all the changes which Sixtus effected, and which just at this time should have been particularized. Nor does the confusion stop here. Leti had probably fallen upon an incorrect manuscript, if he has not himself introduced some arbitrary alterations; at least he has some of the oddest inaccuracies. The *Salara di Roma* produced 27,654 scudi, he puts down 17,654; *tesoreria e salara di Romagna* produced 71,395 scudi, he puts down tesoreria e salario di Romagna 11,395. Enough, his statement is not even for a single year correct, but throughout, in all its parts, it is false and useless.

3. We see already that he compiled without judgment or discrimination: he transcribed but in haste; and how, too, was it possible that, living as he did all his lifetime as a refugee, he could have composed so many books with what could really be called labour. Now, whence did he on this occasion obtain his materials?

A manuscript on the life of Sixtus V., in the Corsini Library at Rome, sufficiently informs us: "Detti e fatti di Papa Sisto V."—[Sayings and doings of Pope Sixtus V.]

It appears at the first glance that this work, in essentials, is throughout Leti's composition. We have only to compare the first best passages.

For example, the Corsini MS. says—

"Il genitore di Sisto V. si chiamava Francesco Peretti, nato nel castello di Farnese, di dove fu costretto non so per qual accidente partire, onde s' incaminò per trovare la sua fortuna altrove: et essendo povero e miserabile, non aveva da poter vivere, essendo solito sostentarsi di quello alla giornata guadagnava grandemente faticando, e con la propria industria viveva. Partitosi dunque da Farnese, se ne andò a trovare un suo zio."

[Sixtus V.'s progenitor was called Francis Peretti, born in the castle of Farnese, from which he was obliged, I know not by what accident, to remove; accordingly he set out to seek his fortune elsewhere: and, being poor and destitute, he had nothing to live upon, being wont to provide for himself by what he got for very hard work as a day labourer, and lived by his own industry. Leaving, therefore, Farnese, he went off in search of an uncle he had.]

Leti has likewise in the first edition—

"Il padre di Sisto si chiamava Francesco Peretti, nato nel castello di Farnese, di dove fu costretto non so per qual' accidente occorsoli di partirsi, ciò che fece volentieri per cercar fortuna altrove, mentre per la povertà della sua casa non haveva di che vivere se non di quello che lavorava con le proprie mani alla giornata. Partito di Farnese la matina, giunse la sera nelle grotte per consigliarsi con un suo zio."

[Sixtus V.'s father was called Francis Peretti, born in the castle of Farnese, from which he was obliged, I know not by what accident that had befallen him, to remove, which he did willingly, to seek his fortune elsewhere, whilst, because of the poverty of his house, he had not wherewithal to live, beyond what he earned by working with his own hands as a day labourer. Having set off from Farnese in the morning, he arrived in the evening at the caves in order to advise with an uncle he had.]

It is evident that this is quite the same, with a slight retouching.

Sometimes we find small interpolations in Leti: and here, too, the MS. and the printed work quite correspond.

And now, if we ask to what source we are to ascribe those additions with which Leti eked out his narrative of the conclave, it appears that these too are taken from the MS. before us. The passage quoted above from Leti runs as follows in the MS.:—

"Montalto se ne stava tutto lasso con la corona in mano et in una piccolissima cella abandonato da ogn' uno, e se pure andava in qualche parte, come a celebrar messa, o nello scrutinio della capella, se ne andava," &c.

[Montalto remained quite dejected, with the chaplet in his hands, and in a very small cell, forsaken by everybody, and if he went anywhere, as to celebrate mass, or to the chapel scrutiny, he went, &c.]

It will be perceived that Leti transcribes this text with slight modifications.

I will add only one passage more, on account of the importance of the subject. The MS. has—

"Prima di cominciarsi il Montalto, che stava appresso al card^{l} di San Sisto per non perderlo della vista o perche non fosse subornato da altri porporati, gli disse alle orec-

[Before commencing (the scrutiny) Montalto, who stood close by cardinal St. Sixtus, in order that he might keep his eye upon him, or that he might not be suborned by

chie queste parole: Faccia instanza V. S^ria ill^ma che lo scrutinio segua senza pregiudicio dell' adoratione: e questo fu il primo atto d' ambitione che mostrò esteriormente Montalto. Non mancò il card^l di San Sisto di far ciò: perche con il Bonelli unitamente principiò ad alzare la voce due o tre volte così: Senza pregiudicio della seguita adoratione. Queste voci atterrirono i cardinali: perche fu supposto da tutti loro che dovesse esser eletto per adoratione. Il card^l Montalto già cominciava a levar quelle nebbie di fintioni che avevano tenuto nascosto per lo spatio di anni 14 l' ambitione grande che li regnava in seno: onde impatiente di vedersi nel trono papale, quando udì leggere la metà e più delli voti in suo favore, tosto allungò il collo e si alzò in piedi, senza attendere il fine del scrutinio, e uscito in mezzo di quella capella gittò verso la porta di quella il bastoncello che portava per appoggiarsi, ergendosi tutto dritto in tal modo che pareva due palmi più longo del solito. E quello che fu più maraviglioso," &c.

others in purple, whispered these words in his ear: Let your most illustrious lordship press that the scrutiny follow without prejudice of the adoration: and this was the first instance of ambition which Montalto outwardly manifested. The cardinal St. Sixtus did not fail to do so, for, together with Bonelli, he began to call aloud two or three times, "Without prejudice of the adoration to follow." These calls alarmed the cardinals: for it was supposed by all of them that he was to be elected by adoration. Cardinal Montalto then began to cast off those mists of dissimulation which had for the space of 14 years concealed the great ambition that reigned in his breast: accordingly, in his impatience to see himself on the papal throne, when he heard that half and more of the votes were in his favour, he immediately raised his head, and stood on his feet, without waiting for the end of the scrutiny, and stepping into the middle of the chapel, he threw towards the door a staff which he had used for leaning upon, holding himself erect in such a manner that he seemed two palms taller than usual. And what was more marvellous, &c.]

With this let us compare the corresponding passage in Leti, i. p. 412. (Edition of 1669.)

"Prima di cominciarsi Montalto si calò nell' orecchia di San Sisto, e gli disse: Fate instanza che lo scrutinio si faccia senza pregiudicio dell' adoratione: che fu appunto il primo atto d' ambitione che mostrò esteriormente Montalto. Nè San Sisto mancò di farlo, perche insieme con Alessandrino cominciò a gridare due o tre volte: Senza pregiudicio dell' adoratione. Gia cominciava Montalto a levar quelle nebbie di fintioni che havevano tenuto nascosto per più di quindeci anni l' ambitione grande che li regnava nel cuore: onde impatiente di vedersi nel trono ponteficale, non si tosto intese legger più della metà de' voti in suo favore che assicuratosi del ponteficato si levò in piedi e senza aspettare il fino dello scrutinio gettò nel mezo di quella sala un certo bastoncino che portava per appoggiarsi, ergendosi tutto dritto in tal modo che pareva quasi un piede più longo di quel ch' erà prima: ma quello che fu più maraviglioso," &c.

[Before commencing (the scrutiny) Montalto went up to the ear of St. Sixtus, and said to him, "Press that the scrutiny be made without prejudice of the adoration;" which was the very first act of ambition that Montalto outwardly displayed. Nor did St. Sixtus fail to do so; for, together with Alessandrino, he began to cry two or three times, "Without prejudice of the adoration." Then Montalto began to throw off those mists of dissimulation that had, for the space of more than fifteen years, concealed the great ambition that reigned in his heart: accordingly, in his impatience to see himself on the papal throne, no sooner did he understand that more than half the votes were in his favour, than, assuring himself of the pontificate, he started to his feet, and without waiting for the end of the scrutiny, tossed into the middle of the hall a certain staff which he had carried to support himself with, holding himself up in such a manner, that he seemed, as it were, a foot taller than he was at first: but what was more marvellous," &c.]

So it appears that all runs quite the same to a few words.

Leti, on one occasion, adduces an authority for his narrative:—

"I ho parlato con un Marchiano, ch' è morto venti (in later editions, trenta) anni sono, et assai caduco, il quale non aveva altro piacere che di parlare di Sisto V., e ne raccontava tutte le particolarità."

[I have conversed with a person from the Mark, who has been dead these twenty years (later editions have, "thirty"), a man frail enough, whose sole delight it was to talk about Sixtus V., and who related all the particulars concerning him.]

It is improbable at once that Leti, who, in 1644, came to Rome at the age of fourteen, should have conversed with persons who intimately knew Sixtus V., and from their conversations should have derived much information for his book; but this, too, is one of the passages that have been transferred from that manuscript:—

"Et un giorno parlando con un certo uomo dalla Marcha, che è morto, che non aveva altro piacere che di parlare di Sisto V."

[And one day, talking with a certain man from the Mark, who is dead, whose sole delight it was to speak about Sixtus V.]

The twenty or thirty years was added by the author to give the greater credibility to what he says.

Here, too, it strikes me that Leti must have fallen upon a faulty copy. The manuscript has, at the very beginning, The boy had often to watch the cattle at night on the open fields: "*in campagna aperta;*" instead of that, Leti has, "in *compagnia d' un altro*" [in another's field], which looks quite like an ill-corrrected error in writing. The M. A. Selleri of Leti would likely have been M. A. Siliaci, according to the manuscript.

In a word, Leti's Vita di Sisto V. is no independent work. It is the reworking of an Italian manuscript, with improvements of style, and some additions that had fallen into his hands.

The whole question now resolves itself into this: What credit may we attach to this manuscript? It is a collection of anecdotes, composed after a considerable lapse of years, altogether of an apocryphal nature. Its account of the conclave, in particular, deserves no credit. Sixtus V. is not the person to whom it was first applied; the same had already been said of pope Paul III. In the preface to the writing intituled, Acta Concilii Tridentini, 1546, an extract from which is to be found in Strobel's Neuen Beiträgen v. 233, it is said of Paul III.:

"Mortuo Clemente valde callide primum simulabat . . . . . vix prae senio posse suis pedibus consistere: arridebat omnibus, laedebat neminem, suamque prorsus voluntatem ad nutum reliquorum accommodabat: . . . . ubi se jam pontificem declaratum sensit, qui antea tarditatem, morbum, senium et quasi formidolosum leporem simulabat, extemplo tunc est factus agilis, validus, imperiosus, suamque inauditam ferociam . . . . coepit ostendere."

[On the death of Clement, he dissembled very cunningly . . . . . that he could hardly stand on his feet from old age. He had a smile for every body, gave offence to none, and indeed accommodated his will to the beck of the rest . . . . when he perceived that he was now declared pontiff, he who had affected slowness, disease, old age, and an almost timorous complaisance, then all at once showed agility, vigour, imperiousness, and began to exhibit . . . . his unheard of ferocity.]

It will be seen that this is the foundation of the narrative as it appears in the manuscript and in Leti.

Leti did not first think of testing the accuracy of his manuscript or of purging it of its defects; he has rather done his best still further to pervert what he found in it.

Not the less did he meet with the greatest acceptance: edition after edition of his book was called for, and it appeared in a multitude of translations.

It is remarkable that history, as it passes into the thoughts of mankind, uniformly touches on the confines of mythology. Personal qualities appear in bolder relief, and stronger; in one way or another they approach a false ideal: occurrences become more signally developed, accessory circumstances and co-operating causes are forgotten and put aside. In this way alone does it appear that the demands of the imagination can be sufficiently satisfied.

Then, long after, comes the man of learning, who wonders how people have happened to adopt such false opinions, does his part in dissipating mistakes, but at last is convinced that this is not so easily to be accomplished. The understanding allows itself to be convinced, the imagination is not to be overcome.

Storia della vita e geste di papa Sisto V. sommo pontefice, scritta dal P^re^ M^ro^ Casimiro Tempesti. Roma, 1755.—[Account of the life and acts of pope Sixtus V., supreme pontiff, written by Father Casimir Tempesti. Rome, 1755.]

We have spoken of the moderate, cheerful, well-meaning pope, Lambertini, Benedict XIV.; his pontificate is remarkable, also, on this account, that almost all works on the internal history of the popes that are in some degree serviceable, fall within that epoch. Then were Maffei's Annals committed to the press; then did Bromato arrange his collection on Paul IV.; the biographies of Marcellus II. and of Benedict XIII. fall within that reign; then it was that Casimir Tempesti, a Franciscan like Sixtus V., undertakes the refutation of Gregory Leti.

For this, every desirable liberty was given him. He made a thorough search in the Roman libraries, and found there the finest harvest—biographies, correspondences, memorials of various kinds, all of which he proceeded to weave into his work. The most important perhaps of all is the nuncio Morosini's correspondence in France, which fills up the greater part of his work. For, generally speaking, he adopts his original materials, with some retouching, into his work.

On this, we have but two remarks to make.

First, he places himself in a singular position as respects his sources of information. He believes them; writes them out; but he thinks that the pope must have fallen out with the authors, that he must have offended them: as soon as they begin to find fault, he renounces them; he endeavours to give a different version of the arraigned proceedings of his hero.

But occasionally he deviates likewise from his authorities, whether because they are not high-church enough for him, or because he has no proper understanding of the matter. Take, for instance, the Mülhausen occurrence in 1587. The manuscript which Tempesti designates under the name "Anonimo Capitolino," which he has, in a great many places, directly transcribed, relates the matter with great clearness: let us observe what use he makes of it. Anonimo notices very properly with the words "Io non so che causa" [I know not what was the cause], the dissension that broke out in Mülhausen, as Laufer in his Helvetic History expresses himself, "about a small wood valued at hardly twelve crowns." Tempesti makes of this, "in urgente lor emergenza" [in their pressing emergency]. The Mülhausen men put some of their councillors in prison, "carcerarono parecchi del suo senato." Tempesti says only, "carcerati alcuni" [some were put into prison], without noticing that they were of the council. People were afraid that the Mühlhäusers might give themselves up to the protection of the Roman catholic cantons of the country, and separate from the protestant: "che' volesse mutar religione e protettori, passando all' eretica fede con raccomandarsi alli cantoni cattolici, siccome allora era raccomandata alli eretici" [that they wished to change religion and protectors, passing to the heretical faith while they recommended themselves to the catholic cantons, as was then recommended to the heretical cantons]: which refers to this, that Mülhausen, at its very first entrance into the Swiss connection, was not admitted by Uri, Schweitz, Lucerne, and Unterwalden, as it was also refused the protection of those territories afterwards, on professing to belong to the reformed church. (Glutz Blotzheim Fortsetzung von Müller's Schweizergeschichte, p. 373.)—[Glutz Blotzheim's continuation of Müller's History of Switzerland.] Tempesti has no perception of this peculiar relation. He very dryly says, "Riputarono che i Milausini volessero dichiararsi cattolici."—[They alleged that the Mülhausers wanted to declare themselves Roman catholics.] Thus this goes farther, there, too, where the author, by typographical marks, gives the reader to understand that he is quoting the words of another. Anonimo Capitolino says, that pope Sixtus had the idea of sending 100,000 scudi to Switzerland, for the purpose of promoting this transition, when he received word that all was composed. Tempesti asserts, nevertheless, that the pope sent the money. For everything must be sacrificed to his hero appearing splendid and liberal, although the latter was certainly not his most brilliant characteristic.

I will accumulate no more examples. Such is his method of proceeding wherever I have compared him with his authorities. He is diligent, careful, furnished with good information, but cramped, dry, monotonous, and wanting in a real insight into affairs. His work is not fitted to counteract the impression produced by Leti's book with a similar one.

II. MANUSCRIPTS.

Let us now return to our manuscripts: we are ever and anon thrown back upon them for proper information.

First of all we meet with a MS. of pope Sixtus himself. It consists of memoranda noted down by himself while still in the monastery.

49.

Memorie autografe di Papa Sisto V. Bibl. Chigi, N. III. 70.—[Autograph Memorials of Pope Sixtus V. Chigi Library, No. III. 70] 158 leaves.

A person, called Salvetti, having found it in a garret, had made a present of it to Alexander VII. In fact, there can be no doubt of its authenticity.

"Questo libro sarà per memoria di mie poche facenducce, scritto di mia propria mano, dove cio che sarà scritto a laude di Dio sarà la ignuda verità, e così priego creda ogn' uno che legge."

[This book is to serve for a memorial of my few small affairs, written with my own hand, whence what shall be written to the praise of God will be the naked truth, and thus I pray every one who reads to believe.]

Now it consists first of accounts, in which, however, one leaf is awanting, if not more.

"E qui sara scritti" [And here shall be written], he goes on to say, "tutti crediti, debiti et ogn' altra mia attione di momento. E così sarà la verità come qui si troverà scritto."—[all things owing to or by me, and every thing else done by me of any moment. And the truth will be as shall be found written here.]

I shall give one example more in addition to what I have put down already in the narrative of the text.

"Andrea del Apiro, frate di San Francesco conventuale, venne a Venetia, e nel partirse per pagar robe comprate per suo fratello, qual mi disse far botega in Apiro, me domandò in prestito denari, e li prestai, presente fra Girolamo da Lunano e fra Cornelio da Bologna, fiorini 30, e mi promise renderli a Montalto in mano di fra Salvatore per tutto il mese presente d'Augusto, come appar in un scritto da sua propria mano il dì 9 Agosto 1557, quale è nella mia casetta. H. 30."

[Andrew of Apiro, conventual friar of St. Francis, came from Venice, and on going away asked me to lend him some money to pay for goods purchased for his brother who, he told me, kept shop in Apiro, and I lent him in the presence of friar Girolamo of Lunano and friar Cornelius of Bologna, 30 florins, and he promised to repay them at Montalto in the hand of friar Salvatore; for the whole of this present month of August 1557, as appears in a writing from his own hand, the 9th of August 1557, which is in my little box. H. 30.]

Here we see these monkish traffickings, how one friar lends money to another, how the borrower gives his aid to the petty business conducted by his brother, how others witness to what passes. Friar Salvatore also appears.

Then there follows a memorandum of books. "Inventarium omnium librorum tam seorsum quam simul ligatorum quos ego Fr. Felix Perettus de Monte alto emi et de licentia superiorum possideo. Qui seorsum fuerit ligatus, faciat numerum: qui non cum aliis, minime."—[Inventory of all the books bound by themselves as well as along with others, which I, friar Felix Peretti of Montalto, have bought and now possess with the leave of my superiors. A volume bound by itself makes a number; that which is not with others, by no means.] I now regret that I took no note of this memorandum: it appeared very insignificant.

Finally, we find at page 144:

"Memoria degli anni che andai a studio, di officii, prediche e commissioni avute."—[Note of the years of my going to study, of the offices, preachings and commissions I have held.]

This I give at full length, although Tempesti has here and there something of it: it is the only diary of a pope that we possess.

"Col nome di dio 1540 il dì 1 settembre di mercoldì intrai a studio in Ferrara, e vi finii il triennio sotto il rdo mro Barto dalla Pergola. Nel 43 fatto il capitolo in Ancona andai a studio in Bologna sotto il rdo maestro Giovanni da Correggio: intrai in Bologna il dì S. Jacobo maggior di Luglio, e vi stetti fino al settembre del 44, quando il costacciaro mi mandò baccellier di convento in Rimini col revmo regente mr Antonio da città di Penna, e vi finii il tempo sino al capitolo di Venezia del 46. Fatto il capitolo andai baccellier di convento in Siena con mro Alexandro da Montefalco, e qui finii il triennio fino al capitolo d'Assisi del 49. Ma il costacciaro mi die' la licentia del magisterio nel 48 a 22 Luglio, e quattro dì dopo me addottorai a Fermo. Nel capitolo generale di Assisi fui fatto regente di Siena 1549 e vi finii il triennio, fu generale monsro Gia Jacobo da Montefalco. A Napoli: nel capitolo generale di Genova fui fatto regente di Napoli 1553 dal revmo generale mr Giulio da Piacenza e vi finii il triennio. A Venezia: nel capitolo generale di Brescia 1556 fui fatto regente di Venezia, e vi finii il triennio, e l'anno primo della mia regeria fui eletto inquisitor in tutto l'illmo dominio 1557 dì 17 di Gennaro. Nel capitolo generale di Assisi 1559 eletto generale mro Giovan Antonio da Cervia, fui confirmato regente et inquisitore in Venezia come di sopra. Per la morte di papa Paolo IIII. l'anno detto d'Agosto partii da Venezia per visitare li miei a Montalto, inquisitore apostolico: mosso da gran tumulti; il 22 di Febbraro 1560 tornai in ufficio col brieve di Pio IIII. papa, et vi stetti tutto 'l Giugno, e me chiamò a Roma: il dì 18 Luglio 1560 fui fatto teologo assistente alla inquisitione di Roma e giurai l'officio in mano del cardl Alessandrino.

"(Prediche.) L'anno 1540 predicai, nè havevo anchor cantato messa, in Montepagano, terra di Abruzzo. L'anno 1541 predicai a Voghiera, villa Ferrarese, mentre ero studente in Ferrara. L'anno 1542 predicai in Grignano, villa del Polesine di Rovigo, e studiavo in Ferrara. L'anno 1543 predicai alla fratta di Badenara, (viveva il Diedo e'l Manfrone) e studiavo in Ferrara. L'anno 1544 predicai alla Canda, villa della Badia, e studiavo in Bologna. L'anno 1545 predicai le feste in Rimini in convento nostro, perche il mro di studio di Bologna ne preoccupò la predica di Monte Scutulo, et ero bacco di convento di Rimini. L'anno 1546 predicai a Macerata di Montefeltro et ero bacco di convento di Rimini. L'anno 1547 predicai a S. Geminiano in Toscana et ero bacco di convento a Siena. L'anno 1548 predicai a S. Miniato al Tedesco in Toscana, et ero bacco di Siena. L'anno 1549 predicai in Ascoli della Marca, partito da Siena per l' ingresso de Spagnoli introdutti da Don Diego Mendozza. L'anno 1550 predicai a

[With the name of God, 1540, on Wednesday the 1st of September, I began my studies at Ferrara, and there finished my three years' course under the reverend master Bartholomew della Pergola. In 1543, after the chapter held at Ancona, I went to study at Bologna under the reverend master John da Correggio. I entered Bologna in July, on St. James the greater's day, and there remained until September of 1544, when the *costacciaro* sent me bachelor of the monastery to Rimini, with the most reverend master Anthony of the city of Penna, and there I completed the time until the chapter of Venice in 1546. After the chapter was over, I went as bachelor of the monastery to Siena, with master Alexander of Montefalco, and there completed the three years until the chapter of Assisi in 1549. But the *costacciaro* gave me the license of master on the 22d of July, 1548, and four days after made me a doctor at Fermo. At the chapter general held at Assisi, I was made regent of Siena, in 1549, and there completed the three years, the general being monsignor Gia Jacobo of Montefalco. At Naples: in the chapter-general held at Genoa, I was made regent of Naples, 1553, by the most reverend general master Julius da Piacenza, and there I finished the three years. At Venice: in the chapter-general of Brescia, 1556, I was made regent of Venice, and there finished the three years, and during the first year of my regentship I was elected inquisitor for the whole most illustrious dominion, on the 17th of January, 1557. In the chapter-general of Assisi, in 1559, master John Anthony da Cervia being elected general, I was confirmed regent and inquisitor in Venice as above. On the death of pope Paul IV., on the said year I set off from Venice to visit my relations at Montalto, as apostolic inquisitor: affected at the great tumults; on the 22d of February, 1560, I returned to office with the brief of pope Paul IV., and there remained during the whole of June, and called myself to Rome on the 18th of July, 1560. I was made assistant theologian to the inquisition at Rome, and took the oaths of office in the hands of cardinal Alexandrino.

(Preachings.) In the year 1540, I preached —nor as yet had I chanted mass—in Montepagano, an estate in Abruzzo. In the year 1541, I preached at Voghiera, a city of Ferrara, while I was a student in Ferrara. In the year 1542, I preached in Grignano, a town of the Polesine di Rovigo, and I studied in Ferrara. In the year 1543, I preached at the *fratta* of Badenara (Diedo and Manfrone were living), and I studied in Ferrara. In the year 1544, I preached at Canda, a town of Badia, and studied in Bologna. In the year 1545, I preached the festival sermons in Rimini in our monastery, because the master of studies

Fano et ero regente a Siena. L'anno 1551 predicai nel domo di Camerino condotto dal r^{mo} vescovo et ero regente a Siena. L'anno 1552 predicai a Roma, in S. Apostoli, e tre ill^{mi} cardinali me intrattennero in Roma, e lessi tutto l'anno tre dì della settimana la pistola a Romani di S. Paolo. L'anno 1553 predicai a Genova, e vi se fece il capitolo generale, et andai regente a Napoli. L'anno 1554 predicai a Napoli in S. Lorenzo, e vi ero regente, e lessi tutto l'anno in chiesa l' evangelio di Giovanni. L'anno 1555 predicai nel duomo di Perugia ad instanza dell' ill^{mo} cardinale della Corgna. L'anno 1556 fu chiamato a Roma al concilio generale, che già principiò la santità di papa Paulo IIII, però non predicai. L'anno 1557 fu eletto inquisitor di Venezia e del dominio, e bisognandome tre dì della settimana seder al tribunale non predicai ordinariamente, ma 3 (?) dì della settimana a S. Caterina in Venezia. L'anno 1558 predicai a S. Apostoli di Venezia e 4 giorni della settimana a S. Caterina, ancorche exequisse l' officio della s^{ta} inquis^{ne}. L'anno 1559 non predicai salvo tre dì della settimana a S. Caterina per le molte occupationi del s. officio. L'anno 1560 tornando col brieve di S. Santità a Venezia inquisitore tardi predicai solo a S. Caterina come di sopra.

"(Commissioni.) L'anno 1548 ebbi da rev^{mo} m^{re} Bartolommeo da Macerata, ministro della Marca, una commissione a Fermò per liberar di prigione del S^{r} vicelegato fra Leonardo della Ripa: lo liberai e lo condussi in Macerata. L'anno 1549 ebbi dal sud^{o} R. P^{re} commissione in tutta la custodia di Ascoli da Febbraro fino a pasqua. L'anno istesso dall' istesso ebbi una commissione nel convento di Fabriano e vi rimisi frate Evangelista dell' istesso luogo. L'anno 1550 ebbi dall' istesso padre commissione in Senegaglia: rimisi fra Nicolò in casa e veddi i suoi conti. L'anno 1551 ebbi commissione dal rev^{mo} p^{re} generale m^{re} Gia Jacobo da Montefalco a visitar tutta la parte de Montefeltro, Cagli et Urbino. L'anno 1552 ebbi dall' ill^{mo} cardinale protettor commissione sopra una lite esistente tra il guardiano fra Tommaso da Piacenza et un fra Francesco da Osimo, che aveva fatto la cocchina in Santo Apostolo. L' istesso anno ebbi commission dal rev^{mo} padre generale m^{ro} Giulio da Piacenza nel convento di Fermo, e privai di guardianato m^{ro} Domenico da Montesanto, e viddi i conti del procuratore fra Lodovico da Pontano, e bandii della provincia fra Ciccone da Monte dell' Olmo per aver dato delle ferite a fra Tommaso dell' istesso luogo. L'anno 1555 ebbi del sudetto r^{mo} generale commissione di andar in Calabria a far il ministro, perche avea inteso quello esser morto, ma chiarito quello esser vivo non andai. L'anno 1557 ebbi commissione sopra il Gattolino di Capodistria, sopra il Garzoneo da Veglia et altre assai commissioni di fra Giulio di Capodistria. L'anno 1559 fui fatto commissario nella provincia di S. Antonio, tenni il capitolo a Bassano, e fu eletto ministro m^{ro} Cornelio Veneso. L'anno 1560 fui fatto inquisitore apostolico in tutto il dominio Veneto, e dell' istesso anno fui fatto teologo assistente alla inquisitione di Roma il dì 16 Luglio 1560.

"Nel capitolo generale di Brescia 1556 fui at Bologna pre-occupied the pulpit of Monte Scutulo, and I was bachelor of the monastery of Rimini. In the year 1546, I preached at Macerata of Montefeltro, and was bachelor of the monastery of Rimini. In the year 1547, I preached at St. Geminiano in Tuscany, and was bachelor of the monastery of Siena. In the year 1548, I preached at St. Miniato al Tedesco in Tuscany, and was bachelor of Siena. In the year 1549, I preached in Ascoli della Marca, having left Siena on account of the entrance of the Spaniards, introduced by Don Diego Mendozza. In the year 1550, I preached at Fano, and was regent at Siena. In 1551, I preached in the cathedral of Camerino, employed by the most rev. bishop, and was regent at Siena. In 1552, I preached at Rome, in the church of the Holy Apostles, and three most illustrious cardinals entertained me in Rome, and I read every year, for three days in the week, St. Paul's Epistle to the Romans. In 1553, I preached at Genoa, and there the chapter-general was held, and I went as regent to Naples. In 1554, I preached at Naples in the church of St. Lawrence, and there I was regent, and read every year in the church the Gospel of John. In 1555, I preached in the cathedral of Perugia, at the instance of the most illustrious cardinal della Corgna. In 1556, I was called to Rome to the council-general, which was already begun by his holiness pope Paul IV., therefore I did not preach. In 1557, I was elected inquisitor of Venice, and of the lordship, and being required to sit in court three days in the week, I did not ordinarily preach but three (?) days of the week at St. Catherine's in Venice. In 1558, I preached at the church of the Apostles in Venice, and four days of the week at that of St. Catherine, although I discharged the office of the inquisition. In 1559, I preached only three days of the week at St. Catherine's, owing to the many engagements of the holy office. In 1560, returning with the brief of his holiness to Venice as inquisitor, I preached late at St. Catherine's only, as above.

(Commissions.) In 1548, I received from the most rev. bishop Bartolommeo of Macerata, minister of the Mark, a commission at Fermo, to liberate friar Leonardo della Ripa from the prison of the lord vice-legate: I delivered him, and conducted him to Macerata. In 1549, I had from the said rev. father a commission in all the *custodia* of Ascoli from February till Easter. In that same year, I had from the same person a commission in the convent of Fabriano, and there I restored friar Evangelista of the same place. In 1550, I had from the same father a commission in Senegaglia: I restored friar Nicolo to the house, and saw his accounts. In 1551, I had a commission from the most rev. father-general monsignor Gia Jacobo of Montefalco, to visit the whole district of Montefeltro, Cagli and Urbino. In 1552, I had a commission from the most illustrious cardinal protector about a lawsuit between friar Thomas, guardian (or superior) of Placentia and a friar Francis of Osimo, who had conducted the cooking in Santo Apostolo. That same year, I had a commission from the most rev. father-general, master Julius, of Placentia, in the

eletto promotor a magisterii con l' Andria e con m[ro] Giovanni da Bergamo, et otto baccalaurei da noi promossi furon dottorati dal rev[mo] generale m[ro] Giulio da Piacenza, cioè da Montalcino, Ottaviano da Ravenna, Bonaventura da Gabiano, Marc Antonio da Lugo, Ottaviano da Napoli, Antonio Panzetta da Padova, Ottaviano da Padova, Martiale Calabrese. Otto altri promossi ma non adottoratti da s. p. r[ma]: Francesco da Sonnino, Antonio da Urbino, Nicolò da Montefalco, Jacobo Appugliese, Antonio Bolletta da Firenze, Constantino da Crema, il Piemontese et il Sicolino. Io però con l' autorità di un cavalier di S. Pietro da Brescia addottorai Antonio da Urbino, il Piemontese e Constantino da Crema. Di Maggio 1558 con l' autorità del cavalier Centani addottorai in Venezia fra Paolo da S. Leo, frate Andrea d' Arimino, Giammatteo da Sassocorbaro e fra Tironino da Lunano, tutti miei discepoli."

monastery of Fermo, and I deprived of the office of guardian master Dominic of Monte Santo, and I inspected the accounts of the procurator friar Lewis of Pontano, and I banished from the province friar Ciccone of Monte dell' Olmo for having struck friar Thomas of the same place. In 1555, I had a commission from the said most rev. general to go into Calabria, to be minister, for he had been given to understand that he was dead; but it appearing that he was alive, I did not go. In 1557, I had a commission about Gattolino di Capodistria, about Garzoneo da Veglia, and enough of other commissions from friar Julius of Capodistria. In 1559, I was made commissary of the province of St. Anthony: I held a chapter at Bassano, and master Cornelius Veneso was elected minister. In 1560, I was made apostolic inquisitor for the whole Venetian dominions, and that same year was made assistant theologian to the inquisition of Rome, 16th of July, 1560.

At the chapter-general of Brescia in 1556, I was elected *promotor a magisterii* along with Andrew and master John of Bergamo; and eight baccalaureats promoted by us were made doctors by the most rev. general master Julius of Placentia, namely of Montalcino, Ottaviano of Ravenna, Bonaventura of Gabiano, Mark Anthony of Lugo, Ottaviano of Naples, Anthony Panzetta of Padua, Ottaviano of Padua, Martial from Calabria. Eight others were promoted but not raised to the degree of doctor by the most reverend father: Francis of Sonnino, Anthony of Urbino, Nicolas of Montefalco, James an Appulian, Anthony Bolletta of Florence, Constantine of Crema, a Piemontese and a Sicilian. I, therefore, with the authority of a knight of St. Peter of Brescia, gave the degree of doctor to Anthony of Urbino, the Piemontese, and Constantine of Crema. In May, 1558, with the authority of a knight Centani, I gave the degree of doctor in Venice to friar Paul of St. Leo, friar Andrew of Ariminum, John Matthew of Sassocorbaro, and friar Tironino of Lunano, all disciples of mine.]

50.

De Vita Sixti V., ipsius manu emendata. Bibl. Altieri.—[On the Life of Sixtus V., corrected with his own hand. Altieri Library.] 57 leaves.

This is but a copy, but one in which the mistakes of the first writer, and the pope's corrections are faithfully taken in. The corrections are seen written over the words that are scored out.

It begins with the poverty of this pope's parents, who prolonged their existence "alieni parvique agri cultura [by the cultivation of a small piece of ground belonging to another person]; he celebrates among the members of the family most of all Signora Camilla, who, at least at the time when he wrote, was extremely moderate in her pretensions:

"Quae ita se intra modestiae atque humilitatis suae fines continuit semper, ut ex summa et celsissima fortuna fratris, praeter innocentiae atque frugalitatis famam et in relictis sibi a familia nepotibus pie ac liberaliter educandis diligentiae laudem, nihil magnopere cepisse dici possit."

[Who always so confined herself within the bounds of her modesty and humility that she might be said to have taken nothing from her brother's most lofty and supreme fortune but the fame of innocence and frugality, and the praise of diligence in piously and liberally educating the grandchildren left to her by the family.]

He proceeds to education, rise in position, and the first period of administration. He is particularly to be noticed because of the prominence he gives to the prevalence of Christian principle in the buildings of Rome.

This small work must have been composed about the year 1587. The author had entertained the prospect of delineating the times that followed also.

"Tum dicentur nobis plenius, cum acta ejus (Sixti) majori parata ordine prodere me-

[We will then speak more fully when we shall attempt to hand down to posterity his

moriae experiemur. Quod et facturi pro viribus nostris, si vita suppetet, omni conatu sumus: et ipse ingentia animo complexus, nec ulla mediocri contentus gloria, uberem ingeniis materiam praebiturus egregie de se condendi volumina videtur."

(Sixtus's) doings arranged on a larger scale. Which thing, if our life be spared, we will do, in so far as we can, with our utmost efforts: and he himself, embracing immense objects in his mind, and not content with any mediocrity of glory, seems likely to supply men of genius with rich materials for writing volumes about him in no ordinary manner.]

Now, with respect to the work at present before us, the most important question that occurs is, whether it was really revised by that pope.

Tempesti, too, who was not acquainted with the copy in the Altieri library, possessed a small work, recommended to him as having been composed by Graziani and revised by pope Sixtus. He makes some objections to it, and in these may be in the right. But it is not identical with the one we have. Tempesti, among other things, notices (p. 30) that Graziani makes the pope begin his first procession from the Church of the Apostles, whereas it had set out from Araceli. This is a blunder which truly would be more apt to escape a man who had become pope, and was immersed in the affairs of the world, than the *padre maestro* Tempesti. But it does not occur in our *Vita*. Here it runs quite correctly:

"Verum ut acceptum divinitus honorem ab ipso Deo exordiretur, ante omnia supplicationes decrevit, quas ipse cum patribus et frequente pupolo pedibus eximia cum religione obivit a templo Franciscanorum ad S. Mariam Majorem."

[But that he might make an honour, which he had divinely received, begin with God, he first of all decreed supplications, which he performed on foot with the fathers and a crowd of people, very religiously going from the church of the Franciscans to that of St. Mary the Greater.]

We have one further testimony to the authenticity of this little work. Another biography —that which we have to speak of next—relates that Sixtus had noted on the margin of certain commentaries, "sororem alteram tenera aetate decessisse" [that another sister had died in early life]. Now we find that this very thing has been done on the writing now in question. The first compiler had written, "Quarum altera nupsit, ex cujus filia Silvestrii profluxisse dicuntur, quos adnumerat suis pontifex," &c.—[Of whom one was married, from whose daughter the Sylvestrii are said to have descended, whom the pope reckoned among his relations, &c.] Sixtus drew his pen through this and some other things, and wrote at the place, "Quarum altera aetate adhuc tenera decessit" [Of whom another died while yet in early life].

A second biography says further:

"In illis commentariis ab ipso Sixto, qui ea recognovit, adscriptum reperi, Sixti matrem Marianam non quidem ante conceptum sed paulo ante editum filium de futura ejus magnitudine divinitus fuisse monitam."

[In those commentaries by Sixtus himself, which he revised, I find it put down, that the mother of Sixtus, not indeed before her son was conceived, but before he was born, had a divine pre-intimation given her of his future greatness.]

This, too, we find in our writing. The author had said that Peretto had received the pre intimation in a dream, "nasciturum sibi filium qui aliquando ad summas esset dignitates perventurus' [that a son was about to be born to him who would one day reach the highest dignities]. The pen is drawn through father, and there is put down, "Ejus uxor partui vicina" [his wife near her confinement].

Thus this little work acquires a great authenticity: it attaches itself directly to that autography of the pope. It well deserved being specially copied.

51.

Sixtus V. Pontifex Maximus. Bibl. Altieri.—[Sixtus V. Supreme Pontiff. Altieri Library.] 80 leaves.

The very writing by which we were enabled to prove the authenticity of the one last described. I do not find that it was known to Tempesti or any one else.

The author wrote after the death of Sixtus. Already he complains that the memory of that pope was misrepresented by many fabrications.

"Sixtus V.," he begins by saying, "memoriae quibusdam gratae, aliquibus invisae, omnibus magnae, cum cura nobis et sine ambitu dicetur: curam expectatio multorum acuit," although the writing was never printed, "ambitum senectus nobis imminens praecidit."

[Sixtus V., of a memory grateful to some, hateful to others, great to all, shall be spoken of by us carefully and without selfish ends; our carefulness has been sharpened by the expectation of many, and impending old age cuts off selfish considerations.]

He deems his object of great importance: "Vix aut rerum moles major aut majoris animi pontifex ullo unquam tempore concurrerunt."—[Hardly has there ever been a concurrence at the same time of a vaster mass of affairs, and of a pontiff of a greater mind.]

In the first part of his little work, he goes through the life of Sixtus V. until the elevation of the latter to the papal see. In this he draws his materials from the above biography, from the correspondences of Sixtus—which he often quotes—and from pieces of information received by word of mouth from cardinal Paleotto, or a confidential domestic of the pope's,

called Capelletto. Wherewithal a great many memorable things besides come to be mentioned.

CHAP. I. "Sixti genus, parentes, patria."—[Sixtus's family, parents, and native country.] Here we find the singular notice that Sixtus had, in his youth, wished himself to be called *Crinitus* [Longhaired], nay, even in the monastery he was for a long time called so. By this he referred to a comet, and chose the name on account of his expectations of good fortune ("propter speratam semper ab se ob ea quae mox exsequar portenta nominis et loci claritatem") [on account of the lustre of name and place always hoped for by him, in consequence of the portents which I shall presently speak of]. To this there is an allusion in the star of his coat of arms. That, at least, is no comet. Moreover he himself told Paleotto that by the pears on that coat of arms his father Peretti was meant, by the hills his fatherland; the lion that carries the pears meant at once magnanimity and beneficence.

II. "Ortus Sixti divinitus ejusque futura magnitudo praenunciatur."—[The rise of Sixtus and his future greatness, is divinely foretold.] Sixtus himself relates that his father once in the night heard a voice call to him: "Vade, age, Perette, uxori jungere; paritura enim tibi filium est, cui Felicis nomen impones: is enim mortalium olim maximus est futurus."—[Go, Peretti, join your wife; for she is about to bring forth to you a son, to whom you shall give the name of Felix: for he is one day to be the greatest of mortals.] He was an odd fellow, however, this Peretti. His wife at the time was in service with the Diana we have spoken of. Pretending to be acting under prophetical encouragement, he visited her under cover of night. By day he durst not venture to let himself be seen from fear of his creditors.—Strange origin! At a time subsequent to this Peretti formally led his creditors to feed their hopes on the good fortune of his son. When he had the child in his arms, he would say indeed that he held a pope in them, and would put out his feet for the neighbours to kiss.

III. "Nomen."—[Name.] Peretto said, on representations being made to him against the name Felix: "Baptismo potius quam Felicis nomine carebit."—[He shall sooner go without baptism than not have Felix for his name.] The bed once took fire from a light that had been left near it: the mother ran to put it out, and found the child unhurt and laughing. Almost like the pre-intimation of his future greatness, to the child of the female slave of Servius Tullius, by a flame that played about his head when asleep. After the lapse of so many centuries, thus is the prodigy, or the belief in it, repeated.

IV. "Studia."—[Studies.] His having herded swine, however, is what he was unwilling to hear: he had forbidden the continuation of the above commentaries, because this was found in them. An account (is given) of his rapid progress at first, so that he occupied the schoolmaster quite too much considering he paid him but five bajocchi. "Vix mensem alterum operam magistro dederat, cum ille Perettum adit, stare se conventis posse negans: tam enim multa Felicem supra reliquorum captum et morem discere, ut sibi, multo plus in uno illo quam in ceteris instituendis omnibus laboranti, non expediat maximam operam minima omnium mercede consumere."—[He had spent another month under the master when the latter went to Peretto, saying that he could not stand to the terms agreed on: for that Felix learned so many things beyond the capacity and custom of the rest that it did not suit him, labouring much more in teaching him than all the others, to give most work where there was least pay.] He was pretty severely treated with friar Salvatore. Many a blow he got for not putting down the meat for him properly. The poor child stood on tiptoes, yet was so little as hardly to be able to reach to the dishes.

V. His monastic life. This we have mentioned in speaking of his manner of study, and the disputation at Assisi. The first fame of his preaching. While on a journey he was laid hold of at Belfort, and not suffered to proceed until he had preached thrice amid an immense concourse from the neighbourhood.

VI. "Montalti cum Ghislerio Alexandrino jungendae familiaritatis occasio."—[The occasion of Montalto's forming an intimacy with Ghisleri Alexandrino.]

VII. "Per magnam multorum invidiam ad magnos multosque honores evadit."—[Through great envy on the part of many, he attains to great and many honours.] Especially at Venice, where he carried through the printing of the Index, he had much to bear. At one time he had to leave the place, and hesitated to return. Cardinal Carpi, his patron ever after the above disputation, intimated to the Franciscans of the place, that either Montalto or none of them should remain in Venice. Meanwhile, however, he could not keep himself there. His brother friars arraigned him before the council of Ten, for raising disorder in the republic by refusing absolution to such as were in possession of forbidden books (qui damnatos libros domi retineant). He had to return to Rome, where he became consultor of the Inquisition.

VIII. "Romanae Inquisitionis consultor, sui ordinis procurator, inter theologos congregationis Tridentini concilii adscribitur."—[Consultor of the Roman Inquisition, procurator of his own order, his name is appended to the list of the divines of the congregation of the council of Trent.] With the Franciscans of Rome too, Montalto found admission only upon the express recommendation of Carpi, and the latter sent him his dinner. He promoted him to that post, he recommended him on his deathbed to cardinal Ghislieri.

IX. "Iter in Hispaniam."—[Journey into Spain.] He accompanied Buoncompagno, afterwards Gregory XIII. Even at that time they were on no very good terms with each other. Montalto had to travel at times on the baggage waggon. "Accidit nonnunquam ut quasi per injuriam aut necessitatem jumento destitutus vehiculis quibus impedimenta comportabantur deferri necesse fuerit."—[It sometimes happened that as if by way of insult

or from necessity, from having no animal to ride, it was necessary to seek a place on the waggons by which the baggage was conveyed.] Many other slights followed.

X. "Post honorifice delatum episcopatum per iniquorum hominum calumnias cardinalatus Montalto maturatur."—[After the episcopate had been honourably conferred upon him, amid the calumnies of unjust men, the cardinalship is hastily given to Montalto.] He was opposed even by the nephew of Pius V., "alium veterem contubernalem evehendi cupidus." —[eager to advance another old chum.] The pope was told, among other things, that there had been taken into Montalto's apartment four well-closed chests, and that he lodged himself very effeminately and sumptuously. Pius went when quite unexpected into the monastery. He found there naked walls, and finally inquired what was in the chests which still stood there. "Books, Holy Father," said Montalto, "which I am going to take with me to St. Agatha,"—that was his bishopric,—and opened one of them. Pius was delighted, and in a short while made him a cardinal.

XI. "Montalti dum cardinalis fuit vita et mores."—[Montalto's life and manners during his cardinalship.] Gregory took from him his pension, which explained to many the future pontificate of Montalto. "Levis enim aulicorum quorundam superstitio diu credidit, pontificum animis occultam quandam in futuros successores obtrectationem insidere."—[For a foolish superstition of some of the persons about the court long led to the belief that the minds of the popes were beset with a certain secret envy of their successors.]

XII. "Francisci Peretti caedes incredibili animi aequitate tolerata."—[The slaughter of Francis Peretto endured with incredible equanimity.]

XIII. "Pontifex M. magna patrum consensione declaratur."—[He is declared supreme pontiff with the great consent of the fathers.]

Then comes the second part.

"Hactenus Sixti vitam per tempora digessimus: jam hinc per species rerum et capita, ut justa hominis aestimatio cuique in promptu sit, exequar."—[Thus far we have gone over the life of Sixtus by dividing it into periods: we shall now pursue the subject according to particulars and heads, in order that every man may readily appreciate the man as he deserves.]

Nevertheless of this part we find but three chapters: "Gratia in bene meritos;—pietas in Franciscanorum ordinem;—publica securitas."—[Favour towards the deserving;—piety towards the order of the Franciscans;—public security.]

The last is by far the most important from his description of the times of Gregory, and not having copied it out at length, I shall at least give an extract:—

"Initio quidem nonnisi qui ob caedes et latrocinia proscripti erant, ut vim magistratuum effugerent, genus hoc vitae instituerant, ut aqua et igne prohibiti latebris silvarum conditi aviisque montium ferarum ritu vagantes miseram anxiamque vitam furtis propemodum necessariis sustentarent. Verum ubi rapinae dulcedo et impunitae nequitiae spes alios atque alios extremae improbitatis homines eodem expulit, coepit quasi legitimum aliquod vel mercimonii vel artificii genus latrocinium frequentari. Itaque certis sub ducibus, quos facinora et saevitia nobilitassent, societates proscriptorum et sicariorum ad vim, caedes, latrocinia coibant. Eorum duces ex audacia vel scelere singulos aestimabant: facinorosissimi et saevissima ausi maxime extollebantur ac decurionum centurionumque nominibus militari prope more donabantur. Hi agros et itinera non jam vago maleficio sed justo pene imperio infesta habebant. . . . . . Denique operam ad caedem inimicorum, stupra virginum et alia a quibus mens refugit, factiosis hominibus et scelere alieno ad suam exaturandam libidinem egentibus presente pretio locare: eoque res jam devenerat ut nemo se impune peccare posse crederet nisi cui proscriptorum aliquis et exulum periculum praestaret. Iis fiebat rebus ut non modo improbi ad scelera, verum etiam minime mali homines ad incolumitatem ejusmodi feras bestias sibi necessarias putarent. . . . . Id proceribus et principibus viris perpetuo palam usurpari. . . . . Et vero graves Jacobo Boncompagno susceptae cum primariis viris inimicitiae ob violatam suarum aedium immunitatem diu fortunam concussere. Procerum plerique, sive quos aes alienum exhauserat, sive quorum ambitio et luxus supra opes erat, sive quos odia et ulciscendi libido ad cruenta

[At first, indeed, those only who had been outlawed on account of murders and robberies, to escape from the grip of the magistrates, had begun this sort of life, that, while debarred from fire and water, they might keep up a wretched and anxious existence, concealed in the coverts of the woods and pathless recesses of the mountains, and subsisting upon almost necessary thefts. But when the charms of rapine and the hope of impunity in wickedness had sent thither more and more men of extreme improbity, robbery began to be followed as a kind of commerce or trade. Accordingly, associated bands of outlaws and assassins were formed for rapine, murder, and robbery, under certain chiefs, ennobled by crimes and deeds of cruelty. Their leaders estimated individuals according to their audacity and criminality: the greatest scoundrels, and those who dared to do the most savage deeds, were most cried up, and, almost in military style, had the titles of captains and sergeants given them. These now infested the fields and highways no longer as wandering malefactors, but almost as if they had a just claim to them. . . . At length they lent out their services for ready money, in the commission of murders, rapes, and other things the mind shudders to think of, to factious men who needed the subornation of crime for the gratification of their own lusts: and matters had proceeded so far that none thought he could sin with impunity but such as some one of the outlaws and exiles undertook to shield from the risk. Thus not only did the wicked come to consider savages of this sort necessary for purposes of crime, but men by no means so, thought them necessary for their safety from danger. . . . . . This was constantly and openly usurped from

consilia rejecerant, non modo patrocinium latronum suscipere, sed foedus cum illis certis conditionibus sancire ut operam illi ad caedem locarent mercede impunitatis et perfugii. Quum quo quisque sicariorum patrono uteretur notum esset, si cui quid surreptum aut per vim ablatum foret, ad patronum deprecatorem confugiebatur, qui sequestrum simulans, utrinque raptor, tum praedae partem a sicariis tum operae mercedem a supplicibus, aliquando recusantis specie, quod saevissimum est rapinae genus, extorquebat. Nec defuere qui ultro adversus mercatores atque pecuniosos eorumque filios, agros etiam et bona ex destinato immitterent, iisque deinde redimendis ad seque confugientibus operam venderent, casum adeo miserantes ut ex animo misereri credi possent. . . . . Lites sicariorum arbitrio privatis intendebantur, summittebantur vi adacti testes, metu alii a testimonio dicendo deterrebantur. . . . . . Per urbes factiones exoriri, distinctae coma et capillitio, ut hi in laevam, illi in dexteram partem vel villos alerent comarum vel comam a fronte demitterent. Multi, ut fidem partium alicui addictam firmarent, uxores necabant, ut filias, sorores, affines eorum inter quos censeri vellent ducerent, alii consanguinearum viros clam seu palam trucidabant, ut illas iis quos in suas partes adlegerant collocarent. Vulgare ea tempestate fuit ut cuique sive forma seu opes mulieris cujuscunque placuissent, eam procerum aliquo interprete vel invitis cognatis uxorem duceret: neque raro accidit ut praedivites nobilesque homines exulum abjectissimis et rapto viventibus grandi cum dote filias collocare vel eorum indotatas filias ipsi sibi justo matrimonio jungere cogerentur. . . . Sceleratisissimi homines tribunalia constituere, forum indicere, judicia exercere, sontes apud se accusare, testibus urgere, tormentis veritatem extorquere, denique solemni formula damnare: alios vero a legitimis magistratibus in vincula conjectos, causa per prôrem (procuratorem) apud se dicta, absolvere, eorum accusatores ac judices poena talionis condemnare. Coram damnatos praesens poena sequebatur: si quid statutum in absentes foret, tantisper mora erat dum sceleris ministri interdum cum mandatis perscriptis riteque obsignatis circummitterentur, qui per veram vim agerent quod legum ludibrio agebatur. . . . Dominos et reges se cujus collibuisset provinciae, ne solennibus quidem inaugurationum parcentes, dixere multi et scripsere. . . . Non semel sacra supellectile e templis direpta, augustissimam et sacratissimam eucharistiam in silvas ac latibula asportarunt, qua ad magica flagitia et execramenta abuterentur. . . . Mollitudo Gregoriani imperii malum in pejus convertit. Sicariorum multitudo infinita, quae facile ex rapto cupiditatibus conniventium vel in speciem tantum irascentium ministrorum largitiones sufficeret. Publica fide securitas vel petentibus concessa vel sponte ablata: arcibus, oppidis, militibus praeficiebantur. Eos, velut ab egregio facinore reduces, multitudo, quocunque irent, spectando effusa mirabatur, laudabat. . . . ."

the nobles and the great. . . . And, indeed, the serious feuds in which James Boncompagno became involved with men of high rank, in consequence of the violated immunity of their houses, long concussed fortune. Several of the nobility, whether overwhelmed with debt, or whose ambition and luxury exceeded their wealth, or whom hatred and revenge had thrown upon bloody counsels, not only undertook the patronage of robbers, but entered into league with them on certain conditions, to hire out their services in committing murder, in return for impunity and an asylum. When it was known who was the patron of each of the assassins, if the person from whom anything had been taken by force or stealth, went to the patron for justice, the latter, pretending to act as umpire, but defrauding both sides, extorted a part of the prey from the brigands, and a gratuity for his trouble from the suppliants, sometimes affecting to refuse it, which is the most barbarous kind of rapine. Nor were there wanting those who of set purpose suborned persons to attack merchants and monied men and their sons, fields, too, and property, and then sold their services to those who applied to them for the redemption of what had been taken, affecting such compassion for the disaster that one might suppose they really felt it. . . . Lawsuits were commenced against private persons at the instance of assassins; witnesses were brought forward who perjured themselves from fear, while others were deterred from giving their testimony. . . . Factions appeared throughout the cities: they were distinguished by particular modes of wearing the hair, some turning it to the left, and others to the right, or combing it down over the forehead. Many, by way of confirming the allegiance given to any of the parties, killed (their) wives, that they might marry the daughters, sisters, and kindred of those with whom they wished to be in league; others secretly or openly slew the husbands of female blood relations, in order that they might marry them to those whom they had brought into their party. It was common at that time for any one who happened to be taken with any woman's person or fortune, to take her to wife, even against the will of her relations, under the mediation of one of the grandees: nor did it rarely happen that very rich and noble men were compelled to give their daughters, with large dowries, in marriage to most abject outlaws, living by rapine, or to marry their undowried daughters. . . . The greatest criminals constituted tribunals, announced the holding of courts, exercised the judicial functions, called the guilty to their bar, pressed them with witnesses, extorted truth with tortures, finally condemned in solemn form: others, again, who had been thrown into prison by lawful magistrates, after hearing their cause pleaded by a procurator before them, they absolved, and condemned their accusers and judges to pay the *poena talionis.* Immediate punishment followed when the condemned were at hand; if anything was decreed against the absent, no farther delay followed than was necessary for the ministers of crime being sent all about, sometimes with orders written out and duly signed, who really enforced proceedings done in mockery of the law. . . . Many called and designed themselves in writing, the lords and kings of whatever province they chose, not even sparing themselves the solemnities of inaugurations. More than once having torn the sacred furniture from the temple, they transported the most august and most sacred eucharist into woods and lurking-places, and then abused it for the most flagitious and execrable magical purposes. . . . The leniency of Gregory's government made the evil worse. There was an infinite number of cut-throats who easily furnished bribes from their plunder for the gratification of ministers of the governments who connived, or were angry only in show. Security from the public faith was either conceded to those who petitioned for it, or taken away spontaneously: they were placed over fortresses, towns, and soldiers. These, wherever they went, were lauded by the multitude who poured out to behold them, as if they were returning from some splendid action. . . .]

52.

Memorie del pontificato di Sisto V.—[Memorials of the pontificate of Sixtus V.] Altieri XIV., a. iv. fol. 480 leaves.

This copious work is not altogether new and unknown. Tempesti had a copy taken from the archives of the capitol, and speaks of its author as the Anonimo Capitolino.

But with respect to this work Tempesti is most unfair. He copies it in countless places, and in the general judgment at the commencement of his history he denies its being worthy of credit.

It is unquestionably, however, the best work to be found on the history of Sixtus V.

The author had the most important documents within his reach. This is seen in his narrative: he himself too says it, for example, in German affairs: "mi risolvo di narrar minutamente quanto ne trovo in lettere e relationi autentiche."—[I am resolved to narrate minutely as much as I find of them in letters and authentic accounts.]

He has the most exact accounts of the financial arrangements of Sixtus V., and follows them out step by step. Yet here he sets to work very discreetly. "Gli venivano," says he, "proposte inventioni stravagantissime ed horrende, ma tutte sotto faccia molto humana di raccor danari, le quali per esser tali non ardisco di metter in carta tutte, ma sole alcune poche vedute da me nelle lettere originali degl' inventori."—[There were proposed to him, says he, the most extravagant and horrible inventions, but all under a very humane appearance for the collecting of money, which being such I dare not put all of them on paper, but only some few seen by me in the original letters of the inventors.]

He had written a life of Gregory XIII., and on that account might have been taken for Maffei: although otherwise I find no reason for identifying him with that Jesuit.

Only, it is a loss that this work is no more than a fragment. At the very first the earlier events are wanting. They were written, but our MS. at least breaks off in the middle of a subject. After this the measures adopted by the popes in his first years are examined, but the compiler comes down only to the year 1587.

We have less to regret the first desideratum, as we have so much sound information elsewhere on that period, but the wanting part of the later portion of the work is extremely annoying. It is a kind of European history which the compiler communicates from pieces of really authentic information. On the year 1588, the *annus climatericus* of the world, we should for a certainty have found in him much sound information.

Mark how intelligently he expresses himself at the commencement of his work.

"Non ho lasciata via per cui potessi trar lume di vero che non abbia con molta diligenza et arte apertami et indefessamente camminata, come si vedrà nel racconto che faccio delle scritture e relationi delle quali mi son servito nella tessitura di questa istoria. Prego Dio, autore e padre d'ogni verità, sicome mi ha dato ferma volontà di non dir mai bugia per ingannare, così mi conceda lume di non dir mai il falso con essere ingannato."

[There is no way of finding the light of truth which I have not with much diligence and skill opened for myself and indefatigably traversed, as will be seen in the abstract I make of the writings and reports of which I have availed myself in the composition of this history. I pray God, the author and father of all truth, that as he has given me the fixed purpose of falsifying nothing for the purpose of deception, so he will give me light to prevent me from stating what is false, in consequence of being myself deceived.]

A prayer very worthy of an historian.

He concludes at the election of cardinals in 1587, with the words "E le speranze spesso contrarie alle proprie apparenze."—[Hopes are often contrary to proper appearances.]

I have adopted a great many of his notices, after comparing them with those from other quarters; what remain, it would exceed the compass of the work to add here.

53.

Sixti V. Pontificis Maximi vita a Guido Gualterio Sangenesino descripta.—[Life of Sixtus V. Supreme Pontiff, by Guido Gualterio of Sangeno.] MS. of the Altieri Library. VIII. F. 1. 54 leaves.

Tempesti speaks of a Journal of the times of Sixtus V., by an author of this name.[1] It is the same that our biographer has composed; in this work he speaks of the previous one. He had been specially rewarded for his endeavours.

The copy in the Altieri palace is very authentic, and perhaps unique. It has notes in the author's handwriting. "Me puero cum in patria mea Sangeno," &c., [While I was a boy in my native place Sangeno, &c.,] he says in these, so that there is no room for doubt.

He wrote it soon after Sixtus's death, in the first times of Clement VIII., whom he often mentions. He mentions that the news of Henry IV.'s transition to catholicism had just arrived, so that we may assume the year 1593 with certainty as the year of the composition.

The author is particularly worthy of credit. He stood closely connected with the Peretti family. Mary Felicia, daughter of Signora Camilla, was educated in Sangeno; the author's daughter was her intimate friend; he himself was intimately acquainted with Anthony Bosto, the secretary of Montalto's first patron, cardinal Carpi: "summa mihi cum eo necessitudo intercedebat."

We see accordingly that he is well informed chiefly on the earlier circumstances in the life of the pope.

To these he devotes the first part of his writing.

He relates how Fra Felice first became acquainted with Paul IV. At the burning of a Minorite church in the Mark, the consecrated wafer remained intact. This must have been connected with some special circumstances. Enough, a serious consultation was held about it. The cardinals of the Inquisition, the generals of the Orders, and many other prelates were present. Cardinal Carpi brought Montalto along with him, and insisted that this favourite of his also should be allowed to express his opinion. Montalto gave an opinion which to all appeared the best: Carpi went away delighted. "In ejus sententiam ab omnibus itum est. Surgens cardinalis Carpensis dixit: Probe noram quem virum huc adduxissem."—[All agreed to his opinion. Cardinal Carpi rising said: I well knew what sort of person I had brought hither.]

The description given of his Aristotelian endeavours is remarkable.

The edition of Postus, who was in fact a disciple of Montalto, is directly ascribed to the latter by Gualterius.

"Aristotelis Averroisque opera ex pluribus antiquis bibliothecis exemplaria nactus emendavit, expurgavit, aptoque ordine in tomos, ut vocant, undecim digessit. Mediam et magnam Averrois in libros posteriorem expositionem apta distributione Aristotelis textui accommodavit: mediam Averrois expositionem in septem metaphysicorum libros invenit, exposuit, ejusdem Averrois epitomata quaesita et epistolas suis restituit locis, solutionibus contradictionum a doctissimo Zunara editis centum addidit."

[Having collected copies of the works of Aristotle and of Averroes from many ancient libraries, these works he amended, expurgated, and collected in fitting order, into eleven *tomes*, as they call them. The middle and the great Averroes he threw into books, and the posterior exposition he by a fitting distribution accommodated to Aristotle's text. He discovered and set forth the middle exposition of Averroes in seven books of metaphysics, and the epitomata quaesita and epistles of the said Averroes, he restored to their proper places, and added a hundred to the solutions of contradictions published by the most learned Zunara (in which the contradictions between Aristotle and Averroes are reconciled).]

He then delineates the character of his hero. "Magnanimus dignoscebatur, ad iram tamen pronus. Somni potens: cibi parcissimus: in ctio nunquam visus nisi aut de studiis aut de negotiis meditans."—[He was distinguished for magnanimity, yet subject to anger. Having great command of sleep; most sparing of food; never seen when at leisure but thinking about study or business.]

So he proceeds to the conclave. Here he begins to describe the deeds of Sixtus V., according to his various virtues: *Religio, Pietas, Justitia, Fortitudo, Magnificentia, Providentia.*

Strange as this classification is, yet it brings out a number of fine things.

Gualterius eagerly endeavours to defend the pope against the complaints that were brought against him on account of the taxes he imposed. But mark how. "Imprimis ignorare videntur, pontificem Romanum non in nostras solum facultates sed in nos etiam ipsos imperium habere."—[First they seem to forget that the Roman pontiff has power not only

1 The commencement of it was printed in the year 1844, in the Archivio storico Italiano. Appendice, No. 8, p. 345.

over our substance, but even over ourselves.] What would people say at the present day to this right on the part of the state?

He devotes his attention particularly to the buildings erected by Sixtus V., and on these is very interesting.

He describes the state of the old Lateran. "Erat aula permagua quam concilii aulam vocabant" [there was a very large hall, which they called the hall of the council], no doubt on account of the Lateran council, until Leo X.'s time,—"erant porticus tractusque cum sacellis nonnullis et cubiculis ab aula usque ad S. Sabae quam S. Salvatoris capellam vocant. Erant s. scalarum gradus et porticus vetustissima e qua veteres pontifices, qui Lateranum incolebant, populo benedicebant. Aedes illae veteres maxima populi veneratione celebrari solebant, cum in illis non pauca monumenta esse crederentur Hierosolymis usque deportata. Sed fortasse res in superstitionem abierat: itaque Sixtus, justis de causis ut credere par est, servatis quibusdam probatioribus monumentis, sanctis scalis alio translatis, omnia demolitus est."—[There were porticoes and passages with some chapels and dormitories reaching from the hall as far as S. Sabae, which is called the chapel of St. Saviour. There were a flight of holy steps and a most ancient portico from which the old pontiffs who occupied the Lateran, blessed the people. These ancient buildings used to be celebrated with the utmost veneration of the people, seeing that they were supposed to contain not a few monuments brought even from Jerusalem. But the thing had perhaps gone into superstition. Sixtus accordingly, for sound reasons we may fairly believe, after preserving some of the more approved monuments, and having transferred the holy steps to another quarter, demolished the whole.]

We see that the author submits, but he feels the wrong done.

No less worth our notice is the description of St. Peter's, as it existed at this period (1593).

"In Vaticano tholum maximum tholosque minores atque adeo sacellum majus quod majorem capellam vocant aliaque minora sacella et aedificationem totam novi templi Petro Apostolo dicati penitus absolvit. At plumbeis tegere laminis, ornamentaque quae animo destinarat adhibere, templique pavimenta sternere non potuit, morte sublatus. At quae supersunt Clemens VIII. persecuturus perfecturusque creditur, qui tholum ipsum plumbeis jam contexit laminis, sanctissimae crucis vexillum aeneum inauratum imposuit, templi illius pavimentum jam implevit, aequavit, stravit pulcherrime, totique templo aptando et exornando diligentissimam dat operam: cum vero ex Michaelis Angeli forma erit absolutum, antiquitatem omnem cito superabit."

[In the Vatican he completely finished the great dome and smaller domes, and also the larger temple which they call the larger chapel, and other smaller temples, and the entire building of the new temple dedicated to the apostle Peter. But death prevented his covering them with leads, and from adding the ornaments he had intended, and from laying the pavements of the temple. But what things are left, it is believed that Clement VIII. will follow out and perfect, who has already covered the dome with leads, has set up the standard of holy cross in gilt brass, has put in, levelled, and beautifully laid the pavement of that temple, and is giving his utmost endeavours to make the whole fitting and beautiful: when indeed it is finished off in the form prescribed by Michael Angelo, it will directly surpass all antiquity.]

We perceive that still people never contemplated anything but the carrying out of the plan of Michael Angelo, and it seems as if all had been by that time actually finished (penitus absolvit).

We have already had a remarkable notice with respect to the Colossuses. I will add here something farther.

The author is speaking of the piazza on the Quirinal. He says of the methods adapted for its beautification by Sixtus V.: "Ornavit perenni fonte et marmoreis Praxitelis et Phidiae equis, quos vetustate cum eorum rectoribus deformatos una cum basi marmorea in pristinam formam concinnavit et e vetere sede ante Constantini thermas in alteram areae partem prope S. Pauli monachorum aedes transtulit."—[He ornamented it with the perennial fountains and marble horses of Praxiteles and Phidias, which as well as the men that hold them, being in a bad condition from their great age, together with their marble pedestal, he repaired according to their old form, and transferred them from their old site before the baths of Constantine, into another part of the area near the buildings of the monks of St. Paul.] In old drawings, too, one of which is copied in Meier (see Gesch. der Kunst II. 229, and accompanying plates, Tafel XV.), the Colossuses appear in a very mutilated state: much as they are described by our Venetians (see p. 473). Evidently they first received their present form under Sixtus V.

54.

Galesini Vita Sixti V.—[Galesini's Life of Sixtus V.] Vatican, 5438. (122 leaves.)

A manuscript without any proper title, and with the following dedication on the first leaf:—

"Sanctissimo patri Sixto V., pontifici maximo, vigilantissimo ecclesiae Dei pastori, providentissimo principi, sapientissimo universae reipublicae christianae moderatori et rectori, commentarium hoc de vita rebusque ab eo in singulos annos diesque publice et

[To the most holy father Sixtus V., supreme pontiff, most vigilant pastor of the Church of God, most prudent prince, most wise moderator and rector of the universal Christian republic, this commentary on the life and achievements publicly and pontifi-

pontificie actis gestisque distributum ac luculenter scriptum Petrus Galesinus magno et summo benignissimoque patrono singularis in illum pietatis atque observantiae ergo in perpetuum dicavit."

cally done and performed by him, from year to year and day to day, after having arranged and clearly written it, Peter Galasini has dedicated to his great, supreme, and most benignant patron, as a perpetual memorial of his singular dutifulness and respect for him.]

These words intimate at once that here we have rather a panegyric than a biography.

The author considers it remarkable that Sixtus V. should have beeen the fourth child born of his parents, "sol enim quarto die creatus est;" [for the sun was created on the fourth day;] and that he was elected (pope) on the day on which Rome was founded.

The account given of the pope's earlier years is very fragmentary. Here too it is proved that a gifted youth usually thrives best in poverty, and under severe discipline. In the family of the Peretti, the mother was severe: "Matris metu, cum aliquid mali se commemisse videret, in omnes partes corporis se excitavit."—[From dread of his mother he trembled all over, on seeing that he had anyhow deserved it.]

Labours in the country. "Opus manu faciebat, ita ut vel hortos coleret, vel arbores sereret, aut aliqua ratione instar diligentissimi agricolae, egregiae insitionis opera consereret, interlocaret."—[He set his hands to work in the cultivation of gardens or the sowing of trees, or after any other way like a most diligent husbandman, in placing them together, or intermingling them by a process of most careful grafting.]

In the proceedings of the popedom, we are particularly struck with that stricter religious tendency to which Sixtus V. devoted himself; for example, in buildings :—

"Ut urbis opera et idolatriae simulacra, inanis et falsae gloriolae insanarumque superstitionum monumenta, adhuc in urbe jam diu nimis inveterata quadam rerum olim Romanarum a Christiano cultu abhorrentium curiositate, . . . ad Christianae pietatis ornamentum pertraheret."

[That he might bring to the adornment of Christian piety the works of the city and the images of idolatry, monuments of an empty and false pretence to glory, and of insane superstitions, still too much rooted in the city, from a certain curiosity with respect to Roman things of days gone by, and abhorrent from Christian worship.]

The origin of the Lateran palace:—

"Pontifex cum vix cubiculum inveniret quo se reciperet, continuo jussit aedes pontificia majestate dignas in Laterano extrui: valde enim absurdum absonumque duxit basilicam Lateranensem, omnium ecclesiarum matrem, proprium pontificis Romani episcopatum, aedes non habere quae cum tanta episcopatus dignitate convenirent."

[The pontiff, when he could hardly find a place to sleep in, forthwith ordered buildings worthy of the pontifical dignity to be reared in the Lateran; for he thought it very absurd and incongruous, that the Lateran basilic—the mother of all the churches, the peculiar bishopric of the Roman pontiff—should not have buildings corresponding to so much episcopal dignity.]

In general, he thinks Rome very pious :—

"Dat magna pietatis et integritatis indicia. Clericorum disciplina fere est ad pristinos sanctissimos mores restituta, ratio divini cultus administratioque sacrarum aedium ad probatum veterem morem plane perducta. . . . Ubique in ipsis ecclesiis genuflexiones: ubique in omni fere urbis regione fideles qui sacra illa sexta feria (Good-Friday) infinitis verberibus miserandum in modum propria terga ita lacerabant ut sanguis in terram usque defluxerit."

[It gives great proofs of piety and integrity. The discipline of the clergy has been almost brought back to the most holy morals of the ancient times, the method of divine worship, and the administration of the sacred edifices, have evidently been restored to the approved old model. . . . Everywhere, in the very churches, you see genuflexions: everywhere, in almost all quarters of the city, there are faithful who, on Good-Friday, so lacerated their own backs with infinite stripes, in a miserable manner, that the blood flowed to the very ground.]

55.

Vita Sixti V. anonyma. [Anonymous Life of Sixtus V.] Vatic. n. 5563.

This consists of only a few leaves on the youthful years of Sixtus V. His name, Felix, is said to have owed its origin to a dream that his father had had.

56.

Relatione al Papa Sisto V. [Report to Pope Sixtus V.] 41 leaves.

From a member of the Curia, who did not frequent the palace, and who knew only as much as everybody else did: originally addressed to a friend who wanted to be informed with respect to the doings of Sixtus V., and afterwards to the pope himself.

In writings such as that before us, written by mediocre people who only occasionally step out from the common crowd, it is worth while to observe what effect a government exercises in general on the mass of the public.

In that before us, which is written throughout in the stricter religious tone which began to predominate towards the close of the sixteenth century, we see first of all what a powerful impression was produced by the conversion of heathen into Christian monuments.

"Le croci santissime in cima delle guglie e le statue delli prencipi apostolici sopra le colonne scancellano la memoria delle antiche idolatrie, . . . come anco che la croce posta in mano della statua sopra la torre di Campidoglio significante Roma ci mostra che hoggi Roma, cioè il papa, non opra la spada per soggiogare il mondo a guisa d' infideli imperatori Romani ma la croce per salutifero giorno dell' universo."

[The most holy crosses on the summits of the obelisks, and the statues of the chief apostles on the columns, obliterate the recollection of the old idolatries, . . . as also the cross placed in the hand of the statue above the tower of Campidoglio, as an emblem of Rome, show to us that now-a-days Rome—that is, the pope—employs not the sword for the subjection of the world, like the infidel Roman emperors, but the cross for the day of salvation to the universe.]

It is striking to see how popular these ideas of spiritual supremacy were, even to people of inferior consideration. The author further denies that the pope, as some say, in order to appear wise—"per esser savione"—thought of making his treasure useful in the way of procuring him consideration among the princes; of this he had no need; his idea rather was, that he would reward obedient princes and punish the refractory. "Col tesoro castigherà i prencipi ribelli di santa chiesa et ajuterà i prencipi obbedienti nelle imprese cattoliche."—[With his treasure he will chastise the rebellious princes of the holy church, and assist the obedient princes in their catholic enterprises.] He lauds Sixtus for having excommunicated Henry IV. "Subito fatto papa ricorse a Dio per ajuto, e poi privò del regno di Navarra quello scellerato re eretico, . . . e con queste armi spirituali principalmente i papi hanno disfatti e fatti imperatori e re."—[Immediately on being made pope, he had recourse to God for aid, and then deprived of the kingdom of Navarre that wicked heretical king, ... and with these spiritual arms chiefly the popes have made and unmade emperors and kings.] That priests and monks are to be considered as a militia belonging to the pope, is here openly maintained even on the Roman catholic side:

"Il papa tiene grossi presidii in tutti regni, che sono frati monaci e preti, in tanto numero e così bene stipendiati e provisti in tempo di pace e di guerra. . . . Nelle cose della religione vuole esser patrone solo et assoluto, sicome Dio vuole: . . . e beati quei populi che avranno prencipi obbedientissimi. . . . Se i prencipi manterranno il pensiero di trattar le cose delli stati prima con li sacerdoti che con i lor consiglieri secolari, credami che manterranno i sudditi obbedienti e fedeli."

[The pope keeps large garrisons in all kingdoms, consisting of friars, monks, and priests, so numerous and so well paid and provided for in peace as well as war. . . . In religious matters he desires to be sole and absolute master, as God would have it: . . . and blessed are those peoples that have the most obedient princes. . . . Would princes but think of treating of matters of state with the priests before they do so with their secular councillors, believe me they would keep their subjects obedient and faithful.]

All the tenets of politico-ecclesiastico doctrine here come out in a popular shape. But what was this secular power on the part of the pope, compared with the authority he possesses of raising a poor servant of God to be a saint? Those canonizations, which Sixtus V. had renewed, our author cannot sufficiently commend:

"A maggior gloria di Dio, ha dedicato alcuni giorni festivi a santi che non erano nel calendario, sì per dare occasioni a' christiani di spendere tanto più tempo in honor di Dio per salute delle anime loro con l'intercessione de' santi astenendosi dell' opere servili, sì perche siano onorati gli amici di Dio."

[For the greater glory of God, he has dedicated some festival days to saints that were not in the calendar, partly to give to Christians opportunities of spending so much the more time in honour of God for the salvation of their souls, with the intercessions of saints and abstinence from servile employments, partly that honour may be done to the servants of God.]

Among other reasons, he adduces also the following:—

"Per far vedere gli infedeli e falsi christiani che solo i veri servi di Christo salvatore fanno camminare i zoppi, parlare i muti, vedere i ciechi, e resuscitare i morti."

[In order to make the infidels and false Christians see that only the true servants of Christ the Saviour can make the lame walk, the dumb speak, the blind see, and raise the dead to life again.]

57.

Relatione presentata nell' ecc^{mo} collegio dal cl^{mo} Signor Lorenzo Priuli, ritornato di Roma, 1586, 2 Luglio.—[Report presented in the most excellent college by the most illustrious Lord Lorenzo Priuli, on his return from Rome, 2d July, 1586.]

From the Roman let us pass to the Venetian memorials.

Lorenzo Priuli lived during the last years of Gregory XIII. and the first of Sixtus V.; he is full on the subject of the contrast between them.

We must not allow ourselves at once to be carried away with this: the first times of a pope generally make a better impression than the last. Whether it be that with advancing years there is necessarily a decline in the talent for government, or because in every man there is gradually found much that people could willingly dispense with.

But Priuli is not unfair. He considers that even Gregory was very useful to the church.

"Nella bontà della vita, nel procurare il culto ecclesiastico, l'osservanza del concilio, la residenza dei vescovi, nell' eccellenza della dottrina, l'uno legale l'altro teologicale, si possono dire assai simili."

[In the goodness of his life, in the attention paid to church worship, the keeping of the council, the residence of the bishops, in the excellency of learning, the one legal, the other theological, they might be said to be much alike.]

He praises God for having given his church such distinguished chiefs.

We observe that the foreign ambassadors also were inspired with the same tone of sentiment that prevailed at court.

Priuli thinks the choice of Sixtus V. (as pope) altogether wonderful, the immediate work of the Holy Ghost. He reminds his native city that it had owed its eminent position to being on a good understanding with the popes: he advises, above all things, the keeping up of the same.

58.

Relatione del cl^{mo} sig^{r} Giov. Gritti ritornato ambasciatore da Roma anno 1589.—[Report of the most illustrious signor Giov. Gritti, on his return as ambassador from Rome, in the year 1589.]

In the Venetian archives we find only a defective copy.

I tried with great eagerness to find another, which I had seen at the Ambrosian library at Milan, but that copy contained just as much, and not a word more than the other.

This is so much the more to be regretted, as the author goes most systematically to work. He is first to treat of the states of the church; then of the person of the pope, whose great admirer he announces himself; third, of the objects he aimed at; and lastly, of the cardinals and the court.

Of the first part only there is now a small part extant. The manuscript breaks off just where the author is about to show how the revenues of Sixtus had increased. Nevertheless I cannot doubt that the work was completed. What we have is at least no sketch, but part of an elaborate work.

But still it is curious that, even in the archives, there is only a defective copy.

59.

Relatione di Roma dell' ambasciatore Badoer K^{r} relata in senato anno 1589.—[Report on Rome, from the ambassador Badoer, knight, given in the senate in 1589.]

This report is wanting in the Venetian archives. It is to be found in the collection of the Orsini family; but it, too, is only fragmentary.

There are eight leaves which contain only a few notices in reference to the rural districts.

Badoer remarks that Venice estranged its partisans in the Mark by either delivering too many of them up to the pope, or causing them to be executed at his request.

The increase of the trade of Ancona had been spoken of, yet the ambassador had no fears that it would prove prejudicial to the Venetians.

"Essendo state imposte allora (bei seiner hinreise) da Sisto V. doi per cento sopra tutte le mercantie, le quali a querelle d' Anconitani furono poi levate, non era gionta in 14 mesi alcuna nave in quel porto."

[Imposts being then (at the time of his journey) laid by Sixtus V. at the rate of two per cent. on all merchandise, which were afterwards taken off on the complaints of the Ancona people, in the space of 14 months no vessel had arrived at that port.]

We see that the two imposts of Gregory and Sixtus V., although they were taken off again, yet owing to the uncertainty of realizing profits, into which the merchants saw themselves suddenly thrown, powerfully contributed to the decline of the trade of Ancona. Most business was done at that time in the articles of camlet and furs, yet the Jews found no proper opportunity for barter in cloth or other wares. The customs were now farmed at 14,000 scudi, and even this was never realized.

Badoer, moreover, remarks, that the example of Spain should be imitated, and that the friends they might have in the Mark should be kept in pay. He breaks off just as he is about to name those friends.

60

Dispacci Veneti—[Venetian Despatches] 1573-1590.

Nobody would believe that, with such abundance of monuments, a deficiency should be felt notwithstanding. Yet this is almost the case here. We see what an evil star presided over the relations with Venice: the Roman written memorials throw light only on the earlier times of this pontificate with any fulness; I should have found myself thrown back at last upon Tempesti for this last year—one of the most important epochs—had not the despatches of the Venetian ambassadors come to my assistance.

I had already excerpted at Vienna the whole series of Venetian despatches from 1573 to

1590, preserved in the archives there, partly in authentic copies, partly in rubricatories made for the use of the state.

There is indeed a certain difficulty in making ourselves masters of the former. Sometimes the despatches for a single month will present 100 leaves: they have been damaged with salt water in coming by sea; they break on being opened; and the breath is affected with a nauseous dust. The rubricatories are more easily handled. They have been protected with covers; and the work of condensation facilitates the separation of matters of importance from the thousand insignificant affairs which two Italian states may have had with each other, and which are quite unworthy of being reproduced in history.

Here now we find the intelligence transmitted by Paul Tiepoli to 1576, by Anthony Tiepoli to 1578, by Zuanne Correr to 1581, Lunardo Donato to 1583, Lorenzo Priuli to 1586, Zuanne Gritti to 1589, Alberto Badoer to 1591.

Among these regular ambassadors there appear now and then extraordinary ones. Zuanne Seranzo from October 1581 to February 1582, who was deputed about the dissensions on the subject of the patriarchate of Aquileja; the congratulatory embassy of the year 1585, sent to Sixtus V., which was composed of M. Ant. Barbaro, Giacomo Foscarini, Marino Grimani, and Lunardo Donato, and had its general correspondence reduced to writing by the secretary Padavino; finally, Lunardo Donato, who was sent anew about the political complications of the year 1589. The despatches of the last are by far the most important: here the relation between the republic and the pope was even of consequence in the history of the world; fortunately, too, they are to be found in all their extent under the title, "Registro delle lettere dell' ill^mo^ signor Lunardo Donato K^r^ ambasciatore straordinario al sommo pontefice: comincia a 13 Ottobre 1589 e finisce a 19 Decembre 1589."—[Register of the letters of the most illustrious signor Lunardo Donato, knight, ambassador extraordinary to the supreme pontiff: it commences at 13th October, 1589, and ends at 19th December, 1589.]

And even therewithal we still do not know the whole of the collective ambassadorial procedure. There is also a special secret correspondence of the ambassador's with the Council of Ten, which is found very beautifully written on parchment: the first volume, under the title of "Libro primo da Roma, secreto del consiglio di X., sotto il serenissimo D. Aluise Mocenigo inclito duca di Venetia."—[First book from Rome, secret of the Council of Ten, under the most serene D. Aluise Mocenigo, renowned duke of Venice]: the subsequent volumes have corresponding titles.

I am quite aware of what may be urged against making use of what is written by ambassadors. It is true that their writings are composed under the impression of the moment; that they are seldom quite impartial, often bear upon certain special objects, and are in no wise to be ever at once adopted. But what memorials, what written documents are there on which we can unhesitatingly bestow full faith? In all quarters the *granum salis* is indispensable. At all events, the ambassadors are contemporary witnesses; they are in the country and at the spot, they are pledged to observe what is passing, and they must indeed be utterly without talent, if their reports, read to any extent, do not communicate the feeling of the present, almost as if we were immediately perceiving it.

Now our Venetians were men of much experience and ability. I find these documents instructive in the highest degree.

But whither would it lead, were I to give extracts here, too, from this long series of volumes?

I shall surely be allowed to abide by my rule of avoiding extracts from despatches in this appendix. A longer consecutive series would be necessary in any measure to give an idea of the contents.

On the other hand I will yet touch upon two important missions that fall within the times of Sixtus V.

61.

Relatione all' ill^mo^ e rev^mo^ cardinale Rusticucci seg^rio^ di N. Sig^re^ papa Sisto V. delle cose di Polonia intorno alla religione e delle azioni del cardinale Bolognetto in quattro anni ch' egli è stato nuntio in quella provincia, divisa in due parti: nella prima si tratta de' danni che fanno le eresie in tutto quel regno, del termine in che si trova il misero stato ecclesiastico, e delle difficoltà e speranze che si possono avere intorno a rimedii: nella seconda si narrano li modi tenuti dal cardinale Bolognetto per superare quelle difficoltà, et il profitto che fece, et il suo negoziare in tutto il tempo della sua nuntiatura: di Horatio Spannocchj, già seg^rio^ del detto sig^re^ card^le^ Bolognetto.—[Report to the most illustrious and most rev. cardinal Rusticucci, secretary to our lord pope Sixtus V., about the affairs of Poland relating to religion, and about the proceedings of cardinal Bolognetto during the four years that he was nuncio in that province, divided into two parts: the first treats of the losses that heresies cause in the whole of that kingdom, of the extremity in which the wretched ecclesiastical state is placed there, and of the difficulties and the hopes that may be entertained as respects remedies; the second relates the methods adopted by cardinal Bolognetto for overcoming those difficulties, and the good he did, and his management of his nuncioship during all that time: by Horatio Spannocchi, secretary at the time to the said lord cardinal Bolognetto.]

Bolognetto's secretary, Spannocchi, who had been with him in Poland, took advantage of the quiet of a winter's residence at Bologna, to compose this report, which not only proves very copious, but highly instructive also.

He first describes the remarkable extension of protestantism in Poland: "non lasciando pure una minima città o castello libero" [not indeed leaving the smallest town or castle free]. This phenomenon he traces, as may be expected, mainly to secular motives: he maintains that the nobles imposed fines on their vassals when they did not attend the protestant churches.

Moreover, here too, as well as in other parts of Europe, a state of indifference had been gaining admission. "La differenza d'esser cattolico o di altra setta si piglia in burla o in riso, come cosa di pochissima importanza."—[The difference between being a catholic or of the other sect becomes a matter of jest or laughter, as a thing of the very least importance.]

The Germans who had settled even in the smallest places, and had married there, had a large share in the spread of protestant doctrine: nevertheless even more dangerous still did the author consider those Italians who brought with them the opinion that, in Italy, under the cloak of catholicism, people doubted even the immortality of the soul: people only waited for an opportunity of declaring themselves wholly against the pope.

He now describes the state of the clergy amid these circumstances.

"Infiniti de' poveri ecclesiastici si trovano privi degli alimenti, sì perche i padroni delle ville, eretici per il più, se non tutti, hanno occupato le possessioni ed altri beni delle chiese o per ampliarne il proprio patrimonio o per gratificarne ministri delle lor sette ovvero per alienarne in varj modi a persone profane, sì ancora perche negano di pagar le decime, quantunque siano loro dovute, oltre alle leggi divine e canoniche, anco per constituzione particolare di quel regno. Onde i miseri preti in molti luoghi non avendo con che sostentarsi lasciavano le chiese in abbandono. La terza è rispetto alla giurisdizione ecclesiastica, la quale insieme con i privilegj del clero è andata mancando, che oggidì altro non si fa di differenza tra' beni sottoposti alle chiese o monasterj e gli altri di persone profane, le citazioni e sentenze per niente. . . . Io medesimo ho udito da principalissimi senatori che vogliono lasciarsi tagliare più presto a pezzi che acconsentire a legge alcuna per la quale si debbano pagar le decime a qualsivoglia cattolico come cosa debita. Fu costituito ne' comizj già sei anni sono per pubblico decreto che nessuno potesse esser gravato a pagar le medesime decime da qualsivoglia tribunale nè ecclesiastico nè secolare. Tuttavia perche ne' prossimi comizj per varj impedimenti non si fece detta composizione, negano sempre di pagare, nè vogliono i capitani de' luoghi eseguire alcuna sentenza sopra dette decime."

[Infinite numbers of poor ecclesiastics are in want of food, partly because the lords of the town, heretics for the most part, if not all of them, have seized on the possessions and other property of the church, either for the purpose of augmenting their own patrimony, or of gratifying the ministers of their sect, or of alienating them in various ways to profane persons, partly, moreover, because payment of tithes is refused, although due by them not only by divine and canonical laws, but further by the particular constitution of that kingdom. Whence the wretched priests, not having in many places wherewithal to live, allow the churches to be forsaken. The third is respect for ecclesiastical jurisdiction, which, together with the privileges of the clergy, has been passing into neglect, so that, now-a-days, there is no other difference put between goods belonging to the churches and monasteries and others belonging to profane persons, than that the citations and sentences go for nothing. . . I myself have heard from the very chiefest senators that they would rather allow themselves to be cut to pieces than consent to any law by which they should be obliged to pay tithes to any catholic whatsoever as a debt. It was settled in the comitia held six years ago, by a public decree, that no one should be sequestered for payment of these tithes by any court whatever, ecclesiastical or secular. Nevertheless, because at the next following comitia, the said composition, owing to various obstacles, was not made, they always refuse payment, and the local magistrates have no wish to follow out any sentence upon the said tithes.]

Now for a nuncio it was a very difficult task to effect a change. It would have been impossible to introduce the Inquisition, or even stricter laws respecting marriage. The name of the pope was already detested; the clergy held themselves bound to uphold the interests of the country against Rome; the king only could be reckoned upon.

The palatine Radziwill had shown the king a call to arms against the Turks, composed by a Zwinglian. The nation was therein recommended to reform itself in the first place, and to put away the images, the worship paid to which the author considered to be idolatry. The king would not allow this reasoning to pass. With his own hands he wrote as follows on the margin:

"Praestat hoc omittere quam falso imputare et orationem monitoriam religionis antiquissimae sugillatione infamem reddere. O utinam faciant novae sectae nos tam diuturna pace florentes atque fecit sancta religio catholica veros secutores suos."

[Better omit this, than make false charges, and render the admonitory address infamous by the slander of the most ancient religion. Oh, how I wish the new sects would make us flourish with as lasting a peace as the holy catholic religion has made its true followers.]

A declaration on which the author of this report builds high expectations.

He now passes to a discussion of Bolognetto's plans, which he reduces to seven heads:

1. The restoration of the papal authority;
2. The persecution of heretics;

3. The reform of the clergy: "modi per moderare la licentiosa vita di sacerdoti scandalosi" [methods for restraining the licentious life of scandalous priests];
4. The establishment of public worship;
5. Union of the clergy;
6. Defence of their rights;
7. Measures bearing on the Christian commonwealth in general.

I have already given a general account of Bolognetto's efficiency according to these notices. By way of example I may give the following more detailed account of his influence on the English negotiation.

"La reina d' Inghilterra domandava al re di Polonia un' indulto per i suoi mercanti Inglesi di poter portar le loro mercanzie e vendere per tutto il regno liberamente, dove ora non possono venderle se non i mercanti del regno in Danzica, domandando insieme che fosse loro concesso aprire un fondaco pubblico in Torogno, ch' è il più celebre porto della Prussia dopo quello di Danzica, e di là poi portar le loro mercanzie eglino stessi a tutte le fiere che si fanno per la Polonia, dove non possono portare ordinariamente se non mercanti del paese, che per il più sono o Tedeschi o Pruteni o Italiani. Domandava dunque con quest' occasione quella pretesa reina che nel decreto di tal concessione si esprimesse, che a questi suoi mercanti non potesse mai esser fatta molestia per conto di religione, ma che potessero esercitarla liberamente a modo loro ovunque andassero per il regno. Piaceva questo partito universalmente a tutta la nobiltà Polacca: solo i Danzicani ostavano gagliardamente, mostrando che da questo indulto saria seguito l' ultimo danno al porto loro, tanto celebre e tanto famoso per tutto il mondo, e che la speranza del minor prezzo era fallace, massimamente perche i mercanti forastieri quando fossero stati in possesso di poter vendere ad arbitrio loro e poter servar la mercanzia loro lungo tempo nelle mani, l' avrebbon venduta molto più cara di quello che la vendono oggi i mercanti del paese. Tuttavia il contraccambio che offeriva la regina a' mercanti di Polonia, di poter fare lo stesso loro in Inghilterra, pareva che già havesse persuaso il re a concedere tutto quello che domandava. Il che non prima venne agli orecchj del Bolognetto, che andò a trovare S. M^{ta}, e con efficacissime ragioni le mostrò quanto esorbitante cosa sarebbe stata che avesse concesso per publico decreto una tanto obbrobriosa setta, e come non senza nascosto inganno e speranza d' importantissime conseguenze quella scellerata donna voleva che si dichiarasse così per decreto potersi esercitar la setta Anglicana in quel regno, dove tutto il mondo pur troppo sa che si permetta il credere in materia di religione quel che piace a chi si sia: con questa ed altre efficacissime ragioni il re Stefano rimase talmente persuaso che promesse non voler mai far menzione alcuna di religione in qualunque accordo avesse fatto con quella regina o suoi mercanti."

[The queen of England asked the king of Poland for an indulgence for her English merchants, enabling them to take and to sell their wares freely throughout the whole kingdom, where at present none can sell them but the merchants of the kingdom in Dantzick, asking at the same time that it might be conceded to them to open a public warehouse in Torogno, which is the most celebrated port of Prussia, next to that of Dantzick, and then from thence to take their merchandise themselves to all the public fairs that are held throughout Poland, to which ordinarily none but the traders of the country can take them, who for the most part are either Pruteni (?) or Italians.[1] That pretended queen then asked on this occasion that in the decree bearing such a concession, it should be laid down that no molestation should ever be given to these merchants on the score of religion, but that they should have it in their power to exercise it freely in their own way wherever they might go throughout the kingdom. This proposed measure gave universal satisfaction to all the Polish nobility: only the Dantzickers vigorously opposed it, showing that such an indulgence would be followed by the utmost loss to their port, so celebrated and famous throughout the world, and that the hope of lower prices would prove fallacious, chiefly because the foreign merchants on being put in possession of a power to sell when they chose and to keep their wares a long while in their own hands, would have them sold at much higher prices than the merchants of the country now sell them at. Nevertheless the reciprocity offered by the queen to the merchants of Poland of their being empowered to do the same thing in England, seems to have at once persuaded the king to yield all that she asked. Which no sooner came to the ears of Bolognetto than he went to his Majesty, and with most effectual reasons demonstrated to him what an exorbitant thing it would have been to acknowledge by so public a decree so opprobrious a sect, and how not without some secret trick and hope of important consequences that wicked woman wished that it should thus be declared by a decree that the Anglican sect might employ themselves in that kingdom, where all the world but too well knew that it was permitted to believe in matters of religion whatever a man pleased: with this and other most efficacious reasons king Stephen rested so satisfied as to promise never to make any mention of religion in any agreement that might be made with that queen or her merchants.]

It will be seen that this report comprises, moreover, purely political notices.

1 In the 2d edition of Pr. Ranke's 3d vol., it runs "o Tedeschi, o Pruteni, o Italiani."—[Germans, or Prutini, or Italians.]—Tr.

At the close the author enters into these still more particularly.

He considers Poland as divided into manifold factions: dissensions even betwixt the different provinces, and then betwixt the clergy and the laity of the same provinces: betwixt the senators and provincial deputies: betwixt the old high nobility and the inferior nobles.

The high-chancellor Zamoisky appears extremely powerful; on him depended all appointments to places; particularly after a vice-chancellor and a secretary of the king's were wholly in his interest; "da che è stato fatto il Baranosky vicecancelliere et il Tolisky segretario del re, persone poco fa incognite."—[since Baranosky has been made vice-chancellor and Tolisky secretary of the king, persons shortly before unknown.]

62.

Discorso del molto illustre e rev^mo mons^r Minuccio Minucci sopra il modo di restituire la religione cattolica in Alemagna, 1588.—[Discourse of the very illustrious and most Rev. monsignor Minuccio Minucci, on the means of restoring the catholic religion in Germany, 1588.]

A very important document, of which I have largely availed myself, particularly I. p. 473.

Minucci served long under Gregory in Germany: he appears often enough in Maffei: here he endeavours minutely to distinguish the state of things, as he says, in order that people from Rome may learn to refuse dangerous medicine to the patients.

He complains all along that so little was done on the Roman catholic side to gain over the protestant princes; thereupon he investigates (for his mission was in the time of keen and still undecided struggle,) the attacks of protestants upon Roman catholicism: "ho pensato di raccontare li pratiche che muovono gli heretici ogni dì per far seccare o svellere tutta la radice del cattolicismo:" [I have thought that I would speak of the devices daily set agoing by the heretics for the wearing out or the utter extirpation of catholicism:] finally, the means by which they might be opposed in doing so.

He shows himself uncommonly well versed in German affairs: yet he cannot suppress a certain feeling of amazement, on comparing the state of matters as they even now were, with the tranquillity and submission to law in Italy and in Spain. We find mention made also of the restless movements of Casimir of the Palatinate. Mark what amazement they produced in a foreigner.

"Il Casimiro dopo aver sprezzata l'autorità dell' imperatore in mille cose, ma principalmente in abbruciare le munitioni presso Spira che si conducevano in Fiandra con salvocondotto imperiale, dopo aver offeso il re di Spagna non solo con quell' atto, ma anco con tanti ajuti dati a ribelli suoi di Fiandra e con l'haver concesso spatio alli medesimi ribelli Fiamenghi per edificare una città (Franchendal) nelli stati suoi, con l'haver portate tante ruine in Francia, tante desolationi in Lorena hor in propria persona, hora mandando genti sue, con l'haver fatto affronto notabile all' arciduca Ferdinando impedendo il card^l suo figliuolo con minaccie e con viva forza nel camino di Colonia, con l'istesso dichiarato nemico alla casa di Baviera, e passato in propria persona contra l'elettore di Colonia, pur se ne sta sicuro in un stato aperto nel mezzo di quelli c'hanno ricevute da lui tante ingiurie: nè ha fortezze o militia che li dia confidenza nè amici o parenti che siano per soccorrerlo e difenderlo, ma gode frutto della troppa pazienza de' cattolici, che li potriano d'improviso et a mano salva portare altre tante ruine quante egli ha tante volte causate nelli stati d'altri, purche si risolvessero et havessero cuor di farlo."

[Casimir after having contemned the emperor's authority in a thousand things, but chiefly in burning the munitions near Spires, that were on their way to Flanders under the imperial safe-conduct, after having offended the king of Spain not only by that act, but further by sending so many aids to his rebellious subjects of Flanders, and by having granted space to the said rebellious Flemings for building a town (Franchendal) in his states, by having carried so many ruins into France, and so many desolations in Lorraine, sometimes in his own person, sometimes by employing his people for the purpose; by having put a marked affront on the archduke Ferdinand, stopping his son the cardinal by threats and actual violence on his way to Cologne; by his being himself a declared enemy of the house of Bavaria, and having passed in his own person against the elector of Cologne, occupied by no means a secure position in an open state in the midst of those who had received so many insults from him: nor had he fortresses or a soldiery which might give him confidence, nor friends or relations who might be ready to succour and defend him, but enjoyed the benefit of the excessive patience of the catholics, who might unawares and without risk bring upon him as many losses as he had so often caused to the states of others, should they resolve and have the courage to do so.]

SECTION FIFTH.

SECOND EPOCH OF THE RESTORATION OF THE CHURCH.

63.

CONCLAVES.

I AM not afraid of being found fault with for not registering at this place every fugitive piece, every less important treatise, that has fallen in my way, in manuscript, in the course of the studies of various kinds that belong to this subject. I seem rather to have already done too much. Many a reader, who has given me his attention thus far, would, besides, feel disgust at a shapeless medley of various tongues; and yet it would not be advisable to give the original communications in German: they would thus lose in point of usefulness and authenticity. On that very account, however, I dare not proceed at once profusely to extend my collectanea in this collection.

Of the conclaves, for example, on which a great many manuscripts are extant, I will make merely a summary mention.

After each election of a pope, especially from the second half of the sixteenth century to the commencement of the 18th, there appeared a report upon it: it is true, never but in manuscript; yet still in such a way that it obtained a wide circulation, and even often called forth counter-statements. These reports are occasionally drawn up by cardinals; ordinarily, however, by their secretaries, who remained in the conclaves under the title of conclavists, and, in the interests of their masters, made it a matter of special concern to watch the course of intrigues, which the conduct required by a respect for their dignity, rendered it not so easy for themselves to do. At times, however, other persons likewise took up the pen.

"Con quella maggior diligenza che ho potuto," says the author of Gregory XIII.'s conclave, "ho raccolto così dalli signori conclavisti come da cardinali che sono stati partecipi del negotio, tutto l'ordine e la verità di questo conclave."

[With the utmost diligence of which I was capable, I have collected both from the lords who formed the conclave, and from cardinals who had had a share in the business, the whole order and truth of that conclave.]

We see that he was not himself present. Sometimes it is diaries that fall in our way, sometimes letters, sometimes, too, elaborate narratives. Each is an independent memoir; yet the generally known formalities are occasionally repeated. They differ much, of course, in value. Sometimes the whole flies off in an inconceivable detail—sometimes, but seldom, we rise to a real view of the prevailing element—yet, fundamentally, we always find information, if we can but bear up against lassitude and fatigue.

One may form some idea of the number of extant works of this sort, from the Marsand catalogue of the Paris library. They have found their way, too, into Germany. The 33d, 35th, and several other volumes of our *Informations,* contain copies in rich abundance. In Joh. Gottf. Geissler's programme of the Bibliotheca Milichiana IV., Gorlitz, 1767, we find the conclaves put down that appear in the 32d, 33d, and 34th codex of the collection. The most copious list that I know of is to be met with in Novaes' "Introduzione alle vite de' sommi pontefici, 1822, I. p. 272." He had access to the library of the Jesuits, in which a tolerably full collection of these works was extant.

It lies in the nature of the case that they very soon, and in another way, to a certain extent at least, reached the public. First of all, they were adopted into the histories of the popes. The conclave of pope Pius V., though not in all that it comprises, yet in its commencement and conclusion, has been transferred into Panvinius's history. Cicarella has in a great measure translated the conclaves of Gregory XIII. and Sixtus V.—the last with all the comments that appear in the Italian. The passage which Schröckh, N. Kirchengeschichte III., 288, quotes as from Cicarella, is taken verbatim from the conclave. De Thou likewise has given a place to these statements, yet, as appears on a closer comparison, from Cicarella, not from the original (lib. 82, p. 27). In the Tesoro politico this conclave is no less adopted, but very incompletely, and in a very hastily made excerpt.

Gradually, however—first indeed in the seventeenth century—people thought of making collections of these conclaves. The first printed collection bears the title, "Conclavi de' pontefici Romani quali si sono potuto trovare fin a questo giorno. 1667."—[Conclaves of the Roman pontiffs, such as could be found to this day. 1667.] It begins with Clement V,. but has one blank interval till Urban VI., and another till Nicolas V.; from thence first, it proceeds regularly to Alexander VII. In publishing it, what was contemplated, ostensibly at least, was to show by example, how little human wisdom availed against the leading of Heaven: "Si tocca con mano che le negotiationi più secrete, dissimulate et accorte . . . per opra arcana del cielo svaniti sortiscono fini tanto difformi."—[It is palpable that the most secret, dissembled, and astute negotiations . . . rendered useless by the secret operation of Heaven, issue only in shapeless conclusions.] This, however, was not what was contemplated by the rest of the world, who preferred having an eager grasp at curious and sometimes scandalous materials. A French edition appeared at Lyons; and as that was soon sold off, it was followed by a re-impression in Holland, revised after the original, and marked,

"Cologne, 1694"—not at all as Novaes gives it, 1594. It has often been repeated, with further additions.

In this way the original memoirs have undergone manifold alterations. If we compare the French collection with the originals, while we shall find it to be the same upon the whole, in particular instances we stumble upon considerable variations. Yet, in so far as I can discover, these arise oftener from mistake than from bad intention.

But there are other collections also that have never been printed. There is one in my hands, which both fills up the blanks which the printed ones had left, and possesses at least no less authenticity than the others. In making use of them for details, it must be confessed that an inspection of the originals is always desirable.

64.

Vita e successi del card[l] di Santaseverina.—[Life and fortunes of cardinal Santaseverina.]

A biography of this important cardinal, of whom we have often had to speak.

It is somewhat prolix, and often runs into minutiae of no consequence: the judgments on persons and things that occur in it, entirely depend on the personal qualities of the man; but we find it communicate very original notices of character.

Nothing remains but to give again here verbatim one of those to which we have occasionally referred.

I. PROTESTANTS IN NAPLES.

"Crescendo tuttavia la setta de' Lutherani nel regno di Napoli, mi armai contro di quella spina del zelo della religione cattolica: e con ogni mio potere e con l' autorità del officio, con le perdiche publiche, scritte da me in un libro detto Quadragesimale, e con le dispute publiche e private in ogni occasione e con l' oratione cercai d' abbattere et esterminare peste sì crudele da i nostri paesi: onde patii acerbissima persecutione dagl' eretici, che per tutte le strade cercavano d' offendermi e d' ammazzarmi, come ne ho fatto un libretto, distintamente intitolato Persecutione eccitata contro di me Giulio Antonio Santorio servo di Gesù Christo per la verità della cattolica fede. Era nel nostro giardino in un cantone una cappelletta con l' immagine di Maria s[ma] con il bambino in braccio, et ivi avanti era nata una pianta d' olivo, che assai presto con maraviglia d' ogn' uno crebbe in arbore grande, essendo in luogo chiuso et ombreggiato da alberi: mi ritiravo ivi a far oratione con disciplinarmi ogni volta che dovevo predicare e disputare contro Lutherani, e mi sentivo mirabilmente infiammare ed avvalorare senza tema di male alcuno e di pericolo, ancorche di sicuro mi fosse minacciato da quelli inimici della croce, e sentivo in me tanta gioja et allegrezza che bramavo d' essere ucciso per la fede cattolica. . . . . . Intanto vedendo crescere contro di me maggiormente la rabbia di quelli eretici quali io avevo processati, fui costretto nel 1563 al fine di Agosto o principio di Settembre passarmene in Napoli alli servitii d' Alfonso Caraffa card[le] del titolo di S. Giovanni e Paolo arcivescovo di Napoli, ove servii per luogotente sotto Luigi Campagna di Rossano vescovo di Montepeloso, che esercitava il vicariato in Napoli: e poiche egli partì per evitare il tumulto popolare concitato contro di noi per l' abrugiamento di Gio. Bernardo Gargano e di Gio. Francesco d' Aloys detto il Caserta, seguito alli quattro di Marzo di sabbato circa le 20 hore, rimasi solo nel governo di detta chiesa: ove doppo molti pericoli scorsi e doppo molte minacce, sassi et archibugiate tirate, mi si ordisce una congiura molto crudele et arrabbiata da Hortensio da Batticchio con fra Fiano (?) di Terra d' Otranto, heretico sacramentario e relapso che io insieme col card' di Napoli e mons[r] Campagna

[As the sect of the Lutherans was constantly increasing in Naples, I armed myself against that thorn with the zeal of the catholic religion; and with all my power and official authority, with public preachings, written by me in a book called Quadragesimale, and with public and private disputations whenever an opportunity offered, and with prayer, I endeavoured to pull down and exterminate so cruel a pestilence from our territories: whence I suffered most bitter persecutions from the heretics, who on all the highways sought to attack and kill me, as I have related in a small book, specially entituled, Persecutions raised against me, Julius Anthony Santorio, servant of Jesus Christ, for the truth of the catholic faith. There was in our garden, in one corner, a small chapel, with an image of the most holy Mary with the child in her arms, and before that there sprang up an olive plant, which very soon, to everybody's amazement, grew to be a great tree, being in a close place and shaded with trees: thither I withdrew to engage in prayer, accompanied with personal discipline, every time that I had to preach and dispute against the Lutherans, and I felt myself wonderfully inflamed and emboldened against all fear of mischief or danger, although I should certainly be threatened with it by those enemies of the cross, and I felt in myself so much joy and gladness as to long to be slain for the catholic faith. . . . Meanwhile, perceiving the fury of those heretics whom I had prosecuted greatly increasing against me, I was constrained, in 1563, about the end of August and the beginning of September, to pass to Naples, into the service of Alfonso Caraffa, cardinal, with the title of St. John and St. Paul, archbishop of Naples, where I served as lieutenant under Lewis Campagna di Rossano, bishop of Montepeloso, who exercised the vicariat in Naples: and on his departure, in order to avoid the popular tumult raised against us at the instigation of John Bernard Gargano and of John Francis d'Aloys, called il Caserta, having followed on the 4th of March, being Saturday, about 2 o'clock (2 o'clock p.m.), I was left alone in the government of that church: where, after many risks had been run, and many threats, stones, and firelocks discharged, there was plotted against me a very cruel and

l' haveva (ssi?) richiesto, di distillare un veleno di tanta forza che poteva infettare l' aria per estinguere papa Pio IV. come nemico de' Carafeschi: e non dubitava l' heretico di far intendere tutto cio al pontefice per mezzo del signor Pompeo Colonna."

rabid conspiracy, by Hortensius da Battichio with friar Fiano (?) of Terra d'Otranto, a sacramentarian heretic, and a relapsed person, (alleging) that I, together with the cardinal of Naples and monsignor Campagna, had asked him to distil a poison of such potency as to infect the air, in order to the killing of pope Pius IV., as the enemy of the Carafeschi, and I did not doubt the heretic's intending to do all this to the pope by means of signor Pompey Colonna.]

II. GREGORY XIII. AND SIXTUS V.

"Appena egli credeva di morire non ostante la longa età, essendo sempre vissuto con molta moderatione e caminato per tutti i gradi della corte. Dopoche lasciò la lettura di Bologna, venne in Roma, fu fatto collaterale di Campidoglio, esercitò l' ufficio di luogotenente di mons^{re} auditore della camera, fu fatto referendario, e la prima volta che propose in segnatura, venne meno: onde tutto pieno di vergogna e di confusione voleva abbandonare la corte, ma fu ritenuto dal card^l Crescentio a non partire. Da Giulio III. nell' auditorato di rota li fu anteposto Palleotto: onde di nuovo confuso di doppio scorno determinò partirsi di Roma, ma dall' istesso card^l Crescentio fu rincorato e trattenuto. Fu da Paolo IV. fatto vescovo di Vieste, fu fatto consultore del sant' officio, fu al concilio di Trento e da Pio IV. fu fatto card^{le} e mandato in Spagna per la causa Toletana: e dopo la morte della santa memoria di Pio V. con ammirabil consenso fu assunto al pontificato. Il quale visse con molta carità, liberalità e modestia, e saria stato ammirabile e senza pari, se in lui fossero concorsi valore e grandezza d' animo senza l' affetto del figlio, che oscurò in gran parte tutte le attioni dignissime di carità che egli usò verso li stranieri e verso tutte le nationi che veramente padre di tutti. Dalli signori cardinali nepoti S. Sisto e Guastavillano fu fatto subito intendere la sua morte al sacro collegio, e doppo celebrate l' esequie e tutte quelle funtioni che porta seco la sede vacante, s' entrò in conclave: ove fu eletto papa il sig^r card^{le} Montalto, già nostro collega e nella causa Toletana e nell' assuntione al cardinalato, per opera speciale del sig^r card^l Alessandrino e sig^r card^l Rusticucci, che tirarono in favore di lui il sig^r card^l d' Este e sig^r card^l de Medici, con non poco disgusto del sig^r card^l Farnese, essendoli mancato di parola il sig^r card^l San Sisto, sul quale egli haveva fatto molto fondamento per ostare alli suoi emoli e nemici, essendosi adoprato contro di lui valorosamente il sig^r card^l Riario, ma con pentimento poi grande, non havendo trovato quella gratitudine che egli si haveva presupposta, sicome anco intervenne al sig^r card^{le} Alessandrino, che tutto festante si credeva di maneggiare il pontificato a modo suo: escendendo in San Pietro lo pregai che dovesse far officio con S. B^{ne} in favore di mons^r Carlo Broglia, rettore del collegio Greco, per un beneficio che egli dimandava: mi rispose tutto gratioso: 'Non diamo fastidio a questo povero vecchio, perche noi saremo infallibilmente li padroni:' al quale sorridendo io all' hora risposi segretamente all' orecchie: 'Faccia Dio che subito che sarà passata questa

[He hardly believed that he was dying, notwithstanding his great age, having always lived with much moderation, and passed through all the gradations of the court. After leaving the lecture at Bologna, he came to Rome, was made *collateral* of Campidoglio, exercised the office of lieutenant of monsignor the auditor of the chamber, was made referendary, and the first time he made a motion in the segnatura, he failed: accordingly, overwhelmed with shame and confusion, he wished to abandon the court, but was prevented from going by cardinal Crescentio. Paleotto was preferred to him in the auditorship of the Rota by Julius III.; accordingly, confounded anew by this second affront, he resolved to leave Rome, but was encouraged and entertained by the same cardinal Crescentio. By Paul IV. he was made bishop of of Vieste, was appointed consultor of the holy office, was at the council of Trent, and by Pius IV. was made cardinal and sent into Spain on the Toledo affair: and after the death of Pius V., of sacred memory, was with wonderful unanimity raised to the pontificate. As pope, he lived with much charity, liberality, and modesty, and would have been admirable and unequalled, had there met in him worth and magnanimity, without affection for his son, which in a great measure obscured the most meritorious instances of charity which he showed towards strangers and towards all, as being truly the father of all. His death was immediately made known to the sacred college by the lords cardinals nephews, St. Sixtus and Guastavillano, and after having celebrated the obsequies and all that is required to be done on the vacancy of the see, the conclave was opened: where there was elected pope cardinal Montalto, who had been our colleague both in the Toledo affair and in his assumption to the cardinalship, through the special exertions of cardinals Alexandrino and Rusticucci, who drew over to his side cardinals d'Este and Medici, to the no small disgust of cardinal Farnese, cardinal St. Sixtus having broken his promise to him—a promise on which he had reckoned a great deal in opposing his rivals and enemies, cardinal Riario having stoutly used his interest against him, but with much repentance afterwards, not having met with that gratitude which he had anticipated, as happened also to cardinal Alexandrino, who in the highest spirits believed he was to manage the popedom as he chose: on going up to St. Peter's, I begged he would use his interest with his beatitude in favour of monsieur Carlo Broglia, rector of the Greek college,

sera, ella non se ne penta:' come appunto in effetto fu, poiche non stette mai di cuore allegro in tutto quel pontificato, sentendo sempre rammarichi, angustie, travagli, affanni, pene et angoscii. E ben vero che esso medesimo se l' andava nella maggior parte procurando o per trascuraggine, inavertenza o altro o pure per la troppa superbia con esprobare sempre esso assiduamente li beneficii, servitii et honorevolezze che haveva fatti a S. Bne. Nelli primi ragionamenti che io potei bavere con S. Sta fu il rallegrarmi dell' assuntione sua al pontificato, con dirli che era stata volontà di Dio, poiche in quel tempo e punto che fu assunto erano finite le 40 hore: quivi ella si dolse della malignità de tempi con molta humiltà e pianse:. l' essortai che cominciasse il pontificato con un giubileo generale, che tenesse parimente cura del sant' officio e delle cose sue, sapendo bene che da quello haveva havuto origine la sua grandezza."

for a benefice which he asked for: he replied very graciously, "We will not weary the poor old man with waiting, since we shall infallibly be the patrons:" smiling at which I then quietly whispered into his ears, "God grant that what shall be done this evening, be not speedily repented of:" which was in fact precisely the case, for he never was happy during all that pontificate, being constantly a prey to griefs, difficulties, travails, vexations, pains, and poignant sorrows. It is true, indeed, that he himself went about for the most part bringing these upon him, whether from negligence, inadvertence, and so forth, or from sheer excess of pride, in constantly boasting of the benefits, services, and marks of honour he had bestowed on his holiness. At the first opportunity I had of exchanging words with his holiness, I congratulated him on his assumption to the popedom, telling him that it had been the will of God, since at the very instant of his assumption the 40 hours were ended: thereupon he lamented the evil state of the times with much humility and tears: I exhorted him to begin his pontificate with a general jubilee; and that he should take care likewise of the holy office and its affairs, well knowing that his greatness had originated from that.]

III. AFFAIRS OF FERRARA.

"Venuto il duca di Ferrara in Roma per l' investitura, della quale pretendeva che li fosse data buona intentione, vi furono di molti garbugli: et avendomi io opposto gagliardamente nelli publici e privati ragionamenti et in concistoro, mi persi affatto la gratia del papa con procurarmi il sdegno del cardl Sfondrato, quale andava parlando per Roma che io sentivo malamente dell' autorità del papa: come anco haveva imputato il cardinale di Camerino, che si mostrava molto ardente in servitio della sede apostolica. Sentendomi pungere in cosa tanto lontana dalla mente mia, io che ero andato incontrando tutti li pericoli per la difensione dell' autorità del papa e della sede apostolica, non potei fare di non alterarmene gravemente, e come si conveniva. Feci una apologia pro Cardinale Sancta Severina contra cardinalem Sfondratum, ove si tratta qual sia la carica e qual sia l' officio di cardinale: benche il papa, che si era mostrato in concistoro molto turbato e collerico in camera, poi nel palazzo di S. Marco mi domandò perdono con lagrime e con humiltà e con havermi anco ringratiato, pentendosi del decreto che egli haveva fatto in pregiudicio della bolla di Pio V. de non alienandis feudis. Partendosi il duca da Roma senza haver fatto effetto alcuno, da quel tempo in poi mi si mostrò sempre nemico, dicendo che io ero stato cagione precipua che egli non havesse ottenuto l'investitura di Ferrara pro persona nominanda, e che io come antico suo amico doveva parlare più mitamente, senza intraprendere l' impresa con tanta ardenza, come che io fossi più obligato agli huomini che a Dio et alla santa chiesa."

[The duke of Ferrara having come to Rome for the investiture, of which he pretended that favourable intentions had been given him, there were many angry meetings, and having shown a vigorous opposition in public and private discussions and in the consistory, I lost forthwith the pope's favour, while I brought upon myself the indignation of cardinal Sfondrato, who went about Rome saying that I thought ill of the pope's authority: as he had blamed also cardinal di Camerino, who showed himself very keen in the service of the apostolic see. Feeling myself slandered in a matter so remote from my sentiments, I who had faced so many dangers in defending the pope and the apostolic see, could not but be offended very seriously, and as it became me to be. I made an apology for cardinal St. Severina against cardinal Sfondrato, where the charge and office of cardinal are discussed: although the pope, who had shown himself in the consistory very much troubled and choleric in the chamber, afterwards asked my forgiveness in the palace, with tears and humility, and further with thanks to me, repenting of the decree that he had made in prejudice of the bull of Pius V. about the non-alienation of feofs. The duke leaving Rome without having effected anything, from that time forward always showed himself my enemy, saying that I had been the chief occasion of his not having obtained the investiture of Ferrara *for a person to be named*, and that I, as his old friend, ought to have spoken more mildly without taking up the matter so keenly, as if I had lain under greater obligations to men than to God and holy church.]

IV. CONCLAVE AFTER THE DEATH OF INNOCENT IX.

"Entrato l' anno 1592 si entrò in conclave, essendosi raddoppiata contro di me la malig-

[At the commencement of the year 1592 the conclave met, the malignity of my ene-

nità de miei nemici, mostrandosi il cardl Sfondrato ardentissimo contro la persona mia, non solamente per tema delle cose sue, ma anco più irato delle parole del cardle Acquaviva, che timoroso et invidioso per l' arcivescovo d' Otranto suo parente et altri signori regnicoli amici miei, moveva ogni pietra contro di me: e s'erano uniti insieme li cardli Aragona, Colonna, Altemps e Sforza, capitali nemici tra essi, ma contro di me concordissimi: Aragona per la continua osservanza et ossequio che io havevo usati, ma pigliava pretesti dell' abbadia che havevo tolta all' abbate Simone Sellarolo; Colonna per li molti servittii che gli bavevo fatti in ogni tempo, ma si raccordava del Talmud impedito da me contro li Giudei, repetendo la morte di Don Pompeo de Monti, con taccia anco di sua sorella; Altems per li favori che gli havevo fatti appresso papa Sisto e monsr Pellicano senatore per conto del figlio rattore della Giulietta, onde ne venne quel galant' huomo in disgratia di Sisto, ma così voleva Galleotto Belardo suo padrone; Sforza per haverlo favorito nel caso del Massaino, quando papa Sisto fulminava contro di lui, havendomi ringratiato con baciarmi la mano in prezenza del buon cardle Farnese vecchio, a cui ancora si era mostrato ingrato havendo avuta da quel buon sigr l' abbadia di S. Lorenzo extra moenia, ma egli diceva che non poteva mancare alli amici suoi, ma in effetto egli temeva sapendo bene la sua coscienza. Palleotto m' usò quell' ingratitudine che ogn' un sa. Venne la notte delli 20 di Gennaro: quivi si rappresentò una tragedia de' fatti miei, mentre Madrucci, già mio caro amico e collega nel sant' officio, consentì tacitamente cogli emoli miei in danno mio, oprando per questa via di conseguire il pontificato, ma egli sentì di quelli bocconi amari che non potendo poscia digerire se ne morì miseramente. Lascio da parte gli andamenti fraudolenti del cardl Gesualdo, che come Napoletano non poteva patire che io gli fossi anteposto, et anche mosso da invidia contro i suoi patriotti: poiche questo e gli altri signori cardinali Napoletani Aragona et Acquaviva havevano questo senso di non voler nessun compagno de' patriotti nel cardinalato. L' atto poi che fece il cardinale Colonna, fu il più brutto che s' havesse sentito già mai, et improbato etiam da suoi più cari, e malissimo inteso nella corte di Spagna. Canano solea prima havermi in tanta riverenza che nullo più, e dovunque m' incontrava, mi voleva baciar la mano: ma all' hora scordato d' ogni amicitia obbediva al suo duca di Ferrara. Borromeo, ajutato da me nell sua promotione per la memoria di quel santo cardinale di S. Prassede et havendo fatto professione di sempre mio caro amico, invischiato dall' interesse d' alcune abbadie che haveva rassegnato Altemps, furiava a guisa di forsennato quello che non professava altro che purità, devotione, spiritualità e coscienza. Alessandrino, autore di tutte le trame, non mancò di fare il suo solito in perseguitare i suoi più cari amici e creature con haversele tutte alienate, e massime doppo l' assuntione di Sisto sentì

mies against me being now redoubled, cardinal Sfondrato showing himself most eagerly opposed to me personally, not only because he was afraid about his own affairs, but furthermore angry at the words of cardinal Aquaviva, who fearful and envious by means of his relation the archbishop of Otranto and other lords of the kingdom, my friends, turned every stone against me, and there combined together cardinals Aragon, Colonna, Altemps, and Sforza, keen enemies among themselves, but most perfectly agreed in opposing me. Aragon, in return for the continual attention and defence I had shown, yet made pretexts of the abbacy which I had taken from the abbot Simon Sellarolo; Colonna in return for all the many services that I had done him at all times yet called to mind the Talmud hindered by me in opposition to the Jews, harping upon the death of Don Pompeo de Monti, together with the stain upon his sister; Altemps, in return for the favours I had obtained for him from pope Sixtus and monsignor Pellicano senator, on account of his son who had ravished Juliet, whence that gentleman fell into disgrace with Sixtus, yet such was the will of his patron Belardo Galleotto; Sforza, in return for my having favoured him in the case of Massaino, when pope Sixtus fulminated against him, he having thanked me and kissed my hand in presence of the good old cardinal Farnese, to whom further he showed his ingratitude, having had from that good lord the abbacy of St. Lawrence in the suburbs, yet said that he could not prove wanting to his friends, but in fact he trembled, knowing well what his conscience told him. Palleotto showed towards me the ingratitude every one knows of. He came on the night of the 20th of January: then there was enacted a tragedy of my affairs, while Madrucci, who had been my dear friend and colleague in the holy office, tacitly consented to join my rivals in perpetrating my ruin,[1] endeavouring in this way to obtain the pontificate, but he felt those bitter morsels, unable to digest which, he died miserably. I leave aside the fraudulent proceedings of cardinal Gesualdo, who as a Neapolitan could not endure my being preferred to him, and was further moved with envy against his fellow-countrymen: seeing he and the other Neapolitan cardinals, Aragon and Aquaviva, had this feeling of being averse to having any of their countrymen in the cardinalship. What was then done by cardinal Colonna was the most brutal thing ever heard of, and was disapproved even by his dearest friends, and taken in the worst part by the court of Spain. Canano used formerly to hold me in such reverence that none showed me more, and wherever he met me he would kiss his hand: but now, forgetting all friendship, he obeyed the duke of Ferrara. Borromeo, who had been aided by me in his promotion on account of the respect felt for the memory of that holy cardinal of St. Prassede, and having professed himself always my dear friend, entangled in the interests of some abbacies which Al-

1 The Venetian ambassador Moro also remarks that S. Severina was not elected, "per mancamento di Gesualdo decano e Madrucci" [owing to dean Gesualdo and Madrucci having failed to support him.]

in conclave quel che non volse per bocca del sig[r] card[l] di Sens che esclamava publicamente contro di lui. Il fervore all' incontro de' miei amici e fautori non fu mediocre, essendosi mostrato ardente più d' ogni altro il sig[r] card[l] Giustiniano : quel suo spirito vivace e coraggioso fu in quella notte et in quel giorno in gravi affanni, essendomi anche stata saccheggiata la cella. Ma la notte appresso mi fu dolorosissima sopra ogn' altra cosa funesta: onde per il grave affanno dell' animo e dell' intima angoscia sudai sangue, cosa incredibile a credere: e ricorrendo con molta humiltà e devotione al sig[re], mi sentii affatto liberato da ogni passione di animo, da ogni senso delle cose mondane, venendo in me stesso e considerandole quanto sono fragili, quanto caduche e quanto miserabili, e che solo in dio e nella contemplatione di lui sono le vere felicità e veri contenti e gaudii."

temps had resigned to him, raged like a mad man, he who professed nothing but purity, devotion, spirituality, and conscience. Alexandrino, who was the author of all that was plotting, was not wanting to his usual course of persecuting his dearest friends and creatures, accompanied with the alienation of all of them, and especially after the assumption of Sixtus, heard in the conclave what he did not like by the mouth of cardinal di Sens, who publicly exclaimed against him. The ardour, on the other hand, of my friends and favourers was not small, cardinal Justiniano showing himself more ardent than any other: that lively and courageous spirit of his, during that whole night and day, was in grievous affliction, my cell having further been emptied of its furniture. But the night that followed was to me most doleful beyond everything else that is dismal: whence owing to profound distress of mind and anguish of heart, I sweated blood, a thing incredible to be believed: and having recourse with much humility and with tears to the Lord, I felt myself entirely freed from all mental suffering, from all sense of mundane things, coming to myself and reflecting how frail, fading, and wretched I am, and that in God alone, and in contemplating him, true happiness, content, and joy are to be found.]

65.

Vita et Gesta Clementis VIII.—[Life and actions of Clement VIII.] Informatt. politt. xxix

Originally designed to be a continuation of Ciaconius, where, however, I do not find it.

An account of the rise of the pope—his first achievements: "Exulum turmas coercuit, quorum insolens furor non solum in continentem sed in ipsa litora et subvecta Tiberis alveo navigia hostiliter insultabat."—[He coerced the troops of exiles, whose insolent fury insulted with their hostilities not only the mainland but the very shores and vessels that had entered the channel of the Tiber.] So far was Sixtus V. from having made an end of them; the opposition Clement made to the king is particularly dwelt upon: how reluctantly he had gone into it: finally the conquest of Ferrara. "A me jam latius coepta scribi opportuniori tempore immortalitati nominis tui consecrabo."—[I will consecrate to the immortality of thy name at a more fitting time what has been already begun to be written by me more at large.] Of this, however, nothing is to be found. As it is, it is of little consequence.

66.

Instruttione al S[r] Bartolomeo Powsinsky alla M[ta] del re di Polonia e Suetia.—[Instructions to S[r] Bartholomew Powsinsky to his Majesty the king of Poland and Sweden.] 1st August, 1593. Subscribed, Cinthio Aldobrandini.

Ragguaglio della andata del re di Polonia in Suetia, 1594.—[Account of the king of Poland's going into Sweden, 1594.]

I know of nothing to be added to the substance of these pieces as adopted in the narrative, except perhaps the assertion in the second, that duke Charles was hated at bottom : "perche egli avea ridotto in se stesso quasi tutte l' incette e mercantie e tutte le cave di metalli e sopra tutto dell' oro e dell' argento" [because he had engrossed to himself almost all purchases and merchandise, and all the vaults (mines ?) of the metals, and most of all, of gold and silver].

67.

Relatione di Polonia.—[Account of Poland.] 1598.

Composed by a nuncio, who even then bitterly laments the unbridled love of liberty among the Poles.

They wanted a weak king, none of warlike sentiments. They say, "che coloro che hanno spirito di gloria, gli hanno vehementi e non moderati e però non diuturni, e che la madre della diuturnità degli imperii è la moderatione [that those who have a spirit of glory have vehement and immoderate and not lasting (spirits), and that the mother of the permanence of empires is moderation].

Neither would they have any alliance with foreigners. They maintain that it never can be difficult for them to defend their kingdom. They should always have 50,000 cavalry to bring into the field, and at the worst would recover in winter what they might lose in summer. They boast of the example of their ancestors.

The nuncio reminds them, "che gli antichi Poloni non sapevano che cosa fosse smaltire il grano nel mar Baltico in Danzig o in Elbing, nè erano intenti a tagliar selve per seminare, nè asciugavano paludi per il medesimo effetto."—[that the ancient Poles knew not what it was to sell grain in the Baltic sea, at Danzig and Elbing, nor eagerly cut down woods in order that they might sow the land, nor drained marshes for the same purpose.]

The nuncio further describes the progress of Roman catholicism, which was in the very best train. I have adopted the more important points.

68.

Relatione dello stato spirituale e politico del regno di Suezia, 1598.—[Account of the spiritual and political state of the kingdom of Sweden, 1598.]

Upon Sigismund's attempts upon Sweden, immediately before his second journey thither. Also made use of in its essential import.

Yet we have some remarkable notices on preceding occurrences

Eric is represented as nothing better than a tyrant. "Per impresa faceva un asino carco di sale a piedi d' una montagna erta e senza via per salirvi sopra, et egli era dipinto con un bastone in mano, che batteva il detto asino."—[For a device he had an ass with a load of salt at the foot of a steep hill, without any way to ascend by, and he was represented with a stick in his hand with which he beat the ass.] The author explains this emblem, which is easily to be understood of itself: the people were to be compelled by force to render even impossible services.

John is considered as a decided Roman catholic.

"Perche era in secreto cattolico, siccome al nuntio ha affirmato il re suo figliulo, usò ogni industria perche il figliulo ritornasse mentre esso viveva in Suetia a fine di dichiararsi apertamente cattolico e ridurre i lregno ad abbracciar essa fede."

[Being in the Roman catholic secret, as the nuncio was informed by the king his son, he used every endeavour that his son might return while he was living in Sweden, in order that he might openly avow himself a Roman catholic, and bring back the kingdom to the adoption of that faith.]

Meanwhile I could not venture to subscribe to these things. The idea probably gradually formed itself in the mind of the worthy Sigismund, that he might have the comfort of thinking that he was sprung from a Roman catholic father.

On the other hand, Sigismund's first expedition is described with the full stamp of the veracity of an initiated person. The hopes that were associated with that second expedition are set before us in their important bearings upon Europe.

INTERCALATION.

Remarks on Bentivoglio's Memoirs.

Cardinal Guido Bentivoglio (born in 1579), when in his sixty-third year—not in 1640, as stated by the edition in the *Classici Italiani*, but in 1642, as Mazzuchelli also has it—after having composed many other memoirs on the history of the world, began to put down personal memorabilia also.

He originally contemplated embracing his first residence at the Roman court, his nuncioships in France and the Netherlands, and the times of his cardinalship. Had he accomplished this, the history of the first half of the seventeenth century would have been enriched with the addition of a beautiful work, full of interesting views.

But he died before he had finished even the first part. His work, Memorie del card[l] Guido Bentivoglio [Memoirs of Cardinal Guido Bentivoglio], reaches only to 1600.

It gives an impression of calmness and comfort such as was enjoyed by the old prelate who, no longer occupied with public affairs, now lived suitably to his rank in his own palace. It forms a very pleasant and at once a cheering and instructive piece of reading: but naturally the cardinal's position lays him under obligations, and it is observable that he does not speak out all that he has to say.

The description, for example, which he gives with tolerable fulness, of the cardinals whom he found about Clement VIII., corresponds but too much in general points with the notices we have of the same persons from other quarters.

The very first, dean Gesualdo, is described by Bentivoglio as "a distinguished man, of amiable manners, who did not seek business, nor yet did he shun it;" but, what others tell us, and which no doubt Bentivoglio knew, of his thwarting the election of Sanseverino from personal aversion, what pretensions of a higher order he made use of towards other cardinals who had given an unwilling adhesion, how all his efforts ever after went to gain over friends in order to be able to attain to the pontificate, and how he particularly attached himself to Spain,—of all this we learn nothing.

The second is Aragona. Bentivoglio remarks of him, "In earlier conclaves he in particular guided the younger cardinals: during the pope's absence he administered the government of Rome in the most brilliant manner; he likes good furniture; he has a fine chapel; he makes exchanges of altar-images. But therewithal the man is not sufficiently described. He was, as we see from Delfino, an old man afflicted with gout, whose death might soon be looked for, but who, on that account, cherished only the more firmly hopes of obtaining the pontificate. He was by no means so much respected by the Spanish court as he could have

wished. He could gain none of his ends in the congregation on French concerns: and it was known that he took this very ill: but not the less did he, with that view, try to maintain the closest intimacy with the Spanish ambassador.

That impression of peace and calmness which the book produces, arises also from the lights being purposely very much subdued, from life not being properly reproduced truly as it appeared.

69.

Relatione fatta all' ill^mo^ sig^r^ card^le^ d' Este al tempo della sua promotione che doveva andar in Roma. Bibl. Vindob. Codd. Foscar. n. 169.—[Report rendered to the most illustrious lord cardinal d' Este, at the time of his promotion, when he had to go to Rome. Vienna Library; Codices Foscarini, No. 169.] 46 leaves.

In consequence of the agreement that Clement VIII. had made with Este at the occupation of Ferrara, he included Alexander, a prince of that house, in the promotion of the 3d of March, 1599.

This is the prince whom it was intended by our paper of instructions to prepare for his entrance into court. Although it bears no date, it is undoubtedly to be placed in the year 1599.

Its very destination at once distinguishes it from a Venetian *relatione.* It was to put the prince in such a position as would enable him, like a good pilot, to steer properly—"per potere come prudente nocchiero prendere meglio l' aura propitia della corte" [to enable him, like a prudent pilot, to catch with better effect the propitious breeze of the court]; it says nothing about political relations: even the calamity that had just befallen the house of Este is passed over in silence: the author's sole aim is to point out the peculiar characteristics of the most important persons.

The pope, his nephews, and the cardinals are described.

Clement VIII. "Di vita incolpabile, di mente retta, di conditione universale. Si può dir ch' abbia in se stesso tutta la theorica e la pratica della politica e region di stato."—[Of blameless life and upright mind, of a nature adapted for everything. It may be said that he comprised in himself the whole theory and the whole practice of politics, and the philosophy of government.] Here we find that Salvestro Aldobrandini stimulated Paul IV. to make war on Naples; yet endeavours were made thereupon to reconcile the family at least with the Medici. "Dicesi che Pio V. volendo promovere il card^l^ Giovanni, fratello di questo pontefice, assicurò il G.D. Cosimo che tutta questa famiglia gli sarebbe fidelissima sempre, e che mandò l' istesso Ippolito Aldobrandino, hora papa, a render testimonio a S. Altezza, della quale fu molto ben visto."—[It is said that Pius V., wishing to promote cardinal Giovanni, brother of this pontiff, assured the grand duke Cosmo that the whole of this family would ever be most faithful to him, and sent this very Hippolytus Aldobrandino, now pope, to give testimony to his highness, by whom he was looked upon very favourably.] At that time John Bardi was in most favour with pope Clement. "Fra i servitori di Clemente il più intimo e favorito è il sig^r^ Giovanni Bardi dei conti di Vernio, luogotenente delle guardie, di molta bontà, virtù e nobiltà."—[Among those in the service of Clement the most intimate and favoured is lord John Bardi, one of the counts of Vernio, lieutenant of the guards, a man of much goodness, virtue, and nobility.] The new cardinal could the more readily attach himself to him, as he wished well to the house of Este.

The Nephews. Peter Aldobrandini's preponderance over San Giorgio was decided. "San Giorgio, accommodato l' animo alla fortuna sua, mortificate le sue pretensioni, non gareggia, non contrasta più, ma o lo seconda o non s' impaccia seco, e si mostra sodisfatto dell' ottenuta segnatura di giustitia."—[San Giorgio, having accommodated his mind to his fortune, having mortified his pretensions, did not contend, did not resist any more, but either seconded him or did not embroil himself with him, and showed himself satisfied with having obtained the segnatura of justice.]

The cardinals went off into two factions—the Spanish, to which Montalto was already attached, and the Aldobrandinish. The former could count at that time on 25, the latter on only 14 decided and staunch members. The author rightly points to that person as the likeliest candidate for the popedom, who afterwards actually obtained it, Alexander Medici. It was not known how the same stood with the grand duke of Tuscany, but on that account he was only the more in favour with Clement: "per patria e conformità di humore" [on account of country and conformity of disposition], the same as if he had been his creature.

The historian of the church, Baronius, makes no bad figure: "molto amato per la dottrina, bontà e simplicità sua: si dimostra tutto spirito, tutto resegnato in dio: si burla del mondo e della propria esaltatione di se stesso."—[much beloved for his learning, goodness, and simplicity: he shows himself all mind, altogether resigned to God: he laughs at the world and his own exaltation.]

70.

Relatione di Roma dell' Illmo Sig^r^ Gioan Delfino K^r^ e Pro, ritornato ambasciatore sotto il pontificato di Clemente VIII.—[Report on Rome from the Most Illustrious Lord John Delfino, Knight and Procurator, on his return as ambassador under the pontificate of Clement VIII.] (1600.)

This too is one of the widely diffused reports; it is very copious—my copy consists of 94 quarto leaves, and is full of information.

I. Delfino begins with a description of the pope: ("il nascimento, la natura, e la vita del papa" [the birth, disposition, and life of the pope]) and his nephews.

"Delli due cardinali (Aldobrandino e S. Giorgio) reputo quasi necessario parlarne unitamente. Questo di età d' anni 45, di gran spirito, altiero, vivace e di buono cognizione nelli affari del mondo: ma temo assai che sia di mala natura, overo che gli accidenti del mondo occorsi, che l' hanno levato dalle gran speranze in che si è posto nel principio del pontificato, lo fanno esser tale, cioè dimostrarsi con tutti non solo severo ma quasi disperato. Questo era grandemente amato e grandemente stimato dal papa avanti che fosse salito al pontificato, e doppo per gran pezzo ebbe la cura principale de' negotii, e si credeva da ogn' uno che egli avesse da esser il primo nipote, perche l' altro era più giovane, assai di poca prosperità e di pochissima cognizione: ma o sia stato la sua poca prudenza nel non essersi saputo governare come averebbe bisognato, sendosi rotto con l' ambasciatore di Spagna quando gittò la beretta, con l' ambasciator di Toscana quando li disse che il papa doveria cacciarlo di corte, oltre i disgusti che ha dato a tutti in mille occasioni, o pur la gran prudenza e destrezza dell' altro, o la forza natural del sangue, questo ha perduto ogni giorno tanto di autorità e di credito che non ha chi lo seguiti e non ottiene cosa alcuna che dimandi. Ha però il carico di tutti li negotii d' Italia e Germania, se bene li ministri publici trattino li medesimi con Aldobrandino, e nelle cose brusche tutti ricorrono a lui. Io con esso sig^{r} card^{le} di S. Giorgio nel principio ho passato qualche borasca, anzi nella prima audienza fui astretto a dolermi apertamente per dignità della republica, e doi o tre volte mi sono lasciato intendere liberamente, in modo tale che so che è stato frutto apresso di lui, et il papa l' ha avuto a carro, e particolarmente nell' ultima occasione di Ferrara: ma doppo sempre è passato tra noi ogni sorte di dimostratione d' amore, et io l' ho onorato sempre come si conveniva. Credo veramente che sia mal affetto alla Serenità Vostra per natura e per accidente: la sua natura l' ho descritta, ma dirò solo delli accidenti. Prima sappia che da un pezzo in qua s' è buttato affatto in braccio de' Spagnuoli, e si è dimostrato poco amico di quelli che sono uniti con Francesi: ha cresciuto ancora quel mal animo suo il vedere che il cardinal Aldobrandino habbi in tutte le occasioni protetto li affari dell' EE. VV., quasi che non sia possibile che concorrino ambidue in alcuna operatione, per giusta e raggionevole che sia. Da che si può conoscere la miseria de' poveri ambasciatori et rappresentanti publici."

[I consider it almost necessary to speak of the two cardinals (Aldobrandino and S. Giorgio) together. The latter is about 45 years of age, a man of much spirit, haughty, animated, and well informed in the affairs of the world: but I much fear that he is of a bad disposition, or that the casualties that he has met with in the world, which have removed him from the high expectations in which he was placed at the commencement of the pontificate, have made him such, so that with everybody his behaviour is not only severe, but almost reckless. The latter was much beloved and much esteemed by the pope before he rose to the pontificate, and for long after he had the chief charge of affairs, and it was thought by every one that he would have to be first nephew, in as much as the other was the younger of the two, and further, not very prosperous, and of very little judgment: but whether it were from his want of prudence in not having known how to govern as was required, having had a rupture with the Spanish ambassador when he threw his cap on the ground, with the ambassador of Tuscany when he said that he ought to drive him away from the court, besides the disgusts he has given to all on a thousand occasions, or from the great prudence and skill of the other, or the natural force of blood, the latter has daily lost so much authority and credit that he has none to follow him, and fails to obtain whatever he may ask. He has, indeed, the charge of all the affairs of Italy and Germany, although the public ministers treat of the same with Aldobrandino, and in untoward matters all apply to him. I had at first some high words with that same signor cardinal di San Giorgio, before I was compelled to complain openly in the first audience, out of respect for the dignity of the republic, and twice or thrice I caused myself to be heard freely, in such wise that I know there has been something gained by it as respects him, and the pope has taken him to task, and particularly on the last occasion of Ferrara: but afterwards there was an exchange betwixt us of every kind of demonstration of love, and I have always honoured him as was befitting. I believe in truth that he is ill affected towards your serenity by nature, and from accidental causes. This I first knew at a time in which he threw himself entirely into the hands of the Spaniards, and he has shown himself little friendly to those who are united with the French: this ill will of his has further been increased by his seeing that cardinal Aldobrandino has on all occasions protected the affairs of your Excellencies, as if it were impossible that they should both concur in the same measure, however just and reasonable it might be. From which one may have an idea of the misery of the poor ambassadors and public representatives.]

II. The second chapter, in our copy at least formally distinguished as such, treats of the form of government, the finances, and the armed force. Delfino is amazed, as he justly might be, at some points in the administration of the finances. "Mentre l' entrate della chiesa sono impegnate al ingrosso ordinariamente e straordinariamente; e quello ch' è peggio,

si comprano castelli e giurisdittioni de' sudditi a $1\frac{1}{2}$ o 2 per cento, (ich verstehe: die sŏ viel abwerfen) e si pagano censi a 9 o 10 per cento, parendo strano agli uomino savj che in tante strettezze si fanno queste compre, e più è che se si vogliono far certe spese, non si facciano per via delli danari del castello, per non ci andar debitando e consumando del tutto."—[While the Church's revenues are mortgaged wholesale, ordinarily and extraordinarily; and which is worse, castles and jurisdictions are purchased from the subjects at $1\frac{1}{2}$ and 2 per cent, (I understand that they yielded as much) and mortgages pay 9 or 10 per cent, it seeming strange to all intelligent men that in such straits such bargains should be made; and what is more, when it is wished that a certain expenditure should be made, the funds are not taken from money in the castle, in order to avoid going there and spending and consuming the whole.] We see that even at that time there were people that were scandalized at the borrowed money in the treasury. For the rest, after the first brief satisfaction felt at Ferrara, much discontentment entered there. "Nobili e popolo si darebbero volentieri a qual principe si voglia, per uscir dalle mani dove si trovano."—[Nobles and people would willingly give themselves to any prince whatever in order to get out of the hands in which they now find themselves.]

III. "Intelligenze."—[Correspondence.] How doubtfully the pope stood with the emperor and with Philip II.—he expected the king's death with a kind of anxiety: how ill he stood with Florence, for it was very well remembered that the house of Aldobrandini belonged to the expatriated party ("le cose passano peggio che con ogn' altro, ricordandosi d'esser andato il papa e la sua casa ramingo per il mondo" [matters go on worse than with any other, it being remembered that the pope and his family have gone roving through the world]): how much better, on the other hand, with France and Poland, particularly with the last, with which he had common interests and plans, ("concorrendo e dall' una e dall' altra parte interessi nel presente e disegni nel tempo a venire" [there being a concurrence of both sides, both in present interests and in plans for the future]). But Clement was prepossessed in favour of nobody so much as the prince of Siebenburg:

"Col prencipe di Transilvania ha trattato il papa con tanto amore, e con tener un nuntio apostolico appresso di lui e con averli dato in mio tempo 60m. scudi in tre volte e con infiniti officii fatti fare con l' imperatore per servitio, che quasi poteva dirsi interessato et obligato alla continua sua protettione: e credo che 'l povero prencipe la meritava, perche s' è risoluto alla guerra con fondamento principale del consiglio et delle promesse di S. Sta: quanto nel principio già tre anni e già due ancora esaltava la virtù e valor di questo prencipe fino al cielo, avendo detto a me più volte ch' egli solo faceva la guerra al Turco, tanto più ultimamente con la cessione che gli fece de' suoi stati restava molto chiarito, et il predicava un gran da poco: onde si vede che se bene aveva promesso all' imperatore di farlo cardinale et a lui ancora, non averebbe però osservato cosa alcuna, e perciò credo che essendo tornato al governo de' suoi stati abbia sentito S. Sta gran consolatione."

[With the prince of Transylvania the pope has conducted himself so affectionately, keeping an apostolic nuncio at his court, and having in my time given him 60,000 scudi on three occasions, and having made infinite good offices to be done with the emperor for service, so that he might be said to be interested and obliged to the continuance of his protection: and I believe that the poor prince deserved it, for he had resolved upon the war, reckoning mainly on the counsel and the promises of his holiness: how much, first three years ago, and further two years ago, he extolled the virtue and worth of this prince to the very heavens, having told me many times that he alone had made war on the Turks, so much more of late, when he made a surrender to him of his states, remained very clear, and he preached, though a great man, such as few: whence it appears, that although he had promised to the emperor to make him a cardinal, and to himself besides, he would not have observed anything, and therefore I believe that his holiness had felt much consoled on his returning to the government of his states.]

IV. "Cardinali."—[Cardinals.] They are all passed severally under review, and more or less favourably pronounced upon.

V. "De' soggetti che cascano in maggior consideratione per lo pontificato."—[On subjects that fall into greater consideration for the popedom.]

VI. "Interessi con Venetia."—[Interests connected wich Venice.] Already a thousand controversies were mooted.

"Quando non si proveda alle pretensioni et ai disordini, un giorno si entrerà in qualche travaglio di gran momento, massime di questi novi acquisti (über die Schiffahrt auf dem Po), che sempre vi penso per cognitione che ho della natura de' preti e della chiesa mi fa temere."

[If no provision be made with respect to claims and irregularities, there will come one day some such embarrassment of great moment, chiefly about these new acquisitions (on the navigation of the Po), which I always remind you that the knowledge I have of the nature of priests and of the church makes me fear.]

This anticipation was but too soon realized.

71.

Venier: Relatione di Roma. 1601.—[Venier's Report from Rome. 1601.]

Already had the dissensions betwixt the pope and Venice become pretty keen. The Ve-

netians refused to send their patriarchs to Rome for the purpose of being approved; bitter contentions had broken out on the subject of the Goro mouth of the Po; and about these very contentions Venier was sent to Rome.

He remained there but a short time: nevertheless the sketch he gives of Clement VIII. is highly useful.

"Della natura et pensieri del pontefice, per quello che a me tocca di considerare nella presente congiuntura per li negotii che giornalmente tratta V. Serenità con S. Beatitudine, dirò che il papa in questa età sua di 65 anni è più sano e più gagliardo di quello che sia stato negli anni adietro, non havendo indispositione alcuna fuoriche quella della chiragra o gotta, che però li serve, come vogliono li medici, a tenerlo preservato da altre indispositioni, e questo molto più di rado e molto meno che per l' inanzi le da molestia al presente, per la bona regola particolarmente del viver, nel quale da certo tempo in qua procede con grandissima riserva e con notabile astinenza nel bere: che le giova anco grandemente a non dar fomento alla grassezza, alla quale è molto inclinata la sua complessione, usando anco per questo di frequentare l' esercitio di camminar longamente sempre che senza sconcio de negotii conosce di poterlo fare, ai quali nondimeno per la sua gran capacità supplisce, intanto che le resta comoda parte di tempo che dispensa admettendo persone private et altri che secondo il solito ricorrono a S. Sta. A negotii gravi si applica con ogni suo spirito, et persiste in essi senza mostrarne mai alcuna fiachezza, et quando li succede di vederli conclusi, gode et fruisce mirabilmente il contento che ne riceve. Nè di cosa maggiormente si compiace che di esser stimato, et che sia rispettata la sua reputatione, della quale è gelosissimo. Et quanto per la complessione sua molto sanguigna e colerica è facile ad accendersi, prorompendo con grandissima vehementia in esagerationi piene di escandescenza et acerbità, tanto anco mentre vede che altri tace con la lingua seben s' attrista nel sembiante, si ravede per se stesso et procura con gran benignità di raddolcire ogni amaritudine: la qual cosa è così nota hormai a tutti li cardinali che ne danno cortese avvertimento agli amici loro, sicome lo diede anco a me nel primo congresso l' illustrissimo sig^{r} card^{le} di Verona per mia da lui stimata molto utile conformatione. Ha S. Sta volti li pensieri suoi alla gloria, nè si può imaginare quanto acquisto facciano li principi della gratia sua, mentre secondano la sua inclinatione. Onde Spagnoli in particolare, che sempre mirano a conservarsi et ad aumentar la gran parte che hanno nella corta di Roma, non trascurano punto l' occasione: et però con tanto maggior prontezza hanno applicato l' animo a far qualche impresa contra Turchi, come hora si vede, et con andar sofferendo non mediocri durezze, che provano anco loro nelli negotii importanti, particolarmente per causa di giurisditione, che vivono alla corte di Roma, si vanno sempre più avanzando nel riportare in molte cose non piccole soddisfattioni. E tenuto generalmente il pontefice persona di gran virtù, bontà et religione: di che egli si compiace far che del continuo se ne veggano segni et importanti effetti. Et se ben li cardinali si vedono nel presente pontefice scemata molto quella autorità che ne' tempi passati sono stati soliti d'havere, res-

[As for the disposition and intentions of the pope, as to what it concerns me to consider in the present conjuncture for the affairs which your serenity daily treats with his beatitude, I shall say that the pope in this his age of sixty-five years, is in better health and more vigorous than what he was some years ago, not having any indisposition except that of chiragra or gout, which indeed serves, as the physicians say, to keep him free from other ailments, and this now troubles him much seldomer and less severely than formerly, owing particularly to the good rules he observes as to diet, to which he allows a certain amount of time, and in which he observes the utmost care, accompanied with notable abstinence in drinking: and this further assists him much in not encouraging a tendency to corpulence, to which he is constitutionally much disposed, employing likewise for this purpose frequent exercise in long walks as often as he can contrive to do so without prejudice to affairs, to which nevertheless he makes compensation by his great capacity, so that he still has left to him a suitable proportion of his time which he spends in admitting private persons and others who, according to custom, apply to his holiness. To serious affairs he applies himself with all his might, and perseveres at them without signs of fatigue; and when he sees them brought to a close, he is delighted, and wonderfully enjoys the satisfaction this gives him. Nor does anything gratify him more than his being much thought of, and having respect paid to his reputation, of which he is most jealous. And whereas from his constitution, which is very sanguine and choleric, he is easily excited, breaking out with immense vehemence into exaggerations full of heat and bitterness, so much the more when he sees the party he addresses silent with his tongue, although his face indicates sadness, does he come to himself again, and try with great kindness to soften down all bitterness: all which is now so well known to all the cardinals, that they have the courtesy to apprize their friends of it, as was done also to me at the first conference by the most illustrious lord cardinal of Verona for my, by him considered, very useful guidance. His holiness has turned his thoughts to glory, nor can it be imagined what advantage princes derive from his favour when they second his inclination. Hence the Spaniards in particular, who are always aiming at the preservation and increase of their great influence at the court of Rome, never neglect a single opportunity: and they have therefore applied their minds with the greater promptitude to the making of such an expedition against the Turks as we now see; and while they go on enduring no small hardships which still try them in matters of importance, particularly in reference to jurisdiction, those who reside at the court of Rome continue making more and more progress in obtaining no small satisfaction in many matters. The pontiff is generally held to be a person of great virtue,

tando quasiche del tutto esclusi dalla partecipatione de negotii più importanti, poiche ben spesso fino al' ultima conclusione di essi non hanno delle trattationi la già solita notitia, mostrano nondimeno di stimare il pontefice, lodano la S[tà] S. con termini di somma riverenza, celebrando la prudenza et l' altre virtù sue con grand' esageratione, affirmando che se fosse occasione hora di elegere pontefice, non elegerebbono altro che questo medesimo, seben son molto reconditi et profondi i loro pensieri, et le parole et le apparenze sono volte ai proprj disegni forse a Roma più che altrove."

goodness, and religion: of which he likes that people should always see signs and important effects. And although the cardinals see themselves, under the present pope, much curtailed of the authority which they used to have in times past, they remaining almost quite excluded from any share in the more important affairs, since, for a long while, negotiations have never been made known to them, as they used to be, until finally closed, yet they showed their esteem for the pontiff by praising his holiness in terms of the utmost reverence, by high-flown eulogies of his prudence and other virtues, affirming that had they to elect a pontiff now, they would elect none but the present, although they are very recondite and profound in their thoughts, and words and appearances are turned to their proper aims perhaps more at Rome than in other places.]

The ambassador succeeded once more in composing the dissensions, although the pope had already been talking of excommunications; yet he thinks him, upon the whole, well disposed. Venice agreed to send her patriarch to Rome.

72.

Instruttione all' ill[mo] et ecc[mo] marchese di Viglienna ambasciatore cattolico in Roma 1603. —[Instructions to the most illustrious and excellent marquis of Viglienna, catholic[1] ambassador in Rome. 1603.] (Informatt. politt. n. 26.)

Viglienna was Sessa's successor. Our author fairly enough leaves it to the ambassador who was leaving the place, to report on the pope and his nearest relations. He himself informs us with respect to the cardinals. He proposes to point out to which faction each belonged. From this, then, we see that the state of things was much changed since 1599. There are now only 10 cardinals adduced as decidedly Spanish. Formerly there was but little said about the French ones; of these there now appear nine—the remainder belonged to no party.

This author, too, is penetrated with the importance of the curia. "Qui le differenze, le pretensioni, le paci, le guerre si maneggiano. . . . Le conditioni invitano i più vivaci e cupidi di grandezza, di maniera che non è meraviglia che qui fioriscano i più acuti ingegni."—[There differences, claims, pacifications, and wars are disposed of. . . . The circumstances of the place invite the most vivacious, and those who court greatness most, in such a manner that no wonder the most acute geniuses flourish there.]

73.

Dialogo di mons[r] Malaspina sopra lo stato spirituale e politico dell' imperio e delle provincie infette d' heresie.—[Dialogue of monsieur Malaspina on the spiritual and political state of the empire and of the provinces infected with heresy.] (Vallic. n. 17. 142 leaves.)

A dialogue between monsignor Malaspina, archbishop of Prague, and the bishops of Lyons and Cordova; also of the clergy of the four leading nations: about the year 1600. Mention is made in it of the occupation of Ferrara.

The particular object of it is to compare what earlier popes with what Clement VIII. had done for the progress of Roman catholicism.

Under the previous popes:

"1. La reduttione delle Indie. 2. La celebratione del concilio. 3. La lega santa e la vittoria navale. 4. L' erettione de' collegii. 5. L' offerta dagli heretici del primato di Pietro al patriarcha Constantinopolitano . . . (?). 6. La constantia del re cattolico in non concedere agli heretici nei paesi bassi cose in pregiudicio della religione."

[1. The reduction of the Indies. 2. The celebration of the council. 3. The holy league and the naval victory. 4. The erection of colleges. 5. The offer of the heretics belonging to the primacy of Peter, to the Constantinopolitan patriarch . . . (?). 6. The firmness of the catholic king in making no concessions to the prejudice of religion in favour of the heretics in the Netherlands.]

From pope Clement VIII.:

"1. Il governo pastorale et universale. 2. Il governo particolare dei dominii del stato ecclesiastico. 3. La vita di S. Beatitudine. 4. Il Turca hora per opera di S. Beatitudine fatto apparire di potersi vincere. 5. Ferrara occupata. 6. L' essersi fatto cattolico il christianissimo re di Francia."

[1. Pastoral and universal government. 2. The particular government of the dominions of the ecclesiastical state. 3. The life of his holiness. 4. The possibility of vanquishing the Turk, now made manifest by what has been done by his holiness. 5. The occupation of Ferrara. 6. The most Christian king of France having become (Roman) catholic.]

1 That is, Spanish, from the catholic king.—TR.

Malaspina concludes that this was of more importance than all that had been done by the rest. Naturally enough. The treatise is dedicated to the papal nephews.

I have been able to find but one point worth noticing in this long piece of writing.

The author was at the electoral diet at Ratisbon in 1575. There he conversed with the electoral prince Augustus of Saxony. That prince was still far from raising any hopes in the Roman catholics of his going over to them. He declared, on the contrary, that he made no account of the pope, whether as pope or as monarch of Rome, or because of his treasures: that the papal treasure-chamber was rather a cistern than a living spring; he was concerned only about this, "that a monk like Pius V. should have united such powerful princes in carrying on a war with the Turks: he might easily do the same thing against the protestants." In fact, Gregory XIII. had projected such a design. Perceiving that France would, from dread of the Huguenots, take no part in the Turkish war, he held that a general league of the Roman catholic princes, alike against Turks and protestants, was necessary. This forthwith became the subject of negotiations with the emperor and the archduke Charles in Steiermark.

74.

Relatione delle chiese di Sassonia. Felicibus auspiciis ill^{mi} comitis Frid. Borromei. 1603. —[Account of the churches of Saxony. Under the felicitous auspices of the most illustrious count Fred. Borromeo. 1603.] Bibl. Ambros. H.,179.

Another of the various projects of Roman catholicism for recovering possession of Germany.

The author is convinced that people in Germany were gradually becoming tired of protestantism. Fathers were already little concerned about bringing up their children in their religion. "Li lasciano in abandono, perche dio gl' inspiri, come essi dicono, a qual che sia per salute dell' anime loro."—[They neglect them altogether, for God prompts them, as they say, to (seek) whatever may be for their salvation.]

In this conviction he forms projects upon two of the leading protestant territories, Saxony and Westphalia.

In Saxony the administrator had already extirpated Calvinism. He was to be gained through the hope of the re-acquisition of the electorate ("mettergli inanzi speranza di poter per la via della conversione farsi assoluto patrone dell' elettorato" [to set before him the hope of being enabled, by the way of conversion, to make himself absolute master of the electorate]). Even the native nobility would willingly see themselves again rendered capable of obtaining the bishoprics.

On the subject of Westphalia he expresses himself as follows:—

"Il Casimiro aveva una sorella vedova, che fu moglie d'un landgravio d'Hassia, la quale suol vivere in Braubach, terra sopra il Rheno, e si dimostra piena di molte virtù morali e di qualche lume del cielo: suol esercitare l'opere di charità per molto zelo, facendo molte elemosine e consolando gl' infermi di quei contorni con provederli di medicine; conversa volentieri con alcuni padri del Giesù e con l'arcivescovo di Treveri. . . . E opinione di molti che mediante una più diligenza o di qualche padre del Giesù amato da lei o di qualche principe cattolico o vescovo saria facil cosa di ridurla totalmente alla vera fede: . . . di che se dio benedetto desse la gratia e che la cosa passasse con conveniente segretezza, sarebbe ella ottimo instrumento per convertire poi il nipote con la sorella di lui et un altra figlia che resta del Casimiro."

[Casimir had a sister, who was a widow, that had been wife of a landgrave of Hesse, which sister usually lives at Braubach (Biberach?), an estate on the Rhine, and shows herself full of many moral virtues and of some light of heaven: she is wont to practise works of charity with much zeal, doing much alms, consoling the infirm of those districts, and also providing them with medicine; she willingly converses with some fathers of the society of Jesus, and with the archbishop of Treves. . . . It is the opinion of many, that by means of more diligence, or of some father of Jesus loved by her, or of some (Roman) catholic prince or bishop, it would be an easy matter to bring her altogether back to the true faith: . . . of which should the blessed God grant the favour, and that the matter pass with convenient secrecy, she will then be the best instrument for the subsequent conversion of her nephew, together with his sister and another daughter left by Casimir.]

The author here alludes to Anna Elizabeth of Westphalia, wife of Philip II. of Hesse Rheinfels, who died so early as 1583. She had previously fallen under suspicion of Calvinism, and on that account was once hurt in a tumult. We see that at a later date, at her jointure residence at Braubach, which she embellished, she made herself suspected of the opposite tendency to Roman catholicism.

Such is the combination on which our author builds. He thinks that on the young count Palatine being then married to a Bavarian princess, the whole country would become Roman catholic.

75.

Instruttione a V. S^ria^ Monsr Barberino arcivescoco di Nazaret destinato nuntio ordinario di N. Sig^ro^ al re christianissimo in Francia, 1603.—[Instruction to your Lordship, Monsignor Barberino, archbishop of Nazareth, appointed ordinary nuncio of our Lord to the most Christian king, in France, 1603.] (MS. Rom.)

Elaborated by cardinal P. Aldobrandino, who often mentions his previous embassy to the French court; and intended for the further promotion of Roman catholicism after the impulse it had received from the conversion of Henry IV., in France.

Let us attend to some of the suggestions that are given to the nuncio (who was afterwards Clement VIII.).

"Ella farà si con il re ch' egli mostri non solamente di desiderareche gli eretici si convertino, ma che dopo che si sono convertiti, gli ajuti e favorisca. .... Il pensare a bilanciare le cose in maniera che si tenghi amiche ambidue le parti è una propositione vana, falsa et erronea, e non potrà esser suggerita a S. M^ta^ che da politici e mal intentionati e da chi non ama la suprema autorità del re nel regno. .... N. Sig^re^ non vuol lasciar di porli (dem König) in consideratione una strada facile (sich der Protestanten zu entledigen) e senza che possa partorir tumulto e che si eseguisca facilmente e fa il suo effetto senza coltivatione: et è quella che altre volte ha S. Sta ricordato alla M^ta^ S. et addotto l' esempio di Polonia, cioè di non dar gradi ad eretici: ......ricorda a S. M^ta^ di dar qualche sbarbatezza alle volte a costoro (den Hugenotten), perche è turba ribelle et insolente. .. .... V. S^ria^ dovrà dire liberamente al re che deve fuggire gli economati et il dar vescovati e badie a soldati et a donne."

[You will so manage with the king that he shall not only show a desire for the conversion of the heretics, but that after conversion they be aided and favoured....... To think of balancing matters in such a manner that both parties shall be held friends, is a vain, false, and erroneous idea, and can be suggested to his Majesty only by politicians and ill-intentioned people, and by those that love not the supreme authority of the king in the kingdom....... Your lordship will not neglect to suggest to his (the king's) consideration an easy method (of ridding himself of the protestants), and without the possibility of there being any tumult, of easy execution, and which produces its effects without husbandry: and this is what his holiness has at other times suggested to his Majesty, and has adduced the example of Poland, that is, not to give preferments to heretics ...... reminds his Majesty to be always reining them (the Huguenots) up, for they are a rebellious and insolent crew. ...... Your lordship ought frankly to tell the king that he ought to avoid the *economati*, and the giving of bishoprics and abbeys to soldiers and women.]

In these *economati* lies the origin of the regalia, which afterwards caused such grievous dissensions. "Il re nomina l' economo, il quale in virtù d' un arresto, inanzi sia fatta la speditione apostolica, amministra lo spirituale e temporale, conferisce beneficii, constituisce vicarii che giudicano, assolvono, dispensano."—[The king nominates the economo, who in virtue of an arrêt, previous to the apostolic expeding being done, administers the spirituality and the temporality, confers benefices, constitutes vicars who judge, absolve, dispense.]

The nuncio was also to endeavour to confirm the king in the Roman catholic faith: during the wars he could not have been duly instructed; he was to urge the appointment of good bishops, and to see to the reform of the clergy: where possible, to effect the publication of the Tridentine council, which the king had promised to the cardinal at his departure to see to within two months, and which he was still delaying after the lapse of several years: he was to recommend the annihilation of Geneva ("di tor via il nido che hanno gli eretici in Ginevra, come quella che è asilo di quanti apostati fuggono d' Italia" [to take away the nest which the heretics have in Geneva, as being the asylum of so many fugitive apostates from Italy]).

The pope has Italy most of all at heart: he declares it intolerable that a Huguenot general should be stationed at Castel Delfino on this side the mountains; his example is deadly.

Clement warmly entered into the idea of a Turkish war. Each monarch was to attack the Turks on a different side: for this the king of Spain was already prepared; only he insisted on having an assurance that the king of France would not raise a war in other quarters.

76.

Pauli V. pontificis maximi vita compendiose scripta. (Bibl. Barb.)—[Compendious Life of Paul V., supreme pontiff.] (Barberini Library.)

A panegyric of no great worth.

The administration of justice and that of the government, and the architectural undertakings of this pope, are eulogized at great length.

" Tacitus plerumque, et in se receptus, ubique locorum et temporum vel in mensa meditabatur, scribebat, plurima transigebat.

" Nullus dabatur facinorosis receptui locus. Ex aulis primariis Romae, ex aedium nobilissimarum non dicam atriis sed penetralibus

[Silent, for the most part, and abstracted; at all times and places, even at table, he meditated, wrote, transacted many things.

No retreat was allowed to criminals. The guilty were dragged out to punishment, by an armed police, from the aristocratic halls of

nocentes ad supplicium armato satellitio educebantur.

"Cum principatus initio rerum singularum, praecipue pecuniarum difficultate premeretur, cum jugiter annis XVI tantum auri tot largitionibus, substructionibus, ex integro aedificationibus, praesidiis exterorumque subsidiis insumpserit, rem frumentariam tanta impensa expediverit, .. nihil de arcis Aeliae thesauro ad publicum tutamen congesto detraxerit, subjectas provincias sublevaverit: tot immensis tamen operibus non modo aes alienum denuo non contraxit, sed vetus imminuit; non modo ad inopiam non est redactus, sed praeter publicum undequaque locupletatum privato aerario novies centena millia nummum aureorum congessit."

Rome, I do not say from the public apartments, but from the private concealments of the noblest houses.

Whereas, at the commencement of his reign, he was oppressed by the difficulties of a singular conjunction of circumstances, particularly in regard to money, whereas he was constantly spending for sixteen years so much gold in so many largesses, repairs on the foundations of some buildings, and on others altogether new, and in garrisons and subsidies to foreign troops, and expedited supplies of corn at such expense . . . . he took nothing from the treasure of the Aelian citadel that had been amassed there for the public defence; he lightened the burthens of the subject provinces: yet, for so many immense operations, he not only did not contract any new debts, but he lessened the old; not only was he not reduced to want, but besides the enrichment of the public treasury on all hands, he amassed in his private treasury 900,000 pieces of gold].

This panegyrist seems not to have considered the creation of so many *luoghi di Monte* as a loan.

77.

Relatione dello stato infelice della Germania cum propositione delli rimedii opportuni, mandata dal nuntio Ferrero vescovo die Vercelli alla S[ta] di N. Sig[re] papa Paolo V. (Bibl. Barb.)—[Account of the unfortunate condition of Germany, together with the suggestion of opportune remedies, transmitted from the nuncio Ferrero, bishop of Vercelli, to his holiness of our lord pope Paul V. (Barberini Library.)]

Probably one of the first more detailed reports that came into the hands of Paul V. The nuncio speaks of the insurrection of the imperial troops against their general Basta in May, 1605, as a thing that had just occurred.

The unfortunate course of the war, under these circumstances, the progress made by the Turks and by the rebels who were in conflict with the emperor, were, no doubt, what chiefly led to his pronouncing the condition of Germany to be unfortunate.

For, besides all this, he was not unaware of the many acquisitions the Roman catholic church was making in Germany.

"Di questi frutti ne sono stati prossima causa gli alunni così di Roma come delle varie città e luoghi della Germania dove la pietà di Gregorio XIII. alle spese della camera apostolica gl' instituì, giunti li collegii e scuole delli padri Giesuiti, alli quali vanno misti cattolici et heretici; perche li alunni sudetti si fanno prelati o canonici."

[Of these fruits, the proximate cause has been the pupils, both from Rome and various other cities and places of Germany where the piety of Gregory XIII. instituted them at the expense of the apostolic chamber, together with the colleges and schools of the Jesuit fathers, which are attended by both catholics and heretics; because the said pupils come to be made prelates or prebendaries.]

He repeatedly asserts that the Jesuit schools had gained over a great many of the younger people to Roman catholicism. Only he finds, especially in Bohemia, an extraordinary want of Roman catholic parish priests.

He enters also into the political state of the country: he considers the danger to be dreaded from the Turks very serious, owing to the bad preparations of the emperor and the internal dissensions of the house of Austria. The archdukes Matthias and Maximilian had become reconciled with each other in opposition to the emperor.

"Hora l' arciduca Mattia e Massimiliano si sono uniti in amore, vedendo che con la loro disunione facevano il gioco che l' imperatore desidera, essendosi risoluto il secondo a cedere al primo come a quello che per ragione di primogenitura toccava il regno d' Ungaria, Boemia e stati d' Austria, et Alberto ha promesso di star a quello che se ne farà, e di comun concerto sollecitano l' imperatore con lettere a prendere risolutione al stabilimento della casa: ma egli è caduto in tanta malinconia, o sia per questa lor unione, e geolosia che non siano per valersi di queste sedizioni, o per altro, che non provede alla casa nè agli stati nè a se stesso."

[The archdukes Matthias and Maximilian are now united in affection, perceiving that with their dissension they were playing the game the emperor wants, the latter having resolved to yield to the former as to the one who, on the ground of primogeniture, obtained the kingdom of Hungary, Bohemia, and the states of Austria, and Albert has promised to stand by the one who will agree to this, and by common concert they solicit the emperor, by letters, to come to some resolution for the stability of the family, but he has fallen into such a state of melancholy, whether from that union of theirs, and from jealousy, lest there should be some to take advantage of these seditions, or from some other cause, that he looks neither to the family, nor to the states, nor to himself.]

Many other remarkable things are withal brought to light: for example, the views of the house of Brandenburg even at that time on Silesia. "Il Brandenburgh non dispera con gli stati che ha in Slesia e le sue proprie forze in tempo di revolutione tirar a se quella provincia."—[Brandenburg does not despair, with the provinces which he has taken in Silesia and his own proper forces, in time of revolution, to draw that province to himself.]

78.

Relatione dell' ill^{mo} Sr Franc. Molino cav^{r} e pro^{r} ritornato da Roma con l' ill^{mi} sig^{ri} Giovanni Mocenigo cav^{r}, Piero Duogo cav^{r} e Francesco Contarini cav^{r}, mandati a Roma a congratularsi con papa Paolo V. della sua assontione al pontificato, letta in senato 25 Genn. 1605 (1606).—[Report from the most illustrious lord Franc. Molino, knight and procurator, on his return from Rome with the most illustrious lords Giovanni Mocenigo, knight, Piero Duodo, knight, and Francesco Contarini, knight, sent to Rome to congratulate pope Paul V. on his assumption to the pontificate; read in the Senate, 25th January, 1605 (1606).]

The outbreak of troubles was already foreseen. The ambassadors had observed Paul V. as closely as possible.

"Sicome pronuntiato Leone XI. penarono doi hore a vestirlo pontificalmente, così il presente pontefice fu quasi creduto prima vestito ch' eletto et pur da altri cardinali: che non fu così presto dichiarato che in momento dimostrò continenza et gravità pontificia tanta nell' aspetto, nel moto, nelle parole et nelli fatti, che restarono tutti pieni di stupore et meraviglia et molti forse pentiti, ma tardi et senza giovamento: perche diversissimo dalli altri precessori, che in quel calore hanno tutti assentito alle richieste così de' cardinali come d' altri et fatte infinite gratie, così il presente stette continentissimo et sul serio, tanto che si dichiarì risoluto a non voler assentire et promettere pur minima cosa, dicendo ch' era conveniente aver prima sopra le richieste et gratie che le erano dimandate ogni debita et matura consideratione: onde pochissimi furono quelli che dopo qualche giorno restassero in qualche parte gratiati. Nè tuttavia si va punto allargando, anzi per la sua sempre maggior riservatezza dubitando la corte di veder anco sempre poche gratie et maggior strettezza in tutte le cose, se ne sta molto mesta. Fra li cardinali non v'è alcuno che si possi gloriar di aver avuto tanto d' intrensichezza o familiarità seco che di certo si possi promettere di ottener prontamente alcuna cosa da lui, e tutti procedono con tanto rispetto che si smarriscono quando sono per andarli a parlar et negotiar seco: perche oltre che lo trovano star sempre sul serio et dar le risposte con poche parole, si vedono incontrar in risolutioni fondate quasi sempre sopra il rigor dei termini legali: perche non admettendo consuetudini, ch' egli chiama abusi, nè esempj de consenso de' pontefici passati, ai quali non solamente dice che non saperia accomodar la sua conscientia, ma che possono aver fatto male et potriano render conto a Dio, o che saranno stati ingannati, o che la cosa sarà stata diversa da quella che a lui viene portata, li lascia per il più malcontenti. Non ha caro che si parli seco lungo per via di contesa o di disputatione, et se ascolta pur una o doi repliche, quello stimando di aver risoluto con le decisioni de' leggi o dei canoni o de' concilj che lor porta per risposta, si torce se passano inanzi, overo egli entra in altro, volendo che sappino che per le fatiche fatte da lui il spatio di trenta cinque anni continuo nel studio delle leggi et praticatele con perpetui esercitii nelli officii di corte in Roma et fuori, possi ragionevolmente pretendere, se bene questo non

[Whereas, on Leo XI. being pronounced (pope), two hours were spent in clothing him pontifically; the present pope was almost believed to be clothed, as such, before his being elected, and that indeed by the other cardinals: for he was no sooner declared to be so, than he showed in a moment such pontifical continency and gravity in his looks, movements, words, and actions, that they were all full of amazement and wonder, and many perhaps repented, but late and to no purpose: for, most different from others his predecessors, who all in the warmth of the moment, granted the petitions both of the cardinals and others, and conferred infinite acts of favour, so the present laid the utmost restraint on himself, and took matters seriously, so much so as to resolve not to assent to, or to promise even the smallest matter, saying that it was fitting that he should first have all due and mature consideration on the petitions and favours that were asked of him: whence those were very few who, after some days, remained anywise gratified. He does not at all go on enlarging his liberality, the court rather dreading to see his constantly increasing reserve followed by a continued paucity of favours, and greater strictness in all things, is very dull on the subject. Among the cardinals there is none that can glory in having had so much intimacy or familiarity with him as certainly to be able to count upon readily obtaining anything from him; and all conduct themselves so respectfully as to lose heart when they are about to speak to or conduct business with him: for besides that they find him always take things seriously, and give his answer in few words, they see themselves thwarted by resolutions almost uniformly founded on the rigour of legal terms: for not admitting customs which he calls abuses, nor examples of consent on the part of past popes, to which he not only says that he cannot accommodate his conscience, but that these popes may have done wrong, and may have to answer to God for it, or that they may have been deceived, or that there may be some difference in the case brought before him, he leaves them for the most part dissatisfied. He does not like to be spoken to long in the way of contention or disputation, and listens to one or two replies, thinking that he has made up his mind according to the decisions of the laws, and canons, and councils which he adduces to

dice tanto espressamente, di aver così esatta cognitione di questa professione che non metti il piede a fallo nelle risolutioni che da et nelle determinationi che fa, dicendo bene che nelle cose dubbie deve l' arbitrio et interpretatione particolarmente nelle materie ecclesiastiche esser di lui solo come pontefice. Et per questo li cardinali, che per l' ordinario da certo tempo in qua non contradicono, come solevano, anzi quasi non consigliano, et se sono ricercati et comandati di parlar liberamente, lo fanno conforme a quell' intentione che vedono esser nelli pontefici, se ben non la sentono, col presente se ne astengono più di quello che habbino fatto con alcun dei suoi precessori: et averanno ogni dì tanto maggior occasione di star in silentio, quanto che manco delli altri ricerca il parere di loro o di alcuno a parte, come soleva pur far papa Clemente et altri: fa fra se stesso solo le risolutioni et quelle de improviso pubblica nel concistoro: in cui hora si duole dei tempi presenti, hora si querela de' principi con parole pungenti, come fece ultimamente in tempo nostro per la deditione di Strigonia, condolendosi et attribuendo la colpa all' imperatore et ad altri principi con parole aculeate et pungenti; hora rappresentando a' cardinali li loro obblighi, li sfodra protesti senza alcun precedente ordine o comandamento, con che li mette in grandissima confusione, come fece significandoli l' obbligo della residenza et, come ho detto, non per via di comando, come facevano li altri pontefici, li quali prefigevano loro ancor stretto tempo di andar alle lor chiese, ma con solamente dirli che non escusarebbe li absenti da esse da peccato mortale et da ricevere i frutti, fondando la sudetta conclusione sopra li canoni et sopra il concilio di Trento: col qual termine solo così stretto et inaspettatamente con molta flamma pronunciato mette tanta confusione nelli cardinali vescovi che conoscendo loro non potersi fermare in Roma più lungamente senza scrupolo et rimorso grandissimo della conscientia, senza dar scandalo et senza incorrer in particolar concetto presso il papa di poco curanti li avvertimenti della S^tà Sua, di poco timorati di Dio et di poco honore ancor presso il mondo, hanno preso risolutione chi di andar alla residenza, et già se ne sono partiti alquanti, chi di rinunciare, et chi di aver dispensa fin che passi la furia dell' inverno per andarvi alla primavera: nè ha admesso per difesa che salvino le legationi delle provincie e delle città del stato ecclesiastico: solo doi poteano esser eccettuati, il card^l Tarasio arcivescovo di Siena vecchissimo et sordo, che non sarà perciò salvato da restar astretta alla renoucia, et il sig^r card^l di Verona, medesimamente per l' età grandissima et per aver già molti anni mons^r suo nipote ch' esercita la coadjutoria et ottimamente supplisce per il zio."

them in reply, he makes wry faces if they proceed farther, or he changes the subject, giving them to understand that by the labours he has undergone during thirty-five years continuously in the study and practice of the laws, with perpetual exercise in the offices of the court of Rome and abroad, he may reasonably pretend, although this may not expressly say as much, to as exact a knowledge of that profession as not to put his foot in the wrong place in the resolutions he gives and the determinations he makes, saying, indeed, that in doubtful matters the power of deciding and the interpretation, particularly in church affairs, should rest with him alone, as pontiff. And owing to this the cardinals who for ordinary, from a certain time, in this way don't oppose as they used to do, rather almost don't counsel, and if asked and commanded to speak freely, do so in conformity with what they see to be the pope's views, even although not of that mind themselves, with the present (pope) refrain more than what they did with any of his predecessors: and have daily the more occasion to remain silent, as he less than others (his predecessors) asks for their opinion, or that of each of them apart, as, indeed, pope Clement and others used to do: he forms his resolutions by himself alone, and then announces them off-hand in the consistory, where he will now complain of the present times, now censures the princes with pungent words, as he did of late, in our time, on account of the surrender of Strigonia, lamenting it and laying the blame upon the emperor and other princes in stinging and pungent expressions; now pressing their duties upon the cardinals, he pulls out protests for them without any preceding order or commandment, with which he utterly confounds them, as he did by intimating the obligation of residence, and, as I have said, not by way of commandment, as other popes have done, who fixed for them beforehand a precise time for going to their churches, but simply telling them that he would not hold those who absented themselves as free from the guilt of mortal sin, and from receiving the fruits (taking the consequences ?), founding the said conclusion on the canons and the council of Trent: with which determination alone, thus strict and pronounced unexpectedly with much fervour, he threw the cardinal bishops into such confusion that knowing that they could not stay in Rome much longer without very great scruple and remorse of conscience, without causing scandal, and without incurring in particular the character with the pope of caring little for his holiness's warnings, of being men of little fear of God, and furthermore of little honour before the world, they have resolved, some to go to their sees, and part of them have already gone thither, some to renounce (their bishoprics), and some to obtain a dispensation until the fury of winter be over, so as to set off in early spring: nor has he admitted as a defence that they have the legations of the provinces and the cities in the ecclesiastical state: two only can be excepted, cardinal Tarasio, archbishop of Siena, very old and deaf, who cannot therefore be held bound to renounce his see; and the lord cardinal of

Verona, likewise on account of his extreme age, and because he has already for many years had monsignor his nephew to administer the coadjutorship, who excellently supplies his uncle's place.]

In spite of this strictness the ambassadors made very good progress at bottom with Paul V. He dismissed them in the most friendly manner. Even the most gracious pope could not have expressed himself more favourably. They are even astonished that matters should have taken so directly opposite and perilous a turn so soon afterwards.

79.

Instruttione a mons^re^ il vescovo di Rimini (C^l^ Gessi) destinato nuntio alla republica di Venetia dalla Santità di N. S. P. Paolo V. 1607 4 Giugno. (Bibl. Alb.)—[Instruction to the bishop of Rimini (C^l^ Gessi), appointed nuncio to the republic of Venice from the holiness of our holy father Paul V. 4th June, 1607. (Alb. Lib.)]

Dating immediately after the close of the contentions, still not yet very pacific.

The pope complains that the Venetians tried to keep the act of absolution concealed: in a declaration to their clergy there appeared an intimation that the pope had removed the censures because he recognised the purity of their views: ("che S. Beat^ne^ per haver conosciuta la sincerità degli animi e delle operationi loro havesse levate le censure" [that his beatitude, having perceived the purity of their minds and proceedings, had taken away the censure]).

Nevertheless Paul V. goes so far as to entertain the hope that the consultors, and even Fra Paolo, would be handed over to the Inquisition. This passage is very important:

"Delle persone di fra Paolo Servita e Gio. Marsilio e degli altri seduttori che passano sotto nome di theologi s'è discorso con V^ra^ Sig^ria^ in voce: la quale doveria non aver difficoltà in ottener che fossero consignati al sant' officio, non che abbandonati dalla republica e privati dello stipendio che s'è loro constituito con tanto scandalo."

[Of the person of Father Paul Servita and John Marsilio, and of the other seducers who pass under the name of divines, your lordship has been talked with by word of mouth: and you ought to obtain without difficulty that they should be handed over to the holy office, not abandoned by the republic, and deprived of the pay which has been appointed for them so scandalously.]

Must not such proposals have had the effect of increasing Fra Paolo's hostile feelings, and making him implacable? The pope knew not what an enemy he was. All his monsignori and illustrissimi are forgotten. The spirit of Fra Paolo lives at least in one part of the internal opposition in Roman catholicism down to this day.

As for the rest the resistance which the pope had met with in Venice, made the greatest impression upon him. "Vuole N. Sig^re^ che l' autorità e giurisdittione ecclesiastica sia difesa virilmente da V. S^ria^, la quale averte non di meno di non abbracciar causa che possa venire in contesa dove non abbia ragione, *perche forse è minor male il non contendere che il perdere.*"—[Our lord desires that the ecclesiastical authority and jurisdiction should be manfully defended by your lordship, and you will no less take care not to undertake a cause which may come into contention where there is not reason, since perhaps it is a minor evil not to dispute a point than to lose it.]

80.

Ragguaglio della dieta imperiale fatta in Ratisbona l' anno del S^r^ 1608, nella quale in luogo dell' ecc^mo^ e rev^mo^ mons^r^ Antonio Gaetano, arcivescovo di Capua, nuntio apostolico, rimasto in Praga appresso la M^tà^ Cesarea, fu residente il padre Filippo Milensio maestro Agostino vicario generale sopra le provincie aquilonarie. All' ecc^mo^ e rev^mo^ sig^re^ e principe il sig^r^ card^l^ Francesco Barberini.—[Report on the Imperial diet held at Ratisbon in the year of our Lord 1608, at which, in the room of the most excellent and most Rev. monsignor Anthony Gaetano, archbishop of Capua, apostolic nuncio, who was left in Prague with his Imperial Majesty, there was resident father Philip Milensio, Augustine master, vicar general over the northern provinces, to the most excellent and most Rev. lord and prince, lord cardinal Francis Barberini.]

When the emperor Rodolph, in 1607, summoned a diet, Anthony Gaetano was nuncio at his court.

Gaetano proposed the more complete introduction of the Tridentinum, to effect the adoption of the Gregorian calendar—to which the three secular electors were already willing to agree, Saxony most decidedly, who had already instructed his ambassador to that effect, and specially to take upon him the Roman catholic interests at the supreme imperial court. The thwarting these experienced is mentioned in the Instructions in the following manner.

"Di questo tribunal essendo presidente supremo l' intruso Magdeburgese heretico, e volendo egli esercitare il suo officio, non fu ammesso, e da quel tempo in qua non essendo state reviste le cause et essendo moltiplicati gli aggravii fatti particolarmente alli catolici, protestando li heretici di volere avere luogo nella detta camera indifferentemente, come

[The supreme president of this tribunal being the intended Magdeburg heretic, and he wishing to exercise his office, was not allowed to do so, and from that time in which there having been no revision of causes, and the grievances done particularly to the Roman catholics having been multiplied, the heretics protesting that they want to have a place in

hanno li catolici, hanno atteso continuamente ad usurpare i beni ecclesiastici." [the said chamber, on the same footing with the (Roman) catholics, have succeeded hitherto in usurping the ecclesiastical estates.]

It was foreseen that this matter would give rise to very keen debates at the diet, yet the nuncio could not attend it. The emperor made the archduke Ferdinand go thither, and would have taken it as an insult had the nuncio left him.

Gaetano sent in his place the Augustinian Fra Milentio. As the latter had already been resident several years in Germany, he could not fail, in some measure, to know how matters stood. But the nuncio farther directed him to Matthew Welser—"per esatta cognitione delle cose dell' imperio" [for an exact knowledge of the affairs of the empire]—and to that very bishop of Ratisbon, a writing by whose pen at that time produced so great an excitement among the protestants. He was also to attach himself to Father Willer, the emperor's confessor.

Unfortunately, this Augustinian first drew up the report of his proceedings several years afterwards. Yet what he relates of his personal doings is extremely interesting: we have already adopted it in the history.

He traces, moreover, the whole of the dispeace that had then broken out in the empire, to the doubtful succession: "essendo fama che Ridolfo volesse adottarsi per figliuolo Leopoldo arciduca, minor fratello di Ferdinando, e che poi a Ferdinando stesso inchinasse."—[It being rumoured that Rodolph wanted to adopt as his son the archduke Leopold, younger brother of Ferdinand, and that then he inclined to Ferdinand himself.] Matthias was exceedingly dissatisfied at this. But he found faithful and influential adherents in Klesel and in prince Lichtenstein, who had so much power in Moravia.

Dietrichstein and Gaetano had a great share, according to this report, in the conclusion of the settlement between the brothers.

81.

Relatione di Roma dell' illustrissimo Sr Giovan Mocenigo Kav^r Amb^r a quella corte l' anno 1612.—[Report from Rome of the most illustrious Signor Giovan Mocenigo, Knight Ambassador to that court in the year 1612.] Inff. politt. tom. xv.

The first ambassador subsequent to the settlement of differences was Francis Contarini: 1607-1609. Our Mocenigo speaks highly of the great advantage he had derived from Contarini's able management. He himself, who had already been employed for eighteen years in embassies, was stationed from 1609 to 1611 in Rome. The quiet tone of his report proves, in the best manner, that he too succeeded in maintaining a good understanding.

In this report it is not his object to repeat what was common and well known, but to confine himself to a discussion of the pope's peculiarities of character and sentiment in reference to the republic: "la qualità, voluntà, dispositione del papa e della republica verso questa republica. Tratterò il tutto con ogni brevità, tralasciando le cose più tosto curiose che necessarie."—[the character, intentions, disposition of the pope and republic towards this republic. I will treat the whole with all brevity, passing over such things as are rather curious than necessary.]

1. Pope Paul V. "Maestoso, grande, di poche parole: nientedimeno corre voce che in Roma non sia alcuno che lo possa agguagliare nelli termini di creanza e buoni officii: veridico, innocente, di costumi esemplari."—[Majestic, tall, of few words: nevertheless it was reported that in Rome there was no one that could match him in civility of expression and good offices: truthful, innocent, of exemplary manners.]

2. Cardinal Borghese. "Di bella presenza, cortese, benigna: porta gran rivereuza al papa: rende ciascuno sodisfatto almeno di buone parole: è stimatissimo e rispettato da ogn' uno."—[Of a fine presence, courteous, benignant: he shows great reverence for the pope: he satisfies everybody at least with good words: he is much esteemed and respected by everybody.] By the year 1611 he had 150,000 scudi of income.

3. Spiritual power. He remarks that former popes sought to procure honour by bestowing favours: that those of the present time rather endeavour to wrest back again favours already bestowed, ("rigorosamente studiano d' annullare et abbassare le già ottenute gratie" [they rigorously study to annul and reduce favours already granted]). Nevertheless people endeavoured to stand well with him, as it was believed that obedience on the part of the people reposed on religion.

4. Temporal power. He thinks the populations of the states of the church still very warlike ("prontissimi alle fattioni, alli disaggi, alle battaglie, all' assalto et a qualunque attione militare;" [most prompt to factions, to troubles, to battles, to assault an enemy, and to all military actions whatsoever;]) the papal military force was not the less in full decline. In former times 650 light horse had been kept up, chiefly against the banditti; these having been suppressed, the cavalry had been sent to the Hungarian war, without being replaced by any other.

5. Form of government, absolute. The cardinal nephew, the Datario and Lanfranco had some influence; in other respects the cardinals were only asked their opinion when the pope wished to have it. Even when he asked it, they answered rather according to his inclination than their own judgment. ("Se pure dimanda consiglio, non è alcuno che ardisca proferir altra parola che d' applauso e di laude, sicche tutto viene terminato dalla prudenza del papa."—[If indeed he ever asks for counsel, there is not one that dares to say a word but

of applause and commendation, so that everything comes at last to be determined by the prudence of the pope.]) That too was at bottom for the best, since the factions of the court had filled it with party spirit.

6. Relation to Spain and France. The pope endeavoured to stand neutral.

"Quando da qualcheduno dipendente da Spagnoli è stato tenuto proposito intorno alla validità et invalidità del matrimonio della regina, si è stato mostrato risoluto a sostenere le ragioni della regina. Li poco buoni Francesi nel medisimo regno di Francia non hanno mancato d' offerirsi pronti a prender l' armi, purche bavessero avuto qualche favore del papa e del re di Spagna.

"Il re di Spagna è più rispettato di qualsivoglia altro principe dalla corte Romana. Cardinali e principi sono consolatissimi, quando possono havere da lui danari et essere suoi dependenti.—Il papa fu già stipendiato da lui, e dall' autorità di S.M., come soggetto confidente, favorito all' assuntione del pontificato con singolare et incomparabile beneficio.—Procura di dar sodisfattione al duca di Lerma, acciò questo le serva per instrumento principalissimo di suoi pensieri presso S. M^a cattolica."

[On anything being said in conversation by any one dependent on the Spaniards, about the validity or invalidity of the queen's marriage, he has shown himself resolute in maintaining that the queen is in the right. The few good French in that same kingdom of France, have not failed to signify their readiness to take up arms, had they had some favour from the pope and the king of Spain.

"The king of Spain is more respected than any other prince whatever by the Roman court. Cardinals and princes feel the greatest comfort when they can have money from him, and be his dependents.—The pope was once in his pay, and by the authority of his majesty, as a trusty subject, was favoured with singular and unparalleled kindness in attaining the popedom. He took care to gratify the duke of Lerma, in order that he might serve him as a chief instrument of his intentions with his catholic majesty.]

7. His counsel: "temporeggiare e dissimulare alcune volte con li pontefici.—Vincitori essercitano le vittorie a modo loro, vinti conseguiscone che conditioni vogliono."—[to temporize and dissemble at times with the popes.—Victors, they make use of their victories in their own way, vanquished, they obtain what terms they please.]

82.

Relatione della nunziatura de' Suizzeri.—[Report of the nuncioship of the Swiss.] Informationi politt. tom. ix. fol. 1-137.

Informatione mandata dal S^r C^l d' Aquino a Monsr Feliciano Silva vescovo di Foligno per il paese di Suizzeri e Grisoni.—[Information transmitted from the lord Cardinal of Aquino to Monsignor Feliciano Silva, bishop of Foligno, for the country of the Swiss and Grisons.] Ibid., fol. 145-212.

In Lebret's Magazin zum Gebrauch der Staaten-und Kirchengeschichte, vol. vii. p. 445, extracts are given from the letters sent by the Roman court, in 1609 and 1614, to the nuncios in Switzerland; it cannot be said that they were very interesting: they are so, but, without answers and reports, not even intelligible.

The first of these nuncios was the bishop of Venafro, the very person of whom Haller (Bibliothek der Schweizergeschichte, vol. v. nr. 783) mentions a report on Switzerland. "The papal nuncio," he says, "Lad. Gr. of Aquino, bishop of Venafro, has in this work given a proof of his penetration and tact, and it is well worth being printed." Haller copied it out with his own hand in Paris, and placed it in the Zurich library.

Now that report is just the one before us; we have it, however, in a more complete state than that in which Haller knew it.

On the bishop of Venafro giving up the nuncioship which he had administered from 1608 to 1612, he not only communicated to his successor, the bishop of Voligno, the instructions which he had received from cardinal Borghese, but he also informed him, in a copious memoir, how he had discharged his functions ("di quanto si è eseguito sino al giorno d' hoggi nelli negotii in essa raccommandatimi" [of all that has been effected till this day in the affairs recommended to me in it]). This is the second of the two MSS. above indicated. It begins with a description of the internal partisanships.

"E seguitando l' istesso ordine dell' instruttione sopradetta, dico che da molti anni in qua si è fatta gran mutatione ne' cantoni cattolici e particolarmente nella buona amicitia e concordia che anticamente passava fra di loro: perche hoggidì non solo per causa delle fattioni Spagnuole e Francesi e delle pensioni, ma ancora per altri interessi, emolumenti e gare vi è fra alcuni tanto poca amicitia che col tempo potrebbe partorire molti danni se tosto non si prende buon rimedio con procurare una dieta particolare non ad altro effetto che a rinuovare le leghe antiche,

[And following the same order of instructions above mentioned, I say that, for many years there has been, in this respect, a great change in the catholic cantons, and particularly in the good friendship and concord that prevailed of old amongst them: for at this day, not only because of the Spanish and French factions and the pensions, but further on account of other interests, emoluments, and contentions, there is so little friendship among some there, as may in time cause many losses if a good remedy be not soon applied, with a special diet to be held for the

l'amicitia, fratellanza et amorevolezza, come io molte volte ho proposto con grandissimo applauso, se bene sin' hora non ho potuto vederne l'effetto. Altorfo è antico emulo di Lucerna, e tira seco gli altri due cantoni Schwitz et Undervalde, e vede mal volontieri preminenza e primo luogo de' signori Lucernesi, e però spesse volte contradice in attioni publiche non ad altro fine che di gara e di poca intelligenza: Lucerna tira seco Friburgo e Soloturno e ancora Zug, e fa un' altra partita. Zug è diviso fra se stesso, essendo in gravi controversie li cittadini con li contadini, volendo ancora essi essere conosciuti per patroni: e così in ogni cantone cattolico vi sono molte publiche e private dissensioni con pregiudicio delle deliberationi e con pericolo di danni assai maggiori se non vi si rimedia, come io procuro con ogni diligenza."

sole purpose of renewing the old leagues, amity, brotherhood, and kindly feeling, as I have often proposed with much applause, albeit indeed to this hour I have not been able to see it accomplished. Altorf is the ancient rival of Lucerne, and draws with it the other two Swiss cantons, Schweitz and Unterwalden, and views with ill-will the preeminence and precedency of the Lucernese lords, and accordingly very often contradicts (them) in public proceedings from sheer emulation and misunderstanding. Lucerne carries with it Friburg and Solothurne and also Zug, and makes another party. Zug is divided within itself, the townsfolk being on very bad terms with the peasantry, they farther desiring to be acknowledged as masters: and thus, in every catholic canton there are many public and private dissensions, to the prejudice of deliberations, and at the risk of much greater evils if there be no antidote, such as I endeavour after with all diligence.]

At the time of his transmitting this piece, the nuncio promises a still fuller report.

"Fra pochi giorni spero di mandarle copia d' una piena e più diffusa relatione di tutti li negotii della nuntiatura."

[In a few days I hope to send a copy of a full and more extensive report on all the affairs of the *nuntiatura*.]

Such is the first-named manuscript: this had become known to Haller.

In it the nuncio proceeds somewhat more methodically. "Cap. I. Della grandezza della nuntiatura." [Of the greatness of the nuncioship.] He first describes the circle embraced by it, which was as extensive as the kingdom of Naples, and moreover extended over peoples speaking the most different languages. He does not forget even the Romanesque tongue, "una favella stravagantissima, composta di otto o dieci idiomi" [a most extraordinary language, composed of eight or ten idioms].

"II. Degli ambasciatori de' principi che resiedono appresso Suizzeri e de' loro fini." [Of the ambassadors of the princes that reside with the Swiss, and of their views.]

"III. Delle diete e del modo, tempo e luogo dove si congregano fra Suizzeri." [Of the diets, and the manner, time, and place where the Swiss hold their meetings.]

"IV. Delli passi che sono nella nuntiatura de' Suizzeri." [Of the passes in the Swiss nuncioship.] For it was just these passes that formed the most important points of controversy with the powers.

"V. Stato spirituale della nuntiatura de' Suizzeri." [Spiritual condition of the Swiss nuncioship.] The most important, and as is reasonable, the most extensive head, p. 28-104; in which information is given on the subject of individual dioceses and abbacies also.

"VI. Officio del nuntio per ajutare lo stato spirituale e de' modi più fruttuosi di farlo." [Office of the nuncio intended to promote the spiritual state (of the country) and of the most fruitful ways of doing so.]

"VII. Che debbia fare il nuntio per dare sodisfattione in cose temporali nella nuntiatura." [What the nuncio ought to do in order to give satisfaction in temporal matters in the nuncioship.]

It will be perceived how carefully the most important elements are distinguished and gone through. The execution shows an acquaintance no less with past than with present time, zeal, tact, and acuteness. The Report naturally repeats the most of what was contained in the Information.

Even all this, however, was not enough for our nuncio. To the Report he adds a "Compendio di quanto ha fatto mons^re^ di Venafro in esecutione dell' instruttione datali nel partire di Roma" [Compendium of what has been done by my lord of Venafro in execution of the instructions that were given him on leaving Rome]: this he had already drawn up on another occasion, and this in particular must have been almost identical with the Information. He himself remarks, You may however lay this short piece of writing aside. When copies came to be taken, no doubt it was very properly left out.

In its place there follows an "Appendice de' Grisoni e de' Vallesani" [Appendix on the Grisons and the Vallesani] no less remarkable than the preceding.

"E questo" [And this], says the author, in concluding his voluminous work, "è il breve summario promesso da me dell stato della nuntiatura Suizzera con le parti che a quella soggiaciono. Deo gratias. Amen."—[is the brief summary promised by me of the state of the Swiss nuncioship, with the parts that are subject to it. Thanks be to God. Amen.]

Still he persists in thinking that he had only given a short review of matters worth being known. So little does the world give itself back in words.[1]

1 Meaning, I suppose, that history never can overtake relating more than a small part of the world's affairs.—Tr.

In vol. ii. p. 176, I have availed myself of the notices found here only in so far as served my object: the publication of the rest must be left to the industry of the Swiss.[1]

83.

Instruttione data a mons^{r} Diotallevi vescovo di S. Andelo destinato dalla Sta di N^{ro} Sig^{ro} papa Paolo V. nuntio al re di Polonia 1614.—[Instruction given to monsignor Diotallevi, bishop of S. Andelo, sent by the holiness of our lord, pope Paul V., as nuncio to the king of Poland in 1614.]

Consisting of general directions to promote the Roman catholic religion, the introduction of the Tridentine council, and the appointment of good Roman catholic persons to public situations, never to give the least toleration to what may prove for the advantage of protestants.

There appear traces, however, of a certain misunderstanding.

The pope had refused to the king to appoint the bishop of Reggio, as the latter proposed, to a cardinalship. The nuncio was to try to soothe the king on that subject.

It was particularly inculcated on him never to promise money:

"Perche o non intendendosi o non vedendosi le stretteze pur troppo grandi della sede apostolica, sono facili i potentati particolarmente oltramontani a cercar ajuto, e se si desse ogni picciola speranza, si offenderebbero poi grandemente dell' esclusione."

[For in consequence of the by far too pressing straits of the apostolic see being either not understood or not perceived, the potentates, particularly those beyond the Alps, are ready to ask assistance, and if the any smallest hope be given them, they will then become mightily offended at being excluded from it.]

Few ecclesiastical memorials are to be found touching the latter years of Paul V. We avail ourselves of this vacant interval to touch upon some others, bearing particularly upon the administration of the state during that period.

84.

Informatione di Bologna del 1595.—[Information respecting Bologna, 1595.] (Ambros. Bibl. at Milan, F. D. 181.)

The position and constitution of Bologna, the kind of independence it asserted, were so remarkable and significant, that even papers and memorials referring to that provincial city were taken into collections.

In the 22d vol. of "Informationi," we find a number of letters, of the year 1580, addressed to Monsignor Cesi, legate of Bologna, and referring to his administration.

They are almost all recommendations, chiefly intercessions.

The grand-duke and grand-duchess of Tuscany intercede in behalf of count Hercules Bentivoglio, whose crops had been sequestered: shortly after, the grand-duchess expresses her thanks for the attention paid to her request. The duke of Ferrara recommends an actress of the name of Vittoria; the cardinal San Sisto some disorderly students of the university: "we, too," says he, "have been school-boys;" Giacomo Boncompagno, son of the pope, a professor whose office had been taken from him; the cardinal of Como, who had the chief direction of affairs at the time; some monks who had been molested in their privileges: in doing so, he in no wise adopts the tone of one who asks a favour. But other petitions likewise occur. A father whose son had been murdered, urgently entreats, even with tears, that justice should be allowed to take its course upon the murderer who had been already taken and was in prison at Bologna.

It is clear that the governor's influence lay chiefly in the department of justice. In everything else the city was very independent.

"I senatori," it runs, in the report before us, "conferiscono ogni cosa importante col superiore, et havendo in mano tutti li datii et entrate della città, dal datio del sale e vino in poi, che è del papa, dispensano li denari publici mediante un scrutinio, che si fa presente il superiore con le mandate sottoscritte dal detto superiore, dal gonfaloniere et assunti deputati secondo li negotii. Hanno cura delle impositioni e gravezze imposte a contadini, reali e personali, come per li buoi e teste: — attendono alle tasse che pagano li contadini, alle muraglie, porte e serragli, a conservare il numero de' soldati del contado: — provedono ch' altri non usurpi il publico e si conservi la bellezza della città: — han cura della fiera della seta: — eleggono ogni mese per la ruota civile 4 dottori forasticri, che bisogna siano almeno dottori di X anni, e questi veggono e determinano ogni causa civile."—[The senators communicate on all important matters with the superior; and having in their hands all the duties and revenues of the city, except the duty on salt and wines, which belongs to the pope, disburse the public money under the control of an audit, which takes place in the presence of the superior, together with a mandate subscribed by the said superior, the *gonfaloniere*, and deputies assumed according to the nature of the business. They have the charge of the imposts and burthens laid upon the rural part of the province, real and personal, as

1 There have been Germans and Swiss who have since made known a translation of the report. Schreiber Taschenbuch für Geschichte und Alterthümer in Süddeutschland, 1840, p. 280. 1841, 289. 1844, 29.

for property and person; they attend to the taxes paid by the peasantry, to the walls, the gates, and enclosures; to keeping up the number of the soldiers of the country; they see to no encroachments being made on the public, and to the preservation of the beauty of the city; they have the charge of the silk fair; they elect, every month, for the civil rota, four foreign doctors, who must be doctors of at least ten years' standing, and who see and determine all civil causes.]

The question now occurs, how far, in such a state of things, the representatives of the papal government still possessed influence. As has been said, this mainly appears in the department of justice.

"Un auditore generale concorre nelli cognitioni delle cause con la ruota, et un' altro particolare delle cause che avoca a se, et uno criminale chiamato auditore dell torrione del luogo ove risiede, qual tiene due sottoauditori per suo servitio; e tutti quelli sono pagati dal publico."

[An auditor-general takes part, along with the rota, in the cognizance of causes, and another individual does this with causes which he advocates to himself, and another criminal (judge), called auditor of the great tower of the place of his residence, who keeps two sub-auditors to assist him; and all these are in the public pay.]

There follow some statistical statements.

"Contado circa miglia 180: semina intorno a corbe 120 m., raccoglie un anno per l' altro 550 m. a 660 m. corbe. Fa da 130 m. anime (la città 70 m., che avanti le carestie passava 90 m.) 16 m. fuochi, consuma corbe 200 m. di formento (la corba 160 libre), 60 m. costolate di vino, 18 m. corbe di sale, 1700 m. libre d' olio, ammazza 8 m. vaccine, 10 m. vitelli, 13 m. porchi, 8 m. castrati, 6 m. agnelli, et abrugia 400 m. libre di candele. . . . Si fa conto che un anno per l' altro moreno nella città 3 m. persone e ne nascono 4 m., che si faccino 500 spose e 60-70 monachi, che siano portati a' poveri bastardini 300 putti l' anno. Ha 400 fra carrozze e cocchj. Vengono nella città ogni anno da 600 m. libre de follicelli da quali si fa la seta, e se ne mette opera per uso della città 100 m. libre l'anno.

[The country is about 180 (square) miles: it sows about 120,000 bushels; reaps, on an average of years, 550,000 to 660,000 bushels. It contains about 130,000 souls (the city 70,000, which before the dearth exceeded 90,000), 16,000 hearths, consumes 200,000 bushels of corn (at 160 lbs. to the bushel), 60,000 *costolate* of wine, 18,000 bushels of salt, 1,700,000 lbs. of oil; there are killed 8,000 cows, 10,000 calves, 13,000 pigs, 8,000 sheep, 6,000 lambs; and there are consumed 400,000 lbs. of candles. . . . It is reckoned that, one year with another, 3,000 persons die in the city, and that there are born 4,000; that 500 marry, and from 60 to 70 become monks; that there are taken to the poor *bastardini* 300 infants in the year. It has 400 carriages and coaches. There are brought to the city every year about 600,000 lbs. of the cones of which silk is made, and of these 100,000 lbs. a-year are worked for the use of the city.]

85.

Instruttione per un legato di Bologna.—[Instructions for a Bologna legate.] (Vallic.)

Of somewhat later date. We note the following pieces of advice.

"Invigilare sopra gli avvocati cavillosi et in particolare quelli che pigliano a proteggere a torto i villani contro li cittadine e gentilhuomini,—accarezzare in apparenza tutti li magistrati, non conculcare i nobili."—[To have a strict eye upon captious advocates, and particularly upon those who take it upon them wrongously to protect rogues against the citizens and gentlemen,—to make a show of caressing all magistrates, not to trample upon the nobility.] The grievance of the bullies had become so flagrant, that some of these were to be found even among the matriculated students.

Other documents take us into the Campagna di Roma, show how the poor peasantry were oppressed, what the barons received, how the land was cultivated.

86.

Dichiaratione di tutto quello che pagano i vassalli de baroni Romani al papa e aggravj che pagano ad essi baroni.—[Declaration of all that the vassals of the Roman barons pay the pope, and what further they pay to those barons.]

"I. Pagamenti diversi che si fanno da vassalli de baroni Romani al papa. Pagano il sale, pagano un quattrino per libra di carne, pagano l' impositione per il mantenimento delle galere posta da Sisto quinto, pagano i sussidii triennali, pagano i cavalli morti, cioè per alloggiamento di cavalleria, pagano una certa impositione che si chiama de soldati, pagano una certa impositione che si chiama l' archivio, pagano un' altra impositione che si chiama S. Felice, pagano la foglietta messa da Sisto quinto, pagano una certa impositione che si chiama sale forastico.

[I. The various payments made by the vassals of the Roman barons to the pope. They pay salt, they pay a farthing per lb. of flesh, they pay the impost for the support of the galley laid on by Sixtus V., they pay the triennial subsidies, they pay the dead horses, that is for the quartering of cavalry, they pay a certain impost which is called the soldiers' (money), they pay another impost called S. Felice, they pay the pint imposed by Sixtus V., they pay a certain impost called *sale forastico*.

"II. Pagamenti che fanno li medesimi vassali a baroni. Pagano poi al barone, ove sono molina, tanto grano, perche è somma molto grave, pagano risposta di vino, pagano risposta d' olio ove ne fa, pagano di mandare i porci nei castagneti e querceti fatta la raccolta che chiamano ruspare, pagano tasse d' hosterie, pagano tasse de pizigaroli, pagano tasse de fornari, pagano de bichierari, pagano quelli che vanno a spigolare come è secato il grano, pagano dei bestiami che vanno a pascere, pagano risposta di grano, pagano risposta di biada. Montano tutti questi aggravii, come si puol vedere dall' entrate dell duca Altemps, computata la portione del molino della molara che si trahe da vassalli, 2803 scudi; questo si cava da vassalli del Montecapuri (?) del ducato Altemps, che sono da 180 e 190 fuochi, e ciò si mette per esempio, onde si possa vedere appresso come sono aggravati i vassalli de baroni Romani dello stato ecclesiastico. Avertasi che qui non ci è quello che si paga alla camera."

[II. Payments which these same vassals pay to the barons. They next pay to the barons, where there are mills, so much grain, because the amount is very great, they pay *risposta* of wine, they pay *risposta* of oil where it is made, they pay for sending their pigs to the chesnut and oak woods after the produce has been gathered in, which they call *ruspare*, they pay a tax on taverns, they pay the tax on pork shops, they pay baker's tax, they pay glass-blower's tax, those pay who come to glean after the corn has been cut, they pay for the cattle that come to feed, they pay *risposta* on wheat, they pay *risposta* on oats. All these burthens, as may be seen from the revenues of the duke of Altemps, reckoning the portion of the grinding-house of the mill tax drawn from the vassals, amount to 2803 scudi; this is got from the vassals of Montecapuri (?) of the duchy of Altemps, numbering from 180 to 190 hearths, and this is given as a specimen from which it may then be seen how the vassals of the Roman barons of the ecclesiastical state are oppressed with burthens. Be it noted that here payments to the chamber are not included.]

87.

Nota della entrata di molti signori e duchi Romani.—[Note of the revenues of many Roman lords and dukes.]

Beyond a doubt, like the preceding piece, from the times of Clement VIII., who is simply called the pope.

The Colonnas are distinguished by the circumstance of their having vassals; others possess more allodical property. The constable Colonna is valued at 25,000, Martio Colonna of Zagarolo at 23,000 scudi of income.

We have seen how the debt-system of the state was imitated by the barons. The Sermonetas about the year 1600, had 27,000 scudi of income, but 300,000 of debts; the duke of Castel Gandolfo, 14,600 scudi of income, 360,000 of debt. The total incomes of the Roman barons were rated at 271,747, and their estates at the value of nine millions gold.

The author thinks that the estates were in no wise neglected.

"Questi terreni di campagna, contrario all' opinione commune e a quel che io pensavo, sono tenuti con grandissima cura e diligenza: perche si arano quattro, sei e sette volte, si nettano d' erbe due o tre, tra le quali una d' inverno, si levano l' erbe con la mano, si seminano, ragguagliati li quattro anni, li due a grano nei sodi luoghi: dove non si semina, vi si fidano le pecore. Le spighe si tagliano alte, onde rimane assai paglia: e quella poi si abbrugia, che fa crescere. E li aratri con che si arano questi terreni, generalmente non vanno molto profondo: e questo avviene perche la maggior parte di questi terreni non son molto fondati e tosto si trova il pancone. Questa campagna è lavorata tutta per punta di denaro (durch Tagelöhner), segata, seminata e sarchiata: in somma, tutti li suoi bisogni si fanno con forastieri: e genti che lavorano detta campagna, sono nutriti della robba che si porta loro con le cavalle. Questa campagna, computati i terreni buoni e cattivi e ragguagliato un' anno per l' altro, si può dir che faccia ogni uno sei, avvertendo che nei luoghi di questi signori dove sono i loro castelli molte fiate non fanno far lavorare, ma li danno a risposta a' vassalli secondo che convengono. E questo basti quanto alla campagna di Roma. S' affitterà ragguagliato il

[These lands, contrary to the common opinion, and to what I thought, are kept with the utmost care and diligence: for they are ploughed four, six or seven times; they are cleared of weeds twice or thrice, whereof once during winter, the weeds are taken up with the hand; they are sown in rotations of four years; wheat is sown twice on stiff lands, when the land is not sown cattle are committed to it. The ears are cut high, so that much straw is left: and that is then set fire to, which makes the ground productive. And the ploughs with which these lands are ploughed generally do not go very deep, and this because the greater part of these lands is not of a deep soil, and because you soon come to the pan (subsoil). This campagna is all laboured by day labourers, cut, sown, and weeded: in short, all that it needs is done by strangers, and the people who labour the said campagna, are fed on what is brought to them with horses. This campagna, reckoning good and bad lands together, and averaging one year with another, may be said to give a return of sixfold, it being to be noted that in the places of those lords where their castles are, in many instances, they are not laboured by themselves, but are given to the vassals for such a rent as may be agreed upon. And let this suffice for the campagna

rubbio di questo terreno 50 giulj, onde a farli grassa verrà il rubbio del terreno cento scudi e dieci giulj."

di Roma. The average rubbio of this land will be rented at 50 julios, whence to make it fertile the rubbio of land will come to (cost?) a hundred scudi and ten julios.]

For the rest, there were reckoned to be in the campagna at that time 79,504 rubbia, and their produce at 318,016 scudi, 4 scudi the rubbio;—of this there belonged to the barons somewhat above 21,000, to pious institutions about 23,000, to foreigners above 4,000, to the other Roman inhabitants 31,000 rubbia. This proportion was afterwards altered, owing to the Roman citizens having sold so much.

Let us rise, however, to more general circumstances.

88.

Per sollevare la camera apostolica. Discorso di Monsr Malvasia. 1606.—[For the alleviation of the apostolic exchequer. A discourse of Monsignor Malvasia. 1606.]

Notwithstanding all the imposts, it was observed with alarm that still nothing was possessed. "The interests," exclaims our author, "consume nearly the whole revenues: a constant concern is felt about how to cover the current expenses; on any extraordinary pressure occurring, nobody knows whither to turn. To lay on new imposts is impossible; new savings are not at all advisable, "magnum vectigal parsimonia [parsimony is a great tax]; nothing remains but to reduce the rate of interest, and also to take money from the castle. Instead of all the different *monti* with different rates of interest, there must only be one, a *monte papale*, with four or at most five per cent., all the rest must be redeemed. This redemption, according to the nominal value of the *luogo*, is perfectly justifiable: generally speaking, the papal see had contemplated such a redemption at the erection of the *monti:* although previous popes, for example Paul IV., had been obliged to redeem sometimes even at 50 per cent. Clement VIII. even had agreed to only $96\frac{1}{2}$. Thereupon he proceeds to inquire how far this is practicable.

"Succederà che stante la larghezza ed abbondanza del denaro che al presente si trova nella piazza di Roma con l' accrescimento che farà il millione estratto, aggiunta la difficoltà e pericolo di mandar fuori la moneta e l' oro per la prohibitione sudetta—die er vorgeschlagen,—che la maggior parte di quelli che hanno monti ed offizj estinti, volontieri entreranno in questo monte papale, ed a quelli che vorranno i lor denari contanti, se gli potranno pagare del detto millione e del prezzo del monte papale che si andrà vendendo. Si può anche considerare che ne' monti non vacabili ne sono gran parte vinculati ed obbligati a reinvestimento per sicurità di eccezione di dote, di luoghi pii ed altri obblighi, che necessariamente entreranno in questo monte papale, e si tarderà assai a ricevere il dinaro, per ritrovare altro reinvestimento o dare altra sodisfattione ed adempimento alle conditioni ed obblighi a quali sono sottoposti, il che anco apporterà molto comodo e facilità a questo negotio.

"Potrà anco la camera accollarsi tutti i monti delle communità e de' particolari, e ridurli come sopra, e godere quel più sino che da esse communità e particolari saranno estinti.

"A tutti quelli che in luogo di altri monti e officj vorranno del detto monte papale, se gli deve dare la spedizione e la patente per la prima volta gratis senza spesa alcuna.

"In questa maniera può la Sta V. in breve tempo sollevare e liberare la sede e la camera apostolica da tanti debiti e tanta oppressione: perche con l' avanzo che si farà dalla detta estinzione e reduzione di frutti ed interesse, che secondo il calcolo dato alla Sta V. dal suo commissario della camera ascende almeno con far la reduzione a 5 per cento a scudi quattro cento trentunmila ottocento cinque l' anno, potrà estinguere ogni anno scudi trecento trentunmila ottocento cinque di debito, oltre alli scudi centomila che sa-

[The result will be that owing to the freeness and abundance of the cash to be found at present in the Roman market, together with the increase from the million abridged, added to the difficulty and risk of sending money and gold abroad, caused by the prohibition undermentioned—which he had proposed—the greater part of those who have extinguished *monti* and offices, will willingly enter this papal *monte*, and to those who would rather have their money in cash, payment can be made from the said million, and from the price of the *monte papale*, which will be in course of sale. It is also to be considered that in the *monti non vacabili* a great part are bound and obliged to a re-investment for the security of surplus dowries, of pious places, and of other obligations, who will necessarily enter the said *monte papale*, and a considerable delay will take place in receiving the money, in looking about for another re-investment, or giving other satisfaction and execution to the conditions and obligations under which they are laid, which will farther give much accommodation and facility to this business.

Further, the exchequer might take to itself all the *monti* of corporate bodies and of individuals, and reduce them as above, and enjoy the surplus until they shall be extinguished by the said corporate bodies and individuals.

To all those who instead of other *monti* and offices would have the said *monte papale*, there ought to be given the transfer and patent for the first time, gratis, without any expense.

In this manner your holiness might in a short time relieve and liberate the apostolic see and exchequer from so many debts and such oppression: for with the amount to be gained by the extinction and reduction of fruits and interests which, according to the calculation given to your holiness by your

ranno assegnati per rimettere in castello il millione estratto a compire la metà del terzo millione che manca."

commissary of the apostolic exchequer, amounts at least, if the reduction be at five per cent., to four hundred and thirty-one thousand, eight hundred and five a-year, might extinguish annually three hundred and thirty-one thousand, eight hundred and five of debt, besides the hundred thousand scudi to be set apart for repayment to the castle of the million which has been taken from it to make up the half of the third million of deficiency.]

It is enough that we here remark how seriously people thought of having a properly regulated financial system. Yet it is unnecessary to give all the calculations. The Roman court did not enter upon proposals of this sort, but pursued the easier and more convenient course.

89.

Nota di danari, officii e mobili donati da papa Paolo V. a suoi parenti e concessioni fatteli.—[Note of the money, offices, and effects bestowed by pope Paul V. on his relations, and the concessions made to them.]

The pope had been advised to retrench the interest—bearing offices and *monti:* here we find, (1.) a "Nota officiorum concessorum excell^{mo} domino M. Antonio Burghesio tempore pontificatus felicis recordationis Pauli V." [Note of the offices granted to the most excellent lord M. Anthony Burghese, in the time of the pontificate of Paul V., of happy memory]: they consist in all of 120 offices, whose value is estimated at the ordinary market price; (2.) "Nota di molte donationi di monti fatte alli sig^{ri} Francesco Gioan Battista e M. A. Borghese da Paolo V., con le giustificationi in margine di qualsivoglia partito."—[Note of many donations of *monti* made to the lords Francis John Baptist and M. A. Borghese by Paul V., with the justifications in the margin of each transaction.] The meaning is, that extracts are adjoined from the official books in which these grants occur. Under similar rubrics lists are given of what accrued to them in bullion, or in other objects of value, and what privileges were granted to them. The justifications are in the following manner.

"Nel libro della thesoreria secreta d' Alessandro Ruspoli fol. 17 e da doi brevi, uno sotto la data delli 26 Genn. 1608 et l' altro delli 11 Marzo, registrati nel libro primo signaturarum Pauli V. negli atti di Felice de Totis fol. 116 et fol. 131.—A dì 23 Dec. 1605 sc. 36 m. d' oro delle stampe donati al sig^{r} G. B. Borghese per pagar il palazzo et il restante impiegarli nella fabrica di quello, quali scudi 36 m. d' oro delle stampe provenivano del prezzo del chiamato di mons^{r} Centurioni ridotti a 24 moneta a ragione di Giulii 13 per scudo sono 46,800 sc."

[In the book of the secret treasury of Alexander Ruspoli fol. 17, and from two letters, one dated 26th Jan. 1608 and the other 11th March, registered in the first book of the signaturas of Paul V. in the acts of Felice de Totis fol. 116 and fol. 131.—23d Dec. 1605, sc. 36,000 of coined gold bestowed on G. B. Borghese to pay for the palace and what remains to be employed in the building thereof, which 36,000 scudi of coined gold are the produce of the price of the chamade of monsignor Centurioni, reduced at 24 money at the rate of 13 julios per scudo, amount to 46,800 sc.

I have already shown to what extraordinary sums these donations amounted, and what influence the rise of the papal families exercised on the capital and the provinces.

90.

Relatione dello stato ecclesiastico dove si contengono molti particolari degni di consideratione.—[Account of the ecclesiastical state, comprising many particulars worthy of consideration.] (1611.) Inform. politt. xi. f. 1-27.

We are told at once that the author was asked for this account in the morning, and now he sends it off in the evening.

It is truly amazing that he should have been capable of dictating within a few hours so copious a statement, which has turned out not so ill, and contains much that is worth notice. In particular, we become aware of the fact, that the number of inhabitants in many parts of Italy was falling off, either owing to pestilence and dearth, or to the murders committed by banditti, or because the imposts also had become excessively severe: it was no longer possible to marry at the proper age or to rear children. Moreover the taxes sucked the very blood from the inhabitants: by the endless restrictions on trade, their minds, too, were paralyzed.

The anonymous author betrays himself for once. He remarks, that he had written a book (called) Ragione di stato. "Ho diffusamente trattato nella ragione di stato."—[I have treated at large in the Philosophy of Government], he says somewhere.

This furnishes a clue to discover who he was. In the year 1589, there appeared at Venice, "Della ragion di stato libri X con tre libri delle cause della grandezza delle città."—[On the philosophy of government, and on the causes of the greatness of cities.] It is dedicated to that Wolf Dietrich von Raittenau, archbishop of Salzburg, who first among the German princes introduced a stricter administration of the government, modelled on that of Italy. Its com piler is the well-known John Bolero, whose *Relationi universali* enjoyed in their day general circulation.

It is clear that we must examine these *Relationi* to see whether that before us may not be among them.

In what is properly the main work, where the church state is summarily mentioned, it is not to be found; but there is also a smaller book, which is frequently attached to the former: *Relationi dal Sigr Giov. Botero Benese,—di Spagna, dello stato della chiesa, del Piamonte, della contea di Nizza, dell' isola Taprobana,* the dedication of which dates in 1611: there it is found word for word.

The introduction only is different. The *Relationi* bears the title, Discorso intorno allo stato della chiesa preso dalla parte dell' ufficio del' cardinale che non è stampata.—[Discourse about the state of the church, taken from that part of the duty of a cardinal which is not printed.] It belongs, as we see, to a work upon the duties of the cardinals.

I shall not take it upon me to say how far any credulous person may have been deceived by the said introduction.

91.

Tarqu. Pitaro sopra la negotiatione maritima. 17 Ott. 1612.—[Tarqu. Pitaro on the maritime negotiation. 17th October, 1612.] (Vallic.)

Botero recommended, among other things, giving an impetus to the trade of the states of the church. In fact, there was projected at that time a plan for excavating a new harbour for the city of Fano. It was hoped by this to attract thither the commerce of the Urbino markets.

Our author, however, sets himself to oppose this plan with the most cogent reasons. He thinks that a lesson might be taken from the example of Ancona, which he represents as much gone down as shortly after (he describes) the Venetians (to be). "Ne sono partiti li mercanti forastieri, i nativi falliti, le genti gl' uomini impoveriti, gli artigiani ruinati e la plebe quasiche dispersa."—[The foreign merchants have left it, the native are bankrupt, the gentlemen impoverished, the artisans ruined, the common people almost dispersed.] Better destroy Fano from the foundation than build a harbour for it with borrowed money. How had it fared with Ascoli, which had made a considerable loan for the purpose of making its maremma arable, but had not succeeded in doing so.

There were, in fact, other reasons which rendered it unadvisable to enter into it, as the Urbino markets were destined, at any event, soon to fall into the hands of the church.

92.

Relatione della Romagna.—[Account of the Romagna.] (Alt.)

About 1615: the year 1612 is expressly mentioned: but of great consequence for the whole period since Julius III. A description is given of the parties that divided the provinces; the change of property, which took place mainly owing to the entrance of papal families, is very well discussed. I have often availed myself of this work: yet let a place be found here for a notice of San Marino, which in those times gradually rose to freedom through progressive exemptions.

"La republica di S. Marino si presume libera, se non in quanto è raccomandata al duca d' Urbino. Del 1612 si propose e si ottenne in quel consiglio che succedendo la mancanza della linea delle Rovere si dichiaravano sotto la protettione della sede apostolica, della quale per ciò ottennero alcuni privilegii et in particolare dell' estrattione de grani e di grascia. Fa questa terra, compresovi due altri castelli annessi, circa 700 fuochi. E situata in monti, è luogo forte et è custodita la porta da soldati proprii. Hanno la libera amministratione della giustizia e della grazia. Si elegono tra di loro ad tempus i magistrati maggiori chiamati conservatori, a quali tra di loro si da il titolo dell' illustrissimo. In qualche grave ecceeso sogliono condurre officiali forestieri per fare processi e cause, et in particolare li ministri dell' Altezza dell duca d' Urbino, con quella autorità che loro pare. Il publico è povero, che non arriva a 500 scudi d' entrada. Ma li particolari alcuni sono comodi et alcuni ricchi rispetto alla pochità del paese. Solevano affittare banditi d' ogni sorte: ma perche alle volte ne nascevano scandali, è stato da loro decretato che non si

[The republic of San Marino presumes itself free, unless in so far as it is recommended to the duke of Urbino. From 1612, it was proposed and carried in that council, that on the failure in the line of Rovere taking place, they declared themselves under the protection of the apostolic see, from which they thereby obtained some privileges, and, in particular, that of the extraction of corn and provisions. This territory, comprehending two other castles annexed to it, makes about 700 hearths. It lies in the mountains, is a strong place, and the entrance is guarded by its own soldiers. The people have the free exercise of justice and mercy. They elect from among themselves for the time being the higher order of magistrates, called conservators, to whom the title of most illustrious is given among themselves. In the case of any very serious offence, they are wont to employ foreign officials to conduct the processes and causes, and, in particular, the ministers of his highness the duke of Urbino, with such authority as they deem fit. The public is poor, not having above 500 scudi of revenue. But some individuals are comfort-

possino affittare banditi se non con certe conditioni: ma non si ne può havere facilmente salvocondotto."

able and some rich, respect being had to the small size of the country. They are wont to hire banditti of all sorts; but as this sometimes causes scandals, they have decreed that there must be no hiring of banditti except under certain conditions; but not if they cannot easily obtain a safe-conduct from them.]

93.

Parole universali dello governo ecclesiastico, per far una greggia et un pastore. Secreto al papa solo.—[Universal words of ecclesiastical government, for making one flock and one shepherd. Intended for the pope alone.] Informatt. xxiv. (26 leaves.)

Notwithstanding the state of the country, which was always getting worse and worse, there still were people who cherished the boldest projects.

More extraordinary or more sweeping measures, however, were never proposed than by Thomas Campanella in the small work before us.

For there can be no doubt that this unfortunate philosopher, who fell under the suspicion of wishing to wrest Calabria from the Spanish monarchy, and of having taken part in the sweeping plans of the duke of Ossuna, was the author of this work. "Questo è il compendio" [This is the summary], says he, "del libro intitolato il governo ecclesiastico, il quale restò in mano di Don Lelio Orsino, et io autore tengo copia in Stilo patria mia" [of the work intituled, the ecclesiastical government which remains in the hands of Don Lelius Orsino; and I, the author, hold a copy in Stilo, my native place]; to this he adds, "Haec et longe plura explicantur in Monarchia Messiae."—[These, and many other things, are explained in the Monarchy of Messiah.] Campanella was from Stilo, the Monarchia Messiae was his work. We cannot doubt that he either composed or retouched the work before us.

The time may be left undecided. Probably he spent his whole life in notions of this sort.

He remarks that the pope had very warlike subjects:

"Li Romagnuoli e Marchiani sono per natura inclinati all' armi: onde servono a Venetiani, Francesi, Toscani e Spagnuoli, perche il papa non è guerriero."

[The people of Romagna and the Mark are naturally inclined to arms: hence they enter the service of the Venetians, French, Tuscans, and Spanish, because the pope is not warlike.]

But he advises the pope, too, to become warlike. The stuff that the Ciceros, the Brutuses, and the Catos were made of was not extinct: nature was not wanting, but art.

He thinks that the pope should raise two armaments, one of St. Peter on the sea, another of St. Paul on the land, something like the Janissaries. An armed religion has never been vanquished, especially if the people are well preached to.

For he no wise leaves this out of account. He recommends a selection of the fittest persons from all the orders; that these should be loosed from their conventual duties, and allowed to devote themselves to the sciences.

In the monasteries, law, medicine, and the liberal arts should be studied as well as theology. People should be preached to about the golden age, when there shall be but one flock and one shepherd; about the felicity of the liberated Jerusalem; patriarchal innocence: the longings of the people after all this must be called forth.

But when was such a blessed state of things to commence? "Then," he replies, "when all secular monarchies shall be vacated, and when Christ's vicar shall rule over the whole earth."

"Sarà nel mondo una greggia et un pastore, e si vedrà il secol d' oro cantato da poeti, l' ottima republica descritta da philosophi, e lo stato dell' innocenza de' patriarchi, e la felicità di Gerusalemme liberata da mano degli eretici et infedeli. E questo fia quando saranno evacuati tutti li principati mondani e regnerà per tutto il mondo solo il vicario di Christo."

[There shall be in the world one flock and one shepherd, and there will be seen the golden age sung by the poets, the best republic described by the philosophers, and the state of innocence of the patriarchs, and the felicity of Jerusalem delivered from the hands of heretics and infidels. And this will be when all mundane principalities shall be vacated, and when the sole vicar of Jesus Christ shall reign throughout the world.]

He recommends that it be preached that the pope is lord in temporal as well as spiritual things, a priest such as Abimelech, not such as Aaron was.

Such notions were still cherished—for I will not determine exactly—towards the close of the sixteenth century, or in the first ten years of the seventeenth. We know already in what an uncommon state of progress the Roman see was at that time. Before I return to the documents bearing on that period, may I be allowed to add a word on the historians of the Jesuits, who at that very time were in the height of their influence.

INTERCALATION.

ON SOME HISTORIANS OF THE ORDER OF THE JESUITS.

Vanity and leisure gradually lead most orders to write their histories at great length. But none of them all have done this so systematically as the Jesuits. The order itself has taken care to present the world with a connected and comprehensive history of its operations.

In fact, the *Historia Societatis Jesu*, known under the name of Orlandino and his continuators, is for the order, nay, we venture to say, for the history of the century in general, a work of the highest importance.

Nicholas Orlandino, a native of Florence, had for some time presided over the college at Nola, the novices of Naples, when he was called, in 1598, by Aquaviva to Rome, and was appointed historian of the order. He was a careful person in the affairs of life, and also ni his style very precise and considerate, but very infirm. He brought down his work, with difficulty, to the death of Ignatius. He died in 1606.

His successor in this occupation was Francis Sacchini, from the Perugian territory, of the Jesuit historians in general certainly the most distinguished. He was the son of a peasant: his father occasionally visited him in the Collegium Romanum, where he taught rhetoric; and it was reckoned to his honour that he was not ashamed of his parentage. For eighteen years he devoted himself to the composition of his history, in the probation house on the Quirinal at Rome, which he hardly ever left. But not the less did he live in the contemplation of the great interests of the world. The restoration of Roman catholicism was still making the greatest progress. What can have a greater charm for an historian than to describe the origin of an occurrence, the development and effects of which he has in actual life before his eyes? Sacchini was fully impressed with the unique character of his subject—that world-conflict achieved in the enthusiasm of orthodoxy. "I describe wars," says he, "not of nations with one another, but of mankind with the monsters and the powers of hell; wars that embrace not single provinces, but all lands and seas; wars in fine, in which not earthly powers but the heavenly kingdom is the reward of the combat." In this feeling of Jesuit ardour, he has described the government of Lainez, 1556-1564, of Borgia to 1572, of Everard Mercuriano to 1580, each in a volume of eight books, and the first ten years of Aquaviva in the same number of books. They form four tolerably large and close printed folio volumes; not the less does he apologize for being so short. Nor can it indeed be said that he falls into diffuseness or produces weariness. Naturally enough he is partial, extremely partial; he passes over what does not please him: from the materials lying before him, he often adopts only what is honourable (to the society), and so forth; but not the less for all that, do we acquire a deal of information from his books. I have here and there compared him with his original; for example, with the *Litterae Annuae*, where they have been printed and are accessible—in our quarter books of this sort are very rare: I was obliged to call to my aid the libraries of Breslau and Göttingen:—every where I have found him make his extracts with judgment, with propriety, even with genius.—Sacchini, however, had, while thus employed, acquired so extensive and intimate an acquaintance with the affairs of the society, that he was called to take a part in these by the general, Mutio Vitelleschi. For us it were to be wished that this had not been the case. For Sacchini would then have finished Aquaviva's government,—one of the most important epochs would have been far better illustrated than it has been done since. Sacchini died in 1625. Even then his last volume was completed and published by Peter Possino.

But with the lapse of time enthusiasm too passed away. The *Imago primi saeculi*, in the year 1640, is already far inferior in the richness of its contents, far more full of the marvellous, and more rugged;—first, in 1710, there appeared a continuation of Sacchini, by Jouvency, comprising the last fifteen years of Aquaviva. Jouvency, too, has undeniable talent: his narrative is graphic and flowing, although not without pretension; but the misfortune is, he took up the term *historia* quite too literally, and would not write annals as Sacchini had done. Hence he distributed the materials that lay before him according to different rubrics; "Societas domesticis motibus agitata—societas externis cladibus jactata—vexata in Anglia—oppugnata—aucta," &c.—[The society agitated with intestine movements—the society tossed about with external disasters—harassed in England—assaulted—augmented, &c.] Now it so happened therewithal that the most important point, beyond a doubt—the re-extension of Roman catholicism in protestant countries—did not obtain from him the attention that it ought to have had. The annalistic method, besides, was by far the best adapted to such a subject as this. With all his historical endeavours, Jouvency produces nothing but fragments.

Nor withal has he met with much acceptance. The order at one time even projected having the history of the whole of this period written according to the model set by Sacchini. Julius Cordara, who continued the history from 1616--1625, kept close to that model. But the spirit of earlier times was irrecoverably lost. Cordara's volume is quite readable, yet it is not to be compared, in point of elevation and power, with the older works that preceded it, or even with Jouvency. It appeared in 1750. From that date the society had too much to do in struggling for its existence, to allow it to think about a continuation of its history. What had now to be related, too, was far less splendid.

Now, besides this general history, there are, as we all know, a great many provincial histories. In these, for the most part, we find the groundwork of the general history. Most evidently, in the case of Socher, *Historia provinciae Austriae*, which Sacchini often copies, even to single turns of expression, and, for example, repeats the "*pudet referre*" of his original in a "*pudet sane referre.*" (Sacchin. iv., vi., 78. Socher vi., n. 23.)

I will not, however, allow myself to run into a criticism of these authors: that field is quite too extensive, and besides they are not very seductive in our times, and people believe them rather too little than too much; let me be permitted to make an observation only on the history of Ignatio Loyola himself.

On comparing Orlandino with Loyola's two other important biographers, it is obvious that he agrees far more with one of them, Maffei—*de Vita et moribus D. Ignatii Loiolae*—than with the other, Peter Ribadeneira. The manner in which this agreement is shown, is likewise remarkable. Maffei's book appeared as early as 1585: Orlandino first began to elaborate his fifteen years later, and from the great similarity between them, one might suppose that Maffei had helped the other. Not the less is Maffei more elaborate and refined in point of style; Orlandino more natural, more simple, and certainly more graphic. The riddle is solved when we perceive that both drew from a common source—the Memoranda of Polanco. Maffei does not name him, yet a particular memoir by Sacchini informs us, "Cujus sit auctoritatis quod in B. Cajetani vita de b. Ignatio traditur" [which is the authority for what is told of St. Ignatius in the life of St. Cajetan], which memoir is found in the later editions of Orlandino, that Everard Mercuriano gave him the use of Polanco's manuscripts. No wonder that they agree. Only we have the original memoranda more genuine in Orlandino than in Maffei:—the former is more industrious, more copious, and better authenticated; the latter seeks his reputation in historical elegance and good Latin.

But whence come Ribadeneira's variations? He drew mainly upon a different manuscript memoir, the Notabilia of Ludovico Gonsalvi.

Both Gonsalvi and Polanco were indebted for their information to verbal communications from Ignatio; nevertheless we perceive thus much, that Polanco took more from the casual and occasional expressions of the general, while Gonsalvi had contrived to induce him to enter at one time into a copious narrative, bearing chiefly upon his first awakening.

It is evident that we have here to distinguish a double tradition—the one, that of Polanco, repeated in Maffei and Orlandino; the other, that of Gonsalvi, repeated in Ribadeneira.

Gonsalvi is by far the most interesting: properly speaking, he gives us, as far as can here be supposed, an authentic tradition of Ignatio himself.

But, as happens in all cases of traditions, here likewise we soon perceive that the original matter is amplified. For example, he took the account of the eight days' ecstasy which Ignatio had at Manresa, and from which he was awakened by the word Jesus, from the tales of the woman Isabella Rosel of Barcelona. Examen Ribadeneirae in comment. praev. AA. SS. Julii, t. vii. p. 590.

But people were not long satisfied with him. He had not even hinted at many of the miracles that were already believed. *Nescio*, says Sacchini, *quae mens incidit Ribadeneirae ut multa ejus generis miracula praeteriret.*—[I know not what had induced Ribadeneira to pass over many miracles of this kind.] It was just on this account that Polanco planned his collection and allowed Mercuriano to have it elaborated by Maffei. Thus too it was transferred into Orlandino.

But even these narratives were insufficient for the satisfaction of the miracle-loving Jesuitism of the 17th century. Even as early as in 1606, people went so far as to attach a peculiar sanctity to a cave at Manresa, which was assumed to be the place in which Ignatio's *Exercitia Spiritualia* were composed, although neither the one nor even the other tradition says a word about it, and the Dominicans, no doubt with perfect justice, maintain that Ignatio's *spelunca* is in their monastery.

This was just as the keenest controversies were waging between Dominicans and Jesuits—presenting quite a sufficient motive for the Jesuits to look about for a different scene for the founding of their order.

And now we return to our manuscripts relating to Gregory XV. and Urban VIII.

94.

Relatione delli ecc^{mi} S^{ri} Hieron. Giustinian K^{r} Proc^{r}, Ant. Grimani K^{r}, Franc. Contarini Proc^{r}, Hieron. Soranzo K^{r}, amb^{ri} estraord. al sommo pontefice Gregorio XV. l'anno 1621 il mese di Maggio.—[Report by the most excellent Signors Jerome Justinian, knight procurator, Ant. Grimani, knight, Franc. Contarini, procurator, Jerome Soranzo, knight, ambassadors extraordinary to the supreme pontiff Gregory XV., in the year 1621, the month of May.]

Like all the reports of this kind, of little importance.

The description of the new pope and of his government can, after so short a stay, be merely a cursory one: some remarks on the journey, the conclave, the ancestry and the previous history of the person chosen, and the first career of the administration, form generally the only matter.

On this occasion something more, indeed, might have been seen, as the ordinary ambassador, Jerome Soranzo, who had resided five years at the Roman court, had a place among the four ambassadors, and had his share in the drawing up of the report.

The interests of the Venetian senate, however, are not what what we have to do with: they were political, not historical. The natural temper and court-management of a deceased prince no longer gratify curiosity, and have no real importance. Soranzo contents himself with a few observations. "Non debbo tralasciare di narrare qualche cosa delle più gravi che mi sono occorse di maneggiare in sì lunga et importante legatione."—[I must not omit a narrative of some of the graver matters which it fell in my way to manage in the course of so long and important an embassy.]

The most important is his examination of the position which had been assumed by Venice, in the negotiations that had been going on shortly before with Spain before the Roman see.

"Gli Spagnuoli facevano considerar a S. Stà quelle sì opportune congiunture di ravvivar le ragioni della chiesa in golfo. L' ambr si affaticò di mostrare il giusto, antico et indubitato possesso del golfo, aggiungendo che la repca per difenderlo ricorrerebbe ad ajuti stranieri, si valerebbe di Inglesi, Olandesi e di Turchi medesimi, e se S. Stà havesse fomentato l' ingiuste et indebite pretensioni di Spagnuoli, arebbe posta tutta la christianità in grandissimo scompiglio. Un giorno S. Stà mi disse, 'Stimiamo necessario che le cose del golfo non si alterino: le novità seguite in esso ci son spiacciute grandemente: lo abbiamo detto a chi ne ha parlato.'"

[The Spaniards submitted to his holiness's consideration that so opportune conjuncture for reviving the rights of the church in the gulph. The ambassador was at pains to prove the just, ancient, and indubitable possession of the gulph, adding that the republic, in order to defend it, would have recourse to foreign assistance, would make use of the English, the Hollanders, and the Turks, and if his holiness had fomented the unjust and unfair pretensions of the Spaniards, he would have thrown all Christendom into the utmost confusion. One day his holiness said to me, 'We think it necessary that no alteration should take place in the affairs of the gulph: the innovations attempted in that matter have given us much displeasure: we have said this to the person who had spoken about it.']

It will be seen that it was but a fresh outbreak of the old oppositions of interest, too open to make hostilities to be apprehended.

Soranzo merely endeavoured to convince Paul V. that the republic did not lean to the protestants. "Lo resi al pieno capace della bontà e del puro zelo della republica."—[I made him fully sensible of the goodness and pure zeal of the republic.]

The ambassadors felt assured likewise that the new pope would not lean to the side of Spain. The mode and manner of his election seemed to admit of this expectation.

"Nella elettione di Gregorio XV. si mostrò l' effetto del spirito santo. Borghese, che aveva per far il papa a sua voglia sei voti oltre il bisogno, era risoluto di far eleggere Campori: ma tre delle sue creature dissentendovi, nascendo più altri inconvenienti, più per motivo et istigatione d' altri che per inclination propria venne alla nominatione di Ludovisio sua creatura. Questo cardinale aveva l' amore di Aldobrandino, fu tenuto da Spagnuoli di placidi pensieri, Francesi suo confidente l' aveano."

[The operation of the Holy Ghost was seen in the election of Gregory XV. Borghese, who for the making of the pope had at his will and pleasure six votes beyond what were necessary, was resolved to have Campori elected: but three of his creatures differing in opinion, other inconveniences arising, led rather by the motives and instigations of others than by his own inclination, he came into the nomination of Ludovisio, his creature. This cardinal enjoyed the affection of Aldobrandino, was considered by the Spaniards as a man of quiet views; the French had him for their confidant.]

The nephew likewise seemed still to keep himself untrammeled. "Mostra sinora genio alieno da Spagnola" [He shows hitherto a disposition averse to the Spaniards], say the ambassadors.

Yet this all too soon underwent a change.

95.

Vita e fatti di Ludovico Ludovisi, di S. R. Ch. vicecanc. nepote di papa Gregorio XV., scritto da Luc Antonio Giunti suo servitore da Urbino.—[Life and doings of Lewis Ludovisi, vice-chancellor of the Holy Roman Church, nephew of pope Gregory XV., written by Luc Antonio Giunti, his servant from Urbino.] (Cors. 122 leaves.)

"Ludovico, ch'è poi stato il cardl Ludovisi, nacque in Bologno dal conte Oratio della famiglia di Ludovisi e dalla contessa Lavinia Albergati l' anno 1595 a 27 d'Ottobre."

[Lewis, who afterwards became cardinal Ludovisi, was born in Bologna, of the count Horatio of the Ludovisi family, and of the countess Lavinia Albergati, on the 27th of October, 1595.]

He was reared at the Jesuit college in Rome, became a doctor in 1615, accompanied his uncle on his nuncioship to Bologna in 1617; in 1619 he entered on the career of the prelature; the day following his uncle's coronation, 16th February, 1621, he became a cardinal, and thus obtained that important position in the world which we have seen him occupy.

"Darò," says the author, "qualche cenno delle cose parte da lui proposte, parte da lui coadjuvate o promosse nel pontificato del suo zio Gregorio."

[I will give some idea of the matters partly proposed by him, partly aided and promoted by him in the pontificate of his uncle Gregory.]

1. Traits of character.

"Ascoltava tutto con flemma più che ordinaria: gli ambasciatori mai si rendevano satii di trattar seco, . . . si dava a tutti, accioche tutti si dassero a lui. Mostrava giustitia e misericordia insieme, senza passione o doppiezza."

[He listened to everything with more than ordinary phlegm: the ambassadors never were tired of transacting business with him, . . . he gave himself to every one, in order that all might give themselves to him. He showed justice and mercy at one and the same time, without passion and duplicity.]

2. Promotions:—of the cardinals who had favoured his uncle's election, to various legations, of Orsini to that in the Romagna, of Pio in the Mark, of Ubaldini to Bologna, of Capponi to the archbishop of Ravenna. Thus were their good services rewarded. Nuncios were sent to all the courts: Massini to Tuscany, Pamfili to Naples, Corsini to France, Sangro to Spain, Caraffa to the emperor, Montorio to Cologne. Aldobrandino served as general, Pino as treasurer, in Germany. We have the greater number of the instructions given to those nuncios still extant. So much the more interesting is the following notice of the manner in which they were drawn up.

"Quantunque fossero distese da m^r Agucchia prelato Bolognese, nondimeno il card^le fece in esse particolar fatica nelle annotationi di capi, di motivi, del senso di S. Beat^ne, de' ripieghi e consigli suggeriti dal suo proprio avvedimento e sapere."

[Whatever might be explained by monsignor Agucchia, Bolognese prelate, nevertheless the cardinal bestowed particular pains on these in the annotations of the heads, of the motives, of the sentiments of his beatitude, of the remedies and counsels suggested by his own judgment and knowledge.]

We see that the cardinal nephew made the draft; Agucchia, a countryman of Ludovisi's, undertook the extending of what was thus sketched.

3. Bulls on the election of the pope. The forms hitherto followed were altered: the secret scrutiny was introduced, the adoration abolished. Giunti mentions the inconveniences caused by the adoration.

"Rendeva i cardinali più timidi nel dire il parer loro, partoriva e fomentava gravi disgusti tra gli escludenti e gli esclusi, cagionava che il pontefice si eleggesse senza la debita premeditatione, mentre i capi delle fattioni manifestavano le loro voluntà, faceva che la somma delle elettioni fosse per il più appoggiata a cardinali giovani."

[It made the cardinals more timid in the expression of their views, it generated and fostered serious disgusts between the excluded and those who excluded them, it led to the pope being elected without the necessary premeditation, while the heads of the factions manifested their wishes, it led to the result of the elections being left for the most part to the young cardinals.]

It is believed, indeed, that Ludovisi had other secret grounds for the change introduced; these, however, do not appear here.

4. The institution of the Propaganda. Canonization of saints.—These we have treated of.

5. Transference of the electorate. Examination of Ludovisi's personal share in that affair.

6. Acquisition of the Heidelberg Library:—

"Per la quale (la biblioteca Palatina) si operò molto il card^le Ludovisio, atteso che riputava uno degli avvenimenti più felici del pontificato del zio di poterla conseguire. Fu destinato il dottor Leon Allaccio, scrittore Greco dell' istessa biblioteca Vaticana, che andasse a riceverla et accompagnarla."

[For which cardinal Ludovisio made great efforts, seeing that he considered that the being able to obtain it was one of the most felicitous events of his uncle's pontificate. Dr. Leon Allaccio, Greek writer of the same Vatican library, was appointed to go to receive and accompany it.]

7. Protection of the Capuchin monks, whom Ludovisio greatly esteemed, and that particularly of the Jesuits. Vitelleschi says that through the special protection that God had bestowed on this society, it so happened that it always had a great cardinal for its protector: Alexander Farnese, Odoardo Farnese, Alexander Orsino, and now Lud. Ludovisi. He had richly supported the Jesuit churches at Rome and Bologna, and finally for the completion of the former, bequeathed 200,000 scudi in his will. During his lifetime he had bestowed upon it 6,000 scudi a-year. The author reckons this among the alms he paid, and which he makes amount to exactly 32,882 scudi.

8. The election of Urban VIII. It is here ascribed to the cardinal, "superando con la sua destrezza le difficoltà che si traponevano" [overcoming by his dexterity the difficulties that lay in the way]. His removal from Rome to his archi-episcopal see in Bologna, was done quite at his own instance.

9. His subsequent life. He sometimes preached in Bologna:—he succeeded in inducing the Bolognese to add Ignatius and Xavier to the number of their celestial guardian-patrons: but the chief matter is that he keenly opposed the tendencies of the government that had been conducted by him consistently with itself, to the fluctuating politics of Urban VIII.

When the victories of Gustavus Adolphus took place in 1631, he offered the Spanish court 100,000 scudi, and the revenue derived from his Spanish abbeys, of which he possessed ten, during the subsistence of the war. Giunti communicates the letter, in which Ludovisi gives as the ground of this proposal the "presenti bisogni della Germania e dell' augustissima casa di S. M^{ta}, base e sostegno della religione cattolica" [the present wants of Germany and of the most august house of his Majesty, the basis and support of the catholic religion]. In Spain it was not at present accepted: Olivarez replied that although the king declined this offer, still that would not prevent his Majesty from giving the cardinal the favours he wanted, and which otherwise might have been considered as interested.

Nothing is to be found here of a project, which a Venetian ascribes to the cardinal, of calling a council against Urban VIII.

For, in general, this biography is written in the tone of an official panegyric. Although it gives us many useful and authentic pieces of information, it communicates nothing of a suspicious character.

The cardinal died soon after. "La cui anima," [whose soul,] says Giunti in conclusion, "riposi in cielo" [may it find rest in heaven].

96.

Instruttione a mons^{r} vescovo d' Aversa, nuutio destinato da N. Sig^{re} alla M^{ta} Cesarea di Ferdinando II. Imperatore. Roma 12 Apr. 1621.—[Instructions to the bishop of Aversa, nuncio appointed by our lord to go to his Imperial Majesty Ferdinand II., emperor. Rome, 12th April, 1621.]

We have seen the importance of Caraffa's exertions: this at once leads us to attend to the instructions communicated to him by Gregory XV. on his entering upon his nuncioship. They are remarkable, however, as revealing the objects contemplated at Rome after the battle of Prague.

Gregory starts from the idea that it was the object of the protestants to extirpate the house of Austria, to seize the empire for themselves, and then to push forward into Italy with the view of conquering and plundering that noblest part of the world.

He directs the nuncio to turn his attention to the following points:—

I. The fixing of the empire on the side of the Roman catholics. He promises the emperor assistance, and urges that the victory should be promptly followed up.

II. Restoration of the Roman catholic religion. The pope is delighted to see how well this promises in Austria and Moravia. He is comforted to think that in Silesia the Calvinists at least are not tolerated; yet he does not approve of furious persecution, if in Hungary the Augsburg confession only were consented to, which makes the nearest approach to Roman catholicism, "la confessione che, quantunque rea, si dilunga assai meno dalla professione cattolica di quello che facciano le più sette cattoliche."—[the confession which, however criminal, is much less remote from the catholic profession than that made by most catholic sects.] But he was chiefly concerned about Bohemia. For the restoration of Roman catholicism there, he suggests the following measures:—

"1. Fondare in Praga un' università cattolica;

"2. Rimettere nelle antiche parrocchie i parrochi cattolici e per le città i maestri di scola parimente cattolici;

"3. L' uso dei catechismi e di buoni libri per tutto, ma per li fanciulli et idioti l' antiche canzoni spirituali in lingua Bohema;

"4. Librarj e stampatori cattolici, facendo visitare le librerie e stampe degli eretici;

"5. L' opera de' padri Gesuiti e di altri religiosi;

"6. Ritornare in piedi li collegii di poveri, assegnando a quelli li beni ecclesiastici alienati."

[1. The founding of a catholic university in Prague;

2. The sending back into the old parishes the catholic parish priests, and in the cities the catholic schoolmasters likewise;

3. The universal use of catechisms and good books, but for children and ignorant persons the ancient canonical hymns in the Bohemian tongue;

4. Catholic booksellers and printers, causing visitations to be made of heretical booksellers' shops and printing presses;

5. The operations of the Jesuit fathers and of other religious orders;

6. To restore the efficiency of the colleges for the poor, by making over to them the alienated church property.]

All methods of instruction and education. But the nuncio was reminded besides this to oppose the appointment of protestants to public offices. "Lasciandosi le menti humane più consigliare dal proprio interesse che da altro, incominceranno a poco a poco massimamente i giovani a piegare l' animo alla religione cattolica, se non per altro, per partecipare di publici honori."—[As the minds of men allow themselves to be more counselled by their own interest than another's, the young in particular will begin by little and little to incline their mind to the catholic religion, were it only for the sake of sharing in public honours.]

III. Re-establishment of the ecclesiastical jurisdiction. The pope had but too much matter of complaint on this point. The bishops uniformly refused to submit to the regulations of Trent: the chapters made bad appointments under their rights of patronage: the prebendaries had pernicious usages; even the emperor allowed himself too much. "L' imperatore istesso sotto varii pretesti di spogli, di juspatronati, di concessioni apostoliche, di avocarie, di incamerationi e di pienezza di potestà trattiene le chiese gli anni vacanti, et in quel mentre se ne prende per se l' entrate."—[The emperor himself, under various pretexts of *spolia*, patronate rights, apostolical concessions, rights of advocation, of confiscation and of plenary power, keeps the churches in vacant years, and meanwhile takes their revenues to himself.]

IV. Restoration of the papal authority. The emperor appears to have been willing to see that the pope durst no more show himself with his excommunication and bulls. The papal court had likewise lost uncommonly in the money revenues it derived from Germany, and which once amounted to 200,000 scudi. The dealing with Klesel Gregory would not approve, yet expresses himself with great moderation on that subject: "non è mai piaciuto troppo quel fatto" [what was done there never pleased me too much]. The auditor of the Rota, Verospi, was sent over to conduct the process.

V. The emperor's relations with Italy. They might become useful, specially in the affair of the Valteline. Consent had not yet been given in Spain to the demolition of the conquered fortresses. "Pare che il duca di Feria et altri ministri di S. M^{ta} Ces. in Italia si opponghino a quel consiglio, come coloro che vorrebbero ritenere i forti e con essi la gloria di quell' acquisto."—[It seems that the duke of Feria and other ministers of his imperial majesty in Italy oppose that advice, as those who would retain the forts, and with them the glory of that acquisition.] But the pope clearly sees how dangerous that would be: the protestants in Germany would like nothing better than to see the sword unsheathed in Italy.

VI. How the nuncio should conduct himself. Before all he was addressed to Eckenberg, as was indeed to be expected; but what is particularly remarkable, is that the nephew expresses himself only with great reserve on the subject of the Jesuits.

"Terrà gran conto del padre Beccano confessore di Cesare, e si valerà con destrezza dell' opera sua, non lasciando intanto di osservare i suoi discorsi e consigli per scoprirne meglio i fini et avvisarmegli. È parimente a' padri Gesuiti ricorrerà con avveduta confidenza."

[You will make much account of father Beccano the emperor's confessor, and will skilfully take advantage of his assistance, not neglecting meanwhile to observe his discourses and counsels, that he may the better discover their objects and advise me of them. And to the Jesuit fathers likewise he will have recourse with a wary confidence.]

With a wary confidence! a very good advice.

Meanwhile we see what bright prospects the pope already aspired to. Even now he contemplated the restoration of all the property of the church. Let the following passage close our extracts:—

"Secondo che s' anderanno acquistando de paesi tenuti avanti dagli eretici, ella faccia grandissima istanza con S. M^{ta} di ricuperare i beni ecclesiastici occupati da loro e di renderli alle chiese et alli veri patroni. Questo officio si fece per ordine di papa Paolo V., quando il marchese Spinola s' impossessò del palatinato, e l' imperatore rispose che non era ancor tempo di trattarne."

[According as progress shall be made in acquiring countries previously held by the heretics, you will make the utmost instance with his majesty to get back the ecclesiastical estates now in their hands, and to restore them to the churches and true patrons. This good office was done by order of pope Paul V., when the marquis of Spinola took possession of the palatinate, and the emperor replied that it was not as yet the time to treat of that.]

We see that the idea of the edict of restitution was conceived by Paul V. in the year 1620, but was at that time still rejected by the emperor as inopportune.

The nuncio was now to press for it anew, and to represent to the emperor the advantages he would derive from it.

97.

Instruttione a mons^{r} Sangro, patriarcha d' Alessandria et arcivescovo di Benevento, per andar nunzio di S. Sta al re cattolico. 1621.—[Instructions to monsignor Sangro, patriarch of Alexandria and archbishop of Benevento, for going as nuncio from his holiness to the catholic king. 1621.]

Sangro is reminded that the government in Spain was now chiefly in the hands of Uzeda and the Grand Inquisitor. He was accordingly to remind the latter especially of his spiritual duties.

In order to make mimself master of the court secrets, he was directed to attach himself to the ambassadors of Venice and Tuscany: "de' quali si suol cavar molto" [from whom much is usually to be got].

The affairs of the immunities, of the ecclesiastical jurisdiction, of the Collettoria, are afterwards more closely discussed. I will only confess that the faulty and illegible copy that I found, has prevented me from farther entering upon these points.

The main affair remains the discussion of political relations. Here the nuncio is specially to demand the renewal of the Dutch war.

He was to remind (the Spanish court) that prince Maurice was already old and weak, and that his death was daily expected:—that the dissension betwixt the Arminians and the Gomarists weakened the provinces: with the help of the former Count Henry, and with that of the latter Count Ernest hoped to obtain the supreme power:—that the Zeelanders were poor, and the Hollanders hated by the rest on account of their encroachments: "Laonde il re non può voltare le sue forze contra di loro in meglior tempo ovvero opportunità."—[Hence the king cannot turn his forces against them in better time or opportunity.]

98.

Instruttione a V. Sig[ria] M[r] di Torres, arcivescovo di Antrinopoli, nuntio destinato da N. Sig[re] in Polonia. 30 Maggio 1621.—[Instructions to your lordship Monsignor di Torres, archbishop of Antrinopoli, nuncio appointed by our lord in Poland. 30th May, 1621.]

The misunderstanding between Paul V. and Sigismund III., was not so insignificant. "Se la pietà del re," [If the king's piety,] says Gregory XV., in these Instructions given to his first nuncio, "e la riverenza che a questa sede egli porta, non havesse ammorzato del tutto o almeno coperte le scintille de' dispiaceri loro, se ne sarebbe per li soffioni altrui acceso alcun fuoco di discordia manifesta" [and the reverence which he bears to this see, have not quite quenched, or at least smothered over the embers of their disagreements, if there shall not be enkindled by suggestions from other quarters the fire of manifest discord].

Gregory is now anxious to have everything settled. He is penetrated with the services of this king who could not have been made a better catholic in Rome itself.

The nuncio is reminded before all things to conduct himself so as to give no scandal:—"perche tutti gli pongono gli occhi adosso e prendono ancora esempio da santi costumi di lui, et il re medesimo il propone a suoi prelati per norma" [because all eyes were turned upon him, and further took an example from his holy manners, and the king himself proposed him as a rule for his prelates]. Assiduously to frequent the banquets of the great, were in itself indeed no unpleasant way of acquiring influence, but in the end would weaken the esteem in which it was necessary that a nuncio should be held.

It were well that the nuncio should again, as before, personally visit the churches.

Education ever remained the grand affair. The institute of the Dottrina Christiana, as it existed in Italy, was to be introduced here also. Attention was to be bestowed on catechisms and spiritual books, and the supplanting of worldly and protestant by Roman catholic songs.

99.

Instruttione a V. S[ria] M[r] Lancellotti, vescovo di Nola, destinato da N. S[re] suo nuntio in Polonia.—[Instructions to your lordship Monsignor Lancellotti, bishop of Nola, appointed by our lord as his nuncio in Poland.]

I know not whether written in 1622 or 1623, but certainly still under Gregory XV.

The instructions received by Torres were communicated to the nuncio. Thereafter, at the command of the Propaganda, all the bishops were called upon to report upon their dioceses; and the nuncio was to consult these reports likewise for information.

The political relations (of the country) appear somewhat more prominently. The nuncio was to do his utmost to preserve the good understanding subsisting between Poland and the house of Austria. That was a check upon the Turks and the rebellious subjects of the emperor.

The Poles would willingly have concluded a peace, or at least a twenty years truce with Gustavus Adolphus: the latter also represented that the Polish line would succeed him in the event of his dying without children, but Sigismund rejected everything of the kind. "Benche Gustavo per conditione expressa offrisse che morendo lui senza figliuoli gli avesse a succedere S. M[tà] e la sua stirpe, s' oppose a questi consigli."—[Although Gustavus by an express condition offered that upon his death without sons his majesty and his line would succeed him, he opposed these counsels.] Solely out of respect for the Poles would he agree to a short truce.

The circumstances of the united Greeks had already been discussed in Torres's Instructions, yet it is done here more clearly and with greater depth.

"I Greci commossi a tempo di Clemente Ottavo per opera di Rupaccio Pacciorio, che fu prima vescovo overo vladica di Vladimiera e poi metropolitano di Chiovia, si contentarono i vescovi o vladici loro, eccettuati quelli di Leopoli e di Premisla, che nella loro ostinatione si rimasero, d' unirsi alla chiesa Romana, e di riconoscere, come fecero l' anno 1595, il papa per loro capo secondo la forma e professione di fede nel concilio Fiorentino contenuta. Ma tante discordie ne nacquero, e così si posero nelle diete a impugnare quella unione li nobili greci, dagli heretici favoriti, che s'è havuto a mettere sossopra il regno: imperocche pochi del clero e molto meno del popolo l'hanno voluto abbracciare, affermando tutti essere per privati disegni e per ambitione di pochi stata fatta e senza loro parte-

[The Greeks, being influenced at the time of Clement VIII. by the exertions of Rupaccio Pacciorio, who was first bishop or vladica of Vladimiera, and then metropolitan of Chiovia, their bishops or vladicas were content, with the exception of those of Leopoli and of Premisla, who persisted in their obstinacy, to unite with the Roman church, and to recognise, as they did in the year 1595, the pope for their head, according to the formula and confession of faith contained in the Florentine council. But so many discords arose out of it, and the Greek nobles, favoured by the heretics, so set themselves to oppose in the diet that union, that it would have turned the kingdom upside down, because few of the clergy, and many fewer of the people, liked to embrace it, all affirming that it had been

cipatione. Onde si conservano bene li vescovi e pastori cattolici, ma questi soli se ne stanno, senza trovare pecorelle che seguitare li vogliano, e di più corrono gran rischio d'essere dalle sedie loro cacciati e che vengano ancor ad essi levate quelle chiese che tolte già alla scismatici furongli concedute. Onde in tutte le diete se ne fa lo strepito grande: e nell' anno passato avvenne che un vescovo o fosse il patriarca scismatico di Gerusalemme mandato in Moscovia et in Russia dal patriarca di Constantinopoli, si fermò fra Russi, e vi creò tanti scismatici quanti sono gli uniti, et eccitò li cosacchi, che sono tutti Greci scismatici, ad addimandare nella dieta con offerte grandissime, perche il regno per la guerra col Turco havesse bisogno di loro, che all' antiche loro pretensioni si sodisfacesse: ma il vescovo di Santo Angelo, all' hora nuntio, ne divertì l'impeto, siche tra per questo e per publiche necessità, che a nuove contese non lasciavano luogo, si pose con l'autorità del re il negotio in silentio. Si vive non di meno dagli uniti nel medesimo timore: e li più prudenti prelati ne pronosticano alla fine de' mali eventi se alcun provedimento non vi si piglia: onde havrebbero alcuni havuto per lo migliore che l'unione non si fosse mai fatta, apportando essi che sarebbe stato più agevole il ridurre li nobili singolarmente e di famiglia in famiglia alla chiesa cattolica, perche si vede per prova che tutti coloro che ad uno abbandonano il rito Greco e lo scisma, stanno nella nostra chiesa perseveranti."

done from private views and the ambition of a few, and without their participation. Whence the catholic bishops and pastors are indeed preserved, but these alone keep their ground without finding flocks willing to follow them, and moreover they run a great risk of being expelled from their sees, and of being again deprived of those churches which, after being taken from the schismatics, had been conceded to them. Hence a great noise is made about it in all the diets: and in the past year it so happened, that a schismatic bishop, or possibly a patriarch, sent into Muscovy and Russia by the patriarch of Constantinople, shut himself up among the Russians, and created there as many schismatics as there are united (Greeks), and stirred up the Cossacks, who are all schismatic Greeks, to demand in the diet, with very great offers, seeing that the kingdom needs them for the war with the Turk, that all their ancient claims should be satisfied· but the bishop of Saint Angelo, present nuncio, turned off the impetus, so as by this and by the public necessities, which allowed no room for new contests, the affair, with the king's sanction, passed off in silence. Not the less do the united Greeks cause the utmost apprehension: and the wisest prelates prognosticate bad results at last, if there be no provision made against them: hence some would have it, that it were better the union had never taken place, these alleging that it would have been easier to bring back the nobles, one by one, and family by family, into the catholic church, since experience proves that all who have singly left the Greek rite and schism, remain steadily attached to our church.]

100.

Relatione fata alla congregatione de propaganda fide da Dionysio Lazari sopra alcune cose che possono essere di servitio alla santa fede cattolica.—[Report made to the congregation de propaganda fide by Dionysius Lazari on some matters that may be of service to the holy catholic faith.] 1622.

Dion. Lazari had been for some time—as he expresses it, "molti mesi" [for many months] —in England, and now suggests how Roman catholicism might be re-established there.

He thinks there were three methods: negotiation with one or many, or violent measures.

He thinks, however, that much might be effected personally with king James. That the king was indifferent in his views and timid. "Per la pratica che ho di lui, lo stimo indifferente in qualsivoglia religione.—[From what I see of him, I consider him indifferent in point of religion.] That it were well to foster his suspicions by means of forged letters.

"Far artificiosamente avisar qualche suo ministro fuori del regno di persona da loro creduta fedele, e nell' istesso regno far trovar qualche lettera a nome supposito che trattasse in forme segrete queste materie."

[So to contrive, that some minister of his, out of the kingdom, should receive advices, apparently from a person believed by them to be faithful, and in the kingdom itself to have some letter drawn up in a fictitious name, which should treat about these matters in secret forms.]

Buckingham, too, might be gained over: his wife was the daughter of a Roman catholic, and herself secretly a Roman catholic (è segreta cattolica figlia anche de secreto cattolico). Buckingham attached much importance to alliances with foreign powers: by means of these he might be most easily gained over; particularly as he was in constant jeopardy from the parliament.

"Essendo composto il parlamento quasi per la maggior parte di puritani, stimarebbe egli specie d' efficace vendetta l' indurre il re al cattolicismo."

[The parliament being composed, for the greater part, almost of puritans, he would think it a kind of efficacious revenge to lead the king to catholicism.]

Influence put forth on the multitude. It would be extremely useful if they could but have liberty of preaching.

"Il che si potrebbe fare per via di danaro, proponendo, per così dire, una gabella di predicatori et auditori, inducendosi il re molte volte per l' interesse a cose contrarie a sua volontà."

[Which might be done by means of money, proposing, so to speak, a tax on ministers and hearers, the king being often led, by a regard to his interest, into things contrary to his will.]

Violent measures, he says, were not to be thought of. But we see well that even the pacific ones he proposes were impracticable.

Lazari belongs to that class of people who imagine that they can operate upon the progress of society by means of intrigue and subtilely contrived measures, but which they can never accomplish.

He has no hopes of the adult generation: it had been brought up entirely in protestant opinions; the prince alone, afterwards Charles I., seemed to give him any hope.

"Io v'ho grandissima speranza, per verderlo d' indole molto ingenua, di costumi assai generosi, molto sobrio nel detestar li cattolici."

[I have the utmost hope of him, from seeing him to be of a very ingenuous disposition, of very noble manners, very temperate in his dislike to the catholics.

101.

Instruttione al dottor Leone Allatio per andare in Germania per la libreria del Palatino. 1622.—[Instructions to doctor Leo Allatio for going into Germany for the library of the Palatine. 1622.] (Library at Vienna, MS. Hohenb.)

Being the instructions wherewith Leo Allatius, at that time scribe to the Vatican, was commissioned to take the Heidelberg library into his possession.

It is to be found not only in Vienna but also in many other libraries; for example, the Chigi library at Rome, among the collections of Gregory XV.'s Instructions. The literary interest attached to the subject, has led likewise to its being known among us. Quade, Baumgarten, and Gerdes, one after another, have had it printed in Latin.

After having once touched the domain of protestant literature, it was destined also at last to become the subject of controversy. In the history of the formation, capture, and annihilation of the old Heidelberg collections of books (Heidelberg, 1817), p. 235, our learned fellow-citizen and friend, Mr. G. R. Fr. Wilken—thus I wrote in 1836—has suggested serious doubts as to its genuineness.

In point of fact, the Latin translation has been made in a manner that must excite distrust. That, however, fortunately disappears when we look at the original manuscript.

In the Latin, for example, it is said with respect to the consecrated medals which had been given to Allatio for Tilly's soldiers:

"Unum adhuc R. T. D. suppeditamus stratagema, ut scilicet sibi magnam nummorum comparet copiam, quos a sanctis canonisatos esse fingat."

[One further stratagem, rev. doctor of theology (?) we suggest, namely, that he should collect a great quantity of pieces of money, which he may pretend to have been canonized by the saints.]

Verily it is incredible that the Roman court should have expressed itself in this manner towards one of its servants.

But let us look to the original, and we find it runs quite otherwise.

"E qui soggiungerò a V. S. che se le darà un grosso numero di medaglie con l' indulgenza della canonizzatione de' santi fatta da N. S."

[And here I will suggest to your lordship that a great number of medals be given them, with the indulgence of the canonization of the saints done by our lord.]

I understand medals struck on the canonization of the saints which Gregory XV. had undertaken, with indulgence.

As little do we find in the original that Allatio addressed the duke of Bavaria in German, as the Latin version would have it. "Tradito," it runs in Baumgarten, "brevi a Sancto Patre fidei ipsius concredito, Germanico idiomate eum affandi."—[Having delivered the brief intrusted by the Holy Father, on the faith of his addressing him in the German idiom.] In the original, on the other hand:

"Presentando a Sua Altezza il breve N. S^re^, le parlerà a nome di Sua S^tà^ conforme al tenore di esso."

[Presenting to his highness the brief from our lord, he will speak to him in the name of his holiness, conformably to it.]

A translation which insults the Italian and all probability.

As, however, we see the original drawn up so much more ably, and in a quarter which leaves no room for doubt, we can no more question its authenticity.

It certainly remains true that Allatio was to spread the report that the library was to go to Munich, not to Rome:

"In ogni caso sarà bene di metter voce che si abbia da condurre solamente a Monaco e non a Roma."

[At all events, it were well to spread the report that you are charged to conduct it only to Munich and not to Rome.]

We have already seen how often the most extreme caution was enjoined as a matter of duty on the papal envoys. Allatio received other similar instructions. For example—

"Massimamente per i paesi sospetti sarà

[In the suspected countries chiefly, it will

sempre meglio di andare in habito corto, come persona negotiante del dominio Veneto."

[It would always be better to go about in a short coat, like a person on commercial business from Venice.]

So much disguise seemed necessary.

That so many directions were thought requisite is not to be wondered at. People were fond of writing at that court, particularly in Ludovisio's chancery. The instructions drawn up by Agucchia are not wanting in important political views, but they are also full of petty matters of this sort. The person who drew them up would have the merit of thinking about everything.

Moreover there was much reason to dread the rage which the loss thus inflicted on their metropolis might excite among the Reformed. The library was to be escorted with a division of cavalry.

102.

Instruttione al padre Don Tobia Corona de' chierici regolari mandato da papa Gregorio XV. al re di Francia e prima al duca di Savoia per l' impresa della città di Ginevra, 1622.—[Instructions to father Don Tobias Corona of the clerks regular, sent by pope Gregory XV. to the king of France, and first to the duke of Savoy, about the city of Geneva enterprise, 1622.] (Library at Frankfort on the Maine. MSS. Glaubarg. tom. 39, n. 1. 26 4to leaves.)

Commencement: "L' Italia che dall' eterna providenza è stata eletta a reggere hora l' imperio temporale, hora lo spirituale del mondo."—[Italy, which by eternal providence has been elected to govern at one time the temporal, at another the spiritual empire of the world.]

To this spiritual empire Geneva is an object of special detestation: "Non solo come piena di huomini appestati, ma come catedra di pestilenza" [not only as being full of infected men, but as being the very seat of the pestilence].

Its punishment and destruction was a task specially befitting both the pope as the vicar of Christ, and the duke of Saxony, who called himself count of Geneva. Often, too, had the popes and dukes attempted this; but their attempts had always misgiven in consequence of the protection given by France to that city.

Now, however, the state of things was altered.

"La Francia tratta il soggetto di domare i ribellati heretici, et ha da ricever piacere che per togliere loro le forze e la riputatione si faccia il medesimo senza suo costo in altre parti."

[France treats the subject of subduing the heretical rebels, and has reason to be pleased that this very thing should be done by depriving them of their force and reputation, without costing her anything in another quarter.]

The pope had from the commencement of his reign conceived the plan, and thought that the accomplishment of it might be furthered by sending a monk.

"Poiche habbiamo un' argumento di religione, si conviene fuggendone il rumore coprirlo più che si puote: vuole inviarvi un religioso. La P. V^{ra} porterà da per tutto questo negotio come nato nell' animo di Sua Sta senza altra origine che dello spirito santo."

[Since we have an argument drawn from religion, it is proper that while rumour is on the wing, it should be dissembled until the thing can be done; he wants to send a monk there. You will conduct the whole of this affair as originating in the mind of his holiness, without having any other source than the Holy Ghost.]

He was first to awaken warlike feelings in the duke of Savoy, and should the duke ask for assistance, to be sure to represent how much the support pledged to the emperor and the league had exhausted the apostolic see, how many claims Poland preferred, how much expense Avignon occasioned; nevertheless he was certainly to allow hopes to be entertained of some assistance being rendered: "che Sua Sta non sarà stretta a S. A. di tutti quelli ajuti che dalle picciole forze uscir potranno" [that his holiness will not be niggardly to his highness in giving him all those aids that may proceed from small resources]. He was also to apply for the necessary information respecting the rights of Savoy to Geneva.

But the main matter is the representations he was to make to the king of France:—1. that he should not even so much as incur the suspicion of persecuting the protestants solely from an eye to political interests; 2. that even these, rightly understood, required the annihilation of Geneva:

"Se Ginevra non fosse stata ricovero di Calvino, la M^{ta} S. non havrebbe di presente da portare l' armi contro l' ostinati e perversi suoi popoli Ugonotti, non si vedrebbe nascere le republiche contro la monarchia. . . . Sono republiche (die hugenottischen) popolari che in ogni palmo di terreno e fino nell' istessa corte e forse nella camera del re hanno lor cittadini e seguaci. . . . Già la republica loro (Ugonotti) è piantata, già ne sono publicate le

[Had Geneva not given shelter to Calvin, his majesty would not now have had to bear arms against his obstinate and perverse people, the Huguenots, republics would not be seen rising against the monarchy. . . . There are democratical republicans (the Huguenots) who, in every handbreadth of territory, and even in the very court, and perhaps in the king's chamber, have their compatriots and followers. . . . Already has their republic

leggi, e già in ogni provincia hanno costituiti i magistrati, i consigli et i governatori dell' armi: più non hanno da fare che da andare eglino a muovere l' armi al re per cacciarlo di casa."

(the Huguenots) been planted, already have their laws been published, and already, in every province, have they magistrates, and military councils, and governors: they have nothing more to do but to go and take up arms for the king's expulsion.]

We see how much the monarchical element appears in the Roman catholic struggles. Geneva is to be destroyed as being the mistress and the counsellor of the Huguenot republicans. It can find no assistance now, for all other protestants were themselves fully occupied, and England was tied up by treaties.

And what will this aggrandizement of Savoy in accord with France amount to? The pass cannot be barred to the Swiss, since the king possesses Bresse.

"I cantoni cattolici, con quali la corona è più congiunta, ne riceveranno e servitio e piacere: certo che il cantone di Friburgo circondato da Bernesi heretici, benche sia valoroso e di loro non tema, haverà nondimeno più caro di confinare per via del lago con quella città divenuta cattolica e posta sotto il dominio di un principe amico e cattolico, che libera et heretica remanente."

[The catholic cantons with whom the crown is most allied, will be served and benefited by it: certainly the canton of Friburg, which is surrounded by the Bernese heretics, although it be valorous and not afraid of them, will not the less like better to be bounded, on the side of the lake, by that city when become catholic and placed under the dominion of a friendly and catholic prince, than remaining free and heretical.]

Cardinal Retz, the constable (Luines), and father Arnour were named to the friar as the persons from whom he might look for special support.

We shall speedily come to the results of this mission.

103.

Relatione di Roma fatta nel senato Veneto dall' ambasciador Rainiero Zeno alli 22 di Nov. 1623.—[Report on Rome, made in the Venetian Senate by the ambassador Rainiero Zeno, 22d Nov. 1623.] Informatt. politt. tom. xvi. 101 leaves.

Ambassadors, on their return, generally express themselves with modesty and deference, both as respects the princes from whom they have come, and as respects their hearers: Rainier Zeno is the first that makes a display of great self-satisfaction. He declares not only that he exhibited a balance-sheet of the papal income and expenditure, which he had made up with assiduous pains (f. 80): he also reminds his hearers, of the warm colours in which he had described this or the other cardinal in his despatches (f. 111). Of pope Urban he states without reserve, "with two words I annihilated his opinion." He says at once that the divine Majesty had given him the talent for penetrating into men's most secret designs; and he makes the cardinal Ludovisio pass an eulogy on the republic for always selecting men of the most approved capacity for the Roman embassy.

Rainier Zeno appears some years after in the Venetian troubles of 1628. There, too, all that proceeds from him, like the report before us, wears the pomposity of the self-conceit that shows itself in so many of the Italians and Spaniards of this century.

Among men of this description there never could fail to occur angry collisions, and Rainier Zeno lived to experience the most unpleasant scenes in the course of his embassy.

These occurred chiefly in the times of Gregory XV. Ludovisio insisted on being treated with a reverence and acknowledgment which Zeno refused to give him: they very soon had a violent quarrel.

In the last part of his report Zeno describes these dissensions. He boasts of his having often spoken sharply to the nephew, and having silenced him. It gave him particular satisfaction that he had by secret means informed himself of things that the nephew believed to have been kept profoundly secret.

"Vedeva," he says, "che appresso di me non poteva restare in quel gran concetto di sapere ch' egli con tutti ascosamente ambiva."

[I saw that before me he could not remain in that great conceit of knowing what he went secretly about with all.]

But it must not be thought that this did much harm: the republic rather acquired thereby the greater reputation. In contemplating the leaving of the Valteline as a deposit in the hands of the Spaniards, Ludovisio dreaded nothing so much as the noise that would be made by the Venetian protests against it ("il fracasso che era per fare io, il rimbombo delle mie proteste" [the noise I was about to make, the redound of my protestations]).

These times meanwhile had passed away. Urban VIII. had mounted the papal throne, and Rainier Zeno makes it his chief business to describe that pope's personal qualities, court and state administration, in so far as they had then developed themselves.

He repeats that the cardinals made it their only concern to speak so as to please the pope: he thinks it all well that no one thought of bringing the finances into order. There is no fitter instrument, says he, for embroiling Christendom than the head of a pope.

After this he gives a sketch of Urban VIII.:—

"E prencipe d' aspetto grave e venerabile, di statura grande, di colore olivastro, di lineamenti nobili, di pel nero che comincia a tirar al canuto. d' uttillatura più che ordinaria, e

[He is a prince of grave and venerable aspect, tall in stature, of an olive complexion, of noble features, his hair black but beginning to turn gray, of more than ordinary

di gratia singolare ne' gesti e ne' moti del corpo. Parla per eccellenza bene, et in qualsivoglia discorso che s' entra seco, ha da difendersi quanto vuole, e d' ogni materia mostra d' haver peritia straordinaria. Ha mostrato sin hora diletto grande della poesia, l' uso della quale non ha mai intermesso, nè pure nelle occupationi e nelli studii più serii: perciò gl' intendenti di questa arte e delle lettere che chiamano di humanità sono stati sempre benveduti da lui, et gli ha favoriti cortesemente in quello che ha potuto: non l' ha però questo diletto astratto da quello che importava più e che era più necessario per li carichi che successivamente li sono passati per le mani, dico dallo studio delle leggi, nel quale ha faticato incessantemente dalla prima gioventù sino a questi ultimi anni con tanta maggiore applicatione, perche così richiedeva la carica del prefetto della signatura di giustitia, magistrato che richiede studio et accuratezza grandissima et esattissima per la varietà delle materie che vi concorrono. Delli affari del mondo e degl' interessi de' prencipi è intendentissimo, quanto che se nelle scuole politiche havesse fatto continua dimora."

elegance, and singularly graceful in his gestures and bodily movements. He speaks well to a proverb, and whatever be the subject of your conversation with him, he has wherewithal to defend himself as much as he pleases, and in all matters displays extraordinary skill. He has shown down to the present time a great love for poetry, the practice of which he has never intermitted, even in the midst of more serious occupations and studies: accordingly the connoisseurs in that art and in what is called humane literature, have always been looked upon by him with a favourable eye, and he has shown them the utmost possible courtesy: this taste in fine has not withdrawn him from what was of more importance and more necessary for the charges that successively passed through his hands, I mean from the study of the laws, in which he has laboured incessantly from his early youth until of these late years with so much the greater application, because this was required by the charge of prefect of the segnatura of justice, a magistracy which requires study and the utmost and most exact accuracy for the variety of matters that concur in it. He is most knowing in the affairs of the world, and in the interests of princes, as much as if he had spen his lifetime in the schools of politics.]

It is nowise necessary to extract more: in general it is all much alike. The finer traits of this intellectual physiognomy, whether because they did not develope themselves till afterwards, or because Zeno was incapable of comprehending them, are not to be found here.

This is just as little the case as respects the subsequent portraits of the pope's relations, or as respects the cardinals whom the author minutely goes through.

This only is to be noticed that he thought no sort of services were to be expected from the Venetian cardinals. "Priuli," says he, "languido di spirito come di corpo" [languid in mind as he is in body]. Thus contemptuously does he speak of them. He will not say a word about Venier, in order to avoid having anything to do with his relations.

He then proceeds to political concerns. He is only well pleased that this time a pope has been elected who does not doat upon the Spaniards. Albuquerque had found the soil uncommonly hard, and his demands had been refused. The relation in which Urban VIII. stood to France, is described by Zeno as follows:—

"Non è da dubitarsi che il pontefice verso il regno di Francia habbi molta propensione d' affetto, additandocelo molte congetture probabilissime: hebbero a quella corte principio le sue grandezze, alle quali se bene ascese per merita proprii, non nega però egli medisimo che di grande ajuto li fossero le attestationi d' Henrico quarto della sodisfattione che haveva del suo modo di negotiare et del gusto che sentirebbe di vederli partecipato l'honor solito a conferirsi alli altri residenti in quella carica: quadra benissimo a Sua Sta il trattare de' Francesi ingenuo et libero, lontano dalli artificii, lontano dalle duplicità proprie delle altre nationi; ha una certa conformità di genio alle qualità de' studii alli quali s' applicano et de' quali si dilettano più li Francesi, ch' è la pulitezza delle lettere, l' eruditione più acconcia, la poesia, la cognitione delle lingue, in che per quanto le permettono le sue attioni, s' è pigliato molto piacere. Stima quel regno, quanto si possa dire, per reputarlo equilibrio dell' ambitione d' altri, li cui fini mirano senza dubbio alla monarchia universale."

[It is not to be doubted that the pontiff has an affectionate leaning to France, this being signified to us by many most probable conjectures: at that court his high preferments commenced, to which, although he rose by merits of his own, he himself does not the less deny that he was greatly helped forward by the attestations of Henry IV., of the satisfaction that monarch had received from his mode of negotiating, and of the gratification he felt at seeing him share in the honours usually conferred on the other residents in that charge: his holiness is very much pleased with the mode of dealing practised by France, so ingenuous and free, far removed from the artifices, far removed from the double dealings peculiar to other nations: he possesses a certain conformity of genius with the kind of studies to which the French are most addicted, and in which they take most delight, that is to say, polite literature, the more elegant kind of erudition, poetry, the knowledge of languages, in which so far as his active engagements will permit, he has taken much pleasure. He thinks of that kingdom as highly as can be said, considering it as the counterweight to the ambition of others, the grand object of whose aims is unquestionably universal monarchy.]

The pope took offence at the Venetians for their being in league with heretics and infidels. He thought they surely might have had some other support.

Zeno concludes, while once more recalling the sweat and toil that his office had cost him, the ceaseless watchings, the bitter vexations by which his health had been impaired. "Nevertheless," he exclaims, "I feel greater satisfaction at having used away my life in my country's service, than I should have felt had it been in my power to live a whole century happily, but unemployed."

104.

Relatione degli ecc^mi signori amb^ri straordinarii Corner, Erizzo, Soranzo e Zeno ritornati ultimamente da Roma, letta all' ecc^mo senato 25 Febr. 1624 (i. e. M. V. 1625).—[Report from the most excellent lords ambassadors extraordinary Corner, Erizzo, Soranzo and Zeno last returned from Rome read to the most excellent Senate 25th February 1624 (that is, M. V. 1625).]

As pope Gregory XV. declared that he would no longer treat with Rainier Zeno, the Venetians sent Jerome Soranzo in his place. Yet as we have just seen, Zeno was still in Rome when Urban VIII. was elected. Both were appointed to the charge of solemnly congratulating the new pope, Corner and Erizzo appear for the purpose of completing the embassy.

The report which they draw up in common, is free from those personal effusions to which Zeno alone was addicted; it acquires a certain importance, owing to the circumstances of the republic having become complicated anew through the affair of the Valteline.

Pope Urban seems to have been much dissatisfied with Venice for having taken part in the attack made by the French on the papal garrisons: "che i cannoni della republica si fossero voltati contra i luoghi tenuti in deposito della S. Sta, che chiamò luoghi dell' istessa chiesa" [that the cannon of the republic should have been turned against the places held in the deposit of his holiness, that are called the places of the church].

"Nè mancano," [there were not wanting,] the ambassadors go on to say, "in Roma soggetti d' ogni grado et d' ogni qualità che proponevano a S. Sta, come ella medesima ci disse, ad usare contra quell' ecc^mo senato le censure ecclesiastiche" [subjects in Rome of every rank and every quality, who proposed to his holiness, as he himself told us, to employ ecclesiastical censures against that most excellent senate].

They endeavour to excuse themselves to the best of their power. They allege that it is the aim of the Spaniards to possess themselves of the sole monarchy: "rendersi patroni di quelli passi, per facilitarsi la monarchia di questa provincia;" [to make themselves masters of those passes, in order to facilitate their having the monarchy of this province;] that religion might even be better secured; that their allying themselves with countries beyond the Alps was the less to be blamed in them, as the raising of troops in the states of the church was forbidden them by the popes themselves.

Urban VIII. had believed that they would make some conciliatory proposals upon the former of these affairs; yet they had no commission to that effect. On his side too, he therefore showed himself on that account inaccessible to their requests. They had to be contented with the mere appeasing of his displeasure—"non si impetrava altro che mitigamento dell' acerbità mostrata del suo animo."

This they could not have found very difficult. Already were there appearances of Urban's anti-Spanish sentiments. He declares, "che non poteva parlar alto, perche troppo era circondato da' Spagnoli, e che a Madrid lo chiamavano heretico, ma che armato si harrebbe fatto rispettare" [that he could not speak high, because he was too much surrounded with Spaniards, and that at Madrid they called him heretic, but that armed he would have made himself respected].

These words involve at once his subsequent views and conduct.

It is mainly with objects of this sort that the report before us is occupied: but there is an attempt made in it besides, to describe the general state of things. Mark the account given of the chiefs of the administration in the first times of Urban VIII.

"Quelle che di presente sono in maggior autorità presso il pontefice nella essentia degli affari, si ristringono nel sig^r cardinale Magalotti e nel sig^r Don Carlo Barberino, fratello della Beat^ne Sua. Mostrano però ambidue di non conoscere e non bavere questa autorità: schifano i congressi, parono non esser informati dei negotii, non gustano di esser frequentemente visitati, e con questa maniera di procedere, differente assai dal costume dei parenti dei pontefici passati, conservano in maggior riputatione la Santità Sua, volendo dar ad intendere che tutto dipende dai soli cenni di lei.

"Era solita la Beat^ne Sua alle volte nelle occorrenze più gravi chiamare anche a se li cardinali Bandino, Melini, Scaglia, Santa Susanna et qualche altro, perche conoscendoli di natura molto severa, procurava con tale apparenza dar segno di stima verso il sacro

[Those who at present are in most authority with the pontiff in the essence of affairs, are confined to the lord cardinal Magalotti and the lord Don Carlo Barberino, his beatitude's brother. Both would have it appear, indeed, that they do not admit and do not possess this authority: they decline holding interviews, they appear not to be informed about affairs, they do not relish being frequently visited, and with this manner of proceeding, very different from what was usual with the relations of past pontiffs, they better maintain his holiness's reputation, desiring that it should be understood that all depends on his sole will.

His beatitude was always wont, in the case of graver occurrences, to call to him cardinals Bandino, Melini, Scaglia, Santa Susanna, and some besides, because being known to be of a very severe temper, he contrived by such

collegio e verso le persone loro, non già perche volentieri inclini o molto si fidi delle loro opinioni: e di questo concetto della Sta Sua, ben noto a detti cardinali et ad altri, tutti se ne dogliono, dicendo che dopo fatte le deliberationi delle cose ella le communica per non admettere il loro consiglio. E si sente anco che va ogni giorno più tralasciando queste comunicationi, anzi omettendo in tutto e per tutto le consultationi con cardinali, così per conservare in se medesimo il solo despotico dominio et autorità, come anco perche conoscendoli dipendenti et interessati chi per l'uno chi per l' altro principe, giudica così convenire al suo servitio maggiormente.

"Nelle occorrentie della Repca sono intervenuti nelle consulte mr Gessi e mr di Montefiascone, come stati nontii in questa città e bene informati delle cose. E talvolta si è introdotto anche Anzolo Badoer, che sotto altro nome e cognome pur si trattiene in Roma positivamente: è fatto sacerdote, et habita per sua maggior sicurezza una casa congiunta con il monasterio de' frati della scalla, nella cui chiesa è solito celebrare la messa. Ma come habbiamo detto, il cardl Magalotti et il sigr Carlo Barberino sono le stelle fisse di quel firmamento: et i negotii ridotti in queste due sole teste passano con molta secretezza, sicche quello che non si può penetrare con la congettura ovvero che non viene riferito dal medesimo pontefice, difficilmente si può sapere per altra via.

"Il sigr Don Carlo mostra la istessa indipendenza da principi nella quale professa conservarsi Sua Sta. E in età di 58 anni, ben complessionato e forte. E inclinato alla sodisfatione de' popoli per conservare la città abbondante di tutte le cose. Nella sua casa è buon economo, et ha mira di far denari assai, sapendo egli molto bene che l' oro accresce la riputatione agli huomini, anzi l' oro gli inalza e li distingue vantaggiosamente nel conspetto del mondo: oltro che si tiene per massima comune non esser conveniente nè ragionevole che chi una volta è stato parente del papa, resti dopo la sua morte in angusta fortuna. E huomo di poche parole, ma sensitivo. Ha mostrato somma riverenza verso la serenissima Republica, et havendo noi nel complir seco detto che auguravamo lunghi anni a Sua Beatne, ci rispose egli con qualche acerbità che quando il papa havesse ad essere rispettato et honorato come papa, alludendo alle cose correnti della Valtellina, li desiderava vita lunga, ma che quando havesse dovuto seguir altrimenti, pregava il sigr dio a chiamarlo a se quanto prima.

"Il cardl Magalotti professa egli ancora vivere indipendente. E huomo sagace et accorto: mostra grande vivacità di spirito e d' inquietezza, et è in concetto di poter esser guadagnato. Crescendo in età et esperienza il cardl nepote si crede che non passeranno d'accordo insieme e che il papa penserà però di valersene in qualche legatione opportunamente."

appearances to give a mark of respect for the sacred college and their persons, by no means because he was willingly inclined to, or had much confidence in, their opinions: and this conceit of his holiness, well known to the said cardinals and others, is matter of grief to all, it being said that after matters have been deliberated upon he then communicates them, so as to leave no room for their advice. And it is perceived also that he is daily more and more leaving off these communications, rather omitting in everything and for everything consultations with the cardinals, both to preserve in himself the sole and absolute dominion and authority, and also because, knowing them to be dependent on and in the interest, one of this and the other of that prince, he considers that this suits his service best.

In matters touching the republic, the consultations are attended by monsignors Gessi and Montefiascone, as having been nuncios in this city and well informed on affairs. And sometimes there has also been introduced Anzolo Badoer, who resides modestly in Rome under another name and surname: he has become a priest, and for his greater security inhabits a house adjoining the monastery of the friars *della scalla*, in whose church he usually says mass. But as we have said, cardinal Magalotti and signor Carlo Barberino are the fixed stars of that firmament: and the affairs referred to these two heads pass with great secrecy, so that what cannot be penetrated by guessing, or does not happen to be told by the pontiff himself, it is hard to find out by any other way.

Signor Don Carlo shows the same independence of princes that his holiness professes himself. He is 58 years old, of a good constitution and strong. He is inclined to the satisfaction of the peoples by keeping the cities well supplied with all things. In his own house he is a good manager, and aims at making a deal of money, knowing very well that gold enhances men's reputation, that gold also raises and distinguishes them advantageously in the eyes of the world; besides that it is most commonly held not to be fitting or reasonable that he who has once been the pope's relation, should be left after his death in narrow circumstances. He is a man of few words, but sensitive. He has shown the utmost reverence for the most serene republic, and on our saying, in interchanging compliments with him, that we wished long years to his beatitude, he answered us with some bitterness that had the pope been to be respected and honoured as pope, alluding to the current affairs of the Valteline, he would have wished that he might live long, but since it had been to be otherwise, he prayed the Lord God to call him to himself as soon as possible.

Cardinal Magalotti professes that he too lives independently. He is a sagacious and prudent man: he shows great mental vivacity and restlessness, and it is thought that he may be gained. Growing in age and experience, the cardinal nephew thinks to himself that they will not go on harmoniously together, and that the pope, therefore, will think of availing himself of his services in case of need in some legation.]

105.

Instruttione a Mre Sacchetti vescovo di Gravina, nunzio destinato di N. Sre per la Mtà cattca. 1624.—[Instructions to monsignor Sacchetti, bishop of Gravina, nuncio appointed from our lord for his catholic majesty. 1624.] (Barber. fol. 26 leaves.)

Sacchetti's commissions relate I. to the internal affairs of Spain, II. to the general affairs of Europe.

I. There were at all times quarrels of various kinds betwixt Rome and Spain. The Roman court, in particular, had taken it ill that a cardinal like Lerma should be deprived of his revenues and arraigned before a secular tribunal. While the pope endeavoured to stay the progress of this proceeding, he made Lerma also be warned to resign all hope of earthly grandeur: that nothing indeed was now to be effected since Olivarez stood so high in favour, and that he should make up his mind, after having lived so long to others, now to live to God. On the other hand, the nuncio was addressed to Olivarez with whom the Roman court was still on good terms. This was attended with the following remarkable result:—"E avvenuto che la gelosia della regina per qualche sospetto d' altri amori del re l' ha provocata a dolersene col re di Francia suo fratello, a segno tale che venne pensiero a questo di far doglianze e querele pubbliche contro il cognato. Di cio scrisse l' antecessore di V. Sria e che vi haveva posto rimedio con far confidente della regina il conte Olivares di diffidentissimo che era prima."—[It so happened that the jealousy of the queen, excited by some suspicion of the king's having other objects of affection, provoked her to complain on the subject to the king of France her brother, to such a degree that the latter had thoughts of making public complaints against his brother-in-law. Your lordship's predecessor wrote of this, and that he had, by way of remedy, restored the queen's confidence in Olivarez, of whom she had been at first most distrustful.]

The nuncio was directed also to the grand inquisitor. He was still further to stimulate him to vigilance against the introduction of heretical books into Spain and the Indies.

II. People in Spain had conceived the idea of putting the German line, by means of two new marriages, in quiet possession of its last acquisitions. The hereditary prince of the Palatinate and Bethlemgabor were both to be married to imperial princesses: thus it was hoped that the Hungarian, and still more the German troubles, might be composed. People would not at first believe this at Rome. Notwithstanding, fresh intelligence left no further room for doubt. The pope hastened to make representations to the kings against it. It was seen from letters that it was nowise the intention of the English, even though the prince of the Palatinate were sent to the imperial court, that he should be allowed to become a Roman catholic. And would people trust to so uncertain a person as Gabor? He could not believe or approve of it. He commissions his nuncio to oppose it with all his might.—"V. Sria, ma con destrezza et a tempo, facci per impedirli (questi due matrimonj) tutto quello che umanamente può."

We know that pope Urban himself took part in causing these, if not very far-seeing, yet well-intended plans to miscarry. The mission of Rota, which we have spoken of, is explained by these expressions.

106.

Instruttione a V. Sria arcivescovo di Damiata e chierico di camera per la nuntiatura ordinaria al re cristmo. 23 Genn. 1624.—[Instructions to your lordship, archbishop of Damiata, and clerk to the chamber, for the ordinary nuncioship to the most christian king. 23d January, 1624.]

Collateral to Sacchetti's instructions.

The pope here also condemns, in the warmest manner, the above plan for the restitution of the Palatinate: he calls upon the king's influence to induce Saxony not to set himself in opposition to the progress of the Bavarian power. Moreover he wished for nothing more than that Orange should be ravaged, which was but a rendezvous for the heretics.

But what is of most importance is the internal affairs. King Louis XIII. is described thus:—

"Il re è fuori di modo virtuoso et abborrisce tutti quei vitii che sogliono accompagnarsi alla dominatione: non è altiero, ma humanissimo; non è amatore della propria opinione, ma più volentieri crede a buoni consigli: non ama il riposo, ma è dedito alle fatiche e le tollera fortemente, senza conoscere altro piacere che quello della caccia: non nutrisce pensieri dimessi, ma è avidissimo di gloria, senza dilungarsi punto dalla pietà. Con la Mtà S. possono i ministri di stato et i serventi nelle caccie, a quali volentieri s' accosta per godere la libertà, che non concede la stretta pratica de' grandi. Il più caro di quelli che hanno l' adito a S. Mtà con occasione delle caccie è il signore di Toiras, huomo cauto e

The king is virtuous beyond measure, and abhors all those vices which usually accompany domination: he is not haughty, but most affable; not self-opinionative, but would rather listen to good advice: he does not love repose, but is devoted to labour, and bears it bravely, relishing no gratification but that of hunting: he does not nourish abject thoughts, but is most greedy of glory, without at all neglecting piety. His majesty is influenced by the ministers of state, and those who attend him to the chase, with whom he likes to enjoy that easy intercourse which is not allowed by the etiquette of high life. The greatest favourite among those who have access to his majesty, on hunting occasions,

prudente, che non si rimescola negli affari di stato per ascondere la sua autorità, ma ne è capace." . . .

is the lord de Toiras, a wary and prudent man, who does not mix himself up with state affairs in order to conceal his authority, but he is capable of conducting them.]

Among these princes, Roman catholicism was now making splendid progress. The nuncio was directed to do his utmost to aid all the famous missions, especially in the south of France, and to defend their interests at the royal court.

But just at this time the opposition of the Gallican principles likewise begins to bestir itself invincibly and with ever-renovated vigour.

Part at least of the members of the Sorbonne propounded the doctrine of the independence of the civil power, and the divine right of bishops. Some were already giving currency to the opinion, that it behoved parish priests to be as powerful in their parishes as bishops in their bishoprics. These opinions the pope thought abominable. He was excessively annoyed that Richer, who defended them with extraordinary zeal, notwithstanding his being excommunicated, should make no account of that, but continue to say mass as usual.

Meanwhile the parliaments endeavoured effectually to limit the church's jurisdiction. The appeals, *come d'abus*, the investigations into the despatch of the dataria, the assaults on the jurisdiction of the bishops, appeared to the pope as so many usurpations.

"Favoriscono chiunque ad essi ricorre, et in questa maniera procurano di soggiogare le provincie a loro non soggette, come la Bretagna, la Provenza e la Borgembrescia."

[They favour all who have recourse to them, and in this manner endeavour to subject provinces not subject to them, such as Brittany, Provence, and Burgundy.]

They interfered, also, in the prohibition of books. The nuncios would willingly have prohibited such works as those of de Thou and Richer, but they found it impossible. The new nuncio was directed rather to prevent the appearance of hurtful books than to wait till they appeared.

"Le stampe de' libri sono il fomite delle false dottrine: et è necessario che ella procuri di tenersi amorevoli i librari, accioche l'avisino di mano in mano de' libri che si stampano: imperoche stampati che sono, porta seco difficoltà di ottenere la prohibitione."

[The printing presses are the nurses of false doctrines: and it is necessary that you endeavour to acquire the favour of the booksellers, in order that they may give notice successively of the books that are sent to press: seeing that, after being printed, difficulties occur in getting them prohibited.]

It is evident that already the entire struggle between the Curia and Gallicism had commenced, that struggle which, in various phases, agitated the different periods of the old Bourbon monarchy.

107.

Instruttione a V. S[ria] mons[r] Campeggi, vescovo di Cesena, destinato da N. Sig[re] suo nuntio al S[mo] Sig[r] duca di Savoia. 1624.—[Instructions to your lordship, monsignor Campeggi, bishop of Cesena, appointed by our lord his nuncio to the most serene duke of Savoy. 1624.]

The interest of these instructions is enhanced by the additional light they throw on the result of Don Tobias Corona's mission. We see that the plan meditated against Geneva misgave, owing especially to the opposition it experienced from Luines and Rohan, who were still powerful, and from the respect commanded by the Huguenots in general; but that it was by no means relinquished on that account.

"Da chi venisse il motivo di tal impresa, dal papa o dal duca, non si sa bene: perche il pontefice lasciò brevi e lettere di esortatione al medesimo sig[r] duca et al principe del Piemonte, donde poteva farsi congettura che il papa ne fosse autore: ma nel ricevere l'esortatione si mostrò tanto pronta l' A. S. che non parve lontano dal vero il credere che havesse indotto il papa a scrivergli. . . . . Le difficultà che incontrò il padre Corona, non furono dalla parte del re e della regina, che piegarono subito alle persuasioni pontificie, ma dalla parte del contestabile Luines, seguitato da principali ministri, o per proprio interresse o per adulatione, e da alcuni grandi del partito Ugonotto. A Luines si crede che instillasse questa aversione all' impresa il duca di Roano, e cercandosi della cagione che ha potuto spignere questo ad opporvisi, altra non se ne trova, fuori della propria inclinatione al mantenimento degli eretici, essendo egli tale, che il timore di perdere il seguito dentro alla Francia, mentre che i seguaci suoi

[It is not well known who first suggested this enterprise, whether the pope or the duke; for the pontiff sent brieves and letters of exhortation to the said lord duke and to the prince of Piedmont, whence it may be conjectured that the pope was its author; but his most serene highness showed so much readiness to receive exhortation, that it does not seem far from the truth to believe that he had induced the pope to write to him. . . . . The difficulties encountered by Father Corona were not on the part of the king and queen, who yielded at once to the pontifical persuasions, but on the part of the constable Luines, followed by the leading ministers, from an eye to their own interests or from adulation, and by some grandees of the Huguenot party. The duke of Rohan is thought to have instilled into Luines this aversion to the enterprise; and if we ask what was the cause that was powerful enough to stimulate him to oppose it, none can be found but his own desire to keep up the heretics, that being tantamount

havessero havuto a soccorrere i Genevrini. Il trattato del padre Tobbia restò a segno che non solamente il re non rimase offeso di questa missione, ma niuno, etiando di quelli che l' intendessero bene, hebbe ardire di biasimarla: e solamente dissero alcuni che non era quello il tempo di intraprendere un tanto affare; altri, che non doveva il duca mettere in queste strette il re se non dopo il fatto, imperciocche allora S. M^ta non havrebbe potuto non dar lode alla pietà e generosità del duca, ma che antecedentemente non doveva la M^ta S. violare quella fede sotto la quale pensano di riposare sicuri i Genevrini. Dall' hora in qua si è creduto che il sig^r duca pensi a tentare la via d'una sorpresa, e adesso non se ne ha più dubbj, imperciocche S. A. se n'è dichiarata con la Sta di N. Sig^re, supplicandola a volerlo assistere. La Sta S. ha risposto che volentieri e con quel medesimo modo che fece papa Gregorio: ma perche il necessario segreto della sorpresa non è capace di questa via, S. A. si è rivoltata a contentarsi che N. Sig^re gli prometta di fare tali ufficii col re christianissimo dopo il fatto che la M^ta S. non habbi a sdegnarsene."

to the dread of his losing a body of followers within France, while his followers would have had to succour Geneva. The negotiation of Father Tobias went so far, that not only the king was not offended at that mission, but none even of those who should have understood it well dared to censure it: and only some said that that was not the time to take in hand so great an affair; others said, that the duke ought not to have placed the king in such a dilemma until after the thing was done, for that then the king could not but have commended the duke's piety and generosity, but that antecedently his majesty was bound not to violate the faith under which the Genevese thought that they securely reposed. It has been believed hitherto that the duke thinks of attempting a surprise, and now this cannot be doubted, since his highness has communicated on the subject with the holiness of our lord, beseeching him to assist him. His holiness has replied, that he will do so willingly, and in the same manner that pope Gregory did: but because the necessary secrecy of a surprise is incompatible with that course, his highness has declined it, and is content that our lord should promise using his influence with the most christian king in such a way after the thing is done, that his majesty shall have no cause to be angry.]

Here, moreover, some matters specially Piemontese, are spoken of. The symptoms of subsequent contentions begin to appear. The duke preferred a claim to the nomination to the episcopal sees: the pope would allow him only the right of recommendation: he shows his dissatisfaction at some burdens imposed on the clergy.

108.

Ragguaglio dello stato di religione nel regno di Boemia e sue provincie incorporate. 1624.—[Account of the state of religion in the kingdom of Bohemia and its incorporated provinces. 1624.]

Charles Caraffa arrived at Prague in 1621, and at once went to the work to which he had been specially commissioned by pope Gregory XV., namely, to superintend the restoration of Roman catholicism in Bohemia.

Eighteen months thereafter, as he himself says—consequently in November 1622—he drew up, under the title *Relatio Bohemica*, a report on his proceedings, which he sent to the newly founded Propaganda. I saw the original of the same which was circulated among the members of the congregation; these were cardinals Sauli, Bandini, Barberini (afterwards Urban VIII.), Borgia (afterwards Urban's keen opponent), Ubaldini, Santa Susanna, Valerio Sagrato, Zollern, and the prelates Vives, Agucchi, Scala. Zollern was to take a copy and report from it.

Caraffa enlarged this first report fourteen months after, consequently in January 1624, and despatched it, under the above title, to Urban VIII., "in order," as he says, "still further to inflame his paternal zeal to love towards Bohemia."

We have a copious printed work of Caraffa's—*Commentaria de Germania sacra restaurata*—one of the most important sources for the history of the first ten years of the Thirty Years' War. But it is evident, that in it he could not enter so fully into the Bohemian proceedings, which he always thinks of with predilection, as in a work specially destined to the subject: and a printed work, too, makes it necessary to have an eye to what may be thought in other quarters. On the other hand, the report is expressed without any restraint in point of fact or feeling.

It comprises, indeed, the commencement only of the Bohemian revolution, but for that it is really of great value.

I have already availed myself of it in my narrative; yet, as the case required, with great conciseness: here I will add some particulars, from which it will appear under what difficulties, created chiefly by the government of the country, the nuncio carried his views into effect.

I. INTRODUCTION OF THE LATIN RITUAL.

"Havendo io tenuto sopra cio proposito col Plateis e considerando, sicome quei pochi Boemi che erano cattolici frequentavano in ogni modo le chiese di nostro rito, dove pure

[Having had a conference on this subject with Plateis, and considering how those few Bohemians that were catholics, frequented in every way the churches of our ritual, where

ascoltavano i divini ufficj in lingua latina, giudicai non essere disperabile che l' istesso potessero fare anche quelli che di nuovo si convertissero, insinuandosi massime loro da predicatori che questa lingua sia quasi in un certo modo d' essenza ne' divini uffici in tutti li paesi cattolici e particolarmente in quelle chiese che si comprendono sotto l' imperio occidentale, per segno della superiorità e maggioranza della chiesa Romana sopra tutte le altre: però diedi ordine ad esso Plateis, che quanto prima havesse potuto, usasse ogni suo studio per restituire l' uso del predetto idioma in quelle chiese che già si erano levate di mano agli eretici. Onde il giorno de' santi apostoli Simone e Giuda dell' anno 1621, con l' occasione di essere stata provista dall' arcivescovo di parroco cattolico la chiesa di Santo Stefano, principale parrocchia di Terra nuova, habitata dal più minuto volgo, tra il quale sono pochissimi cattolici, fu celebrata alla presenza di numero grandissimo di heretici nelli predetta chiesa l' immaculatissimo sacrificio della messa in lingua latina con l' aspersione dell' acqua benedetta, con l' invocatione de' santi e con tutti i riti romani, due secoli dopo che n' era stata esclusa la lingua latina, e che per molti anni non vi si era celebrato nè nell' uno nè nell' altro idioma. Il quale esempio hanno poi seguito con le chiese della città tutti i luoghi del regno senza sentirsi romore o strepito alcuno nel popolo: et io essendo in Praga ho visto detto popolo stare con molta attentione alle funtioni divine."

moreover they heard the divine offices in the Latin tongue, I judged that we should not despair of the same being done by those who should be converted anew, chiefly through having it insinuated in them by preachers, that this tongue is, as it were, in a certain measure, of the essence of the divine offices in all catholic countries, and particularly in those churches that are comprised under the western empire, intimating the superiority and pre-eminence of the Roman church above all the rest: accordingly I gave orders to the said Plateis, that as soon as it should be in his power, he should use his utmost endeavours to restore the use of the said idiom in those churches that had already been taken out of the hands of the heretics. Hence, on the day of the holy apostles Simon and Jude, in 1621, on the occasion of St. Stephen's church being provided by the archbishop with a catholic priest, it being the chief parish church of the New Land, inhabited by the meanest of the common people, among whom there are the fewest catholics, there was celebrated, in the presence of a very great number of heretics in the said church, the most immaculate sacrifice of the mass in the said Latin tongue, together with the sprinkling of holy water, the invocation of saints, and all the Roman rites, two centuries after the Latin tongue had been abolished, and after the lapse of many years in which it had not been celebrated either in the one idiom or the other. Which example was then followed, together with the churches of the city, by all places in the kingdom, without any rumour or tumult being felt among the people: and I, while in Prague, have seen the said people stand with much attention at the divine offices.]

II. TAKING AWAY OF THE CUP.

"Inteso poi da me il senso della sacra congregatione del santo ufficio per le lettere e scritture all' hora mandatemi, risolvei di vietarlo (il calice) onninamente e non dar più orecchie alle ciance e preghiere di detti regnicoli, argomentando che se havessero voluto essere obbedienti figli di santa chiesa, camminerebbero così in questa come in ogni altra cosa di concerto col restante del corpo cattolico; ma se sfuggissero di recedere da questo abuso radicato anche negli animi de' cattolici per la pretesa concessione di Pio quarto, tenerlo per segno di superbia et ostinatione e per indicio di non veri cattolici: onde tralasciato ogni altro rispetto e timore allegato da politici, i quali da questa novità immaginavano sollevationi o ruine irremediabili, feci prohibire a tutti li parrochi che non porgessero ad alcuna persona la specie del vino, comandando loro che a chiunque le domandava ambedue, chiedessero se era cattolico, e confessandosi tale gli enunciassero la necessità di ubbedire al rito Romano il quale esclude i laici dal calice. Così molti che non erano tocchi da vero zelo, sentendo questo si rimanevano nella loro ostinatione, non communicando nè nell' una nè nell' altra forma, e noi intanto conseguivamo l' intento nostro, che non si porgeva il calice: ma non fu però niuno di quei preti tornati all' obbedienza che havevano in cura le chiese reconciliate il quale

[Having afterwards ascertained the sentiments of the sacred congregation of the holy office, by the letters and writings then sent me, I resolved to forbid the cup entirely, and to give no more heed to the prattle and prayers of the natives, arguing with them that if they wished to be obedient children of holy church, they will conduct themselves, both in this and in everything else, in concert with the rest of the catholic body; but should they avoid receding from this abuse which is rooted farther in the minds of catholics by appealing to the concessions of Pius IV., to account it a mark of pride and obstinacy, and as an index of their not being true catholics: hence, laying aside every other consideration and fear, alleged by politicians who imagined that this innovation would produce insurrections and irremediable ruin, I issued a prohibition to all the parish priests, against presenting to any one the species of wine, commanding them to inquire of each that should ask for both, if he was a catholic, and on his confessing as much, to proclaim the necessity of obeying the Roman ritual which excludes the laity from the cup. Thus many who were not touched with a true zeal, perceiving this, persisted in their obstinacy, not communicating in either form, and we meanwhile pursued our purpose that the cup should not be held out: but there was

havesse l' animo di porgere la sola specie del pane in faccia degli heretici che frequentavano dette chiese: sino che il cancelliere Plateis diede intrepidamente principio a questa santa impresa nella parrocchia di San Martino, come di sopra si è notato. Il quale uso introdotto poi a laude di Dio nell' altre chiese si osserva con intera quiete, ancorche mi habbiano in cio dato assai che fare i politici. Perciocche vedendosi gli heretici svanito il disegno fatto di dovere in ogni modo conseguire da veri sacerdoti cattolici il santissimo sacramento sotto l' una e l' altra specie, hebbero l' anno passato 1622 ricorso da politici: e qualunque maniera con loro si tenessero, a me per adesso non importa riferirlo: basta che estorsero una lettera del principe Licchtenstain, che all' hora si trovava qui, in virtù della quale, come se fosse per ordine di Sua M[ta], chiamando i due parrochi della madonna del Tein e di Santo Eurico, stati già predicanti, comandarono loro che nella solennità della pasqua porgessero indifferentemente a ogn' uno, di qualunque rito fosse, la communione sotto l' una e l' altra specie. Così il giovedì in coena domini per mera perfidia di detti politici nella chiesa del Tein fu commessa grandissima abominatione, ricevendo il venerabile corpo del signore consacrato sotto le due specie del pane e del vino da legittimo sacerdote più di mille scellerati heretici, dandosi in tale guisa per colpa d' huomini cattolici il santo a cani. A questo non mancò il Plateis di fare l' oppositione che se li aspettava, ma niente potè contro la temerità loro: onde egli per sostenere la prohibitione dell' uso del calice deliberò fare animo e distribuire il sacramento, come tre giorni dipoi fece, pubblicamente sotto la sola specie del pane, nella parrocchia di San Martino. Ma havendo io havuto notitia di questo empio attentato, fui subito a farne acerba lamentatione con Sua M[ta], dolendomi con ogni più efficace maniera che i suoi ministri si volessero ingerire in quelle cose che concernono la reverenza verso il tremendo sacramento dell' altare, che meramente riguardano lo spirituale e la salute dell' anime, e che senza rispetto niuno s' intromettevano negli affari di religione, non mostrando segno alcuno di obbedienza verso Dio e la santa sede Romana, della quale la Maestà Sua si era sempre mostrata tanto ossequente. Da che fuori di modo commosso l' imperatore diede subito rigidissimi ordini a detti politici, acciò lasciassero la cura delle cose ecclesiastiche e di religione agli huomini di chiesa, facendo loro grave riprensione per la temerità commessa: onde essi gagliardamente si incitarono contro di me e del Plateis, come quelli da quali si persuasero essere proceduto il rabbuffo fattoli da Sua M[ta]: et oltre al minacciare aspramente il Plateis, non si astennero dal manomettere anche l' autorità mia, insinuando a mons[r] arcivescovo che egli s' io non li mostravo sopra cio special breve di Sua Beat[ne], non fosse tenuto ad obbedirmi in una cosa di tanto rilievo come il sopprimere in Prago l uso del calice: e non tralasciando di sollevare i predetti parrocchi e farli animo, persuadendo loro che non havessero timore alcuno di me nè dell' arcivescovo, perche dal governo politico, al quale in quel regno per

none, in fine, of those priests turned to obedience who had the incumbency of the reconciled churches that had the courage to hold out the species of bread alone in the face of the heretics who frequented the said churches: until the chancellor Plateis intrepidly gave a commencement to that holy enterprise in the parish church of St. Martin, as has been noted above. Which custom then introduced to the praise of God in other churches, is observed with internal quiet, although the politicians have given me enough to do in that respect. Accordingly the heretics, seeing the design miscarrying of making it a matter of duty by all means to obtain from true catholic priests the most holy sacrament under both species, last year, 1622, had recourse to the politicians; and in what manner they conducted themselves with them it does not concern me at present to report: enough—they extorted a letter from the prince of Lichtenstein, who was then there, in virtue of which, as if by order of his majesty, calling upon the two parish priests of the Madonna del Tein and of St. Henry, formerly Dominicans, they commanded them that in the solemnity of Easter they should present indifferently to every one, to whatever ritual he belonged, the communion under both kinds. Thus, on Thursday, *in coena domini*, by the mere perfidy of the said politicians, there was committed the greatest abomination, more than two thousand wicked heretics receiving the venerable body of the consecrated Lord, under the two species of bread and wine, from the lawful priest, that which is holy being in this wise given by the fault of catholic men, unto dogs. Plateis failed not to make such opposition to this as might be expected from him, but nothing could avail against their temerity: accordingly, in order to keep up the prohibition of the use of the cup, he thought he would take courage and dispense the sacrament as he did three days after, in public, under the sole species of bread, in the parish church of St. Martin. But having had notice of this impious attempt, I went instantly to make a bitter lamentation about it with his majesty, complaining in every the most efficacious manner, that his ministers should choose to interfere in matters that concern the reverence due to the tremendous sacrament of the altar, which solely regard what is spiritual, and the salvation of souls, and who, without any respect, intermeddle with the affairs of religion, not showing any sign of obedience towards God and the holy Roman see to which his majesty had ever shown himself so obsequious. At which the emperor being affected beyond measure, immediately gave the strictest orders to the said politicians, that they should leave the care of church affairs and of religion to churchmen, severely reproving them for the rashness which they had committed: whence they vigorously rose against me and Plateis, as those with whom, they were convinced, had originated the rebuff given them by his majesty: and besides roughly threatening Plateis, they did not further abstain from destroying my authority, insinuating to the archbishop that if I had not shown him on this subject a special brief from his beatitude,

antiquato stile devono soggiacere gli ecclesiastici, sariano sempre protetti e sostenuti, operarono che il curato del Tein facendo nuova prevaricatione si ridusse in aperta disubbidienza, e prese ardire di predicare al popolo che non volesse tollerare che i papisti, che miravano tiraneggiare il tutto, li togliessero l' uso del calice, e pregassero Dio per lui vero difensore del paterno antico rito: di modo che quel volgo fece un poco di tumulto, rappresentandosi quella sera sino al numero di mille alla casa di detto curato come in sua difesa. Il che venuto a mia notitia, cavai subito da Sua M[ta] Cesarea indignatione e comandamento che il detto prete fosse subito arrestato e consegnato a mons[re] arcivescovo: come fu senza dilatione alcuna eseguito: e quel popolo, che prima si era mostrato così ardente per la sua indennità, non fece motivo alcuno, perche lo vedesse condurre prigione in faccia del giorno e di tutta la gente. Et egli dopo alcune settimane di carcere se ne morì dentro di quella, supplendosi alla cura di detta chiesa, che è la principale di terra vecchia, con altro parroco cattolico e con la predica del canonico Rottua, soggetto insigne per dottrina e zelo, il quale amministra tuttavia questa carica con molto profitto e con grandissimo concorso così di cattolici come di heretici, i quali volentieri ascoltano le prediche di questo buon sacerdote per la sua efficace e grata maniera di dire."

he was not bound to obey me in a matter of such relevancy as the suppression of the use of the cup in Prague: and not neglecting to agitate the said parish priests and to encourage them, persuading them that they should not have any dread of me or of the archbishop, because they would always be protected and upheld by the political government, they effected that the curate of Tein, committing a new prevarication, should return to open disobedience, and dare to preach to the people that they should not suffer papists who aimed at tyrannizing in everything, to take from them the use of the cup, and should pray to God for it, as the true defender of the ancient ancestral rite: in such wise that people made a little of a tumult, showing themselves to the number of about two thousand at the house of the said curate, as if in his defence. Which having come to my knowledge, I instantly obtained from his imperial majesty indignation and command that the said priest should at once be arrested and handed over to the archbishop, as was done without delay: and that people, which at first appeared so eager for his safety, made no movement, for they saw him taken to prison in face of day and of the whole nation. And he, after some weeks of imprisonment, died in prison, the cure of the said parish church, which is the chief one of the old territory, being supplied with another parish priest, and with the preaching of the canon Rottuo, a subject distinguished for learning and zeal, who always administers that charge with much advantage and with the greatest concourse both of catholics and of heretics, who willingly listen to the preachings of this good priest, on account of his effectiveness and pleasing address.]

III. GENERAL PROCEDURE.

"Per decreto di Sua M[ta] in conformità delle risolutioni prese nella congregatione prefata tenuta in Vienna si sono dipoi riformate tutte le città del regno, cacciando da esse e da loro contorni li ministri e predicanti heretici. In ciascuna di esse oltre il parroco si sono messi il capitano, il giudice, il primate del consiglio et un cancelliere cattolico, restandone in eterno bandito l' esercitio heretico, havendo l' imperatore per prova conosciuto, coll' esempio della fedeltà di Budueis e con la perfidia di quasi tutte le altre, quanto importi che le città siano heretiche o cattoliche. Et ancorche il principe Liechtenstain soprasedesse già dalla incominciata riforma rispetto a gran rumori che si spargevano del disgusto di Sassonia, poi la proseguì, havendogliene io fatto reiterare l' ordine: ma però se li sospese circa li circoli di Egra e Culma per essere contigui alla Sassonia e pretendersi che la proprietà loro sia dell' imperio e non della corona di Bohemia. Con tutto ciò resta per ancora nel regno qualche predicante protetto da baroni heretici o da poco buoni cattolici, e particolarmente ne sono nel circolo di Leitmeriz spalleggiati da un barone cattolico, che professando grande strettezza e fratellanza con l' elettore di Sassonia si persuade farli in questa maniera cosa gratissima: et havendolo io esortato a cacciarli e fattogliene parlare ancora da altri, ha promesso mandarli

[By his majesty's decree, in conformity with the resolutions taken in the foresaid congregation held in Vienna, all the cities of the kingdom have since been reformed, heretical ministers and preachers being chased from them and their precincts. In each of these there have been placed besides the parish priests, the captain, the judge, the primate of the council, and a catholic chancellor, the heretical exercise (of worship) remaining under an eternal ban, the emperor having known by experience, by the example of the fidelity of the Buduans, and the perfidy of almost all the rest, how much lay in the cities being heretical or catholic. And although the prince of Lichtenstein had already superseded the reform that had begun, owing to the great rumours in circulation of the disgust of Saxony, and then prosecuted it, from my having reiterated the order for it to him: but finally he suspended it about the circles of Egra and Culm, because of their touching upon Saxony, and it being asserted that they held of the empire and not of the kingdom of Bohemia. With all this there still remain some preachers in the kingdom, protected by heretical barons or by some good catholics, and in particular there are some in the circle of Leitmeriz supported by a good catholic baron, who, professing great intimacy and fraternity with the elector of Saxony, thinks

via, ma dubito che ritenuto dalla moglie, che è heretica, non vorrà farlo se non forzatamente. Ne sono anco rimasti in quelle città nelle quali si trovano acquartierate militie heretiche, non havendo voluto li commissarj regj esporsi col riformarli a pericolo di tumulto: ma hora che i sospetti di guerra vanno scemando, si darà licenza alli soldati heretici, ovvero se li assegneranno altri quartieri, acciò habbai luogho la riforma. Ne resta uno ancora nella città di Kuttembergh, scusando il principe di Liechtenstain di non poter cacciarlo, perche quegli huomini non vorrebbero poi lavorare nelle miniere che ivi sono: tuttavia col ritorno dell' imperatore a Praga spero in Dio che si rimediarà da ogni cosa. Nè devo tralasciare che nel mio passaggio da Ratisbona a Praga, havendo traversato una gran parte della Bohemia, e così da Praga a Vienna ho trovato in ogni luogo la riforma effettuata, eccettoche nella città di Jaromir, dove erano in alloggio alcune fanterie del colonnello duca di Sassonia: ma dipoi ho mandato stretto ordine di Sua M^{ta}, acciò sia riformata, et in ciascuna di esse città s' istruiscano i figliuoli nella dottrina christiana, insegnandoseli orare in lingua latina.

"Sono state sotto rigide pene prohibite dentro e fuori di Praga le conventicole degli heretici, sotto qualunque pretesto le facessero, la qual commissione fu data molti mesi addietro a mai richiesta: ma non ostante che io più volte n' habbia reclamato col governo di Praga, non era stata mai eseguita.

"Dal senato della città di Praga si sono levati tutti gli heretici, supplendo i loro luoghi di persone cattoliche, e se li è tolta ogni essentiale autorità, lasciandogliene solamente qualche apparenza nelle cose che non sono di molto rilievo, annullando in specie tutti li privilegj pregiudiciali alla religione cattolica concessi da re passati, potendo benissimo farlo l' imperatore havendosi per forza d' armi riguadagnato questo regno già apertamente ribellatoseli. L' accademia o collegio di Carlo IV. a gloria divina e della religione cattolica si è restituita alla sua primiera institutione sotto la cura de' padri Gesuiti, li quali hanno ancora la sopraintendenza di tutte le scuole del regno, et a' medesimi l' usare diligenza che non si stampino o vendano libri contrarj alla verità cattolica, essendosi sottoposti alla loro censura i librarj e gli stampatori. Si è havuto intorno alla predetta accademia qualche difficoltà, volendocisi deputare un presidente laico, il che da me non veniva bene inteso, ma finalmente spero che sarà lasciata questa cura a mons^{r} arcivescovo, pretendendo egli per suoi antichi privilegj essere cancelliero del regno.

"Alla casa de' poveri istituita in Praga da Ferdinando Terzo si sono di più assegnati 4 m. talleri annui: onde si è accresciuto il numero loro da ottanta, che prima vi sene alimentavano, fino a duceuto. A padri Gesuiti si sono dati per una volta 20 mila talleri da spendersi nella fabbrica del loro collegio: et in questo non è occorso che si impieghino li miei uffícj, non havendo bisogno di alcun mezzo appresso dell' imperatore l' evidenti utilità che dalle loro attioni si traggono. Per augumento dell' entrate capitolari della cattedrale sono stati assegnati beni che rendono

that he thus does him the utmost favour: and on my exhorting him to drive them away, and farther getting others to speak to him about it, he has promised to dismiss them, but I doubt that, withheld by his wife, who is a heretic, he will not do it until compelled. Farther, some of them have been left in those cities where heretical soldiers are quartered, the royal commissioners not having liked to expose themselves by reforming them at the risk of a tumult: but now that the suspicions of war are diminishing, the heretical soldiers will be disbanded, or other quarters will be assigned them, in order that a reform may take place. One of them still remains in the city of Kuttemberg, the prince of Lichtenstein excusing himself for not being able to banish him, because those men will not then labour in the mines that are there: at all events, with the return of the emperor into Prague, I hope in God that everything will be remedied. I ought not to omit that in my passage from Ratisbon to Prague, having traversed a great part of Bohemia, and so from Prague to Vienna, I found the reform effected everywhere, except that in the city of Jaromir, where was lodged some infantry of the colonel duke of Saxony: but afterwards I sent a strict order from his majesty that it should be reformed, and in each of these cities the children are instructed in the Christian doctrine, being taught to pray in Latin.

Conventicles of heretics are prohibited under rigid penalties both within and without Prague, under whatsoever pretext, which commission was given many months ago at my request: but notwithstanding my having repeatedly made reclamations about it to the government of Prague, it had never been carried into effect.

All the heretics have been removed from the senate of the city of Prague, their places being supplied by catholics, and they have been deprived of all essential authority, there being left to them only some appearance of it in matters of no great importance, and all privileges prejudicial to the catholic religion, conceded by past kings, being formally annulled, the emperor having an excellent opportunity of doing so, having by force of arms regained this kingdom after it was in open rebellion against him. The academy or college of Charles IV. has, to the Divine glory and that of the catholic religion, been restored to its first institution under the care of the Jesuit fathers, who further have the superintendence of all the schools in the kingdom, and who are charged also to see diligently that no books be printed or sold that are contrary to catholic truth, booksellers and printers being subjected to their censorship. There have been some difficulties about the foresaid academy, the appointment of a lay president being thought desirable there, the which was not well understood on my part, but finally I hope that that charge will be left to monsignor the archbishop, he maintaining that by his ancient privileges he is chancellor of the kingdom.

There has been assigned to the house for the poor, instituted at Prague by Ferdinand

6 m. talleri annui, e per le archiepiscopali 24 mila: ma perche questi beni sono assai guasti e rovinati, monsignor arcivescovo desidera ritenersi per qualche tempo il mons[r] d' Ossegg, assegnati già alla mensa archiepiscopale sotto Ridolfo in vece della pensione camerale che veniva difficilmente pagata. Nell' arbitrio di monsignor arcivescovo si è riposta la provincia delle parrocchie di Praga e di tutto il regno, etiam che prima fossero possedute da signori particolari che erano tutti ribelli, essendosi riserbato l' imperatore questo jus, mentre si sono venduti li beni di essi ribelli, havendosi anche havuto riguardo che per molte leghe intorno a Praga siano tutti comprati da cattolici."

III., an additional 40,000 thalers a-year; hence their number has increased from eighty that were at first alimented there, to two hundred. The Jesuit fathers have had given to them at one time, 20,000 thalers, to be spent in the building of their college; and in this there has been no need of their employing my good offices, the evident utility of their proceedings enabling them to dispense with any applications through others to the emperor. For the augmentation of the capitular revenues of the cathedral there has been assigned to it property affording 6000 thalers a-year, and for the archiepiscopal revenues, 24,000: but because these properties are much destroyed and ruined, monsignor the archbishop desires to remain for some time bishop of Ossegg, assigned already to the archiepiscopal revenues under Rodolph, in lieu of the pension from the exchequer, which was paid with difficulty. The province of the parish churches of Prague and of the whole kingdom, has been replaced under the sway of the archbishop, even those that had been possessed by individual nobles who were all rebels, the emperor having reserved this right to himself, meanwhile the properties of these rebels have been sold, regard having also been had to the fact that by many laws relating to Prague, all should be acquired by catholics.]

109.

Relatione alla S[ta] di N. S[re] papa Urbano VIII. delle cose appartenenti alla nuntiatura di Colonia per M[r] Montorio vescovo di Nicastro ritornato nuntio di quelle parti l' anno di N. S[re] 1624.—[Report to the holiness of our lord pope Urban VIII. on the affairs pertaining to the nuncioship of Cologne by monsignor Montorio, bishop of Nicastro, on his return as nuncio from those parts in the year of our Lord 1624.]

In the midst of these warlike commotions Montorio arrived in Germany. He sets forth the danger in which the Roman catholics would have been involved had Mansfeld, who commanded the upper Rhine from Strasburg to Mainz, and the bishop of Halberstadt, who commanded Westphalia, succeeded so far as to unite with Baden Durlach. But all these generals met with defeats. He now describes the advantages that had flowed from these victories, the condition that the German church had reached.

In Fulda the counter-reformation had recommenced in all its vehemence: the Roman catholic party had penetrated into Osnaburg with the Infanta and the army of the League: at Minden hopes were entertained of appointing an archduke bishop: even in Bremen the prebendaries had been wrought upon by special missions to elect a Roman catholic coadjutor, yet for this time a Danish prince was forced upon them: but the nuncio hoped at least to see toleration for the Roman catholic religion admitted into all the Hanse towns: it appeared to him that the emperor might at once command this, especially as those cities drew great advantages from the Spanish and Portuguese trade: already was there a church opened in Altona from which much was to be hoped for, for the north: "per potere in qualche tempo fondarsi un seminario, onde possino pigliarsi operaj, dopo che avranno appreso la lingua Danica e Norvegica, per ridurre al lume della vera fede quei popoli piu settentrionali."—[so as to enable a seminary to be founded ere long, whence there might be taken labourers, after they shall have learned the Danish and Norwegian tongues, to bring back to the light of the true faith those more northern peoples.]

With this progress Montorio thinks a reform likewise in the interior of the German church indispensable. The prelates dressed like laymen, and felt no scruple in going to war; concubinage prevailed openly, and for this fault the nuncio would not allow one Hornberg, in other respects a very fit candidate, to be appointed to the bishopric of Würzburg. The German bishops, too, thought little about the pope: they filled up incumbencies in the reserved months, and through their officials engrossed to themselves many unallowable things. "Dispensano ne' gradi matrimoniali prohibiti, ad sacros ordines et beneficia vacata, super defectu natalium, concedono extra tempora, dispensano super defectu aetatis, anche talvolta hanno dispensato con persone institute in sacris di prender moglie."—[They grant dispensations for marrying within the prohibited degrees, in regard to ordinations and vacant benefices, upon the want of nativities, they make concessions extra tempora, they grant dispensations for the want of the proper age being complied with, they have often too granted dispensations for marrying, to persons ordained to the sacred ministry.] They take the style of by the grace of God, without any mention of the apostolic see, and use

their church property almost as if it were their own. It was no better in the monasteries and convents. The abbots conducted themselves as if they were absolute lords. In the towns there were nothing but banquets, social parties composed of men and women: in the landward monasteries the monks engaged in hunting, and nothing was to be seen but hounds and the attendants of the chase.

The nuncio would willingly have his hand to the work of reform, but was interrupted by contagious diseases, the confusion of war, and political affairs.

Of these also he treats very well. Yet I could not take in all that he says about the transference of the electorship, and will repeat it here.

"Possono esser note a S. Beat^ne le cose all' hora occorse, ed io, benche mi fossero giunti assai tardi i brevi che mi mandava papa Gregorio, acciocche intervenissi alla dieta per tale effetto adunata in Ratisbona, mi mossi nondimeno nel maggior rigore dell' inverno con grandissime spese, disagi e pericoli per comparirvi: e condottomi sino ad Herbipoli da ministri di S. S^tà e da principi elettori ivi congregati, a quali aveva dato avviso della mia mossa, mi fu significato non esser più necessaria la mia persona, poiche la conclusione del negotio era ritardata da più alta cagione che dal mancamento del consenso de' principi ivi adunati, e che il vedersi ivi compariti tanti ministri apostolici havrebbe accresciute le difficoltà, mettendosi in gelosia li protestanti, come che quella traslatione fu trattata più tosto come materia di religione che di stato. Mi rimasi perciò d' andarvi, tanto più che il Magontino, che come degano del collegio elettorale era quasi arbitro del negotio, praticato da me alcuni mesi prima, stava costante nell' offerta fattami di voler secondare la mente del papa e dell' imperatore. Li deputati di Treveri havevano ordine dal suo principe, datoli a mia istanza, di non iscostarsi dalle deliberationi del Magontino e del Coloniceuse. Io non starò qui a divisare a V. Beat^ne le difficoltà che incontrai per disporre il Magontino a consentire a detta traslatione: perche hora diceva abborrire la città di Ratisbona come d' aria nemica alla sua sanità, hora diceva trovarsi esausto di denari e da non potere supplire alle spese che ivi gli saria convenuto di fare, hora che il negotio non era maturo, non essendoci il consenso di Spagna e di Sassonia, hora temeva le minacce del re d' Inghilterra, di Dania e di altri settarj, hora affermava che quella traslatione havrebbe accesa nuova e più cruda guerra in Germania, con danno evidente della religione cattolica, mentre i principi ecclesiastici, che havevano portato fino all' hora e dovevano portare per l' avvenire il peso, esausti per le contributioni passate alla lega, spogliati d' ogni loro bavere dall' insolenze e rubamenti non meno de' nostri che de' nemici soldati, non solo non potevano nè havevano modo di apparecchiarsi a nuova guerra, ma erano ridotti ad estremità tali che erano costretti licentiare le proprie famiglie a vivere quasi privatamente: non lasciava di porre in consideratione il duca di Neoburgh, come più prossimo di sangue al palatino, la cui persona non havrebbe recata tanta gelosia a protestanti, che temeano la grandezza del Bavaro, a cui, conforme le costitutioni imperiali secondo la bolla aurea, come a più prossimo doveasi quella dignità, nella quale il medesimo duca haveva protestato non volere consentire sino all' ultimo spirito che altri fosse a se preferito: basta che in quattro o cinque giorni che mi trattenni con

[The matters that have occurred hitherto might be known to his beatitude, and although the brieves sent me by pope Gregory arrived very late, yet in order that I might take part in the diet met for that effect at Ratisbon, I set off in the utmost rigour of winter at the cost of the greatest expense, inconvenience, and danger, in order to be present: and having proceeded as far as Würzburg it was intimated to me by his holiness's ministers, and by the electoral princes met there, to whom I had given notice of my movements, that my personal presence was no longer necessary, for that the conclusion of the matter was delayed by a higher reason than the consent of the princes there, and that the sight of so many of the pope's ministers would increase the difficulties by making the protestants jealous, as if that transference were more a matter of religion than of state. I therefore abstained from going, the more because Mainz, who, as dean of the electoral college, was almost arbiter of the matter, who had been treated with by me some months before, held to the offer he had made me that he would second the views of the pope and emperor. The Treves deputies had an order from their prince given them at my instance, to adhere to what should be thought right by Mainz and Cologne. I will not waste time in describing to your beatitude the difficulties I encountered in disposing Mainz to consent to the said transference: for now he would say that he disliked the city of Ratisbon as hurtful to his health, at another time that he found his money all spent, and that he could not find means to live as would be thought suitable there; again, that the matter was not yet ripe, the consent of the Spaniards and of Saxony having yet to be obtained; again, that he dreaded the threats of the kings of England and Denmark, and other sectaries; again, he affirmed that that transference would kindle a new and more cruel war in Germany to the evident detriment of the catholic religion, while the leading clergy who had all along borne and would for the future have to bear the expense, exhausted by past contributions to the league, despoiled of all they had by the insolence and robberies not less of our own than of the enemy's soldiers, not only had neither power nor means to prepare for a new war, but were reduced to such extremities that they were compelled to dismiss their own households, and to live almost privately: nor did he omit to bid me consider the duke of Neuberg, as being nearest blood relation to the Palatine, who personally had not infused so much jealousy into the protestants whose dread was the aggrandizement of Bavaria, to whom in conformity with the imperial constitutions according to the golden

lui in Acciaffemburgo, dopo lunghi discorsi fatti in voce et in iscritto, ottenni la risolutione che io desiderava. La traslatione fu fatta, et ancora si mantiene. Il palatinato è in parte occupato dal Bavaro, in parte da Spagnuoli, nè altro resta al palatino che la città di Franchinthal depositata in certo tempo in mano della serenissima infanta di Fiandra con concerto del re Inglese.

"Mentre per detto negotio io era in Acciaffemburgo, giunse ivi la nuova della presa di Adilbergh: et havendo io già fatto officio per commissione di Sua Sta col sig^r duca di Baviera per la libreria Palatina et havendone havuta offerta, mandai subito un' espresso al sig^r conte di Tilly, facendoli istanza per la conservatione di essa, poiche mi veniva affermato per la qualità e quantità de' libri massime manoscritti essere di valore inestimabile: e mi rispose S. E. che il tutto era in poter suo ben conservato per eseguirne l' ordine del sig^r duca: di che havendo dato conto a patroni, havendo essi mandata persona a pigliarlo, fu detta libreria dopo alcuni mesi condotta a Roma."

bull, that dignity was due as to the nearest relation, to which dignity the said duke had protested that to his last breath he never would consent that another should be preferred to him: suffice it to say, that after four or five days' conference with him in Aschaffenburg, after long negotiations by word and writing, I obtained the resolution I wanted. The transference was made and still holds. The palatinate is occupied partly by Bavaria, partly by the Spanish, nor does anything remain to the Palatine but the city of Frankenthal, deposited for a certain time in the hands of the most serene infanta of Flanders in concert with the English king.

While I was on this business at Aschaffenburg, news arrived there of the taking of Heidelberg; and I having by commission from his holiness made interest with the duke of Bavaria for the Palatine library, and having had it offered to me, I instantly sent an express to Count Tilly, urging him to preserve the same, as it had come to my knowledge that it was of inestimable value in respect both of the quantity and quality of books, chiefly manuscript: and his excellency replied, that the whole was in his safe keeping in conformity with the duke's orders: having reported this to (my) masters (and) they having sent a person to remove it, the said library was some months afterwards taken to Rome.]

110.

Instruttione a V. S. Monsr Caraffa vescovo di Tricarico destinato da N. S. suo nuntio in Colonia. 26 Giugno 1624.—[Instructions to your lordship, monsignor Caraffa, bishop of Tricarico, appointed by our lord his nuncio in Cologne. 26th June 1624.]

Lewis Caraffa was Montorio's successor: he was nuncio at Cologne at the same time that Charles Caraffa administered the nunciatura at Vienna.

The pope communicates to him his views on German affairs in a very copious body of Instructions.

In these he discusses all those points relating to interior church discipline which Montorio had started. The apostolic see having by this time suffered so many losses in revenue and respect, the nuncio was to try to recover what had been lost. "V. S. stia attentissima a tutto quello che può sostentare l' autorità apostolica e specialmente a procurare che da essa eschino le dovute provisioni beneficiali."—[Your lordship will be most attentive to all that can sustain the apostolic authority, and specially to see that there issue from it the due beneficial provisions.] It is worth noting that here we find commissions given to the nuncio that were directly founded on the suggestions of Minuccio Minucci. For example, that he should transmit to Rome a list of the German ecclesiastics that deserved promotion: "de' più costumati, de' più dotti, de' più nobili, de' meglio appoggiati all' autorità d' alcun principe cattolico.—Così noi aremo notizie tali che sollecitamente la sede apostolica potrà provedere prima che scorra il suo tempo."—[of the most experienced, of the most learned, of the most noble, of the most attached to the authority of any catholic prince.—Thus we shall have such notices sent us that the apostolic see may make careful provision before it be too late.] This is literally just what Minucci recommended in 1588. Yet time had suggested new measures. The most important is that a Roman catholic coadjutor should be appointed to a bishop on his growing old during his lifetime. This had already been put in operation with the best effects in Paderborn as well as in Munster.

But the main affair now remaining was the wider extension of Roman catholicism.

The league was to be kept up in full vigour; the nuncio was to see to it that every one paid his share. An ecclesiastical society was instituted at Cologne for the conversion of protestants, in which princes of Austria and Bavaria took a part, and which possessed a good treasury: the nuncio was to endeavour to prevent its decline. Some princely houses were made objects of special attention, as first to be gained over, particularly Darmstadt and Saxony. The nuncio was to promote that tendency, "in order that these princes may not resist the grace that God will show them." He was specially to promote the establishment of seminaries and the introduction of the Jesuits. This passage is the most remarkable perhaps of the whole body of instructions, and may be subjoined as it stands in the original.

"Sarà opera degnissima di S. S^ria l' impiegarsi a coltivare i seminarj già fatti et a pro-

[It would be an employment most worthy of your lordship to engage in cultivating the

curare che altri se ne faccino di nuovo: e per queste simili opere chi non vede che i padri della compagnia di Gesù sono maravigliosi? Laonde il predecessore di S. S^ria diede principio a pratticare l' introduttione di quelli in Franchfort, scrivendo sopra di cio caldissime lettere a Cesare, e voleva fare altrettanto l' elettore di Colonia. N. S^re, per sollecitare l' effettuatione di questo buon pensiero, fece scrivere al nuntio presso l' imperatore che non si riscaldi: col quale S. S^ria s' intenderà per quello che restasse da fare, avvisandone le speranze e i successi. L' elettore di Magonza ha fatto rappresentare alla S^tà di N. S^re che per propagare la religione cattolica, che col favore divino piglia piede nel palatinato inferiore, niuna cosa viene giudicata più spediente quanto l' erettione de' seminarj e delle case dove possino convenire i nobili del Reno: e per cio fare, propone a S. B^ne che si potrebbono comodamente applicare i beni d' alcuni monasterj e specialmente di Germershaim, Spanhaim et Odernhaim, posti nella diocesi di Magonza et altre volte occupati da principi Palatini del Reno: la quale proposta è stata stimata da S. B^ne di molto rilievo, e prima di risolvere voleva che l' antecessore di V. S^ria presane diligente informatione avvisasse distintamente lo stato di detti monasterj col suo parere: ma perche la brevità del tempo non gli havrà permesso eseguir tutto, S. B^ne vuole che ella supplisca al rimanente con ogni sollecitudine et accuratezza.

"L' elettore di Colonia ancora vuole instituire un' università nella sua città di Munstero: e di cio è stato ragionato nella sagra congregatione de propaganda fide, inclinando la S^tà di N. S^re che si facci detta università, con conditione però che oltre alle scienze vi si insegnino le leggi canoniche e civili. Serva a S. S^ria per avviso, accioche ella tratti in questa forma con detto elettore, quando S. A. le parlerà d' havere ottenuto per detta erettione il beneplacito apostolico."

seminaries already instituted, and to endeavour to have others founded anew: and who sees not that it is by such works as these that the fathers of the company of Jesus work wonders? Hence your lordship's predecessor began to treat about their introduction at Frankfort, writing about this the warmest letters to the emperor, and wanted the elector of Cologne to do as much. Our lord, in pressing the carrying out of this good idea, caused the nuncio who is with the emperor to be written to that he might not be offended: with whom your lordship will maintain an understanding as to what remains to be done, advising him of hopes and results. The elector of Mainz has caused it to be represented to the holiness of our lord that for the propagation of the catholic religion, which, with the divine favour, is advancing in the Lower Palatinate, nothing has been judged more expedient than the erection of seminaries and of houses in which the Rhenish nobles may meet: and in order to this suggests to his beatitude that the property of some monasteries, and particularly of Germersheim, Spanheim and Odernheim, might be conveniently applied, these being situate in the diocese of Mainz, and having in former times been occupied by the Palatine princes of the Rhine; which suggestion has been thought of much importance by his beatitude, and before coming to a resolution wished that your lordship's predecessor having diligently informed himself on the subject, should distinctly report on the state of the said monasteries, stating his own opinion; but seeing that he was prevented by want of time from doing all this, his holiness wishes you with the utmost care and accuracy to complete what remains undone.

The elector of Cologne further wants to found an university in his city of Munster, and this has been discussed in the sacred college *de propaganda fide*, the holiness of our lord being favourable to the founding of the said university, under the condition, however, that besides other sciences there be taught at it the canon and civil laws. Let it serve as a hint to your lordship in order that you may treat in this form with the said elector, when his highness will tell you of his having obtained the apostolic *beneplacito* for the said erection.]

111.

Relatione dell' ill^mo et ecc^mo sig^r Pietro Contarini K^r ritornato dall' ambasceria ordinaria di Roma, presentata alli 22 Giugno 1627 e letta il medesimo giorno nell' ecc^mo senato.—[Report by the most illustrious and excellent signor Peter Contarini, knight, on his return from the ordinary Roman embassy, presented 22d June, 1627, and read that day to the most excellent senate.]

P. Contarini had spent above three and a half years—44 months—at the court of Urban VIII., when he presented this report.

Dividing it into four parts, he treats in it of the secular and spiritual administration, the most important affairs, and the most influential members of the court.

He is particularly full and instructive on the extension of the spiritual jurisdiction. He thinks that it had never yet been exercised in Italy with such strictness: through the double object of asserting a direct power over spiritual persons, and a free power of disposing of spiritual property, the Roman court became very dangerous to princes. Urban VIII. would often say that were a Venetian nobleman to occupy the Roman see, he could not be more disposed to favour the Venetians than he, the existing pope; nevertheless they never received the smallest favour from him.

In general he has a bad opinion of the Romish system as a whole. The principle of the entire administration was nepotism.

"L' inclinatione dei papi di far grandi i nepoti dà in questi tempi il primo moto all' attioni, dichiarationi e dipendenze con altri principi. Prima si pensa ad imprese contra infideli, ad acquisto di stati, ma come gli anni son brevi, le difficoltà molte, così si ferma il concetto senz' effettuatione alcuna: doppo altra strada si prende più facile, accumulando grandi richezze, comprando stati."

[The leaning of the popes towards the aggrandizement of the nephews, originates nowadays all the actions, declarations, and dependencies with other princes. The first objects contemplated are expeditions against the infidels and the acquisition of states, but as years are short and difficulties many, such ideas are dropt without anything being effected: afterwards another course is more easily taken, by accumulating great wealth, and buying estates.]

He describes the circle that surrounded Urban as follows:—

"Per ordinario si consiglia il pontefice con il card[le] Magalotti, cognato del fratello, e che tiene anco il carico di segretario di stato, per le cui mani passano tutte l' espeditioni. E cardinale d' ingegno grande, vivace: lo stima assai il papa: l'ha voluto sempre appresso di se, et in particolare nella legatione di Bologna, dove le diede la viceregenza di quel governo. E se vi è alcuno che arrivi ad bavere predominio nell' animo della S[tà] Sua, quest' è l'uno, nè si sa se per proprio affetto et inclinatione di lei o se per la grande accortezza del cardinale, che bene conoscendo il genio di chi così lungamente si è servito di lui sa valersi delli mezzi proprj per condursi a questo segno: e può dirsi che negli affari di momento di esso solo si vale. Egli però s' affatica di' aggiustarsi alle inclinationi del pontefice, le contradice meno che può, e nelli suoi sensi procura d' incamminare le proprie attioni per conservare il posto, la confidenza e la riputatione che le apporta l' esser adoperato nelli maneggi più gravi. Procura con allontanarsi da tutte le apparenze, fuggendo l' audienze ordinarie de' ministri di principi, de' cardinali e quasi d' ogni altro (ma solo tratta i negotii ch' espressamente gli sono incaricati), di non acquistar l' odio che per l' ordinario suole cader sopra quelli che si veggono più vicini e participano dell' autorità o gratia del principe: e lo fa maggiormente per non ingelosire il card[le] Barberino, che da principio non mostrò di ricevere intiero gusto di vederlo avanzarsi tanto, e più valersi il pontefice di lui che della sua persona: e percio bene spesso per questa causa s' udirono da Barberino parole che dinotavano il suo sentimento. Hora nondimeno lascia correr le cose come vanno, e mostra confidar nel zio, o per sollevarsi del peso degli affari, o perche non sa o conosce di non poter fermare il corso alla fortuna di questo. Il tutto pure si partecipa col medesimo cardinal Barberino, con S. Onofrio e Don Carlo.

"Il primo, come nipote, è veramente amato. Vorrebbe la S[tà] Sua che non più applicatione attendesse alli negotii: ma egli v' apparisce alieno assai, nè il suo naturale punto si vede inclinato, et pare che quasi a forza assista solo dove per il carico che tiene non può far altrimenti, scaricando il peso degli affari più gravi sopra l' istesso card[le] Magalotti, contentandosi di spogliarsi di quello che dovrebbe esser suo particolare per vestirne il zio, contro la pratica degli passati pontefici, sia o per propria debolezza, o per non saper valersi di quella autorità che gode chi arriva a posto tanto eminente. E di ottimi, virtuosi e lodevoli costumi, di soave natura, e con esempio unico non vuole ricever donativi o pre-

[Ordinarily the pontiff consults with cardinal Magalotti, a connection of his brother's, and who farther holds the office of secretary of state, through whose hands all the public despatches pass. The cardinal is a man of great talents and vivacity: the pope values him much: he has desired that he should be always near him, and in particular in the Bologna legation, where he gave him the viceregency of that government. And if there be any one who has got so far as to have an eminent place in the mind of his holiness, it is he; nor is it known whether it be through a peculiar affection and inclination on the pope's part, or through the great penetration of the cardinal, who, well knowing the temper with which he has so long employed him, knows how to avail himself of the means adapted for the attainment of this degree (of favour): and it may be said that in matters of moment, he alone is made use of. He strives accordingly to conform himself to the inclinations of the pope, contradicts him as little as possible, and according to his views he tries to start things fitted to preserve the position, trust, and reputation arising from his being employed in the more serious concerns of the government. He endeavours, by avoiding all outward appearances, by shunning the ordinary audiences of the ministers of the princes, of the cardinals, and of almost everybody else (but only treats those affairs that are expressly committed to him), not to incur the odium which ordinarily falls upon those who are seen to be most intimate with the sovereign, and to share in his authority and favour: and this he does chiefly that he may not excite the jealousy of cardinal Barberino, who from the first has not seemed quite pleased at seeing him so much advanced, and the pope making more account of him than of his own proper self; and accordingly words indicative of his feelings are on this account very often heard to fall from Barberino. Nevertheless he now allows matters to take their course, and seems to place confidence in his uncle, whether to rid himself of the burthen of business or because he does not know, or professes to be unable to stop, the tide of fortune in his favour. The whole, in a word, is shared with the said cardinal Barberino, with S. Onophrius, and Don Carlo.

The first, as nephew, is truly loved. His holiness would like him to attend with more application to business; but he seems to have no great turn for it, nor do his talents seem naturally to incline that way; and it appears as if it were almost by compulsion that he takes a part only where, from the office he

sente alcuno. Sarà nondimeno vivendo il pontefice al pari d' ogni altro cardinale grande e ricco. Hor deve haver intorno 80 m. scudi d' entrata di beneficj ecclesiastici, e con li governi e legationi che tiene deve avvicinarsi a 100 m. scudi, e tutto il meglio che cava, sarà suo, principiando a farsi delle investite di momento. E poco spendendosi in breve tempo, verrassi ad accumular ricchezze immense.

"Il card[l] S. Onofrio essendo vissuto del continuo nei Cappuccini, seguito tuttavia in una vita religiosissima, non s'ingerisce se non in quello le viene commesso: e degli affari del mondo poco ne sa e meno n' intende: e bene si è conosciuto la sua inabilità in questo nell' absenza di Barberino, mentre fu necessario di trattare e negotiar seco. Hora si ritrova alla residenza della sua chiesa di Sinigaglia.

"Il sig[r] Don Carlo pure, fratello del pontefice, è generale di santa chiesa, e tutto quello che appartiene alle militie, alle fortezze, alle galere, è sotto il suo comando. E signore d' intelligenza, prudente, cauto nello discorrere e trattare, e la cura dell' entrate e maneggi della camera ottimamente l'intende, essendo stato huomo di negotio e versato in queste materie. Qualche cosa ha rilasciato dalla sua prima applicatione agli affari, per non aggravar maggiormente li suoi anni, essendo il più vecchio delli fratelli, e per qualche sua dispositione ancora.

"Due altri nipoti tiene la S[tà] Sua. Il sig[r] Don Taddeo, nel quale si pensa di stabilire la casa, giovane di anni 23 incirca, di nobilissime maniere, di grande ingenuità, et è sommamente amato da tutta la corte. Qualche disegno vi è nel pontefice di farlo prefetto della città dopo la morte del duca di Urbino, che hora gode questo titolo, carico degnissimo, che a tutti precede e dura in vita e dopo la morte anco del pontefice tiene luogo nel solio. E Don Antonio, commendatore di Malta, di anni 18. Ha intorno 14 m. scudi di commende. E di uno spirito pronto, vivace, et a suo tempo vi vorrà esser per la sua parte: desidera egli parimente il cardinalato, e si crede lo compiacerà la S[tà] Sua. Molti che non amano il card[le] Magalotti, lo vedrebbono volentieri quanto prima promosso a quella dignità, con opinione possa egli arrivar dove non giugne il fratello a farle contrasto et oppositione."

holds, he cannot do otherwise, handing over to the same cardinal Magalotti the weight of the more important affairs, being content to divest himself of that which ought to be his own particular (function), in order to invest his uncle with it, contrary to the practice of past pontiffs, whether it be from his own weakness or from not knowing how to avail himself of the authority enjoined by the person who attains so high a position. He is of the best, virtuous, and laudable habits, of a mild temper, and presents a solitary example of one that will take no gift or present. Notwithstanding, during the pontiff's lifetime he will equal any other cardinal in greatness and wealth. At present he should have about 80,000 scudi of revenue from church benefices, and with the governments and legations he holds, ought to have about 100,000 scudi; all the best things that are to be had will be his, and he begins to make important investments. And as he spends little, he will soon come to accumulate immense wealth.

Cardinal S. Onofrio having lived for a continuance with the Capucins, having always pursued a most religious life, intermeddles with nothing that is not committed to him: of the world's affairs he knows little, and understands less, and indeed he confessed his incapacity in this respect during the absence of Barberino, when it was necessary to transact business and negotiate with him. He has now gone back to reside at the church of Sinigaglia.

Signor Don Carlo, in fine, the pope's brother, is general of the holy church, and all that pertains to the army, to fortresses, and to the galleys, is under his command. He is a man of intelligence, prudent, cautious in discourse and negotiation, and admirably understands the management of the revenues and the affairs of the chamber, having been a man of business and versed in these matters. He has so far relaxed from his early attention to business, so as not to bear too hard upon his years, being the elder of the brothers, and further on account of some dislike to it.

His holiness has two other nephews. Signor Don Thaddeus, in whom he proposes to establish his family, a youth of about three and twenty, of the noblest manners, great candour, and exceedingly beloved by the whole court. The pope has some idea of making him prefect of the city after the death of the duke of Urbino, who now enjoys this title, a most dignified office, which takes precedence of all and is held for life, and upon the death of the pope provisionally occupies the throne. Don Antonio, commander of Malta, is 18 years old. He has about 14,000 scudi of revenue from that office. He is of a prompt and vivacious temper, and in his own time would like to have his own share; he wishes to be made a cardinal, and in this it is believed the pope will gratify him. Many who don't like cardinal Magalotti, would willingly see him promoted as soon as possible to that dignity, with the public esteem he may attain to a position where his brother does not approach to contend with and oppose him.]

The Valtelline affair is here discussed once for all in its whole bearings.

"L' altro importante negotio è quello della Valtellina, intorno al quale pure grandemente si travagliò la Santità Sua, ma con fortuna diversa, se bene nel principio vogliono che potesse applicarvi maggiori e più risoluti rimedj. L' esser entrato in affare tanto arduo li primi giorni del pontificato, uscito e non ben ancora rimesso da una grave indispositione, con il pensiero più applicato al primo che a questo negotio, causò forse che si lasciò correr molte cose, che allora il provedervi non era difficile, sicome il rimediarvi poi dopo riuscì impossibile. Fu il deposito della Valtellina fatto dai Spagnoli in mano di Gregorio XV., e Chiavenna con il suo contado la consegnarono con le medesime conditioni al presente pontefice. Le prime negotiationi passarono per mano del commendatore Silleri con tanta cautela e secretezza che il certo d' esse non solo si comunicava alli ministri di V. Serenità, che pure ne doveano aver tanta parte, ma con fatica veniva a loro notitia il vero di quanto si trattava. In niuna altra cosa premeva il pontefice che nel ricevere soddisfattione per il pagamento delli presidj ch' egli teneva nelli forti della Valle, e dopo infinite doglianze et instanze conseguì, credo, fra l' uno e l' altro re intorno 200 m. scudi. Questo danaro andò diminuendo il dispiacere del deposito, che prima e dopo anche dannò sempre grandemente, stimando non esser sollevato dall' interesse niuno pregiudicio potesse apportarle la longhezza et irresolutione di tal maneggio.

"Quelli del Valtellina s' offerivano al papa per vassalli, assicurandolo che li datii che potrebbe imporre sopra li vini e formaggi basterebbono a mantener li presidj ordinarj per difesa di quella Valle. Molti consideravano al pontefice che il ritornar la Valtellina alli Grisoni e rimetter in mano degli heretici li cattolici non si poteva da esso nè si dovea se non con grandissimo scandalo e danno eseguire, che darla ai Spagnoli niuno n' havrebbe assentito, et ai Francesi o ad altri quelli non lo permetterebbono: nè meglio vi fosse che si conservasse alla chiesa la Valtellina, non contenendo alcun altra conditione di momento quel paese che dei passi, che si possono havere o pretender per venirsene et andarsene oltre ai monti: questi restando in potestà del pontefice patre comune, gli havrebbe aperti e concessi sempre secondo il bisogno e necessità d' ogn' uno. Le ragioni se bene poco fondate non lasciano di far impressione, e talvolta anche persuadono dove apparisce alcuna speranza di comodo et utile. Del concetto se ne lasciò intender la Sta Sua, et aggiunse anco, quando vi fosse qualche difficoltà nel restar alla chiesa, ne si potrebbe investir un suo nipote. Era promosso dai Spagnoli il partito, a loro però nè ai Francesi piaceva: in fine si fermò da Silleri il trattato ben noto a V. Serenità, che non fu in Francia approvato dal re, in particolare nella parte che Spagnoli avessero il passo per le genti che andassero in Fiandra e per le medesime solo che ritornassero: poiche il formar della Valtellina una quarta lega, che tanto pretesero Spagnoli, meno il pontefice v' assentì. Fu mutato per questa causa l' ambasciatore, o fosse per la caduta del cancelliere e di Puy-

[The other important affair is that of the Valtelline, on which in fine his holiness has bestowed much labour, but with various success, although at first it were to be wished that greater and more decided remedies had been applied. His having entered upon so arduous an affair during the first days of his pontificate, when just come out of a severe illness, and not quite recovered from it, with his thoughts more occupied with the first than with this affair, was the cause perhaps of his having allowed many things to elapse, which it would not have been difficult to provide against then, whereas to remedy them afterwards became impossible. The deposit of the Valtelline was made in the hands of Gregory XV. by the Spaniards, and they consigned Chiavenna with its territory under the same conditions to the present pontiff. The first negotiations passed through the hands of the commendator Silleri with such caution and secrecy that not only was the certainty of them with difficulty communicated to your serenities' ministers, who indeed ought to have largely shared in them, but it was with difficulty that the real nature of what was transacted came to their knowledge. The pontiff was pressing in nothing but in getting satisfaction for the payment of the garrisons he had kept in the forts of the Valley, and after infinite complaints and entreaties he obtained, I believe, between the two kings, about 200,000 scudi. This money goes to lessen the annoyance of the deposit, which from first to last has caused much loss; reckoning, that as long as no relief could be had from the concern, no prejudice could arise from the length and the irresolution of such management.

The people of the Valtelline offered themselves to the pope as vassals, assuring him that the imposts he might lay on wines and cheeses would suffice to pay the ordinary garrisons for the defence of that valley. Many have suggested to the pope that to restore the Valtelline to the Grisons, and to hand the catholics over to the heretics, could not be done by him, nor ought to be done without the utmost scandal and loss, that nobody would consent to its being given to the Spanish, and these would not have permitted it to be given to the French or any others, nor could there be a better course than for the Valtelline to be retained by the church, the country not comprehending any important peculiarity but that of the passes, which people may have or claim for coming and going beyond the mountains: these remaining in the power of the pontiff as common father, he would keep them always open and free according to every one's wants and necessity. Reasons once urged, although ill-founded, fail not to make an impression, and are often found convincing where there appears any prospect of convenience and utility. His holiness allowed himself to go into the idea and further added, should there be any difficulty in its remaining with the church, one of his nephews might be invested with it. The bargain was favoured by the Spanish, it pleased them indeed, but not the French; in fine there was concluded by Sil-

sieux segretario, l' uno fratello e l' altro nipote del medesimo Silleri. E giunse in Roma mons^{r} di Bettune, ministro di miglior consiglio, di più generosi e risoluti partiti, disautorizzò il negotiato del suo precessore, insistè e parlò sempre per il trattato di Madrid, negò assolutamente il permettere per qualsivoglia maniera a' Spagnoli il passo, e sollecitò in frequenti audienze il pontefice a risolvere alcuna cosa, poiche nè a maggiori lunghezze nè a più tarde dilationi potea la lega assentire.

"Il pontefice, che non stimò mai tanta risolutione nelli collegati nè da questa causa fossero per condursi all' armi, massime che'l suo nuntio in Francia e quello di Suizzeri affermarono del continuo alla Sta Sua con lettere che'l marchese di Covre mai havrebbe presentate l' armi del re dove vi fossero le insegne della Beat^{ne} Sua, s' andò pure continuando nelle irresolutioni, e quanto più accrescevano et apparivano le difficoltà, tanto maggiormente veniva ella a persuadersi (nè vi mancava chi la confermava in questo) che in fine nelle contese essa ne restarebbe posseditrice. E benche Bettune per ultimo significò al papa che il re e la lega insieme la supplicavano di rimettere ai Spagnoli li forti conforme allo obbligo del deposito, accioche essendovi necessità di mover l' armi non s' attribuisca a poco rispetto l' andar contro quelle della Sta Sua, e se all' hora il pontefice si risolvea e prendea partito come dovea, offerendo ai Spagnoli li forti, il tutto veniva ad aggiustarsi con la riputatione sua e soddisfatione degli altri, poiche non gli havrebbono ricevuti li Spagnoli non trovandosi in termine di poterli difendere, e cessava la causa di dolersi mentre in tempo eseguiva il pontefice le conditioni del deposito, nè poteva alcuno contradire lasciandoli a Grisoni: corsero alcuni giorni, in fine surprese il marchese di Covre Plata Mala: allora il pontefice pretese et adimandò tre mesi di tempo, e dopo si ristrinse a tanto che bastasse di scriver in Spagna e farne l' eshibitione, dicendo che li ministri d' Italia non tenevano facoltà di ricever li forti. Ma essendo di già avanzate et ogni giorno procedendo di bene in meglio l' intraprese di Covre, non fu stimato a proposito, anzi sarebbe riuscito dannoso il suspender i progressi, per attender poi di Spagna risposte incerte: e cosi andò il pontefice a poco a poco perdendo tutto quello teneva in deposito, solo restandole Riva e Chiavenna, che sole furono soccorse dai Spagnoli. Si doleva la Sta Sua che questi, se ben ricercati alle prime difese, mai vennero al soccorso, et essi di non essere stati chiamati in tempo, di modo che, mal soddisfatti Spagnoli, non contenti Francesi, ella sommamente disgustata stimando poco rispetto s'havesse portato alle sue insegne, del continuo e grandemente con ognuno se ne querelava: nè altrimenti facevano Spagnoli, mentre attribuivano tutti gl' inconvenienti a lei, e di lei più d'ogni altro si dolevano: et ancorche dopo spedisse il nipote legato in Francia et in Spagna col fine ben noto a V. Serenità, e conoscendo haver preso altra maggior mossa le armi d' Italia, più gravi si rendessero i pericoli se vi applicasse da dovero, con tutto cio non si è potuto levare il primo

leri, the agreement so well known to your serenities, which was not approved in France by the king, particularly in that part which allowed the Spaniards to have the use of the pass for troops on their way to Flanders, and for the same only upon their return: since the forming of the Valtelline into a fourth league, which, as the Spaniards pretend, leads the pope to consent to it. The ambassador was changed on that account, or perhaps on account of the fall of the chancellor and the secretary Puysieux, one the brother, the other the nephew of the said Silleri. And the count of Bethune, a minister who gave better advice, of most generous and resolute manners, disowned his predecessor's negotiation, insisted and spoke always for the treaty of Madrid, absolutely refused to allow the Spaniards the pass in any way whatever, and in frequent audiences solicited the pontiff to come to some resolution, for the league could not consent either to more protracted negotiations or to further delays.

The pontiff, who never thought of finding so much resolution in the members of the league, nor that on that account they would be for appealing to arms, chiefly because his nuncio in France and that of the Swiss continually told his holiness by letters that the Marquis de Coeuvres would never present the arms of the king where there floated the ensigns of his beatitude, went on, in fine, persisting in his irresolutions, and the more that difficulties increased, and became manifest, the more he persuaded himself (nor were there wanting those who confirmed him in this) that at the end of the contest he would remain in possession. And although at last Bethune signified to the pope that the king and the league together besought him to leave the ports to the Spaniards according to the obligation of the deposit, in order that under the necessity that existed for an appeal to arms, one might escape the charge of acting disrespectfully in attacking those of his holiness, and that if the pontiff would now make up his mind and decide as he ought to do, by offering the forts to the Spaniards, all would come to adjust itself to his reputation and the satisfaction of others, for that the Spaniards would not accept of them from not being in a condition to defend them, and the cause of complaint would cease while the pontiff timeously executed the conditions of the deposit, nor could any one oppose their being left to the Grisons: some days elapsed, at last the Marquis de Coeuvres surprised Plata Mala: then the pontiff stood out and required three months time, and afterwards he asked no more than sufficed for writing to Spain and making an offer of them, alleging that the ministers in Italy had no authority to receive the forts. But de Coeuvres' proceedings being already so far advanced, and having daily more and more success, it was not thought to the purpose, but likely to be hurtful to suspend his progress, while an uncertain answer was waited from Spain: and thus the pontiff went on losing by little and little all that he held in deposit, Riva and Chiavenna alone remaining to him, these alone being suc-

concetto che dagli antecedenti mal incamminati principj non siano derivati gl' inconvenienti che si sono dopo visti. Ugualmente Francesi come Spagnoli attribuivano le durezze e difficoltà che si sono incontrate in questa negotiatione, alle pretensioni del pontefice, volendo che ad esso fossero consignati li forti, senza dichiararsi quello che n' havrebbe fatto, negando però assolutamente di volerli demolire. Da che si ha reso sopramodo difficile il trovar ripiego conveniente, si è consumato tanto tempo, fatte tante speditioni, et in fine portato il negotio in Spagna, che in Roma difficilmente s' havrebbe terminato."

coured by the Spaniards. His holiness complained that the latter, although called upon at the first to defend the forts, had never given their assistance, and they again complained of not having been called in time, so that the Spaniards are dissatisfied, the French not content, and the pope extremely disgusted at the thought of so little respect being shown to his flag, has complained of it continually and bitterly to everybody: nor have the Spaniards done aught else, attributing all that had gone wrong to him, and complaining more of him than of any other: and although he afterwards sent his nephew as legate to France and Spain, with the object well known to your serenities, and knowing that the arms of Italy had taken another more important movement, the perils would have been more serious had people there been in earnest, with all this the first idea could not be effaced that, from the antecedent ill-commenced beginnings, had been derived the inconveniences which appeared afterwards. French and Spaniards equally attributed the hardships and difficulties that occurred in that negotiation, to the pretensions of the pope who wanted the forts to be consigned to him without saying what he was to do with them, yet absolutely refusing to demolish them. Hence the excessive difficulty of finding a proper reply, the waste of so much time, the sending of so many despatches, and the business at last taken to Spain, which in Rome would have been wound up with difficulty.]

112.

Relatione dello stato dell' imperio e della Germania fatta da mons' Caraffa nel tempo che era nuntio alla corte dell' imperatore l' anno 1628.—[Report on the state of the empire and of Germany, made by monsignor Caraffa, at the time of his being nuncio at the court of the emperor in the year 1628.]

The fullest report upon the whole that has come into my hands: in a Roman copy it contains 1080 pages. Nor is it rare in Germany. I bought a copy in Leipsic, and another is to be found in a private library at Berlin, in a beautiful folio volume, which one Wynman had presented to the bishop of Eichstadt in 1655, with a splendid title.

It consists of four parts. In the first the German troubles are described; in the second the position, the possessions, and the circumstances of Ferdinand II.; in the third the German principalities, according to circles; in the fourth the alliances that, particularly in the last period, existed in Germany.

The author declares that he would write nothing that he had not himself seen, or at least had perceived on other grounds to be worthy of belief.

"Protestandomi che tutto quello che scriverò, parte n' ho praticato e visto io stesso per lo spatio di 8 anni che sono stato in Germania, parte n' ho intesso di persone degne di fede, parte n' ho cavato della lettura de' libri communi e delle lettere e cancellarie tanto d' amici quanto d' inimici, che sono state intercette in diversi tempi, de' quali alcune sono date alle stampe, altre no."

[Protesting that whatever I shall write I have partly myself transacted and seen during eight years that I was in Germany, partly I have learned from trustworthy persons, partly have got from the reading of common books and letters and papers, including those of both friends and foes, which have been intercepted at various times, and of which some have been printed, others not.]

Here we see at once that a learned compilation was contemplated.

Caraffa's printed Commentaries observe the order of time: this work is drawn up more in the form of a report. In the first part only are occurrences related chronologically.

Yet I will not dissemble that I have often felt doubts as to its genuineness.

It is put together very loosely. Here we have first to re-peruse the Bohemian report with some few omissions: then we find a very remarkable piece on the election of the king of Hungary in 1625, but with an incorrect passage intercalated; finally, which is of still more consequence, a report of the year 1629, presenting not the smallest trace of its being from Caraffa, upon Germany, the emperor and the princes, is here, it is true, enlarged, but moreover adopted word for word. Many other parts also are evidently foreign matter. King James I. of England is spoken of as "presente re d' Inghilterra" [present king of England], which, however, could not be said in 1628.

One would suppose that some mere compiler, without any judgment, had put these documents together.

Yet on farther consideration, this seems not likely to have been the case.

To Caraffa's old "ragguaglio" [statement] there are here added some very important and impressive notices of the later period, of which a compiler must have been utterly ignorant.

There appear in it pieces of information which could have reached none but an initiated person. For instance, the author knew about that secret negotiation of Urban VIII. in England, carried on by a Capuchin friar Rota, which was kept so closely concealed.

The nuncio speaks not unfrequently too in the first person.

I conclude that this work came really from Caraffa, but that it was never properly completed, whether from the author's want of time or of taste for it, or even from want of strength: for his Bohemian report likewise, is at least somewhat diffuse and shapeless. He might, on his return to Aversa, have had some leisure hours to fill up with the putting together of his materials.

At all events, even in its present shape, the work deserves our utmost attention.

The reports which it has embodied, and more or less elaborated, are of high value. The historical remarks too, are always distinct from those that are contained in the printed commentaries.

I select some notices that to me appear particularly interesting.

I. Decline of the order of princes in Germany (lit. of the German principality). For it is to be understood that here there is much more said of German and Austrian circumstances than of Roman and ecclesiastical.

"Per il passato era tanta l' abbondanza che li principi di Germania a pena potevano saper la quantità de regali, datii, argenti et altre dovitie venute da ogni parte, et hora a pena ritrovano il principio per haverle, e pare che vivano solo alla giornata, e quello che dà una giornata, l' altra lo consuma. Non vi è raccolta grande di danaro, se non di cose refiutate da' creditori e che sono più di titolo che di realtà. Di tal negligenza e sì poca economia e di sì fatto errore varie s' assegnano le cause: chi dice ciò venire per la liberalità de' principi, chi per le conditioni de' tempi iniqui, chi per le frequenti guerre, chi per le seditioni de' cittadini, altri finalmente assegnano la causa a' ministri, prefetti e vicarii: veramente si vede tali officii haver voluto abbracciare più di quello che potevano stringere et essere arrivate troppo oltre le comodità prese da governatori: con questo il poco consiglio, l' interesse proprio anteposto al commune, cose che poterono estinguere il gran Romano imperio, perche non ponno estinguere il Germano? Nasce anco la rovina di Germania dall' otio de' principi e dal loro troppo delitiare, o dalla poca forza d' ingegno, o da una precipitosa vecchiaja, o pure per esser tanto nemici del governo che più si contentano di dare in mano d' un' altro il maneggio delle cose publiche, benche riconoschino spesso la poca idoneità di colui, e quasi a foggia di alcuni antichi Eritrei farli secondi principi, da loro solo differenti per nome, ma pari nel total maneggio, come fu Joab appresso David et altri appresso altri principi. I quali maneggiatori, come presi dalla plebe, abusavano et abusano la loro data potestà, e più con la passione che con la moderatione della virtù governandosi e dati in preda a parasiti et adulatori constituivano e constituiscono altri sottoministri indegni, che con prezzo e ragione di parentela et ambitione corrompevano e corrompono la giustitia, et a tale esempio dietro e se tirando altri principi circonvicini facevano commune giustitia cio ch' era proprio interesse."

[In past times there was such plenty that the princes of Germany could hardly know the amount of regalia, reddendos, returns of silver and other riches coming from all quarters, and now they hardly can devise a method of getting them, and it would appear they live from hand to mouth, and what one day gives another consumes. There is no great receipt of money there, unless of things refused by creditors, and that are rather nominal than real. Various causes are alleged for such negligence, and such want of economy, and of such blundering: one says that it arises from the liberality of the princes, another from the peculiar circumstances of evil times, another from frequent wars, another from the seditious of the inhabitants of cities, others, in fine, blame the ministers, prefects, and vicars: in truth such offices (functionaries) are seen eager to lay their hands on more than they can squeeze out of the people, and to exceed too much the emoluments taken as governors: add to this, want of prudence, the interests of individuals preferred to that of the community, things which could extinguish the great Roman empire, and why should they not prove sufficient to extinguish the German? The ruin of Germany further arises from the sloth of the princes and their excessive banquetings, or from the small force of genius, or from a reckless dotage, or, in fine, from the government having so many enemies that more are content to hand over to another the management of public affairs, although they often own his small degree of fitness, and almost after the fashion of some ancient Eritrei, to make them secondary princes, differing from them only in name, but on an equality with them in the general administration, as was Joab with David and others in the courts of other princes. Which managers, being taken from the populace, have abused and do abuse the power given them, and governing rather with passion than with the moderation of virtue, and being preyed upon by parasites and flatterers, have appointed and do appoint other worthless sub-ministers, who have corrupted and do corrupt with venality and motives of regard for kindred and ambition, and

other neighbouring princes following this example, have made common justice that which was private interest.]

II. ELECTION OF A KING OF HUNGARY.

"Sopragiungendo alla dieta li voti del regno di Schiavonia e di Croatia, che erano quasi tutti cattolici, e superando con questa giunta la parte de' cattolici et adherenti di Sua Maestà di non poco la parte degli heretici e non confidenti, la voce sparsa della volontà di S. Mtà dell'elettione veniva giornalmente meglio intesa. Tuttavia li deputati dell' imperatore, per meglio assicurarsi delli voti della dieta, volsero prima di proporre l' elettione dell' arciduca farne esperienza con l' elettione del palatino, che si doveva fare per la morte del Thurzo, desiderando S. Mtà che si facesse un cattolico e particolarmente il sopradetto conte Esterhasi, ancorche secondo le leggi e costitutioni di quel regno havesse proposto alli stati quattro soggetti, due cattolici e due heretici: et il negotio riuscì felicissimamente, poiche detto conte fu eletto con 150 voti, non havendo havuto il contrario più che 60. Fatta questa prova e con essa rincorati maggiormente li confidenti et amici dell' imperatore, parve nondimeno alli ministri di S. Mtà che oltre alli sopradetti voti 150 saria stato bene a superare qualche buona parte delli 60 contrarij con presenti e con doni acciò riuscisse l' elettione con maggior sodisfattione del regno, e collo spendere, per quanto fu detto, da 20 m. fiorini si hebbe l' intento della maggior parte di loro, come si esperimentò nell' altri negotii della dieta. Li Betleniani e suoi adherenti, ancorche non fosse all' hora publicata la volontà dell' imperatore, sebbene si teneva per sicuro che volesse fare eleggere re l' arciduca, non mancavano di contrariare al possibile.

"Soggiungerò un' esempio dell' ardire di una donna in questo proposito, dal quale, si come è straordinario, si conosceranno le forze di detti contrarii. La madre del barone Bathiani, che è de' più principali signori di qualità e di stato e di adherenza d' Ungaria, hebbe ardire di mettere in consideratione all' imperatrice che non doveva permettere che si facesse questa elettione, perche si veniva a pregiudicare a S. Mtà stessa, poiche se fosse venuta qualche disgratia alla vita dell' imperatore, lei per l' interregno, come coronata regina d' Ungaria, finche fosse stato eletto un nuovo re, haveria governato quel regno. Ma l' imperatrice, con somma prudenza dissimulando, le rispose che la ringratiava dell' affetto, ma che lei doppo la morte dell' imperatore, se fosse sopravissuta, non voleva pensare ad altro che all' utile delli figli di Sua Mtà suo marito: al quale subito diede parte della sopradetta proposta.

"Ma ancorche il negotio dell' elettione si stimasse già sicuro, l' impedì tuttavia molti giorni il contrasto grande nato tra ministri più supremi di Sua Mtà, includendosi ancora monsr arcivescovo di Strigonia et il nuovo palatino con monsr cancelliere et altri che vi havevano interessi, come era l' ambasciatore di Spagna et io come indegno ministro apostolico. Il contrasto fu, se seguita detta elettione si doveva far subito la coronatione. Al-

[By superadding to the diet the votes of the kingdom of Sclavonia and of Croatia, which were almost all catholic, and by that addition the party of the catholics and adherents of his holiness exceeding not a little that of the heretics and distrustful, the report circulated of his majesty's wish as to the election came to be daily better understood. Meanwhile the emperor's deputies, in order to be more assured of the votes of the diet, wished, previous to proposing the election of the archduke, to make a trial with the election of the palatine, which had to take place through the death of Thurzo, his majesty wishing that a catholic should be elected, and in particular the count Esterhazy abovementioned, although, according to the laws and constitutions of that kingdom, he had proposed to the states four subjects, two catholics and two heretics: and the business proceeded most felicitously, for the said count was elected with 150 votes in his favour, while there were not more than 60 against him. This trial being made, and the result having greatly encouraged the emperor's confidants and friends, it seemed nevertheless to his majesty's ministers, that, besides the 150 votes, it would be well to gain over some good part of the 60 contrary votes with presents and gifts, so that the election might prove more to the satisfaction of the kingdom; and at the cost, as was said, of 20,000 florins, an attempt was made to gain the greater part of them, as was tried in other matters in that diet. The Betlenians and their adherents, although the emperor's wishes had not then been generally announced, it being considered certain, however, that he wished the archduke to be elected king, failed not to show all possible opposition.

I shall add an instance of the boldness of a lady in this matter, from which, as it is extraordinary, one may perceive the resources of the said opponents. The mother of the baron Bathiani, who is one of the chief of the Hungarian nobles in point of rank and state and followers, had dared to submit to the empress's consideration that she ought not to allow this election to take place, since it might come to prejudice her majesty herself, for were anything to happen to the emperor's life, she, during the interregnum, as crowned queen of Hungary, would have to govern that kingdom until the election of a new king. But the empress, dissembling with consummate prudence, answered that she thanked her for her regard, but that were she to survive the emperor, she would think of nothing but what was most advantageous to the sons of his majesty her husband; to whom she immediately communicated the above suggestion.

But although the business of the election was already thought secure, it was thwarted, nevertheless, for many days, by the grand quarrel that arose between his majesty's highest ministers, including also the arch-

cuni dicevano di sì: perche con questa veniva l'arciduca ad assicurarsi totalmente nel regno, il che non saria stato se fosse stato solamente eletto, per l' accennata di sopra elettione del Gabor, essendo gli Ungari huomini volubilissimi e per lo più infedeli: 2° dicevano che la coronatione, se si fosse fatta, haveria giovato assai nella prima dieta imperiale, se l'imperatore havesse voluto far eleggere Sua Altezza in re de' Romani: 3° per il matrimonio dell' infanta di Spagna, essendosi colà dichiarato di volere l' arciduca prima eletto e coronato re di Ungaria. Altri per il contrario, tra quali ero io et il padre confessore dell' imperatore, dicevano che questa coronatione non si doveva fare all' hora, perche li stati di quel regno non haveriano mai permesso che seguisse detta coronatione se Sua Altezza non havesse promesso loro e giurato, tanto nelli punti politici come di religione, tutto quello che promise il padre stando nelli maggiori pericoli: onde non vi essendo all' hora detti pericoli e potendo con il tempo migliorarsi assai le cose di S. A., o per la morte del Gabor o per li felici successi dell' imperio o per altro, non era bene intrigare la conscienza di questo principe giovane con serrarli la porta a' progressi della religione et impedirgli insieme l' acquisito di maggiore autorità politica e dominio nel regno: 2° dicevano, e questo per lo più li camerali, che nella coronatione vi saria andata una buona spesa, come ancora nell' accrescimento della corte di Sua Altezza, onde stando all' hora imminente la spesa grossa del viaggio d' Ulma, si saria potuto differire in altro tempo, non potendo probabilmente apportare alcun detrimento detta dilatione, perche se il Gabor havesse voluto pigliare pretesti, venendo qualche accidente di morte all' imperatore, tanto l' haveria pigliato ancorche l' arciduca fosse stato coronato, come fece contro l' imperatore ancorche fusse eletto e coronato: che per elettione in re de' Romani e per il matrimonio dell' infanta di Spagna bastava che l' arciduca fusse vero re d' Ungaria, e come tale si potesse intitolare per la sola elettione. Standosi dunque in questo contrasto, ancorche l' ambasciatore di Spagna facesse nuove instanze per la coronatione, dicendo che in Spagna non haveriano fatto il matrimonio dell' infanta con l' arciduca, stimandosi altrimenti la successione nel regno non sicura, Sua M^{ta} con la solita sua pietà si dichiarò che non voleva che si facesse, stimando secondo il consiglio del suo padre confessore che fosse contro conscienza se l' arciduca havesse giurato, come non poteva far di meno, quello che era stata forzata giurare Sua M^{ta} nelli pericoli grandi, quali all' hora non vi erano."

bishop of Strigonia and the new palatine, with the chancellor and others who were interested in the matter, such as the Spanish ambassador and myself as unworthy apostolic minister. The point in dispute was, whether, on the said election taking place, the coronation should immediately follow. Some said, yea; for with that the archduke would come to be firmly seated in the kingdom, which he would not be if merely elected, as was suggested by the above election of Gabor, the Hungarians being most fickle and for the most part faithless men: 2d, they said that the coronation, were it to take place, would be of much assistance in the first imperial diet, if they wished to have his highness elected king of the Romans: 3d, on account of the marriage of the infanta of Spain, a desire being expressed there that the archduke should first be elected and crowned king of Hungary. Others, on the contrary, among whom were myself and the emperor's father-confessor, said that the coronation ought not to take place then, because the states of that kingdom would never allow the said coronation to take place without his highness first promising and swearing to them, alike in political and religious points, all that his father had promised while placed in greater perils: hence, as the said perils did not now exist, and as the affairs of his highness might much improve with time, by the death of Gabor, or by the prosperous events of the empire, or otherwise, it was not well to perplex the conscience of this young prince by shutting the door on the advances of religion, and hindering at the same time the acquisition of greater political authority and dominion in the kingdom: 2dly, It was said, and that most by the exchequer people, that in the coronation there would be a considerable expense, as well as also in the augmentation of his highness's court, whence, with the great expense of the Ulm journey impending, it should be put off to another time, the said delay not being likely to cause any detriment; for if Gabor wished to seize upon pretexts in case of the emperor happening any how to die, he would do as much even were the duke crowned, as he had done against the emperor notwithstanding his having been both elected and crowned: that for his election as king of the Romans and for the marriage of the infanta of Spain, it sufficed that the duke should be really king of Hungary, and that he could assume that title by election alone. Parties being thus at variance, although the Spanish ambassador made new applications for the coronation, saying that in Spain the marriage of the infanta with the duke would not be agreed to, the succession in the kingdom being thought otherwise insecure, his majesty, with his usual piety, declared that he did not wish it to take place, considering, according to the counsel of his father-confessor, that it would be against the archduke's conscience to swear, as he could not avoid doing what his majesty had been forced to swear in the great perils then imminent.]

113.

Relatio status ecclesiae et totius dioecesis Augustanae 1629.—[Account of the state of the church and whole diocese of Augsburg, 1629.]

Of no particular importance. In the main, the circumstances of the city of Augsburg only are brought under consideration.

The author's chief subject is the active influence and final removal of the protestant "pseudo-doctors" from Augsburg.

He hopes that after this being effected through Jerome Imhof and Bernh. Rehlingen, who were with the emperor, all would, in a short time, again become Roman catholic.

114.

Legatio apost^ca^ P. Aloys. Carafae episcopi Tricaricensis sedente Urbano VIII. Pont. M. ad tractum Rheni et ad prov. inferioris Germaniae obita ab anno 1624 usque ad annum 1634. Ad C^lem^ Franc. Barberinum.—[Apostolic legation of P. Aloys. Carafa, bishop of Tricarico, during the pontificate of Urban VIII., to the Rhine country and the provinces of Lower Germany, performed from 1624 to 1634. To cardinal Franc. Barberino.]

A very copious report, of 204 leaves; somewhat diffuse, to be sure, but comprising good things.

First, there comes an account of the journey, where again much space is taken up with matters of no consequence. The nuncio comes, among other places, to Fulda. He takes credit to himself for having reduced to eight the sixteen ancestors[1] whom every candidate had to produce in order to his being capable of enjoying the dignity of abbot.

He is particularly full on the subject of the affair of Liege with the bishop, in which he himself took an active part. He transferred the seat of the nuncioship from Cologne to Liege.

Without doubt, the most remarkable part of the report is a description of the Roman catholic universities of that day in the district of the nuncioship.

We see from it how entirely the higher branches of instruction, at that time, were in the hands of the Jesuits. They were the masters in Treves and Mainz; Paderborn, Münster, and Osnaburg, where a high school had been founded shortly before, were entirely in their hands: yet they taught only humanity, philosophy, and theology. The (civil and canon) laws were altogether neglected. In Cologne, which still held the first place among these universities, medicine was lectured on by only two teachers, and these had few to listen to them. The grand evil in Cologne, in early times, was, that the professors were quite too richly provided with prebends.

"Earum opibus ad vitam clementem et suavem instructi, raro aut nunquam ipsi sacram doctrinam tradebant, sed aliorum vicaria opera passim utebantur. Hinc sine pondere et methodo instruebantur academici, et anni quindeni facile circumagi solebant priusquam universam illi theologiam audirent. Ea res vero antehac non parum incommoda fuerat archidioecesi Coloniensi et praesertim ditionibus Juliae Cliviae ac Montium, quod pro adeunda in iis animarum procuratione reparandisque religionis catholicae ruinis parochi et sacerdotes idonei hoc pacto nisi post longissimum diem non instituebantur."

[Being furnished by the wealth of these (prebends) for an easy and pleasant life, they seldom or never taught theology, but ordinarily availed themselves of the services of substitutes. Hence the students were instructed without weight and method, and fifteen years used easily to be passed before they heard a complete course of theology. This, however, had been formerly no great inconvenience to the archdiocese of Cologne, and particularly to the jurisdictions of Juliers, Cleves, and Mons, because fit parish ministers and priests for engaging in these, in the cure of souls, and in repairing the ruins of the catholic religion, could on this footing be ordained only at a very distant date.]

This the Jesuit fathers abolished. The Three Crowns College, which was handed over to them, enjoyed a great reputation in 1634: it had 1200 students attending it. But it was not so easy to eradicate that taste for the enjoyments of life. The master of the banquets augmented the costs of promotion and the luxury. "Tota quadragesima sunt quotidie academicorum symposia."—[During the whole of Lent there are daily wine parties among the students.] Our bishop gives no bad description of the catholicism and the good living of Cologne.

"Populus Coloniensis religionis avitae retinentissimus est, quam utique semel susceptam nunquam deseruit. Tolerantur quidem in civitate familiae aliquae sectariorum, sed vetitum eis est exercitium omne sectarum suarum, et aere gravi mulctantur si qui clam

[The people of Cologne are most retentive of their ancestral religion, which indeed, since their first adopting it, they have never abandoned. No doubt some families of the sectaries are tolerated in the state, but they are forbidden all exercise of their sects, and those

1 That is, no doubt, the sixteen quarters in heraldry—the armorial bearings of a man's sixteen great-great-great-grandfathers.—Tr.

habere privatos conventus et audire Lutheri aut Calvini buccinatores deprehendantur. In senatum ipsum nulli cooptantur qui catholici non fuerint, et quotquot in eo conscripti ad curiam veniunt, sententiam dicere aut ferre suffragium non possunt nisi prius eodem die intervenerint rei sacrae in proximo palatii senatorii sacello. Noctu ipsi civis excubias habent in potioribus plateis civitatis, nec vis aut injuria metui potest, quia strepitu quovis exciti adsunt et opitulantur, grassatores vero ac sicarios in vincula conjiciunt. Sed et plateae omnes catenis ferreis noctu vinciuntur, ne pateant liberis excursionibus, ideoque populus maxime in tranquillo agit. Inter alia plebis commoda illud imprimis commemorari debet, licere cuique ineunte hieme boves et sues emere eosque fumo arefacere ac in escam anni consequentis, qua vescuntur avide, domi servare. Spatium vero ejusdem anni eis concedi solet ad pretium repraesentandum, dum interim aliqui a senatu constituti mercatoribus solvunt: nec unquam opifices ulli, quamvis inopes, patiuntur suam fidem in ea re desiderari, quia deinceps haud foret integrum eis rursus ejusmodi annonam rei cibariae illo tam insigni subsidio acris publici coemere. Sunt et triclinia tribuum communia, in eisque possunt omnes iis diebus quibus feriantur in hebdomade, constituto pretio admodum facili, convivari."

are heavily fined who may be caught secretly holding private conventicles, and hearing Luther's or Calvin's ranters. None are admitted into the senate itself who have not been catholics, and all who have been enrolled as members and come to the curia, can neither express their opinion nor give their vote, unless they have that same day taken part in the solemnities of religion in the chapel nearest the senatorial palace. At night the citizens themselves keep watch in the larger squares of the city, nor is violence or insult to be dreaded, seeing that the instant they hear a noise, they fly to the spot and render assistance; but robbers and assassins they throw into prison. Moreover, all the streets are closed at night with iron chains, to prevent their being open to loose excursions: the people accordingly live, for the most part, very quietly. Among other advantages enjoyed by the common people, the first to be recorded is that each is allowed, at the commencement of winter, to purchase oxen and pigs, and to dry them with smoke, to be preserved at home during the year following for food, of which they eat greedily. They are allowed the whole of that year, however, for the payment of the price, certain persons meanwhile who are appointed for that purpose by the senate, paying the price; nor is it ever found that any of the artisans, however poor, allow their want of good faith in this matter to be felt, since in that case it would no longer be in their power again to purchase, with such signal aid from the public money, their provision of that kind of food. The public tables of the tribes are common, and in these all, on week-day festivals, may meet in convivial parties, at a fixed and very moderate price.]

But not only cities and universities, but princes and occurrences also are described. Ferdinand of Cologne, "gravitate morum, professione pietatis et ingenii maturitate nulli secundus" [second to none in gravity of morals, the profession of piety, and maturity of genius]; Frederick of Würzburg, "linguarum etiam exterarum peritia, morum suavi quadam gravitate, prudentissima dexteritate omnibus carus" [a man endeared to all by his skill even in foreign tongues, by a certain suavity and seriousness of manner, and by great prudence and tact]; Casimir of Mainz, "eloquens vir in Germanico idiomate, legationibus functus" [eloquent in the German tongue, and one who has discharged embassies].

L. Caraffa adduces also many remarkable things in the way of occurrences. I know not the ground of the opinion that Wallenstein might have taken Stralsund, "si, quod multi existimant, pecuniam quam urbem capere non maluisset" [if, as many think, he had not preferred taking money to taking the city]. He accounts it a great mischance that Tilly, on the first movement of Saxony, had not ventured to throw himself on that country. The account, also, which he gives of the state of Cologne after the battle of Leipsic, and of the French projects that appeared at that critical moment, is very remarkable.

"Ex accepta clade ad Lipsiam fractae vires fuerant et fracti catholicorum animi, et tunc repente imperitia vel metus in propugnandis arcibus aditum hosti victori magnum aperuerunt, ut viscera imperii mox infestis armis invaderet, ex quo Fulda, Herbipolis, Bamberga, Moguntia, Wormatia, Spira aliaeque urbes atque oppida fuerunt exiguo tempore vel expugnata vel dedita. Colonia superfuit principum exulum perfugium, et hi thesauros qua sacros qua laicos in eam civitatem importaverant, si quibus licuerat tamen illos avehere antequam ingrueret ea belli vehemens et subita tempestas. Ibidem anxiae curae principum et dubia consilia erant, an, sicut proposuerat orator Gallus, expediret deinceps neu-

[By the defeat received at Leipsic the forces and the spirits of the catholics were alike broken, and then all at once want of skill, or fear, in the defence of the fortified places, opened a vast entrance for the approach of the victorious enemy, so that he could invade forthwith, with rancorous hostility, the very bowels of the empire, whence Fulda, Wurzburg, Bamberg, Mainz, Worms, Spires, and other cities and towns, were in a short time either taken by storm or capitulated. Cologne remained as the chief refuge of the exiled princes, and these brought treasures, both sacred and secular, into that city, in so far at least as any were allowed to carry these away before that vehement and sudden storm of war came sweep-

tri parti, seu Caesaris seu Gustavi regis, tam arma principum eorundem quam arma ipsiusmet civitatis Coloniensis favere. Id Coloniae suadebat orator christianissimi regis: sed necessarium fore affirmabat ut in eam urbem pariter atque in alias ditiones principum electorum cohortes praesidiariorum ex regis sui legionibus introducerentur: tunc enim reveritus Coloniam Gustavus rex alio arma convertisset, aut si venire hostis nihilominus deliberasset, provocasset merito christianissimum regem, ac foedere extincto inimicitiam et iram ejus experiri coepisset. Gravis nimirum videbatur ea conditio admittendi cohortes praesidiarias regis externi in civitates ac ditiones imperii: sed graviores multo erant conditiones aliae, quibus ut neutri parti faverent deinceps proponebatur, qui in bello tam ancipiti Caesarem non juvare sed quasi deserere videbatur maxime alienum a professione pervetere civitatum ac principum ipsiusmet imperii. Hoc superesse tamen consilii et eum portum securitatis unice adeundum esse judicabat pariter apostolicus nuntius Parisiensis, ad quem scripseram de ingenti clade religioni catholicae templisque et aris illata per Gustavum regem."

ing on. There, too, had the princes anxious thoughts and dubious counsels whether, as the French ambassador had suggested, it were expedient from that time forward, that the arms alike of these princes and those of the city of Cologne should favour neither side, whether that of the emperor or of king Gustavus. This the ambassador of the most Christian king recommended to Cologne: but he stated that it would be necessary that garrison companies from his king's regiments should be introduced both into that city and into other places under the jurisdiction of the electoral princes; for that then king Gustavus, from respect to Cologne, would turn his arms elsewhere, or if the enemy were nevertheless to resolve upon coming, he would deservedly provoke the most Christian king, and the alliance being at an end, would begin to experience his enmity and anger. Serious, indeed, seemed this condition of admitting the garrison troops of a foreign king into the cities and provinces of the empire; but much more serious were those other conditions, by which it was proposed that from thenceforth they should favour neither party, because, in so doubtful a contest, not to aid the emperor but as it were to desert him, seemed most foreign to the ancient profession of the cities and princes of the empire itself. But that this was the only measure that remained, and the sole haven of security that could be reached, was the opinion likewise of the apostolic nuncio at Paris, to whom I had written about the dreadful disaster brought by king Gustavus on the catholic religion and the temples and altars.]

There further follows a full account of Wallenstein's catastrophe, which I will communicate elsewhere.

115.

Relatione della corte di Roma del Sig^r K^r Aluise Contarini dell' anno 1632 al 1635.—[Report on the court of Rome, by Signor Chevalier Aluise Contarini, from 1632 to 1635.] (Arch. Ven.)

A very copious report in thirty-five chapters, written on 140 pages; and doubly important from Aluise Contarini having come immediately from France to Rome, and on that account having been the more capable of passing a judgment on the singular political position assumed at that period by Urban VIII.

He first describes the pope's spiritual and secular system of government.

He considers it quite monarchical. Out of all the old congregations, one only regularly meets, that of the Inquisition; the cardinals have no further privileges beyond people stopping their carriages on meeting them, the purple, and a vote in the election of the pope: the pope is so little disposed to consult them, that on matters of consequence he will resort rather to prelates of inferior rank, whose hopes hang more upon him, than to cardinals, who are already more independent.

But the harder the reins are pulled up, the more does authority become relaxed. "L'antica veneratione sta oggidì molto diminuita."—[The ancient veneration is now-a-days much diminished.]

The inhabitants of Urbino were particularly discontented.

"Quei sudditi si aggravano molto della mutatione, chiamando il governo di preti tirannico, i quali altro interesse che d'arricchirsi e d'avanzarsi non vi tengono."

[Those subjects complain much of the change, calling the government of priests tyrannical, they being influenced by no consideration but that of enriching and advancing themselves.]

The author still laments continually that Urbino should have fallen into the hands of the pope, as involving a great loss to Spain and Venice.

He proceeds in a second part to describe personal characters.

"Nacque il papa Urbano VIII. del 1567 (others say 68) d' Aprile, onde cammina per li 69 di sua età, conservato dal vigore della complessione non soggetta a qualsivoglia ma-

[Pope Urban VIII. was born in 1567 (others say 1568) in April, hence he is in his 69th year, preserved by the vigour of his constitution, which is not subject to any ailment, and

lattia, e dalla vivacità dell' ingegno. La statura mediocre, il color bruno, il pelo bianco, l' occhio vivo, il parlar pronto, la temperatura sanguigna e biliosa. Vive con gran regola. Regola in gran parte le sue attioni coi moti del cielo, dei quali è molto intelligente, ancorche con censure grandissime a tutti gli altri n' babbia prohibito lo studio. Li suoi moti sono subiti e vehementi, tali che alcuna volta confinano con la pazzia, non potendo con la patienza frenarli, se ben egli dice che questa commotione della bile di quando in quando vaglia molto eccitando il calore alla preservatione di sua salute. Cavalca, villeggia, cammina, ama l' esercitio. Non s' affligge per le cose moleste : e tutte queste parti concorrono a predirli qualche anno di vita ancora, non ostante che nel tempo del mio soggiorno assai decaduto sia.

"E arrivato al papato con un servitio continuo di 30 e più anni alla corte. Fu prima prelato di segnatura e poi governatore di Fano. Poco appresso, per opera di Francesco Barberini suo zio paterno, prelato di poco grido ma di gran ricchezze accumulate con parsimonia fiorentina, comprò ufficii in corte e finalmente il chiericato di camera. Clemente VIII. lo impiegò in diverse cariche, ma particolarmente sopra quella del novo taglio del Po, dacche sono arrivate in gran parte le differenze presenti dei confini con la republica, per la cognitione che professa di quell' affare e per il disgusto che allora non si eseguisse a modo suo. Fu poi dall' istesso Clemente mandato nuntio in Francia, prima estraordinàrio per tenere a battesimo il re presente, e poi ordinario di Enrico IV. suo padre, dove si mostrò zelantissimo dell' immunità ecclesiastica. Paolo V. successore di Clemente lo confermò nella medesima legatione di Francia : poi lo fece cardinale, legato di Bologna, e ritornato a Roma prefetto della signatura di giustitia, carico d' onore et impiego ben grande. Finalmente del 1623 fu in luogo di Gregorio XV. con pratiche molto artificiose assonto al pontificato nell' età sua di 56 anni : et oggi corre il XIII. anno, con disgusto di tutta la corte, alla quale non meno che ai principi torna conto i pontificati brevi, perche tanto più tengono conto di tutti, abbondano nelle gratie, non temporalizzano come se fossero hereditarj del papato, e finalmente la corte in generale trova impiego e fortuna nella frequenza delle mutationi.

"In ogni stato hebbe il papa di se stesso grande opinione con affetti di dominio sopra gli altri e disprezzo al consiglio di tutti. Par ch' egli esercita oggidì tanto più liberamente quanto che si ritrova in posto sopra a tutti eminente. Ha ingegno grande, ma non giudicio : ingegno, perche nelle cose che da lui solo dipendono e che riguardano la sua persona e casa, si è sempre condotto ove ha desiderato, senza omettere gl' inganni e gli artificii di lui molto connaturali, come si vide particolarmente nelle pratiche del suo papato, nelle quali seppe far convenire nella sua persona le due fattioni contrarie di Borghese e Ludovisio, solo col far credere all' una d' esser inimico dell' altra : negli affari poi generali, nei quali si richiede il giudicio di saper ben congiungere gl' interessi della sede apostolica con quelli degli altri principi, si è osservato il

by the vivacity of his genius. He is of the middle size, of a brown complexion, white hair, lively eye, prompt utterance, sanguine and bilious temperament. He lives with great regularity. He regulates his actions in a great measure by the motions of the heavens, of which he knows a great deal, although he has prohibited the study of them by the heaviest censures, to all others. His own movements are sudden and vehement, such as sometimes to border upon madness, being unable to restrain them with patience, albeit he says that this commotion of the bile from time to time, by exciting heat, avails much for the preservation of his health. He rides about, enjoys the country, walks, likes exercise. He is not fretted with annoyances; and all these particulars concur in leading one to think he may live some years longer, notwithstanding at the time of my sojourn he had fallen off much.

He came to the popedom after an uninterrupted course of thirty years' service at court. He was first prelate of the *segnatura*, and then governor of Fano. Shortly afterwards, with the assistance of Francis Barberino, his paternal uncle, a prelate of little repute, but of great riches, accumulated with Florentine parsimony, he bought offices at court, and finally the clerkship of the chamber. Clement VIII. employed him in various charges, but chiefly in superintending the new cutting of the Po, from which the present differences about boundaries with the republic have, in a great measure, arisen, owing to the knowledge he professes to have of that affair, and to the disgust he feels at matters not having been conducted at that time as he wished. He was then sent by the same Clement as nuncio into France, first extraordinary, to hold the present king up to baptism, and then as ordinary nuncio of Henry IV., this king's father, where he showed himself most zealous for the ecclesiastical immunities. Paul V., Clement's successor, confirmed him in that French legation; then he made him cardinal, legate of Bologna, and, on his return to Rome, prefect of the segnatura of justice, an honourable charge, and very high office. Finally, in 1623, he was, with many artful intrigues, raised to the pontificate in the place of Gregory XV., at the age of fifty-six; and now he is passing his thirteenth year, to the disgust of the whole court, to which, not less than to the princes, short pontificates prove advantageous, for so much the more do they (the popes) make account of all, abound in favours, do not temporize as if they had inherited the popedom, and, finally, the court in general finds employment and fortune in the frequent recurrence of changes.

In every condition of life, the pope has had a high opinion of himself, indulging airs of superiority over others, and depreciating the counsel of all. It seems that at present he conducts himself more liberally in proportion as he finds himself in a position that places him above all others. He has much genius, but not much judgment: genius, for in matters that depend on himself alone, and that respect his person and family, he has always proceeded to the attainment of the object of his desire, without omitting those

papa esserne per sempre stato manchevole. Tale lo dichiarano il negotio di Valtellina: la guerra di Mantova, che non sarebbe seguita se il papa si fosse dichiarito contro il primo innovatore: la perdita di Mantova, attribuita ai viveri che riceverono gli Alemani dallo stato ecclesiastico, senza quali conveniva loro o dissassediarla o morirsi; la prefettura di Roma data al nipote, privando la sede apostolica dell' assistenza di tanti ministri di principi che sono il più bel fregio di lei, et aggravando lo stesso nipote d' invidia, di riguardi e d' un posto assolutamente insostentabile dopo la morte del pontefice; il mal termine usatosi contro l' ambasciatore di V. Serenità mio precessore, lasciandolo partire senza soddisfattione; l' ultima comprotettione di Francia nel cardinale Antonio nipote prima persuasa et acconsentita, poi ritrattata e prohibita, con nota appresso il mondo di grande artificio, per non dire inganno, e con divisione della propria casa. Tralascio il gran detrimento che sotto il presente pontefice ha fatto la religione cattolica in Fiandra et Alemagna; i pericoli all' Italia per la negata dispensa al duca di Mantova, e molto più per aversi portato il papa in modo che ha disgustato tutti i principi grandi e piccioli, che nessuno gli è amico: onde si è reso incapace di poter esercitar con essi loro quelle parti di autorità e di paterno consiglio che potrebbe pacificarli et unirli insieme alla difesa della religione: parti che sono state così esattamente maneggiate e conosciute proprie de' pontefici che per sostenere il nome di padre comune, dal quale proviene loro ogni veneratione, e per mantenere l' unione tra i principi christiani, che cagiona in essi molta autorità, si sono esposti ad azzardi, a viaggi, a pericoli, non militando nel nome di padre quei puntigli che nel' intromissione degli altri principi possono facilmente incontrarsi.

"Si è sempre professato il papa presente neutrale, attribuendo a sua gloria l' aver arricchita et ingrandita la sua casa senza comprar stati in regno di Napoli nè sottomettersi a favori dei principi grandi. Nell' interno però suo egli è affettionato a Francesi, le loro prontezze e risolutioni essendo più conformi al genio di S. Sta, in ordine di che ha fatto le maggiori dimostrationi quando seguì l' acquisto della Roscella. Persuase la pace con Inglesi, affinche la Francia potesse accorrer al soccorso di Casale allora assediata dai Spagnoli: consigliò ai medesimi l' acquisto e la conservatione di Pinarolo per necessario equilibrio alle cose d' Italia: trovò sempre pretesti di diferir o diminuir i soccorsi in Alemagna, con opinione, la qual vive tuttavia, che a S. Sta sia dispiacciuta la morte del re di Suezia e che più goda o per dir meglio manco tema i progressi de' protestanti che degli Austriaci. Anzi è opinion commune che quando anche fosse portato il papa dal card^l^ Barberino, tutto Spagnolo, a qualche unione con essi, tornerebbe facilmente a maggior rottura di prima. E la causa è questa: perche governandosi al papa con artificio e credendo che Spagnoli facciano il medesimo, saranno sempre tra di loro anzi gelosie d' inganni che confidenza di ben vera unione."

tricks and devices which are inborn with him, as appears particularly in the intrigues of his popedom, in which he has contrived to concentrate in his own person the opposite factions of Borghese and Ludovisio, solely by making the one believe that he is hostile to the other: then in general affairs, which require judgment for knowing well how to conjoin the interests of the apostolic see with those of the other princes, the pope is observed to have been almost always deficient. Such he was declared to be by the business of the Valteline; by the Mantuan war, which would not have followed had the pope declared himself against the first innovator; the loss of Mantua, attributed to the provisions which the Germans received from the ecclesiastical state, without which they must have raised the siege or perished; by the prefecture of Rome being given to the nephew, depriving the apostolic see of the presence of so many ministers of princes which are its finest ornament, and loading the said nephew with envy, with vexations, and with a post absolutely untenable after the death of the pontiff; the ill terms he employed against the ambassador of your serenities, my predecessor, allowing him to depart without satisfaction; the last coprotection of France in the cardinal Anthony, nephew, first advised and consented to, then retracted and prohibited, with marks before the world of great artifice, not to say of deceit, and with the division of his own family. I pass over the great loss that the catholic religion has suffered under the present pope in Flanders and Germany; the perils of Italy by the refusal of the dispensation to the duke of Mantua; and much more by the pope having behaved in such a manner as to have disgusted all princes, great and small, so that none is friendly; whence he is rendered incapable of exercising with them those offices of authority and of fatherly advice which might pacificate them, and unite them together for the defence of religion: offices which have been thus exactly exercised and professed as properly belonging to the pontiffs, both in order to maintain the name of common father, from which there accrues to them much veneration, and to preserve that union among Christian princes which gives them much authority, should they be exposed to hazards, to journeyings, to dangers, by those punctilios which may easily occur in the mutual transactions of other princes, not leading to war in the name of the father.

The present pope has always represented himself as neutral, making it part of his glory to have enriched and aggrandized his family without bargaining for states in the kingdom of Naples, or by meanly seeking favours from great princes. At heart, in fine, he inclines to the French, their promptitude and bold measures being more conformed to his holiness's genius, with respect to which he made great demonstrations when the acquisition of Rochelle took place. He advised peace with the English in order that France might come to the aid of Casale, at that time besieged by the Spaniards: he recommended to the same the acquisition and retention of Pinarolo, as being necessary to the equilibrium of affairs

in Italy: he always found pretexts for delaying or diminishing succours in Germany, while people entertain the notion, which is always prevalent, that the death of the king of Sweden would have been ungrateful news to his holiness, and that he rejoiced more, or to speak more correctly, that he trembled less at the advances made by the protestants than by the Austrians. The opinion is current, also, that even though the pope has been led by cardinal Barberino, who is quite Spanish, to some union with them, he will easily break with them more violently than at first. The reason is this: that as the pope governs by dint of cunning, and believes the Spaniards do the same, there will always be between them rather a jealousy of being over-reached than the confidence of a really sincere union.]

It is unnecessary to introduce here the descriptions of the nephews given by Aluise Contarini. Even Francis Barberino, although the pope liked him best, and although he devoted himself wholly to business, yet was quite dependent on his uncle.

"Nessuno nipote di papa fu giamai alle fatiche del negotio aasiduo come egli è, non avendo minimo divertimento: ma egli è anche vero che nessuno manco di lui ha operato."

[No pope's nephew was ever so assiduous in the labours of business as he is, for he never takes the smallest diversion: but it is also true that none has ever effected less than he.]

He declines any description of the cardinals. In that corporation he finds a general hypocrisy prevalent.

"Sarà tal card[le] sanissimo che per facilitarsi il papato vorrà esser creduto infermo: caminando zoppica, discorrendo tosse, uscendo si sta tutto in una seggietta racchiuso. Tal altro che sarà buon politico, si mostrerà lontano da ogni negotio, nei discorsi s' ammutisce, ne' quesiti si stringe le spalle, nelle risposte generalizza."

[Such a cardinal, though in perfect health, in order to facilitate his getting the popedom, would have it to be believed that he is infirm: in speaking, he coughs; if he goes out, it is only shut up in a sedan chair. Such another, although a good politician, will affect abstaining from all business; while others are talking, he sits mute, shrugs his shoulders when asked questions, and gives general answers.]

One might suppose that here we have the original on which was founded the story told of the elevation of Sixtus V.

The third part follows: on political relations, full of impressive and animated acuteness: as we have said, it is the most important for us.

However disposed pope Urban was to the French, yet the French were never gratified in their ecclesiastical demands.

"Bisogna anche confessare, ch' essi hanno addimandato delle gratie difficili, come la dispositione dell' abbazie di Lorena, la nullità de' matrimonj tanto del duca Carlo di Lorena come di monsieur et altri simili."

[It must further be confessed that they have asked for favours hard to be granted, such as the disposal of the abbacies of Lorraine, the annulling of the marriage both of duke Charles of Lorraine, and of Monsieur, and others like these.]

Francis Barberino, too, was not so much on the French side as his uncle was. Already had the French ceased to hope for any very open declaration in their favour, but they were at the same time aware that the pope would not be against them: that of itself was a great advantage to them, that he was thought to lean to the French, and the opposite party distrusted him.

So much the more dissatisfied were the Spaniards. They blamed cardinal Borgio for having allowed Urban VIII. to be elected; and it was asserted that this cardinal was gained over only by the promise of manifold favours. In the negotiations on the subject of the Valteline, in the policy of the French, in the relations into which Bavaria had entered, they were resolved to see nothing but the influence of the pope's disfavour. On the other hand, even Barberino maintained that the concessions made to them called forth no gratitude on their part. One perceives that the misunderstanding was reciprocal.

Contarini treats most fully of the relations between Rome and Venice. He considers the chief source of difficulty to be this, that whereas other states were dreaded by Rome as more powerful, or slighted as less powerful, Venice was considered and treated as an equal.

Already was it a subject of irritation at Rome that the English and Dutch enjoyed some franchises there. But if once an ecclesiastical person was arrested on the part of the secular jurisdiction, there was immediately a general storm.

The ambassador is, notwithstanding, of opinion, that people durst not allow themselves to be put out of countenance. The nuncio was commissioned directly to maintain the best understanding with the best liked; those who had most confession-children.

"E VV. EE. tengano per constante, che col mezzo di questi tali vengono i nuntii a risapere il midollo delli arcani."

[And your excellencies may hold it for certain, that by means of such as these the nuncios come to know the very marrow of secrets.]

So much the more necessary was it for the republic not to divest itself of its authority.

But over and above this there was a perpetual contention about the boundaries. Urban VIII. was in no wise considered as a favourer of the Venetians. He was particularly set upon advancing the prosperity of Ancona at the expense of Venice.

116.

Discorso della malattia e morte del card[l] Ippolyto Aldobrandino camerlengo di S[ta] Chiesa col fine della grandezza del papa Clemente VIII.—[Account of the illness and death of cardinal Hippolyto Aldobrandino, chamberlain (?) of the holy church with the close of the greatness of pope Clement VIII.] 1638.

An extraordinary impression was produced at Rome by the sudden downfall of the family of the Aldobrandini, which had been founded so shortly before.

The small work before us is written under the influence of this impression. "E stato superato dalla morte quell gran ingegno!"—[Death has at last overcome that great genius!] are the words it begins with. Of the whole family there survived only the daughter of John George Aldobrandino, who necessarily became heiress to immense wealth.

The following passage gives one no bad idea of the state of Roman society: "Il marchese Lodovico Lanti, il conte Gio. Francesco da Bagni, Berlingieri Gessi e Bernardino Biscia, aspettando tutti quattro a gara il pontificato de' loro zii, ambivano le nozze della principessa Aldobrandina."—[The Marquis Lewis Lanti, count George Francis da Bagni, Berlingieri Gessi and Bernardino Biscia, all four looking emulously forward to the pontificate of their respective uncles, intrigued for the marriage of the princess Aldobrandina.] In hope of the pontificate of their uncle the presumptive nephews became rivals with each other for the hand of the richest heiress.

Yet neither this marriage nor the power of a nephew fell to the lot of any of them.

Hippolyta married a Borghese. Our author is in the utmost amazement. Paul V. had persecuted the Aldobrandini, and had imprisoned the father of Hippolyta herself. And now she married his grand nephew.

Subsequently however, she, as we know, fell into the hands of the nephew of a reigning pope, Innocent X., to which the circumstances and conveniences of the Roman court now destined her.

117.

Relatione di q. Zuanne Nani K[r] Proc[r] ritornato di ambasciatore estraordinario da Roma 1641 10 Luglio. (Arch Ven.)—[Report of (?) Zuanne Nani Knight Proc[r] on his return as ambassador extraordinary from Rome 1641, 10th July. (Arch. Ven.)]

There were misunderstandings of various kinds incessantly existing betwixt Rome and Venice: in 1635 there appeared a fresh one of the most extraordinary nature.

A magnificent inscription, in splendid words, set up in the Sala regia of Pius IV., testified to an achievement of the Venetians, of which they were exceedingly proud, and which was paraded in their history: a victory over Frederick Barbarossa, through which they asserted that pope Alexander III. had been saved from destruction.

But already had this inscription gradually come to be thought inadmissible. That it should run thus: "Pontifici Venetae reipublicae beneficio sua dignitas restituta," [By the good office of the Venetian republic his dignity restored to the pontiff,] was declared by the ever-increasing stiffness of orthodoxy to be a sort of insult. The spirit of jealousy with respect to precedence in rank which ruled the world, attached itself to this long past and obsolete occurrence. Over and above this, however, people began generally to question the truth of the account as it appears in the historical books of the Venetians. Writings appeared on both sides.

It involves a question which has been mooted again and again down to our own day.

I cannot see how it should appear doubtful to any one who has the slightest idea of historical criticism.

But however that might be, at all events it was not only conviction but political jealousy also, that prevailed with Urban VIII., to have that inscription first altered and then effaced.

In this light also was it viewed by the republic: as the contentions about the boundaries and about the precedence of the new prefect forthwith became more and more bitter, Venice for a long time sent no regular ambassador to Rome.

Nani even, who went thither in 1638, was only extraordinary ambassador. He remained, however, about three and a half years, and his report shows that he had acquired a considerable knowledge of that court.

The main object contemplated in his mission, was to prevail upon the pope to support the republic in the event of its being attacked by the Turks, a danger which seemed at that time very imminent.

Strange to say, this prayer seemed even desirable to the pope. He could oppose this pressing necessity to the perpetual demands of the house of Austria, then so warmly pressed by the protestants and the French.

The ambassador would willingly have availed himself of his mediation between the belligerent powers; this pope, however, did not enjoy the general confidence necessary for such a task. "Pullulando tante amarezze colle corone, restava fiacca, per non dir quasi odiosa, l' autorità del pontefice."—[So many roots of bitterness springing up with the crowns, the pontiff's authority remained weak, not to say almost hateful.]

For the rest, this ambassador, too, notices Urban's humour for wishing to appear strong in a military point of view. One had to talk with him about his fortifications, if he would be on a good footing with him. He himself would often mention them. He said, indeed, that he could within twenty days bring up more than 20,000 men. He reckoned up the pecuniary resources he possessed. For the most pressing necessities he had laid aside 400,000 scudi: in the castle, it was supposed, there still remained three out of Sixtus's five millions.

Let us mark the description Nani gives us of the pope's mode of conducting the government.

"Il pontefice è nel principio del settantesimo terzo della sua età e nel fine del XVII. del pontificato, dopo un spatio di 324 anni che altro papa non ha goduto così longo governo. E di forze robusto e gagliardo, e per tale li piace di esser creduto: et in effetto, levato qualche dubbio di flussioni e d' accidenti improvisi ai quali pare sottoposto, è in tale costitutione di buona salute che può mantenersi più anni. Usa governo esquisito nella sua cura. Al presente, ch'è più grave l' età, manco s'applica alle faccende, delle quali non suole però prendersi più disturbo di quello che vuole. La mattina è dispensata in audienze et in negotii, il dopo pranzo è riservato alla quiete et alla conversatione domestica, nelle quale è allegro e faceto, come in ogni altro discorso erudito e facondo, e nelle audienze stesse passa volentieri dal negotiare al parlare di cose piacevoli e di studio, al quale è dedito assai. Possede gran talenti e gran qualità. Ha memoria meravigliosa, petto e vigore che lo rende alle volte troppo costante nelli suoi sensi. Ha spiriti grandi accresciuti dall' esperienza del governo e dei negotii. Deferisce assai al suo proprio parere, perciò non ama di consultare nè cura le qualità dei ministri, che possino maggiormente far risplendere le sue risolutioni. Non molto inclina al gratiare. E ardente, et alle volte con li ministri medesimi dei principi non ha potuto dissimulare il suo fervore. Ama che sia trattato seco con destrezza e soavità: e se vi è strada di poter far declinare dai suoi sensi l' animo di Sua Sta, questa è sola la quale, se pure alle volte non può profittare, avanza certo, che se non si piega, almeno non si rompe. . .

"Nel governo presente è desiderata maggior e miglior consulta, perche dove manca il discorso, suole mancar la ragione: e veramente pochissimi sono li ministri e pochi quelli che habbino autorità e confidenza a palazzo. Appresso il pontefice non si sa alcuno che possi, e preponendo S. Sta il proprio parere a quello di tutti, sogliono li altri o lodarlo o secondarlo. Si usò in altri tempi che havevano i papi appresso di se tre e quattro cardinali e con la loro discussione risolvevano i più gravi negotii, e si teneva per arcano dei nepoti medesimi introdurre suoi dipendenti nella confidenza del zio, per condurlo poi e guadagnarlo dove o non potevano essi spuntare o non volevano scoprire gli affetti loro proprj.

"Barberino non ha voluto circuire in tal modo la libertà del papa: ma riservando a se solo il posto più vicino alle orecchie di S. Sta, obbliga gli altri a stare ritirati et al solo parer

[The pontiff is in the 73d year of his age, and at the close of the 17th of his pontificate, an interval of 324 years having elapsed since any other pope has enjoyed so long a government. He is robust and vigorous, and is gratified at being thought so; and, in fact, barring certain fluctions and unlooked-for accidents to which he seems to be subject, he is in such a state of health as may last many years. He usually takes the utmost care in the discharge of his office. At present, as he feels more the effects of age, he applies less to the things that have to be done, with which, in a word, he is wont to trouble himself no more than he pleases. The morning is spent in giving audiences and in business; the time after dinner is reserved for quiet and for domestic conversation, in which he is lively and facetious, as in all other discourse he is learned and eloquent, and even in audiences passes willingly from business to talking on agreeable subjects and study, to which he is much devoted. He possesses great qualities and great talents. He has a wonderful memory, a courage and vigour that make him at all times too constant in his sentiments. He has high aspirations, increased by experience of government and affairs. He defers much to his own opinion, for he loves not to consult, nor cares about the qualities of his ministers, who might impart a greater splendour to his resolutions. He is not much disposed to grant favours. He is ardent, and at all times has been unable to dissemble the warmth of his temper, even with the ministers of the princes. He likes people to treat with him skilfully and mildly: and if there be any way of diverting the mind of his holiness from its purposes, that alone is the way, which, if not always effectual, certainly makes some advances, and if it does not bend, at least does not break. . .

In the present government there is wanted a larger and better consulta, for where discussion is wanting, there reason is wont to be wanting too: and truly very few are the ministers and few those possessed of authority and confidence at the palace. No one is known to have influence with the pope, and as his holiness states his own opinion before that of all others, these are wont either to praise or to second it. It was the practice in other times for the popes to have with them three or four cardinals, and the more serious affairs were brought to a determination after being discussed with them, and it was part of the secret policy of the nephews themselves to introduce their dependants

di lui sottoponere le proprie opinioni, non mostrando gusto che da chi si sia si parli al pontefice di negotio senza sua precedente participatione. Non si serve però nè anco di questa autorità, che gode solo, con quella libertà che per avventura complirebbe al ben publico et al suo proprio interesse: ma non osando respirare contro le risolutioni e li sensi del papa, prende molte volte l' habito della costanza medesima di S. Sta, essendosi in tal maniera sottoposto al disgusto delle corone e d' altri principi e di loro ministri per non divertire e non sopire molti strani accidenti.

"Appresso di questo li cardinali pur si dogliono e massime le creature di non haver apertura nè confidenza. Di pochissimi ministri si serve il sig^r card^{le}, mentre la mole dei negotii et altre circostanze di molti lo possono render bisognevole. Pancirola e Bicchi, auditori di rota, sono li più domestici e li più adoperati.

"Pancirola è soggetto maturo e di molta esperienza, che fu impiegato in Piemonte per la pace sin nel principio delle guerre di Mantova. Serve per li negotii del governo dello stato ecclesiastico, e non havendo havuto che trattar meco, non mi resta che dire delle sue conditioni.

"Bicchi è di gran spirito, pronto et sagace: dirige quasi tutti li negotii dei principi, e particolarmente ha in mano quelli della republica. E dipendentissimo da Barberino, qualità che lo rende oltre modo grato al sig^r cardinale. Ha incontrato disgusto di molti ministri de' principi, nemeno è amato dall' universale. Non ha altra esperienza che quella che li concede l' impiego presente, che è grande. Ha egli sempre trattato meco, e nelle mie lettere e nella forma dei suoi officii l' averanno più volte veduto descritto VV. EE. Tratta con destrezza e con flemma e con altrettanto ingegno e solertia. Della serenissima republica parla con tutte le espressioni di riverenza e divotione. Tiene a cuore certo interesse di pensioni del cardinal suo fratello, del quale ho scritto altre volte.

"A questi aggiungerò mons^r Cecca, segretario di stato, perche assiste al presente alla trattatione della lega. Non ha egli talenti più che ordinarj: ma per la lunga esperienza della sua carica tiene buona informatione de' negotii. E vecchio assai, e si crede vicino al cardinalato, se ben dalli nepoti è poco amato, ma molto rispettato per l' affetto che li porta la Sta Sua. Servì il segretario del pontefice mentre fu nuntio in Francia, e con passaggio mostruoso di fortuna ma solito della corte occupò il luogo del padrone medesimo, e mentre questo vive ancora con poco buona sorte, Cecca gode carico, rendite è speranze più che ordinarie. Appresso Barberino non vi sono altri di credito e di talenti che meritino d' esser osservati.

"Per il governo dello stato vi è consulta dei cardinali e dei prelati, che in due giorni della settimana discute diverse occorrenze. Altre congregationi sono dell' inquisitione, de propaganda fide, del concilio, de' regolari, de' riti e d' altri simili interessi. Tutto però serve a discorso, perche la risolutione resta al gusto di S. Sta e del nipote. Una congregatione di stato si tiene di quando in quando avanti il papa per le occorrenze più gravi,

into the confidence of their uncle, in order to influence and win him over where they could not carry a point themselves, or did not wish to reveal their own wishes.

Barberino has had no idea of thus going about the pope's liberty; but reserving to himself alone the place nearest the ears of his holiness, he obliges the rest to keep at a distance, and to subject their own opinions to his sole judgment, not showing any relish that the pontiff should be spoken to on business by any one, be he who he may, without his preceding participation. He does not indeed any more avail himself of the authority which he alone enjoys, with that freedom which might perhaps be advantageous to the public good and his own interests; but not daring to breathe against the determinations and the sentiments of the pope, he often assumes the habit of the very constancy of his holiness, in this way becoming obnoxious to the dislike of the crowned heads, and of other princes, and their ministers, for not diverting or suppressing many strange casualties.

With him, accordingly, the cardinals, and chiefly those created (by this pope), complain of want of openness and confidence. The lord cardinal takes the services of very few ministers, while the load of affairs and other circumstances might make him feel he required many. Pancirola and Bicchi, auditors of the rota, are the most familiar with him and the most employed.

Pancirola is a person of mature mind and much experience, who was employed in Piemont during the peace till the commencement of the Mantuan wars. He serves in the affairs of the government of the ecclesiastical state, and as I have never had occasion to conduct business with him, it does not rest with me to speak of his personal qualities.

Bicchi is a man of great spirit, prompt and sagacious: he directs almost all the affairs of the princes, and has those of the republic particularly committed to him. He is most dependant on Barberino, a quality which renders him beyond measure agreeable to the lord cardinal. He has met with the dislike of many ministers of the princes, nor is he the less loved upon the whole. He has no experience beyond what he has derived from his present employment, which is great. He has always conducted business with me, and your excellencies have many times seen him described in my letters and in the form of his offices. He treats with skill and coolness, and with as much genius as assiduity. He speaks of the most serene republic with every expression of reverence and devotion. He has at heart a certain interest in the pensions of his brother the cardinal, about which I have written frequently.

To these I shall add monsignor Cecca, secretary of state, as he assists at present at the negotiation of the league. He has no more than ordinary talents, but from the long experience he has had of his charge, he keeps up a good knowledge of affairs. He is pretty old, and thinks himself near getting the cardinalship, although not much liked by the nephews, but much respected on account of the affection with which he is regarded by

e non v' intervengono che le creature e i più confidenti che hanno servito nelle nuntiature: ma anco questa suole servire ad accreditare le deliberationi più che a risolverle, perche nè si discorre nè si forma il decreto che per quell' opinione nella quale si sottragge o si lascia intendere esser S. Sta, et in effetto si querelano i pontefici di non haver di chi confidare, perche tutti li cardinali vivono con li loro interessi e rispetti verso i principi stranieri."

his holiness. He served the pontiff's secretary while he was nuncio in France, and by a monstrous jump of fortune, but not unusual in that court, he obtained the place of his very master, and while the latter still lives in no very good circumstances, Cecca enjoys more than ordinary office, revenues, and hopes. There are no other persons about Barberino of sufficient credit and talents to merit observation.

For the government of the state there is the consulta of the cardinals and prelates, which during two days of the week discusses various matters as they occur. The other congregations are those of the inquisition, of the propaganda, of the council, of the regular clergy, of rites, and of other such like interests. All, however, serves for discourse, for the result remains with the good pleasure of his holiness and the nephews. A congregation of state meets from time to time in the pope's presence for the more serious occurrences, and none intervenes there but the creatures and the most trusted persons who have served in the nunciosships; but even this usually serves rather to accredit the deliberations than to determine their results, for no decree is ever discussed or written out except according to the views that are declared or understood to be those of his holiness, and in fact the pontiffs complain of having none in whom to trust, for all the cardinals live with their interests and views turned towards foreign princes.]

118.

Racconto delle cose più considerabili che sono occorse nel governo di Roma in tempo di mons[r] Gio. Batt[a] Spada.—[Account of the most considerable things that have occurred in the government of Rome in the time of monsignor George Baptist Spada.]

Dating from the last times of Urban VIII., full of sketches of life and manners relating to the department of the police and justice, and here put on record with the utmost authenticity.

Interminable contentions still prevailed among the old clans: for example, between the Gaetanos and the Colonneses: it is not only difficult to institute a comparison between them, but it even requires several days fully to make out a narrative of their quarrel in the legal instrument adopted for such a comparison, which one or other side will not feel itself insulted by.

Contentions betwixt the French and the Spaniards. They meet each other during the Easter holidays; each side drinks to the health of its king; insults are exchanged; yet the weaker party conducts itself with tolerable moderation: but as soon as it has strengthened itself, as soon as they meet upon the public squares, they come to blows: the bargello had the greatest difficulty in separating them.

But even after they are separated, they rival each other on the other hand, in opposing the court and the police of Rome.

The ambassadors are particularly difficult to manage. Those pretensions were gradually set up, which afterwards occasioned such serious broils. They not only declared their palaces to be free towns, so that they permitted forbidden games to be played there, but already they even wanted to take the adjoining houses into their protection. Monsignor Spada was naturally opposed to this.

"Che se si era usata cortesia con i signori ambasciatori di non entrare nelle case loro e delle loro famiglie, era una troppo grande estensione quella che volevano introdurre hora, che nè anche nelle case vicine e comprese nella medesima isola si potesse far esecutione."

[That though it were a usual piece of courtesy shown to the lords ambassadors not to enter their houses and families, it was carrying the matter too far for them to want to introduce it as a principle that no legal writ should be executed even in the houses adjoining, and comprised in the same pile of buildings.]

In an historical point of view, what is of most importance is two attempts upon the life of Urban VIII., that are here reported on with all desirable authenticity.

"1. Del processo di Giacinto Centini, nepote del card[l] d' Ascoli, e d' alcuni complici

[1. The substance of the trial of Hyacinth Centini, nephew of cardinal d'Ascoli and some

. . . . la sostanza era, ch' essendo stato pronosticato ch' al presente pontefice dovesse succedere il cardinal d' Ascoli, invaghito Giacinto del pronostico e desiderando di vederne prestamente l' effetto havesse trattato con fra Serafino Cherubini d' Ancona minor osservante, fra Pietro da Palermo eremita, che si faceva chiamare fra Bernardino, e fra Domenico da Fermo Agostiniano, di procurare con arte diabolica d'abbreviare la vita a N. S^re, et a quest' effetto fu risoluto di fare una statua di cera rappresentante il papa, come si essequì, e dopo molte invocationi di demonii e sacrificii fattigli la fluire, distruggere e consumare al fuoco, con ferma credenza che distrutta quella dovesse terminare la vita di papa Urbano e farsi loco alla successione del card^l d' Ascoli zio di Giacinto.

"2. La confessione di Tomaso Orsolini da Recanate. Che per instigatione di fra Domenico Brancaccio da Bagnarea Augustiniano era andato a Napoli per scoprire al vicerè un supposto trattato di principi d' invadere il regno di Napoli con interessarsi ancora S. Sta, e ch' il rimedio era di far morire uno de' collegati o il papa: al che fare s' offeriva il padre Bagnarea sudetto, mentre se li dessero sc. 3000, quali voleva dare al sagrista di N. S^re, già reso inhabile, e succedendo egli in quel carico, li haverebbe posto il veleno nell' hostia ch' avesse dovuto consegrare S. Sta nella messa, o pure quando non fosse succeduto sagrista, haverebbe operato che lo speciale Carcurasio suo parente, mentre medicava le fontanelle a S. Sta, vi ponesse il veleno: non passò però ad esprimere al vicerè questi particolari, poiche havendogli accennato di dover far morire il papa, vide ch' il vicerè non si applicò."

[. . . . The substance of the accomplices . . . . was this, that it having been prognosticated that card^l d' Ascoli was to succeed the present pope, Hyacinth being excited by the prognostic, and wishing to see it immediately accomplished, had bargained with friar Seraphim Cherubini of Ancona, minor observant, friar Peter of Palermo, a hermit; that friar Bernardino, and friar Dominick da Fermo Agostiniano, were sent for to procure, with diabolical art, the shortening the life of our lord; and for this purpose it was resolved to make an image of wax, representing the pope, as was done, and after many invocations of devils and sacrifices made to them, to melt, destroy, and consume it to smoke, firmly believing that, on its destruction, the life of pope Urban would come to an end, leaving room for the succession of card^l d' Ascoli, uncle of Hyacinth.

2. The confession of Tomaso Orsolini da Recanate. That by the instigation of friar Dominick, Brancaccio da Bagnarea, Augustinian, had gone to Naples to discover to the viceroy a supposititious agreement of the princes to invade the kingdom of Naples, together with his holiness further interesting himself in it, and that the remedy was to effect the death of one of the allies or of the pope: to do which the said father Bagnarea offered himself, provided 3000 scudi were given him, which he wished to give to the sacristan of his holiness, already rendered incapable, and upon his succeeding to that office,[1] was to have put poison in the host which his holiness was to consecrate at the celebration of mass, or in fine, in case of his not succeeding as sacristan, he was to have contrived that the apothecary Carcurasio, his relation, in medicating issues to his holiness, should mix poison with them: he did not, indeed, proceed to explain these particulars to the viceroy, for having hinted to him that the pope should be put to death, he saw that the viceroy did not adopt the suggestion.]

119.

Historica relatione dell' origine e progressi delle rotture nate tra la casa Barberina et Odoardo Farnese duca di Parma e Piacenza.—[Historical account of the rise and progress of the breaches that have arisen between the Barberino family and Edward Farnese, duke of Parma and Placentia.] (Library at Vienna. Historia Prof. n. 899, 224 leaves.)

A party writing, transmitted in the form of a letter, in which the origin of those contentions is attributed altogether to the ill will of the Barberini. This author connects also the monti of the barons with those of the state: that the pope had readily granted the requisite permission: that he had thus made the barons still more subservient to him. ("Nella erettione di simili monti il principe era mallevadore, riservatosi il beneplacito di poterne dimandare l' estintione a suo piacimento."—[In the erection of like monti the prince was security, reserving to himself the power at pleasure of demanding its extinction.])

I do not find that this work, in spite of its size, makes any special revelations, or, as in this case we are not at all in need of such, that it has much merit. The most remarkable part of it consists in its statements in regard to the anti-Austrian, and, in some sense, the anti-catholic leanings of pope Urban.

"Si lasciava tal volta intendere, essergli ben grati li progressi de' cattolici contra li heretici, ma esservi insieme da temere che un giorno queste prosperità cadessero a danno e precipitio de' medesimi per le gelosie che si sarebbero svegliate in tutto il mondo, che

[He often gave it to be understood that the progress made by the catholics against the heretics, was gratifying indeed to him, but that it was at the same time to be feared that this prosperity would one day turn out to the loss and ruin of the same, through

1 It would seem that the sacristan was allowed to sell his office.—Tr.

li imperio dovesse assorbir ogni residuo di libertà che vi rimaneva. Corse fama per tutte le corti che dalli impulsi d' Urbano originassero quelle ombre del duca Massimiliano di Baviera, che apersero una gran scisma nell' unione de' principi cattolici posti su i sbalzi, che domati li heretici fosse per convertirsi lo sforzo delle armi Austriache a danni di quei medesimi che erano stati ministri delle grandezze di quella casa: e per dir tutto, vi fu chi in quei tempi si vantò di sapere che la missione di Ceva, confidente ministro della casa Barberina, in Francia con titolo di nontio straordinario, havesse ne' suoi più reconditi arcani secrete commissioni d' eccitare il re di Francia a mischiarsi nelle turbulenze di Germania, a fine che intendendosi con Baviera si pensasse al modo di alzare qualche argine alla crescente potenza della casa d' Austria."

the jealousy that would be awakened throughout the whole world, lest the empire should absorb every remaining vestige of liberty. It was currently reported in all the courts that from the impulses given by Urban originated those suspicions of duke Maximilian of Bavaria which made a huge breach in the union of the catholic princes that lay exposed to the threatened rebounds, that on the heretics being subdued the force of the Austrian arms would be converted to the loss of those very parties who had ministered to the aggrandizement of that family: and, to say all, there were persons in those times who boasted that they knew that the mission of Ceva, the confidential minister of the Barberini family, to France, with the title of nuncio extraordinary, had in the most profound secrecy concealed commissions to excite the king of France to mix himself up in the turbulent proceedings in Germany, in order that by coming to an understanding with Bavaria, means might be thought of for raising some bulwark against the growing power of the house of Austria.]

It testifies at least to the fact of the diffusion of such views at this time.

120.

Della vita di papa Urbano VIII. e historia del suo pontificato scritta da Andrea Nicoletti.—[Of the life of pope Urban VIII. and the history of his pontificate written by Andrew Nicoletti.] (8 vols. in folio MS.)

It is much to be lamented that there are so few good or even so much as readable biographies of persons that have been distinguished in the history of the world.

We must look for the cause of this desideratum not in any neglect of their memory, which on the contrary, if not over estimated, is wont to be highly appreciated by their relations and friends: its origin is rather as follows.

At first, when the remembrance of the person is fresh in the mind, and materials can still be collected, people stand in awe of contemporaries: they durst not speak out all that might be said: a number of personalities would be compromised, and a thousand animosities would be evoked against the hero himself.

Afterwards, when contemporaries too have quitted the scene, when one may venture to trust himself to speak out, the remembrance of the person has likewise passed away, materials are scattered, interest itself has declined, and is re-awakened only in those who, from the point of view suggested by historical science, wish to obtain information.

Hence we often meet in Italy with the following result.

The materials are handed over to a confidential friend or servant of the family, who in general must be made privy (to facts) and supplied with information: he puts these materials together, duly arranges them, and combines them into a connected narrative; yet this is not destined for the press: it is preserved in manuscript in the family archives.

In this way the susceptibilities of contemporaries are spared, and yet there is obtained the possibility of a future revival of a rapidly fading recollection in all the fulness of truth.

The work of Andrew Nicoletti belongs to those of this sort.

It contains the family recollections of the personal character and the negotiations of Urban VIII.; but what the body of the work presents, what makes up the mass of it, is the incorporation of the collective ambassadorial correspondence, as conducted during the 21 years of Urban's pontificate.

This biography consists essentially of a compilation of nunciatura despatches.

These are not the final reports, the *relationi* properly so called, but the despatches themselves; how then does it adapt itself also to the form of a biography? By the pope always appearing in it as himself regulating, determining, negotiating.

I have noticed that similar compilations have been attempted in Venice, but as the practical efficiency of the republic declines, and only the general mass of intelligence is produced, without the appearance of any visible reaction, the attention is soon distracted and fatigued.

Here it is quite otherwise. The reputation, the complicated political position of Urban VIII., the directly important bearing of all intelligence on a great world-emergency, produces unity and interest.

It is very clear how exceedingly important the pieces of information that are to be met with here, are for the period of the thirty years' war in Germany. They throw light upon it at every conjuncture.

It is true, that whether the author pronounces an opinion or reports in his own person, we must not follow him altogether without reserve. Here and there probably he failed in procuring accurate information: the official colouring does not admit of being dissembled

in the origin and first conception of such a work. I will adduce only one example. In the 3d volume of his work, p. 673, Nicoletti asserts that Urban VIII. had heard of the conclusion of a peace between England and France in 1629 with bitter regret (il rammarico fu acerbissimo); yet from Aluise Contarini, who personally participated in all the negotiations, we see that the pope even recommended that negotiation—that conclusion. Nicoletti's mistake is to be attributed to this notice having escaped him in the immense exuberance of his correspondences, and to his judging of the pope according to his ecclesiastical position. Thus do many other examples occur. Yet this does not prevent the author from being to be believed where he merely excerpts.

His mode of procedure is to transfer the documents directly in all their fulness, only with such alterations as are required by a narrative. At the most it might happen that he may have left out or misplaced some. From the nature of his design, which consisted only in putting together what was given him, and the circumstances of the work, in general, which was not at all intended for the public, this, meanwhile, is not at once to be assumed, and I have perceived no traces of it.

Although I have diligently perused all these volumes, and have not neglected the opportunity of making myself master of such important materials for general history, yet it were impossible to give any further account of them at this place. He who has to occupy himself with correspondences, knows how much must be read before he can get a clear view of any one transaction *(factum)* whatever. Such diffuse materials I cannot adopt and transfer into this work.

There follows, nevertheless, a description of Urban VIII.'s last moments, which is very interesting, and of his personal character, as this author conceives it; taken from the close of the 8th volume.

"Erano in quei giorni," it runs there, "nel fine di Giugno caldi eccessivi in Roma e molto più del solito pericolosi: nondimeno, parendo al papa di essersi alquanto rihavuto, e sapendo che diciasette chiese erano senza i loro vescovi, e non havere il cardinale Grimaldi, tornato dalla nuntiatura di Francia, ricevuto il cappello cardinalizio, si dichiarò di volere tenere il concistoro nel prossimo lunedì. Il cardinale Barberino credette di poterlo indurre anche alla promotione de' cardinali: perciò non gli oppose la pericolosa sua debolezza e la febbre lenta che se gli poteva raddoppiare, anzi lodò il pensiero e confortollo, che fosse quasi in sicuro della sanità. Divulgatasi la voce del futuro concistoro, mentre si teneva il papa da alcuni moribondo e da altri indubitatamente morto ma che per alcuni giorni si fosse la morte di lui occultata, si vide la maggiore parte di Roma impaurita, benche ciascuno fingesse nel viso allegrezza e contento per la ricuperata salute. Accortosi dapoi il cardinale Barberino che il papa non voleva venire alla promotione di alcun cardinale, giacche ne mancavano otto nel sacro collegio, o perche non rimanesse sodisfatto de' soggetti che se gli proponevano, o perche lasciar voleva al successore quella cura, fece con ragioni efficacissime e con preghiere l' ultima pruova di dissuadergli in quei giorni il concistoro, e tanto più si adoperò quanto vedeva, oltre il danno del papa, che egli sarebbe rimasto in discapito della stima e del credito suo, perche non facendosi i cardinali si sarebbe confermata l' opinione che universalmente correva, che egli per cagione delle guerre fosse caduto dalla potenza che haveva appresso il papa, e che se havesse la Sta Sua allungata la vita, havrebbe dominato il cardinale Antonio. Non essendosi a quelle preghiere e ragioni mosso il papa, monsignor Roscioli, conoscendo di dare gusto al cardinale Barberino e di giovare alla vita di Sua Sta col rimuoverlo dalla detta deliberatione, confidato nella benevolenza di Sua B^{ne} verso di se, stabilì di adoperarsi con ogni efficacia possibile, anche a nome pubblico de' cardinali e della città di Roma, di volerlo dissuadere dal concistoro. Preso adunque il tempo opportuno, entrò dal

[There were in those days, in the end of June, excessive heats in Rome, and much more dangerous than usual: nevertheless, the pope thinking that he had somewhat recovered his health, and knowing that seventeen churches were without their bishops, and that cardinal Grimaldi, on his return from the French nuncioship, had not received his cardinal's hat, announced his intention of holding a consistory on the next Monday. Cardinal Barberino believed also that he might further be induced to promote some cardinals: therefore he did not urge upon him his dangerous state of weakness and the slow fever which might return upon him with double violence, but rather commended the idea and comforted him as if he had no need to be anxious about his health. The report of the approaching consistory having spread, while the pope was thought by some to be moribund, and by others to be indubitably dead, but that for some days his death had been concealed, the greater part of Rome seemed frightened, although every body put on a face of joy and content at the recovery of his health. Cardinal Barberino afterwards perceiving that the pope had no wish to proceed to the promotion of any cardinal, seeing eight of them were wanting in the consistory, whether from being dissatisfied with the candidates proposed to him, or because he wished to leave that matter to his successor, he did his very utmost, by reasoning and entreaty, to dissuade him from holding the consistory during those days, and so much the more did he interest himself when he saw that besides the hurt to the pope, he would be left without his estimation and credit, since by the non-creation of the cardinals the opinion universally current would be confirmed, that by reason of the wars he had lost the influence he once had with the pope, and that had the life of his holiness been prolonged, cardinal Anthony would have come into power. The pope being not to be moved by these reasons and entreaties, monsignor Roscioli, professing to gratify cardinal Barberino, and to aid in preserving the life of his holiness, by removing him from that meeting, confiding in

papa, e postosegli inginocchioni gli disse di non volerlo supplicare a nome de' suoi ministri nè per parte de' suoi nipoti nè della cosa Barberina, ma della città tutta di Roma: imperciocche essendo la Sta Sua stata eletta per la salute de' popoli e per governare la chiesa, abbandonando la cura di se medesima con esporsi inferma a pericoloso accidente veniva insieme a lasciare in abbandono la città et il governo commessole della chiesa, non senza grandissimo dolore di tutti: importare più il suo bene o il suo male alla christianità che alla casa Barberina o alla Sta Sua medesima: che percio se non voleva differire quella fatica alle preghiere de' nipoti, lo facesse almeno per l' istanze della città di Roma, che la supplicava. Il papa dopo di essere stato alquanto pensoso rispose di non curarsi di prolungare più la vita, conoscendo il pontificato non esser più peso delle sue forze, et iddio havrebbe proveduto alla sua chiesa. Dopo questa risposta essendosi alquanto trattenuto, si accorse monsignor Roscioli che il papa haveva gli occhi pieni di lagrime e sospirando si rivoltò al cielo e proruppe in ferventi preghiere a dio accioche la maestà sua divina lo volesse liberare dalla vita presente, mostrandosene grandemente annojato.

Venuto finalmente il lunedì determinato per tenere il concistoro, concorse al palazzo gran moltitudine di popolo curioso di vedere il papa, che poco avanti haveva creduto per morto. Appena entrato, i cardinali si accorsero havere egli hormai finita la vita, imperciocche comparve languido, pallido e quasi smarrito nelle parole, e particolarmente nel fine del concistoro mostrava di essere rimasto quasi senza intendimento. Fu data la cagione all' eccessivo caldo della stagione accresciuto dalla calca della gente penetrata dentro: e non andarono senza biasimo i ministri più intimi del palazzo et anche il cardinale Barberino per non havere impedito il papa da quella sì faticosa fontione, non sapendo il popolo le manifatture che si erano fatte per distornelo: imperciocche ognuno dal vederlo in così grande squallore et abbattimento di forze si sarebbe mosso a pietà, poiche chiaramente conoscevasi che il male gli haveva ingombrata la mente et il vero sentimento del governo delle cose. Dopo la propositione delle chiese e dopo bavere dato il cappello al cardinale Grimaldi partissi dal concistoro sommamente aggravato dal male, come gli fu predetto.

Nel dì seguente fece un' attione con la quale si acquistò fama di gran pietà e degna di rimanere per esempio a tutti i principi ecclesiastici. Questa fu di chiamare alla sua presenza alcuni theologi in quella scienza e nella probità riguardevolissimi e dal papa creduti lontani dall' adulatione, a quali fatta prima dare piena cognitione di tutti li beni et entrate ecclesiastiche delle quali in tempo del suo pontificato haveva arricchita la casa Barberina, ordinò che gli riferissero se in alcuna cosa egli haveva trapassato il potere e l' autorità sua: perche era preparato a ripigliare da' nepoti tutto cio che aggravare gli poteva la coscienza avanti al tribunale di dio. Li theologi furono il cardinale de Lugo, il padre Torquato de Cupis della compagnia di

the kindness of his beatitude towards himself, resolved to make his utmost efforts, in the name further of the public and of the city of Rome, to dissuade him from holding the consistory. Availing himself, therefore, of a favourable moment, he entered the pope's apartment, and placing himself on one knee told him that he did not mean to beseech him in the name of his ministers, or on the part of his nephews, or of the Barberini family, but of the whole city of Rome; because as his holiness had been chosen for the welfare of the people, and to govern the church, in neglecting to take care of himself, by exposing himself when infirm to great risks, he at the same time came to neglect taking care of the city and the government committed to him by the church, not without the utmost grief to all men; that his well-being or ill-being was of more importance to Christianity than to the Barberini family or to his holiness himself: that therefore if he would not defer that exertion, in compliance with the prayers of his nephews, he should do it at least at the urgent request of the city of Rome beseeching it. The pope, after musing for a little, replied that he did not care about prolonging his life, being aware that the popedom was no longer a weight adapted to his strength, and that God would provide for his church. After this reply, having been detained a while in conversation, it struck monsignor Rosciol that the pope's eyes were surcharged with tears, and that he looked with a sigh to heaven and broke out into fervent prayers to God that his Divine Majesty would deliver him from this present life, appearing to be grievously tired of it.

The Monday fixed for holding the consistory having at length arrived, a vast concourse of people flocked to the palace, curious to see the pope whom shortly before they had supposed to be dead. Hardly had he entered when the cardinals perceived that life was now over with him, for he looked languid and pale, and almost deprived of the power of utterance, and particularly at the close of the meeting his mind seemed almost entirely gone. This was attributed to the excessive heat of the season, increased by the crowd of people that had found their way in; and the ministers who had most to say in the palace, and cardinal Barberino also, did not get off without blame for not having prevented the pope from attempting so fatiguing a duty, the people not being aware of what had been done to divert him from it: for any one from seeing him so deadly pale and sunk in strength, would have been touched with pity, clearly perceiving that his malady had clouded his understanding and all real consciousness of the direction of affairs. After proposing what should be done for the churches, and having given the cap to cardinal Grimaldi, he left the consistory with his illness extremely aggravated, as had been predicted.

On the day after, he did what brought him the reputation of great piety, and deserved to remain as an example to all ecclesiastical princes. This was to call before him some divines, the most reputed in theology and for

Gesù, et alcuni altri. E si animò il papa a fare questa attione dal sereno che vide in fronte al cardinale Barberino, quando chiamatolo prima di tutti lo fece partecipe di questo suo pensiero, che non ostanti l' ombre passate quasi volle parere di volere da lui prenderne consiglio. Lodò il cardinale la pietà della Sta Sua, e mostrò di haverne particolare contento, sperando maggiori felicità dalla mano liberalissima di dio, mentre solo per sodisfare a Sua Divina Maestà tutto cio si faceva. Dicesi che il parere uniforme de' theologia fu, che havendo Sua Sta arricchiti li suoi nipoti, poteva con sicura coscienza lasciarli godere tutti li beni che haveva loro conceduti, e cio per due ragioni: l' una perche havendo promossi al cardinalato una quantità di soggetti quali non haveva proveduti di entrate secondo il loro grado, li medesimi nipoti havessero comodità di accomodarli secondo il loro bisogno: l' altro motivo per quietare la coscienza del papa fu, che havendo li sopradetti nipoti in sì lungo principato e nelle passate guerre contratto l' odio e l' inimicitie con diversi principi, era ragionevole di lasciarli ben comodi per mantenere il loro grado, anche per riputatione della sede apostolica, e non essere vilipesi, come suole accadere a quelli che dalla cima del dominare si riducono a stato inferiore: onde l' essere bene provisti di ricchezze e di beni di fortuna gli havrebbe fatti maggiormente rispettare: et oltre di cio li medesimi nepoti havevano di loro natura tali viscere di christiana pietà che havrebbero erogate l' entrate in beneficio de' poveri et in altri usi pii. E con queste et altre ragioni mostrò il papa di quietarsi.

Si andava dunque preparando alla morte, che da se stesso conosceva essergli vicina: ma fra questi pensieri e dispositioni si mostrava in tutti i ragionamenti pieno di giusto sdegno contro i principi d' Italia, sentendo immenso dolore che havesse a restare memoria che in tempo del suo pontificato si fossero collegati contro di lui et havessero assalito con eserciti lo stato della chiesa: onde talvolta prorompeva in parole acerbe, come se fossero stati senza pietà, senza religione e senza legge, et implorava dal cielo giusta vendetta per vederli da dio gastigati prima di morire o almeno pentiti. Già, come altrove si è detto, si era con loro fatta la pace, firmata della Sta Sua e sottoscritta: ma in essa non venivano li due cardinali Barberini nè compresi nè nominati: onde le creature più fedeli giudicarono che mentre la casa Barberina era per la vita del papa ancora temuta, si dovesse impiegare ogni industria perche i principi Italiani li dichiarassero inclusi nella medesima pace. Et il cardinal Bicchi, che agli stessi principi andò plenipotentiario per parte di Francio, affermò che per non essere certi della morte del papa non sarebbero stati lontani dal trattarla e dall' accettarla. Ma il cardinal Barberino con ordini precisi vietollo, ordinando al Bicchi che di cio non ne trattasse punto, ancorche i principi spontaneamente gliel' havessero offerto: nè volle mai sopra di cio sentire consigli di alcuno, allegando per ragione che il volere loro essere inclusi ne' capitoli della pace e nominati in essa altro non era che un farsi dichiarare per autori di havere mossa la guerra,

their personal worth, and whom the pope considered most removed from adulation, to whom, after having first seen to their being fully informed of all the church goods and revenues wherewith in the course of his pontificate he had enriched the Barberini family, he gave orders to report to him whether in anything he had exceeded his power and authority: inasmuch as he was prepared to take back from his nephews whatever might burthen his conscience before the tribunal of God. These divines were cardinal de Lugo, father Torquato de Cupis of the company of Jesus, and some others. And the pope was encouraged to act thus by the serenity he saw on the brow of cardinal Barberino, when, having called him first, he communicated to him this thought of his, that notwithstanding past suspicions, he seemed almost to wish to advise with him about it. The cardinal praised his holiness's piety, and seemed to be particularly well pleased with it, hoping to have greater felicities from the most liberal hand of God, seeing all this was done solely for the satisfaction of the Divine Majesty. It is said that it was the unanimous judgment of the divines that his holiness having enriched his nephews, he might with a safe conscience leave them in the enjoyment of the possessions he had granted to them, and that for two reasons: one, because as he had advanced to the cardinalship a number of subjects whom he had not provided with incomes suited to their rank, the said nephews should have it in their power to accommodate them as they might require: the other reason for quieting the pope's conscience was, that as the nephews above said, during so long an enjoyment of power, and in the course of the by-past wars, had incurred the odium and enmity of divers princes, it was reasonable to leave them well provided for the maintenance of their rank, both for the credit of the papal see and that they might not be vilipended, as is wont to happen to those who are reduced to an inferior position from the summit of domination: whereas the being well furnished with wealth and the good things of fortune, would make them more respected: and besides this, the said nephews had naturally such bowels of Christian compassion that they would apply the revenues to the benefit of the poor and other pious uses. And with these and other reasons the pope seemed to be quieted.

He proceeded, accordingly, to prepare for death, which of himself he perceived to be approaching: but amid these thoughts and feelings he seemed, in all his conversations, full of just indignation against the princes of Italy, being hugely afflicted at the thought of history having to record that, in the time of his pontificate, they should have leagued together against him, and attacked the church-state with their armies: hence he often broke out in bitter words, as if they had been without pity, without religion, and without law, and implored the just vengeance of heaven to see them chastised by God before their death, or at least before their repentance. Already, as has been elsewhere said, he had made peace with them, confirmed by his holiness and subscribed: but in that (peace) the two

conciossiacosache ne' trattati di pace non sia mai solito nè si costumi di nominare i ministri, ma i principi e capi che a parte della guerra sono venuti.

Vacavano in quel tempo, come dianzi fu detto, otto luoghi nel sacro collegio de' cardinali: onde grande era l' agitatione in che stava la corte, potendo così gran numero cagionare non picciola mutatione nelle cose de' capi di fattioni già stabilite. Il papa, come più volte disse a noi il cardinale Barberino, desiderando che i cardinali fossero in maggiore estimatione e meglio proveduti di entrate, pensò di ridurre con particolare constitutione tutto il sacro collegio al numero di cinquanta: onde stava fisso in non fare altra promotione. Barberino però, conoscendo che col lasciare tanti luoghi vacanti non havrebbe il papa ottenuto l' intento et havrebbe servito d' ingrandimento alla fattione del successore, più volte supplicollo che si lasciasse vincere dal consentimento comune in promuovere tanti soggetti che vi erano meritevoli della porpora. Ma il tutto gli riuscì vano, rispondendogli il papa di non volere che alcuni de' suoi successori col suo esempio potessero nel fine della vita privatamente senza decoro e stando in letto creare cardinali, e che questo esempio da Gregorio decimoquinto ricevuto haveva e voleva con uguale gloria lasciare a' posteri. Vi si adoperarono altri personaggi e particolarmente il cardinale de Lugo, il quale per render efficaci l' istanze del cardinale Barberino suggerì al papa il decreto concistoriale delli tre cardinali fatti già spedito dopo il concistoro in cui fu fatta l' ultima promotione, e che il cardinale Barberino come vicecancelliere era obbligato a ricordarlo a Sua Sta, non perche promovesse, come fu il caso di Gregorio, ma solo accioche dichiarasse i cardinali già creati e riservati in petto, la quale publicatione a tutto il sacro collegio pareva ragionevole, nè vi era bisogno di altro concistoro. Ma il papa, o che fosse sdegnato perche il cardinale Barberino gli haveva proposti alcuni soggetti che non erano di sodisfattione di Sua Sta, o credesse di lasciare più gloriosa la memoria di se, stette saldo a tutte le istanze, ordinando che niuno più ardisse di parlargli di promotione. . . . .

Era l' aspetto di papa Urbano giocondissimo, ma pieno di maestà: e sebbene nel suo emperamen o vi era alquanto di malinconico, sicche quando si veniva all' emissione del sangue, che per l' ordinario era ne' tempi di primavera, gli uscivano dalle vene pezzetti come gelati di quell' humore, nè senza questo havrebbe potuto profittare tanto nelle lettere, dicendo il filosofo che la malinconia contribuisce assai per apprendere le scienze e ritenerle impresse nel' animo. La dispositione poi del corpo e delle membra era nobilmente compartita. La statura piutosto grande che mediocre: le carni di colore olivastro e piuos o piene di succo che grasse: il capo grande, che dinotava un maraviglioso ingegno et una vivacissima memoria: la fronte spatiosa e serena: gli occhi di colore fra l' azzurro et il bianco · il naso proportionato: le guancie rotonde, ma negli ultimi anni notabilmente estenuate: la bocca piena di gratia: la voce sonora, ma soave, onde con la favella Toscana, che sempre ritenne finche visse, usci-

cardinals Barberini were not included either by name or implication: hence the most faithful of the (pope's) creatures judged that while the Barberini family continued still to be dreaded from the pope being alive, every endeavour should be made to get the Italian princes to declare that they were included in the said peace. And cardinal Bicchi, who went to those princes as plenipotentiary on the part of France, affirmed that owing to their not being sure of the death of the pope they would not be much averse to treating about and agreeing to this. But cardinal Barberino gave express orders forbidding it, enjoining Bicchi not to treat on this point at all, even although the princes should offer it of their own accord: nor would he ever listen to the advice of anybody on that subject, giving as his reason that their wishing to be included in the articles of that peace, and named in it, would be tantamount to their being declared to have been principals in the moving of that war, seeing that in treaties of peace it never was usual, nor the practice, to name the ministers, but the princes and chiefs who have had a part in the war.

There were at that time, as we have said, eight vacancies in the sacred college of cardinals; whence great was the agitation at court, as so great a number might cause no small change in the affairs of the chiefs of factions already established. The pope, as was often told us by cardinal Barberino, wishing the cardinals to enjoy more consideration, and to be better provided with incomes, thought of reducing, by a particular constitution, the whole sacred college to the number of fifty: hence he remained resolved to make no farther promotion. Barberino, in fine, knowing that the pope would not gain his object by leaving so many places vacant, and would only promote the aggrandizement of the faction of his successor, many times besought him to allow himself to be overcome by the common feeling in promoting as many persons as seemed deserving of the purple. But all was in vain, the pope replying that he did not wish that any of his successors should have his example for creating cardinals at the close of life, privately, without decorum, and sitting up in bed, and that he had received this example from Gregory XV., and wished with equal glory to leave it to posterity. Other persons lent their aid to this, and particularly the cardinal de Lugo, who, to give effect to the entreaties of cardinal Barberino, reminded the pope of the consistorial decree of the three cardinals already made on the instant, after the (close of the) consistory in which the last promotion took place, and that cardinal Barberino, as vice-chancellor, had to remind his holiness of it, not that he might promote, as was the case with Gregory, but only declare the cardinals already created and reserved *in petto*, which announcement seemed reasonable to all the sacred college, nor was any other consistory needed. But the pope, either because indignant at cardinal Barberino having proposed some persons to him who were not to the satisfaction of his holiness, or because he thought he should enhance his own glory, stood firm against all these entreaties, com-

vano da essa dolcissime parole piene di eloquenza e sparse di fiori di buone lettere e di eruditioni sacre e di antichi esempj: nutrì infino da prelato la barba honestamente lunga e riquadrata, la quale con la canitie rendeva il suo aspetto più venerabile. . . . .

"Veramente era tanto amabile che da una troppa apertura in poi che dimostrava, se pure l'importanza del negotio non lo ratteneva, non vi era altro che da critici bene attenti vi fosse da tacciare. E se talvolta saliva in collera, ben presto tornava alla giocondità di prima. . . . . L' opinione de' saggi era che con esso lui stimavasi necessario di essere o di alto sapere o di niuno o di poco: poiche sicome non isdegnava di essere guadagnato dalla saviezza dell' uno, così compativa tanto all' altro che egli stesso lo soccorreva e sollevava, se però questo non fosse stato presuntuoso o orgoglioso, abusandosi della humanità e buona conditione del papa, il quale duro et inflessibile fu sempre con gli orgogliosi et arroganti, sicome altrettanto amorevole e benigno mostravasi verso i rispettosi e modesti. . . . . Verso i sopradetti servitori e verso anche i parenti proprj era discretissimo in scegliere i tempi per valersene più comodi a quelli che a se stesso, non isdegnando talvolta di udire con patienza qualche parola o atto di sentimento o di doglienze loro. E nelle sue malattie pareva che pigliasse più dispiacere de' patimenti e vigilie degli assistenti a lui che del proprio male o de' suoi dolori. Così anche non era facile a sfogamenti o lamenti delle persone: ma gli era grave il negare o vedere partire da se alcuno discontento. Coi sui più confidenti servitori era giocondissimo, e talvolta con essi usava de' motti o come si suol dire de' sali ingegnosi. . . . . Non si scordò mai degli amici antichi, o fossero assenti o morti, et in questo fu ammirabile la sua benevolenza: onde ordinò al cardinale Biscia sua creatura, che ero stato uno di quelli suoi più confidenti, accioche havesse la cura di dargli spesso nuova di loro, e se fossero morti, che pigliasse nota de' loro discendenti per provederli all' occasioni. . . . .

"Fiorì in Roma nel suo tempo grandissima abbondanza di tutte le cose: e soleva dire che egli da Firenze haveva havuto il suo nascimento, ma da Roma tutta la sua grandezza, et havrebbe voluto che ogni persona godesse la felicità del suo pontificato, che gli ufficij venali nella cancelleria fruttassero copiosamente, e percio egli era gratiossimo nelle speditioni della dataria, che gli artigiani nelle loro faccende facessero grossi ma leciti guadagni, e lo stesso facessero anche i mercanti di ogni sorte: e quindi era che nel suo pontificato correva tanto il danaro che ogn' uno di qualsivoglia professione rimaneva sodisfatto e contento. Diede tali ordini per l' annona che perdoni a spesa per mantenere l' abbondanza. Così il suo maggiore godimento era che gli agricoltori non restassero privi di quei guadagni che a lui pareva si richiedessero dal pericolo della vita e della facoltà che impiegavano nella vastità delle campagne di Roma e nell' aere insalubre: e quando quasi a niun' altro impiego pareva atta la maritima che della agricoltura, quivi fissò il pensiero, e tenne più volte proposito di seccare le paludi

manding that no one should dare to speak to him any further about promotion. . . . .

The pope had a most agreeable expression, but full of majesty: and although in his temperament there was a tinge of melancholy, so that whenever he was blooded, which was generally about the spring of the year, there came from the veins small pieces as if coagulated by some humour; nor without this could he have made such advances in literature, philosophers telling us that melancholy contributes much to the acquisition of the sciences and to retaining them in the mind. Then the disposition of the body and limbs was nobly proportioned. He was rather tall than of middle size; his flesh olive-coloured, and rather muscular than fat; his head large, denoting a wonderful genius and a most vivacious memory; his forehead spacious and serene; his eyes betwixt azure and white; his nose well proportioned; cheeks round, but in the last years of his life notably shrunk; a mouth full of grace; a voice sonorous but sweet, whence, with the Tuscan accent, which he preserved as long as he lived, there flowed the sweetest words, full of eloquence, and sprinkled with the flowers of polite learning, and sacred erudition, and ancient examples: he cherished, from his rise to the prelacy, a beard of respectable length and cut square, which together with his hoary locks, made him look most venerable. . . . .

Truly he was so amiable, that with the exception of an excessive openness which he showed, unless the importance of the matter restrained him, there was no other blot that observant critics could have detected in him. And if he often sputtered with passion, forthwith he was the first to turn from that to make himself agreeable. . . . . The opinion of the wise was, that with him it was deemed necessary to be either very wise or to be little or nothing in that respect: for as he did not disdain to be gained by the wisdom of the one, so he felt so much for the other that he himself would interpose to encourage him, unless indeed the latter had been presuming and proud, abusing the humanity and good nature of the pope, who was always hard and unbending with the proud and arrogant, as on the contrary he appeared amiable and kind to the respectful and modest. . . . Towards his servants above mentioned, and towards his own relations, he was most discreet in choosing such seasons for employing them as best suited them as well as himself, not thinking it beneath him to listen often with patience to any expression of their feelings or complaints. And in his illness it seemed that he was more annoyed at the sufferings and writhings of those who were with him than at his own ailments and personal sufferings. Thus, too, he had not much patience when people gave way to outbursts of feeling and to lamentations: but it was painful to him to refuse or to see any one leave him dissatisfied. With his most confidential servants he was most pleasant, and often would indulge with them in clever sayings, or as they are called witticisms. . . . . He never forgot his old friends, whether absent or dead, and in this his kindness of heart was admirable: hence he enjoined cardinal Biscia, who had owed his

Pontine, per guadagnare quelle immensità de' paesi che hora sono sott' acqua, e cio per beneficio publico: ma altre cure gravi non gli lasciarono godere l' effetto di sì glorioso disegno. Nè volle mai, per mantenere la detta abbondanza, che si stabilisse il prezzo del grano e dell' altre vittovaglie, ma che ogni cosa fosse libera, ovviando in questo modo ai monopolj: onde i mercanti riempiendo i granari, ciascuno faceva a gara di venderlo a buon mercato, e così la città di Roma diveniva opulenta.

"Se poi nel suo pontificato fiorirono le lettere, non è meraviglia: poiche non haveva migliore divertimento che coi letterati, quali accolse sempre con benignità e rimunerolli. Così anche dell' altre professioni nobili fu amantissimo, come della pittura, scoltura et altre buone arti, sicche non isdegnò più volte, e particolarmente un giorno, andando alla visita delle sette chiese con tutto il sacro collegio, giunto a Santa Maria Maggiore, doppo bavere fatta oratione in quella basilica, di entrare con la stessa comitiva de' cardinali in casa del cavaliere Giovanni Lorenzo Bernino colà vicina, per vedere alcuni lavori di celebre scoltura del suo scalpello.

"L' essere egli stato necessitato per la medesima cagione d' imporre loro le gravezze e le gabelle: onde tal volta a tali avvisi si vide piangere, dicendo che volontieri havrebbe dato il proprio saugue o de' suoi congiunti più tosto che di sentire le affittioni de' popoli e di Roma e gl' incomodi della camera apostolica. Et a monsignore Lorenzo Raggi, tesoriere di essa, il quale in tempo della sua ultima infermità andò alla udienza, disse che desiderava di vivere ancora due soli mesi per tre cagioni: l' una per havere più lungo tempo di penitenza e chiedere a dio il perdono de' suoi peccati: l' altra per finire di rimettere in castel Sant' Angelo tutto il denaro che fu levato per la guerra di Castro: la terza per vedere finita la fabbrica delle mura di Borgo e di Trastevere et asscicurata la città di Roma.

"Se le azioni eroiche del papa per debolezza della mia penna saranno senza eloquenza, senza nobiltà di stile et in somma improportionate per un pontefice sì grande, nondimeno sono state scritte con pura e sincera verità: il che particolarmente mi fu imposto et inculcato da chi teneva sopra di me suprema autorità, cioè *che io scrivessi semplicemente da istorico, e mi tenessi totalmente lontano da ogni adulatione e vanità e da rettorici ingrandimenti, attendendo più alle cose che alle parole.*

"Ma tornando alla sua applicatione intorno alle cose sacre, oltre l' havere fatto emendare e ristampare il ceremoniale Romano, non mancò di dare molti ordini per la cappella pontificia: però o per negligenza de' ministri o per distrattione ad altri gravi affari solo alcune cose principali sono rimaste in osservanza. Vero si fu che riformò anche l' uso delle indulgenze per chiudere la bocca agli heretici.

"Finalmente se Urbano non havesse intrapresa la guerra, o, per meglio dire, se non vi fosse stato provocato e tirato a forza, il che gli accelerò anche notabilmente la morte, non si poteva desiderare nè pontefice più glorioso

elevation to him, and who had been one of those greatest intimates, to see that he was often informed of the news about them, and in case of their death, that a note should be taken of their descendants, that they might be provided for as occasions might occur. . . .

In Rome at that time there was a flush of the greatest plenty in all things: and he used to say that he had his birth from Florence, but owed to Rome all his grandeur, and could have wished that everybody should enjoy the felicity of his pontificate, that the venal offices of the chancery should fructify copiously, and thus it was gratifying to him to expedite affairs in the dataria, in order that artisans in their employments might have full but legitimate gains, and that merchants of every sort should have the same: and hence it was that in his pontificate there was so much money afloat, that everybody, whatever was his profession, remained content and satisfied. He gave such orders for the supply of corn, that he lost money in providing abundance. Thus it was his greatest delight that the tillers of the ground should not be without those gains which he thought were required by the risk of life aud means which they laid out in the waste plains of Rome and in the sickly air: aud since the sea-coast seemed adapted for almost no other use but that of agriculture, on that he fixed his thoughts, and repeatedly proposed the draining of the Pontine marshes, in order to gain that immense tract of lands now under water, and that for the public advantage: but other grave concerns prevented him from enjoying the result of so glorious a design. He never wished, in order to keep up the said abundance, that the price of grain and other victuals should be fixed, but that everything should be free, in this way obviating monopolies: accordingly the merchants filling the granaries, each strove to sell it cheap, and thus the city of Rome became wealthy.

Then if literature flourished in his pontificate, it is no wonder: for he enjoyed nothing in the way of recreation more than the company of men of letters, whom he always received kindly aud remunerated them. Thus too he was exceedingly fond of the other noble professions, such as painting, sculpture, and the other fine arts, so that often he disdained not, and particularly on one occasion, when visiting the seven churches with the whole sacred college, on arriving at St. Mary the Greater, after having delivered an oration on that basilica, to enter along with that train of cardinals the house of the chevalier Giovani Lorenzo Bernino which stood hard by, that he might see some of the results of the celebrated sculpture of his chisel.

It had become necessary for him for the same reason to burthen them with taxes and imposts: hence as often as such measures had to be taken he was observed to lament, saying that he would willingly have given his own blood or that of his kindred, rather than hear of the sufferings of the peoples and of Rome, and the embarrassments of the apostolic chamber. And to monsignor Lorenzo Raggi, its treasurer, who in the time of his last infirmity went to the audience, he said that he wished to live only two months longer, and that for three reasons; one to

nè principe di più egregie qualità, per mezzo delle quali per molti anni del suo pontificato conservò verso di se l' amore universale di tutto il christianesimo, sicche fino ad hora si benedice dai popoli la sua rimembranza per quegli anni felici ne' quali goddettero la tranquillità e la pace."

have longer time for penitence and asking of God the forgiveness of his sins: next, to finish restoring to the treasury the money that had been taken from the castle of St. Angelo for the war of Castro: thirdly, that he might see the building of the walls of the Borgo and of the Trastevere finished, and the city of Rome secured.

If the heroic achievements of the pope, through the weakness of my pen, shall be written without eloquence, without dignity of style, and in a word inadequately to the case of so great a pontiff, they are described nevertheless with pure and sincere veracity: being what was particularly enjoined and inculcated on me by him who had supreme authority over me; that is to say, that *I should write simply as an historian, and should altogether abstain from all adulation, and vanity, and rhetorical flourishes, attending more to things than to words.*

But if we look to his application to sacred things, besides having caused the Roman ritual to be amended and reprinted, he failed not to give out many regulations for the pontifical chapel: in fine, whether from the negligence of ministers or from being called off to other serious affairs only some of the principal things have continued to be observed. It is true that he further reformed the use of indulgences in order that he might shut the mouths of heretics.

Finally, had Urban not engaged in war, or, to speak more correctly, been provoked and drawn into it by force, which circumstance further much hastened his death, there could not be desired either a more glorious pope or a prince of more eminent qualities, by means whereof he for many years of his pontificate attached to himself the universal affection of the whole of Christendom, so that to this day people bless his memory for those happy years in which they enjoyed tranquillity and peace.]

SECTION SIXTH.

LATER EPOCHS.

We have in the preceding section comprised all that immediately relates to Urban VIII.: there still follow some writings which connect his times with those that came after.

121.

Relationi della vita del card[l] Cecchini composta da lui medesimo.—[Account of the life of cardinal Cecchini composed by himself.] (Barb. 275 pages.)

Personal memorabilia which do not directly throw much light on important political concerns, but present a very instructive example of the private life of a clergyman, spent, however, always under important circumstances.

The author intimates that he had composed it for his own gratification. "Tra tutte le cose che apportano all' uomo sommo piacere, una è la memoria della cose passate."—[Among all things that give a man the highest gratification, one is the remembrance of the past.]

At the age of fifteen, Cecchini went, in the year 1604, from Perugia to Rome.

He had placed his hopes on the Aldobrandini, with whom he was distantly connected; but prematurely for him Clement VIII. died, and after his death the power of the Aldo-

brandini was gone. Cecchini, it is true, ventured at the same time to cherish fresh hopes: he had already in Perugia been intimate with Scipio Caffarelli, the same who, under Paul V., contrived to make the position of a nephew so profitable in its results: but Caffarelli did not choose to acknowledge this former acquaintanceship: the youth had to look elsewhere for patronage.

It was now his good fortune to attach himself to two monsignors, both of whom afterwards attained the highest dignities, Ludovisio and Pamfilio.

The opinion very soon prevailed throughout Rome that Ludovisio would obtain the tiara. Accordingly, when his nephew Ludovico in 1619 entered the prelature, many looked upon him as the future cardinal *padrone*. All eyes were fixed upon him; already his friends and servants were endeavouring to supplant each other. Cecchini, too, complains that others had endeavoured to get him out of the way; but he contrived to keep his place; he even had it in his power to perform important services to his master: as a kinsman of the Aldobrandini he was so placed as to be able to negotiate an alliance between the two families. Cardinal Aldobrandino promised his vote to Ludovisio.

Ere long all the requisite measures were taken in contemplation of this. Cardinal Ludovisio scrupled long about accepting a Spanish pension of 1200 scudi, offered him on the conclusion of the peace with Savoy: he dreaded thereby incurring the hostility of the French: our Cecchini had to talk over the matter with the French ambassador, and to disabuse his mind of all the suspicions that might hence arise.

Amid these circumstances cardinal Ludovisio, upon the death of Paul V., came to Rome to attend the conclave, being already in expectation of being elected. Cecchini hastened to meet him. "I conduct the pope to Rome," he said with delighted zeal. "We have only," replied Ludovisio, "to be on our guard against the cardinal of Aquino, and all will go well."

"Ludovisio aveva tal sicurezza del pontificato che domandommi per burla chi saria stato papa: rispondendogli che il papa non era in Roma e che io l' avrei condotto, con gran fiducia mi soggiunse queste parole: 'Guardatemi del card[l] d' Aquino, che faremo bene.' "

[Ludovisio made so sure of obtaining the popedom, that when he asked me in jest who was to be pope, on my replying to him that the pope was not in Rome, and that I was to conduct him thither, he added in the strictest confidence: "Keep me safe from the cardinal of Aquino, that we may succeed."]

Everything went right: Ludovisio was in fact elected. The nephew threw his arms around Cecchini for joy, and made him his auditor.

By this means the latter was now brought into immediate contact with the supreme power. He was not without his share in the affairs of the state, at least not without being admitted to a knowledge of them; but his chief business continued to be the management of the cardinal's money matters. The sums drawn from Avignon and Fermo passed through his hands: the cardinal did not wish it to be generally known how much he spent. For he lived in the most splendid style. On Ludovisio obtaining the chamberlainship, Cecchini, too, was raised to the auditorship of that office.

Singular abuses come before us here. There were issued, in the name of the cardinal nephew, orders called *non gravetur*s. Whoever possessed these could not be sued at law. People sought to secure themselves from their creditors by a *non gravetur*: there were even handicraftsmen that were secured in this way. But our author relates even much worse things than these. Under Paul V., a process was commenced against the prior and the prince Aldobrandini. Cecchini asserts that the fiscal-general availed himself of false witnesses, in order that a condemnatory sentence might be brought out against them. But it was not their death that was wanted; the sole object was to compel the Aldobrandini to deliver up some castles to the Borghese. For this, under Gregory XV., the fiscal-general was thrown into prison.

"Era vivente Gregorio stato carcerato Pier Maria Cirocchi, che vivente papa Paolo fu fiscale generale, per molte imputationi, tra le quali la principale era che nella causa criminale intentata al principe e priore Aldobrandino, nella quale furono condannati in pena della vita e della robba, egli avesse procurato di far esaminar testimonj falsi, sicome in effetto fece. La detta sentenza non fu data per altro se non perche il card[l] Pietro Aldobrandino si disponesse a cedere al card[l] Borghese li castelli di Montefortino e di Olevano, che aveva comprati duca di Zagarolo, sicome se volse la gratia della detta condennatione delli nepoti, lo convenne fare, con farli anco constituir prigioni in castello, dove stettero quattro mesi."

[During Gregory's lifetime there was imprisoned Pier Maria Cirocchi, who during Paul's lifetime was fiscal-general, for many imputed crimes, the chief of which was that in the criminal action brought against the prince and prior Aldobrandino, in which they were condemned to suffer the loss of life and property, he had endeavoured to have false witnesses examined, as in fact was done. The said sentence was pronounced for no reason but that cardinal Peter Aldobrandino might be disposed to cede to cardinal Borghese the castles of Montefortino and of Olevano, which he had bought from the duke of Zagarolo, as was to be done on condition of its being followed by the quashing of the said condemnation of the nephews, together with the constituting them prisoners in the castle, where they remained four months.]

Indignities that are atrocious. The duty of an historian forbids their being passed over,

in silence: although we must remark that Cecchini was naturally an adherent of the Aldobrandini.

After Gregory, Urban VIII. was elected. Already had Cecchini found an opportunity of rendering him signal service, even although it was only by being silent. When a cardinal Urban had once said in a fit of violent excitement, that people would make cardinal Ludovisio pay for something one day, and nothing could have been more hurtful to him in the conclave than this threat, Ludovisio being so powerful there: yet at Magalotto's request Cecchini held his peace.

Urban appears very characteristically on yet another occasion in this biography.

Urban VIII. felt himself profoundly mortified by Borgia's protest: he attributed a share in it to cardinals Ubaldini and Ludovisio, and wanted to punish them accordingly. He would have had Ubaldini thrown into prison, had not the fiscal stoutly opposed him: but that cardinal had at least to remove to a distance; neither was Ludovisio suffered by the pope to remain in Rome. Our Cecchini, who was still in Ludovisio's service, was therefore sent for by him and commanded to tell the cardinal that he must within a fortnight repair to his bishopric of Bologna. This he declared amid violent expressions of his wrath. "A whole hour," says Cecchini, "I had to listen, while with a thousand reproaches he threatened to punish Borgia too: I dared not interrupt him: he then repeated that Ludovisio must be off, else he would have him carried away by the sbirri." On this occasion, too, Cecchini would have done better to have held his peace. But he thought it necessary to mention the matter to his master. It is a very significant symptom of the state of the court that Cecchini thus disobliged everybody. Ludovisio thought that Cecchini should not have submitted to the pope's violent expressions, but would rather that matters had come to an open breach. Cardinal Barberini was angry, for Cecchini ought first to have spoken to him, the cardinal nephew. But Urban himself was most displeased, especially as the true state of the matter was somewhat misrepresented in coming round to him. He sent for poor Cecchini once more, and presented a scene to him in which old resentment against his enemies, and regret for what he had said—his having done the thing and wishing not to have done it—a conviction of his papal power, and the feeling that others notwithstanding had acted not improperly, were strangely mingled. But Urban VIII. was a man who would at last come to himself again. Ludovisio withdrew, and shortly afterwards died. Cecchini, it is true, lost the position he had hitherto filled, but obtained a new one which even allowed him occasionally to see the pope. "Monsignòr Cecchini," the latter began one day to say to him, "forgive us; we went too far against you." Cecchini says that upon this the tears started into his eyes, and he answered with profound submission. The pope's major-domo visited him that same day, and said that the pope had looked forward to that day for four years, and heartily rejoiced that it had come at last.

Cecchini now moreover attached himself to the Aldobrandini: we find him very active on the occasion of the marriage of the wealthy heiress of that family, Olympia. Cardinal Hippolyto died, without having settled anything definitely on the subject, and people were afraid that the Barberini would not allow so rich an inheritance to slip out of their hands: Olympia had to feign illness. With the aid of the Jesuit general, who had to be consulted about everything, the marriage with the young Borghese, as the cardinal at last had wished, was brought about six days after the death of the latter.

The Barberini nevertheless did not on this account allow our prelate to drop: after merely informing themselves whether he maintained any connection with the Farnese, they employed him on the occasion of the arming of Rome.

Cecchini then found for the first time, that the new imposts on the home wines were producing much dissatisfaction. He told cardinal Barberini that it was an impost which the Romans had never endured, and on account of which they had risen against Eugenius IV., and in fact succeeded, although a monte had been already founded upon it, in getting the contractor instantly sent for. He willingly renounced the contract, for he foresaw there would be the utmost difficulty in raising the money. Cecchini hastened to the capitol where the Romans were holding a meeting, and communicated this intelligence to them: they refused at first to believe him, but he caused the contractor to be called, who then confirmed what he had said. All then exclaimed, "Long live pope Urban; long live monsignor Cecchini." People kissed his hands and his clothes.

But Cecchini had not yet attained his highest elevation. He lived to enjoy the felicity of seeing one more of his old favourers, and perhaps the most zealous of them all, cardinal Pamfilio, mount the papal throne.

For some time at first the Barberini remained in favour with Innocent X.; Cecchini obtained an invitation to present himself to the pope along with the two cardinals. "Has cardinal Barberini said anything to you?" he was then asked by Innocent. "No." He turned first to Francis, then to Antonio, and bade them speak. They declined. "We shall no longer keep you in suspense," at last said the pope: "we have appointed you our Datarius: for this you are obliged to the lords Barberini, who have presented a petition to me about it: we have willingly granted their request."

This post meanwhile had much that was unpleasant attending it. The pope was fickle, obstinate, distrustful. From other sources we know that Cecchini's administration was not exempt from censure: Donna Olympia Maidalchina could not endure him, just because her sister-in-law, Donna Clementia, received presents: I have already mentioned these things: she had a certain influence on the administration of Innocent X.: the consequence was scenes of the utmost hatred and deceit. Cecchini had the good fortune at last to see Donna

Olympia removed: he wrote this small work during the period of her disgrace, shortly after the death of Panzirolo, who died in November, 1651, consequently about the commencement of the year 1652.

It strikes me that already there prevails in it, not only in the sentiments, but even in the most isolated expressions, quite a modern cast, the daily life of Roman prelates of the present and immediately preceding times.

122.

Diario veridico e spassionato della città e corte di Roma, dove si legge tutti li successi della suddetta città incominciando dal primo d' Agosto 1640 fino all' ultimo dell' anno 1644, notato e scritto fedelmente da Deone hora Temi Dio, e copiato dal proprio originale.—[A veracious and dispassionate journal of the city and court of Rome, where may be read all the events of the said city, commencing from the 1st of August, 1640, to the end of the year 1644, faithfully noted and written by Deone hora Temi Dio, and copied from the proper original.] Informatt. politt. vol. xl. to the end of 1642; vol. xli. to the end of 1644; vol. xlii., continuation, 1645—1647; vol. xliii. 1648—1650. (Altogether above 2000 pages.)

I have not succeeded in finding out any other notices respecting the author of this so unusually copious a journal, than what he himself here and there communicates.

It appears that he was in the Spanish service, and that he was employed in the affairs of the Netherlanders with Rome, chiefly with the dataria. I should judge that he was a Spaniard, not a Netherlander. At the carnival he translated comedies from Spanish into Italian, and had them performed before a splendid circle by young people. The Spanish monarchy to which he belonged, he treats with religious veneration: he often speaks of the "holy monarchy," without whose aid the bark of Peter would but too soon have been overwhelmed. He attacks adversaries or apostates with vehement and unconcealed hatred. He declares the Catalonians who maintained themselves for some time in a state of independence, to be a nation of barbarians: one or other of them had asked his influence about an order at the dataria; he told them they must first be again good servants of the king. But far less could he bear with patience the Portuguese having even placed another king on the throne of Portugal: his book is full of invectives against that nation. He thinks that all those at least who were settled in Rome, were inclined to fall away into Judaism. Badly as matters went, still he never loses heart. He persists in hoping that Holland in its time would even submit again to the king: heresy has its periods; it must be allowed to run its course. An orthodoxy at once enthusiastic and devoted to the Spanish monarchy!

This spirited servant of Philip IV. dictated every fortnight a writing, a report, on remarkable occurrences of this period, which he then sent to some grandee of the Spanish monarchy. These were originally advices such as are so often to be found at that time: thrown together they form a journal.

Now it is composed altogether in the spirit that was natural to the author. He is displeased at Urban VIII., and puts a bad construction on his leaning to France, and on the whole political position with respect to others in which he had placed himself. Pope Innocent X., on the contrary, who followed a different policy, is regarded with much more favour.

There is nothing left untouched by the author: affairs relating to the church and to learning: the history of (religious) orders and of the court: internal domestic circumstances and the course of policy: general political considerations and the history of cities.

If we look more narrowly into the sources of his communications, we shall find them, as appears to me, to be the following. All who had business to transact at the palace, used to meet on set days in the antechambers of the cardinal nephew: a general conversation ensued: each of the parties present produced his own piece of news: nothing could excite attention that was not talked of there: in so far as I can gather from some hints, there our compiler collected the general mass of the intelligence he communicates.

Therewithal he goes to work with much honest intention; he endeavours to sift matters to the bottom; and often adds corrections.

But he would now and then likewise see the pope, the nephews, the most influential statesmen: he specifies in the most careful manner what he borrows from their conversation: occasionally it is interesting enough.

It cannot be asserted that the reading of so diffuse a piece of writing is exactly very interesting: but even here we are gradually introduced to the knowledge of persons and things almost as if we knew them from a direct view of them; they are presented to us so often, and in so many various positions.

Now it would be impossible to insert an in any measure satisfactory extract from it: it must suffice for me to give passages to which I have particularly referred.

"1. Una delle più belle memorie di questa già dominatrice del mondo è un monumento antico in forma rotonda di circonferenza grandissima e di bellissimo marmo (ohne Zweifel ein Irrthum, das Monument ist von Travertin) presso a San Sebastiano detto Capo di bove. Il Bernino, statuario famo-

[One of the most beautiful memorials of this now queen of the world, is an ancient monument in a round form, of immense circumference, and of the finest marble (no doubt a mistake, that monument is of Travertine) near St. Sebastian called *Capo di bove*. Bernino, a most famous statuary of

sissimo del papa per suo utile, ha posto in consideratione di fare una facciata sontuosa all' Acqua Vergine detta di Trevi: ottenne un breve di poter buttare a terra quella machina sì bella, et incominciò a metterlo in esecutione: ma fu dal popolo Romano avvedutosene impedito, e l' opera cessa per non cagionare rumori.

"2. Martedì mattina tenne concilio generale in Campidoglio il popolo Romano, che fu numerossissimo più che mai, atteso che vi concorsero molti titolati, che per il passato non mai intervennero. La proposta fu che sendo il popolo Romano suppresso dalle gabelle imposte da papa Urbano si dovesse supplicare Sua Sta per levare almeno la gabella della macina, tanto più che fu imposta fin che durasse la guerra all' hora in piedi, la quale hoggi è terminata. Passò il partito, e furono deputati sei gentilhuomini Romani per esporre al papa la petitione incontinente. Comparve Don Cesare Colonna, zio del principe di Gallicano, il quale dimandò udienza da popolo Romano da parte della signora Donna Anna Barberina. Gli fu risposto che venisse, e postosi allo scabelletto trasse dal seno un memoriale, dicendo che era di Donna Anna Colonna, e chiedeva che si legesse. Fu letto, e diceva che non si dovesse mandare al papa per levar gabelle giuridiche e con legitima causa imposte da papa Urbano, il cui zelo verso la giustitia e meriti che ha con questa città non permettono che si ritratti il disposto di lui. Restò ogn' uno meravigliato da simil dimandita, volente impedire il sollevamento del popolo: ma fu però subito penetrato che la buona signora haveva perinteso che si levarebbe la gabella colli beni de' Barberini. Fu risposto al Colonna, che 'l senato e popolo non faceva altro che esporre alla Sua Sta il bisogno della città. Questa risposta il Colonna portò correndo a Donna Anna, che stava aspettando per quest' effetto alla chiesa d' Araceli .... Mercordì il cardinal Colonna havendo inteso la disorbitante proposta della sorella, mandò al senato Romano a farli sapere ch' egli non hebbe in quella sciocchezza parte alcuna, ma che era pronto di assistere alla giusta petitione del popolo...... Venerdì mattina il popolo Romano di nuovo convocò consiglio pieno, e fu riferito che S. Sta s' era contentato di levar la gabella della macina con l' effecto di Don Taddeo Barberini, di modo che fu ben divisata la pretensione di Donna Anna Barberina."

[the pope for his own purposes, had it in contemplation to make a splendid front to the Acqua Vergine called di Trevi: he obtained a brief from the pope to be allowed to throw down that beautiful machinery, and began to execute his design: but it was prevented by the people of Rome coming to be aware of it, and not to occasion disturbances, the operations ceased.

2. On Tuesday morning the people of Rome held a general council in the capitol, which was more numerously attended than it had ever been, seeing that many titled persons flocked thither, who never in past times showed themselves there. What was proposed was that as the Roman people were oppressed with the duties imposed by pope Urban, they ought to supplicate his holiness to take off at least the duty on grinding corn, the more as it was laid on until the termination of the war which was then on foot, but had now come to a close. The resolution was carried, and six Roman gentlemen were deputed to lay the petition forthwith before the pontiff. There appeared there Don Cesar Colonna, uncle of the prince of Gallicano, who asked an audience from the Roman people on the part of signora Donna Anna Barberina. The answer was that he might come, and standing on a footstool he drew from his breast a memorial which he said was from Donna Anna Colonna, and begged that it might be read. It was so, and was to this effect, that the pope ought not to be applied to with the view of procuring the repeal of the taxes laid on lawfully and for legitimate reasons by pope Urban, whose zeal for justice, and whose having so well deserved of this city, did not permit the retractation of what had been arranged by him. Every body was amazed at such a demand, wanting to prevent the disburthening of the people: but at last it was all at once perceived that the good signora had a shrewd guess that the duty would be taken off at the cost of the Barberini. The answer made to Colonna was that the senate and people did nothing but lay before his holiness the wants of the city. This answer Colonna ran with in haste to Donna Anna, who stood waiting for it at the church of Araceli..... On Wednesday cardinal Colonna having heard of the extravagant proposal of his sister, sent to the Roman senate to inform them that he had had no share in that piece of folly, but that he was quite ready to aid the people's just petition..... On Friday morning the Roman people convoked a new and full council, and it was reported to it that his holiness was content to take off the duty on ground corn, compensating the loss with the effects of Don Thaddeus Barberini, so that Donna Anna Barberina's representation was well conceived.]

123.

Del stato di Roma presente.—[Of the present state of Rome.] (MS. Vindob. Fosc. n. 147.) Also under the title Relatione di Roma fatta dall' Almaden.—[Account of Rome by Almaden.]

I will not positively say whether this belongs to the last times of Urban VIII., or to the first of Innocent X.; for indicating the internal state of things in the former period, it is of no small consequence: on the Tiber and the Anio, the increase of the *aria cattiva* (pestilen-

tial air), the incomes of the Romans, money matters in general, the condition of families. It is possible that this small work may have come from the person who composed the Diario itself: some traces would lead us to suppose this.

Yet I will not accumulate extracts, since, if I mistake not, I have seen an old printed copy of it in the possession of the deceased Fea. There only follows the passage to which I have referred above, page 235, vol. II.

"Gregorio XIII. considerando che quantità grande di danaro usciva da Roma e dallo stato per prezzo di grani che venivano per mare da Barberia ed altri luoghi, spesse volte riscaldati e guasti, e tal volta non giungevano a tempo o si restavano affatto, per sostrarsi da tutti questi mancamenti, fece smacchiare per molte miglia riducendo la campagna a coltura, sicche Roma da quel tempo di rado ha havuto bisogno di grano forestiero: ed il buon pontefice Gregorio ha conseguito il suo intento: ma lo smacchiare ha aperto il passo a' venti cattivi, da quali nasce ogni intemperie, che cagiona certo morbo chiamato da Alessandro da Civita medico, trattando de' morbi de' Romani, capiplenium, cosa sopra modo fastidiosa e più alli forestieri ch' alli nativi, morbo anco cresciuto dopo la condotta di tanti fonti, dalli quali Roma, sendo bassa et umida di sua positura, vien resa più umida per la moltitudine dell' acque delle fontane. Siccome Gregorio XIII. smacchiò la campagna sotto Roma verso il mare grassa ed attissima per la coltivatione del grano, così Sisto quinto smacchiò la campagna sopra Roma meno fertile, per torre il ricovero a' masnadieri che infestavano le strade, e ben riusciva il disegno, perchè li sradicò affatto."

[Gregory XIII., taking into consideration that a great quantity of money went out of Rome and from the state, to pay for grain that came by sea from Barbary and other places, very often in a heated and spoiled condition, and sometimes it did not arrive in time or remained altogether, to obviate all these inconveniences, ordered the country to be cleared of wood for many miles and reduced to cultivation, so that Rome since that time has seldom required foreign grain: and the good pontiff Gregory has accomplished his purpose: but the clearance has opened a passage for the pestilential winds, whence there arises such an insalubrity as causes a certain disease called by Alessandro of Civita, a physician, in treating of the diseases of the Romans, capiplenium, an excessively troublesome thing, and more so to foreigners than to natives, a disease further increased since the establishment of so many wells, by which Rome, being low and humid from its situation, is rendered still more so by the multitude of the well waters. As Gregory XIII. cleared the campagna below Rome and towards the sea, a rich country, and very fit for the cultivation of grain, so Sixtus V. cleared the campagna above Rome, which is less fertile, in order to deprive of their retreats the robbers that infested the highways, and succeeded truly in his object, for he utterly rooted them out.]

The author approves indeed of Sixtus V.'s procedure: but how much evil has more recently been alleged to come from the Tramontana! (Cancellieri sopra il tarautismo, p. 88.)

124.

Compendio delli casi più degni e memorandi occorsi nelli pontificati da Gregorio XIII. fino alla creatione di Clemente IX.—[Compendium of the most worthy and memorable cases that occurred in the pontificates from Gregory XIII. to the creation of Clement IX. (50 leaves.)

The author assures us that he saw the clouds that at the death of Sixtus V. darkened the Quirinal (Aug. 1590). Now, as this small work reaches down to 1667, it is clear that it cannot have come from one author: it must have been afterwards continued with the same view with which it was begun, that is, as a collection of Roman remarkable occurrences and anecdotes. For example, we read here how the French monks in Trinita di Monte were at enmity with the Calabrian and others, and expelled these, so that they added Andrea della Fratte to their buildings, which still lay at that time between gardens;—how the Jesuits again aroused all the other orders also, to attend to their duties;—miracles that happened;—notices respecting the buildings of the popes.

In all this information there is much indeed that deserves our notice. For example, the following narrative of the death of Bianca Capello: "Volendo la granduchessa di Toscana, Bianca Capelli, avvelenare il card[l] Ferdinando suo cognato in certa confezione, il G. D. Francesco suo marito ne mangiò prima: il che inteso da lei, ne mangiò essa ancora, e tutti due morirono subito, et il card[l] si fece granduca."—[The grand duchess of Tuscany, Bianca Capelli, wishing to poison cardinal Ferdinand, her brother-in-law, in certain confectionary, the G. D. Francis, her husband, first ate of it: and on understanding from him that he had done so she herself ate also of it, and both died suddenly; and the cardinal became grand duke.] That of the carrying off of Cardinal Clesel from Vienna, which Ferdinand II.'s Jesuit confessor would never consent to: "Verospi ebbe un giorno commodità d' essere coll' imp[re] senza il Giesuita, e con bella maniera fece capace l' imp[re] che non poteva ritenere detto card[le] e solo il papa esser suo vero giudice, e talmente commosse Cesare che lo fece piangere e glielo fece consignare."—[Verospi had one day an opportunity of being with the emperor in the absence of the Jesuit, and with great tact made the emperor understand that he could not retain the same cardinal, and that the pope alone was his own true judge, and so moved the emperor as to make him weep, and cause him to be consigned to him.]

Or traits of manners likewise. A rich prelate inserted a clause in his will, to the effect that his nephew should inherit what he should leave behind him, only in the case of his dying a natural death; otherwise it was to go to pious institutions. Duke Cesarini paid nobody, until people had made arrangements for exposing to auction the mortgaged property he had first allowed them to take. An Orsino threatened to make a pressing creditor be thrown out of the window. The creditor besought him first to allow him to confess to a priest; Orsino replied that people should come to him only after having confessed (che bisognava venirci confessato).—A necromancer entered Rome in a carriage drawn by a pair of dogs: the report spread that they were a pair of devils, with which he could go wherever he pleased. The courier from Milan maintained that he had left him at Milan and found him again in Rome. The supposed sorcerer was arrested and put to death.

Were these notices but a little more spirited, they would be invaluable; they would place before us manners and times without involving the necessity of such fatiguing studies as the above-mentioned journal.

Let us now pass to the writings that immediately relate to Innocent X.

Observations

On Gualdi Vita di Donna Olimpia Maldachina—[on Gualdi's Life of Donna Olympia Maldachina]. 1666.

We no sooner discover that Gregory Leti, whom we have had sufficient means of knowing, was the author of this writing too, than almost all motive ceases for discussing its claim to be believed: it has the strongest presumptions against it.

Yet, as in 1770 a French, and in 1783 a German translation of it appeared, and as our countryman Schröckh thinks he may venture to assume the truth of the general narrative at least, because it has never been controverted, it will not be superfluous to say a word about it. Our author, however, boldly asserts that he is to relate nothing that he has not himself seen, or of which he had not obtained the surest information.

He at once ties his knot (condemns himself) with the story, that the Maldachini family, which he holds to be Roman, had once undertaken a pilgrimage to Loreto, here they had been joined in Borgheto by the young Pamfilia; that he fell in love with the daughter of the family, Donna Olympia, and after the return (of the party) married her; but that very soon Olympia became more intimate with his brother, afterwards pope, at that time a young abbé, than with her husband. That this was the foundation of the influence exercised by Donna Olympia over Innocent X.

But we may confidently say that not a word of this is true.

The Maidalchina family is not from Rome but from Acquapendente. Donna Olympia was a widow when she married Pamfili. Paul Nini at Viterbo, the last of that race, was her first husband: as she succeeded to his property, she brought a rich dowry into the Pamfili family: on this, and not on any imaginary intimacy with the pope, was the authority founded which she enjoyed in the family. When this marriage took place, Innocent X. was far from being a young abbot. In an inscription which the senior member of the family placed in the Villa Maidalchina, at Viterbo, it runs that he had dressed out that villa in the year 1625, before the marriage of his sister into the Pamfili family. "Marchio Andreas Maidalchinus .... villam hanc ante nuptam sororem suam Olympiam cum Innocentii X. germano fratre .... extruxit ornavitque anno Domini MDCXXV.—[Marquis Andrew Maidalchinus .... this villa previous to the marriage of his sister Olympia with the brother-german of Innocent X.... built and beautified in the year of our Lord 1625.] In Bussi's "Istoria di Viterbo, p. 332, the whole inscription is given. Consequently that marriage could have happened at the earliest, in 1626, when Giambattista Pamfili, afterwards Innocent X., was already fifty-four years old, and for twenty years past had been no longer abbé, but prelate. At that very time he was employed in various nuncioships: if we may venture to infer aught from any of his expressions, it will only be the desert of Donna Olympia, in having on these as well as on subsequent occasions, aided him out of her means. He could maintain that splendour which in those days was indispensable to a man's rising in the world. In accordance with such a commencement, her whole relative position afterwards developed itself, as Donna Olympia had supported the prelate, and participated so far in the obtaining of the papal dignity, so did she now desire to make that of use to herself.

In the minute Diario above mentioned, which follows Olympia step by step, and where notice is taken of all the secrets of the pope's domestic life, there is not a trace to be discovered of illegitimate intimacy between the pope and his sister in law.

This little work of Leti's, too, is a romance presenting a tissue of apocryphal information and chimerical tales.

125.

Relatione degli ambasciatori estraordinarj a Roma al sommo pontefice Innocentio X., Pietro Foscarini K^{r}, Zuanne Nani K^{r} Proc^{r}, Aluise Mocenigo I. fu di q. Aluise, e Bertucci Valier K^{r}. 1645, 3 Ott.—[Report from the ambassadors extraordinary at Rome (sent) to the supreme pontiff Innocent X., Peter Foscarini, knight, Zuanne Nani, knight Procurator, Aluise Mocenigo, (?) Aluise, and Bertucci Valier, knight. 1645, October 3d.

A thorough change ensued upon Urban's death. Innocent X. was now viewed with aver-

sion by the French: he would willingly have aided the emperor, had he only had it in his power: he was a friend to the Venetians. Only it was possible that from natural indecision of character he might show symptoms of vacillation in his measures. The ambassadors accordingly find it doubly necessary not to fall out with him from private considerations, and in no wise to slight the papal favour on account of a loose-living monk.

The preceding life of this pope is described in the following manner.

"Nasce il presente sommo pontefice Innocentio X., chiamato prima Gio. Batt. card[le] Pamfilio, dalla famiglia de' Pamfilj originata già in Ugubbio città dello stato d' Urbino. Questa venne habitare in Roma sotto il pontificato d' Innocentio VIII., si apparentò con le prime case della città, visse sempre in molta riputatione et honorevolezza. La madre di S. B[ne] fu della famiglia de' marchesi dal Buffolo, nobile e principale, della quale ne fa il papa hoggidì molto conto, ritrovandosene più d' uno all suo servitio in palazzo. Fu la Sta Sua allevata dal card[le] Gerolamo Pamfilio, suo zio paterno, che visse in gran concetto e fu vicino ad esser papa e che fu fatto card[le] da Clemente VIII., mentre si trovava auditor decano della rota chiaro per la virtù et innocenza de' suoi costumi. Si trova la Sta Sua in età di 72 anni, di statura più che ordinaria, ben proportionata, maestosa nella persona, piena di grande mansuetudine e benignità: onde sempre che esce dalle sue stanze per occasione di concistorj, capelle o altre occasioni, da prontamente e volentieri audienza a tutti di ogni conditione, benche poveri e miserabili, che se gli fanno innanzi, riceve i lor memoriali, e con molta patienza e carità procura di sollevare ognuno, consolar tutti con grande acclamation dei sudditi e con gran differenza dal pontificato antecedente. Fu il papa prima avvocato concistoriale, poi auditor di rota eletto da Clemente VIII. Fu da Gregorio XV. mandato noncio a Napoli e da Urbano VIII. impiegato nelle legationi di Franza e Spagna del card[l] Barberino con titolo di datario, fu dallo stesso Urbano eletto patriarca d' Antiochia, mandato noncio in Spagna, e poi promosso al cardinalato li 9 Novembre 1627. Come cardinale è stato in concetto di natura severa, inclinato al rigore, puntuale nelle cose ecclesiastiche. E stato sempre adoperato in tutte le congregationi principali, e si può dire che ha esercitate tutte le cariche più principali di Roma con universale sodisfattione, havendo nell' animo sua fatta sempre particolar sede la modestia, la patienza, l' integrità, la virtù, la mira di non disgustare alcuno, accarezzando tutti e condonando le ingiurie. Gode una buona salute, ha complessione assai robusta, va sobrio nel cibo, fa volentieri esercitio, assiste alle capelle et altre funtioni con gran maestà, e fa tutte le cose ecclesiastiche con pompa, decoro, particolar godimento suo e puntualità. Va pesato assai in tutti li negotii gravi, vuol tempo ad esaminarli e risolverli. E stato solito nella sua passata fortuna andar tardi e tardi levarsi dal letto, osserva il medesimo stile nel pontificato, onde rare volte è retirato avanti la mezza notte nè levato la mattina avanti qualche hora del giorno. Ha nei tempi andati fatta molta stima dei principi: ha desiderate le loro giuste sodisfattioni: si dichiara preservare ne' stessi concetti, non voler esser partiale d' alcuna delle due corone, ma padre

[The present supreme pontiff Innocent X., called first Gia. Batt. cardinal Pamfilio, was born of the Pamfili family, which has its origin in Ugabbio, a town of the state of Urbino. This (family) came to live in Rome under the pontificate of Innocent VIII., became intimate with the first houses in the city, always lived in much reputation and honour. His beatitude's mother was of the family of the Marquises dal Buffolo, of noble and princely rank, of which the pope makes much account at this day, more than one of its members being in his service in the palace. His holiness was brought up by cardinal Gerolamo Pamfilio, his uncle by the father's side, who lived in great repute, was near being pope, and was made cardinal by Clement VIII., at the time of his being auditor dean of the rota, illustrious by his virtue and the innocence of his manners. His holiness is seventy-two years old, above the common height, well proportioned, of a majestic person, full of the utmost affability and benignity: whence every time he leaves his apartments to attend consistory meetings, chapels, or on other occasions, he gives an audience promptly and cheerfully to all persons of whatsoever condition, though they be poor and wretched, that present themselves to him; he receives their petitions, and with much patience and charity tries to relieve every one, to comfort all with great acclamation on the part of the subjects, and presenting a great contrast to the preceding pontificate. The pope was first consistorial advocate, then auditor of the rota elected by Clement VIII. By Gregory XV. he was sent nuncio to Naples, and by Urban VIII. employed in cardinal Barberino's French and Spanish legations with the title of datario, he was by the same Urban VIII. elected patriarch of Antioch, sent nuncio into Spain, and then promoted to the cardinalship 9th November 1627. As cardinal he had the reputation of being of a severe disposition, inclined to rigour, punctual in ecclesiastical affairs. He has always been employed in all the chief congregations, and it may be said that he has discharged all the most important functions with universal satisfaction, his mind having always been the particular seat of modesty, patience, integrity, virtue, and of the purpose not to do what is disagreeable to any one, caressing all and forgiving injuries. He enjoys good health, has a robust enough constitution, is sober in eating, loves exercise, performs all ecclesiastical things with pomp, decorum, particular enjoyment to himself and punctuality. He is very deliberate in all grave concerns, likes to have time to examine and make up his mind. He has been wont in his past fortune to go late to bed and to rise late, he observes the same habit in the pontificate, hence he has seldom been known to retire before midnight or to have risen in the morn-

universale amorevole di tutti: si risente non incontrar bene nè con l' una nè con l' altra di esse al presente, e se n' è esalata con grande confidenza più d' una volta con noi: crede però che ognuno si dolga per avvantaggiare i proprj interessi, non perchè ambedue non conoscano la necessità della sua indipendenza, e come che sia amica della pace naturalmente e la obblighi a questa il posto di pontefice in cui si trova constituito. Va nutrendosi con simili concetti ricevendo a grande alimento suo la confidenza con la Serenissima Republica, come questa con l' autorità, consigli et amor suo possa esserle del maggior presidio: anzi soggetto di grand' eminenza e della maggior confidenza nostra ha confidato ad alcuno di noi, forse d' ordine della Sta Sua, la intentione ch' ella havrebbe di stringersi con l' EE. VV. con particolare alleanza, quando credesse incontrare la publica dispositione: sopra di che con termini generali ufficiosi fu risposto, nessun nodo poter maggiormente legare i principi che la sincerità e corrispondenza de' cuori e la uniformità de' fini et interessi."

ing before some hour of the day. He has in time past made much account of the princes; he has desired to give them all just satisfaction: he says that he means to keep to the same views, has no wish to be a partisan of either of the two crowns, but to be the universal father, affectionately disposed towards all: he resents his not meeting with friendly feelings from either one or other of them at present, and has allowed his sentiments with regard to them to transpire with great confidence more than once with us: he believes in fine that every one complains for the sake of advancing his own interests, not because each is not aware of the necessity of his independence, and how he is naturally the friend of peace, and obliged to cultivate it by the post of pontiff, to which he has been appointed. He continues to cherish like views, receiving to his great refreshment the confidential friendship of the most serene republic, as that which aided with his authority, councils, and affection, may prove of greater protection to him: even a subject of great eminence and enjoying still more confidence with us, has confidentially told each of us, perhaps by the order of his holiness, the intention he had of connecting himself with your excellencies by a special alliance, since he believed it would meet the public disposition: whereupon in general terms of dutiful respect it was replied that no tie could more effectually bind princes than sincerity and mutual cordiality and uniformity of ends and interests.]

126.

Relatione dell' ambasciatore Veneto Aluise Contarini fatta al senato dopo il ritorno della sua ambasceria appresso Innocentio X.—[Report by the Venetian ambassador Aluise Contarini, given in to the senate after his return from his embassy at the court of Innocent X.] 1648. (22 leaves.)

This pontificate also developed itself not so advantageously by far as had been expected. To the first tolerably honourable report Aluise Contarini, son of Niccolo—the former Aluise was son of Tommaso—adds far less favourable traits.

In his youth Innocent had preferred chivalrous exercises and amorous pastimes (passatempi amorevoli) to studies: he had earned little respect for himself during his nuncioship in France: he had been nick-named, on account of his everlasting evasions, Monsignor Not-get-on (M[r] Non si puol); on the other hand, in Spain, his chariness of his words had procured him the reputation of being a wise man.

What was it that led to his becoming pope? Answer, three things:—speaking little, dissembling much, and doing nothing. "Da corteggiani fu detto che tre cose l' avevano fatto papa, il parlar poco, simulare assai, e non far niente."

"Si fa conoscere hora poco inclinato alle gratie, delicato e vetriolo, (?) . . .riputato da tutti d' ingegno tardo nell' apprendere e poco capace di gran machine, ma ostinato nell' apprensioni: . . . procura di non farsi conoscere partiale di alcuna corona:" [He now makes himself known to be little inclined to favours, delicate and nice (?) . . . thought by everybody to be slow of apprehension and to have little capacity for great machinations, but obstinate in his views: . . . he tries to avoid being thought the partisan of any crown:]—a friend to peace, to righteousness, not blood-thirsty, a good economist.

The circle around the pope: Donna Olympia: dear to him on this account, that she had brought a large dowry into the family, and had supported him out of it: "donna d' ingegno e spirito virile, solo si fa conoscere donna per la superbia e l' avaritia;" [a woman of masculine mind and spirit, only she lets it be known that she is a woman by her pride and avarice;]—Pancirolo: "di tratti manierosi, d' ingegno vivace, cortese di viso e di parole:" [a man of pleasing manners, of a lively turn of mind, courteous in his expression of countenance and words:]—Capponi: "a bocca ridente ricuopre la sua malitiosa industria" [with a smiling mouth he covers his malicious industry]:—Spada: "si pavoneggia delli suoi stimabili talenti" [plumes himself on his estimable talents]. It is easily seen that our author does not just express himself very respectfully. The want of a nephew with a pope of such a nature, became doubly sensible.

There follow some traits of the government.

"Tra li corteggianni si suol dire che chi tratta col papa d' alcuno affare, nelle prime audienze lo reputa quasi perfettionato, nella seconda conosce esser totalmente da farsi, e nella terza si scuopre con stupore sconcluso. . . . Crede disprezzabile quel principe che non conserva appresso di se un buon numero di contanti da valersene in un' urgente bisogno. Per non spendere si contenta di soffrire dell' avversa fortuna ogni più opprobrioso strapazzo. . . Trovandosi l' annata di Roma spogliata di quelli assegnamenti de' quali si valse in altri tempi, come proprii per essere dissipati nella guerra Barberina, Sua Sta conoscendo l' annata presente penuriosa di grano ha più volte assegnato di esser pronto di sovvenirla di grossa somma di cotanti; ma ripugnando la sua natura allo sborso, ha cercato aggiustarlo in altra forma, sebene non a sufficienza. . . . Tutte le communità si trovano talmente esauste e ruinate per cagione della guerra Barberina che gl' è impossibile giammai risorgere e rihaversi. . . . Particolare entrata del papa di 800 m. scudi consistente negli emolumenti delle componende della dataria e nelle vacabilità degli officii di quella e della cancelleria, come ancora di una sorte di monti vacabili dell' auditore e tesoriere di camera, chiericati di essa, et altri simili officii, di tutta questa somma, che entra nella borsa secreta e non nella publica, ne è assoluto patrone S. Sta, potendone disporre al suo arbitrio e donarla a chi più li piace senza temere che siano richieste dal successore."

[Among the courtiers it is wont to be said that he who treats with the pope about any affair, at the first audiences thinks it all but completed, in the second perceives that it has to be begun quite anew, and in the third discovers with amazement that it is concluded. . . . He thinks that prince despicable who does not keep by him a good sum of ready money to avail himself of in case of urgent need. Rather than spend money he is content to suffer from adverse fortune even the most opprobrious insult. . . . The yearly income of Rome happening to have been despoiled of those revenues which were available in other times, as the first likely to be dissipated in the Barberina war, his holiness knowing the present year to be scanty in grain, has repeatedly intimated his readiness to grant relief by the advance of a large sum of money: but as his nature abhors spending, he has sought to adjust the matter in another way, although inadequately. . . . All the corporations are so exhausted and ruined owing to the Barberina war, that their recovery and restoration are for ever impossible. . . . The private revenues of the pope, of 800,000 scudi, consisting of the emoluments of the compositions of the dataria and of the vacabilities of the offices of that department and of the chancery, as also of a sort of *monti vacabili* of the auditor and the treasurer of the chamber, and of the clerks of the same and other similar offices,—that whole sum is at the pope's absolute disposal, to be given to whomsoever he pleases, without any dread of being called to account by his successor.]

His buildings: on the capitol, at St. Peter's, at the Lateran: "in cui rinnovandosi con nuovo modello le tre navate della chiesa, rimane nel suo essere l' adornamento di quel vago e ben inteso soffito," [in which while there were renewed, after a new model, the three naves of the church, there remained all that was essential in the adornment of that elegant and well-conceived entablature],—in the piazza Navona: "con il gettato di alcune case per la parte di S. Giacomo de' Spagnuoli restando in quadro la piazza" [by throwing down some houses in that part where the church of St. James of the Spaniards stands, the place remaining a square].

It will be seen that notwithstanding the bad impression produced by the court, Contarini is, on the whole, impartial and interesting.

127.

Memoriale presentato alla Sta di N. S[re] papa Innocenzo X. dai deputati della città di Fermo per il tumulto ivi seguito alli 6 di Luglio 1648.—[Memorial presented to the holiness of our lord pope Innocent X., from the deputies of the city of Fermo, about the tumult that took place there on the 6th of July 1648.]

In Majolino Bisaccioni's "Historia delle guerre civili di questi ultimi tempi, Ven. 1664" —[History of the civil wars of these last times, Venice 1664], there is to be found, as already remarked, in the midst of the most important events, besides (what relates to) Charles I. and Cromwell, the insurrection of Portugal and Catalonia, also an "Historia della guerra civile di Fermo," that is, a history of a tumult, in which the papal governor, Visconti, was killed.

Here we have the memorial, with which two deputies, Lorenzo Nobile and Lucio Guerrieri, appeared before the pope, to ask his forgiveness for what had been done.

According to its representation, which is much more authentic and graphic than Bisaccioni, and gives a peep at the internal condition of the cities at that time, the crops had failed, and bread was uncommonly dear: nevertheless the governor insisted on exporting corn from the territory of Fermo. He would listen to no warning. With his carabine at his side, and his pistols on the table, he declared that he would rather die like a governor and a soldier, than give way. He forbade the meeting of the council to which deputies from the neighbouring domains even had come, and drew troops together. But these soldiers of his "came from the fields they had tilled, from the thrashing-floors where they had plied the flail:" they knew the want to which the people were exposed, and instead of opposing the riotous populace, they took part with them. The governor saw himself, in spite of his bravadoes, compelled to yield, and to allow his corn to remain within the territory of the city.

But scarcely had the people begun to be quiet, when Corsican militia, called in by the governor, appeared at the gates. The impression prevailed that Visconti would with their assistance carry his purpose into effect. A tumult arose. The cry ran: "We are betrayed; to arms!" the bells were rung, the palace stormed, and the governor slain.

The deputies protest their loyalty, and deplore this event,—the nobles chiefly were afflicted on this account. (di vedere, senza potervi remediare, da persone del popolo ucciso il prelato di V^ra^ Sta datogli per suo governo" [to see, without a possibility of remedying it, a prelate of your holiness given them for their government, slain by persons from among the people].)

128.

Relatione della corte di Roma del cav^re^ Giustiniani data in senato l' anno 1652.—[Report on the court of Rome by the chevalier Guistiniani, presented in the senate, in the year 1652.] (Copy in the Magliabechiana at Florence, 24, 65.)

But from admiration and expectation, people passed under Innocent X., first to doubt and disapprobation, and at last to complaints and reproach.

Zuan Zustinian—for thus do the Venetians pronounce and write this name—came after (having discharged) many other embassies from Vienna to Rome, and resided there from 1648 to 1651. These years fill up his despatches, and to these his report refers.

The description of the court does not give us a very pleasing idea of it.

Whatever is good in the pope, says he, goes to the advantage of the city of Rome and at most of the church-state; his bad qualities are hurtful to the whole of Christendom. Nevertheless, even in the church-state, the remission of the severest punishments for money is a great evil.

"Mi si afferma per massima indubitata che in sette anni di pontificato babbia estratto dalle compositioni di persone processate come ree il valore di 1200 m. scudi, che s' accosta a due milioni di ducati."

[I am told, as an undoubted rule, that in seven years of the pontificate, there had been drawn of compositions paid by persons sued as criminals the value of 1200 scudi, which amounts to about two millions of ducats.]

The influence of Donna Olympia Maidalchima here appears as a sort of public calamity.

"Donna di gran spirito, prepotente per solo titolo di esatta economia. Se vacavano officj nella corte, niente si deliberaba senza il beneplacito de lei: si vi erano beneficj da distribuire, i ministri della dataria tenevano ordine di trattenere ogni spedizione sinche datagli notizia della qualità delle vacanze scegliesse a sua disposizione ciò che più tenesse di gusto: si vi erano chiese episcopali da provedere, ad essa ricorrevano i pretendenti; e quello che rendeva nausea a tutti gli uomini onorati, era il vedere che erano preferiti quelli che più allargavano la mano a donativi."

[A woman of great spirit, very powerful by the sole title of being an exact economist. If offices fell vacant at court, nothing was determined without her approval: if there were benefices there to distribute, the ministers of the dataria held orders to keep all appointments open until, having given her notice of the nature of the vacancies, she should select at her pleasure what best might suit her taste: if there were episcopal churches to be provided for, to her those pretending claims to be appointed had recourse; and what disgusted all honourable men was to see those preferred who were most liberal in offering gifts.]

Thus it proceeds; yet I am not sure if the report is even really genuine.

It does not appear in the Venetian archives: in the Magliabechiana at Florence there are two copies, which however do not tally with each other throughout. I have confined myself to the more moderate one.

Happily it was not necessary for me to take my materials from this report, as the Diarium above mentioned and Pallavicini's notices in the Life of Alexander VII. presented a far better resource.

129.

Relatione dell' ambasceria estraordinaria fatta in Roma alla Sta di N. S^re^ Allessandro VII. dagli Ecc^mi^ SS^ri^ Pesaro, Contarini, Valiero e Sagredo per rendere a nome della Ser^ma^ Republica di Venetia la solita obedienza al sommo pontefice l' anno 1656.—[Report of the extraordinary embassy made in Rome to the holiness of our lord Alexander VII., from the most excellent Signors Pesaro, Contarini, Valiero, and Sagredo, to present in the name of the most serene republic of Venice the customary obeisance to the supreme pontiff in the year 1656.]

The same Pesaro, during whose embassy there occurred the schism between Urban VIII. and the republic, who after that was always held to be rather an adversary of the clergy, was placed at the head of the congratulation ambassadors, and now we find him charged by the rest with the drawing up of the report. Now, whether it be that his temper, as he says, had from the first been very moderate, or that the lapse of years that had passed away had wrought a change in him, his report is very intelligent, well-intended, and instructive.

It is true that on the government of Innocent X. he at once expresses himself disapprovingly, but not with such complete scorn as others.

"Oltre la cupidità insatiabile ch' è regnata in quelli casa, vi si è aggionto che essendo mancato di ministri valevoli al sostentamento di così gran principato, non havendo luogo nell' animo suspicace di quel pontefice la fede di chi si sia, ogni cosa per lo più si regolava secondo gli appetiti immoderati di una donna, che ha aperto largo campo alle penne satiriche di fare comparire i disordini di quel governo maggiori ancora di quel che in fatti si fossero."

[Besides the insatiable cupidity which has reigned in that house, there has been added, that from there being a want of ministers capable of administering so great a principality, for confidence in any one has no place in the suspicious mind of that prince, everything for the most part is regulated according to the immoderate appetites of a woman, which has given wide scope for satirical pens to make the disorders of that government appear still worse than in fact they have been.]

As has been said, however little this may sound like a eulogy, still, compared with the violent expressions of others, it is a very mild judgment.

But the chief object of the report is the new pope, Alexander VII.

Pesaro is of opinion, as was indeed the conviction of the world at large, that the estimate formed of Fabio Chigi's virtues, the fame of his nunciosbip, had promoted him, although the Medici at bottom viewed with dislike the elevation of one of their subjects.

"Più santa elettione non si poteva aspettare da un senato di soggetti che per quanto havessero distratta la volontà da mondani interessi, non potevano di meno di non lasciarsi in fine guidare da quel spirito santo che essi presumono assistere ad un' attione di tanta rilevanza."

[A holier election could not be expected from a senate of subjects, who, however they may have had their intentions distracted by worldly interests, could not fail to allow themselves to be guided at last by that holy spirit which they presume is present at an action of such high importance.]

He describes his rise in life, and in general terms the character of his first proceedings: of economical things he shows little understanding, so much the more does he comprehend ecclesiastical things, and he is not altogether unbending in his ways;—also his relations;—this it is not necessary to repeat; matters too soon developed themselves in a different manner from what was expected.

"Troppo per tempo parmi" [For too long a time it appears to me], says Pesaro, likewise, "che il mondo canonizzi questi sentimenti del papa, e che per farne più accertato giudizio faccia mestiere osservarsi quanto con il tratto del tempo si sia per mostrarsi costante nel resistere alle mantellate dell' affetto"—[the world canonizes these sentiments of the pope, and in order to pass a surer judgment on them, makes a business of observing how far with the lapse of time he is to be seen constant in resisting the specious pretensions of private affection]. Even then so many representations were made to the pope from all quarters that his steadfastness seemed sure to be shaken.

Yet the object of this embassy was not only to congratulate the pope, but much more to apply for the assistance of the Roman court in the Candian war.

The ambassadors explained what efforts Venice had made in opposing the enemy, above all, in order first but to be able to meet the expenses of the war: loans with heavy interests, by way of life annuities or perpetual; the sale of allodial or feudal possessions; the communication to a greater number of the dignities of the state, which had formerly been confined within a narrow circle, even that of the nobility in general, which yet was the more valuable the less it was made common. But now their means were utterly exhausted: nothing could be hoped for from the remaining potentates of Christendom, who were distracted by too many internal animosities among themselves: their sole resource lay in the Roman court.

The pope listened not without showing symptoms of sympathy: he answered them with a glowing eulogy of the republic, which opposed the fury of the barbarians not only with iron but with gold; but as for what regarded the main business, he declared to them that he saw he was not in a condition to do anything for them; that so exhausted was the papal exchequer that he knew not how to assist the city in getting bread.

The ambassadors did not desist from their purpose; they represented that the danger well justified having recourse, on this occasion, to the old treasure of Sixtus V.

"Prima che l' urgenza degli accidenti che possono sopravenire, maggiormente stringa, e per sostentamento della religione e per sicurezza del proprio dominio ecclesiastico."

[First that the urgency of the accidents that might supervene was particularly pressing, both as respected the sustentation of religion and the security of his own ecclesiastical dominion.]

The pope was particularly impressed with the consideration that it would embolden the enemy to see that even a new pope refused the succour which was so much needed. Alexander clearly saw that something must be done: he suggested that ecclesiastical property might be confiscated.

How remarkable to find that the Roman court first appeared with measures of this sort. Already had Innocent X. proposed the abolition of two orders, the canonicals of the Holy Ghost and the Cruciferi. He had it in view to found secular prebends out of their possessions. But the Venetians were at one time afraid that the Roman court would engross to itself the bestowing of them, and then they looked upon these institutions as provisions for the poor nobility. Well, Alexander now proposed this course to them anew.

"Il papa postosi in atto di volerci rappresentare cosa di nostro sollievo, prese a dire che, da qualche tempo in qua essendosi dalla sede apostolica fatto riflesso non meno all' abondanza che alla superfluità degl' instituti religiosi, haveva trovato che alcuni di essi degenerando dalla primiera intentione de' loro fondatori erano trascorsi in una total rilassatione di costumi: che compliva non meno al servitio della chiesa che de' medesimi secolari il pigliare quegli espedienti che sogliono usare gli accorti agricoltori quando vedono in modo lussuriar la vite che la copia de rampolli serve più tosto ad isterilirla che a rendarla più fruttifera: che a ciò s' era dato in qualche parte principio con la soppressione di alcune religioni, ma che ciò non bastava, conoscendosi in tutto necessario restringer questo gran numero a quei solamente che ritengono o che meglio possono ridursi a ritenere la prima forma della loro institutione: che per farsi strada a ciò s' era soppresso un numero grande di conventini piccioli ove con minor riguardo si rallentava il freno alla ritiratezza regolare, e che si persisteva nel primo pensiero di procedere alla finale abolitione d' alcuni altri ordini che con il loro licentioso modo di vivere riempivano il mondo anzi di scandoli e di mormorationi che di buon esempio e di edificatione, ma che si camminava lentamente, perche in negotio di tal rilevanza s' haverebbe voluto incontrare anche nella sodisfattione de principi, i quali, non ben esaminati i veri motivi che inducevano la sede apostolica in questa risolutione, havevano dato segno di qualche repugnanza all' esecutione de brevi ponteficii: ma che sperandosi ad ogni modo che in fine havesse ogn' uno a dar mano al proseguimento di così ben ponderata risolutione, li metteva intanto in consideratione alla Serenissima Republica che abondando il dominio Veneto di questa qualità di religioni, s' apriva un modo facile che venisse dato luogo alla retta intentione di chi ha la suprema direttione degli affari ecclesiastici et insieme a poter somministrare un considerabile ajuto in soccorso della presente guerra contro gl' infideli: che nessuno meglio di noi poteva sapere a che estremità di dissolutezza e di scandoli siano gionti li canonici di San Spirito di Venezia, essendosi la Serenissima Republica veduta in necessità di metter freno alle scorretioni di quel convento, che non contento d' haver postergata ogni osservanza regolare abusava anco sì sconciamente delle ricchezze che haverebbono potuto servire a comodi alimenti di un numero quintuplicatamente maggiore di religiosi, che sempre grossamente si trovava indebitato: che il simile si poteva dire de' Cruciferi, ne' quali apena si discerneva vestigio di vita claustrale: che per tanto anteponeva che procedendosi alla soppressione di queste due religioni, s' haverebbe potuto andar pensando al modo di passare alla vendita de' beni da esse possessi, et il ritratto si convertisse in sostentamento di questa guerra, giacche era diretta contro il nemico fierissimo del nome Christiano."

[The pope, putting himself in the attitude of describing the affair of our relief, began to say that for some time, during which having turned his reflections from the apostolic see to the abundance no less than to the superfluity of the religious orders, he had found that some of them, degenerating from the first intention of their founders, had run into a total relaxation of morals: that it suited no less the service of the church than of the seculars themselves, to adopt those expedients which are usually employed by prudent husbandmen, when they see the vine so luxuriant that the abundauce of branches serves rather to make it barren than to render it more fruitful: that to this effect a commencement had been made in some quarters with the suppression of some religious orders, but that that was not enough, owning, in short, the necessity of restraining that great number to those alone which retain or which might best be brought back to retaining the first form of their institution: that to prepare the way for this there had been suppressed a great number of small religious houses, where the reins of conventual seclusion were relaxed without attracting much notice, and that he persisted in his first idea of proceeding to the final abolition of some other orders, which, with their licentious modes of living, filled the world rather with scandals and murmurs than with good examples and edification, but that he advanced slowly, because in a business of so much importance he could wish further to meet the satisfaction of the princes, who, not having properly examined the true motives that have led the apostolic see to this resolution, have shown symptoms of some repugnance to the execution of the pontifical brieves: hoping, however, that by all means each would finally lend a helping hand to the prosecution of so well-weighed a resolution, he meanwhile submits to the consideration of the most serene republic, that as the Venetian dominion abounds in this kind of religious orders, there was opened up an easy method, which would come into operation upon giving scope to the right intention of him who had the supreme direction of ecclesiastical affairs, and at the same time of being able to furnish considerable aid towards the support of the present war against the infidels: that none better than we could know to what extremes of dissoluteness and scandals the Venetian canonici of the Holy Ghost had come, the most serene republic having seen itself compelled to check the irregularities of that monastery, which, not content with despising all conventual observances, has further so shamefully abused the wealth which might have been made to serve for the suitable alimenting of a five-fold larger number of monks, that it has always been found deeply involved in debt: that the same thing may be said of the Cruciferi, in whom there is hardly to be seen a vestige of conventual life: that thus much he preferred proceeding to the suppression of these two orders, he had thought one might go on to consider in what manner one might pass on to the sale of the property in their possession, and the produce might go to the support of this war, since it was directed against the fiercest enemy of the Christian name.]

On this occasion, it seemed to these ambassadors as if such a proposition was not to be rejected. They calculated what a large capital the sale might bring in with nothing to set against it but inconsiderable and soon to be extinguished annuities; and what an advantage would arise to the prosperity of the country from the secularization of such important possessions. Their reflections, too, upon an undertaking, then so new, and afterwards so common, are worth being noticed verbatim.

"In realtà fatti anche congrui assegnamenti a' frati esclusi per il loro vivere, che non ascenderanno mai fra l' una e l' altra religione 10 m. ducati all' anno, se de' loro beni ascendenti alla summa di 26 m. ducati se ne ritrarranno 600 mila nella vendita, come verismilmente si può credere, non sentirà il publico maggiore interesse di due per cento vitalitii e qualche cosa meno: et ogni altro motivo altre volte portato in dissuasione di negotio simile va per bene, supposti gli alimenti che annualmente si presteranno a superstiti: e così smembrandosi dall' ordine ecclesiastico questa grossa somma di portione di fondi collocati ne' migliori siti di questo dominio, vengono li laici a rimettere in possesso, senza far torto alla pietà di quelle anime grandi che hebbero cuore di spropriare le descendenze loro di così opulenti patrimonii, per fondare e stabilire in questo stato la religione: che se hora veder potessero quanto ella sia ben radicata, altra interpretatione non darebbono a' loro sentimenti se non che se gli fu grato di esser fondatori di tanti monasteri per ricovero di persone sacre, niente meno godérebbono che l' istesse ricchezze, giache sovrabondano, si convertissero in propulsare l' impietà minacciante la distruttione di quella pietà che con le proprie sostanze cercarono di promovere."

[In reality, suitable assignations being made to the excluded friars for their maintenance, which shall never exceed between the one and other order 10,000 ducats a-year, if from their possessions rising to the amount of 26,000 ducats, there should be drawn from them 600,000, as on reasonable grounds might be believed, the public would not have to pay more interest than two per cent. life annuities, and something less: and every other reason preferred at other times in dissuading from such a thing owes all its force to the assumption of the alimentary provision made for the survivors: and thus dissevering from the ecclesiastical order this large amount of property situate in the best localities of this dominion, the laity come to be put in possession, without doing offence to the piety of those great souls who had the hearts to dispossess their descendants of rich patrimonies to found and establish religion in this state: that if they could now see how well it was rooted, they would entertain no other sentiments, but that while it was gratifying to them to be the founders of so many monasteries for affording a retreat to consecrated persons, not the less did they rejoice that the same, seeing they superabounded, should be converted to the repelling of an impiety that threatened the destruction of that piety which with their own proper substance they sought to promote.]

After the concerns of Venice, which here once more present more elevated points of view, European concerns in general are also brought under notice.

The expeditions of Charles X. Gustavus made the greatest impression in Rome, and money was collected for the support of king Casimir.

But what was much more sensibly felt by the Roman court was, that the French not only showed themselves disinclined to conclude a truce with Spain, but that Mazarin even allied himself with England—a cardinal with protestants, the most Christian kingdom with the usurper who had expelled the legitimate princes—and that he did this without there being any need for it, without being led to it by any pressing peril whatever.

But for these troubles, the pope would direct his whole efforts to make Germany again Roman catholic—Germany, where his personal character was in such good repute. The queen of Sweden's change of her faith made men's hopes sanguine in this respect.

The ambassadors saw the splendid preparations that were made for that queen's reception. They could not reconcile to their notions the roving life she led ("fuori forse della convenienza dell' età e dello stato virginale" [incompatible, perhaps, with what is befitting her age and virginal condition], are the very discreet expressions they use), yet they give all justice to the vigour and courage of her determination.

"Ecco in compendio ciò che ci è parso di poter riferire" [Behold in a compendious form what it has seemed proper for us to report], says Pesaro, at this passage.

To this form of conclusion he further adds the good advice, ever to maintain to the utmost a good understanding with the pope.

The pope had fully spoken about the satisfaction it would give him were the Jesuits to be re-admitted into Venice at his request. The ambassador is for this being agreed to.

"Parmi che sia gionto il tempo di decidere se s' habbia a dar luogo a questo regresso, o pure, per non haver di quando in quando ad urtare per questa causa in male sodisfattioni con i pontefici, s' habbia da imporvi perpetuo silentio. . . . . A sodisfare intorno a ciò al desiderio del papa par che possa esser motivo il conoscersi che essendo questi huomini grandi istromenti a sostenere le ragioni della chiesa, i papi pro tempore rinnoveranno le medesime istanze, le quali rejette daranno ne' principj de' pontificati materia a male sodisfattioni."

[It appears to me that the time has arrived for deciding whether one ought to consent to this return, or in fine, in order to avoid occasions recurring from time to time of getting into bad terms with the pontiffs on this account, whether it should be consigned to perpetual silence. . . . It appears that it might be a motive for satisfying the pope's desire with regard to this, to be aware that these men, being great instruments in sustaining the rights of the church, popes for the time being will renew the same solicitations, the rejection of which will furnish matter for dissatisfaction to the principles of those who have been made popes.]

130.

Vita, attioni et operationi di Alessandro VII., opera del C[l] Pallavicini.—[Life, acts, and operations of Alexander VII., by Cardinal Pallavicini.] 2 vols. folio. (Bibl. Cors.)

In the Barberini library at Rome, there was put into my hand, one day, a manuscript, intituled, "*Alexandri VII. de vita propria liber primus et tertius cum fragmentis libri secundi*" [On his own life, by Alexander VII., books first and third, with fragments of book second]: a volume of about 300 leaves, so full of corrections as an autograph only can ever be, but by an unfortunate accident fallen into great confusion. The bookbinder had stitched up the only readable sheets in sets of five each. It was scarcely possible to understand it.

The commencement runs:—

"Res suo tempore gestas literis commendare, quamvis et nunc et olim usitatum, plerisque tamen eo nomine minus probatur quod arduum scriptori sit procul habere spem, metum, amorem, odium animi, nubes quae historiam, lucem veritatis, infuscant."

[Although it has been usual, both now and in former times, to commit to writing the transactions of one's own time, most who pretend to do so make little proof of the difficulty of keeping out the influence of hope, fear, love, hatred, the clouds which obscure history, the light of truth.]

Wherever I cast my eye there appeared interesting notices, and such as had been procured from good sources, on Alexander's youth, the calling of his nephews to Rome, the arrival of Christina: could the pope really, amid the engagements of the supreme spiritual government, have found time to write his life, and so diligently to correct the style throughout?

It soon appeared, in spite of the title, that this could not have been the case.

The author declares, among other things, that he had become capacitated for this work by a close intimacy with the pope.

"Fortunae obsecundantis beneficium fuit ut cum hoc principe inferiores gradus obtinente singularis intercesserit mihi animorum consensio et mutua tum ore tum literis consiliorum communicatio."

[It was the kindness of favouring fortune that with this prince, while passing through the inferior grades of his career, I should have had a singular agreement of sentiment and mutual exchange of counsels, both by word of mouth and letters.]

The ues on remains, who this intimate acquaintance, nay, confidant, of Alexander's might be. ti

Muratori relates, speaking of the year 1656, that the Jesuit Pallavicini had, at the commencement of Alexander's reign, which excited such splendid hopes, set himself to write the life of this pope; but that after the calling for the nephews, and the changes connected with that, the pen had dropt from his hand. Pallavicini was certainly a personal confidant of Alexander VII.; at the commencement of his reign he saw him every day: it seems possible that this may be a fragmentary work of Pallavicini.

After some fresh investigations, there was found in the same library a biography of Alexander VII., ascribed to cardinal Pallavicini. It was written indeed in Italian, yet the matter was worth the trouble of comparison.

The first glance showed that the Italian is the same work as the Latin. The first position runs thus:—

"E opinione di molti che non si debba scrivere historie se non delle cose antiche, intorno alle quali la speranza e la paura, l'amore e l'odio verso le persone commemorate non habbian luogo nè possono infoscare la verità."

[It is the opinion of many that no histories ought to be written but those of ancient things, with regard to which hope and fear, love and hatred towards the persons commemorated, have no place, and cannot mystify the truth.]

The other passage I adduced, runs in Italian:—

"Imperoche m' è toccato a sorte d' haber con questo principe nella sua minor fortuna una singolare e corrispondenza d' affetto e confidenza di communicationi hor con la lingua hor con la penna per lo spatio già di 30 anni."

[Since it fell to my lot to have with this prince, in his less advanced fortune, a singular both correspondence of affection and confidence of communications, at one time with the pen, at another with the tongue, for thirty years.]

Thus it goes on. The Latin copy evidently shows itself to be a translation from the Italian: only somewhat free, with the addition of a slight shade of thought.

Unluckily, however, the likeness between them was greater than I could have wished. As the Latin copy was in the very title announced to be a fragment, the Italian, too, was fragmentary throughout. After some elucidations of his earlier youth, the narrative took a leap at once to the election and first transactions of Alexander in the pontificate.

Seeking and wanting make us only more eager to find: I made inquiries in all quarters. Another copy was found at the Albani library, but that, too, was but fragmentary.

By this time, I thought I must content myself with what I had got, since in an anonymous biography of Pallavicini, I found quoted only a fragment of this history, and from the same books that were already known to me. At last, in the Corsini (library), I was fortunate enough to stumble upon one that was more complete. This is the one whose title I have given above, in two large folio volumes.

Here the work bears Pallavicini's name in the front, and proceeds without a break to the second chapter of the sixth book. In this form it first deserves to be seriously attended to and made use of for the history of that time.

The first book comprises the earlier history of Alexander VII.

"Stirpe, parentelle, natali, fanciullezza di Fabio Chigi:—studj, avvenimenti della pueritia:—studj filosofici e legali: amicitie particolari."

[The family, the kindred, the birth, the infancy of Fabio Chigi:—the studies and occurrences of his boyhood:—his philosophical and legal studies; his private friendships.]

All being chapters which the first copy also contains both in Latin and Italian, but to which the Corsini copy further adds:

"Azioni et esercitii pii:—viceleg:tione di Ferrara sotto Sacchetti:—nunciatura di Colonia."

[Pious deeds and exercises:—vice-legation of Ferrara under Sacchetti:—nuncioship of Cologne.]

The second book then proceeds to relate the government of Innocent X., and the share that Chigi took in it, in fourteen chapters, down to the conclave.

In the third we have the commencement of the pontificate. A general view of the state of Europe, of the church's states, the first economical regulations: referring likewise to the *Monti Vacabili*. The conversion of queen Christina of Sweden, which is handled copiously and *con amore*. I consider as respects this last, that when it has been maintained, as Arckenholtz, in his *Mémoires de Christine*, iv., 39, represents, that Pallavicini had written an *Historia di Christina regina di Suezia*—this assumption rested on an obscure knowledge of this fragment. The conversion is accounted for in the Latin copy in the following manner:

"In libris Tullii de natura deorum animadvertens veram religionem nonnisi unam, omnes falsas esse posse, super hac parte diu multumque cogitando laboravit.[1] Sollicita quoque fuit dubitare de liberorum operum bonorum pravorumque discrimine, nisi quantum alia salubria mundo sunt, alia perniciosa, cujusmodi naturalia sunt, et de divinae providentiae cura vel incuria circa humanas actiones, deque voluntate divina num certum cultum et statutam fidem requirat. Nullus fuit nobilis autor qui ea de re scripsisset, quem illa non perlustraret, non vir apprime doctus harum rerum in borealibus plagis cum quo sermocinari non studeret. Et proclivis interdum fuit ad opinandum, satis esse suae regionis palam colere religionem, caeterum vivere convenienter naturae. Ad extremum in hanc venit sententiam, deum, hoc est optimum, tyranno quovis pejorem fore si conscientiae morsibus acribus sed falsis humanum genus universum cruciaret, si mortalibus ab eodem insita notione communi grata sibi esse eorum sacrificia eorumque votis annuere nihil ea cuncta curaret." . . . .

[Noticing in Tully's books on the nature of the gods, that one religion only could be true but that all might be false, on that part she laboured much and long as the subject of her meditations. She was also led, in her anxiety, to doubt of any difference in free works, good and bad, except what arises from some being salutary to the world, others pernicious, of which sort natural ones are, and concerning the care or indifference of divine providence with respect to human actions, and respecting the divine will, whether it requires a certain worship and fixed faith. There was no great author who had written on that subject whom she did not read, no man excellently learned on those matters in the countries of the north with whom she did not eagerly seek to converse about them. Meanwhile she leant to the opinion that it was enough for her openly to follow the religion of her own country, and for the rest to live according to nature. At last she came to this opinion that God, that is the best of beings, would be worse than any tyrant were he to torture the whole human race with keen but false stings of conscience; and if after having implanted the general notion in mortals that their sacrifices are grateful to him, and that he assents to their vows, he were to pay no regard to these things. . . . .]

In the fourth, which in the Latin and the older copies appears only in part, the author begins with the calling of the nephews. "Raggioni che persuasero al papa di chiamare i nepoti. Discorsi di Roma."—[Reasons that induced the pope to call the nephews. What was said at Rome.] So far is it from being true, that the pen dropt from Pallavicini's hand when he came to this subject, that on the contrary he discusses at full length the occurrence itself, and the opinion entertained respecting it, at Rome.—Queen Christina's circumstances in Rome. The support granted her by the pope.

1 This passage is first made clear on comparing Cic. d. n. d. I., c. ii. (to which Gravert, Christina ii. 32, adverts). The words are "Opiniones (de rebus divinis) cum tam variae sint tamque inter se dissidentes, alterum fieri profecto potest ut earum nulla, alterum certe non potest ut plus una vera sit." [Seeing that opinions (on divine things) are so various and so inconsistent with each other, one thing may be that none of these (opinions) is true, another, it cannot be that more than one is true.] Here, too, we see the character of Pallavicini's historiography; he misleads, as if purposely, yet eludes the error—(lit. plays at bo-peep (*versteckt*) to error: *i. e.*, I suppose, does not allow himself to be convicted of deliberate deception.—Tr.

"La reina, ch' era vissuta con quella prodigalità la quale impoverisce senza il piacere e l' honore di spendere e che si esercita non in dare ma in lasciarsi rubare, nel tempo della sua dimora haveva impegnato tutte le gioje con la speranza delle future rimesse, nè per ciò li restava un scudo onde provedere al destinato viaggio. Però, sicome la necessità vince la vergogna, convenne che ella si facesse violenza in dimandar soccorso al pontefice, ma nelle maniere più lontane che seppe dal limosinare: e perche la lettera non arrossisce, il pregò per mezzo di questa a fare che alcun mercante le prestasse danaro con promessa d' intera restitutione."

[The queen, who had lived with that prodigality which impoverishes without either the pleasure or honour of spending, and who practised not giving away, but allowing herself to be robbed, during the time of her stay pledged all her jewels in hope of future remittances, nor by this did there remain a scudo whence to provide for her appointed journey. Accordingly, seeing that necessity conquers shame, it was necessary that she should do violence to herself by soliciting assistance from the pope, but in the remotest manner she could contrive from asking alms: and because a letter did not make her blush, she besought him by that method to contrive that some merchant should give her money with the promise of complete restitution.]

It did not seem to the pope very honourable to take upon himself the whole burthen of the debt as surety, without further advantage. He preferred causing to be handed over to her, through a confidential member of a religious order, probably Pallavicini himself, together with some golden and silver coins that had been struck at that time on the occasion of her entrance, a purse containing 10,000 sc., as a present, "con escusarne la pochezza per l' angustia dell' erario" [with an excuse for the smallness of the amount on the ground of the straits of the treasury]. "La reina nel ringratiare pianse alle volte per quella mistura d' affetti che sorgono in questi casi."—[The queen in thanking him wept at times from those mingled feelings which such cases usually call forth.] To the restoration of the Jesuit order in Venice also, Pallavicini devotes elucidations, quite in the tone that we have perceived in his history of the council of Trent.

There follows then, in the fifth book, the history of the year 1657. Promotions to the cardinalship. Buildings in S. Maria del Popolo, della Pace, and on St. Peter's Place.—Queen Christina in France. Monaldeschi, whose catastrophe is here related as follows.

"Mentre la regina si tratteneva in Fontanablò, Ludovico, il fratello di lui (Fr. Mar. Sentinelli), emulo nella gratia della padrona di Gian Rinaldo Monaldeschi principal gentil' huomo di questi paesi, per notitie, come si disse, mandategli di Roma dal prenominato fratello, scoperse a lei alcuni trattati del Monaldeschi per cui le appariva poco fedele: onde ella dopo haverlo convinto e trattane dalla sua bocca la confessione gli diede un' hora solamente di spatio per provedere alla coscienza con l' opera d' un sacerdote, e di poi, cio che appena le sarebbe stato permesso in Stocholm quando vi dominava, il fè uccidere per mano dell' istesso suo emulo."

[While the queen was amusing herself at Fontainebleau, Lewis, the brother of him (Fr. Mar. Sentinelli), a rival in the favour of the mistress of Gian Rinaldo Monaldeschi principal gentleman of those countries, by means of intimations, as it was said, sent to him from Rome by his forenamed brother, revealed to her some dealings of Monaldeschi by which he appeared to her far from faithful: accordingly, after having convicted him and drawn a confession from his mouth, she gave him only an hour's time to provide for his conscience with the aid of a priest, and afterwards, what would hardly have been allowed her in Stockholm when she reigned there, she caused him to be slain by the hand of his said rival.]

In the sixth book the author recurs to internal Roman affairs. He breaks off with the institutions with respect to the prelature for which Alexander demanded a fixed amount of revenues.

But even this, the most complete copy of this biography, far from comprises the pope's whole life.

131.

Paolo Casati ad Alessandro VII. sopra la regina di Suecia.—[Paul Casati to Alexander VII. on the queen of Sweden.] (Bibl. Alb.)

Malines and Casati were the two Jesuits who were dispatched by the general of the order to Stockholm, to convert the queen.

A private account of this expedition, written by Malines, is to be found in Arckenholtz, Tom. IV., App. n. 27.

Casati presented a far more copious, and, so to say, official report to Alexander VII.: a document written expressly for the purpose: "Alla Santita di N^{ro} Signore Alessandro VII." [To the holiness of our lord Alexander VII.], dated from the collegio Romano, 5th Dec. 1655,—and subscribed "Della Sta V^{ra} umilissimo servitore ed obedientissimo figlio in X^{to} Paolo Casati della Compagnia di Gesù" [From your holiness's most humble servant and most obedient son in Christ Paul Casati of the Company of Jesus], which brings out more thoroughly and satisfactorily the particular features of the case.

"Per ubbidire" [In obedience to], he begins, "ai cenni di V. Sta, che ha desiderato una breve memoria di quello è passato nella risolutione presa dalla regina Christina di Suecia di rinonciare il regno per rendersi cattolica, sono necessitato farmi un passo a dietro per spiegarne l' occasione, *conforme alle notitie havute dalla bocca della stessa regina*, alla quale mi assicuro non sia per essere se non di gusto che la Sta Vostra sia del tutto sinceramente informata" [the suggestions of your holiness, who have desired to have a brief memoir of what has passed in the resolution taken by the queen of Sweden to renounce her kingdom to make herself a catholic, I am under the necessity of taking a step backwards that I may explain the occasion, *in conformity with the notices had from the mouth of the said queen*, to whom I am sure it will be far from disagreeable that your holiness should be candidly informed of all].

The first notices of the earlier period are not, however, of much importance: the author has no right comprehension of the state of things in Sweden: he first becomes interesting where he speaks of religious matters.

"Havendo acquistato tanto di cognitione, cominciò far riflessione che molte delle cose della setta Luterana, in cui era stata allevata, non potevano sussistere, e cominciando ad esaminarle, più le teneva inconvenienti. Quindi cominciò con più diligenza a studiare nelle cose della religione e delle controversie, e trovando che quella in cui era nudrita non haveva apparenza di vera, si diede con straordinaria curiosità ad informarsi di tutte et a ponderare la difficoltà di ciascuna. Impiegò in questo lo spatio di cinque anni incirca, con grande perturbatione interna d' animo, poiche non trovava dove fermarsi: e misurando ogni cosa con discorso meramente humano, parevale che molte cose potessero essere mere inventioni politiche per trattenere la gente più semplice: e degl' argomenti che quelli d' una setta si servono contro d' un' altra, ella si serviva per ritorcerli contro quella stessa: così paragonava le cose di Mosè nel popolo Ebreo a ciò che fece Maometto negli Arabi. Dal che nasceva che non trovava alcuna religione che vera le paresse. Et io l'ho molte volte udita che s' accusava d' essere stata troppo profana in volere investigare i più alti misterj della divinità: poiche non ha lasciato a dietro alcun mistero della nostra fede che non habbia voluto esaminare, mentre cercava di quietare l' anima sua con trovare finalmente una religione, essendo che ogni sorte di libro che trattasse di cosa appartenente a ciò, ella leggeva, le capitarono anche molte cose degli antichi e de' gentili e d' athei. E se bene ella non giunse mai a tal cecità che dubitasse dell' esistenza di dio e sua unità con farne concetto come di cosa maggiore di tutte le altre, pure si lasciò empire la mente di molte difficoltà, delle quali poi varie volte discorressimo. E finalmente non trovava altra conchiusione se non che nell' esterno conveniva far cio che fanno gl' altri, stimando tutte le cose indifferenti, e non importar più seguir questa che quell' altra religione o setta, e bastar di non far cosa che fosse contro il dettame della ragione e di cui la persona potesse una volta arrossirsi d' haverla fatta. Con questo s' andò qualche tempo governando, e parevale d' haver trovato qualche riposo, massime che haveva scoperte altre persone (anche chiamate di lontano) da lei stimate per dotte e savie essere di poco differente parere, giacche erano fuori della vera religione cattolica da loro riprovata sin dalla fanciullezza. Ma il signore iddio, che voleva havere misericordia della regina nè lasciarla perire negl' errori dell' intelletto, giacche per l' altra parte haveva ottima volontà e desiderio di conoscere il vero e nell' oprare tal-

[Having acquired so much knowledge, she began to reflect that many of the things of the Lutheran sect, in which she had been brought up, could not be, and beginning to examine them, the more she held them to be unsuitable. Hence she began with more diligence to study in matters of religion and controversies, and finding that that in which she had been nursed, had not the appearance of the true, she gave herself with extraordinary curiosity to acquaint herself with all and to weigh the difficulties of each. She spent about five years at this task, with great internal perturbation of mind, seeing she found no settled ground of conviction: and pondering every thing with merely human discourse (of reason), it seemed to her that many things might be mere political inventions for the amusement of the simplest people: and she applied the arguments which those of one sect employ against another, in twisting them against that sect itself: thus she compared the things of Moses among the Hebrews with those done with Mahomet among the Arabs. The result of which was that she found no religion that seemed to her to be true. And I have many times heard her accuse herself of having been too profane in wishing to trace out the deepest mysteries of the divinity: seeing she left no mystery of our faith which she would not fain have examined, in her endeavours to quiet her mind with the final discovery of a religion, it being so that she read every sort of book that treated of matters relating to that, and further, there fell in her way many things of the ancients, and of the heathens and atheists. And albeit she never went so far as to fall into the blindness of doubting of the existence of God and his unity, together with the conception of him as greater than all things else, she yet allowed her mind to be filled with many difficulties, about which afterwards we discoursed at various times. And finally, she found no other conclusion beyond this that in outward things it was fitting to do as others did, considering all things indifferent, and that it mattered not whether one followed this or the other religion or sect, and that it sufficed that one did nothing contrary to the maxims of the country, and which one could at any time blush for having done. With this she went on governing for some time, and seemed to have found some repose, chiefly as she had discovered other persons (called also from a distance) whom she looked upon as learned and wise, to be of much the same opinion, since they were out of the true catholic religion repro-

mente si lasciava guidare dal lume della retta ragione, che più volte m' ha assicurato di non haver mai fatto cosa che guidicasse non doversi fare nè di cui possa arrossirsene (che queste sono le sue formole di parlare), cominciò a farle apprendere che dove si tratta della salute eterna dell' anima, ogn' altro interesse deve cedere e che l' errore in cosa tanto importante è d' eterno pregiuditio: onde ripigliò di nuovo il pensiere che dovea esservi qualche religione, e posto che l' huomo doveva havere pure una religione, tra tutte quelle che si sapeva fossero nel mondo, niuna le sembrava più ragionevole della cattolica: perciò facendosi più attenta riflessione, trovò che li suoi dogmi e istituti non sono così sciocchi come li ministri luterani (li chiamano pastori) vorriano far credere."

bated by them from infancy. But the Lord God, who desired to have mercy on the queen, did not leave her to perish in errors of the understanding, seeing on the other hand that she had the utmost willingness and desire to know the truth, and in acting thus followed the light of right reason, so as often to have assured me that she had never done anything that she judged she ought not to do, or for which she could blush (for these are her own modes of expressing herself), I began to make her apprehend that where the eternal salvation of the soul was in question, every other interest ought to yield, and that error in a matter of so much importance is of eternal prejudice: accordingly she recurred to the idea that there must be some religion, and assuming that man ought certainly to have a religion, among all that were known to be in the world, none seemed to her more reasonable than the catholic: therefore reflecting upon it more attentively, she found that its dogmas and institutions were not so foolish as the Lutheran ministers (they call them pastors) would have her believe.]

Now, as we cannot give admission to the whole work, the following minute account of the first meeting of the Jesuits with the queen, may suffice.

"Partiti d' Hamburg doppo due giornate a Rendsburg ci accompagnammo col signor senatore Rosenhan, che ritornava in Suecia, e con lui andammo sino a Roschilt, dove sono sepolti li re di Danimarca, toltone S. Canuto, il cui capo è a Ringstede. Egli tirò dritto a Elsenor per passare lo stretto, e noi andammo a Coppenhagen. Questa cognitione fatta col sig^{r} Rosenhan ci giovò poi in Stockholm per esser meno sospetti: e la regina un giorno dicendogli che non sapeva che concetto dovesse farsi di quei due Italiani, egli disse che non v' era di che temere, che erano buona gente, e ci usò sempre gran cortesia. Hebbimo pure fortuna nel viaggio d' unirci per alcune giornate col generale Wachtmeister gran scudiere del regno, il quale parimente ci fu di non poca utilità: perche essendo noi giunti in Stockholm alli 24 di Febbraro conforme lo stile antico, et havendo io il giorno seguente cercato di parlare a Gio. Holm, valletto di camera di Sua Maestà, per essere introdotto a presentare la lettera datami in Roma dal padre vicario generale, nè havendolo trovato, la sera detto generale fu occasione che Sua Maestà sapesse il mio arrivo. Mentre stava la regina cenando, due cavalieri si lamentavano che faceva freddo, e il generale Wachtmeister gli sgridò, dicendo che non havevano tanta paura del freddo due Italiani venuti in sua compagnia. Udì la regina questa contesa, e interrogatoli di che contendessero, udito ch' ebbe essere venuti due Italiani, richiese s' erano musici: ma rispondendo il generale che erano due galant' huomini che andavano vedendo il paese, Sua M^{ta} disse che per ogni modo li voleva vedere. Noi subito fummo avvisati di tutto cio ed esortati ad andare il giorno seguente alla corte: anzi dal sig^{r} Zaccaria Grimani nobile Veneto vi fummo condotti la mattina seguente e introdotti a salutare il conte Magnus de la Gardie primo ministro di Sua M^{ta} per ottenere per mezzo suo l' hònore di baciar la mano di Sua M^{ta}: egli con somma cortesia ci

[Setting out from Hamburg after having spent two days at Rendsburg, we went in company with the lord senator Rosenhan who was returning to Sweden, and with him we went as far as Roschilt where the kings of Denmark are buried, with the exception of St. Canute, whose head is at Ringstede. He went direct to Elsinore to pass the straits, and we to Copenhagen. This acquaintanceship made with lord Rosenhan, was of much use to us afterwards in Stockholm by making us less suspected: and the queen happening one day to say to him that she knew not what to think of those two Italians, he said there was no need of being afraid of them, that they were good people, and he always showed us great courtesy. We were fortunate enough on our journey to join company for some days with general Wachtmeister grand armour-bearer of the kingdom, who was equally of no small use to us: for as we reached Stockholm on the 24th of February, old style, and as on the day following, I sought to speak to John Holm, her Majesty's valet-de-chambre, in order to be introduced to present the letter given me in Rome by the father vicar-general, and not having found him, in the evening the said general was the occasion of her Majesty knowing of my arrival. While the queen was at supper, two knights complained of its being cold, and general Wachtmeister called out to them that two Italians who had come along with him, were not so much afraid of cold. The queen overheard this contention, and having asked what they were contending about, on hearing of the arrival of two Italians, asked if they were musicians: but on the general replying that they were two gentlemen who had come to see the country, her Majesty replied that she wished by all means to see them. We were suddenly advised of all this and recommended to go on the day following to the court: also, we were convoyed thither by signior Zaccaria Grimani, a noble Vene-

accolse e ci assicurò che Sua M^{ta} l' havria havuto molto a caro. Era l' hora del pranso, quando la regina usci nel Vierkant, e noi fummo avvisati d' accostarci a Sua M^{ta}, e baciatale la mano fecimo un piccolo complimento in Italiano (che cosi ella haveva comandato, se bene ci aveva fatto avvisare ch' averia risposto in Francese, giacche noi l' intendevamo) proportionato all' apparenza del personaggio che rappresentavamo: et ella con grandissima benignità rispose. Subito s' inviò il maresciallo della corte e con lui tutti li cavalieri verso la sala dove stava preparata la tavola, ed io mi trovai immediatamente d' avanti alla regina. Ella, che la notte ripensando alli due Italiani e facendo riflessione che appunto era il fine di Febbraro, circa il qual tempo da Roma se l' era scritto che saressimo giunti, era venuta in sospetto che noi fossimo quelli che aspettava, quando fossimo poco lontani dalla porta e che già tutti erano quasi usciti dal Vierkant, mi disse sottovoce: 'forse voi havete qualche lettera per me,' ed io senza voltarmi che sì; soggiunse: 'non ne parlate con alcuno.' Mentre noi il dopo pranso stavamo sopra cio che era seguito discorrendo, ecco supragiunge uno che in Francese ci fa varii complimenti, poi s' avvanza a dimandarci se haveriamo lettere per Sua M^{ta}. Io cominciai subito a dar risposte ambigue, che non havevamo negotii, che non havevamo lettere di raccomandatione etc., sin a tanto che egli alla fine disse per ordine tutto quello che nel breve e fortuito colloquio m' haveva detto la regina. Allora m' accorsi che da lei sola poteva esser mandato: pure per maggior sicurezza lo richiesi del suo nome, ed udito che egli era Gio. Holm, gli consegnai la lettera. La mattina seguente, quasi due hore prima del tempo solito d' andar alla corte, ci avvisò Gio. Holm che Sua M^{ta} voleva parlarci. Subito andammo: e appena erano entrati nel Vierkant, dove era solo l' officiale di guardia, quando uscì la regina, e mostrò di meravigliarsi, sì perche non fosse ivi ancora alcuno de' cavaglieri, sì perche noi fossimo stati i primi nell' andare: e dopo haverei interrogati d' alcune poche cose intorno al nostro viaggio, udendo l' officiale, gli dimandò se fosse comparso alcuno de' segretarii, e rispondendo quegli che no, comandolli andasse a chiamare uno di loro, e non tornò che dopo un' hora. Partito che ei fu, cominciò Sua M^{ta} con cortesissime parole a ringratiarci della fatica presa da noi per sua cagione nel viaggio, ci assicurò che qualunque pericolo potesse occorrere d' essere scoperti, non temessimo, perche non haveria permesso havessimo male alcuno. C' incaricò il segreto nè ci fidassimo di persona, additandoci nominatamente alcuni de' quali dubitava potessimo bavere confidenza in progresso di tempo: ci diede speranza che havendo ella sodisfattione il nostro viaggio non saria stato indarno: c' interrogò dell' arrivo del padre Macedo e come noi fossimo stati eletti per andare colà: ci raccontò come fosse succeduta la partenza del padre Macedo... ."

tian, on the following morning, and introduced to pay our respects to Count Magnus de la Gardie, her Majesty's prime minister, in order by his intervention to obtain the honour of kissing her Majesty's hand: he received us with the utmost politeness, and assured us that her Majesty would be very glad of it. It was the hour of dinner, and the queen came out into Vierkant and we were recommended to accost her Majesty, and having kissed her hand, we made a short complimentary address in Italian (for thus she had commanded, although she had caused it to be intimated to us that she would reply in French, since we understood it) suitable to the lustre of the personage whom we represented: and she replied with the utmost kindness. Forthwith she sent the marshal of the court and along with him all the knights towards the hall where the table was set out, and I found myself in the queen's immediate presence. She having thought much during the night of the two Italians and reflecting that it was exactly the end of February, about which time it had been written to her from Rome that we should arrive, began to suspect that we were the persons she was looking for, when we were not very far from the door, and almost all were already gone out of Vierkant, she said to me in a low tone: 'perhaps you have some letter for me,' and I without turning round said, yes; she added; 'say nothing about it to any one.' While after dinner we stood talking over what had taken place, behold there unexpectedly arrived one who paid us various compliments in French, and then stepped forward to ask if we had letters for her Majesty. I began forthwith to make equivocal replies, that we had no affairs to transact, had no letters of introduction, etc., so as that at last he repeated word for word all that in the short casual conversation the queen had said to me. It then struck me that he could have been sent by none but her: yet for greater certainty I asked him his name, and hearing that he was John Holm, I handed him the letter. On the following morning, about two hours before the usual time of going to court, John Holm gave us notice that her Majesty wanted to speak with us. We went to her immediately, and hardly had entered Vierkant, where there was only the officer on guard, when the queen came out, and expressed surprise both because none of the knights as yet were there, and because we were the first to go thither, and after having asked about some little matters relating to our journey, hearing the officer, she asked him if any of the secretaries had made their appearance, and on his answering no, she told him to go and call one of them, and he did not return for an hour. On his departure her Majesty began with the most courteous expressions to thank us for the trouble we had taken in coming, assured us that whatever danger might arise from being discovered, we should not be afraid, for she would not suffer us to be subjected to any harm. She enjoined on us secrecy, and that we should trust ourselves to nobody; pointing out to us by name some of whom she dreaded lest we should give our

confidence to them in progress of time: she led us to hope that in case of her receiving satisfaction, our journey would not be in vain: she asked us about the arrival of father Macedo, and how we had been selected for going there: she related how the departure of father Macedo had taken place. . . . .]

132.

Relatione della corte Romana del Caval. Corraro 1660.—[The Cavalier Corraro's report on the Roman court, 1660.]

In point of fact splendid hopes had been entertained of Alexander VII. Court and state expected their restoration, the church the re-establishment of her ancient discipline from him: accordingly, general wonder and amazement were excited on his beginning so soon to reign just as his predecessors had done. The favourable opinion entertained of him suddenly changed into a vehement dislike to him.

The first ambassador that the Venetians had in Rome after that congratulation embassy, was Jerome Giustiniano. His dispatches fall in the year 1656. He died of the plague.

In his place there was appointed Anzolo Corraro, at the time podesta of Padua. He lingered so long that another had already been chosen instead of him: on this, however, he hastened to Rome, and resided there from 1657 to 1659.

The report which he presented on his return from the court, turned out to be not very favourable. The pope and his family were overwhelmed with censures.

Meanwhile it is unnecessary for us, for the sake of one particular circumstance, to give a copious extract from it.

This report produced so lively an impression that it immediately found its way into the hands of the public.

A French translation of it appeared at Leyden: Relation de la cour de Rome faite l'an 1661 (0), au conseil de Pregadi par l' excell^{mo} Seigneur Angelo Corraro:—chez Lorens, 1663, which, wherever I have compared them, fully gives the meaning of the Italian original, and to this day is not rare.

It was printed at the moment when Chigi's quarrel with Crequi had attracted general attention at Rome: the publication must have served to inflame public opinion against the pope. It is dedicated to Beuningen, who had not yet said, "Sta sol."

133.

Relatione di Roma dell' excellent^{mo} Sig^{r} Niccolò Sagredo.—[Report from Rome from the most excellent Signor Niccolo Sagredo.] 1661.

A report of which I saw no authentic copy, and which is to be found also under the name of Anzolo Correr.

But as there can be no doubt that the last preceding is really to be ascribed to Correr, whose active co-operation in the war against the Barberini is expressly mentioned in it, and as in the one before us, on the other hand, the author expresses a wish that after being relieved from twenty-seven years' wanderings, he might now devote himself at home to the education of his children, which does not truly apply to Correr, who had last been podesta in Padua, I have no hesitation in holding the name of Sagredo to be the right one. Sagredo, as we know, had by that time been once sent as ambassador to Rome and afterwards to Vienna: now he went for a second time to Rome. He was generally one of the most employed of the Venetian statesmen, and at length became doge.

The report is far from being so severe as the previous one, yet no more does it deal in eulogy: it bears the stamp rather of unimpassioned observation.

Speaking of the adoption of the nephews, Sagredo remarks that pope Alexander, oddly enough, even then complained loudly of the riches of the Borghesi, the Barberini, and the Ludovisi, when already he himself was omitting no opportunity of enriching his own nephews.

Description of this pope:—

"Placido e soave: nei negotii nè facile nè molto disposto: per natura è dubbioso nelle risolutioni grandi, osia per timore che non rieschino, o perche mal volontieri s' affatichi nel procurarle, da ogni spina, benche lontana, parendogli sentirsi pungere."

[Placid and gentle: in business neither ready nor much prepared: he is naturally of a hesitating temper in great resolutions, whether from dreading that they may not succeed, or from disliking trouble in promoting them, he feels himself pricked by every thorn, however distant.]

He thought he had done enough for the Venetians by the suppression of the religious orders: in process of time, however, the Candian war did not appear even to him to be formidable. What immediately touched him was that Parma and Modena, with their claims on the church-state, were supported by France. Neither was the Portuguese affair voided.

"Vedutosi quel regno in mancanza assoluta di vescovi e dilapidate le rendite di tutte le

[That kingdom being seen to be in absolute want of bishops, and the revenues of all the

chiese, si sono sentiti molti clamori non solo, ma vivissime l' instanze del card[l] Orsino protettore, perche fossero provedute: ma non si è lasciato condurre il papa mai a farlo."

[churches dilapidated, not only were many clamours heard, but the most urgent entreaties were made on the part of cardinal Orsino that they might be provided for: yet the pope has never allowed himself to be induced to do so.]

In general we find the popedom already engaged in differences with most of the Roman catholic states. There was not one of them which the jurisdictional and pecuniary claims of the curia had not horrified.

First of what had taken place in Rome, the author mentions Alexander's buildings. We see that the general opinion vastly preferred the Cattedra di S. Pietro, in Peter's church, to the colonnades. In the city itself the work of beautification often went violently forward.

"Molte strade della città con getti di case e di palazzi drizzate: levatesi le colonne et impedimenti che stavano avanti le porte di particulari; allargatasi la piazza Colonna del collegio Romano ad istanza de' Gesuiti col abbattimento del nobilissimo palazzo Salviati: ristrettisi tutti i tavolati delle botteghe: opere tutte che come riescono in fine di grand' ornamento della città, così il peso delle medesime su la borsa de' privati cadendo, non puonno che delle mormorationi partorire, il vedersi gittar a terra il proprio nido, il contribuirsi summe rilevanti per l' aggiustamento di strade ch' ai medesimi particulari nulla profittano, sotto colore che le loro habitationi habbiano a godere della vista più bella, non equivalendo all' aggravio che ne risentono et alla forza con cui sono a consentirvi costretti."

[Many streets of the city are made straight by throwing down houses and palaces: the columns and other impediments that stood before the doors of private persons, are removed: the piazza Colonna of the collegio Romano has been enlarged, at the request of the Jesuits, by pulling down of that most noble building, the Salviati palace: the space occupied by the shops has been everywhere restricted: all being operations which, while they result at last in the great ornament of the city, so the burthen thereof falling upon the purse of private persons, cannot fail to cause murmurs at seeing one's own nest thrown down, contributing considerable sums for the proper adjustment of streets that are of no advantage to these same individuals, under the pretext that their dwellings may enjoy the finest views, that being no equivalent for the hardship which they suffer from it, and for the violence done to them in compelling their consent to it.]

134.

Relatione di Roma del K[r] Pietro Basadona.—[Report from Rome, by the Chevalier Peter Basadona.] 1663.

Written in the manner of Corraro, who however is exceeded here. I will introduce some passages.

First, upon the quarrel with France, unquestionably the most important occurrence that took place during this embassy.

"Quanto alle brighe correnti, so di bavere nelle mie successive lettere dispolpate le ossa di tal materia quanto conviene: però non devo tacere che se l' imprudente suberbia fece cadere i Chigi nella fossa, l' ambitiosa mellonagine vi gli babbia miseramente inviluppati. Costoro si persuadevano che Roma fosse il mondo: ma il re di Francia a spese loro gli ha dato a divedere che non havevano bene studiata la geografia. Varie ciarle hanno divolgate le passioni degli huomini circa l'insolenza d' imperiali e di Don Mario contra l' immunità dell ambasciatore Francese. Io non dirò che fossero innocenti, ma effettivamente affermo che congiunta alla loro mala volontà qualche colpa del caso, che accresce o sminuisce non di rado le humane operationi, li constituisca per rei et obligati a rendere puntualmente soddisfatte le pretensioni che il re di Francia può legitimamente fondare sulle ingiurie pur troppo sostenute nella persona del suo ministro: e sicome io conobbi questa verità, così contribuii indefessa applicatione per intepidire le mosse di Crequi, e prima che le cose corressero a manifesta rovina, saldare le scissura col balsamo de' negotiati. Ma erano troppi umori nelle teste Chigiarde e troppa ostinatione per condescendere ad una convenevole humiliatione

[As for the current troubles, I know that in my last successive letters I have given the marrow of such matters as it was fitting that I should write about: in a word, I ought not to conceal that if impudent pride made the Chigi fall into the ditch, ambitious folly has miserably entangled them in it. These persuaded themselves that Rome was the world; but the king of France has made them see to their cost that they have not studied geography well. Men's passions have given rise to much gossipping about the insolence of the imperialists and of Don Mario against the immunities of the French ambassador. I will not say that they are innocent, but positively affirm that there being conjoined to their ill-will some fault of fortune, which not seldom increases or diminishes human proceedings, constituted them guilty persons, and obliged them to see to the punctual satisfaction of the pretensions which the king of France could legitimately found upon the insults, too much sustained, in the person of his minister: and as I know the truth of this, so I contributed with indefatigable application to cool down Crequi's movements, and to salve the schism with the balsam of negotiations ere matters had run into manifest ruin. But there were too many whims in the

verso il re, di cui non si volevano temere le bravate, quasiche fatte in credenza e non durabili più di una effimera Francese. Insino mi hebbe a dire Sua B^ne^ che i cuori Romani non havevano paura delle smargiassate de giovinastri Parigini. Al che risposi, complire tal volta più pigliarsela con gli assennati vecchioni che con giovinastri cervelletti, i quali sogliono per isfogare un favorito capriccio avventurarsi anche sull' orlo de precipitii, e che il trescare con chi ha de grilli in capo, esserciti a fianchi e milioni sotto i piedi, non era buon giuoco per li pontefici, che hanno solamente le due dita alzate. Rappresentai più volte, quando si vide che il re diceva da senno, essersi pur troppo ruinato il dominio ecclesiastico dai quattordeci milioni che spese nella guerra Barberina, che i milioni di cui la camera è debitrice passano cinquanta, e che in somma Sua Sta senza rovinarsi non poteva armarsi, senza perdersi non poteva combattere, anzi che senza combattere il nemico poteva rovinarlo. Ma vane furono queste e cento altre più massiccie ragioni, havendo troppo amore per non alontanarsi i parenti e troppo umore per il puntiglio di Castro. Ed un giorno che lo trovai di vena, mi disse queste formali parole: 'Tutti esclamano che si scameri Castro, e nessuno dice che si restituischi Avignone: tutti espongono che il re merita esser risarcito degli affronti presenti ricevuti, e nessuno parla che si rifacciano gli strapazzi degli ecclesiastici; se fosse vero, come si sa non essere, che imperiali e nostro fratello Mario habbiamo dati gli ordini a Corsi contro l'ambasciatore e potrebbe il re pretendere soddisfattione contro questi due: ma come ci entra Castro? e poi se Mario è innocente, come si ha d' allontanare da noi?'"

Chigi heads, and too much obstinacy withal, to condescend to a kindly humiliation towards the king, whose bravings they did not wish to dread, looking upon them as mere make-believes, that would prove no more lasting than a French ephemeral fit of boasting. So much so, that his Beatitude told me that Roman hearts felt no alarm at the bullyings of Parisian striplings. To which I replied, that it was sometimes more fitting to have to do with wise old men than with hot-brained striplings, who are wont, rather than not humour some favourite whim, to venture to the edge of precipices; and that to play with those who have crotchets in their heads, armies at their sides, and millions under their feet, is no good game for the pontiffs, who have nothing but their two raised fingers. I often represented, when it appeared that the king spoke in earnest, that the ecclesiastical dominion was quite too much ruined by the fourteen millions spent in the Barberini war, that the millions owing by the chamber exceeded fifty, and that, in fine, his holiness could not take up arms without ruining himself, could not fight without being utterly destroyed; on the contrary, without fighting, the enemy could ruin him. But in vain were these, and a hundred other powerful reasons, for he had too much affection to forsake his relations, and was too whimsical about the Castro cavil. And one day that I found him in the humour, he said to me, expressly, "All exclaim that Castro should be taken out (of the church's dominion), but none says that Avignon should be restored: all represent that satisfaction should be made to the king for the present affronts he has received, and none speaks of reparation to be made for what has been snatched from the clergy; were it true, as it is not known to be, that we gave the imperialists and our brother Mario orders for the Corsicans against the ambassador, and could the king claim satisfaction against these two: but what has Castro to do with that? and then if Mario is innocent, why should he have to be removed from us?"]

Thus does it proceed: self-sufficient invectives: a profound contempt for that whole ecclesiastical system: a completely modern tone of feeling. The possibility of the French being able to make themselves masters of Rome was already contemplated. One might doubt, at times, whether such things could really have been ventured to be stated in the senate. But if we consider that, at that very time, violent attacks were raised on all sides (there appeared the wildest satires, for example Le Putanisme de Rome, in which it is directly said that people must give the pope a wife, in order to obviate other evils, and make the popedom hereditary), that this was the epoch in which its credit began generally to decline, it does not appear so unlikely. For the rest, the author was very well acquainted with both court and state. He well deserves to be further heard on the ecclesiastical state.

"Si palpa con mano, l' ecclesiastico dominio essere totalmente aggravato, si che molti possessori non potendo estrarre da i loro terreni quanto basti a pagare le publiche imposizioni straordinariamente aggiunte, trovano di consiglio di necessità l' abbandonare i loro fondi e cercare da paese men rapace la fortuna di poter vivere. Taccio de datii e gabelle sopra tutte le robe comestibili, niuna eccettuata: perche le taglie, i donativi, i sussidii e le altre straordinarie angherie che studiosamente s'inventano, sono tali che eccitarebbono compassione e stupore se i terrabili commissarii che spedisce Roma nelle città suddite con suprema autorità d' inquirere,

[It is a palpable fact, that the ecclesiastical dominions are totally oppressed, so that many proprietors being unable to extract from their lands as much as suffices to pay the public imposts, now that these are extraordinarily increased, find it a matter of necessity to abandon their properties, and to seek a chance of living from countries that are less rapacious. I blame the *datii* and *gabelle* on all eatable commodities, without any exception: for the poll-taxes, the donatives, the subsidies, and the other extraordinary oppressions that are studiously invented, are such as would excite compassion and amazement, if the terrible commissaries sent by Rome into the subject

vendere, asportare, condannare, non eccedessero ogni credenza, non essendo mai mese che non volino su le poste grifoni ed arpie col sopramantello di commissarii o della fabrica di S. Pietro o de legati pii o de spoglii o degli archivii o di venticinque altri tribunali Romani: onde restano martirizzate le borse, benche esauste, de' sudditi impotenti ad ultima prova. E però, se si pongono da parte Ferrara e Bologna, con le quali si usa qualche riguardo e le quali sono favorite dalla natura ed arte di ottimi terreni e di mercatura industriosa, tutte le altre città della Romagna, della Marca, Umbria, Patrimonio, Sabina e Territorio di Roma sono miserabili per ogni rispetto: nè trovasi (oh vergogna de Romani comandanti) in alcuna città l' arte della lana o della seta, non che de panni d' oro, se due o tre picciole bicocche di Fossombrone, Pergola, Matelica, Camerino e Norcia n' eccettuo: e pure facilmente per l' abbondanza della lana e seta si potrebbe introdurre ogni vantagievole mercatura. Ma essendo il dominio ecclesiastico un terreno che si ha ad affitto, coloro che lo noleggiano, non pensano a bonificarlo, ma solamente a cavarne quella pinguedine che può spremersene maggiore che sia del povero campo, che smunto et arido a nuovi affittuali non havrà agio di porgere che sterilissimi suffragj. E pare arso l' erario pontificio da un abisso di voragine: si hebbe per bene armare per due volte, quasi che il primo errore, che costò due milioni, fosse stato imitabile per qualche civanzo alla difesa dello stato, quando alle prime rotture ogni prudenza insegnava a stringere l' accomodamento per (non) dare pretesto a Francia di chieder peggio. Un calcolo, che feci nella mozzatura di quattro e mezzo per cento che rendevano i luoghi de monti, come fanno di sette per cento nella nostra zecca, ridotti a quattro solamente, trovai che a un mezzo scudo per cento in cinquanta milioni effettivi di debito, la camera venne a guadagnare 250 m. scudi di entrata, che a quattro per cento formarebbe un capitale di sei milioni e mezzo."

cities with supreme authority to inquire into, sell, carry off, and condemn, did not exceed all belief, never a month passing that there do not fly on the posts griffons and harpies dressed in the mantles of office of commissaries for the building of St. Peter's, or of pious legacies, or of the *spoglii*, or of the *archivii*, or of the five-and-twenty other Roman tribunals: whence the coffers, however exhausted, of the subjects reduced to the last degree of impotency, are martyrized. And, accordingly, if we set aside Ferrara and Bologna, with which some measure is used, and which are favoured by nature and art with the richest lands and industrious trafficking, all the other cities of the Romagna, of the Mark, Umbria, the Patrimony, Sabina, and the Territory of Rome, are wretched in every respect: there is not to be found (oh, shame of Roman commandants!) in any city woollen or silk manufactures, nor that of cloth of gold, if we except two or three small villages of Fossombrone, Pergola, Matelica, Camerino, and Norcia: and indeed, owing to the abundance of wool and silk, every advantageous merchandise might be easily introduced. But the ecclesiastical dominion being a territory which is let to tenants, those who rent it have no thought of improving it, but only of extracting from it whatever fatness can be squeezed out of it more than from the poor plain, which left exhausted and dried up for new tenants, will not have rest enough to admit of making but the most barren returns. And the pontifical treasury seems burnt up by an all-devouring abyss: it was thought good to arm twice, as if the first error, which cost two millions, should have been to be imitated for some interest in the defence of the state, when at the first ruptures every dictate of prudence taught the propriety of coming to an accommodation, so as (not) to give to give France a pretext for requiring worse terms. Calculating on the reduction of $4\frac{1}{2}$ per cent. given by the *luoghi de monti*, as 7 per cent. is in our mint, to 4 only, I found that at half a scudo per cent. on fifty millions of actual debt, the chamber would come to gain 250,000 scudi of revenue, which, at 4 per cent., would form a capital of six millions and a half.]

135.

Vita di Alessandro VII. Con la descrizione delle sue adherenze e governo. 1666.—[Life of Alexander VII. With the description of his adherents and governments. 1666.]

Not a biography, at least such as Pallavicini's; but a general account of the transactions of this pope, according to the impression they produced in Rome, by a well-informed and, on the whole, well-intentioned contemporary.

"Egli è" [He is], it says of the pope, "veramente d'animo pio, religioso, divoto, e vorrebbe operare miracoli per conservatione del christianesimo: . . . . ma è pigro, timido, irresoluto, e molte volte mal opera per non operare"—[truly of a pious, religious, devout mind, and would work miracles for the preservation of Christianity: but he is slow, timid, irresolute, and many a time does ill by doing nothing. He began by inveighing against nepotism, and yet afterwards practised it to a great extent. All economical arrangements were in the hands of the nephews: they greatly enriched themselves; the contentions with Crequi were absolutely to be imputed to their fault; the pope reserved to himself foreign affairs alone. But to these he paid too little attention. He had literary meetings at home which took away much of his time: in the evening Rospigliosi conversed with him for an hour. In point of fact, business proceeded but very indifferently. The pope answered people in general expressions, yet without there being any minister to whom they might apply.

136.

Relatione di Roma di Giacomo Quirini K^r 1667 (8), 20 Febr.—[The Chevalier James Quirini's Report on Rome, 1667 (8), 20th February.]

J. Quirini was accredited three years and a half with Alexander VII., and thereafter for some time with Clement X.: his report embraces the whole of this period.

He first describes the last years of Alexander VII., not indeed with the animosity of his predecessor, but essentially in the same temper.

"In 42 mesi che servii Alessandro VII., conobbi esservi il solo nome del pontefice, ma non l'uso del pontificato, datosi quel capo alla quiete dell' animo, al solo pensiere di vivere, e con severo divieto ripudiato il negotio, scemate tutte quelle virtù che da cardinale prestantemente teneva con vivacità di spirito, ingegno nel distinguere, prontezza nei partiti, disinvoltura nel risolvere e facilità supragrande dell' esprimersi."

[In the course of forty-two months in which I served with Alexander VII., I could perceive that he had no more than the name of a pope, not the exercise of the popedom; that chief being devoted to quiet of mind, to a purely thoughtful existence, and repudiating business with a severe resolution to avoid it, all the virtues which he possessed so eminently as a cardinal, together with vivacity of spirit, a discriminating judgment, promptness in trying conjunctures, dexterity in resolving difficulties, and extraordinary facility of expression, having disappeared.]

He describes the abuses of nepotism. He even predicts the bad cousequences that would follow from the erection of saltworks (?) at S. Pietro, for which the chevalier Bernini has been blamed.

"Renderà per sempre disabitata la città Leonina, spianate le case, moltiplicate l' acque delle fontane, scemati i fuochi: cagiona in conseguenza la mal' aria."

[It will render the town of Leonina for ever uninhabitable, the houses having been levelled, the waters of the wells having been multiplied, the hearths taken away: the cousequence of which is the mal' aria.]

He discusses the abuses of the pensions, and of the giving away of places, with a special reference to Venice, from which there went every year to Rome 100,000 ducats. It is remarkable that Alexander VII., on his side, was particularly dissatisfied with the cardinals: he complained that they attached themselves to the princes, even in the affair of Castro, that they never on any occasion knew how to advise him well.

"Si lagnava non esser dottrina e virtù sodisfacente in quei porporati, non arricordando mai ripieghi o partiti che prima lui non li sapesse."

[He lamented that there was not a satisfactory amount of learning and virtue among those persons in purple, as they never suggested replies or measures that he was not first himself aware of.]

The declension was general.

The conclave was ruled by Chigi's subserviency to the squadrone volante. Yet it appeared afterwards that in this Chigi had acted very properly. He had to thank this subserviency for Clement IX.'s allowing him a share of the government.

Quirini thinks Clement IX. weakly, oppressed with ailments, firm, nay, obstinate in his opinions: he would, at times, forbid his ministers to speak any more on a subject upon which he had made up his mind. A musician from Pistoja, of the name of Atto, had confidential access to him. His resolving to remit part of the taxes is considered as heroic by Quirini: "Mostrò eroica pietà, levando due giulj di gabella di macinato dei rubiatelli, privandosi di 2 milioni di scudi."—[He showed heroic piety in taking off two julios of multure-tax of the rubiatelli, thus depriving himself of two millions of scudi.]

He proceeds to speak of the family of Clement IX., particularly cardinal Rospigliosi, whom he describes as follows:—

"Tuttoche il giorno innanzi della mia partenza seguisse la promotione, restando al cardinalato promosso l' abate Rospigliosi in età di 38 anni finiti, ciò non ostante, avendolo per due volte conosciuto in Spagna e trattatolo in Roma con negotii diversi come coppiere del cardinal Chigi, posso con distinta cognitione riferire all' EE. VV. che il papa parlando meco frequentemente nelle audienze e lasciandosi con giustizia rapire lo considerava per cauto ministro, e per consentimento comune gli attribuiva merito e lode: et in questo credo che moralmente non si possa ingannare, perche niun nipote di papa è comparso in teatro più informato di lui, mentre in corte cattolica fu sempre a parte della lunga nunciatura del zio. Nella secretaria di stato in Roma era l' unico direttore, for-

[Albeit that on the day previous to my departure the promotion took place, the abbot Rospigliosi at the age of thirty-eight years complete remaining promoted to the cardinalship, notwithstanding this, having twice known him in Spain, and negotiated sundry matters with him in Rome as cup-bearer of cardinal Chigi, I can from a distinct knowledge report to your excellencies that the pope, often talking with me at the audiences, and allowing himself with justice to be highly pleased, considered him as a cautious minister, and with the general consent attributed merit and praise to him: and in this I believe that morally he cannot be deceived, for no nephew of a pope has appeared upon the scene better than he, while in the catholic court he was always connected with his uncle's

mando lettere e risposte negli affari de' principi. Insorti poi li turbini per le pessime risolutioni con l' ambasciatore Crechi fu prima espedito a S. Quirico e poi a Livorno, con intentione più tosto di portar le lusinghe di palazzo che di soddisfare l' ambasciator duca: et aggiustato in fine il negotio fu nella legatione di Chigi spedito in Francia a consultare le formalità del trattamento: e ritornato in Roma col titolo d' internuncio passè in Fiandra: et assunto al pontificato papa Clemente credè con la speranza e con l' opinione di poter conciliare le differenze conservando nello stesso tempo gli ornamenti della pace e rimuovere i pericoli della guerra, dove gli espedì la plenipotenza per aggiustare i dispareri vertenti tra le corone. Nelli di cui viaggi et impieghi siccome nei primi giorni profuse con grande generosità molt' oro: così, caduto mortalmente infermo in Susa, convenne con prodigalità dispensare infinito contante, a segno che 140 m. scudi ne risente d' aggravio la camera apostolica. Nel resto il naturale suo è melanconico: uomo di poche parole e ritirato in se stesso: et in tanti anni di conversationi e d' anticamera si dimostrò con tutti indifferente, non palesando sviscerata amicitia o confidenza con alcuno, essendo più tosto misurato che sostenuto nei discorsi: et hora a causa del patimento sofferto resta per qualche momento predominato da certa fissatione de' pensieri, e tende nel negotio, nelle visite e nell' agitatione della corte s' applica e divertisca: con tutto cio dirige la secretaria di stato il card[l] Azzolini sottoscrivendo lo stesso cardinale gli ordini alle legationi non meno che alle nunciature de' principi. Sin qui resta poi dalla beneficenza del papa proveduto di 3 m. scudi di pensioni e badie che teneva il pontefice, di quattro mila scudi per la morte del card[lo] Palotta, e di dodici m. scudi della legatione d'Avignone come cardinal padrone."

long nuncioship. He had the sole direction at the secretaryship of state in Rome, drawing up the letters and answers to the princes. Then, on the outbreak of the troubles caused by the wretchedly-bad resolutions adopted with respect to the ambassador Crequi, he was first sent to S. Quirico and afterwards to Leghorn, for the purpose rather of carrying with him the coaxings of the palace than of satisfying the ambassador duke: and the matter being finally adjusted he was dispatched to France in Chigi's legation to consult about the formalities of the treaty: and having come back to Rome with the title of internuncio he passed into Flanders: and on Clement IX. being raised to the popedom he trusted with the hope and opinion of being able to reconcile (existing) differences, at once preserving the ornaments of peace and removing the perils of war, he sent him there full powers for adjusting the differences agitated between the crowns. In which journeys and employments as at the commencement he lavished much gold with great generosity; so having fallen mortally ill at Susa, it was found necessary to spend prodigally an immense quantity of cash, to such an extent indeed, that the apostolic chamber feels the burthen of it to the amount of 140,000 scudi. For the rest he is naturally melancholy: a man of few words and self-retired: and in so many years spent in conferring with others and in the ante-chamber he shows no preference for any one, being rather restrained than proud in conversing with others: and now owing to the sufferings he has felt he remains for some time in a sort of abstraction, and cannot get on with business, and spends his time and takes his enjoyment in the visits and bustle of the court. Till now he remains provided by the pope's kindness with 3,000 scudi of pensions and abbacies which the pope held, with 4,000 scudi by the death of cardinal Palotta, and with 12,000 scudi from the Avignon legation as cardinal padrone.]

137.

Relatione della corte di Roma al re christianissimo dal S[r] di Charme 1669.—[Report from the court of Rome to his most Christian Majesty by the seignior di Charme, 1669.]

This report has been printed in both French and Italian, yet, on which very account probably it has been printed, it contains but little that is of importance.

The disorders of the apostolic chamber are here to be discussed: how little it contributed to remedy these, that Clement IX. kept his nephews in straitened circumstances; also, how no congregation did any thing effectual, and a general bankruptcy was to be apprehended.

Grimani's observations on the want of a sufficient supply of capable persons, on Rospigliosi's good intentions and little energy, on the state of the prelature and of the country, are here confirmed.

There are additions in which a good deal has been taken directly out of Grimani.

Yet I may suggest a doubt whether this work really came from a French ambassador: it must have been the duke de Chaulnes, whom we find as ambassador in Rome in the *Négociations relatives à la succession d' Espagne*, II. p. 579: but at all events it is from a not unintelligent contemporary.

138.

Relatione della corte di Roma del sig[r] Antonio Grimani, ambasciatore della republica di Venetia in Roma durante il pontificato di Clemente IX. 1670.—[Report from the court of Rome by seignior Antonio Grimani, ambassador of the republic of Venice in Rome during the pontificate of Clement IX. 1670.]

Quirini expressed himself somewhat doubtfully of the virtues of Clement IX. The experience people had had of Alexander VII. might make him hesitate. Grimani, on the

contrary, breaks out into unbounded commendation, at least, as far as respects morals. "Veramente la mansuetudine, la modestia, la piacevolezza, la moderatione, la clemenza, la candidezza dell' animo, la purità della conscienza sono doti sue particolari."—[Truly meekness, modesty, affability, moderation, clemency, candour, purity of conscience, are his particular endowments.] He asserts that he never knew a better man.

He first speaks of the moderation with which Clement provided for his nephews. Yet it appears that in Rome people found much to say to the contrary. Grimani even thought that the Pistojans would even one day revenge themselves on the nephews for the unexpected neglect with which they were treated.

Therewithal too, it no doubt remains certain that Clement took no serious measures for the removal of remaining abuses: people already exclaimed that if no new Sixtus V. arrived, the pontificate was in danger of being subverted altogether.

Grimani recounts the principal evils: the venality of offices, whence arose the deficiency of capable persons; bad financial arrangements; particularly the neglect of the monks.

"Al presente i religiosi sono tenuti in un concetto si vile che da per loro si allontanano di comparir nella corte per non ricevere affronti da' cortigiani più infimi. Le porpore e vescovadi si tengono vilipesi su le spalle de' religiosi, e nelle concorrenze un pretuccio ignorante e vitioso otteuerà il premio sopra il religioso dotto e da bene. I nipoti non curano de' religiosi: perche non possono da questi esser corteggiati come da' preti. Se si parla di aggravj, i monasterj sono i primi: se di riforma, non si parla di preti, ma di religiosi. In somma, si toglie affatto ad ogni uno la volontà di studiare e la cura di difender la chiesa dalle false opinioni che vanno seminando i nemici di Roma: de' quali moltiplicandosi giornalmente il numero, e deteriorandosi quello de' religiosi dotti et esemplari, potrebbe in breve soffrirne non poco detrimento la corte. Onde al mio credere farebbono bene i pontefici di procurar di rimettere i regolari nel pristino posto di stima, partecipandoli di quando in quando cariche e dignità, tanto più ch' essendo grande il numero possono scegliere i soggetti a loro piacere: e così nelle religioni vi entrarebbono huomini eminenti, dove che tengono a vile hoggidì di coprirsi le spalle d' un cappuccino i più falliti mercanti, nè si veggono entrar ne' monasterj che gente mecanica."

[At present the religiosi (monks) are held in such low estimation that they have of themselves left off appearing at court, to avoid receiving affronts from the meanest people at court. Cardinalships and bishoprics are accounted despicable on the shoulders of the monks, and in competitions of claims an ignorant and vicious priestling is preferred to a religious and moral monk. The nephews pay no regard to monks, because these cannot pay their court to them as the priests do. If wrongs are spoken of, the monasteries are the first (to be blamed): if reform is mentioned, nothing is said of the priests, but only of the monks. In fine every inducement is taken away for any one to wish to study and to defend the church from the false opinions that are in course of circulation by the enemies of Rome: whose numbers multiplying every day, and that of the learned and religious monks diminishing, the court may shortly suffer no small detriment. Hence it is my belief that the pontiffs would do well to endeavour to replace the monks in their old post of estimation, giving them from time to time a share of the charges and dignities, the more as from the number of them being great, they can choose subjects from among them at their pleasure: and thus there will enter eminent men into the religious orders where even bankrupt traders at present consider it ignominious to have a capuchin's dress on their shoulders, nor are any seen to enter monasteries but people of the rank of mechanics.]

Unhappily, however, no redress could be expected from Clement IX.; he was too lukewarm, too good-natured.

After thus describing the pope the ambassador proceeds to speak of his nearest connections. First comes cardinal Rospigliosi of whom it was hoped "quod esset redempturus Israel" [that it was he who should redeem Israel]. He points out how this hope came to be extinguished.

"Tre cose per mio credere sono quelle che fanno camminar col piede di piombo il cardinal predetto, accusato di lentezza di genio e di mancanza d' applicatione. La prima è il gran desiderio di voler far bene ogni cosa e di dar gusto a tutto il mondo, cosa che difficilmente può riuscire ad un' huomo che non è assoluto padrone. La seconda è che la sua volontà viene imbrigliata e trattenuta dal papa, il quale, se bene ama e considera con amore estraordinario questo nipote, gode però di fare il tutto a suo modo: onde dubioso il Rospigliosi d' incontrar nelle sue risolutioni le negative del papa e dall' altra parte volendo sodisfare gl' interessati, fugge le occasioni di concludere cosa alcuna. E finalmente gli noce ancora la capacità del proprio

[There are three things, as I believe, that make the said cardinal proceed with a leaden foot, accused as he is of slowness of wit and want of application. First, there is the great desire to do every thing well, and to give satisfaction to all the world, a thing not easily to be accomplished by one who is not absolute master. The second is that his will is bridled and diverted by the pope, who, albeit that he is very fond of this nephew, and regards him with extraordinary affection, yet delights to do all in his own way: so that Rospigliosi, fearful of meeting with the pope's negative in the resolutions he takes, and desirous on the other hand of satisfying interested persons, avoids the occasions of concluding anything. And finally, he is fur-

intendimento, particolarmente in quelle cose che dipendono da lui: poiche abbondando, come si è detto, di ripieghi capaci da sostenere il posto di nipote, da sì gran copia nasce la gran penuria nelle risolutioni, perdendo la maggior parte dell' hore più pretiose a meditare e crivellare le materie, et intanto che si medita e crivella il modo da eligere senza mancare le più adequate, il tempo vola e le occasioni fuggono."

ther injured by the capacity of his own understanding, particularly in those things that depend upon him: for abounding, as has been said, in endowments adapted to the post of nephew, from such abundance arises great penury in resolutions, as he loses the greater part of the most precious hours in meditating and sifting his materials, and while the method of choosing without fail the most adequate (resolutions) is meditated upon and f , time flies and opportunities are lost.]si ted

Meanwhile people had to do him the justice of admitting that he did not enrich himself: "havendo trascurato molte occasioni d' arrichirsi, e l' havrebbe possuto fare senza scrupolo e con buona coscienza" [having neglected many opportunities of enriching himself, and yet he might have done so without scruple, and with a good conscience]. People thought indeed, that Rospigliosi favoured Chigi mainly for this end, that through his assistance he might one day become pope himself. The ambassador refutes this opinion.

It is remarkable how the temper which we observe in the pope and cardinal patron, is repeated in the other members of this government. They are not destitute of good intentions and capacity, but from one or other cause they can make no important change.

"Di due ministri si serve particolarmente il cardinale nelle cose che corrono alla giornata. L' uno è monsignore Agustini, huomo prudente e di vita esemplare, che può dirsi di lui come di Giobbe, Vir simplex et timens deum, ma del resto lento, lungo e irresoluto e tanto inclinato a voler far bene che fa poco per lo dubbio di non far male: onde con questa natura ha saputo dare così bene nell' humore del padrone che lo decanta per un' oracolo e lo stima il principal ministro della corte, benche quelli che continuamente lo sentono nelle congregationi, ne fanno altro concetto, e lo confessano bene per un soggetto mediocre, ma non più oltre, e della stessa opinione è ancora il papa. L' altro è mons. Fiani, a cui fu dato il carico di segretario della consulta, officio veramente che ricerca gran confidenza col card[l] padrone: onde con ragione Rospigliosi scelse questo huomo che conosce il dovere dell' amicitia e che in effetto non può desiderarsi maggior capacità nel governo, tuttavia inhabile quasi di esercitare il suo officio per esser podagroso e infermo, prolongando per questo ogni cosa con gran rammarico della corte, dalla quale vien poco accettato, tanto più che si è vociferato haver le mani inclinate a ricever presenti, ma per me credo che questa sia una vera malignità di dettatori."

[The cardinal employs two cardinals in particular in affairs of daily occurrence. One is monsignor Agustini, a prudent man and of exemplary life, so that it may be said of him, as of Job, "Vir simplex et timens Deum" [an upright man and one that fears God], but for the rest slow, tardy, and irresolute, and so much inclined to wish to do well, that he does little from the dread of doing ill: hence with this natural temper he has contrived to enter so well into the humour of his patron that he extols him as an oracle, and thinks him the chief minister of the court, albeit that those who for a continuance hear him in the congregations, have a different idea of him, and confess that he is indeed a middling good person, but nothing more, and the pope farther is of this opinion. The other is monsignor Fiani, to whom the charge of secretary of the consulta was given, an office that truly requires great confidence with the cardinal padrone: hence with good reason Rospigliosi has chosen this man, who knows the duties of friendship, and who in fact could not desire for himself greater capacity for government, being almost unfit withal for the discharge of his office from being gouty and infirm, thus drawing out everything to a tedious length, with great complaining on the part of the court, by which he is not very well received, the more as he is loudly said to have his hands inclined to receive presents, but for me I believe this to be a piece of pure malignity on the part of those who say so.]

It is unnecessary to repeat the further details on the subject of the papal family, who, after all, acquired no influence. The pope's brother, Don Camillo Rospigliosi, would, our author says, were this the practice, deserve to be canonized during his life-time. He had five sons, of whom, however, only two used to be spoken of: the second-born, Don Tommaso, who already had the idea of raising the industry of the church-state, and the youngest Giambattista—"giovine di bellissimo aspetto e d' un cervello acuto e penetrante" [a youth of the finest appearance, and of an acute and penetrating brain],—who married a Pallavicini of Genoa, and founded the Rospigliosi family. It is enough for us to quote the general description of the new relative position held by these nephews.

"Fra tutti li pontefici che sono stati nel Vaticano, non se ne è forse veduto mai alcuno più politico e più prudente nel mantenersi con i suoi parenti come fece Clemente IX., il quale godeva di esser con loro, ma non già di darsi in preda di loro: anzi quanto più

[Among all the pontiffs that have been in the Vatican, never perhaps has there been seen any one more politic and more prudent in guiding himself towards his relations than Clement IX., who delights to be with them, but never allows himself to be preyed upon:

li mostrava segni di affetto e di ottima volontà, tanto maggiormente li teneva indietro senza parteciparli in modo alcuno i segreti de' suoi pensieri. Alla buona intentione del papa di torre via dalla chiesa lo scandolo introdotto da lungo tempo mediante la communicatione di quasi tutta l'autorità del Vaticano che i pontefici hanno costumato di partecipare ai loro nipoti, è andata congiunta la bontà del nipotismo: perche si può dire con buona ragione che mai in Roma si sono veduti parenti di papa più modesti, più humili, più caritativi e meno disinteressati de' Rospigliosi, e quel che più importa, tutti dotati d' una stessa bontà e modestia, che però sarebbe stato un disumanarsi di lasciarli d' amare: anzi si può dire giustamente che il papa non li amò mai quanto sarebbe necessario al merito delle loro ottime qualità, havendoli tenuti più tosto come stranieri che come parenti per non comunicare con essi loro alcuna cosa di conseguenza: con che si rendeva infelice, mentre dall' una parte si privava volontariamente della sodisfattione necessaria a' principi di sfogarsi con i congiunti, e dall' altra si vedeva privo di potersi aprire con i domestici, che per lo più erano gente idiota e di spirito ben mediocre. Si crede che il papa non confida le cose più importanti della corte che colla persona del card[l] Chigi, il quale come astuto et accorto ha saputo benissimo guadagnarsi il suo affetto."

on the contrary, the more he shows them signs of affection and good will, the more he keeps them back without any kind of share in the secrets of his thoughts. To the pope's good intention of turning away from the church the scandal introduced from of old through the communication of almost all the authority of the Vatican in which the pontiffs have been accustomed to let their nephews participate, there has gone hand in hand the goodness of the nepotism: for it may be said with good reason that never have there been seen in Rome relations of the pope more modest, more humble, more charitable than the Rospigliosi, and what is of more importance, all endued with such goodness and modesty, that it would have been inhuman not to love them: on the contrary, it may justly be said that the pope has never loved them more than the merit of their admirable qualities called for, having held them rather as strangers than as relations by never communicating with them upon any thing of consequence: whereby he made himself unhappy, while on the one hand he voluntarily deprived himself of the satisfaction necessary to princes of enjoying themselves with their kindred, and, on the other, he saw himself deprived of the possibility of opening his mind to the household servants, who for the most part were silly people, and of a very mediocre spirit. It is believed that the pope does not intrust the most important affairs of the court to any but cardinal Chigi, who being an astute and prudent person, has contrived admirably to gain his affection.]

There follows a description of the cardinals and ambassadors resident at the court. Yet these are not personages of sufficient importance, and the interests are too transitory and evanescent, for us to waste our time upon them.

139.

Relatione dello stato delle cose di Roma del mese di Sett. 1670.—[Report on the state of the affairs of Rome in the month of September, 1670.] (Alt. 9 leaves.)

Spanish reports accompany the Venetian, and such as are ostensibly French. For there is no doubt that this report was drawn up for Spain. Mention is made in it of another that had gone to the Spanish court, on which account the notices contained in it had been omitted in this.

Clement IX.: "la sua natura è placida: perche non viene alcuno a suoi piedi al quale egli non desideri di fare qualche gratia.... Va ristrettissimo nelle spese e parchissimo nel dare a suoi" [he is of a placid nature, for none comes to his feet to whom he does not desire to do some favour..... He is most restricted in his expenses and most parsimonious in giving away to his own relations]. Cardinal Altieri: "opera tutto da se, e poca influenza riceve da altri. Sono secoli che non si è veduto un nepote di pontefice nè di maggior autorità nè d' abilità ed integrità" [he does everything himself, and is little influenced by others. Ages have passed since a nephew of a pope has been seen either of greater authority or of ability and integrity]. We see that even under this government most persons in office left matters as they found them.

But the most important matter mentioned by the author, is the dissension in the court. Chigi, Barberini, and Rospigliosi were on the most intimate footing with Altieri. To this the Spanish ambassador had most of all contributed. Confronting these stood the faction of the Squadronists, that is, of the Innocentian cardinals, who had had so much influence on the last papal elections, and had introduced their adherents into public offices during the two preceding governments. To these belonged Omodei, Ottobono, Imperiali, Borromeo, Azzolino. The queen of Sweden took part with the utmost zeal in the struggles between the two parties. It is known how highly she valued Azzolino. Here she is called his faithful servant. She is charged with a thousand intrigues, entered into for the purpose of promoting the Squadronists.

140.

Memorie per descrivere la vita di Clemente X. Pontefice Massimo, raccolte da Carlo Cartari Orvietano, decano degli avvocati consistoriali e prefetto dell' archivio apostolico di castello S. Angelo di Roma.—[Memorials for describing the life of Clement X., supreme pontiff, collected by Charles Cartari of Orvieto, dean of the consistorial advocates and prefect of the apostolic archives of the castle of St. Angelo of Rome.] (Alt. 211 pages.)

Composed immediately after the pope's death, and finished in October 1676, with an express engagement on the author's part to avoid all flattery, and to keep to the pure truth ("da questi fogli sarà l' adulatione, mia nemica irreconciliabile, affatto sbandita, alla sola verità candida e pura attenendomi" [from these leaves flattery, my irreconcilable enemy, shall be banished entirely, restricting myself to the sole candid and pure truth];) yet, according to the author's design, it is a mere collection, to be made use of at some future time by another.

At first, however, it would appear as if this declaration were but the expression of modesty.

The pope's father, old Lorenzo Altieri, is very quaintly described: Cartari further had known him well: as a man of powerful mind, majestic in his bearing, but withal very modest, as his look at once indicated. Although only a compiler the author does not refrain from adding forthwith a conceit in the spirit of the age in which he lived: "di altrettanto bella canitie nell' esterno ricoperto quanto di una candidezza di costumi, di una rara pietà a meraviglia dotato" [covered externally with as beautifully fair locks as with a fair moral purity, and endowed with a rare piety to a wonder].

Emilio Altieri was born in 1590; was made a doctor in 1611; remained for a long while in the study of Pamfili who was afterwards pope, in 1624 accompanied that bishop of Nola, Lancellotti, whose instructions we have above, to Poland; on his return he became bishop of Camerino in the place of his brother John Baptist, who passed into the college of cardinals; it is asserted, although Cartari does not say it, that Emilio himself had been destined even then for the cardinalship, and that there would have been more willingness in admitting him than his brother: he had the self-command, however, at this conjuncture, to travel away from Rome, and to give place to his elder brother. Innocent X. despatched our Emilio as nuncio to Naples, and it is said that he contributed his share to the settlement of the troubles of Massaniello; Alexander VII. appointed him secretary of the congregation *di vescovi e regolari;* a career which every one found very tiresome. He first came to receive real promotion in his 79th year: on the 29th of November 1669, Clement named him cardinal, yet that pope had not even time to give him the hat: before he had yet received it Altieri entered the conclave, and on the 29th of April, 1670, it ended with his own election as pope. He hesitated for some time: he declared that there were other more deserving persons, and even named cardinal Brancacci; nevertheless he accepted the highest dignity.

Thus advanced in years was the pope already: be had not even any actual nephew: he had to choose one to relieve him so far of the weight of affairs.

"Ritrovavasi S. Beatitudine nell' anno ottantesimo di sua età: onde per questa cagione e per imitare i suoi antecessori, quali ben conoscendo la pesante mole del pontificato stimarono necessario di deputare per proprio sollievo alcuno de' cardinali col titolo di sopraintendente generale dello stato ecclesiastico, si compiacque a dichiarare l' istesso giorno a questa laboriosa carica il card[l] Paluzzo Paluzzi degli Albertoni suo attinente, permutandogli quel cognome coll' altro d' Altieri."

[His Beatitude found himself in the 80th year of his age: accordingly both on that account, and that he might imitate his predecessors, who, well knowing the heavy burthen of the pontificate, thought it necessary to depute affairs for their own relief to some one of the cardinals with the title of superintendent general of the ecclesiastical state, he was pleased that same day to name to that laborious charge cardinal Paluzzo Paluzzi degli Albertoni, a connection of his, changing that name into the other of Altieri.]

On proceeding to what was done by this pope, we find the author first attaches himself to Rome.

The arrival of the ambassadors from Ferrara and Bologna, for the purpose of doing homage,—the discovery of Constantine the Great at the foot of the steps at St. Peter's,—the decoration of the flight of steps at (the castle of) St. Angelo, with ten angels made of Carrara marble,—the building of the Altieri palace, to which there was applied about 300,000 scudi, which, however, was not altogether lost, seeing that the poor reaped the advantage of the outlay,—the erection of a second fountain at Peter's place, but which the pope never saw completed: these are the chief matters on which Cartari dwells. In speaking of the palace he describes the library too. "Vedesi in sito quasi il più alto elevato del medesimo palazzo un vaso per libraria, altrettano capace quanto vago per la veduta della città e della campagna, in maestose scanzie riempite della generosità del card[l] Altieri di pretiosi libri d' ogni scienza, che giungono al numero di 12,000."—[There is seen in almost the most elevated part of the same palace a receptacle for a library, equally capacious and beautiful for the view it affords of the city and country, in magnificent shelves filled by the

generosity of cardinal Altieri with precious books on all the sciences, reaching to the number of 12,000.] I know it right well: how often have I mounted those steps! Of the fountains (he says): "Trasportata la fontana di Paolo V. con machine meravigliose, quasi direi tutte d' un pezzo, dal sito vecchio dove si ritrovava all' altro dove hoggidì si vede stabilita in corrispondenza degl' ingressi laterali del teatro, per accompagnamento della medesima ordinò se ne fabricasse un' altra affatto simile verso il giardino de Cesi, come fu eseguito."—[The fountain of Paul V., with its wonderful machinery, I may almost say all of one piece, being transported from the old site where it stood to the other where it now stands, in correspondence with the lateral entrances to the theatre, as an accompaniment to the same he gave orders for the making another exactly alike towards the Cesi garden, which was done.] The most interesting part, however, is what he relates of that pretended mosaic of Giotto, the navicella di S. Pietro (St. Peter's bark). After having often changed its place since the pulling down of the portico of the old basilica, where it stood originally, brought by Paul V. into the palace, by Urban VIII. into the church, by Innocent X. into the palace again, where it seemed anew unsuitable to Alexander VII., people despaired of bringing it out as it stood, and preferred taking it to pieces, all the small stones belonging to each individual figure being put into a separate bag. Under Clement X., cardinal Barberini proposed its being restored according to a copy that had been made of it in the reign of Urban VIII. Upon this it was put together anew, and inserted in the lunette over the middle entrance of the vestibule. But we must let Cartari's own words explain how this was managed. "Perche il vano non era capace, fu detto che lasciandosi le figure nel proprio essere, potevano restringersi i spatii: come fu diligentemente eseguito."—[Because the empty space was not large enough, it was suggested that leaving the figures just as they were, the spaces might be narrowed; which was done with the utmost care.] It is evident that the new master is not unjustly considered by some to be the author.

Finally, the compiler directs his attention to political matters also. But here he is very defective. He reports that Clement X. had, in spite of all his financial necessity, refused to proceed to any new reduction of the *monti*, out of regard for the many families and particularly for the pious institutions which would have suffered by it:—*ben considerando il danno che a tante famiglie ed in particolare a luoghi pii ne resultarebbe:* he preferred savings, and even prevailed upon a cardinal-nephew to renounce his pay as *sopraintendente dello stato* Yet some money was sent to Poland, then hard pressed by the Turks: at one time 30,000, at another time 16,000, and further at another time 70,000 scudi. The cardinals had arranged that there should be a special collection.

This is all I find upon foreign affairs. Yet those of the church-state are not on that account taken up with an undue minuteness.

"Si adoperò alla libera introduzione delle merci forestiere, e furono rivocate tutte le esenzioni delle gabelle: si diedero ordini circa gli officii vacabili della dataria e frutti di essi:—si estinse la gabella del quatrino degli artisti:—si dicharò che alli Romani et altri nobili dello stato ecclesiastico sia lecito di esercitar commerci senza pregiudizj della nobiltà."

[Efforts were made to introduce foreign merchandise, and all the exemptions from the gabelles were recalled: orders were given respecting the *officii vacabili* of the dataria and the fruits of the same:—the gabelle of the quatrino levied on artists, was repealed:—it was declared that it should be lawful for the Romans and other nobles of the church-state to exercise commerce without prejudice of nobility.]

Properly speaking, that is all that he really says.

He hardly mentions anything done by the pope in reference to the internal state of the Roman catholic church.

141.

Clementis Decimi Pontificis Maximi vita.—[Life of Clement X., supreme Pontiff.] (Alt. 288 pages.)

Cartari was of opinion that many would be found to write the life of Clement X.: and it was just to these that he devoted his materials. Soon there was found an author to undertake the task: but, it must be owned, a Jesuit at the command of his general Oliva. Cardinal Paluzzi Altieri supplied him with the materials for it.

Although this author does not name Cartari, yet it is evident that he had him before him. He frequently does no more than merely translate and enlarge him.

If Cartari purposely avoided flattery, this author in re-constructing his work super-adds it. He will have it that in the year of Clement X.'s birth the Tiber had caused violent inundations: "quasi praesentiret imperantis urbis fluvius augendam ab exorto tum infante Romanam gloriam" [as if the river of the imperial city had a presentiment that the Roman glory would be augmented by the infant that then was born].

Yet he has occasionally more useful additions. He relates the trait of character displayed by Clement X. in spontaneously yielding precedence to his brother.

In subsequent chapters, too, he enters upon a narrative of ecclesiastical occurrences. "Innumeros in callem salutis reduces illo regnante vidit Hungaria, quam catholicam, ut Francisci card[lis] Nerlii verbis utar, pene totam effecit:" [Hungary during his reign saw innumerable persons return to the way of salvation, which country, to use the words of Francis cardinal of Nerli, he made almost wholly catholic:]—truly a strong hyperbole, for not

only was Hungary at that time by no means so Roman catholic, but Clement contributed but little to make it so: "ad veram religionem in Hibernia conservandam ac propagandam solertem industriam contulit: ...... plurimos in Vaticanum regressos Boemia et caetera Boemiae regna atque inter hos magnos principes, plurimos, Rhaeti atque iis finitimae valles, magnam illorum vim Hollandia, majorem vidit Galha" [he applied a clever industry to the preservation and propagation of the true religion in Ireland: ...... Bohemia and the other kingdoms of Bohemia saw very many returned to the Vatican, and great princes among these, the Tyrolese and the neighbouring valleys saw very many, Holland saw a great body of them, and France a still greater]. All, however, much in general terms.

Then, while he praises the pope's fairness and love for his subjects, he exculpates him for having made up the sums sent to help the Poles against the Turks by taxes on the clergy and for having imposed fresh burthens: he had repealed oppressive taxes, and in their stead had taxed articles of luxury, such as wine imported from beyond sea, and tobacco:—in respect to his relations, too, he had shown the utmost moderation. People should not dwell upon that palace, but calculate how few landed estates the Altieri had acquired: "quam minimum in spatium contrahantur Alteriis principibus subjecta oppida et rura, cum latissime pateat aliorum ditio" [into how very small a space the towns and villages subject to the Altieri princes were contracted, while the sway of other (princes) was most extensive].

142.

Nuovo governo di Roma sotto il pontificato di papa Clemente X.—[New government of Rome under the government of Pope Clement X.] (Barb. 17 leaves.)

Discusses the family connection, and the singular elevation of Pauluzzi to the position of papal nephew.

The brother of the pope, the lineal representative of the Altieri family, had left behind him only one daughter, with instructions, that whoever should marry her must take the name of Altieri.

A nephew of cardinal Pauluzzi married this heiress of the house of Altieri. Thus were the two families connected. All other relations, for instance the Gabrielli, who would otherwise have been the nearest, had to withdraw.

For the rest, this government proved, from the first, less mild than the preceding, which arose from Clement IX. having burthened with debt even those revenues which had been always hitherto reserved. A commencement had already been made in the disbanding of the little army. The compiler thinks that the result of the trifling remission of the taxes made by Clement IX. would be the disarming of the whole state.

He laments likewise the form of the government, the recklessness already usual among those who administered it in the church-state.

"Vedendosi odiati et abborriti tanto più s' infierano, e tiratosi il cappello sugli occhi non guardano in faccia a nessuno, e facendo d' ogni erba fascio non pensano che al proprio interesse senza minima apprensione del publico."

[Seeing themselves detested and abhorred the more cruel do they become, and pulling their hair over their eyes, they look nobody in the face; and making a bundle of every herb, they think only of their own interests, without the slightest concern about the public.]

143.

Relatione dello stato presente della corte di Roma, fatta all' ecc^{mo} principe di Ligni governatore di Milano dall' Illmo Sr Feder. Rozzoni inviato straord^{rio} da S. E. alla corte appresso Clemente X.—[Report on the present state of the court of Rome, made to the most excellent prince de Ligny, governor of Milan, by the most illustrious Signor Frederick Rozzoni, envoy extraordinary from his excellency to the court of Clement X.] (24 leaves.)

Written somewhat later than the preceding report.

Already had the position of parties become changed. Rospigliosi and Chigi were neglected by the reigning family: the latter tried to make approaches to the Squadronists.

The mutual relation between the pope and cardinal Altieri is described as follows:—

"Il papa non ha applicatione alcuna, sì per la cadente sua età, come anche per esser suo connaturale attendere alla propria quiete e sottrarsi dalle cure gravi che potrebbero turbare la serenità dell' animo suo, solo inclinato a vivere tranquillamente. Egli perciò non puole sapere le amministrationi della giustitia nè altri negotii politici della corte e dello stato ecclesiastico: onde il ricorrere a lui non giova punto a quelli che da suoi ministri vengono oppressi: e per havere pretesto più colorito di non ingerirsi in simili affari, più volte si fa stimare ammalato, non tralasciando per questo le sue domestiche conversationi,

[The pope has no powers of application, both from his declining years, and also from its being his natural disposition to attend to his own quiet and to withdraw from serious cares that might disturb the serenity of his mind, solely inclined to live in tranquillity. He cannot, on this account, be acquainted with the administration of justice, nor of other political concerns of the court and of the church-state: hence having recourse to him avails not in the least to those who are oppressed by his ministers: and in order to have a more colourable pretext for not interesting himself in such affairs, he often affects being ill, not

che dopo desinato giornalmente si prende con giuochi di carte e godimento di suoni e canti.

"Lascia il governo della chiesa totalmente al cardinale Altieri, et in esso non si ingerisce se non quanto è necessario per la sua approvatione in voce o scritto: nel resto ha rassegnato in tal maniera che più volte l' ha temuto e nascostamente ha fatto fare elemosine, regali e cose simili: ma la collatione de' beneficii, vescovati et elettione de' soggetti alla porpora resta al totale arbitrio di esso cardinale: il quale è uomo flemmatico, e difficilmente si sdegna esternamente, e quando ciò fa, cessa di vendicarsi. Ha molt' attitudine a sostenere la carica che tiene, et in fatti vuol sapere et indrizzare tutti gli affari grandi e piccoli non solo della corte ma ancora di tutto lo stato ecclesiastico, il che da alcuni si attribuisce a grande avidità di suoi interessi, nelli quali è vigilantissimo, non lasciando passare occasione alcuna di non approfittarli: ogni giorno in tal' hore determinate da audienza a tutti i ministri della corte et alli loro segretarj, et esso da le regole et istruttioni non solo generali ma anche particolari, di modo che li giudici et il medesimo governatore non hanno nelle loro cariche arbitrio alcuno.

"Il principale ministro del medesimo cardinale è stato et è l' abbate Piccini, soggetto di deboli parti et inferiori natali, che prima della promotione di Clemente Decimo era suo cameriere: onde per introduttione, anzi per l' arbitrio, conforme la comune stima, che haveva de' voleri di esso cardinale, ha congregato un' annua entrata di 12 m. scudi et un capitale di 200 m., havendo altrettanto empito il capo di fumo quanto la borsa d' oro. Però al presente è cessata tant' aura sua, vogliono alcuni per punti politici e non già perche si sia diminuita la sua gran fortuna dall' unione delli quattro regj ambasciatori: ancorche detto abbate Piccini unitamente col commissario della camera chiamato mons' Zaccaria siano li più intimi del cardinale: quanto a ciò, spetta all' interesse, mostrandosi esso cardinale di questo alieno, volendo lasciar cadere sopra di questi due ministri o torcimanni l' opinione volgare di molto interessato."

omitting on that account his familiar conversations, in which he daily engages after dinner, together with card-playing and the enjoyment of instrumental and vocal music.

He commits the government of the church altogether to cardinal Altieri, and does not interfere in it beyond what is necessary for his approval by word or writing: for the rest, he has surrendered himself in such a manner that he has often felt timid, and has secretly given alms, presents, and such things: but the collation of benefices, bishoprics, and the choice of persons to be raised to the cardinalship, remain at the absolute disposal of the said cardinal; who is a phlegmatic person, and not easily put out of temper externally, and when this does happen, forbears revenging himself. He has much fitness for sustaining the charge he holds, and in fact, wishes to know and direct all affairs, great and small, not only of the court, but further of the whole church-state, which some ascribe to his great eagerness for his own interests, in which he is most vigilant, allowing no opportunity to pass without taking advantage of it: he every day at a set hour gives audience to all the ministers of the court and to their secretaries, and he, too, gives not only general but also particular rules and instructions, in such wise that the judges and the governor himself have no discretion of their own in their charges.

The principal minister of the said cardinal has been and still is the abbot Piccini, a person of weak parts and low parentage, who before the promotion of Clement X. was his chamberlain: whence by introduction, rather from the command, as people commonly think, which he has of the will of the said cardinal, he has amassed an annual revenue of 12,000 scudi and a capital of 200,000, having filled the head as much with smoke as the purse with gold. In fine, for the present, his gale has so far subsided, some will have it, from political causes, and not because his great fortune has already been lessened by the union of the four royal ambassadors: although the said abbot Piccini, together with the commissary of the chamber, called monsieur Zaccaria, are the greatest intimates of the cardinal: as for the latter, he looks to his advantage, the said cardinal being indifferent to that, and desiring that popular opinion, which is much interested, should be allowed to fall upon these two ministers or interpreters.]

144.

Relatione della corte di Roma del N. H. Piero Mocenigo, che fu ambasciatore a papa Clemente X., fatta l' anno 1675.—Report on the court of Rome by N. H. Piero Mocenigo, who was ambassador to pope Clement X., drawn up in the year 1675.] (44 leaves.)

P. Mocenigo had previously been in England; he now came to Rome, which, particularly in a commercial point of view, presented so wholly different an aspect: here he became involved in rather violent dissensions with the Altieri family: he took the lead among the ambassadors, whom there was a wish to deprive of some of their franchises. No wonder if he shows himself not much edified by what he sees and experiences.

He divides his report into three parts.

I. La qualità di quella corte, sua autorità così spirituale come temporale, con aggiunta dell' erario e delle forze. "Tutto il riflesso," he begins, "dei pensieri de' regnanti è rivolto a non lasciare la propria casa

[The nature of that court, its authority as well spiritual as temporal, with the addition of the treasury and (military) forces. The whole drift] he begins by saying [of the thoughts of those in the government, is not

esposta alle persecutioni et al ludibrio della povertà. Di ciò deriva che la tramontana di quella corte è l' interesse privato, e colà non s' applica al publico bene che colla speciosità delle apparenze." [to leave their own family exposed to the persecutions and ridicule of poverty. Hence the pole-star of that court is private interest, and people apply there to the public welfare only with the speciousness of appearances.]

The consequences of the (exclusive) favour shown to the leading families now was, that the middle rank especially, and the inferior nobility, no longer throve in the world. It was too poor in money to rise by its own energy, and yet was too independent to condescend to the subserviency of the really poor.

"Flattery," says P. Mocenigo, "is here at home; but not the less are there many people who, on the failure of their hopes, console themselves with calumny, and cherish the maxim, 'One will never go wrong if he think the worst.'"

The important congregations were those of the Inquisition, of Ecclesiastical Immunities, of the Council, of the Propaganda, of the Bishops and religious orders, of the Index. Did the court mean to refuse anything, it then handed the case over to these: they held to their canons and the practice of preceding centuries: thus the merest trifle would become important. But if the court were favourably inclined, it then took the case into its own hands.

It was particularly in secular concerns that the transmission of its power through others appeared.[1] Cardinals never would have approved of going to war. (For a long time, we may add, even that was no longer the case.)

The condition of the country was daily becoming worse. The author was told that in the course of forty years, the number of inhabitants had fallen off one-third: where formerly there were reckoned one hundred hearths there were now to be found no more than sixty; many houses were pulled down, notwithstanding that the consulta prohibited this being done: every day there was less land cultivated; marriages decreased; people sought for an asylum for their children in monasteries and convents.

He reckons the interests of the state debts, that is, of the monti and officii vacabili, at 2,400,000 scudi, the deficit at several hundred thousand.

II. Il presente governo di Clemente X., sua casa, sacro collegio, e corrispondenze con principi.—[The present government of Clement X., his family, sacred college, and correspondences with the princes.]

Clement X.—He saw, to be sure, the datarius, the clerk to the briefs, the secretary of state, and cardinal Altieri, at set hours, but merely passed through the formality of subscribing his name: disagreeable matters were concealed from him, an object to which cardinal Altieri applied his whole efforts. The ambassador maintains that the pope had no knowledge of the world's affairs; he had never been nuncio. This, as we know, was not the case.—"In Roma si dice che benedicere e sanctificare sia del pontefice, reggere e gubernare sia dell' Altieri."—[In Rome it is said that it is the pope's business to bless and consecrate, cardinal Altieri's to reign and govern.]

Cardinal Altieri.—

"Di complessione delicata: .... la sua natura è ardente, impetuosa e di prima impressione..... Assuefatto alla cortesia Romanesca di non negare cosa alcuna, anzi di concorrere con parole officiose, ad esaudire le instanze facilmente, poi quando ha ponderato il negotio, dà indietro, anco col negare l' impegno, e dà nelle scandescenze..... Da poca speranza vien sollevato, come per contrario da poco timore abbattuto." [Of a delicate constitution: .... his natural disposition is ardent, impetuous, and apt to be carried away by the first impression..... Accustomed to the Romanesque courtesy of not refusing anything, but rather agreeing with officious words, and readily listening to pressing requests, then, after he has weighed the matter, he retracts, still denying any engagement, and goes into calculations. (?) .... He is elevated by slight hopes, as, on the contrary, he is cast down by petty fears.]

In these expressions we clearly see the effect of personal disagreements.

But the remaining characters are described in the same spirit. Laura Altieri, to whom this family owed its good fortune, did not, however, find herself happy in it, and on that account was never allowed to approach the feet of the pope. This, however, I do not quite believe.

What the author says when he describes the union of the court with the Squadronists is less to be suspected: we have seen, ere now, how matters were ready for this: Barberini, Rospigliosi, and Chigi were now sunk in respect and influence: the Squadronists particularly urged the independence of the curia on foreign courts: they had drawn over the Altieri entirely to their side. The author asserts that to them were to be attributed the perplexities in which the court came to be involved.

Into these he enters more minutely, but still in his irritable manner.

The court had occasionally to endeavour to appease the emperor with spiritual presents, *Agnus Dei*, and so forth. People had so many quarrels with France, that they were delighted to see that country involved in war. How, therefore, could the pope be expected to mediate a peace? Spain complained, among other things, that banditti from Naples were admitted into the church-state, and allowed to dispose of stolen property there.

1 Durchfahrende Gewalt, referring, I suppose, to the above employment of the congregations for part of the public business.—TR.

"Ma non segli danno orecchie: perche così comple alla quiete di quei confini, promessa e mantenuta dai medesimi banditi."

[But no attention is paid to them, for it is thus that the peace of the frontiers is secured, which is engaged for and maintained by the said banditti.]

People neglected to spur on Poland with sufficient zeal to prosecute the Turkish war, merely that thus they might escape being obliged to support it. To the czar they would not give that title, for which reason no alliance was entered into with him: from whom, nevertheless, so much assistance might otherwise have been expected against the hereditary enemy. "Per timor d' ingombrarsi in obligatione di rimettere e contribuire soccorsi maggiori si sono lasciate cadere le propositioni fatte da un inviato Polacco, che l' armi del re sarebbero passato il Danubio, entrate nella Bulgaria, e promettevano di portar la guerra nèlle viscere dell' imperio Ottomano."—[From a dread of being embarrassed with an obligation to remit and contribute larger aids, the proposals made by a Polish envoy were allowed to fall to the ground, namely, that the arms of the king should pass the Danube, enter Bulgaria, and promise to carry the war into the bowels of the Ottoman empire.] This I notice merely because it appears from it that such hopes were already entertained. For how the Roman court could have contributed much towards its accomplishment, particularly when so hampered by the state of the papal exchequer and territories as above described, one does not well see. The king of Portugal was refused the patronage of his churches beyond seas, and the duke of Saxony an indult for the filling up of the bishoprics in his territory. In Tuscany, too, in the smaller principalities, this claim to ecclesiastical independence was mooted.

The incameration (annexation of revenues to the exchequer) of Castro proved even a loss. The debts that had been transferred required 90,000 scudi of interest; the farmer of the revenues paid only 60,000. People answered in Rome, it was not thus a prince should reckon.

III. Corrispondenze colla republica [Correspondence with the republic]. But very brief, and chiefly about personal contentions. "Impiego scabrosissimo" [a most difficult employment]. All in the same spirit.

People were already prepared in Venice for a report in this tone. Before P. Mocenigo had as yet returned, there appeared a "Lettera scritta a Venetia da sogetto ben informato sopra l'ambasceria" [Letter written to Venice from a person well-informed, about the (a second hand adds "infame" [infamous] embassy]) "del Sr Kavr Mocenigo" [of Signor Chevalier Mocenigo], in which the little man with the big wig who talked incessantly about England, is very hardly dealt with. He is now sitting day and night with a man of letters, for the purpose of blackening the Roman court in his report: "un governo, migliore del quale per i principi secolari non è stato da S. Pietro in qua, piacevole, moderato, senza puntiglio."—[a government better than which has not been administered by the secular princes from St. Peter till now, peaceable, moderate, and above cavilling.]

Nor can it be doubted that Mocenigo has gone too far: but we are not on that account to reject all that he says.

Every one, after all, gives his opinions on the things that he happens to speak of. We foreigners have to learn to set ourselves right betwixt object and subject.

145.

Scrittura sopra il governo di Roma.—[Writing on the government of Rome.] (MS. Rom.)

Found among writings that refer to the period from 1670 to 1680, and belonging to much about that very period. Just as cheerless as ever were the complaints of Sacchetti.

I. "Sopra il cattivo stato de' popoli. Come mai in ogni pontificato, s' ha da trovar modo di metter 100 et anco 150 m. scudi in una casa, e non è possibile di levarne 50 m. di peso agli aggravati popoli. ...... Il peggio è non voler permettere i modi honesti di riempire le borse con procacciarsi per mezzo di lecite mercantie quei guadagni ch' altri con l' autorità indebitamente s' appropria. II. Sopra la gran povertà et il gran lusso."

I. [On the ill condition of the peoples. How in every pontificate it never fails that means can be found for putting from 100 to 150,000 scudi into the hands of one family, while it is impossible to take off 50,000 of burthens from the oppressed peoples. ...... The worst is the not permitting people to use honest methods of filling their purses by procuring through the medium of legitimate commerce those gains which others appropriate to themselves unduly by (an abuse of) authority. II. On the great poverty and the great luxury (that abound).]

An antithesis rhetorically carried out. III. "Dell' annona e del vino" [On the corn and wine]. Chiefly on the abuses of the annona.

"I ministri del principe vogliono far da mercanti. Quindi tanti fallimenti di mercanti e di fornari, tanti sconcerti nelle case e nelli luoghi pii, il cui loro maggior avere consiste in terreni, e tanti grani lasciati marcire ne' granari a chi non ha voluto soccombere all' estorsione di si detestabil traffico. IV. Del ritardamento della giustitia e de' frutti de' luoghi di monte."

[The ministers of the prince wish to act as merchants. Hence so many failures of merchants and bakers, so many embarrassments in families and pious institutions, the greater part of whose property consists in lands, and such quantities of corn left to spoil in granaries to whoever would not succumb to the extortion of such detestable traffic. IV. On the delays of justice and of the fruits of the *luoghi di monte*.]

Even the *depositarii* of the monti were charged with embezzlement and arbitrary conduct. V. "Sopra l' irreverenza nelle chiese" [On irreverence in the churches]:—as in the theatre, he thinks. VI. "Sopra il fasto de' banchetti palatini" [On the pomp and luxury of the palatine banquets]. VII. "Sopra l' abuso del ceremoniale" [On the abuse of the ceremonial]. The author disapproves of the frequent (recurrence of the) Sanctissimus: he was revolted at people venturing to say at the Corpus Christi procession, "Sanctissimus Sanctissima portat."[1] VIII. "Sopra l' immunità ecclesiastica" [On the ecclesiastical immunities]:—he complains that criminals found an asylum in the churches. IX. "Sopra le lordure delle strade" [On the nastiness of the streets].—Well-intended, graphic upon the whole, but rather superficial.

146.

Vita del servo di dio papa Innocentio XI. raccolta in tre libri.—[Life of the servant of God, pope Innocent XI., collected in three books.] (MS. Rom.)

A very beautiful copy, consisting of 144 leaves, probably put into some subsequent pope's own hands.

The first book comprises the earlier period of Innocent XI.'s life. The author had put himself to the trouble of collecting authentic information respecting it. He denies that the pope ever served during a campaign in his youth: his holiness himself was questioned on the subject. On the other hand he relates that it was cardinal Cueva who had directed the attention of the young man, who had been recommended to him by the governor at Milan, to the superior advantages of the career presented by the curia.

The second book comprises the earlier government transactions of this pope, economy, suppression of useless offices, depreciation of the monti even in the case of communities, restriction of usury which was carried on particularly in Ghetto,[2] new taxes for the ecclesiastical perquisites. His maxim: "essere egli non padrone, ma amministratore delle cose alla santa sede spettanti con l' obbligo rigoroso di distribuirle non secondo la gratia de' parenti ma conforme la legge della giustitia.... Egli medesimo disse che da cardinale haveva cominciato ad esser povero e da papa era divenuto mendico" [that he was not the master, but the administrator of matters belonging to the holy see with the rigorous obligation to distribute them, not for the gratification of relations but according to the rules of justice. . .. He himself said that from the time of his being a cardinal he had begun to be poor, and as pope he had become a beggar]. Moreover, the author speaks of English affairs, and has no hesitation in declaring that king James wanted to make England Roman catholic: "Volendo ricondurre al Romano cortile i suoi sudditi, cominciò a servirsi nel ministero di cattolici."—[Wishing to lead back his subjects to the Roman court, he began by employing catholics in the ministry.]

In the third book we find Innocent XI.'s participation in the Turkish war; his personal qualities are exhibited. He is made to appear what he really was, energetic, disregardless of consequences, dignified. His whole conduct is described with much sagacity, far better than in the small work of Bonamicus which we find in Lebret, and which is, properly speaking, nothing more than a shallow panegyric.

Here, too, we find remarkable proofs of the opposition aroused by the practical efficiency of this pope. What univeral objections were started to the proposal of a bull for the abolition of nepotism. "Il volgo vedendo riformati molti ministri in palazzo et unite le loro cariche ad altri ministerj, che il papa non inclinava a spendere nè a beneficare con gratie, senza pensare più oltre biasimava 'l genio di Innocenzo come incapace della conditione del principe."—[The common people seeing many ministers reformed in the palace, and their charges united to other ministerial offices, that the pope was not inclined to spend, nor to benefit people with favours, without thinking farther, blamed the genius of Innocent as incapable of maintaining the condition of a prince.] This dislike soon revealed itself sometimes in one way, sometimes in another.

147.

Memoriale del 1680 al papa Innocenzo XI. concernente il governo e gli aggravj.—[Memorial of 1680 to pope Innocent XI., concerning the government and the oppressions.] (Bibl. Vallie.)

People acknowledge, this document proceeds to say, the holy zeal of the pope. Unfortunately, however, the consequence of his proceedings is a general dissatisfaction. Many families have been ruined by the reduction of the monti,—the cardinals are not listened to; no favours are granted to princes; the prelates are robbed of their expectations; the poor are without alms; the whole of Rome is one scene of wretchedness.

Who would believe it? Hardly has a pope given heed to the incessant complaints about nepotism, and does away with it, when people demand it back again. "Ond' è" [Hence it is], says our memorial after mentioning some reasons, "che sia una gran fortuna per un principe l' aver parenti buoni e capaci del governo: poiche avendo questo più potenti motivi dei ministri d' interessarsi nella riputatione e gloria di lui, possono anco con maggior sincerità

1 The translation of this puzzles me. As the word Sanctissima begins with a capital S., I presume it means the Virgin Mary, and that the word "portat" [bears] alludes to her carrying in her arms the Most Holy, that is, Christ. But that would require Sanctissimum. Qy. Sanctissimus [papa] sanctissima [symbola] portat.—Tr.

2 Place set apart for the Jews.—Tr.

e franchezza dire i loro pareri" [a piece of great good luck for a prince to have relations of good character and capable of government: in as much as such a one having stronger motives in his ministers to interest themselves in his glory and reputation, they can further speak out their opinions with greater sincerity and frankness].

148.

Ode satirica contra Innocenzo XI.—[Satirical ode against Innocent XI.] (Library at Frankfort on the Maine, MS. Glauburg. n. 31.)

Here the expression of dislike is still tempered in writing as is the preceding: but upon any really committed fault or though no more than a report giving occasion for censure, it vents itself in the most vehement explosions, as is the case in the following lines.

"Io non ritrovo ancor ne' vecchi annali
bestia peggior, che sotto hipocrisia
col sangue altrui tingesse e' l becco e l' ali.
Per altri era zelante, ma concesse
al nepote però che il gran comprasse
due scudi il rubbio e nove lo vendesse."

[Searching old annals nowhere do I find
A worse beast: clothed with hypocrisy
His beak and wings he dabbles with men's
blood.
Zealous for justice otherwise, he lets
His greedy nephew purchase grain at two
Scudi the rubbio, which he sells at nine.]

149.

Discorso sopra la soppressione del collegio de' secretarj apostolici fatta per la Sta di N. Sre Innocenzo XI.—[Discourse on the suppression of the college of the apostolic secretaries by the holiness of our lord Innocent XI.]

In spite of this violent opposition Innocent proceeded with his reforms. This *discorso* shows how people went to work in individual cases.

First, we have described the origin of these secretaries, who are to be found ever since the schism, and the mischiefs that were connected with their existence. The chief source of the evil was there being no administration belonging to the office.

"I possessori degli officii di fatto non hanno amministratione o servitio alcuno nella speditione dei negozj: mentre così il segretario di brevi come quello delle lettere o brevi a principi, come versati nel mestiere, si sogliono deputare ad arbitrio del papa fuori del collegio, nè l' officio porta seco la prelatura conferendosi a persone seculari per lo più inesperte et in età tenera, a guisa di quelli altri officii popolari i quali sono in commercio per il solo commodo et interesse borsale."

[The possessors of the offices, in point of fact, have no administration or service in the expediting of affairs: while both the secretary of briefs, and that of the letters or briefs to the princes, as being conversant with the business, are usually deputed at the pleasure of the pope out of the college, nor does the office carry with it the prelature, being conferred on secular persons, for the most part inexpert, and of tender age, after the manner of those other popular offices which are bought and sold solely for the sake of pecuniary advantages and interests.]

As the interests were enormous, for the chambers had to pay 40,000 scudi of annual interests for 200,000 scudi which it received, Innocent resolved to abolish the college, and appointed a congregation to calculate the claims of those who had a part in it.

The pope wished to repay only what the chamber had actually received: the shareholders demanded at least as much as the current price of the offices drew. The congregation could come to no decision.

Our author is of opinion that the pope was engaged to make good no more than the nominal price: he conceives this to be settled by the practice of the papal see.

Other writings are to be found that belong to this subject, for example, Stato della camera nel presente pontificato d' Innocenzo XI.; but they are made up of calculations, and are incapable of being extracted.

150.

Scritture politiche, morali e satiriche sopra le massime, istituto e governo della compagnia di Gesù.—[Political, moral and satirical writings, on the maxims, institute and government of the company of Jesus.] (Corsini Library.)

The most important is, In nomine Jesu. Discorso sopra la religione de' padri Jesuiti e loro modo di governare [In the name of Jesus. Discourse on the religion of the Jesuit fathers and their method of governing]: of itself about 400 leaves in thickness: composed at the time of the general Noyelle, consequently betwixt 1681 and 1686: unfavourable throughout to the order, yet so, that every word demonstrates that the author was most minutely acquainted with its condition from the middle of the century downwards. He adopts the following course.

I. He enumerates the defects he perceives under some rubrics. 1. "Di alcune loro massime" [Of some of their maxims], for example, of the opinion that their order was the chief, that all their prayers were heard, that all who died in their company were saved beyond a doubt. 2. "Della loro avidità et interesse" [Of their greed and interestedness].

Of their legacy-hunting a number of stories, showing how they contrived to entice people to give them presents,—of their traffic, and many still worse things. The most remarkable was their traffic; the range of view, however, is too narrow, confined as it is for the most part to Rome and the church-state. 3. "Del loro governo" [Of their government]. On the abuses of the monarchical power. On Nickel's deposition: see page 125. 4. "Qualità proprie del governo" [The peculiar characteristics of the government]. For example, Flagello sordo, that is, with respect to those that are punished, their offences are not named properly speaking: denunciation without previous admonition: a superior would often take advantage of the services of an inferior for superintendence which involved the dissolution of all order. 5. "Governo in ordine ai loro convittori e scolari" [The government with regard to their inmates and scholars]. Their defamatory punishments. 6. "La moltitudine delle regole" [The multitude of their rules]. They often ran counter to each other: there was not a single person who knew all of them.

II. After this, the author endeavours, after some repetitions on the causes and effect of this bad state of things, to point out the means of cure. It is remarkable that already he names among the last, above all, the institution of vicar-generalship, which had been so often called for, but to which the order would never allow itself to consent. He says: "Constituire un vicario generale per le provincie della Spagna, Germania, Francia et Indie,—cacciar sangue ad un corpo troppo pingue,—leggi certe a delitti certi" [To constitute a viear-general for the provinces of Spain, Germany, France, and the Indies,—to take blood from a body that is too fat,—certain fixed laws and certain fixed offences].

III. He returns then to his old method of enumerating the defects of the institution under sundry rubrics. Here a number of particulars come to be spoken of which are brought forward with more or less authenticity. Perhaps the last section is the best, "Delle loro Indiche missioni" [On their Indian missions], taken from the correspondences that were found in the papal archives, with great care, so that the individual sources are given: here the acts of disobedience towards the pope of which the Jesuits rendered themselves guilty in India, are adduced; already so long before Father Norbert.

This piece of writing accordingly is throughout unfavourable to the Jesuits: but at the same time extremely instructive. It reveals the faults of the order with such an acuteness and penetration, that one sees into its internal workings far more clearly than would have been possible otherwise. One cannot say that it is directly hostile: it acknowledges the good as well as the evil. Already, however, one perceives, what storms against the order were beginning to gather in the depths of men's minds.

151.

Relatione di Roma di Gio. Lando K^r, inviato straordinario per la ser^ma rep^ca di Venetia ad Innocentio XI. et amb^r straord^rio ad Alessandro VIII. in occasione della canonizzazione di S. Lorenzo Giustiniani.—[Report from Rome by John Lando Knight, envoy extraordinary for the most serene republic of Venice to Innocent XI., and ambassador extraordinary to Alexander VIII., on the occasion of the canonization of St. Lawrence Giustiniani.] 1691. (17 leaves.)

It is a loss that on the important government of Innocent XI. we possess no *relation* that deserves the name; none by which we have impartial elucidations of the results of that pope's exertions. The affairs of the republic were attended to in the first years of his reign, from 1678—1683, by cardinal Ottoboni, a Venetian, afterwards Alexander VIII., who never returned, and hence never reported; after him by John Lando, but without any properly official character. Lando, indeed, not the less gave in a final report, but first only after the conclave had again met; unhappily, moreover, he departs from the tone of Venetian reports.

He begins with discussing the divine dignity of the popedom, and laments that its sway is not universal. Nay, the heretics exceeded the catholics in number. Had not even the profligate Quietists set up their workshop in Rome! People at the Roman court would not believe that they had themselves to blame for this, yet it was really so. Even now, too, a man who contended for the church with deep learning, or with the examp'e of a holy life, was held in far less estimation than the canonists, who write in defence of the papal claims to deference. But the direct result of their over-driving matters, is that the princes set themselves in opposition to the court.

First, after having himself attempted to mark out the limits of spiritual and secular government, he tediously approaches secular affairs. He gives a melancholy description of the condition of the church-state: "desolato negli abitanti, spiantato nella coltura, ruinato coll' estorsioni, mancante d' industria" [desolate in its inhabitants, destroyed in its agriculture, ruined with extortions, wanting in industry]. He reckons the debts at forty-two millions. Alexander VII. had lessened the expenditure about 200,000 scudi, and had thus restored the balance between the expenditure and receipts. The pope had a vein of gold in the dataria. Yet even that money by no means remained in Rome: it came in in small sums, and went out in large: Innocent XI. had, it is true, contributed two millions of scudi towards the Turkish war. Of the above forty-two millions, perhaps fifteen millions had gone to the benefit of christendom.

He still thinks that Rome formed a common country, a trysting-place for all nations. Yet each was led thither purely by motives of interest. Of Germans and French there are few to be seen, in as much as they depend not for promotion on the Roman court, and Spaniards only of the lower class; were each prince in Italy, as well as elsewhere, to have himself the power of appointing to his ecclesiastical offices, the Roman court would fall to the ground. But, to compensate for this, Italy had the enjoyment of the popedom. "Tutta la corte, tutte le dignità, tutte le cariche, tutto lo stato ecclesiastico resta tra gli Italiani" [The whole court, all places of dignity, all the charges, the whole ecclesiastical state remained among the Italians]. And how much did this state of things involve. Owing to the uncertainty of succession in all the Italian families, the safety of Italy was absolutely dependent on the union betwixt Venice and Rome. He takes the opportunity of enlarging upon the necessity for the good understanding between the two. Yet he thinks that much might be conceded in Venice. The protection allowed to be given to disorderly friars—certain jurisdictional pretensions were taken very ill by people in Rome.

Now, these, as we see, are all very good and useful observations, indicative of a candid temper, but they cannot satisfy us who want more positive information upon the administration of the state..... Of the two popes with whom he served, Lando—for the rest a singular author, and who among other forms of speech likes nothing so much as the anacolyth,[1] says only what follows:

"Quando io rifletto a quello che ho sentito a risuonare senza ritegno contro Innocenzio XI., il quale veniva accusato di non dare audienza, d' asprezza, di crudeltà, d' inflessibile nemico di principi, di studioso di controversie, d' irresoluto e tenace, di distruttore delle diocesi e beni ecclesiastici: perche stava molti anni senza provederli, perche aveva calati li monti senza sollevare lo stato coll' avvanzo risultatone, per avere tenuta ferma l' estorsione che chiamano dell' annona, per essere stato indulgente a' quietisti, e tante altre cose con che non vi era persona che non esclamasse contro di lui: e pareva all' ora al volgo indiscreto che non fossero virtù d' alcuna importanza al pontificato, quale memorabilissimo d' una costante alienatione del suo sangue ed un' illibata disinteressatezza per lasciare intatto tutto quello era della camera, fuorche impiegato nelle guerre contro gl' infideli: e s' auguravano all' ora un pontefice che, se bene un poco indulgente alli suoi, lo fosse anco per gl' altri, e che fosse dotato di quelle virtù che all' ora si giudicavano più necessarie, perche pareva mancassero. Ma veduto poi che assonto Alessandro VIII., benche tutto umanità, facile all' audienze, dolce, compassionevole, pieghevole, rispettoso a principi, nemico d' impegni, sbrigativo, franco nei negotii ed in tutte le sorti di speditioni, benefico allo stato, sollevato di 200 mila scudi di gabella e dell' angaria, dell' annona, che ha fulminato li quietisti, che ha finito quietamente il negotio molestissimo del quartiere, ha soccorso lui pure la guerra contro il Turco, ed ha fatto ancora altre attioni importanti nella gran brevità del suo pontificato ad ogni modo, perche all' incontro ha mostrato affetto alli suoi nipoti, perche ha voluto fidarsi di loro più che degl' altri nelle cariche, perche ha voluto provederli con qualche larghezza ma di molto inferiore a quello hanno fatto tanti altri, e perche in questa parte ha mostrato un poco d' umanità e la tolleranza del sangue, è stato anche egli bersaglio d' invettive maligne e continue fin alla morte, ma egualmente ingiuste dell' uno e dell' altro."

[When I reflect upon what I have heard vociferated without reserve against Innocent XI., who was accused of not giving audiences, of rudeness, of cruelty, of being the inflexible enemy of the princes, of being studious of controversies, of being irresolute and tenacious, of being the destroyer of the dioceses and ecclesiastical property: accused of allowing many years to pass without providing for them, of lowering (the interest of) the monti without relieving the state with the advance resulting from it, of refusing to relinquish the extortion called *dell' annona*, of indulgence to the Quietists, and of so many other things with which there was not a person that did not exclaim against him: and then it appeared to the senseless multitude that there was no virtue of any importance to the pontificate, such as that most memorable one of a constant alienation from his own blood (relations) and a pure disinterestedness in leaving untouched everything belonging to the exchequer, excepting only what was employed in the wars with the infidels: and then they would have a pontiff who, although a little indulgent to his own people, should be so also to others, and who should be endued with those virtues which were then thought more necessary, because it appeared they were wanting. But having seen afterwards on the assumption of Alexander VIII., although he was all humanity, easy of access, gentle, compassionate, pliant, respectful to princes, an enemy to engagements, expeditious, frank in business affairs, and in all sorts of matters requiring to be expedited, beneficent to the state, which was relieved of 200,000 scudi of the gabella and of the tax on corn, who fulminated against the Quietists, who quietly finished that most troublesome affair of the (ambassador's?) quarters, who himself gave assistance to the war against the Turks, and further performed other important achievements in the very short time of his pontificate in every way, because on the other hand he showed affection to his nephews, because he had been willing to confide more in them than in others in public charges, because he wanted to provide for them with a certain though with a far inferior liberality to that which others have done, and because in that department he manifested a little humanity and patience of blood, he too became the butt of malignant invectives, and continued to be so till his death, but in both cases with equal injustice.]

1 A figure in grammar, when a word that is to answer to another, is not expressed.—Tr.

Finally, he refers to his own services, how in the course of his official duty he had written more than 700 despatches.

Well, these may comprise so many the more statements of facts. They are to be found partly in Venice, partly in Vienna.

152.

Confessione di papa Alessandro VIII. fatta al suo confessore il padre Giuseppe Gesuita negli ultimi estremi della sua vita.—[Confession of Pope Alexander VIII. made to his confessor father Joseph, Jesuit, in the last moments of his life.] (MS. Rom. 21 leaves.)

G. B. Berini, a clerk of the Vatican archives, seriously reports that he had found this document among other papers of the time of Alexander VIII. This he writes in 1736, when no one could have any interest in slandering a pope, who by that time had had so many successors. Hence, this small work, in spite of its ominous title, is worth consideration. What is it that the pope here acknowledges?

He begins with saying that since 1669 he had never regularly confessed:—assured of absolution by voices from heaven, he wished to do so now. And thereupon he acknowledges having acted as follows:—he had made use of the permission at one time given him by Clement, to subscribe papers for him, for making the most unallowable concessions; he had led Innocent XI. to take the steps he did against France, and yet had secretly conspired with the French against that pope; even after being raised to the popedom, he had knowingly and willingly promoted unfit, nay profligate persons, had thought only of enriching his kindred, and with a view to that, had seen justice and mercy sold in the palace, and what further there is.

One is well aware indeed, that here we have no confession of the pope's; it would have been in quite a different strain, would have revealed quite different details. I believe it is one of those satirical writings which so often appeared at that time, which might represent an opinion, which had been formed with respect to Alexander, but in no wise the truth. It had found its way among the writings of that period, where some zealous Archives official had met with it, and taken it to be genuine. In the Venetian Archives likewise, I stumbled on manifestly spurious pieces.

153.

Relatione di Domenico Contarini K. Roma 1696 5 Luglio.—[Report by Dominick Contarini, Knight, Rome, 5th July, 1696.] (Venetian Arch. 18 leaves.)

Contarini had already been at the French and imperial when he was dispatched to the papal court. He was originally sent to Alexander VIII., whom he found by that time so unwell that he could not be presented to him. His report is devoted to Innocent XII.

Antonio Pignatelli, born in 1615, traced his lineage from the family of the dukes of Monteleone in Naples, and early passed into the prelature. He was vice-legate of Urbino, inquisitor of Malta, governor of Perugia: a career not in itself to be despised, but which presented little to satisfy ambition. Pignatelli felt occasionally inclined to abandon the ecclesiastical course of life altogether. But he succeeded in obtaining a nuncioship, which seemed to him the surest means of promotion. He administered the Florentine, for eight years the Polish, the German, which in the regular course procured the cardinal's hat; but whether, says Contarini, from the influence of unpropitious stars, or from dislike to him on the part of the then government of Clement IX., instead of being rewarded, he was called away and sent off as bishop to Legge, on the extreme frontiers of Naples. Under these circumstances, he had to summon up all the force of his mind, the most masculine firmness, and in fact everybody was amazed at the moderation and resignation he showed. With a serenity above nature, he even expressed his thanks for this appointment, "because he had now no longer to sustain the heavy burthen of that nuncioship." Contarini assumes that Clement IX. sent Pignatelli to that bishopric, and that Clement X. recalled him to Rome: yet we find that, according to the Roman authors, both events took place under Clement X. However that may be—whether it was a wrong done by himself or one done by another, that cardinal Altieri wished to atone for—he placed Pignatelli beside his uncle as *mastro di camera:* in this office Innocent XI. found him and confirmed him in it.

Now, however, his fortune took a sudden rise. In 1681 he became cardinal, immediately thereafter bishop of Faenza, legate of Bologna, archbishop of Naples. Already, on the death of Innocent XI. he was thought of in the conclave: after Alexander VIII.'s departure, what nobody had expected, even the French were for him, a Neapolitan. The reason was this, that they needed a mild and pacific man. So he was elected, though only after that difficult conclave of five months, which wearied out all the cardinals.

Innocent XII., too, confirmed Albano and Panciatichi, the one the secretary of briefs, the other the datarius—whom he found in office, although they had owed their promotion to his predecessor. Spada's appointment to the secretaryship of state met with general approbation: this was done by the advice of cardinal Altieri. The nephews of Alexander VIII. alone were not confirmed in their offices: he kept himself strictly to the example of Innocent XI.

"Andava procurando il papa d'imitare Innocentio XI., di cui è creatura et aveva preso il nome, forzandosi servisse al modello del	[He endeavoured to imitate pope Innocent XI., by whom he was promoted, and whose name he has taken, striving to make the form

suo la forma di quel governo, levandoli però quella parte che nell' austerità e rigidezza non era stata laudata."

[of that government serve as a model for his own, with the exception, however, of that part of it which, on the ground of austerity and rigour, has not been praised.]

As we see, he sought to surpass his model by superior mildness. He gave audiences easily, and owed his good name chiefly to those which were public and for the poor. Although they did not, as these hoped, lead to the rapid decision of their lawsuits, yet they kept the arbitrary violence of the aristocracy in check.

"Tutti confessavano che questo publico ricorso portava un gran freno a tutti li ministri e giudici, mentre era troppo facile la strada di avvicinarsi all' orecchie del principe e di scoprirli quello che in altri tempi era impedito o dalla autorità o dall' astutia di chi s' appressava al papa."

[All confessed that this public recourse (to the pope) formed a powerful check on all the ministers and judges, while the path lay too easy for approaching the ears of the prince, and for detecting that which in other times was prevented from being known, either by the authority or by the astuteness of those who were about the pope.]

An unlucky accident for some time impeded his active exertions: but he soon resumed them again.

The French affair was settled; the most important reforms commenced. The bull upon nepotism made its appearance, in which it was enjoined that the benefices and church revenues which for the future might be conferred upon nephews, were not to exceed the sum of 12,000 scudi. Innocent XII. abolished the power of purchasing such important offices as those of the chierici di camera [clerks of the chamber]; he paid back the price, 1,016,070 scudi: "he by this deprived money of its might, and re-opened to virtue the possibility of rising to higher positions." Forthwith people looked for many other reforms. "The pope," says Contarini, "contemplates nothing but God, the poor, and the reformation of abuses. He lives very abstemiously: he devotes every hour, regardless of his health, to his office. He is blameless in his morals, conscientious, disinterested, uninfluenced by a wish to favour his relations, full of love to the poor, furnished with all the endowments that could be wished for in a chief of the church. Could he but himself do everything, he would be one of the first popes."

Nevertheless this did not please everybody. Contarini regrets that Innocent had no nephews who could feel a personal interest in their uncle's glory; that too much scope was left to his ministers, ("vedendosi offuscate quelle grandi e risplendenti virtù dalla solertia de' ministri troppo pratici dell' arte della corte)" [(those great and resplendent virtues being evidently obscured by the craft of ministers too deeply versed in the arts of the court)]: these were accused of contriving, in order to give the zeal of Innocent XII. another direction, to turn his attention exclusively to the support of the poor. The hospital at the Lateran was proposed. Soon it engrossed all the pope's thoughts. "Questo chiodo fermò l' ardente volontà del papa di riformare."—[That nail arrested the pope's keen desire for reform.]

The author is convinced that the pope might have saved and laid aside two millions of scudi. He is profoundly penetrated with the purity of the pope's sentiments; calling him a man of irreproachable, nay, of blameless life and manners.

154.

Relazione di Roma di Nicolò Erizzo Kr 1702, 29 Ottobre.—[Report on Rome by Nicolo Erizzo, knight, 29th October, 1702.]

N. Erizzo had already accompanied P. Mocenigo on his embassy under Clement X., now he had himself become ambassador: he arrived while Innocent XII. was still reigning; and after that made out the first years of Clement XI. His report derives a double value from his having already been long acquainted with Rome.

He first treats of the preceding popes. After some general observations, he comes to Innocent XI., "that holy man, whose chief merit by no means lay in the sciences, but who, to compensate that, possessed a knowledge of political economy, and not only succeeded in restoring the balance betwixt the expenditure and income, but could also richly support the emperor and the Poles in their contest with the Osmen." Alexander VIII. did not at least give his nephews money belonging to the exchequer. On the other hand he lost immensely by the failure of the house of Nerli, and many are inclined to ascribe his death to that loss. Innocent XII. closed the abyss of nepotism: although he did so much for the poor, remitted a tax, executed buildings for the court, and harbour buildings, yet, after all, he left a considerable sum in the treasury. But he lived too long for the college of cardinals, which he, too, on his side, set at no high value. To them he appeared to sacrifice the interests of the holy see to a spirit of subserviency to the monarchical courts.

At last he died on the 27th of September, 1700, and the cardinals threw themselves with great zeal into the affairs of the conclave. Their object was to elect a pope who should make good again the losses which they considered they had sustained. They destined for this cardinal Marescotti, a man "of strong breast, worthy of the government, obstinate in his purposes, and of inflexible resolution." Erizzo calls him a great man. He was supported by the imperial and Spanish ambassadors. Nevertheless too much zeal often proves hazardous to the election of a pope, and was fatal to Marescotti. The French, who dreaded finding him an open enemy, succeeded in excluding him. Upon that a great many others were proposed: but there were objections to all of them: one was too violent, another was too mild, a third had too many nephews: the friends of the Jesuits opposed cardinal Noris, because he had treated them ill in his history of Pelagianism. The zealous, on this occasion first distinguished as *the zelanti*, would willingly have elevated Colloredo, but the rest considered him too strict: at last, on the arrival of the news of Charles II.'s death, "the cardinals," says Erizzo, "were visibly touched by the hand of God, so as in a moment to be loosed from their passions and from the hopes that each flattered himself with, and turned their eyes to cardinal Albani with that internal movement which is the greatest sign of the divine impulse." Cardinal Albani opposed his being chosen: Erizzo thinks the opposition he made was sincere and seriously felt. He appeared to yield at length, more from the scruples he entertained, and to prevent farther entreaty, than of his own free will.

Erizzo now proceeds to describe the ancestry and the personal character of the pope-elect.

Albani drew his origin from Urbino. When the old Francis Maria of Urbino resolved before his death to hand over his dukedom to Urban VIII., he despatched an Albani who had himself given him that advice, to intimate it to the pope. Twice he sent him off. The first time he repented of what he had done, and recalled his ambassador. Erizzo asserts that the second time, also, he changed his mind, and gave a counter-order, but on that occasion Albani did not return from his mission, and without more ado delivered the act of surrender to Urban VIII. In return, he became senator of Rome, and his son *mastro di camera* with cardinal Barberini. His son again was John Francis Albani, the new pope.

John Francis Albani devoted himself to literature and the ecclesiastical career: fortune favoured him so far, that he soon enjoyed the personal intimacy of the popes of the day. "Under Innocent XI.," says Erizzo, "he learned to be more deliberate in forming his resolutions than he was naturally inclined to be, and to persevere in what he once undertook; under Alexander, he adopted freer and bolder forms of business; he was considered at once prudent and resolute, prompt and thoughtful, and, in outward appearance at least, willing to serve everybody: these accomplishments he afterwards exercised under Innocent XII. That suspicious old man could not bear either his datarius or his secretary of state: Albani alone had access to him, and found means of rendering himself indispensable at once to him and to the court."

Clement XI.'s first step, after his election, was to intimate to the ambassadors that he must do away with many innovations that had crept in under his predecessors: he called the governor to his coronation, which these (ambassadors) did not wish on account of their controversies about precedency:—he recalled all privileges of asylum:—the ambassadors saw that he did all this merely to produce an impression upon the court.

His subsequent appointments to office do not appear very fortunate to Erizzo. Clement surrounded himself with none but weak persons.

"Felicitato il coraggio di questi suoi ordini dal successo e dal rispetto de' regj rappresentanti, non credette Sua Sta d' aver bisogno a palazzo de' ministri di gran valore: onde chiamovvi per segretario di stato il cardinale Paulucci di cortissima esperienza, ed elesse per datario il cardinale Sacripante, infaticabile e diligentissimo per quell' impiego, ma non insignito che della qualità di buon curiale. Indi diede a mons^r^ Olivieri suo parente la segretaria de' brevi, che aveva digià egregiamente esercitata sotto di lui stesso: e pose nelle cariche che più lo avvicinavano, li antichi suoi amici e parenti, come mons^r^ Paracciani gran legista, mons^r^ Origo per segretario delle lettere Latine e Maffei per coppiere confidente, tutta gente di pochissima estrazione, urbinati o delli vicini municipj, che non avendo veduto se non Roma hanno per conseguenza pochissima cognizione delli principi e molto meno poi degli affari del mondo. Non volle presso di se cardinali di grande testa nè ministri che da essi dipendessero, preferendo la sua quiete e la sua autorità a que' consigli, che non gli potevano venire dalle suddette persone domestiche non esercitate nelli maneggi e digià tra loro gelose e discordi. Meno volle Don Orazio suo fratello, padre di tre figlioli di grande aspettazione, uomo d' una singolare modestia ed integrità, lasciatolo alle sue angustie per pompa dell' osservanza della bolla contro il nipotismo, che la Sta Sua giurò nel giorno della sua esaltazione, con aspetto d' evitarne interamente lo scandolo, il quale

[The vigour of these ordinances of his having been happily followed with success, and with the respect of the royal representatives, his holiness did not think he had any need, at the palace, of ministers of great worth: hence he called to the secretaryship of state cardinal Paulucci, whose experience had been very short, and chose for datarius cardinal Sacripante, an indefatigable person, and most assiduous in that employment, but not distinguished for aught beyond the character of a good member of the curia. Hence he gave the secretaryship to the briefs to his relation, monsignor Olivieri, who had already administered it admirably under himself, and placed in the charges that were nearest himself his old friends and relations, such as monsignor Paracciani, a great lawyer; monsignor Origo as the secretary of Latin letters; and Maffei as confidential cup-bearer;—all persons of the lowest extraction, belonging to Urbino or the neighbouring townships, who having never seen anything beyond Rome, have consequently very little knowledge of the princes and much less of the affairs of the world. He had no wish to have about him cardinals of great talents, nor ministers who should be dependent on them, preferring his own quiet and his own authority to those counsels which could never come to him from the said persons of his household who have had no practice in affairs, and already are mutually jealous and disagreed among themselves. Still less would he have Don Horace,

però, per sentimento di molti, *semper vitabitur et retinebitur semper.*"

his brother, father of three sons of great expectation, a man of singular modesty and integrity, having abandoned him to his straitened circumstances by an ostentatious observance of the bull against nepotism, which his holiness swore to on the day of his exaltation, with the look of one who would utterly eschew the scandal, which, however, in the opinion of many, *semper vitabitur et retinebitur* [will always be eschewed and always retained].

Nevertheless, there straightway appeared the greatest difficulties. The quarrel about the Spanish succession became extremely dangerous to the Roman court. Clement XI. at first comported himself very doubtfully. The ambassador thought he could trace his whole behaviour to excessive cunning. When he proposed an Italian league to the Venetians, his chief object was to draw out what were the sentiments of the Venetians.

From these observations bearing on politics and general matters, Erizzo passes to ecclesiastical affairs, particularly to the disputed points that were incessantly agitated betwixt Venice and Rome. Rome, says he, has a double character: the one holy, in so far as the pope is the guardian of christendom and of the rights of God; as such she must be revered; the other secular, in so far as he seeks to extend his power, which has nothing in common with the usage of the first centuries: against this, people must be on their guard. Yet he cannot brook Venice's having been passed over at a promotion of cardinals under the last reign: he laments the republic's not having the right of giving away its bishoprics, as in former times: how many of the poor nobility might she then support: the subjects of Venice now sought, by indirect methods, and through the intercessions of foreign princes, to obtain public appointments: cardinal Panciatichi had introduced into the dataria the maxim that those very persons ought to be favoured who were most independent of the princes in whose territories the benefices lay; he considers it an abuse that the nephews of the popes should participate so largely in the ecclesiastical property of his native country: wherefore, too, was the rank of Venetian nobili so readily conceded to them? Other states, even the grand-duke of Tuscany, had a list of nuncios transmitted to them from which they could choose whom they pleased, the republic enjoyed no such honour; the title of Carissimo [Dearest], too, was refused at Rome to the doge of Venice. We see that the old dissensions were perpetually augmented by the addition of new.

On this account the ambassador recommends the republic seriously to take up the concerns of Rome. Though a pope might not have it in his power to assist any more as in former days, still he had it much in his power to injure, particularly if young, energetic and parsimonious.

155.

Relatione del N. U. Gio. Franc. Morosini K[r] fu ambasciatore al sommo pontefice Clemente XI. 1707, 17 Dec.—[Report of the embassy in which G. F. Morosini, knight, was ambassador to the supreme pontiff Clement XI. 17th December, 1707.] (36 leaves.)

Morosini, Erizzo's successor, was from January 1702 to November 1706 with Clement XI., whose administration now first displayed the whole of its peculiar character.

Morosini minutely describes how zealously this pope imitated his most renowned predecessors. The very tears with which he had refused the (papal) dignity were not without a model. He performed all those external acts by which a man (as was thought) presents a good example to others.

"Vita sobria e regolata: frequenti publiche devotioni alla scala santa, a visite di chiese, al servitio negli hospitali: somma edificatione et accuratezza nei riti sacri e nelle più solenni ed humili funtioni, ai quali vuol supplire anche con pregiuditio della salute. Al paragone pure dell' interesse comparisce egualmente incolpabile: prima consultore, poi esecutore delle bolla del nipotisimo. Con ogni facilità dona ai vescovi poveri le sue propine, e nudrisce del proprio molti operarj ed opere pie. Nella scelta de' vescovi, sopra tutto essentiale al servitio della chiesa, con la debita pesatezza procede, cercando l' informationi dai fonti più sinceri, senza dar luogo che molto parcamente al favore. Ne esamina talvolta alcuno egli stesso ad usanza dei papi antichi. Dell' altre dignità parimenti e beneficj ecclesiastici va così misurato ed attento nella distributione che anche sopra gli stessi suoi congiunti vuol che si scorga giustificata

[A sober and well-regulated life: frequent public devotions at the scala sancta, at the visitations of churches, at the service of the hospitals: eminent edification and exactness in the sacred rites and in the most solemn and humble functions, to which he would even devote himself to the extent of injuring his health. On comparing him with others in point of disinterestedness, he seems equally blameless: first having advised and afterwards executed the bull against nepotism. With the utmost readiness he presents (remits?) his own fees to poor bishops, and nourishes many pious labourers and labours. In the choice of bishops, a matter of essential importance to the service of the church, he proceeds with all due deliberation, seeking information from the purest sources, without giving scope, except very sparingly, to favour. He himself often examines each of them, according to the practice of the ancient popes.

la convenienza d' accomodarli dal requisito di studj e costumi comendabili."

[He proceeds with such measure and attention in the distribution of other such like dignities and church benefices, that even with respect to these his relations desire that the conveniency of accommodating them should be seen to be justified by the requisite degree of studies and commendable manners.]

In this spirit, Clement conducted likewise jurisdictional matters, that is to say, with all the zeal that his office required of him. Here and there he even gained ground. The new king of Spain found himself led to present a petition to him about leave to bring ecclesiastics before the secular court and to demand payment of the tithes. The king of Poland placed certain of the members of the higher clergy (for trial) before the court of the pope. The viceroy of Naples submitted to the papal commands, after a protracted resistance, at the critical moment when the Germans burst into Lower Italy—(" un trionfo che sarà registrato nelli annali della chiesa") [(a triumph which shall be recorded in the church's annals)]; so much the more warmly were Savoy and Lorraine attacked. The pope understood how to take advantage of the most favourable moment ("studiosissimo d' ingrandire con i motivi di pietà la potenza") [(being most studious of aggrandizing his power on grounds of piety)]. Morosini considers the whole court penetrated with a similar spirit. People would not hear of any distinction between church and state: all was church: every congregation would call itself holy, be the object of its consultations what it might: no distinction was made between pastors of the church and prelates of the court: even the former were loosed from their office and busied themselves with state affairs. Piety, moreover, was made use of as a sort of coin which was indispensable to a man's rising in life. Four of the congregations are specially brought forward as being particularly deserving of notice: the inquisition, which deserved all support, in as much as it watched over purity of doctrine, only it was a striking fact that the worst of heresies was to be met with just in Rome itself (he means Quietism); the propaganda: unfortunately few persons were now to be found willing to devote themselves, with absolute self-resignation, to the affairs of missions; of bishops and conventual clergy, which exercised a very necessary superintendence, particularly over the latter; and of immunities: this was posted, like a sentinel, to watch the frontiers of spiritual and secular jurisdiction: were it to succeed in its views, the monarchical power would be utterly annihilated.

Morosini now passes to the state. He repeats the complaints that had been so frequent for some time, of want of inhabitants and cultivation: the pope would willingly have introduced ameliorations, for example, the settlement and cultivation of the campagna, but all ended in mere splendid projects. The ambassador remarks that the (pope's) spiritual authority increased likewise his monarchical power. The power of the senate he considers a laughing-stock for such a title. The barons were put on a level with the meanest of the people in respect of punishments, the pope kept a sharp eye over them, as he well knew that there was something constrained in their condition. At last he comes to political relations. The most important passage, on the relations of the pope with the king of France and the emperor, on which at that time all once more depended, I give as it stands.

"Se il papa abbia avuta mano o partecipatione nel testamento di Carlo II., io non ardirò d'asserirlo, nè è facile penetrare il vero con sicurezza. Bensì addurrò solo due fatti. L'uno che questo arcano, non si sa se con verità, fu esposto in un manifesto uscito alle stampe in Roma ne' primi mesi del mio ingresso all' ambasciata, all' ora che dall' uno e l'altro partito si trattava la guerra non meno con l'armi che con le carte. L'altro che il papa non s'astenne di far pubblici elogj al christianissimo d'essersi ritirato dal partaggio, ricevendo la monarchia intiera per il nipote. Fatto riflesso a tali premesse, non pare che rendano stupore le conseguenze vedutesi di direttione fluttuante e fra se stessa contraria, non potendo mai riuscir uniformi attioni nate da diversi principj: e tali erano l'obbligo da una parte d'ostentar indifferenza propria di padre comune, e l'occulto affetto et impegno preso dall' altra nel giudicare senza maggior pesatezza li vantaggj et il merito della causa. Considerò piamente la Sta Sua il decoro e beneficio della religione nell' escludere gli eretici dall' usurpato. Concepì speranza, facilitata dal genio a Francesi, che o non vi sarebbe guerra o si farebbe inutilmente contro le forze di quell' invitta natione: e dandosi a credere che la monarchia si manterebbe unita, non

[Whether the pope had any hand or share in the testament of Charles II., I will not take it upon me to assert, nor is it easy to penetrate into the truth with safety. Certainly I shall allege two facts only. One is, that this secret, with what truth is not known, was set forth in a manifesto issued at the printing-office at Rome in the first months of my living there as ambassador, at the time when on both sides war was waged no less with arms than with paper. The other is, that the pope did not abstain from passing public eulogies on the most Christian king for having withdrawn from the partition, receiving the entire monarchy for the nephew. Reflecting on these premises, it does not seem that any surprise need be felt at results being seen to take a fluctuating direction and being inconsistent with themselves, it being impossible that uniformity of action should ever proceed from different principles; and such were the duty on the one hand, of showing the indifference that ought to distinguish the common father, and the secret affection and engagement taken on the other hand, in judging without more deliberation the advantages and the merits of the cause. His holiness piously considered the decorum and benefit to religion involved in the exclusion of heretics

stimò in un tal vaticinio meritar disprezzo, errando con la finezza Spagnola, la quale in tal caso ebbe ragioni di necessità più che di politica. L'esito instruì dell' altre ponderationi che dovevano avanzarsi. S'ammassò, scoppiò e tuttavia infuria fatale agl'inimici et agli amici quel fiero nembo che la gelosia, l'astio, l'interesse eccitarono nelle potenze collegate ad abbattere la macchina sospettata nella Francia di monarchia universale. . . . . Riuscì ad ogni modo per molto tempo ai Francesi lo studio di mantenersi nel credito d'invincibili appresso il papa, il quale pieno di confidenza seguendo tacitamente i loro consiglj veniva dagl'incauti lodato d'una condotta che oscurasse quella d'ogni altro: perche dove la Ser^ma Republica in particolare osservando una sincera neutralità pareva, patisce danni nelle sostanze de' sudditi, aggravj al decoro e lo sdegno d'ambi li partiti: egli all' incontro col professare neutralità e minacciare assieme di romperla immantenente contro quel partito che l'offendesse, ma intendendosela occultamente con Francesi, era da questi coltivato et occorrendo difeso senza dispendio, da Cesarei trattato con riguardo per non fornirlo di pretesti a deponer anche l'apparenza di neutrale. Furon immuni per un pezzo li suoi stati: vide rispettate le censure in mezzo all' armi, e comparse flotte di eretici ne' suoi mari senza il minimo oltraggio. Ma il rovesciamento della fortuna Francese, particolarmente in Italia, ha fatto scorgere se meritasse allora encomii o la condotta o la sorte, e se le sane e sincere insinuationi fatteli da VV. EE. replicar spesso col mezzo dei loro ministri di soda indifferenza come padre comune per rendersi arbitro e venerato a beneficio proprio e della cristianità e d'aumentare le sue truppe sotto buoni officiali per appoggiar meglio il rispetto contro l'altrui intemperanza, dovessero sbracciarsi come consiglj infelici, anche nell' esperienza di chi li porgeva. Il frutto d'aver preferite arti più oblique e studj d'economia, la peggior consigliera della politica, fu di soffrir dopo e tutt'ora ciò ch' è noto, ma quel ch' è più, con apparenza di non soffrir senza colpa nel tribunale della fama, ch' è sovrano anche ai principi. Spedì, come adduce in sua difesa, nuncj estraordinarj per la pace universale senza riguardo a spesa et all' ingiuria dell' esclusione incontrata a Vienna: propose leghe, accordi, armistitj per la quiete particolare di questa provincia, ma fuor di tempo e dopo che le dimostrationi di partialità del principio e nel progresso notate introdussero il verme nei migliori semi: onde l'essersi reso una volta sospetto fu un spogliar il zelo di autorità e constituire per sempre impotente il principal instrumento della concordia. Difficile riuscirà in effetto alla Sta Sua il purgar questa imputatione, anzi quella d'aver contribuito a tirare nel suo senso tutti li principi d'Italia appresso quali voleva, notoria essendo la condotta non solo di quelli di Parma, suo feudatario, ma della casa di Fiorenze: onde la sola cautela costante della Ser^ma Republica ha data soggetione al papa e documento agli altri, mercandone però immeritata odiosità appresso Francesi che sopra di lei fu da Sua B^ne scaricata."

from usurpation. He conceived the hope, readily suggested by his natural liking for the French, that either there would not be war, or that it would be waged to no purpose against the forces of that unconquered nation: and giving into the belief that the monarchy would maintain itself united, he did not reckon upon deserving contempt for auguring as much, erring with the subtlety of a Spaniard, which in such a case had reasons of necessity rather than of policy. The result has informed us of the other considerations which ought to have presented themselves. That fierce cloud, which jealousy, envy, and interest had raised in the allied powers with the view of crushing the project suspected to exist in France for establishing an universal monarchy, gathered, burst, and continued to rage, fatal alike to foes and friends. . . . . The French succeeded for a long while every way in their studious endeavours to maintain the credit with the pope of being invincible, who, full of confidence, while tacitly following their counsels, came to be praised by the incautious for a conduct that eclipsed that of everybody else: for where the most serene republic in particular, seemed to observe a sincere neutrality, suffered losses in the substance of its subjects, offences to decorum and the scorn of both parties, he, on the contrary, while professing neutrality, and threatening at the same time to break it immediately against the party which should offend him, but having a secret understanding with the French, had his friendship cultivated by them and met with defence at no cost, and was respectfully treated by the imperialists in order that he might have no pretext for laying down the appearance of neutrality. His states for a time were unassailed; he saw censures respected in the midst of arms; and fleets of heretics appeared in his seas without the least outrage. But the French reverses, particularly in Italy, have showed whether praises were then deserved either by conduct or fortune, and if the sound and sincere recommendations, made to him by your excellencies, repeatedly, through your ministers, to be staunchly impartial as the common father, so as to render himself arbiter and venerated for his own advantage and that of christendom, and to augment his troops under good officers for the better maintenance of respect against the intemperance of others, should be held up as unhappy counsels, even in the experience of those who proffered them. The fruit of having preferred more oblique arts and efforts at economy, the worst political adviser, was the suffering afterwards and till now of what is known, but what is more, with the appearance of not suffering without censure before the tribunal of fame, to which princes themselves must bow. He dispatched, as he adduced in his defence, nuncios extraordinary for universal peace, without regard to the cost and to the insult of the exclusion met with at Vienna: he proposed laws, contracts, armistices for the particular quiet of this province, but out of time and after that the demonstrations of partiality remarked at the beginning and in the progress of affairs, had introduced worms into the best seeds: whence to have rendered himself once suspected was to deprive zeal of authority, and to reduce to perpetual impotency the principal instrument of concord. His holiness, in fact, will find it difficult to clear himself of this imputation, also of that of having contributed to drag, as he thought proper, all the princes of Italy after whom he pleased, the conduct not only of the prince of Parma, his vassal, but of the house of Florence being notorious: hence the constant caution of the most serene republic has given matter of reflection to the pope and proof to the rest, bartering for these indeed unmerited hatred on the part of the French which was discharged upon her by his holiness.]

156.

Lorenzo Tiepolo K^r Proc^r Relatione di Roma, 1712.—[Lorenzo Tiepolo, knight, procurator, Report from Rome.] (40 leaves.)

The rivalry between the spiritual and secular forum (jurisdiction) challenged more and more attention every year. L. Tiepolo begins with it at once.

But this he does with unusual earnestness. The materials, says he, have been purposely complicated; to disentangle them, to allow the secular powers to have all that is their own, and yet not to infringe upon the reverence due to the papal see, one would need have a double measure of the grace of God.

He first describes anew the personal character of Clement XI. He too admires his learning, his zeal, his affability and moderation; yet possibly, says he, they may not have their only allowable aim, virtue itself, apart from human by-considerations, and on that account they may not be blessed by God: possibly the zeal with which he devotes himself to the government is attended with too high an estimate of his own deserts, and is directed less to the thing itself than to the praise and respect that may accrue from it:—praise is all-powerful with him; his physician, for example, takes advantage of this tendency, for the purpose of preserving his influence; flattery inflames him to maintain the honour of the holy see:—hence it follows that he pays so little regard to the rights of princes and states: those who are about him venture so far as to speak of these in so scornful a manner as comports neither with the high position of the pope, nor perhaps even with Christian charity.

From the pope he passes to his minister, whom he as little, as his predecessors, considers particularly distinguished, and thinks him fitted for subordinate services, not for the conduct of affairs. 1. Cardinal Albani.—The pope had twice waited till after his mission before he named him a cardinal. The court approved this nomination, for thus it believed it might find a means of access to the pope, an interest (with him); yet Clement XI. gave him little or no influence.

"E certo che l' autorità del card^le nipote non apparisce a quel segno che per l' ordinario s' haveva veduto in quella corte."

[It is certain that the authority of the cardinal-nephew does not appear to the degree that has been ordinarily seen at that court.]

2. The secretary of state, cardinal Paulucci, good at heart, but not quite a very fit person, dependent on the pope with a kind of fear. 3. Corradini, auditor of the pope:

"Dotto nel dritto, ma di non uguale esperienza negli interessi dei principi:—forte nell' impegno, ma pieghevole alla ragione."

[Learned in the laws, but not equally experienced in the interests of the princes:—strong in keeping engagements, but pliable to reason.]

The only one to whom a man durst thoroughly commit himself: it was useful to bring matters to him where one was unquestionably in the right: less so where the case was doubtful;—he was not on good terms with the nephew; it was even believed that the latter had promoted him to the cardinalship for the purpose of his being removed from being nearer to the pope. 4. Origli, secretary of the Consulta, the rival of Corradini, who, on that account, attached himself more closely to the nephew.

"Pare che più con l' accortezza et adulatione che con la fermezza et ingenuità abbia avanzato la sua fortuna."

[It seems he has advanced his fortune more by penetration and flattery than by firmness and ingenuousness.]

5. Cardinal Sagripante, datarius, who had become rich only by parsimony, strict in his affairs, removed from all politics. The dataria were falling off more and more every day; even in Spain, fraudulent proceedings were no longer tolerated; hence it happened that those cardinals who did not know how to manage their property—"si può dire essere un vero distintivo dell' abbadie de' cardinali il ritrovare le case in abbandono e le chiese dirocate"

1 Meaning, I suppose, for which she, the republic, had to thank his holiness.—Tr.

—[it might be said to be the true distinctive mark of the abbeys of the cardinals, to find the houses in a state of disorder and the churches in ruins]—could no longer maintain their former splendour. Were there to be a papal election, still would the creatures of Clement XI. hardly attach themselves closely to cardinal Albani, just because of his having little influence.

And now Tiepolo proceeds to give an account of political matters. As we have said, his point of view is politico-ecclesiastical; he discusses the controversies betwixt the Roman court and the princes; it was said that the pope had an equal affection for all: but it might better be said, he has an equally cold affection, an equally low esteem for all.

"E' ben vero che se pochi pontefici si hanno preso a tal punto quest' assunto di far pompa di superiorità sopra i principi, è forza di dire che anche pochi pontefici hanno havuto la sfortuna uguale al presente di non poter uscire dagl' impegni volontariamente con gli stessi principi presi, se non con qualche diminutione del suo honore. Pure se ha qualche interna inclinatione, quest' è riposta verso la Francia, benchè quella corte replicatamente si dolga delle sue partialità verso la casa d' Austria, e in fatti in più incontri l' evento ha comprovato i suoi lamenti, ma perchè ha havuto tutta la parte il timore. In ciò la corte di Vienna, o sia a caso o per la cognitione, rilevata del vero temperamento del pontefice ha nel trattar seco fatta la profittevole scielta delle minaccie e delle apprensioni."

[It is true indeed that if few popes have gone to such a point in assuming to make a pompous display of superiority over the princes, there is abundant ground to say that few popes, too, equal to the present, have had the misfortune to be unable to escape from engagements voluntarily contracted with the same princes, unless with some loss of honour. However, if he has any inward leaning, that lies towards France, although that court has repeatedly complained of his partiality towards the house of Austria, and in fact, on most occasions, the event has proved its complaints to be well-founded, but (only) because fear has had everything to do with it. In this the court of Vienna, whether accidentally or knowingly, encouraged by the true temper of the pontiff, has, in treating with him, made the profitable choice of threats and of apprehensions.]

These general remarks he then extends to individual states until he comes to Venice, on whose concerns, though now, it is true, of no importance to the world at large, he dwells at most length.

157.

Relatione di Andrea Corner K^r ritornato dall' amb^ria di Roma, 1724, 25 Luglio.—[Report of Andrew Corner, knight, on his return from the Roman embassy, 25th July, 1724.] (42 leaves.)

Thus keen were the antipathies excited by Clement XI., in spite of the best intentions and a blameless behaviour. Here, where he once more appears on the scene, we see, notwithstanding, that at least after his death the public voice very much changed. Then everybody admired him: even those joined in applauding him who shortly before had censured him. It was found, a thing which had never been believed, that if at times he had promised more than he could perform, it had really been from good nature. It came to light that from his private means he had dispensed the richest alms, the amount of which, during the twenty years of his reign, came to one million of scudi: a sum which, with a good conscience, he might have applied to his family. Corner relates that Clement, shortly before his death, asked cardinal Hannibal, his nephew, to forgive him for having left his family so ill provided for. ("Parera che il pontificato di Clemente sià stato effimero, quando fu de' più lunghi.")—[(It will appear that Clement's pontificate has been ephemeral, although one of the longest.)]

The change that had been expected appeared in the conclave. The whole college had, with few exceptions, been renewed under Clement XI.: but as cardinal Albani had had but little share, as in the government in general, so also in those nominations, the cardinals divided themselves according to their nations. Paulucci, secretary of state, as we know, to the former pope, was first proposed, but count Althan, the imperial ambassador, declared that his master would never acknowledge Paulucci as pope: he threw out this hint for the consideration of their eminences. Now, already previous to this, some friends of the Albani family had cast their eyes on Michael Angelo Conti: one of them, monsignor Riviera, became secretary to the conclave. First, he spoke about it to cardinal Spinola, who, after he had made inquiries, and found that Conti was not disliked, put himself with satisfaction at the head of the party, and proposed him. Count Altban made inquiries at his court. Hence it came to operate in Conti's favour that he had been nuncio in Portugal, and there had obtained the favour of queen Maria Anna of Austria, sister of Charles VI. The Austrian court was in favour of Conti; the whole Austrian connection, Portugal and Poland in particular, might be reckoned upon. The Spanish ambassador likewise sent inquiries to his court; its answer was not favourable, but it arrived too late: meanwhile Innocent XIII. had been already elected (8th May, 1721).

Innocent possessed striking qualifications for the ecclesiastical as well as the secular government. Only he was of a sickly constitution of body, and hence was very sparing in giving audiences. In return, however, it was of importance to have an audience with him: one stood in the place of many. He was very good at the comprehension of a case, and gave definite replies. The Maltese ambassador, says Corner, will remember how, after a somewhat stormy petition for succour, the pope instantly gave him his blessing, and rang the bell for him to go away. When the Portuguese ambassador demanded the elevation of the Bicchi above mentioned to the cardinalship, Innocent would at last no longer listen to him ("non ritrovando merito nel prelato e passando sopra tutti il riguardi che potea avere per una corona di cui era stato protettore") [(not finding merit in the prelate, and passing over all the grounds of respect he could have for a crown of which he had been the protector)].

The Roman families that claimed kindred with Innocent XIII., who hoped to have been promoted by him, found themselves much deceived; even his nephews could only with difficulty come to the enjoyment of 12,000 ducats, which had now become the usual income of a nephew.

The pope's main efforts were directed to the settlement of the controversies on the church's jurisdiction; yet in this he was nowise universally successful. A better mutual relation was formed with the imperial court: as in consequence of the above election was naturally to be expected.

158.

Relatione del N. H. Pietro Capello K[r] ritornato d' ambasciator di Roma, 1728, 6 Marzo.—[Report by N. H. Pietro Capello, Knight, on his return as ambassador from Rome, 6th March, 1728.] (14 leaves.)

Innocent XIII. died so early as the 7th of March, 1724, after a reign of little more than 34 months.

Capello, who further had been sent to Innocent XIII., agrees with his predecessor in the account he gives of that pontiff. He considers him pacific, possessed of a good judgment, considerate, steady in what he undertook. He confirms the rumour that the naming of Dubois as a cardinal, to which he had been induced by a regard to that person's power and influence, had filled this pope with painful scruples in his last moments.

"La di lui morte fu ben un' argomento delle più morali riflessioni: mentre attaccato da scrupoli di coscienza, tarlo che non lascia di rodere anco la mente dei papi, non potè mai lasciarsi persuadere a compire la nomina di quattro cardinali nella vacanza d' altrettanti cappelli: e per quello si è potuto iscoprire, fu giudicato che non sentisse di consumare una tale elettione forse per pentimento d' averne eseguita alcun' altra con maniere atte a turbare la di lui delicata coscienza. Tale non ordinario accidente partorì funeste conseguenze alla di lui casa, a favor della quale non restò alcun partito da disponere dopo la di lui morte: ma con tutto ciò vi fu universale argomento per giudicar molto bene di sua persona, che dimostrò per tali suoi ottimi sentimenti un spirito egualmente nobile che rasseguato."

[His death was truly a theme for the most moral reflections: while attacked by scruples of conscience, a worm which fails not to gnaw the mind of the popes, he would not allow himself to be persuaded to close the nomination of four cardinals for the same number of vacant hats: and in so far as could be discovered, it was judged that he did not like to carry through such an election perhaps from having repented of having made some other in such a manner as was fitted to disturb his delicate conscience. Such an unusual occurrence produced sad consequences to his family, in whose favour there remained no party to make dispositions after his death: but with all that there was there an universal reason for judging very favourably of his character, which showed by such his most excellent sentiments, a spirit equally noble and resigned.]

Benedict XIII. followed on the 29th of May, 1724. Capello thinks him very different from his predecessor: particularly resolute and ardent in all ecclesiastical matters. He remarks that there were few distinguished persons in the college of cardinals, no strong faction, and no prospect of such being formed under Benedict, as already the rivalry between Coscia and Fini was not allowed to go so far. There was indeed a faction of crowns, but it had no proper stability. A great impression was produced at court by the duke of Savoy at length obtaining his objects. Capello concludes from this that with time people may succeed in getting everything here (at Rome). He requires only quietness: the eagerness a man feels for his own affair must never vent itself in complaints.

Capello now goes more closely into properly Venetian interests. First, he demonstrates anew that Venice must enforce a more settled respect for itself at Rome. He once more suggests how the pope should be dealt with. One must endeavour to be always gaining him over with ecclesiastical courtesies, and to influence his inclinations without being observed. After this he passes more minutely into secular circumstances, particularly commerce. It would appear that the Roman state at the commencement of the 18th century, had very seriously contemplated commercial and industrial improvements.

The people of Dulcigno and Ragusa drove a trade in Ancona, which was not very welcome to the Venetians. In particular, they imported a deal of wax which used to be got formerly from Venice, and which people had now begun to manufacture in the church state.

Innocent XII. had commenced the building of St. Michael's a Ripa; Clement XI. had enlarged it: its importance was now enhanced with woollen and silk manufactures: "dalla figura d' un' ospitale, dove per carità alimentavano molti giovani, fu convertita con amplificatione di sito e con grandissima giunta di fabriche in una casa di commercio, nella quale a presente si travagliano le manifatture di lana e di seta" [from the figure of an hospital where many young persons were charitably alimented, it was converted, by enlarging the site, and by a very great addition of buildings, into a house of commerce in which manufactures of wool and silk are at present carried on]. Already were there cloths made which rivalled those of France, and were exported through Ancona to Turkey and Spain. But I will give the whole passage as it stands.

"In questo sontuoso edificio vi si è introdotta la fabrica degl' arazzi con egual perfettione di quelli che si travagliano in Fiandra et in Francia: e vi è fondato un lanificio, nel quale vi entra la lana et escono i panni perfetionati di tutto punto. La fabrica di seta dipendente da questo luogo s' esercita in più contrade di Roma, e quelle della lana sono in tanti generi divise, con idea d' adattarle all' uso del paese per haverne con un spaccio facile il pronto ritratto. Si fabricano in S. Michele tutti li panni per le militie, li scoti per servitio de' monasterj, le tele di tutti i generi per il vestiario delle ciurme, e li panni sonno divisi in varii generi che restano distribuiti per una data quantità, con obligo alli mercanti di farne l' esito. Di recente si è dato anco mano alla fabrica di panni colorati ad uso di Francia, che passano in Ancona e Sinigaglia per concambio alle mercantie che vengono di Turchia. In somma, la casa di S. Michele è una delle più vaste idee che possa esser compita da un principe grande, e sarebbe sicuramente l' emporio di tutta l' Italia, se non fosse costituita in una città dove ad ogn' altra cosa si pensa che al commercio et alla mercatura, essendo diretti questi gran capitali da una congregatione di tre cardinali, tra quali vi è il segretario di stato, sempre occupato e divertito ne' più gravi affari del governo. Con tutto ciò questa casa di commercio sussiste con floridezza, e colli suoi travaglj s' alimentano migliara di persone ricavandosi dalle sue manifatture pronto il ritratto. La fabrica degl' arazzi si mantiene da se stessa, perchè si lavora ad uso de' particolari, et il maggior effetto di questi lavori si è quello desiderabile a tutti li stati, che il danaro non esca ad impinguare l' estere nationi."

[In this sumptuous edifice there has been introduced the manufacture of tapestry, equal to those worked in Flanders and in France: and there has been established a woollen manufactory there, into which wool is introduced, and out of which there come forth cloths perfect in every respect. The manufacture of silk dependent on this place is carried on in many of the territories of Rome, and those of wool are divided into so many different kinds with the idea of adapting them to the use of the countries, in order to have from them a prompt profit with a ready sale. There are manufactured at St. Michael's all the cloths for the soldiers, the *scoti* for the use of the monasteries, linens of all sorts for the use of the common people, and the cloths are divided into various kinds which are distributed by a given quantity, with an obligation on the merchants to make a sale of them.[1] Of late, too, measures have been taken for the manufacture of coloured cloths after the custom of France, which pass into Ancona and Sinigaglia in exchange for wares coming from Turkey. On the whole the establishment of St. Nicholas is one of the vastest ideas that could be executed by a great prince, and would certainly be the emporium of all Italy, had it not been placed in a city where everything is thought of but commerce and trade, these large capitals being directed by a congregation of three cardinals, among whom is the secretary of state, (who is) always occupied, and has his attention drawn off by the gravest affairs of the government. With all that, this commercial establishment is in a flourishing condition, and thousands of people are supported by the employment it gives, a prompt return being received from its manufactures. The weaving of tapestry supports itself, the manufacture being carried on for the advantage of private individuals, and the greatest result of these labours is that most desirable one for all states, that money does not go away for the fattening of foreign nations.]

How extraordinary, that a Venetian should advise his native city to take an industrial establishment of the popes for its model. Already had they also hit upon institutions for the culture of the mind which he recommends for imitation.

"Oltre le arti mecaniche vi sono pure le arti liberali, che servono ad ornamento ed utilità dello stato. Il solo nome di Roma ed il credito degli antichi suoi monumenti attrae a se stessa molte estere nationi et in particolare gli oltramontani. Sono in quella città instituite molte accademie, dove oltre lo studio delle belle lettere non meno fiorisce quello della pittura e scoltura: oltre quella di Campidoglio, che sussiste sotto la protettione di quel rettaglio d' autorità esercitata con tanto credito ne' secoli passati da quella insigne republica. Ve ne sono pure anco dell' altre instituite e governate dall' estere

[Besides the mechanical arts, there are the liberal arts which serve for the ornament and utility of the state. The name alone of Rome, and the renown of its ancient monuments, attract many foreign nations to it, particularly those beyond the Alps. Many academies have been instituted in that city, where, besides the study of literature, there no less flourishes that of painting and sculpture: besides that of Campidoglio, which subsists under the safeguard of that direction on the part of authority, (?) which was exercised with so much credit in past ages by that distinguished republic. There, like-

1 This sentence is obscure, but seems to mean that the merchants had to take a proportion of each different kind of cloth, and obliged themselves to sell all, and return none under the pretext of its not being liked.—TR.

nationi, tra le quali si distingue quella che sussiste col nome della corona di Francia." [wise, there are other institutions besides, governed too by foreign nations, among which that subsisting under the name of the crown of France, is distinguished.]

Now, the author is of opinion, that in Venice likewise, a similar academy should be instituted. In Venice, too, there were the finest monuments of antiquity. Even Bologna had been able to undertake something similar with great success!

Moreover, with the tendencies indicated by Correr, some others of a congenial kind were further associated at that time, upon which other memorials supply us with information.

159.

Osservationi della presente situatione dello stato ecclesiastico con alcuni progetti utili al governo civile ed economico per ristabilire l' erario della rev^da^ camera apostolica dalli passati e correnti suoi discapiti.—[Observations on the present situation of the ecclesiastical state, with some projects useful for the civil and economical government for restoring the treasury of the most reverend apostolic chamber from its past and current losses.] (MS. Rom.)

At the commencement of the eighteenth century a conviction prevailed over the whole south of Europe that matters were in a bad state, that people had unwarrantably neglected themselves; there was a spirit abroad which felt the need of a better state of things, and longed to introduce it. How much was there written and attempted in Spain for the restoration of the finances and commerce! In the church-state the Testamento politico d' un accademico Fiorentino, Colonia, 1734—which suggests the means by which trade, agriculture, and the revenues of the exchequer might be improved—is still held in good repute. In fact, it is a well-intentioned, clever piece of writing, going thoroughly into the subject, and full of sound observations. We find something more, however, than the efforts of mere private persons. In the collections of that time we find a number of projects, calculations, and plans for the same object, more or less official. The above Osservationi, belonging to the period of the Political Testament, form a document of this kind, intended for Clement XII. himself. The author seeks, in particular, to specify the disorders and abuses which had to be removed.

After dwelling for a time on the melancholy spectacle of so many murders taking place in the church-state, even beyond Rome and the four legations still amounting to a thousand—the author thinks people must look to what other princes do against this evil—he comes to the finances. He represents the deficit at 1,200,000 scudi a-year. He proposes as follows: 1. A reform of the officers, who draw large pay without so much as residing at their garrisons. 2. The restriction of the disbursements of the palace. 3. The administration of the dogana by the state itself, instead of farming them, which he condemns for this, among other reasons, that the farmer of the customs opposed the prohibition of foreign manufactures. 4. The limitation of the influence of subaltern officials, who looked upon it as to their advantage that the taxes should be increased. He remarks that the annona (raising of corn) could not maintain itself, for this reason, among others, that there was so much importation from Turkey and the North. What most of all amazes him is, that so much money should go out of the country for cattle, oil, and wine, all which people had even in superabundance at home. Of what consequence was it that people should pay a little dearer for these articles, if, in return, money, "the blood of the state," had but its proper circulation. The owners of stock in the Monti, who draw interest without residing in the country, ought at least to be taxed, as was the case even with the feudatories in the adjoining kingdom of Naples.

The state of the Mark, which fell off in the number of its inhabitants every year, he thinks particularly lamentable. He traces it particularly to the burthens imposed on the exportation of corn. Betwixt June and October it was directly forbidden; then it was permitted only on payment of duties the produce of which was trifling for the exchequer, the effect of which, however, was this, that strangers preferred seeking cheaper corn elsewhere. The Sinigaglia fair proved highly injurious. It made the country round dependent on foreign parts: one needed but to pass through to Urbino, the Mark, and Umbria, where neither skill nor comfort was any longer to be found, but all was in a state of deep decline.

The author conjures the pope to appoint a congregation of a few but select members to find out a remedy for these evils, first of all to appoint none but fit and honest functionaries, but to punish the rest. "These things," he concludes by saying, "are hoped for by the subjects of your holiness."

160.

Provedimento per lo stato ecclesiastico.—[Precautions for the ecclesiastical state.] (MS. Rom. Autograph for the officers of state.)

It will be seen that here two attempts were made to introduce the mercantile system which at that time found so much acceptance in Europe. And had people but vigorously proceeded with it! Industry would probably, in that case, have taken a certain rise. But it was the misfortune of the Roman popes that the subsequent popes did so entirely the opposite of what had seemed good to their predecessors. The paper lying before us gives us an example of this.

In the year 1719, the importation of foreign cloths from Venice and Naples, chiefly too from Germany, made such progress, that Clement felt himself induced directly to prohibit it. Mention is made also in Vergani ("della importanza del nuovo sistema di finanza") [(on the importance of the new system of finance)], of the two decrees of 7th August, 1719, and 7th August, 1720, by which this was accomplished. But when Vergani denies that this did any good, he is unquestionably in error. Pietro Capello remarks the spring that had been made by Roman industry as early as in 1728. In the Provedimento before us, we are expressly assured that directly in consequence of that prohibition the manufactures had taken an important spring. Innocent XIII. and Benedict XIII. confirmed that prohibition.

"In pochi anni si eressero a proprie spese de' particolari in molte città e terre dello stato fabriche nuove di lanificii, di valche, di spurghi, di tintorie et altre, in specie a Roma, Narni, Perugia, Rieti, Tivoli, Alatri, Veroli, Segni, Subiaco, S. Severino, Giulianello."

[In a few years there were erected, at the expense of individuals themselves, in many towns and lands of the state, new manufactories of woollens, of valche,[1] fulling-mills, dyeing-houses, and others, for instance at Rome, Narni, Perugia, Rieti, Tivoli, Alatri, Veroli, Segni, Subiaco, San Severino, Giulianello.]

But a congregation, constituted by Clement XII. in 1735, was led to remove the prohibition, and again to permit the importation of cloth on payment of a duty of 12 per cent. in the provinces and 20 per cent. in Rome. The consequence was, at least as this piece of writing assures us, that the establishments that had just been founded went to ruin. It calculates that a sum of 100,000 scudi went out of the country for cloths. It calls for a renewal of the prohibition, and its extension to silk goods; yet I do not find that it produced any effect.

161.

Altri provedimenti di commercio.—[Other commercial precautions.] (MS. Rom.)

(This presents) a confirmation of the momentary rise of manufacturing prosperity since the above-mentioned prohibition. The old complaints about the prohibition of exportation are renewed. So much came out of Tuscany: but would any one take thither so much as a bushel of corn, he would for that incur the forfeiture of his property, excommunication, aye even risk the loss of life itself. Moreover, here too as in Germany, a very great confusion of coins had come in upon the country. The papal coins were too heavy, although Innocent XI. and Clement XI. had already coined lighter ones. A great quantity of foreign money, subjecting people to much loss, broke in. The pope was called upon, on his side, to strike the lighter sorts, as had already begun to be done with the zechins.

Yet other writings of a like import lie before us: to excerpt them all would lead to too much detail. Enough, if we remark that the church-state also shared in those industrial and economical tendencies which had seized the rest of Europe, although the state of the country, the constitution, and irradicable abuses, would not allow matters to come to any properly successful result:—the tranquillity of the aristocracy; the charm attending a life of enjoyment, and which had no other object: the sweetness of doing nothing. Our countryman, Winkelman, was in ecstasy on coming to Italy soon after this period. The life led there to him seemed a deliverance from the stirring activity and strict subordination of our countries. The learned man was in the right: he wanted ease and leisure, an acknowledged character; he found he must breathe a freer air: and these things, too, for the moment, and for private life, may be allowed to have their weight. But a nation can become prosperous and powerful only by strenuous exertion on all sides.

162.

Relazione 28 Novembre 1737 del N. U. Aluise Mocenigo IV. K^r^ e Proc^r^ ritornato di Roma. —[Report (dated) 28th November, 1737, by the N. U. (?) Aluise Mocenigo IV., knight and procurator, on his return from Rome.] (Arch. Ven.)

Here we see what it was that, on the side of the government, opposed the (general) prosperity. Mocenigo is nowise a fault-finder: he acknowledges the increase of the trade of Ancona, and it even suggests serious considerations to him: he thinks justice to be in a sound state, particularly at the Rota; but he declares the administration to be corrupt from the very foundation: embezzlement was the order of the day: the expenditure exceeded the income: there was no help to be looked for. Pope Clement had availed himself of the establishment of lotteries: but the ambassador considers them as pernicious to the last degree ("l' evidente esterminio e ruina de' popoli") [(the evident destruction and ruin of the people)].

His opinion of pope Clement XII. is, that he was more distinguished by the gifts of a chevalier and of a splendid prelate than by talent or capacity for sustaining the heavy burthen of the popedom. He describes him and his government only in the following sketches:—

"Il pontificato presente influisce piuttosto

[Noble enterprises and magnificence have

1 "Valche." Can this word be from the obsolete German word *walchen*, to be in a state of agitation, and mean waulk-mills, where cloths are purified by violent agitation; or does it mean Walsche, *i.e.* Walloon, from some particular manufacture imported from the Walloon country.—Tr.

le nobili intraprese e la magnificenza, tale essendo stata sempre l' inclinazione del papa sino dalla sua gioventù, e tuttavia nell' età sua cadente e rovinosa sostenuta dal genio e dagli esempj del card[le] Corsini nipote, che più ancora si distingue nell' inclinazione per le belle arti e per il modo affabile di trattare che per un fondo di vera sufficienza negli affari del governo. La serie dei successi nel cadente pontificato, in cui per lo più ha governato l' Eminenza Sua, rende chiara testimonianza a questa verità, e si può dire che i dissapori violenti occorsi quasi con tutte le corti avrebbono dovuto opprimere il card[l] nipote, se egli non fosse stato sostenuto da un credito fondato in un cuore disinteressato e mancante piuttosto per difetto di talento che di cattiva volontà. Vero è che Roma non scusa in lui la premura con cui vuole in ogni caso disporre di tutti gli affari politici, geloso sino all' eccesso dellá sua autorità, e quindi aver egli allontanato dal ministero il card[le] Riviera, il più capace di tutti per gli affari di stato, ed aver ivi sostituito il card[l] Firau per disponerne a piacere e senza contrasto. Per altro, sia inclinazione, sia virtù, certa cosa è che durante tutto il pontificato di Clemente XII. nel corso di sette anni con la disposizione assoluta delli tesori pontificj la casa Corsini non ha aumentate le rendite sue patrimoniali di 8 m. scudi annui, esempio ben raro."

[most favour with the present government, such having always been the pope's inclination from his youth up, and nevertheless in his declining and broken-down age sustained by the genius and examples of cardinal Corsini, the nephew, who further is more distinguished by his turn for the fine arts and for his affability in transacting business, than by any fund of true capacity for the affairs of the government. The course of events in the decline of the pontificate, in which his eminence has governed for the most part, bears clear testimony to this truth, and it may be said that the keen disgusts that have arisen with almost the whole court, must have overwhelmed the cardinal, had he not been sustained by a credit founded in a disinterested heart, and in being wanting rather from defect of talent than from bad intention. True it is that Rome does not excuse in him the eagerness with which he would, in every case, dispose of all political affairs, he being jealous to excess of his authority, and for having therefore removed from the ministry cardinal Riviera, the most capable of all for state affairs, and having put in his place cardinal Firau, in order to dispose of these as he pleases and without wrangling. However, be it inclination or be it virtue, it is certain that, during the whole pontificate of Clement XII., in the course of seven years, with the pontifical treasures at their absolute disposal, the Corsini family has not augmented its patrimonial revenues by 8000 scudi a-year, a very rare example.]

The nephew in return had great power, although he did not enrich himself. The secretary of state was entirely dependent on him, and it was necessary to be on your guard against trusting to what might be said by the former when you are not sure of the latter.

From internal affairs, Mocenigo passes to the relations maintained with the other popes, which, as we have said, daily became more and more unmanageable. I quote at large the following passage because of its important bearing on the history of ecclesiastical contentions.

"La corte di Napoli anela continuamente all' abolimento della solita investitura con argomenti legali, istorici e naturali: nè sarebbe difficile che vi riuscisse, quando il re Don Carlo acconsentisse ad una solenne rinunzia di ogni sua pretesa sopra Castro e Ronciglione. Ma questo non è il tutto: mentre i Napolitani condotti dalle scuole dei loro giurisconsulti sono talmente avversi alla corte di Roma che ogni cosa studiano per sottrarsi dalla dipendenza del papa nel temporale: e quindi ogni giorno escono nuove regolamenti e nuove pretese così ben sostenute dai scrittori loro valenti che la corte Romana n' è più che mai imbarazzata e già si vede nella necessità di rilasciarne una gran parte per mettere in salvo il resto. Il punto si è che queste riforme tendono principalmente ad impinguare l' erario regio e quindi a scemare le rendite e l' autorità pontificia in quegli stati. Il padre Galliani, uomo di profonda dottrina ed erudizione, è in Roma il grande propugnatore per la corte di Napoli, tanto più efficace quanto nelle sue lunghe consuetudini in quella metropoli ha penetrato nel più fondo dei misterj del papato, e proveduto d' una memoria felicissima tutto ha presente per prevalersene nell' opportunità.

"Il grande appoggio della corte di Napoli è quella di Spagna, dove l' irritamento parve tempo fa giunto all' eccesso e dette occasioni

[The court of Naples is continually struggling for the abolition of the usual investment with arguments legal, historical, and natural: nor would it be difficult for it to succeed there if the king, Don Carlo, would consent to a solemn renunciation of all his claims whatsoever upon Castro and Ronciglione. But this is not all; for the Neapolitans, led by the schools of their lawyers, have such an aversion to the court of Rome, that they study every method of disengaging themselves from dependence on the pope in temporal matters: and hence there are, every day, new regulations and new pretensions so well sustained by able writers of theirs, that the Roman court finds itself more embarrassed with them than ever, and already sees the necessity of relinquishing a great part in order that it may keep safe what remains. The main point certainly is, that these reforms tend chiefly to fatten the royal treasury, and hence to curtail the pontifical revenues and authority in these states. Father Galliani, a man of profound learning and erudition, is the great advocate in Rome for the court of Naples, a man so much the more efficient in as much during his long intimacy with the usages of that metropolis, he has penetrated to the very bottom of the mysteries of the papacy, and being endowed with a most felicitous memory, has everything at his fingers'

a quelle strepitose propositioni di riforma della dataria e ristabilimento del juspatronato regio, delle quali ebbi più volte l' onore di trattenere Vra Serenità nei riverenti miei dispaccj, e che ora si vedono già concluse con aggiustamento più utile per la corte di Spagna che per quella di Roma.

"La corte di Torino con costante direzione nel maneggio degli affari politici, protetta dalle bolle e concessioni di Benedetto XIII., non si è mai lasciata rilasciare un momento da quei fondamenti che per essa sono inconcussi e troppo facilmente attaccati dal presente pontificato. Il cardle Albani, uomo per sagacità e risoluzione senza pari, ha sin ora sostenuto con tutta l' efficacia le ragioni di quella corte, a segno che non lasciò mai giungere ad effettuazione le minaccie fatte dal pontefice presente, e secondo tutte le apparenze ne deve sortire fastoso col successore.

"Anco la corte di Francia patì alcuni motivi di querela per le vicende della Polonia: ma furono cose di sì poco momento che può ella sola contarsi affezionata e stabile al presente pontificato, e ciò perchè negli affari ecclesiastici poco o nulla più resta da discutere con Roma, osservandosi pontualmente dall' una e dall' altra parte i concordati e la prammatica, ma principalmente perchè la corte di Roma va con essa più cauta che con qualsivoglia altro nell' introdurre, sostenere e resistere alle novità che intervenir potessero. Il sempre mai lodevole cardle Fleuri, grand' esemplare nel ministero politico, ha saputo tener sempre soggetta la politica alla religione senza mai confondere l' autorità spirituale con la temporale: e questo fa che durante il suo ministero la corte di Roma sia si trattenuta nei limiti dovuti e quasi con una perpetua condescenza, a segno che l' avrebbe costituito l' arbitro di tutte le sue differenze, se gli altri potentati non avessero temuta la grande equità e l' imparzialità di quell' eroe nel ministero politico.

"Gravissimi furono i sconcerti, tuttavia non appianati ancora, con la corte di Portogallo, dove il carattere di quel re fa che acquistano giornalmente vigore ed insistenza le sue pretese quanto più si contrastano: e per dirla con chiarezza, le differenze insorte col Portogallo e con la Spagna avendo da qualche tempo sospese le rendite opulentissime di que' vasti regni, ha quasi scompaginata la corte e la città di Roma, dove migliaja di famiglie da qualche anno in quà sono ridotte dall' opulenza alla povertà e tante altre dalla sufficienza alla miseria. Questo fa che la disposizione d' infiniti beneficj in Spagna, in Portogallo e nel regno di Napoli rimanendo sospesa, anzi correndo apparenza che rimaner possa all' autorità temporale di que' regnanti, gran numero dei loro sudditi secolari e regolari altre volte consacrati a sostenere la corte di Roma presentemente l' abbandonano, e gran numero ancora dei Romani stessi vengono condotti a coltivar le potenze straniere dall' avidità e necessità loro. Particolare e curiosa è stata la condotta della corte di Roma verso le pretese di questo principe di aver il cardinale nato il patriarca di Lisbona. Fu considerato da quel re come condizione indispensabile dell' accommodamento delle vertenze che corrono tra le due

ends, to avail himself of as opportunities offer.

The grand stay of the court of Naples is that of Spain, where the irritation appeared opportunity (?) added to the excitement, and the said occasions to those noisy propositions of reform of the dataria, and re-establishment of the royal right of patronage, which I have many times had the honour to mention to your serenity, in my very respectful dispatches, and which are now seen to be concluded by an adjustment more advantageous to the court of Spain than to that of Rome.

The court of Turin by a steady direction in the management of political affairs, protected by the bulls and concessions of Benedict XIII., has never allowed itself to depart for a moment from those fundamental principles which have never been shaken by it, and have been too readily attacked by the present pontificate. Cardinal Albani, a man without his match for sagacity and resolution, has until now backed the arguments of that court with all efficacy, to such a degree as never to allow the threats made by the present pontiff to be carried into effect, and according to all appearances, is likely to come out of them proudly with his successor.

Further, the court of France suffers from some causes of quarrel through the vicissitudes in Poland; but these were matters of such small moment, that she (France) alone could reckon herself on kindly terms, and firmly established with the present pontificate, and that because in church affairs little or nothing remains to be discussed with Rome, the concordats and the pragmatic being punctually observed on both sides, but chiefly because the court of Rome conducts itself more cautiously with it than with any other whatsoever in the introduction, maintenance and resistance of such innovations as may intervene. The ever to be praised cardinal Fleury, a great example in the political ministry, has contrived to keep politics always subject to religion, without ever confounding the spiritual with the temporal authority: and this brings it about that the court of Rome during his ministry has confined itself within due limits, and as it were with a perpetual condescension, to such a degree as that it would have constituted it the arbiter of all its differences, if the other potentates had not dreaded the great equity and impartiality of that hero in the political ministry.

Most serious were the embroilments, nevertheless, not taken out of the way, with the court of Portugal, where that king's character led to his claims daily acquiring vigour and obstinacy, the more they were resisted: and to speak plainly, the differences that have arisen with Portugal and with Spain, having for some time suspended the most valuable revenues from those vast kingdoms, have almost separated (?) the court and the city of Rome, where thousands of families for some years past till now have been reduced from opulence to poverty, and so many others from sufficiency to absolute want. The consequence of this is, that the disposal of the

corti, di godere una tal distinzione, ed il papa, usando in ciò dell' antico costume Romano, si è dimostrato alcune volte del tutto alieno, altre quasi propenso di soddisfare le premure del re. La cosa non è ancora decisa, ed in ogni maniera che venghi consumata fornirà argomenti non indifferenti di discorsi e forse di querele tra gli altri principi.

"Altre volte il pretendente faceva un' oggetto massimo della corte di Roma, la quale si lusingava molto sopra l' appoggio delle corti di Francia e Spagna, dacchè si riunirono ambedue nella casa di Borbon: ma in oggi scopertasi la gelosia tra la linea primogenita e la cadetta e conosciutosi che la regina di Spagna non ha veramente altre mire che l' ingrandimento dei proprj figlj, l' esule pretendente e la degna sua famiglia divengono presto a molti oggetto più grave ancora che di conforto.

"L' imperatore ha fatto e tuttavia tremare il presente ministero di Roma, vedendosi egli stesso dar mano ad introdurre nei suoi stati d' Italia quelle riforme d' abusi che devono col tempo servire di esempio sommamente pregiudiciale ai Romani: e ciò ch' è peggio per loro, appena ha introdotto le sue truppe nella Toscana, che ivi pure si veggono incamminate le medesime direzioni, a segno che di tutti gli stati esteri al dominio Romano non se ne vede pur uno continuar ciecamente sul piede dei secoli passati. La corte di Vienna professando tempo fa acri motivi di querela per le distinzioni usate a Spagnoli, poco amati dal popolo Romano, si è totalmente attratto il favor d' esso popolo in Roma e nello stato sotto il pontificato presente col maneggio accortissimo de' suoi ministri ed emissarj, ch' è cosa maravigliosa l' udire in universale il popolo Romano dichiarato in favore dell' imperatore. Tuttavia in oggi tanta è la forza dell' interesse della famiglia Corsini che non vi è sagrificio che non si faccia affine di guadagnarsi l' amicizia di Cesare: di che l' Ecc^{mo} Senato ne ha abbondanti prove nelle direzioni de' negozj vertenti."

infinite number of benefices in Spain, in Portugal, and in the kingdom of Naples remaining in suspense, there being even a likelihood of their remaining with the temporal authority of those who govern, a great number of their subjects, secular and regular, at other times devoted to the maintenance of the Roman court, now abandon it, and a great number further of the Romans themselves come to be led by their avarice and by necessity to cultivate the foreign powers. The conduct of the court of Rome has been singular and curious with respect to the claim of that prince to have the cardinal (his) son (made) patriarch of Lisbon. By that king it was considered as an indispensable condition of the accommodation of affairs betwixt the two courts, that such a distinction should be enjoyed, and the pope availing himself in this of the old Roman custom, has shown himself sometimes altogether averse, at others almost inclined to satisfy the king's eagerness. The matter is not yet decided, and in whatever manner it may come to be brought to an issue, will furnish no indifferent arguments for discourses, and perhaps for quarrels among the other monarchs.

At other times the pretender was an object of the utmost importance to the court of Rome, which flattered itself much on the support of the courts of France and Spain, since the two have been united in the Bourbon family; but now that the jealousy between the elder and the cadet branch discovers itself, and that it is known that the queen of Spain has no other aim in truth but the aggrandizement of her own sons, the exiled pretender and his worthy family have forthwith become to most an object rather of grief than of comfort.

The emperor has made, and is always making the present Roman ministry tremble, on seeing that he himself puts his hand to the introduction in his Italian states of those reforms of abuses which must in the course of time serve as an example in the highest degree prejudicial to the Romans: and what is worse for them, hardly has he introduced his troops into Tuscany than the same directions have been commenced there, so that of all the states beyond the Roman dominions, there is not one to be seen that blindly follows in the footsteps of past ages. The court of Vienna, professing that time makes sharp grounds of quarrel on account of the distinctions lavished on the Spaniards, who are in little favour with the Roman people, has entirely drawn to itself the good-will of that same people in Rome, and in the state subject to the present pontificate by a most sagacious management on the part of its ministers and emissaries, which is a most marvellous thing to hear universally that the Roman people are openly in favour of the emperor. Nevertheless, at this day such is the force of the interest of the Corsini family that there is no sacrifice that is not made in order to gain the friendship of the emperor: of which the most excellent senate has abundant proofs in the directions of current affairs.

163.

Relazione del N. H. Franc. Venier K^r ritornato ambasciator da Roma 1744, 24 Apr.—[Report of N. H. Franc. Venier, on his return as ambassador from Rome, 1744, 24th April.]

Unfortunately only two fugitive leaves devoted to Benedict XIV.

Venier assures us that the cardinals of themselves would never have elected this pope: "inalzato anzi dalle sue rare virtù, dalle vicende di quel conclave, dalle sue note lunghezze, che da un' efficace favore de' cardinali che lo esaltarono. Fu opera sola del divino spirito." [elevated rather by his own rare virtues, by the vicissitudes of that conclave, by its notorious delays, than by the effective favour of the cardinals that exalted him. It was the sole work of the Holy Ghost.]

"Il papa," [the pope] he proceeds to say, "dotato di cuore aperto e sincero, trascurò sempre ogn' una di quelle arti che si chiamano romanesche, e lo stesso carattere che fece conoscere senza riserva allora che era prelato, fu quello del card^l Lambertini e si può dire quello del papa" [endowed with an open and sincere heart, always neglected every one of those arts that are called Romanesque, and the same character which he unreservedly disclosed when (only) a prelate, was that of cardinal Lambertini, and if we may say so, that of the pope].

164.

Relazione di Aluise Mocenigo IV. Kav^r ritornato ambasciator di Roma 1750, 14 Apr.—[Report of Aluise Mocenigo IV., on returning as ambassador from Rome, 1750, 14th April.]

This is not at all the ambassador of 1737, appearing again. The former was a son of Aluise Mocenigo the Third: this latter is the son of Aluise Mocenigo the First.

He has unfortunately contented himself with three leaves: as there is a paucity of authentic notices respecting the Roman court at that period, I will give the most important passage verbatim.

"Il regnante Benedetto XIV. non solo non è mai stato nell' impiego di nunziature presso alcuna corte, ma nè pur ha sostenuto alcuna legazione: egli essendo vescovo d' Ancona è stato fatto cardinale, et essendo arcivescovo di Bologna fu assonto al supremo grado in cui regna. Possiede per pratica fatta sin dagli anni suoi più freschi l' ordine della curia, e non se ne scorda certamente, oltre di che si picca d' esser perfetto canonista et ottimo legale, non ammettendo egli in ciò differenza dall' esser suo di decretalista, studio che non lascia al dì d' oggi ancora. Perciò egli è parzialissimo del suo uditore mons^re Argivilliers, perchè si dirige colle stesse dottrine. Conformandosi dunque le massime del papa con quelle del suo uditore, si rende questi nel pontificato presente uomo d' importanza, quando particolarmente per l' esercizio suo, ch' è ristretto alle sole civili ispezioni, non avrebbe altro che il vantaggio di vedere in ogni giorno il monarca ed ora entra a dir parere negli affari di stato. Per dir vero, egli è uomo di probità, ma di nessuna esperienza negl' interessi dei principi, austero ed inaccessibile, scarso di corrispondenza forastiere non solo ma ancora tra li stessi palatini. Per l' aura di favore ch' ei gode sembra che contrasti al card^l Valenti segretario di stato l' accesso vantaggioso presso del papa, che la gran mente di quel porporato, quando voglia gli prema ed a lui convenga, in mezzo alle più difficili determinazioni e massime sempre possiede ed ottiene. Ed eccomi al caso di superfluità e repetizione. Di questo soggetto, perspicace nella coltura degli affari politici e di stato, ministro d' esperienza, accorto e manieroso, avran detto quello conviene li miei eccellentissimi predecessori, e circa questo non altro posso aggiungere se non ch' egli col nuovo posto di camerlengo di S. Chiesa, conferitogli da S. S^tà in tempo della

[The reigning Benedict XIV. not only has never been employed as a nuncio at any court, but he has not even been charged with any legation: while bishop of Ancona he was raised to the cardinalship, and while archbishop of Bologna he was elevated to the supreme rank in which he now reigns. He possesses through the practice he has had since his fresher years, (a knowledge of) the order of the curia, and certainly does not jar with it, besides which he piques himself on being a perfect canonist and excellent lawyer, nor does he admit that in that respect it makes any difference his having in his day been a decretalist, a study which he does not to this day neglect. Accordingly he is most partial to his auditor monsignor Argivilliers, because he directs himself by these same doctrines. Thus, as the pope's maxims agree with those of his auditor, the latter makes himself an important person in the present pontificate, particularly when through his official duty, which is restricted to the inspection of civil matters alone, none but he has the advantage of seeing the sovereign every day, and then he goes in to state his opinion on affairs of state. To say the truth, he is a man of probity, but of no experience in the interests of the princes; he is austere and inaccessible, not only niggardly in foreign correspondences, but further among the courtiers themselves. By the breath of favour he enjoys, it would appear that he disputes with the secretary of state, cardinal Valenti, the advantageous access to the pope, which the great mind of that purpled person, when he pleases, finds matters pressing and thinks it suits him, always possesses and enjoys in the determination of the most difficult and greatest questions. And here I am but indulging in prolixity and repetition. Of this person, so perspicacious in the atten-

mia ambasciata, ha fermato anche dopo la vita del pontefice quel ben onorifico e lucroso posto, che lo renderà ancora necessario e ricercato quando forse dopo di aver dimessa la secretaria di stato l' emulazione, l' invidia e li mal contenti avrebbero potuto spiegar la loro forza ed il loro sdegno. Va ora esente da questi sfoghi, non perchè sia da ogni parte circondato: ma sa egli far fronte e scansar ogni assalto: se a lui giova, cimenta: in caso diverso non cura. Oltre al nominato uditor del papa, poco o niente amico suo vi è ancora mons[r] Millo datario, con il quale benchè a mio tempo apparissero riconciliati in amicizia, in sostanza non lo erano, ed il detto datario è piuttosto del partito dell' uditore. Questi tre soggetti si possono dir quelli che nel presente pontificato abbino ingerenza ed intelligenza negli affari dello stato. Ma se li due prelati sono accetti per l' esposto di sopra ed il card[l] sa rendersi necessario per le tante ragioni ben note, però arrivano dei momenti che il papa ascolta gli uni e l' altro e poscia tutto a sua volontà e talento differentemente risolve. Per questo ancora, se vi sono degli altri ben distinti soggetti tra li palatini, non contano gran cosa nel presente pontificato o almeno in rapporto ai gravi affari dello stato. Uno è il card[le] Passionei, studiosissimo ed amante delle scienze, pratico ministro per le nunziature sostenute, e non ha altra ingerenza che nella secretaria dei brevi. Del giovane prelato mons[r] Marcantonio Colonna maggiorduomo il zio card[l] Girolamo promaggiorduomo è uno tra li prediletti del papa: ma egli non si da pena d'altro che di quelle cose che interessino le particolari sue brame. Il segretario alle zifre mons[re] Antonio Rota, conosciuto dal papa e dall' universale di tutto il sagro collegio ed a parte dalle congregazioni coram sanctissimo per un' uomo della più scelta politica ed un pensamento il più fino, che per l' aggiustatezza dell' estero, dove abbia ad esservi un tratto d' accortezza, altro non ha migliore, talmente conosciuto necessario che con distinto modo si ammette anche podagroso nelle occorrenti congregazioni, non ha però maggiori ispezioni che quelle del suo carico o le avventizie."

tion he devotes to political affairs and to those of the state, an experienced minister, shrewd and mannerly, whatever is fitting has been said by my most excellent predecessors, and about him no other can add aught unless that he, with the new post of camerlengo of Holy Church conferred upon him by his holiness in the time of my embassy, has also secured after the pontiff's death that very honourable and lucrative post, which will further render him necessary and in request, when perhaps, after having laid down the secretaryship of state, emulation, envy, and the discontented will have it in their power to display their force and their spite. He now escapes from these exhalations (of spite) not because he has a rampart all around him, but because he knows how to confront and parry every assault: if it be for his advantage, he hazards an encounter; if the case be otherwise, he does not care. Besides the above-named pope's auditor, who is little if at all friendly to him, there is further monsignor Millo, the datarius, with whom, although in my time they appeared reconciled in friendship, substantially they were not so, and the said datarius is rather of the party of the auditor. These three persons may be said to be those who in the present pontificate have a part in state affairs and understand them. But if the two prelates are acceptable for the reasons above explained, and the cardinal contrives to make himself necessary for so many well-known reasons, there are moments however when the pope hears both the one and the other party, and then determines everything according to his own will and ability, without leaning to either of them. Thus further, if there be other very distinguished persons among those attached to the palace, they are not of much account in the present pontificate, or at least as respects serious matters of state. One is cardinal Passionei, a most studious person and fond of the sciences, a practised minister from the nuncioships he has held, and he has no further to do with the government than the secretaryship of briefs. Cardinal Girolamo, promajordomo, uncle of the young prelate monsignor Marc-antonio, is one of the pope's prime favourites: but he bestows no pains on anything but what concerns his own particular wishes. The secretary to the cypher, monsignor Antonio Rota, known to the pope and to the sacred college at large, and among the congregations *coram sanctissimo* for a man of the choicest political skill and the subtlest thinking, who has not his better for the adjustment of foreign affairs, where a stroke of sagacity is required, and who is known to be so necessary a person that, gouty as he is, he is received in a distinguished manner in the congregations as they occur, yet has no greater affairs to dispatch than those of his own charge, and such as happen to be connected with it.]

165.

Girolamo Zulian Relazione di Roma 15 Decembre 1783.—[Girolamo Zulian, Report on Rome, 15th December, 1783.]

Towards the close of the republic there was a falling off too in the taste for this kind of political activity.

The reports became shorter: the observations they communicate are not to be compared with the older ones in penetration and comprehensiveness.

Zulian, whose report is the last that fell in my way, hardly treats at all of the policy, the foreign affairs, and the personal qualities of Pius VI.: he confines himself to some chief points of the internal civil administration.

He mentions the papal chambers having a large deficit, which was further increased by extraordinary disbursements, the building of the sacristy of St. Peter's, and the operations in the Pontine marshes—both might by that time have cost two millions:—which deficit attempts were made to reduce by anticipations, and the creation of paper money. Much money, too, went otherwise out of the country.

"Le canapi, le sete, le lane che si estraggono dallo stato, non compensano li pesci salati, li piombi, le droghe e la immensa serie delle manifatture che si importano in esso da Genova specialmente e dalla Francia. Il gran mezzo di bilanciar la nazione dovrebbe essere il commercio de' grani: ma la necessità di regolarlo per mezzo di tratte affine di proveder sempre l' annona di Roma a prezzi bassi lo rende misero e spesso dannoso. Quindi resta oppressa l' agricoltura e spesso succedono le scarsezze del genere che obbligano a comprare il formento fuori dello stato a prezzi gravissimi. E comune opinione pertanto che questo commercio cumulativamente preso pochissimo profitto dia alla nazione. Resta essa debitrice con tutte quasi le piazze colle quali è in relazione, e da ciò deriva in gran parte quella rapida estrazion di monete che mette in discredito le cedole e forma la povertà estrema della nazione. Si considera che il maggior vantaggio di Roma sta colla piazza di Venezia per li varj generi che lo stato pontificio tramanda a quelli di Vostra Serenità."

[The hemp, silks and wools that go out of the state, do not compensate for the salt fish, lead, drugs, and the immense series of manufactures that are imported into it from Genoa specially, and from France. The grand means of balancing the nation ought to be the commerce in grain, but the necessity of regulating it by means of licences in order to provide a supply of corn at all times at Rome at low prices, renders that trade a wretched one, and often conducted at a loss. Hence agriculture remains in a low state and there often happen dearths of such a kind as make it necessary to purchase wheat from abroad at the dearest rates. Yet it is the common opinion that this trade, taken cumulatively, gives very little profit to the nation. It remains indebted to almost all the exchanges with which it maintains a connection, and hence arises in a great measure that rapid extraction of money which puts bills at a discount, and forms the extreme poverty of the nation. It is considered that Rome stands at best advantage with the exchange of Venice, owing to the various kinds (of commodities) which the pontifical state consigns to those of your serenity.]

One knows what were the means taken by Pius VI. for the relief of the land. They are discussed here, but not with any particular depth.

Zulian remarks that Pius VI. made the cardinals still more insignificant than they were already. On his return from Vienna he had put them off with obscure and short notices. To this, to be sure, it may be replied that he had little to communicate to them. But the fact was really so. The secretary of state Pallavicini, in other respects a distinguished person, yet could the less carry anything into effect, as he was often in bad health. Rezzonico, the author thinks, had still the greatest influence with this pope.

INDEX.

E

H

I

M

Q

R

V

Lightning Source UK Ltd.
Milton Keynes UK
UKHW010018080219
336804UK00007B/748/P

9 780265 187562